BEA WebLogic® Server Bible

Joe Zuffoletto

Gary Wells, Brian Gill, Geoff Schneider, Barrett Tucker, Rich Helton, Michael Madrid, Sunil Makhijani

est-Selling Books • Digital Downloads • e-Books • Answer Networks • e-Newsletters • Branded Web Sites • e-Learning

New York, NY ✦ Cleveland, OH ✦ Indianapolis, IN

BEA WebLogic® Server Bible

Published by
Hungry Minds, Inc.
909 Third Avenue
New York, NY 10022
www.hungryminds.com

Library of Congress Control Number: 2001118280

ISBN: 0-7645-4854-9

Printed in the United States of America

10 9 8 7 6 5 4 3 2 1

1B/RV/QS/QS/IN

Distributed in the United States by Hungry Minds, Inc.

Distributed by CDG Books Canada Inc. for Canada; by Transworld Publishers Limited in the United Kingdom; by IDG Norge Books for Norway; by IDG Sweden Books for Sweden; by IDG Books Australia Publishing Corporation Pty. Ltd. for Australia and New Zealand; by TransQuest Publishers Pte Ltd. for Singapore, Malaysia, Thailand, Indonesia, and Hong Kong; by Gotop Information Inc. for Taiwan; by ICG Muse, Inc. for Japan; by Intersoft for South Africa; by Eyrolles for France; by International Thomson Publishing for Germany, Austria, and Switzerland; by Distribuidora Cuspide for Argentina; by LR International for Brazil; by Galileo Libros for Chile; by Ediciones ZETA S.C.R. Ltda. for Peru; by WS Computer Publishing Corporation, Inc., for the Philippines; by Contemporanea de Ediciones for Venezuela; by Express Computer Distributors for the Caribbean and West Indies; by Micronesia Media Distributor, Inc. for Micronesia; by Chips Computadoras S.A. de C.V. for Mexico; by Editorial Norma de Panama S.A. for Panama; by American Bookshops for Finland.

For general information on Hungry Minds' products and services please contact our Customer Care department within the U.S. at 800-762-2974, outside the U.S. at 317-572-3993 or fax 317-572-4002.

For sales inquiries and reseller information, including discounts, premium and bulk quantity sales, and foreign-language translations, please contact our Customer Care department at 800-434-3422, fax 317-572-4002 or write to Hungry Minds, Inc., Attn: Customer Care Department, 10475 Crosspoint Boulevard, Indianapolis, IN 46256.

For information on licensing foreign or domestic rights, please contact our Sub-Rights Customer Care department at 212-884-5000.

For information on using Hungry Minds' products and services in the classroom or for ordering examination copies, please contact our Educational Sales department at 800-434-2086 or fax 317-572-4005.

For press review copies, author interviews, or other publicity information, please contact our Public Relations department at 317-572-3168 or fax 317-572-4168.

Credits

Acquisitions Editor
Grace Buechlein

Project Editor
Chandani Thapa

Technical Editors
Wira Pradjinata, Glen Wilcox

Development Editor
Erik Dafforn

Copy Editor
Jeremy Zucker

Editorial Manager
Mary Beth Wakefield

Vice President and Executive Group Publisher
Richard Swadley

Vice President and Executive Publisher
Bob Ipsen

Vice President and Publisher
Joseph B. Wikert

Editorial Director
Mary Bednarek

Project Coordinator
Jennifer Bingham

Graphics and Production Specialists
Melanie DesJardins
Jackie Nicholas
Heather Pope
Jeremey Unger
Erin Zeltner

Quality Control Technicians
Laura Albert
David Faust
John Greenough
Andy Hollandbeck
Angel Perez
Carl Pierce

Proofreading and Indexing
TECHBOOKS Production Services

About the Authors

Joe Zuffoletto is a system architect specializing in application servers and their integration with other host systems. After receiving a computer science degree from Princeton in 1987, he began working with application servers in 1990, when he wrote a number of them for clients in the financial services and technology industries. These servers were based on a C++ framework he developed and enhanced over a five-year span, and they provided server-side execution of business logic, as well as access to embedded and separate relational database systems.

Joe has since left the hard work of writing application servers to others, such as BEA and Sun. He is currently president and co-owner of ZeeWare, Inc. (`www.zeeware.com`), a systems integration firm focused on building J2EE solutions with WebLogic Server. He lives with his wife in Sausalito, California.

Joe wrote Chapters 1-9, 11, 14, 23, and 24.

Gary Wells is a system architect and software project manager with nearly 10 years' experience developing mission-critical applications for the financial services industry. These systems are characterized by high transaction volumes, large user bases, and a requirement for zero downtime. Gary is now leading teams that are building similar systems using WebLogic Server. He is vice-president and co-owner of ZeeWare, Inc.

Gary wrote Chapters 10, 12, 13, and part of Chapter 2.

Brian Gill received his Bachelor of Science in computer science from the University of Wisconsin-Madison in 1998. While at Madison he was the inventor and project-lead to a team that won best prototype in the 1999 Brainstorm, The School's Prize for Creativity competition. He has been a programmer and software architect in the fields of telecommunications, finance, B2B, and Web site load-testing. He specializes in object-oriented architecture and implementation and is an enterprise Java developer at ZeeWare, Inc.

Brian wrote Chapters 15, 19, and part of Chapter 7. He also helps maintain the book's Web site.

Geoff Schneider is a member of the ZeeWare core technologies team that specializes in enterprise applications. A graduate of the University of Wisconsin, he received degrees in computer science and economics. Having previously worked for successful e-commerce companies, Geoff has experience developing scalable applications for large user bases and multiple environments.

Geoff wrote Chapter 26 and part of Chapter 23. He also helps maintain the book's Web site.

Barrett Tucker is a generalist solutions developer who enjoys exploring new computer acronyms. His current favorite is J2EE, but he began his programming life as a GIS programmer developing spatial models of global hydrological systems in ARC/INFO for the NASA EOS project. In the five years since then, he has run the gamut of programmatic and conceptual acronyms to his current favorite, developing OO J2EE EI2 solutions with WebLogic Server for F500 financial institutions. He is an enterprise Java developer at ZeeWare, Inc.

Barrett wrote Chapter 18, the appendix, and part of Chapter 5.

Rich Helton's career with computers and information security spans 20 years. He specialized in secure communications while serving in the U.S. Air Force, and then joined the private sector to further pursue his interests in this area. After receiving a master's degree in computer science from the University of Colorado, he ran his own consulting firm, specializing in network security and the design of large, client/server systems for the telecommunications and cable industries. More recently, he has filled the role of system architect and security architect for firms such as ADP Brokerage and Rhythms NetConnections. He is currently a senior Java architect at Cysive, a provider of enterprise software solutions. Rich wrote Chapters 20-22, 25, and 27.

Michael Madrid is a lead architect at Cysive and has been working in the industry for nine years. He has concentrated on distributed Java-based systems since 1996 and worked with J2EE application servers since 1999. During this time, he has led technical teams, mentored on Java, OO, and design patterns, and helped organizations transition to Java from other technologies.

Michael wrote Chapter 16.

Sunil Makhijani is a senior software engineer specializing in J2EE technologies. He began his career in the defense industry at Northrop Grumman, spending two years developing client/server naval intelligence applications in C/C++, X-Motif, and Oracle. Following that he worked at DLJdirect (now CSFBdirect), developing custom application servers for the financial services industry in C++ and Java. For the past three years, he has worked exclusively with server-side Java technologies, building a number of Web- and wireless-based applications using application servers from BEA, Apple, and Apache. Currently, he works in a pre-sales role at Cysive, working with its J2EE multi-channel software platform, Cymbio.

Sunil wrote Chapter 17.

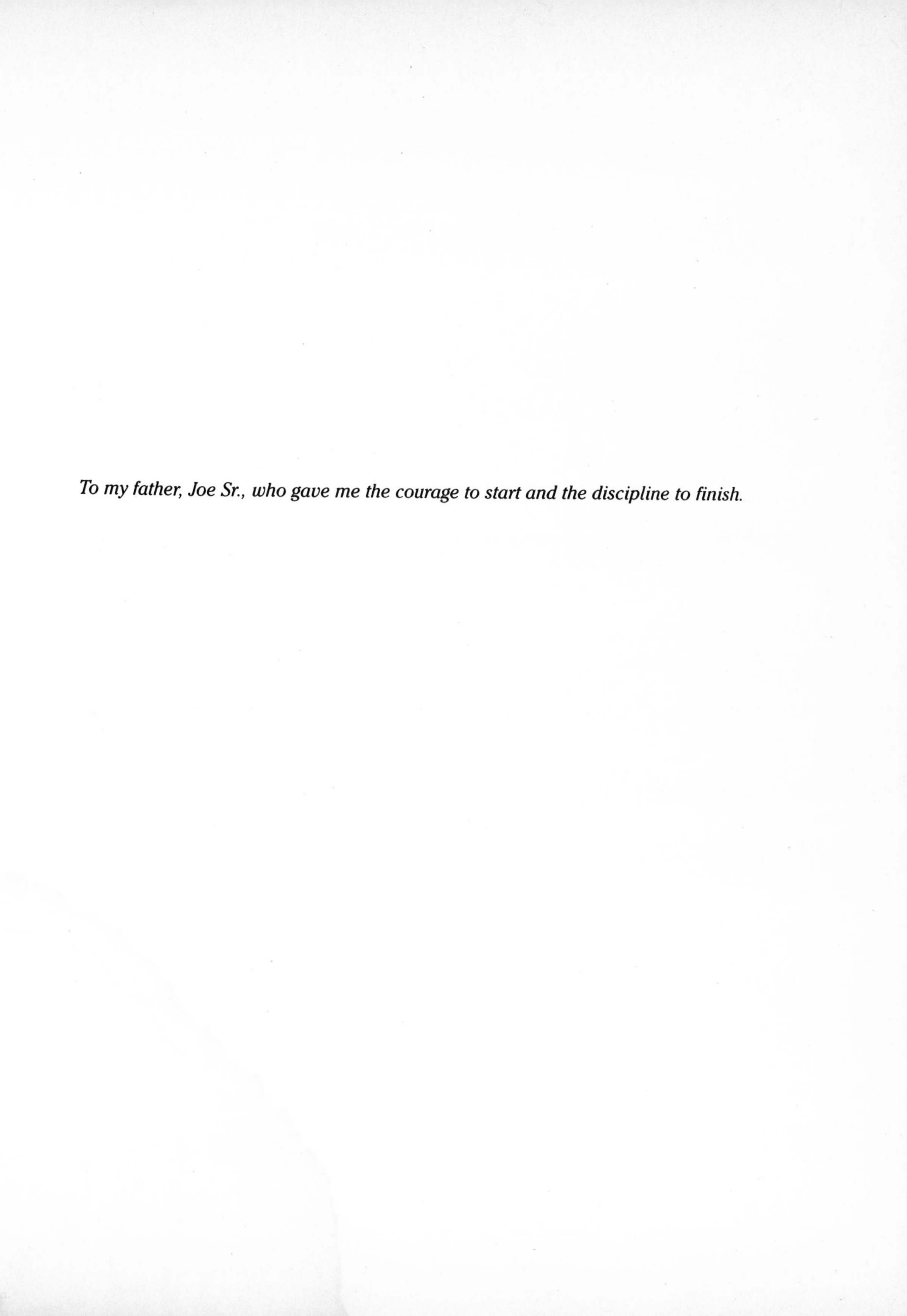

To my father, Joe Sr., who gave me the courage to start and the discipline to finish.

Foreword

As it seems we're all constantly reminded, we live in a world of perpetual, almost maniacal, technology innovation. At every moment, creative destruction is happening, where old paradigms are being rendered obsolete with each successive creation. In most cases, technology innovations render only slight changes in the world around us. In a few cases, changes occur that cause a complete paradigm shift in the way we live. For example, PC computing and the Internet were technology innovations that caused successive waves of worldwide shifts in human existence in the 1980s and 1990s, respectively.

WebLogic is a product riding the wave of several new technology innovations over the past few years: Java/Java 2 Enterprise Edition (J2EE) and the development of the simple Web technologies (HTML/HTTP/SSL) that have changed the world. What started as a small set of database access classes in 1996 for Java has emerged as a complete infrastructure for multitier application development. In five short years, the WebLogic wave has grown enormously. BEA has hundreds of thousands of registered developers and over 12,000 customers. Many of the largest applications on the Internet run on WebLogic. At the same time, this is only the beginning as further changes make the Application Server the central infrastructure for every enterprise application.

Today, we are seeing two momentous occurrences bringing this to fruition. The first is the real standardization of communications between applications. The development of XML and Web Services (SOAP, WSDL, and so on) is enabling developers to build applications that leverage remote services easily and quickly. The second is the development of the Network Effect around J2EE, Web Services, and WebLogic. This Network Effect occurs when a platform (like Microsoft Windows or the Oracle Database) becomes proportionally more valuable (attractive to users) as an ecosystem of partners, community, application developers, and end-users grows.

It is clear that the development of the Internet, standardization of communications, J2EE and Java, and the fact that WebLogic is already a market leader will position it as the ubiquitous infrastructure for enterprise applications. You'll see WebLogic as the single bus for communications in a network to all different types of devices and clients, from PCs to PDAs. WebLogic will be the infrastructure required by every server-side application built, just as Microsoft Windows is a prerequisite for desktop applications.

You are catching the wave at exactly the right moment: when it is apparent what is coming. With Joe's help through this *BEA WebLogic(r) Server Bible,* you've also picked the correct way to become an expert as quickly as possible. With this book, you will learn what's necessary to catch the WebLogic wave and ride it through successful advancement in whatever endeavors you choose.

Good luck!

Michael Girdley
Director, Product Management, BEA WebLogic Server
BEA Systems

Preface

Welcome to *BEA WebLogic Server Bible*, a book designed to help you understand and apply the power of BEA WebLogic Server to help solve your organization's most complex distributed computing problems. This book is written for developers who have a decent knowledge of Java and the Java 2 Platform, Enterprise Edition (J2EE), but are either working with WebLogic Server for the first time or further honing their existing WebLogic skills. In other words, this book assumes you have experience with Java and J2EE, but not necessarily with WebLogic.

Why do You Need this Book?

Perhaps you're thinking of buying this book because you've just downloaded and installed the trial version of WebLogic Server and have no idea what to do next. Or maybe you've become lost in the lush forest of WebLogic documentation on BEA's Web site and you're looking for a trail map. Or perhaps you've been programming WebLogic since the good old Tengah days and you're looking for additional insights on some of the newer features. Whatever your reasons for picking up this book, if you're looking for broad and fairly deep coverage of WebLogic Server, with a healthy balance between theory and hands-on learning, then this book is for you.

WebLogic Server is a large, complex product whose feature set can be positively overwhelming to newcomers. WebLogic's documentation, although excellent, is equally overwhelming, consisting of over 40 manuals and dozens of tutorials and samples. To the uninitiated, just figuring out how to *learn* WebLogic is a difficult job. This book is designed to take some of the pain out of that endeavor.

Although WebLogic Server is based on the Java 2 Platform, Enterprise Edition (J2EE), and although this book covers many of J2EE's features, this book will *not* teach you J2EE programming. In-depth coverage of that topic can be found on Sun's Web site (at `http://java.sun.com/j2ee/tutorial/1_3-fcs/index.html`), or in a number of other books, such as *J2EE Bible*.

Like all software products, WebLogic Server and the J2EE are constantly changing and evolving. This book is based on WebLogic Server 6.1 and the J2EE SDK version 1.3.

Be sure to visit the WebLogic Bible Web site (`www.hungryminds.com/extras`), where you will find the complete source code listings for the book, along with updates, errata, links to other valuable resources, and more!

How this Book is Organized

Most computer scientists are familiar with the "divide-and-conquer" approach to programming, where programmers divide large programming problems into smaller ones that are more easily understood and solved. The same approach works well for learning WebLogic Server, and the organization of this book reflects that.

Part I: Preparing Your Enterprise for WebLogic

The book begins by explaining what WebLogic Server is and what its capabilities are. It goes on to explain how to assemble a WebLogic development team and how to design good WebLogic applications. It closes by showing how to construct an efficient WebLogic development environment on your network. This part of the book is completely nontechnical, directed not only at prospective WebLogic developers, but also to managers who are thinking of adopting WebLogic Server and want to understand the impact it will have on their organization.

Part II: WebLogic and the J2EE APIs

This section begins the technical portion of the book. Its chapters explain, in depth, how WebLogic implements each of the J2EE APIs, including JDBC (database access), JTA (transaction processing), RMI (distributed applications), JNDI (network and directory lookups), JMS (messaging), and JavaMail (electronic mail processing). The approach of each chapter is to explain the background and architecture of each API, show how to write and deploy a simple package in WebLogic Server using the API, and then move on with more advanced examples. Unlike the WebLogic documentation, which often segregates development and administrative information into different manuals, my approach is to put all this information in one place, for easy reference by the developer.

Part III: Developing Web Components

Virtually everyone who buys WebLogic Server uses it to write Web components, which are Java servlets and Java Server Pages (JSPs). This important part of the book shows how to build, deploy, and manage these key components in the WebLogic environment.

Part IV: Developing EJB Components

Enterprise developers will appreciate this section of the book, which shows how to build, deploy, and manage Enterprise JavaBeans (EJBs) in WebLogic Server that conform to the EJB 2.0 specification.

Part V: Deploying and Testing Enterprise Applications

Once you have built a Web application and/or a few EJBs, you'll want to package, deploy, and test your finished product. This section of the book gives insight on how to do so.

Part VI: Implementing Security

WebLogic Server provides a robust security infrastructure that can stand on its own or integrate with outside security architectures. This part of the book explains some of the theory behind securing enterprise computing systems, and then explains WebLogic's security architecture. It closes by showing how to secure WebLogic applications using a variety of approaches and methods.

Part VII: WebLogic Server Administration

This part of the book introduces you to WebLogic's administration tools and shows you how to use them to manage WebLogic domains, servers, clusters, and security.

Part VIII: Enterprise Application Integration

Web Services and SOAP are two of the newest additions to the enterprise developer's toolkit, and WebLogic Server supports them both. This part of the book shows you how to work with these emerging technologies in the context of WebLogic, and it also shows how WebLogic can be used in conjunction with the J2EE Connector Architecture to integrate with existing corporate systems.

Finally, a single appendix explains the major differences between WebLogic 6.1 and earlier versions and gives tips for migrating older WebLogic applications to the newest version.

What You'll Need

To gain the most benefit from this book, you'll need a workstation loaded up with the following software:

- BEA WebLogic Server 6.1 (a free, fully functional trial version is available for download at `http://www.bea.com`).
- Sun's J2EE SDK, version 1.3 (a copy of this is included with the WebLogic Server trial version).

Optional items include the following:

- A relational database, such as Microsoft SQL Server or Oracle. (WebLogic Server ships with a demo version of Informix's Cloudscape database, but if your organization uses one of the other two then you should figure out how to work with it right away.)

- An integrated development environment (IDE) for Java, such as Borland JBuilder (`http://www.borland.com`) or Webgain Studio (`http://www.webgain.com`).
- An SMTP-compliant mail server, if you plan to write applications that will process incoming or outgoing electronic mail.

Conventions Used in this Book

As you go through this book, you will find a few unique elements in nearly every chapter, such as source code listings and special icons that draw your attention to important tidbits of information.

Source Code

Any time you encounter source code, it will be in a special font; this applies to code listings as well as code fragments. This way, it's easy to identify code throughout the book. Whether in a fragment or a numbered listing, code in the text appears in the following style:

```
package bible.servlets;
import javax.servlet.*;
import javax.servlet.http.*;
import java.io.*;
import java.util.*;

public class MyServlet extends HttpServlet {
  public void service(HttpServletRequest request,
                      HttpServletResponse response)
  throws IOException {
    String servletName = this.getServletName();
    response.setContentType("text/html");
    PrintWriter out = response.getWriter();
    out.println("<html>");
    out.println("<head><title>" + servletName +
               "</title></head>");
    out.println("<body>");
    out.println("<p>Welcome to the servlet called " +
             servletName + ".</p>");
    out.println("</body></html>");
  }
}
```

Code elements that appear in the running text, such as the names of objects, classes, variables, methods, and so on, are also shown in the code font — for example, the `MyServlet` class or the `service()` method — as are file and folder names and Web URLs.

Command-line Entries

Any time a command-line entry appears in the book, it will reside on its own line and in the code style to distinguish it from the rest of the text. Command-line entries are "generic;" they don't appear in a certain format such as DOS or Unix. This is because most of the entries will work on either platform, as long as you follow the conventions for the platform you are using.

Icons

A number of special icons appear throughout the book to call your attention to topics of special relevance and interest.

The Note icon is used to bring your attention to things you might otherwise be tempted to highlight with a fluorescent marker.

The Tip icon is used to point out a tip or technique that will save you time, effort, money, or all three!

The Caution icon is used to alert you to potential problems that might wreak havoc in your WebLogic environment. Throughout the text, this icon pinpoints bugs, errors, oversights, gaffes, and anything else that may spoil your WebLogic experience.

The Cross-Reference icon refers you to other sections and chapters in the book, as well as to the book's Web site (`www.hungryminds.com/extras`), and other Web sites that contain additional coverage of the topic being discussed. Often these sites are provided to give you information that can't be squeezed into this book, such as articles, API documentation, source code, or other resources that we hope you'll find valuable in your quest to become a WebLogic expert.

Contacting the Author

I welcome your questions, comments, and constructive criticism regarding the book. You can make submissions at `http://weblogicbible.zeeware.com/feedback`. Please do not submit questions about WebLogic Server or code you're trying to debug — this forum is strictly for the book.

Acknowledgments

I'd like to thank a few people who made it possible for me to realize my career-long dream of writing a technical book. At the top of the list is Michael Rich, who kept my company's developers busy enough to feed me during this project, and without whom ZeeWare might not exist. I owe a similar debt of gratitude to a pair of Michael's lieutenants, Steve Dunn and Carter Smyth, who trusted our brand new company with some important projects, and who were very supportive of our efforts to get this book done.

I would also like to thank my business partner, Gary Wells, who worked double-time to keep our customers satisfied while I worked full-time on the book. Oh, and did I mention he contributed nearly 200 pages to the book as well? I am eternally grateful for his superhuman effort over the past seven months.

Thanks to the ZeeWare developers who contributed to this book: Brian Gill, Geoff Schneider, and Barrett Tucker. They not only wrote chapters, but they provided technical feedback on other peoples' chapters as well. Their hard work and dedication during this project has made Gary and me proud to have them on our team. Thanks also to the Cysive developers who contributed to the book: Rich Helton, Michael Madrid, and Sunil Makhijani.

During the course of this project I received assistance from several people within BEA, but two people in particular stand out: Eric Stahl, who helped me navigate the BEA org chart when I needed help, and Michael "smitty" Smith, who took time to review some of the chapters and answer technical questions along the way. Thanks, guys.

A big thanks to my editors, Grace Buechlein and Chandani Thapa, both of whom did a stellar job shepherding this first-time author through the process of writing and editing a very thick book. I am especially grateful to Grace, who "discovered" me and provided me with a tremendous amount of guidance and moral support during the course of this project.

Finally, I'd like to thank my brand-new wife, Roya, who stuck it out with me through a tough project that robbed her of most of my time and attention. Now we can go on our honeymoon!

Joe Zuffoletto

Sausalito, CA

Contents at a Glance

Contents

Part III: Developing Web Components 311

Part VI: Implementing Security 647

Preparing Your Enterprise for WebLogic

PART I

✦ ✦ ✦ ✦

In This Part

✦ ✦ ✦ ✦

A Quick Tour of WebLogic Server

✦ ✦ ✦ ✦

In This Chapter

Introducing WebLogic Server

Taking WebLogic for a spin

Spotting WebLogic in the real world

Surveying WebLogic's features, services, and architecture

Understanding WebLogic's role in the enterprise

Is WebLogic right for your project?

✦ ✦ ✦ ✦

In this chapter, I take you on a quick tour of WebLogic Server (often referred to as "WebLogic"). I introduce you to WebLogic and fire it up to show you what it looks like. After showing how some of WebLogic's capabilities are used in real-world Web sites, I show you some of WebLogic's components in more detail and discuss how they fit into its overall architecture. The chapter closes with a few questions that you can ask yourself to determine whether WebLogic is right for *your* projects.

Introducing WebLogic Server

WebLogic Server is an industrial-strength application server developed and marketed by BEA Systems, Inc. of San Jose, California. WebLogic is a pure-Java implementation of the *Java 2 Platform, Enterprise Edition*, more commonly known as *J2EE*. J2EE represents Sun's serious effort to make Java a powerful platform for developing enterprise applications. It defines a set of runtime architectures, network services, and application programming interfaces (APIs) that make it easy for developers to write distributed, network-aware software components and applications. WebLogic has long been recognized as one of the best (if not *the* best) J2EE implementations on the market.

Although this book is not intended to be a tutorial on J2EE, WebLogic and J2EE are so tightly bound that you will inevitably learn a great deal about J2EE from this book. For the most part, however, I will assume that you are already familiar with J2EE.

The current shipping version of WebLogic Server is 6.1. Version 6.1 has a lot in common with its immediate predecessors, especially versions 5.1 and 6.0, but there are also significant differences. Therefore, instead of trying to cover multiple versions of WebLogic Server, this book focuses on version 6.1.

Like a database or mail server, WebLogic runs almost invisibly on a computer and provides services to clients that connect to it. The most common use of WebLogic is to deliver secure, data-driven applications to Web clients over corporate intranets or the Internet. But WebLogic can also be used as a general-purpose application server for non-Web clients such as wireless devices and desktop applications. Basically, if you can design it with J2EE, you can build it and run it with WebLogic.

The WebLogic Server family consists of three products:

- WebLogic Server — the focus of this book
- WebLogic Server Enterprise — WebLogic Server plus the BEA Tuxedo transaction engine
- WebLogic Express — WebLogic Server without EJBs, RMI, and CORBA, used for building Web applications only

BEA's WebLogic product line contains several products that run on top of WebLogic Server. Although these products are beyond the scope of this book, you may want to explore them further on your own:

- WebLogic Portal — for managing access to Web-based information by customers, employees, and partners
- WebLogic Personalization Server — for managing customization of Web content delivery based on individual user preferences
- WebLogic Integration — for managing business process, application integration using JCA, and B2B integration
- WebLogic Java Adapter for Mainframe — for bringing mainframe applications and data into the Java fold

These products provide many common capabilities you may not want to write yourself. You can find more information about them at `http://www.bea.com/products/index.shtml`.

The WebLogic product line runs on all of today's popular enterprise computing platforms, including Windows NT/2000, Sun Solaris, HP/UX, IBM AS/400, and Linux. Because WebLogic is a pure Java product, it is installed, configured, and managed almost identically on all platforms.

Companies around the world use WebLogic Server to build large-scale, industrial-strength Web applications for both internal and external use. They choose WebLogic because of its performance, reliability, cross-platform capability, versatility, and strong support for the J2EE standard. With WebLogic Server you can

- Host Web sites for one or more Internet domains on one computer with one IP address, or on multiple computers bundled together in a cluster, or on multiple computers managed by a proxy server

- Deploy server-side Java code written to the J2EE standard, including servlets, JavaServer Pages (JSPs), JavaBeans, and Enterprise JavaBeans (EJBs)
- Integrate disparate computing systems using J2EE's extensive network services, including JDBC for database connectivity, JMS for messaging, JNDI for network directory access, JTA for distributed transactions, and JavaMail for electronic mail
- Deploy Java-only distributed applications by using Remote Method Invocation (RMI)
- Deploy CORBA-accessible distributed applications by using RMI over Internet Inter-ORB Protocol (RMI-IIOP)
- Implement robust security by using Secure Sockets Layer (SSL) and WebLogic's built-in support for user authentication and authorization
- Provide high availability, load balancing, and failover by combining multiple WebLogic servers into a cluster
- Take advantage of Java's cross-platform capabilities by deploying WebLogic servers on Windows NT/2000, Sun Solaris, HP/UX, and other operating systems supported by WebLogic
- Easily manage one or more WebLogic servers on your network, regardless of platform, by using WebLogic's intuitive, Web-based management and monitoring tools

Now that you have some idea of what WebLogic is, let's take it for a spin on a Windows 2000 machine and see what it looks like.

Taking WebLogic for a Spin

WebLogic Server runs either as an application or service on Windows 2000. In this section, you're going to start WebLogic as an application and have a look under the hood by using the WebLogic Administration Console.

I discuss the various options for starting WebLogic Server in Chapter 4.

To start WebLogic on Windows 2000, select Start Default Server from the WebLogic program group. Enter the server's password (defined during the installation process) and the server will start. Figure 1-1 shows the console output from starting WebLogic Server.

```
Start Default Server
*************************************************
*  To start WebLogic Server, use the password    *
*  assigned to the system user.  The system      *
*  username and password must also be used to    *
*  access the WebLogic Server console from a web *
*  browser.                                      *
*************************************************

D:\bea\wlserver6.1>"D:\bea\jdk131\bin\java" -hotspot -ms64m -mx64m -classpath .;
.\lib\weblogic_sp.jar;.\lib\weblogic.jar -Dweblogic.Domain=dev -Dweblogic.Name=a
dmin "-Dbea.home=D:\bea" -Dweblogic.management.password= -Dweblogic.ProductionMo
deEnabled=true "-Djava.security.policy==D:\bea\wlserver6.1/lib/weblogic.policy"
weblogic.Server
<Aug 23, 2001 5:05:14 PM PDT> <Info> <Security> <Getting boot password from user
.>
Enter password to boot WebLogic server:
Starting WebLogic Server ....
<Aug 23, 2001 5:06:24 PM PDT> <Notice> <Management> <Loading configuration file
.\config\dev\config.xml ...>
<Aug 23, 2001 5:06:27 PM PDT> <Notice> <WebLogicServer> <Starting WebLogic Admin
 Server "admin" for domain "dev">
<Aug 23, 2001 5:06:30 PM PDT> <Notice> <Management> <Starting discovery of Manag
ed Server... This feature is on by default, you may turn this off by passing -Dw
eblogic.management.discover=false>
<Aug 23, 2001 5:06:37 PM PDT> <Notice> <Management> <Application Poller not star
ted for production server.>
<Aug 23, 2001 5:06:37 PM PDT> <Notice> <WebLogicServer> <ListenThread listening
on port 7001>
<Aug 23, 2001 5:06:37 PM PDT> <Notice> <WebLogicServer> <SSLListenThread listeni
ng on port 7002>
<Aug 23, 2001 5:06:38 PM PDT> <Notice> <WebLogicServer> <Started WebLogic Admin
Server "admin" for domain "dev" running in Production Mode>
```

Figure 1-1: WebLogic Server 6.1 started and ready for connections

Once you start the server, you must either leave this window open or minimize it. Closing it shuts down the server!

The simple output in the command line window belies the complexity of the engine running beneath. You can gain a better appreciation by looking at the server through the lens of the Administration Console. From the WebLogic program group, select Start Default Console. After entering the username and password for your server, you'll see a Console display in your Web browser, similar to Figure 1-2.

Now it's beginning to look like you got your money's worth. On the left side of the screen is the *domain tree* showing the contents of the WebLogic domain (`mydomain`) to which this Console is pointed.

A WebLogic domain is a collection of one or more WebLogic servers logically bundled together for administrative purposes, and possibly for clustering as well. Every WebLogic server belongs to one and only one domain. `mydomain` and `myserver` are default names set by WebLogic's installer. You can change your domain and server names to anything you want when you install your own servers.

On the right side of the screen is the *entity table* for the last item you clicked in the domain tree. You just started the Console and haven't clicked any items, so the entity table displayed is actually the Console home page, which is just a task-and service-oriented view of the domain tree.

You'll see a lot more of the Administration Console as you work through this book. For now, let's take a quick look at the status of the server started earlier. In the domain tree, expand the Servers node; then click `myserver`.

The entity table for `myserver` is shown in Figure 1-3. It shows basic information about your server, including its name, machine, the TCP/IP port it's listening on, and so on.

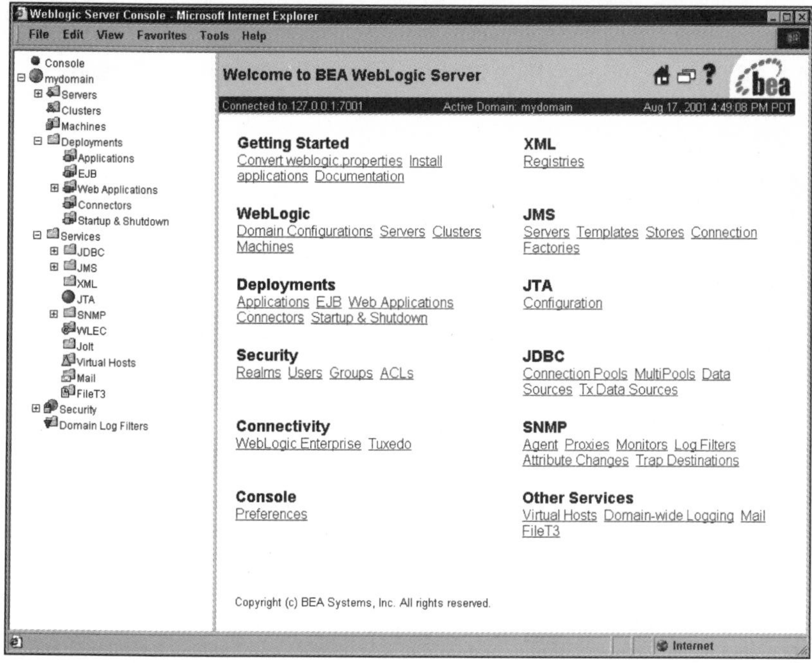

Figure 1-2: WebLogic Server Administration Console start screen

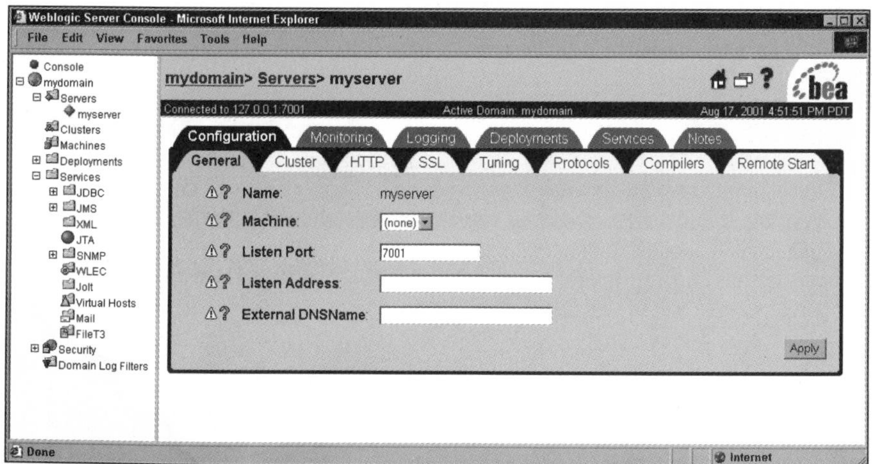

Figure 1-3: The Administration Console's view of your WebLogic Server

This is only one of several sections of data about the server. Notice the dark tabs across the top for Configuration, Monitoring, Logging, and so on. Clicking one of these takes us to a different section of the entity table. Below these are subsections of the selected section. You're now looking at the General subsection of the Configuration section.

To get information about WebLogic Console itself, click Console at the top of the domain tree. The Preferences tab, shown in Figure 1-4, allows you to change the Console's defaults, including which language you want for on-screen displays, refresh intervals, and so on.

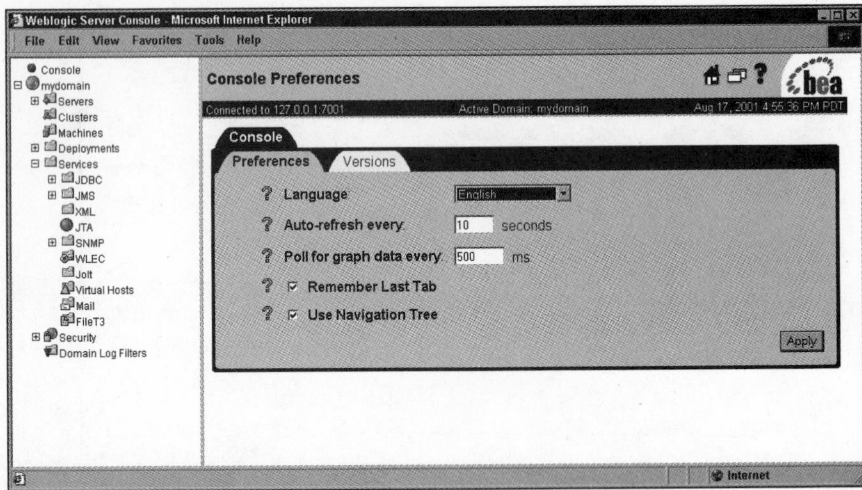

Figure 1-4: The Preferences tab of the Console Preferences page

The Console's Versions tab, shown in Figure 1-5, displays the product versions of the Console and the WebLogic Server to which it is pinned.

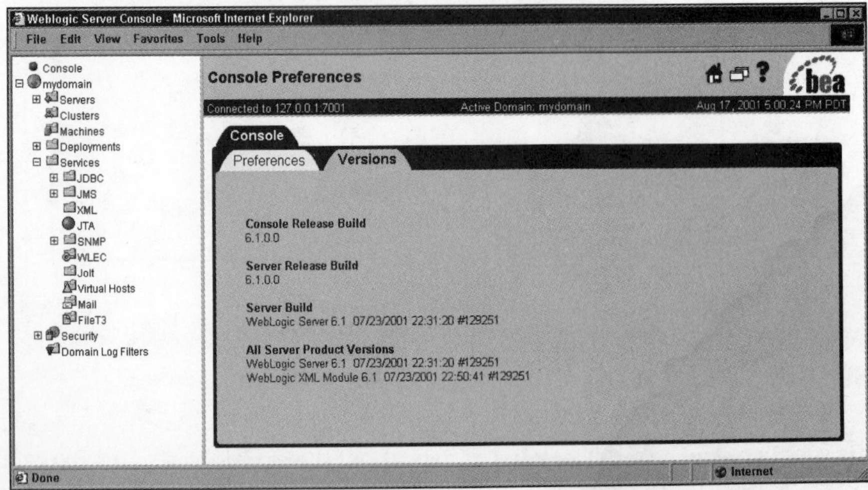

Figure 1-5: The Versions tab of the Console Preferences page

As you can see, the WebLogic Administration Console is an excellent tool for visualizing the innards of your server and understanding how it works. It is also an essential tool for managing your server and keeping it healthy. I explore these topics in greater depth throughout this book.

Spotting WebLogic in the Real World

As I mentioned before, companies around the world use WebLogic Server to build large-scale, industrial-strength Web applications. BEA maintains a partial customer list at `http://www.bea.com/customers/index.shtml`; surfing the Web sites of these companies may give you some idea of how they are putting WebLogic Server to work.

Not surprisingly, BEA itself uses WebLogic Server to drive a number of applications appearing on its corporate Web site at `http://www.bea.com`. In the Education area, for example, you can browse a course catalog provided by BEA Education Services, and then enroll in the WebLogic courses of your choice. Figure 1-6 shows a calendar of upcoming classes, which is generated on the fly from a database. The database stores course dates, locations, prices, and seating availability. If the database indicates that a course is full, the calendar shows "full" in the Availability column, and you cannot enroll in the class. Otherwise, the calendar provides a link to enroll. The developers of this site have even implemented additional business logic that shows when a course has limited seating. Apparently, when the number of empty seats in a course falls below a certain threshold, the "Enroll" link changes to "Limited Seating." This is a great way to motivate procrastinators to enroll before their course fills up!

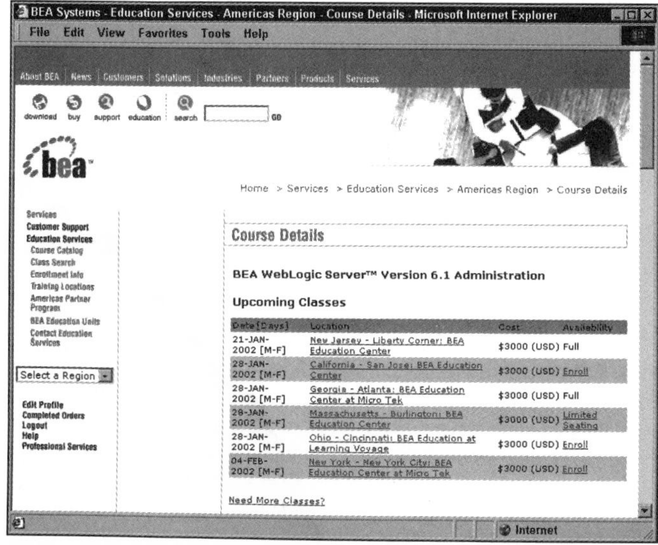

Figure 1-6: WebLogic drives BEA's online course catalog.

Clicking Enroll for a course takes you through a user registration process, which is also database driven. After you have registered, you can enroll in the course. Figure 1-7 shows the enrollment page. This is an input form where you enter your personal contact information to enroll in the given course. When you click the Submit Info button, BEA adds you to the course roster and reduces by one the number of empty seats remaining in the course.

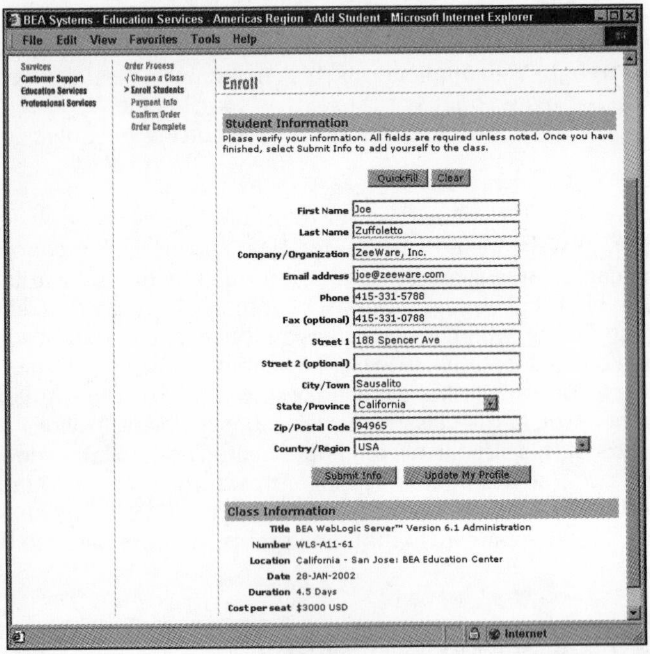

Figure 1-7: Enrolling in a WebLogic class

Notice that you can also use this form to update your personal profile in BEA's database, by clicking the `Update My Profile` button. BEA uses this profile to save you the trouble of re-typing your personal information when using the other applications on their Web site. This is a user-friendly approach you may want to use in your own WebLogic applications.

Sparks.com

One of BEA's customers, Sparks.com (`http://www.sparks.com`), uses WebLogic to drive their online store for paper-based greeting cards, as shown in Figure 1-8. You can search, select, and purchase from a dizzying array of cards on this site. Sparks.com, being a high-volume e-commerce site (especially during the holidays), offers compelling proof that WebLogic applications can scale to support thousands of simultaneous users. The site uses WebLogic clustering to ensure high availability and performance, even under heavy user loads.

Figure 1-8: WebLogic driving a high-volume e-commerce site

Surveying WebLogic's Features, Services, and Architecture

Now that we know the things WebLogic can do, let's examine the components of its architecture to gain a clearer understanding of how it does them.

HTTP server

If you think of WebLogic Server as a big house where your Web applications live, its HTTP server is the front door. All requests made to your applications from Web browsers must pass through it.

WebLogic's integrated HTTP server allows you to host Web sites that contain HTML/XML pages only or HTML/XML pages plus JSPs and servlets. For applications requiring secure connections, WebLogic supports the HTTP-Secure (HTTPS) protocol, which requires you to purchase a certificate for your server from a certifying authority. If your environment requires you to deploy WebLogic behind Apache, Microsoft, or Netscape Web servers, you can do so using WebLogic's proxy plug-ins for those servers.

WebLogic 6.1 supports *virtual hosting,* which allows you to map multiple Web sites to a single WebLogic server. For sites upgrading from earlier WebLogic versions, this may eliminate the need to proxy requests to WebLogic servers from other Web servers, if the only reason for doing so is to support virtual hosting.

J2EE containers

WebLogic Server implements a Web container and an EJB container, which are the two server-side containers mandated by the J2EE standard. These containers give your applications a runtime environment and access to the J2EE APIs. The containers are an integral part of WebLogic Server and are available for use once the server is started.

Web container

WebLogic's Web container hosts servlets and JSPs. These application components are used to service requests originating from Web browsers.

The first time JSPs are invoked, they are automatically compiled into servlets, and the servlet executes instead of the JSP itself. WebLogic manages this process invisibly and automatically as required by the J2EE specification.

EJB container

As you might expect, WebLogic's EJB container hosts EJBs, including session beans, entity beans, and message beans. These application components are used to implement business logic, data access, and asynchronous messaging. They service requests from non-Web clients, such as client applications written in Java, or from Java code living in a servlet or JSP. They generally cannot be accessed directly from Web browsers, unless there is an applet embedded in the page.

The default download for WebLogic Server 6.1 includes J2EE 1.3 and supports the EJB 2.0 and 1.1 specifications. You can also download a version that includes J2EE 1.2, and supports EJB 1.1 only.

Gateway to the J2EE APIs

WebLogic Server provides your Java applications with runtime access to the J2EE APIs, which are JDBC, JMS, JNDI, JTA, RMI, and JavaMail. As mentioned earlier, WebLogic Server includes J2EE 1.3.

Figure 1-9 shows the relationships among WebLogic's HTTP server, J2EE containers, the J2EE APIs, and external systems.

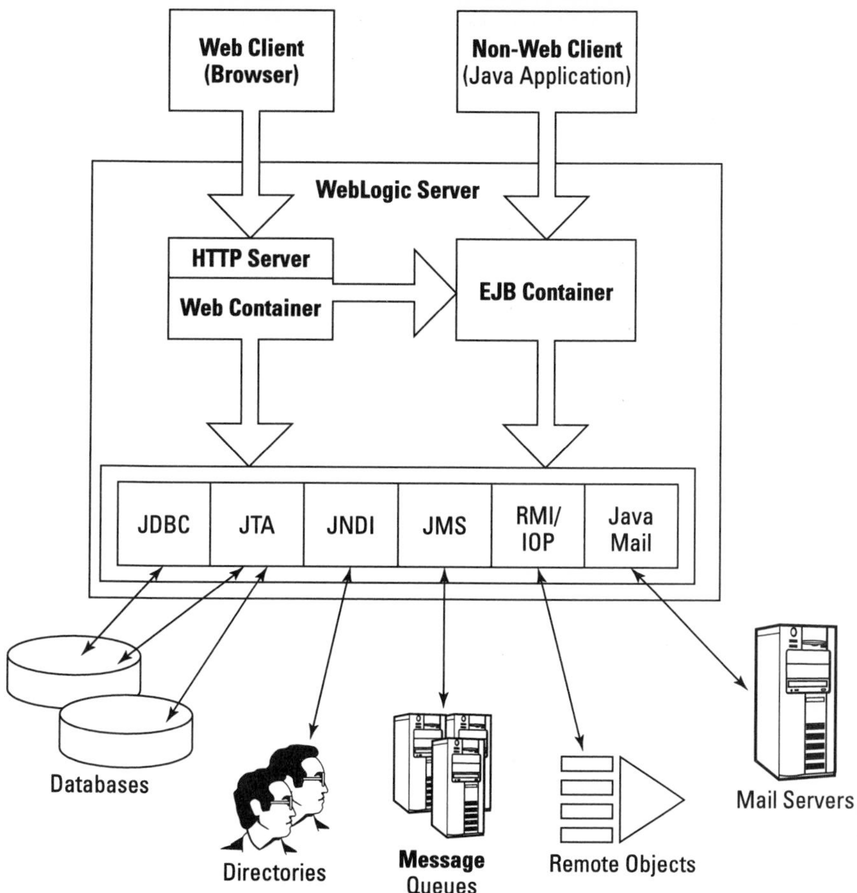

Figure 1-9: WebLogic's J2EE architecture and its relationship to external systems

Web Services

Starting with version 6.1, WebLogic Server supports emerging standards for implementing and deploying *Web Services*. Web Services is an exciting new technology that allows the construction and deployment of self-describing, modular, and reusable application components that can be made available to any other application running on a corporate intranet or the global Internet. WebLogic Server supports Web Services Description Language (WSDL) version 1.1 and Simple Object Access Protocol (SOAP) version 1.1, which are the enabling technologies behind Web Services.

WebLogic's support for Web Services, WSDL, and SOAP is covered in Chapter 26.

J2EE Connector Architecture

Also starting with version 6.1, WebLogic Server supports the J2EE Connector Architecture version 1.0, which defines a portable, open standard for integrating with back-end systems such as Enterprise Resource Planning (ERP) systems, Customer Relationship Management (CRM) systems, and other enterprise-class software and database systems.

WebLogic's support for the J2EE Connector Architecture is covered in Chapter 27.

CORBA support

Many large corporations use CORBA (Common Object Request Broker Architecture) to implement distributed applications on their corporate networks. CORBA provides a means by which software objects can find and call each other remotely over a network. The communication protocol used for this process is IIOP, or Internet Inter-ORB Protocol, which sits on top of TCP/IP.

CORBA is a separate standard that predates J2EE and was indeed the inspiration for RMI, J2EE's remote object protocol. But unlike RMI, CORBA provides support for objects written in many languages, not just Java.

WebLogic Server includes CORBA support in the form of RMI over IIOP. RMI uses a communication protocol that is incompatible with CORBA; RMI/IIOP converts the RMI protocol into IIOP, and vice-versa, so RMI objects can coexist with CORBA objects on a network.

Security services

WebLogic provides a platform for three levels of application security: encryption, user authentication, and user authorization.

Encryption

Data transmitted to and from WebLogic Server can be encrypted by using Secure Sockets Layer (SSL). SSL is implemented for Web applications via HTTP-Secure (HTTPS), and is used in native form over RMI connections.

To use SSL, you must purchase a certificate for your server from a certificate vendor such as VeriSign. When clients request secure connections, the server sends the certificate to the client for validation. Once validated, the client and server exchange encrypted keys and establish the secure connection. WebLogic Server also supports mutual authentication, where the client and server both exchange certificates before establishing a secure connection.

User authentication and authorization

User authentication is the process of ensuring that a user has the proper credentials to gain access to an application. *User authorization* is the process of mapping authenticated users to individual application services, usually at the group level. Sales managers, for example, have access to commission reports in a CRM application, whereas sales representatives do not.

Applications usually authenticate users by prompting them for a login name and password, and then validating these against a database. After the user is authenticated, authorization is performed by matching the user's group membership against a list of resources available to that group. This list is called an Access Control List (ACL).

WebLogic calls authentication/authorization databases *realms* and provides support for five different types. The default realm is the File realm, which is simply a disk file of users, groups, encrypted passwords, and ACL's. The contents of the file are managed by using WebLogic's Administration Console. The other four realms WebLogic supports are

- Lightweight Directory Access Protocol (LDAP), such as Microsoft Active Directory or Netscape Directory Server
- Windows NT/2000 domains
- Unix login service
- Relational databases

If none of these suit your needs, you can create a custom realm by writing Java classes that implement WebLogic's realm interfaces. Any features you don't implement will default to the File realm; you can, for example, write your own realm to handle authentication and let WebLogic handle authorization.

Clustering services

Clustering is the process of combining two or more WebLogic servers on a network into one logical entity for the purpose of increasing an application's *scalability* and *availability*. Scalability is increased because the more CPUs and memory you add to a system, the more users you can support. Availability is increased because if one server crashes, you have other servers available in the cluster to absorb the load.

WebLogic's clustering services are quite flexible and provide many benefits, including the following:

- ✦ Any number of servers can participate, so your site's scalability and availability are limited only by your hardware budget.
- ✦ Clustering is totally transparent to developers and users because the cluster looks like a single WebLogic server on the network.
- ✦ New servers can be added to a cluster dynamically without having to bring the site down.
- ✦ Allocation of resources in the cluster can be controlled by DNS and/or proxy servers, giving administrators tremendous flexibility for handling load balancing and failover.

Clustering is one of WebLogic's best features and a major reason for its popularity in large enterprises.

Management and monitoring tools

You can manage and monitor the servers in your WebLogic installation remotely, using tools supplied by BEA and third-party vendors. Third-party tools allow you to manage WebLogic Server in the context of your entire network installation, leveraging WebLogic's SNMP support to do so.

Tools provided by BEA

As you saw earlier in this chapter, WebLogic Server includes command line and browser-based tools for managing and monitoring the WebLogic servers on your network. These tools make it easy for administrators to configure servers and clusters, delegate services across servers and clusters, configure security, deploy applications, and troubleshoot problems when they occur.

WebLogic servers, whether running independently or as part of a cluster, are grouped into logical units called *domains*. In a domain containing multiple servers, one server is the administration server, and the others are managed servers. WebLogic's command line and browser-based administration tools execute against the administration server, which propagates configuration settings to the managed servers. You decide which servers are which when you construct the domain.

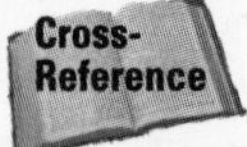

Chapter 4 explains how to construct domains containing administration and managed servers.

WebLogic's browser-based administration tool is called the *Administration Console*. It provides an Explorer-like graphical interface to the WebLogic services available in its domain. As such, it's a great tool for beginners to get a clear mental picture of how a WebLogic installation works, especially if multiple servers are involved. Figures 1-3 and 1-4 show examples of Administration Console screens.

SNMP support

Starting with version 6.1, WebLogic Server can communicate with management systems by using the *Simple Network Management Protocol,* or *SNMP.* This gives network administrators the ability to manage WebLogic installations within the framework of their overall hardware and software infrastructure.

Understanding WebLogic's Role in the Enterprise

WebLogic's long list of features and capabilities make it a powerful and versatile weapon in any company's computing arsenal. Unlike mail and database servers, which fill well-defined and narrow roles in an enterprise's computing infrastructure, WebLogic Server can be made to solve an endless variety of computing problems. Here is a partial list of what you can do with WebLogic:

- Provide a robust, secure, and scalable platform for building intelligent, dynamic Web sites.
- Build enterprise applications that allow Web and non-Web (including wireless) clients to access the same business logic and data stores, reducing development costs.
- Build e-commerce systems that manage customers, product catalogs, orders, payments, order fulfillment, customer service, and electronic marketing via Web or e-mail.
- Give programmers and users secure, friendly access to data locked away in legacy systems.
- Seamlessly display and manipulate data drawn from multiple back-end sources.
- Manage the real-time or batch movement of information from one data store to another, regardless of the types of the data stores or the platforms they run on.
- Build Web interfaces to non-Web applications, such as client/server or mainframe applications.

An investment in WebLogic Server can pay dividends throughout your enterprise in ways you may not yet have imagined. If your business demands big, reliable systems, or if you need to integrate disparate computing systems on multiple platforms, you're likely to see a quick return on your WebLogic investment.

Is WebLogic Right for Your Project?

To determine whether WebLogic and the J2EE platform are a good fit for your project, ask yourself the following questions:

1. Do I need fast, reliable access to my corporate databases from the Web? Are JDBC drivers available for these databases?
2. Do I need to build dynamic, data-driven Web applications for large user populations that expect 24×7 availability?
3. Do I need to automate e-mail or wireless communications with my partners, vendors, employees, or customers?
4. Do I need to implement complex business logic and make it available to all my developers, so they don't have to constantly reinvent the wheel?
5. Do I need to implement message-driven workflows that are tightly bound to database operations?
6. Do I need to provide robust user authentication and authorization for Web resources and other services?
7. Do I need to write applications (Web-based or otherwise) that seamlessly integrate data from disparate sources on multiple platforms?
8. Do I need to execute distributed transactions across multiple data stores?

If you answered "yes" to any of the preceding questions, and if your developers understand object-oriented technology and Java, then WebLogic is probably a good fit for your project.

Summary

WebLogic Server is an industrial-strength implementation of the J2EE platform suitable for developing high-volume, dynamic Web sites and enterprise applications. It gives developers unmatched flexibility in how they design, implement, and deploy these systems on their corporate networks.

WebLogic provides exhaustive support for all aspects of the J2EE standard, making it easy to build Web and enterprise applications that connect to databases, mail systems, messaging systems, CORBA-based systems, and legacy systems on a variety of platforms. Extensive security features are built into WebLogic so you can tightly control access to applications, Web sites, and resources contained within them.

You can cluster WebLogic Server if you need to deploy highly scalable and reliable applications. WebLogic clusters, like the rest of WebLogic, can be easily managed by using command line tools or the browser-based Administration Console application.

Companies around the world use WebLogic to solve a surprising array of difficult computing problems. WebLogic and the J2EE platform make it remarkably easy to build applications that seamlessly integrate data and computing resources from all corners of your organization.

✦ ✦ ✦

CHAPTER 2

Assembling and Managing a WebLogic Development Team

✦ ✦ ✦ ✦

In This Chapter

What WebLogic developers need to know

Project team roles and responsibilities

Project management strategies

✦ ✦ ✦ ✦

For most enterprise developers, the glory days of writing monolithic applications for one operating system and hardware platform are over. Web applications have muscled their way into the enterprise, bringing with them a long list of development and deployment advantages (and an equally long list of challenges). WebLogic Server is a powerful tool for Web application development, but WebLogic developers are not immune to the challenges that all Web developers face. This chapter explores the demands WebLogic places on developers, and then identifies the roles and responsibilities that must be filled by an effective WebLogic development team. It closes by offering some project management strategies you may find useful as you launch your WebLogic projects.

What WebLogic Developers Need to Know

"We are so outnumbered there's only one thing to do. We must attack."

—Sir Andrew Browne Cunningham

Becoming a knowledgeable, well-rounded WebLogic developer is a formidable task because WebLogic, like enterprise Web programming itself, covers a lot of technological ground. Being a good WebLogic developer requires a solid understanding of the J2EE platform, *plus* an understanding of the enhancements and nuances WebLogic brings to J2EE, *plus* an understanding of the systems within your enterprise to which WebLogic will connect. This is a lot of stuff to know!

WebLogic Server's more than 40 manuals contain over 3000 pages of information, most of which assumes some level of knowledge about such diverse topics as networking, databases, e-mail systems, wireless systems, distributed transactions, security, clustering, object-oriented programming, and Java. Sun's library for J2EE occupies a comparable number of pages on its Web site. This is a lot of information for the time-strapped enterprise developer to absorb.

Of course, enterprise developers seldom work alone these days, precisely because there is too much out there for anyone to know, and too little time to learn it. Assuming, then, that WebLogic development is a team effort, what do the members of a WebLogic team need to know?

Object-oriented programming in Java

First and foremost, developing WebLogic applications requires a solid understanding of object-oriented programming in Java. J2EE is written in Java, all J2EE applications are written in Java, and WebLogic itself is written in Java. Therefore, you must know Java.

This book assumes that you have a solid understanding of Java and know how to use its many features. Nevertheless, I'd like to emphasize that mastery of the following Java language features and concepts will save you a lot of time and frustration while working with WebLogic and J2EE:

- Packages
- Interfaces
- Serializable objects
- Classloaders and classpaths
- `.jar` files, `.war` files, `.ear` files, and J2EE application deployment concepts

This book does not contain a tutorial on Java, but J2EE application deployment concepts are covered in Chapter 18.

This book will help you learn more about these topics as they apply to WebLogic and J2EE programming.

J2EE

Once you know Java, you need to understand J2EE. J2EE is a component-based architecture, and you create J2EE applications by building and assembling J2EE components. Therefore, the more you understand the components and their intended use, the better your applications will be.

Understanding J2EE also makes clear the division of labor between J2EE, WebLogic, and your developers. If, for example, your WebLogic developers are writing complex code to handle user session tracking or database transactions, they may not realize that WebLogic and J2EE provide these features for them. Be sure that every member of your team has at least a basic understanding of J2EE before starting your project. You'll save time and build better applications.

Chapter 3 provides an in-depth discussion of J2EE, component software development, and the relationship of these items to WebLogic development.

Object-Oriented Analysis and Design

To design a robust J2EE application that makes effective use of Java and J2EE, your team needs to know Object-Oriented Analysis and Design (OOAD). OOAD is the art of translating complex business requirements into elegant software designs based on reusable objects.

Applying good OOAD techniques to J2EE systems is quite challenging when compared to client/server or desktop systems. When designing client/server and desktop systems, first you model your business logic, and then your data, and then your user interactions; then you're done. But with J2EE, you must also map your design to J2EE's component architecture, deciding what pieces should be implemented as servlets, entity beans, session beans, and so on. Good OOAD for J2EE must also take into account the class frameworks provided by Java and J2EE, so you don't reinvent the wheel with your designs. This is hard work, but a good design more than pays for itself when it comes time to build, maintain, and extend your applications.

Most practitioners of OOAD express their designs using the *Unified Modeling Language,* or *UML.* UML provides a rich visual vocabulary for diagramming complex systems, and it allows you to model them from multiple points of view. Most important, it provides a convenient way to share the design with everyone on the team so it can be understood, improved, and implemented. You can learn more about UML by visiting Rational Software Corporation's UML Resource Center at `www.rational.com/uml/index.jsp`.

Most UML tools on the market today, such as Embarcadero Technologies' Describe, Rational Software's Rational Rose, and TogetherSoft's TogetherJ, provide built-in support for Java and J2EE projects.

Chapter 3 discusses some useful ways to incorporate UML into your WebLogic application designs.

HTML and JavaScript

No matter how much magic you perform on the server side with your JSPs, servlets, beans, and EJBs, you'll probably be pumping out HTML and JavaScript to the Web browser. Most successful Web sites are rendered with little more (with good reason). HTML and JavaScript are the most compatible and widely supported browser languages on the planet, and a good HTML/JavaScript programmer can build some nice front ends if your users are using Netscape/IE 4.0 or higher.

HTML, of course, renders all your static and dynamic data, including text, tables, graphics, hyperlinks, and so on. JavaScript is useful for performing client-side validation of data entry, and also for accomplishing certain GUI tricks. Just be certain that your users' browsers support the versions of HTML and JavaScript you use.

XML

XML is widely used in WebLogic 6.1 for creating properties files, configuration files, and deployment descriptors. WebLogic provides samples and templates for these types of files, so you don't need to be much of an XML expert to create and maintain them.

But XML is being used increasingly for data interchange, especially in domains such as financial services and applied science, because of its extensibility and ability to represent self-describing data. For these more sophisticated applications of XML, your team will need at least one XML expert who also understands Document Type Definitions (DTDs), the Simple API for XML (SAX), and Document Object Models (DOMs).

HTML experts are good candidates for learning XML, given that XML and HTML share syntactical attributes. But database experts should also be involved in the design of custom tags for data interchange.

TCP/IP networking and distributed systems

WebLogic and J2EE applications are almost always distributed systems (they're implemented on multiple computers that communicate with each other over a TCP/IP network). Therefore, having some knowledge of TCP/IP networking and distributed systems on your team is a big plus, if not a requirement.

Helpful TCP/IP knowledge includes

- ✦ TCP/IP addresses, sockets, and ports
- ✦ IP multicasts (used by WebLogic clusters)
- ✦ DNS (used for name resolution and load balancing)

Helpful distributed systems knowledge includes

- ✦ An understanding of clients, servers, and peer-to-peer systems
- ✦ Distributed database transactions and two-phase commit
- ✦ Messaging, e-mail, and wireless protocols
- ✦ Remote method invocation (RMI—used by Java clients and EJBs)
- ✦ CORBA (if you plan to use it)
- ✦ Programming with stubs, skeletons, and Interface Definition Languages (IDLs)—structures used in RMI and CORBA

Relational databases and SQL

Almost all Web applications connect with relational databases. The most popular flavors these days (in alphabetical order) seem to be Microsoft SQL Server, MySQL, and Oracle. Some shops also use the CloudScape object-relational database, a demo version of which ships with WebLogic Server.

Data is selected, inserted, updated, and deleted in a relational database by issuing commands in *Structured Query Language,* or *SQL*. Java's two SQL packages (`java.sql` and `javax.sql`) provide excellent wrappers for performing common database functions with SQL in a vendor-neutral way.

I'd like to emphasize that if an SQL-compliant database is a big part of your Web application's design, then your project's ultimate success will hinge on your team's understanding of that database and SQL. Badly designed and programmed databases are the leading cause of poor performance in Web applications.

If you want to avoid database-related performance problems, make sure that your team includes, or has access to, gurus in your database platform of choice. These people should understand all the intricacies of SQL, your database's query optimizer, indexes, table partitions, caching, and all the other features that make databases sing. Otherwise, you'll be crying the blues later.

Legacy systems

If your WebLogic application will connect with legacy systems, such as a mainframe or a dBase III database running on a noisy old PC/AT, then you'll need some creative people to help you wire them together.

Virtually all access to legacy systems is driven by the need to get to data residing on those systems. Therefore, those who are charged with doing this should know multiple methods of data access for the system at hand and have the ability to devise creative workarounds when things aren't going well.

I recently saw a good example of such creativity at a client site. A WebLogic developer was building an application to process data residing on an AS/400. His WebLogic instance was running under Solaris, and he was using JDBC to move data from DB2 on an AS/400 to Oracle on a Sun machine for processing. But he ran into trouble because of the huge data volumes involved—the millions of rows he was moving were choking the network and his application. After some thought, he realized that he could install a WebLogic instance on the AS/400, do the processing there, and ship only the few thousand rows of results to the Sun machine. In doing so, he reduced the execution time of the job from over an hour to less than a minute. He also did a good job of exploiting the cross-platform capabilities of WebLogic and J2EE.

Collaborative discipline

If a group of people is to work together as a team, they must develop structured, predictable methods for capturing, storing, and sharing their accumulated knowledge and work products. Otherwise, chaos rules the day, valuable information is lost, and productivity goes into the tank. I call this orderly, cooperative behavior among team members *collaborative discipline* because establishing and enforcing consistent team development standards requires discipline, especially in the fast-paced world of Web development.

Collaborative discipline is especially important in WebLogic development because WebLogic applications consist of dozens of components assembled by multiple team members that must fit together like pieces of a jigsaw puzzle—or the application won't work.

Achieving the collaborative discipline required for WebLogic and J2EE development requires, at a minimum, three ingredients: effective content management, continuously updated "living" documentation, and open lines of communication among all team members.

Content management

Although you may try, you will eventually find that you cannot successfully execute a WebLogic project of appreciable size without an effective content management system.

Content management is important because

- ✦ It clearly defines where all the materials for a project are stored
- ✦ It prevents file modification conflicts among multiple users
- ✦ It allows the input of descriptive comments to help document the system
- ✦ It provides backups, revision histories, and version control

What is content? For WebLogic application, content usually includes

- Static Web documents, such as HTML files, XML files, and stylesheets
- Graphics files, such as JPGs, GIFs, and PNGs, and also their source files such as Adobe Illustrator AI files, or PhotoShop PSD files
- Java source code files for servlets, beans, EJBs, and helper classes
- JSP files
- XML descriptors for applications and components
- Relational database scripts written in SQL
- Downloadable files such as Adobe Acrobat PDF files and software installers
- Multimedia files

A content management system stores these elements into a repository, regulates access to them by multiple users, and provides some level of version control.

The type of content management system you choose depends on the size and scope of your project, and the types of users who will be creating and updating the content. If the project is a "pure programming" project, where software developers are creating a Web-based application with no day-to-day involvement by non-programmers, then a source code control system, such as Microsoft Visual SourceSafe or CVS, may adequately meet your content management needs. For larger projects involving developers *and* users, such as large corporate intranets or external Web sites, you may need a dedicated content management system, such as those marketed by Interwoven, Documentum, and others, to manage non-code resources such as brochures, photographs, illustrations, catalog copy, and so on.

Regardless of the product you use, features for check-in/check-out and version control are essential, as is the ability to deploy the content to multiple locations for development, testing, and production.

Living documentation

Web development is an iterative process, and although iterative development has been around since the beginning of programming, Web development raises it to a new level. There are two main reasons for this. First, because Web development requires the assembly of multiple, disparate, and often independent components, the traditional compile-edit-test-debug cycle doesn't apply to the development of a Web site as a whole. Instead, smaller changes are made to pieces of a site and tested independently of the rest. Second, Web sites by their very nature change on a daily, hourly, or even continuous basis. Web sites are indeed "living" systems, always changing and growing, and living systems require living documentation that always changes and grows with them.

Living documentation has three important characteristics:

- ✦ Software developers are the primary authors.
- ✦ It's easy for developers to create and update while they're programming.
- ✦ Changes and updates are easily propagated to the rest of the team.

During the development of Java, Sun was quick to recognize the importance of living documentation and added support for it in the form of JavaDoc. JavaDoc is a flexible documentation tool that addresses the three characteristics of living documentation. First, it recognizes that software developers are the primary authors by being implemented as a code-commenting tool for Java. Second, developers can easily create and update documentation while they're programming by inserting JavaDoc-readable comments directly into their source code. Third, JavaDoc makes it easy to propagate changes to the rest of the team by incorporating a tool that publishes JavaDoc comments to an internal Web site that organizes the documentation the way the code itself is organized. Developers can easily surf and search this Web site to find the information they need.

JavaDoc is a powerful tool for WebLogic developers because it allows them to follow a single documentation standard that easily captures their knowledge and makes it available to the rest of the team.

Information about JavaDoc is available at `http://java.sun.com/j2se/javadoc/index.html`. An excellent example of a JavaDoc-generated Web site is Sun's documentation site for J2EE, which can be found at `http://java.sun.com/j2ee/j2sdkee/techdocs/api/index.html`.

Open lines of communication

Multiple developers working together in a highly iterative fashion must be capable of naturally approaching each other without fear or hesitation to share information and discuss issues that arise during the life of a project. They should be equally comfortable approaching the non-developer members of their team (including management), and vice-versa. Communications may occur in person, via e-mail, or via telephone, and all team members must be conditioned to respond promptly, because time is always of the essence on Web projects.

Web development teams are not the place for those who are unwilling to share information or ask for help when needed. If you can't avoid including one or two of these characters on your team, you'll have to find a way to make them cooperative and approachable. Available methods for doing so are beyond the scope of this book!

Project Team Roles and Responsibilities

The members of a WebLogic development team will be called upon to wear many hats. Several different types of work must be done, sometimes by only a handful of people. Therefore, the best WebLogic teams are composed of experienced, resourceful people who possess the discipline to work well together, to do the job right, and to deliver complex systems that won't break under heavy loads.

Although details vary from project to project, the key roles described in the following sections need to be filled on almost every project.

Project manager

Every project needs a leader who can keep the team on track and assume responsibility for timely delivery of the project. A strong project manager is good at breaking enormous tasks into bite-sized pieces, delegating responsibility for the delivery of those pieces, assigning due dates, and enforcing the project schedule. This person must also be good at communicating with people outside the team, including outside technical resources, corporate management, and members of business units whose interests are at stake.

But there is more to good project management than Gantt charts, delegation, and deadlines. I often compare a good project manager to a good athletics coach. The best coaches know how to size up their teams and combine their players' talents for the best possible outcome. They know how to maximize each player's strengths while minimizing the weaknesses. They know how to keep the team focused and motivated, even in the face of adversity. And they know how to keep the team playing as a *team,* not as a collection of individuals pulling in separate directions. When a good coach pulls all of this together, the team usually wins — and the same goes for software project managers.

Application architect

A project has a much greater chance for success if it has a strong technical leader responsible for the overall architecture of the solution. A veteran with a history of architecting, developing, and implementing distributed systems is invaluable; if that person knows J2EE, so much the better.

The architect's role is to see the "big picture" of the project and map out the solution to the technologies and the surrounding environment. This person must be able to synthesize high-level considerations such as high availability, application and database performance, application and network security, and integration with existing client/server applications or a variety of specialized third-party subsystems. A good architect understands the trade-offs that must be made and chooses the right ones.

To be successful at this role, the application architect must possess the knowledge of both leading edge and proven technologies suitable for developing application solutions. He must understand several technologies, including relational databases, hardware and operating system platforms, the latest enterprise technologies such as J2EE, and the tools and vendor products available to implement solutions. He should have object-oriented design abilities and should know how to express his designs in UML. His designs should draw from a sophisticated awareness of design patterns, including generic object-oriented patterns and patterns specific to J2EE.

The best architects "stir up the pot," forcing a project's developers to consider approaches they may have overlooked, or may not favor. They encourage developers to take calculated risks, seek innovative solutions to problems, and create software systems that exceed users' expectations.

Your organization may have such a person in a management position serving as technical advisor on a variety of projects. Or perhaps this person is someone who has the development lead role, serving as a technical mentor to other team members. Either way, a knowledgeable, opinionated application architect is a vital part of helping your project team achieve success.

Database designer/database administrator

After you gather requirements for your project and select an application architecture, the first person to actually design and build something is usually the database designer. This is because in systems that depend on databases, you must first have a database before you can write code to manipulate it.

A good database begins with a good data model. Data modeling is an art, not a science, because there are several "correct" ways to do it wrong. A relational database design, for example, may conform to all the rules of normalization, but it may not perform well because common queries require too many table joins. Denormalizing the database solves the performance problem but compromises the purity of the design. Good database designers know that these tradeoffs are normal (so to speak) and necessary, and they know how to make wise decisions while designing the system, not after putting it into production.

Good database designers work with users to determine *what* data will be used. Based on this information, they sketch out an initial design that meets project requirements and some level of normalization rules. The best database designers work with users *and* programmers to understand precisely *how* the data will be used. This information is used to bring the model in line with expected data storage and retrieval patterns for maximum throughput and performance. Just as you wouldn't design an interstate highway with hairpin curves because of the wrecks that would surely result, you wouldn't build a database in fifth normal form for a high-volume, online transaction processing system because processing an insert or update would take a prohibitively long time.

In keeping with the trend toward smaller project teams, your database designer may also function as your database administrator. This can work well during development, but usually doesn't fly after a system goes into production. Why? Although these jobs seem similar, they're quite different. Database administrators are tasked with keeping databases alive, healthy, and recoverable in case of disasters. The variables that go into meeting these requirements vary tremendously depending on the database product being used, the size and structure of the database, the database's usage patterns, and even the operating system it is running on. The reservoir of required knowledge is so huge, and the value of experience so great, that people build careers around being Oracle, Sybase, or MS SQL Server DBAs. Being a proficient, responsive DBA is generally not something you can do well on a part-time basis, especially for larger systems.

User Interface (UI) designer

Great UI designers combine artistic ability with technological awareness to create attractive, efficient UIs for Web applications. It's a difficult job for a number of reasons, and good designers are hard to find.

Creating a good-looking site that is easy to use and simplifies the task at hand is no accident. It requires a lot of knowledge, communication, hard work, experimentation, and rework to get it right. The best UI designers know how to work with users *and* developers to create the best possible design. Users provide insight on workflows, daily usage patterns, functionality, and the friendliness of a system, while developers provide feedback on what can actually be built with available technology.

UI design for Web applications is especially challenging — and frustrating. Anyone who has been involved with software development for more than five years knows that Web browsers and HTML are a big step backwards for human-computer interaction. Web UI designers are often asked to render stunning landscapes with the software equivalent of a hammer and chisel. Great designers can actually pull it off to some extent, but the shortcomings and compromises imposed by the environment are many.

From a practical standpoint, the UI designer on your team should be an expert in HTML and, increasingly, XML. She should know how to write JavaServer pages that incorporate JavaBeans and custom tag libraries. She should know JavaScript and how to use it in a browser-neutral manner to perform client-side validations. She should understand HTML forms processing and know how to effectively weave animations and multimedia into a design. And, of course, she should be able to envision and create the artwork necessary to bring a design to life.

Java/J2EE developer

Java developers are the core of a WebLogic team, as the bulk of WebLogic applications are built in Java.

WebLogic development is, by definition, server-side development. Experienced desktop developers, such as those with backgrounds in Visual Basic or client-side Java development, find they have to shift their focus away from UI coding in favor of more "faceless" tasks such as session management and efficient manipulation of back-end data. UI design and implementation is still very important in WebLogic applications, but these tasks are usually assigned to HTML and JSP developers.

Good Java and J2EE developers have a passion for issues involving system architecture and design. They combine their expert knowledge of Java with a deep understanding of object-oriented design. They read, absorb, and apply design patterns, and they recognize the many design patterns employed by J2EE itself (some of which is discussed in the next chapter). Furthermore, they enjoy combining these patterns into tangible solutions, using UML to create, refine, and share their designs.

The best Java and J2EE developers can quickly translate well-designed models into working code, taking advantage of the power and flexibility that Java, J2EE, and WebLogic have to offer. They're willing to try multiple approaches to solving problems, and they're willing to keep plodding away when things don't work right the first time.

Although Java developers are not necessarily database experts, they know enough about databases to write reliable, efficient code by using JDBC. This implies at least a fair knowledge of SQL, which is really a requirement for all server-side developers today.

Finally, great Java developers are also great team players. They collaborate effectively with their fellow server-side developers, with the database team, and with the UI design team to deliver rich, functional solutions in compressed time frames.

Quality Assurance (QA) team

If your organization has a dedicated QA team, consider yourself lucky and try to take full advantage of their unique capabilities and talents.

Every good QA engineer I've worked with derives a unique, almost perverse satisfaction from breaking software. Whereas developers test under the assumption that previously coded sections still work, QA engineers test under the assumption that nothing *ever* works. Developers test applications as they are designed to be used, but QA engineers test applications as they are designed *not* to be used. Developers are under pressure to build software, while QA engineers are under pressure to *break* it. That's why it's best to separate the roles if you can.

Another reason a dedicated QA team is a major asset is that they can devote time to building test scripts and otherwise automating the testing process to maximize productivity and shorten testing cycles. A number of third-party tools exist for testing the functionality and load-bearing capacity of Web applications. None of these tools are easy to learn or use. Having one or more people available full-time to learn and apply these products can be a major boon to your project.

Smaller shops that don't have access to dedicated QA teams almost always task their developers with testing. Getting end users involved can also help in these situations, to help mitigate the previously mentioned developer bias. If your shop falls into this category, you may want to schedule occasional testing events, where employees throughout your organization log on to the system at a predetermined time and try to break it. You may want to provide a script for people to follow, or you may want to just turn them loose on your application to see what breaks when users start poking around. It's important, however, to carefully record what goes wrong so that problems can be relayed back to the development team. A couple observers can walk around and do this, or you can have users record their experiences on feedback forms. The bottom line is that any kind of structured testing approach is better than no testing at all, and if you can dedicate a team of pros to the effort, your software will benefit tremendously.

Documentation team

In these days of rapid development and extreme programming, documentation is one of those things that gets neglected or just doesn't get done at all. Why? Because writing and maintaining accurate system documentation is exceedingly difficult, especially when the system is frequently changing.

A fairly painless way to solve part of the problem is to take advantage of the JavaDoc facility to ensure that, at a minimum, your source code documentation is well organized and available to the team. Of course, this requires that developers do a good job of embedding JavaDoc comments in their code. Enforcing at least this much discipline is a huge improvement over not documenting the system at all, especially when you consider the disruption that can occur when developers are assigned to other projects, or leave the organization entirely.

Tip

On my company's projects, the developers create scripts that automatically run JavaDoc against the company's development servers on a nightly basis. This provides developers and project managers with a central, up-to-date internal Web site with the latest documentation for all code the company has written.

Most large IT organizations have dedicated technical writers. These people work with development teams to create robust documentation for IT system administrators and end users.

Documentation for IT administrators usually includes a brief description of the project and its business purpose, a high level architecture and network topology, detailed installation instructions of all the key software components, troubleshooting and maintenance instructions, and support escalation paths with contact numbers. Such documentation is usually posted in a secure, central location, such as a dedicated intranet site.

User documentation should be minimal but informative. My team has noticed that a quick reference guide (published as a laminated, 8-½ " × 11 " card), context-sensitive online help, or a site navigation map are tools that actually get used. Thick user manuals usually wind up on the shelf, never to be read by anyone!

WebLogic administrator

The WebLogic administrator is the person who deploys applications on your WebLogic Server and keeps the server online and properly tuned. This person could be a Unix or Windows NT/2000 system administrator, or one of the more technical developers.

The WebLogic administrator must have a medium to advanced level of understanding of the operating system upon which you'll be deploying WebLogic Server. This is because the proper installation and tuning of WebLogic differs slightly from platform to platform, and is also affected by the nature of the applications deployed to the server.

A competent administrator is familiar with loading and configuring the hardware, the operating system, and system patches. He should know how to tune the operating system and its usage of available hardware for maximum performance. He should know basic Java concepts such as classpath and how to run a Java program. Remember that WebLogic is written in Java, and a lot of the administration problems encountered when running WebLogic can be more easily solved when the administrator knows Java. He should know how to install and configure WebLogic Server (including multiple server instances and clusters), JDBC drivers, ODBC and native database drivers (if necessary), and messaging and mail interfaces. He should understand and be able to deploy the various types of application packages, including JAR, WAR, and EAR files.

Project Management Strategies

In this section, I share some of the in-the-trenches wisdom that I've accumulated in nearly ten years of managing large, enterprise-class software projects. If you're a senior developer, team leader, or project manager, I'm sure you've gathered some pearls of your own over the years. But if you're like me, you're always willing to share ideas with other experienced people in the industry. So, for what they're worth, here are some of my thoughts on how to effectively manage nontrivial software projects.

I'm not a believer in some of the more extreme methods of project management, nor do I believe in an exhaustive, by-the-book approach. My approach is not based upon any textbook or project management seminar. It's simply what I've discovered has worked well for me in the real world of management, users, developers, technology, and deadlines.

In a nutshell, I believe that proper due diligence in gathering requirements and a well thought out design is a necessity to architecting a good enterprise solution. Documentation should be concise but complete, providing the design and development teams with the critical information they need, but no more. Project management documents during development should also be kept simple, but up-to-date. Therefore, at a moment's notice, you can identify tasks completed or in-progress, those responsible for their completion, and what their priorities are.

You should be able to communicate with management and end users with the same documents, without having to reformat the content to suit them. And finally, throughout all the project stages, documents should be formatted in a way that minimizes the need for maintenance as the project progresses. Let's break these points down into more specifics.

Gathering requirements

The requirements-gathering stage is a necessary evil. Most software project managers hate it, but good work done here pays huge dividends later on.

You and management should have some preliminary agreement about project scope, including budgetary constraints, the definition of the user community, and the business problem to be solved. There should likewise be a clear definition of who and what are *not* part of the scope.

A thorough set of interviews should be conducted with users to gather information about existing systems and proposed solutions. These interviews should cover existing source documents, workflows, demos of existing systems, and a complete understanding of what they desire the solution to be. If you have any preconceived ideas of the solution, run them by the users to get their feedback. But don't make any promises!

Keep notes during these interviews, jot down ideas as they come to you, and highlight issues and questions that come up through these conversations. Start a project binder and include your notes in this. I personally like to type my notes into a Word document to allow me to review the discussion and add more detail as I type. I typically think of more issues and questions at this time.

When you believe you have a good picture of what needs to be done, you'll inevitably need to prepare a Requirements document and present it to management and users. Your organization may have a template for you to use; otherwise, you'll need to deliver the information in a logical order. The document should include a summary description of the project, including the nature of the problem and current workflows. Characteristics of a solution should be discussed, including identification of roles, requirements by role, and proposed phasing. A couple of well thought out diagrams make it easier to help people see the big picture that you've drawn in your head during the requirements gathering process. If everything goes well, you should get sign-off to proceed with a design after one or two rounds of discussions.

Designing the solution

Your organization may require that you complete Design Specifications and Functional Specifications documents, or there may be just one document, or you'll need to make up your own. It doesn't really matter—what does matter is that you do it. A good design enables you to see how the big picture will be accomplished. It also allows you to drill down into the subprocesses that make up the complete system, which is essential for the ensuing software design meetings.

The entire development team should participate in the design. Ultimately, a high level design will show the servers, software components, other interfacing systems, the databases, high-level workflows, and so on. From here you can break down processes and components into detailed workflows, interface designs, report layouts, validation rules, error conditions and user error messages, database diagrams, and Java class diagrams.

Learn UML. Use entity-relationship diagrams to design the data model and Java class structures. Use activity diagrams to document workflows, validations, and exception handling. Use sequence diagrams to map your system to J2EE components.

Chapter 3 walks through an example of applying UML as described in the preceding Tip.

Meanwhile, the UI designer should be creating mock-up pages in HTML and reports in whatever means are appropriate. Effective UI design is an iterative process that involves meeting with users, making modifications based upon feedback, and reviewing changes with the development team.

The format of the documents created during this phase is not important, as long as they present the design as the developer would like to receive it. Another important aspect is that they should deliver enough information, but not too much. Keep it as simple as possible while still getting the information delivered. Maintain these documents only as necessary, such as a major requirements or design change. Don't worry so much about the small things. No design document is ever perfect; no design document ever matches the final product.

Managing development

During the development phase, the intensity of project management activities dies down a little. But a few basic components should be in place.

Source code control

Source control should be implemented and used by all members of the teams at all times—no exceptions. Many products are available to provide source control and, as a result, a few different definitions of source control exist. Here's mine: The purpose of source control is to keep track of who currently "owns" any given source document. If someone needs the source, they check it out, thereby preventing anyone else from changing it until that first person has coded it, tested it, and checked it back in. Throughout the course of the project, all the source documents are in one place—another important aspect of source code control systems.

Periodically, preferably each evening, rebuild your development staging server from the latest version of the source in your source control system. This will provide you with an up-to-date, functioning version of the software (even if it's missing a lot of features). It will also reinforce to the team that this is the master copy of the source.

Task list

You should maintain a simple task list to track completed, in-progress, and outstanding tasks. More importantly, it should become a natural means of communication within the team. Each task should be described at a fairly detailed level, enough so that a developer considers it a single component of work. This typically represents something that can be completed in a week or less. Information about completed tasks should include who did the work and when, along with any important comments. Tasks in progress should describe who is working on what. Anything outstanding should have some sort of priority rating that is understood by the project team.

You can use an elaborate, expensive project-tracking tool, or you can use something as simple as a Microsoft Excel document. Whatever product you use, all members of the team should be able to add tasks to the list as they think of them. The project manager should occasionally meet with the team to discuss outstanding tasks, make assignments, and assign priorities.

Project plan

The task list is a great tool for communicating low-level programming issues among technical team members. But to communicate with management and users, you'll need a higher-level document, the project plan.

The dreaded project plan isn't so bad if you make it a useful management tool. Too often, project managers create excessively detailed plans that are difficult to maintain. Such detailed plans are hardly ever correct, so they become an exercise in futility. Keep the project plan simple and make it work for you. If the project plan is a tool that you can actually use to *manage* your project, then it will become your friend.

The project plan should accomplish two things: It should show concurrent activities and document project progress versus milestones. You don't need multiple levels of detail. If a project is broken down into phases, and those phases have requirements, design, coding, QA, and user acceptance stages, then all you need is one line item for each. If it's important that you track things by team member, then break it down one more level. Or, if you want to track development by major processes, then break down just the development stages one more level. Include only the levels of detail in your plan that you need, no more.

As a result, you now have a usable, easily maintainable document. You won't mind keeping it up to date because you'll find that doing so is an easy way to track the progress of your project. An added bonus is that the plan is at a level that managers and users can understand, so you can discuss it with them without reformatting. You no longer need to reserve the day before a status meeting to update the plan.

Planning the rollout

The rollout phase of a project can almost become a project in itself. To plan the rollout, the entire project team should get together well before the rollout date to discuss the necessary tasks. All aspects of the rollout should be discussed, including hardware, software installations and configurations, database implementation, application server and components, users and roles, application training, initial application support, and support turnover to administrators.

To document and manage this, you may want to create a separate project plan focused only on the rollout. Or you can simply add rollout tasks to your existing project plan if that works better for you and your team.

Keeping morale high

An important part of managing a project is managing your manager and the users. I've found that frequent and regular updates, at least once every week or two, will help boost morale by making everyone feel that requirements are being met and progress is being made. In the IT community, where enterprise projects cost big bucks, no news is *not* good news! Keeping management and users up to date is your opportunity to keep them interested, involved, and supportive of your efforts. You can even assign them tasks from time to time!

One form of communication to managers and end users is the status report. A status report should

- ✦ Relay the status of the major project activities.
- ✦ Divide the project or project phases into major components, and present these components in an organized, tabular format.
- ✦ For each component, provide percentage complete, resource assignments, and a descriptive comment.
- ✦ List accomplishments since the last report.
- ✦ List items to be completed before the next report, along with a date for that report.
- ✦ List outstanding issues, including what they are and what is needed to address them.

A quick note about outstanding issues: They should remain on your status reports until they are completely resolved. After they are resolved, continue to report them for at least one additional cycle to document the resolution and when it was closed.

Throughout the project, whether casually or formally, touch base with managers and end users to let them know your progress and next steps. Typically, status reports and project plans are reviewed at periodic status meetings. Very often, however, these meetings lose audience members over time and therefore don't really do a good job of getting the word out about your project's status. I'm not saying don't have them, but I do suggest that you e-mail everyone a copy of your status report after the meeting is completed. Go a step further by seeking out the people that matter and having a quick, five-minute conversation with them about the project. This could be the most fruitful five minutes of your day.

During development, conduct occasional demos. As components of the application are completed, show them off and gather feedback. The input you receive will be valuable, but more importantly, demonstrating progress gives managers and users .ownership of the system, a stake in seeing it through successfully, and the warm, fuzzy feeling that those mysterious WebLogic developers in the corner are actually getting something done.

Summary

WebLogic development is challenging and demanding. WebLogic development teams must possess multiple talents and skill sets, and they must work hard to work well together. But working on a WebLogic development team is rewarding and enjoyable for developers and project managers alike. After all, solving tough technical problems and delivering complex systems that work well are what being a competent IT professional is all about.

Managing WebLogic projects isn't much different than managing other types of software projects, except that the need to foster teamwork and collaboration, and the need to weave disparate skill sets into a productive whole, is greater. Aside from these differences, WebLogic project management doesn't require any special techniques, documentation, or tricks. It just requires common sense, persistence, and discipline . . . the same ingredients that make any project successful.

✦ ✦ ✦

Designing WebLogic Applications

In This Chapter

Understanding multitier applications

Building multitier applications with J2EE: Containers and components

Organizing components into applications

Deploying components in WebLogic's containers

Designing the example application: ZeeTrade Online Brokerage

In this chapter, I present some background and ideas that should be helpful to you in your quest to become a good J2EE and WebLogic application designer.

J2EE is designed for the construction of distributed applications and is based on the Model-View-Controller (MVC) paradigm, a proven approach for designing multitier, enterprise applications that are scalable and maintainable. A good understanding of MVC and how it relates to J2EE and WebLogic will definitely make you more proficient at designing WebLogic applications.

After explaining the relationship between MVC and J2EE, I'll demonstrate some application design and modeling techniques that may help you shorten your time-to-market. Included is a brief tutorial on how to use Unified Modeling Language (UML) to construct *understandable* and *helpful* models of your J2EE designs, a topic I have found to be conspicuously absent from today's programming literature.

Although this chapter does not contain a lot of WebLogic-specific information, it does contain a wealth of relevant background information and real-world techniques that will help you maximize the return on your WebLogic investment.

Understanding Multitier Applications

A *multitier application* is an application whose code is distributed across multiple logical and physical tiers of execution. Each tier is tied to a specific application function and communicates with the others in well-defined, predictable ways. The application gets its work done by moving signals and data from tier to tier in response to user and program inputs.

J2EE is designed expressly for building multitier applications. In this section you will learn how J2EE's architects accomplished this feat in the context of multitier thinking and design patterns that have been around for over 20 years.

How J2EE separates applications into tiers

Although it may sound complicated, the good news is that the J2EE design is based on only three tiers:

✦ **Client**—This part of the application is seen and manipulated by the user. It can live in a Web browser or be a stand-alone application.

✦ **Middle**—This part of the application contains business logic that controls the flow of information between users and corporate data. In J2EE, the middle tier consists of two subtiers: the Web tier, which handles communications with the client tier, and the Enterprise JavaBeans (EJB) tier, which manages business logic and access to corporate data.

✦ **Enterprise Information System (EIS)**—This part of the application provides access to various corporate data stores, such as relational databases, electronic mail systems, messaging systems, legacy systems, and so on. All such access is accomplished through the use of standard APIs.

The J2EE designers had very good reasons to build their platform around a multitier model. J2EE is designed primarily to build Web systems, and Web systems are inherently multitier. The Web is a world of browsers, Web servers, and database back-ends. In other words, it's a world of clients, middles, and enterprise information systems. This is the world J2EE was created to tame.

The Model-View-Controller design pattern

When the J2EE designers looked at the Web, they saw an environment whose widely distributed nature gave it remarkable power. But the distributed nature of the Web also made it difficult to build Web applications. One of the major challenges was trying to figure out where the code for Web applications should live. Should it live in the browser, or should it live on the Web server? Should pieces of it live in both places? Or should the code live somewhere completely different? There were no clear answers.

Whatever the solution was, it seemed reasonable that the code should be divided up somehow. One sensible approach was to put code for interacting with the user near the user, code for interacting with other systems (such as databases) near those systems, and code for tying the two ends together somewhere in between. This approach reminded the J2EE engineers of a popular, proven, 20-year-old application design pattern that they thought might help them bring order to the chaos. That design pattern is called Model-View-Controller.

Model-View-Controller (MVC) is a widely used and highly successful design pattern for building maintainable applications. Introduced by Xerox researchers in 1980, MVC is especially useful for designing multitier applications, so the architects of J2EE designed the platform with MVC in mind.

MVC revolves around the concept that application logic can be clearly divided into three layers:

- **Model**—This layer of application logic deals with core business entities and their associated business logic. In real-world applications, model objects usually map to rows in database tables and also consist of code for the proper manipulation of that data. Model objects are implemented as a stable set of reusable business objects that are available to developers across the enterprise for use in multiple applications.
- **View**—This layer deals with the presentation of application data and commands to the user. In other words, it is the user's view of the system. View objects can be HTML pages rendered in a browser or the graphical user interface rendered by a Java client application. They are usually application-specific.
- **Controller**—This layer sits between the View and Model layers and implements business logic and workflows. A command initiated by a user in the View layer typically triggers code in the Controller layer, which manipulates one or more objects in the Model layer to complete the command. Controller objects are usually application-specific but can also be designed for use by multiple applications.

Note the resemblance to the J2EE EIS, Client, and Middle layers.

Over the past 20 years, MVC has proven itself to be a resilient, productive model for building distributed applications of all kinds. As you shall see, it turns out to be especially useful for designing Web applications, which is why it became the cornerstone of the J2EE platform.

Model-View-Controller in action: An ATM machine

A simple example of MVC in action is a bank customer interacting with an ATM machine. Figure 3-1 shows how the various components of this system map to MVC.

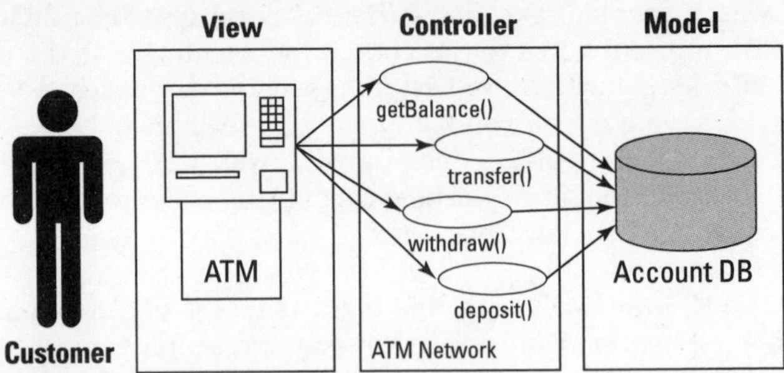

Figure 3-1: An ATM mapped to MVC

Although the paradigm is called Model-View-Controller, I prefer to diagram it from left-to-right as View-Controller-Model, which shows the usual flow of information from user to middle tier to back-end. This is exactly what Sun's team does when they draw Client-Middle-EIS diagrams for J2EE.

Model-View-Controller as a methodology for designing multitier applications

MVC is a powerful model because it cleanly divides code based on its functionality, so changes made in one layer of an application need not affect the other layers. Separating code by functionality is a concept known as *decoupling* and is especially useful in the View layer, which is by far the most changeable layer of an application. Think for a moment about your favorite Web sites, whose appearances often change to keep up with current fashion and browser technology, but whose underlying data remains relatively unchanged. Multitier development organized around MVC is what makes this possible.

Decoupling View code from Controller and Model code pays big dividends over the lifetime of an application because frequent changes can be made to the GUI without rewriting the guts of the application. Some of the dividends accrue in the form of increased developer productivity, because developers can focus on what really needs to be changed without having to worry about the ripple effect their changes have on the rest of the system. This leads, in turn, to reduced development costs. Additional dividends accrue in the form of reduced time to market (and therefore reduced time to revenue) for the Web site or application.

The decoupling concept is what makes MVC useful for designing multitier applications. In a networked environment, decoupling makes it theoretically possible to deploy different parts of an application on different machines. While code in the Client layer, for example, is executing on a user's workstation, code in the Controller and Model layers can be executing on powerful servers, where it can be made easily accessible to all clients and physically close to corporate data stores for increased performance. If you combine this with the cross-platform capabilities of Java, you create an incredibly flexible environment where code can be deployed to the best combinations of hardware *and* operating systems for a given application.

Another strong motivator for MVC is that it cleanly divides development teams by skill set, so GUI design experts can work in the View layer, domain experts can work in the Controller layer, and database experts can work in the Model layer. This clean division of labor capitalizes on the team members' strengths while increasing the productivity of the team as a whole.

Returning to the ATM example, you can see that ATMs are a perfect application for MVC because of their distributed nature and the need for code in each layer to be almost completely independent of the others. Imagine the chaos that would ensue if every little change made to the network required reprogramming all the machines! Thanks to MVC, this is not the case. The guts of the network are completely isolated from the machines, except for the well-defined commands that move between them. Therefore, major changes can be made to the network (such as optimizing the code, or moving it to faster computers) without affecting the machines in any way, as long as the structure of the commands doesn't change. Likewise, banks can upgrade their machines (perhaps by installing graphical operating systems so they can display color advertisements) without affecting the network. And your account data, regardless of the bank in which it resides, is available to every machine on the network — even the ones owned by other banks — because the data formats are also well defined. ATMs, as simple as they seem, are one of the best examples of MVC in practice.

Note An excellent example of MVC at work in the world of personal computers is Microsoft Outlook. Its View layer (the Outlook application) has gone through three revisions since 1997, but all three versions use the same Controller (the MAPI interface) to talk to the same model (Exchange Server). Because of this, all three versions of Outlook can simultaneously connect to the same Exchange Server with no problems.

Building Multitier Applications with J2EE: Containers and Components

Once the J2EE designers decided to embrace MVC as the model for their architecture, the next step was to figure out how to implement it. Their elegant solution was to map a small set of software *components* to the MVC model, and then define specifications for containers that would host those components. The container specifications would be made public, so any application vendor interested in building and marketing J2EE containers could do so. And while vendors would be free to add their own differentiating features to the containers, they would have to meet a strict set of compatibility requirements before their containers would be certified by Sun. This certification process would ensure that components written to the base J2EE standard would run within *any* vendor's container.

As I mentioned earlier, J2EE was designed not only with MVC in mind, but also with the idea that most people would use it to build general-purpose, distributed, enterprise applications. Furthermore, J2EE's designers assumed that most of these applications would run on the Web, either on the Internet, on private corporate intranets, or both. These design principles are readily apparent when you look at how containers and components are defined in J2EE.

Containers

Containers provide runtime support for the types of components they support. J2EE defines four types of containers:

- A *Web container,* for hosting Web components
- An *EJB container,* for hosting EJB components
- An *applet container,* for hosting client-side applets that run within Web browsers
- An *application client container,* for hosting client-side Java applications that run outside of Web browsers

Furthermore, each container must provide support for the following three items:

- Access to container-specific APIs and services (the servlet API for servlets, the EJB API for EJBs, security and transaction services for EJBs, and so on). These services also include life-cycle support for the components themselves; in most cases the container automatically manages the creation and destruction of components in response to user demands on the system.
- Access to the J2EE APIs for interfacing with other systems and components (JDBC, JMS, JNDI, JTA, JavaMail, and RMI).
- Support for runtime configuration of contained components through deployment descriptors, which are implemented as XML files. This allows those who are assembling applications from J2EE components to modify the runtime behavior of those components simply by adjusting entries in the XML files. You may, for example, point an entity EJB to a different database server, or specify that only certain users may invoke a servlet. With deployment descriptors, you can do so without recompiling the component's code, or even having access to the code.

WebLogic Server, being a server-side product, includes Web and EJB containers, but not applet or application client containers.

Components

Components are chunks of application functionality you write that run inside containers. For your components to work, you must follow the specifications and APIs for the types of components you are writing. You must also create default deployment descriptors for your components. This is easy, however, because WebLogic and third-party development tools provide automated support for the creation of deployment descriptors.

J2EE components come in four types:

✦ *Web components* (JSPs and servlets), which run in the Web container

✦ *EJB components* (session beans, message beans, and entity beans), which run in the EJB container

✦ *Applet components* (miniature client-side applications written in Java), which run in an applet container (usually a Web browser)

✦ *Client Application components* (full-featured, client-side applications written in Java), which run in the client application container (usually a Java Virtual Machine on a client computer)

Furthermore, J2EE components share the following characteristics:

✦ They are developed according to the specifications and API's of their containers.

✦ They perform well-defined roles within an application (the rest of this chapter spells these roles out in detail).

WebLogic Server supports deployment of Web and EJB components only.

Organizing Components into Applications

J2EE's creators designed each J2EE component to fill certain roles in the MVC architecture. Therefore, a good recipe for designing an application's components is to

1. Map the application to the MVC model.
2. Decide which J2EE components you need to build, and what functionality they need to provide.

This sounds easy, but it's not. As many project teams have discovered, some MVC roles can be filled by more than one type of J2EE component. This means that you don't need every type of J2EE component to build perfectly functional J2EE applications. In fact, it's sometimes preferable to omit certain types of components, especially for smaller projects, to reduce application complexity, development time, and costs.

Although it may sound like cheating, Sun's own documentation for J2EE endorses this approach. According to *Designing Enterprise Applications with the Java 2 Platform, Enterprise Edition* (Sun Microsystems, Inc., 2000), "The J2EE specifications and technologies, can by definition, make few assumptions about how precisely the API's are going to be used to deliver application-level functionality. . . . The J2EE programming model needs to embrace application scenarios that treat the Web container, and the EJB container, as optional logical entities."

The upshot of all this is that Step 2 is more difficult than it sounds, and the exercise of mapping application functionality to J2EE components often generates lively debate among a project's team members.

As a starting point, most J2EE developers accept the following rules of thumb:

- *Entity EJBs* typically occupy the *Model* layer.
- *JSPs* typically occupy the *View* layer.
- *Servlets, Session EJBs,* and *Message EJBs* typically occupy the *Controller* layer.

What causes debate is when designers and developers "color outside the lines" to solve certain problems under certain circumstances. Nothing in the J2EE specification, for example, prevents you from using a servlet in the View layer, or a session EJB in the Model layer. No technical barriers prevent you from doing so, either. It generally boils down to questions of preference and taste, with no right or wrong answers.

In an attempt to bring consistency to the process, the Sun Java Center recently published a set of application design guidelines known as the *Sun Java Center J2EE Patterns.* These patterns, first released to the public in March 2001, are the most comprehensive guidance available for J2EE application designers. They help designers identify common, recurring problems in J2EE application design, for which they recommend specific solutions by using various combinations of J2EE components. Written by J2EE experts in Sun's consulting division, the patterns represent three years of wisdom accumulated while executing projects for the likes of Ford Motor Company and E*Trade.

The patterns are not "the law," and are themselves open to interpretation and modification. Your team should study the patterns, experiment with them, make appropriate modifications to suit your circumstances, and move on. If the patterns work for you—great. If not, invent your own. But whatever approach you choose, you'll be more productive if you try to apply it consistently from project to project.

The following sections describe commonly used patterns in each layer of MVC. These are just a few of the many patterns available, but they give you a good idea of what the patterns are all about. You can find the full catalog of patterns at `http://developer.java.sun.com/developer/technicalArticles/J2EE/patterns/`.

Model tier patterns

Model tier patterns are designed to facilitate the exchange of data between an application and its data stores. This section describes data access objects and value objects, two of the most commonly used patterns in this tier.

Data Access Object (DAO)

Data access objects (often called DAOs) provide interfaces to persistent data stores, such as relational databases, network directories, messaging systems, e-mail systems, and so on. DAOs encapsulate access to their underlying stores, hiding the details from the rest of the application.

A DAO that connects to a relational database, for example, would handle all the details of connecting to the database server, submitting SQL queries, retrieving results, and returning results to callers. Callers would be presented with a high-level interface to the data that requires no knowledge of the database system or the mechanisms used to manipulate it.

DAOs are an example of a J2EE *helper class.* A helper class supports the processing needs of an application, but is not a formal J2EE component itself. A JavaBean is another example of a helper class.

A common approach is to insert a DAO between an entity EJB and the database, as shown in Figure 3-2.

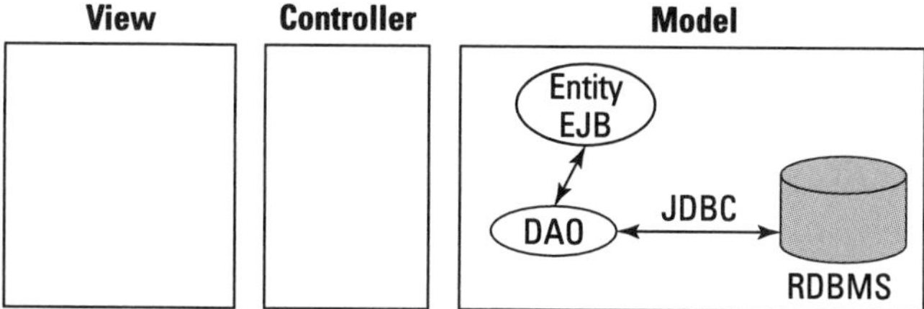

Figure 3-2: DAO managing database access for an entity EJB

By using a DAO this way, you insulate the entity EJB from changes in database platforms, or changes in the mechanisms used to access the database. Such changes would impact the DAO, but would be hidden from the entity EJB, as long as the DAO's public interface didn't change.

Value Object

A *value object* is a helper class that gives components in the View and Controller layers more efficient access to components in the Model layer (usually entity EJBs).

An entity EJB is usually mapped to a row in a database, with getter and setter methods defined for each column in the row. Imagine writing a JSP to display the row of data represented by an entity EJB. The JSP must call every getter method to retrieve the complete row. This means the JSP must have knowledge of the entity EJB's structure. Furthermore, each getter call is a remote method invocation, so the network overhead created by this arrangement is very high.

Value objects are designed to overcome these problems. When a value object is incorporated into the design, the JSP calls a special method in the entity EJB that creates a value object, populates it with the full row of data, and returns it to the JSP. This reduces the number of remote method calls to one, and eliminates the need for the JSP to know the structure of the entity EJB.

Figure 3-3 illustrates this arrangement. Note that in this context, the value object is usually implemented as a JavaBean, allowing the JSP developer to take advantage of the programming linkages between JSPs and JavaBeans.

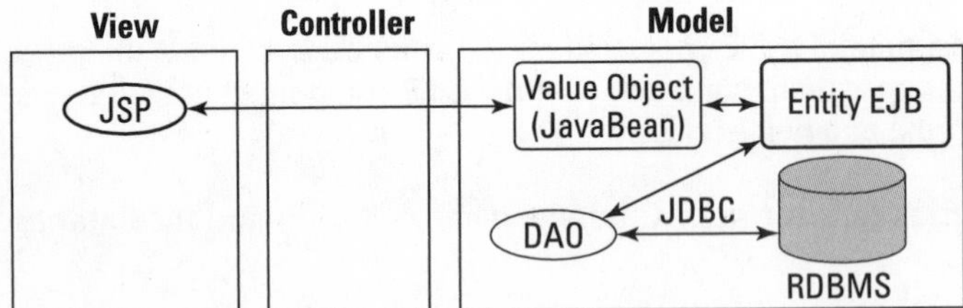

Figure 3-3: Value object providing a JSP with efficient access to an entity EJB

You can write value objects that are *updateable*. In this scenario, the client makes changes to the data in the value object, and then sends the value object back to the entity EJB to be copied to the database. Note, however, that if other clients are holding copies of the same data in value objects of their own, their data will now be stale, so you may need to devise a strategy for dealing with this. Updateable value objects also increase the potential for the old client/server problem of *lost updates*. These occur when user A and user B both get copies of the same data. User A saves changes first, followed by user B. User B's changes overwrite user A's, resulting in user A's updates being lost.

In the diagrams, I represent J2EE components with heavy outlines, and helper classes with regular outlines.

View tier patterns

View tier patterns are designed to support presentation logic and user navigation through an application. The most common such pattern is the *view helper*, which is a class that performs low-level processing for a View component. This pattern is used to enforce the separation of presentation logic from business logic in J2EE.

View helpers are most often used in conjunction with JSPs to prevent the mixing of too much Java code (embedded in scriptlets) with HTML or XML markup code. J2EE provides two types of view helpers for this purpose: JavaBeans (available in JSP 1.0 and higher) and JSP tag libraries (available in JSP 1.1 and higher). Figure 3-4 shows view helpers mapped to MVC.

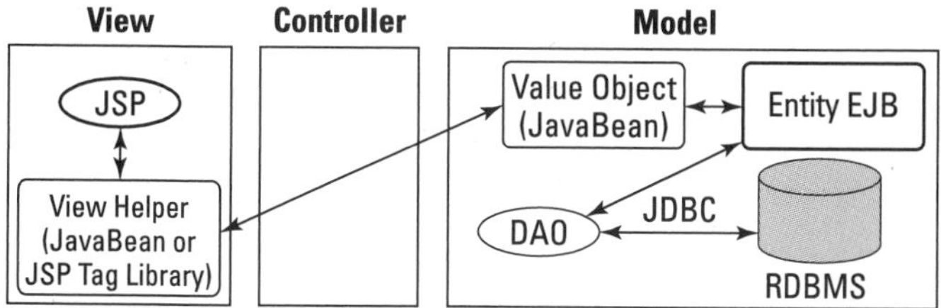

Figure 3-4: JSP with a view helper, implemented as a JavaBean or JSP tag library

Figure 3-4 shows the view helper accessing a database, but this need not be the case. View helpers can perform any kind of low-level processing that you want to isolate from your JSPs.

View helpers provide many benefits. They help separate the View layer from other layers of the application, making the application as a whole more amenable to change. They also provide significant opportunities for code reuse. A well-written JSP tag library, for example, could provide useful functionality for hundreds of JSPs written far into the future. Another benefit of view helpers is that they support a clear division of labor between View developers (working in HTML or XML) and Controller or Model developers (working in Java).

Controller tier patterns

Controller tier patterns support processing that occurs between the View and Model layers. In this section, you will learn about front controllers, dispatchers, and session façades, which manage an application's flow-of-control and access to system resources.

Front controllers and dispatchers

In this pattern, processing initiated by JSPs passes through a *front controller* (implemented as a servlet) that controls access to other system resources via helpers. The servlet also contains code that dispatches requests to other JSPs in the View layer for navigation purposes. This part of the servlet is called a *dispatcher.* Figure 3-5 illustrates this pattern.

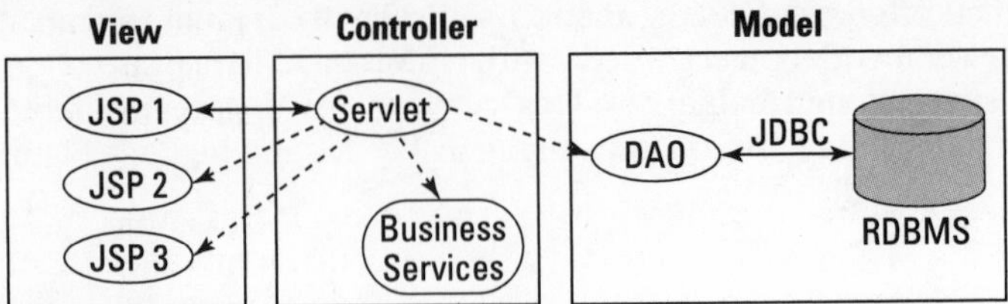

Figure 3-5: Front controller with helpers and an embedded dispatcher

The front controller is usually written as a servlet, because Java code is necessary to implement the required flow-of-control, and the servlet API provides routines designed for this purpose.

The benefit of the front controller pattern is that it centralizes navigation and access to server-side resources. This eliminates code duplication (caused by copying and pasting identical navigation code into multiple JSPs) and allows JSPs in the View layer to focus on presentation.

Session façades

A *session façade* provides clients with uniform, controlled access to business objects in the Controller and Model layers of an application. These business objects are usually implemented as session EJBs, entity EJBs, DAOs, or other types of helpers.

In the absence of a session façade, clients access business objects directly to do their work. This situation is depicted in Figure 3-6.

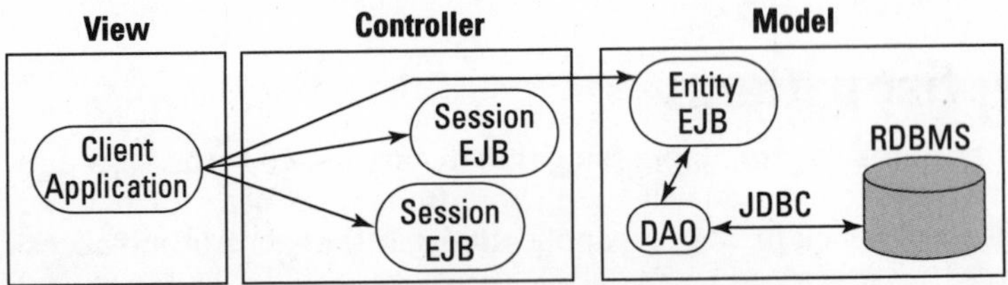

Figure 3-6: Client application accessing business objects directly

This configuration suffers from three major drawbacks:

1. Because the client application manipulates the business objects directly, it is tightly coupled to them. If changes are made to the business objects, or if the rules for using them change, the client application could fail.

2. Business objects implemented as EJBs are accessed via remote method calls, which incur high network overhead. As the number of client applications increases, the number of remote calls increases, and overall system performance suffers.

3. Assume a business process requires the use of three business objects. One client application might invoke the objects in one order, while another client application might invoke them in a different order. Additionally, two or more clients might try to execute their versions of the business process simultaneously. This combination of factors could lead to data synchronization errors and other unanticipated consequences.

Session façades are designed to overcome these drawbacks. A façade, normally implemented as a session EJB, stands between the client applications and business objects and ensures that access to the business objects takes place in an efficient, predictable manner. Figure 3-7 shows the previous application after introducing a session façade:

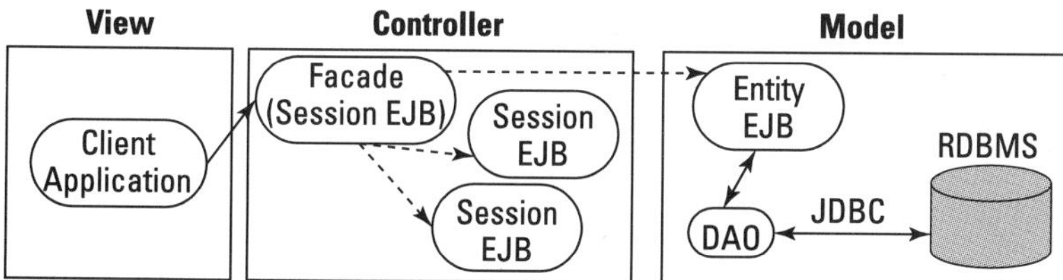

Figure 3-7: Client application accessing business objects through a session façade

The session façade overcomes the drawbacks mentioned earlier as follows:

1. Now that the client calls the facade, it's no longer tightly coupled to the business objects. Changes made to business objects can be absorbed by the façade, decreasing or eliminating the likelihood of breaking the clients.

2. Encapsulating calls to multiple business objects within the façade reduces the high network overhead of remote method calls. The client makes only one remote method call to the façade, which in turn remotely calls the business objects. If the façade and business objects reside in the same EJB container, the network overhead of the calls between them drops to nearly zero.

3. The coding of business processes that require the participation of multiple business objects can be centrally captured in the façade. Any client that wants to execute a business process executes the code for it in the façade. This reduces the likelihood of synchronization errors and other problems, because every client executes the business process identically.

A session façade can be implemented either as a stateful or stateless session EJB, depending on the need to maintain conversational state between the user and the business objects during calls to the façade.

Deploying Components in WebLogic's Containers

Remember that WebLogic Server consists of a Web container and an EJB container. These containers host the Web components and EJB components of an application, as defined in the J2EE component model.

Before WebLogic's containers can do any work, they must have content deployed to them. Figure 3-8 shows how Web components and EJB components are assembled for deployment in WebLogic Server. The boxes enclosing the various objects and components represent special deployment files (known as *archive* files) that contain those items. The boundaries of these boxes are superimposed on the MVC model to show how a complete, deployed J2EE application maps to MVC.

The archive files are copied to deployment directories on your WebLogic Server. WebLogic's containers access the contents of these files at runtime to provide your application's functionality.

Archive files are created with the Java `.jar` utility. These files, referred to as JAR files, are nothing more than slightly modified WinZip files. The `.jar` utility creates files with the extension `.jar`, which you can simply rename to obtain the extensions described in this section. Detailed instructions for creating these archive files appear in later chapters of this book.

The Web Archive (`.war`) file contains the J2EE components (servlets and JSPs) and non-J2EE components that make up a Web application. At runtime, WebLogic's Web container manages the contents of this file.

The Java Archive (`.jar`) file contains the J2EE components (EJBs) that comprise the EJB portion of an enterprise application. WebLogic's EJB container manages the contents of this file.

The Enterprise Archive (`.ear`) file is simply an archive file containing the WAR and JAR files.

The Resource Adapter Archive (`.rar`) file contains classes for interfacing with other enterprise information systems, via the J2EE connector architecture.

Chapter 18 covers the creation and deployment of JAR, WAR, and EAR files. Chapter 27 covers the J2EE Connector Architecture and the creation of RAR files.

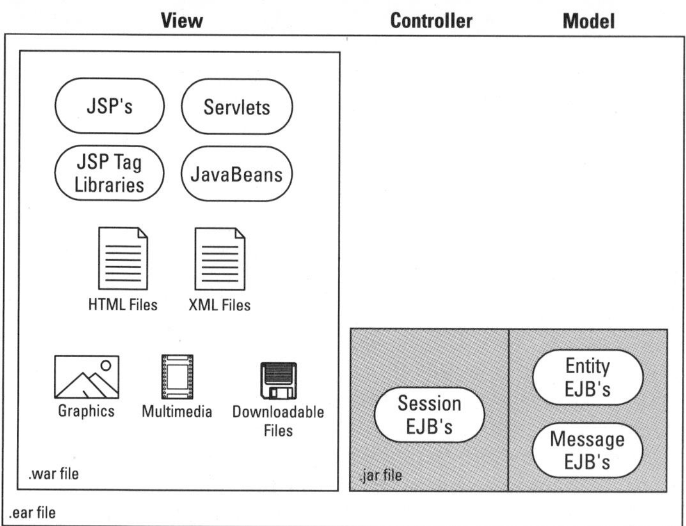

Figure 3-8: WebLogic application components bundled for deployment and mapped to MVC

WebLogic, being a server-side product, does not provide deployment support for client applications and applets. WebLogic does, however, allow you to deploy HTML, XML, graphics, multimedia, and downloadable files with your Web components in the WAR file.

The various archive files are a tremendous convenience when it comes to deploying your application or moving it from one server to another. Instead of having to copy an entire directory structure containing hundreds of files to your server, you simply copy a single archive file, register it with WebLogic Server, and your application is ready to run.

Designing an Example Application: WebLogic Online Brokerage

Now it's time to put theory into practice by designing a WebLogic application. Your application is the J2EE Online Brokerage (JOB), a simplified online stock brokerage system. JOB is a Web application that will be used by a fictitious brokerage firm's customers and employees. Although it will not be as powerful as a real brokerage site, JOB will have enough features to demonstrate the various aspects of designing and building J2EE applications with WebLogic.

Identifying requirements

JOB supports a retail brokerage, one that provides services for individual investors like you and me, as opposed to institutional investors such as mutual funds and pension plans. Each investor's account consists of a mix of cash and securities. To keep the example manageable, you will make a few simplifying assumptions. First, you will only support trading of common stocks on Nasdaq and the New York Stock Exchange (NYSE)—no options, warrants, or derivatives, and no trading on commodities exchanges or foreign exchanges. Second, you will only support cash purchases of securities on the expectation that their prices will rise; stocks cannot be bought on margin or sold short. Third, each customer can have only one brokerage account.

Before diving into the design of the application, it's helpful to understand who will be using it. The brokerage's clients, the individual investors, are certainly one group of users, but why stop with them? Customers interact with a company's employees, so it might be worthwhile to make the site useful to the employees as well. After all, J2EE and WebLogic give you the power to build much more than a pretty Web site—you can build a full-featured *application* disguised as a Web site, which serves an entire community of users.

With this in mind, you will design JOB to serve five different types of users:

- *Customers*—The individual investors who form the brokerage's client base. These are the only users who are not brokerage employees.
- *Brokers*—Registered stockbrokers who manage one or more customer accounts.
- *Managers*—The stockbrokers' bosses. Each broker reports to one manager, and each manager supervises one or more brokers. Managers do not directly manage customer accounts.
- *Research Analysts*—These people examine promising companies and industry trends and write reports about their findings. The reports are made available to customers to help them make intelligent stock purchase decisions.
- *System Administrators*—These people are charged with managing the brokerage's Web site, including the JOB application.

Next, you need to decide in broad terms what functionality you want to deliver to your users. You do this by imagining what options should appear in the application's main menu. These options for JOB will be the following:

- *Portfolio tracking*—Where users can see how much cash they have, and how much their securities are worth based on current prices.
- *Real-time quotes*—Where users can enter a ticker symbol for a stock and get back its current price.
- *Online trading*—Where users buy and sell stocks.

✦ *Investor's Library*—A searchable database of useful documents for investors.

✦ *Report Center*—Where employees can run reports on client trading activity, account status, and sales commissions.

✦ *User Profile Editor*—Where users of all types can securely update their mailing address, e-mail address, password, and other personal information.

A good online brokerage not only supports the mechanics of trading, but also provides timely information to guide investors' trading decisions. Trading activity often regulates access to such information; the more you trade, the more information you can obtain. This common feature would be interesting to implement in your example, so you will invent a scheme to partition the contents of the Investor's Library into tiers of increasing value. JOB's Investor's Library will contain the following types of documents, arranged in order from lowest value to highest:

1. *Annual Reports*—Detailed reports of business activity and financial results for the past year, filed by publicly traded companies. These are posted to the library as they become available.
2. *Industry Outlook Reports*—In-depth studies of entire industry segments (such as semiconductors or healthcare), written by the brokerage'sresearch analysts. These are posted to the library on a quarterly basis.
3. *Research Reports*—In-depth studies of publicly traded companies, written by the brokerage's research analysts. These are posted to the library on a weekly basis.
4. *Morning Meeting Notes*—Late-breaking news stories and a daily assessment of market conditions, written by the brokerage's research analysts. These are posted to the Investor's Library every weekday morning before the stock markets open.

To govern access to material in the Investor's Library, each JOB user shall be granted varying access privileges, based on his or her recent trading activity:

✦ *Bronze*—The default level, granted to all customers regardless of trading activity. Bronze customers can access annual reports and industry outlook reports.

✦ *Silver*—A higher level, granted to customers who made at least five trades in the preceding month. Silver customers can access annual reports, research reports, and industry outlook reports.

✦ *Gold*—The highest level, granted to customers who made at least ten trades in the preceding month. Gold customers can access annual reports, research reports, industry outlook reports, and morning meeting notes.

Brokerage employees have Gold level access to all areas of the site, regardless of their trading activity.

You now have enough background information about your online brokerage to proceed with a detailed design.

Organizing requirements by user role

JOB's development team has interviewed management and customers to discover what features they would like to see in an online brokerage system. They have also surveyed the competitive landscape to see what services other online brokerages provide. The result of these efforts is the following list of high-level site requirements, broken down by the type of site user.

Customer

- View portfolio (cash and stocks)
- Make a trade (buy or sell shares of a stock)
- Get real-time quotes
- Browse, search, and download content in the Investor's Library, subject to access privileges (Gold, Silver, or Bronze)
- Edit personal profile

System administrator

Customer privileges, plus:

- Enable/disable Web access for all users
- Run reports on system activity

Research analyst

Customer privileges, plus:

- Post annual reports, industry outlook reports, research reports, and morning meeting notes to the Investor's Library
- Delete previously published information from the Investor's Library

Broker

Customer privileges, plus:

- View portfolios of their customers
- Make trades for their customers
- Edit personal profiles of their customers

- ✦ Run commission reports for themselves (At ZeeTrade, each customer trade generates a $10 commission for the customer's broker, unless the trade is made online, in which case the trade generates a $5 commission for the "house account.")

Manager

Broker privileges, plus:

- ✦ View portfolios of all customers
- ✦ Make trades for all customers
- ✦ Edit personal profiles of all customers and brokers
- ✦ Run commission reports for all brokers

Expressing requirements in use case diagrams

The Unified Modeling Language (UML) provides a number of ways to express various aspects of system designs visually. A useful tool for visualizing system requirements is the UML use case diagram. Use case diagrams show, at a high level, who the users of a system are, and what functionality they have available to them. Figure 3-9 is a use case diagram that illustrates the system requirements for ZeeTrade.

A detailed discussion of UML is beyond the scope of this book, but UML diagrams are used occasionally throughout the book. A number of resources are available for learning UML. A good place to start is *The Unified Modeling Language User Guide,* by Grady Booch, James Rumbaugh, and Ivar Jacobsen (Addison Wesley).

The use case diagram shows functionality available to the Customer as a series of ovals (Log in, View portfolio, Make a trade, and so on). Arrows pointing from other users to the Customer show that those users inherit the Customer's functionality (but not the other way around), while separate use cases attached to the other users show the functionality available only to them. A Research Analyst, for example, can do everything a Customer can do, plus post reports to the Investor's Library.

The value of use case diagrams is that they provide concise, visual representations of textual requirements that are easy to read and share. They also serve as a starting point for more detailed UML diagrams of various types.

Exploding use cases into activity diagrams

One such detailed diagram is an activity diagram, which illustrates a workflow. Figure 3-10 is a high-level activity diagram for the Log In use case. I say "high-level" because the diagram captures the essential aspects of the workflow, but omits most of the details, which will be filled in later.

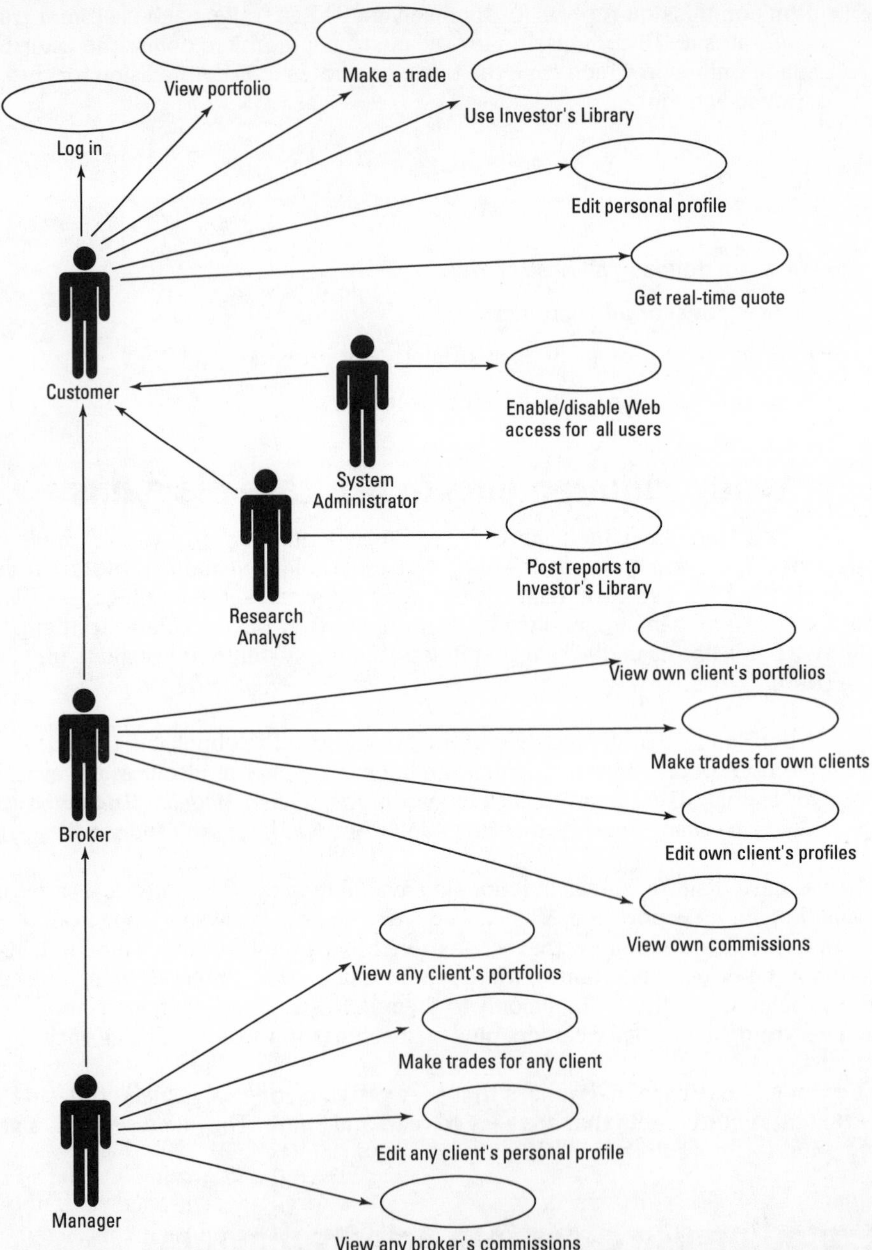

Figure 3-9: UML use case diagram for ZeeTrade online brokerage system

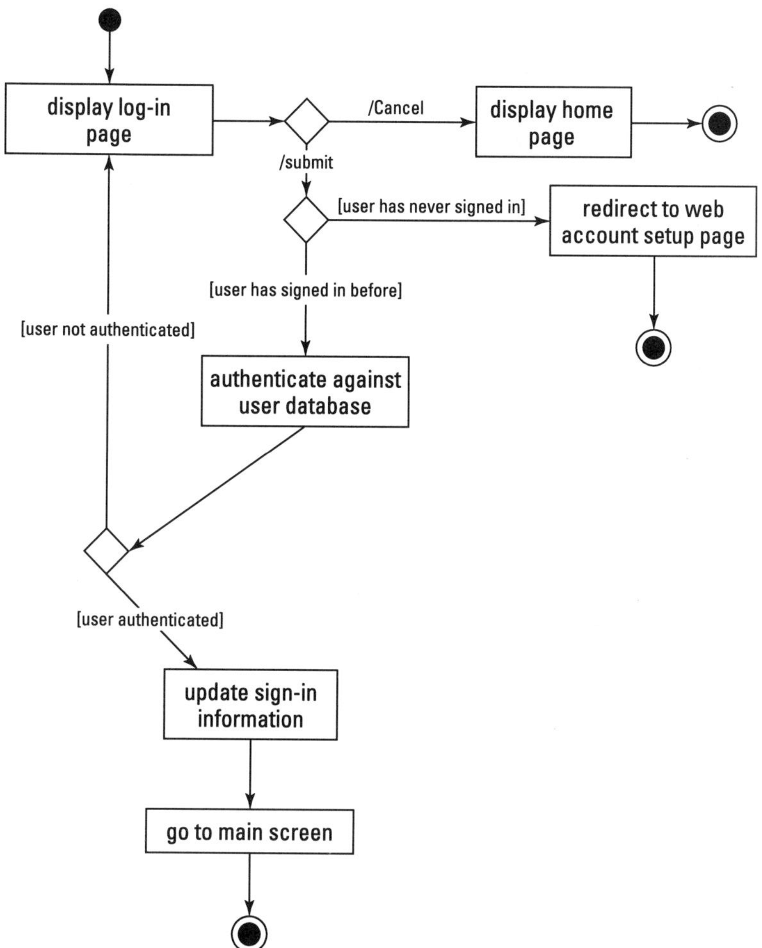

Figure 3-10: Activity diagram for the Log In use case

The workflow begins with the solid black dot in the upper-left corner, which leads to the Display Log In Page activity state. The user presumably supplies a username and password. If the user hits Cancel, he returns to the home page and the workflow ends (as indicated by the solid black dot with the circle around it). If the user hits Submit, the workflow proceeds to the diamond-shaped decision point, where you check to see if the user has ever signed in before (the diagram does not specify how). If so, you authenticate him against the user database, update his sign-in information, take him to the main screen, and the workflow ends. If not, you set up his

Web account. No details are given about this process; it's probably a good candidate for a separate activity diagram. During the course of setting up the user's account, you will authenticate him. Afterwards, you update his sign-in information, take him to the main screen, and the workflow ends.

High-level activity diagrams are a valuable tool for modeling workflows in Web applications. But they don't provide enough detail to determine what components a system needs. Adding more detail to the diagram — say, by expanding each activity into multiple subactivities — doesn't help either, because then you simply have more information about the workflows with no additional insight on how to build them.

Mapping functionality to MVC with swimlanes

The key to unlocking this puzzle is to remember that J2EE applications are Model-View-Controller applications. Is it possible to draw an activity diagram of your system mapped to MVC?

The answer is yes. UML defines a refinement to activity diagrams called *swimlanes* that will do the trick. Swimlanes divide a workflow into multiple roles of responsibility. A vertical column running down the page depicts each role, and the role's name appears on top. Activities are drawn in the columns that have responsibility for them, and arrows link activities as before. Activity diagrams with swimlanes show the clear division of labor among the various participants in a workflow.

For the purpose of designing J2EE applications, I like to create an activity diagram with three swimlanes: View, Controller, and Model. This forces me to map the system's workflows to MVC, which I try to do in more detail than in the high-level diagram. Figure 3-11 shows an expanded activity diagram for the Log In use case with MVC swimlanes added.

As I mentioned before, I prefer to diagram MVC from left-to-right as View-Controller-Model, and I do so in my swimlane diagrams as well.

Here are some tips for drawing MVC swimlane activity diagrams:

- ✦ The View layer should only contain activities initiated by users and pages displayed to users.
- ✦ The Model layer should only contain atomic actions against data stores, such as selects, inserts, updates, deletes for databases, and posts and retrieves for message queues.
- ✦ If you're modeling activities triggered by users, then all begin and end states should appear in the View layer. The *begin* state shows that the user initiated the process. The *end* state, which usually appears immediately after a concluding page is displayed, shows that the user knows the process has ended.

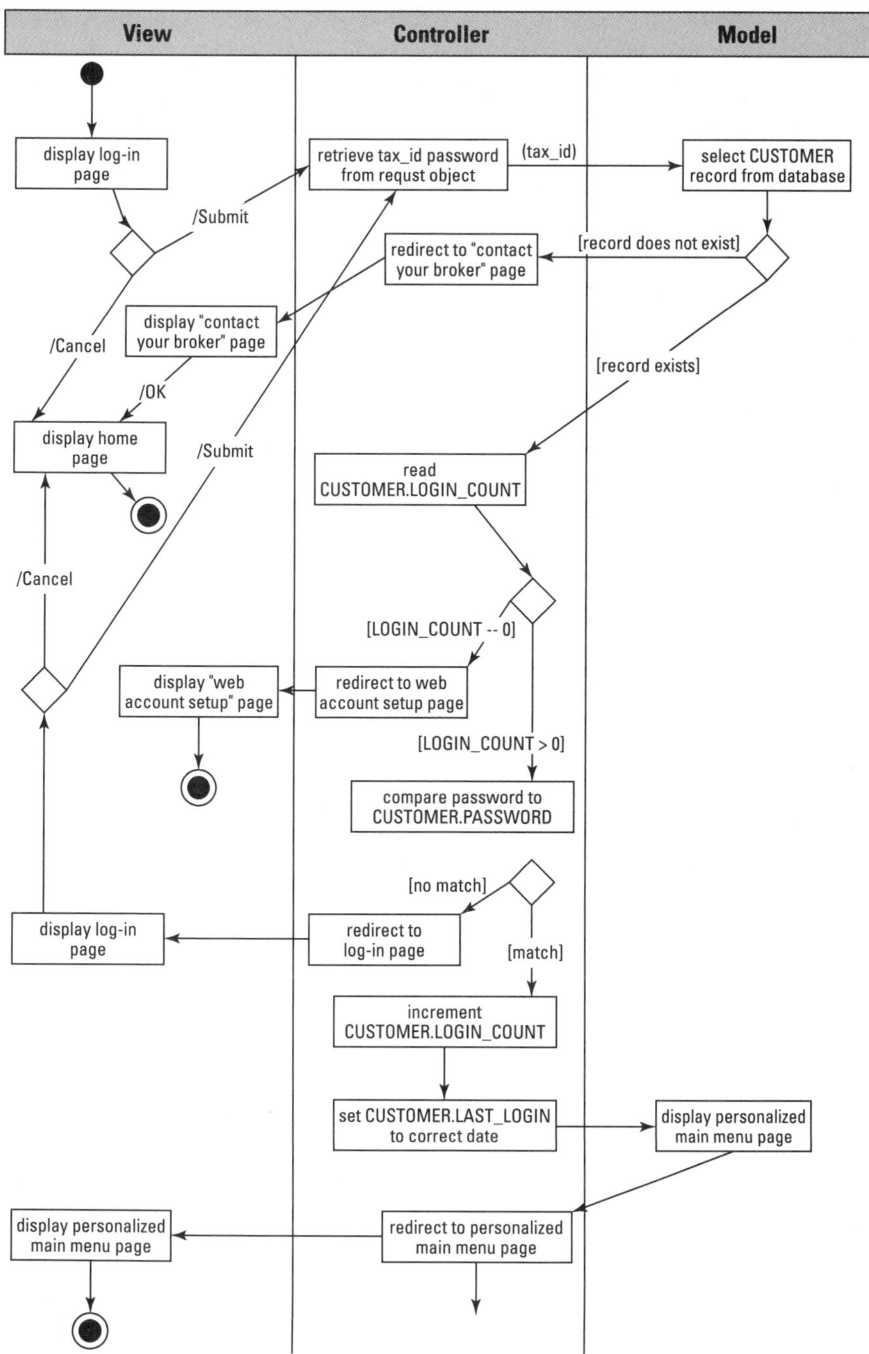

Figure 3-11: Activity diagram for the Log In use case, with MVC swimlanes added

✦ In the View layer, use actions that correspond to button presses or menu selections to label state transitions. In UML, leading forward slashes (/) denote actions. Examples in Figure 3-11 include `/Submit` and `/Cancel`, to indicate what happens when the user clicks these buttons in their Web browser.

✦ Choose verbs for activity states that are appropriate to the layer. In the View layer, I use *display* to indicate the display of a page to the user. In the Controller layer, I use *redirect* to indicate a page transition, and for data manipulations I use verbs such as *read, compare, increment, decrement,* and *set.* In the Model layer, I use the SQL verbs *select, insert, update,* and *delete* to generically describe database operations.

Selecting appropriate J2EE components and modeling their interactions

If you study the diagram in Figure 3-11 with the J2EE design patterns in mind, you should be able to see possible ways to implement the login process with J2EE components. One option is to use a front controller with a JavaBean helper and an embedded dispatcher. In this scenario, you see from the View swimlane that you need five JSPs: a login page, a home page, a contact your broker page, a setup your Web account page, and a main menu page. You see from the Model swimlane that you need one database table: Customer. At a minimum, the Customer table must contain columns for the customer's tax ID, password, total number of logins, and last login date. The Controller swimlane shows that you need code to process requests, manipulate data from the Customer table, and display different JSPs depending on the results. You can use a servlet controller to handle requests and dispatching to the JSPs, and a JavaBean DAO to front-end the Customer table. Figure 3-12 is a class diagram showing the required entities, including the Customer relational database table.

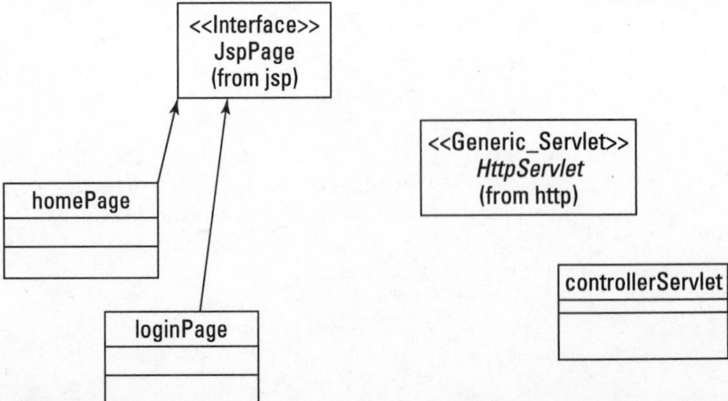

Figure 3-12: Class diagram showing components to implement the Log In use case

The class diagram provides a static view of the application; it shows what pieces must be built. To get a better idea of what the pieces of a system must do, UML defines a *sequence diagram.* A sequence diagram is similar to an activity diagram, but it shows workflows expressed in terms of actual system components, not generic activities.

Figure 3-13 is a sequence diagram that shows how the components in the class diagram work together to accomplish the Log In use case.

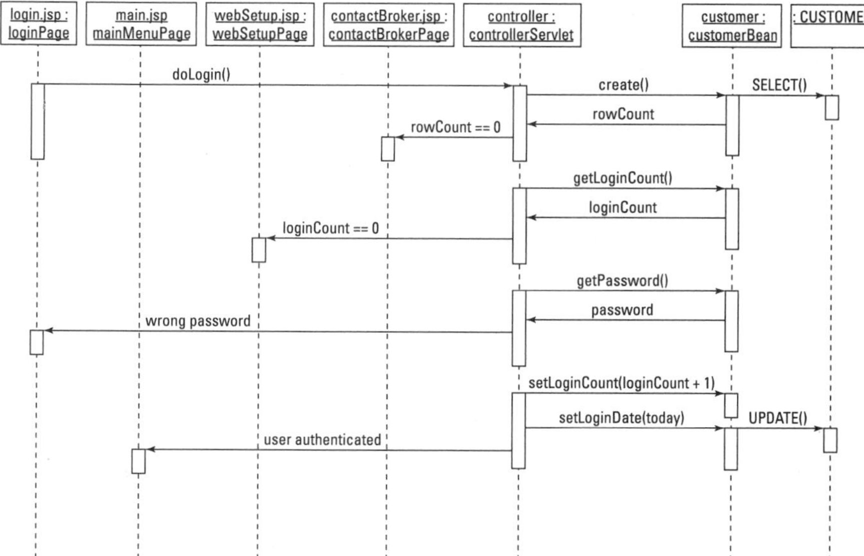

Figure 3-13: Sequence diagram showing component interactions for the Log In use case

Notice the structural similarities between Figures 3-5, 3-11, and 3-13. These are three completely different views of the system, but they are remarkably consistent. Figure 3-5 is the J2EE design pattern used to model the Log In use case, molded around MVC. Figure 3-11 is an activity diagram of the Log In use case, also molded around MVC. What's remarkable is that Figure 3-13, the sequence diagram showing the J2EE component interactions, is *not* explicitly molded around MVC, yet the same overall structure comes shining through. This diagram makes it strikingly obvious that J2EE was designed with MVC in mind.

Other considerations

Besides pure J2EE issues, there are other issues to consider when designing WebLogic applications that will have an impact on how you design your applications.

Databases

One of the most important non-J2EE considerations is the database (or multitude of databases) with which your WebLogic applications will interact. If you are using a modern RDBMS such as Oracle or Microsoft SQL Server, remember that these products are powerful servers in their own right. Don't assume that all the advances made in RDBMS technology over the past 15 years should be thrown out the window in favor of the wanton use of session or entity EJBs. On the contrary, such a design approach is likely a recipe for disaster. In almost every case, you will achieve maximum performance if you leave database processing to the database.

Operations on large sets of data

Take advantage of stored procedures, packages, views, and other RDBMS features that specialize in bulk operations on sets of data. A stored procedure that uses SQL to apply a formula to a set of rows, for example, will execute orders of magnitude faster than a session EJB that reads the rows out of the database, applies the formula in memory, and then writes the rows back.

Operations embedded in transactions

Likewise, a business rule that makes small changes to multiple database tables runs faster and more reliably if it is coded into a stored procedure, especially if the entire process is embedded in a transaction.

I believe that database transactions against a single data source should never be started or stopped outside of the database engine, even if the external code resides on the same machine as the RDBMS. The penalty for failures is simply too high. If the code crashes in the middle of a transaction, or if the network connection between the code and the database is lost, then operations against the database may block until the transaction is somehow forced to complete—usually by rolling it back and losing the changes.

The absolute worst offense is to have user input determine the boundaries of a transaction. Imagine a JSP that begins a transaction when the user puts a record into Edit mode in their browser. If the user saves changes, the transaction is committed; otherwise, it is rolled back. What if the user hits the Back button on their browser, or goes home for the night without saving? The affected database tables will be locked until the transaction is somehow completed. This sounds like a ridiculous case, but I have seen it happen. Beware!

The only exception to my "transactions-stay-inside-the-database" rule are operations involving two-phase commit (transactions spanning multiple databases). It is obviously impossible for such transactions to stay inside any single database.

See Chapter 6 for a complete discussion of transactions.

Security

The log in scenario explored in this chapter is based on a simple design where usernames and passwords are transmitted across the network and validated against a database. Thousands of such systems exist in production today. In many cases, the usernames and passwords are transmitted in clear text (no encryption), and the passwords are stored unencrypted in a relational database. Such a “security” system is hardly secure!

Fortunately, a number of better options are available. As mentioned in Chapter 1, WebLogic provides several different types of security realms for user authentication and authorization, or you can roll your own within WebLogic’s robust security infrastructure. Several approaches for doing this are demonstrated in Chapter 21, including an approach that securely incorporates a relational database.

WebLogic startup and shutdown classes

WebLogic allows you to deploy Java classes that execute when WebLogic Server starts up and shuts down. Such classes can perform housekeeping tasks for any or all J2EE applications deployed on your server, such as verifying connections to databases, file servers, message queues, credit card processing services, and so on.

Startup and shutdown classes fall outside the realm of normal J2EE design, but they are useful tools you should keep in mind as you design your applications.

Summary

This chapter has covered a lot of background material that should give you a much clearer understanding of J2EE and how to design multitier, component-based applications for the J2EE platform. Because WebLogic applications are in fact J2EE applications, you are now a more informed WebLogic application designer as well!

J2EE is heavily predicated on the Model-View-Controller (MVC) application design pattern. Quite simply, if you understand MVC and thoroughly embrace it during your application’s design phase, you will save valuable time. You will also design a much better application that takes advantage of all the power J2EE has to offer.

The Unified Modeling Language (UML) can be a powerful ally in helping you chart out your application’s design. Unfortunately, today’s programming literature contains very little information on how to use UML effectively when designing J2EE applications. I have tried to remedy this situation somewhat by showing how to combine use cases, activity diagrams, swimlanes, class diagrams, and sequence diagrams into a concise package of J2EE design documents that clearly show you *what* to build, *why* to build it, and *how* to hook it together.

This chapter concludes the discussion of how to prepare your enterprise for WebLogic. Now, whether you think you're ready or not, it's time to dive into WebLogic!

✦ ✦ ✦

Creating a WebLogic Environment

✦ ✦ ✦ ✦

In This Chapter

Configuring a computer for development

Obtaining a copy of WebLogic Server

Installing WebLogic Server

Installing JDBC drivers

Selecting an IDE to use with WebLogic Server

✦ ✦ ✦ ✦

My goal in this part of the book has been to introduce you to WebLogic Server's many capabilities and to help you understand how to field a team that can effectively take advantage of them. I've also given you some ideas on how to design J2EE applications that can be deployed with WebLogic.

The rest of this book is hands-on, showing you in great detail how to configure WebLogic's features, how to write code that uses those features, and how to deploy and test that code. To derive the most benefit from this book, you need to install WebLogic Server and create a WebLogic environment to play in. This chapter shows you how to do so.

I start by showing you how to install the simplest possible WebLogic development environment on a computer and verify that it is working correctly. I then show you how to connect WebLogic to two popular relational database systems, Oracle and Microsoft SQL Server, so that you can write and test database code. Finally, I give you some tips and techniques on how to create a WebLogic development environment that supports a complete application development workflow, from development to testing to final deployment.

I want to make this chapter concrete without making it too long, so I limit my discussion to WebLogic Server 6.1 running under the Windows 2000 Server operating system. WebLogic runs on a multitude of platforms, including several flavors of Unix, but showing how to install and configure WebLogic on each platform would take too much space. Many developers, especially individual developers, start with Windows 2000 anyway, so I think the greatest number of readers will benefit if I focus on that platform. Knowledgeable Unix developers can easily adapt the instructions I give here to the version of Unix that they are using. The steps to install WebLogic on those platforms are fairly similar and well-documented in the WebLogic manuals.

After you have finished reading this chapter, you will have a fully functional copy of WebLogic Server running on your machine, ready to conquer the material in the rest of this book. So let's get to work!

Configuring a Computer for Development

WebLogic Server's published hardware requirements are modest and sufficient for one developer working with one computer. The minimum requirements for an Intel-based, Windows system are the following:

- Hardware: Pentium 200MHz or faster, 85MB free disk space, 64MB RAM
- Operating System: Microsoft Windows NT 4.0 or Microsoft Windows 2000

Obviously, the more capable your computer, the more productive you will be. I run WebLogic on a laptop running Windows 2000 Server. This machine has a 750MHz Pentium III chip, a 20GB hard drive, and 256MB of RAM. In addition to WebLogic Server, it comfortably supports my Oracle 8i and Microsoft SQL Server 7 installations, so I can develop and test database code no matter where I go.

Note that the stated minimums are not at all sufficient for large, production systems. Requirements for those will vary, depending on user traffic, application complexity, clustering configurations, and so on.

In addition to the hardware and software requirements, WebLogic Server 6.1 requires the following be installed on the computer running WebLogic Server:

- Java Development Kit (JDK) 1.3. At this writing, JDK 1.3.1 is bundled with WebLogic 6.1 and is automatically installed by WebLogic's installer.
- Microsoft Internet Explorer 5.*x* or Netscape 4.7.*x*. You need one of these Web browsers to run the WebLogic Console application (used to administer WebLogic).

Obtaining a Copy of WebLogic Server

The quickest way to get a copy of WebLogic Server is to download it from the BEA Web site. BEA provides complete, fully functional copies of all its products on its Web site. The download URL for WebLogic Server 6.1 is `http://commerce.bea.com/downloads/weblogic_server.jsp`. Beware—the download for the Windows 2000 version of WebLogic Server is approximately 75 megabytes.

In addition to the product itself, you need a valid license file under which to run WebLogic Server. BEA controls distribution of WebLogic Server through the use of XML license files. These files contain encrypted keys that enable the product to varying degrees, depending on the type of license you purchase. The free download of WebLogic Server includes a license key for a 30-day evaluation that allows up to five simultaneous connections to the server. This is sufficient for most evaluations and is certainly sufficient for use with this book.

Another factor you need to consider is which version of the J2EE you plan to use for development. The default download of WebLogic Server supports J2EE 1.3, which includes EJB 2.0, JSP 1.2, Servlet 2.3, and J2EE Connector Architecture 1.0. A separate download is available that supports J2EE 1.2 only. But the default download is backward-compatible with J2EE 1.2, so if you're installing WebLogic Server for the first time, the default download is probably your best bet. It's also the version you need for this book.

All WebLogic Server downloads include the jDriver for Oracle, the jDriver for Microsoft SQL Server, and the jDriver for Informix. You can, therefore, connect to any of these databases after installing WebLogic Server. The drivers include 30-day evaluation licenses that support up to two simultaneous database connections each.

Finally, you may want to download your own copy of the WebLogic documentation set, which is available in PDF format. You can find the documentation at `http://edocs.bea.com/wls/docs61/pdf.html`.

Installing WebLogic Server

This section walks you through the procedure for installing WebLogic Server 6.1 on a computer running the Windows 2000 operating system. The steps for installing on Windows NT 4.0 are exactly the same. Before continuing, you may also want to read the *BEA WebLogic Server Installation Guide* included with the WebLogic documentation set.

I will perform what BEA calls a GUI-mode installation; in other words, I will interactively install WebLogic by using its GUI-based installer program rather than perform a script-based or silent installation.

Script-based and unattended modes for installing WebLogic Server are available for use by system administrators. See the *WebLogic Server Installation Guide* for details.

Running the installer

Downloading WebLogic Server 6.1 places a file called `weblogic610_win.exe` on your computer. This executable is the installer program. To begin the installation, run this program. After a few moments, the installation screen appears, as shown in Figure 4-1.

Figure 4-1: WebLogic Server 6.1 installation start screen

Choose a language (the options are English, French, German, and Spanish) and then click OK. The installer walks you through a series of screens where you can set your installation options. One option is to install the server with examples, or just the server only, as shown in Figure 4-2.

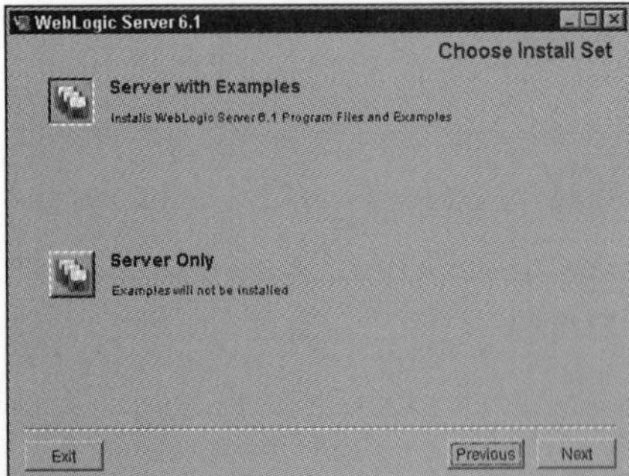

Figure 4-2: Installing WebLogic Server with examples

I recommend installing the examples for two reasons. First, you can see how multiple WebLogic Server instances are configured on one computer, because separate instances are installed for the default server, the BEA examples, and the Java Pet Store application. It's instructive to see how these servers are configured. Second, you can use the examples to accelerate your learning of WebLogic.

The next step is to choose or define a BEA Home Directory, as shown in Figure 4-3. If you have never installed WebLogic on your computer before, your only option is to create a new BEA Home Directory, which is where information about the installation and configuration of your installed BEA products is kept.

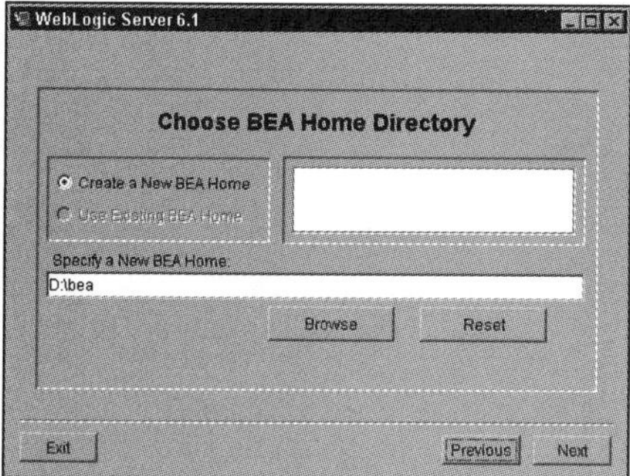

Figure 4-3: Creating a new BEA Home Directory

You can install *one* copy of each *different* version of every BEA product in the BEA Home Directory. You can, for example, install WebLogic 6.0 *and* WebLogic 6.1 in the same BEA Home without any ill effects. As such, BEA recommends you create only one BEA Home per computer.

Enter a directory path for your BEA Home (it can reside on any drive that has enough room) and click Next. From Figure 4-3 you can see that I elected to specify `D:\bea` as my BEA Home.

The next step is to choose a directory into which the WebLogic Server product will be installed. This directory need not be a subdirectory of the BEA Home Directory, but the default option is to put it there in a directory called `wlserver6.1`, as shown in Figure 4-4. Choosing this option is fine for now.

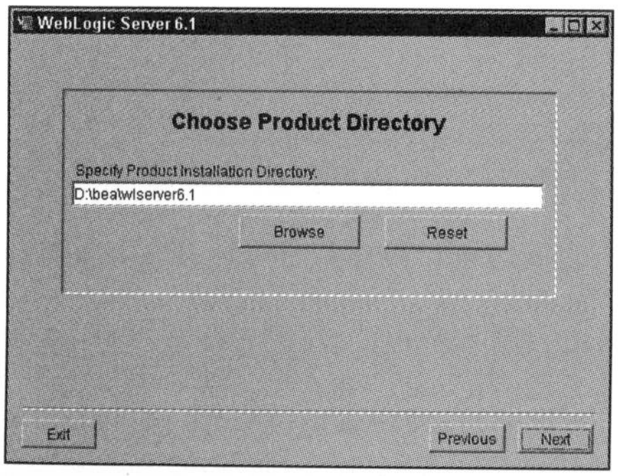

Figure 4-4: Choosing a product directory for WebLogic Server

The next step is to specify a default server configuration. Figure 4-5 shows the default options.

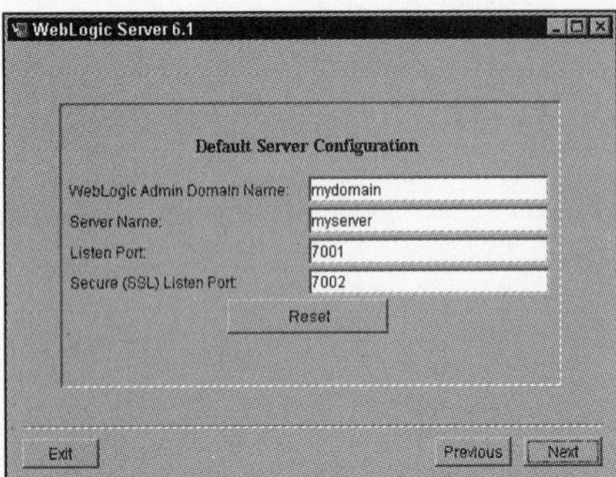

Figure 4-5: Default server configuration screen

The meanings of the entries on this screen are as follows:

✦ *WebLogic Admin Domain Name*: The name of the WebLogic domain into which this WebLogic Server instance will be installed. It can be the name of a new or existing domain. A WebLogic domain is a collection of one or more WebLogic servers (or clusters) grouped for administrative purposes and sharing common configuration parameters. The servers in a domain are managed as a group, using the WebLogic Console administrative application. WebLogic domains are completely independent of Windows NT, Windows 2000, and Internet domains. They exist only to facilitate the management of multiple WebLogic Server instances.

✦ *Server Name*: The name of this WebLogic Server, which must be unique within its domain.

✦ *Listen Port*: The TCP/IP port on which WebLogic's HTTP server listens for requests. The default port is 7001, but you can change it to any valid port. It is common to change this to port 80 if you plan to use WebLogic as your default HTTP server.

✦ *Secure (SSL) Listen Port*: The TCP/IP port on which WebLogic's HTTPS server listens for requests. The default is 7002, but you can change it to any valid port. You can change it to port 443, for example, if you plan to use WebLogic as your default HTTPS server.

A useful strategy for creating a WebLogic development environment is to create separate domains for development, testing, and production. This enables you to stage your applications on the appropriate servers as they move through the development life cycle. It also enables you to protect production code from experiments you may be conducting in the development area, because each domain has its own distinct configuration.

To create such an environment, define three domains: `dev`, `test`, and `prod`. Within each domain, create a server called `admin`, which is the default, administrative server for that domain. Later, you can add additional servers to each domain with different names and purposes.

In this example, I take the first step toward creating such a structure by calling the domain `dev` and the server `admin`, as shown in Figure 4-6. I keep the default settings for the ports, 7001 and 7002.

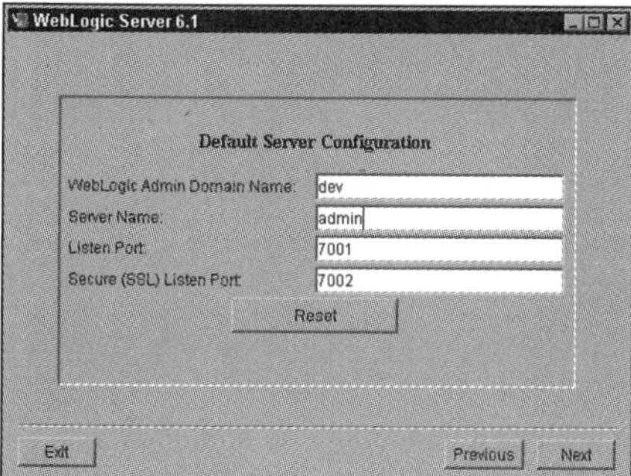

Figure 4-6: Creating the admin server of my dev domain

Administration Servers versus Managed Servers

WebLogic Server contains an implementation of the Java Management Extension (JMX) standard called the *Administration Service.* Management of a WebLogic domain's configuration occurs through the Administration Service, and the WebLogic Console is your window into its features.

WebLogic is designed so that only one WebLogic server in a domain can run the Administration Service. This server is called the *administration server.* All other servers in the domain are managed by the administration server and obtain their runtime configuration from it. These servers are called *managed servers.*

The administration server is the single point of control for the entire domain, and it must be running for you to make changes to the configurations of any of the managed servers running beneath it. If you run only one server for development purposes, you must run it as an administration server or you can't configure it.

By default, when you execute the class `weblogic.Server` to create a server instance, the server starts up as an administration server. To start a server as a managed server, you must specify its administration server by using the `-Dweblogic.management.server=URL` command line option. In the absence of this option, the server starts as an administration server.

For more details about how to use administration servers and managed servers, see the *BEA WebLogic Server Administration Guide.*

Next, the installer asks whether you want to install the default WebLogic Server as a Windows service, as shown in Figure 4-7. For development purposes, it's usually better not to do this, so you can explicitly control the starting and stopping of your server. But in a production environment, installing WebLogic Server as a service provides two key benefits:

- ✦ WebLogic Server restarts automatically whenever the machine restarts.
- ✦ You can start and stop WebLogic Server from a remote machine by using the server management tools included with Windows 2000.

Because I am installing a development environment, I elect not to install WebLogic Server as a service.

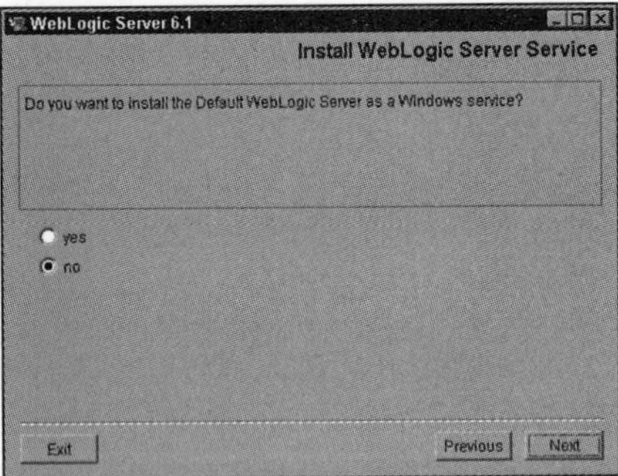

Figure 4-7: The option to install WebLogic Server as a Windows service

The final step is to define a password for WebLogic's built-in `system` account, as shown in Figure 4-8. This password is required to start the server and also to log into the server by using the WebLogic Console administrative application. Choose a password (between 8 and 20 characters), enter it twice, and then click Install.

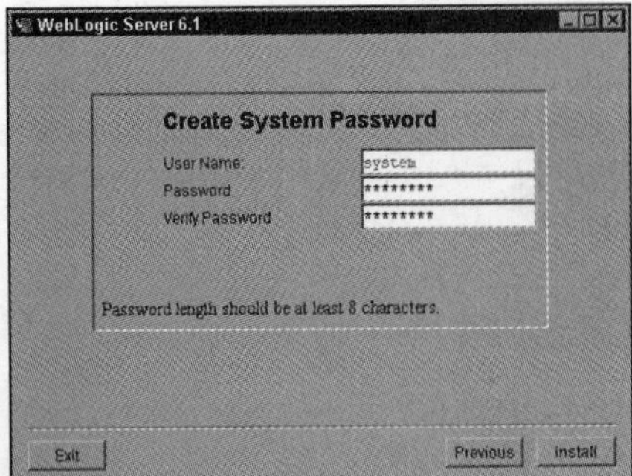

Figure 4-8: Defining a password for WebLogic's system account

After a few moments, installation is complete, and your WebLogic Server is ready for use. You don't need to reboot the computer.

Starting WebLogic Server

The best way to tell whether installation succeeded is to start WebLogic Server. To do so, choose Start ➪ Programs ➪ BEA WebLogic Business Platform ➪ WebLogic Server 6.1 ➪ Start Default Server. A command window opens, and the startup sequence begins. You are prompted to enter a password to boot WebLogic Server; enter the password you defined during the installation process and then press Enter. After a few moments, WebLogic Server starts and is ready to go, and the command window looks something like Figure 4-9.

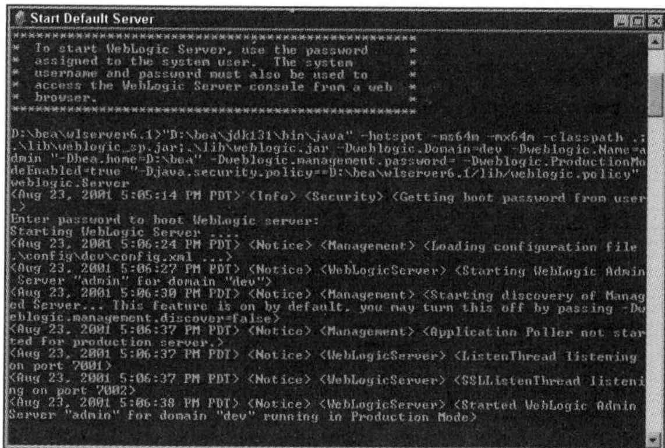

Figure 4-9: WebLogic Server up and running

Running the WebLogic Console

After the server is up and running, start the WebLogic Console by choosing Start ➪ Programs ➪ BEA WebLogic Business Platform ➪ WebLogic Server 6.1 ➪ Start Default Console. You are prompted for a username and password. Type **system** for the username and enter the password you defined during installation. After a few moments, the Console's main screen appears, as shown in Figure 4-10.

The WebLogic Console is simply a Web application deployed on WebLogic Server. It presents its user interface by using the default Web browser on your computer. You can exit the WebLogic Console by closing its browser window, but leave it open for now.

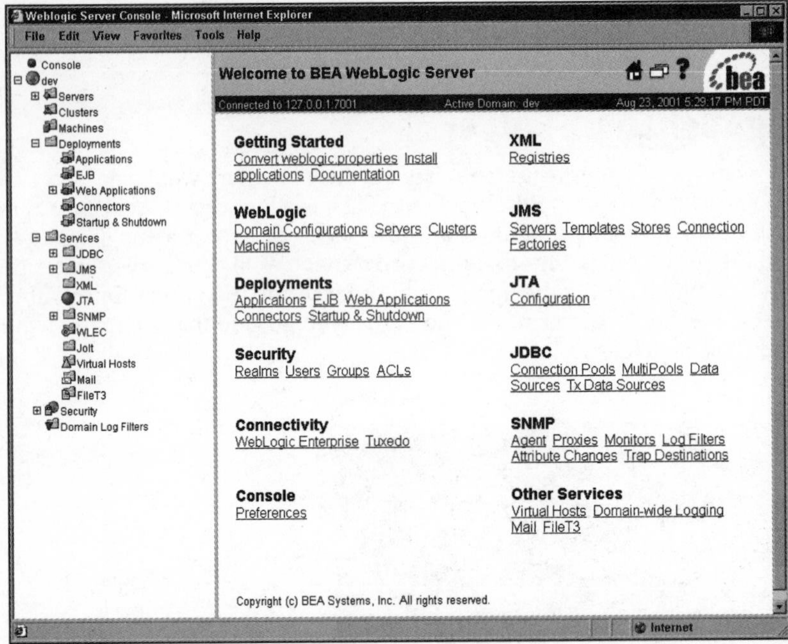

Figure 4-10: The WebLogic Console

Shutting down WebLogic Server

To perform an orderly shutdown of WebLogic Server, right-click the server's entry in the domain tree of the WebLogic Console and then choose Stop this Server, as shown in Figure 4-11.

After the server is shut down, Console commands against it no longer work; you need to restart the server as described earlier in this chapter before you can execute Console commands against it.

Optimizing the WebLogic Server startup process for development

Because you will likely be starting and stopping your development WebLogic Server frequently, you may want to perform the following steps to optimize your development environment.

Add the password to the startup script

Having to enter a password every time you start WebLogic Server becomes tedious after a while. You can short-circuit this by storing the system password in WebLogic's startup script. Then the server starts without prompting for the password.

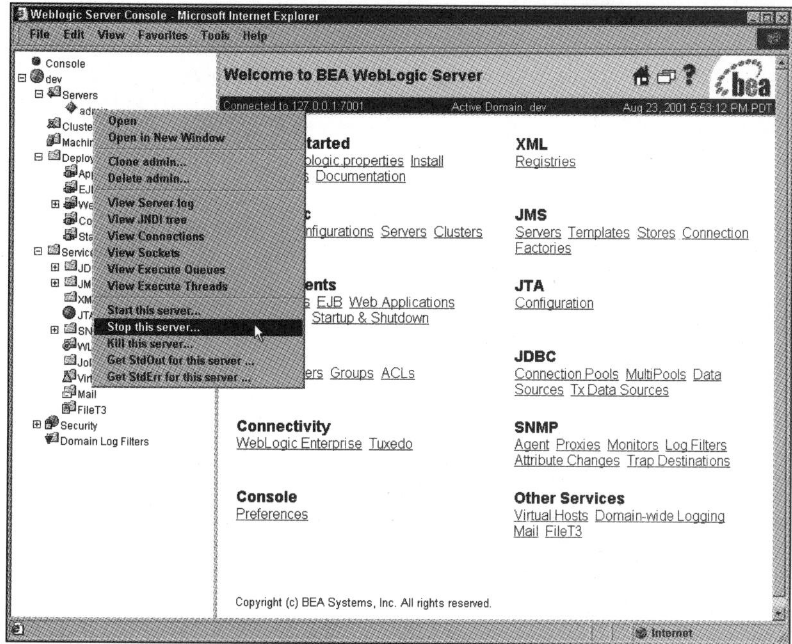

Figure 4-11: Stopping a WebLogic Server from the WebLogic Console

Of course, doing so exposes your password in clear text to anyone who has access to the startup script. For one developer working on one computer, this isn't usually a problem (especially if you choose an innocuous password), but larger shops with several developers sharing machines in a lab may not want to do this.

To add the password to the startup script, edit the following file:

```
wlserver6.1\config\<servername>\startWebLogic.cmd
```

If your password is *password*, for example, add it to the indicated line, as follows:

```
@rem Set WLS_PW equal to your system password for no password prompt server
startup.
set WLS_PW=password
```

Start the server in development mode

While you have `startWebLogic.cmd` open, let's make a few more changes. The first is to change WebLogic Server's startup mode to development mode.

WebLogic Server's startup modes are a new feature in version 6.1. By default (if you don't start WebLogic with the `-Dweblogic.ProductionModeEnabled` option), WebLogic Server starts in development mode, which enables the autodeployment feature. With autodeployment enabled, WebLogic polls the /applications subdirectory of the active domain to detect changes in deployed applications. This is a useful feature during development, because it means you don't have to restart WebLogic Server every time you make changes to your code. But the feature incurs additional overhead that you probably want to avoid in production systems, which should not change except in rare and controlled circumstances.

To change the startup mode to development mode, change the indicated line in startWebLogic.cmd as follows:

```
@rem Set Production Mode.  When set to true, the server starts up in production
mode.  When
@rem set to false, the server starts up in development mode.  The default is
false.
set STARTMODE=false
```

Disable the discovery of managed servers

Recall that WebLogic Server can run either as an administration server for a domain or a managed server within the domain. If you are running only one WebLogic instance for development purposes, you always run it as an administration server, and it has no managed servers running beneath it.

By default, when WebLogic Server is started as an administration server, it attempts to discover which, if any, of its managed servers are running. It does so by consulting a file called running-managed-servers.xml, which is a list of the managed servers that the administration server knows about. This file is created on the fly when you run an administration server and start another instance with the startManagedWebLogic command. The file is stored in the configuration directory for the domain.

When you set -Dweblogic.management.discover=false, you disable the capability of the administration server to detect the presence of managed servers that may be running. You may want to do this to save a little time at startup if you know you will be running an administration server, but no managed servers, in your domain. To do so, open startWebLogic.cmd and change the command line to start WebLogic as shown:

```
"%JAVA_HOME%\bin\java" -hotspot -ms64m -mx64m -classpath %CLASSPATH% -
Dweblogic.Domain=dev -Dweblogic.Name=admin "-Dbea.home=D:\bea"
-Dweblogic.management.password=%WLS_PW% -
Dweblogic.ProductionModeEnabled=%STARTMODE% "-
Djava.security.policy==D:\bea\wlserver6.1/lib/weblogic.policy" -
Dweblogic.management.discover=false weblogic.Server
```

Examining the environment

Figure 4-12 shows the directory structure of the WebLogic installation I just performed. At the top level of this structure is the `bea` directory, which is my BEA Home Directory. Within this directory are directories containing JDK 1.3.1, installation logs, and Java utilities. The contents of these directories are shared by all BEA products installed to this BEA Home Directory.

My BEA Home Directory also contains a directory called `wlserver6.1`, which is the product directory for WebLogic Server 6.1. Although I elected to install WebLogic Server inside my BEA Home Directory, I could have installed it anywhere on my computer. The installer would have linked it to my home directory via classpath settings and the installation log file.

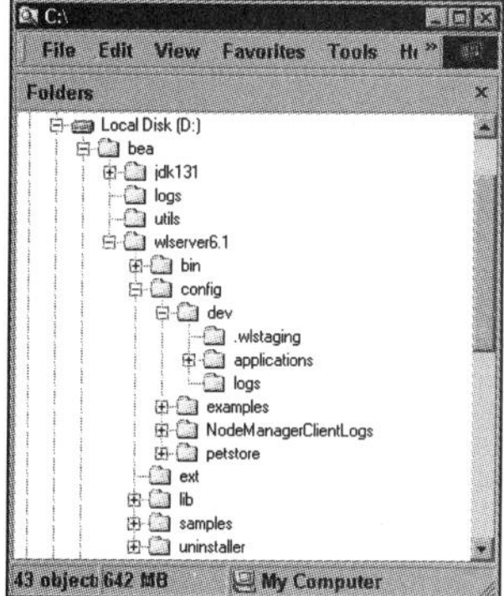

Figure 4-12: WebLogic directory structure

Inside the `wlserver6.1` directory are several subdirectories. Table 4-1 explains their contents.

Table 4-1
WebLogic Server Directory Structure

Directory	*Contents*
`/bin`	Executable programs, plus Windows libraries to support JDBC drivers, Apache plug-ins, Internet Server (IS) API plug-ins, Netscape Server (NS) API plug ins, and other native code packages.

Continued

Table 4-1 (continued)

Directory	Contents
`/config`	Configuration data for each domain in the configuration. Each domain is defined in a separate subdirectory, the name of which is the name of that domain. When you install WebLogic Server with the examples, three subdirectories are created in the `/config` directory: 1. A directory for the domain specified in the installer (`mydomain` is the default; the one I installed is called `dev`). 2. `examples`. 3. `petstore`. Each subdirectory contains the Extensible Markup Language (XML) configuration file (`config.xml`) and the security resources for that domain.
`/ext`	XML JAR files.
`/lib`	The JAR files to run WebLogic Server, plus Unix libraries to support JDBC drivers, Apache plug-ins, Internet Server (IS) API plug-ins, Netscape Server (NS) API plug-ins, and other native code packages.
`/samples`	Sample code and resources. The samples directory contains the following subdirectories: 1. `examples`. A collection of simple applications that demonstrate WebLogic's features. 2. `petStore`. The WebLogic Server Pet Store application, which is a full-blown e-commerce application based on the Sun Microsystems, Inc., J2EE Blueprint example. The J2EE Blueprint example has been slightly modified to demonstrate WebLogic's features and capabilities. 3. `eval`. An evaluation copy of the Cloudscape relational database management system (RDBMS), which is included so that you can run the examples and Pet Store applications with a live database.
`/uninstaller`	Code required to uninstall WebLogic Server 6.1.

Additional directories related to service packs may be present if you have installed WebLogic Server service packs. Service packs contain bug fixes and improvements to WebLogic Server and become available from time to time. At this writing, there are no service packs for WebLogic Server 6.1.

Adding domains for testing and production

I mentioned earlier that a useful strategy for creating a WebLogic development environment is to create separate domains for development, testing, and production so that you can isolate the effects of your development from code that is being tested or is already in production. I have already created a domain for development (`dev`), so in this section I show you how to create additional domains for testing (`test`) and production (`prod`).

Start WebLogic Server and the WebLogic Console. From the Console home page, click the Domain Configurations link, located under the WebLogic heading on the right side of the screen. The screen shown in Figure 4-13 appears.

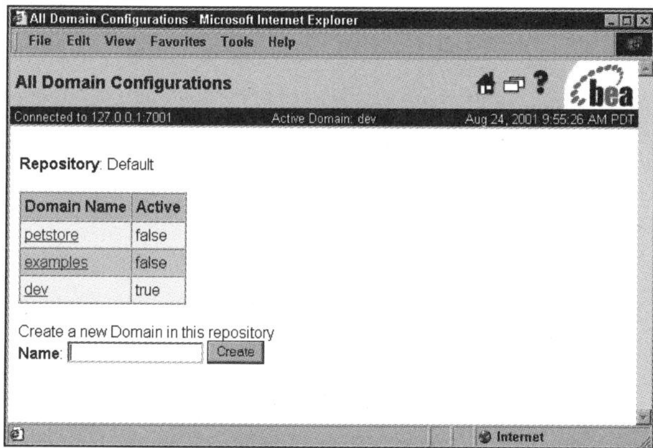

Figure 4-13: Configuring a new domain

Type **test** for the domain name, and then click Create. You immediately return to the Console home page, except now the domain tree is pointed to the test domain, as shown in Figure 4-14.

The next step is to create an administration server for the new domain. To do so, right-click the Servers node in the domain tree and choose Configure a New Server from the menu. The screen in Figure 4-15 appears. To save space, I have already filled in values for the server Name (`admin`) and Listen Port (`7011`).

Note

You can choose any value you want for Listen Port, but make sure that it is different from the other WebLogic Servers on your computer so that they can all run at the same time.

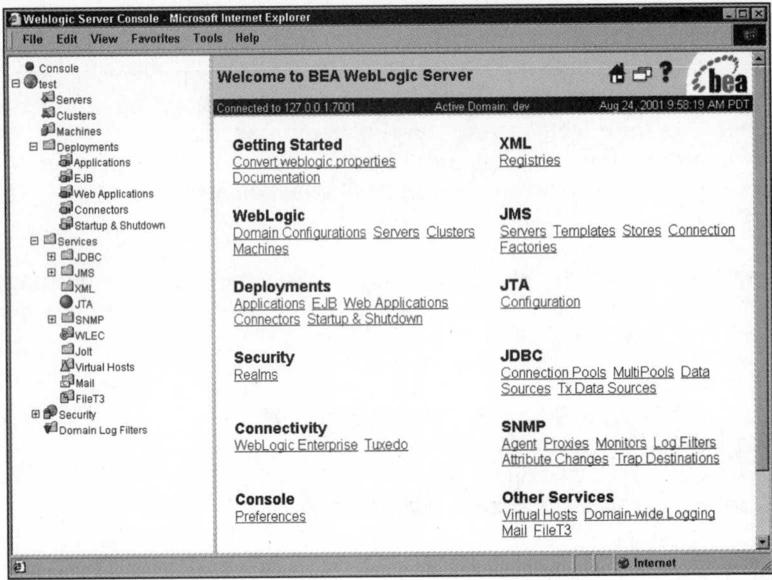

Figure 4-14: The test domain

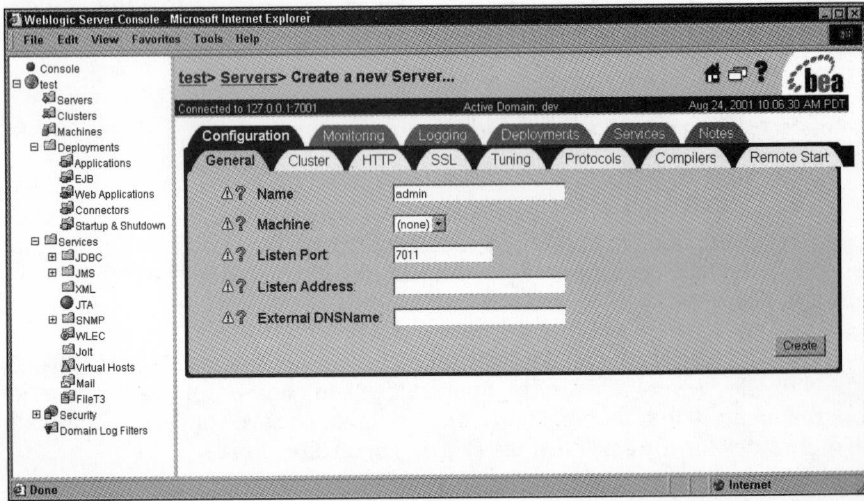

Figure 4-15: Creating a new WebLogic server

The data I have provided in Figure 4-15 is all that is needed to create a new server. Click Create.

At this point, the Console has created a new subdirectory in the `wlserver6.1/config` directory with the name of the new domain, `test`. Initially, the directory contains only a `config.xml` file for the domain. Using Windows Explorer or another disk management utility, find this directory on your hard drive and create a subdirectory within it called `applications`, as shown in Figure 4-16.

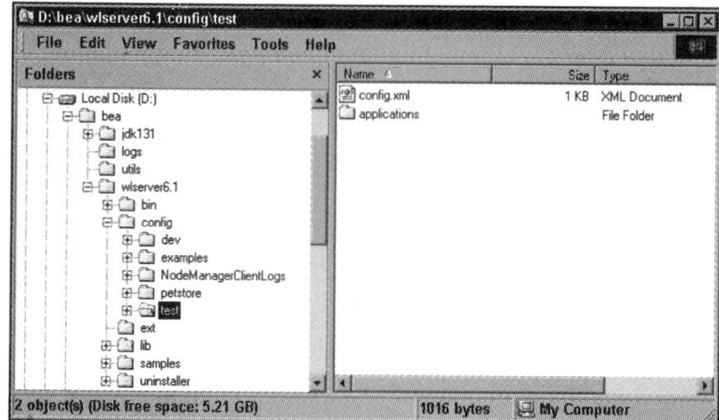

Figure 4-16: Preparing the new domain's directory for use

Next, copy the scripts `startWebLogic.cmd` and `startManagedWebLogic.cmd` from the `/config/dev` directory to the `/config/test` directory. You need to edit the new copies so that they work for the new domain. In each copy, change the command line to start WebLogic (near the bottom of the script) so that the name of the new domain, `test`, replaces that of the old domain, `dev`, in the following entry:

```
-Dweblogic.Domain=test
```

Change the `cd` command at the end of the scripts to read as follows:

```
cd config\test
```

At the beginning of `startWebLogic.cmd`, find the line that reads as follows:

```
echo startWebLogic.cmd must be run from the config\dev directory
```

Change it to the following:

```
echo startWebLogic.cmd must be run from the config\test directory
```

A similar line is in `startManagedWebLogic.cmd`; change it as well.

Finally, copy the files `SerializedSystemIni.dat` and `fileRealm.properties` from the `/config/dev` directory to the `/config/test` directory. (These files are related to security and are discussed later in the book.) After you have done this, you can start the new server. Then repeat the steps in this section to create the production domain, `prod`. After you finish, your WebLogic environment should resemble the one shown in Figure 4-17.

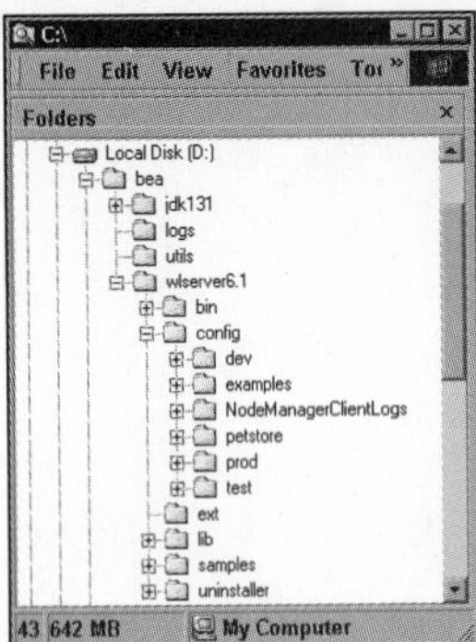

Figure 4-17: WebLogic installation with domains for dev, test, and prod

Installing JDBC Drivers

One of the most common uses of WebLogic Server is to Web-enable data residing in relational database management systems (RDBMSs), such as Oracle, Microsoft SQL Server, Cloudscape, and others. Access to such data is enabled through the Java Database Connectivity (JDBC) API, which is part of J2EE.

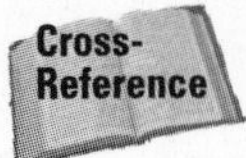

JDBC is covered fully in Chapter 5.

JDBC is implemented with drivers provided by BEA, database vendors, and others. As I mentioned earlier, WebLogic Server is bundled with the jDriver for Oracle, jDriver for Microsoft SQL Server, and jDriver for Informix.

Correct installation and configuration of JDBC drivers depends on the database you are using, the drivers you are using, and how your database and network are configured. You can find detailed instructions for installing the BEA-provided drivers in the following locations:

✦ *Installing and Using WebLogic jDriver for Oracle*, available at `http://edocs.bea.com/wls/docs61/oracle/index.html`

✦ *Installing and Using WebLogic jDriver for Microsoft SQL Server*, available at `http://edocs.bea.com/wls/docs61/mssqlserver4/index.html`

✦ *Installing and Using WebLogic jDriver for Informix*, available at `http://edocs.bea.com/wls/docs61/informix4/index.html`

Selecting an IDE to use with WebLogic Server

Many developers today use an *integrated development environment* (IDE) to facilitate the rapid prototyping, development, and deployment of applications. These environments contain a number of labor-saving features that automate redundant tasks, such as generating EJB templates, XML deployment descriptors, and so on. They also provide source code management and build support, further increasing developer productivity.

Two of the most popular IDE products on the market today are WebGain Studio and Borland JBuilder. Both products contain hooks for integrating with WebLogic Server that may increase the productivity of your team. If you don't use one of these products already, I recommend you evaluate them to see whether they have a place in your shop.

You can find more information about WebGain Studio at `www.webgain.com/products/webgain_studio` and more information about Borland JBuilder at `www.borland.com/jbuilder`.

Summary

Installing and configuring WebLogic Server is relatively easy, considering the complexity of the product. This chapter has shown you how to download, install, and configure a flexible WebLogic development environment. I have also pointed you to additional steps you may want to take, such as installing JDBC drivers and using an IDE with WebLogic, to make your development environment as complete and productive as possible.

The rest of this book is spent playing in the sandbox you have just created. So grab your pail and shovel and prepare to dive in!

✦ ✦ ✦

P A R T

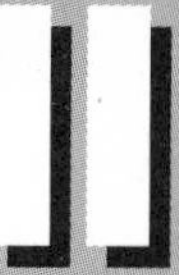

WebLogic and the J2EE APIs

✦ ✦ ✦ ✦

In This Part

✦ ✦ ✦ ✦

Working with WebLogic JDBC

✦ ✦ ✦ ✦

In This Chapter

Understanding JDBC

Understanding WebLogic JDBC

Configuring WebLogic JDBC

Programming WebLogic JDBC

✦ ✦ ✦ ✦

Java Database Connectivity, or JDBC, is the standard API used by Java programs to communicate with database systems. JDBC provides a uniform programming interface to any JDBC-compliant database system, and provides powerful features for solving enterprise-level database management tasks.

WebLogic, of course, provides excellent support for JDBC, and contains a number of features that allow you to write portable, maintainable, available, and efficient JDBC code.

This chapter begins with an overview of JDBC, introducing you to important JDBC concepts and terms. It then dives into WebLogic's JDBC features, showing you in great detail how to configure and program them.

It is not my intent to provide a comprehensive JDBC tutorial in this chapter. Plenty of other resources are available for this purpose, including Sun's JDBC tutorial at `http://java.sun.com/docs/books/tutorial/jdbc/index.html`. My goal is to show you how to use JDBC in the WebLogic environment, focusing on how to configure and use WebLogic's drivers, connection pools, data sources, and transaction support. When you are finished with this chapter, you will have a solid understanding of how to combine WebLogic with today's leading database engines to build fast, reliable, data-driven applications.

Understanding JDBC

This section explains "generic" JDBC architecture, focusing on issues independent of vendor implementations (including BEAs). A clear understanding of these concepts allows you to take firm control of database access issues in your applications, and helps you take better advantage of WebLogic's excellent support for JDBC.

JDBC versions and packages

WebLogic 6.1 runs on top of JDK 1.3, which contains JDBC Version 2.0. JDBC 2.0 consists of two sets of calls: the JDBC 2.0 Core API, and the JDBC 2.0 Standard Extension API. The Core API includes all the functionality of JDBC 1.0, plus enhancements for handling query results, batch updates, Java object persistence, and advanced SQL data types. The Standard Extension API includes additional enterprise features, such as support for connection pools, distributed transactions, and sophisticated result set handling.

JDBC is implemented in two packages:

- `java.sql`, the Core API
- `javax.sql`, the Optional Package API

To work with JDBC in your WebLogic applications, simply import these packages into your code. You don't need to import special WebLogic packages because the JDBC API simply routes calls to whatever JDBC driver is in use.

JDBC architecture

The JDBC API encapsulates relational database access into a hierarchy of Java classes and interfaces. JDBC is a fairly low-level API; in other words, it doesn't magically make a relational database look like a set of Java objects, but it gives you the tools to do so yourself if you wish. After explaining JDBC drivers, which contain database-specific implementations of the AII, this section explains the major components of the API and how they are related.

Drivers and driver types

JDBC *drivers* manage data interchange between Java applications and relational database management systems (RDBMSs). To understand how these drivers work, it's helpful to know how databases exchange data with outside systems in general.

All major databases, such as Oracle, Sybase Adaptive Server, Microsoft SQL Server, and others, ship with *network libraries* that are used to communicate with the database over a network. Network libraries typically consist of a client-side component that communicates with applications running on a client machine, and a server-side component that communicates with the database server itself. The client-side and server-side components in turn communicate with each other over the network. Figure 5-1 shows database access through a typical network library.

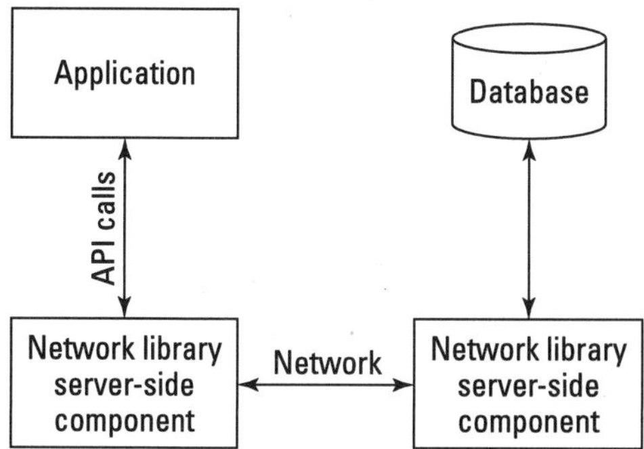

Figure 5-1: Accessing a database through its network library

Network libraries expose their functionality through APIs that are callable from C, C++, and other programming languages. On the Windows platform, network libraries usually ship as dynamic link libraries (DLLs). Examples of network libraries include the Oracle Call Interface (OCI), Sybase Open Client, and DBLibrary, a legacy network library used both by Sybase and Microsoft SQL Server.

Note

BEA has licensed OCI for distribution with WebLogic Server. On Windows machines, you can find the OCI DLLs in the `\bea\wlserver6.1\bin\oci816_7`**,** `oci816_8`**, and** `oci817_8` **directories.**

Figure 5-2 shows an application accessing databases from different vendors through their respective network libraries.

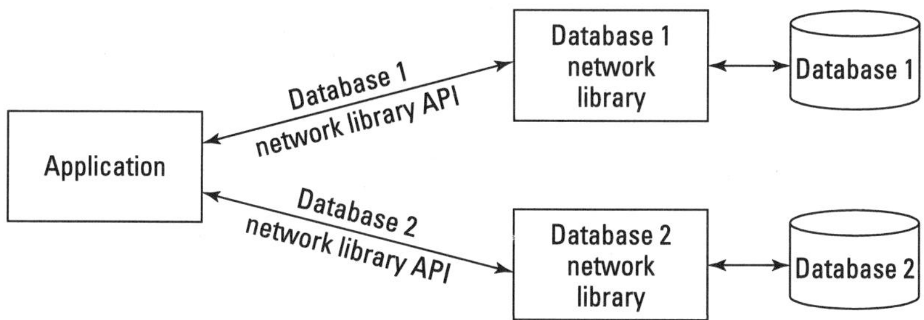

Figure 5-2: An application accessing multiple databases through their native drivers

Because they're written to exploit the special features of a vendor's database, and because their programmers have intimate knowledge of that database's inner workings, network libraries offer the best performance of any type of remote database access. But every network library API is different, so code written to one vendor's API will not work with any other vendor's database, and vice-versa. This makes it difficult and time-consuming to write applications that support multiple databases.

To solve this problem, several vendors came up with the idea of abstracting network library functionality into a high level API that sits on top of the various network libraries. Developers write to the high level API, which makes calls to network libraries behind the scenes. At the same time, database vendors make sure that their network libraries provide support for the calls in the high level API. Through this mechanism, access to vendor-specific functionality is possibly reduced, but this is offset by the developer's ability to write one set of code to access any database.

The most well-known solution of this type is Microsoft's Open Database Connectivity (ODBC) API. Over a period of several years, ODBC has become the de facto standard for accessing databases from applications running on the Microsoft Windows platform, and other platforms as well. As a result, virtually all major database vendors offer ODBC drivers for their products. Figure 5-3 shows an application accessing different vendors' databases through ODBC.

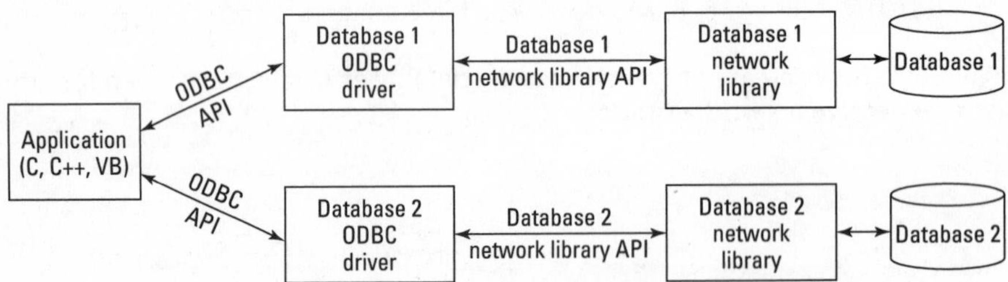

Figure 5-3: An application accessing multiple databases through ODBC

JDBC is an ODBC-like solution designed for Java developers. But unlike ODBC, which supports applications written in multiple programming languages, JDBC is designed exclusively for Java, and supports applications written only in Java.

Sun has divided JDBC drivers into four different types, based on how they're implemented.

Type 1 drivers

A type 1 JDBC driver provides a bridge between Java applications and ODBC drivers, as shown in Figure 5-4 (in fact, this type of driver is called a *JDBC-ODBC bridge*). Type 1 drivers are good for development purposes, but because of the multiple driver layers involved, their performance is generally not sufficient for production systems.

Figure 5-4: An application accessing a database through a type 1 JDBC driver

Type 2 drivers

Type 2 JDBC drivers link applications directly to network libraries, as shown in Figure 5-5. Because of this, you must install the network libraries on computers that use the drivers, such as the one hosting WebLogic Server. Most database vendors provide type 2 drivers for their products. Type 2 drivers provide better performance than type 1 drivers because they bypass the ODBC layer. As a result, they are commonly used in both development and production systems. The WebLogic jDriver for Oracle is an example of a type 2 JDBC driver.

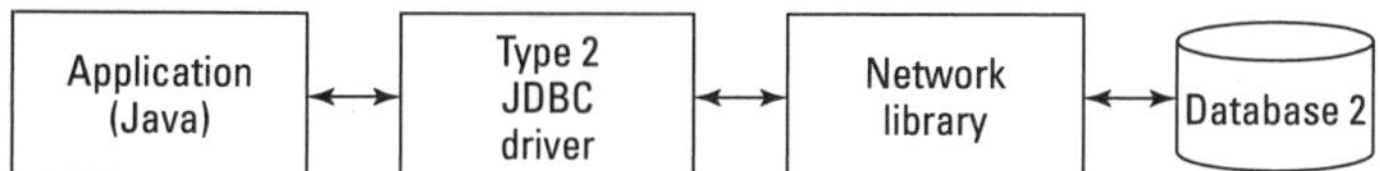

Figure 5-5: An application accessing a database through a type 2 JDBC driver

Type 3 drivers

Type 3 JDBC drivers link applications to middleware servers that allow easy client connections to multiple database back ends (see Figure 5-6). To achieve this, the middleware server maps the application's JDBC calls to appropriate drivers, which are installed on the middleware server, not on the client. The advantage of this approach is that it removes the necessity to install network libraries on client machines. The WebLogic Pool driver is an example of a type 3 JDBC driver, as is the WebLogic RMI driver.

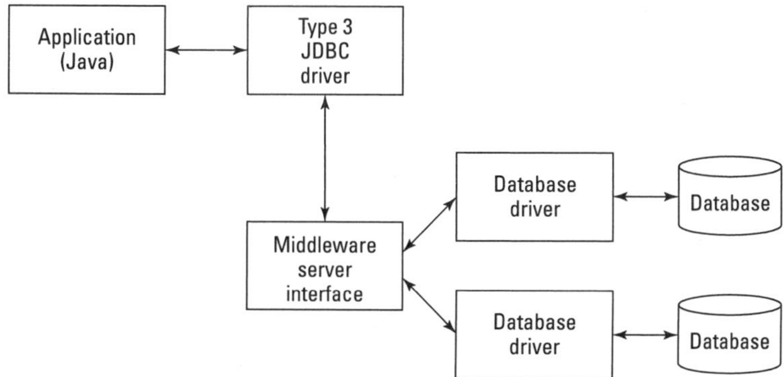

Figure 5-6: An application accessing a database through a type 3 JDBC driver

Type 4 drivers

The final type of driver is the type 4 JDBC driver, which is implemented completely in Java and requires no additional drivers or client-side network libraries to function (in fact, the client-side network libraries are incorporated into this type of driver). Figure 5-7 shows a type 4 driver. Type 4 drivers, like network libraries, are vendor- and database-specific. As such, they provide maximum, optimal access to the vendor's database features, but cannot be used with databases from any other vendor. The Sybase jConnect driver is an example of a type 4 JDBC driver.

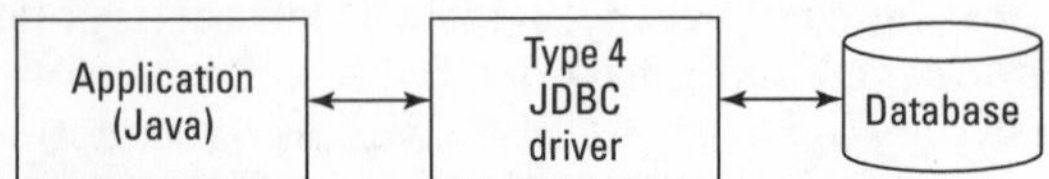

Figure 5-7: An application accessing a database through a type 4 JDBC driver

Choosing the right driver for your application is a complex decision that depends on several factors, including the version of JDBC you plan to use (1.0 vs. 2.0), the availability of drivers that support the desired JDBC version, and your database server, desired application performance, requirements for transaction support, software licensing issues for the JDBC driver and database, the overall topology of your application, and your application's expected patterns of database access. You may find it advantageous to test several candidate drivers and topologies before arriving at a final decision. You may even find that your final design should use different drivers for different tasks.

Sun maintains a directory of JDBC drivers on the Internet and currently contains over 150 different drivers. You can find the directory at `http://industry.java.sun.com/products/jdbc/drivers`.

Connections

A *connection* is a communication link between client-side Java code and the database server, established via the JDBC driver. It forms the context for all calls made against that database server. Before working with a database in your code, you must open a connection (unless you're using RowSets, but more on that later in this chapter).

In JDBC, connections are represented by the `java.sql.Connection` interface. Connections are obtained by calling the driver's `connect` method. After a connection is created, you can call its methods to get and set connection options, manage transactions, and create statement objects.

There are two major types of connections: *direct connections* and *pooled connections*.

Direct connections

Direct connections are opened and maintained directly in code, against a type 1, 2, or 4 JDBC driver that physically exists in the calling code's classpath. Code that opens direct connections is fully responsible for managing those connections, and must remember to close them when it's finished using them. Otherwise, the database server's connection limit may be exceeded, or the overall performance of the system may suffer due to too many open connections.

Pooled connections

Pooled connections are opened and maintained by J2EE servers, against one or more type 1, 2, or 4 JDBC drivers that physically exist in the server's classpath. Pooled connections are direct connections that are available to potentially any code running within the J2EE server's containers. Connection sharing is managed by a *pool driver,* which is a type 3 JDBC driver used to obtain pooled connections (pooled connections follow the access scheme shown in Figure 5-6).

At startup, the J2EE server is configured to open some number of pooled connections (five for this example). This becomes the pool's minimum size; the pool will always maintain at least five open connections to the database.

When a software module needs a connection, it requests it from the pool driver instead of from a two-tier JDBC driver. The pool driver returns a connection that is not being used, and marks that connection as busy. If all pooled connections are busy, the pool driver opens additional connections, the number of which is determined by its configuration parameters. When the caller is finished with a connection, it is marked as unused by the pool driver and returned to the pool for use by other callers.

If a large number of pool connections remain unused for a configurable period, and if the pool size is greater than the minimum, the pool can be configured to shrink itself in predetermined increments by physically closing connections. The pool, however, never shrinks below its minimum size.

Pooled connections are generally preferable to direct connections because they improve performance while conserving precious resources (such as database connections). In most applications, database connections are typically opened, used briefly (usually within the scope of a method), and then closed. This kind of usage pattern makes the idea of sharing connections a good one. Opening a database connection is a CPU- and network-intensive task. Repeatedly opening direct connections during the lifetime of an application is therefore a performance killer. Pooled connections are opened only once at server startup, eliminating this performance problem. Connections can be effectively shared because they're only used for short periods. And privileged information about connection parameters, such as database usernames and passwords, is available only to the pool driver, increasing system security and manageability.

Statements

A *statement* is used to issue a command to a database for the manipulation of data. Statements (also known as *queries*) are almost always written in Structured Query Language, or SQL. SQL is an industry standard language for database commands that is supported by all leading database products. SQL includes commands for retrieving, adding, modifying, and deleting data from a database.

Relational databases store data in *tables*. A table is a collection of zero or more rows of data, each with identical structure. Each row contains one or more columns that define the structure of the table. Oracle, for example, defines an example table called `EMP` (for employee) that contains the columns `EMPNO`, `ENAME`, `JOB`, and `HIREDATE`, among others. The table contains one row of data for each employee, as shown in Figure 5-8.

EMP			
EMPNO	**ENAME**	**JOB**	**HIREDATE**
7369	SMITH	CLERK	12/17/1980
7499	ALLEN	SALESMAN	02/20/1981
7521	WARD	SALESMAN	02/22/1981
7566	JONES	MANAGER	04/02/1981
7654	MARTIN	SALESMAN	09/28/1981

Figure 5-8: Oracle's EMP database table

SQL statements operate on database tables. SQL commands that retrieve data return some number of rows, depending on the query. For example, the SQL statement

```
SELECT * FROM EMP
```

returns all five rows of the `EMP` table, whereas the SQL statement

```
SELECT * FROM EMP WHERE ENAME = "MARTIN"
```

returns only the last row.

SQL statements are represented in JDBC by the `java.sql.Statement`, `java.sql.CallableStatement`, and `java.sql.PreparedStatement` interfaces. Statement objects are created by requesting them from an open connection. After creating a statement, you call its methods to define the SQL command, execute the command, and retrieve the results (if any).

A Statement object is used to execute simple SQL commands. A PreparedStatement can be precompiled (or prepared) for increased performance (statement preparation is performed by the database). A PreparedStatement can also be defined to accept runtime parameters, and the PreparedStatement interface includes methods for setting the values of these parameters. A CallableStatement is used to execute stored procedures that are defined within the database. Stored procedures are blocks of SQL code that perform repetitive, well-defined tasks. They execute more quickly than equivalent SQL generated on the fly because the database stores them in a compiled, optimized format.

ResultSets

After a statement executes, its results are available in a *ResultSet,* which is represented in JDBC by the java.sql.ResultSet interface. If, for example, you execute a statement to retrieve all employees in your employee database, you use the ResultSet to retrieve the results for use within your Java program.

A ResultSet contains all rows returned by an SQL statement. To retrieve the information in each row, you traverse the ResultSet using a while loop. In JDBC 1.0, a ResultSet can be traversed only once from beginning to end. JDBC 2.0 introduces scrollable ResultSets, which can be traversed any number of times, in any order.

The following code shows how to obtain a connection, a statement, and a ResultSet, and how to traverse the ResultSet to display its data:

```
// Create a connection
Connection conn = DriverManager.getConnection(connectionURL);

// Create a statement
Statement statement = conn.createStatment();

// Execute a query
ResultSet resultSet =
    statement.executeQuery("SELECT * FROM EMPLOYEE");

while (resultSet.next()) {
  // Output the results in last name, first name format
  System.out.println(resultSet.getString("LAST_NAME") +
    ", " + resultSet.getString("FIRST_NAME");
}

// Close the statement and the connection
statement.close();
conn.close();
```

RowSets

A RowSet is a JDBC 2.0 feature that combines connections, statements, and ResultSets into one interface. RowSets extend the `java.sql.ResultSet` interface and are represented in JDBC by the `javax.sql.RowSet` interface. Note that `javax.sql.RowSet` is an abstract interface that cannot be used directly; you must use a vendor's implementation of this interface.

The most distinctive feature of RowSets is that they are JavaBean-compliant, so they can be used by tools or components that rely on the JavaBeans specification to do their job.

The best way to illustrate the difference between ResultSets and RowSets is to rewrite the preceding example using a RowSet. In this example, I use Sun's reference implementation of the RowSet interface, which you can find in the `sun.jdbc.rowset` package:

```
// Create a RowSet
JdbcRowSet rowSet = new JdbcRowSet();

// Do the rest
rowSet.setUrl(connectionURL);
rowSet.setCommand("SELECT * FROM EMPLOYEE");
rowSet.setUserName("sa");
rowSet.setPassword("password");
rowSet.execute();

while (rowSet.next()) {
  // Output the results in last name, first name format
  System.out.println(rowSet.getString("LAST_NAME") +
    ", " + rowSet.getString("FIRST_NAME");
}

rowset.close();
```

In contrast with the previous example, you can now do all the work with a single interface, the RowSet. Some developers may find this easier.

Because RowSets extend ResultSets, you lose no functionality by using RowSets. The choice of which interface to use boils down to personal preference, unless the ability to use RowSets as JavaBeans is a big win for your project.

Transactions

Transactions provide a means of encapsulating multiple, related database operations into one logical unit of work. If all the operations succeed, the transaction succeeds, and the effects of the operations are stored in the database. If any of the operations fail, the transaction fails, and no changes are written to the database.

WebLogic and its JDBC drivers provide comprehensive support for transactions, and Chapter 6 is devoted to this large and complex topic.

Understanding WebLogic JDBC

Now that you understand the basics of JDBC, it should be much easier for you to understand WebLogic's implementation of it, which is the focus of this section.

WebLogic and third-party drivers

WebLogic provides a number of JDBC drivers for use by developers. Some are strictly for database connectivity, while others provide support for transactions, database access via RMI, and pooled connections.

WebLogic two-tier drivers (types 2 and 4)

The drivers discussed in this section are two-tier drivers. This means that you can use them to make direct database connections from any Java application. For the type 2 drivers, you must also have the appropriate client-side libraries installed.

The most common use of the drivers is to make direct connections from code running within WebLogic Server, or to use them in conjunction with WebLogic's three-tier driver (discussed in the next section) to create connection pools usable from within WebLogic Server.

These drivers are included with WebLogic Server and do not require separate installation. But they do require separate software license agreements with their respective vendors.

WebLogic jDriver for Oracle

The WebLogic jDriver for Oracle is a type 2 driver for connection to Oracle databases. As such, it requires Oracle's client-side network libraries to be installed on the computer that will connect to the Oracle database. The driver supports JDBC 2.0.

Proper installation and configuration of the jDriver for Oracle depends on your Oracle installation. For detailed installation instructions, see *Installing and Using WebLogic jDriver for Oracle,* available at `http://edocs.bea.com/wls/docs61/oracle/index.html`.

WebLogic jDriver for Microsoft SQL Server

The WebLogic jDriver for Microsoft SQL Server is a pure Java, type 4 driver for connecting to Microsoft SQL Server. Two separate versions of the driver exist. One is for connecting to SQL Server versions 6 and 6.5, and the other is for versions 7.0 and 2000. Both versions support JDBC 2.0.

Proper installation and configuration of the jDriver for Microsoft SQL Server depends on your SQL Server installation. For detailed installation instructions, see *Installing and Using WebLogic jDriver for Microsoft SQL Server,* available at `http://edocs.bea.com/wls/docs61/mssqlserver4/index.html`.

WebLogic jDriver for Informix

This driver is also a pure Java, type 4 driver for connecting to Informix databases. It supports JDBC 2.0.

WebLogic multitier drivers (type 3)

WebLogic provides a number of multitier drivers that sit on top of their two-tier drivers, increasing their reach and functionality.

WebLogic pool driver

The WebLogic pool driver enables container-managed connection pooling as specified in the JDBC 2.0 Optional API, and as described earlier in the section about pooled connections.

The pool driver is a "pass-through" driver; it receives JDBC calls from clients and passes them directly through to the drivers used to create the pooled connections. Therefore, the pool driver's level of JDBC compliance is the same as the underlying driver(s) it uses.

The pool driver can be used in conjunction with any WebLogic or third-party JDBC driver that is certified to work with WebLogic Server (I discuss the precise meaning of this in the next section about third-party drivers).

Connection pools are configured by using the WebLogic console, and become active when WebLogic Server starts up.

WebLogic RMI driver

The WebLogic RMI driver allows Java client applications to connect to a database via RMI. Like the pool driver, the RMI driver uses a separate JDBC driver to connect WebLogic Server to the database. But all client-to-server communication takes place via RMI.

Additionally, WebLogic uses the RMI driver for clustered JDBC, allowing JDBC connections to be shared among the participants in a WebLogic cluster.

The RMI driver replaces the deprecated T3 database driver, which used the proprietary WebLogic T3 protocol for communication.

You can access RMI drivers by looking up their associated `DataSource` object in the JNDI tree. I discuss this further when I talk about DataSources later in this chapter.

Transaction-aware drivers

WebLogic and other vendors provide a number of drivers that are transaction-aware — they support the execution of transactions across one or more data stores. Details about these drivers and their usage appear in Chapter 6.

Third-party drivers

In addition to the drivers provided by BEA, you can use JDBC drivers written by database vendors and other third parties. When evaluating such drivers, be sure they meet the following criteria, or they won't work with WebLogic:

- ✦ They must be thread-safe.
- ✦ They must be EJB-accessible (they support JDBC transaction calls).

To get the most out of WebLogic and your JDBC driver, you should consider two additional criteria for selecting third-party JDBC drivers:

- ✦ Prefer drivers that support JDBC 2.0. Its advanced transaction and DataSet features are indispensable for serious database applications.
- ✦ Prefer drivers that support JNDI lookups via the `DataSource` interface. This allows you to completely decouple your database connection parameters from your Java code, resulting in applications that are more portable and easier to maintain.

For more information about WebLogic Server's support for third-party JDBC drivers, visit `http://e-docs.bea.com/wls/docs61/jdbc/thirdparty.html`.

MultiPools

MultiPools are a new feature of WebLogic 6.1. They allow single-server WebLogic configurations to create pools of pools, for one of two reasons:

1. To provide redundancy in case of database connectivity failures. This type of pool is called a *backup* or *high availability* pool.
2. To provide database load balancing for heavy usage scenarios. This type of pool is called a *load balancing* pool.

The type of pool to use is determined when the pool is configured in the WebLogic console. Like connection pools, MultiPools become active when WebLogic Server starts.

Although WebLogic's documentation calls the first type of pools *backup* pools, the WebLogic console calls them *high availability* pools. Keep this in mind when you configure MultiPools in the console.

Backup (high availability) pools

Database connection redundancy is achieved through the use of a backup pool (also known as a high-availability pool). A backup pool consists of an ordered list of connection pools. When a database connection request is made, the first pool in the list serves the request. If the connection fails for some reason—perhaps the server is down, or the network connection is broken—the connection request is passed to the next pool on the list (I call this a failover event). This sequence continues until the connection is successfully made.

Simply exceeding the capacity of a connection pool does not trigger a failover event in a backup pool. Failover events in backup pools are triggered only by database connectivity failures.

An example of an application that would benefit from a backup pool is an online catalog that uses a read-only product database. Assume the product database consists of a primary instance and a backup, configured for one-way replication from the primary to the backup. Assume also that the primary database is updated once per day. During the update, which is disk-intensive, the DBA brings down the primary database. Thanks to the backup pool, catalog users are automatically redirected to the backup database when connections to the primary database fail. After the primary database is returned to service, catalog users once again get connections to the primary database, giving them access to the latest information. Meanwhile, replication from the primary to the backup occurs in the background, so by the time tomorrow's update occurs, the backup database once again mirrors the primary.

Load balancing pools

Load balancing pools distribute connection requests evenly to every pool in the list, using a simple "round-robin" algorithm. Each successive connection request goes to the next pool in the list, with the rotation going back to the first pool after the last pool is used.

Using the online catalog example from before, assume site traffic is heavy, and therefore multiple instances of the read-only product database are put into service to handle demand. A load balancing pool is configured to round-robin requests among all the instances. Under this scenario, the site would go down during updates, unless the programmers and DBAs devise a clever scheme to combine both types of MultiPools simultaneously!

DataSources

DataSources are new in JDBC 2.0 and are fully supported in WebLogic 6.1. The `javax.sql.DataSource` interface is a factory for `java.sql.Connection` objects and can be registered with a JNDI service. This allows information about database connections to be completely separated from your Java code, making the code more portable and the database connections more secure and manageable.

In WebLogic, DataSources are fully integrated with the WebLogic pool driver, the WebLogic RMI driver, and the WebLogic JTS driver. `DataSource` objects are configured by using the WebLogic console.

Clustered JDBC

Clustered JDBC provides a means for JDBC connections to be shared among participants in a WebLogic cluster. One important feature is that it allows clients to restore database connections that are lost when a participating server in a WebLogic cluster fails. Clustered JDBC requires the use of DataSources and WebLogic RMI.

Configuring WebLogic JDBC

Now that you have a good grasp of JDBC concepts and WebLogic's implementation of JDBC, it's time to learn how to configure WebLogic's JDBC features.

Configuring connection pools

Almost all JDBC code you write for deployment on WebLogic Server will use connection pools. Therefore, understanding how to configure a connection pool is essential. It's easy to do, assuming you've properly installed WebLogic, the JDBC drivers you plan to use, and the database systems to which you plan to connect.

Creating a new pool

The following example shows how to create a connection pool by using the WebLogic jDriver for Oracle. This pool will open connections to an Oracle instance running on the same machine as WebLogic Server.

Note

Before performing the steps in this section, be sure the path to Oracle's OCI driver appears in your system's PATH variable. In Windows NT/2000, this setting is made in the System control panel. On my computer, the path is `D:\bea\wlserver6.1\bin\oci816_8`.

1. Start WebLogic Server and open the WebLogic Console. In the domain tree, choose Services ➪ JDBC ➪ Connection Pools. This shows a list of connection pools, as shown in Figure 5-9.

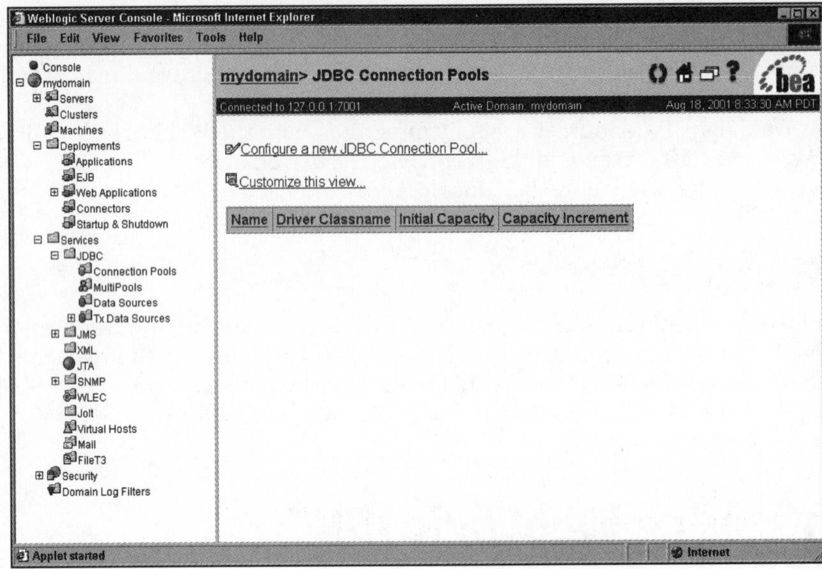

Figure 5-9: The JDBC Connection Pools page in the WebLogic console

2. Click Configure a New JDBC Connection Pool. The screen to create a pool appears, as shown in Figure 5-10.

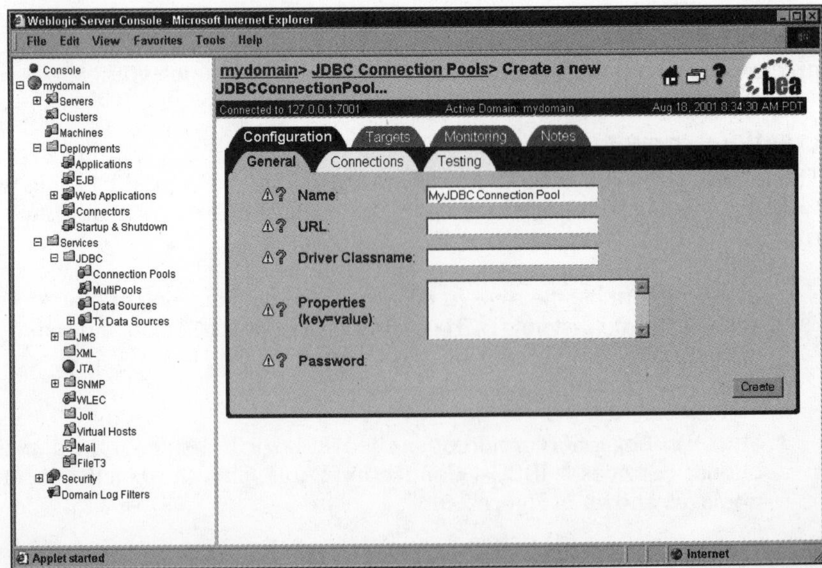

Figure 5-10: JDBC Connection Pool configuration screen

3. In the Name box, type **OraclePool** (you can use any name you want, as long as it's not being used by any other connection pool on the server).

4. In the URL box, type **jdbc:weblogic:oracle:<serverName>**, where `serverName` is the name of the desired Oracle instance, as defined in `TNSNAMES.ORA`. On my network, the Oracle instance is called `JOEVAIO.ZEEWARE.COM`. The URL tells the pool driver where to find your database on the network.

For whatever driver you are using, supply the same URL that you would use in code to open a direct connection with that driver yourself. To use the WebLogic jDriver for Microsoft SQL Server, set the URL to `jdbc:weblogic: mssqlserver4`. To use the jDriver for Informix, set the URL to `jdbc:weblogic: informix4`. To use a third-party driver, set the URL according to the vendor's instructions.

5. In the Driver Classname box, type **weblogic.jdbc.oci.Driver**. This instructs the pool driver to use the WebLogic jDriver for Oracle to create its connections.

For whatever driver you are using, supply the same Driver Classname that you would use in code to open a direct connection with that driver yourself. To use the WebLogic jDriver for Microsoft SQL Server, set the Driver Classname to `weblogic.jdbc.mssqlserver4.Driver`. To use the jDriver for Informix, set the Driver Classname to `weblogic.jdbc.informix4.Driver`. To use a third-party driver, set the Driver Classname to the full class name of whatever type 2 or type 4 driver you are using. Whatever driver you use, be sure the driver is in the Java classpath used to run WebLogic.

6. In the Properties text box, type **user=SCOTT**. This instructs the jDriver to connect to Oracle's sample schema (the database owned by `SCOTT`, the sample user).

You can also specify the property `server=<serverName>`, where `serverName` is the name of the desired Oracle instance, as defined in `TNSNAMES.ORA`. But when you stop and restart WebLogic Server to initialize the pool, you will find that WebLogic appends `serverName` to the URL, as described in Step 4, and removes it from the properties. Therefore, I usually just append it to the URL.

You can separate the properties by semicolons or carriage returns. I prefer carriage returns because it makes the property entries more readable.

7. Click Create to create the pool. A new link called Change appears next to Password. Click this link.

8. Enter the password, as shown in Figure 5-11. Oracle's default password for `SCOTT` is `tiger`. Click Apply.

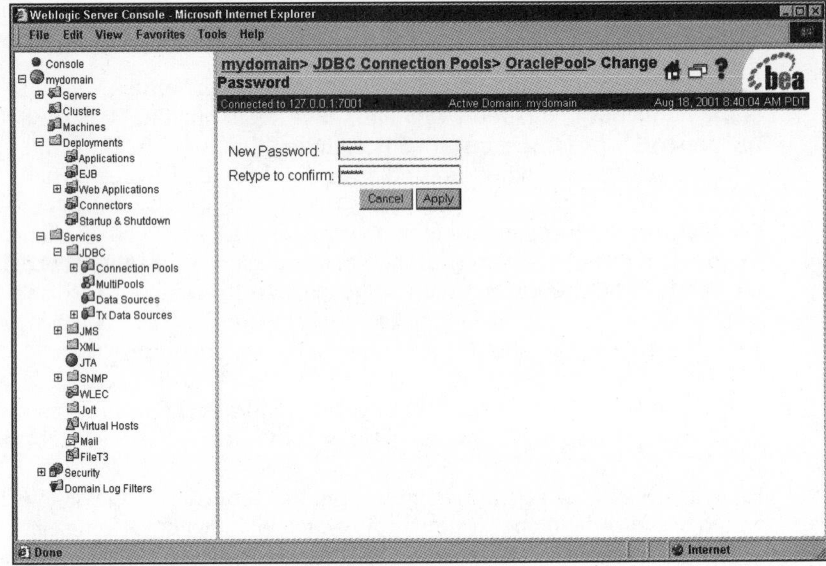

Figure 5-11: Specifying the database password for the connection pool

9. Click Continue to return to the main configuration screen, which should now look similar to Figure 5-12. Verify that your settings are correct, and then click Apply.

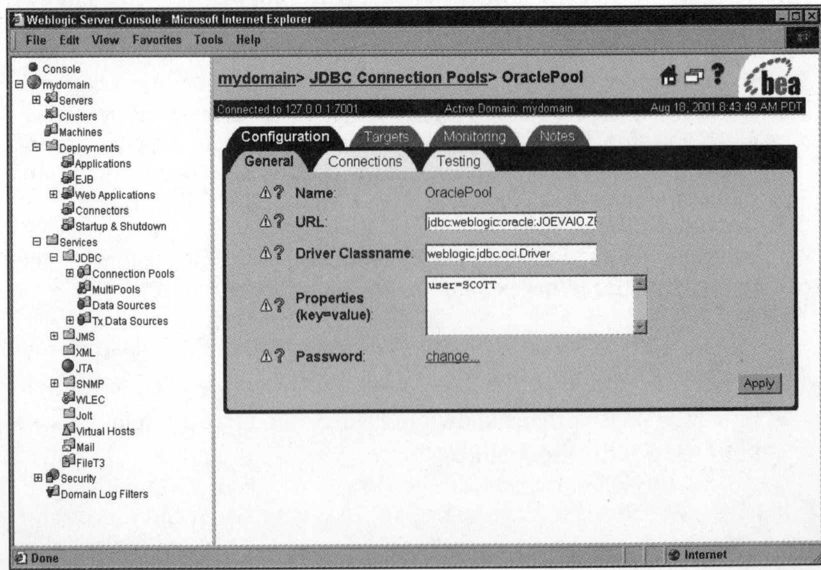

Figure 5-12: A connection pool configured to connect to Oracle's sample database schema

10. Click the Connections tab to configure the pool driver's connection parameters. Set the parameters as shown in Figure 5-13, and then click Apply.

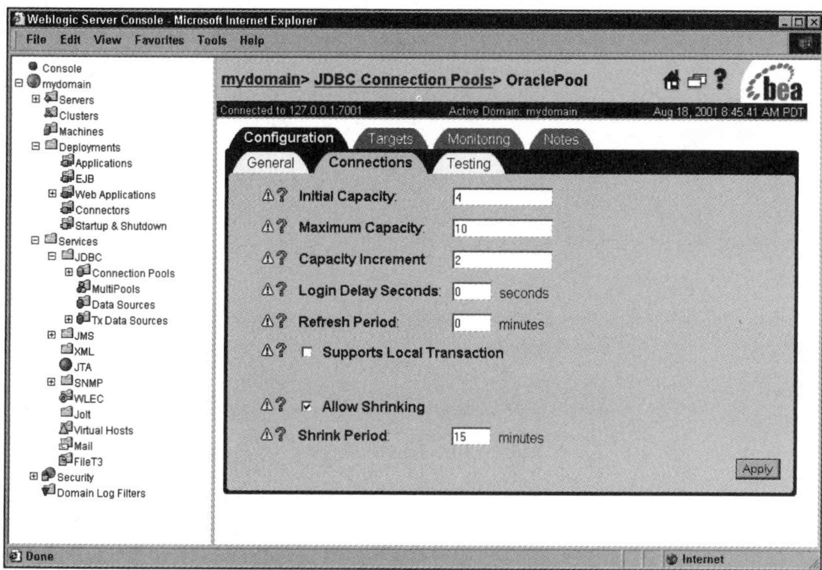

Figure 5-13: Connection parameters for the Oracle connection pool

The parameters have the following meanings:

- *Initial Capacity:* This is the number of connections to Oracle the pool will create at startup. You can enter any number that's within the maximum supported by your WebLogic jDriver for Oracle license and/or your Oracle server.
- *Maximum Capacity:* This is the maximum number of Oracle connections the pool will open, regardless of client demand.
- *Capacity Increment:* If a new connection is requested and all open connections are busy, the pool will add this number of new connections to the pool, subject to the limits imposed by your license and the Maximum Capacity. Because opening a database connection is time consuming, it's wise to open connections in bunches.
- *Login Delay Seconds:* The amount of time the pool driver waits between opening each new connection at startup.
- *Refresh Period:* Open connections are closed and reopened at this interval, unless they're in use, to ensure the database is still available, or to restore lost connections in case the database is shut down and then restarted again.

✦ *Supports Local Transaction:* This attribute applies to XA connection pools only, and is ignored for non-XA drivers. Check it if you're using an XA driver that supports SQL with no global transaction. For this example, however, leave it unchecked, because you're not using the Oracle XA driver.

✦ *Allow Shrinking and Shrink Period:* If the size of the pool is greater than its initial capacity, and if any of the connections are idle for the duration of the shrink period, then the idle connections will be closed at the end of the shrink period.

Click the Testing tab. In the Test Table Name box, type **dual**, which is the name of Oracle's built-in test table. You can leave the other testing parameters unchecked, as shown in Figure 5-14. Click Apply.

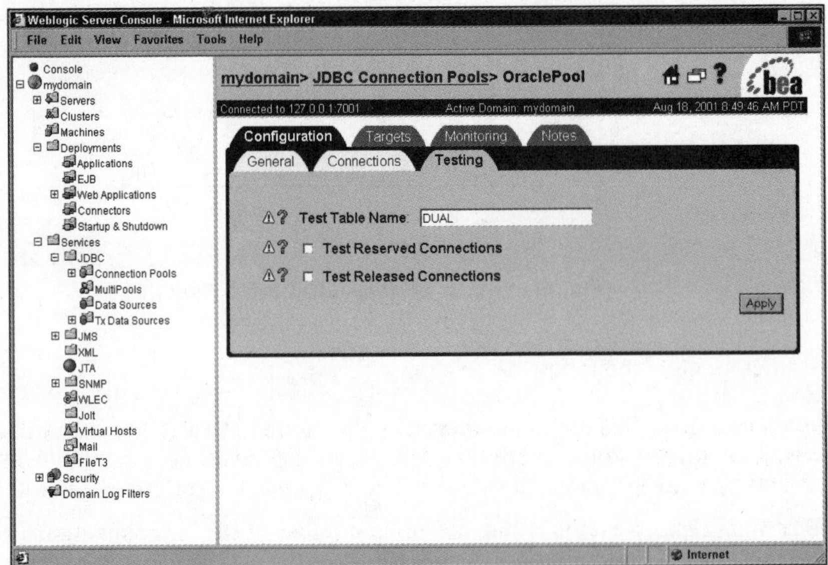

Figure 5-14: Testing parameters for the Oracle connection pool

Caution If you leave the Test Table Name box blank, the connection pool will not work—only if you do testing. I have also found this to be true for connections to Microsoft SQL Server, which doesn't even have a test table like Oracle does. I found by trial and error that entering "dual" for the Test Table Name works for both Oracle and Microsoft SQL Server.

The other parameters on this screen have the following meanings:

✦ *Test Reserved Connections:* Checking this option instructs WebLogic Server to briefly test a connection every time a client requests (or *reserves*) one from the pool. This test incurs a slight performance hit every time a connection is requested.

✦ *Test Released Connections:* Checking this option instructs WebLogic Server to test a connection every time a client releases it back to the pool.

Now that you have configured the connection pool, you must pin it to a WebLogic server. Click the Targets tab and specify the WebLogic Server under which the pool will run, as shown in Figure 5-15. Click Apply.

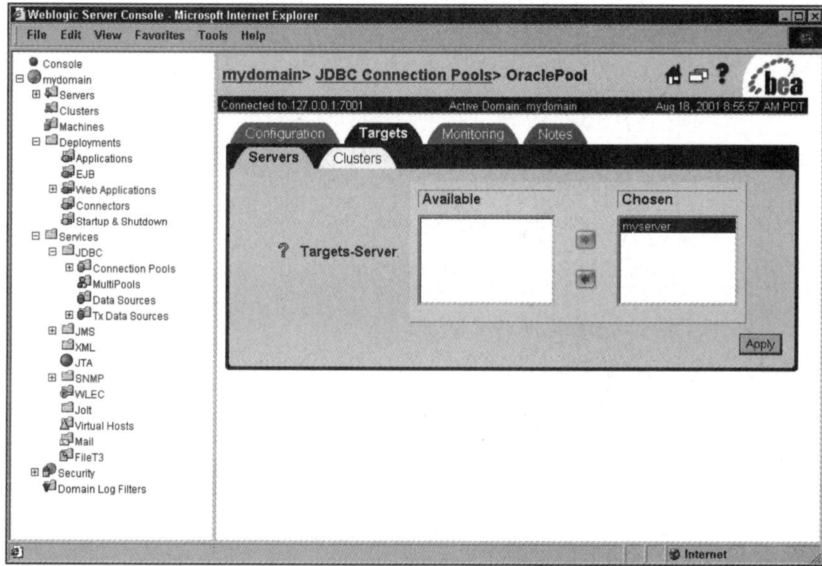

Figure 5-15: Pinning the connection pool to a WebLogic Server instance

As soon as you click Apply, WebLogic Server activates the connection pool by creating the initial number of Oracle connections you specified. If all goes well, you will see an indication in the WebLogic command window that the jDriver for Oracle is being loaded for use by the connection pool, as shown in Figure 5-16.

```
Select Start Default Server
*  username and password must also be used to    *
*  access the WebLogic Server console from a web *
*  browser.                                      *
**************************************************

D:\bea\wlserver6.1>"D:\bea\jdk131\bin\java" -hotspot -ms64m -mx64m -classpath .;
.\lib\weblogic_sp.jar;.\lib\weblogic.jar -Dweblogic.Domain=dev -Dweblogic.Name=a
dmin "-Dbea.home=D:\bea" -Dweblogic.management.password=password -Dweblogic.Prod
uctionModeEnabled=false -Dweblogic.management.discover=false "-Djava.security.po
licy==D:\bea\wlserver6.1/lib/weblogic.policy" weblogic.Server
Starting WebLogic Server ....
<Nov 28, 2001 2:52:49 PM PST> <Notice> <Management> <Loading configuration file
.\config\dev\config.xml ...>
<Nov 28, 2001 2:52:55 PM PST> <Notice> <WebLogicServer> <Starting WebLogic Admin
 Server "admin" for domain "dev">
<Nov 28, 2001 2:53:12 PM PST> <Notice> <Management> <Application Poller started
for development server.>
<Nov 28, 2001 2:53:12 PM PST> <Notice> <WebLogicServer> <ListenThread listening
on port 7001, ip address 127.0.0.1>
<Nov 28, 2001 2:53:12 PM PST> <Notice> <WebLogicServer> <SSLListenThread listeni
ng on port 7002, ip address 127.0.0.1>
<Nov 28, 2001 2:53:13 PM PST> <Notice> <WebLogicServer> <Started WebLogic Admin
Server "admin" for domain "dev" running in Development Mode>
Starting Loading jDriver/Oracle .....
```

Figure 5-16: WebLogic Server's command window after successful initialization of the connection pool

You can further verify the pool's health in the WebLogic console. In the domain tree, choose Services ➪ JDBC ➪ Connection Pools. The list should contain the pool you just created. Click the name of the pool to go to the monitoring page, and then click Monitor All Instances of OraclePool. You should see a screen similar to Figure 5-17.

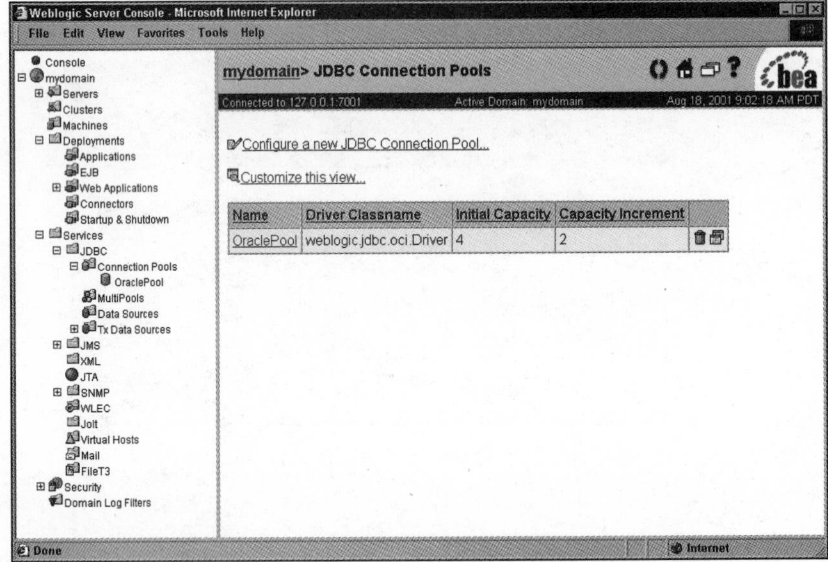

Figure 5-17: Verifying the connection pool's health in the WebLogic console

The connection pool is now ready to accept connection requests. Later in this chapter, you'll see how to obtain a connection to this pool from within your Java code.

Cloning a connection pool

Next you're going to clone the pool you just created so that you have two pools available for your MultiPool example later. To clone a pool, follow these steps:

1. In the domain tree, choose Services ➪ JDBC ➪ Connection Pools to display the list of available connection pools (see Figure 5-17).
2. Click the Clone Pool icon, which appears on the right side of the screen, to the right of the trash can. The pool cloning screen appears, as shown in Figure 5-18.
3. You can give the clone any name you like, as long as it's unique within your WebLogic Server or cluster. The default cloned pool name, Clone of OraclePool, is fine for this example. Click Clone.

If you try to change the password before clicking Clone, a bug in the WebLogic Console takes you to the password configuration screen for OraclePool. Therefore, you must clone the pool first, and then change the password.

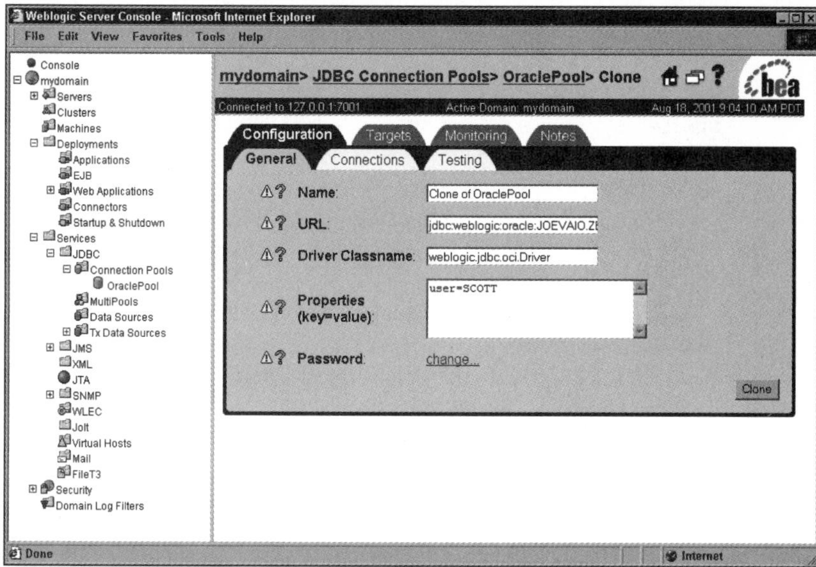

Figure 5-18: Cloning a connection pool

4. When you clone a pool, WebLogic does not clone the password, for security reasons. Therefore, set the password to `tiger`, following the same steps you did when you created the initial pool. After setting the password, click Apply.

You must stop and restart WebLogic Server to activate the cloned pool connections.

Configuring MultiPools

Creating a MultiPool is very similar to creating a connection pool. In this example, you'll create a MultiPool containing the two Oracle connection pools you just created.

1. In the domain tree, choose Services ➪ JDBC ➪ MultiPools. The screen shown in Figure 5-19 appears.
2. Click Configure a New JDBC MultiPool and complete the MultiPool configuration screen, as shown in Figure 5-20 (for this example, you'll create a Load Balancing MultiPool). Click Create.
3. Click the Pools tab and move both Oracle connection pools into the Chosen list, as shown in Figure 5-21. Click Apply.
4. Click the Targets tab and move your instance of WebLogic Server into the Chosen list, as shown in Figure 5-22. Click Apply.

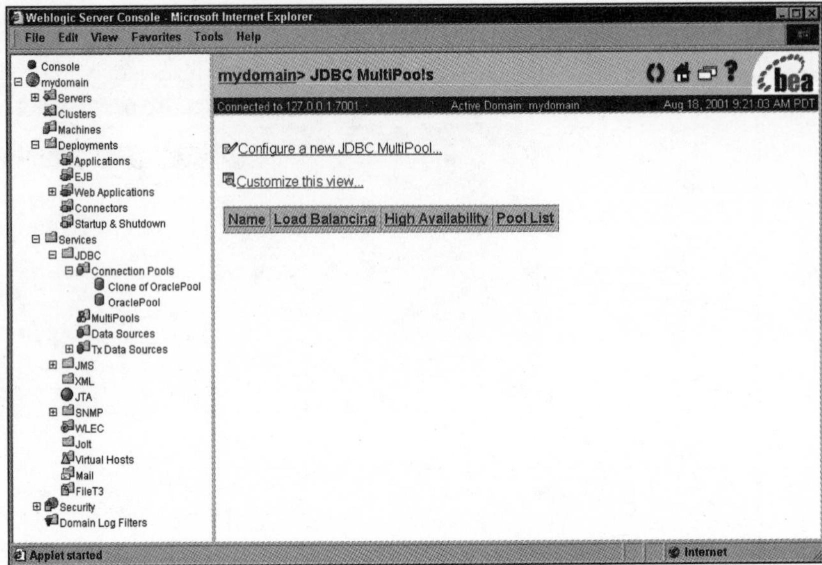

Figure 5-19: Preparing to configure a WebLogic MultiPool

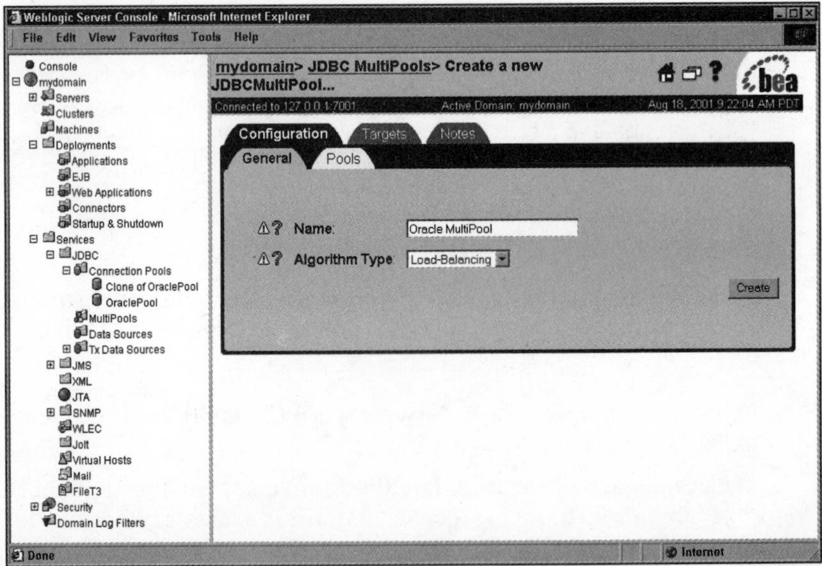

Figure 5-20: Configuring a WebLogic MultiPool as a Load-Balancing MultiPool

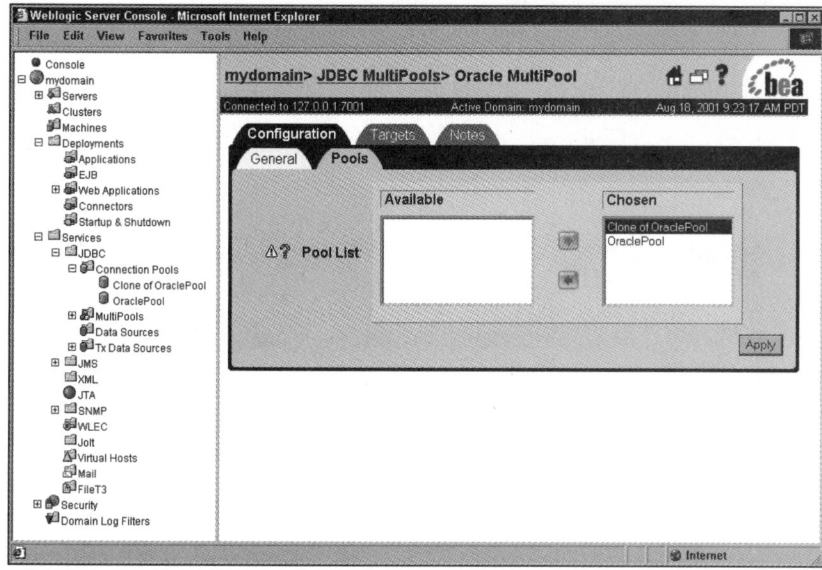

Figure 5-21: Choosing connection pools to include in the MultiPool

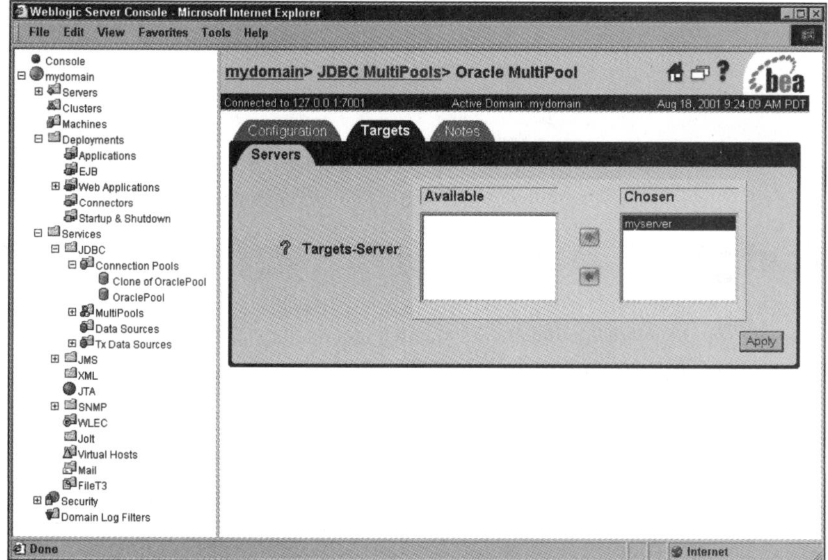

Figure 5-22: Assigning the MultiPool to a WebLogic Server instance

5. Stop and restart WebLogic Server to activate the MultiPool; then confirm proper creation of the MultiPool by viewing it in the WebLogic console, as shown in Figure 5-23.

Due to an apparent bug in WebLogic Console, the Load Balancing and High Availability attributes on this screen always display as false.

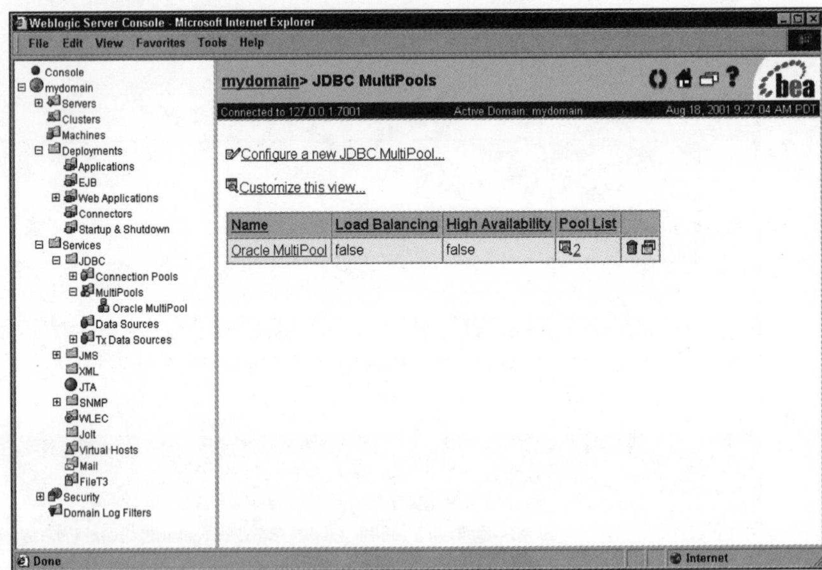

Figure 5-23: Confirming the existence of a MultiPool in the WebLogic console

Configuring DataSources

Now you're going to create a DataSource for the OraclePool connection pool. This enables your server applications to obtain connections by looking up the DataSource in WebLogic's JNDI tree.

1. In the domain tree, choose Services ➪ JDBC ➪ Data Sources. The screen shown in Figure 5-24 appears.

2. Click Configure a New JDBC Data Source to display the DataSource configuration screen, as shown in Figure 5-25.

   The entries on this page are as follows:

   - *Name*: A name for the DataSource, which must be unique within the WebLogic Server instance or its cluster. Type **DataSource for OraclePool** for this value.

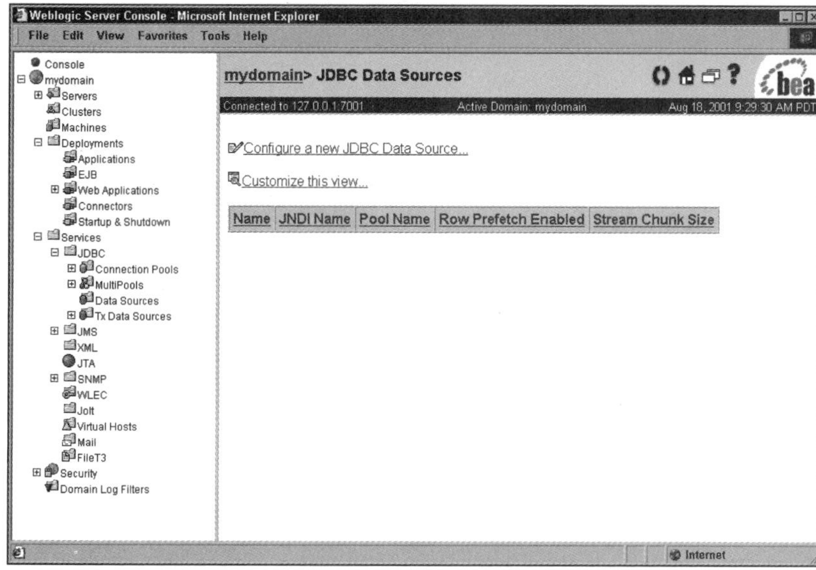

Figure 5-24: Preparing to configure a JDBC DataSource

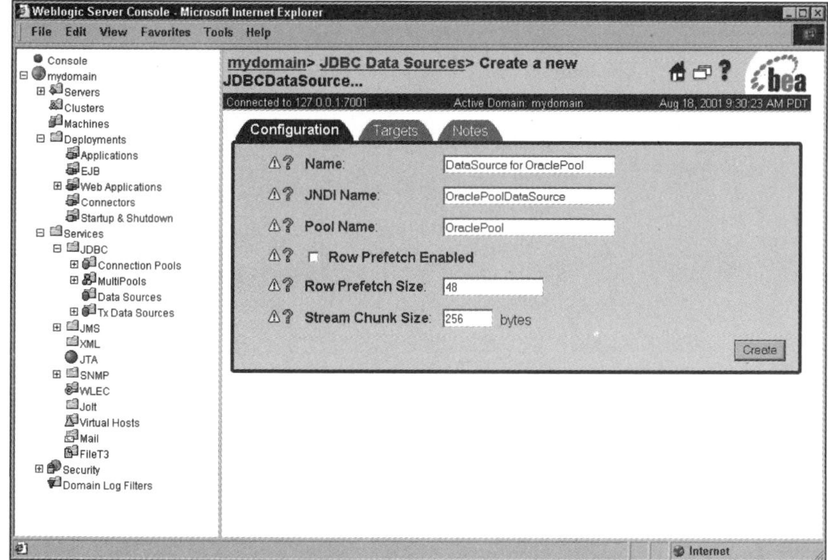

Figure 5-25: Configuring a JDBC DataSource for OraclePool

- *Pool Name:* The name of the existing JDBC connection pool to which this DataSource is mapped. Type **OraclePool** for this value.
- *JNDI Name:* The JNDI name for the DataSource, which must conform to the rules for Java identifiers and be unique within the WebLogic Server instance or its cluster. Type **OraclePoolDataSource** for this value.
- *Row Prefetch Enabled:* Check this option if the JDBC DataSource will be used by external Java clients, such as RMI clients, that are not executing within WebLogic's JVM. It increases performance by automatically prefetching a given number of rows and sending them to the client when it opens a JDBC ResultSet, thereby reducing the number of network roundtrips between the client and WebLogic Server.
- *Row Prefetch Size:* The number of rows that will be automatically prefetched and sent to an external client when it opens a ResultSet. The optimal value for this parameter depends on your application and database.
- *Stream Chunk Size:* When multiple rows are prefetched from the server, the data is streamed to the client in chunks whose size is determined by this parameter. Generally speaking, larger values increase performance by reducing network roundtrips between the client and server.

After completing the configuration screen, click Create.

3. Click the Targets tab and move your WebLogic Server instance into the Chosen list, as shown in Figure 5-26. Click Apply.

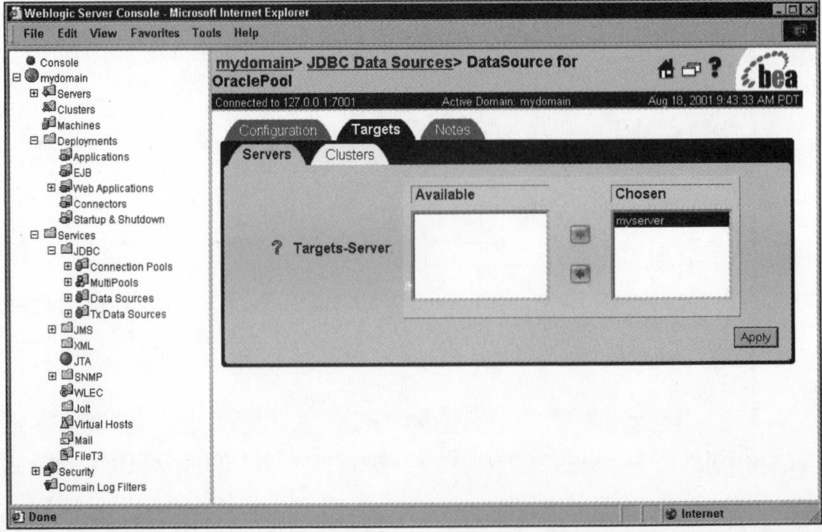

Figure 5-26: Assigning the DataSource to a WebLogic Server instance

4. Stop and restart WebLogic Server to activate the DataSource.

Configuring Tx DataSources

I discuss the configuration of Tx DataSources (Transactional DataSources) in Chapter 6.

Programming WebLogic JDBC

The rest of this chapter is devoted to code examples that show how to program WebLogic JDBC. Each example shows how to perform the same tasks by using Microsoft SQL Server and Oracle, which are the databases most WebLogic programmers work with on a daily basis.

Because the RowSet interface is youthful and still evolving, the examples focus on the use of Connections, Statements, and ResultSets.

The local network you built for these examples is quite simple. It consists of only two machines, as shown in Figure 5-27.

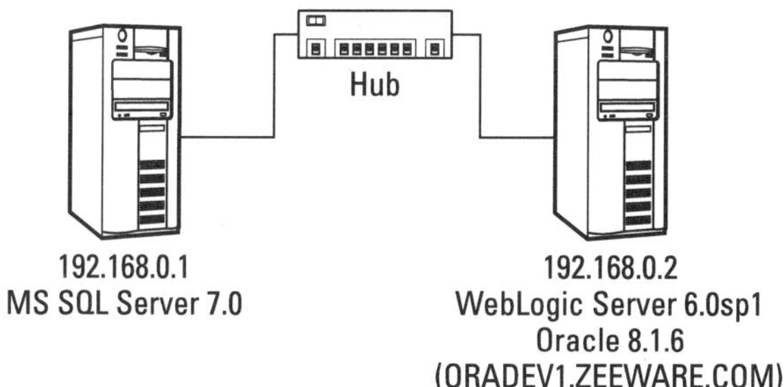

Figure 5-27: The simple network used for the JDBC examples

Obtaining connections

This section shows how to obtain JDBC connections from a variety of sources, including type 2 and 4 JDBC drivers, the WebLogic pool driver, and DataSources (including Tx DataSources). Keep in mind that all connections are used the same way, regardless of how they are obtained.

Obtaining direct connections from type 2 or type 4 JDBC drivers

To obtain a direct connection from a type 2 or type 4 JDBC driver, perform the following steps:

1. Obtain an instance of the JDBC driver you will be using. This is done with the following code:

```
import java.sql.*;

Driver myDriver =
  (Driver)Class.forName(driverName).newInstance();
```

where `driverName` is one of the following:

`weblogic.jdbc.oci.Driver` for the WebLogic jDriver for Oracle

`weblogic.jdbc.mssqlserver4.Driver` for the WebLogic jDriver for Microsoft SQL Server

`weblogic.jdbc.informix4.Driver` for the WebLogic jDriver for Informix

or the full class name of whatever type 2 or type 4 driver you are using. Be sure the driver is in your WebLogic classpath.

2. Obtain a Connection by calling the driver's `connect` method, providing a username, password, server name, and other necessary parameters for accessing the database. These parameters are loaded into a `Properties` object and passed to the `connect` method, along with a URL to the database you're using. The URL is one of the following:

`jdbc:weblogic:oracle` for the Oracle driver

`jdbc:weblogic:mssqlserver4` for the Microsoft SQL Server driver

`jdbc:weblogic:informix4` for the Informix driver

or the URL of whatever other type 2 or type 4 driver you are using. Note that the components of the URL are separated by colons, not periods.

The following code shows how to obtain a connection to an Oracle database, using the WebLogic jDriver for Oracle:

```
import java.sql.*;
import java.util.*;

String driverURL = "weblogic:jdbc:oracle";
Properties myProperties = new Properties();

// The Oracle server name should match the entry in
// the tnsnames.ora file
myProperties.put("server", "ORADEV1.ZEEWARE.COM");

// The db property is not needed for Oracle connections,
// because the schema (i.e. "SCOTT") determines the
// database used. You can omit setting this property, or
// simply set it to an empty string as shown.
myProperties.put("db", "");
myProperties.put("user", "SCOTT");
myProperties.put("password", "tiger");

Connection myConnection =
  myDriver.connect(driverURL, myProperties);
```

Similarly, to obtain a connection to Microsoft SQL Server, write this code:

```
import java.sql.*;
import java.util.*;

String driverURL = "weblogic:jdbc:mssqlserver4";
Properties myProperties = new Properties();

// IP addresses work best for MS SQL Server. Simply
// provide the IP address of the SQL Server host.
// You can omit the port if SQL Server is running on
// its default port of 1433.
myProperties.put("server", "192.168.0.1");

// The db property is not needed for MS SQL Server or
// Sybase connections, but if you don't use it then
// you'll need to execute a "use database" statement
// elsewhere in your code. It's simpler to just use
// the property, as shown here.
myProperties.put("db", "pubs");
myProperties.put("user", "sa");
myProperties.put("password", "password");

Connection myConnection =
  myDriver.connect(driverURL, myProperties);
```

Note

You must provide hard-coded IP addresses for your SQL Server hosts, even if you have installed the SQL Server Client Network Utility on your WebLogic machine and defined SQL Server host names. The WebLogic jDriver for Microsoft SQL Server, being a type 4 driver, does not communicate with the Client Network Utility.

When specifying the IP address of an SQL Server host, you can omit the port number if SQL Server is running on its default port of 1433. Otherwise, specify the port by adding a colon and the port number to the IP address, as in `192.168.0.1:7005`.

Obtaining pooled connections from the WebLogic pool driver

To obtain a pooled connection from the WebLogic pool driver, follow these steps:

1. Obtain an instance of the WebLogic pool driver with the following code:

```
import java.sql.*;

String driverName = "weblogic.jdbc.pool.Driver";
Driver myDriver =
  (Driver)Class.forName(driverName).newInstance();
```

Note that this is always the driver name used for pooled connections, regardless of whether the underlying database is Oracle, Sybase, Informix, or something else.

2. Obtain a connection by calling the driver's `connect` method, providing the name of the pool from which you want a connection. You don't need to provide a username, password, or database name, because these details are handled by the pool when it creates its connections.

   You can either pass the pool name in a `Properties` object, or append it to the URL. To pass it in a `Properties` object, write the following code:

```
import java.sql.*;
import java.util.*;

String driverURL = "jdbc:weblogic:pool";
Properties myProperties = new Properties();
myProperties.put("connectionPoolID", "OraclePool");

Connection myConnection =
  myDriver.connect(driverURL, myProperties);
```

   The preceding code obtains a connection from `OraclePool`, the pool you configured in the WebLogic console earlier in this chapter.

   To do the same thing by appending the pool name to the URL, write the following code:

```
import java.sql.*;

String driverURL = "jdbc:weblogic:pool:OraclePool";

Connection myConnection =
  myDriver.connect(driverURL, null);
```

   Neither method is better than the other—the one you choose is a matter of personal preference.

Obtaining pooled connections from predefined DataSources or Tx DataSources

To obtain a pooled connection from a predefined DataSource or Tx DataSource, follow these steps:

1. Obtain an instance of the DataSource by performing a JNDI lookup on it, passing the full JNDI name of the DataSource as defined in the WebLogic console. To obtain, for example, an instance of `OraclePoolDataSource`, the DataSource defined in the earlier example, write the following code:

```
import javax.naming.*;
import java.sql.*

javax.sql.DataSource myDataSource = null;

try {
```

```
    Context myContext = new InitialContext();
    myDataSource =
      (javax.sql.DataSource)
      myContext.lookup("OraclePoolDataSource");
  }
  catch {NamingException e) {
  }
```

2. Obtain a connection by calling the DataSource's `getConnection` method:

```
  try {
    myConnection = myDataSource.getConnection();
  }
  catch (SQLException e) {
  }
```

Using Connections to execute Statements and process Results

After you obtain a connection to a database, you make the same standard JDBC calls against it, no matter which method you used to get the connection. In other words, a connection is a connection is a connection, whether it's direct, pooled, obtained via a driver, or obtained via a DataSource. The only caveat is that the underlying source of the connection (the JDBC driver that physically connects to the database) must support whatever version of JDBC calls you plan to make.

To illustrate this, consider the following method to select and display all rows of the `EMP` table in the Oracle schema `SCOTT`:

```
public static void getData(Connection theConnection) {
  try {
    Statement myStatement = theConnection.createStatement();
    ResultSet rs =
      myStatement.executeQuery("SELECT * FROM EMP");
    while (rs.next()) {
      System.out.println(rs.getInt("EMPNO") +
      "     " + rs.getString("ENAME") +
      "     " + rs.getString("JOB"));
    }
  }
  catch (SQLException e) {
  }
}
```

You can pass this method any valid database connection, regardless of how the connection was obtained. In fact, the connection doesn't even have to be to an Oracle database, as long as `getData`'s SQL is valid for the database described by the connection.

Incidentally, when executed against the `SCOTT` schema in Oracle, the output from `getData` is the following:

```
7369    SMITH    CLERK
7499    ALLEN    SALESMAN
7521    WARD    SALESMAN
7566    JONES    MANAGER
7654    MARTIN    SALESMAN
7698    BLAKE    MANAGER
7782    CLARK    MANAGER
7788    SCOTT    ANALYST
7839    KING    PRESIDENT
7844    TURNER    SALESMAN
7876    ADAMS    CLERK
7900    JAMES    CLERK
7902    FORD    ANALYST
7934    MILLER    CLERK
```

You can obviously do much more with JDBC than open connections and select data from tables, but providing demonstrations of generic JDBC programming techniques is beyond the scope of this book. In addition to the many books written on the subject, a great way to learn more is to take Sun's online JDBC tutorial, which you can find at `http://java.sun.com/docs/books/tutorial/jdbc/index.html`.

Closing connections

After using a connection, it's a good idea to close it to release unused database resources. The code to close a connection is the same regardless of how the connection is obtained. The following code closes a connection:

```
public static void closeConnection(Connection theConnection) {
  try {
    theConnection.close();
  }
  catch (SQLException e) {
    System.out.println("A SQLException occurred: " +
                       e.getMessage());
    e.printStackTrace();
  }
}
```

If you pass this method a direct connection, the connection's driver physically closes the connection, rendering the connection unusable. If you pass a pooled connection, the WebLogic pool driver does not physically close the connection. Instead, it marks the connection as unused and returns it to the pool of available connections.

Summary

This chapter provided you with a thorough understanding of how WebLogic implements JDBC. JDBC is a complex API sitting on top of an even more complex architecture. This chapter shows how the pieces of this architecture fit together, and how to properly configure and use them in the WebLogic environment. Specifically, you learned about the various types of JDBC drivers, how to use them directly or in WebLogic connection pools, and how to extend their functionality by accessing them through data sources.

Chapter 6 digs deeper into the Java Transaction API (JTA), showing how to program user transactions by using J2EE and transaction-aware database drivers.

✦ ✦ ✦

Working with WebLogic JTA

✦ ✦ ✦ ✦

In This Chapter

Understanding transactions

Understanding JTA

Configuring WebLogic JTA

Programming WebLogic JTA

✦ ✦ ✦ ✦

Transactions provide an "all-or-nothing" way of making permanent changes to data residing in one or more data stores, such as relational databases and messaging systems. Transactions are an essential component of enterprise computing because they help enforce data integrity. This feature becomes even more important in the context of distributed systems, where network failures, server outages, and a host of other unexpected problems can wreak havoc on your business logic.

In a networked computing environment, where enterprise systems consist of multiple application servers, databases, messaging systems, and other resources working together, the concept of transactions is essential because of the possibility that components might fail in the overall system. If unexpected errors occur, for example, in a database that is participating in a complex sequence of business logic, developers must have a reliable way to reverse all the other effects of the business logic. This not only allows them to ensure that the system as a whole remains consistent, but it also gives them the ability to retry the entire sequence of operations later, after the offending system has been repaired or brought back online.

The *Java Transaction API,* or *JTA,* gives Java developers the ability to control transactions easily and reliably from within Java code by using a simple set of transaction-oriented commands. Such transactions can include EJB method calls, JDBC database operations, JMS messaging operations, and operations against any other computing source that provides transaction support. WebLogic, working in concert with transaction-enabled drivers for the participating data sources, handles the considerable load of back-end processing that transactions require.

This chapter introduces you to essential transaction concepts. I then explain JTA, showing you how to properly configure and program it in the WebLogic environment.

Understanding Transactions

As I mentioned, transactions are a critical part of the enterprise computing equation, but they are difficult to program correctly, and even more difficult to troubleshoot when something goes wrong. A solid understanding of the theory behind transactions will help you become a more effective transactions programmer.

What is a transaction?

A *transaction* is a means of encapsulating multiple, related operations against one or more data stores into one logical unit of work. If all the operations succeed, the transaction succeeds, and the effects of the operations are permanently written to the data stores. If any of the operations fail, the transaction fails, and the effects of the operations on the data stores are reversed.

The first step in transaction processing is notifying the data stores that you wish to begin a transaction. This tells the data stores to batch subsequent commands into the transaction until you either *commit* the transaction (indicating success) or *roll back* the transaction (indicating failure).

Performing a funds transfer at an ATM is a good example of a transaction. Suppose you step up to an ATM and try to transfer $1,000 from your savings account to your checking account. It's one button for you, but in the background a program must first remove $1,000 from your savings account (that's one operation) and then update your checking account by adding $1,000 (that's another operation). Let's say the first operation occurs, but then a rolling blackout hits and prevents completion of the second operation. You now have $1,000 floating around in electronic limbo! But when power is restored, the database will automatically roll back the incomplete transaction, restoring $1,000 to your savings account. Without transactions, that money would be gone forever.

Transactions and the ACID test

For a logical unit of work comprising a transaction to be considered transactional, it must meet the *ACID* test. ACID is an acronym describing the essential characteristics of a transaction; its letters stand for *atomic, consistent, isolated,* and *durable.*

- ✦ *Atomic* means that the operations comprising the unit of work succeed or fail as a group. In other words, a transaction is an "all-or-nothing" operation.
- ✦ *Consistent* means that all data stores affected by a transaction are left in a state consistent with the business logic of the system, whether the transaction succeeds or fails.

✦ *Isolated* means that multiple transactions occurring simultaneously against the data stores will not interfere with each other, or get tangled up in each other's effects. If two transactions, for example, each successfully deposit $1,000 into a bank account at the same time, the account balance must increase by $2,000, not $1,000.

✦ *Durable* means that if a transaction succeeds, its effects will be permanently and reliably written to the data stores. In practical terms, this means that all database changes are flushed to disk.

Resources and resource managers

Each participant in a transaction is called a *resource.* A resource can be a database system, persistent messaging store, or any other transaction-enabled entity.

For a resource to be transaction-enabled, it must have a transaction-aware *resource manager,* which coordinates communications between the resource and the transaction manager (transaction managers are defined in the next section). Resource managers can be implemented as drivers, as is the case with transaction-aware JDBC drivers, or they can be integrated with the resource they control, as is the case with WebLogic JMS.

Local and distributed transactions

Transactions can be *local* or *distributed.* A local transaction is confined to one resource, while a distributed transaction spans multiple resources, including resources of different types (such as databases and messaging systems), possibly provided by multiple vendors.

Local transactions

A *local transaction* is the simplest type of transaction. It involves a single resource and resource manager. Multiple inserts into a single database, for example, could be contained within a local transaction, as could multiple messaging operations against a JMS queue.

Note

Most relational database systems have the capability to manage local transactions themselves, without involving an external resource manager. Sybase's Transact-SQL language and Oracle's PL/SQL language, for example, both contain commands to manage local transactions. These commands execute more quickly and potentially with greater reliability than those issued from external resource managers. In addition, they support additional features such as transaction nesting, which is not available in WebLogic's transaction manager. For these reasons, it's better in almost every case to control local transactions from within the databases themselves, rather than from Java code.

Distributed transactions

A *distributed transaction* involves multiple resources and resource managers. A transaction spanning inserts into a database, followed by messages being written to a JMS queue, for example, would be contained within a distributed transaction. Distributed transactions are managed by a *transaction monitor,* which runs outside the participating databases and coordinates transactions among them.

Transaction isolation levels

As I mentioned before, one of the ACID properties of transactions is isolation—the effects of simultaneously occurring transactions are isolated from one another. But maintaining perfect transaction isolation can be costly in terms of application performance. Additionally, certain real-world situations don't require perfect isolation in order to function acceptably. To accommodate these realities, many transactional resource managers support *isolation levels* that give developers some degree of control over how strictly perfect isolation is enforced.

In J2EE, developers set transaction isolation levels by using the `java.sql.Connection` interface. This interface provides getter and setter methods for the connection's isolation level:

```
int getTransactionIsolation() throws SQLException;
void setTransactionIsolation(int level) throws SQLException;
```

Additionally, the `java.sql.DatabaseMetaData` interface provides methods to discover the level of isolation level support provided by a data store. An instance of an object that implements this interface is obtained by calling `Connection.getMetaData()`, and the methods relevant to transaction isolation levels are:

```
int getDefaultTransactionIsolation() throws SQLException;
boolean supportsTransactionIsolationLevel(int level)
  throws SQLException;
```

The `java.sql.Connection` interface defines five integer constants for transaction isolation levels:

- `TRANSACTION_READ_UNCOMMITTED`
- `TRANSACTION_READ_COMMITTED`
- `TRANSACTION_REPEATABLE_READ`
- `TRANSACTION_SERIALIZABLE`
- `TRANSACTION_NONE`

These isolation levels are designed to address specific data inconsistency scenarios defined by the ANSI/ISO 92 standard. Let's explore these scenarios in more detail.

Dirty read

A *dirty read* occurs when a transaction is allowed to read data affected by another transaction before the other transaction commits. Suppose, for example, that transaction 1 (T1) updates a row in the database. Immediately afterwards, transaction 2 (T2) reads the row, retrieving the change made by T1. If T1 then issues a rollback, the data previously read by T2 becomes inconsistent with the state of the database.

Non-repeatable read

A *non-repeatable read* occurs when a transaction attempts to select the same row twice, but a second transaction has modified or deleted the row in the interim. This situation may lead to unpredictable or incorrect results in the first transaction.

Phantom read

A *phantom read* occurs when a transaction reads all rows that meet certain criteria, but then a second transaction inserts a new row that meets the same criteria. If the first transaction rereads the rows, the new, phantom row appears in the results.

Table 6-1 shows JTA's transaction isolation levels across the top, and data inconsistency scenarios on the left. Check marks indicate that the given isolation level prevents the given inconsistency scenario.

Table 6-1
JTA Transaction Isolation and Data Inconsistency

	Uncommited	*Committed*	*Repeatable*	*Serializable*
Dirty read		✓	✓	✓
NR read			✓	✓
Phantom read				✓

As you can see, `TRANSACTION_READ_UNCOMMITTED` is the most lenient of the isolation levels (it essentially does nothing), and therefore performs the best. The remaining isolation levels are listed in ascending order of strictness, with `TRANSACTION_SERIALIZABLE` providing "perfect" isolation. Which isolation level you choose will depend on your databases (because different databases support different levels), your system's data integrity requirements, and your performance requirements.

Note

Some databases do not support the `TRANSACTION_SERIALIZABLE` attribute. Oracle, for example, throws an exception if you try to commit a transaction this way. Consult the WebLogic Server documentation and the documentation for your database to learn how you can work around this limitation.

Keep in mind that a distributed transaction operating against multiple stores must execute at the same isolation level across all stores, or unpredictable results may occur. Consult the documentation for your databases and drivers for more information.

Transaction demarcation

Transaction demarcation is the process of specifying when a transaction is started, suspended, resumed, committed, and rolled back. With J2EE, transactions can be manually demarcated in code, using calls to the JTA, or they can be automatically demarcated, using declarative rules stored in XML deployment descriptors.

Automatically demarcated transactions are called *container-managed transactions,* and are available for session, message-driven, and entity EJBs. The EJB container reads the declarative rules in the deployment descriptors and executes the affected methods in the appropriate transaction context.

When writing servlets, RMI applications, and JavaBeans, you must manually demarcate transactions by using the JTA. You can also manually demarcate transactions in session and message-driven EJBs; these are called *bean-managed transactions.* The EJB 2.0 specification, however, prohibits the use of bean-managed transactions in entity EJBs; entity EJBs must always use container-managed transactions.

Container-managed transaction demarcation attributes

The EJB specification defines several attributes for container-managed transactions that control how EJB methods participate in transactions. EJB developers must specify these attributes in the deployment descriptors of EJBs that use container-managed transactions. In this section, I will summarize how the EJB 2.0 specification defines the container's behavior for each attribute, but you should consult the EJB 2.0 specification for more details (available at `www.java.sun.com`).

NotSupported

This attribute applies to EJB methods that do not support transactions. The container invokes the EJB method with an unspecified transaction context. If the caller has a transaction in progress when such a method is invoked, the container suspends the transaction before invoking the method, and then resumes it when the method completes.

Required

The container must establish a valid transaction context before invoking an EJB method with this attribute. If a transaction is already underway, the container will associate the method with that transaction. If not, the container will start a new transaction, invoke the method, and then commit the transaction when the method completes.

Note, however, that message-driven EJB methods never execute within the context of an existing transaction, so the container always creates a new transaction context for them, prior to executing the `onMessage()` method. After `onMessage()` completes, the container commits the transaction. If the container rolls back the transaction, the message is marked for redelivery in accordance with the JMS specification.

Supports

This attribute is a cross between `NotSupported` and `Required`. If the EJB method is invoked with a transaction in progress, the container proceeds as in the `Required` case. If not, the container proceeds as in the `NotSupported` case.

RequiresNew

This attribute always forces the new container to start a new transaction for the EJB method, and to commit that transaction when the method completes. If the caller has a transaction underway, that transaction is suspended until the method completes, and then is resumed again.

Mandatory

The caller is required to have a transaction underway before calling EJB methods with this attribute set, and the container executes the methods within the context of the caller's transaction. If no transaction is underway, the container throws an exception.

Never

This attribute is the opposite of `Mandatory`. The caller must invoke the EJB method with no transaction underway. If a transaction is underway, the container throws an exception; otherwise, it proceeds as in the `NotSupported` case.

Two-phase commit and the XA interface

Two-phase commit is a protocol used to control distributed transactions. It specifies a series of states and commands that travel between the transaction manager and resource managers during the course of a transaction.

In the first phase of the two-phase commit process, updates that will be written to the resources are sent to those resources and saved in a transaction log file. Each resource is then asked if it can guarantee the successful completion of its portion of the transaction. The second phase of the process depends on the results of the first. If all resources answer yes, the transaction manager notifies all resource managers to commit, and the effects of the transaction are permanently saved to all participating resources. If one or more resources answers no, the transaction manager notifies all resource managers to roll back, and the effects of the transaction are reversed.

The WebLogic transaction manager uses the Open Group's XA interface to implement two-phase commit.

The XA interface is simply a realization of the XA specification, which is a standard for distributed transaction protocols that was developed by the Open Group. This standard has been adopted by many database vendors. The specification is available at `http://www.opengroup.org/products/publications/catalog/c193.htm`.

If a resource manager is XA-compliant, WebLogic will issue XA commands to it directly. If not, WebLogic automatically maps XA commands to the resource manager's native commands as the transaction proceeds.

Understanding JTA

While the JavaSoft implementation of JTA gives Java developers programmatic control over transactions, the WebLogic JTA gives developers access to WebLogic's robust transaction manager. The WebLogic transaction manager fully supports local and distributed transactions, transaction isolation levels, two-phase commit via the XA interface, and complete monitoring, diagnostics, and logging to facilitate performance tuning and troubleshooting.

JTA versions and packages

WebLogic 6.1 supports version 1.0.1 of the JTA specification. JTA is implemented in the following packages:

- `javax.transaction`, which contains the API for managing local transactions.
- `javax.transaction.xa`, which contains the API for managing distributed transactions by using the X/Open XA interface.
- `weblogic.transaction`, which contains WebLogic extensions to some of the classes and interfaces defined in `javax.transaction` and `javax.transaction.xa`.

You can download the JTA 1.0.1 specification from the Sun Web site at `http://java.sun.com/products/jta/`.

JTA architecture

The JTA architecture follows the familiar, layered pattern common to most J2EE APIs. Figure 6-1 shows the major components of the architecture.

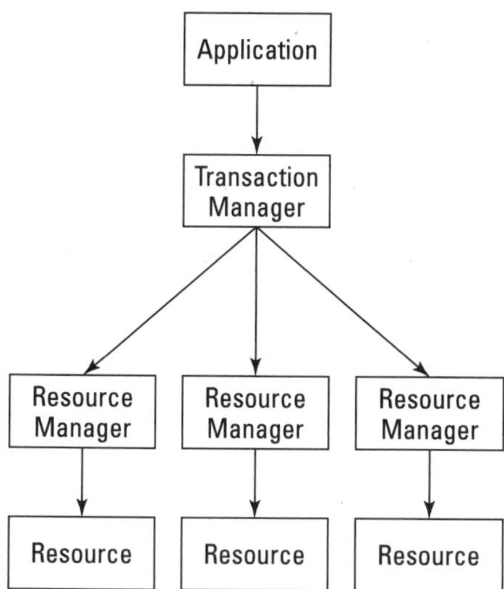

Figure 6-1: Components of the JTA architecture

The top layer of the architecture is the *application,* which can be implemented as a servlet, JSP, RMI application, EJB, or stand-alone Java application. The application makes calls to the *transaction manager,* which manages communications between the application and the transaction's resource managers. WebLogic Server has embedded within it a transaction manager that is fully J2EE compliant.

Transaction-aware resource managers

WebLogic Server works in tandem with a number of transaction-aware resource managers, including JDBC drivers provided by BEA and others, and the WebLogic built-in messaging broker, which serves as the resource manager for WebLogic's Java Message Service (JMS) implementation.

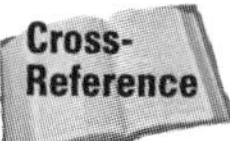

For more information about JDBC drivers, see Chapter 5. For more information about JMS, see Chapter 9.

WebLogic Java Transaction Services (JTS) driver

The WebLogic JTS driver is a special-purpose, type 3 JDBC driver that supports local transactions spanning one or more blocks of server-side code. Transactions are controlled by using the `javax.Transaction.UserTransaction` interface.

A transaction can be initiated, for example, by a servlet running on WebLogic server A, continued by an RMI server running on WebLogic server B, and concluded by a session EJB running back on server A. The only requirement is that all three code modules execute in the same thread, and draw their database connections from the same connection pool.

Under the covers, the JTS driver does some fancy bookkeeping to make things work. After a thread initiates a transaction against a pooled connection, the JTS driver ensures that the *same connection* is delivered to that thread for all subsequent connection requests made against the *same pool*, until the transaction is either committed or rolled back. Only then does it return the connection to the pool.

Therefore, to program with JTS, you simply ensure that all code participating in a transaction executes in the same thread, and requests connections from the same connection pool. JTS handles the rest.

Distributed transactions using XA and non-XA drivers

Distributed transactions require *XA drivers* that implement the X/Open XA interface for distributed transactions. The Oracle driver referenced by `weblogic.jdbc.oci.xa.XADataSource` is an example of such a driver, as is the driver referenced by `COM.cloudscape.core.XADataSource`. Both drivers are included with WebLogic.

Note You can also use a non-XA driver (such as the WebLogic jDriver for Oracle), in conjunction with a Tx DataSource, to perform distributed transactions. For this combination to work, however, the Tx DataSource must be configured with two-phase commit enabled. This essentially wraps stubbed-out XA calls around the non-XA driver. Don't worry if you accidentally enable two-phase commit for an XA driver—the Tx DataSource is smart enough to ignore this setting if the underlying driver is XA. I'll demonstrate how to configure Tx DataSources later in the chapter.

Caution Although WebLogic can manage both local and distributed transactions, local transactions are best handled within the databases themselves, using their embedded transaction management commands. The reason for this is simple. Suppose that Java code running on WebLogic begins a local transaction against a database located elsewhere on the network. If the transaction updates a table, it will gain a lock on that table, which prevents other users from using that table until the transaction completes. Now suppose the network link goes down, or a bug in the Java code crashes WebLogic Server. The transaction is now in limbo, the table remains locked indefinitely, and other users are blocked until a DBA steps in and kills the suspended transaction. By confining local transactions to the database server, you eliminate the possibility of database disruption due to unanticipated network or programming errors.

Note that distributed transactions must *always* be managed from outside the affected databases, because a separate transaction monitor (in this case, WebLogic Server) is required to coordinate transaction processing among all involved data sources.

Configuring WebLogic JTA

Configuring WebLogic JTA is quite simple — all you need to do is define transaction-aware DataSources mapped to existing JDBC connection pools. In this section, I'll create a Tx DataSource (Transactional DataSource) for the `OraclePool` connection pool created in the preceding chapter. This is the type of data source that must be used for applications wishing to perform distributed transactions.

Like DataSources, Tx DataSources are bound to the JNDI tree, where calling applications can look them up by using the `javax.naming` interface.

Here are the required steps to define a Tx DataSource against the `OraclePool` connection pool:

1. In the domain tree, choose Services ⇨ JDBC ⇨ Tx Data Sources. The screen shown in Figure 6-2 appears.

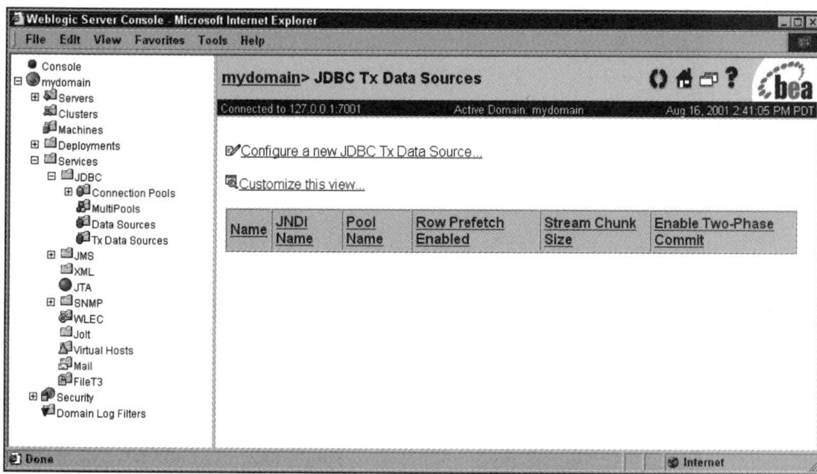

Figure 6-2: Preparing to configure a JDBC Tx DataSource

2. Click Create a New JDBC Tx Data Source to display the DataSource configuration screen. Fill out the fields on the screen, as shown in Figure 6-3; then click Create.

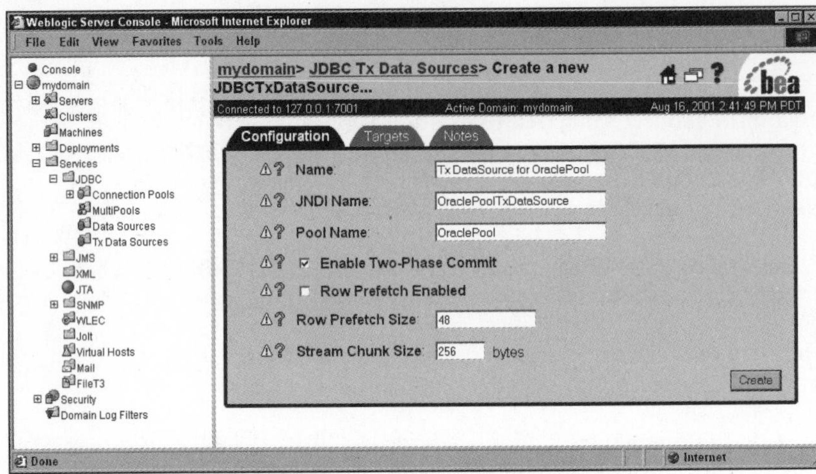

Figure 6-3: Configuring a JDBC Tx DataSource for OraclePool

Check the Enable Two-Phase Commit box only if the JDBC driver used by the underlying connection pool is not XA, which is the case for the following drivers:

```
weblogic.jdbc.oci.Driver
weblogic.jdbc.mssqlserver4.Driver
weblogic.jdbc.informix4.Driver
```

Do not check the box if the underlying pool was created with any of the following XA drivers:

```
weblogic.jdbc.oci.xa.XADataSource
oracle.jdbc.xa.client.OracleXADataSource
COM.cloudscape.core.XADataSource
```

If you are using a third-party driver that does not appear in these lists, check your driver's documentation to determine whether or not it is XA, and check the box accordingly.

3. Click the Targets tab and move your WebLogic Server instance into the Chosen list, as shown in Figure 6-4. Click Apply.
4. Stop and restart WebLogic Server to activate the Tx DataSource.

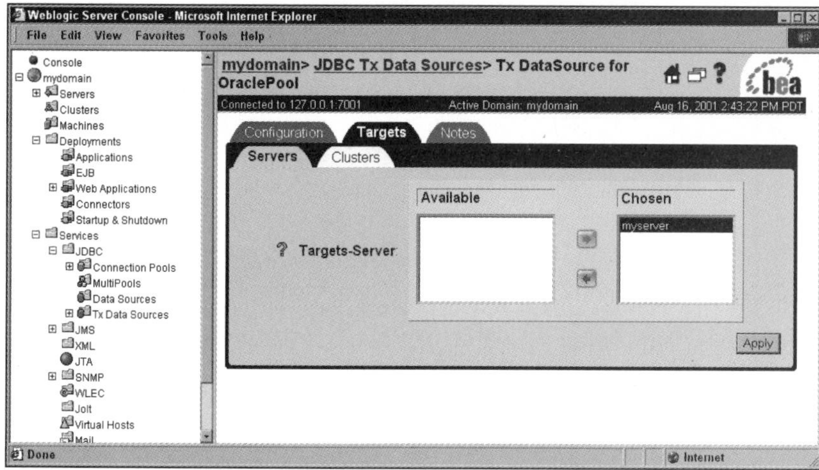

Figure 6-4: Assigning the Tx DataSource to a WebLogic Server instance

Programming WebLogic JTA

This section provides two examples of how to manually program transaction demarcation by using the Java Transaction API.

Programming a local transaction with the WebLogic JTS driver

Recall from Chapter 5 that the WebLogic JTS driver is a special-purpose, type 3 JDBC driver that supports local transactions spanning one or more blocks of server-side code. In this example, I'll show you how to use the JTS driver in a single block of server code to control multiple inserts into a table of a single Oracle database. I'll use the `EMP` table described in the preceding chapter.

First, write two utility methods to perform important tasks. The first is to obtain a reference to an object that implements the `javax.transaction.UserTransaction` interface. WebLogic provides this object as part of its runtime environment. Calling the `begin` method of this object tells it to associate a transaction with your thread and begin controlling it. Note that the `UserTransaction` object does not represent a single transaction in memory. Rather, it's a service class that might be controlling several transactions running in multiple threads of execution.

The `UserTransaction` object reference is obtained via a JNDI lookup. The following method performs the lookup and returns a reference to the object:

```
public static UserTransaction getUserTransaction() {
  Context ctx = null;
  Hashtable env = new Hashtable();
  UserTransaction tx = null;

  try {
    // Get the context of the WebLogic runtime environment.
    env.put(Context.INITIAL_CONTEXT_FACTORY,
            "weblogic.jndi.WLInitialContextFactory");
    env.put(Context.PROVIDER_URL, "t3://localhost:7001");
    env.put(Context.SECURITY_PRINCIPAL, "system");
    env.put(Context.SECURITY_CREDENTIALS, "password");
    ctx = new InitialContext(env);

    // Obtain a reference to its UserTransaction class.
    tx = (UserTransaction)
           ctx.lookup("javax.transaction.UserTransaction");
  }
  catch (Exception e) {
    e.printStackTrace();
  }
  finally {
    // Return the UserTransaction reference to the caller.
    return tx;
  }
}
```

The second task is to get a JTS connection bound to the connection pool you want to use. This is accomplished by using the following method:

```
public static Connection getJTSConnection(String poolName) {
  Connection myConnection = null;

  try {
    Driver myDriver =
     (Driver)
     Class.forName("weblogic.jdbc.jts.Driver").newInstance();

    myConnection = myDriver.connect("jdbc:weblogic:jts:" +
      poolName, null);
  }
  catch (Exception e) {
    e.printStackTrace();
  }
  finally {
    return myConnection;
  }
}
```

After incorporating the utility methods into a class, add another method to the class, demoJTS, which demonstrates how to perform a transaction with JTS by using OraclePool, the connection pool to Oracle defined earlier:

```
public static void demoJTS(String demoMode) {
  Connection myConnection = null;
  UserTransaction tx = null;
  Driver myDriver = null;

  try {
    // Get a reference to the UserTransaction class
    // and associate a new transaction with our thread.
    tx = getUserTransaction();
    tx.begin();

    // Obtain a JTS-enabled connection from OraclePool.
    myConnection = getJTSConnection("OraclePool");

    // Insert 6 new employees into the SCOTT.EMP table.
    insertEmp(8000, "ZUFFOLETTO", "WRITER");
    insertEmp(8001, "WELLS", "MANAGER");
    insertEmp(8002, "TUCKER", "ENGINEER");
    insertEmp(8003, "GILL", "ENGINEER");
    insertEmp(8004, "SEKANDER", "SALES");
    insertEmp(8005, "SCHNEIDER", "ENGINEER");

    // Commit the transaction
    tx.commit();
  }
  catch (Exception e) {
    // Something went wrong - roll back the transaction.
    // In this case, no employees will be inserted.
    tx.rollback();
    e.printStackTrace();
  }
  finally {
    try {
      // Close the database connection, returning it
      // to the pool.
      myConnection.close();
    }
    catch (Exception e) {
      e.printStackTrace();
    }
  }
}
```

As you can see, coding a JTS transaction is straightforward. First you get a UserTransaction reference, and then a transaction-enabled connection from the JTS driver. Next you perform your data manipulations. If no exceptions occur, you commit the transaction. Otherwise, you roll it back.

The code that makes JTS interesting appears in the `insertEmp` method, shown here:

```
public static void insertEmp(int empNo,
                             String empName,
                             String empJob)
                             throws SQLException {

  // Obtain a JTS-enabled connection from OraclePool
  Connection myConnection = getJTSConnection("OraclePool");

  // Define a SQL statement to insert an employee into EMP
  String sql = "INSERT INTO EMP (EMPNO, ENAME, JOB) " +
               "VALUES (?, ?, ?)";

  // Bind the SQL statement to a PreparedStatement
  PreparedStatement myStatement =
    theConnection.prepareStatement(sql);

  // Load the input variables into the INSERT statement
  myStatement.setInt(1, empNo);
  myStatement.setString(2, empName);
  myStatement.setString(3, empJob);

  // Perform the INSERT
  if (myStatement.executeUpdate() == 1) {
    System.out.println("Employee inserted.");
  } else {
    System.out.println("Employee not inserted.");
  }
  myStatement.close();
}
```

Notice that `insertEmp` does not receive a JTS-enabled connection as an input parameter. Instead, it seemingly obtains its own JTS-enabled connection to `OraclePool`, by calling `getJTSConnection`, just as `demoJTS` did. How can this possibly work?

The answer lies in the way the JTS driver works. Recall that once a thread initiates a transaction against a pooled connection, the JTS driver ensures the *same connection* is delivered to that thread for all subsequent connection requests made against the *same pool,* until the transaction is either committed or rolled back. Only then does it return the connection to the pool. The preceding code shows this feature of the JTS driver at work.

Nevertheless, if you prefer, you can pass a JTS-enabled connection as a parameter to `insertEmp`, and simply use that connection instead of calling `getJTSConnection`. The results will be the same.

Note that `insertEmp` could have been a method residing in a JavaBean, EJB, RMI server, or any other component callable by `demoJTS`. As long as `insertEmp` executes in the same thread as `demoJTS` and uses the same connection pool, it will correctly participate in the transaction.

If you rely on the Java exception handling mechanism to either commit or roll back transactions (as I do in these examples), be sure any methods you call that participate in the transaction throw exceptions to the calling method. In this example, `insertEmp` throws an SQLException, rather than catching it itself. If `insertEmp` caught its own SQLExceptions, the caller would never know about them, and transaction processing would continue, possibly terminating with a bogus commit.

Programming a distributed transaction with the Oracle XA driver

This example implements a "brute force" database replication engine that inserts identical data into the `EMP` tables of two different Oracle databases. It does so by performing a distributed transaction across the two databases by using the Oracle XA driver.

Getting distributed transactions to work is tricky business, so I'll walk through the complete configuration and programming steps required to make it work.

I have two Oracle instances on my network: `ORADEV1.ZEEWARE.COM` (residing in Denver, CO) and `JOEVAIO.ZEEWARE.COM` (residing in Sausalito, CA). Both are standard Oracle 8.1.6 installations.

The first step is to create connection pools to each of these databases by using the Oracle XA driver. These are the specifications of the two pools:

```
Configuration of pool 1
  Pool Name = DenverPool
  URL = jdbc:weblogic:oracle:ORADEV1.ZEEWARE.COM
  Driver Classname = weblogic.jdbc.oci.xa.XADataSource
  Properties
    user=SCOTT
    password=tiger
    dataSourceName=DenverPool
    serverName=ORADEV1.ZEEWARE.COM

Configuration of pool 2
  Pool Name = SausalitoPool
  URL = jdbc:weblogic:oracle:JOEVAIO.ZEEWARE.COM
  Driver Classname = weblogic.jdbc.oci.xa.XADataSource
  Properties
    user=SCOTT
```

```
password=tiger
dataSourceName=SausalitoPool
serverName=JOEVAIO.ZEEWARE.COM
```

Both pools have the following additional settings:

```
Connections
  Initial Capacity = 4
  Maximum Capacity = 10
  Capacity Increment = 2
  Login Delay Seconds = 0
  Refresh Period = 15 minutes
  Allow Shrinking = true
  Shrink Period = 15 minutes

Testing
  Test Table Name = dual
  Test Reserved Connections = false
  Test Released Connections = false

Targets
  Chosen = myserver
```

The next step is to create a Tx DataSource for each pool. These are the specifications for the data sources:

```
Configuration of Tx Data Source 1
  Name = DenverTxDS
  JNDI Name = DenverTxDS
  Pool Name = DenverPool
  Enable Two-Phase Commit = false

Configuration of Tx Data Source 2
  Name = SausalitoTxDS
  JNDI Name = SausalitoTxDS
  Pool Name = SausalitoPool
  Enable Two-Phase Commit = false

Targets (both pools)
  Chosen = myserver
```

Note that you do not enable two-phase commit because you are using an XA-enabled driver.

The code that uses these data sources and does the distributed transaction is fairly simple. I enclosed it in a method called `demoXA`:

```
public static void demoXA() {
  javax.sql.DataSource ds1 = null;
  javax.sql.DataSource ds2 = null;
  Connection conn1 = null;
  Connection conn2 = null;
```

```
InitialContext ctx = null;
UserTransaction tx = null;
Driver myDriver = null;

try {
  // Get a reference to the UserTransaction class
  // and associate a new transaction with our thread.
  tx = getUserTransaction();
  tx.begin();

  // Get a context for making JNDI calls.
  ctx = new InitialContext();

  // Use JNDI to lookup references to the two data sources.
  ds1 = (javax.sql.DataSource)ctx.lookup("DenverTxDS");
  ds2 = (javax.sql.DataSource)ctx.lookup("SausalitoTxDS");

  // Obtain database connections from the data sources.
  conn1 = ds1.getConnection();
  conn2 = ds2.getConnection();

  // Insert employee records into the Denver database.
  insertEmp(conn1, 8000, "ZUFFOLETTO", "WRITER");
  insertEmp(conn1, 8001, "WELLS", "MANAGER");
  insertEmp(conn1, 8002, "TUCKER", "ENGINEER");
  insertEmp(conn1, 8003, "GILL", "ENGINEER");
  insertEmp(conn1, 8004, "SEKANDER", "SALES");
  insertEmp(conn1, 8005, "SCHNEIDER", "ENGINEER");

  // Insert identical records into the Sausalito database.
  insertEmp(conn2, 8000, "ZUFFOLETTO", "WRITER");
  insertEmp(conn2, 8001, "WELLS", "MANAGER");
  insertEmp(conn2, 8002, "TUCKER", "ENGINEER");
  insertEmp(conn2, 8003, "GILL", "ENGINEER");
  insertEmp(conn2, 8004, "SEKANDER", "SALES");
  insertEmp(conn2, 8005, " SCHNEIDER ", "ENGINEER");

  // All's well and the databases are in sync, so commit
  // the transaction. This causes the data to be
  // permanently written to each database.
  tx.commit();
}
catch (Exception e) {
  try {
    // Something went wrong - roll back the transaction.
    // In this case, no employees are inserted into either
    // database.
    tx.rollback();
    e.printStackTrace();
  }
  catch (Exception ex) {
    ex.printStackTrace();
```

```
      }
    }
    finally {
      try {
        // Close the database connections, returning them
        // to the pool.
        conn1.close();
        conn2.close();
      }
      catch (Exception e) {
        e.printStackTrace();
      }
    }
  }
```

After getting a `UserTransaction` reference (using the same `getTransaction` method as in the previous example), it begins the transaction. Then it gets references to the data source instances by performing JNDI lookups on `DenverTxDS` and `SausalitoTxDS`, the data sources defined in the console. The transaction uses these data sources to get transaction-enabled connections to the databases, and then passes these connections to a version of `insertEmp` that accepts a connection as a parameter. After performing identical calls to `insertEmp` for each database, it commits the transaction. But if `insertEmp` throws an exception, or if any of the other code throws an exception, the transaction is rolled back. The following is the code for this new version of `insertEmp`:

```
public static void insertEmp(Connection theConnection,
                             int empNo,
                             String empName,
                             String empJob)
                             throws SQLException {

  // Define a SQL statement to insert an employee into EMP
  String sql = "INSERT INTO EMP (EMPNO, ENAME, JOB) " +
               "VALUES (?, ?, ?)";

  // Bind the SQL statement to a PreparedStatement
  PreparedStatement myStatement =
    theConnection.prepareStatement(sql);

  // Load the input variables into the INSERT statement
  myStatement.setInt(1, empNo);
  myStatement.setString(2, empName);
  myStatement.setString(3, empJob);

  // Perform the INSERT
  if (myStatement.executeUpdate() == 1) {
    System.out.println("Employee inserted.");
  } else {
    System.out.println("Employee not inserted.");
  }
  myStatement.close();
}
```

This concludes the discussion of database transaction programming with WebLogic. If you're a relative newcomer to database programming, you probably don't fully appreciate the wonder of what these examples have accomplished. I have been programming databases for nearly 15 years, and I find the distributed transaction support provided by Sun, WebLogic, and the database vendors to be just slightly short of miraculous. The simplicity of the transaction calls belies a monstrous amount of very difficult work that is going on behind the scenes.

Summary

Transactions are an essential tool for maintaining data integrity in distributed computing systems. WebLogic's implementation of JTA gives Java programmers access to a robust transaction manager that supports manual or automatic transaction management in accordance with the J2EE specification. The WebLogic transaction manager also fully supports the EJB 2.0 specification, including container-managed transaction semantics for session, message-driven, and entity EJBs.

Transactions can be local (spanning one data store) or distributed (spanning multiple data stores). Out of the box, WebLogic supports distributed transactions that can span operations against multiple relational databases and/or Java Message Service stores.

Considering their underlying complexity, programming transactions with JTA is quite simple, requiring the use of only a handful of methods in the `javax.Transaction.UserTransaction` interface. Configuring transactions in WebLogic Server is equally easy, requiring only the configuration of transaction-enabled data sources that are mapped to existing database connection pools.

✦ ✦ ✦

CHAPTER 7

Working with WebLogic JNDI

✦ ✦ ✦ ✦

In This Chapter

Understanding JNDI

Programming WebLogic JNDI

Using WebLogic JNDI in a clustered environment

✦ ✦ ✦ ✦

The *Java Naming and Directory Interface,* or *JNDI,* provides a mechanism for linking Java programs to external naming and directory services, such as file systems, network resources, and corporate directories. JNDI enables Java programmers to find objects and data registered in these services, and to register their own objects and data for use by others.

In this chapter, an overview of JNDI is provided, as well as details on how JNDI is used in WebLogic. You will learn how to register and look up objects in the WebLogic JNDI tree, which is a simple, JNDI-accessible naming service built into WebLogic. You will also learn how to use JNDI to access an external directory based on the Lightweight Directory Access Protocol (LDAP).

Understanding JNDI

To use JNDI effectively, you need to understand its package structure, architecture, and a few key concepts. JNDI is easy to understand and use, especially if you use it only to access WebLogic's JNDI tree. Keep in mind, however, that you can use JNDI to access other directory structures as well.

JNDI versions and packages

WebLogic 6.1 runs on top of JDK 1.3, and supports JNDI version 1.2.1. JNDI is implemented in the following packages:

- `javax.naming`, which contains classes and interfaces for accessing naming services, such as the WebLogic JNDI tree
- `javax.naming.directory`, which contains classes and interfaces for accessing directories, such as LDAP directories

- `javax.naming.ldap`, which contains classes and interfaces that extend those in `javax.naming.directory` and support LDAP v3 extensions
- `javax.naming.event`, which contains classes and interfaces for event notification in naming and directory services

You can find complete documentation for these packages on Sun's FTP site at `ftp://ftp.javasoft.com/docs/j2se1.3/jndi.pdf`.

In addition to the core JNDI packages, Sun provides the package `javax.naming.spi` for those implementing service provider interfaces (SPIs). I'll discuss the role of SPIs in the next section. You can find complete documentation for this package at `ftp://ftp.javasoft.com/docs/j2se1.3/jndispi.pdf`.

JNDI architecture

Figure 7-1 shows the layers of the JNDI architecture. At the top is Java application code, implemented as a servlet, EJB, or other component, which makes calls to the JNDI API. These calls are routed by the naming and directory manager (in your case, WebLogic Server) to the appropriate JNDI service provider interface (SPI), which translates the JNDI calls into native commands for the naming or directory resource being accessed. This resource can be the JNDI tree built into WebLogic, an external LDAP directory, an RMI registry, a file system, or virtually any other resource for which an appropriate JNDI SPI can be written.

<table>
<tr><td colspan="5">Application</td></tr>
<tr><td colspan="5">JNDI API</td></tr>
<tr><td colspan="5">JNDI Naming and Directory manager (WebLogic)</td></tr>
<tr><td colspan="5">JNDI Service Provider Interfaces</td></tr>
<tr><td>WebLogic JNDI tree</td><td>LDAP</td><td>RMI</td><td>File System</td><td>Others</td></tr>
</table>

Figure 7-1: JNDI architecture

JNDI service providers are similar in concept to JDBC drivers; they convert JNDI API calls into protocol-specific commands for underlying services. An LDAP service provider, for example, converts JNDI calls into LDAP calls, while a file system service provider converts JNDI calls to local file system calls, and so on.

A full understanding of JNDI requires an understanding of a few key concepts, which I cover next.

Naming services

Naming services enable Java programmers to assign meaningful names to computing resources of various types, and to perform lookups on those resources by name. Names are easier for humans to deal with, and they insulate programmers from changes that might be made to the associated resources. As long as the name doesn't change, the programmer will always get the correct resource when finding it by name.

The most ubiquitous naming service on Earth is the Internet's Domain Name System, or DNS, which associates network host names (such as `www.zeeware.com`) with IP addresses (such as `204.56.46.11`). Thanks to DNS, you can surf the Internet by using easily remembered names such as `www.yahoo.com`, `www.cnn.com`, and `www.bea.com`. Your browser performs lookups on these names by using DNS, and then uses the IP addresses DNS returns to communicate with the Web sites. Imagine how difficult surfing the Internet would be if you had to remember the IP addresses yourself! Worse, suppose Yahoo reorganized its network, causing their IP addresses to change. You wouldn't be able to find Yahoo at all, unless you knew the new addresses. DNS insulates you from this problem because it always returns the correct address if you provide the correct name (assuming Yahoo correctly updates its DNS records, of course).

The WebLogic JNDI tree is another naming service. It enables programmers to publish Java classes into the tree, such as RMI stubs, JDBC connection pools, JDBC data sources, or any other class that implements the `java.io.Serializable` interface, and then retrieve instances of them by name for use in their programs. This makes it easy for developers to create a server-side code repository available to code running on the server and also to any authorized user accessing the naming service over the network.

Directory services

Directory services are like naming services, but allow additional attributes beyond names to be associated with objects, and allow object lookups based on any combination of the attributes.

A common directory example is that of an e-mail directory, which allows lookups by a person's name, and returns the name along with one or more e-mail addresses for that person. Such directories may also include information about the person's address, telephone numbers, corporate department, and so on.

LDAP is a standard protocol for accessing directories and performing lookups on their contents. Industry support for LDAP is steadily increasing, making LDAP a preferred method for communicating with directory services. The Windows 2000 Active Directory, for example, which replaces Windows NT domains and integrates with Microsoft Exchange's e-mail directory, is fully LDAP-compliant.

Service providers

A *service provider* is simply the underlying service being accessed via JNDI. It can be a naming service, directory service, native file system, RMI registry, LDAP-compliant directory, or any other service for which a JNDI-compliant SPI exists.

Sun's Web site contains service provider interfaces for accessing LDAP directories, CORBA naming services, the Windows registry, native file systems, Novell directory services, DNS, and more. You can find it at `http://java.sun.com/products/jndi/serviceproviders.html`.

Contexts

Contexts provide the programmatic link between your Java code and the JNDI service provider you wish to use. A JNDI context is analogous to a JDBC connection—it's the pipe through which your code's commands to the naming or directory service flow, and through which data from the service provider is received.

When obtaining a context, your code passes properties to JNDI specifying which *context factory* to use. This determines, in turn, which SPI to use. You must also provide a URL specifying the location of the naming or directory resource to be used. Optional parameters include a username, password, and various configuration parameters, as shown in Table 7-1.

Table 7-1
Properties for Creating JNDI Contexts

Property	*Comments*
`INITIAL_CONTEXT_FACTORY`	The fully qualified name of the class used to create the JNDI context. Example: `weblogic.jndi.WLInitialContextFactory`
`PROVIDER_URL`	The protocol, host, and port used to connect to the naming or directory service provider. Example: `t3://localhost:7001`
`SECURITY_PRINCIPAL`	The identity of the user in the WebLogic security realm with whom to associate the context. Defaults to the WebLogic `guest` account, unless the current thread is already associated with a different user.
`SECURITY_CREDENTIALS`	The password of the user defined by the `SECURITY_PRINCIPAL` property, or an object that implements the `weblogic.security.acl.UserInfo` interface. Defaults to the password of the WebLogic `guest` account, unless the current thread is already associated with a different user.
`SECURITY_PROTOCOL`	Specifies which security protocol to use, such as SSL.

Property	*Comments*
SECURITY_AUTHENTICATION	Specifies the level of authentication to use. Values include none, simple, strong, or a provider-specific string.
AUTHORITATIVE	If true, then the naming or directory service being accessed is deemed the ultimate authority for JNDI lookups, and lookups will bypass any caches or replicas that may exist.
REFERRAL	A value of follow specifies that the service provider should automatically follow referrals generated by the naming or directory service. A value of ignore means the service provider should not follow referrals.
OBJECT_FACTORIES	A colon-separated list of class names specifying which object factories to use.
STATE_FACTORIES	A colon-separated list of class names specifying which state factories to use.
CONTROL_FACTORIES	A colon-separated list of class names of response control factory classes to use.
URL_PKG_PREFIXES	A colon-separated list of package prefixes to use when loading URL context factories.
DNS_URL	Specifies the DNS host to use for looking up addresses associated with JNDI URLs.
BATCHSIZE	Specifies the size of the buffer the service provider should use to return data. If a lookup generates more data than BATCHSIZE accommodates, the data will be returned in multiple chunks, each the size of BATCHSIZE.
LANGUAGE	A colon-separated list of languages to use with the service provider. Acceptable values are the tags defined by RFC 1766, such as en-US, fr, and ja-JP-kanji.
APPLET	An instance of java.applet.Applet to use to obtain the values of some environment properties. Almost never used with WebLogic.
REPLICATE_BINDINGS	If true, replicate this bound object to all JNDI trees in a cluster. Otherwise, bind it only to its home server. This property is WebLogic-specific and available only when using the WebLogic context factory to bind objects to the WebLogic JNDI Tree.

Programming WebLogic JNDI

When you write JNDI code, it is to perform one or more of the following tasks:

- ✦ Obtain a reference to WebLogic server's context
- ✦ Bind objects to WebLogic's JNDI tree
- ✦ Look up objects already bound to WebLogic's JNDI tree
- ✦ Perform binds and lookups against other JNDI-compliant resources, such as LDAP servers

In this section, you learn how to write Java code to do all these things.

Obtaining a reference to WebLogic's context

Before making any JNDI calls, you must obtain a reference to WebLogic Server's context. You can do this in one of two ways:

- ✦ Use the `javax.naming.InitialContext` class, which is the portable, J2EE way of doing it
- ✦ Use the `weblogic.jndi.Environment` class, which is the non-portable, WebLogic-specific way of doing it

To obtain a context using `javax.naming.InitialContext`, you must provide values for the properties `INITIAL_CONTEXT_FACTORY` and `PROVIDER_URL`. You may optionally provide values for `SECURITY_PRINCIPAL` and `SECURITY_CREDENTIALS`, but if you don't, the context will be obtained by using the WebLogic `guest` account. Listing 7-1 shows how to obtain a WebLogic context by using the WebLogic `system` account:

Listing 7-1: Obtaining a WebLogic Context Using the `javax.naming.Initial`Context Class

```
import javax.naming.*;
import weblogic.jndi.*;
import java.util.*;

Context ctx = null;
Hashtable ht = new Hashtable();

ht.put(Context.INITIAL_CONTEXT_FACTORY,
       "weblogic.jndi.WLInitialContextFactory");
ht.put(Context.PROVIDER_URL, "t3://localhost:7001");
ht.put(Context.SECURITY_PRINCIPAL, "system");
```

```
ht.put(Context.SECURITY_CREDENTIALS, "password");

try {
  ctx = new InitialContext(ht);
  // do something with the context
}
catch (NamingException e) {
}
finally {
  try {
    // close the context when finished with it
    ctx.close();
  }
  catch (Exception e) {
  }
}
```

BEA recommends using the Java Authentication and Authorization Service (JAAS) instead of JNDI to associate a user with a security context. Nevertheless, the preceding example shows how to do it with JNDI, and is provided as a reference.

The WebLogic-specific way to obtain a context is to use the `weblogic.jndi.Environment` interface. This interface provides defaults for the context's properties that reduce the amount of code you need to write, especially if the code is running within WebLogic Server. With this interface, `INITIAL_CONTEXT_FACTORY` defaults to `weblogic.jndi.WLInitialContextFactory`, `PROVIDER_URL` defaults to `t3://localhost:7001`, `SECURITY_PRINCIPAL` defaults to WebLogic's `guest` account, and `SECURITY_CREDENTIALS` defaults to the `guest` account's password.

If you want to set the context properties to different values, the `Environment` interface provides `set` methods for this purpose. The code in Listing 7-2 reimplements the preceding example, using the `Environment` interface and two of its `set` methods to change the security context to the `system` account.

Listing 7-2: Obtaining a WebLogic Context Using the `weblogic.jndi.Environment` Interface

```
import javax.naming.*;
import weblogic.jndi.*;
import java.util.*;

Context ctx = null;
Environment env = new Environment();
```

Continued

Listing 7-2 *(continued)*

```
env.setSecurityPrincipal("system");
env.setSecurityCredentials("password");

try {
  ctx = env.getInitialContext();
  // do something with the context
}
catch (NamingException e) {
}
finally {
  try {
    // close the context when finished with it
    ctx.close();
  }
  catch (Exception e) {
  }
}
```

Binding objects to the WebLogic JNDI tree

After you obtain a context, you can use it to bind objects to the WebLogic JNDI Tree. The following code snippet shows how to bind an instance of a hypothetical `Person` class to the JNDI Tree, under the logical name `Person Object`:

```
try {
  ctx = env.getInitialContext();
  Person myPerson = new Person();
  ctx.bind("Person Object", myPerson);
}
catch (NamingException e) {
}
```

Note that if an object is already bound to the tree with this name, the call to `InitialContext.bind()` will throw a `NamingException`. If you don't want an exception thrown in this case, call `InitialContext.rebind()` instead, which overwrites any previous bindings with the new one:

```
try {
  ctx = env.getInitialContext();
  Person myPerson = new Person();
  ctx.rebind("Person Object", myPerson);
}
catch (NamingException e) {
}
```

You can use the WebLogic console to view bound objects in the JNDI Tree. Expand the Servers node in the domain tree, and then right-click myserver (or whatever server you are using). From the pop-up menu of server-related operations, select View JNDI Tree. The JNDI Tree appears in a new browser window, as shown in Figure 7-2.

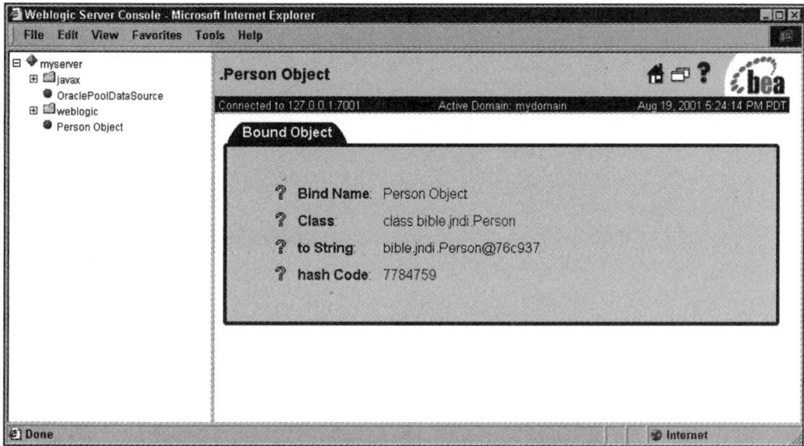

Figure 7-2: A Person object bound to the WebLogic JNDI Tree

Using subcontexts to organize the JNDI tree

Notice that the `Person` object was bound to the root level of the JNDI Tree. If you are binding a lot of objects, or if you want to organize your bound objects by application, you may want to bind your objects into *subcontexts*, which are simply folders in the JNDI Tree. In Figure 7-2, there are subcontexts called `javax`, `weblogic`, and `Weblogic`. Subcontexts can nest to any number of levels, similar to directories in a file system, and are case-sensitive (which explains why there are `weblogic` and `Weblogic` subcontexts in Figure 7-2).

The following example shows how to create a subcontext called `JNDI Chapter` and bind a `Person` object into it:

```
try {
  ctx = env.getInitialContext();
  Context subctx = ctx.createSubContext("JNDI Chapter");
  Person myPerson = new Person();
  subctx.bind("Person Object", myPerson);
}
catch (NamingException e) {
}
```

Figure 7-3 shows the result of this binding in the WebLogic JNDI Tree.

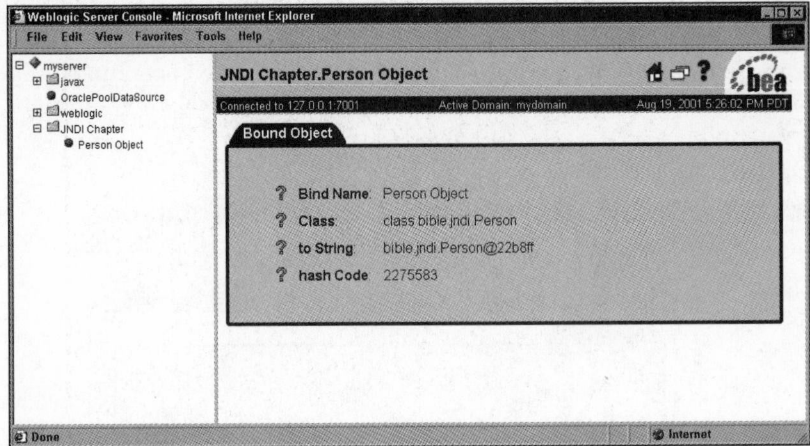

Figure 7-3: A Person object bound to a subcontext in the WebLogic JNDI Tree

Performing lookups on objects bound to the WebLogic JNDI tree

After you bind objects to the WebLogic JNDI Tree, you can obtain references to them by performing lookups. You accomplish this by calling the `Context.lookup()` method, which returns a Java `Object`, and casting the result to the proper object type. The following code shows how to obtain a reference to the `Person` object you stored in the preceding example:

```
try {
  ctx = env.getInitialContext();
  Person myPerson =
    (Person) ctx.lookup("JNDI Chapter/Person Object");
  // You can now call myPerson's methods
}
catch (NamingException e) {
}
```

Recall from Chapter 7 that classes used in this manner (`Person`) must implement the `java.io.Serializable` interface.

Another shortcut is to call `Environment.getContext()` instead of `Environment.getInitialContext()`, passing the name of the subcontext you want to use for the lookup. `getInitialContext()` always returns a reference to the root context, while `getContext()` returns a reference to any valid subcontext:

```
try {
  ctx = env.getContext("JNDI Chapter");
  Person myPerson = (Person) ctx.lookup("Person Object");
  // You can now call myPerson's methods
```

```
}
catch (NamingException e) {
}
```

Performing lookups against an LDAP directory

In this section, I show you how to use JNDI to obtain a context to an external LDAP directory, and then perform simple lookups on its contents. Before proceeding with the example, however, I will give you a brief overview of LDAP. LDAP directories are hierarchical, usually organized from the top down using geographical or organizational divisions. The design of an LDAP directory (the way it's organized and the items it tracks) is called its *schema;* LDAP schemas are completely user-definable. To find an entry in the directory, you provide a *distinguished name* (DN), which consists of one or more *relative distinguished names* (RDNs) that fully specify the entry. Table 7-2 lists the standard LDAP RDNs found in all LDAP directories.

Table 7-2
Standard LDAP RDNs

RDN Type	*Description*
C	Country name
ST	State or province name
L	Locality or city name
STREET	Street address
O	Organization name
OU	Organizational unit name
CN	Common name

To perform a lookup in an LDAP directory, you construct a DN from one or more RDNs. The more RDNs you supply, the more specific the query becomes. Here is an example of a DN constructed from the RDNs in the preceding table:

```
CN=Joe Zuffoletto, OU=Management, O=ZeeWare, L=Sausalito,
ST=California, C=US
```

When passed as a query to an LDAP server, the preceding DN, which specifies a person, will probably return only one entry. You can pass less specific DNs to retrieve multiple entries; for example, the following DN retrieves the entries for all members of management at ZeeWare's offices in California: OU=Management, O=ZeeWare, ST=California, C=US.

You now have enough background to understand the examples. For these examples, I installed iPlanet Directory Server v5.0 on the same Windows 2000 machine as my WebLogic Server (you can download iPlanet Directory Server, along with installation instructions, from `http://www.iplanet.com/downloads/download/index html`). After downloading, I expanded the zip file and ran the default setup. The installer created a directory instance with a root suffix of `dc=JMZ,dc=local` (derived from my Windows 2000 domain name).

After completing the installation, I used the iPlanet Console to add sample organizational units and users to the directory tree, organized as follows:

```
dc=JMZ (root)
  ou=Management
    uid=GWells
    uid=JZuffoletto
  ou=Developers
    uid=BGill
    uid=GSchneider
    uid=BTucker
  ou=Clients
    uid=SJohnson
    uid=MJones
    uid=DMiller
    uid=NSmith
```

Figure 7-4 shows the iPlanet Console after I added this information.

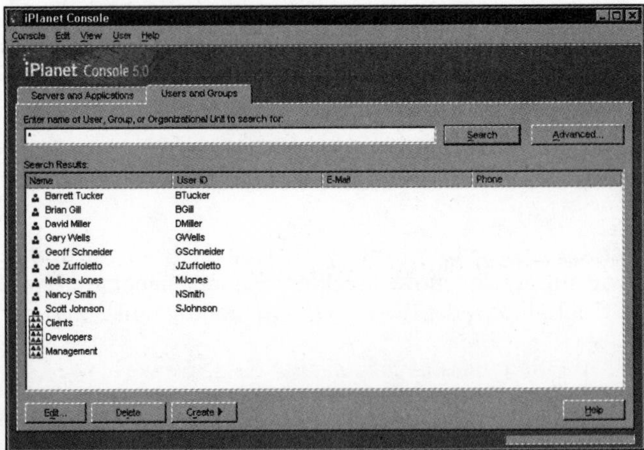

Figure 7-4: iPlanet Console showing sample organizational units and users

Accessing Microsoft's Active Directory

One popular topic on the newsgroups these days is how to use JNDI to access Microsoft's Active Directory. Active Directory is Microsoft's LDAP-compliant replacement for Windows NT domains that ships with Windows 2000 servers. Being able to access the Windows 2000 directory from Java is a major boon for many enterprise programmers. The question is: How do you do it?

It turns out to be fairly easy if Active Directory and DNS are properly configured for your Windows 2000 domain. Assuming they are, the following code snippet will get you a `DirContext` to Active Directory:

```
DirContext ctx = null;
Hashtable ht = new Hashtable();

ht.put(Context.INITIAL_CONTEXT_FACTORY,
      "com.sun.jndi.ldap.LdapCtxFactory");

ht.put(Context.PROVIDER_URL, "ldap://pdc.mycompany.com:389");
ht.put(Context.SECURITY_AUTHENTICATION, "simple");
ht.put(Context.SECURITY_PRINCIPAL, "MYCOMPANY\\Administrator");
ht.put(Context.SECURITY_CREDENTIALS, "password");

ctx = new InitialDirContext(ht);
```

In this example, `PROVIDER_URL` contains the DNS hostname of the Active Directory server (`pdc.mycompany.com`), plus the (optional) port of 389. You must specify a `SECURITY_AUTHENTICATION` of simple, or Active Directory will expect Windows 2000 authentication, which Java does not support. The `SECURITY_PRINCIPAL` can be the Windows Administrator account (shown), or any other account with access to the directory. To make your code location-independent, include the Windows 2000 domain name before the account name, using the usual Windows 2000 syntax, as in `MYCOMPANY\\Administrator`. The `SECURITY_CREDENTIALS` simply contain the password for the account given by `SECURITY_PRINCIPAL`.

After you obtain a `DirContext` to Active Directory, you can use it like any other LDAP directory. The following code dumps all the `Person Objects` in the directory:

```
SearchControls cons = new SearchControls();
cons.setSearchScope(SearchControls.SUBTREE_SCOPE);
NamingEnumeration results = ctx.search("dc=zeeware,dc=com",
                                      "objectclass=person",
                                      cons);
```

Continued

Continued

```
while (results.hasMore()) {
  System.out.println("\n\n");
  SearchResult result = (SearchResult) results.next();
  Attributes rAttrs = result.getAttributes();
  for (NamingEnumeration ne = rAttrs.getAll(); ne.hasMore();) {
    Attribute nAttr = (Attribute) ne.next();
    String sID = nAttr.getID();
    for (Enumeration vals = nAttr.getAll();
         vals.hasMoreElements();) {
      System.out.println(sID + ": " + vals.nextElement());
    }
  }
}
```

Beware! Active Directory contains a lot of administrative information, so you'll need to experiment and tune your queries so they return only the information you need.

Obtaining a directory context

Now that the directory is up and running, the first programming step is to write a method that obtains the LDAP directory's context. But rather than obtaining an instance of `javax.naming.Context`, it's necessary that you obtain an instance of `javax.naming.directory.DirContext`. A `DirContext` contains methods that enable you to access the attributes of entries in the directory, which is essential when working with LDAP.

The following method returns a `DirContext` to the LDAP directory specified by `providerUrl`:

```
public static DirContext getLDAPContext(String providerUrl)
throws javax.naming.NamingException {
  DirContext ctx = null;
  Hashtable ht = new Hashtable();

  ht.put(Context.INITIAL_CONTEXT_FACTORY,
         "com.sun.jndi.ldap.LdapCtxFactory");
  ht.put(Context.PROVIDER_URL, providerUrl);

  ctx = new InitialDirContext(ht);
  return ctx;
}
```

Notice that you're using a different `INITIAL_CONTEXT_FACTORY`—Sun's default LDAP context factory, contained in the factory class `com.sun.jndi.ldap. LdapCtxFactory`. This class should already be in your Java/WebLogic classpath, so there's no need to install it. Note also that you're creating a new `InitialDirContext`, which returns a `DirContext`, rather than `InitialContext`, which returns a regular `Context`.

The following call obtains a context to the local iPlanet directory I installed:

```
try {
  DirContext ctx = getLDAPContext("ldap://localhost:389");
}
catch (NamingException e) {
}
```

Authenticating a user

Once you have obtained the LDAP directory's context, you can do some useful work with the directory. A common task is to authenticate users by comparing a given name and password (such as those keyed into a login page) against the entries in the directory. The following code performs this task:

```
Properties p = new Properties();
p.put(Context.INITIAL_CONTEXT_FACTORY,
  "com.sun.jndi.ldap.LdapCtxFactory");
p.put(Context.PROVIDER_URL, LdapURL);
p.put(Context.SECURITY_AUTHENTICATION, "simple");
p.put(Context.SECURITY_PRINCIPAL, "cn=" + strUserName);
p.put(Context.SECURITY_CREDENTIALS, strPassword);
try {
  DirContext ctx = new InitialDirContext(p);
} catch (Exception e) {
  System.out.println("Login failed.");
}
```

Retrieving user attributes

Another important task is to retrieve attributes for selected users, perhaps to support a system administrator's ability to manage the user list. The following code retrieves a list of all users in the organizational unit `Clients`, then iterates through the list to print the full name of each user:

```
Attributes match = new BasicAttributes();
match.put("cn", username);
try {
  NamingEnumeration list = dctx.search("ou=Clients", match);
  if ((list != null) && (list.hasMore())) {
    SearchResult sr = (SearchResult) list.next();
    Attributes attrs = sr.getAttributes();
    if (attrs != null) {
      System.out.println("Full Name: " +
        attrs.get("cn")).get());
      System.out.println("E-mail: " +
        attrs.get("mail")).get());
```

```
          System.out.println("");
        }
      } else {
        System.out.println("No clients found.");
      }
    } catch (NamingException ne) {
      System.out.println("Error finding clients.");
    }
```

Here is what the output might look like:

```
Full Name: David Miller
E-mail: dmiller@somecompany.com

Full Name: Melissa Jones
E-mail: mjones@someothercompany.com

Full Name: Nancy Smith
E-mail: nsmith@another.com

Full Name: Scott Johnson
E-mail: sjohnson@yetanother.com
```

Using WebLogic JNDI to Deploy Objects in a Clustered Environment

Because of the way WebLogic JNDI works in a clustered environment, additional planning is required when designing and deploying resources that will be bound to the JNDI Tree of a cluster. This section explains how JNDI works in a WebLogic cluster, and then provides a set of strategies you can choose from to make your design and deployment decisions.

By default, when a WebLogic Server instance joins a cluster, the contents of its JNDI Tree are merged with the contents of the cluster's tree, and the resulting tree is replicated to every server in the cluster. Figure 7-5 shows the effects of this process.

As you might imagine, the two-way replication that takes place among all participants in a cluster to synchronize the JNDI Tree generates a potentially large amount of network traffic. Fortunately, BEA recognized this problem and designed two features into WebLogic to help programmers cope with it.

First, BEA designed WebLogic RMI in such a way that WebLogic RMI stubs are incredibly compact. Therefore, replicating RMI stubs across a cluster generates relatively little network traffic.

Cluster		
WebLogic Server A	**WebLogic Server B**	**WebLogic Server C**
JNDI Tree	**JNDI Tree**	**JNDI Tree**
JDBC	JDBC	JDBC
Pool A	Pool A	Pool A
Pool B	Pool B	Pool C
RMI	RMI	RMI
Stub A	Stub A	Stub C
Stub B	Stub B	EJB
EJB	EJB	Bean B
Bean A	Bean A	Bean C
Custom	Custom	Custom
Object A	Object A	Object B
Object B	Object B	Object C

Before adding server C to the cluster

Cluster		
WebLogic Server A	**WebLogic Server B**	**WebLogic Server C**
JNDI Tree	**JNDI Tree**	**JNDI Tree**
JDBC	JDBC	JDBC
Pool A	Pool A	Pool A
Pool B	Pool B	Pool B
Pool C	Pool C	Pool C
RMI	RMI	RMI
Stub A	Stub A	Stub A
Stub B	Stub B	Stub B
Stub C	Stub C	Stub C
EJB	EJB	EJB
Bean A	Bean A	Bean A
Bean B	Bean B	Bean B
Bean C	Bean C	Bean C
Custom	Custom	Custom
Object A	Object A	Object A
Object B	Object B	Object B
Object C	Object C	Object C

After adding server C to the cluster

Figure 7-5: Adding WebLogic Server C to a 2-server cluster causes the combined JNDI Tree to be replicated to all three servers in the cluster.

Second, the BEA JNDI context factory, `weblogic.jndi.WLInitialContextFactory`, supports the use of an additional property, `REPLICATE_BINDINGS`, which allows the programmer to decide which objects will be replicated to the cluster tree, and which ones will not. This reduces network overhead during JNDI Tree replications, at the cost of reduced load-balancing and failover capability for nonreplicated objects.

Non-RMI, custom objects (such as the `Person` object implemented earlier) are the ones that require the most attention when binding to a cluster-wide JNDI tree. This is because custom objects can be potentially large, and are replicated in their entirety across the cluster. If you have created a large, custom object, and want to minimize network traffic when deploying it to a cluster, you can choose from a number of strategies to do so.

Write an RMI proxy for the custom object

The first strategy is to write an RMI proxy for the object, creating stubs for the methods you want to be made available across the cluster. Then you bind the custom object to the JNDI tree with `REPLICATE_BINDINGS = false`. During JNDI tree replication, only the stubs will be replicated, and they will all point back to a single instance of the custom object.

The shortcoming of this strategy is that you give up a certain amount of availability for the object. If the server hosting the custom object goes down, none of the stubs will work, and the object will be rendered completely unavailable.

To overcome this, you can deploy the object to more than one server in the cluster. In this case, WebLogic creates a replica-aware stub that knows how to locate all instances of the object that you have deployed to the cluster. If one of the servers goes down, the replica-aware stub traverses the remaining instances until it finds one that's available. During JNDI tree replication, copies of the replica-aware stub are distributed to all participants in the cluster.

Pin the custom object to one server

In this strategy, you set `REPLICATE_BINDINGS=false` for the custom object, which causes it to appear only in the JNDI tree of its home server. Then, whenever you call the object, you must explicitly specify its home server in the context's `PROVIDER_URL`, or you will get `javax.naming.NamingException` when you perform a lookup on the object.

The downside of this strategy is that you give up both failover and availability for the custom object. Failover doesn't exist because the object is only available via its home server. Availability is compromised because if the home server goes down, the custom object goes down with it.

Deploy the custom object separately to all servers

The final strategy is to manually deploy the custom object to all servers in the cluster, binding it to each server's JNDI tree with `REPLICATE_BINDINGS=false`. Then each server will have a copy of the object, and it will not be replicated.

One problem with this strategy is that it creates a maintenance headache. Whenever the custom object is changed, programmers must remember to redeploy it to every server in the cluster. If the object cannot be hot-deployed, then the entire cluster must be brought down while the object is copied around. Also, if additional servers are added to the cluster later on, someone must remember to copy the custom object to them. In a rapidly changing runtime environment, this is certain to cause problems.

Another weakness of this strategy is that you might sacrifice performance if the object caches data at runtime. If, for example, user A invokes the copy on server A during his first call, but then invokes the copy on server B on his next call, any performance gain he might have seen from the data cached with object A is lost, because the data must be refetched by object B.

Summary

WebLogic JNDI is a convenient way to publish code resources for easy lookup and use across the distributed enterprise. Combined with a WebLogic cluster, WebLogic JNDI allows these code resources to be made available in a fault-tolerant way.

JNDI is easy to use and provides an extensible, vendor-independent way to access resources other than code, including corporate directories, file systems, e-mail systems, and even databases.

JNDI includes features that make it easy to interface with LDAP-compliant directory services. These features will become indispensable in the near future, especially for programmers who are integrating WebLogic with the Active Directory component of Microsoft Windows 2000.

✦ ✦ ✦

Working with WebLogic RMI

In This Chapter

Understanding RMI

Comparing WebLogic RMI to JavaSoft RMI

Writing your first WebLogic RMI application

Remote Method Invocation, or RMI, is the standard Java facility for distributed, object-oriented computing over a network. RMI allows code in one Java virtual machine (JVM) to execute methods against objects in other JVMs as if those objects were available locally. This enables developers to write powerful, network-aware applications without writing complex networking code or designing bidirectional communications protocols.

RMI provides an efficient, Java-centric way to write distributed applications. Java client applications can use RMI to invoke methods residing in servers, and application servers can use RMI to invoke methods residing in other application servers. With WebLogic RMI, clients can even invoke methods in other clients, with the remote calls being routed through WebLogic Server.

Many Java developers find RMI intimidating, probably because it reminds them of the bad old days when network programming was exceedingly difficult. But RMI is really quite easy—once you figure it out. This chapter will make it much easier for you to do so.

RMI is a powerful weapon in the J2EE arsenal. Knowing it enables you to easily write applications you might have otherwise considered too difficult to attempt. Another good reason to learn and understand RMI is because RMI is used behind the scenes to call methods in EJBs.

Understanding RMI

To effectively use RMI within the WebLogic environment, you need to understand that Sun and WebLogic provide separate implementations of the RMI specification, with WebLogic's implementation being highly tuned for the WebLogic environment. You can use either vendor's implementation in your WebLogic applications. This section explains the class packages required for each implementation, then discusses RMI's architecture and the optimizations that have been coded into WebLogic's implementation.

RMI versions and packages

RMI is included with the Java 2 Platform, Standard Edition (J2SE) and also with J2EE. WebLogic's documentation refers to this as *JavaSoft's RMI.* WebLogic provides its own version of RMI as well, called *WebLogic RMI.* WebLogic RMI is implemented as a drop-in replacement for JavaSoft's RMI, and is fully compatible with JavaSoft's RMI specification. But WebLogic RMI is optimized to take advantage of the WebLogic environment, and provides some features and extensions not available in the standard implementation.

JavaSoft's RMI is implemented in seven packages:

- `java.rmi`, the core API
- `java.rmi.activation`, the API for activatable objects
- `java.rmi.dgc`, the API for the distributed garbage collector (DGC)
- `java.rmi.registry`, the API for RMI's network naming service
- `java.rmi.server`, the API for server-side operations
- `javax.rmi`, the core API for RMI over Internet Inter-Orb Protocol (RMI-IIOP)
- `javax.rmi.CORBA`, additional portability APIs for RMI-IIOP to provide a standard interface between the generated stubs and ties and the RMI-IIOP runtime

WebLogic RMI replaces the five `java.rmi` packages with its own packages as follows:

- `weblogic.rmi`
- `weblogic.rmi.activation`
- `weblogic.rmi.dgc`
- `weblogic.rmi.registry`
- `weblogic.rmi.server`

You can write WebLogic applications by using either RMI implementation. To switch implementations, you only need to switch Java import statements for RMI. To switch from JavaSoft's RMI to WebLogic's, for example, just replace all occurrences of

```
import java.rmi.<packageName>
```

with:

```
import weblogic.rmi.<packageName>
```

or vice-versa. Of course, this will work only if you adhere to the JavaSoft specification and do *not* use WebLogic's RMI extensions, which I explain later in this chapter.

You cannot mix and match the Java and WebLogic RMI packages in your application, due to major differences in their low-level implementations.

RMI architecture

RMI employs a layered architecture that makes use of the proxy design pattern and serialization to do its work.

Clients and servers

In an RMI system, code executing in one JVM (the RMI client) executes methods belonging to objects residing in a different JVM (the RMI server). The client need not be a client in the normal client/server sense. Code executing in one WebLogic server, for example, can act as an RMI client, invoking methods on a different WebLogic server (which in this case is the RMI server as well). In fact, the client can even make "remote" calls to objects running in its own JVM, as is usually the case when session EJB's invoke methods on entity EJB's.

Stubs and skeletons

To make the process of invoking server-side objects appear transparent to the client, RMI employs *stubs* on the client side; these stubs function as proxies for the server-side code. From the perspective of the client, the stubs look exactly like the server-side methods, with the same method names, parameter lists, and return values. But instead of containing the actual method code, the stubs contain code that transmits the client-side calls to the server, processes the results sent back from the server, and returns the results back to the client.

On the server side, proxies called *skeletons* are used to perform the inverse operations of receiving remote calls from clients, converting them into local calls on the server, making the local calls, and transmitting the results back to the clients.

Stubs and skeletons are automatically generated by an *RMI compiler*. This piece of software analyzes the server-side classes you write and creates the appropriate code fragments for the stubs and skeletons. You deploy these fragments along with your RMI server. Sun and BEA both provide RMI compilers for their implementations of the RMI specification. Be sure to use the correct compiler; if your code uses WebLogic RMI, you must use WebLogic's RMI compiler to generate your stubs and skeletons.

Figure 8-1 shows the layered architecture that makes up an RMI client and server.

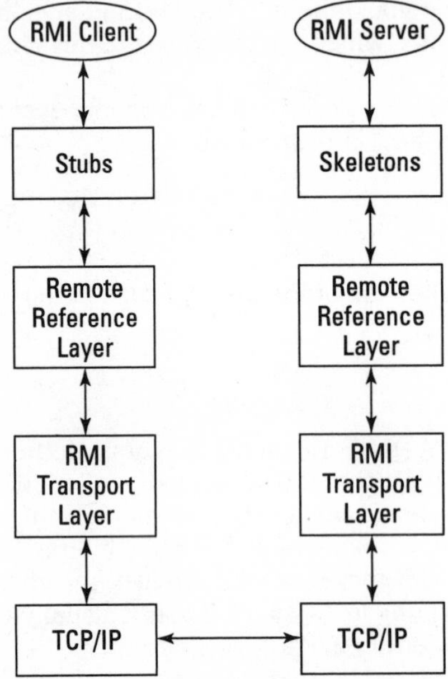

Figure 8-1: RMI's layered architecture

Serialization, marshalling, and unmarshalling

The stubs and skeletons work their magic by using Java serialization. Stubs convert client-side calls of server methods into serialized byte streams; this process is called *marshalling*. During this process, each object is checked to see if it implements the `java.rmi.Remote` (or `weblogic.rmi.Remote`) interface. If so, its remote reference is added to the marshalled byte stream. If not, the object itself is serialized and added to the byte stream.

When an object is serialized, its fields (including arrays, collections, and references to other objects) are serialized recursively, assuming all such nested objects themselves implement the Serializable interface. This is an important point to remember—if you don't watch the size of your objects and the objects they contain, you may find yourself generating far more network traffic than you want, while impairing the performance of your application.

The stub forwards the marshalled calls to the Remote Reference Layer for transmission to the server. Skeletons receive these serialized byte streams from the Remote Reference Layer and convert them back into method calls. This is called *unmarshalling*. After the method calls complete on the server machine, the skeletons marshal the results and send them back to the stubs. The stubs unmarshal these results and return them to the calling thread on the client.

Objects that will be marshalled by RMI must implement either the `java.rmi.Remote`, `weblogic.rmi.Remote`, or `java.io.Serializable` interface. This applies to objects embedded in the marshalled objects as well.

You can prevent certain fields in your objects from being serialized by marking them as `transient`. For example:

```
private transient boolean myBoolean;
public transient Connection myConnection;
```

This technique can be used to protect sensitive information in your objects or to suppress the transmission of unnecessary data, such as local network connections or file references.

Note that `static` fields will not be serialized and marshalled either. For example:

```
private static String serverName;
```

This is because `static` fields are class fields, and RMI is concerned with object instances, not classes.

Registries and naming

If you're wondering how a client finds a server object on the network, the answer is by using a naming service. WebLogic programmers have access to two RMI naming services: the default RMI registry, and the WebLogic RMI registry.

The default RMI registry

JavaSoft's RMI registry is a server process that returns remote references to objects that have been registered with it. This registry is started simply by executing the `rmiregistry` command on the command line, with an optional port number on which to listen for client lookups. If you don't specify a port, the registry will listen on the default port of 1099.

You must explicitly start the default RMI registry before using it. You can find copies of `rmiregistry.exe` in either the `/bea/jdk131/bin` directory or the `/bea/jdk131/jre/bin` directory. You can also start a registry instance in code by calling `java.rmi.Registry.LocateRegistry.createRegistry(intport)`.

Remote references are stored in a hash table, mapped to unique logical names of type `String`. Servers create entries in the registry by making calls to a running registry process. They can do so by using the `java.rmi.registry.Registry` interface, the `java.rmi.registry.LocateRegistry` class, or the `java.rmi.Naming` class. Clients look up entries in the registry by using the `java.rmi.Naming` class. Code examples appearing later in this chapter show how to perform these operations.

The WebLogic RMI registry

The WebLogic RMI registry is a drop-in replacement for the default registry that runs automatically when WebLogic Server starts up. Registry and naming calls made to the `weblogic.rmi` packages operate against this registry. Unlike the default RMI registry, only one WebLogic RMI registry can run per WebLogic server. Calls to create additional registries, even on different ports, simply return references to the existing registry.

The WebLogic RMI registry is fully integrated with WebLogic JNDI. In fact, it makes calls to WebLogic JNDI methods when it registers and looks up remote references. If you prefer, you can use JNDI directly to do the same, bypassing the WebLogic RMI registry calls completely. This enables you to set up meaningful namespaces for your applications, and also allows you to publish RMI objects to enterprise directories such as NDS or LDAP. I demonstrate how to take advantage of these features in the examples.

Chapter 7 covers WebLogic JNDI.

Comparing WebLogic RMI to JavaSoft RMI

Although WebLogic RMI and JavaSoft RMI are functionally identical, the WebLogic implementation has a number of advantages over the JavaSoft implementation. Most of these advantages boil down to ease-of-use for the programmer and application performance and scalability.

Ease-of-use

The WebLogic RMI is much easier to use than the JavaSoft RMI because there is less administrative overhead. When you start WebLogic Server, the supporting infrastructure for RMI starts up automatically, including the runtime environment, a security environment, and a JNDI-enabled RMI registry. This saves you from writing code to start RMI servers, manage security, and configure JNDI-enabled registries yourself.

From a coding standpoint, WebLogic's RMI runtime environment is set up so your remote classes aren't required to inherit from `UnicastRemoteObject`. This allows you to implement a proper class hierarchy instead of conforming to this arbitrary runtime requirement of the reference implementation that throws a wrench into your class tree.

You can code around the requirement to extend `UnicastRemoteObject`, even if you're using the JavaSoft RMI. A discussion of the techniques for doing so is beyond the scope of this book, but you can learn more by reading *Mastering RMI*, by Rickard Öberg (John Wiley & Sons).

Another handy WebLogic RMI feature is that remote methods need not declare `RemoteExceptions`. This gives developers additional flexibility in how they design their applications. With JavaSoft RMI, client calls to remote methods must be enclosed in try/catch blocks that handle the `RemoteExceptions`. This means that if the server crashes, can't marshal a call, or is simply down, an exception gets thrown to the client. In come cases, you may find that these events happen so infrequently that you don't want to deal with the possibility on every call. Or, you may simply want your code to handle all runtime exceptions the same way, regardless of their origin. WebLogic RMI gives you this flexibility.

After you deploy your RMI application, the WebLogic Console provides a graphical interface to the state of your RMI environment. You can easily see which remote implementations are deployed, where in the JNDI tree they're deployed, and how much usage they're experiencing. This information is a big help when you're trying to optimize or troubleshoot an installation.

With WebLogic 6.1, you don't even need to run the RMI compiler, because WebLogic automatically generates stubs and skeletons at runtime. The only time you must run the RMI compiler yourself is when you are creating clusterable or Internet Inter-Orb Protocol (IIOP) clients; see the WebLogic documentation for more information.

Performance and scalability

WebLogic RMI incorporates a number of optimizations that increase performance and scalability.

Efficient network communications

One of WebLogic RMI's most significant optimizations is the way it handles network connections between RMI clients and WebLogic Server. JavaSoft RMI opens separate socket connections for communication between the client and the server, and also between the client and the RMI registry. WebLogic RMI, on the other hand, multiplexes all this network traffic over a single socket connection, which is also used for other client-to-server communications such as JDBC, JMS, and so on. Sockets are a relatively expensive and limited networking resource; by minimizing socket use, WebLogic makes it possible for more clients to communicate with the server. Figure 8-2 shows the difference in TCP/IP port usage between JavaSoft RMI and WebLogic RMI.

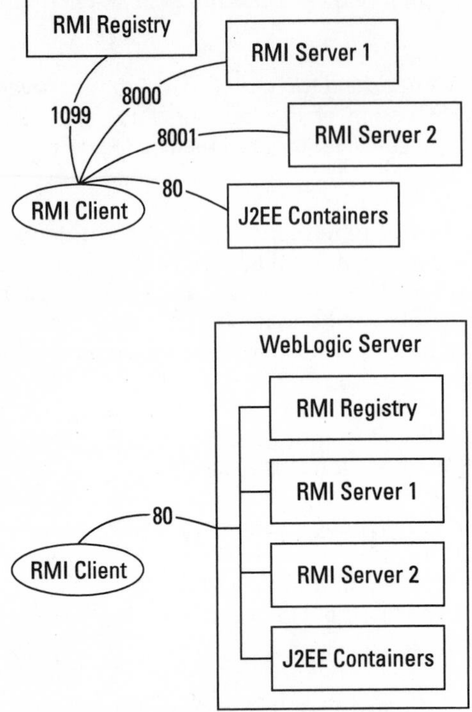

Figure 8-2: TCP/IP socket use by JavaSoft RMI (top) and WebLogic RMI (bottom)

Optimized remote method calls within the same JVM

Another important difference is the way that WebLogic handles remote method calls made within the same JVM. JavaSoft RMI makes no distinction in this regard; the full method invocation process always occurs, complete with the loading of stubs and skeletons, object serialization, marshalling and unmarshalling of parameter lists, and so on. WebLogic, however, short-circuits this process by directly calling remote methods that are resident in the same JVM. Figure 8-3 illustrates this concept.

WebLogic's approach yields significant performance improvements when RMI servers and EJBs are deployed on the same WebLogic server as the code that calls them. Keep this in mind when you're deploying facades, DAOs, and view helpers that access entity EJBs.

Note, however, that when WebLogic refers to objects in the same JVM, it does so by reference—not by value, as does the JavaSoft implementation. Although this subtle difference shouldn't matter in most cases, it's an important semantic difference of which you should be aware.

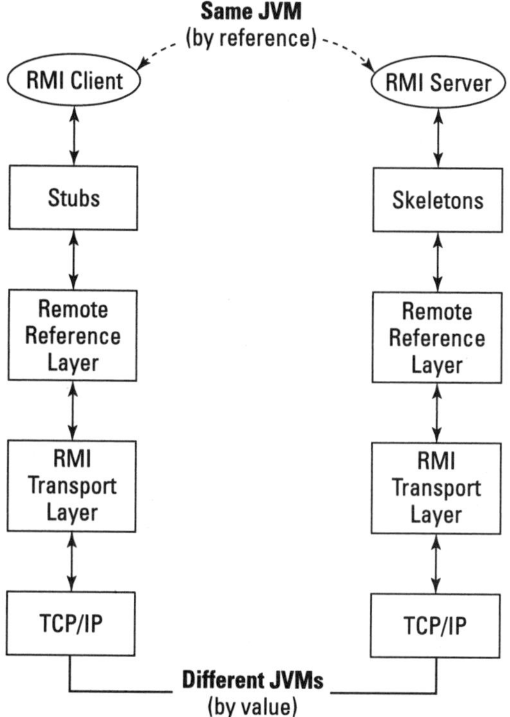

Figure 8-3: WebLogic remote method calls in the same versus different JVMs

Client-to-server, server-to-client, and client-to-client method invocation

Another unique feature of WebLogic RMI is its support for various remote method invocation schemes. WebLogic allows RMI clients to invoke remote methods not only on RMI servers, but also on other RMI clients that have published their remote interfaces to the WebLogic RMI registry. RMI servers hosted by WebLogic can invoke remote methods published by clients as well. This enables programmers to create flexible applications that support peer-to-peer processing schemes, as well as bidirectional processing schemes between clients and servers. Because of the way WebLogic optimizes remote method calls made within the same JVM, clients incur no performance penalty for invoking their own methods.

Writing Your First WebLogic RMI Application

Now that you have a good understanding of the WebLogic RMI architecture, it's time to write and deploy a WebLogic RMI application. You'll start with a simple example that shows how to create the required software components, install them in WebLogic, verify the installation, and then test them out. Later in the chapter, you'll develop a more complex example.

The first example is an adaptation of the Hello sample that appears in the WebLogic documentation. You'll keep the coding to a minimum for now so that you can focus on the steps required to make the application work.

To write and deploy a WebLogic RMI application, follow these steps:

1. Write the remote interface. This interface exposes the methods on the server that are available to RMI clients. It must extend the `weblogic.rmi.Remote` interface, which contains no method signatures.
2. Write the server. The server is a class that implements the remote interface. The server may also contain additional methods, not exposed through the interface, for its internal operations and housekeeping. One such method is the `main` method (or a method called by `main`), which registers the server in the RMI registry.
3. Compile the remote interface and the server with the Java compiler.
4. (Optional) Compile the server with the WebLogic RMI compiler to generate the stub and skeleton classes. If you don't do it, WebLogic will do it for you at runtime, but you must do it yourself if you're writing clusterable or IIOP clients.
5. Write a client that makes remote calls to the server.
6. Compile the client with the Java compiler.
7. Run WebLogic Server and use the console to configure the RMI server class as a WebLogic startup class.
8. Stop and restart WebLogic Server so it executes the RMI server class at startup. This will cause the RMI server to register itself in the WebLogic RMI registry.
9. Use the WebLogic console to verify that the RMI server is correctly deployed and visible in the JNDI tree (remember that WebLogic RMI is integrated with WebLogic JNDI, so all RMI registrations are written to the JNDI tree).
10. Run the client and see if it works!

These instructions assume you are working with the default WebLogic Server (`myserver`), or a clone of it that has been configured to run these examples. Chapter 4 shows how to install and configure such a server on Windows NT/2000 or Solaris.

Now that you know the steps to follow, you can get to work. You're going to write an RMI server with one remote method that returns the string `Hello, remote world!` Then you'll write an RMI client that invokes the method and writes the returned string to standard output.

Write the remote interface

The remote interface exposes the methods on the server that are available to RMI clients. The interface may have any number of methods but it must extend the `weblogic.rmi.Remote` interface. What follows is the remote interface for the simple example, `HelloInterface.java`:

```
package bible.rmi.example1;
import weblogic.rmi.*;// as opposed to java.rmi.*

public interface HelloInterface extends weblogic.rmi.Remote {
  // This method is called by clients and is implemented
  // by the server class.
  public String sayHello() throws RemoteException;
}
```

This interface exposes only one method, `sayHello`, to RMI clients. Note that it extends the `weblogic.rmi.Remote` interface as required. The interface and the method are both declared to be `public`, which they must be in order to be remotely accessible. You've also defined the method to throw a `RemoteException`, which is required in JavaSoft RMI but not in WebLogic RMI—this ensures that your interface is compatible with both.

Write the server

The server is a class that provides the guts behind the method signatures in the remote interface. The server should also know how to install itself in the RMI registry. Here's the code for your server, `HelloServer.java`, which performs these functions.

```
package bible.rmi.example1;
import weblogic.rmi.*;

public class HelloServer implements HelloInterface {

  // This method is called by remote clients.
  public String sayHello() throws RemoteException {
    // Write a status message to the server's console
    System.out.println("HelloServer.sayHello()" +
                       "has been remotely invoked.");

    // Return a message to the client
    return "Hello, remote world!!";
  }

  // The main() method registers our server in the
  // WebLogic RMI registry, which by default resides
  // in the WebLogic JNDI tree.
  public static void main(String[] argv) {
```

```
        try {
          // Create a remote object instance
          HelloServer obj = new HelloServer();

          // Register the server with the naming service
          Naming.rebind("HelloServer", obj);

          // Write a status message to the console
          System.out.println("HelloServer was created and " +
                             "bound in the registry " +
                             "to the name HelloServer");
        }
        catch (Exception e) {
          System.out.println("HelloServer error: " +
                             e.getMessage());
          e.printStackTrace();
        }
      }
    }
```

This most basic server class implements only two methods: the `sayHello` method defined in the remote interface, and a `main` method to register the server in the RMI registry. `sayHello` first writes a message to standard output indicating that it has been invoked; this message will appear on the console of the JVM hosting the server. `sayHello` then returns the `Hello, remote world!` message to the client.

`main` creates an instance of the remote object, and then registers it with the naming service under the name `HelloServer`. In this example, you use the `weblogic.rmi.Naming.rebind` method to register the object. That way, if you need to stop and restart the RMI server for some reason, the new binding will overwrite the old one. If you had used `weblogic.rmi.Naming.bind` to register the object, the new binding would fail if a previous binding already existed by that name. Note also that it is the remote object's *stub* that is bound to the registry, not the remote object itself. This is convenient for clients doing registry lookups for the remote object, because the stub is what they need.

Note

In JavaSoft RMI, you must perform the additional step of *exporting* the server object to the RMI implementation. Exporting creates a reference to the server object that is used by the stubs at runtime to forward calls to the server. One way to export a server object is to write a default constructor for the server class that simply calls `super()` on its parent class — `UnicastRemoteObject`. Another way is to call the static method `java.rmi.server.UnicastRemoteObject.exportObject` from the default constructor.

Neither step is required with WebLogic RMI — WebLogic Server automatically exports objects that implement the remote interface. But if you're porting existing RMI code to WebLogic, or if you just want to write your WebLogic code to be compatible with JavaSoft RMI, you can export by using either technique with no ill effects.

Compile the remote interface and the server

The next step is to compile the Java classes for the remote interface and the server. For development and testing, simply output the `.class` files to your Web server's `serverclasses` directory.

The WebLogic Bible Web site (`http://www.zeeware.com/wlbible`) shows how to set up a WebLogic development environment for compiling and running the examples, including how to set up environment variables for classpath, compiler output directories, and so on.

Assuming your environment variables are set as explained in The WebLogic Bible Web site (`http://www.zeeware.com/wlbible`), the DOS commands to build these classes are similar to the following:

```
> javac -classpath %classpath% -d %outputdir%
bible.rmi.example1.HelloInterface

> javac -classpath %classpath% -d %outputdir%
bible.rmi.example1.HelloServer
```

These commands result in `HelloInterface.class` and `HelloServer.class` being written to the `\bea\wlserver6.1\config\myserver\serverclasses` directory, a location that puts them in the classpath for that instance of WebLogic Server.

Generate stubs and skeletons for the server

To generate the RMI server's stubs and skeletons, run `weblogic.rmic`, WebLogic's RMI compiler, against the `HelloServer` class, outputting the generated classes to the same `serverclasses` folder as before:

```
> java -classpath %classpath% weblogic.rmic
bible.rmi.example1.HelloServer -d %outputdir%
```

This causes two additional classes, `HelloInterface_WLStub.class` and `HelloInterface_WLSkel.class`, to be written to the output directory. The stub class is the one that is marshalled and sent to remote clients invoking the server. The skeleton class is the one used by the server to handle communications between the client stub and the server.

When the WebLogic RMI compiler runs, it generates intermediate Java source files for the stubs and skeletons, compiles those source files into classes, and then deletes the source files. If you want to examine the source files, you can instruct the WebLogic RMI compiler to keep them by using the `-keepgenerated` option, as shown in the following code:

```
> java -classpath %classpath% weblogic.rmic -keepgenerated
bible.rmi.example1.HelloServer -d %outputdir%
```

Now when you look in the output directory, you will see HelloInterface_WLStub.java and HelloInterface_WLSkel.java, in addition to the generated class files. A discussion of the contents of these files is beyond the scope of this book, but feel free to study them on your own.

Write a client that remotely calls the server

Now that the server, stubs, and skeletons are successfully built, you can build a simple client application that calls the server's remote method. Following is the code for such a client, HelloClient.java:

```
package bible.rmi.example1;

import weblogic.rmi.*;
import weblogic.common.*;

public class HelloClient {

  public final static String SERVERNAME =
    "rmi://localhost:7001/HelloServer";

  public static void main(String[] argv) {
    try {
      HelloInterface obj =
        (HelloInterface)Naming.lookup(SERVERNAME);
      System.out.println("Connected to HelloServer.");
      String message = obj.sayHello();
      System.out.println(message);
    }

    catch (Throwable t) {
      t.printStackTrace();
      System.exit(-1);
    }
  }
}
```

Compile the client

Assuming your environment variables are set as explained in Chapter 4, compile HelloClient.java as follows:

```
> javac -classpath %classpath% -d %outputdir%
bible.rmi.example1.HelloClient
```

This command results in HelloClient.class being written to the \bea\wlserver6.1\config\myserver\serverclasses directory, along with the server, stub, and skeleton classes built earlier.

Configure the RMI server as a WebLogic startup class

Start the WebLogic Server that will run the classes you've created. Then start the default WebLogic Console (recall from Chapter 1 that you do this by selecting Start Default Console from the WebLogic program group).

In the domain tree on the left side of the console, expand the Deployments node and click Startup and Shutdown. The console should look like Figure 8-4.

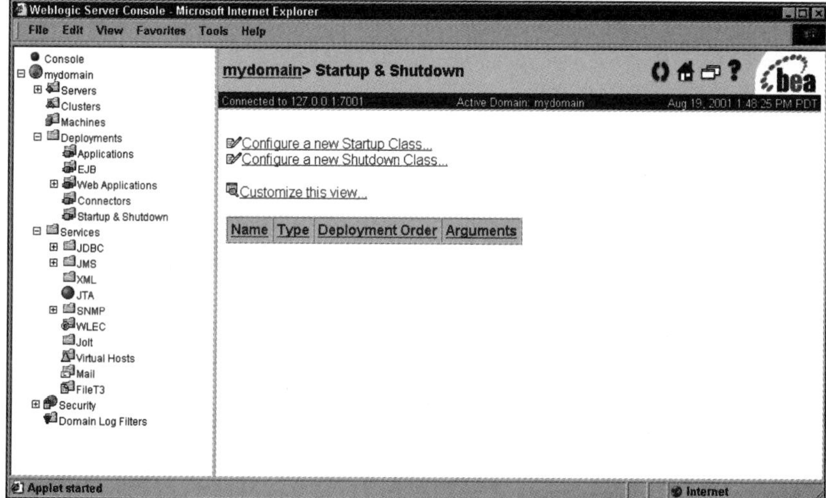

Figure 8-4: Configuring startup and shutdown classes in the WebLogic Console

Click Configure a New Startup Class to bring up the startup class configuration page, as shown in Figure 8-5.

Fill out the configuration page as shown. The name of the startup class is simply the name of the class that implements the RMI server — in this case, `HelloServer`. The `ClassName` is the fully qualified name of the class, including its package name. `HelloServer` takes no arguments, so leave that field blank. Also elect *not* to abort startup on failure for now. Click Create.

After the class is created, click the Targets tab. Figure 8-6 shows the resulting display.

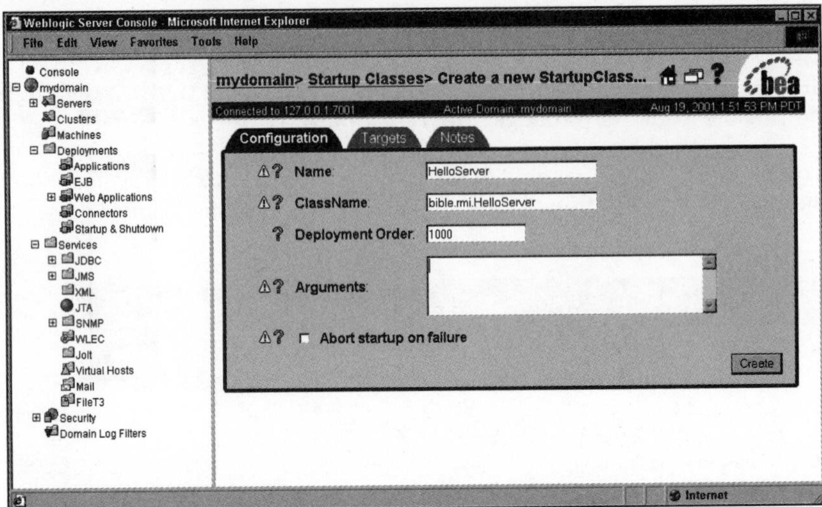

Figure 8-5: Startup class configuration page with entries for your RMI server

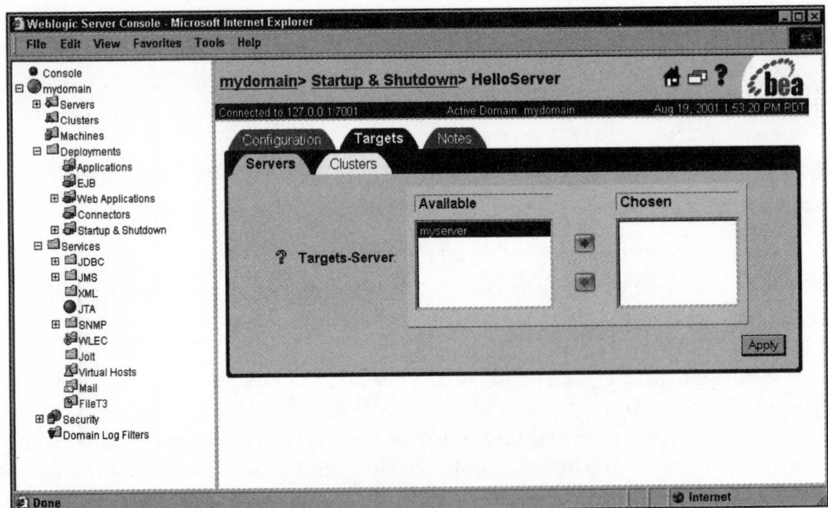

Figure 8-6: Choosing a target WebLogic server for the RMI server

This page enables you to select any WebLogic server in your domain to host the startup class. Because only one server is available (`myserver`), that's the server you'll choose. Click `myserver` in the Available list, and then click the right-pointing arrow to move it into the Chosen list, as shown in Figure 8-7. Click Apply.

You should now be able to expand the Startup & Shutdown node in the domain tree; `HelloServer` deploys within that node, as shown in Figure 8-8.

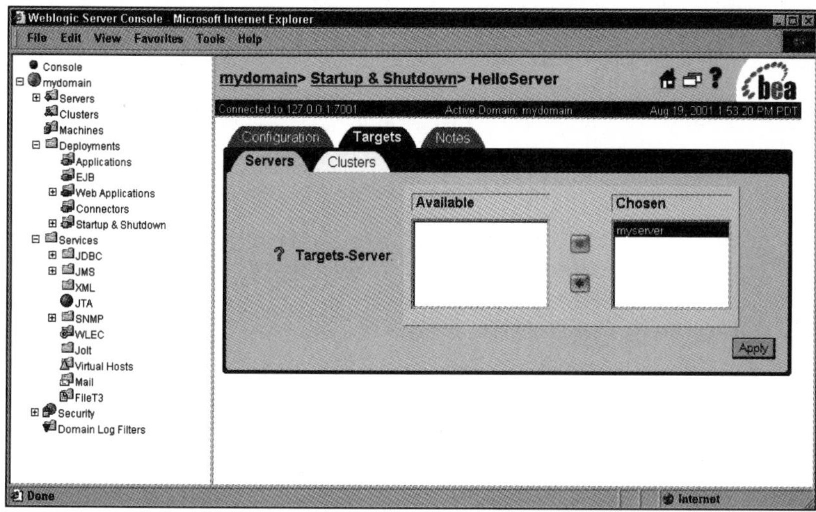

Figure 8-7: HelloServer will be deployed as a startup class in myserver.

HelloServer has been deployed to the domain tree

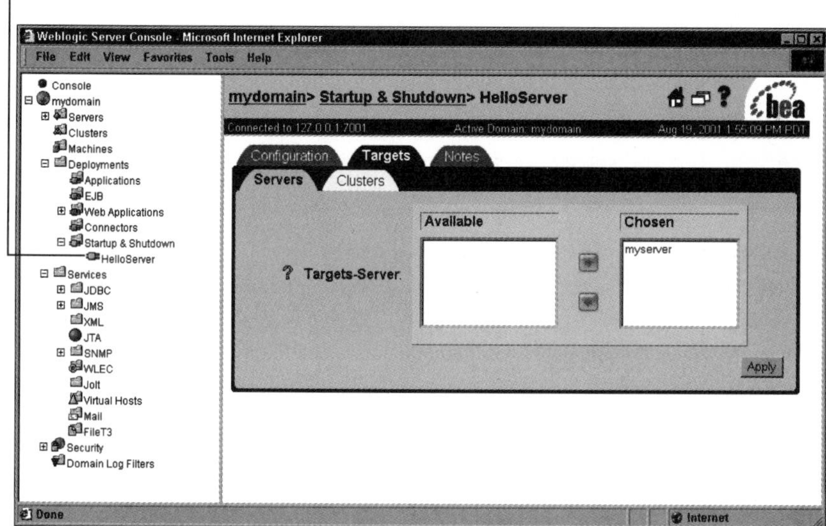

Figure 8-8: Confirm the deployment of HelloServer in the domain tree.

Now that you've deployed the startup class, exit the console.

Stop and restart WebLogic Server

You've used the WebLogic Console to specify a startup class and pin it to a target server. But the class will not deploy until you stop and restart WebLogic Server. Go ahead and do so. When WebLogic Server restarts, it will call the `main` method of your `HelloServer` class. It will also cause `HelloServer` to register itself in the WebLogic RMI registry.

Recall that you wrote your main method to write a startup message to standard output. When you start WebLogic Server, you should see the message `HelloServer was created and bound in the registry to the name HelloServer` appear while the server is starting, as shown in Figure 8-9.

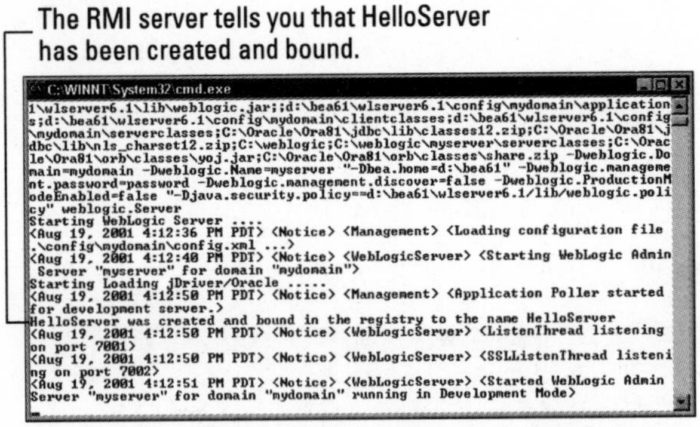

Figure 8-9: WebLogic Server after restarting, with the message from your RMI server appearing in its window

Verify correct deployment of the RMI server

After WebLogic Server restarts, restart the console. In the domain tree, expand mydomain, and then Servers. Right-click myserver to display a pop-up menu of server-related operations. From this pop-up menu, select View JNDI tree, as shown in Figure 8-10.

A new browser window opens, displaying the JNDI tree. Expand the weblogic node, and then expand the rmi node. `HelloServer` should appear within this node, as shown in Figure 8-11.

You can now feel reasonably confident that your RMI server is deployed correctly. The ultimate test is to call its remote method, which you will do next.

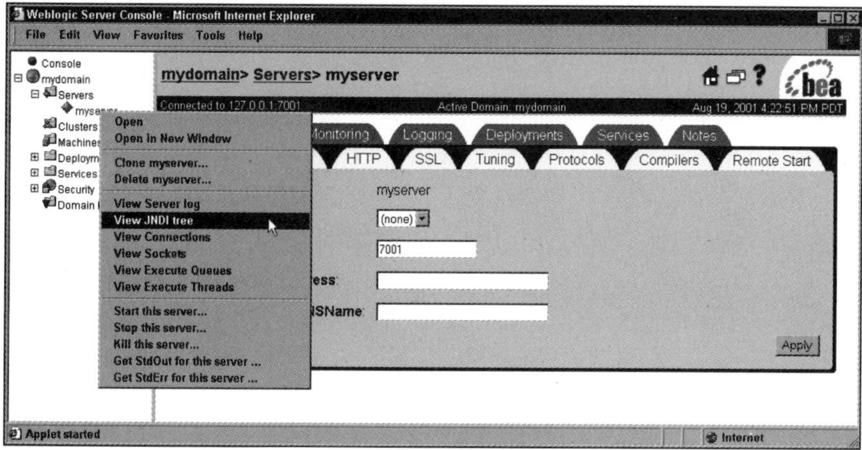

Figure 8-10: Viewing the WebLogic Server JNDI tree

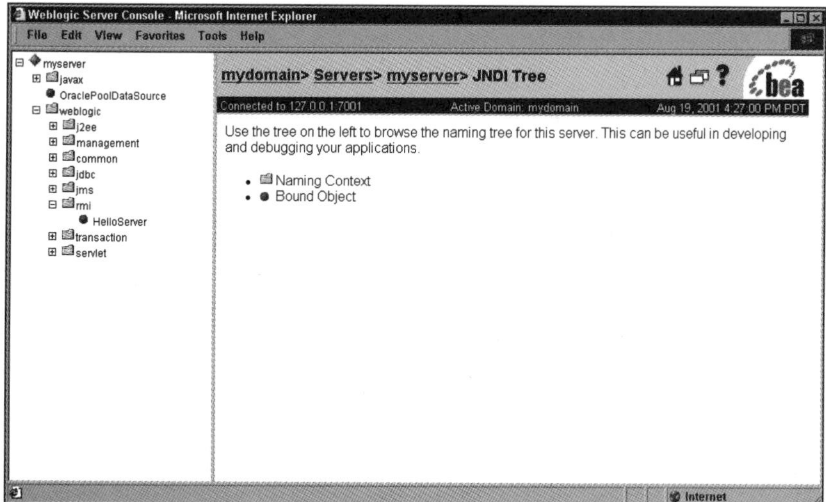

Figure 8-11: HelloServer displayed in the JNDI tree under weblogic.rmi

Run the client and test the server

On a new command line, run `HelloClient.java`. The command to do so resembles the following:

```
> java -classpath %classpath% bible.rmi.example1.HelloClient
```

After a few seconds, you should see the following on your screen:

```
> Connected to HelloServer.
> Hello, remote world!!
```

Additionally, you should see the message `HelloServer.sayHello() has been remotely invoked` written to the WebLogic command window by the remote method on the server (see Figure 8-12).

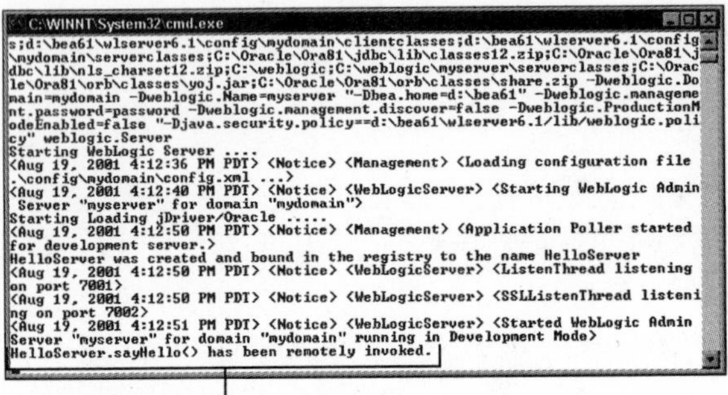

The message from the RMI server, telling you that HelloServer has been created and bound.

Figure 8-12: Message written to the WebLogic Server command window indicating that the RMI server's remote method has been invoked

Congratulations! You've successfully written, deployed, and tested your first WebLogic RMI application. In the rest of this chapter, you'll explore additional features and coding techniques applicable to WebLogic RMI.

Using WebLogic RMI with JNDI and Multiple Clients

Now that you know how to write and deploy an RMI application, it's time to try some additional variations. The remaining examples in this chapter implement a simple stock trading system while demonstrating important features of WebLogic RMI, including its integration with JNDI, support for client callbacks, and integration with EJBs.

Building a server

The first piece of software we'll build is an RMI server called `PriceServer`. `PriceServer` maintains a database of stock ticker symbols and prices (stored in memory as a Java HashTable) and provides methods to get and set stock prices for stocks with given symbols. PriceServer also provides a method to retrieve all stock symbols in the database. A remote interface that meets this specification is defined in PriceServer.java:

```
package bible.rmi.example2;

import weblogic.rmi.Remote;

public interface PriceServer extends weblogic.rmi.Remote {

  // Used to locate or register a PriceServer via RMI.
  public static final String PRICESERVERNAME = "priceserver";

  // Return the current price of the given security.
  public float getPrice(String symbol);

  // Set the price of the given security.
  public void setPrice(String symbol, float price);

  // Return all ticker symbols in this server's database.
  public String[] getSecurities();
}
```

Following the RMI programming methodology established in the preceding section, we next write the implementation of the remote interface. This class will be called PriceServerImpl. PriceServerImpl manages a Hashtable of securities and prices, so a good job for the default constructor is to initialize this Hashtable:

```
// Declare a Hashtable for the stock price database.
private Hashtable stockTable = null;

// Default constructor - creates a stock price database
// with three stocks and their starting prices for the
// session.
public PriceServerImpl() {
  stockTable = new Hashtable();
  Float f = new Float(0);
  stockTable.put("SUNW", f.valueOf("20"));
  stockTable.put("INTC", f.valueOf("30"));
  stockTable.put("BEAS", f.valueOf("40"));
}
```

getPrice takes a stock ticker symbol (such as SUNW or BEAS) as input, finds the stock in the database, and returns the stock's price:

```
public float getPrice(String symbol) {
  Float f = (Float)stockTable.get(symbol);
  return f.floatValue();
}
```

`setPrice` takes a stock ticker symbol and price as input, finds the symbol in the database, and updates its price. Because the database is a `Hashtable`, a new entry is automatically created if the symbol does not exist in the database:

```
public void setPrice(String symbol, float price) {
  Float f = new Float(price);
  stockTable.put(symbol, f);
}
```

`getSecurities` returns a string array containing all the symbols in the database:

```
public String[] getSecurities() {
  if(stockTable.size() > 0) {
    String[] securities = new String[stockTable.size()];
    Enumeration enum = stockTable.keys();
    int i = 0;

    while(enum.hasMoreElements()) {
      securities[i] = (String)enum.nextElement();
      i++;
    }
    return securities;
  }
  return null;
}
```

With all the remote methods implemented, it's time to think about how to register the RMI server with WebLogic. Unlike the first example, which used the WebLogic RMI interface to register itself, `PriceServerImpl` will register itself using JNDI calls. This turns out to be quite simple, requiring only three lines of code:

```
PriceServerImpl server = new PriceServerImpl();
Context ctx = new InitialContext();
ctx.bind(PRICESERVERNAME, server);
```

This code binds a reference to the `PriceServerImpl` stubs to the root of the WebLogic JNDI tree. We'll put it in the `main` method of the `PriceServerImpl` class.

The advantage of using JNDI directly is that you can register your servers anywhere you want in WebLogic's JNDI tree, creating your own hierarchy of registrations (WebLogic RMI always registers classes in the weblogic.rmi node). These registrations might be organized by functionality, application, or some other criteria. Also, you can use JNDI to register RMI servers in other JNDI-accessible directories, such as LDAP directories or other external naming services.

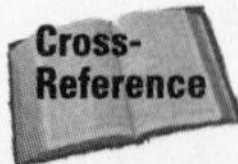

This chapter presents the JNDI calls necessary for RMI registration and lookup, but does not explain them in great detail. For in-depth information about using WebLogic JNDI, see Chapter 7, "Working with WebLogic JNDI."

Listing 8-1 shows `PriceServerImpl.java`, the complete implementation of the `PriceServerImpl` class. The code has gained some minor enhancements to write status messages to the WebLogic Console and also to deal with exceptions.

Listing 8-1: PriceServerImpl.java, an RMI Server to Manage Securities Transactions

```
package bible.rmi.example2;

import java.util.*;
import javax.naming.*;
import weblogic.rmi.*;

public class PriceServerImpl implements PriceServer {

  // Stock price database, implemented as a Hashtable.
  private Hashtable stockTable = null;

  // Default constructor - creates the stock price database.
  public PriceServerImpl() {
    stockTable = new Hashtable();
    Float f = new Float(0);
    stockTable.put("SUNW", f.valueOf("20"));
    stockTable.put("INTC", f.valueOf("30"));
    stockTable.put("BEAS", f.valueOf("40"));
  }

  // Return the price of the given security.
  public float getPrice(String symbol) {
    Float f = (Float)stockTable.get(symbol);
    System.out.println("PriceServer: Call to getPrice " +
                       "for symbol : " + symbol);
    return f.floatValue();
  }

  // Set the price of the given security.
  public void setPrice(String symbol, float price) {
    Float f = new Float(price);
    stockTable.put(symbol, f);
    System.out.println("PriceServer: Call to setPrice " +
                       "for " + symbol + " to " + price);
  }

  // Return all ticker symbols in this server's database.
  public String[] getSecurities() {
    if(stockTable.size() > 0) {
```

Continued

Listing 8-1 *(continued)*

```
      String[] securities = new String[stockTable.size()];
      Enumeration enum = stockTable.keys();
      int i = 0;

      while(enum.hasMoreElements()) {
        securities[i] = (String)enum.nextElement();
        i++;
      }
      return securities;
    }
    return null;
  }

  // Main method - registers the RMI server using JNDI.
  public static void main (String [] args) {
    try {
      PriceServerImpl server = new PriceServerImpl();
      Context ctx = new InitialContext();
      ctx.bind(PRICESERVERNAME, server);
      System.out.println("PriceServer was created and bound " +
                         "in the registry " +
                         "to the name " + PRICESERVERNAME);
    }
    catch(Exception e) {
      e.printStackTrace();
      System.exit(1);
    }
  }
}
```

This completes the coding of the server. The next step is to write some clients that call its methods.

Building the clients

Instead of writing just one client to call `PriceServer's` remote methods, we'll write two. One, called `MarketMakerClient`, will be responsible for updating securities prices on a periodic basis; it simulates (in a very rudimentary way) a pricing feed from an exchange such as Nasdaq. The other, called `QuoteClient`, retrieves the latest prices of stocks on a periodic basis; it simulates (also in a very rudimentary way) a stock portfolio tracking system.

Using WebLogic JNDI to find the RMI server

Both clients will find `PriceServer` by making JNDI calls. To support this functionality, we'll create a class called `Environment` that stores the server access paths and makes the JNDI call to return the server's context to the clients. The advantage of this approach is that if the server ever moves, only the `Environment` class needs to be changed.

Listing 8-2 contains `Environment.java`, the code to implement the `Environment` class.

Listing 8-2: Environment.java, a WebLogic JNDI Lookup Class

```
package bible.rmi.example2;

import javax.naming.*;
import java.util.*;

public class Environment {

  // Specify that we'll be using WebLogic JNDI
  public final static String JNDI_FACTORY =
    "weblogic.jndi.WLInitialContextFactory";

  // Specify the location of our WebLogic server
  public final static String WEBLOGIC_URL =
    "t3://localhost:7001";

  public static InitialContext getInitialContext()
   throws NamingException {

    // Load a Hashtable with the factory and URL information,
    // then use it to retrieve the WebLogic server's context.
    Hashtable env = new Hashtable();
    env.put(Context.INITIAL_CONTEXT_FACTORY, JNDI_FACTORY);
    env.put(Context.PROVIDER_URL, WEBLOGIC_URL);
    return new InitialContext(env);
  }
}
```

Chapter 7 contains a more detailed explanation of JNDI, but notice that `Environment.getInitialContext` is implemented as a static method. This is done as a convenience for clients; it allows them to invoke the method without creating an instance of the class, as in:

```
InitialContext ctx = Environment.getInitialContext();
```

Once the client retrieves the InitialContext, only one additional call is required to obtain a reference to the RMI server we wrote earlier:

```
PriceServer server =
 (PriceServer) ctx.lookup(PriceServer.PRICESERVERNAME);
```

where `PriceServer.PRICESERVERNAME` is the name under which the RMI server registered itself, defined as a `public static final String` in the `PriceServer` interface.

As you can see, using JNDI to register and lookup RMI servers is quite simple, and gives you more control over how registrations are organized. Using JNDI gives you access to the full capabilities of your naming service, whether it's WebLogic Server or an LDAP directory such as Netscape Directory Server. This allows you to partition your RMI namespaces in meaningful ways to ease the administration and use of a large server.

Implementing MarketMakerClient

The `MarketMakerClient` generates random price fluctuations for the securities tracked by `PricesServer`, and posts these to `PriceServer` every few seconds. To accomplish this, `MarketMakerClient` extends `java.util.TimerTask`, and is scheduled for periodic execution using `java.util.Timer`.

After retrieving a remote reference to `PriceServer`, `MarketMakerClient` invokes the server's `setPrice` method for each of the three securities, adjusting their prices in random increments. The code to do this appears in the `MarketMakerClient.run` method, which is invoked every 5 seconds by the timer:

```
InitialContext ctx = Environment.getInitialContext();
PriceServer server =
  (PriceServer)ctx.lookup(PriceServer.PRICESERVERNAME);

// Remote call to get securities tracked by server
securities = server.getSecurities();
for(int i = 0; i < securities.length; i++) {
  // Randomly increase or decrease each security's
  // price by 0, 0.25, or 0.5
  boolean increase = rand.nextBoolean();
  Float amount = new Float(0.25 * rand.nextInt(2));
  if (increase) {
    server.setPrice(securities[i],
    server.getPrice(securities[i]) + amount.floatValue());
  } else {
    server.setPrice(securities[i],
    server.getPrice(securities[i]) - amount.floatValue());
  }
}
```

In the `main` method of `MarketMakerClient`, we simply create a timer and schedule the periodic execution of the security price updating code:

```
Timer t = new Timer();
MarketMakerClient client = new MarketMakerClient();
```

```
//Starting in 5 secs, update prices every 5 seconds.
t.schedule(client, 5000, 5000);
```

Listing 8-3 contains the complete implementation of `MarketMakerClient`. In addition to the code discussed above, it contains code to write status messages to standard output, close the JNDI contexts we open, and handle exceptions.

Listing 8-3: MarketMakerClient.java

```
package bible.rmi.example2;

import weblogic.rmi.*;
import java.util.*;
import javax.naming.*;

public class MarketMakerClient
  extends TimerTask
  implements Runnable {

  private Random rand = new Random();
  private String[] securities = null;

  // Get a reference to PriceServer, get its list of
  // securities, and adjust their prices.
  public void run() {
    // Write a status message to standard output
    System.out.println("MarketMakerClient setting prices.");
    System.out.println(" Time: "
                       + new Date(System.currentTimeMillis()));

    InitialContext ctx = null;
    try {
      // Obtain a reference to the RMI server using JNDI
      ctx = Environment.getInitialContext();
      PriceServer server =
       (PriceServer) ctx.lookup(PriceServer.PRICESERVERNAME);

      // Remote call to get securities tracked by server
      securities = server.getSecurities();
      for(int i = 0; i < securities.length; i++) {
        // Randomly increase or decrease each security's
        // price by 0, 0.25, or 0.5
        boolean increase = rand.nextBoolean();
        Float amount = new Float(0.25 * rand.nextInt(2));
```

Continued

Listing 8-3 *(continued)*

```
          if (increase) {
            server.setPrice(securities[i],
            server.getPrice(securities[i]) +
              amount.floatValue());
          } else {
            server.setPrice(securities[i],
            server.getPrice(securities[i]) -
              amount.floatValue());
          }
        }
      }
      catch (Exception e) {
        e.printStackTrace();
      }
      finally {
        try {
          ctx.close();
        }
        catch (Exception e) {
          e.printStackTrace();
        }
      }
    }

    // Create a new client and schedule it to
    // execute periodically.
    public static void main(String [] args) {
      Timer t = new Timer();
      MarketMakerClient client = new MarketMakerClient();

      //Starting in 5 secs, update prices every 5 seconds.
      t.schedule(client, 5000, 5000);
    }
  }
```

There is one non-optimal aspect of this design that is worth discussing. Rather than calling `server.setPrice` repeatedly for each individual security, which generates a lot of excess network traffic for the RMI calls, it would be more efficient to transmit an entire data structure of symbols and prices to the server, using only one remote method call. We won't redesign our example code for this, but you should keep these kinds of issues in mind when you design your own RMI systems.

Implementing QuoteClient

`QuoteClient` is even simpler than `MarketMakerClient`. Like `MarketMakerClient`, it extends `java.util.TimerTask` and executes on a periodic basis, every 20 seconds. Every time it runs, it retrieves a list of securities being tracked by `PriceServer`, then retrieves the prices of those securities. And, of course, it performs these queries using remote method calls to `PriceServer.getSecurities` and `PriceServer.getPrice`, respectively. The code for `QuoteClient`, much of which is identical to `MarketMakerClient`, appears in Listing 8-4.

Listing 8-4: QuoteClient.java

```
package bible.rmi.example2;

import weblogic.rmi.*;
import java.util.*;
import javax.naming.*;

// Periodically ask PriceServer for prices
// of all securities.
public class QuoteClient
  extends TimerTask
  implements Runnable {

  // Get a reference to PriceServer, get a list of securities,
  // and display prices.
  public void run() {
    System.out.println("QuoteClient getting quotes.");
    System.out.println("Quote time: " +
                       new Date(System.currentTimeMillis()));

    try {
      // Get the remote stub for the Price server via JNDI.
      InitialContext ctx = Environment.getInitialContext();
      PriceServer server =
        (PriceServer) ctx.lookup(PriceServer.PRICESERVERNAME);

      // Remote call to get the list of securities
      String securities[] = server.getSecurities();

      if(securities != null) {
        for(int i = 0; i < securities.length; i++) {
          // Remote call to get each security's price
          System.out.println("Security: " + securities[i] +
              " Price: " + server.getPrice(securities[i]));
        }
      }
      else {
        System.out.println("No securities registered " +
                           "with the server at this time.");
      }
    }
```

Continued

Listing 8-4 (continued)

```
    catch(Exception e) {
      e.printStackTrace();
    }
    finally {
      try {
        ctx.close();
      }
      catch (Exception e) {
        e.printStackTrace();
      }
    }
  }

  // Create a new client and schedule it to
  // execute periodically.
  public static void main(String [] args) {
    Timer t = new Timer();
    QuoteClient client = new QuoteClient();
    System.out.println("QuoteClient started.");

    //Starting in 10 secs, get prices every 20 seconds.
    t.schedule(client, 10000, 20000);
  }
}
```

Building and deploying the example

Follow the instructions in the first example to build and deploy this RMI application. You'll need to compile the Java source files first:

```
> javac -classpath %classpath% -d %outputdir%
bible.rmi.example2.PriceServer

> javac -classpath %classpath% -d %outputdir%
bible.rmi.example2.PriceServerImpl

> javac -classpath %classpath% -d %outputdir%
bible.rmi.example2.Environment

> javac -classpath %classpath% -d %outputdir%
bible.rmi.example2.MarketMakerClient

> javac -classpath %classpath% -d %outputdir%
bible.rmi.example1.QuoteClient
```

Next, you'll need to run the RMI compiler on `PriceServerImpl`:

```
> java -classpath %classpath% weblogic.rmic
bible.rmi.example2.PriceServerImpl -d %outputdir%
```

Deploy `PriceServerImpl` as a WebLogic startup class. Then you can run the clients against it in their own JVM's by executing the following commands:

```
> java -classpath %classpath%
bible.rmi.example2.MarketMakerClient

> java -classpath %classpath% bible.rmi.example2.QuoteClient
```

The output from `MarketMakerClient` will look something like the following:

```
> MarketMakerClient setting prices.
>  Time: Mon Apr 30 13:33:29 PDT 2001

> MarketMakerClient setting prices.
>  Time: Mon Apr 30 13:33:59 PDT 2001
```

The output from `QuoteClient` will look something like this:

```
QuoteClient started.
QuoteClient getting quotes.
Quote time: Mon Apr 30 13:33:44 PDT 2001
Security: SUNW Price: 20.25
Security: INTC Price: 30.5
Security: BEAS Price: 39.75
QuoteClient getting quotes.
Quote time: Mon Apr 30 13:34:04 PDT 2001
Security: SUNW Price: 20.5
Security: INTC Price: 30.25
Security: BEAS Price: 40
```

Meanwhile, the output from `PriceServerImpl`, displayed in the WebLogic Server command window, will look something like this:

```
PriceServer: Call to setPrice for SUNW to 20.25
PriceServer: Call to setPrice for INTC to 30.5
PriceServer: Call to setPrice for BEAS to 39.75
PriceServer: Call to getPrice for symbol : SUNW
PriceServer: Call to getPrice for symbol : INTC
PriceServer: Call to getPrice for symbol : BEAS
PriceServer: Call to setPrice for SUNW to 20.5
PriceServer: Call to setPrice for INTC to 30.25
PriceServer: Call to setPrice for BEAS to 40
PriceServer: Call to getPrice for symbol : SUNW
PriceServer: Call to getPrice for symbol : INTC
PriceServer: Call to getPrice for symbol : BEAS
```

Invoking Client Methods from RMI Servers

Now that we have our stock market up and running, let's make a further enhancement that demonstrates WebLogic RMI's support for server-to-client remote method invocation.

Consider the code we have already written. `PriceServerImpl`, the RMI server, simultaneously services requests from `MarketMakerClient` and `QuoteClient`. However, these communications occur in only one direction, from the clients to the server, as shown in Figure 8-13.

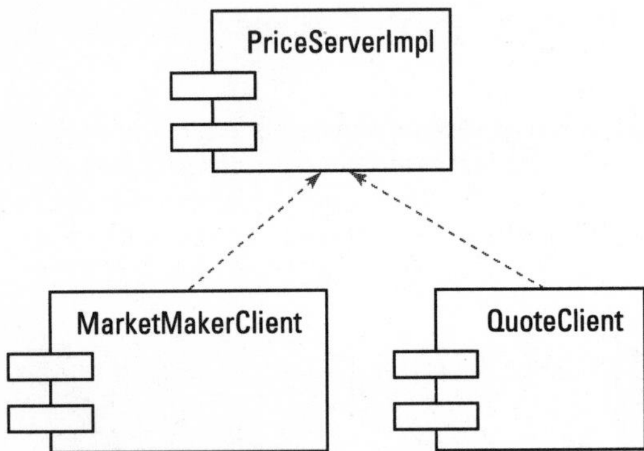

Figure 8-13: One-way communications from the clients to the server

This architecture works well most of the time, but for some designs it has weaknesses. For example, what happens if a client invokes a long-running method on the server? If the call is made synchronously, the invoking client thread will be blocked until the server method returns. If the call is made asynchronously, the client has no way of knowing when the server method completes. This creates a problem if subsequent client processing depends on the server method's results, or if the client would like to be notified when the server has finished.

WebLogic RMI provides a solution for this problem. It allows clients to register remote interfaces of their own with WebLogic Server. These methods can then be invoked by server-side code, or even by code running on other clients, just as if it resided on the server.

To illustrate the usefulness of this feature, we'll create another client for our securities system called `TradingClient`. `TradingClient` will asynchronously place market orders for stocks with `PriceServerImpl` (a market order is an order to purchase stock at the prevailing market price). After an artificial delay, `PriceServerImpl` will execute the orders, then notify `TradingClient` of the executions. This requires two-way communications between `PriceServerImpl` and `TradingClient`, as shown in Figure 8-14.

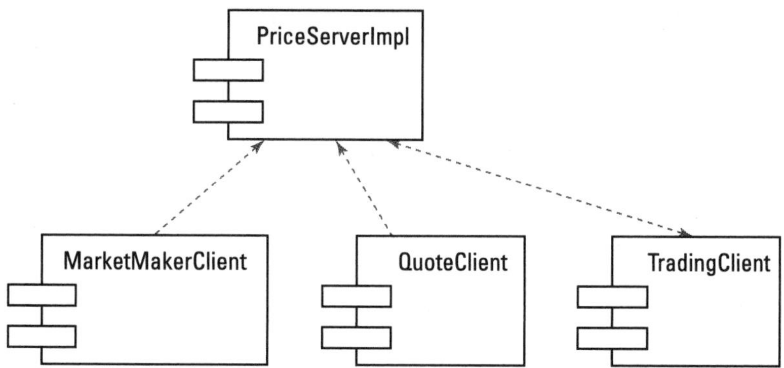

Figure 8-14: Two-way communications between PriceServerImpl and TradingClient

To facilitate these communications, we will create two new classes: `Order` and `Execution`. These nearly identical classes will transmit information concerning the security being purchased, the number of shares, and the price. Because we plan to transmit instances of them across the wire via RMI, they must implement the `java.io.Serializable` interface. These class definitions appear below (the methods have been omitted to save space):

```
public class Order implements java.io.Serializable {
  private int number;      // unique order number
  private String symbol;  // ticker symbol
  private int shares;      // number of shares to purchase
  // plus method definitions
}

public class Execution implements java.io.Serializable {
  private int number;      // copied from order number
  private String symbol;  // ticker symbol
  private int shares;      // number of shares purchased
  private float price;     // price per share at execution
  // plus method definitions
}
```

Much of the code in `TradingClient` is the same as the code in our other clients. `TradingClient` extends `java.util.TimerTask` and submits a new order every 30 seconds. When submitting an order, `TradingClient` uses JNDI to get a remote reference to `PriceServer`. Then it calls `PriceServer.getSecurities` to get the list of securities `PriceServer` knows about:

```
// Get the list of securities managed by the server.
String securities[] = server.getSecurities();
```

Next, `TradingClient` creates a new `Order` instance and populates it with the order specifications. The order number (an integer class field) is incremented, so each order has a unique number. This allows us to match the returning executions against the orders. The security to be purchased is chosen at random from those available, and the number of shares to purchase is randomly chosen as well. Finally, a remote call is made to `PriceServerImpl.enterMarketOrder` to place the order. The interesting aspect of this call is that `TradingClient` passes a reference to itself (`this`) that the server will use to call it back. Here is the code to implement these steps:

```
// Create a new Order instance
Order order = new Order();
Random rand = new Random();

// Increment the order number
order.setNumber(++orderNumber);

// Choose one of the available securities at random
order.setSymbol(securities[rand.nextInt(securities.length)]);

// Choose a random number of shares
order.setShares(rand.nextInt(1000) + 1);

// Enter the order via a remote call to the server.
// Pass a reference to ourselves so the server can call back.
server.enterMarketOrder(order, this);
```

On the server side, `PriceServerImpl.enterMarketOrder` accepts two input parameters: the order being submitted by the client, and the client's reference to itself. This reference is of type `ExecutionAlert`, which is the remote interface the client implements.

`enterMarketOrder` does its work asynchronously by spawning a separate thread to handle the execution of the order. It passes the order and the client reference to the new thread, then returns control to the caller, which is `TradingClient`. Here is the code for `enterMarketOrder`:

```
public void enterMarketOrder(Order order,
                             ExecutionAlert clientRef) {
  // Receives an order from a client, and also a
  // reference to the client. Spawns a new thread
  // to execute the trade (which may take some time),
  // then returns.
  System.out.println("A client has placed an order!");
  System.out.println("Time: " + new Date());
  System.out.println(order + "\n");
  DoExecution exec = new DoExecution(order, clientRef);
  new Thread(exec).start();
}
```

`DoExecution` is implemented as an inner class. Its default constructor copies the `Order` and `ExecutionAlert` references to instance fields, and its `run` method executes the order. To do this, the `run` method first sleeps for 10 seconds (this simulates the time it might take for the order to be filled). Upon awakening, the code creates an `Execution` instance and copies the relevant data from the incoming order to it. Then it gets the current price of the requested security by calling `PriceServerImpl.getPrice`. This is the price at which the order is filled. Finally, it calls the `notifyOfExecution` method of the `ExecutionAlert` remote interface, using the incoming client reference to do so. This causes the notification code to execute remotely on the client that submitted the order.

Listing 8-5 shows the complete implementation of `PriceServerImpl.enterMarketOrder`.

Listing 8-5: PriceServerImpl.enterMarketOrder

```
public void enterMarketOrder(Order order,
                              ExecutionAlert clientRef) {
  // Receives an order from a client, and also a
  // reference to the client. Spawns a new thread
  // to execute the trade (which may take some time),
  // then returns.
  System.out.println("A client has placed an order!");
  System.out.println("Time: " + new Date());
  System.out.println(order + "\n");
  DoExecution exec = new DoExecution(order, clientRef);
  new Thread(exec).start();
}

// Inner class to handle order executions.
private class DoExecution implements Runnable {
  private Order order;
  private ExecutionAlert client;

  public DoExecution(Order ord, ExecutionAlert clientRef) {
    order = ord;
    client = clientRef;
  }

  public void run() {
    try {
      // Wait 10 seconds to simulate submission of the order
      // to a stock exchange.
      Thread.currentThread().sleep(10000);
      // Create an Execution instance and execute the order.
      Execution execution = new Execution();
      // Copy order data into the execution.
      execution.setNumber(order.getNumber());
      execution.setSymbol(order.getSymbol());
      execution.setShares(order.getShares());
      // Execute at the stock's current price and write a
      // status message to standard output.
```

Continued

Listing 8-5 *(continued)*

```
            execution.setPrice(getPrice(order.getSymbol()));
            System.out.println("An order has been executed!");
            System.out.println("Time: " + new Date());
            System.out.println(execution + "\n");
            // Make a remote call to the client to notify them
            // of the execution.
            client.notifyOfExecution(execution);
         } catch (Exception e) {
            e.printStackTrace();
         }
      }
   }
```

`TradingClient.notifyOfExecution` is a simple method; it merely writes a status message to standard output, along with the execution data:

```
public void notifyOfExecution(Execution exec) {
   System.out.println("An order has been executed!");
   System.out.println("Time: " + new Date());
   System.out.println(exec + "\n");
}
```

To recap: `TradingClient` creates an order and transmits it to `PriceServer` by invoking a remote method on `PriceServer`. `PriceServer's` remote method receives the order, hands it off to a new server thread for execution, and then exits. As soon as the order is executed, `PriceServer` transmits the execution data back to `TradingClient` by invoking a remote method on `TradingClient`. This remote method receives the execution data, displays it onscreen for the user, and exits.

Keep in mind that `TradingClient` could have just as easily invoked a remote method in a different client, or vice-versa. All that's required is that the clients implement interfaces that extend `weblogic.rmi.remote`, and that stubs are available in WebLogic's classpath for the clients' remote methods. To create these stubs, simply run the WebLogic RMI compiler on the client classes.

You might be wondering why there is no code to register the `TradingClient` class in the RMI registry, or at least the `TradingClient.notifyOfExecution` method. The reason is because instead of doing a registry lookup to find this code, we simply use the client reference passed to us by the client to do it. This allows us to ensure that the correct client gets notified of the execution This being the case, how does WebLogic know that a remote call must be made, and therefore the stub must be used? The answer is because the client reference is of type `ExecutionAlert`, which extends `weblogic.rmi.remote`. Recall that WebLogic will always use a remote reference (stub) to call methods that extend this interface, unless they live in the same JVM. If the stub is not available, the method call will fail with a `ClassDefNotFound` exception for the stub.

You could, however, register `TradingClient` (or any other client) in the RMI registry, and look it up in the usual way from the server or another client. To register `TradingClient` in WebLogic Server's RMI registry, you would write this code in `TradingClient`:

```
TradingClient client = new TradingClient();
Context ctx = Environment.getInitialContext();
ctx.bind("TradingClient", client);
System.out.println("TradingClient was started and bound " +
                   "in the registry to the name " +
                   "TradingClient");
```

This causes a remote reference to `TradingClient` to appear in the WebLogic JNDI tree, alongside `PriceServer`. Take careful note of the second line, where we obtain a `Context`. Recall that in `PriceServer` we did this as follows:

```
Context ctx = new InitialContext();
```

In `TradingClient`, we must use the `Environment` class to get the `Context` because `TradingClient's` code is not executing in WebLogic's JVM. Therefore, we must explicitly specify the JNDI factory and provider URL for WebLogic Server, which the `Environment` class does for us (we use the `Environment` class for the same reason when clients look up remote references registered on WebLogic Server).

To invoke a remote method in `TradingClient` from another client, you would write the following code:

```
InitialContext ctx = Environment.getInitialContext();
ExecutionAlert tc = (ExecutionAlert)
  ctx.lookup("TradingClient");
Execution exec = new Execution();
tc.notifyOfExecution(exec);
```

Notice that this is no different from invoking remote methods on the server. The remote reference lookup and the method call are routed through WebLogic Server, but the invoked method executes in `TradingClient's` JVM, not WebLogic's.

Calling EJBs from RMI Servers

Our final example introduces a session EJB into the design. It shows how to invoke the EJB's remote methods from the RMI server, and how to invoke the RMI server's and RMI client's remote methods from the EJB. EJBs are essentially RMI servers, but because they live in the EJB container and support a great deal of additional functionality (such as pooling and transaction support), they are used somewhat differently. This example highlights the differences and allows you to leverage your newly-acquired RMI knowledge to better understand EJBs.

Part IV, "Developing EJB Components," covers EJBs in detail. The intent of this section is to show you how RMI and EJBs are related.

The change we'll make in the application is to move the execution code out of `PriceServerImpl` and into a session bean called `ExecuteTrade`. We'll modify `PriceServerImpl.enterMarketOrder` so it invokes the bean method, as shown below:

```
public void enterMarketOrder(Order order,
                             ExecutionAlert client) {
  // The ExecuteTrade bean returns immediately and calls back
  // the client when the trade has been executed.
  try {
    // Create a context with which to lookup the bean
    Hashtable ht = new Hashtable();
    ht.put(Context.INITIAL_CONTEXT_FACTORY,
           Environment.JNDI_FACTORY);
    ht.put(Context.PROVIDER_URL, Environment.WEBLOGIC_URL);
    Context ctx2 = new InitialContext(ht);
    // Get a reference to the bean object
    Object objref = ctx2.lookup("ExecuteTrade");
    // Get a reference to the bean's home interface
    ExecuteTradeHome home = (ExecuteTradeHome)
      javax.rmi.PortableRemoteObject.narrow(objref,
      ExecuteTradeHome.class);
    // Get a reference to the bean's remote interface
    ExecuteTradeRemote executionBean = home.create();
    // Invoke the bean's remote method to execute the trade
    executionBean.executeTrade(order, client);
  } catch (Exception e) {
    e.printStackTrace();
  }
}
```

Notice the differences in the way remote references are obtained for EJBs as opposed to RMI servers. A JNDI lookup is used to get a reference to the session EJB's *object*, not its remote references:

```
Object objref = ctx2.lookup("ExecuteTrade");
```

This object reference is cast to an instance of the EJB's home interface:

```
ExecuteTradeHome home = (ExecuteTradeHome)
  javax.rmi.PortableRemoteObject.narrow(objref,
  ExecuteTradeHome.class);
```

Finally, a remote reference to the bean is obtained by calling the home interface's `create` method:

```
ExecuteTradeRemote executionBean = home.create();
```

At this point, we are finally able to invoke one of the bean's methods.

The reasons for these differences are due to the architecture of the EJB container and the EJB API. Although the EJB is an RMI server, the EJB API must do a lot more work behind the scenes beyond simply dealing with RMI issues. We'll explore this further later in the book when we learn about EJBs, but for now it's interesting to see the coding differences side by side.

The `ExecuteTrade` session bean exposes the following remote interface. Note we have put the bean in a separate package, which would likely be the case in a real application:

```
package biblermiexample4;

import java.rmi.*;
import javax.ejb.*;
import bible.rmi.example4.*;

// Remote interface for the ExecuteTrade Session EJB.
public interface ExecuteTradeRemote extends EJBObject {

  // Execute an order and alert the client of the execution.
  public void executeTrade(Order order, ExecutionAlert alert)
    throws RemoteException;
}
```

The bean's `executeTrade` method looks like this:

```
public void executeTrade(Order order, ExecutionAlert alert)
    throws RemoteException {
  DoExecution exec = new DoExecution(order, alert);
  new Thread(exec).start();
}

private class DoExecution implements Runnable {
  private Order order;
  private ExecutionAlert client;

  public DoExecution(Order ord, ExecutionAlert alert) {
    order = ord;
    client = alert;
  }

  public void run() {
```

```
        try {
          Thread.currentThread().sleep(15000); //sleep 15 seconds.

          // Get a remote reference to the PriceServer RMI
          // server so we can invoke its getPrice() method
          // to get the latest price for the security
          InitialContext ctx = Environment.getInitialContext();
          PriceServer server = (PriceServer)
            ctx.lookup(PriceServer.PRICESERVERNAME);

          // Create and populate an Execution instance
          Execution execution = new Execution();
          execution.setNumber(order.getNumber());
          // Remote method call to the server to get the price
          execution.setPrice(server.getPrice(order.getSymbol()));
          execution.setShares(order.getShares());
          execution.setSymbol(order.getSymbol());
          System.out.println("An order has been executed!");
          System.out.println("Time: " + new Date());
          System.out.println(execution + "\n");
          // Remote method call to the calling instance of
          // TradingClient to notify it of the execution
          client.notifyOfExecution(execution);
        } catch (Exception e) {
          e.printStackTrace();
        }
      }
    }
```

This code is almost identical to `PriceServer's executeTrade` code in Example 3. The only difference is that our bean must invoke `PriceServer.getPrice()` remotely, whereas `PriceServer` was able to call its own method locally.

Summary

You should now have a strong understanding of RMI, and the advantages of WebLogic RMI over the JavaSoft implementation. You have learned, step-by-step, how to write, deploy, and test WebLogic RMI applications, and you have seen the various ways in which RMI servers and clients can work together in a WebLogic-hosted environment to solve difficult distributed computing problems. Finally, you have seen a glimpse of how RMI and EJBs work together, which should give you a better understanding of how EJBs work

✦ ✦ ✦

Working with WebLogic JMS

✦ ✦ ✦ ✦

In This Chapter

✦ ✦ ✦ ✦

The *Java Message Service,* or *JMS,* provides a mechanism for Java processes to send synchronous or asynchronous messages to each other. These processes can run in the same or different JVMs, and on the same or different computers on a network or the Internet.

In this chapter, I provide an overview of the JMS architecture. Then I show you how to configure WebLogic JMS, which involves a large number of important, interrelated steps. After you configure a working JMS infrastructure, I provide several code examples showing how to use the many powerful JMS features. I conclude by showing you how to build reliable, fault-tolerant applications by using JMS, JDBC, and the Java Transaction API (JTA).

Understanding JMS

I will begin this chapter by introducing you to the organization, architecture, and features of JMS, before moving on to its configuration and programming in the WebLogic environment.

JMS versions and packages

WebLogic 6.1 runs on top of JDK 1.3 and supports JMS version 1.0.2. JMS is implemented in a multitude of packages; the following list shows the packages you'll most commonly import:

- `javax.jms`, which contains the JMS API
- `weblogic.jms.ServerSessionPoolFactory`, which contains WebLogic extensions for server-side JMS session pools

✦ `weblogic.jms.extensions`, which includes WebLogic extensions for creating XML messages, dynamically creating message queues and topics, creating session exception listeners, managing message multicasting, and converting between WebLogic 6.0 and pre-6.0 JMS message ID formats

You can download the latest JMS specification from the Sun Web site at. `http://java.sun.com/products/jms/docs.html`.

JMS architecture

Like JNDI, JMS has a multilayered architecture, as shown in Figure 9-1. A Java application (or application component) accesses a JMS-enabled message server through the JMS API. References to the message server are obtained via JNDI lookups. WebLogic Server contains a complete, feature-rich message server of its own; third-party message servers that run outside of WebLogic Server (such as IBM MQSeries) can also be used if their vendors provide JMS API implementations for them.

WebLogic JMS interfaces with WebLogic JTA to transaction-enable the delivery of messages, and it interfaces with the file system and/or JDBC to provide persistent storage of messages when desired by the developer.

Chapter 6 discusses WebLogic JTA.

<table>
<tr><td colspan="2">Application</td></tr>
<tr><td colspan="2">JMS API</td></tr>
<tr><td colspan="2">JNDI</td></tr>
<tr><td colspan="2">Message Server
(WebLogic)</td></tr>
<tr><td>Transaction Services
(via JTA)</td><td>Persistent Message Store
(file or JDBC)</td></tr>
</table>

Figure 9-1: JMS architecture

A full understanding of JMS requires an understanding of a few key concepts, which I cover next.

Messages

A *message* is an object containing the information being sent from one application (or part of an application) to another. JMS provides the `Message` interface as the base interface for all messages in JMS. Five distinct JMS message types, plus one type specific to WebLogic, extend this interface, as shown in Figure 9-2.

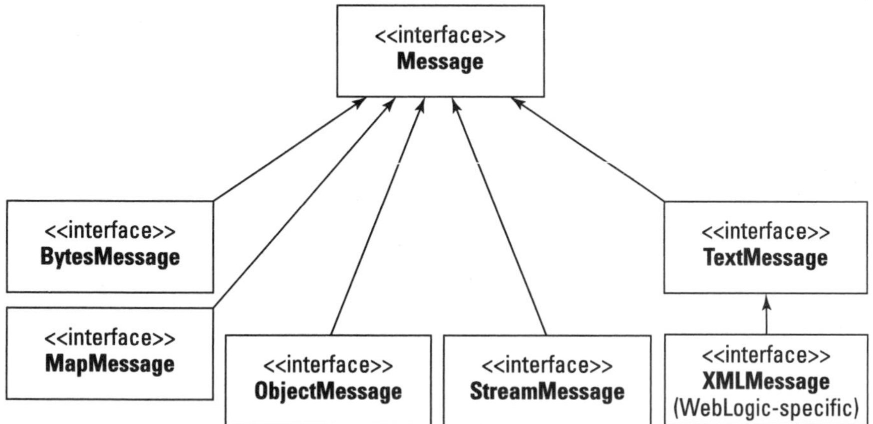

Figure 9-2: The JMS Message interface hierarchy

A message consists of a fixed set of header fields, a user-configurable set of optional properties fields, and a message body that carries the content of the message (see Figure 9-3).

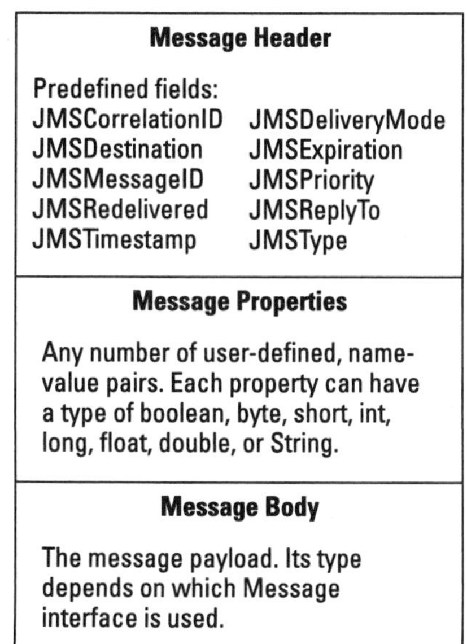

Figure 9-3: The structure of a JMS message

Message producers and consumers

A *message producer* is a Java application or component that creates and sends messages. A *message consumer* is a Java application or component that receives messages. Between them lives the message server, which manages the delivery of messages between the two.

Point-to-point (PTP) messaging

Point-to-point messaging occurs when a message producer sends a message to exactly one message consumer. Point-to-point messaging is managed by JMS message *queues*. The message producer is called a *queue sender*, and the message consumer a *queue receiver*. Any number of message producers may send to a queue, and any number of consumers may listen to a queue, but only one can be the queue receiver, as shown in Figure 9-4. JMS selects the listener who has been listening the longest to be the receiver. JMS removes incoming messages from queues as soon as the receiver has received them.

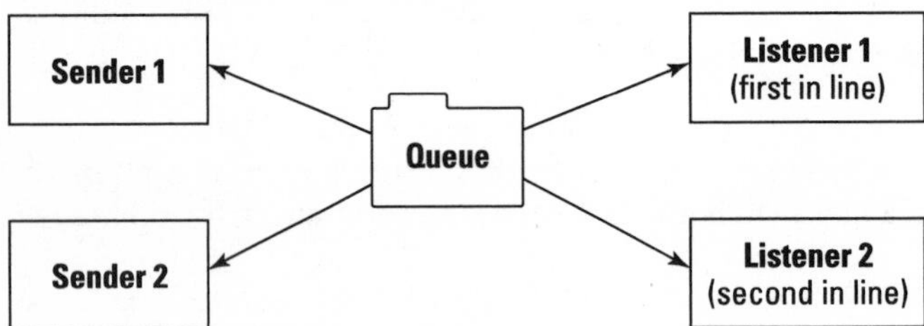

Figure 9-4: Point-to-point messaging is accomplished in JMS by using Queues.

Publish-and-subscribe (Pub/Sub) messaging

Publish-and-subscribe messaging occurs when a message producer sends a message to multiple message consumers. Publish-and-subscribe messaging is managed by JMS message *topics*. The message producer is called a *topic publisher*, and the message consumer a *topic subscriber*. Any number of message producers may publish to a topic, and any number of consumers may subscribe to a topic. JMS delivers published messages to all topic subscribers and removes incoming messages from topics only after *all* subscribers have received them. Figure 9-5 illustrates publish-and-subscribe messaging.

Message persistence

A message is classified as being either *persistent* or *nonpersistent*. A persistent message is guaranteed to be delivered at least once. It is considered to be delivered after it has been successfully written to a persistent message data store, which in WebLogic is either a disk file or JDBC-enabled database. A nonpersistent message is also guaranteed to be delivered at least once, but messages may be lost if there's a system failure. Nonpersistent messages are considered to be delivered when a recipient acknowledges their receipt.

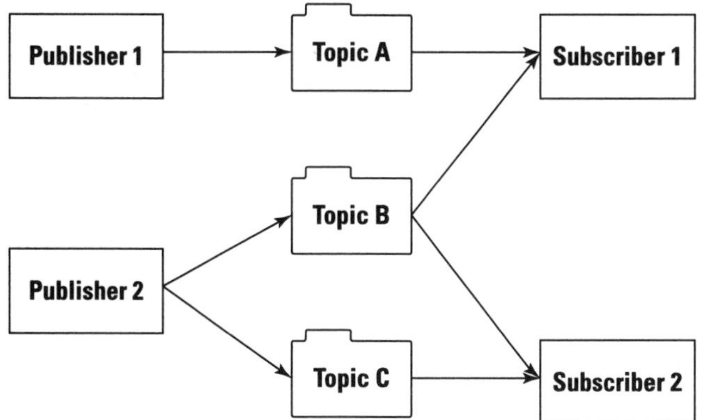

Figure 9-5: Publish-and-subscribe messaging is accomplished in JMS by using topics.

Connection factories

A *connection factory* is a class that spawns JMS connections for a given message server and system configuration. Connection factories are the developer's first line of interaction with JMS. Once the developer obtains a reference to a connection factory (via JNDI lookup), he can use that reference to obtain a connection, and from there a reference to a queue, a topic, and so on.

In WebLogic, system administrators use the WebLogic Console to define connection factories with predefined characteristics. Developers can also create connection factories in code if they prefer to define connection factory characteristics at runtime.

Connections

A *connection* is an application's communication link with JMS. Connections are obtained from connection factories and create the client-side and server-side resources necessary to manage messaging interactions. User authentication may also be embedded in connections, so applications can be sure that only authorized users are sending and receiving messages.

Connections can be *started*, *stopped*, or *closed*. This is accomplished by calling `Connection.start()`, `Connection.stop()`, and `Connection.close()`, respectively. Connections are in stopped mode when they are first created. Messages can be sent or received only through started connections, so you must call `Connection.start()` before using the connection. Calling `Connection.stop()` pauses message delivery for that connection, without releasing the connection's system resources. To completely tear down a connection and release its system resources, call `Connection.close()`.

Separate Connection subclasses exist for each type of messaging. A `QueueConnection` is used for point-to-point messaging, and a `TopicConnection` is used for publish-and-subscribe messaging.

Sessions

Sessions handle the actual production and consumption of messages by applications and application components. After creating a message, a Java application uses a session to send it. Similarly, an application listening for messages retrieves them through a session.

Separate session subclasses exist for each type of messaging, and are created by the corresponding `Connection` classes. A `QueueSession` is used to send and receive point-to-point messages, and a `TopicSession` is used to send and receive publish-and-subscribe messages.

Configuring WebLogic JMS

Before writing code to send or receive messages, you must configure WebLogic JMS by using the WebLogic Console. Configuring JMS involves performing a series of interrelated steps. This section shows you how to perform the required steps in the correct order and helps you understand the meanings and implications of your configuration choices.

Here is the list of configuration steps, which you should perform in the following order:

1. Create a connection factory and assign it a JNDI name.
2. Define *backing stores* for your messages (optional). Backing stores are disk files or JDBC-accessible databases that provide persistent storage for messages. You need to create backing stores only if you want to support persistent messages or durable subscribers.
3. Define *destination keys* (optional). Destination keys are a WebLogic extension to JMS that allow you to control the order in which messages are delivered.
4. Define *templates* (optional). Templates are another WebLogic extension that allow you to group several destination keys together, giving you the ability to send messages that are sorted by multiple criteria.
5. Create a JMS server, which is a logical container for queues and topics, and which optionally maps queues and topics to backing stores.
6. Create one or more queues or topics and map them to the JMS server you created in step 5.

You can change certain configuration settings later. For example, you can define backing stores, destination keys, or templates at any time, and assign them to existing JMS servers, queues, and topics. You can also create or delete queues and topics whenever you want.

Creating a connection factory

Start WebLogic Server and open the WebLogic Console. In the domain tree, expand the JMS node, and then click Connection Factories. At the top of the page, click Create a New JMS Connection Factory. Figure 9-6 shows the connection factory configuration page with the data I provided for my factory.

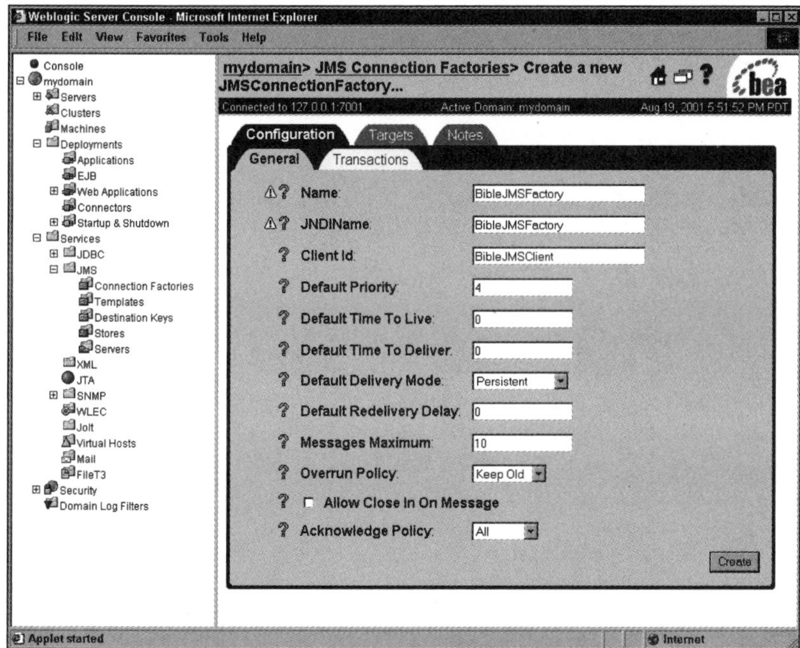

Figure 9-6: Configuring a JMS connection factory in the WebLogic Console

The entries on this page are as follows:

✦ **Name:** A name for the connection factory, which must conform to the rules for Java identifiers and be unique within the WebLogic Server instance or its cluster. Type **BibleJMSFactory** for this value.

✦ **JNDIName:** This name will be used to look up instances of the connection factory with JNDI. It must be a valid Java identifier and be unique within the JNDI namespace of the server or cluster. Type **BibleJMSFactory** for this value as well.

✦ **Client ID:** Leave this blank unless you want to use the connection factory to support a durable subscriber for pub/sub messaging. Durable subscribers are explained later in this chapter in the section, "Creating durable subscribers to topics."

- **Default Priority:** When sending messages, you can assign them numeric priorities between zero (lowest) and 9 (highest). Higher priority messages are delivered first. The default priority defined here is automatically assigned by JMS to messages for which no priority is specified. WebLogic sets this value to `4` (medium), which is fine for this example.
- **Default Time To Live:** This is the default maximum time in milliseconds that undelivered messages are allowed to exist in the system before being destroyed. The value applies only to messages for which the programmer did not assign a priority. A value of zero indicates undelivered messages are allowed to exist indefinitely, which is fine for this example.
- **Default Time To Deliver:** This is the default time in milliseconds that elapses between the time that a message is delivered and the time it appears at its destination. A value of zero indicates messages appear at their destinations immediately after being delivered, which is fine for this example.
- **Default Delivery Mode:** Allows you to choose between persistent and non-persistent message delivery, as described in the "Message persistence" section earlier. If you select persistent, you must specify a backing store for the messages; I show how to do this shortly. Select Persistent.
- **Default Redelivery Delay:** Default time delay, in milliseconds, before rolled back or recovered messages are redelivered. A value of zero indicates such messages are redelivered immediately, which is fine for this example.
- **Messages Maximum:** This is the maximum number of messages that may exist in an asynchronous session that have not been forwarded to a message listener. A value of `-1` indicates there is no limit, in which case messages will be held on the server up to the limit of available virtual memory. If a positive value is specified and then exceeded at runtime, WebLogic handles the situation according to a complex set of rules that I discuss later in the chapter. Type **-1** for this example.
- **Overrun Policy:** This instructs WebLogic what to do if Messages Maximum is exceeded for this factory. I explain this parameter later in the chapter; select Keep Old for this example.
- **Allow Close in On Message:** Checking this box means that asynchronous message handlers are allowed to close the connection in their `onMessage()` methods and an acknowledgement of message receipt will still be sent. Leave this unchecked.
- **Acknowledge Policy:** This parameter is new in WebLogic 6.1 and is included as a workaround for a change that took place in the JMS specification between versions 6.0 and 6.1 of WebLogic. Setting the value to All causes all messages to be acknowledged, which is the behavior specified in the latest JMS specification. Setting the value to Previous causes all messages previously received to be acknowledged, which used to be the behavior specified by the JMS specification. You should set this value to All, unless you need to provide backward compatibility with an application written to the old JMS specification.

After completing the configuration screen, click Create.

The next step is to attach the connection factory to a server or cluster. Click the Targets tab, and then move the desired server into the Chosen list of the desired server or cluster. Click Apply. Figure 9-7 shows my connection factory attached to my local WebLogic server instance.

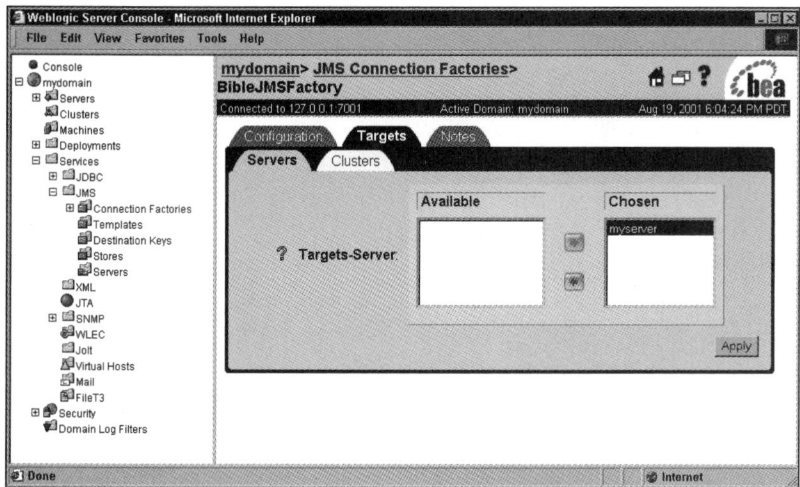

Figure 9-7: Attaching the connection factory to a WebLogic server

This completes configuration of the connection factory. Next I show how to define backing stores.

Defining a file backing store

In the domain tree of the WebLogic Console, expand the JMS node, and then click Stores. At the top of the page, click Create a New JMSFile Store. Figure 9-8 shows the resulting configuration page.

The entries on this page are as follows:

- **Name:** A name for the file store, which must conform to the rules for Java identifiers and be unique within the WebLogic Server instance or its cluster. Type **BibleJMSFileStore** for this value.
- **Directory:** A pathname to a valid file system directory where the store will be kept. This directory must exist on your system, so be sure to create it before completing this page.

After completing the configuration screen, click Create.

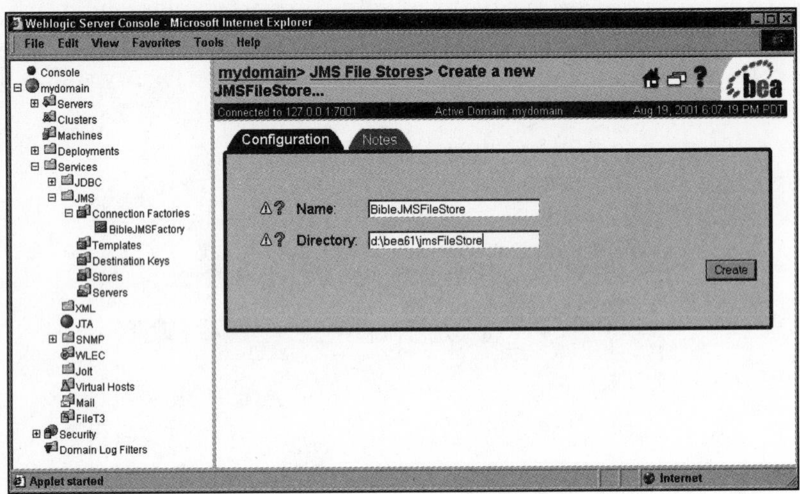

Figure 9-8: Creating a JMS file store

WebLogic creates the JMS file store automatically the first time that messages are sent to a queue or topic backed by the store. The structure of this file is private and undocumented.

Defining a JDBC backing store

In the domain tree of the WebLogic Console, expand the JMS node, and then click Stores. At the top of the page, click Create a New JMSJDBCStore. Figure 9-9 shows the resulting configuration page.

The entries on this page are as follows:

✦ **Name:** A name for the JDBC store, which must conform to the rules for Java identifiers and be unique within the WebLogic Server instance or its cluster. Type **BibleJMSJDBCStore** for this value.

✦ **Connection Pool:** A valid JDBC connection pool already defined on your server (the drop-down menu will be populated with available pool names). See Chapter 5 for instructions on how to configure JDBC connection pools.

✦ **Prefix Name:** A string value that is prepended to all table names whenever JMS makes JDBC calls to the JDBC store. Enter a value if your RDBMS requires fully qualified table names. Some instances of SQL Server or Sybase, for example, require `dbo` to be prepended to all table names. Check with your database administrator if you have any doubts. My instance does not, so I'm leaving this attribute blank.

After completing the configuration screen, click Create.

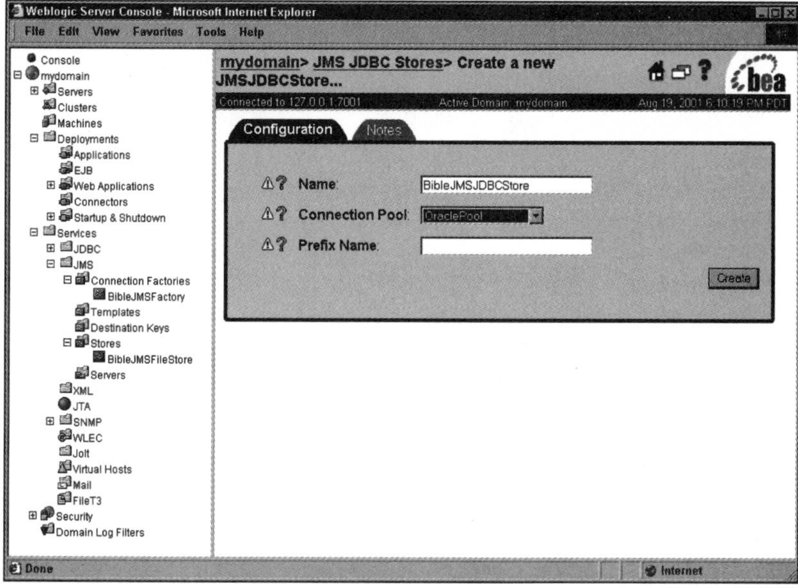

Figure 9-9: Creating a JMS JDBC store

The connection pool you specify must use a non-XA driver, because the WebLogic classes that manage the JMS system tables are not XA-aware.

When you restart WebLogic Server, it automatically adds two system tables to the database specified by your JMS connection pool, if they don't already exist (note the contrast with file stores, which are not created until they are actually used). Each table contains one nonclustered index. The following code is the resulting DDL for Oracle. I created a schema called JMS to hold the tables, but you can put them in any schema you want:

```
CREATE TABLE JMS.JMSSTATE
(
    RECORDHANDLE     NUMBER     NULL,
    RECORDSTATE      NUMBER     NULL,
    RECORDGENERATION NUMBER     NULL
);

CREATE INDEX JMS.JMSMSG_X
    ON SCOTT.JMSSTATE(RECORDHANDLE);

CREATE TABLE JMS.JMSSTORE
(
    RECORDHANDLE NUMBER      NULL,
    RECORDSTATE  NUMBER      NULL,
```

Continued

```
    RECORD       LONG RAW     NULL
);

CREATE INDEX JMS.JMSMSGQ_X
    ON SCOTT.JMSSTORE(RECORDHANDLE);
```

Next is the DDL for Microsoft SQL Server:

```
CREATE TABLE dbo.JMSState
(
    recordHandle     numeric(12,0) NULL,
    recordState      int           NULL,
    recordGeneration int           NULL
)
go
CREATE NONCLUSTERED INDEX JMSMSG_X
    ON dbo.JMSState(recordHandle)
    ON [PRIMARY]
go
CREATE TABLE dbo.JMSStore
(
    recordHandle numeric(12,0) NULL,
    recordState  int           NULL,
    record       image         NULL
)
go
CREATE NONCLUSTERED INDEX JMSMSGQ_X
    ON dbo.JMSStore(recordHandle)
    ON [PRIMARY]
go
```

The structure of these tables is private and undocumented. But it's worth noting that the table `JMSStore` contains persisted messages, which remain in this table until they are delivered. After delivery, the messages are automatically deleted from the table by WebLogic JMS.

Defining destination keys

Destination keys are a WebLogic-specific feature that control the order in which messages are delivered to a queue or topic. Destination keys operate on the user-definable properties that are stored in a message.

Suppose, for example, that my application sends error messages to an error queue. I can define an `int` property called `severity`, whose values range from 1 (least severe errors) to 10 (most severe), and attach it to my messages. By default, messages are delivered to destinations in the order in which they're sent. But if I want the most severe errors delivered first, I can define a destination key that delivers error messages in descending order by `severity`.

To create such a destination key, expand the JMS node in the WebLogic Console, and then click Destination Keys. At the top of the page, click Create a New JMS Destination Key. Figure 9-10 shows the resulting configuration page.

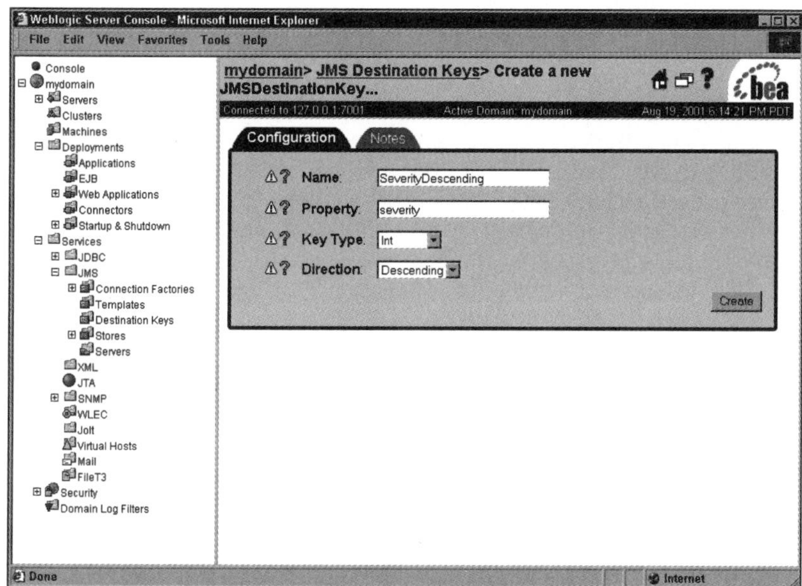

Figure 9-10: Defining a destination key

The entries on this page are as follows:

✦ **Name:** A name for the destination key, which must conform to the rules for Java identifiers and be unique within the WebLogic Server instance or its cluster. Type **SeverityDescending** for this value.

✦ **Property:** The name of the message property to which the key applies. The name must match the property name you use in your Java code and is case-sensitive. Type **severity** for this value.

✦ **Key Type:** The Java type of the key (one of: `boolean`, `byte`, `short`, `int`, `long`, `float`, `double`, or `String`). Select `Int`.

✦ **Direction:** The sort direction of the key (Ascending or Descending). Select `Descending`.

After completing the configuration screen, click Create.

Defining templates

Templates are collections of one or more destination keys that can be applied to JMS servers, queues, or topics. Use templates to create a set of message delivery attributes once and apply it to multiple queues and topics. You can also use templates to deliver messages sorted by multiple criteria.

Returning to the application error log example, suppose that my error queue receives messages from every application in my company. Suppose that I have also prioritized my applications by order of importance, and am storing this attribute in an `int` property called `appPriority`, whose values are `1` (high), `2` (medium), and `3` (low). I create a destination key for `appPriority`, sorted in ascending order, and then I create a template containing the `severity` and `appPriority` keys. This template, when applied to my queue, will cause messages to be delivered in descending order by `severity`, and ascending order by `appPriority`.

To create this template, expand the JMS node in the WebLogic Console, and then click Templates. At the top of the page, click Create a New JMS Template. Figure 9-11 shows the resulting configuration page.

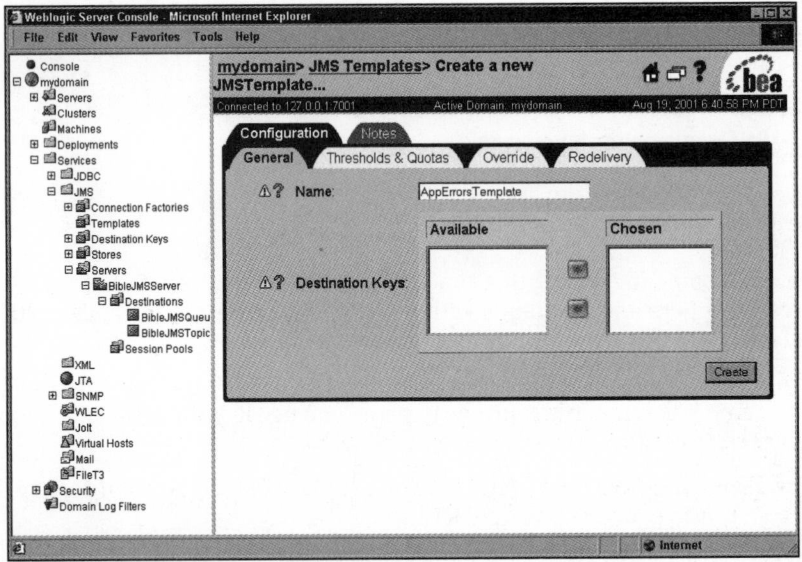

Figure 9-11: Defining a template

The entries on this page are as follows:

✦ **Name:** A name for the template, which must conform to the rules for Java identifiers and be unique within the WebLogic Server instance or its cluster. Type **AppErrorsTemplate** for this value.

✦ **Destination Keys:** Available destination keys for the template. Even if you have already defined some keys, none will be shown until you create the template. Click Create to create the template with no keys; the available keys will appear. Move the desired keys from the Available list to the Chosen list, and then click Apply.

Defining a JMS server

In the domain tree of the WebLogic Console, expand the JMS node, and then click Servers. At the top of the page, click Create a New JMS Server. Figure 9-12 shows the resulting configuration page.

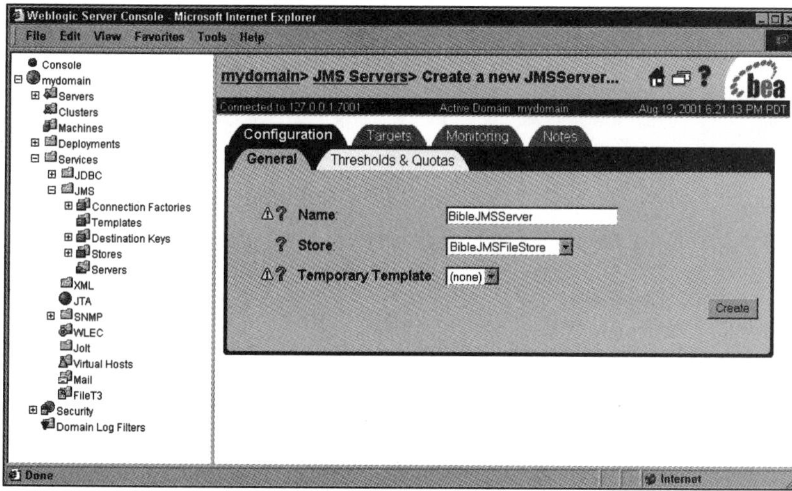

Figure 9-12: Defining a JMS server

The entries on this page are as follows:

✦ **Name:** A name for the JMS server, which must conform to the rules for Java identifiers and be unique within the WebLogic Server instance or its cluster. Type **BibleJMSServer** for this value.

✦ **Store:** The name of an existing JMS file or JDBC store to use for this JMS server. Select `BibleJMSFileStore`, the file store you created earlier.

✦ **Temporary Template:** The name of the JMS template (if any) that will be applied to all temporary destinations created against this server. Select `(none)`.

After completing the configuration screen, click Create. Then click the Targets tab and move your server or cluster into the Chosen list so it will be the target for the JMS server you just defined.

Creating a message queue

Before you can use your JMS server, you must create message queues or topics for applications to use.

In the domain tree of the WebLogic Console, expand the JMS node, and then click Servers. BibleJMSServer, the server you just created, should appear. Click BibleJMSServer to expand it; you will now see entries for Destinations and Session Pools. Click Destinations.

At the top of the page, click Create a New JMSQueue. Figure 9-13 shows the resulting configuration page.

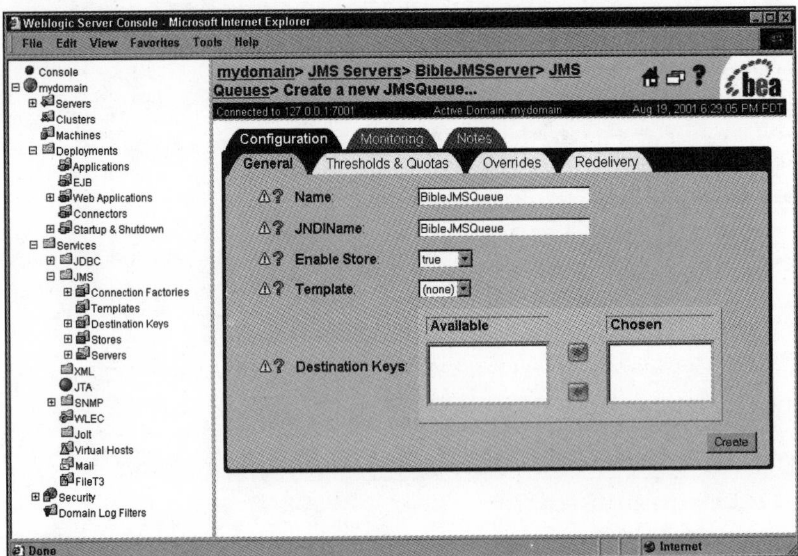

Figure 9-13: Configuring a JMS queue

The entries on this page are as follows:

- ✦ **Name:** A name for the JMS queue, which must conform to the rules for Java identifiers and be unique within the WebLogic Server instance or its cluster. Type **BibleJMSQueue** for this value.
- ✦ **JNDIName:** Programs will use this name to perform JNDI lookups on the queue at runtime. The name must be unique within the server's or cluster's JNDI namespace. Type **BibleJMSQueue** for this value.

✦ **Enable Store:** If `true`, messages sent to the queue will be written to the backing store defined for the JMS server. If `false`, they will not. If `default` is selected, messages will be written to the backing store if one is defined; otherwise they will not.

✦ **Template:** The JMS template that controls the order in which messages are delivered to the queue. Select `(none)`.

✦ **Destination Keys:** JMS destination keys that control the order in which messages are delivered to the queue. These can be chosen in lieu of, or in addition to, a template. Even if you have already defined some keys, none will be shown until you create the queue. Click Create to create the queue with no keys; the available keys will appear. Move the desired keys from the Available list to the Chosen list, and then click Apply.

Creating a message topic

In the domain tree of the WebLogic Console, expand the JMS node, and then click Servers. BibleJMSServer, the server you just created, should appear. Click BibleJMSServer to expand it; you will now see entries for Destinations and Session Pools. Click Destinations.

At the top of the page, click Create a New JMSTopic. Figure 9-14 shows the resulting configuration page.

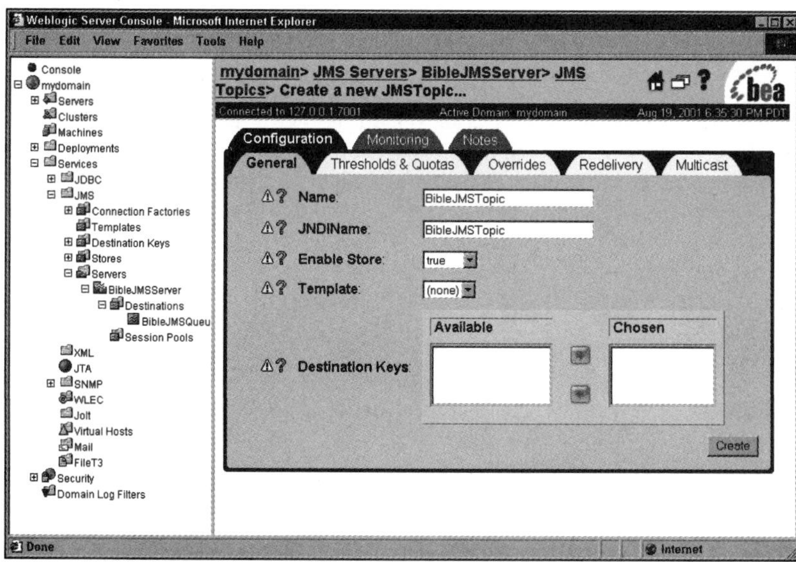

Figure 9-14: Configuring a JMS topic

The entries on this page are as follows:

- ✦ **Name:** A name for the JMS topic, which must conform to the rules for Java identifiers and be unique within the WebLogic Server instance or its cluster. Type **BibleJMSTopic** for this value.
- ✦ **JNDIName:** Programs will use this name to perform JNDI lookups on the topic at runtime. The name must be unique within the server's or cluster's JNDI namespace. Type **BibleJMSTopic** for this value.
- ✦ **Enable Store:** If `true`, messages sent to the topic will be written to the backing store defined for the JMS server. If `false`, they will not. If `default` is selected, messages will be written to the backing store if one is defined; otherwise they will not. `Enable Store` must be true if the topic will have durable subscribers. See the "Creating durable subscribers to topics" section later in this chapter for more details.
- ✦ **Template:** The JMS template that controls the order in which messages are delivered to the topic. Select `(none)`.
- ✦ **Destination Keys:** JMS destination keys that control the order in which messages are delivered to the topic. These can be chosen in lieu of, or in addition to, a template. Even if you have already defined some keys, none will be shown until you create the topic. Click Create to create the topic with no keys; the available keys will appear. Move the desired keys from the Available list to the Chosen list, and then click Apply.

Programming WebLogic JMS

After you finish configuring JMS on your server, you can write Java code that uses your messaging infrastructure. This section shows you how to write code to send and receive messages, using both the point-to-point and publish-and-subscribe models, for the messaging infrastructure we created in the previous section.

Sending messages

Whether you're sending messages to a queue, or publishing them to a topic, the programming steps are the same. You'll use different classes, however, depending on whether you're working with queues or topics. Here is a summary of the steps:

1. Obtain a reference to WebLogic Server's context.
2. Use the context and JNDI to obtain a reference to a connection factory.
3. Use the connection factory to create a connection.
4. Use the connection to create a session.

5. Use the connection to create an instance of the type of message you wish to send, then populate the message with data.
6. Use the connection to create a queue sender or topic publisher, then use the sender or publisher to send the message.

Obtaining a server context

Programming JMS requires the use of JNDI to look up connection factories and other resources. Therefore, the first step in any JMS session is to obtain the server context of the WebLogic server in question.

For more information about JNDI and obtaining server contexts, see Chapter 7.

The following code obtains the context of the local WebLogic server:

```
import javax.naming.*;
import java.util.*;

Context ctx = null;
Hashtable ht = new Hashtable();

ht.put(Context.INITIAL_CONTEXT_FACTORY,
       "weblogic.jndi.WLInitialContextFactory";
ht.put(Context.PROVIDER_URL, "t3://localhost:7001");

try {
  ctx = new InitialContext(ht);
}
catch (NamingException e) {
  e.printStackTrace();
}
```

I'll refer to the `Context` you obtained, stored in the variable `ctx`, in subsequent code examples.

Sending messages to a queue

To send messages to a queue, follow these steps:

1. Use the server context to look up a reference to a connection factory that has been defined in the WebLogic Console. Cast this reference to the `QueueConnectionFactory` type. The following code obtains a reference to `BibleJMSFactory`, the factory you defined earlier in this chapter:

```
import javax.jms.*;

QueueConnectionFactory qConnectionFactory =
  (QueueConnectionFactory) ctx.lookup("BibleJMSFactory");
```

2. Use the `QueueConnectionFactory` to create a `QueueConnection` instance. You can call one of two methods to do this, depending on whether a username and password (both strings) are required for your application:

```
QueueConnection qConnection =
  qConnectionFactory.createQueueConnection();
```

or:

```
QueueConnection qConnection =
  qConnectionFactory.createQueueConnection(userName,
                                          password);
```

3. Use the `QueueConnection` to create a `QueueSession` instance:

```
QueueSession qSession =
  qConnection.createQueueSession(TRANSACT_MODE,
    ACKNOWLEDGE_MODE);
```

`TRANSACT_MODE` is a Boolean specifying whether or not the session will operate in transactional mode. If `true`, then you can bundle a series of messages into a JMS transaction and send them as an atomic unit. Committing the transaction sends all the messages; rolling it back sends none. Also, when `TRANSACT_MODE` is `true`, `ACKNOWLEDGE_MODE` is ignored.

I demonstrate how to manage JMS transactions later in this chapter, in the section "Working with transactions."

`ACKNOWLEDGE_MODE` is an `int` specifying how your application will acknowledge the receipt of messages for nontransacted sessions. Table 9-1 describes its different values and their meanings.

Table 9-1
JMS Nontransacted Acknowledge Modes

Mode	*Description*
AUTO_ACKNOWLEDGE	The Session object automatically acknowledges receipt of the message after the application processes it.
`CLIENT_ACKNOWLEDGE`	The `Session` object relies on the application to explicitly call `Message.acknowledge()` from time to time to acknowledge one or more messages. Calling this method acknowledges all messages received since the last call, which allows applications to acknowledge large batches of messages with one call.

Mode	Description
DUPS_OK_ACKNOWLEDGE	Similar to AUTO_ACKNOWLEDGE, except the Session is notified that duplicate acknowledgements are allowed, so duplicate messages may be sent if the first attempt to send fails. This is the most efficient mode in terms of JMS resource overhead, but use it only if your application can handle the receipt of duplicate messages.
NO_ACKNOWLEDGE	Notifies the Session that no acknowledgement is required. Messages sent this way are immediately deleted from the server on receipt. If receipt fails, the message is lost. Duplicate messages may be sent if the first attempt to send fails. Use this mode only if your application can cope with lost or duplicate messages.
MULTICAST_NO_ACKNOWLEDGE	This mode is the same as NO_ACKNOWLEDGE, but is used for WebLogic message multicasting.

4. Use the server context to look up a reference to the desired JMS Queue. To look up a reference to BibleJMSQueue, for example, write this code:

```
Queue q = (Queue) ctx.lookup("BibleJMSQueue");
```

5. Use the QueueSession object to create a QueueSender instance for the Queue:

```
QueueSender qSender = qSession.createSender(q);
```

6. Use QueueSession to create an instance of the desired Message type (BytesMessage, MapMessage, ObjectMessage, StreamMessage, TextMessage, or XMLMessage). To create a TextMessage, for example, write this code:

```
TextMessage textMsg = qSession.createTextMessage();
```

7. Populate the message with data. Set its header information and properties as well, if your application requires it. The following code sets a user-defined int property called severity to a known value, and then populates the body of a TextMessage:

```
textMsg.clearBody();
textMsg.setIntProperty("severity", 1);
textMsg.setText("The mail server is down!");
```

8. Use the QueueSender object to send the following message:

```
qSender.send(textMsg);
```

When this call completes, the message will have been delivered to the queue.

The class BibleQueueSender, shown in Listing 9-1, illustrates the preceding steps. This class sends ten messages, plus a "stop" message signaling the transmission is complete.

You are not required to send "stop" messages. I am doing it in the examples for demonstration purposes only.

Listing 9-1: BibleQueueSender.java

```
package bible.jms;

import javax.jms.*;
import javax.naming.*;
import java.util.*;

public class BibleQueueSender {

  public static void main(String[] args) {
    Context ctx = null;
    Hashtable ht = new Hashtable();
    QueueConnectionFactory qConnectionFactory = null;
    QueueConnection qConnection = null;
    QueueSession qSession = null;
    QueueSender qSender = null;
    Queue q = null;
    TextMessage textMsg = null;
    String msg;

    try {
      // Obtain references to JMS queue components.
      ht.put(Context.INITIAL_CONTEXT_FACTORY,
             "weblogic.jndi.WLInitialContextFactory");
      ht.put(Context.PROVIDER_URL, "t3://localhost:7001");
      ctx = new InitialContext(ht);
      qConnectionFactory =
        (QueueConnectionFactory)
        ctx.lookup("BibleJMSFactory");
      qConnection =
        qConnectionFactory.createQueueConnection();
      qSession = qConnection.createQueueSession(false,
        javax.jms.QueueSession.AUTO_ACKNOWLEDGE);
      q = (Queue) ctx.lookup("BibleJMSQueue");
      qSender = qSession.createSender(q);

      System.out.println("Sending messages...");
      textMsg = qSession.createTextMessage();
      for (int i=1; i<=10; i++) {
        msg = "Message #" + i;
```

```
          textMsg.clearBody();
          textMsg.setIntProperty("severity", i);
          textMsg.setText(msg);
          System.out.println("  Sending message: " + msg);
          qSender.send(textMsg);
        }
        msg = "Stop";
        textMsg.clearBody();
        textMsg.setIntProperty("severity", 0);
        textMsg.setText(msg);
        System.out.println("  Sending message: " + msg);
        qSender.send(textMsg);
      }
      catch (Exception e) {
        e.printStackTrace();
      }
      finally {
        try {
          // Release JMS resources.
          qSender.close();
          qSession.close();
          qConnection.close();
        }
        catch (Exception e) {
          e.printStackTrace();
        }
      }
    }
  }
```

After starting WebLogic Server, running `BibleQueueSender.main()` in its own JVM yields the following output:

```
Sending messages...
  Sending message: Message #1
  Sending message: Message #2
  Sending message: Message #3
  Sending message: Message #4
  Sending message: Message #5
  Sending message: Message #6
  Sending message: Message #7
  Sending message: Message #8
  Sending message: Message #9
  Sending message: Message #10
  Sending message: Stop
```

The result is that the preceding 11 messages are waiting in `BibleJMSQueue`. The first queue receiver to read this queue will receive the messages.

Publishing messages to a topic

Publishing messages to a topic is analogous to sending messages to a queue—only the data types change. To publish a message to a topic, follow these steps:

1. Use the server context to look up a reference to a connection factory that has been defined in the WebLogic Console. Cast this reference to the `TopicConnectionFactory` type. The following code obtains a reference to `BibleJMSFactory`, the factory you defined earlier in this chapter:

   ```
   import javax.jms.*;

   TopicConnectionFactory tConnectionFactory =
     (TopicConnectionFactory) ctx.lookup("BibleJMSFactory");
   ```

2. Use the `TopicConnectionFactory` to create a `TopicConnection` instance. You can call one of two methods to do this, depending on whether a username and password (both strings) are required for your application:

   ```
   TopicConnection tConnection =
     tConnectionFactory.createTopicConnection();
   ```

   or:

   ```
   TopicConnection tConnection =
     tConnectionFactory.createTopicConnection(userName,
                                               password);
   ```

3. Use `TopicConnection` to create a `TopicSession` instance:

   ```
   TopicSession tSession =
     tConnection.createTopicSession(TRANSACT_MODE,
       ACKNOWLEDGE_MODE);
   ```

   `TRANSACT_MODE` and `ACKNOWLEDGE_MODE` have the same meanings in `TopicSessions` as they do in `QueueSessions`. Refer to Table 9-1 for a list of valid acknowledge modes.

4. Use the server context to look up a reference to the desired JMS `Topic`. To look up a reference to `BibleJMSTopic`, for example, write the following code:

   ```
   Topic t = (Topic) ctx.lookup("BibleJMSTopic");
   ```

5. Use the `TopicSession` object to create a `TopicPublisher` instance for the `Topic`:

   ```
   TopicPublisher tPublisher = tSession.createPublisher(t);
   ```

6. Use `TopicSession` to create an instance of the desired `Message` type (`BytesMessage`, `MapMessage`, `ObjectMessage`, `StreamMessage`, `TextMessage`, or `XMLMessage`). To create a `TextMessage`, for example, write the following code:

   ```
   TextMessage textMsg = tSession.createTextMessage();
   ```

7. Populate the message with data. Set its header information and properties as well, if your application requires it. The following code sets a user-defined `int` property called `priority` to a known value, and then populates the body of a `TextMessage`:

   ```
   textMsg.clearBody();
   textMsg.setIntProperty("priority", 1);
   textMsg.setText("The mail server is down!");
   ```

8. Use the `TopicPublisher` object to send the message:

   ```
   tPublisher.publish(textMsg);
   ```

   When this call completes, the message will have been published to the topic.

The class `BibleTopicPublisher`, shown in Listing 9-2, illustrates the preceding steps, again by publishing ten messages, plus a "stop" message.

Listing 9-2: BibleTopicPublisher.java

```
package bible.jms;

import javax.jms.*;
import javax.naming.*;
import java.util.*;

public class BibleTopicPublisher {

  public static void main(String[] args) {
    Context ctx = null;
    Hashtable ht = new Hashtable();
    TopicConnectionFactory tConnectionFactory = null;
    TopicConnection tConnection = null;
    TopicSession tSession = null;
    TopicPublisher tPublisher = null;
    Topic t = null;
    TextMessage textMsg = null;
    String msg;

    try {
      // Obtain references to JMS Topic components.
      ht.put(Context.INITIAL_CONTEXT_FACTORY,
             "weblogic.jndi.WLInitialContextFactory");
      ht.put(Context.PROVIDER_URL, "t3://localhost:7001");
      ctx = new InitialContext(ht);
      tConnectionFactory =
        (TopicConnectionFactory)
        ctx.lookup("BibleJMSFactory");
      tConnection =
        tConnectionFactory.createTopicConnection();
      tSession = tConnection.createTopicSession(false,
```

Continued

Listing 9-2 *(continued)*

```
          javax.jms.TopicSession.AUTO_ACKNOWLEDGE);
        t = (Topic) ctx.lookup("BibleJMSTopic");
        tPublisher = tSession.createPublisher(t);

        System.out.println("Publishing messages...");
        textMsg = tSession.createTextMessage();
        for (int i=1; i<=10; i++) {
          msg = "Message #" + i;
          textMsg.clearBody();
          textMsg.setIntProperty("severity", i);
          textMsg.setText(msg);
          System.out.println("  Publishing message: " + msg);
          tPublisher.publish(textMsg);
        }
        msg = "Stop";
        textMsg.clearBody();
        textMsg.setText(msg);
        textMsg.setIntProperty("severity", 0);
        System.out.println("  Sending message: " + msg);
        tPublisher.publish(textMsg);
      }
      catch (Exception e) {
        e.printStackTrace();
      }
      finally {
        try {
          // Release JMS resources.
          tPublisher.close();
          tSession.close();
          tConnection.close();
        }
        catch (Exception e) {
          e.printStackTrace();
        }
      }
    }
  }
```

After starting WebLogic Server, running `BibleTopicSender.main()` in its own JVM yields the following output:

```
Publishing messages...
  Publishing message: Message #1
  Publishing message: Message #2
  Publishing message: Message #3
  Publishing message: Message #4
  Publishing message: Message #5
  Publishing message: Message #6
```

```
Publishing message: Message #7
Publishing message: Message #8
Publishing message: Message #9
Publishing message: Message #10
Publishing message: Stop
```

The result is that the preceding 11 messages are published to `BibleJMSTopic`. But if no durable subscribers are registered with the topic, and there are no active, nondurable subscribers, the messages are immediately lost.

I describe durable and nondurable subscribers later in this chapter, in the section "Creating durable subscribers to topics."

Receiving messages synchronously

Receiving messages synchronously, while sometimes useful, is usually the least efficient way to process incoming messages. Synchronous code spends most of its time in loops waiting for messages to arrive, consuming precious CPU cycles and server threads in the process. On a busy server, large numbers of synchronous messaging threads can deadlock the entire server. Therefore, before writing synchronous code to receive messages, take a hard look at your application to make sure that an asynchronous approach isn't better.

Nevertheless, situations exist where synchronous message processing makes sense, especially for queues — this section shows you how to do so.

Receiving messages synchronously from a queue

Receiving messages synchronously from a queue is useful for batch applications that connect to the queue on a periodic basis, download the queue's contents, and then disconnect until the next scheduled batch session. A log analyzer program, for example, could retrieve log entries from a queue on a nightly basis, add them to its database, perform statistical analysis on the day's entries, and e-mail the results to a system administrator. As a side effect of this operation, the queue would be emptied in preparation for the next day's activity.

To receive messages synchronously from a queue, follow these steps:

1. Obtain `QueueConnectionFactory` and `QueueConnection` instances, and then call `QueueConnection.start()` to start the connection.
2. Use the `QueueSession` to create a `QueueReceiver` instance for the `Queue`.
3. Use the `QueueReceiver` to retrieve messages from the queue.
4. After retrieving all desired messages, call `QueueConnection.stop()` to stop the connection.
5. Release JMS resources by calling the `close` method of the `QueueReceiver`, `QueueSession`, and `QueueConnection`.

The class SyncQueueReceiver, shown in Listing 9-3, illustrates the preceding steps. The function of this class is to retrieve messages synchronously from a queue until the queue is empty.

Listing 9-3: SyncQueueReceiver.java

```
package bible.jms;

import javax.jms.*;
import javax.naming.*;
import java.util.*;

public class SyncQueueReceiver {

  public static void main(String[] args) {
    Context ctx = null;
    Hashtable ht = new Hashtable();
    QueueConnectionFactory qConnectionFactory = null;
    QueueConnection qConnection = null;
    QueueSession qSession = null;
    QueueReceiver qReceiver = null;
    Queue q = null;
    TextMessage textMsg = null;
    String msg;

    try {
      // Obtain references to JMS queue components.
      ht.put(Context.INITIAL_CONTEXT_FACTORY,
             "weblogic.jndi.WLInitialContextFactory");
      ht.put(Context.PROVIDER_URL, "t3://localhost:7001");
      ctx = new InitialContext(ht);
      qConnectionFactory =
        (QueueConnectionFactory)
        ctx.lookup("BibleJMSFactory");
      qConnection =
        qConnectionFactory.createQueueConnection();
      qSession = qConnection.createQueueSession(false,
        javax.jms.QueueSession.AUTO_ACKNOWLEDGE);
      q = (Queue) ctx.lookup("BibleJMSQueue");
      qReceiver = qSession.createReceiver(q);

      // Start a connection to the queue, retrieve all
      // messages in the queue, then stop the connection.
      System.out.println("Receiving messages...");
      qConnection.start();
      textMsg = (TextMessage)qReceiver.receiveNoWait();
      while (textMsg != null) {
        System.out.println("  Receiving message: " +
                           textMsg.getText());
        textMsg = (TextMessage)qReceiver.receiveNoWait();
      }
```

```
        qConnection.stop();
      }
      catch (Exception e) {
        e.printStackTrace();
      }
      finally {
        try {
          // Release JMS resources.
          qReceiver.close();
          qSession.close();
          qConnection.close();
        }
        catch (Exception e) {
          e.printStackTrace();
        }
      }
    }
  }
```

After starting WebLogic Server and running `BibleQueueSender.main()`, running `BibleTopicSender.main()` in its own JVM yields the following output:

```
Receiving messages...
  Receiving message: Message #1
  Receiving message: Message #2
  Receiving message: Message #3
  Receiving message: Message #4
  Receiving message: Message #5
  Receiving message: Message #6
  Receiving message: Message #7
  Receiving message: Message #8
  Receiving message: Message #9
  Receiving message: Message #10
  Receiving message: Stop
```

Now the queue is empty.

The line of code that synchronously examines the queue is as follows:

```
textMsg = (TextMessage)qReceiver.receiveNoWait();
```

`QueueReceiver.receiveNoWait()` returns the next message in a queue, or `null` if there are no messages. The call returns immediately; it does not wait for messages to arrive, nor does it wait for any predetermined period of time. Therefore, if you know a queue contains messages and you just want to grab them, `receiveNoWait()` is the way to go. In the example, I repeatedly call `receiveNoWait()` in a `while` loop until the queue is empty.

A variation of this call is `QueueReceiver.receive()`, which comes in two forms. Calling `receive()` with no arguments results in `receive()` waiting (and therefore blocking its thread) until a message arrives, at which time it returns the message. If a message never arrives, `receive()` blocks indefinitely. An alternative is to call `receive(long timeout)`, which causes `receive()` to wait the number of seconds given by `timeout` before returning, regardless of whether a message arrives. If no message arrives within the timeout period, `receive()` returns `null`; otherwise, it returns the message.

Receiving messages synchronously from a topic

Topic subscribers can retrieve synchronously messages published to a topic. But a topic subscriber will receive only those messages published *after* the subscriber registers with the topic. (Contrast this with queues, where a queue receiver receives messages sent before *or* after the receiver reads the queue, as long as the messages published before are persistent, have a long enough time-to-live, and haven't been retrieved by any other receivers.)

To receive published messages synchronously, follow these steps:

1. Obtain `TopicConnectionFactory` and `TopicConnection` instances, and then call `TopicConnection.start()` to start the connection.
2. Use `TopicSession` to create a `TopicSubscriber` instance for the `Topic`.
3. Use `TopicSubscriber` to retrieve messages from the topic.
4. After retrieving all desired messages, call `TopicConnection.stop()` to stop the connection.
5. Release JMS resources by calling the `close` method of the `TopicSubscriber`, `TopicSession`, and `TopicConnection`.

The class `SyncTopicSubscriber`, shown in Listing 9-4, illustrates these steps. The function of this class is to receive messages synchronously from a topic until a "stop" message is received. Looking for a "stop" message is necessary because receiving a message from a topic doesn't necessarily remove it from the topic—if other subscribers exist, the message will remain until they receive it.

Listing 9-4: SyncTopicSubscriber.java

```
package bible.jms;

import javax.jms.*;
import javax.naming.*;
import java.util.*;

public class SyncTopicSubscriber {

  public static void main(String[] args) {
    Context ctx = null;
    Hashtable ht = new Hashtable();
    TopicConnectionFactory tConnectionFactory = null;
```

```
      TopicConnection tConnection = null;
      TopicSession tSession = null;
      TopicSubscriber tSubscriber = null;
      Topic t = null;
      TextMessage textMsg = null;
      String msg;

      try {
        // Obtain references to JMS Topic components.
        ht.put(Context.INITIAL_CONTEXT_FACTORY,
               "weblogic.jndi.WLInitialContextFactory");
        ht.put(Context.PROVIDER_URL, "t3://localhost:7001");
        ctx = new InitialContext(ht);
        tConnectionFactory =
          (TopicConnectionFactory)
          ctx.lookup("BibleJMSFactory");
        tConnection =
          tConnectionFactory.createTopicConnection();
        tSession = tConnection.createTopicSession(false,
          javax.jms.TopicSession.AUTO_ACKNOWLEDGE);
        t = (Topic) ctx.lookup("BibleJMSTopic");
        tSubscriber = tSession.createSubscriber(t);

        System.out.println("Receiving messages...");
        tConnection.start();
        textMsg =
          (TextMessage)tSubscriber.receive();
        while (true) {
          msg = textMsg.getText();
          System.out.println("  Receiving message: " + msg);
          if (msg.equals("Stop")) {
            break;
          }
          textMsg = (TextMessage) tSubscriber.receive();
        }
        tConnection.stop();
      }
      catch (Exception e) {
        e.printStackTrace();
      }
      finally {
        try {
          // Release JMS resources.
          tSubscriber.close();
          tSession.close();
          tConnection.close();
        }
        catch (Exception e) {
          e.printStackTrace();
        }
      }
    }
  }
```

After starting WebLogic Server and running `BibleTopicSubscriber.main()`, running `BibleTopicPublisher.main()` causes messages to be published to the topic. The messages are immediately received by `BibleTopicSubscriber`, which displays the following output:

```
Receiving messages...
  Receiving message: Message #1
  Receiving message: Message #2
  Receiving message: Message #3
  Receiving message: Message #4
  Receiving message: Message #5
  Receiving message: Message #6
  Receiving message: Message #7
  Receiving message: Message #8
  Receiving message: Message #9
  Receiving message: Message #10
  Receiving message: Stop
```

The topic is now empty if no durable subscribers registered with the topic, or if there are no active, nondurable subscribers. Otherwise, the messages remain in the topic for delivery to other subscribers.

Notice that in this example I call the blocking version of `receive()` to retrieve messages. This is because a topic, by definition, is initially "empty" to a new subscriber; messages delivered to that topic before the new subscriber comes online are not available to that subscriber. Therefore, you must wait for a subsequent message to arrive before beginning message processing. For this reason, it's almost always better to write asynchronous topic subscribers, which I discuss in the next section.

Receiving messages asynchronously

Receiving messages asynchronously is almost always the preferred approach because it consumes fewer resources, doesn't block threads, and doesn't deadlock WebLogic Server. For this reason, JMS and WebLogic make it very easy to write asynchronous message listeners, and this section shows you how.

Receiving messages asynchronously from a queue

Receiving PTP messages asynchronously is useful for real-time applications that need to process incoming messages as they arrive. A stock trading application, for example, might receive messages about a stock's price movements that would immediately trigger trades in that stock.

To receive PTP messages asynchronously, you must write a class that implements the `javax.jms.MessageListener` interface. This interface defines an `onMessage()` method that is automatically called when a message arrives in the subject queue. The code you write for `onMessage()` defines how you respond to messages arriving in that queue.

Another wrinkle is that the message listener cannot use the same JMS connection factory as code writing to the queue if both are connected to the queue at the same time *and* the connection factory has a nonblank `Client ID`. Doing so leads to a `javax.jms.InvalidClientIDException`, which results in the offending code being disconnected from the queue. To avoid this, either use a connection factory with a blank `Client ID`, or configure a second connection factory for use by the asynchronous queue receiver.

Client IDs are not used with queues anyway—they're designed to support durable subscribers to publish-and-subscribe topics. But I'm alerting you to this issue because you may encounter it someday on a busy server, and unless you know the reason, it can be difficult to troubleshoot.

The class I wrote to receive messages asynchronously is called `bible.jms.AsyncQueueReceiver`, which appears in Listing 9-5. Its `main()` method creates an instance of `AsyncQueueReceiver` and calls its `init()` method to initialize JMS structures and register it as a listener for the queue. Next, `main()` calls `AsyncQueueReceiver.wait()` (inherited from `java.lang.Object`) to suspend execution of its thread. This puts `AsyncQueueReceiver` into a state where it can wait for incoming messages.

Listing 9-5: AsyncQueueReceiver.java

```
package bible.jms;

import javax.jms.*;
import javax.naming.*;
import java.util.*;

public class AsyncQueueReceiver implements MessageListener {

  // Instance variables.
  private boolean finished = false;
  private Context ctx = null;
  private Hashtable ht = null;
  private QueueConnectionFactory qConnectionFactory = null;
  private QueueConnection qConnection = null;
  private QueueSession qSession = null;
  private QueueReceiver qReceiver = null;
  private Queue q = null;

  public void init() {
    try {
      // Obtain references to JMS queue components.
      ht = new Hashtable();
      ht.put(Context.INITIAL_CONTEXT_FACTORY,
           "weblogic.jndi.WLInitialContextFactory");
      ht.put(Context.PROVIDER_URL, "t3://localhost:7001");
```

Continued

Listing 9-5 *(continued)*

```
      ctx = new InitialContext(ht);
      qConnectionFactory = (QueueConnectionFactory)
        ctx.lookup("BibleJMSFactory");
      qConnection =
        qConnectionFactory.createQueueConnection();
      qSession = qConnection.createQueueSession(false,
        javax.jms.QueueSession.AUTO_ACKNOWLEDGE);
      q = (Queue) ctx.lookup("BibleJMSQueue");
      qReceiver = qSession.createReceiver(q);
      qReceiver.setMessageListener(this);
      // Must start the connection in order to listen.
      qConnection.start();
    }
    catch (Exception e) {
      e.printStackTrace();
    }
  }

  public void close()
       throws JMSException
  {
    try {
      // Release JMS resources.
      qReceiver.close();
      qSession.close();
      qConnection.close();
    }
    catch (Exception e) {
      e.printStackTrace();
    }
  }

  public void onMessage(Message message) {
    if (message instanceof BytesMessage) {
      BytesMessage bytesMessage = (BytesMessage) message;
      //Process bytesMessage here
    }
    else {
      if (message instanceof MapMessage) {
        MapMessage mapMessage = (MapMessage) message;
        //Process mapMessage here
      }
      else {
        if (message instanceof ObjectMessage) {
          ObjectMessage objectMessage =
            (ObjectMessage) message;
          //Process objectMessage here
        }
        else {
          if (message instanceof StreamMessage) {
```

```
                StreamMessage streamMessage =
                  (StreamMessage) message;
                //Process streamMessage here
              }
              else {
                if (message instanceof TextMessage) {
                  try {
                    TextMessage textMessage =
                      (TextMessage) message;
                    //Process textMessage here
                    String msg = textMessage.getText();
                    System.out.println("Received message: " +
                                       msg);
                    if (msg.equals("Stop")) {
                      synchronized(this) {
                        finished = true;
                        // Notify main thread to quit
                        this.notifyAll();
                      }
                    }
                  }
                  catch (Exception e) {
                    e.printStackTrace();
                  }
                }
              }
            }
          }
        }
      }

      public static void main(String[] args) {
        try {
          AsyncQueueReceiver qr = new AsyncQueueReceiver();
          qr.init();
          System.out.println("Ready to receive messages....");

          // Receive text messages until one is equal to "Stop"
          synchronized(qr) {
            while (!qr.finished) {
              try {
                qr.wait();
              } catch (InterruptedException ie) {}
            }
          }
          qr.close();
        }
        catch (Exception e) {
          e.printStackTrace();
        }
      }
    }
```

When a message arrives in BibleJMSQueue, JMS invokes AsyncQueueReceiveer.onMessage(), which resumes execution in AsyncQueueReceiver's thread until onMessage() completes. If a TextMessage is received whose contents are "Stop," onMessage() sets the instance variable finished to true, and then calls notifyAll() to awaken the main thread, which closes all JMS connections and quits.

Notice that onMessage() is written to handle incoming messages of any type. It's good programming practice to check incoming message types, so your code will be less likely to break if you change your messaging protocols later.

Receiving messages asynchronously from a topic

The code for receiving pub/sub messages asynchronously is nearly identical to the code for receiving PTP messages asynchronously. The only difference is that topics are substituted for queues. In case you skipped the PTP section, I'll describe the process again.

To receive pub/sub messages asynchronously, you must write a class that implements the javax.jms.MessageListener interface. This interface defines an onMessage() method that is automatically called when a message is published to the topic. The code you write for onMessage() defines how you respond to messages published to the topic.

The class I wrote to receive messages asynchronously is called bible.jms.AsyncTopicSubscriber, which appears in Listing 9-6. Its main() method creates an instance of AsyncTopicSubscriber and calls its init() method to initialize JMS structures and register it as a subscriber to the topic. Next, main() calls AsyncTopicSubscriber.wait() (inherited from java.lang.Object) to suspend execution of its thread. This puts AsyncTopicSubscriber into a state where it can wait for incoming messages.

Listing 9-6: AsyncTopicSubscriber.java

```
package bible.jms;

import javax.jms.*;
import javax.naming.*;
import java.util.*;

public class AsyncTopicSubscriber
  implements MessageListener {

  // Instance variables.
  private boolean finished = false;
  private Context ctx = null;
```

```
private Hashtable ht = null;
private TopicConnectionFactory tConnectionFactory = null;
private TopicConnection tConnection = null;
private TopicSession tSession = null;
private TopicSubscriber tSubscriber = null;
private Topic t = null;

public void init() {
  try {
    // Obtain references to JMS queue components.
    ht = new Hashtable();
    ht.put(Context.INITIAL_CONTEXT_FACTORY,
          "weblogic.jndi.WLInitialContextFactory");
    ht.put(Context.PROVIDER_URL, "t3://localhost:7001");
    ctx = new InitialContext(ht);
    tConnectionFactory =
      (TopicConnectionFactory)
      ctx.lookup("BibleJMSFactory");
    tConnection =
      tConnectionFactory.createTopicConnection();
    tSession = tConnection.createTopicSession(false,
      javax.jms.QueueSession.AUTO_ACKNOWLEDGE);
    t = (Topic) ctx.lookup("BibleJMSTopic");
    tSubscriber = tSession.createSubscriber(t);
    tSubscriber.setMessageListener(this);
    // Must start the connection in order to listen.
    tConnection.start();
  }
  catch (Exception e) {
    e.printStackTrace();
  }
}

public void close() throws JMSException {
  try {
    // Release JMS resources.
    tSubscriber.close();
    tSession.close();
    tConnection.close();
  }
  catch (Exception e) {
    e.printStackTrace();
  }
}

public void onMessage(Message message) {
  if (message instanceof BytesMessage) {
    BytesMessage bytesMessage = (BytesMessage) message;
    //Process bytesMessage here
  }
```

Continued

Listing 9-6 *(continued)*

```
        else {
          if (message instanceof MapMessage) {
            MapMessage mapMessage = (MapMessage) message;
            //Process mapMessage here
          }
    else {
            if (message instanceof ObjectMessage) {
              ObjectMessage objectMessage =
                (ObjectMessage) message;
              //Process objectMessage here
            }
            else {
              if (message instanceof StreamMessage) {
                StreamMessage streamMessage =
                  (StreamMessage) message;
                //Process streamMessage here
              }
              else {
                if (message instanceof TextMessage) {
                  try {
                    TextMessage textMessage =
                      (TextMessage) message;
                    //Process textMessage here
                    String msg = textMessage.getText();
                    System.out.println("Received message: " +
                                       msg);
                    if (msg.equals("Stop")) {
                      synchronized(this) {
                        finished = true;
                        // Notify main thread to quit
                        this.notifyAll();
                      }
                    }
                  }
                  catch (Exception e) {
                    e.printStackTrace();
                  }
                }
              }
            }
          }
        }
      }

      public static void main(String[] args) {
        try {
          AsyncTopicSubscriber ts = new AsyncTopicSubscriber();
```

```
        ts.init();
        System.out.println("Ready to receive messages....");

        // Receive text messages until one is equal to "Stop"
        synchronized(ts) {
          while (!ts.finished) {
            try {
              ts.wait();
            } catch (InterruptedException ie) {}
          }
        }
        ts.close();
      }
      catch (Exception e) {
        e.printStackTrace();
      }
    }
  }
```

When a message is published to `BibleJMSTopic`, JMS invokes `AsyncTopicSubscriber.onMessage()`, which resumes execution in `AsyncTopicSubscriber's` thread until `onMessage()` completes. If a `TextMessage` is received whose contents are "Stop," `onMessage()` sets the instance variable `finished` to `true`, then calls `notifyAll()` to awaken the main thread, which closes all JMS connections and quits.

Notice that `onMessage()` is written to handle incoming messages of any type. It's good programming practice to check incoming message types, so your code will be less likely to break if you change your messaging protocols later.

Receiving from a topic using a multicast session

WebLogic's JMS implementation supports *multicasting*, in which messages are simultaneously delivered to multiple hosts, and then forwarded by these hosts to subscribers. Multicasting provides increased messaging throughput at the expense of reliability, because not all messages are guaranteed to be delivered to all hosts. This makes multicasting useful for applications where large numbers of messages must be delivered to large numbers of recipients, and where the negative impact of lost messages is minor. Multicasting can be used for publish-and-subscribe messaging only.

To receive messages from a topic that participates in a multicast session, simply change the call to create the `TopicSession` as follows:

```
tSession = tConnection.createTopicSession(false,
           WLSession.MULTICAST_NO_ACKNOWLEDGE);
```

Then create a topic subscriber as usual:

```
tSubscriber = tSession.createSubscriber(t);
```

Receiving messages concurrently using session pools

WebLogic session pools provide a convenient way to deploy asynchronous message listeners to WebLogic Server without having to set up and tear down the JMS infrastructure. For each session pool you create, WebLogic allocates a thread and JMS session for the message listener you provide.

Receiving messages by using session pools is identical to receiving messages asynchronously. Simply write a class that implements the `MessageListener` interface, implement the `onMessage()` method, deploy it to the server bound to a session pool, and you're in business. In fact, the `onMessage()` method is *all* you need to write—WebLogic handles the JMS infrastructure for you, so there's no need to obtain server contexts, connections, sessions, or any other JMS structures.

Before using session pools, consider the following caveats:

- ✦ Participants in a session pool consume messages concurrently, so message ordering is not guaranteed.
- ✦ There is no way to predict which participant in a pool will receive any given message, so session pools should be used only for "stateless" conversations, in which the identity of a message's recipient doesn't matter.

Listing 9-7 shows the code for `SessionPoolConsumer.java`, a class that can be used in conjunction with session pools to consume messages for queues or topics.

Listing 9-7: SessionPoolConsumer.java

```
package bible.jms;

import javax.jms.*;

public class SessionPoolConsumer implements MessageListener {

  public void onMessage(Message message) {
    if (message instanceof BytesMessage) {
      BytesMessage bytesMessage = (BytesMessage) message;
      //Process bytesMessage here
    }
    else {
      if (message instanceof MapMessage) {
        MapMessage mapMessage = (MapMessage) message;
        //Process mapMessage here
```

```
        }
        else {
          if (message instanceof ObjectMessage) {
            ObjectMessage objectMessage =
              (ObjectMessage) message;
            //Process objectMessage here
          }
          else {
            if (message instanceof StreamMessage) {
              StreamMessage streamMessage =
                (StreamMessage) message;
              //Process streamMessage here
            }
            else {
              if (message instanceof TextMessage) {
                try {
                  TextMessage textMessage =
                    (TextMessage) message;
                  //Process textMessage here
                  String msg = textMessage.getText();
                  System.out.println("Received message: " +
                                     msg);
                  if (msg.equals("Stop")) {
                    synchronized(this) {
                      finished = true;
                      // Notify main thread to quit
                      this.notifyAll();
                    }
                  }
                }
                catch (Exception e) {
                  e.printStackTrace();
                }
              }
            }
          }
        }
      }
    }
  }
```

Notice that `SessionPoolConsumer` is nothing more than the `onMessage()` method you implemented earlier in both the `AsyncQueueReceiver` and `AsyncTopicSubscriber` classes (Listings 9-5 and 9-6, respectively).

After deploying this class to your WebLogic classpath, the next step is to configure a session pool in the WebLogic Console to which you can bind `SessionPoolConsumer`. To do this, expand the Servers node under JMS in the domain tree, and then expand the node for BibleJMSServer (the server created earlier in this chapter). Click Session Pools, and then click Create a New JMS Session Pool. The session pool configuration screen appears, as shown in Figure 9-15.

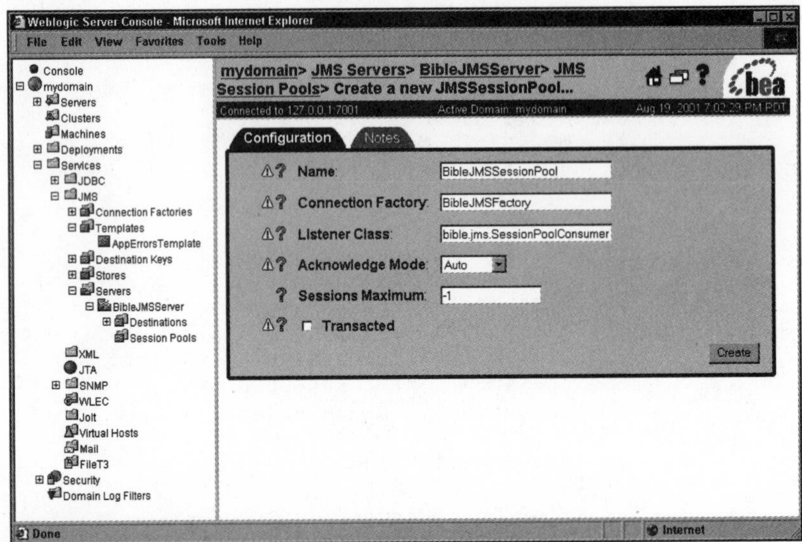

Figure 9-15: Configuring a JMS session pool

The entries on this page are as follows:

✦ **Name:** A name for the session pool, which must conform to the rules for Java identifiers and be unique within the WebLogic Server instance or its cluster. For this example, type **BibleJMSSessionPool**.

✦ **Connection Factory:** The name of a connection factory that has already been defined for the server or cluster. Type **BibleJMSFactory**, the factory you created earlier in this chapter.

✦ **Listener Class:** The fully qualified name of the class that provides the `onMessage()` method for listening on the session. For this example, type **bible.jms.SessionPoolConsumer**, the class shown in Listing 9-7.

You must correctly deploy the listener class to the WebLogic classpath, or creation of the session pool will fail.

✦ **Acknowledge Mode:** The mode you want the session pool to use to acknowledge messages, chosen from the list in Table 9-1. Choose Auto for this example.

✦ **Sessions Maximum:** The maximum number of sessions you want WebLogic to allocate to this session pool. A value of `-1` means no limit, which is fine for this example.

- **Transacted:** Check this box if you want message processing in the session to occur in the context of JMS transactions. For this example, leave the box unchecked.

After completing the configuration screen, click Create.

After you create the session pool, you must create a consumer within that pool that binds the listener class to a queue or topic defined on the server. To do so, expand the pool you just created in the domain tree, and then click Consumers. Click Create a New JMS Connection Consumer at the top of the page; the configuration screen shown in Figure 9-16 appears:

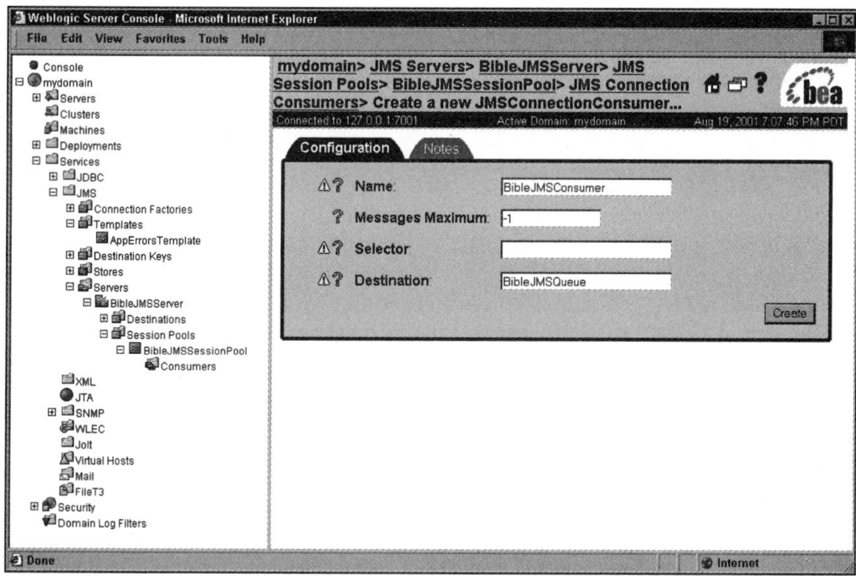

Figure 9-16: Configuring a connection consumer for a session pool

The entries on this page are as follows:

- **Name:** A name for the connection consumer, which must conform to the rules for Java identifiers and be unique within the WebLogic Server instance or its cluster. For the example, type **BibleJMSConsumer**.
- **Messages Maximum:** The maximum number of messages you want this consumer to manage. A value of `-1` means no limit, which is fine for this example.
- **Selector:** A valid message selector statement used to filter messages. For more details, see the next section in this chapter, "Filtering incoming messages."
- **Destination:** The queue or topic, already defined on your WebLogic Server, to which the message listener should be bound. For this example, type **BibleJMSQueue**, the queue you defined earlier in this chapter.

After completing the configuration screen, click Create. The session pool is now ready for use. In this example, sending messages to `BibleJMSQueue` with the `BibleQueueSender` class you wrote earlier (Listing 9-1) results in the session pool writing the following output to the WebLogic command window:

```
Receiving messages...
  Receiving message: Message #1
  Receiving message: Message #2
  Receiving message: Message #3
  Receiving message: Message #4
  Receiving message: Message #5
  Receiving message: Message #6
  Receiving message: Message #7
  Receiving message: Message #8
  Receiving message: Message #9
  Receiving message: Message #10
  Receiving message: Stop
```

Filtering incoming messages

By default, a queue receiver or a topic subscriber retrieves all incoming messages on a queue or topic. But you may want to filter messages based on various criteria to accomplish certain tasks. You may, for example, want to write an asynchronous queue receiver or topic subscriber that immediately acts on log messages with high severity, leaving the rest in the queue for overnight batch processing.

To activate a filter, you specify a *message selector* when you create the queue receiver or topic subscriber. A message selector is a conditional expression, written using SQL-92 syntax and stored in a `String`, which JMS applies to incoming messages in the queue or topic. The message selector is compared against the properties of incoming messages. Therefore, to use message selectors, you must set the properties in your messages to known values.

To understand how message selectors work, recall the code from `BibleQueueSender` (Listing 9-1) that set an `int` property called `severity` for each message to the value of the `for` loop counter. The property is also set to zero for the “stop” message:

```
for (int i=1; i<=10; i++) {
  msg = "Message #" + i;
  textMsg.clearBody();
  textMsg.setIntProperty("severity", i);
  textMsg.setText(msg);
  System.out.println("  Sending message: " + msg);
  qSender.send(textMsg);
}
msg = "Stop";
textMsg.clearBody();
textMsg.setIntProperty("severity", 0);
```

```
textMsg.setText(msg);
System.out.println("  Sending message: " + msg);
qSender.send(textMsg);
```

You can filter this property by using a message selector. To include only messages with severity less than 5, for example, I can modify SyncQueueReceiver (Listing 9-3) by creating a queue receiver with the appropriate message selector attached:

```
qReceiver = qSession.createReceiver(q, "severity < 5");
```

This results in the following output from SyncQueueReceiver:

```
Receiving messages...
  Receiving message: Message #1
  Receiving message: Message #2
  Receiving message: Message #3
  Receiving message: Message #4
  Receiving message: Stop
```

Consider a few more examples of message selectors. To select messages whose severity is between 3 and 7 inclusive, write a message selector like this:

```
"severity >= 3 and severity <= 7"
```

Or, equivalently:

```
"severity between 3 and 7"
```

To select messages whose severity is equal to 7 or 9, write this:

```
"severity = 7 or severity = 9"
```

If you're filtering on String properties, note that strings are enclosed in single quotes and are case-sensitive, as in:

```
"strProperty = 'hello world'"
```

To select messages containing the string pattern #3, write this:

```
"strProperty like '%#3%'"
```

You can find additional message selector examples in the WebLogic manual, *Developing a WebLogic JMS Application,* which is part of the WebLogic documentation set.

Just as queue receivers can filter incoming messages on their queues, topic subscribers can filter incoming messages on their topics, using the same mechanism. The only exception is that the filter is applied when creating the topic subscriber:

```
tSubscriber =
  tSession.createSubscriber(t, "severity < 5", true);
```

The variant of `TopicSession.createSubscriber()` used in this code also requires a Boolean value specifying whether to exclude locally generated messages from the topic (messages published to the topic by the subscriber). If `noLocal` is `true`, locally generated messages are excluded.

Browsing messages in a queue

When a `QueueReceiver` receives messages from a queue, it removes them from the queue. In some cases, however, it might be convenient to examine a queue's contents *before* receiving messages, perhaps to allow a user to interactively choose which messages to remove and when. JMS provides two methods in the `QueueSession` interface for this purpose:

```
public QueueBrowser createBrowser(Queue queue)
                               throws JMSException

public QueueBrowser createBrowser(Queue queue,
                               java.lang.String messageSelector)
                               throws JMSException
```

The first version of `createBrowser` takes a `Queue` as input and returns a `java.util.Enumeration` listing the messages in that queue, in the order in which they will be delivered. The second version takes a `Queue` and a `String` as input, allowing you to filter the browse results with a message selector. Both methods return a snapshot of the queue at moment of the method call. If you expect the queue has changed and you want to update the browse list, you must call `createBrowser` again. Neither method removes messages from the queue.

Listing 9-8 contains a simple class, `BrowseQueue`, to browse a queue. It provides no message selector, so it simply prints all messages in the queue to standard output.

Listing 9-8: BrowseQueue.java

```
package bible.jms;

import javax.jms.*;
import javax.naming.*;
import java.util.*;

public class BrowseQueue {

  public static void main(String[] args) {
    Context ctx = null;
    Hashtable ht = new Hashtable();
    QueueConnectionFactory qConnectionFactory = null;
    QueueConnection qConnection = null;
    QueueSession qSession = null;
    QueueBrowser qBrowser = null;
```

```
      Queue q = null;
      TextMessage textMsg = null;
      String msg;

      try {
        // Obtain references to JMS queue components.
        ht.put(Context.INITIAL_CONTEXT_FACTORY,
               "weblogic.jndi.WLInitialContextFactory");
        ht.put(Context.PROVIDER_URL, "t3://localhost:7001");
        ctx = new InitialContext(ht);
        qConnectionFactory =
          (QueueConnectionFactory)
          ctx.lookup("BibleJMSFactory");
        qConnection =
          qConnectionFactory.createQueueConnection();
        qSession = qConnection.createQueueSession(false,
          javax.jms.QueueSession.AUTO_ACKNOWLEDGE);
        q = (Queue) ctx.lookup("BibleJMSQueue");
        qBrowser = qSession.createBrowser(q);

        System.out.println("Browsing messages...");
        Enumeration enum = qBrowser.getEnumeration();
        while (enum.hasMoreElements()) {
          textMsg = (TextMessage) enum.nextElement();
          System.out.println("    " + textMsg.getText());
        }
      }
      catch (Exception e) {
        e.printStackTrace();
      }
      finally {
        try {
          // Release JMS resources.
          qBrowser.close();
          qSession.close();
          qConnection.close();
        }
        catch (Exception e) {
          e.printStackTrace();
        }
      }
    }
  }
```

The resulting output is:

```
Browsing messages...
    Message #2
    Message #3
    Message #4
```

```
        Message #5
        Message #6
        Message #7
        Message #8
        Message #9
        Message #10
        Stop
```

To filter the results, simply modify the line that creates the `QueueBrowser` as follows:

```
qBrowser = qSession.createBrowser(q, "severity > 8");
```

This changes the output to the following:

```
Browsing messages...
    Message #9
    Message #10
```

Browsing is available only for queues. You cannot browse the contents of a publish-subscribe topic.

Creating durable subscribers to topics

Recall that messages are delivered to topic subscribers only when subscribers are actively listening for messages. If a subscriber quits and restarts later, messages published in the interim are never delivered to that subscriber. Such a subscriber is called a nondurable subscriber, and is the default subscriber type in JMS.

You can, however, create a subscriber that receives all messages published to a topic, even if the subscriber is not actively listening when the messages are sent. Such a subscriber is called a durable subscriber. Durable subscribers receive all messages posted to a topic *after* the subscriber's initial registration with the topic.

The "preferred" way to support durable subscriptions is to configure WebLogic JMS as follows:

1. Specify a connection factory with a defined `Client ID` for each durable subscriber. The `Client ID`, a `String`, must be unique within the WebLogic server or cluster in which it resides. For information on how to do this, see the section, "Creating a connection factory," which appears earlier in this chapter.
2. Define a file or JDBC backing store to hold undelivered messages. Instructions for doing so appear earlier in this chapter in the sections, "Defining a file backing store" and "Defining a JDBC backing store."
3. Define a JMS server that uses the backing store you create. Instructions for doing so appear earlier in this chapter in the section, "Defining a JMS server."
4. Define a message topic for which `Enable Store` is `true`. Instructions for doing so appear earlier in this chapter in the section, "Creating a message topic."

After you configure JMS for durable subscribers, call one of the following `TopicSession` methods to create a durable subscriber:

```
public TopicSubscriber createDurableSubscriber(
  Topic topic,
  String name) throws JMSException

public TopicSubscriber createDurableSubscriber)
  Topic topic,
  String name,
  String messageSelector,
  boolean noLocal) throws JMSException
```

Where `myTopic` is a reference to the appropriate `Topic`, `myName` is a `String` that is unique for the given `Client ID`, `messageSelector` is a valid filter expression, and `noLocal` is `true` if the subscriber should not receive messages it publishes itself.

You can also support durable subscriptions by dynamically setting a `Client ID` for the subscriber in code, without reconfiguring JMS. To do so, you must call the following `TopicConnection` method immediately after creating a connection:

```
public void setClientID(String clientID) throws JMSException
```

Problems may arise if you specify a `Client ID` that is already in use, or if two blocks of code are trying to specify the same `Client ID` at the same time. In the latter case, `setClientID` will not throw a connection, but the durable subscriber will not work. To avoid this, test for a duplicate `Client ID` by first calling `TopicConnection.getClientID()`:

```
public String getClientID() throws JMSException
```

Working with Transactions

Transactions enable you to send and receive messages in logical groups that represent units of work. Committing a group of messages results in all messages being sent or received, while rolling back a group of messages results in none of them being sent or received.

JMS sessions that manage transactions are called JMS transacted sessions. WebLogic also supports transactions that span JMS and other components, such as EJBs. The Java Transaction API (JTA) manages these transactions.

Chapter 6 covers JTA.

Working with JMS transacted sessions

The first step in working with JMS transacted sessions is to make sure that the connection factory you intend to use has a transaction timeout period long enough to support the expected maximum length of your transactions. This parameter is set in the WebLogic Console page for the connection factory, under the `Transactions` tab, as shown in Figure 9-17:

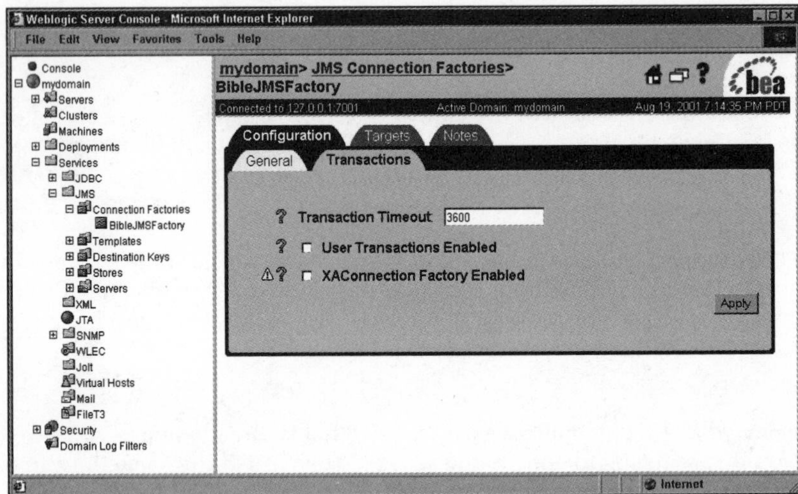

Figure 9-17: Configuring the transaction timeout for JMS transacted sessions

By default, a connection factory's `Transaction Timeout` is set to 3600 seconds (one hour). This should be more than long enough for most applications. If a transaction is held open beyond the timeout period, JMS automatically rolls it back.

The User Transactions Enabled check box makes the connection factory JTA-aware. Leave it unchecked for now; I discuss JTA transactions in the next section.

To use a JMS transacted session, you simply set the `transacted` Boolean variable to `true` when you create a `QueueSession` or `TopicSession`:

```
qSession = qConnection.createQueueSession(true,
           javax.jms.QueueSession.AUTO_ACKNOWLEDGE);

tSession = tConnection.createTopicSession(true,
           javax.jms.TopicSession.AUTO_ACKNOWLEDGE);
```

Recall that `ACKNOWLEDGE_MODE` is ignored for transacted sessions, so the value you provide (in this case, `AUTO_ACKNOWLEDGE`) doesn't matter.

The following code snippet, adapted from `BibleQueueSender.java` (Listing 9-1), illustrates how to create a JMS transacted session, and how to commit and roll back transactions:

```
qSession = qConnection.createQueueSession(true,
           javax.jms.QueueSession.AUTO_ACKNOWLEDGE);
q = (Queue) ctx.lookup("BibleJMSQueue");
qSender = qSession.createSender(q);

System.out.println("Sending messages...");
textMsg = qSession.createTextMessage();
for (int i=1; i<=10; i++) {
  msg = "Message #" + i;
  textMsg.clearBody();
  textMsg.setIntProperty("severity", i);
  textMsg.setText(msg);
  System.out.println("  Sending message: " + msg);
  qSender.send(textMsg);
}
// Cancel the 10 messages sent so far.
qSession.rollback();
msg = "Stop";
textMsg.clearBody();
textMsg.setText(msg);
textMsg.setIntProperty("severity", 0);
System.out.println("  Sending message: " + msg);
qSender.send(textMsg);
// Commit the "Stop" message.
qSession.commit();
```

The result of this code is that the ten messages sent in the `for` loop will not be sent, but the "stop" message will. The output from running this program is therefore the following:

```
Receiving messages...
  Receiving message: Stop
```

Note that JMS transactions execute back-to-back; transaction boundaries are set by calls to `commit()` and `rollback()`. These calls also reset the transaction timeout counter for the active session. The first transaction in a program, however, is implicitly made active when the transacted session is created.

Working with JTA transactions

The Java Transaction API (JTA) supports transactions spanning multiple data sources. You can use JTA, for example, to manage a transaction that involves receiving a JMS message, writing a row to a JDBC database, invoking a method in an EJB, and then sending a different JMS message elsewhere. If all four operations succeed, the transaction is committed; otherwise, it is rolled back, and the effects of the operations are reversed as if they never happened.

JTA and JMS transactions are independent of each other and do not cooperate in any way. The effects of JMS transactions are ignored by JTA, and vice versa. Also, JTA transactions work only within the context of synchronous messaging; asynchronous message listeners cannot participate in JTA transactions, unless they are implemented by using message-driven EJBs.

Chapter 17 covers using JTA with message-driven EJBs.

Consider an example where an online brokerage client wishes to purchase 1000 shares of BEA stock. The client enters his order on the brokerage's Web site, which causes a message to be written to an order queue. After the market closes, a Java application settles the transaction by performing these steps:

1. Initiates a JTA transaction.
2. Retrieves the client's purchase order synchronously from the queue.
3. Calculates the amount of cash required to purchase the stock.
4. Retrieves the client's cash account balance from an account database.
5. If the client has enough cash for the purchase, deducts the amount required from the account database. If not, it throws an insufficient funds exception.
6. Adds the shares purchased to the client's portfolio database. If this operation fails for any reason, it throws an exception.
7. If no exceptions were thrown, it commits the transaction. Otherwise, it rolls back the transaction, and the effects the above operations are reversed.

Listing 9-9 is `ClientHandler.java`, an application that performs the preceding tasks. The `main()` method starts by loading `BibleJMSQueue` with a "test" trade. Then it initiates a JTA transaction, within which it removes the trade from the queue, updates the client's account data in Oracle, and updates the client's portfolio in Oracle. If all operations succeed, it commits the transaction. Otherwise, it rolls back the transaction, which has the following effects:

1. JMS returns the trade to the queue.
2. Oracle reverses the update to the account data.
3. Oracle reverses the update to the portfolio data.

Listing 9-9: ClientHandler.java

```
package bible.jms;

import java.util.*;
import java.sql.*;
import javax.jms.*;
```

```
import javax.naming.*;
import javax.transaction.UserTransaction;

public class ClientHandler {

  // Unique client ID for
  // database operations
  private String clientID = null;

  // Data structure describing a trade
  private class Trade {
    String clientID = null;
    String side = null;
    String ticker = null;
    int shares = 0;
    double sharePrice = 0.0;
  }

  public ClientHandler() {
  }

  public ClientHandler(String id) {
    clientID = id;
  }

  // Get the WebLogic server's context
  public Context getServerContext() {
    Context ctx = null;
    Hashtable ht = new Hashtable();
    ht.put(Context.INITIAL_CONTEXT_FACTORY,
      "weblogic.jndi.WLInitialContextFactory");
    ht.put(Context.PROVIDER_URL,
      "t3://localhost:7001");

    try {
      ctx = new InitialContext(ht);
    }
    catch (NamingException e) {
      e.printStackTrace();
    }
    finally {
      return ctx;
    }
  }

  // Load the queue with a single trade:
  // BUY 1000 shares BEAS at $30/share
  public void loadQueue() {
    Context ctx = null;
    QueueConnectionFactory qConnectionFactory = null;
    QueueConnection qConnection = null;
    QueueSession qSession = null;
```

Continued

Listing 9-9 *(continued)*

```
QueueSender qSender = null;
Queue q = null;
TextMessage textMsg = null;

try {
  // Obtain references to JMS structures
  qConnectionFactory =
    (QueueConnectionFactory)
    getServerContext().lookup("BibleJMSFactory");
  qConnection =
    qConnectionFactory.createQueueConnection();
  qSession = qConnection.createQueueSession(false,
    javax.jms.QueueSession.AUTO_ACKNOWLEDGE);
  q = (Queue) getServerContext().lookup("BibleJMSQueue");
  qSender = qSession.createSender(q);
  textMsg = qSession.createTextMessage();

  // Pass a human-readable trade summary
  // in the message's body
  textMsg.clearBody();
  textMsg.setText("BUY 1000 BEAS 30.0");

  // Pass essential trade data in
  // user-defined message properties
  textMsg.setStringProperty("client_id", clientID);
  textMsg.setStringProperty("side", "BUY");
  textMsg.setStringProperty("ticker", "BEAS");
  textMsg.setIntProperty("shares", 1000);
  textMsg.setDoubleProperty("sharePrice", 30.0);

  // Send the message
  qSender.send(textMsg);
}
catch (Exception e) {
  e.printStackTrace();
}
finally {
  try {
    if (qSender != null) {
      qSender.close();
    }
    if (qSession != null) {
      qSession.close();
    }
    if (qConnection != null) {
      qConnection.close();
    }
  }
  catch (Exception e) {
  }
```

```
    }
  }

  // Synchronously read a single trade from
  // the queue for the given client
  public Trade getNextTrade() throws Exception {
    QueueConnectionFactory qConnectionFactory = null;
    QueueConnection qConnection = null;
    QueueSession qSession = null;
    QueueReceiver qReceiver = null;
    Queue q = null;
    Trade trade = null;

    try {
      // Obtain references to JMS structures
      qConnectionFactory =
        (QueueConnectionFactory)
        getServerContext().lookup("BibleJMSFactory");
      qConnection =
       qConnectionFactory.createQueueConnection();
      qSession = qConnection.createQueueSession(false,
        javax.jms.QueueSession.AUTO_ACKNOWLEDGE);
      q = (Queue) getServerContext().lookup("BibleJMSQueue");

      // Note the use of a message filter - we
      // only want the next trade for the client
      // represented by this ClientHandler instance
      qReceiver = qSession.createReceiver(q,
        "client_id = '" + clientID + "'");

      // Start the connection
      qConnection.start();

      // Grab the next trade, if there is one,
      // and copy its data from the message
      // properties to a Trade data structure
      TextMessage textMsg =
        (TextMessage) qReceiver.receiveNoWait();
      if (textMsg != null) {
        trade = new Trade();
        trade.clientID = clientID;
        trade.side = textMsg.getStringProperty("side");
        trade.ticker = textMsg.getStringProperty("ticker");
        trade.shares = textMsg.getIntProperty("shares");
        trade.sharePrice =
          textMsg.getDoubleProperty("sharePrice");
      }

      // Stop the connection
      qConnection.stop();
    }
```

Continued

Listing 9-9 (continued)

```
      catch (Exception e) {
        throw e;
      }
      finally {
        try {
          if (qReceiver != null) {
            qReceiver.close();
          }
          if (qSession != null) {
            qSession.close();
          }
          if (qConnection != null) {
            qConnection.close();
          }
        }
        catch (Exception e) {
        }
        return trade;
      }
    }

    // Update the cash balance remaining in
    // the client's account. Account data is
    // stored in an Oracle table. For simplicity,
    // this code handles BUY transactions only.
    public void updateAccountBalance(Trade trade)
    throws Exception {
      javax.sql.DataSource ds = null;
      java.sql.Connection conn = null;
      PreparedStatement statement1 = null;
      PreparedStatement statement2 = null;
      String sql = null;
      double balance = 0.0;

      try {
        // Obtain a JDBC connection from a transaction-enabled
        // DataSource. I'm using the Oracle OCI driver
        // with two-phase commit enabled, rather than
        // the Oracle XA driver.
        ds = (javax.sql.DataSource)
          getServerContext().lookup("OracleTxDataSource");
        conn = ds.getConnection();

        // Execute a query to obtain the client's current
        // account balance from the database.
        sql = "SELECT BALANCE FROM ACCOUNT " +
              "WHERE CLIENT_ID = ?";
        statement1 = conn.prepareStatement(sql);
        statement1.setString(1, clientID);
        ResultSet resultSet = statement1.executeQuery();
        if (resultSet.next()) {
```

```
          balance = resultSet.getDouble(1);
        } else {
          Exception ex = new Exception("No such account");
          throw ex;
        }

        // Calculate the cash required to buy the stock
        double cost = trade.sharePrice * trade.shares;

        // If the client has enough money, deduct the
        // cost from their account balance and update
        // their account in the database.
        if (balance > cost) {
          balance -= cost;
          sql = "UPDATE ACCOUNT SET BALANCE = ? " +
                "WHERE CLIENT_ID = ?";
          statement2 = conn.prepareStatement(sql);
          statement2.setDouble(1, balance);
          statement2.setString(2, clientID);
          if (statement2.executeUpdate() != 1) {
            Exception ex =
              new Exception("Error updating account balance");
            throw ex;
          }
        } else {
          Exception ex = new Exception("Insufficient funds");
          throw ex;
        }

      }
      catch (Exception e) {
        e.printStackTrace();
        throw e;
      }
      finally {
        statement1.close();
        statement2.close();
        conn.close();
      }
    }

    // Add an entry for stock purchased to
    // the client's portfolio, which is stored
    // in an Oracle table.
    public void updatePortfolio(Trade trade) throws Exception {
      javax.sql.DataSource ds = null;
      java.sql.Connection conn = null;
      PreparedStatement statement = null;
      String sql = null;

      try {
        // Obtain a JDBC connection from a transaction-enabled
```

Continued

Listing 9-9 (continued)

```
      // DataSource. I'm using the Oracle OCI driver
      // with two-phase commit enabled, rather than
      // the Oracle XA driver.
      ds = (javax.sql.DataSource)
        getServerContext().lookup("OracleTxDataSource");
      conn = ds.getConnection();

      // Execute a query to insert the client's stock
      // purchase into the portfolio table.
      sql = "INSERT INTO PORTFOLIO " +
            "(CLIENT_ID, SIDE, TICKER, SHARES, PRICE) " +
            "VALUES (?, ?, ?, ?, ?)";
      statement = conn.prepareStatement(sql);
      statement.setString(1, clientID);
      statement.setString(2, trade.side);
      statement.setString(3, trade.ticker);
      statement.setInt(4, trade.shares);
      statement.setDouble(5, trade.sharePrice);
      if (statement.executeUpdate() != 1) {
        Exception ex =
          new Exception("Error updating client's portfolio");
        throw ex;
      }
    }
    catch (Exception e) {
      e.printStackTrace();
      throw e;
    }
    finally {
      statement.close();
      conn.close();
    }
  }

  // Method to test our example
  public static void main(String[] args) {

    UserTransaction tx = null;

    try {
      // Create a ClientHandler instance for fictitious
      // customer "joe." Load the queue with a hard-coded
      // trade for this client.
      ClientHandler ch = new ClientHandler("joe");
      ch.loadQueue();

      // Obtain a reference to WebLogic Server's context.
      // Use it to perform a JNDI lookup on the server's
      // UserTransaction object.
```

```
          Context ctx = ch.getServerContext();
          tx = (UserTransaction)
            ctx.lookup("javax.transaction.UserTransaction");

          // Begin the transaction
          tx.begin();
          // Grab the trade from the message queue
          Trade trade = ch.getNextTrade();
          // Update the client's account balance
          ch.updateAccountBalance(trade);
          // Update the client's portfolio
          ch.updatePortfolio(trade);
          // If no exceptions, commit the transaction
          tx.commit();
        }
        catch (Exception e) {
          try {
            // Something went wrong... roll back
            // the transaction
            tx.rollback();
          }
          catch (Exception ee) {
            ee.printStackTrace();
          }
        }
      }
    }
```

Listing 9-10 shows the simple tables I added to Oracle's SCOTT schema to support the example.

Listing 9-10: Trading System Table Definitions

```
CREATE TABLE SCOTT.ACCOUNT
(
    CLIENT_ID VARCHAR2(10) NOT NULL,
    BALANCE   NUMBER(10,2)     NULL
);

CREATE TABLE SCOTT.PORTFOLIO
(
    CLIENT_ID VARCHAR2(10) NOT NULL,
    SIDE      CHAR(4)          NULL,
    TICKER    VARCHAR2(10)     NULL,
    SHARES    NUMBER(10)       NULL,
    PRICE     NUMBER(10,2)     NULL
);
```

To connect to the database in a transaction-enabled mode, I created a JDBC connection pool with the following properties:

```
Pool Name = OraclePool
URL = jdbc:weblogic:oracle:JOEVAIO.ZEEWARE.COM
Driver Classname = weblogic.jdbc.oci.Driver
Properties
  user=SCOTT
  password=tiger
  serverName=JOEVAIO.ZEEWARE.COM
Connections
  Initial Capacity = 4
  Maximum Capacity = 10
  Capacity Increment = 2
  Login Delay Seconds = 0
  Refresh Period = 15 minutes
  Allow Shrinking = true
  Shrink Period = 15 minutes
Testing
  Test Table Name = dual
  Test Reserved Connections = false
  Test Released Connections = false
Targets
  Chosen = myserver
```

I also created a `TxDataSource` with these properties:

```
Name = OracleTxDataSource
JNDI Name = OracleTxDataSource
Pool Name = OraclePool
Enable Two-Phase Commit = true
Targets
  Chosen = myserver
```

See Chapter 5 for more information on configuring JDBC connection pools and transaction-enabled data sources.

Finally, I made sure that my JMS connection factory, `BibleJMSFactory`, was JTA-enabled. To do so, I edited the factory in the WebLogic Console. On the factory's Transaction tab is a check box, `User Transactions Enabled`, which I checked, as shown in Figure 9-18.

Study Listing 9-9 carefully. It's well commented, and gives a good, real-world example of JMS and JDBC in action in a transacted environment. Considering the incredible amount of work that is being done (messaging and database operations controlled by a transaction manager using two-phase commit), the amount of code required is very small . . . yet another testament to the power of WebLogic and J2EE.

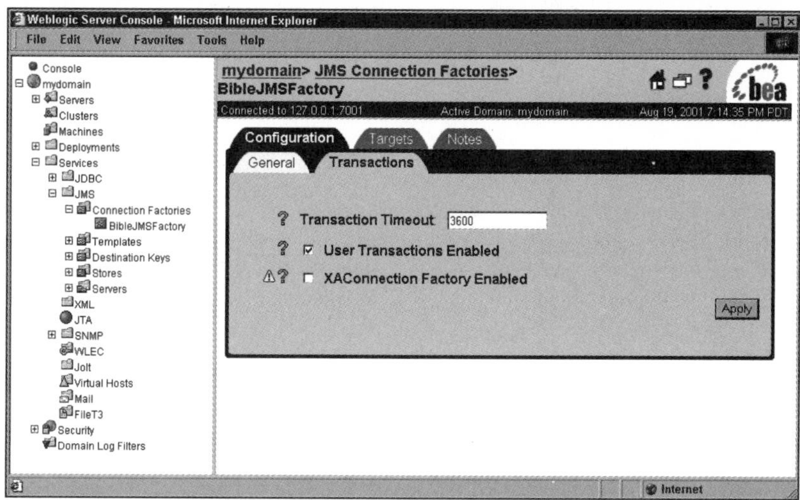

Figure 9-18: A JMS connection factory with user transactions enabled

Summary

WebLogic JMS is a powerful messaging system that enables you to build flexible communications into your distributed applications. WebLogic JMS supports two messaging models: point-to-point (using queues), and publish-subscribe (using topics). Within each mode, you can easily send many types of messages, as well as receive them either synchronously or asynchronously.

Although JMS code is easy to write, the WebLogic JMS infrastructure requires a fair amount of configuration before it can be used. Fortunately, the WebLogic Console provides an intuitive interface for performing the multitude of configuration tasks, which this chapter has shown you how to do in significant detail.

JMS derives a significant amount of its power from its integration with the rest of J2EE. Foremost in this regard is the ability of JMS to participate in transactions that incorporate messaging, database operations (using JDBC), and business logic (using EJBs). The JMS transactional abilities, which result from its seamless integration with the Java Transaction API (JTA), allow developers to incorporate messaging into robust, fault-tolerant applications that work with a multitude of enterprise data sources.

✦ ✦ ✦

Working with WebLogic JavaMail

✦ ✦ ✦ ✦

In This Chapter

Understanding JavaMail

Configuring WebLogic JavaMail

Sending messages with WebLogic JavaMail

Navigating stores with WebLogic JavaMail

Retrieving and displaying messages with WebLogic JavaMail

✦ ✦ ✦ ✦

The JavaMail API provides interfaces and abstract classes that developers can use to write functionally complete mail clients by using a variety of mail transfer protocols. Sun and third-party vendors have extended the API to provide protocol-specific implementations.

In the first half of this chapter, I provide an overview of the JavaMail architecture and show you how to configure WebLogic JavaMail for various protocols. In the second half of the chapter, I provide several code examples showing how to send mail via SMTP, navigate folders, and receive mail via IMAP or POP3.

Understanding JavaMail

In this section, I explain JavaMail's organization, architecture, and features. A firm understanding of these concepts makes programming JavaMail much easier.

JavaMail versions and packages

WebLogic 6.1 runs on top of JDK 1.3, and `weblogic.jar` contains JavaMail version 1.1.3. But JavaMail 1.2 is the latest version supported by Sun. JavaMail 1.1.3 includes support for SMTP and IMAP (discussed later in this chapter), while JavaMail 1.2 also supports POP3. You can download JavaMail 1.2 from the Sun Web site, and then insert it into your classpath ahead of `weblogic.jar` to suppress the 1.1.3 API. Instructions for doing so appear later in this chapter, in the section "Configuring WebLogic JavaMail."

The intention of the Sun JavaMail specification is to describe a generic interface for mail network servers regardless of the mail protocol used by that server. The API is not a mail server application, but rather a Java interface to network mail servers that support SMTP, IMAP, and POP.

JavaMail is implemented in the following packages:

- `javax.mail`, which contains the first part of the JavaMail API and provides abstract implementations of addresses, messages, parts, stores, transports, and related classes.
- `javax.mail.internet`, which contains the remainder of the JavaMail API and provides abstract implementations of Internet addresses and MIME messages and body parts.

JavaMail also requires the `javax.activation` package, which contains the JavaBeans Activation Framework (JAF), to handle access to data based on data type, and to facilitate the addition of data types and commands on those data types. The JavaMail API provides convenience functions to simplify these coding tasks.

You can find the JavaMail 1.2 specification, API, and tutorial on the Sun Web site at `http://java.sun.com/products/javamail/index.html`. You can find more information about the JavaBeans Activation Framework at `http://java.sun.com/products/javabeans/glasgow/jaf.html`.

JavaMail architecture

JavaMail has a multilayered architecture, as shown in Figure 10-1.

Mail-handling functions are provided in the abstract layer interfaces, abstract, and concrete classes. You can extend mail-handling functions as necessary in order to support standard data types, and to interface with message access and message transport protocols.

RFC822 and MIME Internet standards are implemented as part of the abstract layer. The JAF is used to encapsulate message data and to handle commands intended to interact with message data.

Service providers implement the JavaMail API, which in turn is utilized by a JavaMail client. The layered design architecture enables clients to use the same JavaMail API calls to send, receive, and store a variety of messages by using different data types from different message stores and by using different message transport protocols.

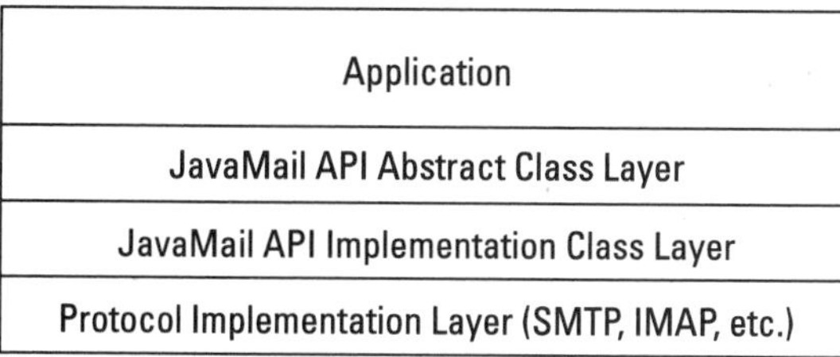

Figure 10-1: The JavaMail architecture

Mail protocols

Three major protocols are used to send mail messages around the Internet: SMTP, POP, and IMAP. Although other protocols exist, these three are the most commonly used, and therefore the focus of this chapter.

- *SMTP* stands for *Simple Mail Transfer Protocol,* and is the protocol used by mail servers to send messages to each other. It is also used by mail clients to send messages to mail servers. When you send a mail message, it travels first from your mail client to your mail server. From there, it is sent to one or more destination mail servers, depending on the number of recipients and the configurations of the mail servers involved.
- *POP* stands for *Post Office Protocol,* and is used by mail clients to retrieve incoming messages from mail servers. Two versions of POP exist. The first is POP2, which emerged in the mid-1980s and requires SMTP to function. The second is POP3, which became widespread in the 1990s and can function with or without SMTP. POP3 is used almost exclusively by POP clients today.
- *IMAP* means *Internet Message Access Protocol.* Like POP, IMAP is used by mail clients to retrieve messages from servers. The latest version, IMAP4, is similar to POP3, but it includes additional features that allow you to inspect messages on the server before downloading them to the client.

JavaMail services, transports, and stores

The JavaMail API represents mail protocols as services, transports, and stores. Classes representing these entities are used to send and receive messages. The abstract class `javax.mail.Service` is at the top of the hierarchy, and is extended by `javax.mail.Transport` and `javax.mail.Store`.

The `javax.mail.Transport` class is used to send messages. The `Transport` class included in the Sun JavaMail distribution is a fully functional SMTP implementation, and is the class you will almost always use to send messages.

The `javax.mail.Store` class is used to retrieve messages. JavaMail 1.1.3 contains a `Store` class that implements IMAP4, while JavaMail 1.2 contains a `Store` class that implements both IMAP4 and POP3.

Messages

Figure 10-2 shows the relationships among the classes and interfaces that comprise JavaMail messages.

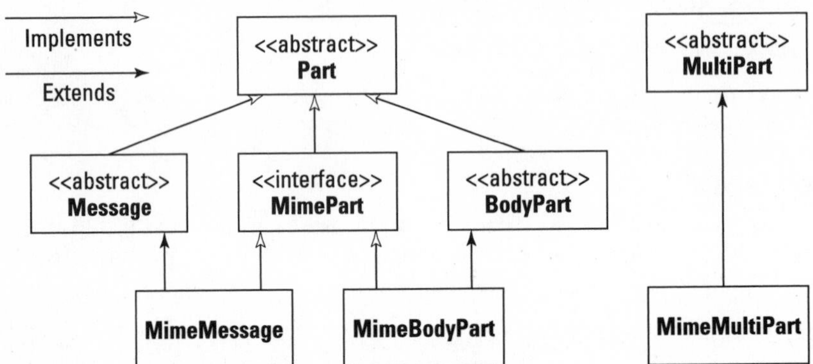

Figure 10-2: The relationships among JavaMail's Part Interfaces and Message classes

At the core of JavaMail are `Message`, `BodyPart` and `Multipart` objects. `Message` objects can be simple, containing only header information and content, or more complex, with a nested set of `Multipart` and `BodyPart` objects to support nested messages or multiple enclosures.

The `Message` class is an abstract class that implements the `Part` interface. It declares content and attributes of a message. Subclasses of the `Message` class implement several standard message formats such as the `MimeMessage` class, which implements the RFC822 and MIME standards.

A `Message` object declares message content, addresses for the sender and the recipients, structural information about the message, and the content type of the message body. `Message` objects also contain a set of flags that describe the state of the message within the folder. A `DataHandler` object contains the actual content data.

The `BodyPart` class is an abstract class that implements the `Part` interface. It is intended to be stored as part of a `Multipart` container; therefore, it only declares attributes and content. The class does not declare addressing header information, as a `Message` object does. Because a `BodyPart` object is an instantiation of the `Part` interface, it can contain either a new `Multipart` object or a `DataHandler` object.

The `Multipart` class is an abstract class that extends `java.lang.Object`. A `Multipart` object is a container class that holds multiple `BodyPart` objects. It provides methods to retrieve and set its subparts.

The JavaMail API documentation has multiple examples of how to create messages implementing this structure. To understand one way, an example later in the chapter uses a `MimeMessage` object with a `MimeMultiPart` object as its content. The `MimeMultiPart` object will contain multiple `MimeBodyPart` objects, the first holding message text and the second holding an enclosure.

Folders

Folders are where mail messages are stored, either on the mail server or on the client's device. They are similar to file system directories in that they are hierarchical in structure. A folder may contain messages or other folders. The default folder is the parent folder in the structure. A special folder named INBOX exists as a child of the default folder and is the recipient of incoming messages. To read incoming mail, you establish a connection, get the store from the session, get the default folder from the store, and then get the INBOX folder from the default folder.

An IMAP mail server stores message folders directly on the mail server, including folders that contain incoming messages and archived messages. A POP3 mail server only provides a folder for incoming messages. It's the mail client's responsibility to retrieve the messages and transfer them to a message store via WebLogic Server, possibly using a database or file system to represent folders.

Figure 10-3 is a diagram showing the relationships among messages, protocols, mail servers, stores, and folders.

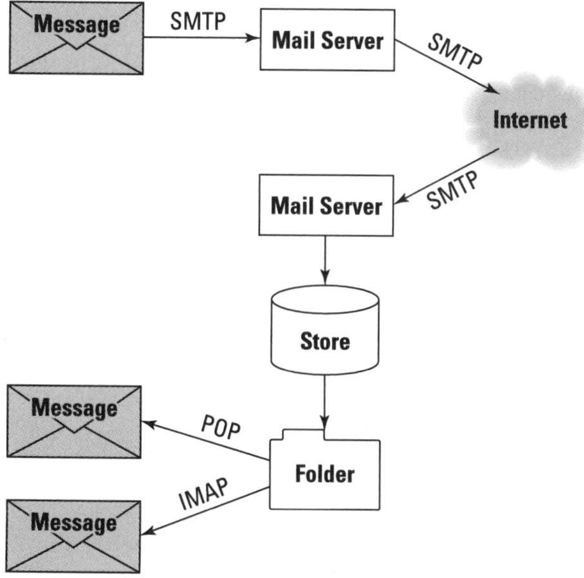

Figure 10-3: The JavaMail message handling process

Sessions and properties

The `Session` class is a concrete class that extends `java.lang.Object`. It acts as a factory for the installed `Transport` and `Store` implementations and is the way providers are associated with a particular set of user mail configuration settings. A `Session` also manages user authentication for the `Transport` and `Store` services.

WebLogic provides the facility for predefining various mail sessions for use by any of your WebLogic applications. They are associated with default session properties and named for easy accessibility via JNDI.

When a session is instantiated, it uses a `Properties` object to define the configuration information. The following list describes the properties that you can set along with their default values. You should expect that at least the `mail.store.protocol`, `mail.transport.protocol`, `mail.host`, `mail.user`, and `mail.from` properties are set.

If necessary, you can override the properties in your Java code when establishing a session for connecting to a transport or a store. But it's recommended that you take full advantage of predefining your mail sessions in WebLogic and avoid hard-coding them in your application.

✦ `mail.store.protocol`—Name the protocol to use to retrieve mail. The `Session.getStore()` method returns a `Store` object that implements this protocol. Note that the JavaMail library bundled within the `weblogic.jar` has support for IMAP.

```
mail.store.protocol=imap
```

✦ `mail.transport.protocol`—Specify the protocol to use to send mail. The `Session.getTransport()` method returns a `Transport` object that implements this protocol. Note that the JavaMail library bundled within the `weblogic.jar` has support for SMTP.

```
mail.transport.protocol=smtp
```

✦ `mail.host`—Specify the name of the mail host machine. If not specified, the default is the local machine name.

```
mail.host=mail.mycompany.com
```

✦ `mail.user`—Specify the name of the user for retrieving mail. If not specified, the default is the `user.name` Java system property.

```
mail.user=userid
```

✦ `mail.protocol.host`—Specify the mail host for a specific protocol. This is useful if you are using multiple protocols to connect to multiple hosts. If not specified, the default is the value of the `mail.host` property.

```
mail.imap.host=mail.mycompany.com
mail.pop3.host=pop3.mycompany.com
```

✦ `mail.protocol.user`—Specify the protocol-specific default username for logging into a mail server. If not specified, the default is the value of the `mail.user` property.

```
mail.pop3.user=pop3userid
```

✦ `mail.from`—Specify the default return address. If not specified, the default is the value of the `mail.user` property.

```
mail.from=custserv@mycompany.com
```

✦ `mail.debug`—Specify `true` if you want to see debug information on the console and in the WebLogic system log. If not specified, the default is `false`.

```
mail.debug=true
```

Configuring WebLogic JavaMail

Before writing code to send or receive messages, you must configure WebLogic JavaMail by using the WebLogic Console. Configuring JavaMail for the first time is quite simple, requiring only a couple of steps. This section shows you how to perform the required steps, and helps you understand the meanings and implications of your configuration choices.

Creating a mail session

Start WebLogic Server and open the default console. In the domain tree, click Mail. At the top of the page, click Create a New Mail Session. Figure 10-4 shows the mail session configuration page with the data I provided for this session.

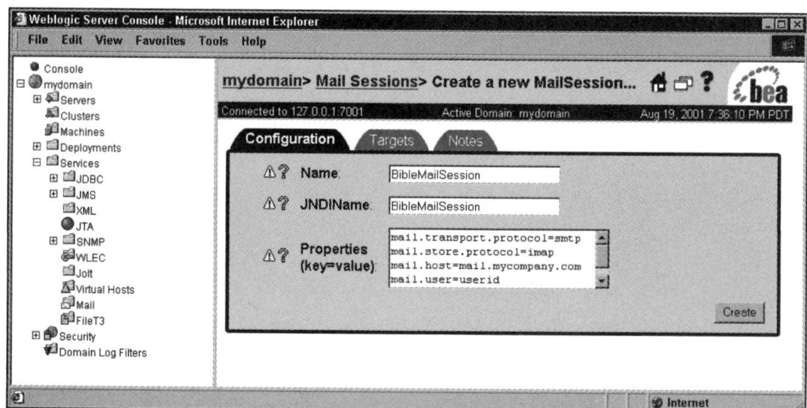

Figure 10-4: Creating a mail session in WebLogic Console

The entries on this page are as follows:

✦ **Name:** A name for the mail session, which must conform to the rules for Java identifiers and be unique within the WebLogic Server instance or its cluster. Type **BibleMailSession** for this value.

✦ **JNDIName:** You use this name to look up instances of the session with JNDI. The name must be a valid Java identifier and be unique within the JNDI namespace of the server or cluster. Type **BibleMailSession** for this value as well.

✦ **Properties:** This defines the properties that will be used when WebLogic returns an instance of this mail session. For these examples, I define the protocols `mail.transport.protocol=smtp` and `mail.store.protocol=imap`. I also define the host and user, `mail.host=mail.mycompany.com` and `mail.user=userid`. I want to see debug messages on the console, so for these examples only I define `mail.debug=true`.

You can override these properties in your Java code, but it makes sense to define everything here. If multiple types of connections are needed to multiple mail servers, define multiple mail sessions.

After completing the configuration screen, click Create.

The next step is to attach the mail session to a server or cluster. Click the Targets tab, and then move the desired server into the Chosen list of the desired server or cluster. Click Apply. Figure 10-5 shows my mail session attached to my local WebLogic server instance.

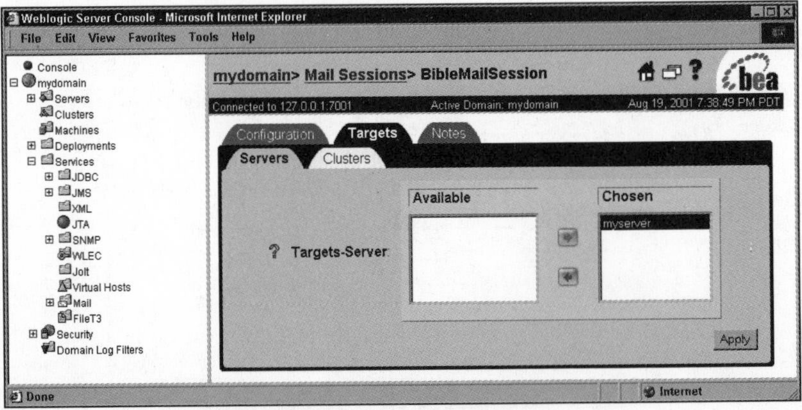

Figure 10-5: Targeting the mail service to a WebLogic Server

After you add the mail session to WebLogic Server, you see debug messages regarding the providers being loaded. The messages should appear as shown in Figure 10-6:

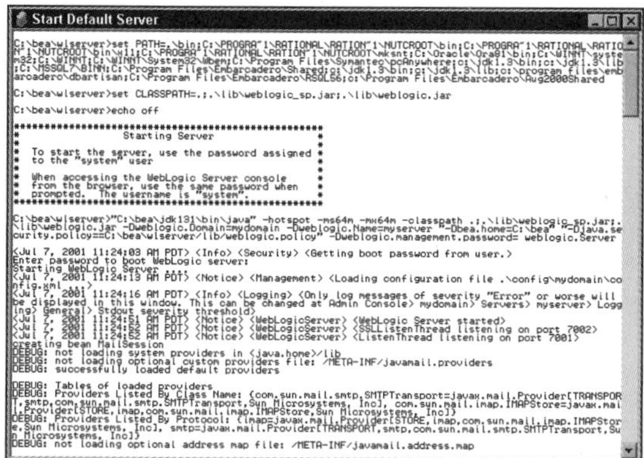

Figure 10-6: The WebLogic Server command display with JavaMail debug messages

I don't cover any of the debug messages in this chapter, but because you have the option turned on, watch the console during the execution of the examples. You'll find it interesting to see what's happening under the covers.

This completes configuration of a mail session. Next I cover how to install the additional POP3 provider from Sun.

Adding POP3 to WebLogic

Sun includes a separate POP3 provider for JavaMail, which is not included in `weblogic.jar`. You need to download the JavaMail 1.2 API provider from Sun and add it to the WebLogic if you intend on using the POP3 protocol.

You can download the JavaMail 1.2 API from the Sun Web site at `http://java.sun.com/products/javamail/index.html`. After you download the file `javamail-1_2.zip`, you must unzip it to a directory called `javamail-1.2`. Copy `mail.jar` to your WebLogic library directory (mine is `C:\bea\wlserver\lib`). Edit the `startWebLogic.cmd` file in your WebLogic domain directory (mine is `C:\bea\wlserver\config\mydomain`) to add the `mail.jar` file to the WebLogic classpath. It's important that it be listed before the `weblogic_sp.jar` and `weblogic.jar` files. The new classpath statement should look similar to the following:

```
set CLASSPATH=.;.\lib\mail.jar;.\lib\weblogic_sp.jar;.\lib\weblogic.jar
```

I tried adding only the `pop3.jar file`, but I received ClassNotFoundException messages when I tried certain operations. Apparently, there are some dependent classes in `mail.jar`.

Save the changed command file and restart WebLogic. The command window displays messages indicating that the POP3 provider is now loaded, as shown in Figure 10-7.

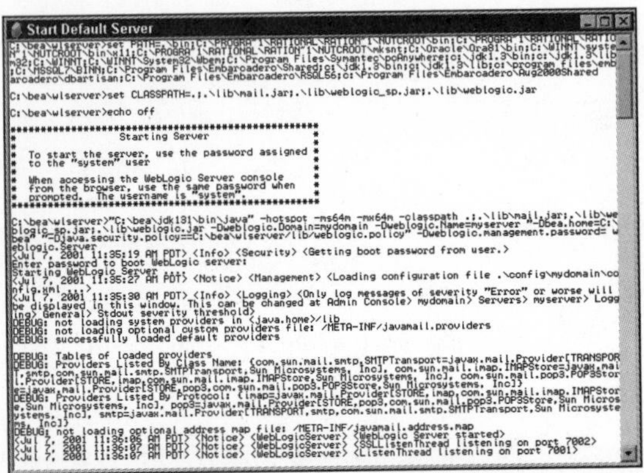

Figure 10-7: WebLogic Server after installing POP3. Note the references to POP3 classes in the "Providers Listed By Class Name" section of the display.

This completes the installation of the POP3 provider package. The next section covers how to send messages with JavaMail.

Sending Messages with WebLogic JavaMail

If you plan to use JavaMail in your application, then you probably want to send outgoing mail messages, so I'll dive into that topic first.

Obtaining a mail session via JNDI

For the examples, you must import the packages for JavaMail, JAF, and JNDI. After that's done, the first step is to create a new `InitialContext` and use it to look up a mail session by its JNDI name.

For more information about JNDI and contexts, see Chapter 7. Otherwise, just understand that successful execution of this code will result in your program having a handle to a JavaMail session.

```
import javax.activation.*;
import javax.mail.*;
import javax.mail.internet.*;
import javax.naming.*;

try {
  InitialContext context = new InitialContext();
  Session session = (Session)
    context.lookup("BibleMailSession");
} catch (NamingException e) {}
```

Sending a simple message

The next step is to construct a message (I'm using a `MimeMessage`) and set its attributes. Notice that I use the static `InternetAddress.parse()` convenience method to take a list of addresses either separated by commas or spaces and parse it into recipients of the message.

In this example, I use the static `Transport.send ()` convenience method. First, it saves the changes to the message via the `Message.saveChanges()` method. Then it connects to the default transport, sends the message, and closes the transport via the `Transport.connect()`, `Transport.sendMessage()`, and `Transport.close()` methods, respectively.

```
try {
  Message msg = new MimeMessage(session);
  msg.setFrom();
  msg.setRecipients(Message.RecipientType.TO,
    InternetAddress.parse(to, false));
  msg.setSubject(subject);
  msg.setSentDate(new Date());
  msg.setText(messageText);
  Transport.send(msg);
} catch (AddressException e) {
} catch (MessagingException e) {}
```

Deployment descriptor for the examples

For all examples, I'm using servlets to keep things simple and to keep all the code for each example in one source file.

See Chapter 11 for more information about servlets and how to program them.

Of course, the example code will work in whatever J2EE component you choose to use, whether it's servlets, JavaBeans, or EJBs. Listing 10-1, `web.xml`, defines the servlets and servlet mappings necessary to run all the examples in this chapter.

Listing 10-1: web.xml

```
<?xml version="1.0" ?>
<!DOCTYPE web-app PUBLIC "-//Sun Microsystems, Inc.//DTD Web Application
1.2//EN"
  "http://java.sun.com/j2ee/dtds/web-app_2_2.dtd">
<web-app>
  <servlet>
    <servlet-name>SendMailServlet</servlet-name>
    <servlet-class>bible.javamail.SendMailServlet</servlet-class>
  </servlet>
  <servlet>
    <servlet-name>SendMailServlet2</servlet-name>
    <servlet-class>bible.javamail.SendMailServlet2</servlet-class>
  </servlet>
  <servlet>
    <servlet-name>DisplayFolders</servlet-name>
    <servlet-class>bible.javamail.DisplayFolders</servlet-class>
  </servlet>
  <servlet>
    <servlet-name>DisplayMessages</servlet-name>
    <servlet-class>bible.javamail.DisplayMessages</servlet-class>
  </servlet>
  <servlet>
    <servlet-name>DisplayMessage</servlet-name>
    <servlet-class>bible.javamail.DisplayMessage</servlet-class>
  </servlet>
  <servlet-mapping>
    <servlet-name>SendMailServlet</servlet-name>
    <url-pattern>/sendmail</url-pattern>
  </servlet-mapping>
  <servlet-mapping>
    <servlet-name>SendMailServlet2</servlet-name>
    <url-pattern>/sendmail2</url-pattern>
  </servlet-mapping>
  <servlet-mapping>
    <servlet-name>DisplayFolders</servlet-name>
    <url-pattern>/folders</url-pattern>
  </servlet-mapping>
  <servlet-mapping>
    <servlet-name>DisplayMessages</servlet-name>
    <url-pattern>/messages</url-pattern>
  </servlet-mapping>
  <servlet-mapping>
    <servlet-name>DisplayMessage</servlet-name>
    <url-pattern>/message</url-pattern>
  </servlet-mapping>
</web-app>
```

Example: Send Mail servlet

Listing 10-2 contains the code for `SendMailServlet.java`, a servlet that supports the composing and sending of e-mail messages.

`SendMailServlet.java` is structured as follows:

1. Its `doGet()` method displays an HTML form in the user's browser, prompting for a message recipient's e-mail address, a message subject, and a message body. The form also contains a Submit button that, when clicked, posts the form's contents to the server. Figure 10-8 shows this form rendered in a Web browser.
2. Its `doPost()` method retrieves the user's input for the message recipient, subject, and body, then makes JavaMail calls to build and send the message, using the messaging infrastructure I defined in the section "Configuring WebLogic JavaMail."

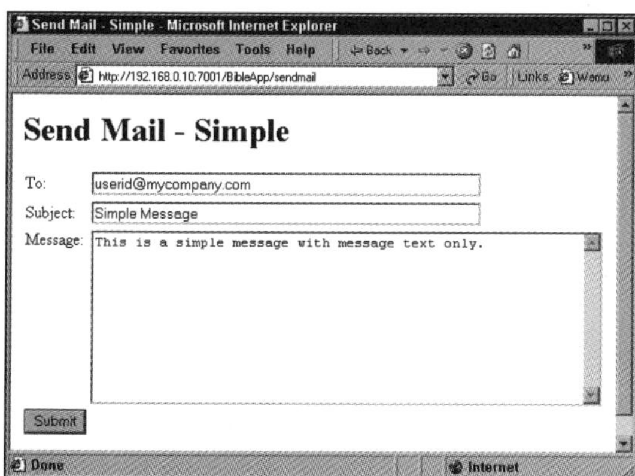

Figure 10-8: Send Mail servlet – simple version

Listing 10-2: SendMailServlet.java

```
package bible.javamail;

import java.io.*;
import javax.servlet.*;
import javax.servlet.http.*;

import java.util.*;
import javax.activation.*;
```

Continued

Listing 10-2 (continued)

```
import javax.mail.*;
import javax.mail.internet.*;
import javax.naming.*;

public class SendMailServlet extends HttpServlet {

  private String to = "";
  private String subject = "";
  private String messageText = "";
  private String successMessage = "";

  public void doGet(HttpServletRequest req, HttpServletResponse res)
  throws ServletException, IOException {

    PrintWriter pw = res.getWriter();
    res.setContentType("text/html");

    pw.println("<HTML><HEAD><TITLE>Send Mail - Simple</TITLE></HEAD>");
    pw.println("<BODY><H1>Send Mail - Simple</H1>");
    pw.println("<FORM ACTION='sendmail' METHOD=post><TABLE>");
    pw.println("<TR><TD>To:</TD><TD><INPUT NAME=to size=60></TD></TR>");
    pw.println("<TR><TD>Subject:</TD>" +
      "<TD><INPUT NAME=subject size=60></TD></TR>");
    pw.println("<TR><TD VALIGN>Message:</TD>");
    pw.println("<TD><TEXTAREA NAME=messageText rows=10 cols=60>" +
      "</TEXTAREA></TD></TR>");
    pw.println("<TR><TD>" +
      "<INPUT TYPE=SUBMIT NAME=Submit VALUE=Submit></TD></TR>");
    pw.println("</TABLE></FORM>");
    pw.println("<STRONG>" + successMessage + "</STRONG>");
    pw.println("</BODY></HTML>");
  }

  public void doPost(HttpServletRequest req, HttpServletResponse res)
  throws ServletException, IOException {

    to = req.getParameter("to");
    subject = req.getParameter("subject");
    messageText = req.getParameter("messageText");
    sendMessage();
    doGet(req, res);
  }

  public void sendMessage() {

    try {
      // lookup mail session in JNDI
      InitialContext context = new InitialContext();
      Session session = (Session) context.lookup("BibleMailSession");

      // set message with to, subject, and message text
```

```
      Message msg = new MimeMessage(session);

      // set message with to, subject, and message text
      msg.setFrom();
      msg.setRecipients(Message.RecipientType.TO,
                        InternetAddress.parse(to, false));
      msg.setSubject(subject);
      msg.setSentDate(new Date());
      msg.setText(messageText);

      // send message
      Transport.send(msg);
      successMessage = "Message sucessfully sent.";
      session = null;
    }
    catch (Exception e) {
      successMessage = e.getMessage();
    }
  }
}
```

Overriding mail session properties

You can override mail session properties in your Java code by creating a `Properties` object containing the properties you want to override. Then call the `Session.getInstance()` method with your `Properties` to get a customized `Session`. The `getInstance()` method also takes an `Authenticator` object to create an authenticated session (if your SMTP mail server does not require authentication to send mail, then specify `null` for the `Authenticator` object). The following code snippet demonstrates the technique:

```
Properties mailProps = new Properties();
mailProps.put("mail.transport.protocol", "smtp");
mailProps.put("mail.host", "mail.mycompany.com");
mailProps.put("mail.user", "userid");
mailProps.put("mail.from", "custserv@mycompany.com");
mailProps.put("mail.debug", "true");
Session mySession = session.getInstance(mailProps, null);
```

Authenticating a mail session

If your SMTP mail server does require authentication to send mail, then you'll need to pass an `Authenticator` object to the `Session.getInstance()` method to get an authenticated mail session.

To do this, you must first create your own `MailAuthenticator` class that extends `Authenticator`. Listing 10-3 gives a simple example of such a class. I'm creating this as a class that gets instantiated and set by some other process, perhaps by prompting the user or retrieving user information from a database. The important part is that it must have a `getPasswordAuthentication()` method that returns a `PasswordAuthentication` object.

If you are wondering how this works, the `getInstance()` method creates a new `Session` object and associates it with the `Authenticator`. The `Session` object has a package level method it calls, which in turn calls the `getPasswordAuthentication()` method on the `Authenticator`. The result is that only the `requestPasswordAuthentication()` method can use the `Authenticator` to obtain an authenticated session.

Listing 10-3: MailAuthenticator.java

```
package bible.javamail;

import javax.mail.*;

public class MailAuthenticator extends Authenticator {

  private String user;
  private String password;

  public void setUser(String s) {
    user = s;
  }
  public String getUser() {
    return user;
  }
  public void setPassword(String s) {
    password = s;
  }
  public String getPassword() {
    return password;
  }
  public PasswordAuthentication getPasswordAuthentication(){
    return new PasswordAuthentication(user, password);
  }
}
```

The next step is to specify that you're requesting SMTP authentication by setting the `mail.smtp.auth` property to `true`:

```
Properties mailProps = new Properties();
mailProps.put("mail.transport.protocol","smtp");
mailProps.put("mail.host","mail.mycompany.com");
mailProps.put("mail.user","userid");
```

```
mailProps.put("mail.from","custserv@mycompany.com");
mailProps.put("mail.debug","true");
mailProps.put("mail.smtp.auth","true");
```

Now create a new MailAuthenticator and set the values. Then I'll get an authenticated session by calling the getInstance() method with the Properties and Authenticator objects as parameters.

I set the user and password values here for this example only. In real life, you get the Authenticator object as a result of a user login or from accessing a database or descriptor.

```
MailAuthenticator mailAuth = new MailAuthenticator();
mailAuth.setUser("userid ");
mailAuth.setPassword("password");
Session authSession = session.getInstance(mailProps,
  mailAuth);
```

Finally, after creating a message, you can send it. But there are some additional steps to do this. In the preceding example, you called the static Transport.send() convenience method. Instead, manually save the message changes, get a new transport from the authenticated session, connect, send the message, and disconnect.

```
msg.saveChanges();

// get transport and send a message
Transport authTransport = authSession.getTransport();
authTransport.connect();
authTransport.sendMessage(msg, msg.getAllRecipients());
authTransport.close();
```

Sending an enclosure using a MimeMultipart

To send a message with attachments, a multipart message is used with multiple body parts. The first part contains the message text and the other parts contain the attachments. The multipart message is then stored set as the content of the message.

In the following example, I use a MimeMultipart with multiple MimeBodyParts. I only have one enclosure, which is set into the second MimeBodyPart. Additional enclosures can be set in multiple MimeBodyParts as necessary. The raw data from the FileDataSource is wrapped in a DataHandler object and stored in the MimeBodyPart. I also set the file name in the MimeBodyPart. Finally, I set the message content to the MimeMultipart.

```
// set with message text via a mime multipart
Multipart mp = new MimeMultipart();

MimeBodyPart mbp1 = new MimeBodyPart();
mbp1.setText(messageText);
```

```
mp.addBodyPart(mbp1);

MimeBodyPart mbp2 = new MimeBodyPart();
FileDataSource fds = new FileDataSource(filename);
mbp2.setDataHandler(new DataHandler(fds));
mbp2.setFileName(fds.getName());
mp.addBodyPart(mbp2);

msg.setContent(mp);
```

Example: Send Mail servlet 2

The second example, shown in Figure 10-9, expands upon the first servlet to send more complex messages. This example will prompt for the To, Cc, and Bcc addresses; Subject; the file name of an enclosure, the message text, and an indication of whether the message text is HTML.

This example also demonstrates how to override the session's default properties, use an authenticator to get an authenticated SMTP session, use a `MimeMultipart` to optionally include an enclosure, optionally flag the message text as HTML, and manually execute the steps to send the message through a transport obtained from the authenticated session.

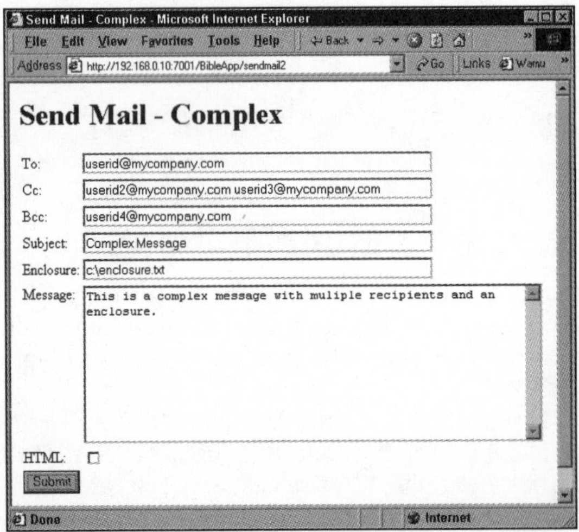

Figure 10-9: Send Mail servlet – complex version

In Listing 10-4, the Java code to store an enclosure in a message gets the file from the local file system. Because my example is a servlet, the file must be in the local file system of the server running WebLogic. You need to explore further if you wish to get the file from the client's file system.

Listing 10-4: SendMailServlet2.java

```
package bible.javamail;

import java.io.*;
import javax.servlet.*;
import javax.servlet.http.*;

import java.util.*;
import javax.activation.*;
import javax.mail.*;
import javax.mail.internet.*;
import javax.naming.*;

public class SendMailServlet2 extends HttpServlet {

  private String to = "";
  private String cc = "";
  private String bcc = "";
  private String subject = "";
  private String filename = "";
  private String messageText = "";
  private boolean isHTML;
  private String successMessage = "";

  public void doGet(HttpServletRequest req, HttpServletResponse res)
  throws ServletException, IOException {

    PrintWriter pw = res.getWriter();
    res.setContentType("text/html");

    pw.println("<HTML><HEAD><TITLE>Send Mail - Complex</TITLE></HEAD>");
    pw.println("<BODY><H1>Send Mail - Complex</H1>");
    pw.println("<FORM ACTION='sendmail2' METHOD=post><TABLE>");
    pw.println("<TR><TD>To:</TD><TD><INPUT NAME=to size=60></TD></TR>");
    pw.println("<TR><TD>Cc:</TD><TD><INPUT NAME=cc size=60></TD></TR>");
    pw.println("<TR><TD>Bcc:</TD><TD><INPUT NAME=bcc size=60></TD></TR>");
    pw.println("<TR><TD>Subject:</TD><TD><INPUT NAME=subject size=60>" +
      "</TD></TR>");
    pw.println("<TR><TD>Enclosure:</TD><TD>" +
      "<INPUT NAME=filename size=60></TD></TR>");
    pw.println("<TR><TD VALIGN>Message:</TD>");
    pw.println("<TD><TEXTAREA NAME=messageText rows=10 cols=60>" +
      "</TEXTAREA></TD></TR>");
    pw.println("<TR><TD>HTML:</TD><TD><input type=checkbox NAME=isHTML>" +
      "</TD></TR>");
    pw.println("<TR><TD><INPUT TYPE=SUBMIT NAME=Submit VALUE=Submit>" +
      "</TD></TR>");
    pw.println("</TABLE></FORM>");
    pw.println("<STRONG>" + successMessage + "</STRONG>");
```

Continued

Listing 10-4 *(continued)*

```
  pw.println("</BODY></HTML>");
}

public void doPost(HttpServletRequest req, HttpServletResponse res)
throws ServletException, IOException {
  to = req.getParameter("to");
  cc = req.getParameter("cc");
  bcc = req.getParameter("bcc");
  subject = req.getParameter("subject");
  filename = req.getParameter("filename");
  messageText = req.getParameter("messageText");
  isHTML = "on".equals(req.getParameter("isHTML"));
  sendMessage();
  doGet(req, res);
}

public void sendMessage() {

  try {
    // lookup mail session in JNDI
    InitialContext context = new InitialContext();
    Session session = (Session) context.lookup("BibleMailSession");

    // override mail session properties
    Properties mailProps = new Properties();
    mailProps.put("mail.transport.protocol","smtp");
    mailProps.put("mail.host", "mail.mycompany.com");
    mailProps.put("mail.user", "userid");
    mailProps.put("mail.from", "userid@mycompany.com");
    mailProps.put("mail.debug", "true");
    mailProps.put("mail.smtp.auth", "true");

    // get an authenticated session
    MailAuthenticator mailAuth = new MailAuthenticator();
    // For testing, set the values here. The user should be prompted or
    // retrieved from a database or descriptor
    mailAuth.setUser("userid ");
    mailAuth.setPassword("password");
    Session authSession = session.getInstance(mailProps, mailAuth);

    // set message with to, subject, and message text
    Message msg = new MimeMessage(authSession);

    // set message with to, cc, bcc, and subject
    msg.setFrom();
    msg.setRecipients(Message.RecipientType.TO,
      InternetAddress.parse(to, false));
    msg.setRecipients(Message.RecipientType.CC,
```

```
          InternetAddress.parse(cc, false));
        msg.setRecipients(Message.RecipientType.BCC,
          InternetAddress.parse(bcc, false));
        msg.setSubject(subject);
        msg.setSentDate(new Date());

        // set with message text via a mime multipart
        Multipart mp = new MimeMultipart();

        MimeBodyPart mbp1 = new MimeBodyPart();
        if (isHTML) {
          mbp1.setContent(messageText, "text/html");
        } else {
          mbp1.setText(messageText);
        }
        mp.addBodyPart(mbp1);

        if (!filename.equals("")) {
          MimeBodyPart mbp2 = new MimeBodyPart();
          FileDataSource fds = new FileDataSource(filename);
          mbp2.setDataHandler(new DataHandler(fds));
          mbp2.setFileName(fds.getName());
          mp.addBodyPart(mbp2);
        }

        msg.setContent(mp);
        msg.saveChanges();

        // get transport and send message
        Transport authTransport = authSession.getTransport();
        authTransport.connect();
        authTransport.sendMessage(msg, msg.getAllRecipients());
        authTransport.close();
        successMessage = "Message sucessfully sent.";
        session = null;

      } catch (Exception e) {
        successMessage = e.getMessage();
      }
    }
  }
```

Sending a message to multiple recipients (bulk mail)

JavaMail is commonly used to add automated e-mail notification to applications. The application typically sends an e-mail message to multiple recipients based upon a list of addresses retrieved from a database. Often, the e-mails are tailored to the recipient with name and other personal information. In this case, it's inefficient to repetitively connect to a transport, send, and disconnect, because connecting is a time-consuming, network-intensive operation. A more efficient way is to connect, customize and send multiple messages, and disconnect. The following code snippet demonstrates this technique:

```
Transport transport = session.getTransport();
transport.connect();

// personalize message and send
for (int i = 0; i < recipients.length, i++) {
  // personalize message here ...
  msg.saveChanges();
  transport.sendMessage(msg, recipients[i]);
}
transport.close();
```

Navigating stores

Most e-mail clients provide a mechanism for organizing messages into folders and browsing the folders. To provide this functionality with JavaMail, you must use the JavaMail `Store` object to drive the display of and interaction with the folder hierarchies your users define. The next four sections provide several examples of how to work with stores.

Obtaining a mail session via JNDI

Before working with stores, you must obtain a mail session via a JNDI lookup, just as you did when sending messages:

```
import javax.activation.*;
import javax.mail.*;
import javax.mail.internet.*;
import javax.naming.*;

try {
  InitialContext context = new InitialContext();
  Session session = (Session)
    context.lookup("BibleMailSession");
} catch (NamingException e) {}
```

Connecting to a store and the default folder

Next you must connect to a store by using the protocol defined in the mail session (in this case, `mail.store.protocol=imap`), and get the default folder. As described earlier, the default folder is the root folder of a user's default folder hierarchy.

```
try {
  // get store and create an authenticated session
  Store store = session.getStore();
  store.connect("mail.mycompany.com", "userid", "password");
  defaultFolder = store.getDefaultFolder();
} catch (NoSuchProviderException e) {
} catch (MessagingException e) {}
```

Listing folders

After you have a reference to the default folder, you can retrieve the user's entire folder hierarchy and navigate through it. In this example, I specifically include only folders that hold messages and explicitly exclude the Public Folders folder. For each folder, I display its name and some information about it, such as total number of messages, number of new messages, and number of unread messages. Several other folder attributes are available as well; see the J2EE documentation for a complete list of information available for a folder.

Some implementations of certain folder methods may not return expected data if the folder is not opened first. In this example, the folder is opened and closed. If your implementation works without these steps, it's more efficient to omit them.

```
try {
  Folder[] allFolders = defaultFolder.list();
  for (int i = 0; i < allFolders.length; i++) {
    String name = allFolders[i].getName();
    if (allFolders[i].HOLDS_MESSAGES ==
        Folder.HOLDS_MESSAGES &&
        !name.equals("Public Folders")) {
      allFolders[i].open(Folder.READ_ONLY);
      System.out.print ("Name: " + allFolders[i].getName());
      System.out.print("  Messages: " +
        allFolders[i]. getMessageCount());
      System.out.print("  New: " +
        allFolders[i]. getNewMessageCount());
      System.out.println("  Unread: " +
        allFolders[i].getUnreadMessageCount());
      allFolders[i].close(false);
    }
  }
} catch (MessagingException e) {}
```

Example: Display folders

The next example displays a list of folders in the user's folder hierarchy. After obtaining a mail session via JNDI, the code establishes an authenticated connection to the store, opens the default folder, retrieves a list of folders, and displays the folders with some basic information about them.

Figure 10-10 shows a list of folders and their attributes retrieved by using the IMAP protocol.

Folders - Microsoft Internet Explorer

http://192.168.0.10:7001/BibleApp/folders

Folders

Folder	Messages	New	Unread
Calendar	0	0	0
Contacts	4	4	0
Deleted Items	4	4	2
Drafts	0	0	0
INBOX	2	0	2
Journal	0	0	0
Notes	0	0	0
Outbox	0	0	0
Sent Items	23	23	0
Tasks	0	0	0

Figure 10-10: Displaying folders by using IMAP

Figure 10-11 shows a list of folders and their attributes retrieved by using the POP3 protocol. Notice that there is only one folder, the `INBOX`. This is a prime example of how the JavaMail API provides a common interface for all protocols. POP3 doesn't actually support the concept of folders, but the JavaMail API ensures that the POP3 container for storing messages is presented as the `INBOX` within the default folder.

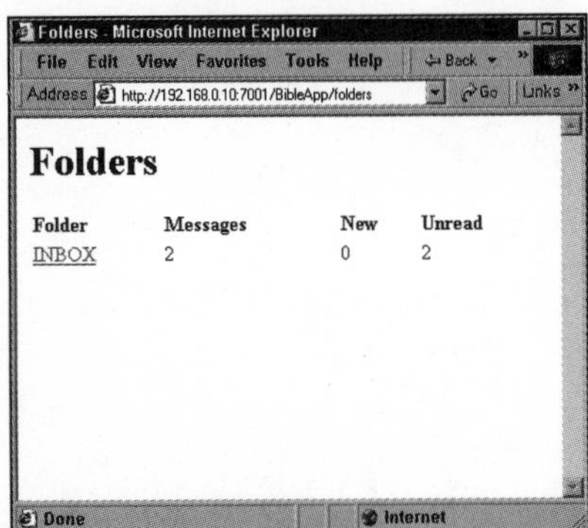

Figure 10-11: Displaying folders by using POP3

Listing 10-5 contains the code that generates Figures 10-10 and 10-11.

Listing 10-5: DisplayFolders.java

```
package bible.javamail;

import java.io.*;
import javax.servlet.*;
import javax.servlet.http.*;

import javax.activation.*;
import javax.mail.*;
import javax.mail.internet.*;
import javax.naming.*;

public class DisplayFolders extends HttpServlet {

  private PrintWriter pw;
  private Session session;
  private Store store;
  private Folder defaultFolder;

  public void doGet(HttpServletRequest req, HttpServletResponse res)
  throws ServletException, IOException {

    pw = res.getWriter();
    res.setContentType("text/html");

    pw.println("<HTML><HEAD><TITLE>Folders</TITLE></HEAD>");
    pw.println("<BODY><H1>Folders</H1>");

    try {
      getDefaultFolder();
      displayFolders();
      store.close();
    } catch (Exception e) {
      pw.println("<BR><BR><STRONG>" + e.getMessage() + "</STRONG>");
    }

    pw.println("</BODY></HTML>");
  }

  private void getDefaultFolder()
  throws NamingException, NoSuchProviderException, MessagingException {

    // lookup mail session in JNDI
    InitialContext context = new InitialContext();
    Session session = (Session) context.lookup("BibleMailSession");

    // get store and create an authenticated session
```

Continued

Listing 10-5 (continued)

```
    store = session.getStore();
    store.connect("mail.mycompany.com", "userid", "password");

    // get the default folder
    defaultFolder = store.getDefaultFolder();
  }

  private void displayFolders() throws MessagingException {
    Folder[] allFolders = defaultFolder.list();
    if (allFolders.length > 0) {

      pw.println("<TABLE width='100%'>");
      pw.println("<TR><TD><STRONG>Folder</STRONG></TD>");
      pw.println("<TD><STRONG>Messages</STRONG></TD>");
      pw.println("<TD><STRONG>New</STRONG></TD>");
      pw.println("<TD><STRONG>Unread</STRONG></TD></TR>");

      for (int i = 0; i < allFolders.length; i++) {
        String name = allFolders[i].getName();

        if (allFolders[i].HOLDS_MESSAGES == Folder.HOLDS_MESSAGES &&
            !name.equals("Public Folders")) {
          allFolders[i].open(Folder.READ_ONLY);
          pw.println("<TR><TD><A HREF='messages?folder=" + name +
            "'>" + name + "</A></TD></TD>");
          pw.println("<TD>" + allFolders[i].getMessageCount() + "</TD>");
          pw.println("<TD>" + allFolders[i].getNewMessageCount() +
            "</TD>");
          pw.println("<TD>" + allFolders[i].getUnreadMessageCount() +
            "</TD></TR>");
          allFolders[i].close(false);
        }
      }
      pw.println("</TABLE>");
    }
  }
}
```

Retrieving and Displaying Messages with WebLogic JavaMail

If you plan to write the Next Great J2EE E-mail Client, you will need to know how to retrieve and display e-mail messages using JavaMail. This section shows you how to do it.

Listing messages

Before you can retrieve a list of messages from a folder, it must first be opened via the `Folder.open()` method. This method takes an integer as a parameter corresponding to the mode in which to open the folder. Two modes, `READ_ONLY` and `READ_WRITE`, are provided as public static final variables. For the following example, I use `READ_ONLY` because I'm only retrieving information about the messages, not changing their state or their content.

To obtain a list of messages, simply call the `getMessages()` method against a folder, and it will return an array of `Messages`. You can then loop through the messages and retrieve information about them or the data they contain. Notice that I bypass messages flagged as deleted.

```
try {
  // open folder and get messages
  folder.open(Folder.READ_ONLY);
  Message[] messages = folder.getMessages();

  // loop through messages
  for (int i = 0; i < messages.length; i++) {
    // skip deleted messages
    if (!messages[i].isSet(Flags.Flag.DELETED)) {
    System.out.print ("MessageNumber: " +
      messages[i].getFrom());
    System.out.print ("From: " +
      messages[i].getFrom());
    System.out.print ("Subject: " +
      messages[i].getSubject());
    System.out.print ("Received: " +
      messages[i].getReceivedDate());
  }
  folder.close(false);
} catch (MessagingException e) {}
```

Example: Display messages

A basic function of an e-mail client is to display a list of incoming messages. This is done in JavaMail by opening a folder, retrieving the messages it contains, and writing their attributes to the screen. These attributes usually include the sender of the message, the subject of the message, the date and time the message was received, the size of the message in bytes, whether or not the message has an enclosure, and whether or not the message has been read. Figure 10-12 shows what such a display might look like. It is the result of retrieving a list of messages using the IMAP protocol.

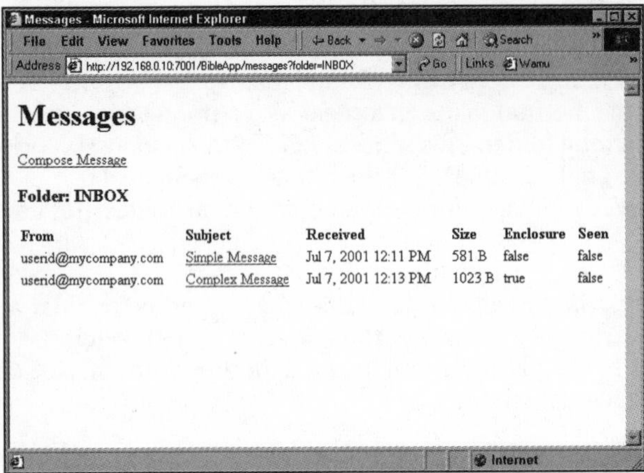

Figure 10-12: Displaying messages by using IMAP

Figure 10-13 shows the results of retrieving a list of messages and their attributes by using the POP3 protocol. Notice that there are a few differences in the output. First, there is no *received* date. Also, the size of each message is different from that in the IMAP execution. This is because, according to the JavaMail API documentation, "the size may not be an exact measure of the content size and may or may not account for any transfer encoding of the content. The size is appropriate for display in a user interface to give the user a rough idea of the size of this part." In other words, don't count on `Message.getSize()` to return 100 percent accurate message sizes if you are using POP3 to retrieve messages

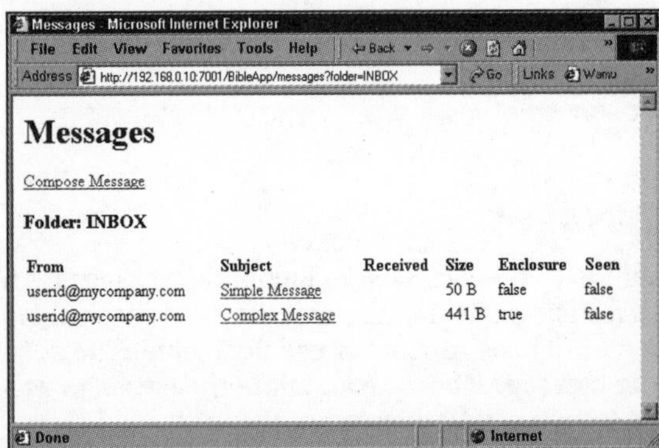

Figure 10-13: Displaying messages by using POP3

Listing 10-6 shows the Java code used to generate Figures 10-12 and 10-13.

Listing 10-6: DisplayMessages.java

```
package bible.javamail;

import java.io.*;
import javax.servlet.*;
import javax.servlet.http.*;

import java.util.*;
import java.text.*;
import javax.activation.*;
import javax.mail.*;
import javax.mail.internet.*;
import javax.naming.*;

public class DisplayMessages extends HttpServlet {

  private PrintWriter pw;
  private Session session;
  private Store store;
  private Folder defaultFolder;
  private Folder folder;
  private String folderName;
  private Message message;

  public void doGet(HttpServletRequest req, HttpServletResponse res)
  throws ServletException, IOException {

    pw = res.getWriter();
    res.setContentType("text/html");

    folderName = req.getParameter("folder");

    pw.println("<HTML><HEAD><TITLE>Messages</TITLE></HEAD>");
    pw.println("<BODY><H1>Messages</H1>");

    try {
      getDefaultFolder();
      displayMessages(folderName);
    } catch (Exception e) {
      e.printStackTrace(pw);
      pw.println("<BR><BR><STRONG>" + e.getMessage() + "</STRONG>");
    }

    pw.println("</BODY></HTML>");
  }

  private void getDefaultFolder()
```

Continued

Listing 10-6 *(continued)*

```
throws NamingException, NoSuchProviderException, MessagingException {

  // lookup mail session in JNDI
  InitialContext context = new InitialContext();
  Session session = (Session) context.lookup("BibleMailSession");

  // get store and create an authenticated session
  store = session.getStore();
  store.connect("mail.mycompany.com", "userid", "password");

  // get the default folder
  defaultFolder = store.getDefaultFolder();
}

private void displayMessages (String folderName)
throws MessagingException, IOException {

  pw.println("<A HREF='sendmail2'>Compose Message</A><BR>");
  pw.println("<H3>Folder: " + folderName + "</H3>");

  folder = defaultFolder.getFolder(folderName);
  folder.open(Folder.READ_ONLY);
  Message[] messages = folder.getMessages();

  if (messages.length > 0) {
    pw.println("<TABLE width='100%'>");
    pw.println("<TR><TD><STRONG>From</STRONG></TD>");
    pw.println("<TD><STRONG>Subject</STRONG></TD>");
    pw.println("<TD><STRONG>Received</STRONG></TD>");
    pw.println("<TD><STRONG>Size</STRONG></TD>");
    pw.println("<TD><STRONG>Enclosure</STRONG></TD>");
    pw.println("<TD><STRONG>Seen</STRONG></TD></TR>");

    // loop through messages
    for (int i = 0; i < messages.length; i++) {

      // skip deleted messages
      if (!messages[i].isSet(Flags.Flag.DELETED)) {
        message = messages[i];
        pw.println("<TR><TD>" + getFrom() + "</TD>");
        String subject =
          ("".equals(getSubject()) ? "None" : getSubject());
        pw.println("<TD><A HREF='message?cmd=display&folder=" +
          folderName + "&msgid=" + getMessageNumber() + "'>" +
          subject + "</A></TD>");
        pw.println("<TD>" + getReceived() + "</TD>");
        pw.println("<TD>" + getSize() + "</TD>");
        pw.println("<TD>" + hasEnclosure() + "</TD>");
```

```
        pw.println("<TD>" + hasBeenSeen() + "</TD></TR>");
      }
    }
    pw.println("</TABLE>");
    folder.close(false);
    store.close();
  }
}

public String getFrom() throws MessagingException {
  Address[] addresses = message.getFrom();
  return addresses[0].toString();
}

public String getSubject() throws MessagingException {
  return message.getSubject();
}

public int getMessageNumber() throws MessagingException {
  return message.getMessageNumber();
}

public String getReceived() throws MessagingException {
  String date = "";
  Date receivedDate = message.getReceivedDate();
  if (receivedDate != null) {
    date = DateFormat.getDateTimeInstance(DateFormat.MEDIUM,
           DateFormat.SHORT).format(receivedDate);
  }
  return date;
}

private String getSize() throws MessagingException {
  int size = message.getSize();
  String sizeDesc = size + " B";
  if (size >= 1024) {
    size /= 1024;
    sizeDesc = size + " KB";
    if (size >= 1024) {
      size /= 1024;
      sizeDesc = size + " MB";
    }
  }
  return sizeDesc;
}

private boolean hasEnclosure() throws MessagingException, IOException {
  boolean b = false;
  if (message.isMimeType("multipart/*")) {
    Multipart mp = (Multipart)message.getContent();
```

Continued

Listing 10-6 (continued)

```
        int count = mp.getCount();
        for (int j = 0; j < count; j++) {
          BodyPart bp = mp.getBodyPart(j);
          if (bp.getFileName() != null) {
            b = true;
          }
        }
      }
      return b;
    }

    private boolean hasBeenSeen() throws MessagingException {
      boolean b = false;
      if (message.isSet(Flags.Flag.SEEN))
        b = true;
        return b;
    }
  }
```

Analyzing message flags

Flags describe the state of a message within its containing folder. The `Message.getFlags()` method returns a `Flags` object that holds all the flags currently set for that message. Messages can contain multiple flags, both system and user-defined.

The system flags are defined as public static final fields in the public static final class `Flags.flag`. They include `ANSWERED`, `DELETED`, `DRAFT`, `FLAGGED`, `RECENT`, `SEEN`, and `USER`. The mail server can automatically set system flags as operations are executed against the message, or they can be manually set by your Java code. The `getPermanentFlags()` method in a folder returns a `Flags` object that contains all the system flags supported by that folder. Each mail server is not guaranteed to support all flags and may use them somewhat differently, so you'll need to experiment to understand how your particular mail server behaves.

The presence of the special `USER` flag indicates that the client can set arbitrary user-definable flags on any message belonging to this folder.

The following code defines a method, `getFlags()`, that returns a `String` containing all of a message's flags:

```
private String getFlags() throws MessagingException {

  Flags flags = message.getFlags();
```

```
    StringBuffer sb = new StringBuffer();
    Flags.Flag[] sysFlags = flags.getSystemFlags();
    for (int i = 0; i < sysFlags.length; i++) {
      if (sysFlags[i] == Flags.Flag.ANSWERED)
        sb.append("Answered ");
      else if (sysFlags[i] == Flags.Flag.DELETED)
        sb.append("Deleted ");
      else if (sysFlags[i] == Flags.Flag.DRAFT)
        sb.append("Draft ");
      else if (sysFlags[i] == Flags.Flag.FLAGGED)
        sb.append("Flagged ");
      else if (sysFlags[i] == Flags.Flag.RECENT)
        sb.append("Recent ");
      else if (sysFlags[i] == Flags.Flag.SEEN)
        sb.append("Seen ");
      else if (sysFlags[i] == Flags.Flag.USER)
        sb.append("User ");
      else
        sb.append("Unknown ");
    }

    String[] userFlags = flags.getUserFlags();
    for (int i = 0; i < userFlags.length; i++) {
      sb.append(userFlags[i].toString() + " ");
    }
    return sb.toString();
  }
```

Deleting a message

To delete a message, simply set its `DELETED` flag to `true` via the `setFlag()` method. The message is flagged as deleted, yet it still exists with its current message number. It can still be retrieved, displayed, and have its `DELETED` flag set back to `false`. It's not until the folder containing the messages is *expunged* that the messages are permanently deleted—I discuss the expunging of messages in the next section.

```
  try {
    getMessage();
    message.setFlag(Flags.Flag.DELETED, true);
  } catch (MessagingException e) {}
```

Expunging messages

As mentioned in the preceding section, messages flagged as `DELETED` still exist and maintain their message number. Expunging a folder permanently deletes all messages flagged as `DELETED`. Additionally, all remaining messages in the folder are assigned new message numbers.

You can expunge messages in one of two ways. The first is to call the expunge() method against the folder:

```
try {
  folder.expunge();
} catch (MessagingException e) {}
```

The other is to specify that the folder should be expunged when it is closed. To do so, you must pass true to the folder.close() method:

```
try {
  folder.close(true);
} catch (MessagingException e) {}
```

Example: Displaying message details

In the final example, I display the details of a message. The folder name and message number are passed as request parameters from the previous Display Messages servlet. I open the folder in READ_WRITE mode, retrieve the message by its message number, and display information about the message, including sent, received, reply to, to, cc, subject, size, flags, the message text, and the name of the enclosed file. A link appears that enables the user to delete the message.

Figure 10-14 shows the results of displaying a message's content and attributes by using the IMAP protocol.

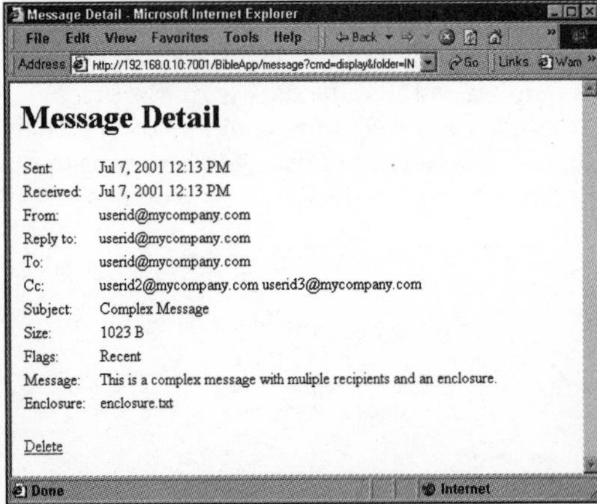

Figure 10-14: Displaying message details by using IMAP

Figure 10-15 shows the results of displaying a message's content and attributes by using the POP3 protocol. Again, notice the protocol differences by comparing the received date, size, and flags to the IMAP execution.

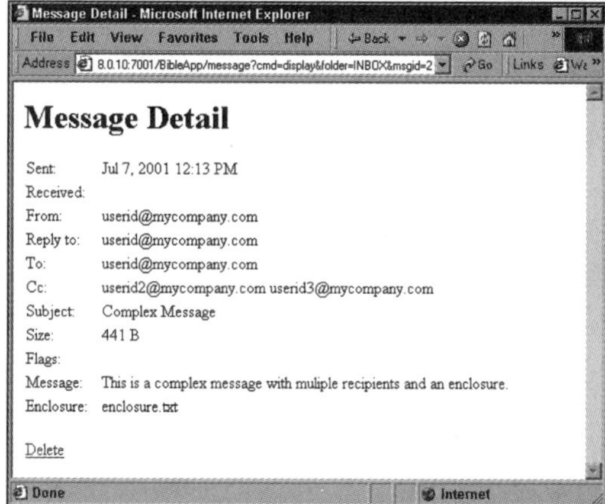

Figure 10-15: Displaying message details by using POP3

Listing 10-7 contains the Java code for displaying message details that generated Figures 10-14 and 10-15.

Listing 10-7: DisplayMessage.java

```
package bible.javamail;

import java.io.*;
import javax.servlet.*;
import javax.servlet.http.*;

import java.util.*;
import java.text.*;
import javax.activation.*;
import javax.mail.*;
import javax.mail.internet.*;
import javax.naming.*;

public class DisplayMessage extends HttpServlet {

  private PrintWriter pw;
  private Session session;
  private Store store;
  private Folder defaultFolder;
  private Folder folder;
  private String folderName;
  private int msgid;
  private Message message;

  public void doGet(HttpServletRequest req, HttpServletResponse res)
```

Continued

Listing 10-7 *(continued)*

```
throws ServletException, IOException {

  pw = res.getWriter();
  res.setContentType("text/html");

  String cmd = req.getParameter("cmd");
  folderName = req.getParameter("folder");
  msgid = new Integer(req.getParameter("msgid")).intValue();

  // display message
  if (cmd.equals("display")) {
    displayMessage();

  // delete message
  } else if (cmd.equals("delete")) {
    deleteMessage();
    RequestDispatcher rd =
      getServletContext().getNamedDispatcher("DisplayMessages");
    rd.forward(req, res);
  }
}

private void getDefaultFolder()
throws NamingException, NoSuchProviderException, MessagingException {

  // lookup mail session in JNDI
  InitialContext context = new InitialContext();
  session = (Session) context.lookup("BibleMailSession");

  // get store and create an authenticated session
  store = session.getStore();
  store.connect("mail.mycompany.com", "userid", "password");

  // get the default folder
  defaultFolder = store.getDefaultFolder();
}

private void getMessage() throws MessagingException, NamingException {

  // try to open folder read/write otherwise read-only
  getDefaultFolder();
  folder = defaultFolder.getFolder(folderName);
  try {
    folder.open(Folder.READ_WRITE);
  } catch (MessagingException ex) {
    folder.open(Folder.READ_ONLY);
  }

  // get message
```

```
    message = folder.getMessage(msgid);
  }

  private void displayMessage() {

    pw.println("<HTML><HEAD><TITLE>Message Detail</TITLE></HEAD>");
    pw.println("<BODY><H1>Message Detail</H1>");

    try {
      getMessage();

      // display the message
      pw.println("<TABLE width='100%'>");
      pw.println("<TR><TD>Sent:</TD><TD>" + getSent() + "</TD></TR>");
      pw.println("<TR><TD>Received:</TD><TD>" + getReceived() +
        "</TD></TR>");
      pw.println("<TR><TD>From:</TD><TD>" + getFrom() + "</TD></TR>");
      pw.println("<TR><TD>Reply to:</TD><TD>" + getReplyTo() +
        "</TD></TR>");
      pw.println("<TR><TD>To:</TD><TD>" + getTo() + "</TD></TR>");
      pw.println("<TR><TD>Cc:</TD><TD>" + getCc() + "</TD></TR>");
      pw.println("<TR><TD>Subject:</TD><TD>" + getSubject() +
        "</TD></TR>");
      pw.println("<TR><TD>Size:</TD><TD>" + getSize() + "</TD></TR>");
      pw.println("<TR><TD>Flags:</TD><TD>" + getFlags() + "</TD></TR>");
      pw.println("<TR><TD VALIGN>Message:</TD><TD>" + getMessageText() +
        "</TD></TR>");
      String enclosure = getEnclosureName();
      pw.print("<TR><TD>Enclosure:</TD><TD>" + enclosure + "</TD></TR>");
      pw.print("<TR><TD><BR><A HREF='message?cmd=delete&folder=" +
        folderName + "&msgid=" + msgid + "'>Delete</A></TD></TR>");
      pw.println("</TABLE>");
      folder.close(false);
      store.close();
    } catch (Exception e) {
      pw.println("<BR><BR><STRONG>" + e.getMessage() + "</STRONG>");
    }

    pw.println("</BODY></HTML>");
  }

  private void deleteMessage() {
    try {
      getMessage();
      message.setFlag(Flags.Flag.DELETED, true);
    } catch (Exception e) {}
  }

  public String getSent() throws MessagingException {
  private int msgid;
    Date sentDate = message.getSentDate();
    return DateFormat.getDateTimeInstance(DateFormat.MEDIUM,
```

Continued

Listing 10-7 *(continued)*

```
    DateFormat.SHORT).format(sentDate);
  }

  public String getReceived() throws MessagingException {
    String date = "";
    Date receivedDate = message.getReceivedDate();
    if (receivedDate != null) {
      date = DateFormat.getDateTimeInstance(DateFormat.MEDIUM,
      DateFormat.SHORT).format(receivedDate);
    }
    return date;
  }

  public String getFrom() throws MessagingException {
    Address[] addresses = message.getFrom();
    return addresses[0].toString();
  }

  public String getReplyTo() throws MessagingException {
    StringBuffer sb = new StringBuffer();
    Address[] addresses = message.getReplyTo();
    if (addresses != null) {
      for (int j = 0; j < addresses.length; j++) {
        sb.append(addresses[j].toString() + " ");
      }
    }
    return sb.toString();
  }

  public String getTo() throws MessagingException {
    StringBuffer sb = new StringBuffer();
    Address[] addresses = message.getRecipients(Message.RecipientType.TO);
    if (addresses != null) {
      for (int j = 0; j < addresses.length; j++) {
        sb.append(addresses[j].toString() + " ");
      }
    }
    return sb.toString();
  }

  public String getCc() throws MessagingException {
    StringBuffer sb = new StringBuffer();
    Address[] addresses = message.getRecipients(Message.RecipientType.CC);
    if (addresses != null) {
      for (int j = 0; j < addresses.length; j++) {
        sb.append(addresses[j].toString() + " ");
      }
    }
    return sb.toString();
```

```
}

public String getSubject() throws MessagingException {
  return message.getSubject();
}

private String getSize() throws MessagingException {
  int size = message.getSize();
  String sizeDesc = size + " B";
  if (size >= 1024) {
    size /= 1024;
    sizeDesc = size + " KB";
    if (size >= 1024) {
      size /= 1024;
      sizeDesc = size + " MB";
    }
  }
  return sizeDesc;
}

private String getFlags() throws MessagingException {
  Flags flags = message.getFlags();
  StringBuffer sb = new StringBuffer();
  Flags.Flag[] sysFlags = flags.getSystemFlags();
  for (int i = 0; i < sysFlags.length; i++) {
    if (sysFlags[i] == Flags.Flag.ANSWERED)
      sb.append("Answered ");
    else if (sysFlags[i] == Flags.Flag.DELETED)
      sb.append("Deleted ");
    else if (sysFlags[i] == Flags.Flag.DRAFT)
      sb.append("Draft ");
    else if (sysFlags[i] == Flags.Flag.FLAGGED)
      sb.append("Flagged ");
    else if (sysFlags[i] == Flags.Flag.RECENT)
      sb.append("Recent ");
    else if (sysFlags[i] == Flags.Flag.SEEN)
      sb.append("Seen ");
    else if (sysFlags[i] == Flags.Flag.USER)
      sb.append("User ");
    else
      sb.append("Unknown ");
  }

  String[] userFlags = flags.getUserFlags();
  for (int i = 0; i < userFlags.length; i++) {
    sb.append(userFlags[i].toString() + " ");
  }
  return sb.toString();
}

public String getMessageText() throws IOException, MessagingException {
```

Continued

Listing 10-7 *(continued)*

```
    String text = "";
    if (message.isMimeType("text/plain")) {
      text = (String)message.getContent();
    } else if (message.isMimeType("multipart/*")) {
      Multipart mp = (Multipart) message.getContent();
      BodyPart bp = mp.getBodyPart(0);
      if (bp.isMimeType("text/plain") | bp.isMimeType("text/html")) {
        text = (String)bp.getContent();
      }
    }
    return text;
  }

  private String getEnclosureName()
  throws MessagingException, IOException {
    StringBuffer sb = new StringBuffer();
    if (message.isMimeType("multipart/*")) {
      Multipart mp = (Multipart)message.getContent();
      int count = mp.getCount();
      for (int i = 0; i < count; i++) {
        BodyPart bp = mp.getBodyPart(i);
        if (bp.getFileName() != null) {
          sb.append(bp.getFileName() + " ");
        }
      }
    }
    return sb.toString();
  }
}
```

Summary

WebLogic Server and the Sun J2EE make adding electronic mail capabilities to your applications easy. The JavaMail API defines classes and interfaces that enable you to solve the most simple or complex requirements in a protocol-independent manner. You can add a send mail facility or create a complete, fully functional mail client.

This chapter covered the most commonly used JavaMail functionality, but a great deal more exists. The JavaMail API documentation covers the remainder in detail and gives examples of how to list providers, pre-fetch message headers, search for messages by using search terms, copy and move messages to other folders, and much more. Now that you've read this chapter, you should have no problem implementing the rest . . . have fun!

✦ ✦ ✦

P A R T

Developing Web Components

✦ ✦ ✦ ✦

In This Part

✦ ✦ ✦ ✦

Developing Servlets

✦ ✦ ✦ ✦

In This Chapter

Understanding servets

Programming servlets

Advanced servlet programming techniques

Building an advanced application with servlets

✦ ✦ ✦ ✦

Now that you have learned how to program the J2EE APIs, it's time to learn about how you are most likely to put them to use: by writing Web applications. This chapter (about servlets) and Chapter 12, which covers JavaServer pages (JSPs), show you how to use two important J2EE technologies in conjunction with WebLogic Server to build and deploy dynamic, scalable Web applications.

What is a Web application? Quite simply, it's a collection of pages, delivered to a Web browser, that provide useful functionality to a community of users. A Web application might be as simple as a personal photo album deployed on the World Wide Web, or as complex as an employee benefits application running on a corporate intranet. You can write both kinds of applications with servlets and JSPs, but you are more likely to use these technologies to write the complex type; this requires effective security as well as the capability to handle substantial user input, to make decisions based on that input, and to interface with databases and other back-end systems to do "real" work.

Servlets are especially important because they bridge the gap between Web browsers and the power of J2EE. A *servlet* is a Java class that receives HTTP requests from a Web server, processes them, and then sends a response back to the HTTP server for transmission to the client's Web browser. In effect, a servlet is a seamless extension of a Web server that can perform any task you are capable of programming in Java. In the case of WebLogic, a servlet is a seamless extension of a Web server that also has complete access to the power of J2EE. From within a WebLogic-hosted servlet, you can

- ✦ Access databases by using JDBC and JTA.
- ✦ Make calls to RMI servers.
- ✦ Perform JNDI lookups.

- Send messages by using JMS.
- Process e-mail by using JavaMail.
- Invoke Enterprise JavaBeans (EJBs).
- Dynamically generate HTML (or any other kind of client-side script) for transmission back to the client.
- Use session tracking to conduct an extended conversation with a client.
- Use security to authenticate users and control their access to content.
- Transfer control to other servlets and JSPs.

That's a lot of power!

Another reason servlets are important is because they are the foundation of JSPs. As you will see in Chapter 12, when a JSP is invoked for the first time, a J2EE-compliant Web container (such as WebLogic) automatically compiles the JSP into a servlet and then executes the servlet any time a request comes in for that JSP (unless the JSP is subsequently changed). Understanding servlets will give you a better understanding of JSPs.

In this chapter, I introduce you to the basics of servlets and show you how to write, deploy, and test a simple servlet for WebLogic Server. Then I cover a number of advanced servlet programming topics, including session tracking, database access, access to the J2EE APIs, security, clustering, and more.

Understanding Servlets

To program servlets effectively, you need to understand the Servlet API, how servlets function within WebLogic's Web container, and how servlets interact with HTTP requests and responses.

The servlet API: Versions and packages

Servlets are Java classes written to the Java Servlet API. WebLogic Server 6.1 implements version 2.3 of the Servlet API, which was released in fall 2001. Version 2.2 of the Servlet API is in common use today, and WebLogic Server 6.1 fully supports this version as well. You can find copies of both versions of the specification at `http://java.sun.com/products/servlet/download.html#specs`.

The Servlet API is implemented in two packages:

- `javax.servlet`, the generic package for servlets that respond to requests using any network protocol

- `javax.servlet.http`, the package for servlets that respond to requests using the HTTP protocol. These are known as *HTTP Servlets* and are the only type of servlets supported by WebLogic Server. I focus on HTTP servlets for the remainder of this chapter.

The Sun JavaDocs for both packages are available at the following locations:

- `http://java.sun.com/products/servlet/2.2/javadoc/` (version 2.2)
- `http://java.sun.com/products/servlet/2.3/javadoc/` (version 2.3)

Every servlet must implement the `javax.servlet.Servlet` interface, and the servlet API contains a class called `javax.servlet.http.HttpServlet` that does so. This is the class you extend when you write HTTP servlets of your own, as in

```
import javax.servlet.*;
import javax.servlet.http.*;

public class MyServlet extends HttpServlet {
  // your class implementation here
}
```

Before diving further into the code, let's examine how servlets are deployed within the WebLogic Web container and how they function in general.

The Web container and Web applications

Recall from Chapter 1 that servlets execute within the WebLogic Web container, as mandated by the J2EE standard. This container provides a runtime environment that includes life cycle support, access to server resources (usually through JNDI lookups), and access to the J2EE APIs. Servlets can also access EJBs and RMI servers that are hosted by WebLogic or other servers, as long as the objects are J2EE-compliant and can be located on the network via JNDI lookups.

In WebLogic 6.1, a servlet exists within the context of a *Web application*. A Web application is a collection of resources that implements a desired functionality. These resources can include servlets, static HTML pages, images, movies, sounds, templates, and so on. The resources are organized into a predefined directory structure on disk, which is defined by the J2EE standard. The application must also contain one or more deployment descriptors, written in XML, that define various properties of the application, including the servlets it contains and the URL patterns required to access them. Web applications deployed in WebLogic Server require two deployment descriptors: `web.xml`, the descriptor required by J2EE, and `weblogic.xml`, a descriptor that provides WebLogic-specific deployment information. Figure 11-1 shows the required directory structure for a Web application. The `Application Root` folder is usually located in the `wlserver6.1/config/<domain name>/applications` folder but can be located anywhere on the server computer.

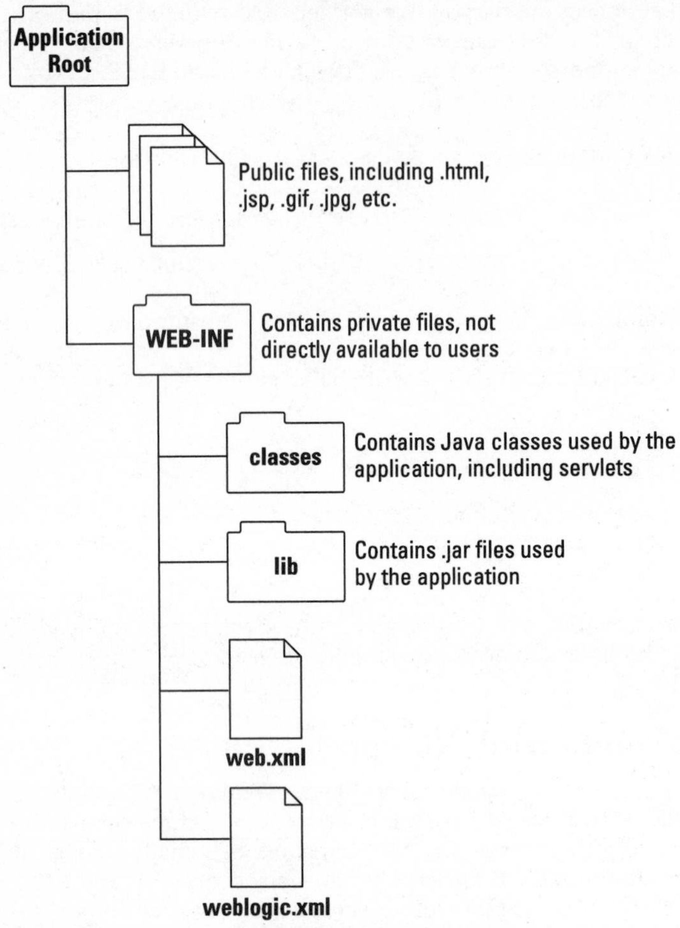

Figure 11-1: Web application directory structure

You can have any number of applications, each inside its own `Application Root` folder. You can name each `Application Root` folder anything you like, but I recommend using names that don't contain spaces.

When developing servlets, you must copy the compiled class files to the `/wlserver6.1/config/<domain name>/<application root>/WEB-INF/classes` directory for your application, or they won't work.

To see an example of a deployed Web application, go to your BEA Home directory (see Chapter 4), and then go to `/wlserver6.1/config/<domain-name>/applications/DefaultWebApp`. Inside this folder is the application that comes up when you point your Web browser to WebLogic Server (by typing **http://localhost:7001**).

To make Web applications more manageable and portable, you can bundle them into an archive, similar to a JAR file, and deploy the archive instead. The archive is called, fittingly enough, a *Web application archive* and is bundled into a WAR file—using the JAR utility, no less. I show you how to create and deploy WAR files later in this chapter.

During development, it's common to deploy to the full directory structure, without creating a WAR file. This makes it easy to replace files with newer versions as development proceeds. Then when you're ready to go into production, you can create a WAR file that can be easily moved to a different box or deployed on multiple boxes in a cluster.

Web applications deployed to a full directory structure will work only if WebLogic Server is running in Development mode. When WebLogic Server is running in Production mode, your Web applications must be deployed in WAR files.

How servlets work

Servlets bridge the gap between two worlds: HTTP and J2EE. The Servlet API is designed to make it easy to work with HTTP requests and responses in a Java-friendly way. And because servlets are ordinary Java classes running within WebLogic, they have complete access to the power of J2EE. In this section, I'll explain how servlets interact with HTTP requests, how servlets are structured programmatically, and how they are managed by WebLogic Server.

HTTP requests

When a client requests data from an HTTP server, it does so by using an HTTP request method. The most commonly used methods are `GET` and `POST`. The `GET` method is used to retrieve information from the server (such as a Web page), while the `POST` method is used to transmit data to the server (such as the data required to complete a credit card transaction).

Even though the `GET` method is used to retrieve data, you can include in your request parameters that specify what to get. These parameters are appended to the request URL in the form of a *querystring*. The querystring is separated from the rest of the URL by a question mark, as in `http://localhost:7001/myWebApp/myServlet?name=Joe+Zuffoletto`.

Parameters are passed as `name=value` pairs. Note that plus signs are used in place of spaces; URLs cannot contain spaces. Multiple parameters are separated by the ampersand (&) character.

Querystrings are visible to users (in the address boxes of their browsers), so make sure that they don't contain privileged information, such as passwords, or information that can be easily hacked. Also, you should only use querystrings for simple requests containing up to a handful of parameters, because some Web servers truncate incoming URLs that exceed 240 characters or so. WebLogic doesn't do this, but if your querystrings contain 100 characters or more, you should consider using the POST method (discussed later in this section) to avoid shipping large URLs around.

Querystrings pose other hazards as well. URLs containing querystrings can be bookmarked; they can also be revisited by clicking the browser's Back button. Therefore, servlets that respond to these types of requests should be designed to perform read-only tasks, such as displaying account activity or the contents of an electronic mailbox. Otherwise, you may cause users to inadvertently make multiple purchases or delete multiple records from a database, which in turn would reduce your marketability as a Java developer.

The POST method sends information to the server in a different way as part of its HTTP request body. This enables you to send long lists of parameters to the server, or parameters of great length, such as graphics or long blocks of text. The data being posted is invisible to the user; it doesn't appear in the URL, so it's slightly more secure. Unlike GET requests, POST requests cannot be bookmarked, e-mailed, or resent with the Back button. Therefore, POST requests are better for transmitting sensitive data, such as the user's approval to purchase something, because there is less chance the user will erroneously duplicate the request.

Other request methods include HEAD, which the client sends when it only wants to see the headers of the response. The PUT method is used to copy documents to the server, and the DELETE method is used to remove documents. The TRACE method is a debugging tool that returns to the client the exact contents of its request, and the OPTIONS method is used to ask the server which methods it supports or what other types of options are available. All these methods are far less commonly used than GET and POST, and I don't cover them any further in this chapter.

How servlets are structured

An *HTTP servlet* is a Java class that extends javax.servlet.http.HttpServlet. It includes methods you can override that map to the various HTTP request methods. These methods are doGet(), doPost(), doHead(), doPut(), doDelete(), doTrace(), and doOptions(). Each of these methods accepts two input parameters. The first is an object of type HttpServletRequest, which contains the client's request data and methods to retrieve it. The second is an object of type HttpServletResponse, into which your response to the request is written. When your servlet finishes executing, WebLogic transmits the data contained in this object back to the client.

HttpServlet also contains a generic service() method that is invoked by the Web container whenever a request comes in for a servlet. This method also receives the HttpServletRequest and HttpServletResponse objects as parameters, and its default behavior is to simply turn around and call the appropriate doXXX() method, based on the HTTP request method received from the client.

When you write a servlet, you can structure your implementation in one of three ways:

- *Override the* `service()` *method.* This causes your servlet to respond to all requests in the same way. This is usually sufficient and is the path most WebLogic developers take.
- *Override one or more of the* `doXXX()` *methods.* This enables you to respond to different types of requests in different ways. But your servlet will return an error message if you receive a request type that you do not support.
- *Override the* `service()` *method and one or more* `doXXX()` *methods.* This technique enables you to respond to different types of requests in different ways while also performing processing common to all types. For this to work, you must call `super.service()` from your `service()` method, or the `doXXX()` methods will not be called.

How WebLogic Server invokes servlets

When WebLogic Server receives a request for a Web page, it examines the incoming URL to see if it maps to a Web application and/or servlet deployed on the server. It makes this determination by examining the `web.xml` file of all deployed applications. These deployment descriptors contain entries that map URL patterns to servlets and other resources.

If the URL maps to a servlet, WebLogic loads the HTTP request information into an `HttpServletRequest` object. It also creates an instance of an `HttpServletResponse` object. It then invokes the servlet's `service()` method, passing the `HttpServletRequest` and `HttpServletResponse` objects as parameters. The servlet does its work, writing data to the `HttpServletResponse` object along the way, and then returns the `HttpServletResponse` object back to WebLogic Server for transmission back to the client. This object usually contains a stream of HTML data, so from the client's perspective, the server simply returned an HTML document. But instead of returning static HTML data from a disk file, the server returns HTML that was dynamically constructed by the servlet — usually in response to one or more input parameters sent by the client — and therein lies the power of servlets.

When to use servlets

When servlets first arrived on the scene, they were used not only to perform server-side processing in response to requests, but also to generate extensive amounts of markup language (usually HTML) for transmission back to the client. A common example is for a servlet to perform a database search based on the contents of its input parameters, and then to render possibly hundreds of rows of results as an HTML table.

Although there is nothing technically wrong with this approach, it creates application maintenance headaches because it causes client-side markup code to be tightly bound with server-side Java code. If a change is desired in the client-side display, even something as simple as a font size or color, a server-side Java developer must be called upon to recode and recompile one or more servlets. This undermines the clean separation J2EE strives to achieve between business and presentation logic.

The designers of J2EE responded to this problem by introducing JSPs. Since the advent of JSPs, the proper way to structure Web applications is to embed presentation logic in JSPs, and business logic in servlets and/or JavaBeans. This allows client-side developers to focus on coding markup language into JSPs and server-side developers to focus on coding Java into servlets and JavaBeans.

JSPs are the topic of Chapter 12.

The upshot of this is that the "proper" use of servlets these days is as server-side controllers and dispatchers that do not generate client-side markup. As a controller, a servlet is called upon to manage access to server-side resources, such as EJBs, JMS message queues, and so on in response to client-side requests. As a dispatcher, a servlet is called upon to forward requests to other servlets or JSPs based on the current state of the application; in other words, the servlet provides server-side support of client-side navigation and workflow.

See Chapter 3 for a more detailed discussion about servlets as controllers and dispatchers.

The early examples in this chapter break the rules a bit and use servlets to generate markup so that you can see how it's done. The later examples, however, try to demonstrate the proper use of servlets as controllers and dispatchers.

The servlet life cycle

A deployed servlet exists in one of five states, which comprise the servlet life cycle:

✦ **Instantiation:** The Web container loads the servlet into memory and calls its default constructor. This happens once in the servlet's lifetime — either the first time a client invokes the servlet or at server startup (if the servlet is configured to load at server startup).

✦ **Initialization:** The Web container calls the servlet's `init()` method to perform initialization tasks. This also happens once: immediately after instantiation. Overriding the `init()` method is your opportunity to perform one-time initialization of data structures, database connections, class variables, and other infrastructure that will be used by the servlet during its lifetime.

✦ **Service:** A client invokes the servlet, resulting in the Web container calling its `service()` method. In HTTP servlets, the `service()` method automatically calls the appropriate `doXXX()` method, which is the method you override to make the servlet do its work.

✦ **Destruction:** The Web container is removing the servlet instance from memory. Before doing so, it calls the servlet's `destroy()` method. You can override this method to perform cleanup tasks, such as closing database connections and reversing tasks you performed in the initialization state.

✦ **Unavailable:** The servlet is destroyed and awaiting garbage collection.

After a servlet is loaded into the JVM, the same instance of the servlet is used to respond to all client requests for that servlet, until either the servlet is modified or WebLogic Server restarts. When either of those events happens, WebLogic calls the servlet's `destroy()` method before unloading it from the JVM.

The exception to this rule is when the servlet implements the `javax.Servlet.SingleThreadModel` interface. By default, each incoming request for a servlet spawns its own execution thread in the JVM, and multiple threads simultaneously execute the servlet if traffic is heavy. You can support heavy concurrent loads if you have your servlet implement the `SingleThreadModel` interface, in which case WebLogic Server spawns a pool of servlet instances, the size of which you specify in the WebLogic Console. WebLogic guarantees that only one thread executes each servlet instance at a time. For more information, see the "Threading Issues in HTTP Servlets" section of the BEA *Programming WebLogic HTTP Servlets* guide.

To detect whether a servlet has been modified, WebLogic periodically compares the timestamp of the servlet instance loaded into memory with that of the servlet's class file on disk. If the timestamps are different, WebLogic assumes the servlet has been modified. When this happens, WebLogic calls the `destroy()` method of the servlet loaded in memory before unloading that instance. Upon loading the modified version from disk, WebLogic calls its `init()` method.

Programming Servlets

To see how to program servlets and deploy them within Web applications, you're going to develop a simple Web application from the ground up that starts with a static HTML document, and then adds a servlet. This will help you understand how Web applications are deployed in WebLogic, and how servlets fit into the picture.

For the rest of this chapter, I develop to the WebLogic domain called `dev` created in Chapter 4. You may want to create the same domain on your machine to follow along with the examples. Also, I am working with WebLogic Server set to Development mode, as explained in Chapter 4.

Creating a simple Web application

Before writing a servlet, let's create and deploy the simplest possible Web application — one that contains a home page implemented as static HTML. This application will become the shell into which you deploy your servlets later.

1. Use your favorite file manager to navigate to the applications directory of your WebLogic domain. On my system, the path is `d:\bea\wlserver6.1\config\dev\applications`. Within this directory, create a directory called `BibleApp`. Then, within `BibleApp`, create empty directories called `WEB-INF` (must be all caps, with a hyphen in the middle and no spaces), `classes`, and `lib`. In other words, create the directory structure shown in Figure 11-1, with the root directory called `BibleApp`.

2. Create a simple home page in HTML using Notepad or your favorite text editor. Here's the code for mine:

```
<html>
<head>
<title>WebLogic 6.1 Bible</title>
<meta http-equiv="Content-Type" content="text/html">
</head>
<body>
Hello, Bible reader!
</body>
</html>
```

   Save this to the `BibleApp` directory as `index.html`.

3. Create a J2EE deployment descriptor, also in your favorite text editor, that matches the following:

```
<!DOCTYPE web-app PUBLIC "-//Sun Microsystems, Inc.//DTD Web
Application 2.3//EN" "http://java.sun.com/dtd/web-app_2_3.dtd">

<web-app>
  <welcome-file-list>
    <welcome-file>index.html</welcome-file>
  </welcome-file-list>
</web-app>
```

   Save this file in the `WEB-INF` directory as `web.xml`. This file tells WebLogic that `index.html` is the welcome file for your Web application; if a user navigates to your Web application without specifying a file in the URL, then `index.html` will be displayed.

The `web.xml` deployment descriptor begins with a reference to the Sun DTD (Document Type Definition) for Web applications. Use the one shown if you want your Web applications to support the features of the Servlet 2.3 specification. If you want to support the Servlet 2.2 specification, use the following DTD instead:

```
<!DOCTYPE web-app PUBLIC "-//Sun Microsystems, Inc.//DTD
Web Application 2.2//EN"
"http://java.sun.com/j2ee/dtds/web-app_2.2.dtd">
```

4. Start WebLogic Server in Development mode. Open your Web browser and go to `http://localhost:7001/BibleApp`. The Web page created in Step 2 should appear, as shown in Figure 11-2.

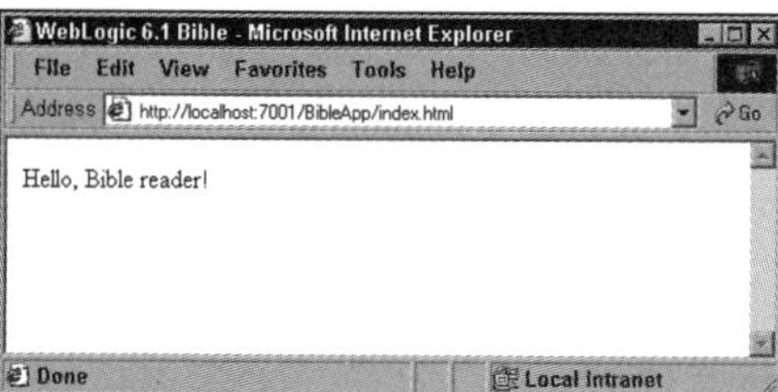

Figure 11-2: BibleApp home page, implemented as HTML

Notice that although the full URL of the home page is `http://localhost:7001/BibleApp/index.html`, you don't need to specify the `index.html` part; it was previously defined in the deployment descriptor as the welcome page.

A peek inside the WebLogic Console shows how WebLogic automatically deployed the application in my domain, as shown in Figure 11-3.

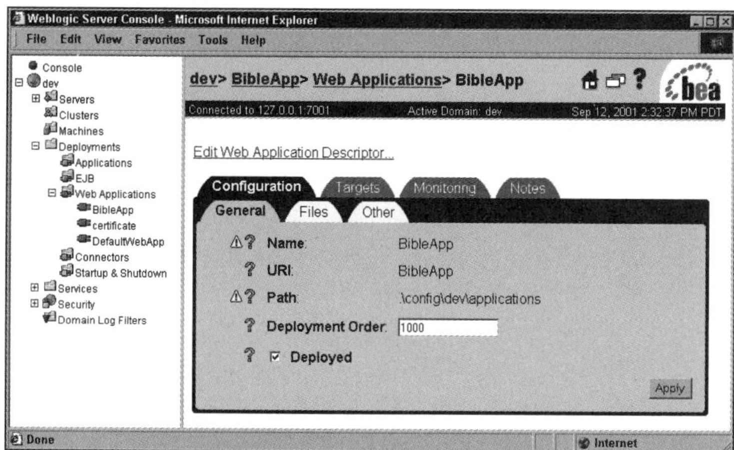

Figure 11-3: The WebLogic Console view of the Web application

Writing a simple servlet

Next you're going to write a simple servlet called `HelloServlet` and add it to the application. This servlet accepts a username as an input parameter, and then outputs that name as part of the HTML page that it creates on the fly. It also keeps count of how many times it has been called. Listing 11-1 shows the Java code for the servlet.

The code begins by importing the `javax.servlet` packages. You also import `java.io.*` so you can work with output streams. You declare an instance variable called `counter`, of type `int`, to keep track of how many times the servlet has been called.

This servlet includes a "do-nothing" default constructor that simply writes a message to the WebLogic command window by using `System.out.println()`. This enables you to follow the servlet's movement through its life cycle when it is invoked. The `init()` method does the same thing, but it also initializes the hit counter by resetting it to zero. A `destroy()` method appears at the end of the listing that writes a message to the command window in support of your life-cycle tracking. Obviously, your production servlets wouldn't waste cycles with methods like `HelloServlet()` and `destroy()` that simply write messages to WebLogic's command window—I've only included them for instructional purposes.

The `service()` method does the servlet's work. Its input parameters enable you to work with the request and response objects associated with the servlet. The first step is to increment the servlet's hit counter, and then to call the `getParameter()` method of the request object to find out what username was provided in the querystring. Recall that querystrings consist of name-value pairs, separated by the `&` character. When you pass one of the names in your querystring to `getParameter()`, it returns a string containing the corresponding value. The name of my parameter is `username`, so I get its value with this line:

```
String userName = request.getParameter("username");
```

The next step is to use the response object to construct an HTML response to the client's request. Begin by calling the response object's `setContentType()` method to tell it you will be returning text formatted as HTML. Then use the `getWriter()` method to obtain a reference to the response object's output stream. It's to this stream that you must send your properly formatted HTML, which you do with a series of `println()` calls. These calls construct, in the proper sequential order, the set of HTML tags that make up your response. Notice in particular the statements that read

```
out.println("<p>Hello, " + name + "!</p>");
out.println("This servlet has been invoked " +
        counter + " times.");
```

This is the *dynamic* portion of the servlet; these statements insert into the HTML the name you received as an input parameter, and the number of times the servlet has invoked. Therefore, if the name changes, so does the HTML that is sent back to the client. The HTML also changes when the counter changes.

Notice how cumbersome it is to generate HTML from within a servlet by using a succession of `PrintWriter.println()` calls. You can imagine the difficulty of maintaining this code for pages that are very complex. This is why JSPs were invented!

The `service()` method closes by writing a message to the WebLogic command window indicating the servlet was invoked.

Listing 11-1: HelloServlet.java

```
package bible.servlets;

import javax.servlet.*;
import javax.servlet.http.*;
import java.io.*;

private int counter = 0;

public class HelloServlet extends HttpServlet {

  public HelloServlet() {
    // Perform instantiation tasks here (rare).
    super();
    System.out.println("HelloServlet instantiated.");
  }

  public void init() throws ServletException {
    // Perform one-time initialization tasks here.
    System.out.println("HelloServlet initialized.");
  }

  public void service(HttpServletRequest request,
   HttpServletResponse response) throws IOException {
    // Do the servlet's work here.
    counter++;
    String userName = request.getParameter("username");
    response.setContentType("text/html");
    PrintWriter out = response.getWriter();
    out.println("<html>");
    out.println("<head><title>HelloServlet</title></head>");
    out.println("<body>");
    out.println("<p>Hello, " + userName + "!</p>");
    out.println("This servlet has been invoked " +
      counter + " times.");
    out.println("</body></html>");
    System.out.println("HelloServlet.doGet() invoked.");
  }

  public void destroy() {
    // Perform cleanup tasks here.
    System.out.println("HelloServlet destroyed.");
  }
}
```

Deploying and testing the servlet

To deploy this servlet, you must compile it (saving the class file to your application's `WEB-INF/classes` directory) and create an entry for it in your `web.xml` deployment descriptor.

Compiling the servlet

A command similar to the following (depending on your classpath and system settings) compiles the servlet and copies the class file into the proper directory:

```
javac -d /BibleApp/WEB-INF/classes HelloServlet.java
```

Adding the servlet to the web.xml deployment descriptor

Modify the `web.xml` deployment descriptor (as shown by the bolded text in the following code sample) to deploy the servlet:

```
<!DOCTYPE web-app PUBLIC "-//Sun Microsystems, Inc.//DTD Web Application
2.3//EN" "http://java.sun.com/j2ee/dtds/web-app_2.3.dtd">

<web-app>
  <welcome-file-list>
    <welcome-file>index.html</welcome-file>
  </welcome-file-list>

  <servlet>
    <servlet-name>helloservlet</servlet-name>
    <servlet-class>bible.servlets.HelloServlet</servlet-class>
  </servlet>

  <servlet-mapping>
    <servlet-name>helloservlet</servlet-name>
    <url-pattern>/helloservlet</url-pattern>
  </servlet-mapping>
</web-app>
```

Studying this file, you can see that the `<welcome-file-list>` has not changed — it still points to `index.html`. But now you have added `<servlet>` and `<servlet-mapping>` tags that tell the Web container the name of my servlet, the class that implements it, and what incoming URL pattern should invoke it. Note that the string you give for `<url-pattern>` should *not* include the name of your Web application; the Web container handles this for you.

After compiling the servlet and updating `web.xml`, stop and restart WebLogic Server. It's best to restart WebLogic Server after changing a deployment descriptor.

Testing the servlet

To invoke a servlet, you provide a URL that matches the following pattern:

```
http://host:port/web-application-name/servlet-name?query-string
```

An example of a URL that invokes `HelloServlet` follows:

```
http://localhost:7001/BibleApp/helloservlet?username=Joe+Zuffoletto
```

Of course, you can provide any value for `username` you like; this is a good thing, because typing my long name gets old in a hurry. The servlet simply retrieves the name provided as an input parameter and inserts it into the HTML it generates in response. Figure 11-4 shows my browser window after invoking the servlet with the preceding URL. If you call the servlet again, the counter will increase until either the servlet's class file changes on disk (causing WebLogic to destroy the in-memory version and load the new disk version) or WebLogic Server is restarted.

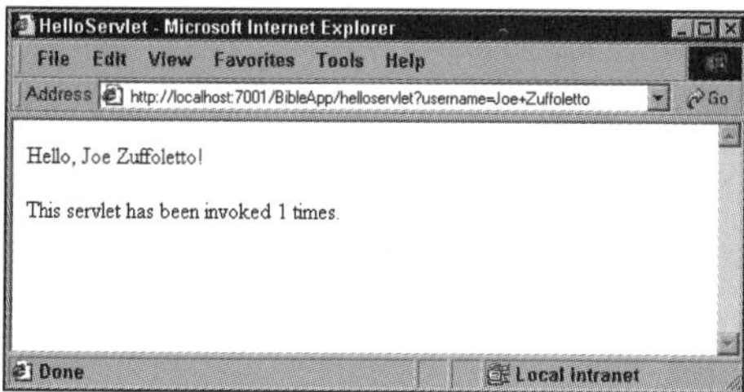

Figure 11-4: Output from HelloServlet

Advanced Servlet Programming Techniques

Now that you've mastered the basics of servlets, it's time to learn about advanced servlet programming techniques that make it possible to build useful applications. These techniques involve working with sessions, working with servlet context, dispatching requests to other application resources, and implementing servlet security.

Working with sessions

A *session* is a prolonged conversation between a server and a client, during which time the client's state is updated and used to drive the client's flow through the application.

As almost every Web developer knows, HTTP is a stateless protocol. Web servers receive requests from clients (usually Web browsers), fulfill those requests, and then move on, completely forgetting about the clients they have served and the requests they have fulfilled in the past.

In traditional client/server systems, clients establish network connections with servers that remain open from the time users start the application until the time they quit. This length of time, which can span from minutes to hours, corresponds to each user's session. During the course of a session, the server and the client can keep track of each other's state and pass that information back and forth at will. As a result, many complex applications have been built by using the client/server model, because it's easy to track a user's progress through the system.

Building such systems with HTTP is more difficult. The problem is that when you interact with a Web server, even for an extended period of time (such as when you're using an online shopping cart), there is no persistent network connection held open between you and the server. Every time you call up a new page, a new network connection is opened. After the page is delivered to you, the network connection is closed. Therefore, the user's concept of a single session with a Web application is actually a multitude of HTTP sessions that are completely independent of each other, and across which no state is maintained.

Note

The HTTP 1.1 specification introduces the notion of connections being held open to service multiple requests from the same client. But the purpose of this feature is strictly to improve performance. It has no impact on HTTP's inability to maintain state.

Fortunately, this limitation of HTTP is easily overcome. Think for a moment about how client/server applications work. When you start such an application, the first thing it does is prompt you for a username and password. This serves two purposes: It makes the system secure, and it gives the server a token that it can use to identify you in order to establish a stateful session. To accomplish the latter, the server matches this token (your unique username) against its user profile database and retrieves your profile for use during the session. This profile might include personal information, such as your name, address, and phone number, as well as application-specific information, such as your access privileges and search preferences. As you move through the application, your profile is updated as necessary. When you quit the application, your updated profile is saved back to the database so it can be reused during your next session.

The next day, you log in to the application again. This new session with the application is completely independent of the last, yet the server is able to restore your state, just as it did the day before, by matching your login token to your user profile.

This same technique is used to achieve the effect of a stateful session with HTTP. A token is created and exchanged between the Web browser and the Web server, uniquely identifying you as a user. The server uses this token to work with your profile on the server. The only differences are that the sessions are shorter and more numerous, and that the token is created by the server instead of the client.

Session-tracking methods

Over the past few years, three methods for tracking sessions and state in Web applications have emerged:

- ✦ URL rewriting
- ✦ Cookies
- ✦ Hidden form fields

All three methods can be used to exchange one or more tokens of the developer's choosing between the Web server and the browser. The server can then use these tokens to retrieve, update, and save a session's state on the server.

URL rewriting

URL rewriting uses querystrings to pass tokens between the browser and server. After a user named John, for example, is identified by the server, the server can dynamically rewrite all URLs served to John so they include his name in the querystring

```
http://myBank.com/reports?type=creditReport&user=John

http://myBank.com/reports?type=accountSummary&user=John
```

and so on. Now whenever John clicks a link in the Web application, his name is transparently sent to the server, where it can be retrieved with a `request.getParameter()` call.

The J2EE specification takes this one step further by requiring that the client-specific token be called `jsessionid`, and that it be automatically generated by the server, as in

```
http://myBank.com/reports?jsessionid=3T78X90W225PQ46&type=creditReport
```

WebLogic Server generates long, random `jsessionids`. This increases security by reducing the chances a user will masquerade as someone by faking their `jsessionid`. Furthermore, you don't use `request.getParameter()` to manipulate `jsessionids` yourself. Instead, you use other methods in the servlet API to work with the session. I explain these in the next section.

Chapter 23 discusses configuring `jsessionid` length in the WebLogic Console.

Because rewritten URLs are different for each user, URL rewriting cannot be used in static HTML pages. The server must dynamically generate pages that include rewritten URLs, either by using servlets or JSPs. To specify that a URL is to be rewritten, use the `javax.servlet.http.HttpServletResponse.encodeURL()` method. The following statement in a servlet, for example, generates a non-encoded URL:

```
out.println("<a href=\"/reports?type=creditReport\">Credit Report</a>");
```

To encode the same URL, write the following:

```
out.println(<a href=\"" + response.encodeURL("/reports?type=creditReport) +
         "\">Credit Report</a>");
```

Cookies

Cookies are the most popular technology used for session tracking. A *cookie* is a token sent to a Web browser as part of an HTTP response header. The cookie is saved by the browser and then resubmitted to the server the next time the browser connects to that server.

A cookie consists of a name, a value, and optional attributes. The attributes include the following:

- ✦ The Internet domain to which the browser should present the cookie, and optionally a path within that domain. The default is the domain that issued the cookie.
- ✦ The cookie's lifetime, after which the cookie expires and is no longer valid
- ✦ A security setting that determines whether the cookie must be presented using a secure protocol, such as SSL
- ✦ The cookie's version
- ✦ A short comment stating the cookie's purpose

In J2EE, cookies are created and sent by servlets and JSPs by using the `javax.servlet.http.Cookie` class. The following code shows how to do this.

```
// Create a new cookie, providing a name and value
// to its constructor.
Cookie cookie = new Cookie("userID", "John");

// Set the cookie's lifetime in seconds.
// This one expires in 2 hours.
cookie.setMaxAge(7200);

// Set the cookie's domain. Note the leading dot.
cookie.setDomain(".myBank.com");

// Set the cookie's path within the domain. The cookie
// is presented only to URLs in that path.
cookie.setPath("/myWebApp");

// Add the cookie to the HTTP response.
response.addCookie(cookie);
```

Corresponding methods exist to read the values and attributes of cookies.

You can learn more about cookies by reading RFC 2109, available at `http://www.faqs.org/rfcs/rfc2109.html`.

The problem with cookies is that some users perceive them to be a security risk, so they disable cookies in their browser. Obviously, if a user has disabled cookies, you cannot use them to track sessions.

Hidden form fields

Hidden form fields are similar in concept to URL rewriting, except that tokens are embedded in HTML forms as hidden fields, as in the following:

```
<input type="hidden" name="userID" value="John">
```

The tokens are invisible to the user but are posted to the server when the form is submitted. The server can then read the values of the hidden fields and act on them.

Like URL rewriting, this approach requires the affected pages to be dynamically generated by the server. But this approach is more restrictive than URL rewriting, because it can only be used on pages that employ HTML forms.

How J2EE implements session tracking

J2EE implements session tracking through the servlet API by using a collection of methods that are intuitive and easy to use. Behind the scenes, the servlet API uses cookies and URL rewriting to implement the session-tracking calls. Hidden form fields are not used at all.

Creating a session

To enable session tracking in your Web application, you must first create a session, which is an instance of `javax.servlet.http.HttpSession`. To do so, you call `HttpServletRequest.getSession()`:

```
HttpSession session = request.getSession();
```

Sessions are bound to users. If a session already exists for the current user, `getSession()` returns the existing session. Otherwise, it creates a new one.

To create a session, `getSession()` transparently creates a cookie *and* rewrites your URLs. These are transmitted to the browser in the next response, at which time the browser may or may not join the session. If the browser accepts cookies, it sends the cookie back with the next request and is said to have *joined the session.* The servlet API detects this and automatically uses cookies for the remainder of the session. But if a cookie is not returned, the servlet API assumes the browser has rejected the cookie, and it automatically uses URL rewriting instead. In this case, the browser has not joined the session, but if your application uses URL rewriting, you'll still be able to perform session tracking. Therefore, if you want your applications to work with or without cookies, you must use URL rewriting.

Working with session attributes

You can store any number of named attributes into a session and retrieve them later. Each attribute must have a unique name. The following code shows how to do this.

```
HttpSession session = request.getSession();
session.setAttribute("userID", "John");
session.setAttribute("accountNo", "1234-345-456");
session.setAttribute("phoneNo", "555-1212");
...
String userID = (String) session.getAttribute("userID");
String accountNo = (String) session.getAttribute("accountNo");
String phoneNo = (String) session.getAttribute("phoneNo");
```

`setAttribute()` creates the attribute if it doesn't exist; otherwise, it overwrites its value. `getAttribute()` returns null if the given attribute doesn't exist.

You can also permanently remove an attribute from a session:

```
session.removeAttribute("phoneNo");
```

By default, WebLogic caches session attributes in memory, so they don't persist across server restarts. You can, however, configure WebLogic to support persistent sessions by using either a disk file or JDBC data source as a backing store. For more information, see the section "Making Sessions Persistent," in the *Programming WebLogic HTTP Servlets* guide.

Invalidating a session

When a user's session has ended, you can invalidate it. This removes all attributes bound to the session and effectively kills the session:

```
session.invalidate();
```

You normally call `invalidate()` when a user explicitly logs off your Web application, or when you choose to log the user off.

If you don't explicitly invalidate a session, WebLogic will automatically invalidate it after it expires. All sessions expire after a certain period of time, which you can configure in the WebLogic Console. The default is 60 minutes.

Working with the servlet context

While sessions allow your application's servlets to maintain state with users, the *servlet context* allows your servlets and JSPs to maintain state with each other across the entire Web application. Every Web application has its own servlet context, which you can think of as a global storage area for the application.

You access an application's servlet context through the `javax.servlet.ServletContext` interface, which provides methods for storing and retrieving attributes, obtaining information about the servlet container and the servlet's runtime environment, logging events to the application log file, and more.

To obtain a reference to the servlet context, call `ServletContext.getServletContext()`:

```
ServletContext ctx = this.getServletContext();
```

where `this` refers to your class that extends `HttpServlet`.

After you have a reference to the servlet context, you can set and get attributes much like you would with a session:

```
ctx.setAttribute("myAttribute", myObject);
myObject = (myObjectType) ctx.getAttribute("myAttribute");
```

`setAttribute()` takes a string containing a unique name for the attribute and an object containing the attribute's data. `getAttribute()` returns the object corresponding to the given name or null if no attribute by that name exists.

You can remove attributes with the `removeAttribute()` method:

```
ctx.removeAttribute("myAttribute");
```

`ServletContext` contains a number of other useful methods; see the JavaDocs for more information.

A Web application contains only one servlet context. The servlet context exists for the lifetime of the application and cannot be invalidated or destroyed by the programmer.

Dispatching requests to other resources

One of the most important features of servlets is their capability to act as traffic cops for your application. Instead of responding to HTTP requests themselves, servlets can dispatch the requests to other servlets, JSPs, or even static HTML pages residing on the same server. Thus, servlets can manage the flow of control through the application based on decisions made in the business logic.

Two types of dispatching are available: *forwarding* and *redirecting*. Forwarding is achieved through the `javax.servlet.RequestDispatcher` interface, and redirecting through the `javax.servlet.http.HttpServletResponse` interface.

When should you forward, and when should you redirect? Behind the scenes, the two function quite differently. When you forward, the Web container makes a direct call to the target resource without the browser's knowledge. Therefore, the URL in the browser's address window does not change. If users refresh the display or otherwise cause the page to reload (in some browsers, merely resizing the window will do it), they get the page you forwarded from, not the page you forwarded to.

Redirecting, on the other hand, forces the browser to issue a completely new request to the target page, as if users had requested it themselves.

To forward a request, you call `javax.servlet.RequestDispatcher.forward()`, passing the request and response objects as parameters. You obtain a reference to the `RequestDispatcher` interface either from the `ServletContext` or the `HttpServletRequest`. The following code snippet shows how to obtain a `RequestDispatcher` from the `ServletContext` and then forward the request to a servlet called `registerServlet` located at the root of the servlet context (at the application root):

```
if (!user.isRegistered) {
  ServletContext ctx = this.getServletContext();
  RequestDispatcher dispatcher =
    ctx.getRequestDispatcher("/registerServlet");
  dispatcher.forward(request, response);
}
```

Note that you can also forward to a JSP by using its file name, such as `/register.jsp`.

The next snippet shows how to obtain a `RequestDispatcher` from the `HttpServletRequest` and then forward to the same servlet:

```
if (!user.isRegistered) {
  RequestDispatcher dispatcher =
    request.getRequestDispatcher("/registerServlet");
  dispatcher.forward(request, response);
}
```

These methods work identically in this example, but there is a key difference between them. In the `ServletContext` version, the path you provide for the `RequestDispatcher` must begin with a / and is always relative to the context root. In the `HttpServletRequest` version, you can omit the leading /, in which case the path is interpreted to be relative to the servlet doing the forwarding.

The next code snippet shows how to redirect. In this example, users indicate they want to log off of your application, so you invalidate their session and redirect them to your home page:

```
if (request.getParameter("action").equals("logoff")) {
  session.invalidate();
  response.sendRedirect("/myApp/home.html");
}
```

The rules for URL rewriting apply for both versions of `forward()` and `redirect()`, so be sure to encode your target URLs in case cookies are turned off, as in

```
response.sendRedirect(response.encodeURL("/myApp/home.html"));
```

Securing your application

Security is an essential part of many Web applications, as it is often necessary to restrict access to a site to authorized users or to provide different levels of access to different groups of users. WebLogic supports a number of basic security mechanisms that you can incorporate into your Web applications. You can also roll your own security by using J2EE facilities such as the Java Authentication and Authorization Service (JAAS). The following sections focus on the basic security mechanisms available to WebLogic Web applications. JAAS and other advanced security topics are covered in Part VI.

Application security consists of two elements: *authentication* and *authorization.* Authentication is the process of verifying a user's identity, usually by prompting for a username and password, or perhaps a digital certificate, and checking that against a user database. Authorization is the process of granting a user access to various parts of an application based on that person's level of access privileges. The WebLogic Web security mechanisms support both authentication and authorization.

To secure a Web application, perform the following steps:

1. Use the WebLogic Console to define the users and groups that will have access to your application.
2. Select an authentication method. WebLogic supports three methods, which I explain in the next section. Each Web application uses only one of these methods. You specify your method in the application's deployment descriptor, `web.xml`.
3. Define one or more security constraints, also in `web.xml`. Each security constraint protects a set of resources (HTML pages, servlets, JSPs, and so on) that share a common URL pattern. The presence of a security constraint on a resource automatically triggers the authentication method you selected whenever a user tries to access that resource.
4. Define one or more security roles in `web.xml` and map them to your security constraints. Security roles define the different types of users who use the application. You can define any number of roles, such as administrator, manager, and normal user, and map any number of them to each security constraint. You can, for example, specify that administrative screens are available only to administrators, reporting screens only to managers, and everything else to adminstrators plus managers plus normal users.
5. Create security role assignments, which map the users and groups you defined in Step 1 to the security roles you defined in Step 4. These mappings go into the `weblogic.xml` file, which is the WebLogic-specific deployment descriptor for Web applications. You must create `weblogic.xml` in a text editor (if it doesn't exist already) and put it into your application's `WEB-INF` folder.

I demonstrate these five steps later in this chapter when I show you how to create and deploy a secured Web application.

WebLogic supports three methods of authentication for Web applications: *basic, form-based,* and *client certificates.* You can also devise your own authentication mechanism, but that's beyond the scope of this chapter.

Basic authentication

Basic authentication is the oldest form of Web authentication. In this scheme, the Web browser displays a pop-up window prompting for a username and password whenever the user encounters a protected resource. This is the method employed by the WebLogic Console, as shown in Figure 11-5.

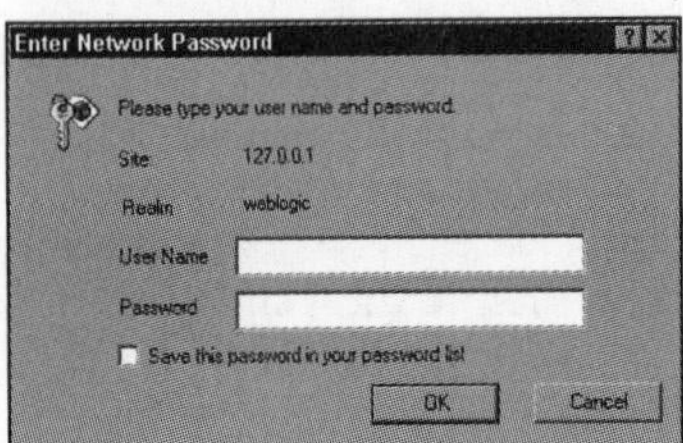

Figure 11-5: Pop-up window that appears in a Web browser for applications that employ basic authentication

To specify basic authentication as the method to use in your application, make the following entries to `web.xml`:

```
<web-app>
  ...
  <login-config>
    <auth-method>BASIC</auth-method>
    <realm-name>default</realm-name>
  </login-config>
  ...
</web-app>
```

The realm-name entry specifies that the WebLogic default File realm is to be used for authenticating users. Security realms, including the File realm, are covered in Part VI of this book.

Form-based authentication

With form-based authentication, you provide an HTML page, JSP, or servlet that renders a login screen. Additionally, you provide an error screen to which the user is redirected if the login fails. This gives you complete control over the appearance and navigation on these screens, so you can make them fit into the rest of your application.

The login screen you provide must follow certain rules so that the container can accurately retrieve its data to perform authentication. The form should only prompt for a username and password, and must return them in form elements named `j_username` and `j_password`, respectively. Additionally, the form action attribute must be called `j_security_check`.

The following HTML renders the simplest possible login form:

```
<html>
  <head>
    <title>My Web Application</title>
  </head>
  <body>
    <p>Welcome to my Web application! Please log in.</p>
    <form method="POST" action="j_security_check">
      <p>User name: <input type="text" name="j_username"></p>
      <p>Password: <input type="password" name="j_password"></p>
      <p><input type="submit" name="Submit" value="Login"></p>
    </form>
  </body>
</html>
```

Figure 11-6 shows the form as it appears in a Web browser.

Figure 11-6: Login screen for form-based authentication

The error page has no design requirements; you can design it any way you want.

The following entries in `web.xml` demonstrate how to specify static HTML pages as the login and error pages:

```
<web-app>
  ...
  <login-config>
```

```
    <auth-method>FORM</auth-method>
    <realm-name>default</realm-name>
    <form-login-config>
      <form-login-page>login.html</form-login-page>
      <form-error-page>loginError.html</form-error-page>
    </form-login-config>
  </login-config>
  ...
</web-app>
```

Note that you use servlets and/or JSPs for the login and error pages, as long as they render the login form according to the rules described earlier.

Authenticating with client certificates

Client certificates enable you to authenticate users in a highly secure manner by using digital certificates and Secure Socket Layers (SSL). Configuring WebLogic to support client certificates is a complex, multistep process that is beyond the scope of this chapter. You can find more information about it in the WebLogic documentation, under "Configuring the SSL Protocol." This information is available on the Internet at `http://e-docs.bea.com/wls/docs61/adminguide/cnfgsec.html#cnfgsec015`.

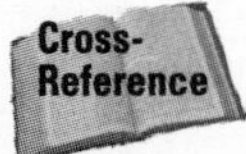

You can also refer to Part VI of this book for more information about securing Web applications with client certificates.

Building an Advanced Application with Servlets

In this section, you're going to build a Web application that uses the advanced features just discussed, including sessions, the servlet context, request dispatching, and security. In the process, I demonstrate how to properly configure and deploy such an application in WebLogic Server, and how to configure a simple security scheme by using the WebLogic Console and the application's deployment descriptors.

Gathering the requirements

The application, called `BibleServlets`, has two entry points: one for normal users and one for administrators. The application's home page welcomes users to the application and provides hyperlinks to the two entry points.

Clicking either entry point brings up the login form, where the user is prompted for a name and password. An error page is displayed if the login is invalid; otherwise, the user gains entry to their chosen entry point.

The normal user area is a simple succession of five Web pages that the user can traverse in forward or reverse. Each page displays the user's name and the number of the page they are on (1 through 5), as well as hyperlinks to the previous and next pages. Each page also contains a hyperlink to log off, which returns the user to the home page.

The administrator area is a Web page that lists the names of all users who are navigating through the normal user area, along with what page numbers they are on. If no one is logged on, the page indicates that as well. The page also provides a hyperlink to log off.

Once users have logged into the application, they cannot log in again from a different Web browser. If they attempt to do so, their login attempt is rejected.

Finally, the application must work even if cookies are turned off in the client's browser.

Figure 11-7 shows a flow diagram for the application.

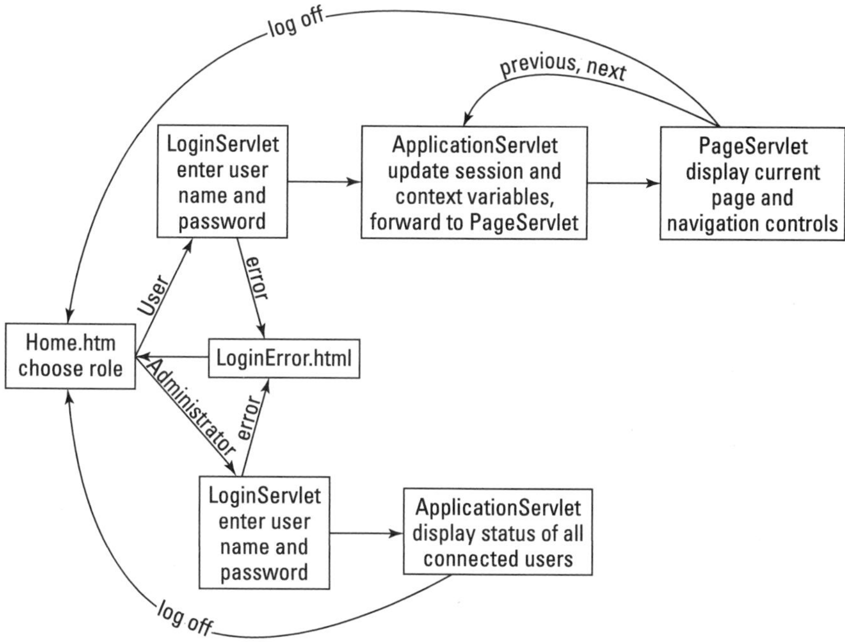

Figure 11-7: Flow diagram for the advanced servlet application

Brainstorming a design

You will implement the meat of the application with two servlets: one to manage the normal user pages, and one for the administrator page. Call the first servlet `ApplicationServlet` and the second `AdminServlet`.

If you think about it for a moment, you can see that `ApplicationServlet` is a dispatcher. It sends users to one of five pages based on the page they're on and the direction in which they want to go (forward or backward). Therefore, you need to keep track of who each user is and which page they're on. This is the perfect kind of information to store in the session. You also need to know the direction in which the user wants to go. This is a good job for a parameter passed as a querystring, so you'll design `ApplicationServlet` to accept and act on such a parameter.

The five application pages themselves must be dynamically generated if they are to display the user's name and current page, and also if they are to support URL rewriting to meet the cookies/no cookies requirement. Therefore, you will implement these pages as servlets.

In a real-world application, you would implement these pages as JSPs because they consist mostly of markup language. But JSPs are the topic of the next chapter, so stick with servlets for now.

Closer study of the requirements reveals that the five application pages are identical except for the page number displayed. Therefore, you can easily write a single servlet, which you will call `PageServlet`, to generate these pages. After updating the application's business logic, `ApplicationServlet` will forward to `PageServlet`, which will render the appropriate page. This will give a nice demonstration of request dispatching.

Now let's turn to `AdminServlet`. Its purpose is to display the current state of all active sessions. Somehow it must be able to communicate with all instances of `ApplicationServlet` to discover what pages the users are on. This is a job for the servlet context. You'll add code to `ApplicationServlet` to store each user's name and page number into the servlet context, and code `AdminServlet` to retrieve this information and render it as HTML in the browser.

The home page will be implemented as static HTML with links to the two servlets.

You will use form-based authentication to control access to the application, and you will define security roles to differentiate between administrators and normal users. Only administrators are allowed to execute `AdminServlet`, and all authenticated users are allowed to execute `ApplicationServlet`. For the sake of illustration, you will implement the login page as a servlet called `LoginServlet`. The login error page, however, will be straight HTML.

Wow! You gathered your requirements and documented your design. Now you can start coding!

Building the application

In this section, I'll show you how to build the advanced servlet application, step by step.

Creating the directory structure and home page

The first thing you need to do is set up a directory structure for your application in the WebLogic domain. Create a directory in the domain's `applications` directory called `BibleServlets`, and create another directory within that called `WEB-INF`. Then populate `WEB-INF` with directories called `classes` and `lib`, as discussed earlier in this chapter.

Next create a static HTML home page for your application. Listing 11-2 shows the code.

Listing 11-2: Home.html, the home page for BibleServlets

```
<html>
<head>
<title>WebLogic 6.1 Bible</title>
<meta http-equiv="Content-Type" content="text/html">
</head>

<body>
<p>Welcome to BibleServlets! Please choose your role:</p>
<p><a href="/BibleServlets/ServletDemo/ApplicationServlet">User</a></p>
<p><a href="/BibleServlets/ServletDemo/AdminServlet">Administrator</a></p>
</body>
</html>
```

This code contains instructions for the user, along with hyperlinks to the servlets. Notice the links are fully qualified, starting with `/BibleServlets`. This is necessary for static HTML pages in a WebLogic application.

Save the home page into the `BibleServlets` directory, where it is available to all users. Also create a `web.xml` file, add a `<welcome-file>` tag that points to `Home.html`, and save it into the `WEB-INF` directory. Here are the initial contents of `web.xml`:

```
<!DOCTYPE web-app PUBLIC "-//Sun Microsystems, Inc.//DTD Web Application
2.3//EN" "http://java.sun.com/j2ee/dtds/web-app_2.3.dtd">

<web-app>
  <welcome-file-list>
    <welcome-file>Home.html</welcome-file>
  </welcome-file-list>
</web-app>
```

Now you can start WebLogic Server and test your application by navigating to `http://localhost:7001/BibleServlets`. Figure 11-8 shows the resulting display in a Web browser.

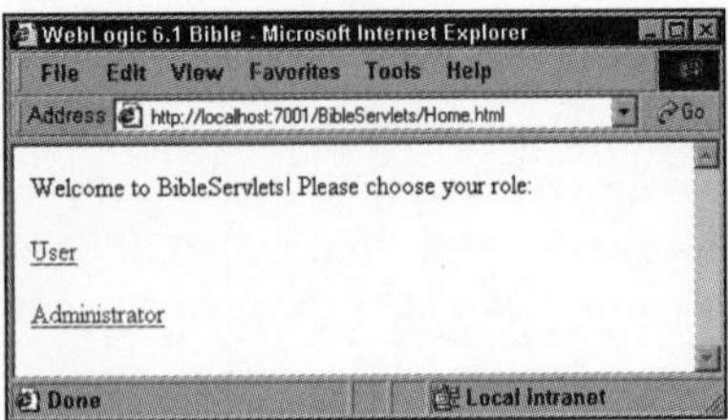

Figure 11-8: The home page for the BibleServlets application

Implementing form-based authentication

Now you're going to create the pages to implement form-based authentication. The first is `LoginServlet`, which generates an HTML form that follows the rules for accepting a username and password (as discussed earlier in this chapter). Listing 11-3 shows the code for `LoginServlet`.

Listing 11-3: LoginServlet

```
package bible.servlets;

import javax.servlet.*;
import javax.servlet.http.*;
import java.io.*;
import java.util.*;

public class LoginServlet extends HttpServlet {

  public void service(HttpServletRequest request,
                      HttpServletResponse response)
  throws IOException {
    response.setContentType("text/html");
    PrintWriter out = response.getWriter();
    out.println("<html>");
    out.println("<head><title>BibleServlets</title></head>");
    out.println("<body>");
    out.println("<p>Welcome to BibleServlets! Please log in.</p>");
    out.println("<form method=\"POST\" action=\"" +
          response.encodeURL("j_security_check") + "\">");
    out.print("<p>User name: ");
    out.println("<input type=\"text\" name=\"j_username\"></p>");
```

```
        out.print("<p>Password: ");
        out.println("<input type=\"password\" name=\"j_password\"></p>");
        out.print("<p><input type=\"submit\" ");
        out.println("name=\"Submit\" value=\"Login\"></p>");
        out.println("</form>");
        out.println("</body></html>");
    }
}
```

If you refer to the HTML code for a simple login page earlier, you'll notice that LoginServlet does little more than spit out that code. The only difference is that you rewrite the URL for the j_security_check page by using response.encodeURL(). This ensures that the login page will function with cookies turned off and is also the reason you implemented the page as a servlet.

After compiling this servlet to the WEB-INF/classes directory, create the login error page called LoginError.html. The HTML for this page appears in Listing 11-4. This page notifies users of a problem with their login and includes a button that returns them to Home.html.

Listing 11-4: **LoginError.html**

```
<html>
<head>
<title>BibleServlets Login Error</title>
<meta http-equiv="Content-Type" content="text/html">
</head>

<body>
<p>An error occurred trying to log you in. Please double-check your user name
and password.</p>
<form method="POST" action="Home.html">
<input type="submit" name="submit" value="Start Over">
</form>
</body>
</html>
```

The next piece of the login puzzle is to add a <login-config> tag to web.xml, which tells the Web container that you're using the form-based authentication method. It also specifies which security realm to use for authentication, and which resources to use for the login page and error page. The security realm is default, which corresponds to the WebLogic default File realm.

I will defer an involved discussion about WebLogic security until later in the book. Chapters 20 and 21 explain the various types of security realms supported by WebLogic, including the File realm.

```
<login-config>
  <auth-method>FORM</auth-method>
  <realm-name>default</realm-name>
  <form-login-config>
    <form-login-page>ServletDemo/LoginServlet</form-login-page>
    <form-error-page>LoginError.html</form-error-page>
  </form-login-config>
</login-config>
```

Defining users in the WebLogic File realm

Because your application requires authentication, you need to define a set of authorized users. The place to do it is the WebLogic Console. Create users in the File realm named `Joe`, `Gary`, and `Roya`. To do so, expand the Security node in the domain tree, and then click Users. This presents you with the page to add a new user. Figure 11-9 shows the Users page after you enter the information for `Joe`.

Figure 11-9: Adding a new user to the File realm

Click Create, and `Joe` is added to the list of existing users at the bottom of the page. Figure 11-10 shows the state of your File realm after adding all three users.

This is all the work you need to do in the WebLogic Console. The remainder of the security setup takes place in the application's deployment descriptors. I'll come back to that later in the chapter.

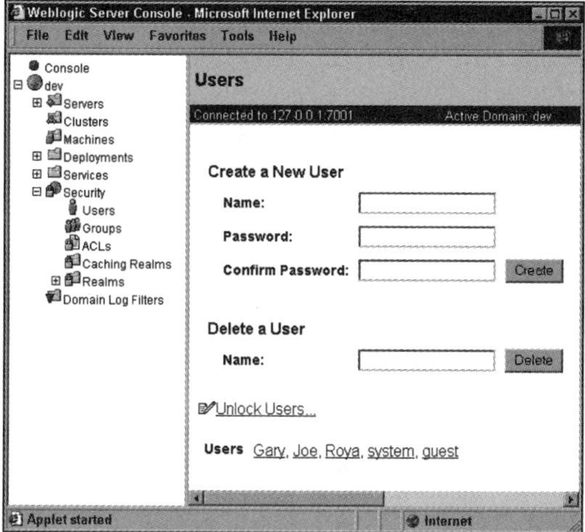

Figure 11-10: The state of your user list after adding Gary, Joe, and Roya

Writing the dispatcher servlet

The next step is to write `ApplicationServlet`, your application's dispatcher.

Creating the servlet shell

Listing 11-5 shows the shell for this servlet. You will implement a `service()` method only, so the servlet will respond to all types of HTTP requests.

Listing 11-5: ApplicationServlet shell

```
package bible.servlets;

import javax.servlet.*;
import javax.servlet.http.*;
import java.io.*;
import java.util.*;

public class ApplicationServlet extends HttpServlet {

  public void service(HttpServletRequest request,
                      HttpServletResponse response)
  throws ServletException, IOException {
  }

}
```

ApplicationServlet's job is to track the user's state through a series of five sequential Web pages. Therefore, it might be handy to define some class variables to track the first and last pages of this sequence. These variables are simply integer constants:

```
private static final int FIRST_PAGE = 1;
private static final int LAST_PAGE = 5;
```

The servlet will work with the session in order to track each user's state. It will also work with the servlet context in order to share that state with AdminServlet. Therefore, kick off the service() method by obtaining references to these structures:

```
ServletContext ctx = this.getServletContext();
HttpSession session = request.getSession();
```

Retrieving the username

Another piece of information you need is the name of the user, because you plan to use that as part of the unique key that identifies each session in the servlet context. You also need the user's name to enforce the "one user, one session" rule spelled out in the requirements.

The problem is that the Web container handles form-based authentication automatically, so there's no obvious way for you to obtain the username from the login screen. One thing to notice is that the Web container automatically creates a session for users if they're authenticated. So maybe it copies the j_username attribute into the session, where you can retrieve it with the following call:

```
String userName = session.getAttribute("j_username");
```

Unfortunately, this is not the case. Even if it were, this code would not be portable, because the j_username and j_password attributes are WebLogic-specific.

The good news is that the ServletRequest interface contains a call that gets the username for you: getRemoteUser(). And it just so happens that when a user logs in successfully, WebLogic stuffs its j_username attribute into the Web container, where it can be returned by getRemoteUser():

```
String userName = request.getRemoteUser();
```

This is the perfect solution, because it is completely vendor-independent.

Tracking state in the session and in the servlet context

Now that you know who the user is, you can start tracking their state as they move through the application. At the session level, you do this with an attribute called sessionInfo, which you stuff with a Hashtable containing the user's name and current page. This attribute can have the same name for every session, because every session is different.

At the servlet context level, things are slightly different. You stuff the same Hashtable into the context, but you must ensure the attribute you map it to has a unique name, because you're stuffing Hashtables for all users into the same context. You must also devise a way of naming your attributes that makes them distinguishable from attributes stuffed into the context by the Web container. Otherwise, you won't be able to reliably retrieve them later.

One other item: ApplicationServlet must be able to distinguish a new user from a returning user, because its behavior is slightly different for the two groups. If users are new, ApplicationServlet must establish their initial state and save it to the session and servlet context. Then it sends them to the first page. If users are returning, ApplicationServlet must retrieve their state from the session, update their page number, and forward them to that page.

So how can ApplicationServlet tell a new user from a returning user? You can't do it by checking for a null versus non-null session, because form-based authentication passes you a valid session for every authenticated user. A new session, however, does not contain any of the attributes you've defined. Therefore, you can detect if the user is new by checking for a sessionInfo attribute in the session. If it doesn't exist, session.getAttribute() returns null, and then you know the user is new.

The first half of ApplicationServlet initializes a sessionInfo structure for a new user and then saves it to the session and servlet context. It uniquely names sessionInfo structures in the servlet context with the value session_ plus the user's name, so you can reliably retrieve them later. And it checks to see if a returning user is already logged in, in which case it invalidates the second user's session, redirects that user to the home page, and exits the servlet.

The second half of ApplicationServlet updates the state variables for your session based on the value of the query parameter passed to the servlet. It then forwards the request to PageServlet, which draws a Web page that reflects the state of the session.

The query parameter for ApplicationServlet is called action, and its legal values are previous, next, logoff, and null (if the session is new). The following URL, for example, invokes ApplicationServlet with an instruction to go to the next page:

```
http://localhost:7001/BibleServlets/ApplicationServlet?action=next
```

Listing 11-6 contains the full implementation of ApplicationServlet.

Listing 11-6: ApplicationServlet.java

```
package bible.servlets;

import javax.servlet.*;
import javax.servlet.http.*;
import java.io.*;
import java.util.*;

public class ApplicationServlet extends HttpServlet {

  private static final int FIRST_PAGE = 1;
  private static final int LAST_PAGE = 5;

  public void service(HttpServletRequest request,
                      HttpServletResponse response)
  throws ServletException, IOException {

    ServletContext ctx = this.getServletContext();
    HttpSession session = request.getSession();
    String userName = request.getRemoteUser();
    Hashtable sessionInfo = null;

    if (session.getAttribute("sessionInfo") == null) {
      // New user. Create a Hashtable to track their
      // session state.
      sessionInfo = new Hashtable();
      sessionInfo.put("userName", userName);
      sessionInfo.put("pageNumber", new Integer(FIRST_PAGE));
      session.setAttribute("sessionInfo", sessionInfo);
      // See if the new user is already logged in by checking
      // for their sessionInfo in the servlet context.
      if (ctx.getAttribute("session_" + userName) == null) {
        // Not already logged in. Save their sessionInfo to
        // the servletContext and continue.
        ctx.setAttribute("session_" + userName, sessionInfo);
      } else {
        // Already logged in elsewhere. Invalidate this session
        // and kick this user out.
        session.invalidate();
        response.sendRedirect(
          response.encodeURL("/BibleServlets/Home.html"));
        return;
      }
    } else {
      // Returning user. Retrieve their state from the session.
      sessionInfo = (Hashtable) session.getAttribute("sessionInfo");
      Integer pageNumber = (Integer)sessionInfo.get("pageNumber");
      int nextPage = pageNumber.intValue();
      pageNumber = null;
```

```
        // Read the query string to determine the user's desired
        // action. Update their state in the session accordingly.
        if (request.getParameter("action").equals("next")) {
          // Go to the next page. Wrap around to the
          // first page after passing the last page.
          nextPage++;
          if (nextPage > LAST_PAGE) {
            nextPage = FIRST_PAGE;
          }
          sessionInfo.put("pageNumber", new Integer(nextPage));
        } else if (request.getParameter("action").equals("previous")) {
          // Go to the previous page. Wrap around to the last page
          // after passing the first page.
          nextPage--;
          if (nextPage < FIRST_PAGE) {
            nextPage = LAST_PAGE;
          }
          sessionInfo.put("pageNumber", new Integer(nextPage));
        } else if (request.getParameter("action").equals("logoff")) {
          // User wants to log off. Invalidate their session,
          // remove their session info from the servlet context,
          // redirect them to the home page, and then quit.
          session.invalidate();
          ctx.removeAttribute("session_" + userName);
          response.sendRedirect(
            response.encodeURL("/BibleServlets/Home.html"));
          return;
        }
      }
      // Forward all non-logoff requests to the PageServlet.
      request.getRequestDispatcher("PageServlet").forward(request, response);
    }
}
```

Writing the page-rendering servlet

Listing 11-7 contains the full implementation of `PageServlet`, which simply renders HTML for the browser that reflects the user's current position within the application.

Listing 11-7: PageServlet.java

```
package bible.servlets;

import javax.servlet.*;
import javax.servlet.http.*;
```

Continued

Listing 11-7 *(continued)*

```
import java.io.*;
import java.util.*;

public class PageServlet extends HttpServlet {

  public void service(HttpServletRequest request,
                      HttpServletResponse response)
  throws ServletException, IOException {
    HttpSession session = request.getSession();
    Hashtable sessionInfo =
      (Hashtable) session.getAttribute("sessionInfo");
    String userName = (String) sessionInfo.get("userName");
    Integer pageNumber = (Integer) sessionInfo.get("pageNumber");

    response.setContentType("text/html");
    PrintWriter out = response.getWriter();
    out.println("<html>");
    out.println("<head><title>ApplicationServlet</title></head>");
    out.println("<body>");
    out.println("<p>Welcome to the ApplicationServlet.</p>");
    out.println("<p>Your name is " + userName + " and you are on page " +
      pageNumber.intValue() + ".</p>");
    out.println("<p></p>");
    out.println("<p><a href=\"" +
      response.encodeURL("ApplicationServlet?action=next") +
                         "\">Next Page</a></p>");
    out.println("<p></p>");
    out.println("<p><a href=\"" +
      response.encodeURL("ApplicationServlet?action=previous") +
                         "\">Previous Page</a></p>");
    out.println("<p></p>");
    out.println("<p><a href=\"" +
      response.encodeURL("ApplicationServlet?action=logoff") +
                         "\">Log Off</a></p>");
    out.println("</body></html>");
  }
}
```

Writing the administrative servlet

Listing 11-8 contains the full implementation of `AdminServlet`. This servlet loops through all the attributes stored in the servlet context. If it recognizes an attribute as one of our sessions, it writes a single line of HTML describing that session. After `AdminServlet` loops through all the sessions, the HTML is returned to the browser. The user may also elect to log off, in which case `AdminServlet` sends a redirect to `Home.html`.

Listing 11-8: AdminServlet.java

```
package bible.servlets;

import javax.servlet.*;
import javax.servlet.http.*;
import java.io.*;
import java.util.*;

public class AdminServlet extends HttpServlet {

  public void service(HttpServletRequest request,
                      HttpServletResponse response)
  throws IOException {

    ServletContext ctx = this.getServletContext();
    HttpSession session = request.getSession();
    String servletName = this.getServletName();

    if (request.getParameter("action") == null) {
      // Generate an HTML page listing all active sessions.
      // This servlet does NOT store data into the session
      // or the servlet context.
      response.setContentType("text/html");
      PrintWriter out = response.getWriter();
      out.println("<html>");
      out.println("<head><title>" + servletName + "</title></head>");
      out.println("<body>");
      out.print("<p>Welcome to the " + servletName + ". ");
      out.print("Click your browser's Refresh button ");
      out.print("to update the display.</p>");
      // Get the names of all attributes in the servlet context.
      Enumeration sessions = ctx.getAttributeNames();
      int numSessions = 0;
      // Loop through the attributes, rendering the ones we recognize
      // as our sessions to the HTML output.
      while (sessions.hasMoreElements()) {
        String sessionName = (String) sessions.nextElement();
        if (sessionName.startsWith("session_")) {
          Hashtable sessionInfo =
            (Hashtable) ctx.getAttribute(sessionName);
          String userName = (String) sessionInfo.get("userName");
          Integer pageNumber = (Integer) sessionInfo.get("pageNumber");
          out.println("<p>" + userName + " is on page " +
                      pageNumber.intValue() + ".</p>");
          numSessions++;
        }
      }
      // If there are no sessions, indicate that as well.
      if (numSessions == 0) {
```

Continued

Listing 11-8 (continued)

```
        out.println("<p>There are no active sessions.</p>");
      }
      out.println("<p></p>");
      out.println("<p><a href=\"" + response.encodeURL(servletName +
                  "?action=logoff") + "\">Log Off</a></p>");
      out.println("</body></html>");
    } else if (request.getParameter("action").equals("logoff")) {
        // User wants to log off. Invalidate their session and
        // redirect them to the home page.
      session.invalidate();
      response.sendRedirect(
        response.encodeURL("/BibleServlets/Home.html"));
    }
  }
}
```

Creating the deployment descriptors

You will now create the two deployment descriptors required for a Web application in WebLogic Server: web.xml, and weblogic.xml.

web.xml

Listing 11-9 shows web.xml, the J2EE deployment descriptor for your application. It begins with the <welcome-file-list> and <login-config> entries you created before.

The four <servlet> entries define your application's servlets. They give a logical name for the servlet, and then the fully qualified name of the servlet's class.

Next come four <servlet-mapping> entries that map the logical names of the servlets to URL patterns in the browser. To invoke a servlet, you enter a URL that follows this pattern:

```
http://<host-name>/<app-name><servlet-url-pattern>
```

In this example, LoginServlet is invoked as follows:

```
http://localhost:7001/BibleServlets/LoginServlet
```

The <security-role> entries define the security roles recognized by your application. In this case, you recognize two classes of users: normal users and administrators. The role names can be anything you want.

Finally, the <security-constraint> entries define which roles are allowed to access which servlets. The constraints you've defined specify that ApplicationServlet and PageServlet are available to normal and administrative users, while AdminServlet is available only to administrators. The restrictions apply for HTTP GET and POST requests alike, and you're not requiring a secure sockets connection to access any of these resources.

Notice that there is no <security-constraint> entry for LoginServlet. This is because LoginServlet is available to everyone; it sits outside the security perimeter of your application. The same applies for Home.html and LoginError.html.

Listing 11-9: web.xml

```
<!DOCTYPE web-app PUBLIC "-//Sun Microsystems, Inc.//DTD Web
Application 2.3//EN" "http://java.sun.com/dtd/web-app_2_3.dtd">

<web-app>

  <welcome-file-list>
    <welcome-file>Home.html</welcome-file>
  </welcome-file-list>

  <login-config>
    <auth-method>FORM</auth-method>
    <realm-name>default</realm-name>
    <form-login-config>
      <form-login-page>LoginServlet</form-login-page>
      <form-error-page>LoginError.html</form-error-page>
    </form-login-config>
  </login-config>

  <servlet>
    <servlet-name>LoginServlet</servlet-name>
    <servlet-class>
      bible.servlets.LoginServlet
    </servlet-class>
  </servlet>

  <servlet>
    <servlet-name>ApplicationServlet</servlet-name>
    <servlet-class>
      bible.servlets.ApplicationServlet
    </servlet-class>
  </servlet>

  <servlet>
    <servlet-name>PageServlet</servlet-name>
    <servlet-class>
      bible.servlets.PageServlet
```

Continued

Listing 11-9 *(continued)*

```
    </servlet-class>
  </servlet>

  <servlet>
    <servlet-name>AdminServlet</servlet-name>
    <servlet-class>
      bible.servlets.AdminServlet
    </servlet-class>
  </servlet>

  <servlet-mapping>
    <servlet-name>LoginServlet</servlet-name>
    <url-pattern>/LoginServlet</url-pattern>
  </servlet-mapping>

  <servlet-mapping>
    <servlet-name>ApplicationServlet</servlet-name>
    <url-pattern>/ApplicationServlet</url-pattern>
  </servlet-mapping>

  <servlet-mapping>
    <servlet-name>PageServlet</servlet-name>
    <url-pattern>/PageServlet</url-pattern>
  </servlet-mapping>

  <servlet-mapping>
    <servlet-name>AdminServlet</servlet-name>
    <url-pattern>/AdminServlet</url-pattern>
  </servlet-mapping>

  <security-role>
    <role-name>admin_user</role-name>
  </security-role>

  <security-role>
    <role-name>normal_user</role-name>
  </security-role>

  <security-constraint>
    <web-resource-collection>
      <web-resource-name>
        ApplicationServlet
      </web-resource-name>
      <description>
        Security constraint for ApplicationServlet.
      </description>
      <url-pattern>/ApplicationServlet</url-pattern>
      <http-method>POST</http-method>
      <http-method>GET</http-method>
    </web-resource-collection>
    <auth-constraint>
```

```
    <description>
      Constraint for all users
    </description>
    <role-name>admin_user</role-name>
    <role-name>normal_user</role-name>
  </auth-constraint>
  <user-data-constraint>
    <description>SSL not required</description>
    <transport-guarantee>NONE</transport-guarantee>
  </user-data-constraint>
</security-constraint>

<security-constraint>
  <web-resource-collection>
    <web-resource-name>
      PageServlet
    </web-resource-name>
    <description>
      Security constraint for PageServlet.
    </description>
    <url-pattern>/PageServlet</url-pattern>
    <http-method>POST</http-method>
    <http-method>GET</http-method>
  </web-resource-collection>
  <auth-constraint>
    <description>
      Constraint for all users
    </description>
    <role-name>admin_user</role-name>
    <role-name>normal_user</role-name>
  </auth-constraint>
  <user-data-constraint>
    <description>SSL not required</description>
    <transport-guarantee>NONE</transport-guarantee>
  </user-data-constraint>
</security-constraint>

<security-constraint>
  <web-resource-collection>
    <web-resource-name>
      AdminServlet
    </web-resource-name>
    <description>
      Security constraint for AdminServlet.
    </description>
    <url-pattern>/AdminServlet</url-pattern>
    <http-method>POST</http-method>
    <http-method>GET</http-method>
  </web-resource-collection>
  <auth-constraint>
    <description>
      Constraint for admin users
```

Continued

Listing 11-9 *(continued)*

```
      </description>
      <role-name>admin_user</role-name>
    </auth-constraint>
    <user-data-constraint>
      <description>SSL not required</description>
      <transport-guarantee>NONE</transport-guarantee>
    </user-data-constraint>
  </security-constraint>

</web-app>
```

If you study the <url-pattern> tags within the security constraints, you'll see they map directly to the protected servlets. This is because your servlets all reside within the root of your application. Suppose that your application was much larger, and that you had several administrative servlets instead of just one. You could map all these servlets to an administrative area called /admin and then protect them all in one stroke, as shown by the bold lines in the following code sample:

```
<servlet>
  <servlet-name>AdminServlet</servlet-name>
  <servlet-class>
    bible.servlets.AdminServlet
  </servlet-class>
</servlet>

<servlet-mapping>
  <servlet-name>LoginServlet</servlet-name>
  <url-pattern>/Admin/AdminServlet</url-pattern>
</servlet-mapping>

//and so on for the other admin servlets

<security-constraint>
  <web-resource-collection>
    <web-resource-name>
      Administrative resources
    </web-resource-name>
    <description>
      Security constraint for administrative resources.
    </description>
    <url-pattern>/Admin/*</url-pattern>
    <http-method>POST</http-method>
    <http-method>GET</http-method>
```

```
    </web-resource-collection>
    <auth-constraint>
      <description>
        Constraint for admin users
      </description>
      <role-name>admin_user</role-name>
    </auth-constraint>
    <user-data-constraint>
      <description>SSL not required</description>
      <transport-guarantee>NONE</transport-guarantee>
    </user-data-constraint>
  </security-constraint>
```

weblogic.xml

Listing 11-10 shows `weblogic.xml`, your application's WebLogic-specific deployment descriptor. This file serves as a bridge between `web.xml` and features specific to WebLogic, for which there is no support in the `web.xml` DTD. In the `BibleServlets` application, `weblogic.xml` uses security role assignments to map WebLogic users from the File realm to role names in `web.xml`. This enables you to specify which users belong to which roles. In this example, `Joe` is an administrator, while `Gary` and `Roya` are normal users.

User and role names are case sensitive. The users must match exactly those you defined in the WebLogic Console, and the role names must match exactly those you defined in `web.xml`.

Listing 11-10: weblogic.xml

```
<!DOCTYPE weblogic-web-app PUBLIC "-//BEA
Systems, Inc.//DTD Web Application 6.0//EN"
"http://www.bea.com/servers/wls610/dtd/
weblogic-web-jar.dtd">

<weblogic-web-app>

  <description>
    Demo of servlet features.
  </description>

  <security-role-assignment>
    <role-name>admin_user</role-name>
    <principal-name>Joe</principal-name>
  </security-role-assignment>

  <security-role-assignment>
    <role-name>normal_user</role-name>
```

Continued

Listing 11-10 *(continued)*

```
      <principal-name>Gary</principal-name>
      <principal-name>Roya</principal-name>
    </security-role-assignment>

  </weblogic-web-app>
```

The application is now complete. Let's try it out!

Running the application

Figure 11-8 shows the application home page you receive when you point your browser to `BibleServlets`. If you click User, you're taken to the login page, as shown in Figure 11-11.

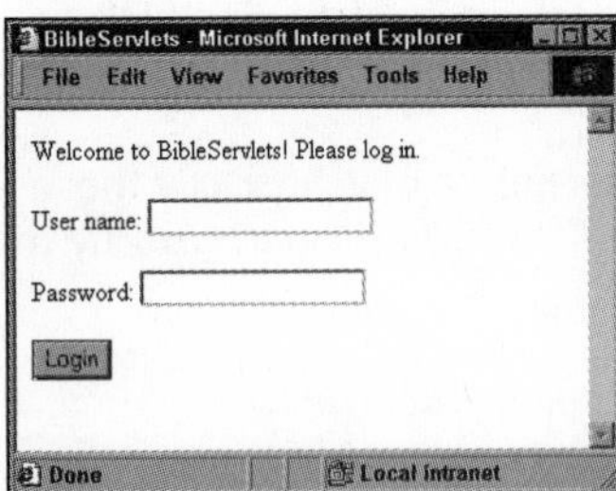

Figure 11-11: The BibleServlets login page

First log in as `Roya`. At this point, `ApplicationServlet` creates a session for `Roya` and dispatches her to the first page, as shown in Figure 11-12.

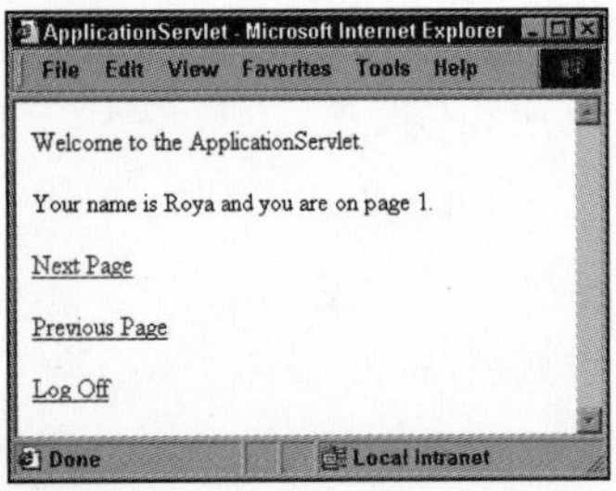

Figure 11-12: Roya on Page 1

Leave this browser window open and point a second browser window to `BibleServlets`. This time, enter the `Administrator` area and log in as `Joe`. Figure 11-13 shows the resulting administrative screen.

Figure 11-13: The BibleServlets administrative screen

Next log into the User area as `Gary` and advance to Page 4, as shown in Figure 11-14.

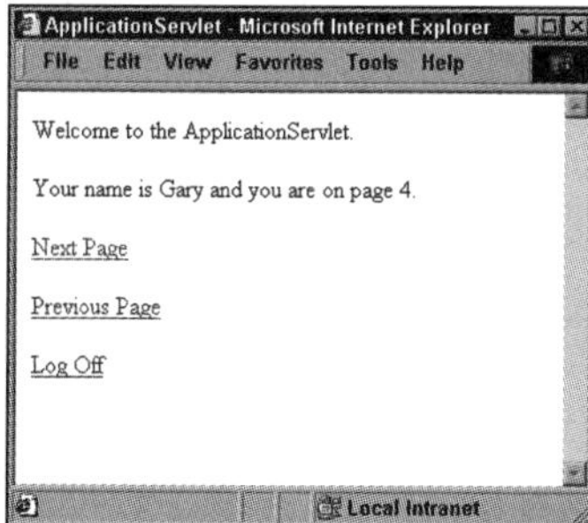

Figure 11-14: Gary on Page 4

Return to your administrative window and click the browser's Refresh button to update the display, as shown in Figure 11-15.

Figure 11-15: Admin screen showing two active sessions

This is a very simple example, but it gives you a good idea of the power behind servlets.

Deploying the application as a WAR file

When you finish the development and testing of an application, you'll want to convert it to a WAR file for easy deployment. WAR files are essential for two reasons:

✦ WebLogic Server, when running in Production mode, recognizes only WAR files. It will not recognize or deploy exploded directory structures.

✦ To deploy a Web application to a WebLogic cluster, you must copy the application to every machine in the cluster. This is easier and quicker to do with a WAR file.

To deploy the `BibleServlets` application as a WAR file, follow these steps:

1. In the WebLogic Console, delete the `BibleServlets` application from the list of deployed Web applications. Exit from the Console and stop WebLogic Server.
2. Open a command window and change to the `BibleServlets` directory.
3. Use the WebLogic `setenv.cmd` utility to set your classpath; then enter the following command:

   ```
   jar cv0f BibleServlets.war *
   ```

   This instructs the JAR utility to create a WAR file called `BibleServlets.war`, and to copy every file in the `BibleServlets` directory into it. The third parameter is a zero, and it instructs the JAR utility not to compress the file. WebLogic can load resources from uncompressed files more quickly, so this is a good option if you need maximum performance.
4. Move `BibleServlets.war` out of the `BibleServlets` directory and into the applications directory of your WebLogic domain.
5. Move the `BibleServlets` directory to another location outside of the applications directory, or simply delete it.
6. Start WebLogic Server. `BibleServlets.war` will automatically deploy, and you can use the application exactly as before.

Summary

Servlets are one of the most important features of J2EE because they enable you to deliver the full power of J2EE, as well as your organization's critical data, to any user with a Web browser. Most companies buy WebLogic Server precisely because of this capability. If you master the concepts behind servlets and learn how to exploit their many capabilities, there is no almost no limit to the power and functionality you can deliver to your browser-based users.

✦ ✦ ✦

CHAPTER 12

Developing JavaServer Pages

In This Chapter

Understanding JavaServer Pages

Configuring WebLogic Server for JSPs

Programming JSPs

Programming JSPs with JavaBeans

The JavaServer Pages API defines a mechanism for server-side scripting within the J2EE environment. WebLogic Server provides an implementation of the API in the form of its JSP container.

In the first part of this chapter, I provide an overview of the JavaServer Pages architecture and the coding syntax. I show how to configure WebLogic deployment descriptors and deploy JSPs within the WebLogic environment. Next, I provide several code examples demonstrating the various features available, including using JSPs with JavaBeans.

Understanding JavaServer Pages

To gain a full appreciation of why JavaServer Pages exists, and what advantages the JSP API brings to J2EE development, you should know something about how server-side scripting was done before JSPs.

Product of evolution

Server-side scripting is not a new concept to Web development. Once static content was being delivered to the browser, developers were already looking to deliver dynamic content and make the user experience more robust.

Along came server-side scripting in the form of Common Gateway Interface (CGI). CGIs are either interpreted scripts or compiled executables that can be accessed on the Web server, access databases, and generate dynamic responses. The downside of using CGIs is performance. Because every CGI runs as a separate process, every request to the server would result in a CGI process being created and destroyed. This is very resource-expensive and does not scale.

Microsoft introduced Active Server Pages (ASP), which allowed for inline scripts using either VBScript or JScript commingled with HTML for generating dynamic content. ASPs are interpreted on the Microsoft IIS server (plug-ins are available for other platforms) and allow access to Component Object Model (COM) objects for external functions such as database calls. Even though ASPs were great leaps in developer usability, because of their interpretive environment, the downside was again performance and scalability. Good or bad, you are also tied to the Microsoft environment.

Sun Microsystems introduced the first draft of the JavaServer Pages API specification in 1998. It, too, provided a means of inline scripting utilizing Java, but it excelled in performance by leveraging its powerful and very successful servlet technology. From the developer's point of view, it provided the desired level of ease of use by providing the ability to embed HTML-like tags and Java scriptlets. It also enabled the developer to take full advantage of Java as an OO language. Sun addressed scalability concerns by precompiling JSPs into servlets, therefore inheriting all the performance benefits of executing as "lightweight processes," or threads within the Java Virtual Machine.

JavaServer Pages scripting is typically done in Java, but the JSP specification allows for alternative scripting languages. Later in the chapter I'll show you how to specify the language you want to use, but I'll assume it's Java.

WebLogic Server 6.1 supports the JSP 1.2 specification and the Servlet 2.3 specification. You can download copies of these specifications at `http://java.sun.com/products/jsp/download.html` and `http://java.sun.com/products/servlet/download.html`, respectively.

How JSPs work

In the simplest case, users request JSPs by requesting files ending in `.jsp`. For example:

```
http://www.bigbank.com/mystatement.jsp
```

The first time a JSP is requested, WebLogic forwards the JSP to the JSP compiler, which converts the JSP to a servlet, then compiles the servlet.

By default, the Java compiler is Sun Microsystems' `javac` compiler, but WebLogic lets you configure a different Java compiler. This is covered later in the chapter.

Assuming the JSP compiles successfully, WebLogic Server executes the corresponding servlet and returns its response to the user. For all subsequent requests for the JSP, WebLogic automatically executes the servlet, unless WebLogic detects the JSP's code has changed since it was last compiled. In this case, WebLogic resubmits the JSP for compilation, then executes the new version of the servlet.

The code in your JSPs is not visible to users; i.e., they cannot see it with the "View Source" command in their browsers. Users can only see the HTML your JSP (actually, its servlet) generates.

JSPs are converted into servlets for performance reasons, but an important by-product of this design is that anything you can program in a servlet, you can also program in a JSP. This makes JSPs very powerful and flexible.

Figure 12-1 illustrates the full cycle of JSP requests, compilation, execution, and response.

Tip

You can configure WebLogic Server to precompile your JSPs when starting WebLogic Server by setting the precompile parameter to `true` in the `weblogic.xml` deployment descriptor. You can also run the JSP compiler yourself from within your build scripts. Either approach saves your users from having to wait for JSPs to compile. The latter approach is better, however, because it won't increase the startup time of your WebLogic Server, and it also ensures that the JSPs are recompiled only when they change, instead of every time the server restarts. I'll cover both techniques later in the chapter.

Model-View-Controller

JSPs are a great way of implementing the Model-View-Controller design pattern. Separating code by functionality is a concept known as *decoupling* and is especially useful in the View layer, which is by far the most changeable layer of an application. JSPs allow you to do just that — separate the presentation or View layer from the implementation or Controller layer.

See Chapter 3 for a complete discussion of Model-View-Controller.

JSPs provide the ability to decouple the View layer by providing you with all the capabilities of the Java language. You can embed Java scriptlets within HTML or other markup languages to generate dynamic content, access the Controller layer, or anything else desired. As a result, JSPs enjoy all the benefits of Java: an object-oriented language with strong typing, encapsulation and polymorphism, exception handling, automatic memory management, platform independence, and portability of code, to name a few.

JSPs are for generating markup, not just HTML. You can, for example, generate XML with JSPs. In this chapter, however, I will generate HTML only.

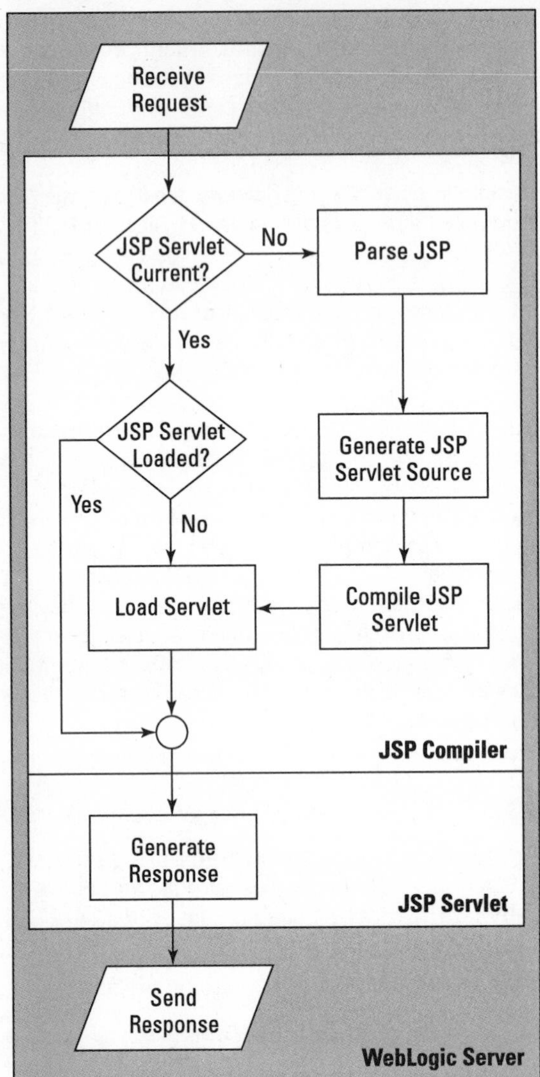

Figure 12-1: WebLogic's JSP request and compilation process

JSPs also provide access to other Java-based objects such as JavaBeans. JavaBeans are objects written in Java that encapsulate data and behavior in a way that allows them to be reused. JSPs access JavaBeans via standard tags in an HTML-like syntax to request data or services, but without regard for how they are implemented. A typical bean might have a set of values or properties. The JSP will request these properties for the sake of displaying them as dynamic content. Because the properties were set by some other process with its own methodology, the JSP does not know nor need to know how the properties were derived.

JSPs also can use custom tag extensions in an HTML-like syntax. Tag extensions are a mechanism that enables developers to create libraries of custom tag classes written in Java that can be used in a JSP page. This is a great way of "separating presentation from implementation" by minimizing the Java code in the JSP. Tag extensions allow you to minimize the amount of programming logic commingled with your code by enabling you to call Java objects that encapsulate that logic.

With a robust collection of JavaBeans and tag library extensions, JSPs provide an even greater level of layer separation — syntax. JSPs provide the ability to minimize code and give user interface designers a language format with which they are familiar. A traditional UI developer proficient in HTML doesn't need to learn the Java syntax, but needs only to become familiar with a new set of tags. A traditional Java developer can create reusable routines for the UI developer to leverage or standard objects encapsulating display data. This perfectly matches division of labor sought by most development teams.

You may be wondering if anything can stop you from using Java code in your JSPs. Is there anything wrong with JavaBeans or tag library extensions generating HTML? Well, no, not really. It will work, but you don't achieve the level of separation as defined by the Model-View-Controller design pattern.

By using a significant amount of Java code in your JSPs, you force your UI developer to learn Java and potentially introduce controller level logic. You may end up with the need to make logic changes in your JSP every time you make logic changes in your controller layer.

You give up the reusability of your JavaBeans or tag library extension classes if they generate HTML. Maybe some other server-side Java classes would benefit from using them, but they have no need for HTML. Likewise, your UI developer now needs to ask your Java developer to make changes to modify the presentation layer.

You can be quite successful by implementing JSPs without regard for the MVC design pattern, but sticking with the pattern pays dividends in programmer productivity and code maintainability.

Configuring WebLogic Server for JSPs

Before using JSPs with WebLogic Server, you should configure the server to handle JSPs exactly the way you want. This section explains the various aspects of configuring WebLogic Server to handle JSPs, and shows you how to do so.

The JSP compiler

As discussed earlier, the JSP compiler is provided by WebLogic Server. It's responsible for converting JSP source into JSP servlet source. WebLogic Server automatically invokes the compiler when a requested JSP's source is new or has changed.

In some scenarios, such as debugging, it might be useful to access the JSP compiler directly. To start the JSP compiler, enter the following command:

```
java weblogic.jspc -options fileName
```

Replace `fileName` with the name of the JSP file to compile. You can specify any options before or after the target `fileName`. For information on the compile options, see the WebLogic Server documentation on compiling JSPs at `http://edocs.bea.com/wls/docs61/jsp/reference.html`.

The location of the generated JSP servlet source file (`.java`) and the compiled JSP servlet file (`.class`) depend upon the working directory and package prefix settings in the WebLogic Application Extension Deployment Descriptor (`weblogic.xml`). Whether to keep the source file depends upon the `keepgenerated` setting; this is discussed further in the next section.

Configuring the WebLogic Application Extension Deployment Descriptor

WebLogic Server allows you to configure the JSP container by setting the WebLogic Application Extension Deployment Descriptor (`weblogic.xml`). This descriptor is located in the `WEB-INF` directory of your Web application. It is defined by and verified against the BEA Web Application Document Type Definitions (DTD) file (`http://www.beasys.com/j2ee/dtds/weblogic-web-jar.dtd`).

After starting the default WebLogic Server and the default WebLogic Console, expand the Web Applications branch on the navigation tree. For this example, you'll define the deployment descriptor associated with the `DefaultWebApp`. After clicking the `DefaultWebApp` Web application node, the page shown in Figure 12-2 appears.

Next click the Edit Web Application Descriptor link. A new window opens, displaying the page shown in Figure 12-3.

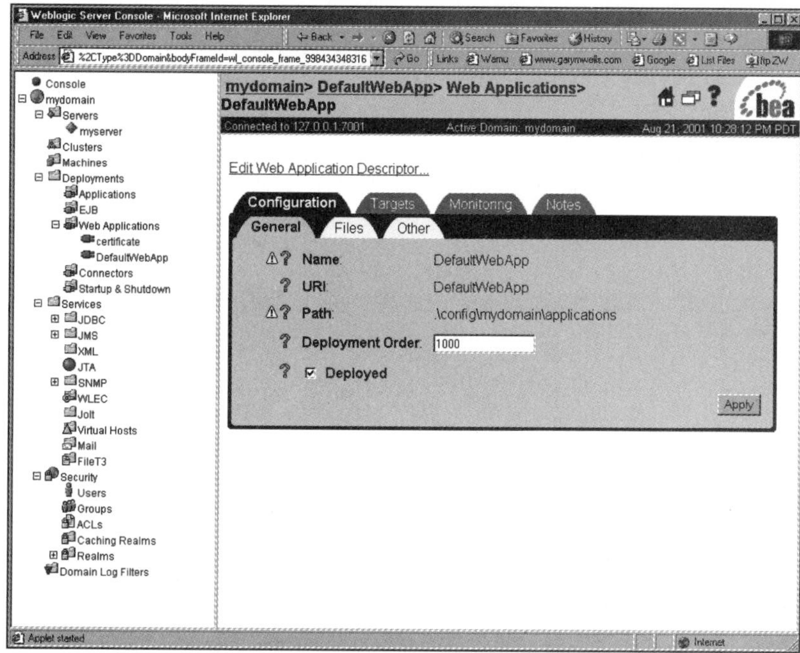

Figure 12-2: WebLogic Server console for the default server instance

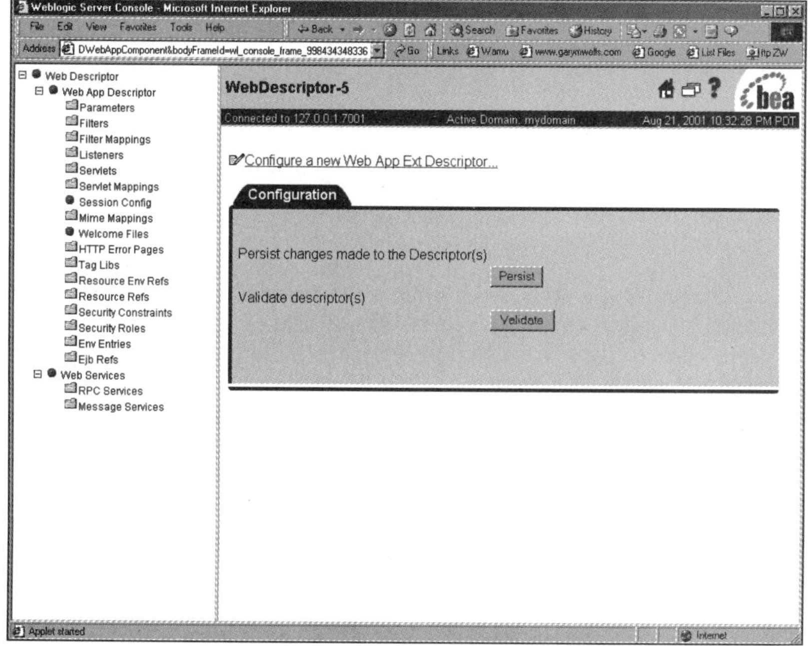

Figure 12-3: Web Descriptor editing navigation

Notice that the left navigation pane has a navigation tree of the various categories of descriptors that can be defined. The right pane provides you with a couple of buttons to persist the changes made to the descriptors and to validate the descriptors. I use these a few steps later.

Since you have not yet created a Web App Ext Descriptor, the `weblogic.xml` file, for this application, click the Configure a new Web App Ext Descriptor link to instruct the console to create one. The page shown in Figure 12-4 appears.

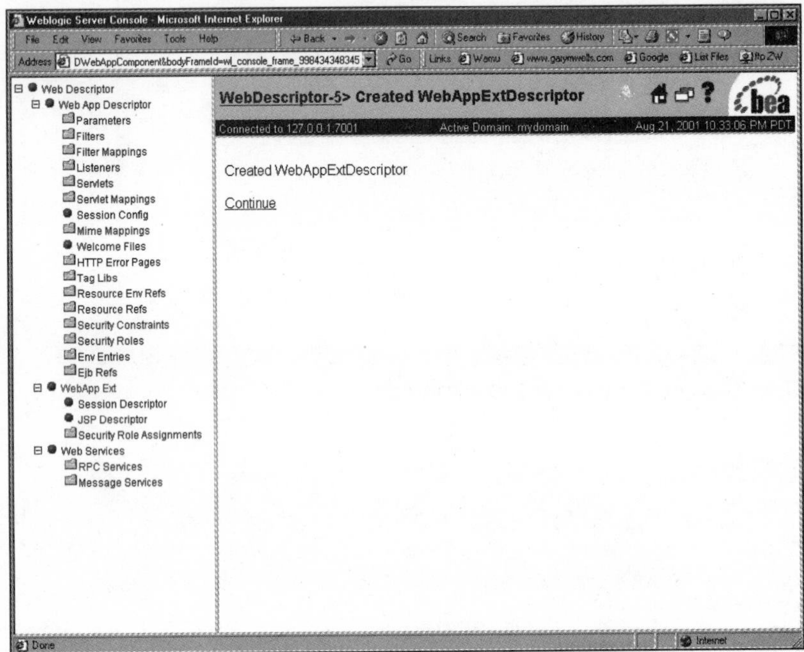

Figure 12-4: Confirmation that the Web App Ext Descriptor was created

This page confirms that the console was successful. Notice that there is a new branch of nodes in the left navigation pane. The Continue link will forward you back to the previous page, but you want to configure the JSP descriptor. Click that node. The page shown in Figure 12-5 appears.

Here's the page you've been waiting for. A whole series of options is available to configure the WebLogic Server JSP container. I'll describe each option for you.

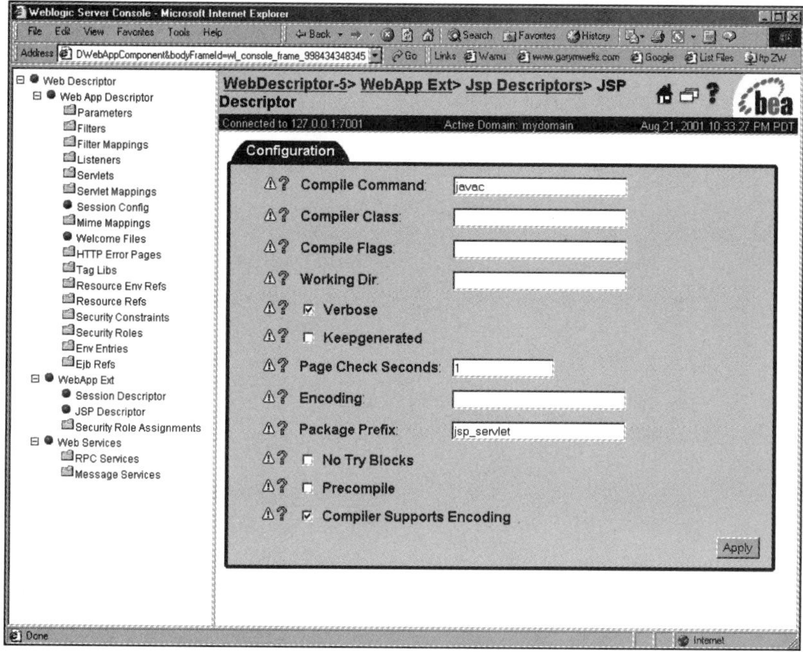

Figure 12-5: Configuring the JSP Descriptor

Compile Command

This option specifies the full pathname of the standard Java compiler used to compile the generated JSP servlets. The default value is `javac`, or the Java compiler defined for a server under the Configuration/Tuning tab of the WebLogic Server Administration Console.

Compiler Class

This option specifies the name of a Java compiler that is executed by WebLogic Server. This is used in place of an executable compiler such as `javac`. This class must reside within the WebLogic Server classpath. If not specified, there is no default value.

Compile Flags

This option specifies one or more command-line flags for the JSP compiler. If specifying multiple, enclose them in quotes and separate them by a space. If not specified, there is no default value.

Working Dir

This option specifies the name of a directory where WebLogic Server saves the generated JSP servlet source file (`.java`) and the compiled JSP servlet file (`.class`). If specified, it is either located or created within the `WEB-INF` directory of the Web application. If not specified, WebLogic Server uses an internally generated directory. WebLogic Server, for example, will generate a directory named `_tmp_war_myserver_myserver_ DefaultWebApp` in the `WEB-INF` directory of the `DefaultWebApp` Web application. Within that directory, both servlet Java source and compiled class files will be placed in a subdirectory named `jsp_servlet` based upon the Package Prefix value.

Verbose

This instructs WebLogic Server to output debugging information to the browser, the command prompt, and the WebLogic Server log file. If not specified, the default value is `true`.

Keepgenerated

This option specifies that the JSP compiler keep the generated JSP servlet source file upon completion of the JSP compilation process. Otherwise, the intermediate Java files are deleted after they are compiled. If not specified, the default value is `false`.

Page Check Seconds

This option specifies the interval, in seconds, which WebLogic Server will check the JSP files to determine if they have changed and need recompiling. Dependent JSPs are also checked and recompiled if changed. If not specified, the default value is 1. If set to 0, JSPs are checked on every request. If set to -1, page checking and recompiling is disabled.

Encoding

This option specifies the default character set used in the JSP page. Note that the `contentType` attribute of the page directive overrides this setting for that particular JSP page. See `http://java.sun.com/j2se/1.3/docs/guide/intl/encoding.doc.htm` for more information. If not specified, the default value is the encoding for your platform.

Package Prefix

This option specifies the package into which all JSP pages are compiled. If not specified, there is no default value.

No Try Blocks

If a JSP file has numerous or deeply nested custom JSP tags and you receive a `java.lang.VerifyError` exception when compiling, use this flag to allow the JSPs to compile correctly. If not specified, the default value is `false`.

Precompile

This option specifies whether WebLogic Server should automatically compile all JSPs on startup. If not specified, the default value is `false`.

Compiler Supports Encoding

This option specifies the encoding used by the JSP compiler to create the intermediate JSP servlet source file. To use the encoding as defined in this descriptor (see "Encoding" above) or overridden by the JSP's page directive, then specify `true`. To use the default encoding for the JVM, specify `false`. If not specified, the default value is `false`.

Suggested settings for development

When developing, I like to have as much information about what's happening as possible; I'm not too worried about the performance of the JSP container. Therefore, I usually use the following settings:

```
Verbose = true
Keepgenerated = true
Page Check Seconds = 1
Precompile = false
```

Suggested settings for production

In production, however, performance is critical, so I want to turn off unwanted processing steps. I am not in development mode, so I have no need for verbose messages. Also, I am deploying an Enterprise Application Archive (`.ear`) file with all the JSP files already compiled, so there is no need to check for new versions of JSPs and to set compiling options. Therefore, I usually use the following settings:

```
Verbose = false
keepgenerated = false
Page Check Seconds = -1
Precompile = false
```

After setting the descriptors according to your needs, click the Apply button. The page shown in Figure 12-6 appears.

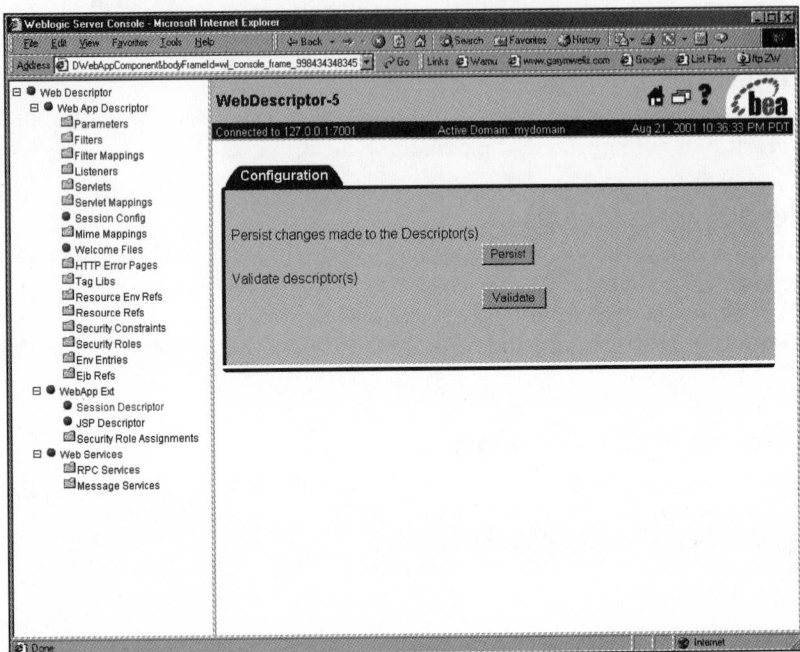

Figure 12-6: Validating the Web Descriptor

This is essentially the same page as Figure 12-3, but there's no longer a Configure link and the left navigation tree shows the WebApp Ext branch that you created. Next instruct the WebLogic Console to validate your descriptor against the DTD file (`www.beasys.com/j2ee/dtds/weblogic-web-jar.dtd`) by clicking the Validate button. The page shown in Figure 12-7 appears.

After receiving validation that your Web Descriptor is correct, click the Web Descriptor node to redisplay the following page, as shown in Figure 12-8.

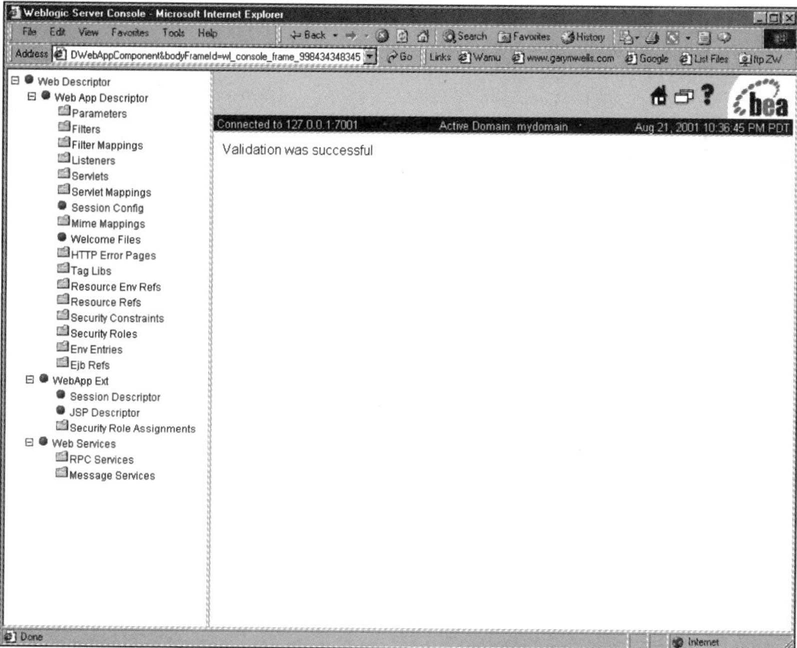

Figure 12-7: Web Descriptor Validation confirmation

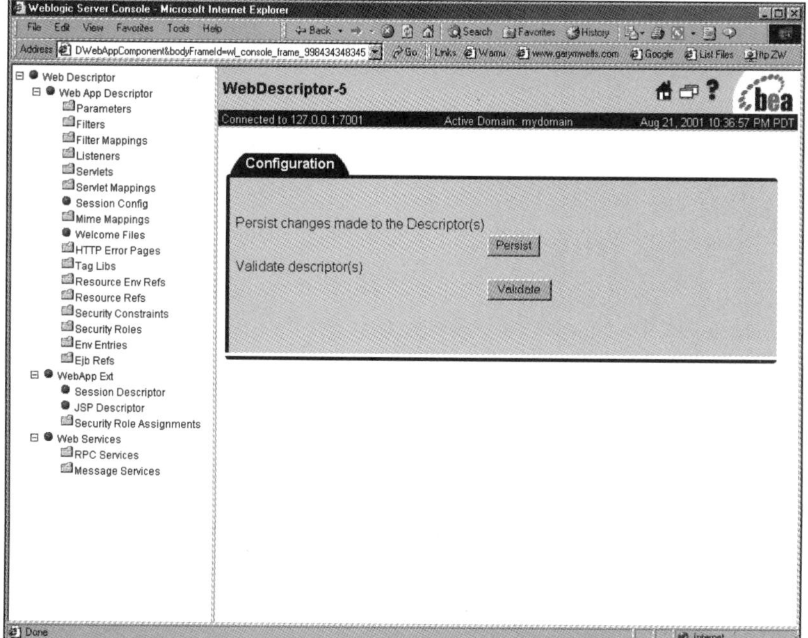

Figure 12-8: Persisting the Web Descriptor

Next click the Persist button to persist your changes to the `weblogic.xml` file. Additionally, WebLogic Server loads these changes immediately for the JSP container. The page shown in Figure 12-9 appears.

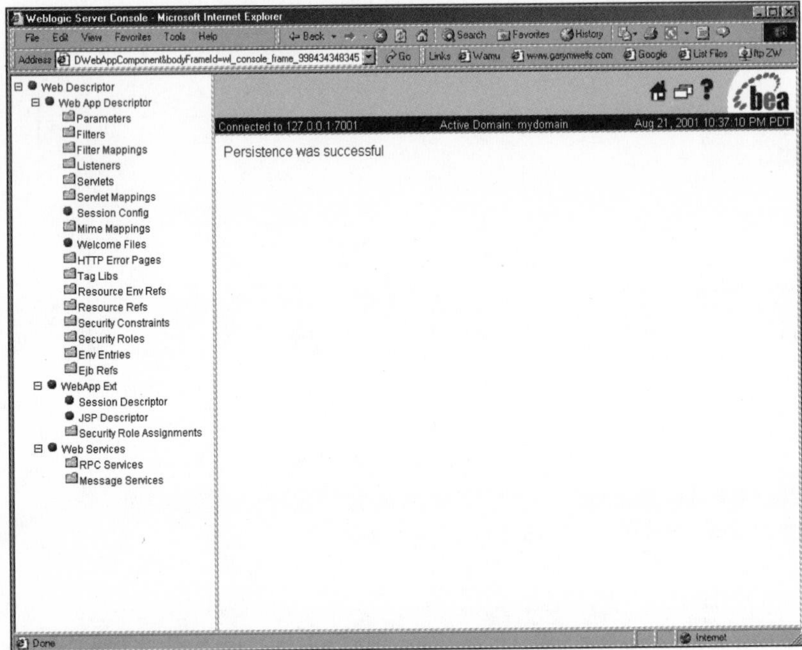

Figure 12-9: Successful persistence of the Web Descriptor

The changes have been persisted to the file system and loaded in WebLogic Server. Listing 12-1 is a listing of the `weblogic.xml` file that was created in my Web application's `WEB-INF` directory.

Listing 12-1: weblogic.xml

```
<!DOCTYPE weblogic-web-app PUBLIC "-//BEA Systems, Inc.//DTD Web Application
6.0//EN" "http://www.beasys.com/j2ee/dtds/weblogic-web-jar.dtd">
<weblogic-web-app>
  <jsp-descriptor>
    <jsp-param>
      <param-name>compileCommand</param-name>
      <param-value>javac</param-value>
    </jsp-param>
    <jsp-param>
      <param-name>verbose</param-name>
```

```
      <param-value>true</param-value>
    </jsp-param>
    <jsp-param>
      <param-name>keepgenerated</param-name>
      <param-value>true</param-value>
    </jsp-param>
    <jsp-param>
      <param-name>pageCheckSeconds</param-name>
      <param-value>1</param-value>
    </jsp-param>
    <jsp-param>
      <param-name>packagePrefix</param-name>
      <param-value>jsp_servlet</param-value>
    </jsp-param>
    <jsp-param>
      <param-name>noTryBlocks</param-name>
      <param-value>false</param-value>
    </jsp-param>
    <jsp-param>
      <param-name>precompile</param-name>
      <param-value>false</param-value>
    </jsp-param>
    <jsp-param>
      <param-name>compilerSupportsEncoding</param-name>
      <param-value>true</param-value>
    </jsp-param>
  </jsp-descriptor>
</weblogic-web-app>
```

Deploying your first JSP in WebLogic Server

In this section, I show you how to deploy and run your first JSP. Because this will be the first time you call it, the JSP will be converted to a servlet and compiled. Then it will be loaded and executed, generating output to the browser. Finally, I show you how to find the generated JSP servlet source so you can look at it.

Start with a simple JSP, named `First.jsp`, as shown in Listing 12-2. If you take a close look, you'll see that it's a simple HTML page with a small scriptlet to get the current date from the server and output it.

Listing 12-2: First.jsp

```
<html>
<head>
  <title>First JSP</title>
```

Continued

Listing 12-2 *(continued)*

```
</head>

<body>
Welcome! It is currently: <%= new Date() %>
</body>
</html>
```

Place the servlet in the root level of your Web application directory (named `BibleApp`), like you would an HTML document. Unlike servlets, there are no deployment descriptor entries necessary to register the JSP. WebLogic Server looks for the document based upon the URL in the client's request.

Configure your Web application's JSP deployment descriptor for a development environment. As a result, WebLogic Server will compile your JSP and retain the generated JSP servlet source file.

The generated servlet source files (`.java` files) are written to `WEB-INF/tmp_war_X_Y_Z/jsp_servlet`, where X is the name of the administrative server for your WebLogic domain, Y is the name of the WebLogic server to which the JSP is deployed, and Z is the name of your application.

Type `http://localhost:7001/BibleApp/First.jsp` to run the JSP. After a few seconds in which to create the JSP servlet and compile it, the page shown in Figure 12-10 appears.

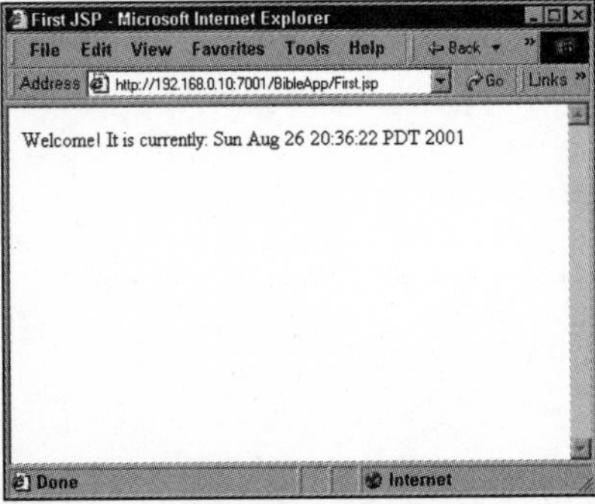

Figure 12-10: Executing First.jsp

Within the `BibleApp` Web application directory, in the `WEB-INF` directory, there is now a `_tmp_war_myserver_myserver_BibleApp` directory, and within that a jsp_servlet directory. Again, these directory names are based upon the settings in your JSP deployment descriptor.

If you examine the contents of the jsp_servlet directory, there are now two files: _first.class and _first.java. The .java file is the generated JSP servlet source, and the .class filed is the compiled JSP servlet. If you open the _first.java file in an editor, then the source shown in Listing 12-3 appears.

Listing 12-3: _first.java

```
/* compiled from JSP: /First.jsp
*
* This code was automatically generated at 4:27:02 PM on Aug 25, 2001
* by weblogic.servlet.jsp.Jsp2Java -- do not edit.
*/

package jsp_servlet;

import java.io.*;
import java.util.*;
import javax.servlet.*;
import javax.servlet.http.*;
import javax.servlet.jsp.*;
import javax.servlet.jsp.tagext.*;

// User imports


// built-in init parameters:
// boolean            _verbose -- wants debugging

// Well-known variables:
// JspWriter out                     -- to write to the browser
// HttpServletRequest  request       -- the request object.
// HttpServletResponse response      -- the response object.
// PageContext pageContext           -- the page context for this JSP
// HttpSession session               -- the session object for the client (if any)
// ServletContext application        -- The servlet (application) context
// ServletConfig config              -- The ServletConfig for this JSP
// Object page                       -- the instance of this page's implementation
class (i.e., 'this')

/**
* This code was automatically generated at 4:27:02 PM on Aug 25, 2001
* by weblogic.servlet.jsp.Jsp2Java -- do not edit.
*
* Copyright (c) 2001 by BEA Systems, Inc. All Rights Reserved.
*/
```

Continued

Listing 12-3 *(continued)*

```
public final class _first
extends
weblogic.servlet.jsp.JspBase
implements weblogic.servlet.jsp.StaleIndicator
{

    // StaleIndicator interface
    public boolean _isStale() {
        weblogic.servlet.jsp.StaleChecker sci
=(weblogic.servlet.jsp.StaleChecker)(getServletConfig().getServletContext());
        java.io.File f = null;
        long lastModWhenBuilt = 0L;
        if (sci.isResourceStale("/First.jsp", 998782020000L, "WebLogic Server
6.1  07/23/2001 22:31:20 #129251 ")) return true;
        return false;
    }

    public static boolean _staticIsStale(weblogic.servlet.jsp.StaleChecker sci)
{
        java.io.File f = null;
        long lastModWhenBuilt = 0L;
        if (sci.isResourceStale("/First.jsp", 998782020000L, "WebLogic Server
6.1  07/23/2001 22:31:20 #129251 ")) return true;
        return false;
    }




    public void _jspService(javax.servlet.http.HttpServletRequest request,
javax.servlet.http.HttpServletResponse response) throws java.io.IOException,
javax.servlet.ServletException
    {

        // declare and set well-known variables:
        javax.servlet.ServletConfig config = getServletConfig();
        javax.servlet.ServletContext application = config.getServletContext();
        javax.servlet.jsp.tagext.Tag _activeTag = null;
        // variables for Tag extension protocol

        Object page = this;
        javax.servlet.jsp.JspWriter out;
        javax.servlet.jsp.PageContext pageContext =
        javax.servlet.jsp.JspFactory.getDefaultFactory().getPageContext(this,
request, response, null, true, 8192, true);

        out = pageContext.getOut();
```

```
        JspWriter _originalOut = out;

        javax.servlet.http.HttpSession session = request.getSession(true);


        try { // error page try block

            out.print("<html>\r\n<head>\r\n\t<title>First
JSP</title>\r\n</head>\r\n\r\n<body>\r\nWelcome! It is currently: ");
            out.print(weblogic.utils.StringUtils.valueOf( new Date() )); //[
/First.jsp; Line: 7]
            out.print("\r\n</body>\r\n</html>\r\n");
        } catch (Exception __ee) {
            while (out != null && out != _originalOut) out =
pageContext.popBody();
            pageContext.handlePageException(__ee);
        }


        //before final close brace...
    }


}
```

Wow, a lot of code was generated from a relatively small JSP! If you read through the servlet code, you'll see there is a lot there to support the variety of functionality a JSP can contain.

Take some time to examine this source. Pay particular attention to the package name, import statements, parent class and interface, method names, declaration of implicit objects, and so on. Also notice that the lines of the servlet that directly correlate to the JSP are commented and reference line numbers in the JSP.

Support for JSP 1.2

As of this writing, Sun Microsystems has released JavaServer Pages API specification Version 1.2. WebLogic Server 6.1 has added support for the following features of JSP 1.2:

- ✦ **<jsp:include flush="false">** — Allows you to buffer the page output and then flush the buffer before including another resource.
- ✦ **TryCatchFinally** — Allows you to catch exceptions thrown from within a tag by implementing the `doCatch()` and `doFinally()` methods of the `javax.servlet.jsp.tagext.TryCatchFinally` interface.

✦ **Tag Library Validator**—Allows you to write a Java class that you can use to perform custom validation on a JSP page. The validator class takes the entire JSP page as an input stream, and you can validate the page based on criteria that you write into the validator class.

✦ **Iteration Tag Class**—Allows tag handler classes to implement a new `javax.servlet.jsp.tagext.IterationTag` interface to conditionally reevaluate the tag body.

✦ **Scripting Variables**—Allows you to define scripting variables within a Tag Library Descriptor (TLD).

A JSP page can be written directly as an XML document, so you can use XML authoring tools. The XML document can be delivered to a JSP container for processing.

Programming JavaServer Pages

Now that I've covered what JSPs are and how to deploy them in WebLogic Server, I'm going to cover the rules and syntax to build them. In this section, I cover tag conventions, directives, scripting, comments, implicit objects, and actions. Then I provide you with a simple example that uses a little bit of everything. Finally, I talk about error handling and debugging.

Tag conventions

JSP pages have two styles of syntax. Both always enclose their statements in angle brackets (< >). This is the obvious reason why JSP tags are said to be like HTML.

The first syntax style is used for scripting and always begins with `<%` and ends with `%>`. Those familiar with Microsoft's ASP will recognize this syntax style. An additional character may appear after the `<%` to further identify the type of tag. These characters are `@` for directives, `!` for declarations, and `=` for expressions. Following are some examples:

```
<%@ include file="header.jsp" %>
<%! int lineNumber = 0 %>
<% if (lineNumber % 2 > 0) { lineClass = "detailLineOdd";
} else { lineClass = "detailLineEven"; } %>
<%= lineClass %>"
```

The second syntax style is based upon the XML syntax. They are case-sensitive, all values must appear in single or double quotes, and belong to the `jsp` namespace. They also make the distinction between those that contain a body versus those that don't.

An XML-based tag with body content (enclosed statements) has both a starting tag `<jsp: ... >` and ending tag `</jsp: ... >`. For example:

```
<jsp:useBean id="testBean" class="bible.jsp.TestBean">
<jsp:setProperty name="testBean" property="*"/>
</jsp:useBean>
```

An XML-based tag without a body begins with a `<jsp:` and ends with `/>`. For example:

```
<jsp:include help="helpMain.htm" />
```

Directives

Directives are a set of tags with specific instructions to the JSP container about the JSP page. They do not affect request processing nor produce any output that is visible to the end user. Instead, they change the way the JSP container processes the page.

Directives support both styles of syntax, but it's a good idea to choose one and stick with it to make your code more readable. The scripting syntax uses an at-sign (@) to uniquely identify directives. The XML syntax uses the directive action. These two tag styles are interchangeable. Following are some examples:

```
<%@ page import="java.util.*, bible.jsp.*" %>
<jsp:directive.page import="java.util.*, bible.jsp.*" />
```

page directive

The `page` directive defines attributes that apply to an entire JSP page. For convenience, you are allowed to specify multiple `page` directives on a single page. But no individual attribute of the `page` directive can be specified multiple times on a page. Any attempt to do so will result in a JSP-to-servlet translation-time error.

The basic syntax of the directive in both script-based the XML-based syntax is

```
<%@ page attribute="value" attribute="value" ... %>
<jsp:directive.page attribute="value" attribute="value" ... />
```

The `page` directive supports a number of attributes, which are listed and described in the following sections.

info

The `info` attribute enables the developer to include textual information about the page. The `String` is then available to the JSP container and any other object that has access to the JSP servlet. If not specified, there is no default value.

```
<%@ page info="Application Main Page" %>
<jsp:directive.page info="Application Main Page" />
```

language

The `language` attribute identifies the scripting language to be used by the JSP. JSP containers are required to support Java, but they allow for other languages to be used based upon a set of rules defined in the JSP API specification. If not specified, the default value is `"java"`. This is typically not specified unless a unique situation warrants it.

```
<%@ page language="java" %>
<jsp:directive.page language="java" />
```

contentType

The `contentType` attribute identifies the MIME type of the generated response. If not specified, the default value is `"text/html"`. A common alternative would be `"text/xml"`.

```
<%@ page contentType="text/xml" %>
<jsp:directive.page contentType="text/xml" />
```

extends

The `extends` attribute identifies the class by which the generated JSP servlet will extend. If not specified, then WebLogic Server will extend `weblogic.servlet.jsp.JspBase`. This attribute is typically not specified unless a unique situation warrants it.

```
<%@ page extends="bible.jsp.myParentJspClass" %>
<jsp:directive.page extends="bible.jsp.myParentJspClass" />
```

import

The `import` attribute identifies Java classes and packages to be imported for successful compilation of the generated JSP servlet. This works identically to the Java import statement. Multiple packages and classes can be specified separated by a comma. As a convenience, WebLogic will automatically import the following packages: `java.lang`, `java.io`, `java.util`, `javax.servlet`, `javax.servlet.http`, `javax.servlet.jsp`, `javax.servlet.jsp.tagext`. If not specified, there is no default value.

```
<%@ page import='bible.jsp.*, bible.jsp.taglib.*" %>
<jsp:directive.page
  import="bible.jsp.*, bible.jsp.taglib.*" />
```

session

The `session` attribute indicates the page's participation in session management. In other words, the JSP servlet will either use URL rewriting or cookies to maintain state. Note that the implicit object `session` is only available if this attribute is set to `"true"`. If not specified, the default value is `true`.

```
<%@ page session="false" %>
<jsp:directive.page session="false" />
```

buffer

The `buffer` attribute indicates whether or not the generated response should be buffered, and if so, the buffer size. Because WebLogic Server actually uses a pool of buffers and may allocate more if needed, consider this more of a minimum size. The valid values are either `none` or the buffer size in kilobytes. If not specified, the default value is `"8kb"`.

```
<%@ page buffer="12kb" %>
<jsp:directive.page buffer="12kb" />
```

autoFlush

The `autoFlush` attribute is used for controller buffered output and indicates if the output should automatically be flushed or sent when the buffer is full. If set to `"false"`, then WebLogic Server will raise an exception. Note that once a buffer has been flushed, it is no longer possible to set HTTP headers or forward the request to another JSP for processing. If not specified, the default value is `"true"`.

```
<%@ page autoFlush="false" %>
<jsp:directive.page autoFlush="false" />
```

isThreadSafe

The `isThreadSafe` attribute indicates whether the generated JSP servlet is capable of running multiple threads successfully. If set to `"false"`, then WebLogic Server will queue requests for this servlet and process them sequentially. If not specified, the default value is `"true"`.

```
<%@ page isThreadSafe="false" %>
<jsp:directive.page isThreadSafe="false" />
```

errorPage

The `errorPage` attribute identifies the URL of an alternate JSP to display if an uncaught exception occurs. After output has been flushed and an exception occurs, it is no longer possible to forward the request. If not specified, there is no default value.

```
<%@ page errorPage="/BibleApp/Error.jsp" %>
<jsp:directive.page errorPage="/BibleApp/Error.jsp" />
```

isErrorPage

The `isErrorPage` attribute indicates that the current JSP is behaving as an error page for another JSP. Note that the implicit object "exception" is only available if this attribute is set to `"true"`. If not specified, the default value is `"false"`.

```
<%@ page isErrorPage="true" %>
<jsp:directive.page isErrorPage="true" />
```

include directive

The `include` directive defines a file to be included by the JSP compiler. The file is identified by either a relative or explicit URL or path to the file. The end result is the tag replacing itself with the contents of the specified file.

No restrictions exist on the number of `include` directives nor on the number of nesting levels. The included file can contain any combination of static HTML and JSP tags. It is the final combined source that is parsed and compiled, and therefore must follow all JSP rules to compile successfully. Additionally, because you are logically combining the source, it's perfectly legal to reference a variable in the child file from the parent file, and vice versa.

As described earlier in the chapter, WebLogic Server will automatically rebuild and recompile the JSP when it determines that the JSP source has changed. This is, of course, based upon the deployment descriptor settings detailed above. WebLogic Server is able to determine when an included file has changed, and as a result will rebuild and recompile all parent JSPs.

```
<%@ include file="header.jsp" %>
<jsp:directive.include file="header.jsp" />
```

taglib directive

The `taglib` directive defines a tag library and prefix for the custom tags used in the JSP page. The `uri` attribute is the logical name to identify the location of the Tag Library Descriptor (TLD) as defined by the Web application deployment descriptor (`web.xml`). The `prefix` is the XML namespace identifier used by all custom tags referencing classes in the tag library.

```
<%@ taglib uri="BibleTagLib" prefix="bible" %>
<jsp:directive.taglib uri="BibleTagLib" prefix="bible" />
```

Scripting

Scripting tags are used to embed programming code within the body of a JSP to be executed during the process of each request. They are written in the designated processing language, which is typically Java. Note that the language can be changed in the `language` attribute of the `page` directive.

Declarations

Declarations are used to define instance level or class level variables and methods. Subsequently, they may be referenced by other scripting elements on the page.

Declarations support both styles of syntax. The scripting syntax uses an exclamation (!) to uniquely identify declarations. The XML syntax uses the `declaration` action. These two tag styles are interchangeable. Following are some examples:

```
<%! int x = 0; %>
<jsp:declaration> int x = 0; </jsp:declaration>
```

Variable declarations

Variable declarations have the net effect of defining instance level variables within the JSP servlet. Multiple variables can be declared within a single tag. Keep in mind that your JSP servlets are running multithreaded, and therefore if one thread changes an instance level variable, any other thread that has a reference to that variable may be affected. This is not a consideration, however, if you have set the `isThreadSafe` attribute of the `page` directive to `"false"`. Another option is to use local variables, which are always thread safe and usually the better choice, anyway.

```
<%! int x = 0; int y = 1; %>
<jsp:declaration> int x = 0; int y = 1; </jsp:declaration>
```

Class level variables can also be defined by using the static keyword within the declaration. Because this is defined at the class level, any thread of any instance of this JSP servlet may be affected by changes to this value regardless of the `isThreadSafe` attribute setting.

```
<%! static public boolean validate = true; %>
<jsp:declaration>
  static public boolean validate = true;
</jsp:declaration>
```

Method declarations

Method declarations define methods of the JSP servlet class. They can be called from any scripting element within the page. Multiple method declarations can be declared within a singe tag.

```
<%@ page import="java.text.*" %>

<%!
// Get a formatted current date and time
public String getCurrentDateTime() {
  Date date = new Date();
  DateFormat dateFormat =
    DateFormat.getDateTimeInstance(DateFormat.FULL,
    DateFormat.SHORT);
  return dateFormat.format(date);
}
%>
```

A very specific usage for method declarations is to define logic associated with the initialization and destruction of a JSP servlet. By defining methods `jspInit()` and `jspDestroy()`, the corresponding `_jspInit()` and `_jspDestroy()` methods of the JSP servlet are defined.

See Chapter 11 for a complete discussion of servlet initialization and destruction.

```
<%!
public void jspInit() {
  // initilization logic ...
}
public void jspDestroy() {
  // destruction logic ...
}
%>
```

Expressions

Expressions are used to output the evaluated value of an individual variable, calculation, or method call. All expression results are converted to character strings before being added to the page's output. Java primitives are converted via the static `toString()` method on the corresponding Java object (for example, an integer uses the `Integer.toString()` method, and so on). Java objects use their own `toString()` method.

Note that no semicolon is required at the end of an expression because the JSP compiler is concerned with evaluating the code and not with its side effects.

Expressions support both styles of syntax. The scripting syntax uses an equal sign (=) to uniquely identify expressions. The XML syntax uses the `expression` action. These two tag styles are interchangeable. Following are some examples:

```
<%= 365 * 24 %>
<%= x %>
<%= getDate() %>
<jsp:expression> 365 * 24 </jsp:expression>
<jsp:expression> x </jsp:expression>
<jsp:expression> getDate() </jsp:expression>
```

Conditional output is usually handled by using scriptlets in combination with expressions, but expressions do support the tertiary condition operator.

```
<%= hours < 12 ? "am" : "pm" %>
<jsp:expression> hours < 12 ? "am" : "pm" </jsp:expression>
```

Scriptlets

Scriptlets are tags that contain code fragments of one or more lines. Whereas all the tags that I've covered are for specific purposes, scriptlets are general purpose and allow you to embed Java code within your JSP. Each line of code within a scriptlet must be a complete line of code and therefore should end with a semicolon where appropriate.

Variables can be declared and set, methods can be called, return values can be evaluated, implicit objects can be referenced—virtually any Java code you want to embed within your JSP is valid. This is because scriptlets undergo no translation at all during the creation of the JSP servlet source, but are simply inserted as-is into the `_jspService()` method.

Scriptlets support both styles of syntax. The scripting syntax doesn't use any specific character to uniquely identify it, therefore all scriptlet tags begin with the base `<%` designation. The XML syntax uses the `scriptlet` action. These two tag styles are interchangeable. Following are some examples:

```
<% String fullName = firstName + " " + lastName; %>
<jsp:scriptlet>
  String fullName = firstName + " " + lastName;
</jsp:scriptlet>
```

Conditional processing

One of the strengths of a scriptlet is JSP's support of code blocks left open across multiple statements. In other words, scoped blocks of code can be broken into multiple tags with HTML or any other valid code text intermingled. A good example of using this is conditional output based upon a dynamic variable. Look at the following example:

```
<% Random rand = new Random();
if (rand.nextBoolean()) { %>
<strong>Do something.</strong>
<% } else {  %>
<strong>Do nothing.</strong>
<% } %>
```

Notice the if/else statement with two blocks of code based upon a random Boolean value. Through use of the begin and end scope notations using curly braces `{}`, you can span the logic across three scriptlet tags. In addition, notice that intermingled with the scriptlet tags is basic HTML code. Execution of this code will randomly output "Do something." or "Do nothing."

Iterative processing

Another way to take advantage of this technique is with iterative processing. Java provides for loops, while loops, and do/while loops as iterative constructs. Again, by using the scope notations, blocks can be left open across multiple statements to create the desired results. The following code iteratively computes a table of squares and cubes for the integers between 1 and 10:

```
<table>
  <tr>
    <td>Number</td>
    <td>Squared</td>
    <td>Cubed</td>
  </tr>

<% for (int i = 1; i <= 10; i++ ) { %>
  <tr>
    <td><%= i %></td>
    <td><%= i * i %></td>
    <td><%= i * i * i %></td>
  </tr>
<% } %>

</table>
```

Comments

Comments are used to document various types of code that can be found in a JSP page. You can use three styles of comments in JSPs.

Content comments

Content comments are an HTML-style comment that is converted by the JSP compiler and is output as a `String` by the corresponding JSP servlet. Subsequently, the comment is sent to the client in the viewable page source. Any JSP statement in an HTML comment is still evaluated, thereby allowing the comment to contain dynamic content.

```
<!-- HTML comment -->
<!-- Table line number <%= lineNumber %> -->
```

JSP comments

A JSP-style comment is filtered out during the JSP conversion process and therefore cannot be found in the JSP servlet source. It is only viewable in the original JSP source. Any JSP statement between the beginning and end tags of a JSP comment is ignored by the JSP compiler.

```
<%-- JSP comment --%>
<%-- <jsp:getProperty name="bean" property="newAttribute" />
not yet implemented -->
```

Scripting comments

Scripting comments are comments within the scriptlets themselves. They are in the style as defined by the scripting language. Java, for example, supports multiline comments beginning with /* and ending with */ as well as line level comments beginning with //. They are converted by the JSP compiler into the corresponding JSP servlet as a Java comment.

```
<% /* Scripting comment */ %>
<% int workHours = 178 /* number of workdays */ * 8 %>
<%  int hours = 365 * 24; // number of hours per year %>
```

Implicit objects

To expose all the capabilities of executing as servlets, WebLogic Server exposes a number of internal objects to the JSP developer. They are referred to as implicit objects because their availability is automatic and they're referenced by reserved names. Implicit objects are always either an instance of a class or interface adhering to the specific API and always scoped at the same level. The following sections provide the details of each of the nine implicit objects.

page

The `page` object represents an instance of the JSP Servlet class corresponding to the JSP page. It can be used to call any of the methods defined by the servlet class. But because these methods will be accessible automatically, this object is typically not implicitly referenced in the body of the JSP.

Type: `java.lang.Object`

Scope: `page`

Some useful methods: Not typically referenced

Scope is discussed in the "Programming JSPs with JavaBeans" section of this chapter.

config

The `config` object represents the JSP servlet configuration data accessible in the form of initialization parameters.

Type: `javax.servlet.ServletConfig`

Scope: `page`

Some useful methods: `getInitParameter`, `getInitParameterNames`

request

The `request` object represents the request received by WebLogic Server to initiate processing. It provides information regarding the requested URL, HTTP headers, parameters, and cookies associated with the request.

Type: `javax.servlet.ServletRequest` or `javax.servlet.http.HttpServletRequest`

Scope: `request`

Some useful methods: `getAttribute`, `getParameter`, `setParameterNames`, `getParameterValues`, `setAttribute`

response

The `response` object represents the response that will be returned by WebLogic Server upon completion of processing.

Type: `javax.Servlet.ServletResponse` or `javax.servlet.http.HttpServletResponse`

Scope: `page`

Some useful methods: `setHeader`, `addHeader`, `encodeURL`

out

The `out` object represents the output stream for the page. The contents of the `out` object will be sent as the body of the response.

Type: `javax.servlet.jsp.JspWriter`

Scope: `page`

Some useful methods: `clear`, `clearBuffer`, `flush`, `getBufferSize`, `getRemaining`

session

The `session` object represents an individual user's current session. The session persists as long as that user continues to send requests to the server frequently enough that it does not time out. It is only available if the `session` attribute of the `page` directive indicates that this JSP is participating in session management.

Type: `javax.servlet.http.HttpSession`

Scope: `session`

Some useful methods: `getAttribute`, `getId`, `setAttribute`

application

The application object represents the application to which the JSP belongs and is an instance of the ServletContext. It can be used to share information with other JSPs and servlets running as part of other sessions within an application.

Type: javax.servlet.ServletContext

Scope: application

Some useful methods: getAttribute, getMimeType, getRealPath, setAttribute

pageContext

The pageContext object is an instance of the servlet PageContext and provides programmatic access to all the other implicit objects as well as methods for forwarding requests to or including responses from other URLs.

Type: javax.servlet.jsp.PageContext

Scope: page

Some useful methods: findAttribute, getAttribute, getAttributesScope, getAttributeNamesInScope, setAttribute

exception

The exception object represents the exception that is thrown as the result of execution of another JSP. It can be used to retrieve and display information about the exception. It is only available if the isErrorPage attribute of the page directive indicates that the JSP page is an error page.

Type: java.lang.Throwable

Scope: page

Some useful methods: getMessage, getLocalizedMessage, printStackTrace, toString

Actions

Actions are the final type of JSP tag. They are used to transfer control between pages, support applets in a browser-independent manner, and interact with JavaBeans. Unlike the other types of tags, actions support only the XML-based syntax. Following are some examples:

```
<jsp:forward page="<%= nextPage %>">
  <jsp:param name="cmd" value="load"/>
</jsp:forward>
<jsp:include page="Header.jsp" flush="true">
```

```
  <jsp:param name="helpTag" value="help_Main.htm"/>
</jsp:include>
<jsp:plugin type="applet" codebase="plugins"
  code="bible.jsp.myplugin.class"/>
<jsp:useBean id="account" class="bible.jsp.AccountBean"/>
<jsp:setProperty name="account" property="accountNumber"
  value="110-12345"/>
<jsp:getProperty name="account" property="accountNumber"/>
```

forward

The `forward` action permanently forwards a client request to another server location for processing. The recipient can be an HTML file, CGI, JSP file, or servlet.

A new `pageContext` object will be assigned to the forwarded page. The `request` and `session` objects remain the same. The `application` object will be shared only if both the from and to pages are part of the same Web application.

Because the same `request` object is available to the forwarded page, the URL remains the same and the request parameters are still available. Additional parameters can be specified via the `param` tag within the body of the tag to add name-value pairs to the request. The number of parameters that you can specify in this manner is unlimited. Larger amounts of data are typically stored in the `request` or the `session` objects. Note that to reference the `session` object, both pages need to participate in session management. See the `session` attribute of the `page` directive for more information.

Once control is passed to the new page, processing of the originating page is immediately terminated. If the originating page buffered any data for output, and that output has not yet been flushed, then it can be cleared. But if output has already been flushed and an attempt to clear the buffer is made, an `IllegalStateException` will be thrown.

Following are some examples:

```
<jsp:forward page="Main.jsp"/>
<jsp:forward page="Confirm.jsp">
  <jsp:param name="cmd" value="load"/>
</jsp:forward>
```

For dynamic flow of control, embedding expressions within the body of the `forward` tag is supported. This allows the request to be forwarded to a location that is derived or passed as a parameter. Following is an example:

```
<% if (rows == 1) {
     nextPage = "Detail.jsp";
   } else {
     nextPage = "List.jsp";
   } %>

<jsp:forward page="<%= nextPage %>"/>
```

include

The include action allows the generated content of another file to be included into the output of the current JSP. Control is temporarily passed to the other location, where upon completing, returns to continue processing immediately after the action tag.

Unlike the include directive, the include action is resolved during the processing of the request. The included page's output is resolved and added to the output buffer, as opposed to processing the commingled the source.

The flush attribute controls whether the output buffer is flushed prior to transferring to the included file's location. JSP 1.1 restricted usage of this attribute to only allow false. WebLogic supports some prerelease features of JSP 1.2, including support for this attribute's value as true. This allows the page output to be buffered and then flush the buffer before including another resource.

As with the forward action, a new pageContext object is assigned, the request and session objects remain the same, and the application object is shared only if both the from and to pages are part of the same Web application. Likewise, an unlimited number of additional parameters can be specified via the param tags. In addition, expressions may be embedded for dynamic includes.

Following are some examples:

```
<jsp:include page="<%= helpTag %>"/>
<jsp:include page="Header.jsp" flush="true">
  <jsp:param name="helpTag" value="help_Main.htm"/>
</jsp:include>
```

plugin

The plugin action downloads plug-in software to the browser to execute an applet or bean. Because this book focuses on the development of server-side applications using WebLogic Server, this is outside of the scope of this book. See the complete JavaServer Pages specification at http://java.sun.com/products/jsp/download.html for more information.

Bean tags

Three additional tags exist for interacting with JavaBeans. They are useBean, setProperty, and getProperty, and I cover them later in the section, "Programming JSPs with JavaBeans." The following, however, is provided as a quick reference:

useBean

The useBean action locates or instantiates a bean with a specific name and scope. Example:

```
<jsp:useBean id="account" class="bible.jsp.AccountBean"
  scope="request" />
```

setProperty

The `setProperty` action sets a property value or values in a bean. Example:

```
<jsp:setProperty name="account" property="accountNumber"
  value="110-12345"/>
```

getProperty

The `getProperty` action gets the value of a bean property so that you can display it in a result page. Example:

```
<jsp:getProperty name="account" property="accountNumber"/>
```

JSP example

Now that I've covered all the different types of tags and their syntax, let's dive into a fairly meaty example and try to use a little bit of everything. I'll keep it simple by writing a JSP that prompts for the high value of a range of numbers, calculates the square and cube values of all the numbers in the range, and displays them in a table.

`Simple.jsp`, as shown in Listing 12-4, is the JSP to do exactly that. I'll walk you through this JSP and point out the various features.

First, I'll define my page directive and state that I'm not participating in session management and to define my error page as `Error.jsp`.

Next, I'll make a variable declaration for the integer variable I'll use to store the end of my range.

In this example, I wanted to use stylesheets and JavaScript to make sure everyone is clear on how to commingle the various technologies necessary to build a robust application. Therefore, further down I define my stylesheet and include a function to open a new window to display help text. Note that I am using Microsoft's Internet Explorer version 5.5, and therefore using Microsoft stylesheet syntax and JavaScript 1.2.

Next of note is the `include` directive including my application's standard header, `Header.jsp`. In this case, it is a JSP file because it contains JSP tags to dynamically retrieve the server's current date and time for display.

An HTML anchor tag displays a Help link. This link calls `Help.jsp` passing the document name containing the help text for this page.

Next is a scriptlet that gets a parameter "end" from the request. Note that all parameters are of type `java.lang.String`, therefore it is parsed by using the static `Integer.parse()` method before being set as the "end" variable.

Immediately after that is an HTML form tag enclosing an input prompt for the end of the range. Note that the value of the input field uses an expression tag to substitute the value of the "end" variable. Also note that upon submittal, this form calls `Simple.jsp` again using the `get` method.

Now that I have all the information I need, I have a scriptlet with a conditional if statement checking for a valid value for the end of my range. If it's not 0 and not greater than 20, then I'll proceed with displaying the result table. Otherwise, I'll bypass that and display a validation error message. Notice how the end variable is referenced within the scriptlet. Also notice how I use the scope notations to create the blocks of code necessary for this logic.

After I've passed my validation check, I have another scriptlet with an iterative for loop, looping from 1 through my end number. Again, notice the usage of the end variable and the code block created by the scope notations.

Now that I've either output my result table or issued a validation error, I want to end my output with my application's standard footer, `Footer.htm`. This time I include an HTML document because the footer is static.

Finally, I'll inline some JavaScript to set the focus on my input field and end my HTML.

Listing 12-4: **Simple.jsp**

```
<%-- Page Directives --%>
<%@ page session="false" errorPage="Error.jsp" %>

<%-- Declarations --%>
<%! int end; %>

<html>
<head>
  <title>Simple JSP</title>
  <link href="jsp.css" type=text/css rel=stylesheet>
  <script language=JavaScript1.2>
  function openHelp(url) {
    var winname = "help"
    var winprops = "toolbar=0, location=0, status=1, menubar=0, scrollbars=1,
resizable=1, width=450, height=300"
    var win = window.open(url , winname, winprops);
    win.window.focus();
  }
  </script>
</head>

<body>
```

Continued

Listing 12-4 *(continued)*

```
    <%@ include file="Header.jsp" %>

<table width="100%">
  <tr>
    <td>
      <span class="sectionTitle">Simple JSP</span>
</td>
    <td align=right><A href="Help.jsp?helpdoc=help_simple.htm"
onclick="javascript:openHelp(this.href);return false;">Help</A>
    </td>
  </tr>
 </table>

<%
// get the request parameter for the input field
String endParm = request.getParameter("end");
if (endParm != null) end = Integer.parseInt(endParm);
%>

<form action="Simple.jsp" method="get" name="prompt" id="prompt">
  <span class="prompt">Last number: </span>
  <input type="text" name="end" size="10" maxlength="2" value="<%= end %>">
  <span class="prompt">(1 - 20)</span>
</form>

<% // only output table if valid value
if (end > 0 && end <= 20) { %>
<table>
  <tr>
    <td>Number</td>
    <td>Squared</td>
    <td>Cubed</td>
  </tr>

  <% // Share square and cube of 1 through 10
  for (int i = 1; i <= end; i++ ) { %>
  <tr>
    <td align=center><%= i %></td>
    <td align=center><%= i * i %></td>
    <td align=center><%= i * i * i %></td>
  </tr>
  <% } %>
</table>

<% // otherwise display error message
} else if (endParm != null) { %>
<span class="errorText">Only values between 1 and 20 are allowed.</span>
<% } %>
```

```
<%@ include file="Footer.htm" %>

<script language=JavaScript1.2>
// set focus
document.prompt.end.focus();
</script>

</body>
</html>
```

Listing 12-5 is the `jsp.css` stylesheet source I'm using for this example. Note that I am using Internet Explorer syntax.

Listing 12-5: jsp.css

```
TD {
  FONT-WEIGHT: normal;
  FONT-SIZE: 9pt;
  COLOR: #000000;
  FONT-FAMILY: 'Arial', 'Helvetica';
  TEXT-DECORATION: none
}
.pageTitle {
  FONT-WEIGHT: bold;
  FONT-SIZE: 11pt;
  COLOR: #000000;
  FONT-FAMILY: 'Arial', 'Helvetica';
  TEXT-DECORATION: none
}
.sectionTitle {
  FONT-WEIGHT: bold;
  FONT-SIZE: 10pt;
  COLOR: #000000;
  FONT-FAMILY: 'Arial', 'Helvetica';
  TEXT-DECORATION: none
}
.prompt {
  FONT-WEIGHT: normal;
  FONT-SIZE: 10pt;
  COLOR: #000000;
  FONT-FAMILY: 'Arial', 'Helvetica';
  TEXT-DECORATION: none
}
.footer {
  FONT-WEIGHT: normal;
  FONT-SIZE: 8pt;
  COLOR: #666666;
```

Continued

Listing 12-5 *(continued)*

```
  FONT-FAMILY: 'Arial', 'Helvetica';
  TEXT-DECORATION: none
}
.errorText {
  FONT-WEIGHT: bold;
  FONT-SIZE: 9pt;
  COLOR: Red;
  FONT-FAMILY: 'Arial', 'Helvetica';
  TEXT-DECORATION: none
}
```

`Header.jsp`, as shown in Listing 12-6, is the standard header for the application. It first uses the `page` directive to import the `java.text` package. Note that even though `Simple.jsp` already defined a `page` directive, this second `page` directive is valid. Next is the declaration of method `getCurrentDateTime()`, which gets the current date and time and formats it by using the `java.text.DateFormat` class. Finally, it outputs an HTML table by using an expression to call the `getCurrentDateTime()` method.

Listing 12-6: Header.jsp

```
<!-- Standard Header ------------------------------------------------------->
<%@ page import="java.text.*" %>

<%!
// Get a formatted current date and time
public String getCurrentDateTime() {
  Date date = new Date();
  DateFormat dateFormat =
    DateFormat.getDateTimeInstance(DateFormat.FULL,
    DateFormat.SHORT);
  return dateFormat.format(date);
}
%>

<table cellSpacing=0 cellPadding=0 border=0 width="100%">
  <tr>
    <td align=middle class="pageTitle">WebLogic Bible JSP Examples</td>
  </tr>
  <tr>
    <td align=middle><%= getCurrentDateTime() %></td>
  </tr>
</table>
<hr>
<!-- End Header ------------------------------------------------------------>
```

Footer.htm, as shown in Listing 12-7, is a simple HTML document representing the application's standard footer. HTML comments surround the code and will be included in the source output to the browser.

Listing 12-7: Footer.htm

```
<!-- Standard Footer ----------------------------------------------------->
<hr>
<table cellSpacing=0 cellPadding=0 border=0 align=center>
  <tr>
    <td class=footer>Copyright (c)2001 Your Company  All rights reserved.</td>
  </tr>
</table>
<!-- End Footer ---------------------------------------------------------->
```

Help.jsp, shown in Listing 12-8, is the standard help page for the application. This design allows for a standard help page with dynamic help text through the usage of the JSP include action. Because it is resolved at request time, the help text document to be displayed can vary from page to page but continue to have the same look. Putting the finishing touches on this approach is the usage of the standard application header and footer JSPs.

Listing 12-8: Help.jsp

```
<%-- Page Directives --%>
<%@ page session="false" errorPage="Error.jsp" %>

<html>
<head>
  <title>Help Page</title>
  <link href="jsp.css" type=text/css rel=stylesheet>
</head>

<body>
<%@ include file="Header.jsp" %>

  <span class="sectionTitle">Help</span>
  <br><br>
<% String helpdoc = request.getParameter("helpdoc"); %>
<jsp:include page="<%= helpdoc %>" />

  <br>
  <form>
```

Continued

Listing 12-8 *(continued)*

```
    <input type="button" value="Close" onClick="window.close()">
  </form>

<%@ include file="Footer.htm" %>
</body>
</html>
```

The help text for the `Simple.jsp` is found in an HTML document, `help_simple.htm`, as shown in Listing 12-9. The nice thing about this approach is not only does it allow for a standard help page, but it also enables nondevelopers using tools such as Microsoft Word to create the online help.

Listing 12-9: help_simple.htm

```
This is sample help text for the Simple.jsp example. This is a good way to
provide simple online help text while demonstrating the <em>jsp:include</em>
action. Any changes made to this page will take effect immediately without
recreating or recompiling the JSP.
```

Each of these files is placed in the root level of my Web application directory, `BibleApp`. I'll run the example by typing **http://localhost:7001/BibleApp/Simple.jsp** in the address field of my browser. The first time, it takes a few seconds while WebLogic Server combines `Simple.jsp`, `Header.jsp`, and `Footer.htm` into one source file, `_simple.java`, and compiles it into a servlet, `_simple.class`.

Because there is no parameter named "end" in the request, the page will not display a table the first time it appears. I'll type the number **6** in the entry field and press Enter. The page shown in Figure 12-11 appears.

If I enter a value of 0 or greater than 20, such as 25, then the entry does not pass validation and an error message is shown, as in Figure 12-12.

If I click the Help link, a new window opens displaying the help text for this page (see Figure 12-13). Again, this will take a few seconds the first time around so that `Help.jsp`, `Header.jsp`, and `Footer.htm` can be combined into one servlet and compiled. The help document, `help_simple.htm`, is included at request time.

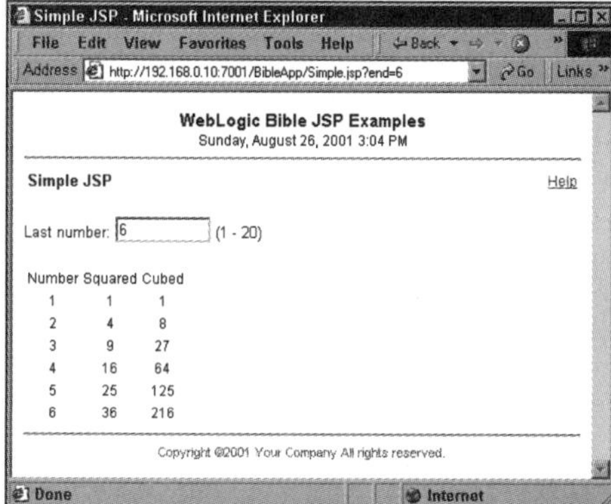

Figure 12-11: A simple calculator of squared and cubed values

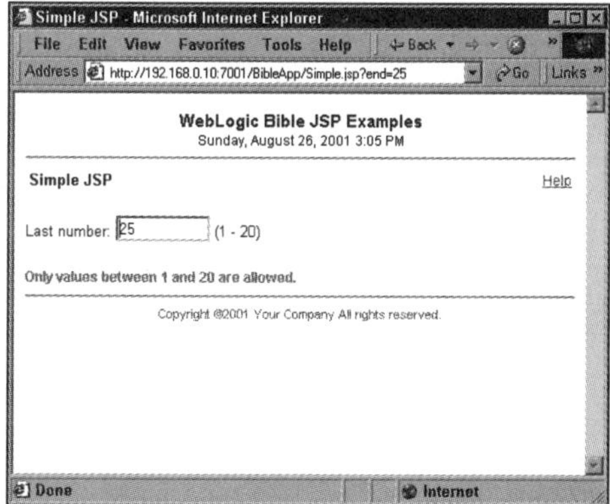

Figure 12-12: Displaying validation error text using conditional scriptlets

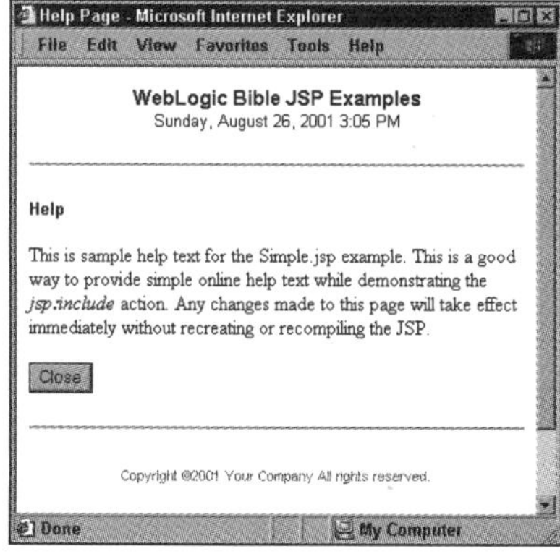

Figure 12-13: Displaying a dynamic help page

Error handling

As described earlier in the chapter, JavaServer Pages have built-in support for error handling. A JSP can be set to automatically forward to another page by setting the `errorPage` attribute of the `page` directive. Upon an uncaught error being thrown, processing is forwarded to the JSP defined in the `errorPage` attribute.

```
<%@ page errorPage="Error.jsp" %>
```

The page to receive the request as a result of an error also uses a `page` directive to set the `isErrorPage` to `true`. By defining this attribute, the implicit object `exception` is available to the page.

```
<%@ page isErrorPage="true" %>
```

Then anything can be done within that error page to elegantly handle the error, log it, and report it as required. Listing 12-10 of `Error.jsp` is my error page for this application.

I've defined an error page to display the exception message, the stack trace, and the URL to the browser. A lot more information is available that could also be displayed, such as request header information, request parameters, and cookie information. The information could also be logged or e-mailed. I suggest you take time to develop an error page that will work for all your applications and that provides you with all the information you need.

Listing 12-10: Error.jsp

```
<%@ page isErrorPage="true" %>

<html>
<head>
  <title>Error Page</title>
</head>

<body>
  <strong>There was an error processing this request ...</strong><br><br>
  <strong>Error Message:</strong><br>
<%= exception %>
  <br><br><strong>Stack Trace:</strong><br>
<% exception.printStackTrace(response.getWriter()); %>
  <br><br><strong>Request URL:</strong><br>
<%
out.print(HttpUtils.getRequestURL(request));
String query = request.getQueryString();
if (query != null) out.print("?" + query);
%>
</body>
</html>
```

I've intentionally left a bug in the code so that I could demonstrate JSP error handling. When running the `Simple.jsp` example in Listing 12-10, blank out the input field and press Enter. As a result, the "end" parameter exists, but with an empty `String`. The `Integer.parseInt()` method throws a `NumberFormatException`. The JSP error handling catches this and forwards the request to `Error.jsp`.

The error page, `Error.jsp`, receives the request and takes control of the processing. It uses the `exception` object to display the exception message, stack trace, and URL. The page shown in Figure 12-14 appears.

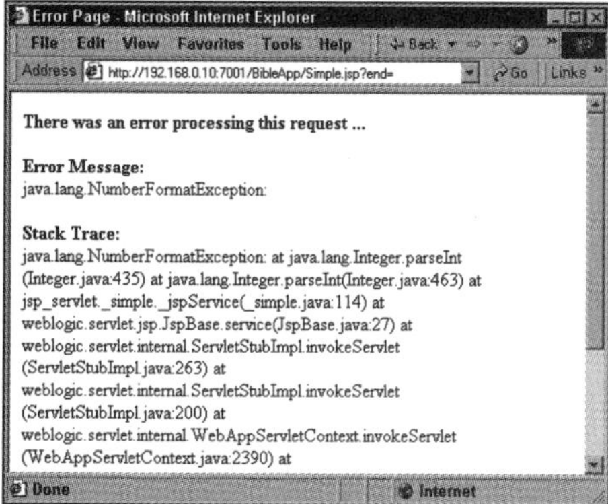

Figure 12-14: Displaying the error page

Another way that this could have been handled, assuming the developer expected this type of exception to be thrown, is through the use of Java's try/catch statements. JSP scriptlets also support the definition of try/catch blocks, and therefore the `NumberFormatException` could have been caught and handled within `Simple.jsp`.

In fact, it's good practice to eliminate the error or use the try/catch methodology to avoid the error page in future requests.

Debugging

During the course of JSP development, every developer inevitably encounters syntax errors or logic errors. These errors could result in compile errors or undesirable execution results.

Compilation errors are reported to the browser and the WebLogic Server console. Both the JSP and the servlet compilers write error messages, referencing line numbers in your code or in the generated servlet code when appropriate. Each compiler identifies the error situation and tries to point out exactly where and why the error may have occurred.

Here's an example of a compile error. If I change line 11 of `Header.jsp` to misspell the `date` variable, then this statement should no longer be able to compile properly.

```
return dateFormat.format(dat);
```

Figures 12-15 and 12-16 show the browser and WebLogic Console display of the compilation errors.

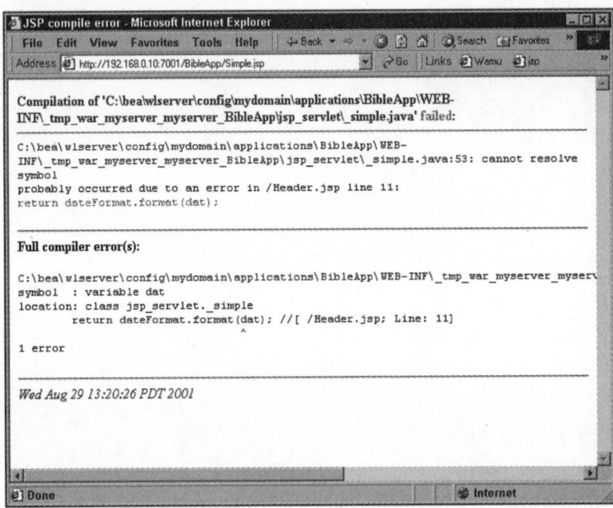

Figure 12-15: Compile errors displayed to the browser

Figure 12-16: Compile errors displayed to the WebLogic Server console

To determine the exact cause of the compilation error, sometimes it's necessary to examine the JSP servlet source that was created. As mentioned earlier, the `keepgenerated` tag of the JSP descriptor can be set to retain the generated JSP servlet source. The `package prefix` tag determines where the source will be located. I'm using the default, therefore the source can be found in my Web application's `WEB-INF\_tmp_war_myserver_myserver_BibleApp\jsp_servlet` directory.

Execution or logical errors are debugged as usual. Most developers use the standard `System.out.println()` or `out.println()` methods to display variables and informational text.

```
<%
boolean debug = true;

System.out.println("Debug mode = " + debug);
out.println("Debug mode = " + debug);
%>
```

The `weblogic.logging.NonCatalogLogger.info()` method can also be used to log information messages to the WebLogic Server log or a custom application log. See `http://e-docs.bea.com/wls/docs61/programming/topics.html` for more information on logging.

```
<%@ page import="weblogic.logging.NonCatalogLogger" %>

<%
NonCatalogLogger mylogger = new NonCatalogLogger("BibleApp");
boolean debug = true;

mylogger.info("Debug mode = " + debug);
%>
```

Programming JSPs with JavaBeans

The JavaBeans API specification version 1.01 describes the core specification for the JavaBeans component architecture. JavaBeans are Java objects whose implementation conforms to a set of conventions designed to promote modularity and reusability. They encapsulate data and behavior in a way that allows them to be reused without knowing how they are implemented. In fact, their implementation can be changed completely as long as their public methods provide the same interface. Separating presentation from implementation is the primary goal of JavaBeans.

The benefit is simple: developer productivity. Because JavaBeans are modular, they can be reused by multiple JSP pages or other server-side objects as necessary.

When a bean object is defined for use by a JSP, the JSP container searches for an existence of the bean instance in the defined scope. If not found, a new bean is instantiated with that scope. JavaBeans are scoped to the page, request, session, or application level just like implicit objects.

When scoping beans to the session or application, it is then up to WebLogic Server to determine how to manage those beans and its own internal resources. It may choose to temporarily persist a dormant object such as the bean or the session to disk to free memory resources. For this reason, it's a good convention to make your beans serializable. This means the bean should implement the `java.io.Serializable` interface. It also means that the bean properties should use either primitives or object types that likewise implement the `java.io.Serializable` interface.

For more information on JavaBeans, download the JavaBeans 1.01 specification at `http://java.sun.com/products/javabeans/docs/spec.html`.

Deploying your first JavaBean

Listing 12-11 is a simple JavaBean that represents a brokerage account. It has three properties with their corresponding accessor methods — getter and setter. It implements the `java.io.Serializable` interface, and each of its properties is serializable.

Basing your JavaBeans on a custom interface and/or partially implemented abstract class is good development practice. This enables you to code your Java code to the interface while enforcing that the beans have a common methodology. The `AccountBean` also implements a custom `ValueBean` interface (see Listing 12-12), and therefore defines another method for setting the bean with static test data.

Because the package name is `bible.jsp`, I'll compile both files into the `WEB-INF\classes\bible\jsp` of my `BibleApp` Web application.

Listing 12-11: AccountBean.java

```
package bible.jsp;

/**
 * Title:        AccountBean
 * Description:  JavaBean value object for Brokerage Accounts
 * Copyright:    Copyright (c) 2001
 * Company:      ZeeWare Inc.
 * @author Gary Wells
 * @version 1.0
 */

public class AccountBean implements ValueBean, java.io.Serializable {

  // private properties
```

```
  private String accountNumber;
  private String accountName;
  private String status;

  /**
   * Account Number
   */
  public String getAccountNumber() {
    return accountNumber;
  }
  public void setAccountNumber(String accountNumber) {
    this.accountNumber = accountNumber;
  }

  /**
   * Name
   */
  public void setAccountName(String accountName) {
    this.accountName = accountName;
  }
  public String getAccountName() {
     return accountName;
  }

  /**
   * Status
   */
  public void setStatus(String status) {
    this.status = status;
  }
  public String getStatus() {
    return status;
  }

  /**
   * Sets the bean with static test data
   */
  public void setTestData() {
    setAccountNumber("110-12345");
    setAccountName("Martin Moneybags");
    setStatus("Active");
  }
}
```

Listing 12-12, `ValueBean.java`, is the ValueBean interface.

Listing 12-12: ValueBean.java

```
package bible.jsp;

/**
 * Title:        ValueBean
 * Description:  JavaBean interface beans with only properties and accessor
methods
 * Copyright:    Copyright (c) 2001
 * Company:      ZeeWare Inc.
 * @author Gary Wells
 * @version 1.0
 */

public interface ValueBean {

  /**
   * Sets the bean with static test data
   */
  public void setTestData();

}
```

JSP bean tags

As described earlier in the chapter, there are three action tags that exist for interacting with JavaBeans. They allow the JavaBean object to be instantiated and used within a JSP. I explain each of these tags in detail so that you understand how it all works.

useBean

The `useBean` action tag is used to locate an existing bean instance or instantiate a new bean. That bean is assigned a logical name as it is known and referenced throughout the JSP. The lifetime or scope of the object is also specified. Depending upon the scope, the object may also be referenced by other JSPs. Following are some examples:

```
<jsp:useBean id="account" class="bible.jsp.AccountBean" scope="request"/>
<jsp:useBean id="pageBean" class="AccountPageBean" type="PageBean" />
<jsp:useBean id="userBean" class="UserBean" scope=session />
```

The attributes of the `useBean` tag are described in the following sections:

id

The `id` attribute identifies the name assigned to the bean object instance. It is referenced by this name throughout the JSP. This attribute is required.

scope

The `scope` attribute identifies the lifespan of the object. It is implemented by actually binding the bean object to the implicit object representing that level of scope. Possible values are `page`, `request`, `session`, and `application`. If not specified, the default value is `page`.

The different scope values are explained as follows:

- **page:** the bean instance is associated with this page for the processing of this particular request. An object with `page` scope is bound to `javax.servlet.jsp.PageContext`.
- **request:** the bean instance is associated with the processing of this particular request. The bean will be available to any JSP upon which control has been transferred using the `forward` or `include` action. An object with `page` scope is bound to `javax.servlet.ServletRequest`.
- **session:** the bean instance is available during any requests made by the same client in the same session.
- **application:** the bean instance is available to any JSP with the same Web application. An object with `page` scope is bound to `javax.servlet.jsp.ServletContext`.

class

The `class` attribute identifies the fully qualified class name.

beanName

The `beanName` attribute specifies the name of the bean as it would be supplied to the `Java.beans.Beans.instantiate()` method.

This attribute supports request time evaluation through the use of an expression.

type

The `type` attribute specifies the object type to which an existing bean should be cast. It must be the bean's class, a superclass of the bean's class, or an interface implemented by the bean's class. If not, a `ClassCastExeption` will be thrown. This attribute is optional, and if not specified, will default to the value of the `class` attribute.

JavaBean instantiation

WebLogic Server uses the following logic to instantiate a new or locate an existing JavaBean instance:

1. An attempt is made to locate an object that has the same `id` in the specified `scope`.

2. If the bean instance is found, and the `type` attribute has been specified, the object is cast to the specified type. If the cast fails, a `ClassCastException` is thrown.

3. If the bean instance is not found in the specified `scope`, and no `class` or `beanName` attribute is specified, an `InstantiationException` is thrown.

4. If the bean instance is not found in the specified `scope` and the `class` attribute is specified, then the bean specified in the `class` attribute is instantiated associating it with the `id` in the specified `scope`. Upon failure, an `InstantiationException` is thrown.

5. If the bean instance is not found in the specified `scope` and the `beanName` attribute is specified, the `java.beans.Beans.instantiate()` is invoked, associating it with the `id` in the specified `scope`. Upon failure, either a `ClassNotFoundException` or `IOException` is thrown.

6. If a bean is instantiated, the `useBean` tag is processed intializing the variable. It is now available for scriptlets, the `setProperty` action, and the `getProperty` action to reference.

getProperty

The `getProperty` action tag returns the value of a bean property so that it can be displayed in a result page. The bean property is accessed by using the corresponding getter method, converted to a `String`, and returned. Following are some examples:

```
<jsp:getProperty name="account" property="accountNumber"/>
<jsp:getProperty name="position" property="shares"/>
```

When properties are returned from a bean, the value is converted to a `String`. If the property is an object, that object's `toString()` method is used. If it is a primitive, the `valueOf()` method of the corresponding wrapper class is used. If the bean property is an integer primitive, for example, then the `Integer.valueOf()` method is used.

The `getProperty` tag has the following attributes:

name

The `name` attribute identifies the name assigned to the bean object instance in the `useBean` tag. This attribute is required.

property

The `property` attribute identifies the name of the bean property to be returned. This attribute is required.

setProperty

The `setProperty` action tag sets a property value or values in a bean. It is used to map the data from the request to the bean. Bean properties, such as arrays, can be simple or indexed.

Bean properties are set at request time from request parameters, evaluated expressions, or hard coded Strings. Following are some examples:

```
<jsp:setProperty name="account" property="*"/>
<jsp:setProperty name="account" property="accountNumber"/>
<jsp:setProperty name="position" property="shares"
  param="quantity"/>
<jsp:setProperty name="account" property="status"
  value="Active"/>
```

One method for setting bean properties is to set them at request time from parameters in the request object. A single property can be set by simply specifying the bean name and the property to be set. Note that the param attribute needs to be specified only if the request parameter name doesn't match the bean property name.

```
<jsp:setProperty name="account" property="accountNumber"/>
```

The JSP can also set all the properties of a bean by specifying an asterisk (*). It will automatically map all the properties in the request to those in the bean. Note that this will only work when the request parameter name matches the bean property name.

```
<jsp:setProperty name="account" property="*"/>
```

It's important to note that no exception will be thrown if there are request parameters that do not have matching bean properties. Therefore, pay special attention that you achieve the desired results.

When properties are assigned from request parameters or String constants, the value is converted to the appropriate type if the bean property is not of type String. This is done by using the valueOf() method of the corresponding wrapper class. If the bean property is an integer primitive or Integer, for example, the Integer.valueOf() method is used. No conversion is performed if the property is being set from an evaluated expression. Indexed properties must be set with an array.

The setProperty tag has the following attributes:

name

The name attribute identifies the name assigned to the bean object instance in the useBean tag. This attribute is required.

property

The property attribute identifies the name of the bean property to be set. If this property has a value of *, all the parameters of the request are mapped to the bean attributes and the appropriate setter methods are called. If the request parameter is "", the bean property is left unaltered. This attribute is required.

param

The `param` attribute is used to specify the name of the request parameter to be mapped to the specified property. This attribute is unnecessary if the request parameter name is identical to the bean property name. If there is no request parameter with this name, the bean property is left unaltered. This attribute cannot be specified if the value of the `property` attribute is *.

value

The `value` attribute specifies the value to assign to the bean property. This can be a request time attribute or an expression. A tag cannot have both the `param` and `value` attributes.

Introspection

You may be wondering how the `setProperty` and `getProperty` action tags know what methods to call against the bean to set and return values. How do they determine the property type and therefore when to perform data type conversions?

These tags use a process called *introspection* to discover the bean's properties, whether they are simple or indexed, their type, and their accessor methods. Because the JSP container does not have any common interface or base class to rely upon for interaction with a bean, it must rely upon conventions to establish properties.

Introspection uses *reflection* to examine the bean class at request processing to determine its methods. Through detailed examination of each method, introspection can determine the corresponding private or protected variable and its type. Therefore, bean properties are defined by simply creating the appropriate accessor methods for them. Note that only one method needs to exist to define the existence of a bean's property.

Accessor methods are defined as the corresponding setter and getter methods for a property. They must be defined as public and named as the property with the word `get` or `set` prefixed. The setter should be declared void and accept one argument of the appropriate type. The getter should return the appropriate type and doesn't accept any arguments. The declaration of a property named `description` and its accessor methods are as follows:

```
private String description;

public void setDescription(String description) {
  this.description = description;
}
public String getDescription() {
  return description;
}
```

The corresponding `getProperty` and `setProperty` action tags are as follows:

```
<jsp:setProperty name="bean" property="description" />
<jsp:getProperty name="bean" property="description" />
```

Invoking bean methods

Note that it is valid to directly invoke the accessor methods or any other methods in a bean. To refer to the bean object, the same name as in the id attribute of the useBean tag is used. Other than that, it's the same as invoking a method in any other instantiated object. Note, however, that because the JSP compiler simply transfers the scriptlet code to the JSP servlet, there is no introspection or type conversion that takes place when using the accessor methods.

```
<% positions.next();
   position.getSymbol();
   position.getShares();
%>
```

JSP and JavaBean example

Now I'll walk you through an example of a JSP using a JavaBean. AccountEdit.jsp in Listing 12-13 represents a page that displays the details of a brokerage account for the purposes of editing the information.

This is not a complete example because I want to keep it simple and show you a JSP that demonstrates only the bean tags recently discussed. I'm not going to provide the implementation of creating and setting the bean. Instead, I'll use the setTestData() method of the AccountBean and/or specify the name-value pairs in the URL request.

Looking at the source example, the first thing to notice is the import attribute of the page directive. The bible.jsp package is needed for the bean and any helper classes that may potentially be needed.

A useBean tag identifies a bean named account of class bible.jsp.AccountBean scoped to the request. Again, if the bean of this name and type is not found in the request, a new bean will be instantiated and bound to the request.

The setProperty tag immediately following will set the bean properties with the parameters in the request.

Next is little scriptlet for use in development only. It looks for a parameter indicating that the JSP is being run in test mode, and if so, it instructs the bean to set itself with test data. This is nice to have for UI design and debugging the JSP tags.

Further down are JSP tags that get account number and name from the bean for display in the input text boxes. Note how these tags are used with the value attribute of the HTML input tag. Also notice that I name the input fields the same at the bean properties so that when this page is submitted, the receiving JSP can successfully use property="*" in the setProperty tag.

To set the HTML select list with the proper status value is a bit trickier. First, I'll use a scriptlet to set a local status variable directly via the bean's get method. Next I'll use an expression with a tertiary statement with each option tag to determine if it should be flagged as selected. Again, the select list is named the same as the bean property.

Normally, when the request is submitted, it's sent to a servlet of JSP that exists to process the request and forward to the next page to be displayed. But for the sake of easily demonstrating this example, this JSP submits the request to itself. This means that the new request gets created and forwarded to the JSP page. Because the `account` bean is scoped to the `request`, a new instance is created and set from the request parameters. The form submits the request by using the `get` method so that you can see the name-value pairs in the URL.

Listing 12-13: **AccountEdit.jsp**

```
<%-- Page Directives --%>
<%@ page session="false" errorPage="Error.jsp" import="bible.jsp.*"%>

<%-- Bean Tags  --%>
<jsp:useBean id="account" class="bible.jsp.AccountBean" scope="request"/>
<jsp:setProperty name="account" property="*" />

<%  // Test Mode
if ("true".equals(request.getParameter("testmode"))) {
  account.setTestData(); // Create test data
} %>

<html>
<head>
  <title>Edit Account Information</title>
  <link href="jsp.css" type=text/css rel=stylesheet>
</head>

<body>
<%@ include file="Header.jsp" %>

  <form action="AccountEdit.jsp" method="get" name="prompt" id="prompt">
    <table cellSpacing=1 cellPadding=0 border=0 width="100%">
      <tr>
        <td colspan=2 class="sectionTitle">Edit Account Information</td>
      </tr>
      <tr>
        <td class="columnHead" align=right width="20%">Account Number: </td>
        <td><input type="hidden" name="accountNumber" size="9" maxlength="9"
          value="<jsp:getProperty name="account" property="accountNumber"/>">
          <jsp:getProperty name="account" property="accountNumber"/></td>
      </tr>
      <tr>
        <td class="columnHead" align=right width="20%">Name: </td>
        <td><input type="text" name="accountName" size="40" maxlength="40"
```

```
            value="<jsp:getProperty name="account" property="accountName"/>"></td>
        </tr>
        <tr>
          <td class="columnHead" align=right width="20%">Status: </td>
          <td><select name="status">
<% String status = account.getStatus(); %>
          <option value="A" <%= status == "A" ? "selected" : "" %>>Active
          <option value="I" <%= status == "I" ? "selected" : "" %>>Inactive
          </option></select>
          </td>
        </tr>
      </table>

      <br>
      <input type="Button" value="Submit" onclick="javascript:submit(); return
false;">
    </form>

<%@ include file="Footer.htm" %>

</body>
</html>
```

First, request the `AccountEdit.jsp` with the `testmode` parameter. The JSP will look at this parameter and instruct the bean to set itself with test data. This enables you to display the JSP with data.

```
http://localhost:7001/BibleApp/AccountEdit.jsp?testmode=true
```

The page shown in Figure 12-17 appears.

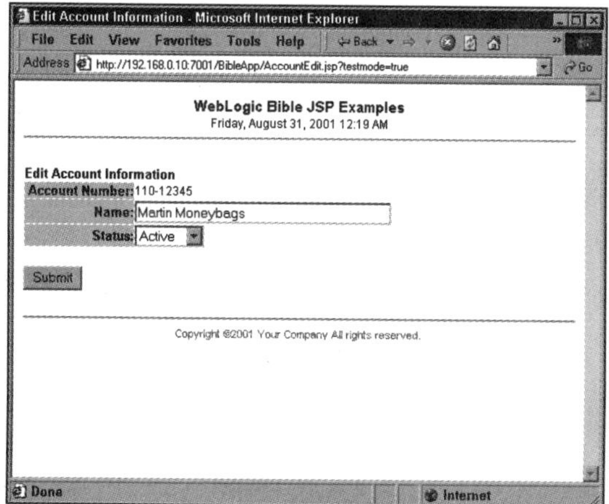

Figure 12-17: Displaying the account edit page with test data

Now change the account name and status. When you submit this request, the request is actually submitted to the same JSP. The HTML form uses the `get` method, therefore you can see the name-value pairs in the URL.

Another way to test this same JSP is by typing in the complete URL with a complete set of parameters. Either way, the parameters from the request are mapped to the `AccountBean`'s properties, so the values are properly displayed on the page (see Figure 12-18).

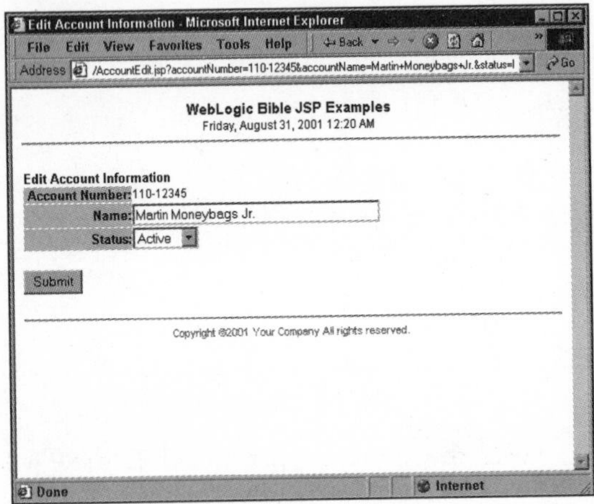

Figure 12-18: Displaying the account edit page with the request data

Using servlets to handle requests

A common methodology is to use servlets to receive and process requests and control navigation. Upon receiving a request for data, a servlet might get a connection from a JDBC connection pool, request data from the database, and forward the request to the next JSP.

In order to get the requested data to the JSP, the servlet could map all the data into the parameter portion of the URL before calling the bean. The bean would then map the parameters to the bean properties as seen previously. Sounds a bit cumbersome, doesn't it?

A simpler and more elegant solution is for the servlet to actually use the bean to send the data to the JSP. It could instantiate the bean, map the data from the result set to the bean's properties, and manually bind the bean to the proper scope.

The bean must have the same name, be the same type, and have the same scope in order for the JSP to locate the bean via the `useBean` tag. If the JSP scoped the bean to the `request`, for example, the servlet would bind the bean to the `request` object. It would do this by creating the bean of the proper type and setting it in a parameter in the `HttpServletRequest` object. The parameter would have the same name as specified by the `id` attribute in the `useBean` tag.

To demonstrate this, I'll introduce the new `AccountSearch.jsp` in Listing 12-14. It prompts for the account and provides the option of editing it or viewing the details. The request is sent to the `AccountServlet`, as shown in Listing 12-15. The servlet loads the selected account information into an `AccountBean` instance, binds the bean to the request object, and forwards the request to `AccountEdit.jsp`. Listing 12-16 provides the `web.xml` application deployment descriptor to deploy the `AccountServlet`.

Listing 12-14: **AccountSearch.jsp**

```
<%-- Page Directives --%>
<%@ page session="false" errorPage="Error.jsp" import="bible.jsp.*"%>

<html>
<head>
  <title>Account Search</title>
  <link href="jsp.css" type=text/css rel=stylesheet>
</head>

<body>
<%@ include file="Header.jsp" %>

  <form action="loadaccount" method="get" name="prompt" id="prompt">
    <input type="hidden" name="cmd" value="">
    <table cellSpacing=1 cellPadding=0 border=0 width="100%">
      <tr>
        <td colspan=2 class="sectionTitle">Account Search</td>
      </tr>
      <tr>
        <td class="columnHead" align=right width="20%">Select Account: </td>
        <td><select name="accountNumber">
          <option value="">--Choose One--
          <option value="110-12345">Martin Moneybags
          <option value="110-98765">Lois Lottamoney
          <option value="110-13579">Greg Goinbroke
          </option></select>
         </td>
```

Continued

Listing 12-14 *(continued)*

```
      </tr>
    </table>

    <br>
    <input type="Submit" name="btnEdit" value="edit" >
    <input type="Submit" name="btnDetail" value="detail">
  </form>

<%@ include file="Footer.htm" %>

</body>
</html>
```

Listing 12-15: **AccountServlet.java**

```
package bible.jsp;

/**
 * Title:        AccountServlet
 * Description:  Loads an account from the database
 * Copyright:    Copyright (c) 2001
 * Company:      ZeeWare Inc.
 * @author Gary Wells
 * @version 1.0
 */

import java.io.*;
import javax.servlet.*;
import javax.servlet.http.*;

public class AccountServlet extends HttpServlet {

  private AccountBean account;
  private String accountNumber;

  public void service(HttpServletRequest request, HttpServletResponse response)
    throws ServletException, IOException {

    // get the account number from the request
    accountNumber = request.getParameter("accountNumber");

    // create the band, set its properties, and scope it to the request
    account = new AccountBean();
```

```
    loadAccount();
    request.setAttribute("account", account);


    // determine next page based upon cmd
    String nextPage = "AccountSearch.jsp";
    if ("edit".equals(request.getParameter("cmd"))) {
      nextPage = "/AccountEdit.jsp";
    } else if ("detail".equals(request.getParameter("cmd"))) {
      nextPage = "/AccountDetail.jsp";
    }

    // forward the request to the next page
    try {
      RequestDispatcher rd = getServletContext().getNamedDispatcher(nextPage);
      rd.forward(request, response);
    } catch (Exception e) {
      throw new ServletException(e);
    }
  }

  private void loadAccount() {
    // connect to the database here and load bean from account data, however
    // this example with set the static data baase upon the request parameter

    if (accountNumber.equals("110-12345")) {
      account.setAccountNumber("110-12345");
      account.setAccountName("Martin Moneybags");
      account.setStatus("A");

    } else if (accountNumber.equals("110-98765")) {
      account.setAccountNumber("110-98765");
      account.setAccountName("Lois Lottamoney");
      account.setStatus("A");

    } else if (accountNumber.equals("110-13579")) {
      account.setAccountNumber("110-13579");
      account.setAccountName("Greg Goinbroke");
      account.setStatus("A");
    }
  }
}
```

Listing 12-16: **web.xml**

```
<!DOCTYPE web-app PUBLIC "-//Sun Microsystems, Inc.//DTD Web Application
2.2//EN" "http://java.sun.com/j2ee/dtds/web-app_2.2.dtd">
```

Continued

Listing 12-16 (continued)

```
<web-app>
  <servlet>
    <servlet-name>AccountServlet</servlet-name>
    <servlet-class>bible.jsp.AccountServlet</servlet-class>
    <load-on-startup>0</load-on-startup>
  </servlet>
  <servlet-mapping>
    <servlet-name>AccountServlet</servlet-name>
    <url-pattern>/loadaccount</url-pattern>
  </servlet-mapping>
  <welcome-file-list>
    <welcome-file>index.html</welcome-file>
  </welcome-file-list>
</web-app>
```

To execute this example, type `http://localhost:7001/BibleApp/AccountSearch.jsp` to request the account search. The page shown in Figure 12-19 appears. Choose one of the accounts and press Enter. The account information appears for edit, as shown in Figure 12-20.

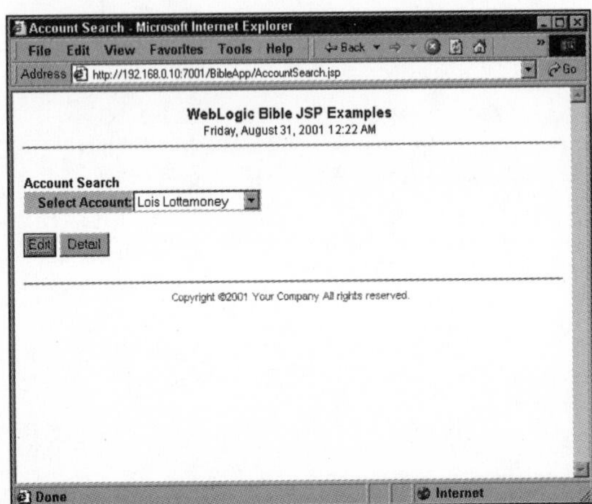

Figure 12-19: Selecting an account to edit

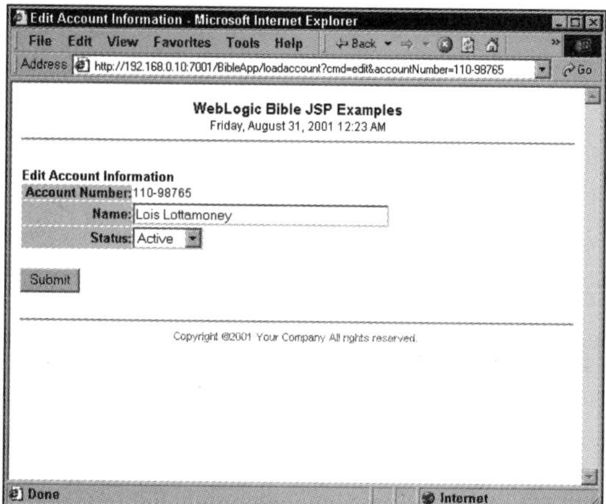

Figure 12-20: Displaying the selected account

Summary

JavaServer Pages represent the next generation of Web development architecture. Because they leverage the existing servlet technology, they offer excellent performance due to highly optimized use of processing and memory resources. WebLogic Server's implementation adds container management of JSP servlets and JavaBeans to optimize the handling of requests.

JSPs are also positioned perfectly for today's developers. They map better to the Model-View-Controller design pattern than to any other technology. They allow the User Interface and Server Side developers to separate tasks cleanly and cooperate at the highest levels of efficiency. They allow for the development of reusable JavaBeans that take advantage of the OO strengths of Java. They allow the UI developer to utilize XML-like tags to interact with JavaBeans and tag extensions.

This chapter covered the basics of JSPs and used them with JavaBeans and servlets. Chapter 13 takes a look at tag extensions.

✦ ✦ ✦

CHAPTER 13

Developing Tag Libraries

In This Chapter

Understanding tag libraries

Programming and using a tag extension

Programming a TagExtraInfo class

WebLogic tag libraries

WebLogic EJB-to-JSP integration tool

The JavaServer Pages API defines tag libraries that contain reusable and modular functionality that can be invoked by custom tags within a JSP page. They reduce the necessity to embed large amounts of Java code in JSP pages by moving the functionality into tag implementation classes.

In the first part of this chapter, an overview of the interfaces, convenience classes, and support classes that are the core of the tag extension architecture is provided. You learn how to program tag handler classes, create a descriptor for the tag library, and deploy the tag handler class and tag library within WebLogic Server. Finally, you learn how to access your tag library with custom tag extensions in JSPs.

Understanding Tag Libraries

The JavaServer Pages API version 1.1 was the first version to define tag extensions or custom tags that can be used in a JSP. Tag extensions reference custom tag handlers to extend the functionality of a page. Tag handlers are custom Java classes that provide additional functionality to the JSP page.

JavaServer Pages API version 1.2 offers additional interfaces and convenience classes that provide base implementations of commonly coded functionality such as iteration and validation.

Four components are required to define and utilize tag extensions in a JSP:

- A Java class called a tag handler with the desired functionality of a tag extension
- An XML document call a Tag Library Descriptor (TLD) containing information about a library and one or more tag handler classes
- An entry in the Web Application Deployment Descriptor (`web.xml`) defining the tag library to the Web application
- Taglib directive and tag extension statements referencing the tag handlers within the JSP

Tag handler lifecycle

The tag handler interfaces define methods that are invoked by the JSP engine at specific points during the processing of the JSP page. As shown in Figure 13-1, they signify points in the lifecycle of the tag. Therefore, understanding this lifecycle is important for proper implementation of your tag handlers.

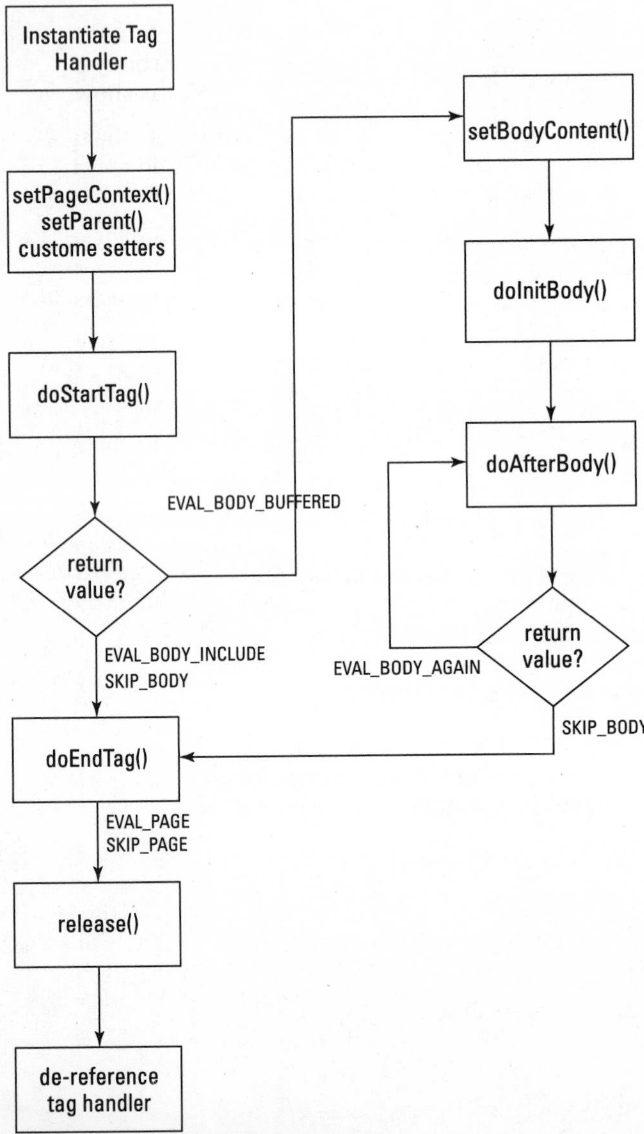

Figure 13-1: The tag handler lifecycle

1. When the JSP engine encounters a tag in a JSP page, a new tag handler is initialized. The `setPageContext()`, `setParent()`, and custom setter methods of the class are invoked to set up the environment context for the tag handler.

2. The `doStartTag()` method is invoked. At the end of the `doStartTag()` method, one of the following constants is returned:

   `SKIP_BODY` directs the JSP engine to skip the processing of the tag's body content and continue to the `doEndTag()` method (as shown in Step 6).

   `EVAL_BODY_INCLUDE` directs the JSP engine to evaluate and include the content of the tag body but skip the processing of the body content. Processing continues with the `doEndTag()` method (as shown in Step 6).

   `EVAL_BODY_BUFFERED` directs the JSP engine to evaluate the tag body content and invoke the `doInitBody()` method. This is valid only if the tag handler implements the `BodyTag` interface or extends `BodyTagSupport`.

3. If the body is to be processed by the tag handler, the tag content is evaluated and appended to a `BodyContent` object's buffer. The `setBodyContent()` method is invoked to store a reference to the object in the tag handler.

   At this point in the cycle, if the tag is to output to the JSP page, the `BodyContent.getEnclosingWriter().write()` method should be used to gain access to the parent-scoped `JspWriter`.

4. The `doInitBody()` method is invoked to allow for processing before the tag body is evaluated for the first time.

5. The `doAfterBody()` method is invoked to perform some work based on the evaluated tag body. If the tag handler extends the `BodyTagSupport` convenience class, the `getBodyContent()` method can access the evaluated body. At the end of the `doAfterBody()` method, one of the following constants is returned:

   `SKIP_BODY` directs the JSP engine to end any iteration of body evaluation and continue to the `doEndTag()` method (Step 6).

   `EVAL_BODY_AGAIN` directs the JSP engine to append evaluated body to the `BodyContent` object and begin another iteration of the body by invoking `doAfterBody()` again.

   The `BodyContent` is appended to the existing `BodyContent` upon each iteration through the body. Care must be taken to avoid repeating the content of each subsequent iteration in the output. A common approach is to hold the evaluated body content in a `StringBuffer` while iterating through the body content. The content of the `StringBuffer` should be written to the `JspWriter` only after it is determined that iteration is complete and `SKIP_BODY` will be returned.

At this point in the cycle, output needs to be written to the surrounding scope by using either the `BodyTagSupport.getPreviousOut().write()` method or the `BodyContent.getEnclosingWriter().write()` method. Either method obtains the same enclosing writer.

6. The `doEndTag()` method is invoked to perform processing at the end tag, such as writing output in a noniterative tag or cleaning up resources. At the end of the `doEndTag()` method, one of the following constants is returned:

   `EVAL_PAGE` directs the JSP engine to continue processing the rest of the JSP page.

   `SKIP_PAGE` directs the JSP engine to skip the rest of the JSP page. Caution should be taken when using this return value as it can be complicated to debug.

   At this point in the cycle, output needs to be written to the surrounding scope by using the `pageContext.getOut().write()` method.

7. The `release()` method is invoked to release state. This occurs just before the tag handler instance is dereferenced by the JSP page and made available for garbage collection.

Tag handlers and the Tag Extension API

A tag handler is a request-time, container-managed, Java object that evaluates tag extensions or custom tags during the execution of a JSP page. It must implement or extend a set of interfaces and convenience classes provided by Sun within the `javax.servlet.jsp.tagext` package. These interfaces ensure that the custom tag handler classes are capable of supporting a protocol to interact with the JSP container.

This protocol provides for passing of parameters, the evaluation and reevaluation of the body content of a tag extension, and for getting access to objects and other tag handlers in the JSP page.

A tag extension can contain attributes that, in turn, set properties on a tag handler by the JSP container (Figure 13-2). Similar to JavaBeans, the JSP container uses introspection to discover the properties and setter methods of the tag handler. It then generates the appropriate code during JSP servlet generation to interact with the tag handler.

WebLogic manages tag handlers much like JavaBeans, in that it will create and manage a pool of tag handlers to handle requests. Unlike JavaBeans, tag handlers do not need to be threadsafe. WebLogic will only choose a tag handler that is not being used to process a request. If none is available, WebLogic will either add new tag handler to the pool or queue up the request.

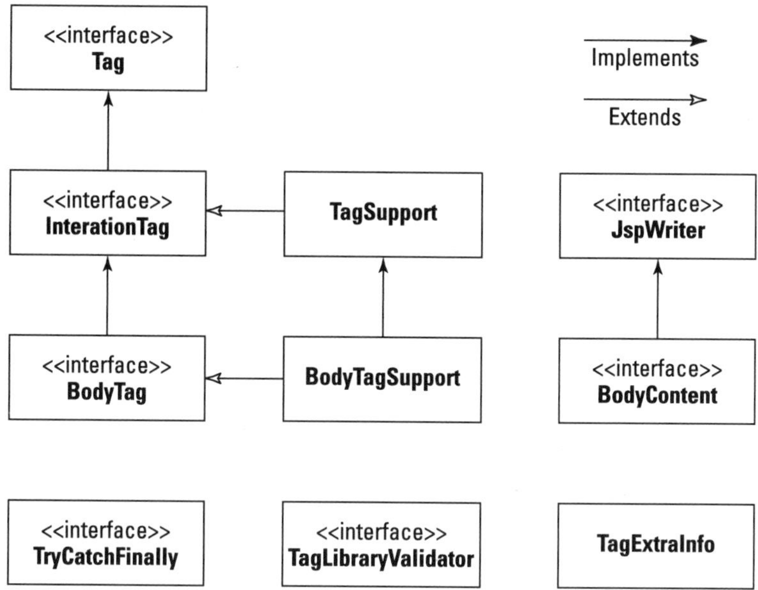

Figure 13-2: The Tag Extension API

Main interfaces

A tag handler class must implement one of three main interfaces: `Tag`, `InterationTag`, or `BodyTag`. They define methodology that the JSP container expects to invoke upon encountering a tag extension.

Tag interface

The `javax.servlet.jsp.tagext.Tag` interface is used by tag handlers that don't contain body content or desire to process the body content.

Any tag handler class implementing the `Tag` interface must define the following methods: `doStartTag()`, `doEndTag()`, `getParent()`, `setPageContext()`, and `release()`. Complete descriptions of these methods are provided in the upcoming section describing the `TagSupport` class.

IterationTag interface

Tag handlers that need to iteratively process the body content of the tag without manipulating its content use the `javax.servlet.jsp.tagext.IterationTag` interface. It extends the `Tag` interface and defines one additional method, `doAfterBody()`, to handle body-content iteration. This method will be covered in detail in the upcoming section describing the `TagSupport` class.

BodyTag interface

Tag handlers that want access to the body content of the tag and the capability to manipulate it use the `javax.servlet.jsp.tagext.BodyTag` interface. It extends the `IterationTag` interface and defines two additional methods to process and set the body content.

Any tag handler class implementing the `BodyTag` interface must define the following methods: `doInitBody()` and `setBodyContent()`. Complete descriptions of these methods are provided in the upcoming section describing the `BodyTagSupport` class.

Convenience classes

The API also provides two convenience classes: `TagSupport` and `BodyTagSupport`. They are provided as base classes for your tag handler classes. They are concrete classes that provide properties, convenience methods, and default implementations of the methods defined in the interfaces.

These classes are provided with the intent that they be extended to develop your own custom tag handler classes. Because they provide a set of default properties and methods, only the methods that need custom definition need to be coded.

TagSupport

The `TagSupport` convenience class implements both the `Tag` and `InterationTag` interfaces. Therefore, this class supports both simple tags and tags that desire tag body iteration. This is the base class that should be used for most tag handlers unless they need to access and manipulate the body content. In this case, see the `BodyTagSupport` convenience class described in a later section.

The `TagSupport` class provides a lot of base functionality that should be useful for most tag handlers. It provides convenience methods for getting, setting, and managing the tag handler's attributes. It also provides access to the `pageContext` object and methods for coordination among cooperating tags.

Tag extensions are typically used to write dynamic content to the page, replacing the start and end tags. To do this from a class that extends the `TagSupport` class, the `pageContext.getOut().write()` method should be used. This accesses and uses the `JspWriter.out` object.

The most commonly used `TagSupport` methods are described in the following sections. See the JSP API specification for a complete reference of its fields and methods.

doStartTag()

The `doStartTag()` method is called at request time when the start tag has been encountered and initialized. You should override this method if you want processing to occur before the body content and end tag are processed.

This method assumes that the properties pageContext and parent have been set. It also assumes that any properties exposed as attributes have been set as well. The TagSupport convenience class provides a default implementation that automatically takes care of these prerequisites.

This method can throw a JspException if an error condition occurs that the JSP should know about and perhaps handle through its error page. Otherwise, it's recommended that the JspException should be handled within the tag handler.

This method should return Tag.EVAL_BODY_INCLUDE or Tag.SKIP_BODY class constants. EVAL_BODY_INCLUDE indicates that upon return to the JSP, the body content should be evaluated and the end tag should be processed. SKIP_BODY indicates that the body content should be ignored and processing should continue and process the end tag only. If the action is an empty action, the doStartTag() method must return SKIP_BODY.

The default implementation of this method returns SKIP_BODY.

doEndTag()

The doEndTag() method is called by your JSP page servlet at request time when the end tag has been encountered and following execution of the doStartTag() method. The developer can override this method with whatever processing is desired by the tag extension after processing the start tag and body content.

This method can throw a JspException if an error condition occurs that the JSP should know about and perhaps handle through its error page. Otherwise, it's recommended that it should be handled within the tag handler.

This method should return either the Tag.EVAL_PAGE or Tag.SKIP_PAGE class constants. EVAL_PAGE indicates that upon return to the JSP, processing should continue evaluation of the page. SKIP_PAGE indicates that processing should terminate evaluation of the page. This should only be used with very good reason. Because it's not immediately apparent to the JSP developer why execution is being stopped, it can be confusing to determine what is happening.

The default implementation of this method returns EVAL_PAGE.

getParent()

The getParent() method gets the parent or enclosing tag handler for this tag handler. This method is used by the findAncestorWithClass() method in TagSupport.

The default implementation of this method is typically sufficient for most developers' needs.

setParent()

The setParent() method sets the parent or enclosing tag handler for this tag handler. This method is automatically invoked by your JSP page servlet prior to doStartTag(). Note that this value is not reset by the doEndTag() method and must be explicitly reset by a JSP if it changes between calls to the doStartTag() method.

The default implementation of this method is typically sufficient for most developers' needs.

setPageContext()

The setParent() method sets the current page context and a default implementation is provided by the class. This method is automatically invoked by your JSP page servlet prior to doStartTag().Note that this value is not reset by the doEndTag() method and must be explicitly reset by a JSP if it changes between calls to the doStartTag() method.

The default implementation of this method is typically sufficient for most developers' needs.

release()

The release() method is invoked by your JSP page servlet to release state. Therefore, the developer would override this method if special processing related to the tag handler's state is required. Note that the doStartTag() and doEndTag() methods may be invoked multiple times in between initial invocation and release.

The default implementation of this method is typically sufficient for most developers' needs.

doAfterBody()

The doAfterBody() method allows you to conditionally reevaluate the body of the tag. It is invoked by your JSP page servlet after every evaluation of the body, so it's not invoked if there is no body. The developer would override this method with whatever processing is desired upon each iteration of the body content. This method is defined as a result of implementing the IterationTag interface.

This method can throw a JspException if an error condition occurs that the JSP should know about and perhaps handle through its error page. Otherwise, it's recommended that it should be handled within the tag handler.

This method should return either the IterationTag.EVAL_BODY_AGAIN or Tag.SKIP_BODY class constants to control the iteration. EVAL_BODY_AGAIN indicates that a new evaluation of the body should occur, followed by another invocation of doAfterBody(). SKIP_BODY indicates that no more body evaluations should occur and processing should continue and evaluate the end tag.

Note that the BodyTag.EVAL_BODY_TAG constant has been deprecated in JSP version 1.2 to encourage the use of the more descriptive term EVAL_BODY_AGAIN.

The JSP container will resynchronize any variable values that are indicated as such in TagExtraInfo after the invocation of doAfterBody().

The default implementation of this method returns SKIP_BODY.

BodyTagSupport

The BodyTagSupport convenience class implements the BodyTag interface. BodyTagSupport supports tags that need to access and manipulate the body content.

In addition, it extends the TagSupport convenience class and has access to its fields and convenience methods. It provides two new methods to set the body content and define body initialization processing.

A BodyContent object is available to any tag handler class implementing the BodyTag interface or extending the BodyTagSupport class. The JSP page servlet will create a BodyContent object at request time that contains the evaluation of the body content. This is only done if the doStartTag() method returns a EVAL_BODY_BUFFERED. The BodyContent instance remains available until completion of the doEndTag() method. An upcoming section gives a complete description of the BodyContent class.

Tag extensions that extend BodyTagSupport are used to write dynamic content to the page, iterating through the body content, modifying the body content along the way. The doAfterBody() method, as described in the previous TagSupport section, is the appropriate place to do this. The main difference is that the BodyContent object is available to alter and output new body content.

The BodyContent is appended to the existing BodyContent upon each iteration through the body. Care must be taken to avoid repeating the content of each subsequent iteration in the output. A common approach is to hold the evaluated body content in a StringBuffer while iterating through the body content. The content of the StringBuffer should be written to the JspWriter only after it is determined that iteration is complete and SKIP_BODY will be returned.

The BodyContent object extends JspWriter. Therefore, to write output to the page while processing the body, the bodyContent.getEnclosingWriter().write() method should be used to access the enclosing JspWriter.out object. But after the body content processing has completed and processing continues with the doEndTag() method, output needs to be written to the surrounding scope by using the pageContext.getOut().write() method.

The most commonly used BodyTagSupport methods are described in the following sections. See the JSP API specification for more information about TagSupport's fields and methods.

doStartTag()

The `doStartTag()` method is as described earlier in the `TagSupport` convenience class. But this method can also return `BodyTag.EVAL_BODY_BUFFERED` as a constant value. `EVAL_BODY_BUFFERED` indicates the body content should be evaluated and buffered in a `BodyContent` object and the body processing should be initiated.

Note that the `BodyTag.EVAL_BODY_TAG` constant has been deprecated in JSP version 1.2 to encourage the use of the more descriptive term `EVAL_BODY_BUFFERED`.

The default implementation of this method returns `EVAL_BODY_BUFFERED`.

doEndTag()

The `doEndTag()` method is as described earlier in the `TagSupport` convenience class. Likewise, the default implementation of this method returns `EVAL_PAGE`.

setBodyContent()

The `setBodyContent()` method is the setter for the `bodyContent` field and supplies the class with the `BodyContent` object. This method is automatically invoked by your JSP page servlet prior to `doInitBody()`.

The default implementation of this method is typically sufficient for most developers' needs.

doInitBody()

The `doInitBody()` method is invoked immediately after `setBodyContent()` and just before the first body evaluation. It can be overridden to include processing to prepare for evaluation of the body. This method is only invoked if `doStartTag()` returns `EVAL_BODY_BUFFERED`.

This method can throw a `JspException` if an error condition occurs that the JSP should know about and perhaps handle through its error page. Otherwise, it's recommended that it should be handled within the tag handler.

Unlike the other methods that allow processing of tags or tag bodies, this method does not return any value to control processing.

doAfterBody()

The `doAfterBody()` method is as described earlier in the `TagSupport` convenience class. Likewise, the default implementation of this method returns `SKIP_BODY`.

This method should be overridden to define processing associated with body content iteration. The `BodyContent` object is available to manipulate its content.

Supporting interfaces and classes

The Tag Extension API also provides supporting interfaces and classes, some of which have been mentioned previously. They are described in detail in the following sections.

BodyContent class

The `BodyContent` class is an object that contains the body content of the tag extension to be accessible for a tag handler. It extends `JspWriter` and has additional methods to convert the tag body into a `String`, manage its contents, and ensure that buffer size will never be exceeded.

A `BodyContent` object is available to any tag handler class implementing the `BodyTag` interface or extending the `BodyTagSupport` class. The JSP page servlet will create a `BodyContent` object at request time that contains the evaluation of the body content. This is only done if the if the `doStartTag()` method returns a `EVAL_BODY_TAG`. The `BodyContent` instance remains available until completion of the `doEndTag()` method.

Note that a `BodyContent` object contains the evaluation of the body content, rather than the body text itself. The significance of this is that it will not contain actions but their evaluated results.

A `BodyContent` object is enclosed within the JSP `JspWriter` object. It could also be enclosed in another `BodyContent` object if the JSP defines the body tag nested within another body tag. Instances of `BodyContent` are created by invoking the `pushBody()` and `popBody()` methods of the `PageContext` class.

clearBody()

The `clearBody()` method clears the body content.

flush()

The `flush()` method is redefined from `JspWriter` to be invalid. It is not valid to flush a `BodyContent` object because there is no backing stream behind it. It can throw an `IOException` if an error situation occurs.

getEnclosingWriter()

The `getEnclosingWriter()` method gets the enclosing `JspWriter`. This can either be a `JspWriter` object or another `BodyContent` object. This is set at the time the `BodyContent` object is constructed.

getReader()

The `getReader()` method returns the value of the `BodyContent` object as a `Reader` object.

getString()

The `getString()` method returns the value of the `BodyContent` object as a `String` object.

writeOut()

The `writeOut()` method writes the contents of the `BodyContent` object into a `Writer`. The `Writer` is passed as a parameter. It can throw an `IOException` if an error situation occurs.

TagExtraInfo class

The `TagExtraInfo` class is an optional class provided by the tag library author to describe additional translation-time information not described in the TLD file. It is used to define scripting variables used by the tag or to provide translation-time validation of the tag attributes. In other words, it does not create markup but rather provides information to the JSP compiler about the tag handler class.

The `TagExtraInfo` class is an abstract class that must be extended by your custom extra info class. It is associated with a tag extension by the `teiclass` attribute in the TLD file.

The most commonly used `TagExtraInfo` methods are described in the following sections. See the JSP API specification for a complete reference of its fields and methods.

setTagInfo()

The `setTagInfo()` method sets an object of type `TagInfo` that contains the tag information from the TLD. This information is available to the JSP translator at translation time and is invoked by the JSP translator to set its initial value. This invocation is prior to any invocation of `isValid()` or `getVariableInfo()`.

Note that if an explicit call is made to `setTagInfo()`, the object passed will be returned in subsequent calls to `getTagInfo()`.

The default implementation of this method is typically sufficient for most developers' needs.

getTagInfo()

The `getTagInfo()` method returns an object of type `TagInfo` that contains the tag information from the TLD.

The default implementation of this method is typically sufficient for most developers' needs.

getVariableInfo()

The `getVariableInfo()` method is used to introduce new or use existing variables to return data to the JSP. This allows the JSP to use expressions to access the returned variables as opposed to receiving generated markup.

The `getVariableInfo()` method receives a `TagData` object as input and returns an array of `VariableInfo` objects. Each `VariableInfo` object represents a variable to be returned to the JSP.

`VariableInfo` objects are created using its single constructor, which takes the variable name, class name, a Boolean indicating whether this is a new variable to be declared, and the variable's scope.

A variable's scope can be defined as one of three values. If `VariableInfo.NESTED` is specified, the variable is available to the calling JSP only within the body of the tag. If `VariableInfo.AT_BEGIN` is specified, the variable is available to the calling JSP from the start tag through the end of the page. If `VariableInfo.AT_END` is specified, the variable is available to the calling JSP from the end tag through the end of the page.

See the JSP API specification for more information. A working example of a `TagExtraInfo` class introducing a new scripting variable into a JSP is provided later in this chapter.

isValid()

The `isValid()` method provides translation-time validation of the attributes of a tag extension. It receives a `TagData` object as a parameter and returns a Boolean indicating if the tag instance is valid.

Validation occurs subsequent to the validation performed by a `validator` class implementing the `TagValidator` interface. Upon completion of the `validator` class processing, the `TagExtraInfo` classes for all tags will be consulted by invoking their `isValid()` method. The order of invocation is undefined. See the section below for an explanation of the `TagValidator` interface.

This method should be defined if validation on a custom tag extension is desired.

TryCatchFinally interface

A new interface defined in the JSP version 1.2 API is the `TryCatchFinally` interface. It allows for exceptions thrown from within a tag to be caught and handled by a custom tag handler implementing the `doCatch()` and `doFinally()` methods of the `javax.servlet.jsp.tagext.TryCatchFinally` interface.

doCatch()

The `doCatch()` method is invoked if a `Throwable` exception occurs while evaluating the body inside a tag or in any of the `doStartTag()`, `doEndTag()`, `doAfterBody()`, and `doInitBody()` methods. It is not invoked if an exception occurs during one of the setter methods.

This method is intended to handle the exception. But it can throw a Throwable exception if it is determined that there are exceptions that should still be thrown to the JSP.

doFinally()

The doFinally() method is invoked after doCatch() if a Throwable exception occurred or after doEndTag() if not. But as with doCatch(), it is not invoked if an exception occurs during one of the setter methods.

A JSP servlet that implements the TryCatchFinally interface looks something like this:

```
setPageContext(pc);
setParent(null);
...
try {
  doStartTag()...
  ...
  doEndTag()...
} catch (Throwable t) {
  doCatch(t);
} finally {
  doFinally();
}
...
release();
```

TagLibraryValidator interface

Another new interface defined in the JSP version 1.2 API is the TagLibraryValidator interface. Whereas the TagExtraInfo class allows for a specific action to be validated, a Java class that implements the javax.servlet.jsp.tagext.TagLibraryValidator interface can perform custom validation on the entire JSP page. A common use of a validator class is to use an XML parser to validate the page against a Document Type Definition (DTD) file.

The validator class is invoked by the JSP compiler. It presents the entire JSP page via the PageData object, which abstracts the XML view of the JSP page and provides a read-only InputStream on the page. The validator class then utilizes its custom internal logic to validate the page. It returns a null String if the page is valid or a String with error information if it is determined to be invalid.

The validator class must be defined within the TLD. Initialization parameters for the class can also be defined.

Methods defined by the interface are setInitParameters(), getInitParameters(), validate(), and release(). The getter and setter methods are used in conjunction with the initialization parameters defined in the TLD. The validate() method is intended to be used for the validation logic of the JSP. The release() method is used to release any resources referenced during processing. See the JSP API specification for more information.

Programming and Using a Tag Extension

Now that I've covered the architecture, let's build and deploy a custom tag extension and utilize it within a JSP. For my example, I'll write a tag extension that will set the appropriate selected values in a HTML select list based upon a value or list of values.

Programming a tag handler class

The `SelectOption` tag handler, shown in Listing 13-1, is the tag handler class that will alter the contents of an HTML select list. The begin and end tags will enclose the option tags of the select list; therefore, the tag handler will process the body and modify it according to the selected values. The tag handler will extend the `BodyTagSupport` convenience class, which enables me to modify body content.

A private `String` array is declared to hold a list of values to be selected. A getter method is defined for this property along with two setters. My tag will accept either a `String` with a single value or a `String` array with multiple values, so the setter has an overloaded method.

A `doStartTag()` method is not defined because the default method from the `BodyTagSupport` class is sufficient. It will return `BODY_TAG_BUFFERED`, which will trigger the creation of the `BodyContent` object and invoke the `setBodyContent()` method. Again, the `BodyTagSupport`'s default implementation of this method is sufficient.

The `doInitBody()` and `doAfterBody()` methods are not defined as well because I'm not iterating through the body content. Instead, I'm processing it once as a whole, modifying it as I go, and writing back to the JSP once completed. I, therefore, use the `doEndTag()` method because it still has access to the `BodyContent` object.

The `doEndTag()` method sets the body content into a `String`, uses a `StringTokenizer` to assist in finding each option tag's value, compares it to the value array, and sets `"SELECTED"` in the appropriate option tags. The significant thing to note is that the output is written to a `StringBuffer` while processing, and then written to the enclosing JSP's out object upon completion.

No `release()` method is necessary because no resources were acquired that need to be dereferenced.

Listing 13-1: SelectOption.java

```
package bible.jsp.tags;

import java.io.*;
import java.util.*;
```

Continued

Listing 13-1 *(continued)*

```
import javax.servlet.jsp.*;
import javax.servlet.jsp.tagext.*;

/**
 * Title:        SelectOption
 * Description:  Tag extension to set selected option(s) in a select list
 * Copyright:    Copyright (c) 2001
 * Company:      ZeeWare Inc.
 * @author Gary Wells
 * @version 1.0
 */

public class SelectOption extends BodyTagSupport {

  /** Array of values to be selected */
  String[] values;

  /**
   * Returns an array of selected values.
   * @return    the array of selected values.
   */
  public String[] getValue() {
    return values;
  }

  /**
   * Sets the array of selected values to the array parameter.
   * @param     newArrayValues  the desired array of selected values.
   */
  public void setValue(String[] newArrayValues) {
    values = newArrayValues;
  }

  /**
   * Creates an array of selected values from the single value parameter.
   * @param     newValue  the desired array of selected values.
   */
  public void setValue(String newValue) {
    if (newValue != null) {
      values = new String[1];
      values[0] = newValue;
    }
  }

  /**
   * Creates an array of selected values from the single value parameter.
   * @return    the desired character.
```

```
 * @exception JspTagException
 *              if an error occurs while writing to the JSP writer.
 * @see       javax.servlet.jsp.JspWriter#write()
 */
public int doEndTag() throws JspTagException {

  // get body content
  String bodyString = bodyContent.getString();

  if(values != null && values.length > 0) {

    // make a string array of option tags
    StringTokenizer bodyTokens = new StringTokenizer(bodyString,"\n");
    ArrayList optionsList = new ArrayList();
    while (bodyTokens.hasMoreTokens()) {
      optionsList.add(bodyTokens.nextToken());
    }
    String[] optionsArray = new String[optionsList.size()];
    optionsArray = (String[])optionsList.toArray(optionsArray);

    // declare work fields
    String optionBeforeValue;
    String optionAfterValue;
    String optionValue;
    String opt;
    StringBuffer optionsOut = new StringBuffer();
    boolean found = false;

    // parse through the array looking for selected values
    for (int i = 0; i < optionsArray.length; i++) {
      opt = optionsArray[i];
      if (opt.trim().length() > 0) {

        // before option value
        optionBeforeValue = opt.substring(0,opt.indexOf("value="));

        //option value
        optionValue = opt.substring(opt.indexOf("value=")+6,opt.indexOf(">"));
        if (optionValue.startsWith("\""))
          optionValue = optionValue.substring(1,optionValue.length());
        if (optionValue.endsWith("\""))
          optionValue = optionValue.substring(0,optionValue.length()-1);

        // after option value
        optionAfterValue = opt.substring(opt.indexOf("value="),opt.length());

        // if a selected value is found, add to the buffer with "SELECTED"
        found = false;
        for (int j = 0; j < values.length ; j++) {
```

Continued

Listing 13-1 *(continued)*

```
            if (optionValue.equals(values[j])) {
              found = true;
              optionsOut.append(optionBeforeValue + "SELECTED " +
optionAfterValue + "\n");
}
          }

          // if not found, add to the buffer as is
          if (found == false) {
            optionsOut.append(opt + "\n");
          }
        }
      }

      // write the buffer
      try {
        pageContext.getOut().write(optionsOut.toString());
      } catch (IOException ex) {
        throw new JspTagException("Fatal IO error");
      }

    // no values, write the body content as is
    } else {
      try {
        pageContext.getOut().write(bodyString);
      } catch (IOException ex) {
        throw new JspTagException("Fatal IO error");
      }
    }
    return EVAL_PAGE;
  }
}
```

Defining a Tag Library Descriptor

The Tag Library Descriptor (TLD) is a file that defines the tag library and all the details of its tag extensions and corresponding tag handler classes. It's essentially an XML document with a `.tld` extension that is defined and validated against a DTD definition file provided by Sun. The latest version can be found at `http://java.sun.com/dtd/web-jsptaglibrary_1_2.dtd`.

The main element of the TLD is `taglib`:

```
<!ELEMENT taglib (tlib-version, jsp-version, short-name,
                  uri?, display-name?, small-icon?,
                  large-icon?, description?, validator?,
                  listener*, tag+) >
```

The meanings of the `taglib` attributes are as follows:

tlib-version

The `tlib-version` attribute represents the version of the tag library implementation as defined by the developer. This attribute is optional.

jsp-version

The `jsp-version` attribute identifies the version of the JSP specification the tag library depends on. This attribute is now mandatory.

short-name

The `short-name` attribute identifies a short name for the tag library. This should be specified as the prefix used by JSPs. This attribute is optional.

uri

The `uri` attribute uniquely identifies this tag library. If used, the value will be the URL of the definitive version of the tag library descriptor. This attribute is optional.

display-name

A short name for the tag library intended for use by development tools.

small-icon

An optional small icon (16x16 pixels) for use by development tools. Each icon must be a stand-alone file in either JPEG or GIF format, and with either a `.jpg` or `.gif` extension. The file name is given as a relative path within the tag library.

large-icon

An optional large icon (32x32 pixels) for use by development tools.

description

An arbitrary text string describing the tag library.

validator

An optional reference to a class that verifies correct usage of the tag library from within the calling JSP page.

listener

An optional event listener class that is instantiated and registered automatically.

tag

The `tag` attribute defines and describes a tag extension and its corresponding tag handler. This attribute is required and is defined as follows:

```
<!ELEMENT tag (name, tag-class, tei-class?, body-content?,
               display-name?, small-icon?, large-icon?,
               description?, variable*, attribute*,
               example?) >
```

The meanings of these attributes are as follows:

name

The `name` attribute identifies the tag. It is the same name used in the tag extension following the prefix. This attribute is required.

tag-class

The `tag-class` attribute identifies the fully qualified name of the tag handler class. It is expected that this class either implements the `javax.servlet.jsp.tagext.Tag` interface directly or extends one of its support classes. This attribute is required.

tei-class

The `tei-class` attribute identifies the `TagExtraInfo` class that will provide extra information about this tag at runtime to the JSP. It is expected that this class extends the `javax.servlet.jsp.tagest.TagExtraInfo` class. This attribute is optional.

body-content

The `body-content` attribute specifies the type of body content the tag contains. This attribute instructs the JSP engine on how it should process the body content upon completing execution of the tag handler class. This attribute can contain only one of three acceptable values. A value of `JSP` indicates that the tag content will be evaluated at runtime like any other JSP content. A value of `tagdependent` signifies that the JSP engine should pass the content to the tag handler unchanged and not attempt to evaluate it. A value of `empty` is useful when a tag should not have any body content. JSP translation will fail if this tag is used and the tag is not empty. If not specified, the default value is `JSP`.

display-name

An optional, short name for the tag intended for use by development tools.

small-icon

An optional small icon for use by development tools.

large-icon

An optional large icon for use by development tools..

description

An arbitrary text string describing the tag.

variable

Scripting variable information, which is optional.

attribute

A list of all attributes accepted or required by the tag. Each attribute contains the following elements:

- **name:** The name of the attribute as it is referenced in the tag extension.
- **required:** A Boolean indicating whether or not the attribute is required. JSP translation will fail if `true` is specified and the attribute is not defined in the tag extension.
- **rtpexprvalue:** A Boolean specifying whether the attribute can be the result of an expression or whether it must be a fixed value. JSP translation will fail if `false` is specified and the tag extension attribute is an expression. If not specified, the default value is `false`.
- **type:** The Java type of the attribute value. Those determined at JSP translation time are assumed to be `java.lang.String`.
- **description:** A text description of the attribute for use by development tools.

example

An optional example demonstrating usage of the tag.

Listing 13-2 contains the TLD for my sample application. I'll explain the important components of a TLD by referencing this example.

First, I define the tag library by indicating that this is version 1.0 of my example and that I'm using JSP version 1.2. I use the same `short-name` as my prefix to document to others that this is the suggested prefix for tag extensions using this tag library.

Next I describe my tag extension and handler. I specify the name that matches the name in my JSP tag. The tag class is the fully qualified name of the tag handler class. This class evaluates standard HTML code and modifies it, so I specify that the body content is JSP. I use the `info` attribute to provide a short description of this tag.

This tag uses one attribute named `value`. It's required and allows a value evaluated from an expression.

Listing 13-2: bible.tld

```
<?xml version="1.0" encoding="ISO-8859-1"?>
<!DOCTYPE taglib PUBLIC "-//Sun Microsystems, Inc.//DTD JSP Tag Library 1.2//EN"
"http://java.sun.com/dtd/web-jsptaglibrary_1_2.dtd">
<taglib>
  <tlib-version>1.2</tlib-version>
  <jsp-version>1.2</jsp-version>
  <short-name>bibleTags</short-name>
  <tag>
    <name>selectOption</name>
    <tag-class>bible.jsp.tags.SelectOption</tag-class>
    <body-content>JSP</body-content>
    <description>Set selected option in select list</description>
    <attribute>
      <name>value</name>
      <required>true</required>
      <rtexprvalue>true</rtexprvalue>
    </attribute>
  </tag>
</taglib>
```

Configuring the WebLogic Web application deployment descriptor

The final step is to configure the Web application deployment descriptor in WebLogic Server by using the WebLogic Console. For this example, I'll define the deployment descriptor associated with the `BibleApp`. I click the `BibleApp` Web application node and then the Edit Web Application Descriptor link. Refer back to Figures 12-2 and 12-3 if you want a reminder on how to do this. I click the Tag Libs node, and the page shown in Figure 13-3 appears.

Next I click the Configure a new Tag Lib link. The page shown in Figure 13-4 appears.

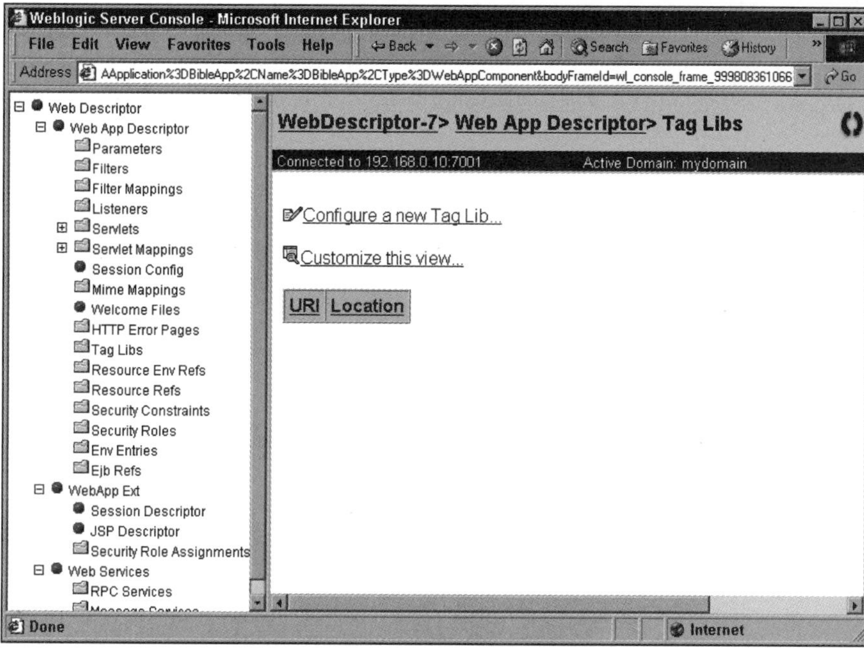

Figure 13-3: Configuring a new Tag Library Descriptor

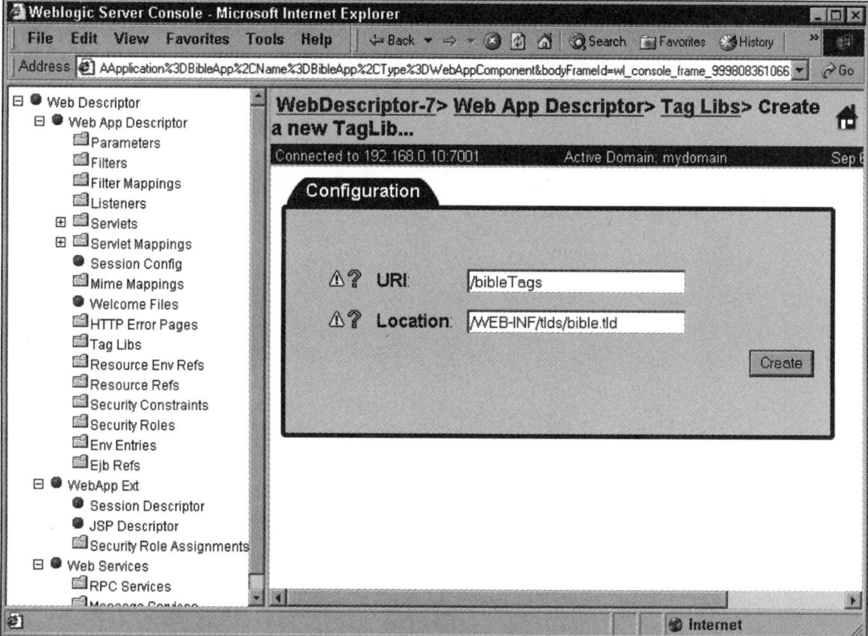

Figure 13-4: Tag library configuration page

I type `/bibleTags` as the URI, which directly corresponds to the `uri` property of the `taglib` directive. The Location is entered as `/WEB-INF/tlds/bible.tld`, which is the path within the Web application directory to the Tag Library Descriptor file. Next I click the Create button. The page shown in Figure 13-5 appears.

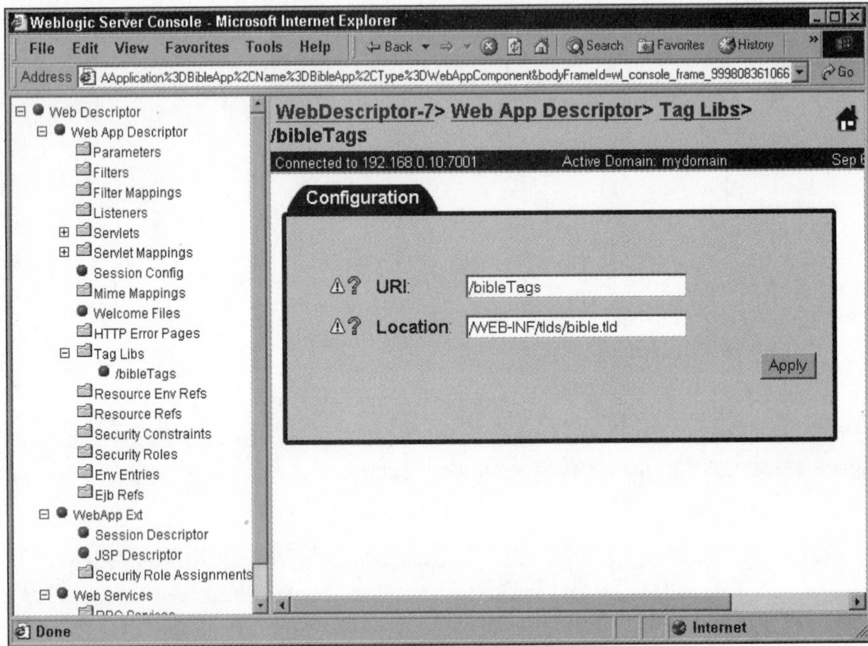

Figure 13-5: Successfully created tag library configuration.

To complete this process, I validate and persist my Web descriptor. Refer back to Figures 12-6 through 12-9 for a reminder on how to do this.

If I look at before and after versions of the Web application's `web.xml` deployment descriptor, I'll see that the following lines were added.

```
<taglib>
  <taglib-uri>/bibleTags</taglib-uri>
  <taglib-location>/WEB-INF/tlds/bible.tld</taglib-location>
</taglib>
```

Using a tag extension within a JSP

You must use two types of statements in a JSP to utilize a tag handler from within a JSP. First, a `taglib` directive statement must define the tag library and indicate the prefix by which it will be referred. Second, a custom tag extension references the tag library prefix and the logical name of the tag extension.

taglib directive

The `taglib` directive defines a tag library and prefix for the tag extensions used in the JSP page. It allows a JSP page to use tag handler classes by naming the tag library that contains the compiled Java code defining the tags to be used.

```
<%@ taglib uri="/bibleTags" prefix="bible" %>
<jsp:directive.taglib uri="="/bibleTags" prefix="bible" />
```

The `taglib` directive supports two attributes, which are described in the next two sections.

uri

The `uri` attribute identifies the Uniform Resource Identifier (URI) to for the Tag Library Descriptor (TLD) file. This value is matched against the `taglib` entries in the Web application deployment descriptor (`web.xml`) to physically locate the corresponding TLD file. This attribute is required.

prefix

The `prefix` attribute identifies the XML namespace identifier used by all tag extensions referencing classes in the tag library. It directly corresponds to the tag extensions in the JSP to associate those tags with this tag library definition. The prefixes `jsp`, `jspx`, `java`, `javax`, `servlet`, `sun`, and `sunw` are reserved. This attribute is required.

Tag extensions (or custom tags)

To actually reference a tag handler class within a JSP, tag extensions are used. The JSP compiler interprets the tag extension statements by replacing the tags with method calls to your tag handler class. The tag handler class is a Java class that actually performs the work. I'll cover tag handler classes shortly.

Tag extensions use an XML format similar to the standard JSP tags described earlier in this chapter. But instead of using the `jsp` prefix, the prefix identified in the `taglib` directive is used. This `prefix` identifies the XML namespace used by all tag extensions referencing classes in the tag library.

Immediately following the prefix is the logical name of the tag handler class. This name is matched against entries in the Tag Library Descriptor (TLD) file to identify the location of the class file.

Tag extensions can have any number of attributes that can be specified. Attributes are the means by which information is passed to the tag handler class. They are defined in the TLD as part of tag definition.

These attributes are what allow tag extensions to be dynamic. They are essentially input parameters for the tag handler class that allows it to respond with different results. The most powerful way of leveraging this is in combination with expressions. Attributes are allowed to contain an evaluation of an expression statement, thereby allowing request-specific data to be used.

Because tag extensions follow XML conventions, an end tag is required. This can be specified by either ending the begin tag with />or with a separate end tag specifying prefix and tag name. Following are some examples:

```
<bible:debugData/>
<bible:selectOption value="<%= color %>">
</bible:selectOption>
```

JSP example

Now let's bring it all together with a JSP that uses the tag handler class just created and configured. The TestTags.jsp in Listing 13-3 represents a simple JSP that exists merely to test the tag in two different scenarios: an option list with only one selected value and an option list with multiple selection values.

The first thing to notice is the taglib directive. It defines the uri and prefix as described earlier.

Next there is an options list with a selection of five colors. The options tags are surrounded by begin and end tag extensions for the tag handler. The correct prefix and tag are referenced to call the extension class. The value passed is a String; therefore, the extension class's overloaded getValue() method that expects to receive a String will be called. This String is initialized with a valid value for testing purposes.

Finally, there is another options list with five colors. But the tag extension passes a String array as its value, thereby calling the other getValue() method. This String array is initialized with two values for testing purposes.

Listing 13-3: TestSelectOptionTag.jsp

```
<%-- Page Directives --%>
<%@ page session="false" errorPage="Error.jsp" %>

<%-- Taglib Directives --%>
<%@ taglib uri="/bibleTags" prefix="bible" %>

<html>
<head>
  <title>Test Select Option Tag</title>
</head>

<body>
```

```
<%@ include file="Header.jsp" %>

  <h3>SelectOption with single value</h3>
<%-- Set color for testing purpose only --%>
<% String color = "2"; %>
  Color: 
  <select name="color">
    <bible:selectOption value="<%= color %>">
      <option value="0">--Select One--</option>
      <option value="1">Red</option>
      <option value="2">Green</option>
      <option value="3">Blue</option>
      <option value="4">Yellow</option>
      <option value="5">Orange</option>
    </bible:selectOption>
  </select>
   (value selected = <%= color %>)

  <h3>SelectOption with multiple values</h3>
<%-- Set colors for testing purpose only --%>
<%
String[] colors = new String[2];
colors[0] = "1";
colors[1] = "4";
%>
  Colors: 
  <select name="colors" size="6" multiple>
    <bible:selectOption value="<%= colors %>">
      <option value="0">--Select Multiple--</option>
      <option value="1">Red</option>
      <option value="2">Green</option>
      <option value="3">Blue</option>
      <option value="4">Yellow</option>
      <option value="5">Orange</option>
    </bible:selectOption>
  </select>
   (values selected =
<%
boolean needComma = false;
for (int i = 0; i < colors.length; i++) {
  if (needComma) out.print(", ");
  out.print(colors[i]);
  needComma = true;
} %>
)

<br><br>

<%@ include file="Footer.htm" %>

</body>
</html>
```

My WebLogic Server is running on a machine with an IP address of 192.168.0.10, so I type `http://192.168.0.10:7001/BibleApp/TestSelectOptionTag.jsp` to run the JSP. After a few seconds to create the JSP servlet and compile it, the page shown in Figure 13-6 appears.

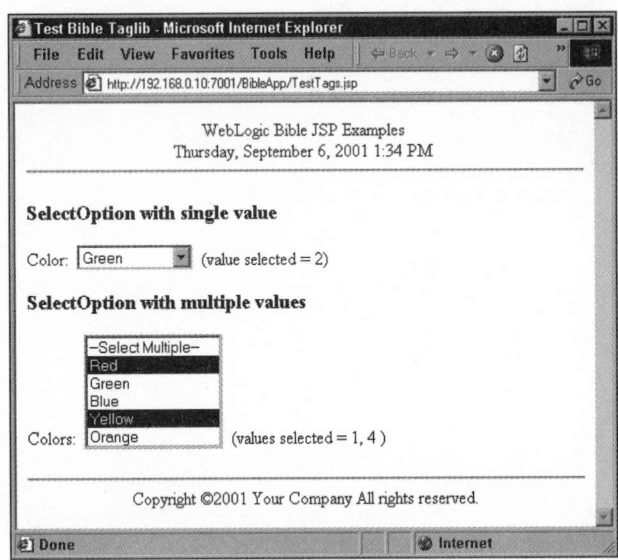

Figure 13-6: Testing the tag extension

Notice that both tags worked as expected, selecting the appropriate values for display. Viewing the source from the browser shows the select list tags generated as a result processing the tag extension. Listing 13-4 shows a subset of this source.

Notice that the tag extensions are not present in the output. Also notice that the appropriate values are selected.

Listing 13-4: Generated source from selectOption tag

```
<h3>SelectOption with single value</h3>

Color: 
<select name="color">
<option value="0">--Select One--</option>
<option value="1">Red</option>
<option SELECTED value="2">Green</option>
<option value="3">Blue</option>
<option value="4">Yellow</option>
<option value="5">Orange</option>
```

```
</select>
 (value selected = 2)


<h3>SelectOption with multiple values</h3>

Colors: 
<select name="colors" size="6" multiple>
<option value="0">--Select Multiple--</option>
<option SELECTED value="1">Red</option>
<option value="2">Green</option>
<option value="3">Blue</option>
<option SELECTED value="4">Yellow</option>
<option value="5">Orange</option>

</select>
 (values selected =
1, 4
)
```

Resolving a tag extension

Let's review how a tag extension is resolved by the JSP engine to find the tag handler class.

1. A JSP encounters a tag extension and looks at the prefix to determine the tag library and the logical tag name (following the colon).
2. The `taglib` directive of the JSP defines the tag library by a logical name that is defined by the Web application deployment descriptor (`web.xml`).
3. The Web application deployment descriptor (`web.xml`) defines the tag library by a logical name and identifies the location of the tag library descriptor (TLD).
4. The tag library descriptor defines the tag by identifying its logical name as referred by the JSP. It also defines the location of the tag handler class file. The tag handler's attributes, `TagExtraInfo` class, and `TagValidator` class can also be defined.
5. The JSP engine instantiates the tag handler class and begins invoking methods against it.

Programming a TagExtraInfo Class

One useful way to use this class is to introduce new scripting variables into the page. This allows the JSP to have variable content while externalizing the processing to define the new scripting variables. To do this, there are three major steps.

First, add the following lines to the TLD file to describe a new tag named `lineClass`. Notice that the `tei-class` attribute must define the `TagExtraInfo` class, as described earlier in this chapter.

```
<tag>
  <name>lineClass</name>
  <tagclass>bible.jsp.tags.LineClass</tagclass>
  <tei-class>bible.jsp.tags.LineClassTEI</tei-class>
  <bodycontent>JSP</bodycontent>
  <info>Determine stylesheet class based upon line#</info>
  <attribute>
    <name>lineNumber</name>
    <required>true</required>
    <rtexprvalue>true</rtexprvalue>
  </attribute>
  <attribute>
    <name>oddClass</name>
    <required>true</required>
    <rtexprvalue>true</rtexprvalue>
  </attribute>
  <attribute>
    <name>evenClass</name>
    <required>true</required>
    <rtexprvalue>true</rtexprvalue>
  </attribute>
</tag>
```

Next you need to write a custom class that extends `TagExtraInfo`. The only method that needs to be overridden is the `getVariableInfo()` method. This method returns an array of `VariableInfo` objects. Therefore, your class should create and add to the array a new `VariableInfo` object for each new variable being introduced.

An example is shown in Listing 13-5. This class defines a new scripting variable named `className` of type `java.lang.String`. It is being declared by this class and has a scope available from the end tag onward.

Listing 13-5: LineClassTEI.java

```
package bible.jsp.tags;

import javax.servlet.jsp.tagext.*;

/**
 * Title:        LineClassTEI
 * Description:  Extra info class for tag handler LineClass
 * Copyright:    Copyright (c) 2001
 * Company:      ZeeWare Inc.
```

```
 * @author Gary Wells
 * @version 1.0
 */
public class LineClassTEI extends TagExtraInfo {

  /**
   * Returns an array of VariableInfo objects defining new scripting
   * variables.
   * @return    the array of scripting variables.
   * @see       javax.servlet.jsp.tagext.TagExtraInfo#getVariableInfo()
   */
  public VariableInfo[] getVariableInfo(TagData tagData) {

    // return VariableInfo array with the new scripting variable
    return new VariableInfo[] {
      new VariableInfo("className", "java.lang.String", true,
VariableInfo.AT_END)
    };

  }
}
```

Finally, the tag handler class must add the new variables to the `PageContext` by using the `pageContext.setAttribute()` method. They cannot be available to the JSP unless this occurs. A good place to do this is in the `doStartTag()` method of the tag handler.

Listing 13-6 is an example of tag handler class that uses the `Extra info` class defined in Listing 13-5. It extends the `TagSupport` class because that listing only requires processing of the tag and not the body content. It is invoked by the JSP and passed a line number and two class names. Based upon the line number, the stylesheet class is determined, based, and set in the `PageContext`. The JSP uses an expression to output the returned class name to the browser, as shown in Listing 13-7.

Listing 13-6: **LineClass.java**

```
package bible.jsp.tags;

import javax.servlet.jsp.*;
import javax.servlet.jsp.tagext.*;

/**
 * Title:        LineClass
 * Description:  Tag extension to set determine stylesheet class
 *               based upon line number
```

Continued

Listing 13-6 (continued)

```
* Copyright:    Copyright (c) 2001
* Company:      ZeeWare Inc.
* @author Gary Wells
* @version 1.0
*/
public class LineClass extends TagSupport {

 /** tag properties */
 private int lineNumber;
 private String oddClass;
 private String evenClass;

 /** getters and setters */
 public int getLineNumber() {
   return lineNumber;
 }
 public void setLineNumber(int lineNumber) {
   this.lineNumber = lineNumber;
 }
 public String getOddClass() {
   return oddClass;
 }
 public void setOddClass(String oddClass) {
   this.oddClass = oddClass;
 }
 public String getEvenClass() {
   return evenClass;
 }
 public void setEvenClass(String evenClass) {
   this.evenClass = evenClass;
 }

 /**
  * Returns the stylesheet class based upon the HTML table line
  * number.
  * @return    the desired stylesheet class.
  * @exception JspException
  * @see       javax.servlet.jsp.tagext.TagSupport#doStartTag()
  */
 public int doStartTag() throws JspException {
   String className = (lineNumber % 2 == 0 ? evenClass : oddClass);
   pageContext.setAttribute("className", className);
   return EVAL_BODY_INCLUDE;
 }
}
```

Now that everything is in place, the JSP can use the tag and is able to refer to the new scripting variable in an expression without ever declaring it within the JSP itself. An example is shown in Listing 13-7. Notice that the variable `className` isn't declared anywhere within the JSP.

Listing 13-7: TestLineClassTag.jsp

```
<%-- Page Directives --%>
<%@ page session="false" errorPage="Error.jsp" %>

<%-- Taglib Directives --%>
<%@ taglib uri="/bibleTags" prefix="bible" %>

<html>
<head>
  <title>Test Line Class Tag</title>
</head>

<body>
<%@ include file="Header.jsp" %>

  <h3>LineClass with odd value</h3>
  <% int lineNumber = 5; // for testing purposes only %>
  <bible:lineClass lineNumber="<%= lineNumber %>" oddClass="oddLine"
   evenClass="evenLine"/>
  Line Number = <%= lineNumber %>  Stylesheet Class = <%= className %>

  <h3>LineClass with even value</h3>
  <% lineNumber = 8; // for testing purposes only %>
  <bible:lineClass lineNumber="<%= lineNumber %>" oddClass="oddLine"
   evenClass="evenLine"/>
  Line Number = <%= lineNumber %>  Stylesheet Class = <%= className %>

  <br><br>

<%@ include file="Footer.htm" %>

</body>
</html>
```

I type `http://192.168.0.10:7001/BibleApp/TestLineClassTag.jsp` to run the JSP. After a few seconds to create the JSP servlet and compile it, the page shown in Figure 13-7 appears.

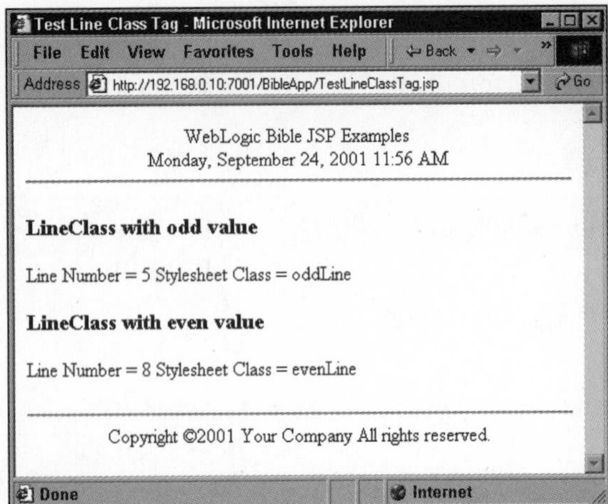

Figure 13-7: Declaring a new scripting variable using the TagExtraInfo class

WebLogic Tag Libraries

WebLogic Server provides a library of custom tag extensions that you can access and use in your JSP pages. In this section, I provide a quick overview of these tags along with a link to WebLogic's documentation Web site with more detailed descriptions and JavaDocs of the tag handler classes.

WebLogic JSP form validation tags

WebLogic JSP form validation tags are used with HTML forms to validate user entry. They can validate required fields, text fields against regular expressions, compare fields on a form, and allow custom validation logic.

You can find this tag library in a `.jar` file named `weblogic-vtags.jar`, which is in the `ext` directory of your WebLogic implementation. To use these tags, copy this JAR file to your Web application and define it in the Web application deployment descriptor (`web.xml`).

Validator classes

Three `validator` tag handler classes are provided in the `weblogicx.jsp.tags.validators` package. They are fully implemented and invoked directly by the validation tags in the JSP. A custom tag handler class that implements a WebLogic provided interface or abstract class must handle custom validation.

Required field validator

The `weblogicx.jsp.tags.validators.RequiredFieldValidator` class is used to validate that a required field has been entered. It is invoked directly from the JSP via the `<wl:validator>` tag.

Regular expression validator

The `weblogicx.jsp.tags.validators.RegExpValidator` class is used to validate text in a form field against a regular expression. It is invoked directly from the JSP via the `<wl:validator>` tag.

Compare validator

The `weblogicx.jsp.tags.validators.CompareValidator` class is used to validate a form field against another form field. They must be `String`s. It is invoked directly from the JSP via the `<wl:validator>` tag.

Custom validator

Custom `validator` classes can be written to implement any logic that needs to be performed to complete form field validation. To write a custom `validator`, the tag handler must implement the `weblogicx.jsp.tags.validators.Customizable` interface or extend the `weblogicx.jsp.tags.validators.CustomizableAdapter` abstract class. The `validate()` method must be defined to implement the custom validation logic and return a Boolean indicating if it passed.

Validator tags

Three `validator` tags are provided for use within a JSP page. They are nested within each other to reference attributes defined by the parent tag. Each tag has a set of attributes required for proper use.

Summary tag

The `summary` tag, `<wl:summary>`, wraps the HTML code and subsequent `validator` tags. It is used to define attributes to be used across all page validation. This could include a vector of error messages to be used, header text to be displayed only when there is an error, or a page that a request is directed when there are no errors.

Form tag

The `form` tag, `<wl:form>`, is similar to the HTML form tag. It is used to define attributes associated with a form. This could include the `GET` or `POST` methods, the action or URL if there are no errors, and the form name (significant if there are multiple errors).

Validator tag

The validator tag, <wl:validator>, is used to define a validation rule for a form field. Multiple validator tags may exist for any form field. A blank text field, for example, will always be evaluated as valid by the regular expression validator. Therefore, the required field validator may need to be used in conjunction if entry is required. Attributes associated with this tag define the error message text, the regular expression if using the regular expression validator, the field to validate, and the validator class to use for validation.

When a validation tag determines that data in a field is not been input correctly, the page is redisplayed and the fields that need to be reentered are flagged with text or an image to alert the end user. After the form is correctly filled out, the end user's browser displays a new page specified by the validation tag.

The preceding information is intended to provide you with just an overview of the tag library. For more information, see http://e-docs.bea.com/wls/docs61/jsp/validation_tags.html.

WebLogic custom JSP tags

WebLogic provides a library of three custom tags that you can use to code your JSPs. They include a cache, process, and repeat tag.

You can find this tag library in a .jar file named weblogic-tags.jar in the ext directory of your WebLogic implementation. To use these tags, you copy this JAR file to your Web application and define it in the Web application deployment descriptor (web.xml).

Custom tags

Three custom tags are provided for use within a JSP page. They are completely independent of each other and can be used as necessary within the same JSP. Each tag has a set of attributes required for proper use.

Cache tag

The cache tag, <wl:cache>, provides the capability to cache data during processing of the tag body. It supports caching of the evaluated body prior to processing and the transformed body upon completion. This can be useful if the page needs to display either the evaluated or transformed body content based upon some other criteria.

Process tag

The process tag, <wl:process>, provides the capability to conditionally execute the statements between start and end tags based upon attribute values. It can also declaratively process the results of form submissions.

Repeat tag

The `repeat` tag, `<wl:repeat>`, provides the capability to iterate over many different types of sets, including Enumerations, Iterators, Collections, Arrays of Objects, Vectors, ResultSets, ResultSetMetaData, and the keys of a hashtable. It can also loop base upon a counter.

The preceding information is intended to provide you with just an overview of the tag library. For more information, see `http://e-docs.bea.com/wls/docs61/jsp/customtags.html`.

WebLogic EJB-to-JSP Integration Tool

WebLogic provides an EJB-to-JSP integration tool, which can generate a JSP tag extension library based upon an EJB JAR file. By referencing the EJB's remote interface, tags are created for invoking methods of an EJB. The generated tag libraries support stateless and stateful session beans, and entity beans.

Traditionally, a JSP would contain Java code within a scriptlet to invoke the EJB directly. Through the use of this tool, JSPs can use custom XML tags to access EJBs through the associated tag handler objects. The tag handler encapsulates the code to invoke the EJB and its methods.

See `http://e-docs.bea.com/wls/docs61/jsp/ejb2jsp.html` for more information.

Summary

Tag libraries can help to dramatically reduce or even eliminate Java scriptlets from within your JSPs. At the same time, they provide a powerful mechanism to produce reusable components for your JSPs. A rich set of tag libraries can increase a JSP developer's productivity and efficiency.

In this chapter, I covered the basics of JSP tag libraries and deployed a couple of examples to transform HTML and introduce new scripting variables. Definitions of the appropriate XML descriptors and deployment in WebLogic were also covered. Finally, an overview was given of two tag libraries and a generation tool provided by WebLogic.

I'm sure you've thought of many ideas along the way on how tag libraries can improve your Web applications. Go to it!

✦ ✦ ✦

PART

IV

Developing EJB Components

✦ ✦ ✦ ✦

In This Part

✦ ✦ ✦ ✦

Understanding Enterprise JavaBeans

✦ ✦ ✦ ✦

In This Chapter

EJB architecture

EJB types

EJB client access models

EJB components

WebLogic's EJB container services

EJB 1.1 versus 2.0

✦ ✦ ✦ ✦

Enterprise JavaBeans (*EJBs*) are software components written in Java that encapsulate a system's business logic and data access and make it available to Java clients running anywhere on the network. When you consider the architecture of EJBs plus the runtime services they provide — high availability, transactions, session management, persistence, and security — no other technology comes as close to delivering on the promise of reusable software components for the distributed enterprise. EJBs are at the heart of what J2EE is all about; in fact, whenever developers think of J2EE, they usually think of EJBs.

EJBs come in four different varieties:

✦ *Stateless session EJBs* execute business logic on behalf of any client, usually performing relatively quick and simple tasks, such as returning a current stock price given a ticker symbol.

✦ *Stateful session EJBs* execute business logic on behalf of a specific client with whom they are maintaining conversational state; the classic example of a stateful session EJB is an online shopping cart that tracks a user's purchases until checkout.

✦ *Entity EJBs* manage low-level database storage and retrieval and also provide some degree of related business logic. They are usually used in conjunction with session EJBs. A good example is an entity EJB that manages a customer's stock portfolio.

✦ *Message-driven EJBs*, which are new with the EJB 2.0 specification, work hand-in-hand with JMS (see Chapter 9) to provide asynchronous processing capabilities to any client that sends them a message. A good use for a message-driven EJB would be to handle the confirmation and settlement of a securities trade.

The J2EE specification mandates that EJBs run within an *EJB container* that not only provides a runtime environment for them, but also provides the enterprise-class services that I mentioned before: high availability, transactions, session management, persistence, and security. The container must also provide support for *declarative services*, which allow the users of EJBs (referred to in J2EE parlance as *application assemblers*) to configure many aspects of EJB runtime behavior through the use of XML deployment descriptors. WebLogic Server's EJB container provides all these services and more, as you will see in the rest of this chapter.

Enterprise JavaBeans are different from "plain" JavaBeans, which are written to a completely different specification (originally intended for implementing client-side GUI components) and which do not participate in the EJB container architecture. You can learn more about JavaBeans in Chapter 12.

The next four chapters of this book guide you through the complex world of EJB development and deployment with WebLogic Server. This chapter begins by giving you an overview of EJB technology, explaining issues that pertain to all four types of EJBs. The other three chapters cover the different types of EJBs in detail, with Chapter 15 devoted to stateless and stateful session EJBs, Chapter 16 to entity EJBs, and Chapter 17 to message-driven EJBs.

EJB Architecture

Enterprise JavaBeans are simply Java classes written to the EJB specification and deployed within a J2EE-compliant EJB container. The J2EE standard mandates that the EJB container must provide well-defined deployment support, as well as certain runtime services and behavior. The EJB container, in turn, runs within a J2EE-compliant Application Server. This allows it to provide the required access to the J2EE APIs, while making the EJBs available to Java clients over the network via JNDI and RMI. Figure 14-1 shows the interactions among the EJB container, the Web container, the J2EE APIs, the Application Server, and EJB clients.

Application software vendors, such as BEA, implement EJB containers, while end-user developers, like you and me, implement EJBs and their clients. The container, the EJBs, and the clients each have certain roles and responsibilities within the overall system, which the J2EE specification spells out in the form of contracts. If an EJB container is written to fulfill *its* responsibilities with the contract, and if I write my EJBs to fulfill *their* responsibilities, then my EJBs will work within the container.

One of the most powerful aspects of EJB architecture is that the services provided by the container—transactions, persistence, security, and so on—are completely transparent to EJBs deployed within the container. In other words, it's possible to write an EJB that is fully transactional, secure, and persistent without writing a single line of Java code in support of these services. This is a tremendous boon for developers, because writing code to support these services is notoriously difficult. Nevertheless, the EJB standard and the J2EE APIs still make it possible for developers to code these services themselves, but it's generally better to avoid doing so if you can.

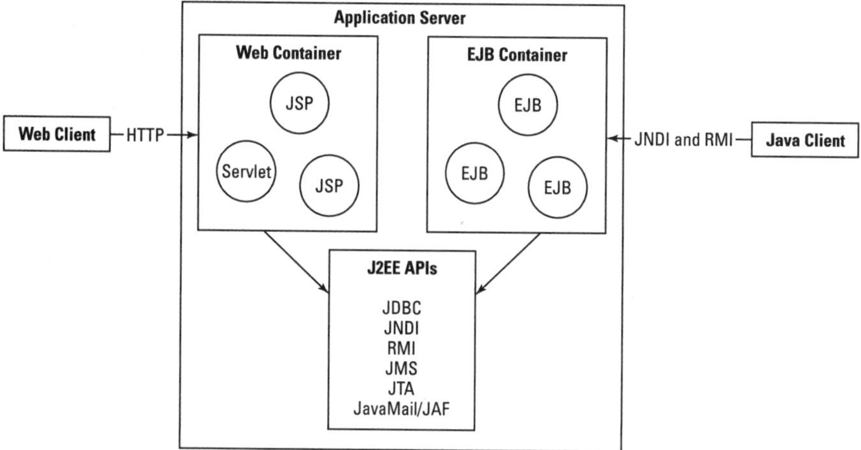

Figure 14-1: EJB architecture

EJB Types

The J2EE specification defines four different types of EJBs, each designed to meet a specific category of software development challenges.

Session beans

Session beans are generally used to implement control, process, and workflow in an application. In the Model-View-Controller world, session beans almost always live in the Controller realm.

Session beans come in two flavors: *stateless* and *stateful.* These beans are so named because they are commonly invoked directly by clients in the context of a client session. But their usage and treatment by the EJB container are completely different.

Stateless session beans

As their name implies, stateless session beans do not maintain client state across method calls — when a method call completes, the bean's state is exactly the same as it was before the call. Multiple instances of the same session bean are, therefore, identical to each other and can be shared or pooled among multiple clients.

Stateless session beans are used to perform simple, self-contained tasks that don't require the preservation of state, such as verifying a user's identity, returning the current time from an atomic clock, performing a database search, and so on.

Stateful session beans

Stateful session beans, on the other hand, do preserve state across method calls, and execute on behalf of a single client. As the client performs tasks supported by the bean, the bean's state changes as needed to reflect the current status of the interaction. The bean maintains its state by using Java instance variables.

Stateful session beans are used to support prolonged interactions between individual clients and the system. The most common example is an online shopping cart. A client might use a stateless session bean to find products in an online catalog, but when he adds an item to his cart, a stateful session bean is created for his exclusive use that tracks the items he has added to his cart. The same bean might also track the overall state of his visit (shopping, checkout pending, checkout completed, and so on).

Entity beans

Entity beans are Java representations of items stored in a database. Most often, the database is relational, and the entity bean represents a row in a relational table. Entity beans make programming easier because they allow developers to work with Java objects and methods, rather than using JDBC or some other protocol to interact with the underlying data store.

Entity beans possess the quality of *persistence*—they work in conjunction with the EJB container and the database to keep the bean's state in memory synchronized with the data in the store. In most cases, this is accomplished by making JDBC calls to select, insert, update, or delete the row represented by the bean in a relational database. These calls can be hand-coded by the developer directly in the bean (an approach called *bean-managed persistence,* or *BMP*), or they can be automatically generated by the EJB container (an approach called *container-managed persistence,* or *CMP*). I'll have more to say about BMP and CMP later in this chapter in the section called "WebLogic's EJB Container Services."

Message-driven beans

Message-driven beans are deployed as listeners for JMS queues and topics, and execute their business logic in response to incoming JMS messages. This enables developers to write beans that can be invoked asynchronously.

JMS, the Java Messaging Service, is covered in Chapter 9.

Unlike session and entity beans, client code cannot obtain references to message-driven beans, nor can it invoke the methods of message-driven beans directly. Instead, the client invokes the beans' methods indirectly, by posting JMS messages to the queues or topics to which the beans are listening.

Message-driven beans are well suited for deferred processing or the completion of time-consuming tasks that don't require the client's attention. You can use message-driven beans, for example, to queue up overnight processing tasks, or to implement logging functions, or to process orders for online purchases. In the last case, the message-driven bean can transmit a pick list and shipping instructions to the warehouse, a credit card transaction to the bank, and a confirmation e-mail to the customer, without requiring the customer to wait for any of these tasks to complete.

EJB Client-Access Models

EJBs can be called from Java code running with the same JVM as the EJB, or from a different JVM elsewhere on the network. The first form of access is called *local* access, and the second is called *remote* access. With either form of access, the initial reference to an EJB is obtained in client code by performing a JNDI lookup on one of the EJB's home interfaces, which I discuss in the next section.

In the EJB 1.1 specification, there is no difference in the way an EJB is programmed to accommodate local versus remote access. EJBs are implemented as RMI objects, so access to their methods always takes place through the bean's remote interface, and traverses RMI's server and client stacks. Note, however, that WebLogic Server short-circuits the access path, if the client code and EJB code both reside within WebLogic's JVM, by transparently replacing remote calls with local calls. This increases performance by eliminating the overhead of building serialized remote method calls.

See Chapter 7 for a complete description of this process. Specifically, see Figure 7-3 for a diagram comparing the two access methods.

Unlike the EJB 1.1 specification, the EJB 2.0 specification defines separate programmatic interfaces for local and remote access to EJBs. This allows developers to formally design and implement EJBs whose calling semantics explicitly support the two types of access. When developing EJBs under the 2.0 specification, developers can implement the remote interface only, the local interface only, or both.

EJB Components

With the exception of message-driven beans, EJBs are deployed as RMI objects, and therefore possess many of the same structural elements as RMI servers. As a result, programming EJBs is much like programming RMI servers with some important differences.

In this section, I explain the components common to all EJBs, which are

- ✦ The home interface
- ✦ The remote interface
- ✦ The implementation class
- ✦ The deployment descriptor

To make the explanations concrete, I present the code and deployment descriptors for a simple session EJB that implements business logic surrounding a company's revenues. Such an EJB might be part of an accounting package or an executive reporting system.

Home interface

An EJB's *home interface* controls the bean's lifecycle within the EJB container, including creating, removing, and locating the bean. You, as the bean developer, don't need to implement the interface; its implementation is provided by the EJB container. The home interface merely identifies to the container the type of bean it is dealing with; it has nothing to do with actual bean instances. Think of the home interface as a factory for the type of bean you seek to create.

When deploying a bean to WebLogic Server, you register the home interface with JNDI. Then, when client code wants to work with the bean, it obtains a reference to the bean's home interface, via a JNDI lookup, and uses this to work with the bean.

JNDI lookup is too slow for repeated lookups of EJBs. If you want your applications to be fast and scalable, you should avoid doing a JNDI lookup for the home interface in every page or every client of your application.

A better solution is to implement a *service locator class* that keeps a cache (implemented as a static Hashtable or something similar) of all EJB home interfaces. When a client requests a home, the service locator checks the cache to see if it has already been looked up. If so, it simply returns the cached copy. If not, it performs a JNDI lookup and adds the home interface to its cache before returning it to the client.

You can learn more about the service locator design pattern at `http://developer.java.sun.com/developer/restricted/patterns/ServiceLocator.html`.

For remote clients, the EJB's home interface extends from the `javax.ejb.EJBHome` interface. For local clients, the home interface extends from `javax.ejb.EJBLocalHome`. The latter interface is new with EJB 2.0.

The following is the "remote" home interface for my Revenue EJB, intended for use by remote clients:

```
package bible.ejb;

import java.rmi.*;
import javax.ejb.*;

public interface RevenueHome extends EJBHome {
  public Revenue create()
  throws RemoteException, CreateException;
}
```

Here is the "local" home interface, intended for use by local clients:

```
package bible.ejb;

import java.rmi.*;
import javax.ejb.*;

public interface RevenueLocalHome extends EJBLocalHome {
  public RevenueLocal create()
  throws CreateException;
}
```

Note that the only differences between these two interfaces are their base classes, the type of objects their `create()` methods return, and the types of exceptions they throw. With regard to exceptions, the "remote" home interface throws a `RemoteException`, whereas the "local" home interface does not. Otherwise, the interfaces are identical—they simply provide a `create()` method that clients can use to obtain a runtime reference to the appropriate underlying bean.

Remote interface

The EJB's *remote interface* is where you define the signatures of business methods that are visible to clients using the EJB. The `create()` method of the home interface returns a reference to this remote interface, which clients use to invoke methods on the bean.

As with the home interface, you can write separate remote interfaces for remote and local clients. For remote clients, the remote interface extends the `javax.ejb.EJBObject` interface, and for local clients, it extends the `javax.ejb.EJBLocalObject` interface. Again, the latter interface is new with EJB 2.0.

The following is the "remote" remote interface for my Revenue EJB:

```
package bible.ejb;

import java.rmi.*;
import javax.ejb.*;
import java.util.Date;

public interface Revenue extends EJBObject {
  double getYTD() throws RemoteException;
  double getForPeriod(Date startDate, Date endDate)
  throws RemoteException;
}
```

In this interface, I've exposed two business methods to clients: `Revenue.getYTD()`, and `Revenue.getForPeriod()`. Note that these methods must throw `javax.rmi.RemoteExceptions` because `EJBObject` extends the `java.rmi.Remote` interface.

You can define any number of business methods to your remote interface, just as you would in a normal Java class.

The “local” remote interface for my Revenue EJB is as follows:

```
package bible.ejb;

import javax.ejb.*;
import java.util.Date;

public interface RevenueLocal extends EJBLocalObject {
  double getYTD();
  double getForPeriod(Date startDate, Date endDate);
}
```

In most cases, the business methods in your “remote” and “local” remote interfaces will be identical. The only difference is that the “local” methods will not throw `RemoteExceptions`. Another difference, not reflected in the code itself, is that arguments are passed to “remote” methods by value, and to “local” methods by reference.

Implementation class

The EJB’s *implementation class* is where you provide the code behind the methods defined in the remote interfaces. The interface you implement depends on the type of bean you are writing:

- ✦ Session beans (stateful and stateless) implement `javax.ejb.SessionBean`
- ✦ Entity beans implement `javax.ejb.EntityBean`
- ✦ Message-driven beans (new with EJB 2.0) implement `javax.ejb.MessageDrivenBean`

For session beans, you must implement the `ejbCreate()` method. Implementing the other lifecycle methods—`ejbRemove()`, `ejbActivate()`, and `ejbPassivate()`—is optional.

For session beans, you must also define a private instance variable of type `javax.ejb.SessionContext` and a setter method called `setSessionContext()` the container can call to set it. Entity beans and message-driven beans have similar methods—for entity beans the method is called `setEntityContext()`, and for message-driven beans it is called `setMessageDrivenContext()`. All three methods perform the same function: to provide the bean instance with information about its container that can be used by the bean or its clients at runtime. Each method accepts an extension of the `javax.ejb.EJBContext` interface as a parameter—for session beans it is `javax.ejb.SessionContext`, for entity beans it is `javax.ejb.EntityContext`, and for message-driven beans it is `javax.ejb.MessageDrivenContext`.

In my example, I will not provide implementations for the lifecycle methods, relying instead on the default implementations provided by WebLogic's EJB container.

Listing 14-1 shows the implementation class for my Revenue bean, including the lifecycle methods and business methods. But instead of providing code for the business methods, I've merely written comments explaining what they might do so that you can focus on the structure of the class rather than the details of its implementation.

If you want your implementation class to support both local and remote clients, as mine does, you may have to duplicate some of your business methods — one for each case. The only difference is that the implementations for local clients must not throw `RemoteExceptions`. As you can see from the code, my local implementations simply call the remote implementations and catch the `RemoteExceptions`. This saves me from writing the same code twice.

Listing 14-1: RevenueEJB.java

```
package bible.ejb;

import java.rmi.*;
import javax.ejb.*;
import java.util.*;
import javax.naming.*;
import java.sql.*;

public class RevenueEJB implements SessionBean {

  // Mandatory instance variable.
  private SessionContext sessionContext;

  // Mandatory setter for the SessionContext.
  public void setSessionContext(SessionContext sessionContext)
{
    this.sessionContext = sessionContext;
  }

  // Mandatory bean lifecycle methods.
  public void ejbCreate() throws CreateException {
  }

  public void ejbRemove(){
  }

  public void ejbActivate(){
  }

  public void ejbPassivate(){
  }
```

Continued

Listing 14-1 *(continued)*

```
  // Business method to return YTD revenues.
  public double getYTD(){
    double revenue = 0.0;
    // Insert code here to read revenues from
    // a data source, such as a relational database.
    return revenue;
  }

  // Local version of getYTD(). Calls getYTD() but does not
  // throw the RemoteException.
  public double getYTDLocal() {
    double revenue = 0.0;
    try {
      revenue = getYTD();
    }
    catch (RemoteException re) {
    }
    finally {
      return revenue;
    }
  }

  // Business method to return revenues realized between
  // the given date range.
    public double getForPeriod(java.sql.Date startDate,
      java.sql.Date endDate) throws RemoteException {
    double revenue = 0.0;
    // Insert code here to read revenues from
    // a data source, such as a relational database.
    return revenue;
  }

  // Local version of getForPeriod(). Calls getForPeriod()
  // but does not throw the RemoteException.
  public double getForPeriodLocal(java.sql.Date startDate,
    java.sql.Date endDate) {
    double revenue = 0.0;
    try {
      revenue = getForPeriod(startDate, endDate);
    }
    catch (RemoteException re) {
    }
    finally {
      return revenue;
    }
  }
}
```

Deployment descriptors

The EJB's deployment descriptors define how the EJB should be deployed within WebLogic Server. Every EJB deployed to WebLogic requires two deployment descriptors:

- `ejb-jar.xml` — the deployment descriptor required by J2EE. This descriptor defines the bean's deployment structure and maps its internal dependencies and application assembly information.
- `weblogic-ejb-jar.xml` — the WebLogic-specific deployment descriptor, which specifies the bean's caching, clustering, and performance behavior. This descriptor also defines the bean's JNDI identity, security roles, and dependencies on other WebLogic Server resources such as JMS connection factories, JDBC connection pools, and other deployed EJBs.

Notice that EJB deployment descriptors are analogous to Web application descriptors, consisting of a J2EE-specific descriptor, plus a WebLogic-specific descriptor. Unlike Web applications, however, you cannot omit the WebLogic-specific descriptor — *all* EJBs require *both* deployment descriptors.

Listing 14-2 shows `ejb-jar.xml` for my sample session bean. Note that it is based on the XML DTD for EJB 2.0. The DTD for EJB 1.1 is

```
<!DOCTYPE ejb-jar PUBLIC '-//Sun Microsystems, Inc.//DTD
Enterprise JavaBeans 1.1//EN'
'http://java.sun.com/j2ee/dtds/ejb-jar_1_1.dtd'>
```

Listing 14-2: ejb-jar.xml for the Revenue bean

```
<?xml version="1.0"?>

<!DOCTYPE ejb-jar PUBLIC '-//Sun Microsystems, Inc.//DTD
Enterprise JavaBeans 2.0//EN' 'http://java.sun.com/dtd/
ejb-jar_2_0.dtd'>

<ejb-jar>
  <enterprise-beans>
    <session>
      <ejb-name>Revenue</ejb-name>
      <home>bible.ejb.RevenueHome</home>
      <remote>bible.ejb.Revenue</remote>
      <local-home>bible.ejb.RevenueLocalHome</local-home>
      <local>bible.ejb.RevenueLocal</local>
      <ejb-class>bible.ejb.RevenueEJB</ejb-class>
      <session-type>Stateless</session-type>
```

Continued

Listing 14-2 (continued)

```
      <transaction-type>Container</transaction-type>
    </session>
  </enterprise-beans>
  <assembly-descriptor>
    <container-transaction>
      <method>
        <ejb-name>Revenue</ejb-name>
        <method-name>*</method-name>
      </method>
      <trans-attribute>Required</trans-attribute>
    </container-transaction>
  </assembly-descriptor>
</ejb-jar>
```

From top to bottom, the elements of this deployment descriptor are as follows:

- `<ejb-jar>`: The top-level document type.
- `<enterprise-beans>`: A listing of all the enterprise Java beans contained in this deployment. It can include any number of `<session>`, `<entity>`, or `<message-driven>` descriptors.
- `<session>`: The descriptor for the session bean included in this deployment.
- `<ejb-name>`: A descriptive name for the bean.
- `<home>`: The fully qualified class name of the home interface used for remote clients.
- `<remote>`: The fully qualified class name of the remote interface.
- `<local-home>`: The fully qualified class name of the home interface used for local clients.
- `<local>`: The fully qualified class name of the local interface.
- `<ejb-class>`: The fully qualified name of the class implementing the bean, including its lifecycle methods and the business methods defined in the local and remote interfaces.
- `<session-type>`: This tag applies to session beans only and indicates whether the bean is stateless (as mine is), or stateful.
- `<transaction-type>`: Indicates how transactions are demarcated. In this example, transaction demarcation is handled by the EJB container. I discuss transactions and EJBs later in this chapter in the section called "WebLogic's EJB Container Services."
- `<assembly-descriptor>`: This tag defines transaction control on a method-by-method basis for the bean.

✦ <container-transaction>: Indicates that attributes for container-managed transactions are now being defined.

✦ <method>: The list of EJBs and methods to which a a container-managed transaction attribute applies.

✦ <ejb-name>: The name of the EJB owning the method(s).

✦ <method-name>: The method(s) to be controlled by the transaction attribute. An asterisk (*) indicates the attribute applies to all methods of the EJB.

✦ <trans-attribute>: The transaction attribute to apply to the methods just listed. In this example, my methods all require a transaction context to be established by the EJB container before they are called.

See Chapter 6 for a complete description of transaction attributes and their meanings.

Listing 14-3 shows weblogic-ejb-jar.xml for my sample session bean.

Listing 14-3: weblogic-ejb-jar.xml for the Revenue bean

```
<?xml version="1.0"?>

<!DOCTYPE weblogic-ejb-jar PUBLIC '-//BEA Systems, Inc.//DTD
WebLogic 6.0.0 EJB//EN'
'http://www.bea.com/servers/wls600/dtd/weblogic-ejb-jar.dtd'>

<weblogic-ejb-jar>
    <weblogic-enterprise-bean>
        <ejb-name>Revenue</ejb-name>
        <jndi-name>Revenue</jndi-name>
        <local-jndi-name>RevenueLocal</local-jndi-name>
    </weblogic-enterprise-bean>
</weblogic-ejb-jar>
```

This deployment descriptor simply maps EJB names (as defined in ejb-jar.xml) to JNDI names corresponding to the local and remote implementations of the beans. Clients invoke the EJBs by performing lookups against these JNDI names.

For each bean, you should only define JNDI names for the type(s) of beans you're deploying; don't define a local JNDI name for a bean unless it actually contains a local home interface, and so on.

My simple sample bean contains no descriptors for caching, clustering, or other WebLogic services. You'll see examples of those in upcoming chapters.

WebLogic's EJB Container Services

Maximizing the performance and scalability of your EJBs requires a clear understanding of how WebLogic's EJB container works. This section gives you an overview of the services WebLogic's EBJ container provides. These services are highly configurable and tunable; consult the WebLogic Server documentation for more information on the multitude of options available.

Lifecycle management

WebLogic Server's EJB container, like all J2EE-compliant EJB containers, provides full lifecycle management for the beans you deploy. This means the container assumes responsibility for the following tasks:

- Creating new bean instances, either in response to demand from clients or to populate predefined bean pools at startup time.
- Passivating bean instances that are still in use, but idle. This involves serializing the contents of the bean and saving it to disk.
- Activating bean instances that have been passivated. In this case, the passivated beans are deserialized from disk and restored to active memory, where they are once again available for use.
- Destroying bean instances that are no longer in use, usually to make memory available for other functions or to prepare for a shutdown of WebLogic Server.
- Handling the create, load, store, and delete operations for entity EJBs.
- Binding message-driven EJBs to the appropriate JMS queues and topics.
- Managing failover operations in clustered environments.

Transaction support

EJBs, by definition, operate in a transactional environment. When you deploy EJBs, you specify the level of transaction support you expect from the EJB container in your `ejb-jar.xml` deployment descriptor.

Recall from Chapter 6 that *transaction demarcation* is the process of specifying when a transaction is started, suspended, resumed, committed, and rolled back. With J2EE, transactions can be manually demarcated in code, using calls to the JTA; or they can be automatically demarcated, using declarative rules stored in XML deployment descriptors.

Because writing transaction code is such a difficult and error-prone process, it is almost always better to take advantage of automatic transaction demarcation. Nevertheless, you can manually demarcate transactions in session and message-driven EJBs; these are called bean-managed transactions. The EJB 2.0 specification, however, prohibits the use of bean-managed transactions in entity EJBs; entity EJBs must always use container-managed transactions (which, of course, are available to the other bean types as well).

Container-managed transactions

The EJB specification defines several attributes for container-managed transactions that control how EJB methods participate in transactions. You specify the attributes you want in `ejb-jar.xml` by using the `<trans-attribute>` element of the `<assembly-descriptor>` tag.

The following sections summarize how EJB 2.0 specification defines the container's behavior for each attribute, but you should consult the EJB 2.0 specification for more details (`http://www.java.sun.com`).

NotSupported

This attribute applies to EJB methods that do not support transactions. The container invokes the EJB method with an unspecified transaction context. If the caller has a transaction in progress when such a method is invoked, the container suspends the transaction before invoking the method and then resumes it when the method completes.

Required

The container must establish a valid transaction context before invoking an EJB method with this attribute. If a transaction is already underway, the container will associate the method with that transaction. If not, the container will start a new transaction, invoke the method, and then commit the transaction when the method completes.

Note, however, that message-driven EJB methods *never* execute within the context of an existing transaction, so the container *always* creates a new transaction context for them, prior to executing the `onMessage()` method. After `onMessage()` completes, the container commits the transaction. If the container rolls back the transaction, the message is marked for redelivery in accordance with the JMS specification.

Supports

This attribute is a cross between `NotSupported` and `Required`. If the EJB method is invoked with a transaction in progress, the container proceeds as in the `Required` case. If not, the container proceeds as in the `NotSupported` case.

RequiresNew

This attribute always forces the new container to start a new transaction for the EJB method and to commit that transaction when the method completes. If the caller has a transaction underway, that transaction is suspended until the method completes; it is then resumed again.

Mandatory

The caller is required to have a transaction underway before calling EJB methods with this attribute set, and the container executes the methods within the context of the caller's transaction. If no transaction is underway, the container throws an exception.

Never

This attribute is the opposite of `Mandatory`. The caller must invoke the EJB method with no transaction underway. If a transaction is underway, the container throws an exception; otherwise, it proceeds as in the `NotSupported` case.

Bean-managed transactions

To use bean-managed transactions, you omit the `<trans-attribute>` tag for the affected bean methods, and you write your own transaction demarcation code as explained in Chapter 6.

Persistence

The EJB container provides persistence services for stateful session beans and entity beans. For stateful session beans, the container automatically serializes the bean's state to disk when the bean is passivated, assuming the bean is still in use (and the client session with the bean has not expired or otherwise ended). When the same bean is activated later, the container reloads its state from disk into main memory.

Persistence services for entity beans, which almost always represent data in relational or object-relational databases, are far more advanced. Here, the programmer has two persistence models to choose from:

- ✦ Container-managed persistence (CMP), where the container automatically synchronizes the bean instance in memory with the underlying data it represents
- ✦ Bean-managed persistence (BMP), where the developer writes code to maintain this synchronization

In theory, it is always better for developers to use CMP. This allows developers to focus on implementing business logic, while leaving the details of entity persistence to the container. It also enables developers to write code that is independent of the underlying data source used because the container correctly manages persistence for any data source with a compliant JDBC driver.

In practice, it's not always that easy. With EJB 1.1, CMP has a lot of usability and performance problems that force developers to use BMP almost exclusively. EJB 2.0, however, promises to be a different story. Sun has completely rewritten CMP in EJB

2.0 to address developer concerns with the previous version. It's too early to tell if they did a good job, but you should probably give CMP a try in EJB 2.0 to see if it works for your project before taking on the formidable task of implementing BMP.

Clustering support

WebLogic Server provides full clustering support for EJBs. This allows you to deploy your EJBs in an environment that requires high scalability and availability. WebLogic uses cluster-aware stubs for bean home interfaces, along with cluster-aware EJBObjects, to implement clustering for EJBs. These cluster-aware entities are aware of the locations of all other instances of the bean in the cluster. Drawing from this information, the stub manages load balancing and failover for bean invocations, whereas the EJBObjects manage failover to bean instances on healthy servers if the servers on which the beans are executing go down.

Security

You can control user access to the methods of your EJBs by using the same mechanisms available for controlling access to Web applications. In your deployment descriptors, you can declare users, roles, and security role assignments; at runtime, the EJB container automatically restricts access to EJB method calls based on your security role assignments.

EJB 1.1 versus 2.0

Two versions of the EJB specification are now in use:

- ✦ EJB 1.1, which was released in December, 1999
- ✦ EJB 2.0, which was released in September, 2001

A detailed discussion of the features of the two versions is beyond the scope of this book, but this section alerts you to some of the most important additions and enhancements Sun introduced with the EJB 2.0 specification. To fill in the blanks, you should download copies of both specifications at `http://java.sun.com/products/ejb/docs.html` and study them carefully. You should also carefully review *Programming WebLogic Enterprise JavaBeans,* which is part of WebLogic's documentation set.

According to the EJB specification, EJB 2.0-compliant containers must support beans written to the EJB 1.1 specification, and WebLogic's does. But you must write each of your beans to one version of the specification or the other; you cannot mix and match features from both versions in the same bean.

EJB 2.0 expands and improves upon the EJB architecture, in response to suggestions from developers, vendors, and customers. What follows are some of the most important changes.

New: Message-driven beans

Message-driven beans, discussed in a previous section, are completely new with EJB 2.0, and have no counterpart in EJB 1.1. Message-driven beans attach themselves to JMS queues and topics and provide a component-based solution for managing messaging.

Chapter 17 covers message-driven beans.

Improved: CMP for entity beans

As mentioned earlier, container-managed persistence is dramatically improved in EJB 2.0. These improvements are embodied in the following new features:

- Abstract accessor methods
- Container-managed relationships
- Local interfaces and local home interfaces
- Enterprise JavaBeans Query Language (EJB QL)

Abstract accessor methods

Abstract accessor methods are abstract getters and setters that manipulate an object's persistent state. All access to the persistent state passes through these accessors, so the container can interpose code of its own that efficiently manages exchanges between the bean and its underlying data store.

Container-managed relationships

With EJB 2.0, you can now represent various types of data relationships with collections of entity beans that work together at runtime. These relationships map to the same ones that have been modeled in relational databases for years:

- One-to-one, unidirectional
- One-to-one, bidirectional
- One-to-many
- Many-to-many

Such relationships were difficult, if not impossible, to model in EJB 1.1, both for technical and performance reasons.

Local interfaces and local home interfaces for session and entity beans

The concept of local interfaces (and corresponding local home interfaces), which I demonstrated earlier in this chapter, is new with EJB 2.0. In EJB 1.1, all access to EJBs was through their remote interfaces, whether the client code resided in the same JVM as the EJB or not. Now, developers can write separate interfaces to explicitly support clients that are local *or* remote relative to the bean, thereby maximizing performance.

Enterprise JavaBeans Query Language (EJB QL)

The *Enterprise JavaBeans Query Language,* or *EJB QL,* is used to define queries for entity beans with container-managed persistence (for *all* entity beans in EJB 2.0). Because it's based on the SQL 92 standard, EJB QL makes it possible to shift the parsing and execution of queries from the runtime representations of data in beans to the underlying data stores. This results in greater portability and performance, as well as enhanced functionality, for clients who want to query schemas of entity beans based on arbitrary criteria.

Summary

In this chapter, you learned the basics of EJBs, including what they are, how they are constructed, the extensive runtime services that are available to them, and how some of those services are implemented in WebLogic Server. You've also learned about the two versions of the EJB specification now in use, 1.1 and 2.0, and how to properly structure your EJBs to support either version.

The next three chapters explore the three types of EJBs in detail, starting with session EJBs, and then entity EJBs, and finally, message-driven EJBs — J2EE's newest bean type.

✦ ✦ ✦

CHAPTER 15

Developing Session Beans

✦ ✦ ✦ ✦

In This Chapter

Understanding session beans

Stateless and stateful beans

Programming session beans

Clustering session beans

Programming transactions in session beans

✦ ✦ ✦ ✦

In Chapter 14, you learned that session EJBs are used to represent control, process, and workflow in an application. This chapter provides concrete examples of this theory in action and shows how to build and deploy session EJBs in WebLogic Server.

Session EJBs come in two flavors: *stateful* and *stateless*. Stateful session beans maintain ongoing conversations with clients, whereas stateless beans do not. The classic example of a stateful session bean is the online shopping cart, which keeps track of the items a customer intends to purchase until the customer checks out or otherwise concludes the shopping session. Stateless beans, on the other hand, are used to perform simple, one-off tasks, such as updating the customer's mailing address or adding an item to her wish list. These are atomic functions that do not require an ongoing dialogue between the client and the server.

Stateful session beans maintain their state in memory, not in a database. Therefore, if the WebLogic EJB container crashes or destroys a session bean instance for some reason, the state of the bean is lost. But stateful beans can be clustered, which provides a failover capability for applications that need it.

WebLogic's EJB container manages the lifecycle of session EJBs, including their creation, caching, and destruction. For the most part, WebLogic's bean lifecycle management occurs automatically, in response to client demand for beans. In this chapter, I show how this occurs and I discuss steps that you can take to override the container's behavior in certain situations.

Before you can invoke a session EJB's methods, you must obtain a reference to either its local or remote interface. The first step is to perform a JNDI lookup to obtain a reference to the bean's home interface. This, in turn, is used to retrieve a reference to the bean's local or remote interface. The local or remote interface is then used to invoke the bean's methods.

Which interface you'll use (local or remote) depends partially on where the client code lives in relationship to the bean, and partially on how portable you want your application's components to be. If the client code is a Java class, servlet, or another EJB, it can use the local interface as long as it is deployed in the same EAR file as the EJB, or as part of a standalone JAR that is loaded into the same JVM as the EJB. The local interface is more efficient than the remote interface because method calls are made directly within the same JVM, with parameters being passed by reference instead of by value. Local calls, however, are location-specific — if you decide to move the calling code or the EJB to a different server, you will have to rewrite your code to use the EJB's remote interface.

Chapter 7 discusses WebLogic's implementation of RMI as an alternative to the Sun implementation. Although it's possible to have your EJBs use the `weblogic.rmi` package instead of the standard `java.rmi` implementation, it is not recommended. By using Sun's RMI, your beans will be easily portable to non-WebLogic application servers, which is one of the most profound benefits of using EJBs. When writing remote EJBs, your developers will never need to worry about method invocations passing parameters by reference — when using `java.rmi` they can count on parameters being passed by value. If a developer wishes to increase the efficiency of his EJBs and knows his EJBs will be accessed from clients within the server, he can now write a local EJB.

Common session bean uses

Any business logic that will be used by clients in your WebLogic applications can be encapsulated in session EJBs. Session EJBs can update and fetch shared data as long as they do not directly represent that data. In other words, you could write `FooDataFactory` as a session EJB to obtain references to a non-EJB `Foo` class. They can be used to do business calculations, obtain references and call other EJBs, or even help facilitate the model role in the MVC design architecture. Session beans can be used instead of entity beans to persist objects representing data in your business model, but this approach is not recommended. This scenario is often seen when an application has an existing object database or developers have been using an object-relational mapping tool.

Using session EJBs to model workflow

Many good reasons exist for choosing to model workflow and business processes in session EJBs instead of normal Java classes.

Client-server architecture

When you encapsulate business logic in a session EJB, you maximize the benefits of client-server computing. Logic implemented in session EJBs is executed inside the

WebLogic EJB Container on the server. Client code not running on the server can remain lightweight and avoid the expense and details of local method invocations.

EJB Container functionality

By choosing session EJBs to model workflow, a good deal of complex functionality is provided by the EJB Container. Security issues, transactional capabilities, and other complicated issues will be easier to implement than if you had to start from scratch. Because the WebLogic EJB Container has been built with lots of these issues in mind, you only need to implement your EJBs correctly, leaving these complex details to the WebLogic Server. This also ensures that your security and transactional issues will be standardized across your application, making your application easier to support over time.

No synchronization issues

The WebLogic EJB Container, as part of implementing the EJB specification, ensures that no EJB instance will be accessed by multiple clients across method invocations. Thus, application developers don't need to deal with somewhat complicated threading details.

Inherently reusable

The logic session EJBs contain can be reusable across many applications in the WebLogic application environment or even in non-WebLogic J2EE applications. Session beans can be deployed with different security settings and environment settings across many applications or even servers with no change to the underlying Java classes. This is accomplished by using the bean's deployment descriptors to encapsulate environment-specific information.

Scalability

The WebLogic EJB Container provides a runtime environment that scales exceptionally well. WebLogic Server provides the capability to have a pool of session EJBs that dynamically grow and shrink with the real-time needs of your application. This concept is a powerful one, especially when you look closely at how WebLogic Server handles pools of stateless session EJBs.

Comparing Stateless and Stateful Beans

Stateless and stateful session beans are completely different, both in terms of the way they are used and the way they are managed by WebLogic Server.

Stateless session beans are used to perform simple, one-off tasks that are not client-specific and often involve only a single method call. Stateful session beans, on the other hand, are used to maintain conversational state with clients, and the conversation may span several method calls against the bean.

When a client uses a stateless session bean, it's not pinned to a specific instance of that bean because the bean doesn't care who the client is. The beans are all alike, and any bean is capable of servicing any client. Because of this, the client-to-bean ratio for stateless session beans is potentially many-to-many.

When a client uses a stateful session bean, it's pinned to a specific instance of the bean for the duration of its conversation with that bean. No two beans are alike because each bean represents the unique state of its client. Because of this, the client-to-bean ratio for stateful session beans is always one-to-one.

Figure 15-1 illustrates these client-to-bean relationships for the two types of session beans.

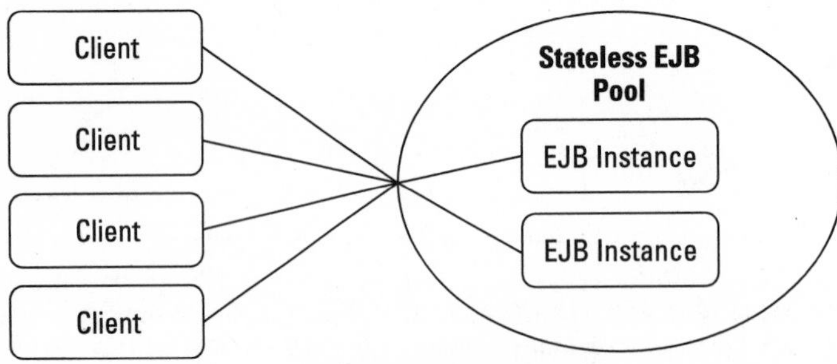

Stateless EJB Clients
Remote reference actually a proxy to pool of EJB instances

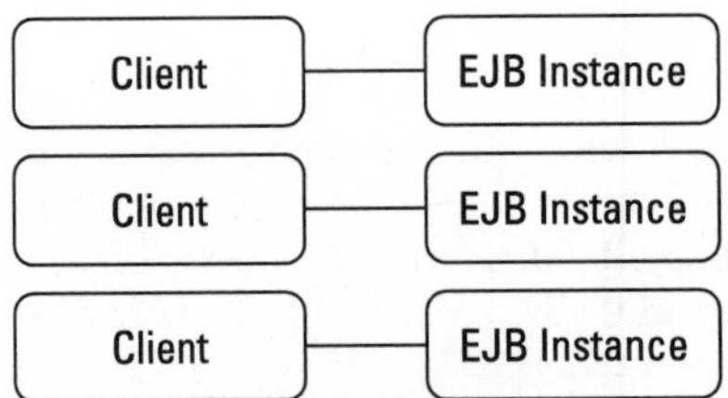

Stateful EJB Clients
One to One Relationship with EJB instances

Figure 15-1: Client-to-bean relationships for session beans

WebLogic Server takes these session bean usage patterns into account and manages the two types of session beans within the EJB container in completely different ways.

Stateless session beans are managed like connections in a JDBC connection pool. WebLogic creates a pool of bean instances, and when a client requests a bean, WebLogic hands it an unused (or *unbound*) bean from the pool. If no unbound beans are available, WebLogic creates one or more new bean instances, depending on how the pool is configured. When a client is finished with a bean, it is returned to the pool. This is illustrated in Figure 15-2.

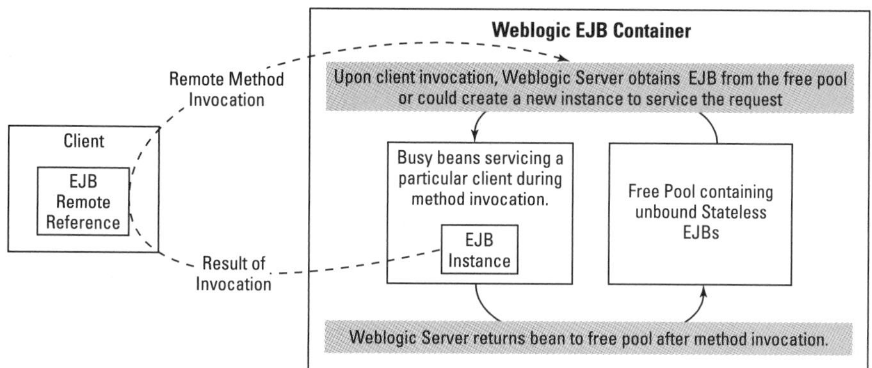

Figure 15-2: WebLogic Server stateless session bean lifecycle

When a client requests a new stateful session bean, WebLogic Server creates a brand new instance of the bean for that client. Every subsequent method call the client makes to the bean is funneled to the same bean. The bean remains in WebLogic's stateful session bean cache either until the client removes it (by calling its `remove()` method), or until WebLogic *passivates* it to free up memory for other needs. Passivating a bean involves serializing its contents and writing them to disk. If a client calls a method on a passivated bean, WebLogic *activates* it by reading it from disk back into the cache. Passivation and activation are completely transparent to clients. Figure 15-3 illustrates the lifecycle of stateful session beans.

When programming stateful session beans, you must ensure that their internal member variables are serializable, and you must respond intelligently when WebLogic passivates and activates your beans. WebLogic Server calls your bean's `ejbPassivate()` method when passivation occurs; this is your opportunity to perform cleanup tasks, such as closing open network sockets or database connections, before the bean instance is written to disk. Likewise, you should code the `ejbActivate()` method to reverse these operations when the bean is read back into the cache.

Refer to Chapter 7 for more details on object serialization.

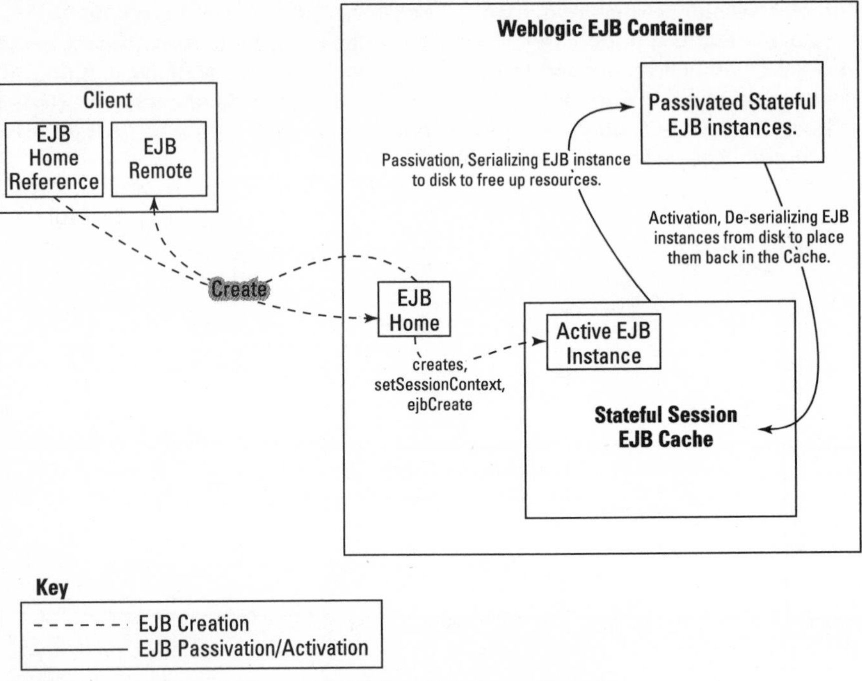

Figure 15-3: WebLogic Server stateful session bean lifecycle

Programming Session Beans

Now I'll discuss the EJB components that you will have to create in your session EJB development process. The mandatory components that you must provide the WebLogic Server during a session EJB deployment are a home interface, a local or remote interface to interact with a client of the bean, an implementation class, and two deployment descriptors.

I'll examine each piece of the session EJB development process in detail, and give an example in the form of two stateless session EJBs. The first session EJB you will develop will be called `RequestResearch` and will be used by a remote client to request research on a particular security. The second example session EJB, `RequestDataManager`, is a local EJB that will act as a helper bean to the remotely accessible `RequestResearch`.

Home interfaces

Home interfaces are the conduits that allow clients to communicate with the WebLogic EJB Container to obtain references to session EJBs. All stateless session beans must supply a `create()` method with no parameters as they have no state to initialize.

When developing a home interface, the first decision that you must make is whether the home is remote or local. As the home interface is what clients use to obtain EJBs, your client's location is the major factor in determining which to use. If you don't know where your clients will be located, or don't want to mandate that the clients will be living locally on the WebLogic Server, simply choose to use a remote home interface.

The decoupling of a bean's functionality and access location is a powerful design concept that you inherit by implementing a remote session EJB. It enables you to reuse a session EJB in many applications without worrying about where the client is located.

Example remote home: RequestResearchHome

As shown in Listing 15-1, this remote home interface has a `create()` method that returns a remote reference, `RequestResearchRemote`, to the `RequestResearch` session EJB. Because the bean home is being accessed remotely, the `create` method throws a `java.rmi.RemoteException` and will also throw `CreateException` if a problem occurs during creation.

Listing 15-1: RequestResearchHome.java

```
package request;

import java.rmi.*;
import javax.ejb.*;

public interface RequestResearchHome extends EJBHome {
  public RequestResearchRemote create() throws RemoteException,
CreateException;
}
```

Example local home: RequestDataManagerLocalHome

As shown in Listing 15-2, this local home interface has a single `create()` method that returns a local reference, `RequestDataManagerLocal`. Notice how there's no need to import the `java.rmi` package because the bean is accessing a local interface that isn't passed via RMI.

Listing 15-2: RequestDataManagerLocalHome.java

```
package request;

import javax.ejb.*;
```

Continued

Listing 15-2 *(continued)*

```
public interface RequestDataManagerLocalHome extends
EJBLocalHome {
  public RequestDataManagerLocal create() throws
CreateException;
}
```

Session EJB interfaces

The second component to develop is the bean's client interfaces. Remote and local interfaces to session beans are essentially the client's view of the bean, and contain the methods that define those session beans. These methods represent the business logic supplied by the session EJBs. If you've chosen a remote home, you must use a remote interface here, and vice-versa.

Remote session EJB interfaces

Remote interfaces are what clients will actually obtain and use from remote home interfaces. Remote interfaces extend from `javax.ejb.EJBObject`. As this is a remote reference to an object living on the WebLogic Server, you must adhere to proper RMI standards. Methods must throw `java.rmi.RemoteExceptions`, and all method parameters, return-types, and application exceptions must be serializable.

See Chapter 7 for further details on object serialization.

Listing 15-3 shows `RequestResearchRemote.java`, a sample remote interface. Note how `RequestResearchRemote` extends `EJBObject` because it's a remote interface. Also note that the return types and parameters are of type `String`, which are serializable and therefore RMI-compliant.

Listing 15-3: RequestResearchRemote.java

```
package research;

import java.rmi.*;
import javax.ejb.*;

public interface RequestResearchRemote extends EJBObject {

  /**
   * Fetches and returns research for a security.
```

```
     */
    public String requestResearch(String symbol)
        throws RemoteException;
}
```

Local session EJB interfaces

Local interfaces are obtained by clients from the local home EJB interface. Local interfaces extend `javax.ejb.EJBLocalObject`. Because local objects live within the same JVM, they are passed by value, not by reference.

Listing 15-4 shows `RequestDataManagerLocal.java`, a sample local interface. To demonstrate that parameters are passed by reference with local EJBs, note that I pass a `StringBuffer` as a parameter to the local EJB and have that EJB alter it. Note also that the methods in this interface need not throw `java.rmi.RemoteException`, as they cannot be invoked remotely.

Listing 15-4: RequestDataManagerLocal.java

```
package request;

import javax.ejb.*;

public interface RequestDataManagerLocal
  extends EJBLocalObject {

  /**
   * Returns research data about a particular security.
   */
   public String getResearchData(String symbol);

  /**
   * Appends research data about a particular security
   * to this buffer.
   */
   public void appendResearchData(StringBuffer buffer,
                                   String symbol);
}
```

Implementation class

The next component to define after the home and client interfaces is the implementation class. These classes must implement the `javax.ejb.SessionBean` so that the container can notify them of the bean's lifecycle events. They will also implement `create()` methods matching the signatures of the `create()` methods in the their home interfaces. Finally, they will implement all the methods defined in their local or remote interfaces.

The SessionBean lifecycle methods in `javax.ejb.SessionBean` are as follows:

✦ `ejbActivate()`: called when the instance is activated from its passive state. Stateless session beans will have nothing to activate as they have no state, whereas stateful beans will contain logic to refresh their states and obtain necessary external resources.

✦ `ejbPassivate()`: called before the instance enters the passive state. Stateless session beans should have nothing to passivate and should implement an empty `ejbPassivate` method. Stateful beans should deallocate any external resources here.

✦ `ejbRemove()`: called before the WebLogic EJB Container ends the life of the session object.

✦ `setSessionContext()`: WebLogic Server will call this to set the associated session context.

During activation and passivation, the WebLogic Server may serialize and deserialize your instance, so it will be necessary that any internal variables are serializable. It is also legal to mark members *transient* although those members will be lost upon serialization.

See Chapter 14 for discussion of the EJBContext.

RequestResearch implementation

The implementation class for the remote stateless session bean must provide methods for all the previously discussed components. First, it will implement the `ejbCreate()` method from `RequestRequestHome`. Then it will implement all the necessary lifecycle methods as defined by the `SessionBean` interface. Because this is a stateless session bean that doesn't use any external resources, note how the `ejbActivate()` and `ejbPassivate()` methods are empty. Don't forget that you must provide these methods, even if they are empty. Finally, the implementation class provides the functionality for `RequestResearchRemote` that the remote clients will use.

The implementation class does not directly implement the home or the remote interfaces. The WebLogic Server will use our deployment descriptors to make the logical connection.

Note how the implementation class clients will call the `requestResearch()` method that returns a `String` containing research for a particular security. When this method is invoked, it will first call a private method `useRequestDataManager()`

to determine how it will process the request. If `useRequestDataManager()` returns `false`, the bean itself will generate test research with the private method `createRandomResearch()`. Otherwise, it will call the `RequestDataManager` EJB to obtain the research for the client.

The `useRequestDataManager()` method actually will do an environment entry lookup in order to determine whether to use the `RequestDataManager`. I'll discuss how this works in more detail a little later when I cover the bean's deployment descriptor.

Note that because the `RequestResearch` EJB lives inside the WebLogic Server, it can use the default empty constructor for `InitialContext`. This is different from client code, where you must use the Environment configuration class to obtain the `InitialContext`.

Listing 15-5 contains `RequestResearch.java`, the code for the implementation class.

Pay special interest below in the `getResearchFromDataManager()` method, where the `RequestDataManagerLocalHome` reference is obtained through a normal casting operation on the object it obtains via the JNDI lookup. When obtaining a reference to a remote interface, it's necessary to invoke `javax.rmi.PortableRemoteObject.narrow` on the object obtained through JNDI, which is less efficient than simply casting.

Listing 15-5: **RequestResearch.java**

```
package request;

import java.rmi.*;
import javax.ejb.*;
import java.util.*;
import javax.naming.*;

public class RequestResearch implements SessionBean {
  //Implemented create method required by RequestResearchHome.
  public void ejbCreate() {
  }

  //Implemented methods required by SessionBean.
  private SessionContext sessionContext;
  public void ejbRemove() throws RemoteException {
  }
  public void ejbActivate() throws RemoteException {
  }
  public void ejbPassivate() throws RemoteException {
  }
  public void setSessionContext(
```

Continued

Listing 15-5 (continued)

```
    SessionContext sessionContext) throws RemoteException {
    this.sessionContext = sessionContext;
  }

  //Methods for processing requests for research as required
  //for the RequestResearchRemote interface.
  /**
   * Fetches and returns research for a security.
   */
  public String requestResearch(String symbol)
  throws RemoteException {
    //CheckEnvironment flag here to see whether to route
    // the call to the internal system.
    String research = null;

    if (this.useRequestDataManager()) {
      System.out.println("Locally calling RequestDataManager
for research.");
      research = getResearchFromDataManager(symbol);
    }
    else {
      System.out.println("Randomly generating research for this
symbol.");
      research = createRandomResearch(symbol);
    }
    return research;
  }

  /**
   * Randomly creates 'research' for this security.
   */
  private String createRandomResearch(String symbol) {
    Random rand = new Random();
    int x = rand.nextInt();
    x = x % 3;
    String research = null;
    switch(x) {
      case 0:
        research = "Zeetrade recommends you buy "+ symbol;
        break;
      case 1:
        research = "Zeetrade recommends you hold "+ symbol;
        break;
      default:
        research = "Zeetrade recommends you sell "+ symbol;
        break;
    }
    return research;
```

```
  }

  /**
   * Does an environment entry lookup to determine where or not
to use
   * the DataManager or randomly generate data here. This field
can be edited in
   * the ejb-jar.xml before EJB deployment.
   */
  private boolean useRequestDataManager() {
    System.out.println("Checking the env-entry for
useRequestDataManager");
    InitialContext ctx = null;
    boolean useManager = false;

    try {
      //Because Request Research is a bean living in the EJB
container,
      //no need to specify server parameters to obtain the
correct context.
      ctx = new InitialContext();
      Boolean useManagerBool =
(Boolean)ctx.lookup("java:comp/env/useRequestDataManager");
      useManager = useManagerBool.booleanValue();
    } catch (Exception e) {
      e.printStackTrace();
    } finally {
      try {
        ctx.close();
      } catch (Exception e) {}
    }
    return useManager;
  }

  /**
   * Calls local EJB RequestDataManager to get research.
   */
  private String getResearchFromDataManager(String symbol) {
    InitialContext ctx = null;
    StringBuffer sb = new StringBuffer();

    try {
    //Because Request Research is a bean living in the EJB
container,
    //no need to specify server parameters to obtain the
correct context.
    ctx = new InitialContext();
    Object objref = ctx.lookup("RequestDataManager");

    //No need to do narrow, simply cast as this is a local
object to this JVM.
```

Continued

Listing 15-5 *(continued)*

```
    RequestDataManagerLocalHome home =
(RequestDataManagerLocalHome)objref;

    RequestDataManagerLocal dataBean = home.create();

    sb.append("**Data Retreived from the local datasource**");
    //Call the dataBean, this is not pass by value as in RMI
(Remote
    //beans included) Instead the stringbuffer is passed by
reference,
    // and therefore when the local session EJB
RequestDataManager
    //appends to it, the appends are altering this buffer (sb).
    dataBean.appendResearchData(sb, symbol);

    } catch (Exception e) {
      e.printStackTrace();
    } finally {
      try {
        ctx.close();
      } catch (Exception e) {}
    }

    return sb.toString();
  }
}
```

RequestDataManager implementation

Listing 15-6 is the implementation of the local helper bean. It's similar to the previous implementation in that it defines methods in its home interface and also implements nearly empty methods to fulfill its `SessionBean` interface requirements. It defines two business methods, `getResearchData()` and `appendResearchData()`. Both simply call the private method `checkResearchDatasource()`, which checks a hard-coded list of securities. This example could be extended to do a symbol lookup on an external data-source like a database. Note how in `appendResearchData()` the results are returned through the client by appending to a `StringBuffer` the client provides as a parameter, thus showing that parameters are passed by reference when invoking methods on local EJBs.

Listing 15-6: RequestDataManager.java

```
package request;

import javax.ejb.*;
```

```
import java.util.*;

public class RequestDataManager implements SessionBean {
  private SessionContext sessionContext;
  public void ejbCreate() {
  }
  public void ejbRemove() {
  }
  public void ejbActivate() {
  }
  public void ejbPassivate() {
  }
  public void setSessionContext(SessionContext sessionContext)
{
    this.sessionContext = sessionContext;
  }

  /**
   * Returns research data about a particular security.
   */
   public String getResearchData(String symbol) {
     return checkResearchDatasource(symbol);
   }

  /**
   * Appends research data about a particular security to this
buffer.
   */
   public void appendResearchData(StringBuffer buffer, String
symbol) {
     buffer.append(checkResearchDatasource(symbol));
   }

  /**
   * Checks a hard-coded list of securities for a match and
returns recommendations.
   * This has been kept simple for the sake of the example, but
potentially
   * could be doing a database lookup here.
   */
  private String checkResearchDatasource(String symbol) {
    if(symbol.equals("BEAS"))
      return "(Zeeware Internal System Lookup) BEAS is rated at
a Strong Buy";
    else if(symbol.equals("YHOO"))
      return "(Zeeware Internal System Lookup) YHOO is rated at
a Buy";

    return "(Zeeware Internal System Lookup Failed) No research
available for security: "+ symbol;
  }
}
```

Session EJB deployment descriptors

Because the deployment descriptors for session beans are the same deployment descriptors used by entity beans, you should review the previous chapter for an overview of weblogic-ejb-jar.xml and ejb-jar.xml. Here I'll discuss a few of the deployment descriptors important to deploying session beans in WebLogic, and look at the two deployment descriptors for the two session beans.

ejb-jar.xml

Both beans declare a <session-type> with value stateless as they are stateless session EJBs. Note that you're declaring a Boolean environment entry useRequestDataManager in the RequestResearch deployment descriptor. This flag tells RequestResearch whether or not to use the data manager bean. Also of note is that RequestResearch declares <home> and <remote> tags whereas the local EJB RequestDataManager has <local-home> and <local> tags.

Notice that an environment entry has been declared in the RequestResearch descriptor marked by the <env-entry> flag. The entry type is defined by the <env-entry-type> tag, and must be a fully qualified object relating to the eight Java primitives. In the sample application (see Listing 15-7), the RequestResearch EJB uses the entry useRequestDataManager to decide whether or not to route a method call to the local helper EJB, RequestDataManager.

Listing 15-7: ejb-jar.xml

```
<!DOCTYPE ejb-jar PUBLIC '-//Sun Microsystems, Inc.//DTD
Enterprise JavaBeans 2.0//EN' 'http://java.sun.com/dtd/
ejb-jar_2_0.dtd'>

<ejb-jar>
  <enterprise-beans>
    <session>
      <ejb-name>RequestResearch</ejb-name>
      <home>request.RequestResearchHome</home>
      <remote>request.RequestResearchRemote</remote>
      <ejb-class>request.RequestResearch</ejb-class>
      <session-type>Stateless</session-type>
      <transaction-type>Container</transaction-type>
      <env-entry>
        <env-entry-name>
          useRequestDataManager
        </env-entry-name>
        <env-entry-type>java.lang.Boolean</env-entry-type>
        <env-entry-value>true</env-entry-value>
      </env-entry>
    </session>
    <session>
      <ejb-name>RequestDataManager</ejb-name>
      <local-home>
        request.RequestDataManagerLocalHome
```

```
      </local-home>
      <local>request.RequestDataManagerLocal</local>
      <ejb-class>request.RequestDataManager</ejb-class>
      <session-type>Stateless</session-type>
      <transaction-type>Container</transaction-type>
    </session>
  </enterprise-beans>

  <assembly-descriptor>
    <container-transaction>
      <method>
        <ejb-name>RequestResearch</ejb-name>
        <method-name>*</method-name>
      </method>
      <method>
        <ejb-name>RequestDataManager</ejb-name>
        <method-name>*</method-name>
      </method>
      <trans-attribute>Required</trans-attribute>
    </container-transaction>
  </assembly-descriptor>
</ejb-jar>
```

weblogic-ejb-jar.xml

This is the WebLogic-specific deployment descriptor. Table 15-1 shows some of the more important properties relating to session EJBs. For a complete list, see the WebLogic documentation.

Table 15-1
Session EJB Properties

Property	*Description*	*Default Value*
allow-concurrent-calls	If this is set to `true`, the WebLogic Server will not throw `RemoteExceptions` when a client tries to make concurrent calls to the EJB, instead blocking the second call until the first has completed.	FALSE
idle-timeout-seconds	The maximum amount of time a stateful EJB should stay in the cache.	600s
initial-beans-in-free-pool	Amount of stateless beans in the free pool on initialization.	0
max-beans-in-cache	The maximum number of stateful bean instances allowed in memory.	100
max-beans-in-free-pool	Maximum number of stateless session beans allowed in the pool.	max Int

See Chapter 14 for a more detailed look at this deployment descriptor.

Note that the `RequestResearch` EJB declares a `<jndi-name>` tag while `RequestDataManager` uses a `<local-jndi-name>` tag (see Listing 15-8).

Listing 15-8: weblogic-ejb-jar.xml

```
<!DOCTYPE weblogic-ejb-jar PUBLIC '-//BEA Systems, Inc.//DTD
WebLogic 6.0.0 EJB//EN'
'http://www.bea.com/servers/wls600/dtd/weblogic-ejb-jar.dtd'>

<weblogic-ejb-jar>
  <weblogic-enterprise-bean>
    <ejb-name>RequestResearch</ejb-name>
    <stateless-session-descriptor>
      <pool>
        <max-beans-in-free-pool>1000</max-beans-in-free-pool>
        <initial-beans-in-free-pool>
          0
        </initial-beans-in-free-pool>
      </pool>

      <stateless-clustering>
        <stateless-bean-is-clusterable>
          True
        </stateless-bean-is-clusterable>
        <stateless-bean-methods-are-idempotent>
          False
        </stateless-bean-methods-are-idempotent>
      </stateless-clustering>

    </stateless-session-descriptor>

    <transaction-descriptor>
      <trans-timeout-seconds>0</trans-timeout-seconds>
    </transaction-descriptor>

    <enable-call-by-reference>True</enable-call-by-reference>
    <jndi-name>RequestResearch</jndi-name>
  </weblogic-enterprise-bean>

  <weblogic-enterprise-bean>
    <ejb-name>RequestDataManager</ejb-name>
    <stateless-session-descriptor>
      <pool>
        <max-beans-in-free-pool>1000</max-beans-in-free-pool>
        <initial-beans-in-free-pool>
          0
        </initial-beans-in-free-pool>
      </pool>
```

```
        <stateless-clustering>
          <stateless-bean-is-clusterable>
            True
          </stateless-bean-is-clusterable>
          <stateless-bean-methods-are-idempotent>
            False
          </stateless-bean-methods-are-idempotent>
        </stateless-clustering>

      </stateless-session-descriptor>

      <transaction-descriptor>
        <trans-timeout-seconds>0</trans-timeout-seconds>
      </transaction-descriptor>

      <enable-call-by-reference>True</enable-call-by-reference>
      <local-jndi-name>RequestDataManager</local-jndi-name>
    </weblogic-enterprise-bean>
  </weblogic-ejb-jar>
```

Client example – Using RequestResearch EJB

The client will periodically obtain a reference to a `RequestResearch` session EJB, ask it about a couple securities, and dump those results to standard out. Because the simple client will be running in its own Java Virtual Machine (JVM), it will need to do a little more work to access the proper `InitialContext`. The `Environment` class is used to accomplish `InitialContext` lookup. The `Environment` class makes assumptions about your WebLogic configuration, including listening ports and URL. You may need to edit this file to match your exact configuration.

The client extends `TimerTask` and implements the `Runnable` interface so that it will continue to poll the WebLogic Server over time.

Because the client code shown in Listing 15-9 is running outside the server, the client code must obtain a reference to the `RequestResearchHome` by using `javax.rmi.PortableRemoteObject.narrow()`, instead of simply casting..

Listing 15-9: **ResearchClient.java**

```
package request;

import java.rmi.*;
import java.util.*;
import javax.naming.*;

/**
```

Continued

Listing 15-9 *(continued)*

```
 * ResearchClient periodically asks server for research.
 */
public class ResearchClient extends TimerTask implements
Runnable {

  private Random rand = new Random();
  private String[] securities = null;

  /**
   * Initializes an InitialContext, gets a reference to a
remote EJB on the server,
   * and asks that EJB for research.
   */
  public void run() {
    System.out.println("ResearchClient calling remote EJB.");
    System.out.println(" Time: "+ new
Date(System.currentTimeMillis()));

    try {
      InitialContext ctx = Environment.getInitialContext();

      Object objref = ctx.lookup("RequestResearch");
      RequestResearchHome home = (RequestResearchHome)
javax.rmi.PortableRemoteObject.narrow(objref,
RequestResearchHome.class);

      RequestResearchRemote requestResearchBean =
home.create();

      StringBuffer sb = new StringBuffer();

sb.append(requestResearchBean.requestResearch("YHOO")+"\n");

sb.append(requestResearchBean.requestResearch("BEAS")+"\n");

sb.append(requestResearchBean.requestResearch("WAG")+"\n");

      System.out.println(sb.toString());
    }
    catch(Exception e) {
      e.printStackTrace();
    }
  }

  /**
   * Declare a new client and schedule it on a timer.
   */
  public static void main(String [] args) {
    Timer t = new Timer();
    ResearchClient client = new ResearchClient();
```

```
      //Starting in 5 secs, run every 5 seconds.
      t.schedule(client, 5000, 5000);
    }
  }
```

Because the simple client will be running in its own Java Virtual Machine(JVM), it will need to do a little more work to access the InitialContext. This Environment class has a static method getInitialContext, which returns a InitialContext. The Environment class makes assumptions about your WebLogic configuration, including listening ports and URL. You may need to edit this file shown in Listing 15-10 to match your exact WebLogic Server configuration.

Listing 15-10: **Environment.java**

```
package request;

import javax.naming.*;
import java.util.*;

public class Environment {

  public final static String
JNDI_FACTORY="weblogic.jndi.WLInitialContextFactory";
  public final static String WEBLOGIC_URL =
"t3://localhost:7001";

  public static InitialContext getInitialContext()
   throws NamingException {

    Hashtable env = new Hashtable();
    env.put(Context.INITIAL_CONTEXT_FACTORY, JNDI_FACTORY);
    env.put(Context.PROVIDER_URL, WEBLOGIC_URL);
    return new InitialContext(env);
  }
}
```

Figure 15-4 shows how the components of the application work together. The research client, running in its own JVM, accesses a RequestResearch EJB via the RequestResearchRemote remote interface. Client method invocations on RequestResearchRemote are proxied to a pool of RequestResearch EJB instances by the Weblogic Server. The RequestResearch EJB then acts as a client and accesses a RequestDataManager EJB through RequestDataManager's local interface. Method invocations on the local interface are again proxied to a pool of RequestDataManager instances. Non-remote invocations are possible because all EJB instances in this example live within the same JVM.

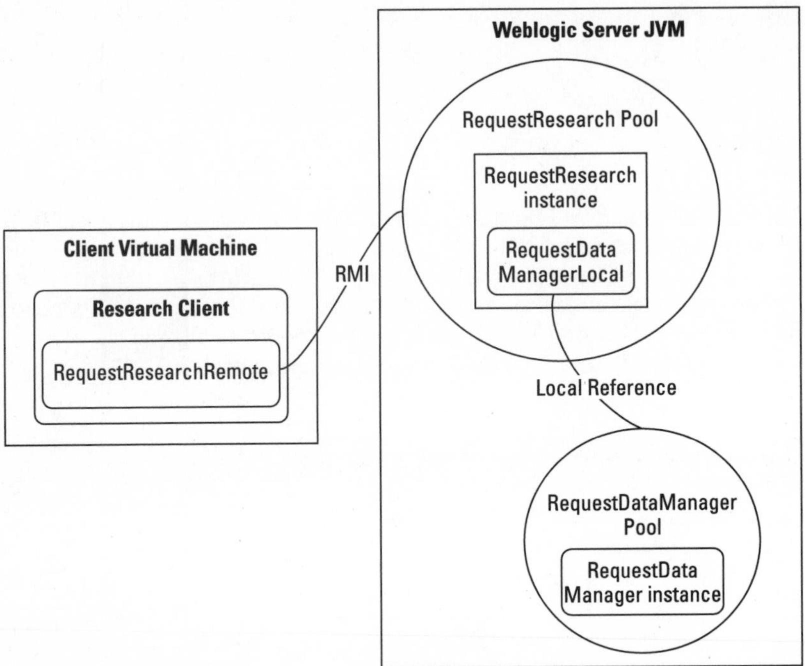

Figure 15-4: RequestResearch design diagram

Build, deploy, and run RequestResearch example

Now let's build and deploy the EJBs to the WebLogic Server, and run the client.

Create the EJB JAR file

First, you must build the JAR file to deploy to the server (see Figure 15-5). This JAR file will contain all the EJB components for the two beans.

```
C:\WINNT\System32\cmd.exe

C:\statelessexample>jar -cvf RequestBeans.jar *
added manifest
ignoring entry META-INF/
adding: META-INF/ejb-jar.xml(in = 1462) (out= 445)(deflated 69%)
ignoring entry META-INF/MANIFEST.MF
adding: META-INF/weblogic-ejb-jar.xml(in = 1762) (out= 418)(deflated 76%)
adding: request/(in = 0) (out= 0)(stored 0%)
adding: request/Environment.class(in = 1016) (out= 603)(deflated 40%)
adding: request/RequestDataManager.class(in = 1779) (out= 793)(deflated 55%)
adding: request/RequestDataManagerLocal.class(in = 311) (out= 190)(deflated 38%)

adding: request/RequestDataManagerLocalHome.class(in = 282) (out= 187)(deflated
33%)
adding: request/RequestResearch.class(in = 3646) (out= 1752)(deflated 51%)
adding: request/RequestResearchHome.class(in = 291) (out= 200)(deflated 31%)
adding: request/RequestResearchRemote.class(in = 278) (out= 184)(deflated 33%)
adding: request/ResearchClient.class(in = 2968) (out= 1478)(deflated 50%)
```

Figure 15-5: Building the EJB JAR file

Deploy the beans to the WebLogic Server

Create a new `EJBComponent` and deploy it to the server, as shown in Figure 15-6. Don't forget to go to the `Targets` tab and move your WebLogic server into the `Chosen` list for the bean deployment.

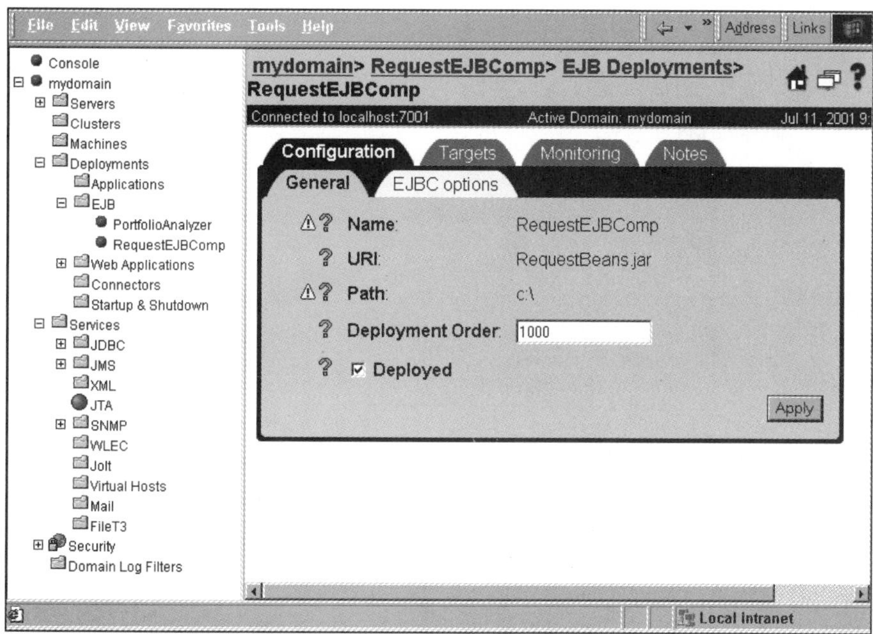

Figure 15-6: EJB deployment

Run the client

Run the client from the command-line, as shown in Figure 15-7. Ensure that you have the `weblogic.jar` in your classpath, as this is required to get access to the JNDI tree.

```
C:\WINNT\System32\cmd.exe

C:\>java -classpath .;RequestBeans.jar;./weblogic.jar request.ResearchClient
ResearchClient running.
 Time: Wed Jul 11 10:11:22 PDT 2001
Zeetrade recommends you sell YHOO
Zeetrade recommends you sell BEAS
Zeetrade recommends you hold WAG

ResearchClient running.
 Time: Wed Jul 11 10:11:27 PDT 2001
Zeetrade recommends you buy YHOO
Zeetrade recommends you buy BEAS
Zeetrade recommends you buy WAG

ResearchClient running.
 Time: Wed Jul 11 10:11:32 PDT 2001
Zeetrade recommends you buy YHOO
Zeetrade recommends you buy BEAS
Zeetrade recommends you buy WAG
```

Figure 15-7: Client running with environment entry set to false, not routing calls to the RequestDataManager EJB

Change the useRequestDataManager env-entry in ejb-jar.xml to true

Change the environment entry that tells the bean to use the local helper bean, `RequestDataManager`. Rebuild your JAR file and redeploy the bean, as shown in Figure 15-8.

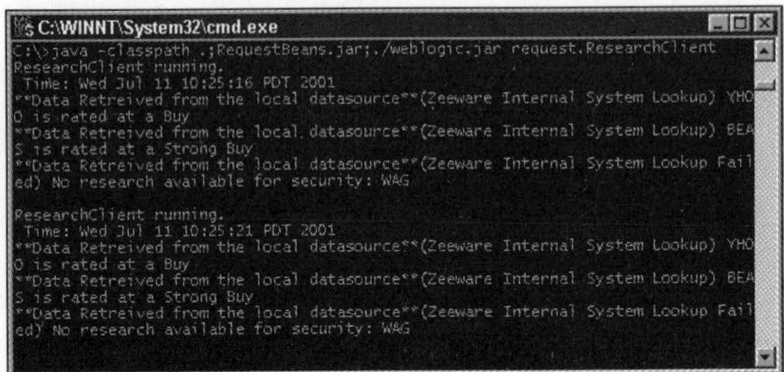

Figure 15-8 Client running with environment entry set to true, routing calls to the RequestDataManager EJB

Stateful EJB example – AnalyzePortfolio

Now that you're familiar with all the components of session beans, let's create a stateful session bean. The `AnalyzePortfolio` bean, whose remote and local interfaces are given in Listings 15-11 and 15-12, is a stateful session bean to which you can pass holdings and debts. As you add to the bean by invoking `addHolding()` and `addDebt()`, the bean will keep track of all client holdings in internal state variables. At any time, a client may ask for a summary of his account, including whether or not he has enough assets to qualify for a gold plan. The minimum assets required to qualify are set in the `ejb-jar.xml` deployment descriptor of the bean.

Listing 15-11: AnalyzePortfolioRemote.java

```
package portfolioanalyzer;

import java.rmi.*;
import javax.ejb.*;

public interface AnalyzePortfolioRemote extends EJBObject {

  /**
   * Adds a holding.
   */
  public void addHolding(String name, Integer amount) throws
RemoteException;

  /**
   * Adds a debt.
   */
```

```
    public void addDebt(String name, Integer amount) throws
  RemoteException;

    /**
     * Returns a detailed analysis of the current state.
     */
    public String getAnalysis() throws RemoteException;

    /**
     * Returns true if they have the financial strength to
  qualify for
     * a gold account.
     */
    public boolean qualifiesForGoldAccount() throws
  RemoteException;
  }
```

Listing 15-12: AnalyzePortfolioHome.java

```
package portfolioanalyzer;

import java.rmi.*;
import javax.ejb.*;

public interface AnalyzePortfolioHome extends EJBHome {
  public AnalyzePortfolioRemote create() throws
RemoteException, CreateException;
}
```

AnalyzePortfolio

Note that in the stateful bean, you now declare some internal variables to maintain state. Note that `java.util.Hashmap`, `Integer`, and `String` all implement `java.io.serializable`, so you're okay for passivation and activation (see Listing 15-13).

Listing 15-13: AnalyzePortfolio.java

```
package portfolioanalyzer;

import java.rmi.*;
import javax.ejb.*;
import java.util.*;

public class AnalyzePortfolio implements SessionBean {
```

Continued

Listing 15-13 *(continued)*

```
  private SessionContext sessionContext;
  public void ejbCreate() {
  }
  public void ejbRemove() throws RemoteException {
  }
  public void ejbActivate() throws RemoteException {
  }
  public void ejbPassivate() throws RemoteException {
  }
  public void setSessionContext(SessionContext sessionContext)
throws RemoteException {
    this.sessionContext = sessionContext;
  }

  //Internal state variables
  private HashMap holdings = new HashMap();
  private HashMap debts = new HashMap();

 /**
   * Adds a holding.
   */
  public void addHolding(String name, Integer amount) throws
RemoteException {
    holdings.put(name, amount);
  }

  /**
   * Adds a debt.
   */
  public void addDebt(String name, Integer amount) throws
RemoteException {
    debts.put(name, amount);
  }

  /**
   * Returns a detailed analysis of the current state.
   */
  public String getAnalysis() throws RemoteException {
    StringBuffer sb = new StringBuffer();
    sb.append("**Current Portfolio Analysis**\n");

    sb.append(analyzeMap("Your Holdings", holdings));
    sb.append(analyzeMap("Your Debts", debts));

    sb.append("  Total Cash Value: " + this.getTotalCash());
    sb.append("Currently qualifies for Zeetrade Gold plan: "
      + this.qualifiesForGoldAccount());

    return sb.toString();
```

```
  }

  /**
   * Returns true if they have the financial strength to
qualify for
   * a gold account.
   */
  public boolean qualifiesForGoldAccount() throws
RemoteException {
    if(this.getGoldAccountMinimum() > this.getTotalCash())
      return false;
    else
      return true;
  }

 /**
   * Checks the deployment descriptor for the minimum amount of
   * total cash is needed to qualify.
   */
  private int getGoldAccountMinimum() {
    InitialContext ctx = null;
    Integer minimum = new Integer(10000); //10000 for default.

    try {
      ctx = new InitialContext();
      minimum =
(Integer)ctx.lookup("java:comp/env/goldAccountMinimum");
    } catch (Exception e) {
      e.printStackTrace();
    } finally {
      try {
        ctx.close();
      } catch (Exception e) {}
    }
    return minimum.intValue();
  }

  private int getTotalCash() {
    return getTotalHoldings() - getTotalDebt();
  }

  private int getTotalHoldings() {
    return calculateTotal(holdings);
  }

  private int getTotalDebt() {
    return calculateTotal(debts);
  }

  private int calculateTotal(HashMap map) {
    Iterator iter = map.values().iterator();
```

Continued

Listing 15-13 *(continued)*

```
    int total = 0;
    Integer tmp = null;
    while(iter.hasNext()) {
      tmp = (Integer)iter.next();
      total += tmp.intValue();
    }
    return total;
  }

  private String analyzeMap(String name, HashMap map) {
    StringBuffer sb = new StringBuffer();
    sb.append("  **" + name + "**\n");
    Iterator iter = map.keySet().iterator();
    String key = null;
    Integer tmpInt = null;
    int total = 0;

    while(iter.hasNext()) {
      key = (String)iter.next();
      tmpInt = (Integer)map.get(key);
      sb.append("    " +key + ": "+ tmpInt.intValue() + "\n");
      total += tmpInt.intValue();
    }
    sb.append("  Total: " + total+ "\n\n");
    return sb.toString();
  }
}
```

ejb-jar.xml

Listing 15-14 shows `ejb-jar.xml` for `AnalyzePortfolio`. Note that the session-type property is now *stateful*. Also take notice of the environment entry where you're setting the minimum portfolio value to qualify for a gold account.

Listing 15-14: ejb-jar.xml

```
<!DOCTYPE ejb-jar PUBLIC '-//Sun Microsystems, Inc.//DTD
Enterprise JavaBeans 2.0//EN' 'http://java.sun.com/dtd/
ejb-jar_2_0.dtd'>

<ejb-jar>
  <enterprise-beans>
    <session>
      <ejb-name>AnalyzePortfolio</ejb-name>
      <home>portfolioanalyzer.AnalyzePortfolioHome</home>
```

```
      <remote>portfolioanalyzer.AnalyzePortfolioRemote</remote>
      <ejb-class>portfolioanalyzer.AnalyzePortfolio</ejb-class>
      <session-type>Stateful</session-type>
      <transaction-type>Container</transaction-type>
      <env-entry>
        <env-entry-name>goldAccountMinimum</env-entry-name>
        <env-entry-type>java.lang.Integer</env-entry-type>
        <env-entry-value>15000</env-entry-value>
      </env-entry>
    </session>
  </enterprise-beans>

  <assembly-descriptor>
    <container-transaction>
      <method>
        <ejb-name>AnalyzePortfolio</ejb-name>
        <method-name>*</method-name>
      </method>
      <trans-attribute>Required</trans-attribute>
    </container-transaction>
  </assembly-descriptor>

</ejb-jar>
```

Listing 15-15 shows `weblogic-ejb-jar.xml` for `AnalyzePortfolio`.

Listing 15-15: weblogic-ejb-jar.xml

```
<!DOCTYPE weblogic-ejb-jar PUBLIC '-//BEA Systems, Inc.//DTD
WebLogic 6.0.0 EJB//EN'
'http://www.bea.com/servers/wls600/dtd/weblogic-ejb-jar.dtd'>

<weblogic-ejb-jar>
  <weblogic-enterprise-bean>
    <ejb-name>AnalyzePortfolio</ejb-name>
    <stateful-session-descriptor>
      <stateful-session-cache>
        <max-beans-in-cache>1000</max-beans-in-cache>
        <idle-timeout-seconds>600</idle-timeout-seconds>
        <cache-type>NRU</cache-type>
      </stateful-session-cache>

      <lifecycle>
        <passivation-strategy>Default</passivation-strategy>
      </lifecycle>

      <stateful-session-clustering>
```

Continued

Listing 15-15 *(continued)*

```
      </stateful-session-clustering>

      <allow-concurrent-calls>False</allow-concurrent-calls>
    </stateful-session-descriptor>

    <transaction-descriptor>
      <trans-timeout-seconds>0</trans-timeout-seconds>
    </transaction-descriptor>

    <enable-call-by-reference>True</enable-call-by-reference>
    <jndi-name>AnalyzePortfolio</jndi-name>
  </weblogic-enterprise-bean>
</weblogic-ejb-jar>
```

PortfolioClient

Notice that the bean maintains state by remembering the holdings and debts passed to it. Additionally, because the stateful EJB is tied to this client and not to a free-pool, it's imperative that you call the `remove()` method on your EJB to free it when you're done with it (see Listing 15-16).

Listing 15-16: PortfolioClient.java

```
package portfolioanalyzer;

import java.rmi.*;
import java.util.*;
import javax.naming.*;

/**
 * ResearchClient periodically asks server for research.
 */
public class PortfolioClient extends TimerTask implements
Runnable {

  public void run() {
   System.out.println("PortfolioClient running:" + new Date());

    try {
      InitialContext ctx = Environment.getInitialContext();

      Object objref = ctx.lookup("AnalyzePortfolio");
```

```
      AnalyzePortfolioHome home = (AnalyzePortfolioHome)
javax.rmi.PortableRemoteObject.narrow(objref,
AnalyzePortfolioHome.class);

      AnalyzePortfolioRemote analyzer = home.create();

      //Add some debts and some holdings.
      analyzer.addHolding("BEAS", new Integer(20000));
      analyzer.addHolding("WAG", new Integer(10000));
      analyzer.addHolding("MSFT", new Integer(150));
      analyzer.addDebt("Car Loan", new Integer(20000));
      analyzer.addDebt("Mortgage", new Integer(30000));

      //Ask for first analysis.
      System.out.println(analyzer.getAnalysis());

      //Add a big holding and ask for second analysis.
      analyzer.addHolding("PETS", new Integer(200000));
      System.out.println(analyzer.getAnalysis());

      analyzer.remove();
    }
    catch(Exception e) {
      e.printStackTrace();
      return ;
    }
  }

  /**
   * Declare a new client and schedule it on a timer.
   */
  public static void main(String [] args) {
    Timer t = new Timer();
    PortfolioClient client = new PortfolioClient();
    //Starting in 5 secs, run every 5 seconds.
    t.schedule(client, 5000, 5000);
  }
}
```

Because the simple client will be running in its own Java Virtual Machine(JVM), it will need to do a little more work to access the `InitialContext`. This `Environment` class has a static method `getInitialContext()`, which returns a `InitialContext`. The `Environment` class makes assumptions about your WebLogic configuration, including listening ports and URL. You may need to edit the file shown in Listing 15-17 to match your exact WebLogic Server configuration.

Listing 15-17: **Environment.java**

```
package portfolioanalyzer;

import javax.naming.*;
import java.util.*;

public class Environment {

  public final static String
JNDI_FACTORY="weblogic.jndi.WLInitialContextFactory";
  public final static String WEBLOGIC_URL =
"t3://localhost:7001";

  public static InitialContext getInitialContext()
   throws NamingException {

    Hashtable env = new Hashtable();
    env.put(Context.INITIAL_CONTEXT_FACTORY, JNDI_FACTORY);
    env.put(Context.PROVIDER_URL, WEBLOGIC_URL);
    return new InitialContext(env);
  }
}
```

Figure 15-9 shows the results of running PortfolioClient. The client makes multiple calls to the stateful session bean `AnalyzePortfolio` and outputs them via standard out. Notice that the EJB remembers the client's portfolio details from previous method invocations.

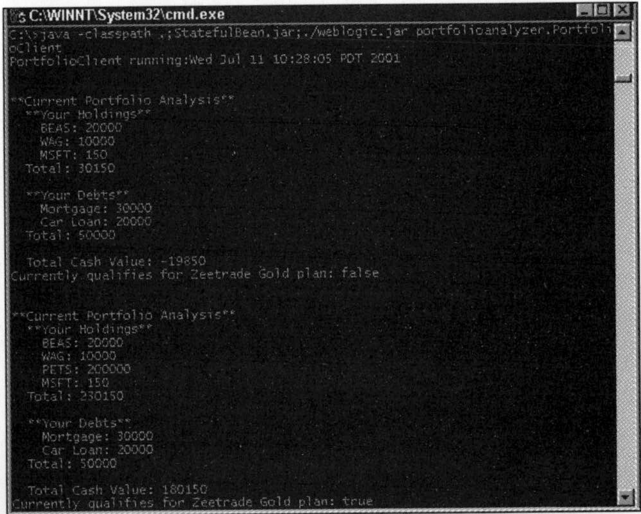

Figure 15-9: Running the PortfolioClient

Clustering Session Beans

The WebLogic Server provides failover services for all stateless session bean method calls, but only if the failure occurs between those method calls. That is, if there is a failure during a method call, that method call will not failover to a replica stateless session bean on another server. This default behavior will prevent potential errors in most systems by ensuring that a failure does not cause a unit of work to be done more than once accidentally. WebLogic does allow you to configure this setting in the `stateless-bean-methods-are-idempotent` property of the `weblogic-ejb-jar.xml` file. If this property is set to `true`, the methods are assumed to be repeat-safe and the WebLogic Server will provide failover when a failure occurs during a method call.

With stateful session EJBs, the WebLogic Server only provides failover for stateful EJB lookups. Unlike stateless session EJBs, there is no failover service for method calls to stateful session EJBs unless those stateful session EJBs have been in-memory replicated to another server.

For more information on in-memory replication for stateful session EJBs, see Chapter 24.

Programming Transactions in Session Beans

If one or more of your beans is used as part of a larger transaction, and you want those beans to be notified of events about that transaction, you can have your session EJBs implement the `javax.ejb.SessionSynronization` interface. Using this interface, you can provide necessary functionality or efficiently allocate/deallocate resources in the context of that external transaction. To implement the interface, you must program the following methods:

`public void afterBegin()`—This method will be called on the bean to notify it that a new transaction has started and that it can expect further method invocations in the context of that transaction. You could use this method to obtain necessary resources during the transaction.

`public void beforeCompletion()`—This method will be called on the bean to notify it that the transaction is about to be committed. You could put logic in this method to push any cached data to a database.

`public void afterCompletion(Boolean committed)`—This method will be called on the bean to notify it the transaction has completed and will pass true if the transaction has successfully completed.

Session beans can also manage transaction demarcation themselves using the `javax.transaction.UserTransaction` interface. For information regarding this interface and transactions, see Chapter 6.

Summary

Session EJBs encapsulate business logic and workflow in your WebLogic applications. They do not represent data like entity beans, but they can manipulate data and interact with entity beans. They are not persisted to disk and will be lost when the EJB container crashes or the server shuts down. From the bean's client perspective, the bean was obtained by creation through the bean's home interface. The client gets a reference to the bean's home interface through a JNDI lookup.

Stateless session beans do not maintain state between a client's method invocations. They are shared in a pool and never assigned to a particular client. They are the most efficient type of EJB.

Stateful session beans maintain a conversational state with a client, but not a transactional state. They cannot be pooled, but the WebLogic Server does maintain a cache to increase efficiency. The server may choose to passivate these beans, which is the process of serializing a bean to disk to free up memory. Upon the next client invocation, the bean can be deserialized from disk and put back into memory during the process of activation.

✦ ✦ ✦

Developing Entity Beans

In This Chapter

Understanding entity beans

EJB 2.0

Entity bean component files

Programming BMP

Programming CMP

Deployment to WebLogic

Advanced WebLogic settings for entity beans

CMP, BMP, and other options

Tools

Session beans represent business processes. Although they can be used to persist data, they do not represent persistent data. This is the role of entity beans, which may be used to represent things such as orders, products, and employees — things that you want to keep track of across sessions and server crashes.

Entity beans are much more complex than session beans, and a full discussion would have to go into the intricacies of object-relational mapping and transactions, among other things. In this chapter, I provide an overview of basic entity bean development and discuss some WebLogic-specific features relating to them.

Unless otherwise noted, this discussion will deal with the WebLogic 6.1 EJB 2.0 implementation.

Understanding Entity Beans

I'll begin by discussing basic entity bean concepts, including persistence, entity bean types, and the entity bean lifecycle within the EJB container.

Entity beans and persistence

Representing and accessing persistent data in an OO system is always a major effort. Some of the approaches include using something like SQL (in the case of relational databases) or a mapping tool, such as an object-relational mapping tool (again in the case of relational databases). Another approach is to use an object-oriented database (OODBMS), which reduces the impedance of trying to map one paradigm to another. Although this approach has much to offer, most OO systems still use relational databases.

Entity beans offer a uniform way to represent persistent objects in Java. The type of storage in which the persistent entities reside does not matter. In the case of container-managed entities (more later), this should make it easier to port from one type of storage to another.

Types of entity beans

Two types of entity beans exist: those with bean-managed persistence (BMP) and those with container-managed persistence (CMP). With BMP entities, the developer codes data access functionality in the bean by using SQL, an O/R mapping tool, or whatever other programmatic tools are available in Java to access the persistent store. With CMP, beans and their attributes are mapped to objects in the persistent store by using deployment descriptors, not code.

Don't confuse bean- and container-managed persistence with bean- and container-managed transactions. Entity beans, whether BMP or CMP, use container-managed transactions.

Entity bean lifecycle

The lifecycle of an entity bean, like all enterprise beans, is controlled by its container. This allows the container to optimize performance and memory-usage through techniques such as reusing pooled objects and passivating objects. Most servers allow a certain amount of configuration of the object pool. WebLogic, for example, allows you to set bean cache sizes and the number of beans to create on startup.

An entity bean instance is first created through a call to `newInstance()`, followed by a call to `setEntityContext()`. It is said to be in the pooled state and is not yet associated with an entity in the persistent store. Thus, you may have an entity bean of type `Employee`, but this bean will not be associated with any specific employee.

Before the bean instance can be useful, it must be associated with a persistent entity, after which it is said to be in the ready state. This can happen in two ways. The first is when a client calls a create method on the home interface. This results in the container picking an entity instance and calling its `ejbCreate()` and `ejbPostCreate()` methods. This results in creation of a new entity in the persistence store, with which the bean instance is associated.

The second way for a bean instance to enter the ready state is if a business method is called on an entity for which no suitable bean instance currently exists. In this case, the container takes an entity instance and calls its `ejbActivate()` method followed by its `ejbLoad()` method. Then it calls the business method.

As an example, suppose that you have configured your Application Server to put three `Employee` bean instances (call them A, B, and C) in the bean pool on startup. They are not associated with actual employees in your database. At this point, the personnel department inputs information on John Smith, who has just joined the company. When the `create()` call comes to the container, it plucks bean instance A from anonymity in the pool and calls its `ejbCreate()` and `ejbPostCreate()` methods. It is now associated with John Smith (or at least his data).

Next, personnel must update data on Sally Johnson, who has just gotten a raise. They do a search that results in a call to a finder method. The finder method itself does not result in the bean being put in the ready state, but when personnel updates the salary, the container chooses bean instance B, calls `ejbActivate()`, and then `ejbLoad()`, followed by the call to the business method, say `setSalary()`. Now A and B are associated with entities in the persistent store, with C in reserve for when another employee needs to be created or have its data updated.

A bean instance in the ready state can transition back to the pooled state if any of three actions take place. First, the container may call `ejbPassivate()`, which disassociates the bean instance from the persistent entity (while maintaining the persistent entity in storage). Second, the container may call `ejbRemove()` as a result of a client `remove()` call, which will remove the entity from persistent storage. Finally, the bean instance may return to the pooled state if the `ejbCreate()`, `ejbPostCreate()`, or `ejbRemove()` method is called from within a transaction that rolls back.

When the instance is back in the pool, the container can assign it to a new persistent entity as before. If it decides it no longer needs the instance, it can remove it from the pool by calling the instance's `unsetEntityContext()` method.

EJB 2.0

This section provides a brief overview of the major features in EJB 2.0 in relation to entity beans.

CMP relationships

The EJB 2.0 spec fills a major void in CMP development with support for relationships. Previously, this could only be done with a nonstandard O/R mapping tool such as TopLink or Cocobase. Now, relationships are specified explicitly in the EJB deployment descriptor (`ejb-jar.xml`). Relationships can be one-to-one, one-to-many, or many-to-many. In addition, relationships can be unidirectional or bidirectional, depending on if only one or both beans have references to one another.

CMP entities in a relationship must be local to each other and access each other through local interfaces (discussed in the next section). WebLogic 6.1 actually supports both local and remote CMP relationships but, according to the documentation, "relationships in CMP that use remote interfaces should probably not be used in new code."

Local interfaces

EJB 2.0 adds local interfaces, originally intended only for session beans, to entity beans. A local interface exposes methods that can only be called from a client residing in the same Java virtual machine (including another bean). Local methods calls are, needless to say, quicker and less resource-intensive than remote methods, which involve network calls.

Local interfaces were extended to entity beans to provide support for relationships, especially between beans and fine-grained objects. Previously, it was not efficient to code fine-grained objects as entity beans. If modeling an order and line items, for example, it was recommended that you implement the line item as an ordinary Java class, not an entity bean. Otherwise, remote calls between remote order and line item beans would generate too much network traffic. The problem then became how to model the line item. One solution was serialization, but then the line item became a monolithic blob in the database, which was not ideal.

Local interfaces solve the problem by lowering the overhead for fine-grained objects. Now, instead of modeling a line item as a regular object, it's recommended that you model it as an entity bean with all the advantages that go with this. Also, because beans with relationships will generally be accessing each other frequently, all entities with relationships must be local to one another and must access each other through each other's local interfaces.

CMP abstract persistence schema

In EJB 1.1, a CMP entity bean class was a concrete class that specified its fields as instance variables. This has changed in 2.0. Now the entity bean class is an abstract class that specifies abstract getter and setter methods for the persistent fields and relationships declared in its EJB deployment descriptor. The container is responsible for generating the concrete class that implements the abstract entity bean class.

EJB QL

EJB 2.0 also features the introduction of EJB Query Language (EJB QL), an SQL-like language for querying entities and related objects. This serves two functions. The first is to specify the expressions the container uses to fulfill finder methods. This takes the place of proprietary finder query languages such as WebLogic Query Language (WLQL), which vendors supplied for lack of a standard facility. EJB QL also enables developers to express query methods, which are used for queries the bean may use internally. These are not exposed to the client.

EJB QL methods take the following form:

```
select_clause from_clause [where_clause]
```

You will see some EJB QL in the example CMP beans.

Entity Bean Component Files

As with session beans, entity beans are composed of both Java classes and deployment descriptors. Chapter 14 explains the various remote, local, and home interfaces that apply to all EJBs. Entity beans have an additional requirement for a *primary key class* and *finder methods* that live in the home interface and return one or more bean instances matching search criteria given by clients.

Every entity bean must have a primary key class. This may be specific to that entity bean type, but doesn't have to be. Any class that is a legal `Value` type in RMI-IIOP will do, and different entity bean types may have the same primary key. The primary key must implement `java.io.Serializable`. A custom primary key class is needed for a compound primary key (consisting of more than one data field), whereas an ordinary Java type such as `String` or `Integer` may be used when the key has only one data field.

A finder method called `findByPrimaryKey()`, which takes a primary key class instance as an input parameter, is also required. This method allows clients to retrieve specific, existing data elements. You can optionally write additional finder methods that return individual bean instances, similar to the `findByPrimaryKey()` method, or collections of instances. You can write any number of finder methods to match the needs of your application.

CMP entity beans also require an additional deployment descriptor: `weblogic-cmp-rdbms-jar.xml`. The name and content of this descriptor depend on the persistence-mapping framework being used, and this can be configured in the WebLogic deployment descriptor.

Programming BMP

In this section, I describe the steps needed to implement a BMP entity bean. As an example, I use a `Student` entity, perhaps part of an online learning system.

Define the home interface

As with session beans, the home interface of an entity bean contains factory methods for obtaining beans. Two types of methods exist: creation methods and finder methods.

Creation methods

Creation Methods take the form

```
public void create(<args>)
  throws CreateException, Remote Exception;
```

where <args> are arguments. As with session beans, the create method corresponds to an ejbCreate() method in the bean class (along with an ejbPostCreate() method to be discussed later). In the example, you have one create method that takes a value object as a parameter.

```
public Student create(StudentVO student)
  throws CreateException, RemoteException;
```

Finder methods

Finder methods are used to retrieve existing objects from persistent storage. They are analogous to database queries. There must always be a finder method called findByPrimaryKey(<arg>), which takes the entity's primary key class as an argument. The example has two custom finders:

```
public Student findBySSNum(String ssNum)
  throws FinderException, RemoteException;

public Collection findByLastName(String lastName)
  throws FinderException, RemoteException;
```

The first returns an instance of the remote interface—in this case an instance of Student. The second finder can potentially return more than one object. In this case, the return type must be specified as a Collection (this has changed since 1.1, when an Enumeration was also allowed).

The complete remote home interface is as follows:

```
package bible.entitybeans.bmp;

import javax.ejb.*;
import java.rmi.RemoteException;
import java.util.Collection;

public interface StudentHome extends EJBHome
{
  public Student create(StudentVO student)
    throws CreateException, RemoteException;

  public Student findByPrimaryKey(StudentPK key)
    throws FinderException, RemoteException;

  public Student findBySSNum(String ssNum)
    throws FinderException, RemoteException;

  public Collection findByLastName(String lastName)
    throws FinderException, RemoteException;
}
```

Define the local home interface

You'll see examples of local home interface in the CMP example, but the `Student` entity does not have one.

Define the remote interface

The entity's remote interface is used to define business methods accessible by remote callers. These can be a variety of things, but as entity beans deal with state, you will usually have getter and setter methods for accessing state.

One way to do this is to have a getter and setter for each attribute. The disadvantage of this is that it can result in many fine-grained calls. Although this is okay for a regular Java object, one must remember that entity beans are remote objects, and remote method calls are expensive. For this reason, value objects are often used to aggregate state and effectively batch remote calls, as explained in Chapter 3. The example bean has both fine-grained methods and value object methods.

The complete remote interface is as follows:

```
package bible.entitybeans.bmp;

import javax.ejb.EJBObject;
import java.rmi.RemoteException;

public interface Student extends EJBObject
{
  public String getFirstName() throws RemoteException;

  public void setFirstName(String firstName)
    throws RemoteException;

  public String getLastName() throws RemoteException;

  public void setLastName(String lastName)
    throws RemoteException;

  public String getEMailAddr() throws RemoteException;

  public void setEMailAddr(String eMailAddr)
    throws RemoteException;

  public String getPhone() throws RemoteException;

  public void setPhone(String phone) throws RemoteException;

  public String getSSNum() throws RemoteException;

  public void setSSNum(String ssNum) throws RemoteException;

  public void setStudentData(StudentVO student)
```

```
    throws RemoteException;

  public StudentVO getStudentData() throws RemoteException;
}
```

Define the local interface

The example bean will not define a local interface, which you will see in the CMP example.

Create the bean

The bean file contains the code to persist entity state. The developer must code both callback methods and any bean business methods.

The ejbCreate() methods

The bean class must contain an `ejbCreate()` method for each `create()` method on the remote interface (the argument list must be the same).

In the `ejbCreate()` method, you typically set bean attributes, and then manually persist the bean. If using SQL, this will involve an `INSERT` statement. As with any `INSERT` statement, all constraints, such as field uniqueness and nullability, must be respected or an exception will by thrown.

The `ejbCreate()` method returns an instance of the entity's primary key class. Note that this differs from the home interface `create()` method, which returns an instance of the remote interface.

The ejbPostCreate() methods

Each `ejbCreate()` method has a corresponding `ejbPostCreate()` method, which is called after the `ejbCreate()`. The `ejbPostCreate()` method differs from `ejbCreate()` in that the entity's object identity is available. This allows a reference to a remote interface instance to be passed during the creation process, as shown in the following code:

```
EntityContext context;
...
public void ejbPostCreate(StudentVO) {
  Student thisStudent = (Student) context.getEJBObject();
  SchoolEJB schoolEJB = getSchoolEJB();
  schoolEJB.addStudent(thisStudent);
}
```

The ejbLoad() method

The `ejbLoad()` method is called to synchronize the bean's state with the persistent store. Generally, it's called whenever a new transaction involving the entity begins, but may be configurable depending on the application server.

When using SQL and JDBC, `ejbLoad()` generally involves executing a `SELECT` statement and setting entity attributes based on the values returned in the `ResultSet`.

The ejbStore() method

This method is called to update the persistent store with the entity's current state. It's generally called at transaction commit, but may be configurable based on the application server. When using SQL, this involves an `UPDATE` statement.

The ejbRemove() method

The `ejbRemove()` method gets called by a client to remove an entity from persistent storage. With SQL, this involves a `DELETE` statement.

Finder methods

Finder methods are used by the container to service calls to the finder methods on the entity's home interface. Each `findBy<someCriteria>(<args>)` in the home interface will have a corresponding `ejbFindBy<someCriteria>(<args>)` with matching parameters. Note that finders returning a single object do not return an instance of the remote interface, but an instance of the primary key. This is used by the container to get the instance of the remote interface that is returned to the client. Finders returning collections are similar — the finder returns a collection of primary key instances that the container uses to return a collection of remote interface instances.

The ejbActivate() and ejbPassivate() methods

These methods serve the same purpose as in stateful session beans. The `ejbActivate()` method should be used to initialize any resources (such as socket connections) needed by the bean before being activated, while `ejbPassivate()` should be used to release these resources on passivation.

Business methods

Business methods correspond to methods in the entity's remote interface. In your case, these are getter and setters for the entity's attributes and for `StudentVO`, its value object.

Note that the `setStudentData()` method does not set the primary key field (ID). According to the EJB 2.0 spec, the primary key field should not be reset. This suggests that any field that may change, even if unique, should not be used as a primary key. You may, for example, have a `UserProfile` bean with a `userName` field.

You may require this to be unique, but allow users to change it. If so, you should not use this field as a primary key. One commonly used technique is to have a separate field whose sole purpose is to serve as a primary key and generate unique primary keys. This is the purpose of the ID field in the `Student` entity.

The complete bean class is given in Listing 16-1.

Listing 16-1: StudentEJB.java

```
package bible.entitybeans.bmp;

import javax.ejb.*;
import java.sql.*;
import javax.sql.DataSource;
import javax.naming.InitialContext;
import java.util.Collection;
import java.util.Vector;

public class StudentEJB implements EntityBean
{
  private EntityContext context;
  private static final String DATASOURCE
    = "java:comp/env/jdbc/connectionPool";

  public String id;
  public String firstName;
  public String lastName;
  public String eMailAddr;
  public String phone;
  public String ssNum;


  public void setEntityContext(EntityContext ec) {
    context = ec;
  }

  public void unsetEntityContext() {
    this.context = null;
  }

  public StudentPK ejbCreate(StudentVO student)
      throws CreateException
  {
    this.id = student.getId();
    setStudentData(student);

    Connection con = null;
    PreparedStatement ps = null;
    StudentPK key = null;
    try {
      con = getConnection();
```

```
      ps = con.prepareStatement("insert into STUDENT (ID,
              FIRST_NAME, LAST_NAME, EMAIL_ADDR, PHONE,
              SSNUM) values (?, ?, ?, ?, ?, ?)");
      ps.setString(1, id);
      ps.setString(2, firstName);
      ps.setString(3, lastName);
      ps.setString(4, eMailAddr);
      ps.setString(5, phone);
      ps.setString(6, ssNum);
      int ret = ps.executeUpdate();
      if (ret != 1) {
        throw new CreateException("Create failed");
      }
      key = new StudentPK();
      key.id = id;
      return key;
    }
    catch (Exception e) {
      throw new CreateException(e.getMessage());
    }
    finally {
      cleanup(con, ps);
    }
  }

  public void ejbPostCreate(StudentVO student) {
  }

  public void ejbLoad()
  {
    StudentPK key = (StudentPK)context.getPrimaryKey();

    try {
      readData(key);
    }
    catch(Exception e) {
      throw new EJBException(e.getMessage());
    }
  }

  public void ejbStore()
  {
    Connection con = null;
    PreparedStatement ps = null;
    try {
      con = getConnection();
      StudentPK key =
        (StudentPK)context.getPrimaryKey();

      ps = con.prepareStatement("update STUDENT set
              FIRST_NAME = ?,LAST_NAME = ?,EMAIL_ADDR = ?,
              PHONE = ?,SSNUM = ? where ID = ?");
```

Continued

Listing 16-1 (continued)

```
      ps.setString(1, firstName);
      ps.setString(2, lastName);
      ps.setString(3, eMailAddr);
      ps.setString(4, phone);
      ps.setString(5, ssNum);
      ps.setString(6, key.id);
      int ret = ps.executeUpdate();
      if (ret == 0) {
        throw new EJBException("ejbStore failed");
      }
    }
    catch (Exception e) {
      throw new EJBException(e.getMessage());
    }
    finally {
      cleanup(con, ps);
    }
  }

  public void ejbRemove() throws RemoveException
  {
    Connection con = null;
    PreparedStatement ps = null;
    try {
      con = getConnection();
      StudentPK key =
          (StudentPK) context.getPrimaryKey();

      ps = con.prepareStatement("delete from STUDENT where
               ID=?");
      ps.setString(1, key.id);
      int result = ps.executeUpdate();
      if (result == 0) {
        throw new RemoveException("Remove failed");
      }
    }
    catch (Exception e) {
      throw new RemoveException(e.getMessage());
    }
    finally {
      cleanup(con, ps);
    }
  }

  public void ejbActivate() {
  }

  public void ejbPassivate() {
  }

  public StudentPK ejbFindByPrimaryKey(StudentPK key)
```

```
      throws FinderException
  {
    try {
      readData(key);
      return key;
    }
    catch (Exception e) {
      throw new FinderException(e.getMessage());
    }
  }

  public StudentPK ejbFindBySSNum(String ssNum)
    throws FinderException
  {
    Connection con = null;
    PreparedStatement ps = null;
    try {
      con = getConnection();
      ps = con.prepareStatement("select ID, FIRST_NAME,
               LAST_NAME,EMAIL_ADDR,PHONE,SSNUM from STUDENT
               where SSNUM = ?");
      ps.setString(1, ssNum);
      ResultSet rs = ps.executeQuery();
      if (!rs.next()) {
        throw new FinderException("Record not found");
      }
      else {
        loadAttributes(rs);
      }
      rs.close();
      StudentPK key = new StudentPK();
      key.id = id;
      return key;
    }
    catch (Exception e) {
      throw new EJBException(e.getMessage());
    }
    finally {
      cleanup(con, ps);
    }
  }

public Collection ejbFindByLastName(String lastName)
    throws FinderException
  {
    Connection con = null;
    PreparedStatement ps = null;
    try {
      con = getConnection();
      ps = con.prepareStatement("select ID from STUDENT where
```

Continued

Listing 16-1 *(continued)*

```
                LAST_NAME = ?");
      ps.setString(1, lastName);
      ResultSet rs = ps.executeQuery();
      Vector students = new Vector();
      StudentPK key = null;
      while (rs.next()) {
        key = new StudentPK();
        key.id = rs.getString(1);
        students.addElement(key);
      }
      rs.close();
      return students;
    }
    catch (Exception e) {
      throw new FinderException(e.getMessage());
    }
    finally {
      cleanup(con, ps);
    }
  }

  private void loadAttributes(ResultSet rs)
      throws SQLException
  {
    id = rs.getString(1);
    firstName = rs.getString(2);
    lastName = rs.getString(3);
    eMailAddr = rs.getString(4);
    phone = rs.getString(5);
    ssNum = rs.getString(6);
  }

  private void cleanup(Connection con, PreparedStatement ps)
  {
    try {
      if (ps != null) {
        ps.close();
      }
      if (con != null) {
        con.close();
      }
    }
    catch (Exception e) {
      throw new EJBException (e);
    }
  }

  public StudentVO getStudentData()
  {
```

```
    StudentVO student = new StudentVO();
    student.setFirstName(firstName);
    student.setLastName(lastName);
    student.setPhone(phone);
    student.setEMailAddr(eMailAddr);
    student.setSSNum(ssNum);
    return student;
  }

  public void setStudentData(StudentVO student)
  {
    firstName = student.getFirstName();
    lastName = student.getLastName();
    eMailAddr = student.getEMailAddr();
    phone = student.getPhone();
    ssNum = student.getSSNum();
  }

  public String getFirstName() {
    return(firstName);
  }

  public void setFirstName(String firstName) {
    this.firstName = firstName;
  }

  public String getLastName() {
    return lastName;
  }

  public void setLastName(String lastName) {
    this.lastName = lastName;
  }

  public String getEMailAddr() {
    return eMailAddr;
  }

  public void setEMailAddr(String eMailAddr) {
    this.eMailAddr = eMailAddr;
  }

  public String getPhone() {
    return phone;
  }

  public void setPhone(String phone) {
    this.phone = phone;
  }

  public String getSSNum() {
```

Continued

Listing 16-1 *(continued)*

```
    return ssNum;
  }

  public void setSSNum(String ssNum) {
    this.ssNum = ssNum;
  }

  private Connection getConnection() throws EJBException
  {
    try {
      InitialContext ic = new InitialContext();
      DataSource ds = (DataSource)ic.lookup(DATASOURCE);
      return ds.getConnection();
    }
    catch (Exception e) {
      throw new EJBException(e.getMessage());
    }
  }

  private void readData(StudentPK key) throws
        FinderException, EJBException
  {
    Connection con = null;
    PreparedStatement ps = null;
    try {
      con = getConnection();
      ps = con.prepareStatement("select ID, FIRST_NAME,
              LAST_NAME,EMAIL_ADDR,PHONE,SSNUM from STUDENT
              where ID = ?");
      ps.setString(1, key.id);
      ResultSet rs = ps.executeQuery();
      if (!rs.next()) {
        throw new FinderException("Record not found");
      }
      else {
        loadAttributes(rs);
      }
      rs.close();
    }
    catch (Exception e){
      throw new EJBException(e.getMessage());
    }
    finally {
      cleanup(con, ps);
    }
  }
}
```

Create the primary key class (optional)

Entities must have a primary key class, which is used to find a unique entity. The primary key class may be a special-purpose class (required if the key has multiple fields) or an ordinary Java class such as `String` or `Integer`.

If constructing a specific primary key class, the class must have a public no-argument constructor. The fields in the primary key class must be public and must be some subset of the attributes of the bean (every primary key class field must have the same name as that of a field of the bean).

Though not strictly necessary, the example bean uses a custom primary key class, which is given in Listing 16-2.

Listing 16-2: Student primary key class

```
package bible.entitybeans.bmp;

import java.io.Serializable;

public class StudentPK implements Serializable
{
  public String id;

  public int hashCode() {
    return id.hashCode();
  }

  public boolean equals(Object that)
  {
    if (that == null || !(that instanceof StudentPK))
      return false;

    String otherId = ((StudentPK) that).id;
    return id.equals(otherId);
  }
}
```

Create value object class (optional)

As mentioned, the `Student` class uses a value object to minimize network calls. The value object contains attributes corresponding to the fields of the entity. As the value object is passed over the wire, it must implement `java.io.Serializable`. Listing 16-3 shows a value object implementation for the Student class.

Listing 16-3: Value object for the Student class

```
package bible.entitybeans.bmp;

public class StudentVO implements java.io.Serializable
{
  private String id;
  private String firstName;
  private String lastName;
  private String eMailAddr;
  private String phone;
  private String ssNum;

  public StudentVO() {
  }

  public String getId() {
    return id;
  }

  public void setId(String id) {
    this.id = id;
  }

  public String getFirstName() {
    return firstName;
  }

  public void setFirstName(String firstName) {
    this.firstName = firstName;
  }

  public String getLastName() {
    return lastName;
  }

  public void setLastName(String lastName) {
    this.lastName = lastName;
  }

  public String getEMailAddr() {
    return eMailAddr;
  }

  public void setEMailAddr(String eMailAddr) {
    this.eMailAddr = eMailAddr;
  }

  public String getPhone() {
    return phone;
  }

  public void setPhone(String phone) {
```

```
      this.phone = phone;
    }

    public String getSSNum() {
      return ssNum;
    }

    public void setSSNum(String ssNum) {
      this.ssNum = ssNum;
    }
  }
```

Create the deployment descriptors

As with all EJB, BMP entities have an EJB deployment descriptor. BMP beans developed with WebLogic will also have a WebLogic deployment descriptor. I'll discuss the properties in each relevant to BMP entities.

The EJB deployment descriptor (ejb-jar.xml)

The following sections discuss the properties specific to entity beans.

<persistence-type>

For BMP, this is set to `Bean`

<prim-key-class>

This is the bean's primary key class. In your case, it's the fully qualified class name of the custom class you developed.

<reentrant>

This indicates whether the bean is reentrant or not. Reentrant means that a thread can enter the bean more than once within a method call. In a loopback call, for example, bean A may call bean B, which then calls bean A again.

Whenever possible, loopback calls should be avoided and `<reentrant>` should be set to `false`. This is because it's difficult for containers to distinguish loopback calls from calls from other threads, which are illegal and, as the specification warns, may lead to unpredictable results.

<resource-ref>

The `<resource-ref>` element is not specific to entity beans, but this element is where you specify the `DataSource` for use within the bean. This, in turn, is mapped to a connection factory supplied by the container using container-specific mappings.

The complete EJB deployment descriptor for the Student bean is as follows:

```
<?xml version="1.0"?>

<!DOCTYPE ejb-jar PUBLIC '-//Sun Microsystems, Inc.//DTD
Enterprise JavaBeans 2.0//EN' 'http://java.sun.com/dtd/ejb-
jar_2_0.dtd'>

<ejb-jar>
  <enterprise-beans>
    <entity>
      <ejb-name>Student</ejb-name>
      <home>bible.entitybeans.bmp.StudentHome</home>
      <remote>bible.entitybeans.bmp.Student</remote>
      <ejb-class>bible.entitybeans.bmp.StudentEJB</ejb-class>
      <persistence-type>Bean</persistence-type>
      <prim-key-class>
bible.entitybeans.bmp.StudentPK
      </prim-key-class>
      <reentrant>False</reentrant>
      <resource-ref>
        <res-ref-name>jdbc/connectionPool</res-ref-name>
        <res-type>javax.sql.DataSource</res-type>
        <res-auth>Container</res-auth>
      </resource-ref>
    </entity>
</enterprise-beans>

<assembly-descriptor>
  <container-transaction>
    <method>
      <ejb-name>Student</ejb-name>
      <method-intf>Remote</method-intf>
      <method-name>*</method-name>
    </method>
    <trans-attribute>Required</trans-attribute>
  </container-transaction>
</assembly-descriptor>
</ejb-jar>
```

The WebLogic deployment descriptor (weblogic-jar.xml)

The weblogic-ejb-jar.xml file contains WebLogic-specific deployment settings.

<reference-descriptor>

This element is what WebLogic uses to map a connection pool to the DataSource required by your bean in the EJB deployment descriptor. The <resource-descriptor> corresponds to a <res-ref-name> in the EJB deployment descriptor, whereas the <jndi-name> is used to look up a connection pool set up in a WebLogic Server instance by an administrator.

The complete WebLogic deployment descriptor is as follows:

```
<?xml version="1.0"?>

<!DOCTYPE weblogic-ejb-jar PUBLIC '-//BEA Systems, Inc.//DTD
WebLogic 6.0.0 EJB//EN'
'http://www.bea.com/servers/wls600/dtd/weblogic-ejb-jar.dtd'>
<weblogic-ejb-jar>
  <weblogic-enterprise-bean>
    <ejb-name>Student</ejb-name>
    <reference-descriptor>
      <resource-description>
        <res-ref-name>
          jdbc/connectionPool
        </res-ref-name>
        <jndi-name>
          schoolDbPool
        </jndi-name>
      </resource-description>
    </reference-descriptor>

    <jndi-name>bible.entitybeans.bmp.Student</jndi-name>
  </weblogic-enterprise-bean>
</weblogic-ejb-jar>
```

Database table

To run this example, you need to create a table on your database. You can use the following:

```
CREATE TABLE STUDENT
   (
      ID VARCHAR(50) NOT NULL,
      LAST_NAME VARCHAR(50) NOT NULL,
      FIRST_NAME VARCHAR(50) ,
      EMAIL_ADDR VARCHAR(50) ,
      PHONE VARCHAR(20) ,
      SSNUM VARCHAR(50)
   )
```

In practice, it is a good idea to define indexes on columns used by the finder methods in your EJBs. In this case, you (or your DBA) would create indexes on `ID`, `LAST_NAME`, and `SSNUM` to improve the performance of the EJB's finder methods.

Notes

In the example, you used straight SQL to persist your entity to a relational database. If using another type of persistent store, you would use whatever persistent layer that store had available in Java. Also, an RBDMS does not limit you to SQL. Within your BMP entity, you can also use any technique available to a regular Java program, such as SQLJ or an O/R mapping tool.

Programming CMP

In this section, you find out about programming CMP beans. As you will see, there is a less coding, but more configuration.

In order to demonstrate relationships (and local interfaces), you will develop two beans: `Department` and `Course`. `Department` will encapsulate information about departments at your online educational institution, whereas `Course` will represent courses offered. `Department` will be in a one-to-many relationship with `Course`. `Course` will not expose a remote interface but will instead use `Department` as a façade for remote access.

I'll discuss the bean classes of `Department` and `Course` separately, and then look at the deployment descriptors.

Create the Department bean

For the Department bean, I will implement remote home and remote interfaces, local home and local interfaces, and an abstract bean class. I will also write a value object (optional) for the bean.

Define the remote home interface

Your remote home interface will have a `create` method that takes a value object. In addition, it will have two custom finder methods, `findAll()` which returns a collection, and `findByName()`, which returns the bean's remote interface.

The remote interface is as follows:

```
package bible.entitybeans.cmp;

import java.util.Collection;
import java.rmi.RemoteException;
import javax.ejb.CreateException;
import javax.ejb.EJBHome;
import javax.ejb.FinderException;

public interface DepartmentRemoteHome extends EJBHome
{

  public DepartmentRemote create(DepartmentVO Department)
    throws CreateException, RemoteException;

  public DepartmentRemote findByPrimaryKey(Integer
      primaryKey) throws FinderException, RemoteException;

  public Collection findAll()
```

```
    throws FinderException, RemoteException;

  public DepartmentRemote findByName(java.lang.String name)
    throws FinderException, RemoteException;
}
```

Define the remote interface

You have dispensed with individual field access methods in this interface and instead will rely on value objects to retrieve and update `Department` fields. This is a design decision, which will depend on your application's needs. You will also allow callers to add courses and retrieve course data from a `Department` through value objects.

The remote interface is as follows:

```
package bible.entitybeans.cmp;

import java.rmi.RemoteException;
import javax.ejb.*;
import javax.naming.*;

public interface DepartmentRemote extends EJBObject
{
  public DepartmentVO getDepartmentData()
    throws RemoteException;

  public void setDepartmentData(DepartmentVO dept)
    throws RemoteException;

  public void addCourse(CourseVO courseData)
    throws NamingException, CreateException, RemoteException;

  public CourseVO[] getAllCourses() throws RemoteException;
}
```

Define the local home interface

According to the EJB 2.0 spec, beans must refer to each other through their local interfaces. Because the `Course` beans will reference `Department` beans, the `Department` bean must have a local and local home interface. The latter must have a `findByPrimaryKey()` method, which is the only method you will need.

The local home interface is as follows:

```
package bible.entitybeans.cmp;

import javax.ejb.*;

public interface DepartmentLocalHome extends EJBLocalHome
```

```
{
  public DepartmentLocal findByPrimaryKey(Integer primaryKey)
    throws FinderException;
}
```

Define the local interface

As noted, this interface exists so that the `Course` bean can reference the `Department` bean. It doesn't have any methods.

The local interface is as follows:

```
package bible.entitybeans.cmp;

import javax.ejb.*;

public interface DepartmentLocal extends EJBLocalObject
{
}
```

Create the abstract bean class

Unlike BMP, the bean developer does not write the actual bean class used by the container. Instead, the developer writes an abstract bean class, for which the container generates a concrete class based on the bean's abstract persistence schema.

Specify abstract methods for persistent fields and relationships

Persistent fields and relationships are not declared in the bean class. Instead, abstract getter and setter methods are declared, which are implemented in the concrete class generated by the container at deployment. The abstract getter and setter methods must be named to correspond to fields specified in the deployment descriptor. In the deployment descriptor, the field name must be lowercase. In the bean class, the method names will be `get` and `set` followed by the field name with the first letter capitalized. The pattern should be familiar — if the field were `name`, for example, the methods would be declared as `getName()` and `setName()`.

The ejbCreate() methods

In your sole `ejbCreate()` method, you call the `setDepartmentData()` method, which uses the abstract set methods (actually only one in our case) to set persistent fields. Note, also, that you're not setting the ID field — you'll see why shortly.

The ejbPostCreate() methods

Nothing is needed here.

Business methods

In addition to a getter and setter, you have two methods relating to `Course`: `addCourse()` and `getAllCourses()`.

The addCourse() finds Course's local home interface through its local JNDI name, which is defined in the WebLogic deployment descriptor.

```
public void addCourse(CourseVO courseData)
    throws NamingException, CreateException
{
  Context ctx = new InitialContext();
  CourseLocalHome courseHome = (CourseLocalHome)
  ctx.lookup("cmp.Course");
  CourseLocal course = courseHome.create(courseData);
      getCourses().add(course);
}
```

The getAllCourses() method obtains a Collection of Courses by using the getCourses() method, which is abstract in the bean class and implemented in the concrete class generated by the container. It iterates over the returned collection and creates an array of value objects.

```
public CourseVO[] getAllCourses()
{
  Collection courses = getCourses();
  CourseVO[] courseArray = new CourseVO[courses.size()];
  Iterator courseIterator = courses.iterator();
  for (int i=0; courseIterator.hasNext(); i++) {
    CourseLocal course = (CourseLocal) courseIterator.next();
    courseArray[i] = course.getCourseData();
  }

  return courseArray;
}
```

That's it for code. The other methods, ejbLoad, ejbStore, and ejbRemove are left blank and handled by the container. Finder methods will be configured in the EJB deployment descriptor using EJB QL.

The complete bean class is given in Listing 16-4.

Listing 16-4: **DepartmentEJB.javapackage**

```
bible.entitybeans.cmp;

import java.util.*;
import javax.ejb.*;
import javax.naming.*;

abstract public class DepartmentEJB implements EntityBean
```

Continued

Listing 16-4 (continued)

```
{
  private EntityContext ctx;

  public void setEntityContext(EntityContext ctx) {
    this.ctx = ctx;
  }

  public void unsetEntityContext() {
    this.ctx = null;
  }

  abstract public Integer getId();
  abstract public void setId(Integer id);

  abstract public String getName();
  abstract public void setName(String val);

  abstract public Collection getCourses();
  abstract public void setCourses(Collection courses);


  public void ejbActivate() {
  }

  public void ejbPassivate() {
  }

  public void ejbLoad() {
  }

  public void ejbStore() {
  }

  public void ejbRemove() throws RemoveException
  {
  }

  public Integer ejbCreate(DepartmentVO dept)
    throws CreateException
  {
    setDepartmentData(dept);
    return null;
  }

  public void ejbPostCreate(DepartmentVO dept)
    throws CreateException
```

```
    {
    }

    public void addCourse(CourseVO courseData)
        throws NamingException, CreateException
    {
      Context ctx = new InitialContext();
      CourseLocalHome courseHome = (CourseLocalHome)
      ctx.lookup("cmp.Course");
      CourseLocal course = courseHome.create(courseData);
          getCourses().add(course);
    }

    public CourseVO[] getAllCourses()
    {
      Collection courses = getCourses();
      CourseVO[] courseArray = new CourseVO[courses.size()];
      Iterator courseIterator = courses.iterator();
      for (int i=0; courseIterator.hasNext(); i++) {
        CourseLocal course = (CourseLocal)
            courseIterator.next();
        courseArray[i] = course.getCourseData();
      }

      return courseArray;
    }

    public DepartmentVO getDepartmentData()
    {
      DepartmentVO dept = new DepartmentVO(this.getId());
      dept.setName(this.getName());
      return dept;
    }

    public void setDepartmentData(DepartmentVO dept) {
      setName(dept.getName());
    }
  }
```

Create the value object (optional)

The `Department` value object has two constructors: a default constructor and one that takes an `Integer` and sets the ID field. The latter is so that the bean can set the ID when returning `DepartmentVO` objects for existing beans. You don't have a `setId()` method to emphasize the fact that clients will not set the ID field. Client programmers should be made aware of this fact through documentation or other means.

The `Department` value object's value object is given in Listing 16-5.

Listing 16-5: Value object for the Department class

```
public class DepartmentVO implements java.io.Serializable
{
  private Integer id;
  private String name;

  public DepartmentVO() {
  }

  public DepartmentVO(Integer id) {
    this.id = id;
  }

  public Integer getId() {
    return id;
  }

  public void setName(String name) {
    this.name = name;
  }

  public String getName() {
    return name;
  }
}
```

Define the Course bean

For the Course bean, I will implement local home and local interfaces, and an abstract bean class. I will also write a value object (optional) for the bean.

Define the local home interface

Because your `Course` bean is in a relationship, it must be accessible through a local home interface. You will have one `create` method, which takes a value object in addition to the required `findByPrimaryKey`. Both methods return a reference to `Course`'s local interface.

```
package bible.entitybeans.cmp;

import javax.ejb.*;

public interface CourseLocalHome extends EJBLocalHome
```

```
{
  public CourseLocal create(CourseVO course)
    throws CreateException;

  public CourseLocal findByPrimaryKey(Integer primaryKey)
    throws FinderException;
}
```

Define the local interfaces

Your local interface will include methods for accessing `Course` data and establishing the relationship with a `Department` bean.

The local interface is as follows:

```
package bible.entitybeans.cmp;

import javax.ejb.*;

public interface CourseLocal extends EJBLocalObject
{
  public CourseVO getCourseData();
  public void setCourseData(CourseVO course);

  public void setDepartment(DepartmentLocal dept);
  public DepartmentLocal getDepartment();
}
```

Create the abstract bean class

Creating the abstract bean class requires a few simple steps.

Specify abstract methods for persistent fields and relationships

You specify the abstract getters and setters for persistent fields and your reference to `Department`.

The ejbCreate method

As with `Department`, you pass in a value object and let WebLogic set the ID field.

The ejbPostCreate methods

You don't need to do anything special here.

Business methods

There's nothing new here. You have a getter and setter by using value objects.

The complete `Course` bean is given in Listing 16-6.

Listing 16-6: CourseEJB.java

```
package bible.entitybeans.cmp;

import java.io.Serializable;
import java.util.*;

import javax.ejb.*;
import javax.naming.InitialContext;
import javax.naming.NamingException;
import javax.sql.DataSource;

abstract public class CourseEJB implements EntityBean
{
  private EntityContext ctx;

  public void setEntityContext(EntityContext ctx) {
    this.ctx = ctx;
  }

  public void unsetEntityContext() {
    this.ctx = null;
  }

  abstract public Integer getId();
  abstract public void setId(Integer id);

  abstract public String getName();
  abstract public void setName(String name);

  abstract public double getCredits();
  abstract public void setCredits(double credits);

  abstract public void setDepartment(DepartmentLocal dept);
  abstract public DepartmentLocal getDepartment();

  public void ejbActivate() {
  }

  public void ejbPassivate() {
  }

  public void ejbLoad() {
  }

  public void ejbStore() {
  }

  public void ejbRemove()
```

```
    throws RemoveException {
  }

  public Integer ejbCreate(CourseVO course)
    throws CreateException
  {
    setCourseData(course);
    return null;
  }

  public void ejbPostCreate(CourseVO course) {
  }

  public CourseVO getCourseData()
  {
    CourseVO course = new CourseVO(this.getId());
    course.setName(this.getName());
    course.setCredits(this.getCredits());
    return course;
  }

  public void setCourseData(CourseVO course)
  {
    setName(course.getName());
    setCredits(course.getCredits());
  }

}
```

Create the value object (optional)

The `CourseVO` value object, which is similar to the `DepartmentVO` value object, is given in Listing 16-7.

Listing 16-7: Value object for the Course class

```
package bible.entitybeans.cmp;

public class CourseVO implements java.io.Serializable
{
  private Integer id;
  private String name;
  private double credits;
```

Continued

Listing 16-7 (continued)

```
    public CourseVO() {
    }

    public CourseVO(Integer id) {
      this.id = id;
    }

    public Integer getId() {
      return id;
    }

    public void setName(String name) {
      this.name = name;
    }

    public String getName() {
      return name;
    }

    public void setCredits(double credits)   {
      this.credits = credits;
    }

    public double getCredits() {
      return credits;
    }
}
```

Create the deployment descriptors

Our CMP entity beans require three deployment descriptors: `ejb-jar.xml`, `weblogic-ejb-jar.xml`, and `weblogic-cmp-rdbms-jar-.xml`.

ejb-jar.xml

The `ejb-jar.xml file`, or EJB deployment descriptor, has two sections with properties relating specifically to CMP entity beans. The `<enterprise-beans>` section contains an `<entity>` element for each entity bean and describes, among other things, persistent fields and queries. The `<relationships>` section, new in EJB 2.0, describes logical relationships between CMP entities. The `<assembly-descriptor>` section doesn't contain any entity-specific properties. Following is a discussion of elements that pertain to CMP beans.

<entity>

Each entity bean must be declared in an <entity> element, which contains a number of other elements, such as those relating to the classes of the bean and interfaces, persistent fields, and queries.

<local-home>

This element is where you specify the bean's local home interface. It isn't specific to entity beans, but I mention it because you will need to use it if using CMP entities with relationships.

<local>

This element is where you specify the bean's local interface. I mention it for the same reason as the <local-home> interface.

<persistence-type>

For CMP, this is set to `Container`.

<prim-key-class>

As with BMP, this is where the type of the primary key class is specified.

<cmp-version>

This specifies which EJB CMP version this bean uses. Possible values are 1.x and 2.x, with the latter being the default.

<abstract-schema-name>

This element specifies a name for the bean that can be used in EJB QL queries. In the example, the `Department` bean has an abstract schema name of `DepartmentSchema`; the choice of schema name is entirely up to you. The query below demonstrates how the abstract schema name is used.

```
<entity>
...
  <abstract-schema-name>
    DepartmentSchema
  </abstract-schema-name>
...
  <query>
   ...
    <ejb-ql>
      <![CDATA[SELECT OBJECT(d) FROM DepartmentSchema AS d
         WHERE d.name = ?1]]>
    </ejb-ql>
  </query>
...
</entity>
```

<cmp-field>

The complete syntax for the `<cmp-field>` element is

```
<cmp-field><field-name>name</field-name></cmp-field>
```

This element is where persistent entity fields are declared. Field names must begin with a lowercase letter and have corresponding get and set methods within the bean class. For example

```
<cmp-field>
  <field-name>name</field-name>
</cmp-field>
```

will correspond to the following methods within the bean:

```
abstract public String getName();
abstract public void setName(String name);
```

`<cmp-field>` elements may be serializable dependent classes as well as simple attributes.

<primkey-field>

This element specifies which field is the bean's primary key field. It must be a field declared in a `<cmp-field>` element. It is not used if the primary key consists of multiple CMP fields.

<query>

Query elements map EJB QL statements to queries on the bean's home interface and bean select methods. The `<query>` element has two subelements: `<query-method>` and `<ejb-ql>`.

<query-method>

This element has two subelements, `<query-method>` and `<method-name>`, which map the query to a method on the bean's home interface.

<ejb-ql>

This element is where the query's EJB QL statement is specified.

To illustrate a `<query>` element, the home interface method

```
findByName(java.lang.String name)
```

is mapped to an EJB QL statement as follows:

```
<query>
  <query-method>
    <method-name>findByName</method-name>
```

```
    <method-params>
      <method-param>java.lang.String</method-param>
    </method-params>
  </query-method>
  <ejb-ql>
    <![CDATA[SELECT OBJECT(d) FROM DepartmentSchema AS d
         WHERE d.name = ?1]]>
  </ejb-ql>
</query>
```

The EJB QL statement in this case returns all Departments where the name field equals the value of the String passed in to the method.

<relationships>

The <relationships> element is the other major section pertaining to entities and describes the logical relationship between them. The <relationships> section consists of <ejb-relation> elements.

<ejb-relation>

This element describes the relationship between two entity beans. It in turn consists of an optional <ejb-relation-name> element and two <ejb-relationship-role> elements, one to describe each side of the relation.

<ejb-relation-name>

This is the name given to the relation. Although it's optional from the J2EE spec point of view, it is used by WebLogic, which refers to it in its persistence descriptor.

<ejb-relationship-role>

As mentioned, each <ejb-relation> has two <ejb-relationship-role> elements, each describing the relationship from one entity's point of view. This is specified with the <multiplicity> and <relationship-role-source> elements. This element also has optional <ejb-relationship-role-name>, <cascade-delete>, and <cmr-field> elements.

<ejb-relationship-role-name>

As with <ejb-relation-name>, this element is optional from the J2EE spec point of view, but is used by WebLogic to map the relationship in the database.

<multiplicity>

This element specifies the multiplicity of the entity in this <ejb-relationship-role> and can have values of one or many. In the example, Department and Course are in a one-to-many relationship, so the <ejb-relationship-role> describing Department will have a <multiplicity> of one, whereas Course will have a <multiplicity> of many.

<cascade-delete>

This element can be used to specify that any deletes of entities should be cascaded to related entities. It can only be used for beans where the related bean has a multiplicity of one. In the example, `Course` has `<cascade-delete>` set, which is allowable because `Department` has a multiplicity of one.

<relationship-role-source>

This element specifies which entity this `<ejb-relationship-role>` describes. It has an `<ejb-name>` subelement whose value must correspond to an `<ejb-name>` element of an `<entity>` element declared in the `<enterprise-beans>` section.

<cmr-field>

This element specifies what field will store the reference to the other bean in the relationship. Each element listed here will have corresponding abstract getter and setter methods using the same naming pattern as with `<cmp-field>` elements.

The complete EJB deployment descriptor is given in Listing 16-8.

Listing 16-8: ejb-jar.xml

```
<?xml version="1.0"?>
<!DOCTYPE ejb-jar PUBLIC '-//Sun Microsystems, Inc.//DTD
Enterprise JavaBeans 2.0//EN'
'http://java.sun.com/j2ee/dtd/ejb-jar_2_0.dtd'>

<ejb-jar>
  <enterprise-beans>
    <entity>
      <ejb-name>DepartmentEJB</ejb-name>
      <home>bible.entitybeans.cmp.DepartmentRemoteHome</home>
      <remote>bible.entitybeans.cmp.DepartmentRemote</remote>
      <local-home>
        bible.entitybeans.cmp.DepartmentLocalHome
      </local-home>
      <local>bible.entitybeans.cmp.DepartmentLocal</local>
      <ejb-class>
        bible.entitybeans.cmp.DepartmentEJB
      </ejb-class>
      <persistence-type>Container</persistence-type>
      <prim-key-class>java.lang.Integer</prim-key-class>
      <reentrant>False</reentrant>
      <cmp-version>2.x</cmp-version>
      <abstract-schema-name>
        DepartmentSchema
      </abstract-schema-name>
      <cmp-field>
        <field-name>id</field-name>
      </cmp-field>
      <cmp-field>
```

```
        <field-name>name</field-name>
      </cmp-field>
      <primkey-field>id</primkey-field>
      <query>
        <query-method>
          <method-name>findByName</method-name>
          <method-params>
            <method-param>java.lang.String</method-param>
          </method-params>
        </query-method>
        <ejb-ql>
          <![CDATA[SELECT OBJECT(d) FROM DepartmentSchema AS d
            WHERE d.name = ?1]]>
        </ejb-ql>
      </query>
    <query>
      <query-method>
        <method-name>findAll</method-name>
        <method-params>
        </method-params>
      </query-method>
      <ejb-ql>
        <![CDATA[SELECT OBJECT(d) FROM DepartmentSchema AS
            d]]>
      </ejb-ql>
    </query>
  </entity>

  <entity>
    <ejb-name>CourseEJB</ejb-name>
    <local-home>
      bible.entitybeans.cmp.CourseLocalHome
    </local-home>
    <local>bible.entitybeans.cmp.CourseLocal</local>
    <ejb-class>bible.entitybeans.cmp.CourseEJB</ejb-class>
    <persistence-type>Container</persistence-type>
    <prim-key-class>java.lang.Integer</prim-key-class>
    <reentrant>False</reentrant>
    <cmp-version>2.x</cmp-version>
    <abstract-schema-name>CourseSchema</abstract-schema-name>
    <cmp-field>
      <field-name>id</field-name>
    </cmp-field>
    <cmp-field>
      <field-name>name</field-name>
    </cmp-field>
    <cmp-field>
      <field-name>credits</field-name>
    </cmp-field>
    <primkey-field>id</primkey-field>
    </entity>
  </enterprise-beans>
```

Continued

Listing 16-8 *(continued)*

```
<relationships>
  <ejb-relation>
    <ejb-relation-name>
      Department-Course</ejb-relation-name>
    <ejb-relationship-role>
      <ejb-relationship-role-name>
        Department-Has-Courses
      </ejb-relationship-role-name>
      <multiplicity>one</multiplicity>
      <relationship-role-source>
        <ejb-name>DepartmentEJB</ejb-name>
      </relationship-role-source>
      <cmr-field>
        <cmr-field-name>courses</cmr-field-name>
        <cmr-field-type>
          java.util.Collection
        </cmr-field-type>
      </cmr-field>
    </ejb-relationship-role>
    <ejb-relationship-role>
      <ejb-relationship-role-name>
        Course-Has-Department
      </ejb-relationship-role-name>
      <multiplicity>many</multiplicity>
      <cascade-delete/>
      <relationship-role-source>
        <ejb-name>CourseEJB</ejb-name>
      </relationship-role-source>
      <cmr-field>
        <cmr-field-name>department</cmr-field-name>
      </cmr-field>
      </ejb-relationship-role>
  </ejb-relation>
</relationships>

<assembly-descriptor>
  <container-transaction>
  <method>
    <ejb-name>DepartmentEJB</ejb-name>
    <method-name>*</method-name>
  </method>
  <trans-attribute>Required</trans-attribute>
  </container-transaction>
  <container-transaction>
  <method>
    <ejb-name>CourseEJB</ejb-name>
    <method-name>*</method-name>
  </method>
  <trans-attribute>Required</trans-attribute>
```

```
    </container-transaction>
  </assembly-descriptor>
</ejb-jar>
```

weblogic-jar.xml

The WebLogic deployment descriptor allows you to specify the JNDI name for your beans as well as use value-added WebLogic features. Many of these will be discussed in the "Advanced WebLogic Features for Entity Beans" section.

<entity-descriptor>

This section is used to specify options for the entity bean named by the `<ejb-name>` parent element.

<persistence-type>

This element specifies a persistent service that the container can use to persist an entity. I specify WebLogic's (`WebLogic_CMP_RDBMS`), but you can specify others such as DataIntegrator (formerly TopLink) as well.

Multiple `<persistence-type>` elements can be defined. The one actually used is specified in the `<persistence-use>` element. The `<type-identifier>` and `<type-version>` specify the persistent service, whereas the `<type-storage>` element specifies the location of a persistence descriptor used by this persistence service.

<persistence-use>

This element specifies which persistence type to use to persist the entity. Its `<type-identifier>` and `<type-version>` elements must correspond to those of one of the `<persistence-type>` elements.

<local-jndi-name>

Although not specific to entities, I mention this element because entities may need it to obtain a reference to one another's home interface.

The WebLogic deployment descriptor is given in Listing 16-9.

Listing 16-9: weblogic-ejb-jar.xml

```
<?xml version="1.0"?>

<!DOCTYPE weblogic-ejb-jar PUBLIC
'-//BEA Systems, Inc.//DTD WebLogic 6.0.0 EJB//EN'
'http://www.bea.com/servers/wls600/dtd/weblogic-ejb-jar.dtd'>
```

Continued

Listing 16-9 *(continued)*

```
<weblogic-ejb-jar>

  <weblogic-enterprise-bean>
    <ejb-name>DepartmentEJB</ejb-name>
    <entity-descriptor>
      <persistence>
        <persistence-type>
          <type-identifier>
            WebLogic_CMP_RDBMS
          </type-identifier>
          <type-version>6.0</type-version>
          <type-storage>
            META-INF/weblogic-cmp-rdbms-jar.xml
          </type-storage>
        </persistence-type>
        <persistence-use>
          <type-identifier>
            WebLogic_CMP_RDBMS
          </type-identifier>
          <type-version>6.0</type-version>
        </persistence-use>
      </persistence>
    </entity-descriptor>
    <jndi-name>cmp.Department</jndi-name>
    <local-jndi-name>cmp.Department-Local</local-jndi-name>
  </weblogic-enterprise-bean>

  <weblogic-enterprise-bean>
    <ejb-name>CourseEJB</ejb-name>
    <entity-descriptor>
      <persistence>
        <persistence-type>
          <type-identifier>
            WebLogic_CMP_RDBMS
          </type-identifier>
          <type-version>6.0</type-version>
          <type-storage>
            META-INF/weblogic-cmp-rdbms-jar.xml
          </type-storage>
        </persistence-type>
        <persistence-use>
          <type-identifier>
            WebLogic_CMP_RDBMS
          </type-identifier>
          <type-version>6.0</type-version>
        </persistence-use>
      </persistence>
    </entity-descriptor>
```

```
    <local-jndi-name>cmp.Course</local-jndi-name>
  </weblogic-enterprise-bean>
</weblogic-ejb-jar>
```

weblogic-cmp-rdbms-jar-.xml

The EJB deployment descriptor specifies entities' abstract persistence schemas. But it does not specify how entities map to an underlying persistent store. This must be done by the persistence service specified in the WebLogic deployment descriptor. I discuss the descriptor used by WebLogic's default implementation in the following sections.

Like the EJB deployment descriptor, the WebLogic persistence descriptor contains a section dealing with beans and their fields (`<weblogic-rdbms-bean>`) and another dealing with relationships (`<weblogic-rdbms-relation>`).

<weblogic-rdbms-bean>

There is one `<weblogic-rdbms-bean>` element for each CMP bean declared in the EJB deployment descriptor. This element maps the entity to a table and its persistent fields to table columns. It also specifies the database connection pool to use.

<ejb-name>

This element maps the entity to this `<weblogic-rdbms-bean>` description. It must correspond to the `<ejb-name>` of an `<entity>` element in the EJB deployment descriptor.

<data-source-name>

This element specifies which database connection pool to use to persist the bean. It must be a connection pool set up on the WebLogic Server instance used.

<table-name>

This is the name of the database table to which to persist the bean.

<field-map>

This element maps an entity field to a column in the table specified in `<table-name>` through its `<cmp-field>` and `<dbms-column>` subelements. There is one of these elements for each of the entity's persistent fields.

```
<field-map>
  <cmp-field>id</cmp-field>
  <dbms-column>id</dbms-column>
</field-map>
```

<automatic-key-generation>

WebLogic 6.1 includes a useful feature for generating primary keys for CMP entities. You can use this feature by including an `<automatic-key-generation>` element in the `<weblogic-rdbms-bean>` section. There are two types of generation. One involves using native facilities of supported databases, which are Oracle using Oracle sequences or Microsoft SQL Server using its `IDENTITY` column. For more information on using these facilities, consult the WebLogic documentation.

The other method, which can be used with any database, involves setting up a sequence table with a single column and single record that serves as a counter. All entities using this facility will get keys from this field. This is the method your example beans use.

The SQL to create the sequence table is

```
CREATE table_name (SEQUENCE int)
INSERT into table_name VALUES (0)
```

where *`table_name`* is specified by the user.

The `<automatic-key-generation>` setting you use in your example is as follows:

```
<automatic-key-generation>
  <generator-type>NAMED_SEQUENCE_TABLE</generator-type>
  <generator-name>SEQUENCE</generator-name>
  <key-cache-size>10</key-cache-size>
</automatic-key-generation>
```

The `<generator-type>` element can have values of `NAMED_SEQUENCE_TABLE` when using a user-specified table, or `ORACLE` or `SQL-SERVER` if using the native facilities of those databases.

The `<generator-name>` element specifies the name of the sequence table (or the Oracle sequence object if using Oracle).

The `<key-cache-size>` allows WebLogic to cache primary key values so that it doesn't have to call the database every time a new primary key in needed. In your example `<key-cache-size>` is set to 10, so a database call will be needed only after every tenth primary key is requested.

Here are a couple of notes about using automatic primary key generation. Your primary key must be a single field and it must be of type `Integer`. This means that you have about 4 billion unique primary keys shared among all the entities that use this facility. This may not be sufficient for all applications. Also, to get all 4 billion IDs, you should start your counter (in the sequence table) at -2147483648 (the value of `Integer.MIN`), because going from 0 to `Integer.MAX` only gives you half your potential values.

It should be stressed that this facility is specific to WebLogic. If you switch to another Application Server, you will have to find another way to generate your primary keys.

<weblogic-rdbms-relation>

The `<weblogic-rdbms-relation>` section handles persisting bean relationships to the database. In databases, relationships are expressed using foreign keys, so this section specifies what columns in what tables that foreign keys are stored.

<relation-name>

This element maps this WebLogic relation to an `<ejb-relation>` in the EJB deployment descriptor. Its value must be the same as the `<ejb-relation-name>` element of the mapped `<ejb-relation>`.

<weblogic-relationship-role>

This element is used to map any keys needed by the relationships expressed in the EJB deployment descriptor. For each relationship needing a key mapping, there is an element of this type. Specifically, this element's `<relationship-role-name>` value will be the value of an `<ejb-relationship-role>` element's `<ejb-relationship-role-name>` value in the EJB deployment descriptor.

In your example, you have a one-to-many relationship between `Department` and `Course`. In relational tables, a one-to-many relationship is implemented by the many table having a column to store a foreign key to the one table. In your example, `dept_id` in `Course` (the many table) will be a foreign key corresponding to an ID in `Department` (the one table). This mapping is expressed in the `<column-map>` element through the `<foreign-key-column>` and `<key-column>` subelements.

```
<column-map>
  <foreign-key-column>dept_id</foreign-key-column>
  <key-column>id</key-column>
</column-map>
```

Tables 16-1 and 16-2 give an example of how this might look in the database.

Table 16-1
The Department Table within the Database

Id	*name*
1	English
2	Computer Science

Table 16-2
The Course Table within the Database

Id	*dept_id*	*Name*
1	1	Composition
2	1	Creative Writing
3	2	Data Structures

The complete `weblogic-cmp-rdbms-jar.xml` file is given in Listing 16-10.

Listing 16-10: weblogic-cmp-rdbms-jar.xml

```
<!DOCTYPE weblogic-rdbms-jar PUBLIC
 '-//BEA Systems, Inc.//DTD WebLogic 6.0.0 EJB RDBMS
Persistence//EN'
 'http://www.bea.com/servers/wls600/dtd/weblogic-rdbms20-
persistence-600.dtd'>
<weblogic-rdbms-jar>

  <weblogic-rdbms-bean>
    <ejb-name>DepartmentEJB</ejb-name>
    <data-source-name>
      schoolDbPool
    </data-source-name>
    <table-name>department</table-name>
    <field-map>
       <cmp-field>id</cmp-field>
       <dbms-column>id</dbms-column>
    </field-map>
    <field-map>
      <cmp-field>name</cmp-field>
      <dbms-column>name</dbms-column>
    </field-map>

    <automatic-key-generation>
      <generator-type>NAMED_SEQUENCE_TABLE</generator-type>
      <generator-name>SEQUENCE</generator-name>
      <key-cache-size>10</key-cache-size>
    </automatic-key-generation>

  </weblogic-rdbms-bean>

  <weblogic-rdbms-bean>
    <ejb-name>CourseEJB</ejb-name>
    <data-source-name>
      schoolDbPool
```

```
      </data-source-name>
      <table-name>Course</table-name>
      <field-map>
        <cmp-field>name</cmp-field>
        <dbms-column>name</dbms-column>
      </field-map>
      <field-map>
        <cmp-field>id</cmp-field>
        <dbms-column>id</dbms-column>
      </field-map>
      <field-map>
        <cmp-field>credits</cmp-field>
        <dbms-column>credits</dbms-column>
      </field-map>

      <automatic-key-generation>
        <generator-type>NAMED_SEQUENCE_TABLE</generator-type>
        <generator-name>SEQUENCE</generator-name>
        <key-cache-size>10</key-cache-size>
      </automatic-key-generation>
    </weblogic-rdbms-bean>

    <weblogic-rdbms-relation>
      <relation-name>Department-Course</relation-name>
      <weblogic-relationship-role>
        <relationship-role-name>
          Course-Has-Department
        </relationship-role-name>
        <column-map>
          <foreign-key-column>dept_id</foreign-key-column>
          <key-column>id</key-column>
        </column-map>
      </weblogic-relationship-role>
    </weblogic-rdbms-relation>
  </weblogic-rdbms-jar>
```

Deployment to WebLogic

Deployment to WebLogic is much simplified in WebLogic 6.1. You just put the JAR file containing the bean's classes into the applications directory of your application, and then you are done. WebLogic generates all the implementation classes.

With entities, you must also make sure that you have properly set up your connection pool and any tables that you might need.

Before running (deploying) the bean, the database tables to which the bean maps must be created.

DDL for your tables using Cloudscape are as follows:

```
CREATE TABLE DEPARTMENT
  (
    NAME CHAR(50) NOT NULL,
    ID INT NOT NULL
  )

CREATE TABLE COURSE
  (
    CREDITS DECIMAL(2) NOT NULL,
    NAME CHAR(50) NOT NULL,
    DEPT_ID INT ,
    ID INT NOT NULL
  )
```

Advanced WebLogic Features for Entity Beans

This section discusses some advanced features WebLogic offers for entity beans. Most are performance enhancements. For a complete list, see the WebLogic documentation.

Concurrency and locking

By default, WebLogic calls ejbLoad on an entity when a transaction is initiated on that entity, and ejbStore when the transaction commits. This behavior can be modified by using the features discussed in this section.

<concurrency-strategy>

WebLogic offers several ways to optimize concurrency by using the <concurrency-strategy> element. This element has three options: Exclusive, Database, and ReadOnly, which can be set for each entity bean type in the WebLogic deployment descriptor as follows:

```
<weblogic-enterprise-bean>
  <ejb-name>AccountBean</ejb-name>
  <entity-descriptor>
    <entity-cache>
      <concurrency-strategy>ReadOnly</concurrency-strategy>
    </entity-cache>
  </entity-descriptor>
</weblogic-enterprise-bean>
```

Exclusive locking places an exclusive lock on an entity instance until transaction commit, meaning other requests, including read requests, block until transaction completion. This was the default up through 5.1.

Database locking defers locking requests to the underlying datastore. It is the current default and can increase throughput over exclusive locking.

The ReadOnly option can be used in cases where bean clients are only reading, perhaps because updates are performed by an external system. Your system, for example, may have stock quotes streamed from an external system. Bean clients will use this data but will never change it. In this case, it's unnecessary to ever call ejbStore(). You can turn this off by setting your bean's <concurrency-strategy> to ReadOnly. Note that this also requires a transaction-attribute setting of NotSupported.

<read-timeout-seconds>

Setting a bean's concurrency strategy to ReadOnly not only affects calls to ejbStore(), but also to ejbLoad(). The ejbLoad() method only gets called at bean startup, and then at an interval defined in the <read-timeout-seconds> element. In the stock quotes example, you might update quotes every second or few seconds (depending on requirements). For a quote being requested multiple times a second, this could offer a large performance savings.

WebLogic has also introduced a feature called *read-only multicast invalidation*, which can be a more efficient way to update cached data when updates to read-only beans occur infrequently. This involves programmatically calling an invalidate() method on the CachingHome interface, which gets implemented by the concrete class WebLogic generates to implement the home interface of read-only entities.

Calling invalidate() invalidates the read-only entity bean on the local server and, if the bean is clustered, causes a multicast message to be sent out which invalidates copies of the bean on the other servers in the cluster. A call to an invalidated read-only entity causes ejbLoad() to be called on that bean.

The invalidate() method can take an entity's primary key object or Collection of primary keys as parameters. There is also an invalidateAll() method. An example of calling invalidate() is:

```
((CachingHome) home).invalidate(someBeansPrimaryKey)
```

<invalidate-target>

This subelement of the <entity-descriptor> enables you to automatically invalidate a read-only entity when the CMP entity bean in whose descriptor this element appears gets modified.

```
<invalidate-target>
  <ejb-name>SomeReadOnlyEntity</ejb-name>
</invalidation-target
```

<db-is-shared>

This is another way to optimize calls to `ejbLoad()`. By default, WebLogic Server calls `ejbLoad()` at the beginning of each transaction. This is to avoid missing any updates to the database from other database clients (including other WebLogic instances). But if a single (nonclustered) WebLogic instance is the only client updating the database, the data cached in the entity will always be synched with the database, and the calls to `ejbLoad()` will be unnecessary. You can configure this behavior by setting `<db-is-shared>` to `false` (the default is `true`).

<delay-updates-until-end-of-tx>

This property enables you to control the timing of when updates can be read by other transactions. By default, WebLogic only writes data (calls `ejbStore()`) when a transaction commits. But there may be cases where you want to allow other database users to see uncommitted data. If so, you can set this property to `false`, which will cause `ejbStore()` to be called whenever there is an update. The data will not actually be committed after each `ejbStore()` call, only when the transaction commits.

Automatic table creation

WebLogic enables you to specify that tables be automatically created for beans and relationship join tables if they don't already exist. This feature is meant to the used only in development because production tables will probably need more precise table schemas than WebLogic can generate. To turn this feature on, add the following line to the WebLogic persistence deployment descriptor:

```
<create-default-dbms-table>True</create-default-dbms-table>
```

CMP, BMP, and Other Options

I'll briefly discuss trade-offs between BMP and CMP and discuss some other alternatives.

Trade-offs between BMP and CMP

Which should you use BMP or CMP? It depends on what you are doing. Following are some guidelines to help when choosing:

- ✦ BMP may be more efficient if well coded.
- ✦ BMP allows you greater scope for customization, although EJB 2.0 greatly extends what you can do with CMP.

✦ CMP is easier to program and maintain.

✦ CMP is more easily ported because persistence-related functionality is configured, not hard-coded.

Session beans

Entity beans are slower than session beans, and in database-intensive applications, entity beans may not be suitable. One alternative is to put persistence code in session beans. The trade-off here is that, like BMP, you have a lot of code to manage. Using an O/R tool or other persistence-mapping framework can mitigate this.

Java Data Objects

Java Data Objects (JDO) is a new specification from Sun, which seeks to offer developers a standard view of persistent entities in Java, regardless of what type of persistent store those objects reside in. It is similar to O/R mapping frameworks, but allows mapping schemes to different persistent storage types to be plugged in without changing code.

Before local interfaces, a major difference between JDO objects and entity beans was that JDO objects are not remote objects. Many seized on this and were advocating a pattern where session beans provide a façade to allow remote access to JDO objects. With local interfaces, the gap is much less, but JDO proponents argue it is simpler to use.

Third-Party Tools

Tools should be an integral part of EJB development to help ease the burden of the countless configuration details and patterns to which developers must adhere. The spec explicitly acknowledges the role of tools. I discuss some of the major EJB tools with the caveat that most offer little if any EJB 2.0 CMP support at the time of this writing. This probably has something to do with the newness of the spec. The tools' arena is constantly changing, so it's a good idea to check sites like `theServerside.com` and vendor Web sites for new developments.

WebGain Studio

WebGain Studio is a conglomeration of a number of tools including Visual Café, StructureBuilder, and DataIntegrator (formerly TopLink). Visual Café is an IDE that has features to automate creation, configuration, and deployment of EJB. There is a beta version of DataIntegrator with support for EJB 2.0 CMP.

JBuilder

JBuilder is Borland's general purpose Java IDE with features to create, configure, and deploy EJB. It also includes an O/R mapping tool for entity beans, but at the time of this writing no support for EJB 2.0 CMP.

Cocobase Enterprise O/R

Enterprise O/R is a mapping tool from Thought Inc. that enables you to do complex entity bean mappings. Other features include auto-generation of entity beans from database tables and integration with IDEs such as JBuilder. As of this writing, there was no support for EJB 2.0 CMP or WebLogic 6.1.

TogetherSoft Control Center

Control Center is a modeling and code generation tool which allows you to model EJB and their configurations in UML diagrams. It does not currently support EJB 2.0 CMP.

Summary

Entity beans are used to offer an object representation of persistent objects. Two types of entity beans exist: bean-managed (BMP) and container-managed (CMP). BMP entities require the developer to handle bean persistence in code, whereas CMP beans use deployment descriptors that get interpreted by the EJB container. A key benefit of entity beans is that they are transaction-aware. WebLogic offers bean developers a variety of configuration settings to optimize performance. Tools can greatly simplify bean development, but for the most part, they haven't caught up to EJB 2.0.

✦ ✦ ✦

17

CHAPTER

Developing Message-Driven Beans

✦ ✦ ✦ ✦

In This Chapter

Understanding message-driven beans

Programming message-driven beans

Deploying message-driven beans in WebLogic Server

Building an application using message-driven beans and XML

✦ ✦ ✦ ✦

In Chapters 15 and 16, you examined the features of session beans and entity beans. The EJB 2.0 specification introduces *message-driven beans,* which are essentially Java Message Service (JMS) clients that live within the EJB container, benefiting from its component-based architecture and transactional services.

This chapter begins with an introduction to message-driven beans, showing you the advantages of this new technology. It then dives into message-driven bean development and deployment, showing you all the essentials you need to program message-driven beans. Finally, the chapter explores a real-world application of message-driven beans, a B2B application that makes use of XML and a message-driven bean. When you're finished with this chapter, you will have a complete understanding of how to implement message-driven beans, enabling you to build transactional components that are tied into asynchronous messaging.

Message-driven beans rely on the Java Message Service (JMS) to function. Therefore, before beginning this chapter, you should read Chapter 9. The remainder of this chapter assumes you are familiar with the material in Chapter 9.

Understanding Message-Driven Beans

Message-driven beans are a significant addition to the EJB 2.0 specification. They provide a simple, component-based way to process asynchronous messages. Recall that an asynchronous message is a message that does not require an immediate response. But most Web applications respond to requests synchronously. A request, for example, is sent to a servlet, and the servlet immediately returns a response. To send a message to a server that requires no response, you can use JMS. A message-driven bean is an EJB that can consume asynchronous JMS messages, either by listening to a queue or by subscribing to a topic.

Versions and packages

EJB 2.0, released mid-September 2001, is not just an updated version of the EJB specification, but a new release altogether. It's nearly twice as long as the EJB 1.1 specification. The largest changes in the specification are the introduction of message-driven beans, and several changes to container-managed beans (see Chapter 14 for a comparison of EJB 1.1 and 2.0).

As discussed in Chapter 4, WebLogic Server 6.1 ships in two versions: one that supports the EJB 1.1 *and* 2.0 specifications, and one that supports EJB 1.1 only. To use message-driven beans in your application, you must be sure to obtain the WebLogic distribution that supports both versions of the specification.

How message-driven beans differ from other EJBs

Unlike session beans and entity beans, clients cannot directly invoke a message-driven bean's methods. The only way to invoke a message-driven bean is to send it a JMS message. For this reason, there are no home or remote interfaces for message-driven beans, and message-driven beans are always invoked asynchronously. Figure 17-1 shows how client code accesses the different types of EJBs.

Deciding whether to write a message-driven bean or a JMS client

Developers familiar with WebLogic JMS may wonder: When should I write conventional JMS applications, and when should I write message-driven beans?

The answer depends partly on how much control over the environment your application requires, and partly on how much coding you want to do. Conventional WebLogic JMS, for example, provides features such as load balancing and stability, but taking advantage of these features is left up to you, the application developer. This is fine if you need fine-grained control over the JMS infrastructure, transactions, and data access. But if you're simply writing queue listeners and topic subscribers that perform relatively simple processing, you should seriously consider implementing them as message-driven beans. This way, you'll benefit from the EJB container's transparent support for managing the JMS infrastructure, controlling transactions, enforcing security, and managing database access. You'll also be able to make certain changes to your code's runtime behavior, such as changing the target queue or topic, simply by modifying the beans' deployment descriptors.

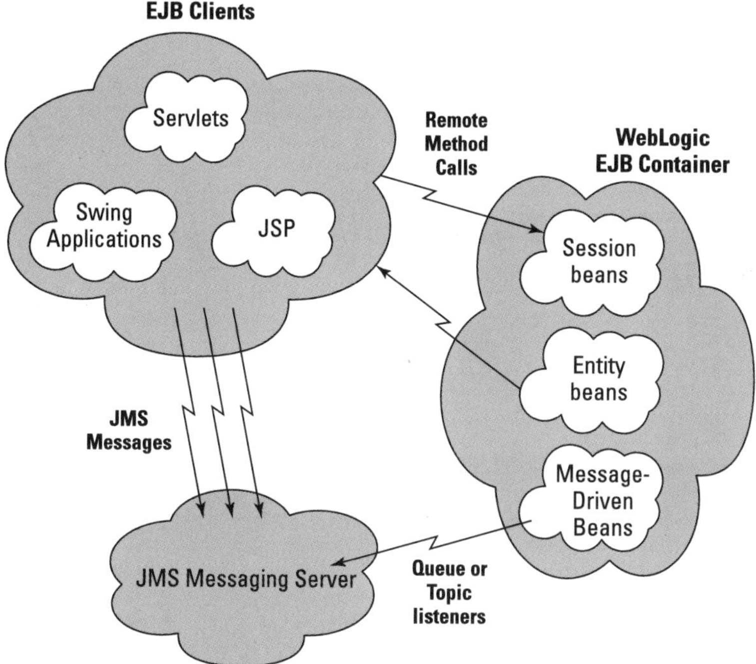

Figure 17-1: Client access to the three types of EJBs

Table 17-1 gives a list of key differences between message-driven beans and JMS clients. Consider these differences before writing your code, so you can be sure to choose the right approach for your project.

Table 17-1
Message Beans versus JMS Clients

Feature	*Message Bean*	*JMS Client*
Transaction support	Built-in transaction support (via the EJB container)	Transaction support must be coded by the developer
Binding	Can bind to only one JMS topic or queue	Can bind to any number of JMS topics or queues
JMS infrastructure management	JMS infrastructure (references to connection factories, sessions, queues, and topics) managed by the EJB container	JMS infrastructure managed by the developer
Runtime JMS behavior	Runtime JMS behavior controlled by deployment descriptors	Runtime JMS behavior controlled by code and WebLogic Console settings

Programming Message-Driven Beans

Now that you have learned some basics about message-driven beans, let's look at them in more detail. Just like entity beans and session beans, there are a few programming constructs you must follow when developing message-driven beans.

The MessageDrivenBean interface – javax.ejb.MessageDrivenBean

Just like entity beans and session beans, message-driven beans require you to implement standard interfaces. The methods defined in the `javax.ejb.MessageDrivenBean` interface are shown in Table 17-2.

Table 17-2
The javax.ejb.MessageDrivenBean Interface

Method Name	*Purpose*
`onMessage (javax.jms.Message messageName )`	This method is called when a message is received by a bean from a topic or queue. Most of the business logic for your bean should be implemented in this method.
`ejbCreate()`	This method is called when the MDB is created by the EJB container.
`ejbRemove()`	This method is called when the MDB is removed from the EJB container.
`setMessageDrivenBeanContext (MessageDrivenContext context`	This method is called before `ejbCreate()`, and is invoked by the EJB container. The `MessageDrivenContext` object describes the environment-specific information for the MDB. If you want to obtain any type of environment- or transaction-specific information in your bean, you should do it in this method by invoking the methods in the context object (this will be explained further in the next section).

The message-driven bean context

When an instance of a message-driven bean is created, the EJB container passes it an instance of the `MessageDrivenContext`. Table 17-3 shows methods for obtaining useful information from this context.

Table 17-3
MessageDrivenContext Methods

Method Name	*Purpose*
`setRollbackOnly()`	If transaction demarcation is container-managed, `setRollbackOnly()` will mark a transaction so that it will not be able to commit.
`getRollbackOnly()`	If the transaction demarcation is container-managed, `getRollbackOnly()` will return a Boolean indicating whether the transaction will be able to be committed.
`getUserTransaction()`	If the transaction demarcation is bean-managed, `getUserTransaction()` will return the User Transaction interface, which can allow the bean to explicitly manage transaction boundaries.

Implementing business logic

Recall that message-driven beans cannot be accessed directly by client code; the only way to trigger the business logic in message-driven beans is to send them JMS messages. Such logic resides in the bean's `onMessage()` method, a simple example of which is given in Listing 17-1.

Listing 17-1: A Simple onMessage() Method

```
public void onMessage(Message incomingMsg) {
  TextMessage msg = null;
  String msgType = null;
  String msgPayload = null;

  try {
    if (incomingMsg instanceof TextMessage) {
      msg = (TextMessage) inMessage;
      msgType = msg.getStringProperty("messageType");
      msgPayload = msg.getText();

      if (msgType.equals("PriceAlert"))
        processAlert(msgPayload);
      else if (msgType.equals("FullQuote"))
        processFullQuote(msgPayload);
    } else {
```

Continued

Listing 17-1 (continued)

```
        log.append("Only accepting text messages");
      }
    } catch (JMSException e) {
      log.append("Exception: " + e.printStackTrace());
    } catch (Throwable te) {
      log.append("Throwable: " + te.printStackTrace());
    }
  }
```

Notice the similarity between this code and the code for asynchronous message listeners discussed in Chapter 9. In fact, the code is functionally identical. A message-driven bean is nothing more than an asynchronous message listener implemented within the EJB container.

It's important to note that if any bean method throws an exception, WLS immediately removes the bean instance from the EJB container without calling `ejbRemove()`, and creates a new one. This behavior may be undesirable for your application, especially if the bean instance must reestablish database connections or perform other time-consuming setup tasks. A more serious problem is that beans removed in this manner don't get a chance to clean up after themselves, which could lead to memory leaks and wasted resources. To prevent these problems, program the bean to catch its own exceptions, so they don't propagate to WebLogic. The code in Listing 17-1 accomplishes this by embedding its logic in a `try-catch` block.

Deploying Message-Driven Beans in WebLogic Server

Before deploying a message-driven bean, you must create its deployment descriptors, then bundle the bean's classes and deployment descriptors into a `jar` file.

Deployment descriptors

Just like entity beans and session beans, message-driven beans use XML-based deployment descriptors. WebLogic requires two deployment descriptors: a JavaSoft-compliant message-driven bean descriptor, and a WebLogic-specific descriptor.

ejb-jar.xml

The JavaSoft deployment descriptor, `ejb-jar.xml`, gives basic information about the message-driven bean's deployment, such as its class name, type of transaction support, and so on. The DTD for the generic message-driven bean descriptor is shown in Listing 17-2.

Listing 17-2: DTD for the Message-Driven Bean's Deployment Descriptor

```
<!ELEMENT message-driven (description?,
 display-name?, small-icon?,
 large-icon?, ejb-name?, ejb-class,
 transaction-type, transaction-scope?,
 jms-message-selector?, jms-acknowledge-
 mode?, message-driven-destination?,
 env-entry*, ejb-ref*, security-
 identity?, resource-ref*, resource-
 env-ref*)>
```

As you can see, the deployment descriptor for a message-driven bean is similar to the entity and session bean deployment descriptors discussed in the last two chapters. One new field is the `message-driven-destination` field, which specifies the type of messaging destination (queue or topic) to which the message-driven bean will be bound. The value of this field should be the fully qualified class name of the destination type; for example, `javax.jms.Queue` or `javax.jms.Topic`.

If a JMS `topic` is specified, a `subscription-durability` tag must also be added. The two values for this field are either `durable` or `nondurable`. See Chapter 9 for more information on durable and nondurable topic subscribers.

Listing 17-3 is an example of a completed deployment descriptor.

Listing 17-3: ejb-jar.xml

```
<!DOCTYPE ejb-jar PUBLIC "-//Sun Microsystems, Inc.//DTD
Enterprise JavaBeans 2.0//EN" "http://java.sun.com/dtd/ejb-
jar_2_0.dtd">
<ejb-jar>
  <enterprise-beans>
    <message-driven>
      <ejb-name>prescriptionConsumer</ejb-name>
      <ejb-class>bible.chapter17.PrescriptionBean</ejb-class>
      <transaction-type>Container</transaction-type>
      <message-driven-destination>
        <destination-type>
          javax.jms.Queue
        </destination-type>
      </message-driven-destination>
    </message-driven>
  </enterprise-beans>
</ejb-jar>
```

weblogic-ejb-jar.xml

The WebLogic-specific deployment descriptor, `weblogic-ejb-jar.xml`, is used to specify WebLogic-specific bean behavior, such as cache pool behavior, the name of the WebLogic JMS queue or topic to which the bean will listen, and so on. To map a message-driven bean to a topic or queue, simply specify the JNDI name of the topic or queue in the bean's WebLogic deployment descriptor. Listing 17-4 shows an example of a WebLogic-specific message bean deployment descriptor. The JMS mapping information is in bold type.

Listing 17-4: weblogic-ejb-jar.xml

```
<?xml version="1.0"?>
<!DOCTYPE weblogic-ejb-jar PUBLIC "-//BEA Systems, Inc.//DTD WebLogic 6.0.0
EJB//EN" "http://www.bea.com/servers/wls600/dtd/weblogic-ejb-jar.dtd">
<weblogic-ejb-jar>
  <weblogic-enterprise-bean>
    <ejb-name>prescriptionConsumer</ejb-name>
    <message-driven-descriptor>
      <pool>
        <max-beans-in-free-pool>50</max-beans-in-free-pool>
        <initial-beans-in-free-pool>10</initial-beans-in-free-pool>
      </pool>
      <destination-jndi-name>PrescriptionQueue</destination-jndi-name>
    </message-driven-descriptor>
    <jndi-name>prescriptionConsumer</jndi-name>
  </weblogic-enterprise-bean>
</weblogic-ejb-jar>
```

Transaction attributes

Like entity and session beans, message-driven beans can either have container-managed transactions or bean-managed transactions. For container-managed transactions, two transaction attributes are supported: `Required` and `NotSupported`. By indicating `Required` as the transaction type, WebLogic Server makes the JMS message receipt "required" as part of the bean's transaction. This transactional attribute is useful to use if the `onMessage` method invokes other enterprise beans. Because the container passes the transaction context with the invocation, the transaction started at the `onMessage` method execution may involve several operations such as accessing a database (via entity bean or JDBC calls), or sending messages (by using a connection factory resource). By indicating `NotSupported`, the message receipt will be "NotSupported" as part of the transaction. This should be used when enterprise beans are not accessed from your `onMessage()` method.

The following assembly descriptor specifies that all methods of the `prescriptionConsumer` bean must be executed within the scope of a transaction. The assembly descriptor appears in `ejb-jar.xml`:

```
<assembly-descriptor>
  <container-transaction>
    <method>
      <ejb-name>prescriptionConsumer</ejb-name>
      <method-name>*</method-name>
    </method>
    <trans-attribute>Required</trans-attribute>
  </container-transaction>
</assembly-descriptor>
```

When using bean-managed transactions, WebLogic server allows message-driven beans to use one of two acknowledge modes: `AUTO_ACKNOWLEDGE` or `DUPS_OK_ACKNOWLEDGE`. See Table 9-1 for a complete listing of JMS non-transacted acknowledge modes. If your message bean was designed to handle duplicate JMS message requests, use the `DUPS_OK_ACKNOWLEDGE` mode. An example of specifying bean-managed transactions in the deployment descriptor is the following:

```
<transaction-type>Bean</transaction-type>
<acknowledge-mode>Auto-acknowledge</acknowledge-mode>
```

Deploying message-driven beans using WebLogic Console

After you successfully compile your message beans, you must deploy them to WebLogic Server. The deployment process has two steps:

1. Create a standard JAR file.
2. Deploy the EJB JAR file to WebLogic Server.

Create a standard JAR file

The first step in this process will be to create a `META-INF` directory in the same directory your compiled message-bean classes are stored. After you create this directory, move the `ejb-jar.xml` and `weblogic-ejb-jar.xml` deployment descriptors into the directory. The command below creates the file, `message-bean.jar`, which you will deploy to WebLogic Server:

```
d:\MYBEANS> jar cvf message-bean.jar *.*
```

Deploy the EJB JAR file to WebLogic Server

The final step in the deployment process is to deploy the EJB JAR file to WebLogic Server. First, open the WebLogic Console and click Deployments%%>EJB. Select the EJB JAR you created in the last step by using the Browse button, and then click Upload. Figure 17-2 shows the appearance of the WebLogic Console after performing these steps. Your message bean will now be deployed to WebLogic Server.

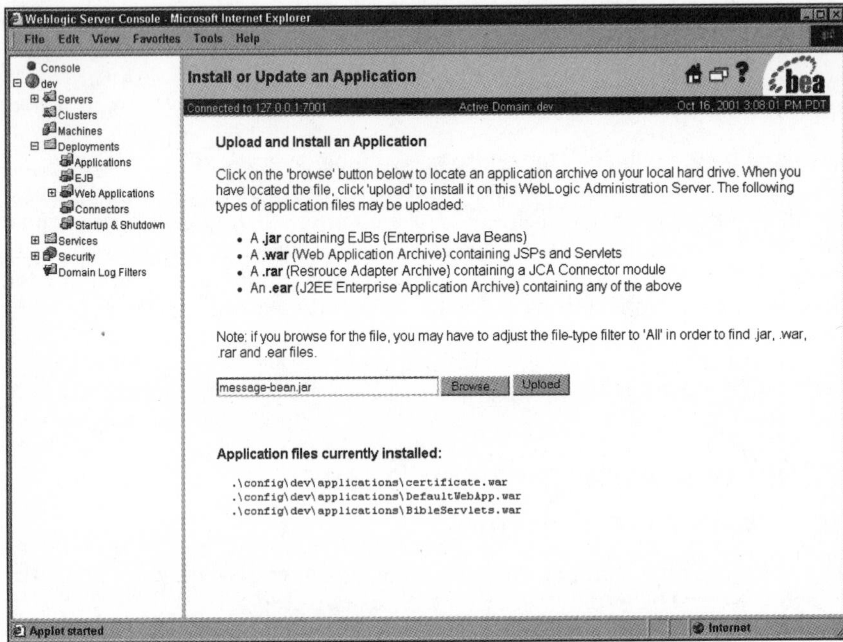

Figure 17-2: Deploying a message bean by using the WebLogic Console

Building an Application Using Message-Driven Beans and XML

Recall that message-driven beans are used exclusively for asynchronous message processing. One application domain that relies heavily on asynchronous messaging is that of wireless services. Therefore, to demonstrate the use of message-driven beans in the real world, I will show how to include them as part of a wireless application solution.

Because current wireless transfer rates are still too unreliable to host mission-critical applications, asynchronous messaging plays an important role in application development for wireless devices. By making use of JMS and message-driven beans, you can design an application with quick response times that can still connect to enterprise resources and business partners.

This example makes use of a number of different J2EE technologies, including servlets, XML, and JMS. If you are unfamiliar with these topics, you may want to review Chapters 9 and 11 through 13 before continuing.

The business problem: Sending medical prescriptions over a wireless network

A physician examining patients is always on the move, whether traveling from one examining room to the next, or, in the case of family practitioners in rural areas, making house calls. Having immediate access to medical history or drug information while writing the prescription is a clear benefit, as is the ability to transmit the prescription immediately to a pharmacy. Finally, writing a prescription requires quick response time, because a physician's time is of the essence. Your challenge is to write a wireless application that caters to the mobile physician's need to quickly and reliably transmit prescriptions to a remote pharmacy.

Application design issues

Processing a prescription on the server side is a rather time-consuming task: It must be logged to a database, and information about the prescription must be sent to various pharmaceutical companies. Because it's possible that these transactions might take 20 to 30 seconds to complete, you must devise a way to handle this processing asynchronously, so you don't keep busy physicians waiting.

Figure 17-3 shows the architecture of a possible solution. The physician uses a palmtop device to write and submit a prescription request, which is transmitted via a radio or cellular network to the Internet. A URL embedded in the prescription request routes it to a servlet running on a designated Web server. The servlet parses the data in the `HttpRequest` object and constructs an XML document from the information. The XML document is then embedded in a `TextMessage` and published to a predefined JMS queue. After this completes, the servlet forwards the `HttpRequest` to a JSP, which renders an acknowledgement message that is returned immediately to the physician.

Although the physician has received acknowledgement of a successful transmission, processing continues asynchronously on the server. A message-driven bean retrieves the `TextMessage` from the queue and processes the XML embedded within it according to the pharmacy's business rules, which may include checking the patient's medical background, routing the prescription to a fulfillment center, and sending a bill to the patient's insurance carrier. The system is designed so that the physician does not have to wait for any of this back-end processing to finish; all he or she is concerned with is that the prescription request was successfully sent and received.

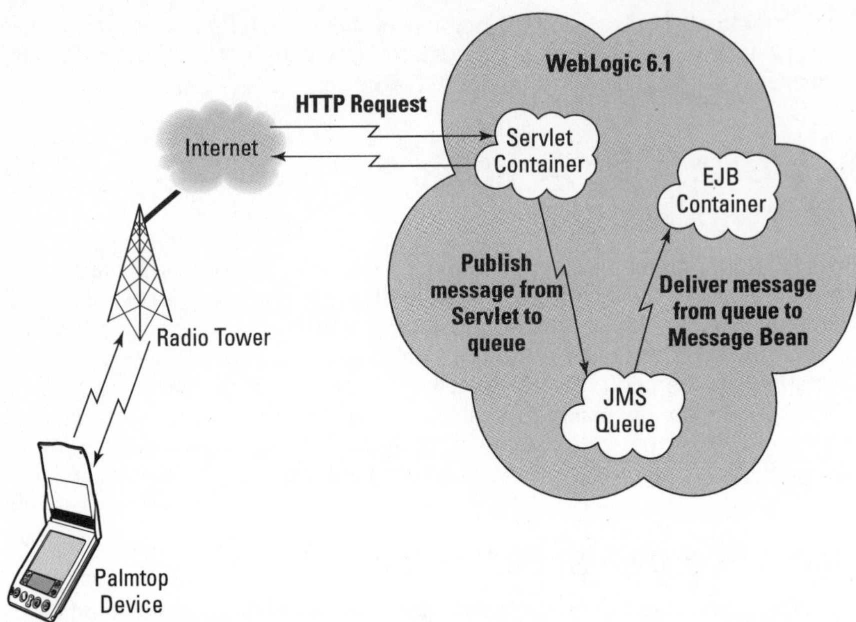

Figure 17-3: An HTTP servlet sending JMS messages to a message-driven EJB

Source code

Listing 17-5 displays the code for `SendPrescriptionServlet`. Notice the initialization of the JMS queue in the `init()` method of the servlet.

Listing 17-5: SendPrescriptionServlet.java

```
package bible.chapter17;

import java.io.*;
import javax.servlet.*;
import javax.servlet.http.*;
import java.rmi.RemoteException;
import java.util.*;
import javax.naming.*;
import javax.jms.*;


public class SendPrescriptionServlet extends HttpServlet {
  SessionContext sc = null;
  ServletContext context = null;
  QueueConnection qConnection = null;
  Queue q = null;

  public void init(ServletConfig config)
```

```
throws ServletException {
  super();

  Context context = null;
  QueueConnectionFactory qConnectionFactory = null;
  context = getServletContext();

  try {
    q = (Queue) context.lookup("PrescriptionQueue");

    // Create a TopicConnection
    qConnectionFactory = (QueueConnectionFactory)
      context.lookup("PrescriptionConnectionFactory");
    qConnection =
      qConnectionFactory.createQueueConnection();

  } catch (Throwable t) {
    log.append(t.toString());
  }
}

public void service(HttpServletRequest req,
                    HttpServletResponse res)
throws ServletException, IOException
{

  QueueSession qSession = null;
  QueueSender qSender = null;
  TextMessage message = null;

  try {
    // retrieve parameters from request
    String physicianId =
      (String)req.getParameter("physicianId");
    String patientId =
      (String)req.getParameter("patientId");
    String drug = (String)req.getParameter("drug");
    String note = (String)req.getParameter("note");

    // create a jms session
    qSession = qConnection.createQueueSession(true, 0);
    qSender = qSession.createSender(queue);

    // create a message
    message = qSession.createTextMessage();
    message.setStringProperty("necessity", "immediate");
    message.setText(
      generatePrescriptionXML(physicianId,
                              patientId,
                              date,
                              drug,
                              note));
```

Continued

Listing 17-5 *(continued)*

```
// send the message to the queue
      qSender.send(message);
    } catch (Exception e) {
      pageToReturn = "error.jsp";
      e.printStackTrace();
      context.getRequestDispatcher(pageToReturn).forward(req,
        res);
    }
  }

  // generate XML for a prescription

  private String generatePrescriptionXML(String physicianId,
    String patientId, String drug, String note )
  {
    StringBuffer sb = new StringBuffer();

    sb.append("<?xml version=\"1.0\" ?>");
    sb.append("<PRESCRIPTION>");
    sb.append("<PHYSICIAN_ID>" + physicianId +
      "</PHYSICIAN_ID>");
    sb.append("<PATIENT_ID>" + patientId + "</PATIENT_ID>");
    sb.append("<DRUG>" + drug + "</DRUG>");
    sb.append("<NOTE>" + note + "</NOTE>");
    sb.append("</PRESCRIPTION>");

    return sb.toString();
  }

  // close the queue connection here
  public void destroy()
  {
    if (qConnection != null) {
      try {
        qConnection.close();
      } catch (Exception e) {
        e.printStackTrace();
      }
    }
  }
}
```

Now that the prescription message was sent successfully, it's time to process the information sent. Listing 17-6 shows the code for `PrescriptionBean`, which listens for prescription requests on `PrescriptionQueue`. As I mentioned earlier, the onMessage() method is the central location for developing your business logic. In this case, you are only going to process JMS messages that were sent with the tag immediate. This is accomplished by reading the JMS properties. After a message is processed, the processPrescription() method is called, with the message payload as a parameter. Using the SAX parser shown in Listing 17-7, a Java Prescription object, defined in Listing 17-8, is generated from the data in the XML document.

Listing 17-6: PrescriptionBean.java

```
package bible.chapter17;


import java.rmi.RemoteException;
import javax.ejb.EJBException;
import javax.ejb.MessageDrivenBean;
import javax.ejb.MessageDrivenContext;
import javax.ejb.CreateException;
import javax.jms.*;


public class PrescriptionBean
implements MessageDrivenBean ,javax.jms.MessageListener {

  public MessageBean() {
  }

  public void setMessageDrivenContext(
    MessageDrivenContext mdc)
  {
  }

  public void ejbCreate() {
  }

  public void onMessage(Message incomingMsg) {
    TextMessage msg = null;
    String msgType = null;
    String msgPayload = null;

    try {
      if (incomingMsg instanceof TextMessage) {
        msg = (TextMessage) inMessage;
        msgType = msg.getStringProperty("necessity");
        msgPayload = msg.getText();

        if (msgType.equals("immediate"))

          processPrescription(msgPayload);
```

Continued

Listing 17-6 *(continued)*

```
        } else {
          System.out.println("Only accepting text messages");
        }
      } catch (JMSException e) {
        e.printStackTrace();
      } catch (Throwable te) {
        te.printStackTrace();
      }
    }

    public void ejbRemove() {
    }

    public void processPrescription(String prescriptionXmlDoc)
    {
      PrescriptionXmlParser parser =
        new PrescriptionXmlParser(
          handlerContext.getConnection());

      // Create SAX 2 parser...
      XMLReader xr =
        XMLReaderFactory.createXMLReader(
          "org.apache.xerces.parsers.SAXParser");

      // Set the ContentHandler...
      xr.setContentHandler(parser);
      xr.parse(prescriptionXmlDoc);

      Prescription currentPrescription =
        parser.getPrescription();

      // Now that you have the prescription object
      // you can make calls to various backend order
      // management systems
    }
  }
```

Listing 17-7: PrescriptionXmlParser.java

```
import org.xml.sax.*;
import org.xml.sax.helpers.*;

import java.io.*;
import java.util.*;
```

```
import java.text.ParseException;


public class PrescriptionXmlParser extends DefaultHandler {

  private Prescription prescription = new Prescription();

  public void startElement(String namespaceURI,
    String localName,
    String qName,
    Attributes attr ) throws SAXException {

    contents.reset();
  }

  public void endElement(String namespaceURI,
    String localName,
    String qName ) throws SAXException{

    try {
      if (localName.equals("physician_id")) {
        prescription.setPhysicianId(
          Integer.parseInt(contents.toString()));
      }

      if (localName.equals("patient_id")) {
        prescription.setPatientId(
          Integer.parseInt(contents.toString()));
      }

      if (localName.equals("note")) {
        prescription.setNote(contents.toString());
      }

      if (localName.equals("drug")) {
         prescription.setDrug(contents.toString());
      }
    } catch (ParseException p) {
      System.out.println("Here" + p.toString());
    }
  }

  public void characters(char[] ch, int start, int length)
  throws SAXException {
    contents.write( ch, start, length );
  }

  public Prescription getPrescription() {
    return prescription;
  }
}
```

Listing 17-8: **Prescription.java**

```
package bible.weblogic.chapter17;


public class Prescription {
  private int physicianId;
  private int patientId;
  private String note;
  private String drug;

  public void setPhysicianId(int physicianId) {
    // SBgen: Assign variable
    this.physicianId = physicianId;
  }

  public int getPhysicianId() {
    // SBgen: Get variable
    return(physicianId);
  }

  public void setPatientId(int patientId) {
    // SBgen: Assign variable
    this.patientId = patientId;
  }

  public int getPatientId() {
    // SBgen: Get variable
    return(patientId);
  }

  public void setDrug(String drug) {
    // SBgen: Assign variable
    this.drug = drug;
  }

  public String getDrug() {
    // SBgen: Get variable
    return(drug);
  }
}
```

Deploying the message-driven bean

Now that the message-driven bean is written, it's time to deploy it. For instructions on how to deploy the servlet and set up the JMS queue, refer to the chapters on servlets (Chapter 11) and JMS (Chapter 9).

The first step is to create a deployment descriptor for your bean. As with entity and session bean deployment descriptors, the file must be called `ejb-jar.xml` and it must be in the directory `META-INF`, which resides in the directory where your compiled classes are stored. Listing 17-9 shows `ejb-jar.xml` for `PrescriptionBean.java`.

Listing 17-9: ejb-jar.xml

```
<!DOCTYPE ejb-jar PUBLIC "-//Sun Microsystems, Inc.//DTD
Enterprise JavaBeans 2.0//EN" "http://java.sun.com/dtd/ejb-
jar_2_0.dtd">

<ejb-jar>
 <enterprise-beans>
    <message-driven>
      <ejb-name>prescriptionConsumer</ejb-name>
      <ejb-class>bible.chapter17.PrescriptionBean</ejb-class>
      <transaction-type>Container</transaction-type>
      <message-driven-destination>
        <jms-destination-type>
          javax.jms.Queue
        </jms-destination-type>
      </message-driven-destination>
    </message-driven>
 </enterprise-beans>
</ejb-jar>
```

Looking at the file, you can see that the JNDI name for `PrescriptionBean` will be `prescriptionConsumer`, the transaction type will be `container-managed`, and the destination type will be a JMS queue. To specify the exact queue to which the bean will listen, you must modify the WebLogic-specific deployment descriptor (`weblogic-ejb-jar`), which is shown in Listing 17-10. This file also belongs in the `META-INF` directory mentioned earlier.

Listing 17-10: weblogic-ejb-jar.xml

```
<?xml version="1.0"?>
<!DOCTYPE weblogic-ejb-jar PUBLIC "-//BEA Systems, Inc.//DTD
WebLogic 6.0.0 EJB//EN"
"http://www.bea.com/servers/wls600/dtd/weblogic-ejb-jar.dtd">
<weblogic-ejb-jar>
```

Continued

Listing 17-10 (continued)

```
    <weblogic-enterprise-bean>

      <ejb-name>prescriptionConsumer</ejb-name>
      <message-driven-descriptor>
      <pool>
        <max-beans-in-free-pool>
          50
        </max-beans-in-free-pool>
        <initial-beans-in-free-pool>
          10
        </initial-beans-in-free-pool>
      </pool>
      <destination-jndi-name>
        PrescriptionQueue
      </destination-jndi-name>
      </message-driven-descriptor>
      <jndi-name>prescriptionConsumer</jndi-name>
    </weblogic-enterprise-bean>
  </weblogic-ejb-jar>
```

Now that the deployment descriptors are ready, the next step is to create a standard JAR file that contains the class and interface files of each message-driven bean. The command below creates the file, `ch17-mdb.jar`, which will be used by the EJB compiler:

```
d:\MYBEANS> jar cvf ch17-mdb.jar *.*
```

The next step is to run the EJB compiler on the JAR file you just created. The following command invokes the EJB compiler and creates a JAR file that is ready for deployment:

```
D:\wls60\utils\wlserver6.0\lib>java -classpath weblogic.jar
weblogic.ejbc  ch17-mdb.jar ch17-mdb-deploy.jar
```

The final step in the deployment process is to deploy the message-driven bean's JAR file by using the WebLogic Console. Under the WebLogic Server's name, select Deployments%%>EJB from the domain tree. Click Install a New EJB, and upload the JAR file you created, as shown in Figure 17-4.

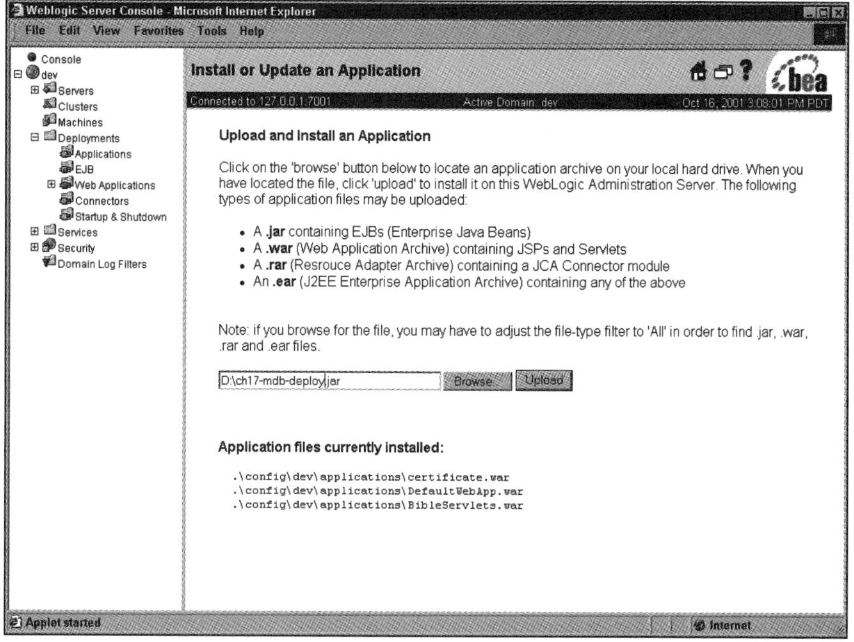

Figure 17-4: Deploying the message-driven bean by using the WebLogic Console

Summary

This chapter explained the fundamental concepts behind message-driven EJBs, which are a new type of EJB introduced in the EJB 2.0 specification.

Message-driven beans enable you to easily write asynchronous message-handling code that lives within the EJB container, and benefits from the services the container provides, such as automatic caching, transaction control, and management of the JMS infrastructure.

Message-driven beans are for asynchronous message-handling only. They can listen to any JMS queue or subscribe to any JMS topic defined in your WebLogic Server.

Unlike other types of EJBs, the business logic in message-driven beans can only be invoked by sending the bean a JMS message. You cannot directly invoke any of the bean's methods from code living outside the bean.

Writing a message-driven bean is as simple as writing an `onMessage()` method, creating deployment descriptors, and deploying the bean's JAR file to WebLogic Server. Of course, you must also create the JMS queue or topic to which the message-driven bean will be attached.

✦ ✦ ✦

Deploying and Testing Enterprise Applications

PART

V

✦ ✦ ✦ ✦

In This Part

✦ ✦ ✦ ✦

CHAPTER 18

Assembling and Deploying WebLogic Applications

✦ ✦ ✦ ✦

In This Chapter

Packaging J2EE applications

Web applications structure and packaging

Packaging Enterprise JavaBeans

Packaging Enterprise Applications

Classloading in Enterprise Applications and WebLogic Server

Third-party and utility classes

✦ ✦ ✦ ✦

The J2EE specification gives us a number of packaging formats for wrapping up everything from Java client applications to JSPs and servlets to Enterprise JavaBeans in standardized formats that are generic and portable to all platforms.

Packaging J2EE Applications

Proper packaging enables you to configure your applications via deployment descriptors, which are text documents written in XML. This allows you to change

- the URL a browser uses to point to a servlet in a Web application
- database connection pools for a container-managed entity EJB
- security constraints on any part of an application

without rewriting a single line of code. Simply change the deployment descriptors and redeploy the application from WebLogic Console. In most cases, you don't even have to restart the server if it is running in Development mode because every application in WebLogic gets its own area of memory to work in; that is, each is loaded by a separate ClassLoader — more on this later. An application can be destroyed and recreated without affecting anything else on the server.

In addition to the J2EE standard package and descriptors, each application Server usually adds deployment descriptors of its own to a package. Sometimes these descriptors are optional; in other cases, they're required by the server for proper deployment of the package. In some cases, WebLogic requires additional files used by the container to be included. Usually a WebLogic-specific compiler like the EJB or the RMI compiler generates these files; you just have to feed them your package.

Deployment descriptors

Table 18-1 shows the different application types supported by WebLogic, and the names and locations of J2EE and WebLogic-specific deployment descriptors that go with them.

Table 18-1
Deployment Descriptor Files and Locations

Application	*J2EE*	*WebLogic*
Web applications	`WEB-INF/web.xml`	`WEB-INF/weblogic.xml`
Enterprise JavaBeans	`META-INF/ejb-jar.xml`	`META-INF/weblogic-ejb-jar.xml` `META-INF/weblogic-cmp-rdbms-jar.xml`
Enterprise applications	`META-INF/application.xml`	`META-INF/application.xml`
Client applications	`application-client.xml`	`client-application.runtime.xml`
Resource adaptors	`META-INF/ra.xml`	`META-INF/weblogic-ra.xml`

Writing deployment descriptors can be confusing at first. The order of elements in the XML files is important, and translating examples from a book into a working descriptor for your application involves a lot of cutting and pasting, which is a time consuming and trial-and-error process. Luckily, WebLogic 6.1 simplifies this process by including deployment descriptor editors for each of the application types listed in the table. You still must create the basic descriptor, but tweaking settings and configuration from the WebLogic Console makes these descriptors much more manageable.

If you choose to create all your descriptors by hand, there are many good XML editors available, including ones that will let you check your files against the Document Type Definition (DTD—a set of rules for what constitutes a valid form of that type of XML document) for validity. Many Java IDEs also include auto-generation of deployment descriptors for your application, complete and ready to go.

WebLogic also provides a number of Java-based utilities for generating deployment descriptors by scanning your application directory. This is a best-effort attempt at creating your deployment descriptors. The files generated may be syntactically correct, but you should review the files to make sure the content is correct. In any case, it saves a lot of typing.

Table 18-2 lists the utility names and the applications for which they generate descriptors.

Table 18-2
Deployment Descriptor Utility Classes

Application	*Java Utility*
Enterprise JavaBeans 1.1	`weblogic.ant.taskdefs.ejb.DDInit`
Enterprise JavaBeans 2.0	`weblogic.ant.taskdefs.ejb20.DDInit`
Web applications	`weblogic.ant.taskdefs.war.DDInit`
Enterprise Applications	`weblogic.ant.taskdefs.ear.DDInit.messages`

An example of using this on a Web application located at `c:\testwebapp` is the following:

```
$ java weblogic.ant.taskdefs.war.DDInit c:\testwebapp
```

This command generates the `web.xml` and `weblogic.xml` files and places them in the `c:\testwebapp\WEB-INF` directory.

JAR — Java archive format

The Java `.jar` utility allows you to bundle files together into a single `.jar` (Java ARchive) file. This format maintains the directory structure of your application, and by default, uses ZIP compression to reduce the amount of space the application takes up. WebLogic does not require that you deploy applications in the `.jar` format, because the Classloader can read both “exploded” directory structures and JAR files with equal ease.

Developing your applications in the exploded directory makes life easier, as WebLogic can detect when single files have been changed and load them individually without reloading the application. But when it comes time to deploy your application into production, bundling it into a JAR file saves space and ensures a neat package.

To get WebLogic 6.1 to automatically deploy "exploded" or JAR'd applications, you must be running your server in development mode. For more about development and production modes on your WebLogic server, see Chapter 4.

The `.jar` format is not always optional either. If you are deploying your application from an administration server that manages a domain with many WebLogic servers (clustered or not), you have to deploy your file in the `.jar` format.

The `.jar` utility is included in the `bin` directory of any Java Development Kit. And because the JDK 1.3 is included with the WebLogic distribution, you probably have it available to you. I'll go into details of how to use the `.jar` utility when I talk about how to build each package format.

Web Applications Structure and Packaging

Web applications provide a J2EE-standard application structure (defined in the servlet 2.2 + 2.3 specification) for deploying resources for availability via HTTP, WAP, and other network protocols. The application structure

- ✦ can contain an application's resources such as servlets, JavaServer Pages (JSP), JSP tag libraries, and static resources such as HTML pages and image files.
- ✦ can contain links to resources outside of the application, such as Enterprise JavaBeans (EJB).
- ✦ is described by a J2EE `web.xml` file and a Weblogic `weblogic.xml` file.
- ✦ can be standalone or part of an Enterprise Application (more on this later).
- ✦ have a standard directory structure, known as the exploded directory form (handy during development). You can also run JAR (Java ARchive file. creator) on the directory to create a `.war` file (recommended for production).

Steps to create a Web application

Web applications are fairly simple structures, requiring only a single subdirectory (`WEB-INF`) and a single file (`web.xml`) to become a valid application. Now a Web application with out any content would be pretty boring, so this is where a little help getting set up is useful. Here's a rough sketch of where to put things and what you need to do to get a typical J2EE Web application up and running.

1. Arrange files in the proper directory structure. JSPs and tag libraries, Servlet classes, helper classes and libraries, static files, and deployment descriptors all have their proper place in a Web app, some dictated by the J2EE Servlet specification, some only by convention.

2. Create the `web.xml` deployment descriptor. It is in this file that you register servlets and map them to URLs, define servlet initialization parameters, register JSP tag libraries, define security constraints, and so on.

3. Create the `weblogic.xml` deployment descriptor (optional). This file allows you to configure WebLogic-specific Web application features such as JSP properties and HTTP session parameters. It also maps `web.xml` configurations into WebLogic-specific configurations, which includes EJB and JNDI resources and security role mappings.

4. JAR the directory structure into a `.war` file (optional). Using the Java `jar` utility, you can package your Web application into a single file (giving it a `.war` extension instead of a `.jar` extension). As mentioned, this is not always necessary for WebLogic Server to deploy the application.

5. Deploy the Web application to your WebLogic server. During development this is as easy as dropping the folder structure or `.war` file in the applications directory under your domain root (for example, on Windows `c:\bea\wlserver\config\mydomain\applications\webapp.war`). For clustered or managed WebLogic Server this changes, but I'll get to that in good time.

Web application directory structure

In a Web application, all your documents are arranged as part of directory hierarchy. Files must be in their proper places for WebLogic to be able to deploy the application properly.

The root of this hierarchy is called the document root. In "exploded" directory format, the name of the document root folder is also the name of your Web application when it is deployed, so choose carefully. In the case where you `jar` the Web application, the deployed name is the name of the `.war` file (sans extension). Directory or file names should not contain spaces.

With the exception of two special directories, `WEB-INF` and `META-INF` directly under the document root (these directories are private), anything under the document root can be served to a client browser. So, in a manner similar to static content Web servers, you can create an orderly directory structure to help in the management of files.

The `META-INF` directory is not used in the Web application specification, but it is created to hold the manifest file when you `jar` a Web application. This folder can also be handy for storing files that you want to package with a Web application but do not want to be available to the client. Good examples of this are documentation about the application and source files. Files not directly accessed by the server for deployment and running of the Web application are not loaded into memory, so you don't have to worry about using up valuable RAM by putting some potentially handy documentation here.

The WEB-INF directory contains many files necessary to the working of the Web application. These files are not served directly to client, but many are mapped via the web.xml file to resources available to the client.

Here's the basic directory structure of a Web application.

```
WebAppName/
        | All static files and JSP pages are placed
        | here or in subdirectories of your choosing.
        WEB-INF/web.xml (required)
        WEB-INF/weblogic.xml (optional)
        WEB-INF/classes (
        | Contains server-side classes such as HTTP servlets
        | and utility classes. All class files under this
        | directory are loaded automatically by the web
        | application classloader.
        WEB-INF/lib
        | By convention, this is the area you should put any
        | jar files referenced by the Web Application (jars
        | must be referenced in the web.xml file to be
        | loaded by the web application class loader)
        WEB-INF/tlds
          Again by convention this is where JSP tag library
          definition files often go. The actual java classes
          go in either the lib or classes directory as
          appropriate.
```

Here's a sample Web application directory structure with "real" files. You'll build and deploy this application in the following pages.

```
accountManager/
    login.jsp
    /errors
        login_error.jsp
    /accounts
        myAccount.jsp
    /images
        logo.gif
        navbar.gif
    /WEB-INF
        web.xml
        weblogic.xml
        /lib
            jspTagLibrary.jar
        /classes
            /bible
                /deployment
                    AcctReport.class
        /tlds
            jspTags.tld
```

Configuring your Web application

In WebLogic, a Web application is configured via two XML deployment descriptor files. One is the `web.xml` file specified by the J2EE servlet specification; the second is specific to WebLogic and is named `weblogic.xml`. This optional file is used to configure WebLogic-specific features.

Note that the document type definitions (DTDs) of the XML deployment descriptors specify a certain order to the XML file's contents. You'll walk through some parts of the descriptors in order, but this is not the venue for an exhaustive description of all the portions of the `web.xml` file. You can view Sun's DTD for web.xml at `http://java.sun.com/dtd/web-app_2_3.dtd`.

Table 18-3 gives a simple listing of the elements in a `web.xml` file and their use. The order that the tags appear in the list is the order that should be in your `web.xml` file.

Table 18-3
web.xml elements

Element	*Description*
`<icon>`	An optional icon for the Web application. Not used by WebLogic.
`<display-name>`	An optional display name for the application. Not used by WebLogic.
`<description>`	An optional, short description of the application. Not used by WebLogic.
`<distributable>`	Indicates the Web application can be deployed into a distributed servlet container. Not used by WebLogic.
`<context-param>`	Servlet context initialization parameters
`<filter>`	Filters can intercept servlet requests and response objects and examine or modify the object before passing it on (part of the Servlet 2.3 spec)
`<filter-mapping>`	Maps a filter to a URL pattern
`<listener>`	Application listeners fire events when the servlet context changes state (part of the Servlet 2.3 spec)
`<servlet>`	Defines servlets available to the Web application
`<servlet-mapping>`	Maps a servlet or JSP to a URL pattern
`<session-config>`	Only used to set the session time out

Continued

Table 18-3 *(continued)*

Element	*Description*
`<mime-mapping>`	Allows association between a mime extension and return mime type associating .txt with text/plain
`<welcome-file-list>`	Defines default file names when a URL request is a directory
`<error-page>`	Allows mapping between HTTP error codes and error handling pages
`<taglib>`	Defines JSP tag libraries available to the Web application
`<resource-env-ref>`	Declares a Web application's reference to another administered entity on the server, such as a JMS queue or topic
`<resource-ref>`	Used with the `<resource-description>` element in the `weblogic.xml` file, it maps resources used in your Web application to objects listed in the JNDI tree
`<security-constraint>`	Used with the `<security-role-assignment>` element in the `weblogic.xml` file, it defines the access privileges for a `<security-role>` element to a group of resources via their URL pattern
`<login-config>`	Defines how a user is authenticated in a Web application
`<security-role>`	Used with the `<security-role-assignment>` element in the `weblogic.xml` file, maps role names to principal in the WebLogic security domain
`<env-entry>`	Declares an environment entry for the Web application
`<ejb-local-ref>`	Declares a reference to an EJB's local home interface
`<ejb-ref>`	Used with the `<ejb-reference-description>` element in the `weblogic.xml` file, it creates references to EJB resources used within the Web application

Although the `weblogic.xml` file is optional, many features defined in the `web.xml` will not work without corresponding entries in a `weblogic.xml`. These include security constraints and roles and EJB and resource references. Table 18-4 shows the elements of a `weblogic.xml` deployment descriptor. I'll talk about a couple of the features available, but for a complete explanation, you should refer to the WebLogic documentation.

Table 18-4
weblogic.xml elements

Element	*Description*
`<description>`	Description of the Web application
`<weblogic-version>`	The WebLogic version for which the application is designed. This element is no longer used.
`<security-role-assignment>`	Used with the `<security-contraint>` element in the `web.xml` file, it maps between a role defined in the `web.xml` file to principals in the WebLogic security realm
`<reference-descriptor>`	Used with the `<resource-ref>` element in the `web.xml` file to map resources used in the Web application to objects listed in the JNDI tree
`<session-descriptor>`	Contains parameters for how WebLogic configures the session
`<jsp-descriptor>`	Contains parameters for how WebLogic handles JSPs
`<auth-filter>`	This is the fully qualified name of a servlet that extends the AuthFilter abstract servlet; methods on this servlet are called just before and after authentication and authorization
`<container-descriptor>`	Contains the `<check-auth-on-forward/>`, `<redirect-content>`, and `<redirect-content-type>` flags to force reauthentication on forwarded requests.
`<charset-params>`	This element is used to define character set mappings from incoming POSTs and GETs to the Java character set

Creating the web.xml deployment descriptor

First, you need to create the basic framework of the deployment descriptor, and then you can begin to add elements in the proper order. As mentioned earlier, you can do this by hand by using a text editor, use an editor specifically made for XML, or you can have WebLogic generate a descriptor for you using its ANT deployment descriptor utilities.

After you create the basic descriptor, you can deploy your application and use the WebLogic Console's deployment descriptor editors to add references and configurations to all parts of your application.

The basic outline of a `web.xml` file begins with a header declaring the type of XML file and showing where to find the definition.

```
<!DOCTYPE web-app PUBLIC
"-//Sun Microsystems, Inc.//DTD Web Application 2.3//EN"
"http://java.sun.com/dtd/web-app_2_3.dtd">
```

If your WebLogic server resides behind a firewall, make sure that either your server has access to the public DTD, or make a copy of the DTD onto a stable Web server (not the WebLogic server where the application is being deployed) and point your header to that location.

All of your following entries should be contained between a pair of opening and closing `<web-app>` tags.

```
<web-app>
  <!-- All other elements between these two elements -->
</web-app>
```

For the example Web application, you'll begin with the `web.xml` file, as this is required for any Web application to work. After, you'll walk through the options available to you by creating a `weblogic.xml` file.

Deploying your basic Web application

Because you're developing a new application, you should be running your WebLogic server in development mode (see Chapter 4 for an explanation of how to do this). By doing so, applications you place in the applications folder under your domain root will be automatically deployed.

You'll deploy the Account Manager Web application by placing the `accountManager` folder in your applications folder.

On Windows NT, the path might look something like this:

```
C:\bea\wlserver6.1\config\mydomain\applications\accountManager
```

As discussed earlier, the bare minimum required for WebLogic to recognize a Web application is a directory root and a subfolder called `WEB-INF` containing a well-formed `web.xml` file.

You'll start out with a deployment descriptor that looks like the following:

```
<!DOCTYPE web-app PUBLIC
"-//Sun Microsystems, Inc.//DTD Web Application 2.3//EN"
"http://java.sun.com/dtd/web-app_2_3.dtd">
```

```
<web-app>
</web-app>
```

Let's go to WebLogic Console and edit your deployment descriptor from there. Figure 18-1 shows the console screen for doing so.

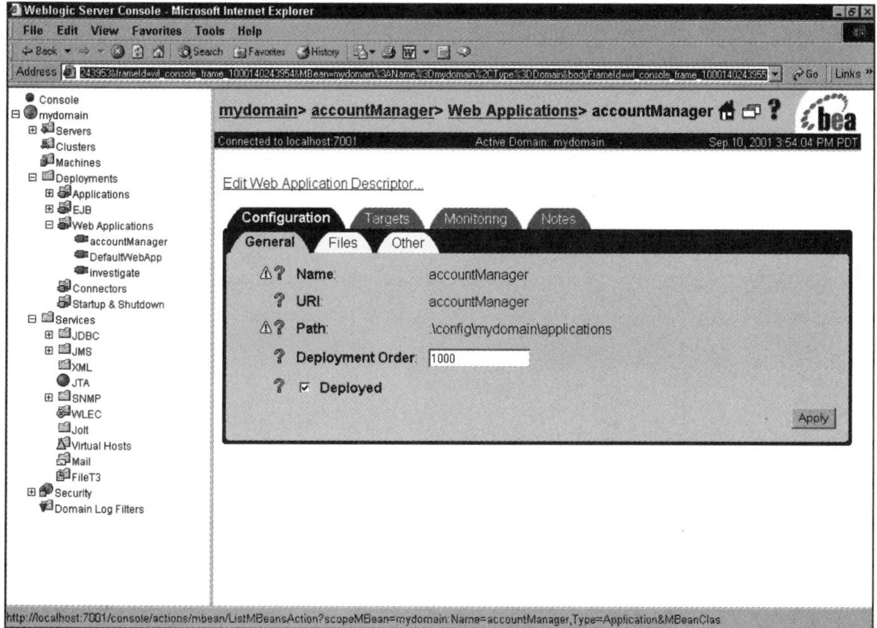

Figure 18-1: Editing a Web application's deployment descriptor

Click the Edit Web Application Descriptor link and a new window pops up with all the possible settings for your Web application.

Servlet configuration

Because your Web application contains an HTTP servlet, you need to put in several references to the Java class in order for clients to be able to access it. You'll only put in the required subelements, but be aware that for most deployment descriptor tags, there are many optional elements (see the references at the end of the chapter for links to the full servlet specification for information on all tags).

Click the Servlet folder in the left frame, followed by the Configure a New Servlet link. Figure 18-2 shows the resulting screen.

From here, you'll fill in information about your servlet. `Servlet Name` is the name by which the servlet will be referred to throughout the deployment descriptor. `Servlet Class` is the fully qualified name of the Java servlet class. Usually the class is in `WEB-INF/classes`, but this location is not required. The class should be in the classpath at deployment.

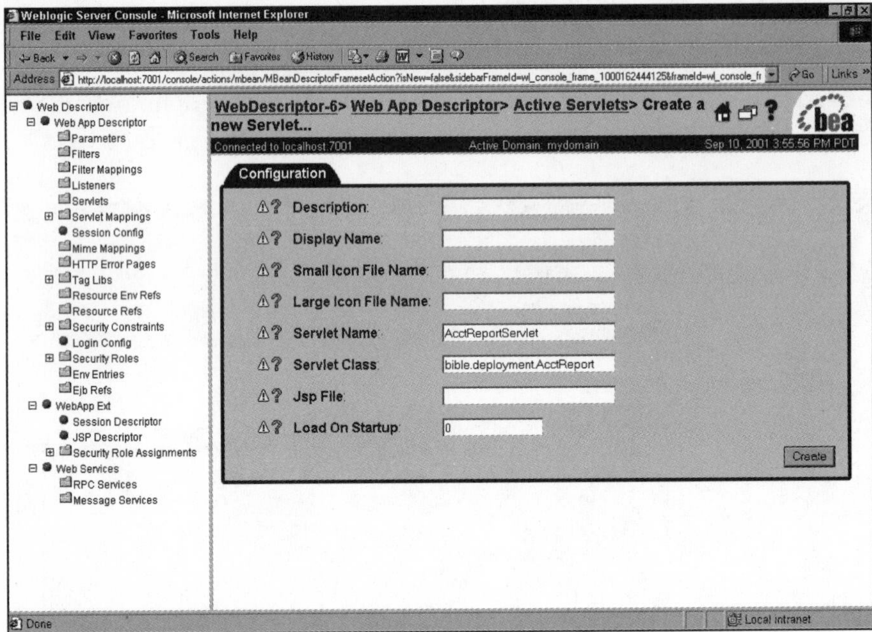

Figure 18-2: Configuring a new servlet

Now you need to map your servlet reference to a URL pattern so that the browser can connect to it. Again, `Servlet Name` is the name defined in the servlet declaration, and the URL pattern is the portion of the URL that comes after `http://server:port/WebApplicationName` (more on URL patterns in a bit).

Click the Servlet Mappings folder in the left frame, followed by the Configure a New Servlet Mapping link. Figure 18-3 shows the resulting console screen.

What this accomplishes is that when a client connects to the following URL

```
http://www.zeetrade.com/accountManager/acct_report
```

he is directed to the `AcctReport` servlet class. You can also have as many `<servlet-mapping>` elements per `<servlet>` element as you want. It is worthwhile to play around with the `<url-pattern>` subelement of `<servlet-mapping>` as you can be quite flexible with what client requests get mapped to your servlet.

Table 18-5, for example, lists changes to the `<url-pattern>` element associated with the `Login` servlet and the HTTP requests that could connect to them.

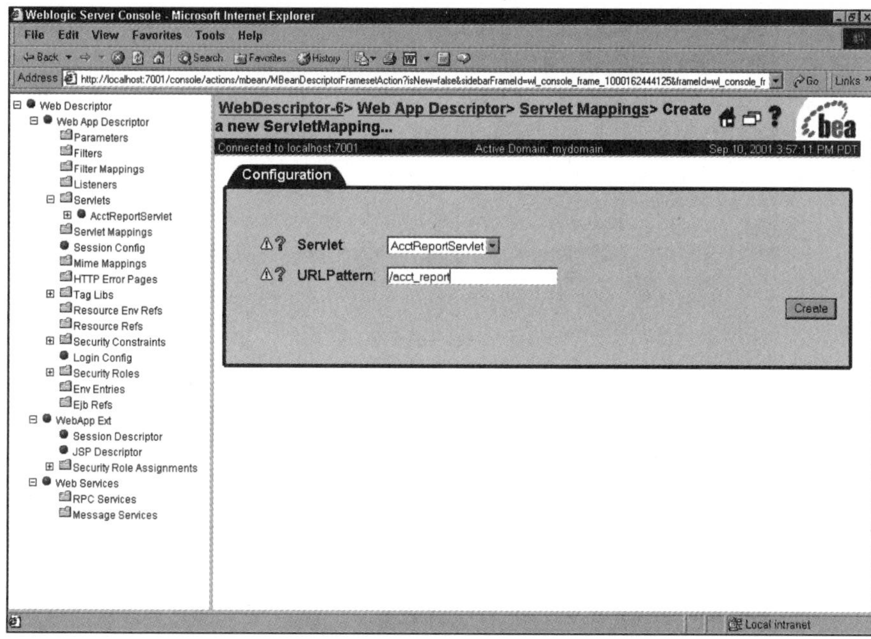

Figure 18-3: Configuring the servlet mapping

Table 18-5
URL Patterns

URL pattern	*HTTP request*
`/acct_report/*`	`http://www.zeetrade.com/accountManager/acct_report/index.html`
`/myaccount/report`	`http://www.zeetrade.com/accountManager/myaccount/report`
`/*.report`	`http://www.zeetrade.com/accountManager/anypage.report`
`/`	`http://www.zeetrade.com/accountManager/`

JSP tag libraries

The example includes a JSP tag library, so you have to put a reference for that in your deployment descriptor for your JSPs to be able to use those custom tags.

Click the Tag Libs folder in the left frame, followed by the Configure a New Tag Lib link. Figure 18-4 shows the resulting console screen.

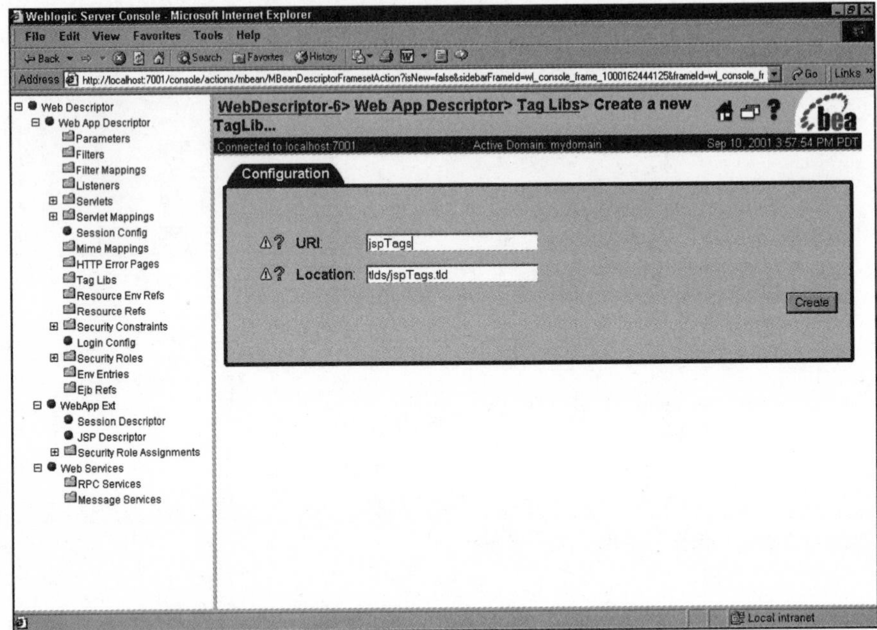

Figure 18-4: Creating a new TagLib

The URI that you enter is the URI that you will refer to in the `<%@ taglib %>` declaration in your JSP pages. The Location is the location of the tag library definition file (`.tld` file) relative to the `WEB-INF` directory.

For more on how to write `.tld` files, see Chapter 12.

In this case, your JSP pages might reference the tab library this way:

```
<%@ taglib uri="/jspTags" prefix="bible" %>
```

Application security

Now let's tighten up the security on your Web application. First, create some roles for your applications. Think of roles as groups of users who have similar privileges in your application. They may be administrators, general users, managers — whatever titles and descriptions make sense for your environment. You'll create the roles in your Web application, and then you'll map them to WebLogic-specific principals in the WebLogic extension descriptor (`weblogic.xml`).

To create a security role, click the Security Roles folder in the left frame, followed by the Configure a New Security Role link.

You'll create a single group (Users) that represents the users who are allowed access to the application. Figure 18-5 shows the Create a New SecurityRole page.

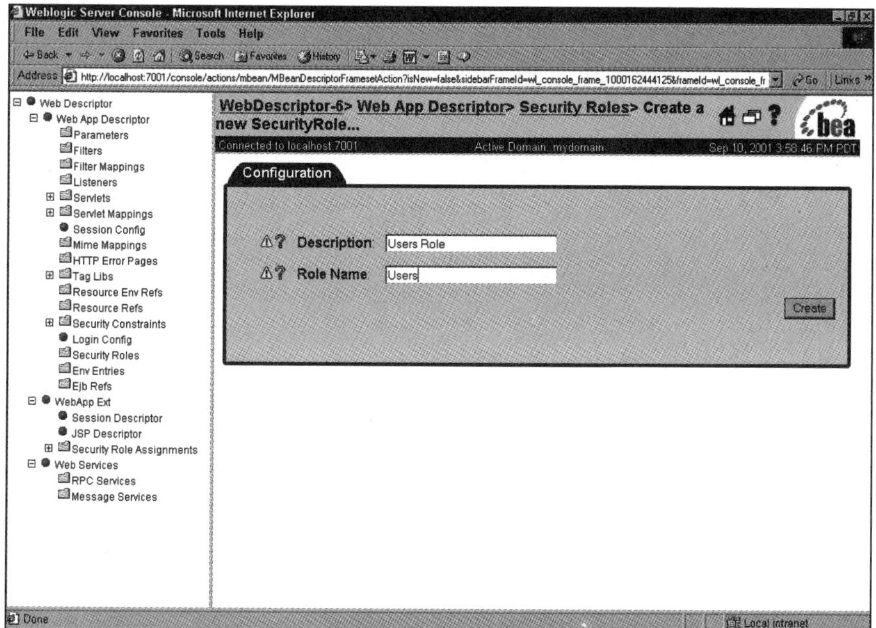

Figure 18-5: Creating a new security role

Now you need to map this security role to actual principals (either users or groups) with a WebLogic security realm.

For more information on configuring a WebLogic security realm, see Chapter 22.

If you haven't already created the WebLogic Web application extension descriptor (`weblogic.xml`), create it now.

Click the Web Descriptor link at the top of the left frame, click the Security Roles folder, and then click the Configure a New Web App Ext Descriptor link.

You will now have a new link in the left frame called WebApp Ext (see Figure 18-6). Inside the WebApp Ext folder, click the Security Role Assignments folder, and then click the Configure a New Security Role Assignment link.

On this screen, choose the Users role you just created. In the Principal Names text area, type the names of the users and groups that are part of the WebLogic security realm that you are using. (Asking a user for validation of a particular security realm by using the `login-config` element is discussed in a following section.)

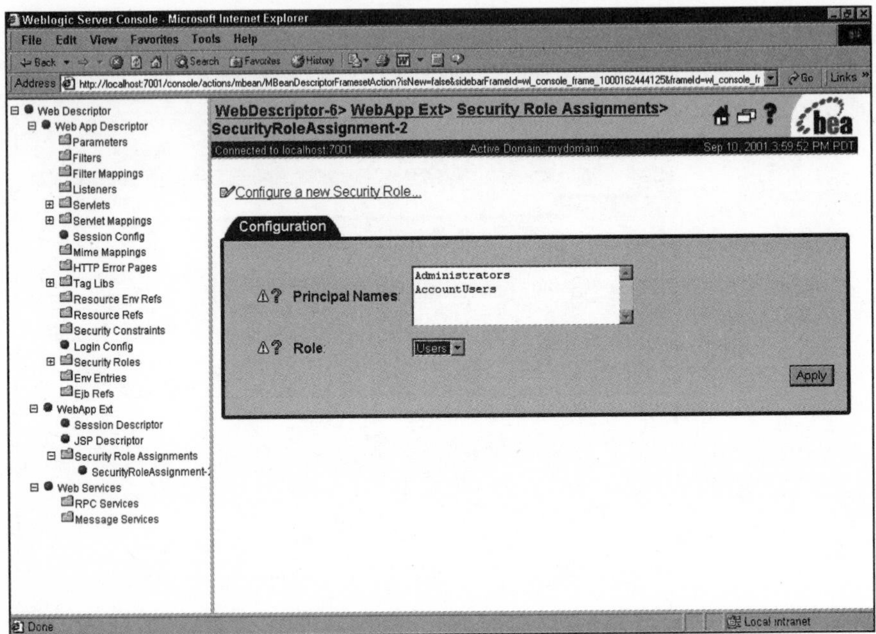

Figure 18-6: Creating a security role assignment

Because WebLogic 6.1 Web applications are running on the same server and share user authentication information, you don't necessarily need to have a login page associated with this Web application. The user may have been authenticated in a different application altogether. Just in case, you'll make one of your own.

To create a new login configuration element to your deployment descriptor, click the Web App Descriptor link in the left frame, and then click the Configure a New Login Config link. The screen in Figure 18-7 appears.

You have now specified that you want to use your own login form page, that you want to authenticate against the WebLogic file realm, and that your login page will be `login.jsp`. Upon errors in the login process, you will send browsers to the `login_error.jsp` file.

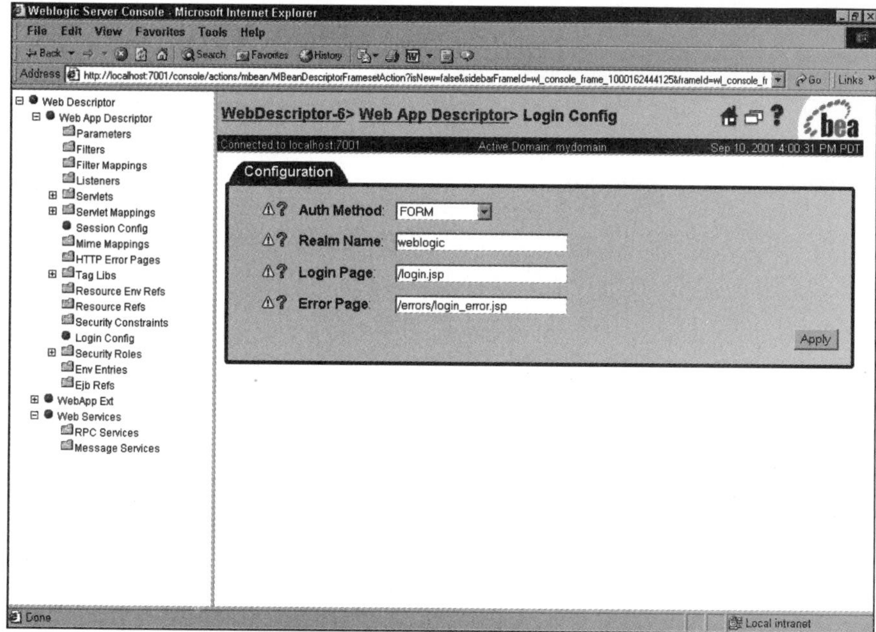

Figure 18-7: Creating a LoginConfig

Validation using an HTML form and WebLogic requires that the field names of the form's input boxes be as follows:

```
<form method="POST" action="j_security_check">
    Name: <input type="text" name="j_username"><br>
    Password: <input type="password" name="j_password"><br>
              <input type="submit" name="login">
</form>
```

Now you must create a security constraint to define which resources of your Web application you want to protect. To do so, click the Security Constraints link in the left frame, and then click the Configure a New Security Constraint link. Figure 18-8 shows the resulting page.

After creating the constraint, you need to add some URL patterns to determine which resource on the site gets restricted.

Click the Web Resource Collections folder under the newly created Accounts Security Constraint, and then click the Configure a New Web Resource Collection link.

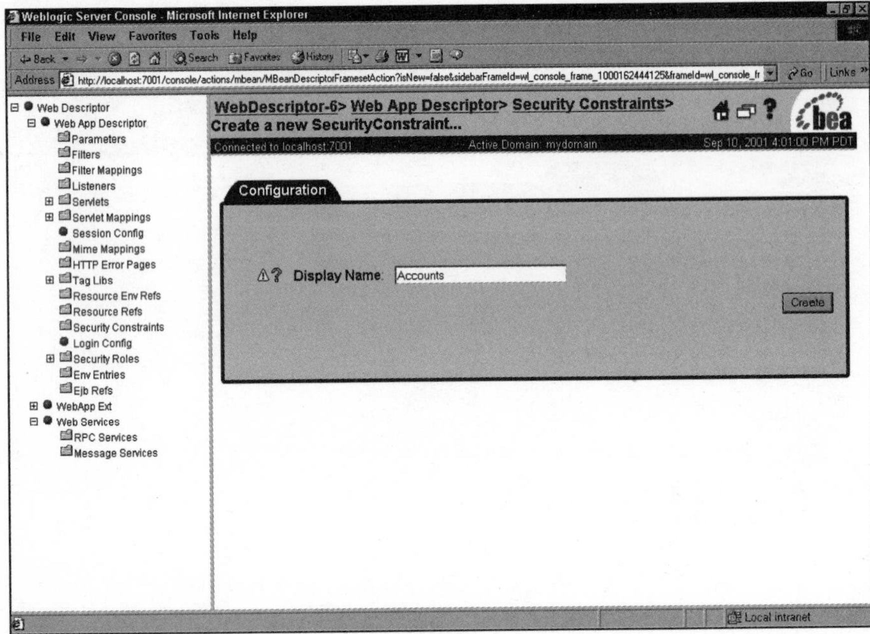

Figure 18-8: Creating a security constraint

On this screen, pick the URL pattern you want to protect (see the earlier section on URL patterns for more help choosing an appropriate pattern). In this case, you're going to protect everything under the accounts folder in your Web application. You may also choose the HTTP protocols that will be allowed, which includes the standard GET and POST, but can also include other HTTP methods such as PUT and DELETE (useful for managing upload folders) (see Figure 18-9).

Now you need to assign the security roles that will be allowed access to this particular Web resource.

Click the Account Security Constraint in the left frame, and then click the Configure a New Auth Constraint link. Type in the auth constraint name, click Create, and then choose the role you want to include. Figure 18-10 shows the resulting screen.

Well, that should secure our application a bit.

Suppose that you're going to test this out by pointing your browser to

```
http://localhost:7001/accountManager/accounts/myAccount.jsp
```

You would get redirected to your simple login page at

```
http://localhost:7001/accountManager/login.jsp
```

This page is shown in Figure 18-11.

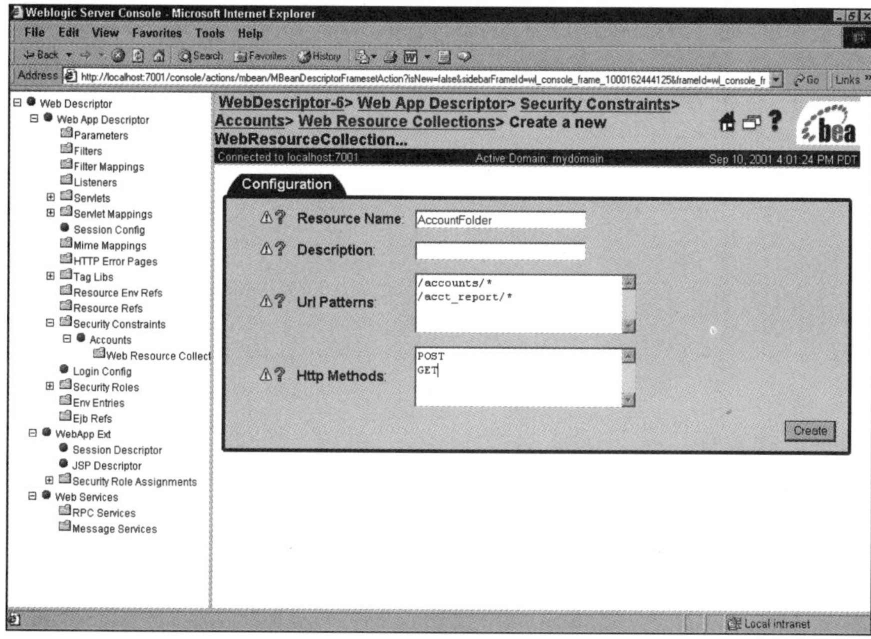

Figure 18-9: Creating a Web resource definition

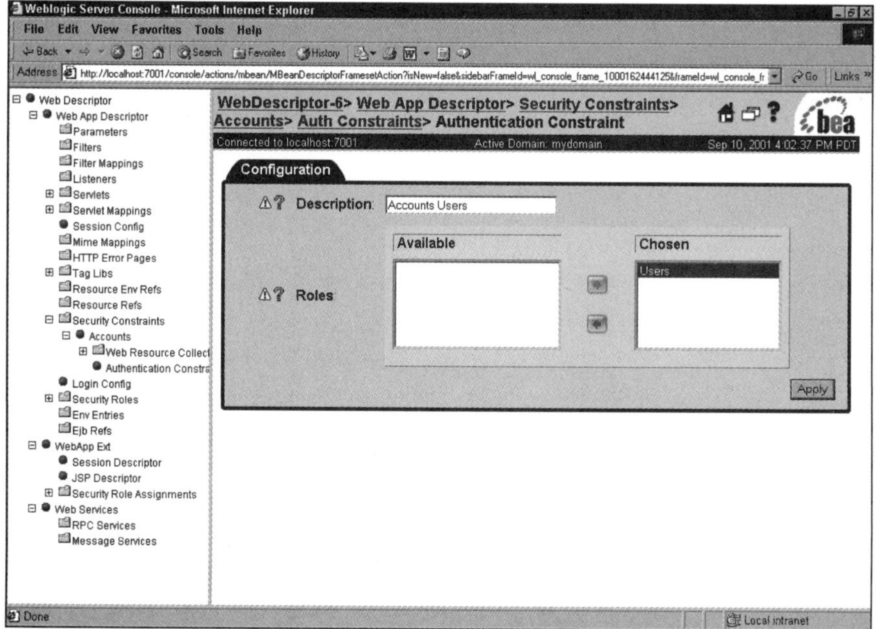

Figure 18-10: Creating an authentication user constraint

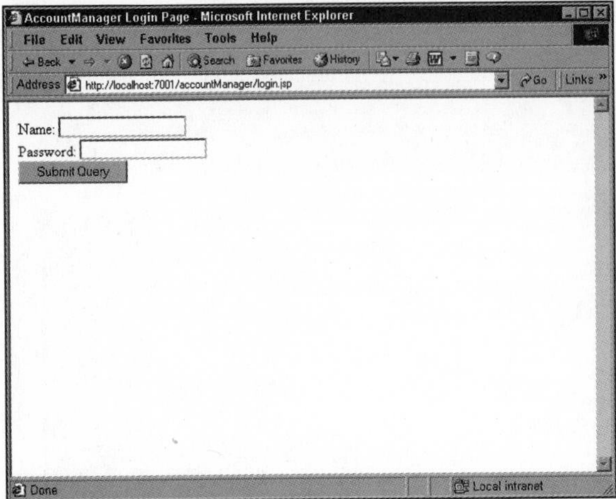

Figure 18-11: The Login page

After your login is successful, you are forwarded to your original request page. If the login is invalid, you are redirected to the defined error page, `errors/login_error.jsp`.

Packaging Enterprise JavaBeans

Enterprise JavaBeans (EJBs) beans are server-side Java components created according to the EJB specification. WebLogic 6.1 supports the EJB 2.0 specification, which includes three types of Enterprise beans: session beans, entity beans, and message-driven beans.

Like Web applications, the deployment of EJBs is handled via XML deployment descriptors, and they are bundled up in JAR format for deployment.

Chapters 14-17 explain how to package and deploy the various types of EJBs, and I will not repeat that information here.

Upon deployment, WebLogic's EJB compiler, `weblogic.ejbc`, is run to generate the RMI stub and skeleton classes that allow remote access to the EJBs. You may run the EJBC compiler separately if you wish, but when you deploy the EJB, WebLogic will run the compiler if you have not already.

It's a good habit to run `ejbc` yourself when you build EJBs, so you can catch errors in your code or deployment descriptors *before* deploying the EJBs to WebLogic Server.

Packaging Enterprise Applications

The Enterprise Application format can contain Web- and EJB-application components, as well as other supporting Java classes and files.

The files are bundled into an Enterprise Archive (`.ear`) file. This file has a `META-INF` directory, which contains the `application.xml` deployment descriptor. `application.xml` contains an entry for each EJB and Web application. You may also describe security roles and other application resources here.

You can configure your Enterprise Application via the console. WebLogic provides a convenient XML deployment descriptor editor. Or if you choose to create one by hand the, DTD is

```
<!DOCTYPE application PUBLIC "-//Sun Microsystems,
Inc.//DTD J2EE Application 1.3//EN"
"http://java.sun.com/dtd/application_1_3.dtd">
```

The XML file has five sections that are contained within the `<application></application>` tags. They are as follows:

Web Modules:

```
<module>
  <web>
    <web-uri>webapp.war</web-uri>
    <context-root>mywebapp</context-root>
  </web>
</module>
```

EJB modules:

```
<module>
  <ejb>myEJB.jar</ejb>
</module>
```

Java Client Modules:

```
<module>
  <java>clientApp.jar</java>
</module>
```

Enterprise Connector Modules:

```
<module>
  <connector>myConnector.rar</connector>
</module>
```

Security Roles:

```
<security-role>
  <description>All Users</description>
  <role-name>Users</role-name>
</security-role>
```

Classloading in Enterprise Applications and WebLogic Server

Classloading can be a frustrating topic for J2EE programmers. Your Enterprise Application may contain many EJBs, servlets, JSPs, utility classes, third-party packages, and more. How do you make sure that your Java classes have appropriate access to each other without putting everything everywhere?

A *classloader* is a Java class that locates a requested file and loads it into the memory space of the Java Virtual Machine (JVM) for use by the requestor. A classloader finds these files by looking though the JARs and directories listed in its classpath.

WebLogic, in complying with the Enterprise Application specification, creates a number of classloaders to deploy an Enterprise Application:

- ✦ An Enterprise classloader (effectively the EJB classloader) that contains all the EJBs in an Enterprise Application
- ✦ Any number of "children" Web application classloaders, loaded beneath the EJB classloader. There is one such class loader for each Web application in the Enterprise Application.

WebLogic creates the separate children classloaders so that the server may dynamically deploy and undeploy any one particular application without affecting any other on the server (thus avoiding having to reboot the entire server to change one application).

These classloaders are created in a specific hierarchy where resources at any one level may only see the resources at their own level and above, as shown in Figure 18-12. What this means in practical terms is that Web applications can see files in their own classloader and those in its parent EJB classloader, but not those files in other sibling Web applications within the Enterprise Application. EJBs in the EJB classloader can only see files listed in the EJB classloader. And, of course, all levels can see files listed in the WebLogic classloader created at server startup. It is important to note that when a resource is requested, the topmost classloader will be queried first (for an identically named resource, the copy in the root classloader will be returned in preference to a copy in the EJB classloader).

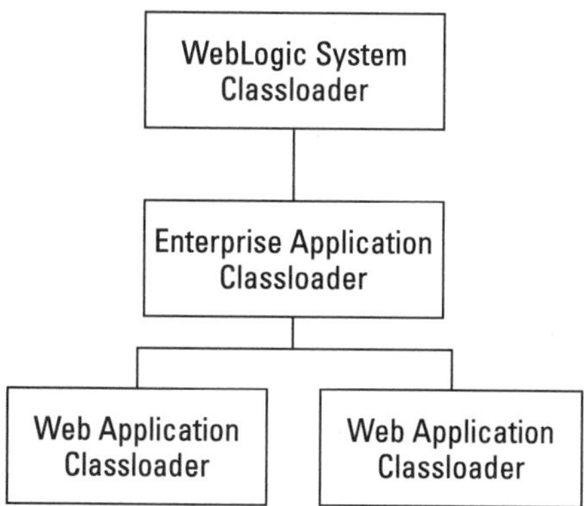

Figure 18-12: Classloader hierarchy

Third-Party and Utility Classes

Dealing with third-party classes is another area that can be quite frustrating. You have your favorite third-party package, `randomWords.jar`, which you use all over your Enterprise Application, in EJBs, and Web applications alike. Where should you put it? Here are some choices and their pros and cons.

Root classloader

One place that would guarantee its universal availability is in the root system level classpath that is used when WebLogic starts up (`java -cp`).

Pros: Files placed here would be available to everything in the entire server.

Cons: One downside is that to change files here you would have to reboot the entire server. Also, you potentially face the problem of versioning. Suppose that three different Enterprise Applications on the server use three different versions of the Xeres XML parser. Placing `xerces.jar` in the root classloader will not work for you then.

Keep in mind, too, that classes in the root classloader are, by nature, not distributed as part of your application. Maintaining boot scripts for all your applications on multiple clustered servers could be a hassle.

Put it everywhere

This means placing the JAR in every Web application's `WEB-INF/lib` directory, and placing dependant files in every EJB JAR file.

Pros: You know that any particular application will have access to the files it needs no matter how you slice and dice your application. This makes for very portable components.

Cons: Without meticulous care and/or good build scripts. versioning can become a nightmare.

Suppose that you've always used one version of `xerces.jar` in your Web application. But any EJB new to your Enterprise Application has a more recent version of the `xerces.jar` bundled in its JAR file. Due to the hierarchical nature of classloading, the EJB version will be loaded by your Web app before the version actually contained in the Web application.

The JAR manifest file class-path header

This is a handy way to reference dependency classes without having to leave copies of them everywhere. The manifest file (`manifest.mf`) contained in the `META-INF` directory of every JAR-packaged application can contain numerous bits of meta information about the package, useful for security, versions, and many other things. For your purposes though, you are interested in the class-path entry in the manifest file. This entry is a space-delimited list of JARs and folders (either absolute or relative to the location of the JAR file) that the deploying application container should make available to the files in the JAR.

WebLogic makes good use of the class-path entry (the implementation of which is left to the application vendor). Within an Enterprise Application, should any `.jar` file (including `.war` files) refer to a file in its manifest class-path entry, that file will be loaded at the Enterprise Application classloader level. This means that if a Web applications refers to a file in its class-path entry, not only will EJBs be able to reference it, but other Web applications will as be able to load it as well.

Here's an example of how you could structure your Enterprise Application to efficiently use this.

Place all third-party and utility classes in a `lib` directory under the root of your Enterprise Application directory. An example application might look like the following:

```
EntApp/
        accountEJB.jar
        accountManager.war
        /lib/
            xerces.jar
            xalan.jar
            myFormat.jar
        /META-INF/
                  application.xml
```

Now you'll create a manifest update file that contains the classpath listings for your utility files located in your `lib` directory and call it manifest.update. Note that classpath listings should be space-delimited and all on the same line as the class-path header (though you may have as many class-path header lines as you like).

```
Manifest-Version: 1.0
Class-Path: lib\xerces.jar lib\xalan.jar lib\myFormat.jar
```

As part of whatever build method you are using for your application, ensure that the following command is run on every `.jar` or `.war` file:

```
jar -umf myJarlib.jar manifest.update
```

Summary

The capability to configure the runtime behavior of applications and components at deployment time is one of J2EE's greatest strengths. In this chapter, you learned how to configure J2EE Web applications, EJBs, and Enterprise Applications using XML deployment descriptors, and how to package these entities into WAR files, JAR files, and EAR files for easy deployment to one or more WebLogic Server instances.

✦ ✦ ✦

CHAPTER 19

Testing and Tuning WebLogic Applications

✦ ✦ ✦ ✦

In This Chapter

Understanding performance tuning

WebLogic Server performance monitoring

Tuning the WebLogic Server

Tuning the WebLogic Server's JVM

Tuning WebLogic Server applications

Tuning process example

✦ ✦ ✦ ✦

Building your J2EE application and testing its functionality in a development environment is only half the battle. Having constructed a logical and sound business application for your clients, the next step is to ensure that your application yields acceptable performance in a production environment. WebLogic Server enables you to tailor its internal settings to your application's needs.

In this chapter, I provide an overview of monitoring your application's performance by using the WebLogic Console. I define load testing and profiling tools that may help you simulate users and analyze performance. I explain many possible environment settings for your WebLogic Server and Java Virtual Machine. I also mention various tips on tuning your application, touching on JDBC, EJB, and other WebLogic J2EE features. I then provide an overview of profiling, load testing, and clustering. Finally, I wrap things up with an example WebLogic server and application tuning process.

Understanding Performance Tuning

The first step of performance tuning is to define what you are trying to achieve. A developer's time is expensive to any business. A clear understanding of performance goals is necessary to ensure that developers don't waste time unnecessarily tuning applications that already perform well enough. After performance goals are defined, the next step is to determine if your application is meeting those goals through testing. By monitoring your application and server when under simulated load, you can analyze your server's performance. If you determine that your application is falling short of its performance goals, it's time to tune the application and potentially tweak the server itself, the JVM, or even change the amount or configuration of your hardware environment. Tuning is the process of changing various aspects of your application and its environment to achieve those goals.

Determining performance goals

Before spending a lot of time tuning and tweaking your application, you should first identify your client's needs and performance expectations. The foundation for performance tuning is examining performance expectations and expected user population and behavior.

Identify critical user actions

Rather than setting broad goals of having fast search queries or quick file downloads, look at specific user actions. Find the most time-critical and the most frequently used user actions in your application. Write these actions down and prioritize performance in these core pieces of your application. Come up with a list of performance goals in a scientific manner. Perhaps one of your goals is to ensure that a customer running a search query on your product database never has to wait more than five seconds for a response. This goal could take priority over another piece of your application, such as a user downloading documentation.

Later in this chapter I discuss how you can focus the WebLogic server to prioritize specific mission-critical facets of your application by assigning a group of server threads, called an *execute queue,* to specific servlets or JSPs.

Determine user population

After you come up with a prioritized list of client expectations, you must then study your expected user population. What is the maximum and average amount of users that will be using your application simultaneously?

Study user behavior

After determining the maximum number of simultaneous users, you must then focus on the users' behavior. Maybe the most users you will ever expect to see is 1,000, but that doesn't necessarily mean that those users are all doing performance-intensive activities. Perhaps most of your users spend time browsing static content, while only a few run expensive queries. The second thing to keep in mind is how active your users are during their application sessions. Some applications may see users that have a request from the server every 30 seconds of their session, while other applications may see fairly inactive users that hit the server only once every couple of minutes.

Finalize performance goals

Now that you have at least roughly identified your user population and behaviors, you should finalize your application performance goals. These goals consist of various user actions and usage scenarios. You can now, for example, define a goal of product queries taking a maximum of five seconds each, while 1,000 users simultaneously run these queries at one-minute intervals.

Knowing performance goals will help you determine your performance testing needs. If you determine that you require the use of commercial load-testing software or service, this information will help you pick one to best suit your needs. Having well-defined goals can also help you determine in which area of performance tuning to start your tuning efforts.

Load testing

Load testing is the process of simulating your user base for the purposes of testing your application performance and finding bottlenecks.

A performance bottleneck occurs when a facet of your application environment is found to be responsible for performance degradation. Generally, you will be able to see only the very worst bottlenecks during a load test, as they will tend to mask smaller issues. For instance, an improper network configuration between the database server and your WebLogic server could be a huge bottleneck. Only after you fix the largest problem, the network latency, will you be able to determine whether your database queries are well designed.

Load testing is therefore a fairly iterative process of pounding the server with users, finding a performance bottleneck, fixing that bottleneck, and again pounding the server. Depending on the amount of users who will be using your application, it can become a critical piece of your development process. You will sleep better at night knowing that you have tested your applications under a load similar or even more extreme than you will see in production. This process is over when your application has met its performance goals.

Simulating hundreds or thousands of simultaneous users, and recording performance results from these simulated users, is not an easy task. There are many commercial and some non-commercial tools available for this purpose. Knowing your load testing needs before entering into a commercial agreement for load testing tools is truly important, because you can identify specific things to look for in your tool. How important is it to you to simulate real user behavior? How many users do you need to simulate to feel comfortable moving into a production environment? Will the service allow you to iteratively run tests and tune your servers? Will it require purchasing extra hardware to simulate the load? Will it require one of your developers or QA engineers to install and run the software?

To further your understanding of these tools and what they do, I have provided a simplistic class that illustrates load testing behavior. Listing 19-1 shows `CheapLoadTester.java`, a class that uses internal WebLogic classes to test a system's response to heavy bursts of HTTP requests. `CheapLoadTester` simulates users by making multiple HTTP connections to URLs defined in the `main()` method. When run, the class creates a number of "users" equal to `NUM_CLIENTS`, and waits `SLEEP_INTERVAL` milliseconds between initiating user requests.

Note that this class provides only a first-order approximation to actual Web browser behavior. For example, it does not spawn multiple threads for downloading images and framesets, as real browsers do; nor does it handle cookies or sessions. Nevertheless, it might be useful for testing certain parts of your application, and it might help you determine whether you really need more realistic (and expensive) load testing tools. Many commercially available load testing suites simulate real browsers, and also install performance monitoring hooks into your systems while the tests are running. Some vendors will sell you software, and some will perform the tests over the Internet from their own data centers.

One important point is to run `CheapLoadTester` on separate hardware from the system you are testing, so it doesn't affect the results of the tests.

Listing 19-1: CheapLoadtester.java

```
package bible.performance;

import java.io.*;
import java.net.*;
import java.util.*;
import weblogic.net.http.HttpURLConnection;

/**
 * This class uses the WebLogic HttpURLConnection
 * class to do a HTTP request and time the contents. It does not
 * do a good job of simulating a real browser's behavior; real
 * browsers are far more complex. Many testing suites do a much
 * better job of simulating browsers by doing multi-threaded
 * image downloading, paying attention to cookies, etc.
 * Remember to run load testing software on separate hardware from
```

```
 * your WebLogic server so you don't taint testing results.
 */
public class CheapLoadtester
    extends TimerTask implements Runnable {

  /**
   * Milliseconds of sleeps between requests, used for initializing
   * the timertask and as sleeps between URL hits during the run
   * method.
   */
  private static final int SLEEP_INTERVAL = 1000*10;

  /**
   * Number of users to simulate.
   */
  private static final int NUM_CLIENTS = 10;
  private ArrayList urlsToHit = null;
  private String testerName;

  /**
   * Instanciates a new CheapLoadtester.
   * @param name Name this tester for display purposes.
   */
  public CheapLoadtester(String name) {
    urlsToHit = new ArrayList();
    this.testerName = name;
  }

  /**
   * Adds a URL to iteratively test.
   */
  public void addURL(URL url) {
    urlsToHit.add(url);
  }

  public String getName() {
    return testerName;
  }

  /**
   * Hits all this tester's URLs and pushes timing info to standard
   * out.
   */
  public void run() {
    URL[] urls = new URL[urlsToHit.size()];
    urls = (URL[]) urlsToHit.toArray(urls);

    long start = 0;
    String contents = null;
    float runtime, total = 0;
    for(int i = 0; i < urls.length; i++) {
```

Continued

Listing 19-1 *(Continued)*

```
      start = System.currentTimeMillis();
      try {
        contents = getPage(urls[i]);
        System.out.println(
          testerName + " contents returned: " + contents);
      } catch (Exception e) {
        System.out.println(testerName +
          testerName + ": Exceptions occurred attempting to hit URL.");
        e.printStackTrace();
      }

      runtime = (float)(System.currentTimeMillis() - start)/1000;
      total += runtime;
      System.out.println(testerName + " took " + runtime +
        " seconds to process: " +  urls[i].toString());

      try { //Sleep between requests.
        Thread.sleep(CheapLoadtester.SLEEP_INTERVAL);
      } catch(Exception e) {
        e.printStackTrace();
      }
    }
    System.out.println("*****************************************");
    System.out.println("** " + testerName +
      ": Total time (not including sleeps) to process " +
      urls.length + " URLs: " + total + " seconds **");
    System.out.println("*****************************************");
  }

  /**
   * Opens a HttpURLConnection to the URL and returns the contents.
   */
  private String getPage(URL url) throws Exception {
    StringBuffer sb = new StringBuffer();

    HttpURLConnection conn = new HttpURLConnection(url);
    conn.connect();
    DataInputStream dis = new DataInputStream(conn.getInputStream());
    String nextline;

    while((nextline = dis.readLine()) != null) {
     sb.append(nextline);
    }
    dis.close();
    return sb.toString();
  }

  /**
```

```
     * Declares multiple new 'clients' and schedules them on a timer.
     */
    public static void main(String[] args) {
      ArrayList clients = new ArrayList(); //holds clients.
      try {
        for(int i = 0; i < NUM_CLIENTS; i++) {
          CheapLoadtester client = new CheapLoadtester("User"+i);
          //Add URLs for client to hit.
          URL tmpURL = new URL("http://servername:7001/APP/index.html");
          client.addURL(tmpURL);
          tmpURL = new URL(
           "http://servername:7001/APP/ProductDetail.jsp?productID=12345");
          client.addURL(tmpURL);
          tmpURL = new URL(
           "http://servername:7001/APP/ProductSearch.jsp?searchName=Potter");
          client.addURL(tmpURL);
          clients.add(client);
        }
      } catch(Exception e) {
        System.out.println("Exceptions occurred building clients, exiting.");
        e.printStackTrace();
        System.exit(1);
      }

      CheapLoadtester[] testerArray = new CheapLoadtester[clients.size()];
      testerArray = (CheapLoadtester[]) clients.toArray(testerArray);
      for(int i = 0; i < testerArray.length; i++ ) {
        Timer t = new Timer();
        t.schedule(testerArray[i], 500, CheapLoadtester.SLEEP_INTERVAL);
        //Start clients a second off from each other.
        try {
          Thread.sleep(1000);
        } catch(Exception e) {}
      }
    }
}
```

If you would like to investigate more sophisticated load testing tools, the Jakarta Foundation has a Jmeter project for performance testing. Information can be found at `http://jakarta.apache.org/jmeter/index.html`. Mercury Interactive also has performance testing solutions, which you can find at `http://www-svca.mercuryinteractive.com`.

During load testing you may find many client connections are being dropped. This could be because the server is bogged down and you have the accept backlog attribute set too low (refer to Figure 19-7).

Areas of performance tuning

Many different factors can degrade application performance. This chapter focuses on some different options for configuring and tuning your WebLogic Server environment. I will touch on the tuning hardware and operating systems, but extensive coverage of these topics is beyond the scope of this book.

If there are configuration problems with your hardware, operating system, or JVM, it may be that no amount of WebLogic server or application tuning will increase application performance. For instance, if you have only allotted 64 megabytes of RAM to your JVM when much more is available, WebLogic Server may be forced to use massive amounts of CPU swapping from memory to disk in its internal operations. Rather than start your tuning efforts at the lowest application level, it is wise to familiarize yourself with the bigger picture.

WebLogic Server tuning

You can configure the WebLogic Server to suit your application's needs. I examine many of these settings later in the chapter. One example of tuning WebLogic Server's environment is that you can modify the total amount of threads the server is allowed to spawn. Another example of WebLogic Server tuning is tweaking a JDBC connection pool to have a different initial size or maximum size.

Java Virtual Machine tuning

All instances of WebLogic Server run inside a Java Virtual Machine, or JVM. WebLogic Server 6.1 is distributed with and runs on the Java HotSpot JVM. One example of tuning the JVM is the ability to change the algorithm the JVM uses for garbage collection.

WebLogic application tuning

In your application code are many potential performance improvements. One example of improving your WebLogic application's performance is by using value objects to create an entity EJB, instead of calling individual setters to decrease network and database traffic.

See Chapter 3 for information about using value objects with EJBs.

Hardware and operating system tuning

Some of the most important performance tuning of your production environment will be in ensuring a proper amount of CPU power, memory, throughput, and other hardware tuning. Also, your choice of operating system and its settings will drastically affect the performance of your applications. Be sure to read your platform's performance tuning documentation and work with your IT-Operations team to ensure your environment is properly tuned for your needs.

As I mentioned, WebLogic Server runs on the HotSpot JVM, and your applications run on the WebLogic Server. In a clustered environment, you will have multiple servers running on multiple JVMs. Figure 19-1 is a reminder that performance tuning for WebLogic applications must occur on several fronts.

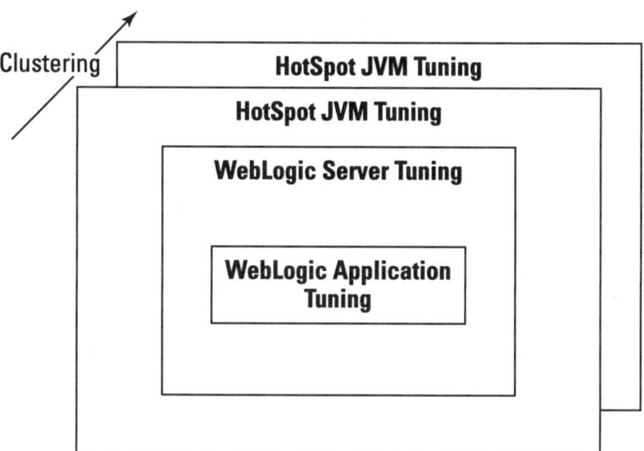

Figure 19-1: Performance tuning occurs on several fronts for WebLogic applications.

WebLogic Server Performance Monitoring

The key to making your WebLogic Server environment faster and more efficient is being able to quickly identify bottlenecks in WebLogic Server's performance. There are also different command-line arguments to your JVM that can provide some performance monitoring information. Finally, I'll mention some popular commercial tools that interface with the WebLogic Server to assist in performance monitoring.

Monitoring WebLogic Servers with the console

Understanding the WebLogic Console will be critical to helping you identify exactly why you may or may not be meeting your performance needs. The console will also be critical in providing evidence that a performance bottleneck has been solved.

Monitoring performance graphs from the console

The WebLogic Console provides a great tool for monitoring application performance. From the console, go to your domain and select a server. Click the Monitoring tab, and then the Performance tab, as shown in Figure 19-2.

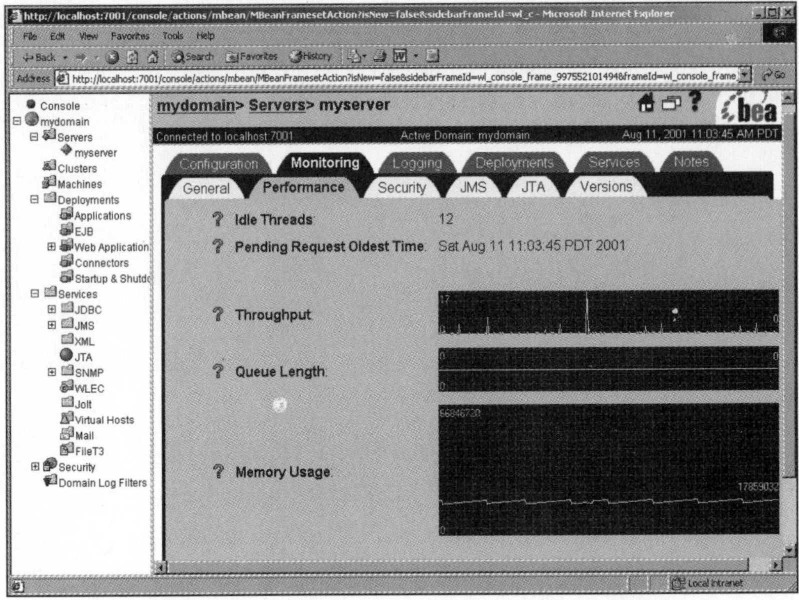

Figure 19-2: WebLogic Console performance monitoring graphs

These graphs provide visual real-time performance monitoring of some aspects of your server's performance. Table 19-1 describes the attributes shown on the screen.

Table 19-1
WebLogic Console Performance Monitoring Attributes

Attribute	***Description***
Idle Threads	The amount of the server's threads that are currently sitting idle.
Pending Request Oldest Time	The amount of time the oldest server request has been waiting to be serviced.
Throughput	The rate at which this server processes requests.
Queue Length	The total number of requests waiting to be serviced.
Memory Usage	The amount of memory currently being used by this server.

These graphs are ideal for easily understanding how your WebLogic Server is performing. If the amount of idle threads approaches zero, this reflects a potential server performance bottleneck. New client requests coming to the server in this state will be queued, as the server will not have available threads to immediately service the requests. Alternatively, if the number of idle threads is very high when your server is at its peak usage, this could also hurt performance. Each server thread costs a certain amount of server resources to keep around and alive. Therefore, having more server threads than you require may hurt performance.

The queue length and pending oldest request times provide a great insight into your server's performance. A growing queue implies that your server is receiving more requests than it can handle. As this queue gets larger, the amount of lag-time before new requests can be serviced will increase. You'll notice that when your queue is growing, the oldest pending request time will also tend to increase.

If your memory usage is approaching 60 to 70 percent of the total available, it may start to degrade performance. As the server starts running out of memory it will start pushing in-memory pieces of your applications to disk to free up memory, and also run the garbage collector more frequently than it would normally.

Later in the chapter, I explain how to allocate more memory to the JVM, as well as how to tweak the number of threads available to the server.

Monitoring active queues, connections, and sockets

Still having your server selected on the console, choose Monitoring ➪ General (see Figure 19-3).

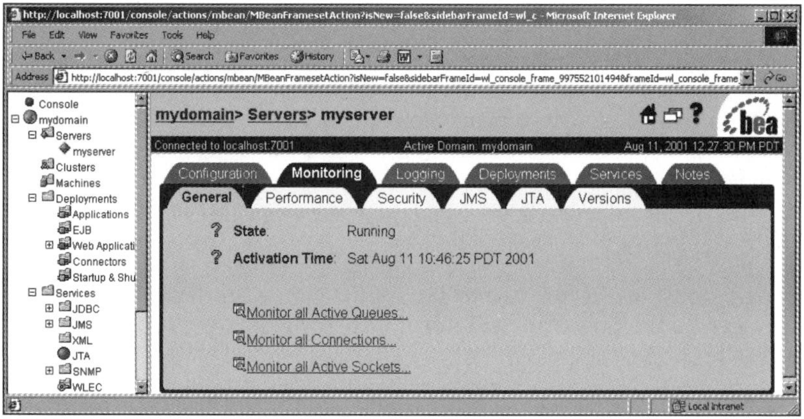

Figure 19-3: General server monitoring options

From the page shown in Figure 19-3, you can get a more detailed look at the server queues, connections, and sockets by clicking those links. If you noticed that your request queues were getting large from the graph, you could come here to determine which execute queues were having poor performance.

Execute queues in the WebLogic server are essentially a group of execute threads that the server has at its disposal to assign work. New execute queues can be created and assigned to particular servlets of your application. Each queue has a configurable amount of threads assigned to it, and also a configurable thread priority. The normal WebLogic configuration is to have one execute queue named default that all JSPs and servlets share. I will discuss the implications of creating and modifying execute queues later in this chapter.

As seen in Figure 19-3, clicking the Monitor Active Queues link takes you to the Active Execute Queues page. In Figure 19-4, you can see the total number of server threads allocated, idle threads, request queue length, and throughput of each execute queue. Clicking a particular queue will allow you to see the threads and the latest actions they have performed.

The first thing to check when monitoring execute queue performance is the idle thread count. This is the number of execute threads that aren't currently doing anything and are waiting to process requests.

If the number of idle threads in the queue is zero, all the execute threads in this queue are busy and the next request to this queue will be blocked until one becomes available. This isn't necessarily a bad thing, as long as requests aren't being timed out and are being processed within an acceptable time frame. On this page you can see how many requests are currently waiting for an execute thread to become available. You can also see the time the oldest request was made, to give you an idea of how long a client is waiting for a response from the server. If an HTTP request from a servlet is waiting for an execute thread for too long, as defined by your Web-server and HTTP configuration, the client's request will timeout.

Having too many idle threads in an execute queue, especially when your server is under maximum load, can also potentially lead to performance problems. With each execute thread comes a performance cost, as each thread owns its own stack and some system resources are required for its creation and maintenance. If your server is under maximum load and execute threads are still available, you may have assigned too many to this queue and you may see a performance increase when reducing the number of threads available to it.

The WebLogic Console enables you to see performance bottlenecks at a high level, and then gives you the power to drill-down into low-level details of your server performance.

Monitoring CPU utilization

Another important metric for monitoring your server's performance is CPU utilization. Familiarize yourself with your operating system and research the performance monitoring tools you have at your disposal. For example, knowing that your server has a good amount of idle CPU under maximum load might be a sign that you can add a few more execute threads to the server. Alternatively, if you see that the server does not have any idle CPU and is consistently above 90 percent utilization, that's a good sign that you will not be able to improve performance by adding additional threads and could even hinder performance by doing so. Under these circumstances, it might be time to add another CPU to your server computer, or possibly another computer.

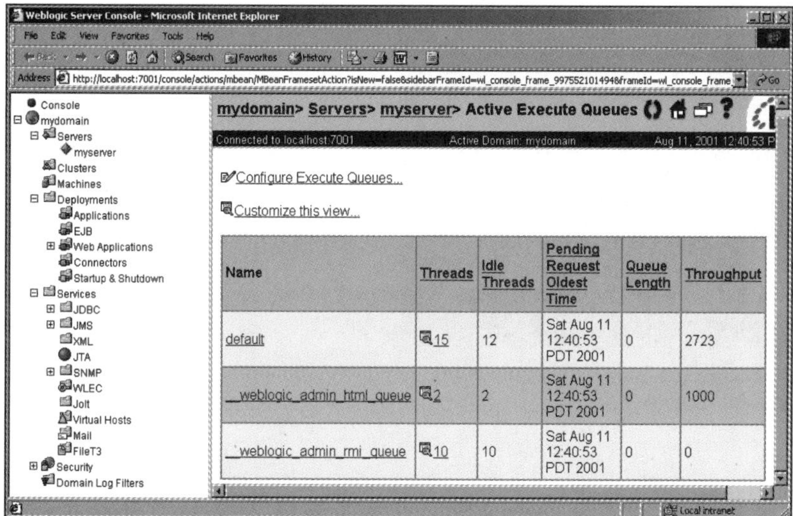

Figure 19-4: Examining active execute queues

JVM options for performance monitoring

The Java HotSpot JVM provides some command-line flags that you may find useful. While complete analysis of their output data is outside the scope of this book, I will briefly mention them and point you in the right direction if you choose to investigate further.

Garbage collection monitoring

Garbage collection can sometimes cause noticeable pauses in Java applications. The Hotspot JVM allows you to tune garbage performance behavior and get garbage collection information. To get detailed analysis of your JVM's garbage collecting behavior, use the option for verbose garbage collection, `-verbosegc`. See your JVM documentation for detailed analysis and explanation of the output.

Be sure to turn off verbose garbage collection when you move to a production environment, as there is a performance hit associated with using it.

-Xprof JVM profiling

Edit your scripts to start WebLogic by adding an `-Xprof` to the server startup call. This flag tells the JVM that you want to get some JVM profiling information, as shown in Figure 19-5.

```
Start Default Server

Flat profile of 1.50 secs (101 total ticks): Thread-1

  Interpreted + native   Method
 20.8%     0  +    15    weblogic.management.snmp.agent.ServerMap.<clinit>
 18.1%     0  +    13    java.lang.ClassLoader.defineClass0
  1.4%     1  +     0    java.util.Hashtable$Enumerator.<init>
 40.3%     1  +    28    Total interpreted

     Compiled + native   Method
  1.4%     1  +     0    java.lang.String.equals
  1.4%     1  +     0    java.lang.String.substring
  2.8%     2  +     0    Total compiled

         Stub + native   Method
 25.0%     0  +    18    java.lang.Class.forName0
  6.9%     0  +     5    java.util.zip.Inflater.inflateBytes
  5.6%     0  +     4    java.util.zip.ZipFile.getEntry
  2.8%     0  +     2    java.util.zip.ZipFile.read
  2.8%     0  +     2    java.lang.ClassLoader.findLoadedClass
  1.4%     0  +     1    java.lang.Throwable.fillInStackTrace
 44.4%     0  +    32    Total stub

  Thread-local ticks:
 28.7%    29             Blocked (of total)
 12.5%     9             Unknown: thread_state
```

Figure 19-5: Sample standard output from running your JVM with -Xprof

Running your JVM with `-Xprof` will push some profiling information to standard out. (You can find more information on `-Xprof` output at `http://java.sun.com/docs/hotspot/PerformanceFAQ.html`.)

-Xrunhprof JVM profiling

Another way to get more profiling information about your JVM is to put the `-Xrunhprof` flag in your WebLogic Server startup scripts, as shown in Figure 19-6.

```
C:\WINNT\System32\cmd.exe

Z:\>java -Xrunhprof:help
Hprof usage: -Xrunhprof[:help]|[<option>=<value>, ...]

Option Name and Value  Description                Default
---------------------  -----------                -------
heap=dump|sites|all    heap profiling             all
cpu=samples|times|old  CPU usage                  off
monitor=y|n            monitor contention         n
format=a|b             ascii or binary output     a
file=<file>            write data to file         java.hprof(.txt for ascii)
net=<host>:<port>      send data over a socket    write to file
depth=<size>           stack trace depth          4
cutoff=<value>         output cutoff point        0.0001
lineno=y|n             line number in traces?     y
thread=y|n             thread in traces?          n
doe=y|n                dump on exit?              y

Example: java -Xrunhprof:cpu=samples,file=log.txt,depth=3 FooClass

Z:\>
```

Figure 19-6: -Xrunhprof JVM profiling options

Running your WebLogic Server with the `-Xrunhprof` flag can give you a lot more detailed JVM information, including heap profiling and CPU usage. You can have this information pushed to an ASCII text file for later review. Again, you can find more information on `-Xrunhprof` profiling at `http://java.sun.com/docs/hotspot/PerformanceFAQ.html`.

When moving your WebLogic applications into production, be sure to remove these profiling flags from your server startup scripts.

Commercial tools for performance monitoring

If you need more detailed or easier-to-understand performance analysis, there are a number of commercially available Java profilers. Many of them even integrate easily with the WebLogic Server. Intuitive Systems' profiler Optimizeit and Sitraka's Jprobe are just a few you may want to research for your WebLogic Server profiling needs.

Tuning WebLogic Server

Now you have put some thought into performance expectations of your WebLogic application and also learned some methods to monitor WebLogic Server's performance. You can use these skills to find critical bottlenecks. I will now address methods to solve these bottlenecks.

Basic server configuration

A number of basic configuration options are available from the WebLogic Console tuning page. Enabling native I/O using performance packs, creating and adjusting WebLogic's internal execute queues, and configuring connection buffer sizes are just a few.

WebLogic Server performance packs

WebLogic provides performance packs for certain platforms. These performance packs tie I/O operations more closely to the platform and thereby increase application performance, because platform-independent I/O is not as efficient. Depending on which platform you are running WebLogic Server, you may be able to enable these platform-native I/O operations, which will yield a significant performance boost. See the WebLogic documentation to see whether your platform has a performance pack available. If one is available for your platform you should use it.

To activate the native I/O performance pack, go to the WebLogic Console, click Configuration, and then click the Tuning tab, as shown in Figure 19-7.

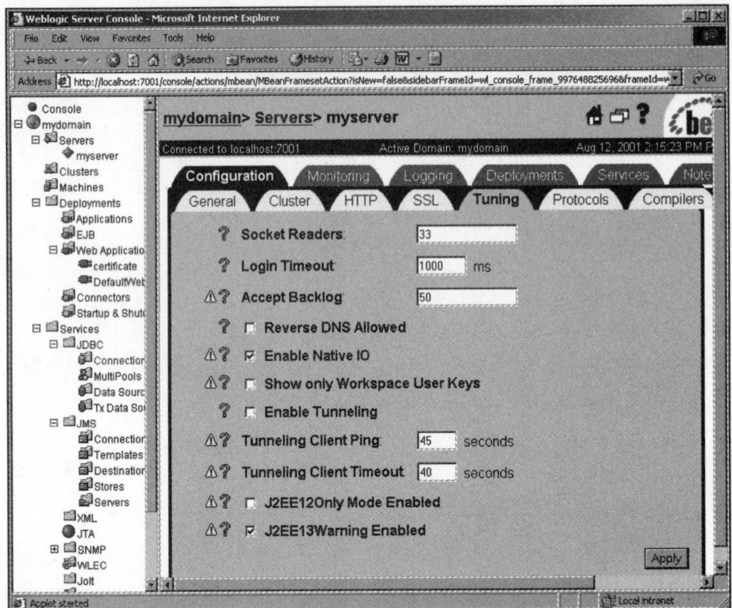

Figure 19-7: Enabling native I/O in the WebLogic Console

Select the Enable Native IO check box and click Apply. When you restart your server, you will now be using native I/O.

If no performance pack is available for your platform, WebLogic Server will allocate a certain percentage of its execute threads to be available as socket readers. This percentage is also available for adjustment on the console, also seen in Figure 19-7. If your application heavily uses I/O, you may get a performance boost by raising this percentage.

Modifying execute thread counts

The number of execute threads WebLogic Server has allotted to it affects its internal operations and your applications drastically. The more threads allotted, the more simultaneous actions can take place within the server. During the course of your testing, look for the situation where the waiting request queues are building up and your CPU utilization isn't 100 percent. This implies that while there is CPU time available to the server, all the threads are potentially blocked and not available to service a new request. This is a situation where raising the execute thread count could improve your server's performance.

You can adjust the number of threads from the WebLogic Console. From the Examining Active Execute Queues page (see Figure 19-4) click the link to Configure Execute Queues. This will bring up a list of all the execute queues, as shown in Figure 19-8. Click one to configure it.

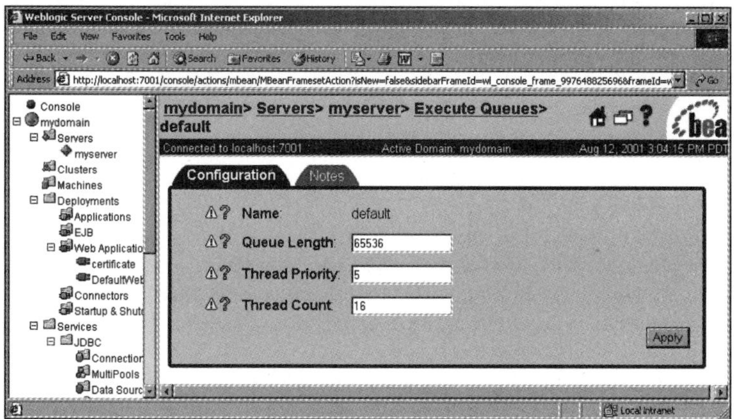

Figure 19-8: Modifying thread count on execute queues

Adjusting the thread count will take effect after restarting your WebLogic Server. The queue length is the maximum length of the execute queue. Raising thread priority will result in this queue taking CPU-priority over threads with lower priority.

Raising the server thread count can sometimes increase application performance, but there are many factors to consider before raising the count. Setting the count too high will degrade server performance. The number of simultaneous actions that can happen on your server is dependent on the number of CPUs on your server hardware. The more processors available, the more threads you can give the server and expect a performance boost.

Another factor to consider when deciding to modify the thread counts is what operating system you are running. Some operating systems can handle higher numbers of threads than others. Also, keep in mind that the more threads you allocate to the server, the more context-switching will occur. Context-switching occurs when one thread stops and another takes over on the CPU — and you pay a performance price when that happens. Also, by increasing the number of server threads, you're increasing the amount of memory the server uses, which can degrade performance.

Accept Backlog attribute

The WebLogic server will allow a certain number of connections, 50 by default, to be placed in the connection backlog when all execute threads in the queue are busy. The amount is configurable by changing the accept backlog attribute on the Server Tuning page of the console, as seen in Figure 19-7. If you notice that many of your clients are having their connections refused by your WebLogic server, you could increase this number accordingly to allow the buffer to grow larger.

Creating new execute queues

The WebLogic server allows you to create new execute queues as well. This is generally only a good idea if you have pieces of your application that you can define as far more or far less critical than the rest of your application. Even in that case, use extreme caution when configuring new queues as taking this step unnecessarily could easily create new performance issues.

For example, imagine there is a certain set of JSPs that your company provides free of charge that see lots of traffic. You may need to take steps to ensure that these users don't interfere with a set of pages your customers use during payment. This is because you have found that there is a good chance customers will not proceed with a purchase if the pages are taking too long. In this case, you could create a new execute thread with a small number of execute threads at a low priority, and assign the freely available JSPs to use that execute thread. This way, the JSPs or servlets will only get so much attention from the WebLogic server, and will not directly interfere with the execute queues of the mission-critical JSPs. Alternatively, you could create a new execute queue with threads at a higher priority and assign your mission-critical pages to that thread.

To bind servlets or JSPs to a specific execute queue, you must alter the `web.xml` file entry to set the `wl-dispatch-policy` initialization parameter to the proper execute queues name. An example of this is seen in Listing 19-2.

Listing 19-2: Binding Servlets or JSPs to Execute Queues

```
<servlet>
  <servlet-name>ServletName</servlet-name>
  <jsp-file>/applicationname/dopayment.jsp</jsp-file>
  <init-param>
    <param-name>wl-dispatch-policy</param-name>
    <param-value>NewExecuteQueueName</param-value>
  </init-param>
</servlet>
```

JDBC tuning considerations

Correctly configuring your JDBC connection pools and using the correct drivers can increase the performance of your WebLogic Server applications. Using pre-compiled prepared statements is another method of increasing performance. Also, sometimes the best way to improve database performance is to avoid the database as much as possible through the use of object caches.

Connection pool settings

Making your database connection pool too small can drastically degrade application performance. In most applications, the ideal number of maximum connections in a pool is equal to the amount of simultaneous users using the application, assuming those users could cause database hits. If your pool has reached its maximum number of connections, and all connections are in use by other users, a new database connection request will block until one becomes available.

Alternatively, if the number of database connections is set too high, this could also cause performance issues. Each database connection you create has a performance cost in terms of memory, and also in ongoing maintenance as the WebLogic server pool will monitor its connections.

Also, some databases will kill idle connections, causing the WebLogic server to recreate the connections at a high performance cost. You must work with your DBAs to determine your connection pool settings in production and development.

Driver-type considerations

Not all JDBC drivers perform alike. Much like how using a performance pack can use native I/O, some drivers are more optimized and closely tied to the platform. If your application is database intensive, be sure and research what driver you are using and what other drivers are available to you.

See Chapter 5 for more detailed information on driver-types, pool settings, and general JDBC concerns.

EJB tuning considerations

You can find many potential performance improvements by correctly tuning the EJB pools for your applications. This section discusses a few of them, but be sure to look at Part IV for information on database locking issues, detailed analysis of deployment descriptors, and other performance-related information.

EJB pool settings

As with JDBC connection pools, the WebLogic Server saves the cost of allocating some types of EJBs by using pooling. If you set the maximum size of the pools too low, you will degrade application performance. The maximum size of these pools is found in the `weblogic-ejb-jar.xml` descriptor under the attribute `max-beans-in-free-pool`. If all of a pool's EJBs are in use by a client and a new client requests an EJB from the pool, the client must wait until one becomes available. You have the option of setting the initial size of these pools high as well; at server startup, a certain number will be created, increasing memory usage but potentially improving performance.

Stateful and entity EJB caching

Another potential area to focus your tuning efforts is in the caching of the stateful session EJBs. Stateful session EJBs are never persisted to a database, so the server must keep them in a memory cache or push them to disk for temporary storage. The process of pushing these beans to disk and retrieving them when needed — called activation and passivation — is expensive. The most stateful session EJBs that the server will keep in the cache are set in the `weblogic-ejb-jar.xml` file under the attribute `max-beans-in-cache`. If this attribute is set too low, your server may do an excessive amount of passivation of these EJBs, which will degrade performance. Excessive raising of the maximum cache size could cost your server in memory availability.

Defer locking to database with entity EJBs

By default, the WebLogic server will defer entity locking to the database, which is more efficient than having the EJB container do it.

Tuning the WebLogic Server's JVM

The Hotspot Java Virtual Machine (JVM) is highly tunable for boosting your server performance. I'll discuss a few common options for tuning your JVM when launching your WebLogic Servers. Be sure to research in more detail in the documentation for the Hotspot JVM. Pay particular attention to options available to the platform on which you are running WebLogic as they vary. You will tune the JVM by editing the server startup scripts.

Heap sizes

One of the most important steps when starting the WebLogic Server in your production environment is setting the maximum and minimum sizes of the memory heap, as shown in Figure 19-9. It's a good general practice to set the minimum and maximum equal to each other as this ensures the JVM will not waste resources resizing the heap. Tuning the size of this heap will greatly affect server performance. You want to set this as high as your hardware will allow, but at a point prior to reaching that maximum you may encounter performance degradation. Having too much memory allocated can sometimes cause garbage collection to be overly slow. To change these sizes, adjust the JVM options `-ms` and `-mx` by modifying the allotted memory in your scripts that start the WebLogic server JVM. In Figure 19-9 you can see that the startup script has set the minimum and maximum memory to be 64 megabytes.

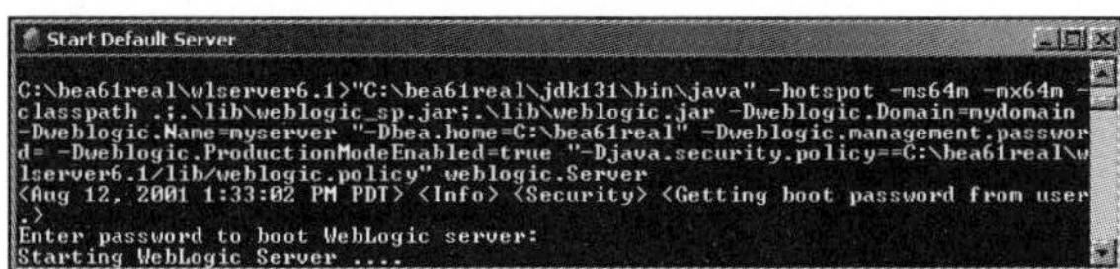

Figure 19-9: Starting the WebLogic Server JVM with heap sizes of 64 megabytes

Garbage collection

The Hotspot JVM uses a generational garbage collection algorithm. Rather than scan the entire heap for all dereferenced objects, it keeps track of the age of the objects and uses the information to increase its efficiency. You may see a performance boost by playing with more options for setting the heap. The options `-XX:NewSize` and `-XX:MaxNewSize` set the size of the portion of the heap that will house relatively new objects. These objects are the most frequently garbage collected, and this area will be garbage collected more than some other areas of the heap. WebLogic recommends setting these sizes to approximately one-fourth the total size of the heap. If your application tends to allocate large quantities of objects only to have them dereferenced shortly thereafter, you may want to tune this number higher. For a more complete discussion of the Hotspot Garbage Collector and settings, go to `http://java.sun.com/docs/hotspot/PerformanceFAQ.html`.

Client/Server JVM options

Multiple JVMs come with Hotspot. By running with a `-hotspot` flag or a `-client` flag, you are running the client version. The client version is optimized for a small scope. Alternatively, running your server with a `-server` flag will run the Hotspot JVM that has been optimized for a server environment.

Be sure to retest your applications if you choose to try and switch JVMs in this manner. Changing the JVM is a fundamentally radical change in environment and should be taken seriously.

Tuning WebLogic Server Applications

Now that you know about tuning your WebLogic Server and also its JVM, let's look at some performance considerations for your applications.

Tuning JDBC modules within your application

Not only must you properly set up your WebLogic server connection pools and datasources, but you must also make sure your applications use those resources intelligently. Here are a few simple JDBC tuning considerations when examining your application code.

ResultSet concurrency and direction

Make sure that when you are doing normal forward-only and read-only processing that you are using the most efficient ResultSet concurrency and direction modes. When the statements are initialized to return forward moving and read-only results, they are generally far more efficient. See the `java.sql.Statement` and static constants on the `java.sql.ResultSet` interface documentation and your database driver documentation for further details.

Prepared statements

Use JDBC optimizations like prepared statements whenever possible, including in your session EJBs that perform database operations. To learn more about what prepared statements are, research the `java.sql.PreparedStatement` interface as defined by Sun.

Java object caches

Caching information in memory on the server can prevent unnecessary database hits. Oftentimes, these caches are loaded on application startup and are serializable objects registered with JNDI. For example, an application may be able to keep its entire product catalog in memory, in a collection keyed by a unique product identifier. This would be an alternative to doing a database query to load product information on demand.

Depending on the type and configuration of the database you are using, it's possible that it is doing some complex caching on its end to improve query performance. However, no matter how fast the JDBC queries come back from the database, you still will have to parse the ResultSet into a Java object at some point in order to use it. Also, it's possible that your database lives on a separate piece of hardware and must communicate over a network. This network communication will use bandwidth and also increase the latency of the queries. For those reasons there is always a performance gain from keeping some commonly used objects in a cache.

EJB considerations

When developing EJBs that you know will not be accessed remotely via Remote Method Invocation (RMI), define local interfaces for those EJBs. This is a new option in the EJB 2.0 specification.

The WebLogic Server is extremely efficient at supplying stateless session EJBs to clients, far more efficient than when you use stateful beans. Clients do not actually hold onto a reference to a stateless session EJB, but a proxy to the pool of EJBs.

Use value objects to populate entity EJBs rather than individual setters. Each set method call is potentially a remote method call, as well as a database hit! By passing a serializable object that represents all the values to set, you can accomplish this all at once.

See Part IV for more detailed discussion of these types of EJB considerations.

Asynchronous components

By keeping your application components asynchronous, you often increase performance, or at least response times, to the client. Research some of the different J2EE technologies that can help achieve this, including JMS messaging and message-driven EJBs.

For instance, let's say one result of a user's action is that an e-mail should be sent to an administrator. Instead of doing that processing synchronously, where the user doesn't receive confirmation until the e-mail has been sent, you could post the user's message to some JMS destination and then immediately respond to the user. A message-driven EJB could be listening on the JMS destination and kicking off the e-mail asynchronously. So if the WebLogic server was very busy and it takes lots of time to build and kickoff that e-mail, the user would not notice that performance issue. This is only one example of improving performance via asynchronous behavior.

Singletons

A singleton is a design pattern in which only one of a certain facet of your application exists. This pattern can be useful when making performance tuning decisions. Let's say there is a certain process, doing a massive data conversion, that takes an enormous amount of CPU and memory to run. You want to make a design decision to enforce that this process can only be running by one thread at any given moment in time to limit the amount of server resources it can take up. You would therefore implement this class as a singleton.

Transaction considerations

In general, make sure you keep your transaction scopes as small as possible. Don't have unnecessary systems or modules inside a transaction as large scope and duration can be extremely expensive. Also, make it a rule to never have a transaction spanning a user's input.

See Chapter 6 for more information about transaction scopes.

Logging considerations

Anyone who has coded in Java is familiar with the tendency to put lots of `System.out.println` lines in code for debugging purposes. It's important to try and limit these logging messages when you move to production as there is a performance cost to this extra messaging to the standard output stream.

Even if you use WebLogic Server's logging subsystem, or some configurable logging system like log4j, there may be a cost in the very method call to those subsystems, regardless of priority of the log message. It is possible that in your strings you are calling lots of `toString()` methods during those log statements. Even if there is no I/O cost relating to the logging call because you have logging turned off, you still will be using CPU with the unnecessary method calls and string building.

Compiler settings

You can configure your EJBC and JSP compiler settings to use more efficient compilers if you have them. These optimizing compilers may create more efficient Java classes. Also, you can configure your JSPs to pre-compile on server startup to avoid situations where a JSP compiler causes brief but noticeable spikes in your CPU utilization when compiling JSPs.

Nonsynchronized collections

You can achieve some significant performance boosts by using nonsynchronized collections, like `java.util.HashMap`, instead of synchronized collections like `java.util.HashTable`. This, of course, assumes that you don't have concurrent access of these collections.

Placing objects in sessions

Placing Java objects in a client session can drastically improve performance. For example, it's a much better idea to place a user's personal data in her session than to load it from a database on every one of her page clicks. However, there is a server-side cost relating to placing objects in the session.

Every object you keep in the session has a performance cost related to the object's in-memory size. Every data member of the object increases the amount of memory it will take to store it in the session. Say when monitoring your server's performance you notice the server is using near its maximum allotted memory, and you detect a direct correlation between the number of users logged in and the amount of memory used, regardless of user behavior. This would indicate a large memory cost per client session, and could point to a case with large data objects, or large numbers of objects in session.

Before putting a large object into the session, take the time to think of potential design alternatives. For example, let's look at an e-commerce site's decision of placing of a UserBean object into all user sessions. The UserBean contains other data members relating to the user's preferences, request-history, general account information, and a product wish list. Perhaps all those data members are loaded when a user logs in and then placed into that user's session. Instead of keeping a user's wish list in memory as a UserBean data member, perhaps you want that information to be loaded from the database on every HTTP request, or only get loaded into memory when they visit a specific subset of application pages relating to the wish-list functionality. With these alternatives, when the user is not building or viewing a wish list, the data members relating to the wish list aren't eating up precious memory resources.

You also want to analyze all the objects you put in the session to see if they are holding redundant information. Perhaps you are actually storing product names and descriptions in the user's wish list, when you only need to keep around the product's unique integer identifier.

Make sure that your application is intelligent enough to remove objects from the session when it is no longer necessary to keep them around. Instead of letting the user's entire product history in the session, you will keep around data relating only to the last four products he viewed. This would cut down the amount of memory the product history takes up in the session and free valuable server resources.

To summarize, placing objects in the session can improve performance if there is enough available memory on the server. Realize that a developer's abuse of the session can cause a server to run low on memory and drastically reduce server performance.

WebLogic Server clustering overview

At some point in your load testing and tuning process you may realize that you've made lots of improvements but you are still unable to meet your performance goals. You've worked with IT to ensure the hardware is properly configured and has a good amount of memory and fast CPUs. All your execute queues are busy and requests are still being dropped. There is no idle CPU and available memory is running low, so creating extra execute threads or object caches don't seem like good solutions.

No matter how tuned, there is only so much one WebLogic Server can do. If your application has a large audience whose performance demands have your single server peaked, clustering is the answer. Instead of running one server, you run your applications on many servers, and WebLogic is intelligent enough to distribute the load across the different servers. Clustering also has the added bonus of providing failover. When one of your servers goes down, there are more to fill in and your clients may not even notice. Assuming you wrote your application components in a somewhat standard J2EE fashion, using EJBs, JSPs, Servlets, and so on, there is a good chance your application performance will improve linearly as you add hardware and servers.

Take special care when tuning WebLogic servers in a cluster. A WebLogic server in a cluster will tend to use more execute threads as socket readers than a non-clustered server. This is due to the overhead of the clustered servers interacting via socket communication. As seen in Figure 19-7, you can adjust the number of execute threads and also increase the percentage of those threads available as socket readers. If you are encountering performance problems with your cluster under load, pay special attention to the number of idle execute threads. If there are a good number of idle execute threads available to the server, you may increase performance by increasing the percentage available. If there are no execute threads idle, you may need to increase the overall number of execute threads on the server, taking into consideration your hardware and platform constraints.

It is generally best to performance tune and test your applications in a single-server environment before adding the complexity of a server cluster into the mix.

See Chapter 24 for more information about clustering WebLogic Server.

Tuning Process Example

Here I'll examine the steps a fictitious development took in its iterative tuning, load testing, and analysis process. This case study will not contain code, specific details about load testing suites, profilers, or hardware. It is of a walkthrough of simple tuning steps and high-level tuning thoughts. The purpose is to illustrate a simple process that may be similar to those used in many development shops.

Define performance goals

After the project team had completed the project's functional specifications, it was time to for the software engineers to focus on the design specifications and high-level architecture. Before starting this design, they laid out detailed thoughts on user behavior, expected user populations, and application performance goals in specific application modules.

For this example, we will focus on three of the project team's goals. The first goal is to be able to support 1,000 concurrent users, which is twice as many as they have ever seen in production. By overshooting the amount of users they expect to see, they should be able to develop their application and tune their environment to handle a potential unexpected growth in users.

The second goal is to return "critical" Web pages; i.e., pages central to the user's purpose for using the application, in two seconds or less. On an online brokerage site, for example, such pages might include forms to buy and sell securities, or pages that display individual account statements.

The third goal is to return "non-critical" Web pages to users in five seconds or less. Considering again an online brokerage site, such pages might include the brokerage firm's quarterly financial statements, delivery of lengthy research reports, explanations of trading regulations, and so on.

Now that the project team has laid down goals, they must define what they mean by 1,000 users. When analyzing user behavior of similar sites and of their own current user population, the team has estimated that the average user will do one request every 45 seconds. Forty percent of the requests are for portfolio analysis or to view breaking news about companies. Forty percent of the requests are for research on specific stocks and mutual funds, including getting real-time quotes of stocks. Twenty percent of the requests are directly related to the trading of stocks, such as a request to enter an order to buy a security.

The application tuning process

Having a great iterative tuning process is no substitute for good initial architecture and engineering practices. Many of the performance problems seen in the testing phase of applications reflects a poor initial architecture or an architecture that was created without detailed performance goals and scalability in mind. For this example, let's assume the application's architects did a mediocre job, so during their tuning process we'll see some architecture decisions rethought, as well as tweaking of the server, JVM, database, and EJB settings.

The process employed by the project team is to load test the application with an accurate portrayal of the user population. During the testing, developers will monitor the server's performance from the WebLogic Console and by monitoring the hardware's CPU metrics. After analyzing the test data to see if they met their performance objectives, the team will decide when it's time to end the tuning process and proceed to staging the application in production.

Load testing

The development team leverages its knowledge of expected user behavior and performance goals to create its load testing suite. The team configures its load testing suite to create a user population that is similar to the one it will see in production. The team also has configured the testing suite to gradually increase users over time, until it reaches the 1,000-user limit. Starting small and increasing the amount of users over time allows the team to monitor the performance at a wide range of stresses and help it pinpoint an approximate number of maximum users with the current application and server configuration.

The team will then correlate data returned from its simulated users with data gained from monitoring the server. When the simulated users start to see large response times, server timeouts, or refusing connections, that is the time to closely inspect the WebLogic Console and the CPU Utilization for evidence of where the bottlenecks are occurring. Once they have theorized where the bottleneck lies, they will attempt to fix the issue and then move forward with the next load testing phase to see if the server performance has improved, stayed the same, or become worse.

Now let's examine the specific iterations of load testing and taking a WebLogic server and application configuration to production.

Iteration 1

Test results: At the first run of the load testing, the test got up to 40 users before the users started to experience response times slower than five seconds. At 60 users, many user connections were getting dropped and an inspection of the WebLogic Server logs indicated out of memory exceptions. Meanwhile, the WebLogic Console performance graph showed that the server had indeed consumed its entire memory allocation of 64 megabytes.

Solution: After checking the staging server's hardware and speaking with IT-Operations, the team decided to give the server's JVM maximum and minimum heap size to 512 megabytes of memory.

Iteration 2

Test results: This time, the team started encountering "connection refused" errors when the test got to 100 total users. All of the users previous to that moment had been getting server responses within acceptable time frames.

Solution: Because all the users who got any responses got acceptable ones, and the rest of the user connections were refused, the engineering team thinks that the server could accept more connections and increases the Accept Backlog attribute on the WebLogic Console tuning page from 50 to 100. This forces the server to allow the backlog to grow so it can continue to service those requests.

Iteration 3

Test results: This time the test got up to 250 users, at which point server response times on a specific page fell below acceptable limits, taking over five seconds. This page is related to looking up a detailed view of a stock's metrics.

Solution: The engineers looked at the code for looking up the stock metrics, and noticed that it was a JDBC query against the stock database. They worked with the DBAs to create indexes on the columns of data that the users could search on, and changed their result sets to be forward moving and read-only.

Iteration 4

Test results: This time the test got up to 300 users, at which point server response times on all JDBC-related pages fell below acceptable limits, taking over five seconds. The engineers inspected the JDBC connection pools and noticed that all the connections were busy, and therefore all new database requests started to queue up waiting for connections from the pool.

Solution: The engineers worked with the DBAs and decided to triple the amount of maximum database connections. They also decided to build an in-memory cache of objects encapsulating data about the top 1,000 stocks.

Iteration 5

Test results: The test got up to 400 users before users started to get unacceptable response times on all pages. Using the WebLogic Console to examine the execute queues, the engineers noticed that there were no available execute threads and requests had started piling up. Inspection of the CPU Utilization at the same moment shows that there is still 50 percent CPU idle time.

Solution: The engineers researched WebLogic documentation about their operating system and hardware configurations, and decided to increase the number of threads on the default execute queue from 15 to 40.

Iteration 6

Test results: The test approached 700 users before server response times fell well below acceptable limits. The idle CPU time was less than one percent, free memory available to the server was also less than one percent, no free database connections were seen, and the backlog had overflowed. The engineers had cached everything possible, inspected the user sessions for unnecessary objects, and worked with DBAs to build all the necessary database tuning.

Solution: The engineers now feel it is time to cluster and add hardware. Not only will this provide another server to disperse the load to, but it has the added bonus of giving the Web site some measure of failover. They decide to purchase two additional boxes. The current server seems to be able to service 700 users before peaking out. By purchasing two additional servers, they estimate they will be able to service almost 2,000 simultaneous users. And if one server happens to go down, they will still be able to service the performance goals with the other two. A three-server cluster is implemented.

Iteration 7

Test results: The test approached 900 users before the performance on the mission-critical pages fell below acceptable range, and trades started approaching three-second response times. All other page requests were well within acceptable range. There was plenty of memory available across the cluster, and CPU Utilization was relatively low. Examining the execute queues the engineers realized all execute threads were busy.

Solution: The mission-critical pages are using the same execute queues as the rest of the pages. The engineers decide to create separate execute queues for the mission-critical pages. These new queues are assigned 15 threads each, while moving the default queues down to 25 execute threads. The priority of the mission-critical execute queues is set higher than the default queues.

Iteration 8

Test results: The test approached 1,800 users before performance was unacceptable. Engineers then dropped one server from the cluster and ran the test again to simulate a server crash at a critical time. The test was still within acceptable parameters, allowing 1,300 users.

Summary

WebLogic Server supplies you with lots of help in measuring and monitoring its performance. The real-time graphing and thread-queue monitoring from the console are especially helpful. You must also familiarize yourself with tools to monitor performance in your operating system in order to help you tune applications.

Load testing is the process of simulating a user base in order to measure your application and server performance during development. Profiling is the process of using tools to inspect the application and server environments and help you troubleshoot bottlenecks. Many commercial tools are available to help you load test and profile your server's performance. Define your application testing needs before investigating these potentially commercial solutions. Look for tools that easily interface with the WebLogic Server.

Because your WebLogic Server has many components, when improperly tuned, they can cause performance bottlenecks. Use the console to investigate and tailor these components for your platform and application.

WebLogic Server runs on the Java Hotspot JVM. Hotspot gives you many options for tuning it to your particular operating system and hardware.

WebLogic Server clustering, assuming your application was written with scalability in mind, scales almost linearly by adding new server instances to the cluster.

✦ ✦ ✦

Implementing Security

PART

VI

✦ ✦ ✦ ✦

In This Part

✦ ✦ ✦ ✦

CHAPTER 20

Understanding Security Fundamentals

✦ ✦ ✦ ✦

In This Chapter

Security principles and layers

Security perimeters

Security attacks

Ciphers, keys, and secure sockets

✦ ✦ ✦ ✦

Almost all Enterprise Applications today, especially those being deployed to the Internet, require some level of security and protection. Sometimes the requirement is to protect consumers from fraud (such as credit card theft); other times the requirement is to protect internal corporate data (such as payroll information) from access by unauthorized persons; other times the requirement is something completely different. This chapter helps you understand the need for Enterprise Application security, the fundamental concepts of Enterprise Application security, and the properties of effective security solutions. In Chapters 21 and 22, you'll learn how to apply these concepts in the context of WebLogic Server to build secure WebLogic applications.

Enterprise security concepts closely parallel the security concepts you encounter in daily life. Security is the capability to enforce some level of trust among people, organizations, and systems, including the capability to protect assets belonging to those entities. Just as people have different levels of trust, so do organizations. You encounter different levels of trust in your daily lives. When getting change from a cashier, for example, do you count it? Do you trust your daughter with the car keys? Do you lock up your jewelry and cash when a maid cleans your hotel room? Do you believe your co-worker about the layoff rumors without asking anyone else? All these questions imply some form of security layering. The more valuable you believe an object is, the more security you apply to it. You may, for example, forget about change on the nightstand in a hotel room, but you will pick up fifty dollars before you leave the room.

Just as you apply different levels of security to items of different perceived value, so do organizations. An online trading firm's home page, for example, is visible to everyone; whereas only customers can view their accounts. The firm's internal mail system is protected from everyone except employees. The question becomes how valuable is the Enterprise data?

Customers and their data are at the mercy of how an organization manages that data. When a credit card number is stored into the Web site for an order, that number is now stored by the system that the customer placed the order in. If that same customer places many orders at different systems, his credit card number is managed by each of them, and the security of that important data depends on the security of those systems. The question is, how secure must Enterprise data be, and how do you go about securing it?

Security Layers

Security principles are the answers to the questions of how secure and how valuable the Enterprise data needs to be. *Security layers* refer to how those answers are modeled in the system. Before you give access to your objects (*authorization*), you first have to know the person (*authentication*). If you have any doubts about the state of something you own, you check up on it (*integrity*). If the person seems untrustworthy, you keep mental notes on what to trust to him, what to double-check, and what not to share (*auditing*). A typical security layering system may look like Figure 20-1.

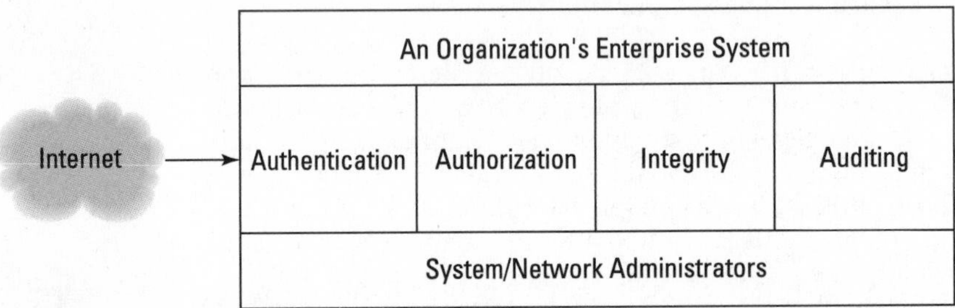

Figure 20-1: Security layers

You apply security levels throughout your everyday life. The first level is authentication. You use authentication whenever you answer a phone and give a name, or whenever you try to recognize someone's face. Authentication knows with whom you are communicating to determine how much access you will give that person. If a telemarketer calls me in a cold call, for example, I'm unlikely to give him my credit card number. Yet, sometimes I find myself ordering from a site without truly knowing the company at the other end. Even if I know the company, such as ABCD.com, how do I know that it is the one at the other end? How do I know that ABCD.com, instead of someone pretending to be, is getting my credit card number? If I ask

ABCD.com to verify itself by answering some questions about the company that only it would know, it's called *one-way authentication.* If it finishes answering my questions and starts asking me questions, such as my mother's maiden name, to also verify me, the authentication becomes *mutual authentication.*

After a customer talks to ABCD.com and believes it is who it says it is, and if he needs to purchase something, he might give it access to his credit card, one of his objects. Now ABCD.com has entered the authorization layer. It's like a person who has entered my house after I let them through my front door. Now I have given that person permission to touch something that I own. Depending on how much I trust that person, I may allow him to pick it up and look at it (read permission), I may allow him to modify it (write permission), or I may allow him to use it (execute permission).

Another example is when I give my car keys to my daughter. After she has access to the car, she can lend the keys to a friend. But if I wanted to limit her access to the car, I might only give her the keys when she asks for them. Not giving users access to resources unless they ask for them is a common idea in a lot of organizations— this is known as the *least privileged method.*

To continue with the car scenario, let's look at the next layer of security, integrity. After my daughter drives my car for the first time, I might go outside and look at it to ensure that the car is the same. That is called integrity. If you upload a file to an FTP site, and later download it, how do you know the file has not changed? You trust that no one has gone into your Web site; but that might not be true. You might check the byte size and date/time of the file, and if it is the same, you might assume that the file has not been modified. But changing the file and setting the original file information is a trivial exercise. The same could hold true with my daughter. She may have banged up the car over the weekend but then repaired it. Because I know my car well, I can tell the difference—or so I hope.

If my car seems different and I'm unsure what is different about it, I would have to figure it out. I might not even know the extent of the damage unless I examined the car in detail. I may have to take it to a mechanic and get an estimate of the damage. That is the next layer, auditing. In this layer, not knowing the extent of the damage is the worst thing that could happen. It could be that the brakes on the car are only good for another 40 miles. I cannot blame my daughter for not knowing the extent of the damage of the car; she isn't a mechanic. The same applies to hackers. Many hackers use tools that someone else invented, and they're not even sure about the extent of damage that they might do to a system. If a hacker is caught and questioned about what is now wrong with the system, it's possible that he wouldn't know the answer.

Therefore, there should always be monitoring techniques to detect changes in the system and the system's data. If a hacker intercepted your credit card, for example, you could cancel the credit card. If the hacker found a hole in the firewall, you could plug it up next time, setting a redirector to fake him out, while monitoring and tracking his moves to find out where he's originated. For every enhancement to security, there have been enhancements to hacking skills to break these securities. If it weren't for auditing records, nobody would know how hackers break in.

Some organizations see security in a negative light — as something that must be accomplished to protect their data. But I have seen many instances in day-to-day development where security could have helped the development process. Not long ago, there were some issues at an organization where it could have easily applied some of these concepts. The organization was using properties files inside Java Archive (JAR) files, and developers were changing these files at will without regard to how they would affect other programs. Because of this incident, the organization decided to avoid properties files. The organization could have saved a lot of time and trouble by just changing the permissions on the file to be read-only. Auditing records could have been applied to find out who was changing the file. In the end, applying security could have saved more time than changing the architecture based on security issues.

The following sections explore each of the four security layers — authentication, authorization, integrity and auditing — in greater detail.

Authentication layer

As mentioned earlier, authentication is simply asserting the originator of a message. When a client needs to assert that the server is who it claims to be, it is a one-way authentication. Sometimes, especially in Business-to-Business (B2B), it's necessary for both parties to ensure that they have verified each other's identification as the originator. Mutual authentication occurs when both parties need to know that the other is the originator.

An important issue with Internet authentication is that you cannot see exactly whom you are authenticating. An attacker could intercede and try to pass for the other party. In the B2B world, for example, if a party such as ABCD.com was placing a batch of orders into XYZ.com, and competitor company DEF.com interceded and deterred the batch process, it would be bad business for XYZ.com.

Before discussing how you can establish a counter defense, you need to understand some terms. You can find some of these terms in the *Java Authentication and Authorization Service* (JAAS). The term *subject* refers to any user of computing services; it's a user or another computing service. Because of issues with using straight subjects across systems, principals are further defined in JAAS. A *principal* is a name associated with a subject. A set of principals might exist for one subject across an enterprise in case the same name does not exist for the same subject. Principals are associated to a subject only after it has a successful authentication into a system, but principals solve the issue of resolving name issues across systems. Some services may want to associate more security-related information. These generic security attributes are credentials. *Credentials* may include passwords, Kerberos tickets, and other types of data used for verifying the principal throughout the system.

JAAS uses principals and credentials to authenticate throughout an Enterprise system. Another form of principal authentication is incorporated into the Java Servlet v2.2 and EJB v1.1 specifications to pass principal information through Java Naming and Directory Interface (JNDI) context. This authenticates the original user through the Java Enterprise systems.

These techniques help authentication throughout the enterprise; however, there are still issues of getting into the system. When a user tries to authenticate to a proprietary system, he still runs the risk of an attacker intercepting his call, especially in getting the exchange of public keys for encryption. This attack is called the man-in-the-middle attack. For this reason, digital certificates were invented to thwart potential attackers. *Digital certificates* are remote documents that are maintained through a trusted third party to uniquely identify the user, or principal, over the Internet to another party.

The trusted third party is a *Certificate Authority* (CA). The primary standard for certificates is X.509, which has been around since 1988. The X.509 scheme has a public key associated with each CA. The recipient of the certificate uses this public key from the CA to decrypt a digital signature. If he can decrypt it, it follows that it was encrypted with the CA's private key in the key pair algorithm. In the certificate is the public key of the owner of the certificate that the recipient wishes to communicate with by using ciphers. This ensures that a valid key pair matches the certificate from the CA and that the public key of the owner is valid. A chain of responsibility can grow here, because a certificate can contain another certificate, and so on. Then the signature can be matched with another signature of another authority and so on. When the certificate is a top-level certificate, implying a self-signed signature, it's called the *root certificate;* thus, no public key is needed to certify it. Root certificates are used to check with other third parties for trust of the CA itself.

The application server receives only a copy of the certificate; the original remains with and can be modified by the CA. The CA ensures that no changes can be made in the user's certificate, and the CA is responsible for ensuring that you receive the correct public key for that user. The certificate will contain several elements, including the owner of the certificate, the key associated with this owner, and a digital signature to verify the integrity of the certificate. If there is any doubt from the CA that tampering may appear or integrity is lost, the CA can revoke the certificate and inform the owner of the certificate revocation. The CA can identify the owner of the certificate through the owner's key pair and IP address. For specific information about a CA, two companies come to mind, Verisign and Entrust. For more information in the Java API for X.509, refer to the `java.security.cert` package from the JAAS distribution or JDK 1.4 distribution.

To get a certificate, you have to contact a CA. After paying money, in most cases, and sending the machine name and IP address of the authentication server to the CA, you will receive information about your certificate, including a directory on the CA where it will be located and the key to access it. You can then configure your Web and application servers to communicate with the CA via HTTPS.

The Web Server protocol that uses these certificates for authentication is called HTTPS, or HTTP Secure. HTTPS is also referred to as HTTP over SSL and HTTP over TLS (Transport Layer Security). TLS is the successor of SSL v3 after the IETF (Internet Engineering Task Force) created it as an Internet standard when they took it over from Netscape.

An example of when to use HTTPS is when you log on to a secure Web site to upload a chapter to a book using a URL such as `www.hungryminds.com`. After accessing the URL, a login prompts you for secure authentication. In this scenario, only one certificate is used at the Hungry Minds Web site to pass you the encryption keys through the HTTPS protocol on port 443. This messaging is encrypted by using the public keys that the CA distributes to the SSL handshaking.

For this application, you need to provide confidentiality for the data passing between client and server, and the user needs to be sure that his client is connected to the correct server and is using the correct key pair. Behind the scenes, a digital certificate is being received through the X.509 protocol, the handshaking and socket encryption is being handled by SSL, and the overall protocol for the Web interfacing is being handled through HTTPS.

Authorization layer

Authentication verifies that the correct user is logged into the system; but after the user is logged in, there's still a need to ensure that the user is only allowed certain resources.

Authorization entails applying security policies to regulate which resources specific users, or groups of users, can access in the system. In order to access any given resource, the user needs privileges for that resource. The privilege is the level of access granted to that user for a particular resource. Each user will have a collection of privileges for the system, which is the user's role. The basic system usually consists of four roles: user, group, other, and super-user. As the system grows, more and more roles will be added, such as network and database administrator.

The Unix operating system has always accessed resources in this way. The owner of the resource determines who has access to the resource. The Unix system has three privilege levels of interest to most users: read access, write access, and execute access. Each of these levels must be set from the owner for it to be allowed for a particular user or group. A group is a logical set of users. Groups are used because they are more efficient to manage than individual users. It's simply easier to set the accesses to groups and to have all the users that need that access to belong to that group. This security follows the *Discretionary Access Control* (DAC) model in which the owner of each file can determine who else can access it by setting the file's permission bits. One of the issues with this model is that anyone who has read access to a file can copy the file and give it to another user. DAC is called discretionary because it is up to the owner's discretion to give others permission to that file or resource. DAC is also sometimes referred to as the owner-based model.

Another authorization model is the *Mandatory Access Control* (MAC) model. In the MAC security model, each user and resource is assigned a security level, such as classified, secret, and top secret. These security levels are usually ordered, thereby creating a *lattice*. Top secret, for example, is higher than secret, which is higher than classified. Each user has a security clearance, such as secret. If the user has a secret clearance, he only has access to resources that are classified and secret, but not top secret. This security model follows how sensitive data is used in the military and other Department of Defense organizations. Many systems, however, are not currently supporting this type of security model.

Access Control Lists

The DAC model has been enhanced over the years. From the structure of Unix files and directories, it has moved into the Java world of Enterprise development for EJB and JSP resources. For Enterprise systems, DAC policies are implemented in the form of *Access Control Lists* (ACL), where each resource has an ACL administered by its owner. The purpose of the ACL and its entries is to ensure that a user can perform an action on a resource, based on the action and user having the correct permission on the resource. Because this model is very generic, it can easily suit access control requirements for any system. The biggest issue is that as the number of users grows, so does the administration of the DAC model. An ACL is a data structure that guards access to resources. Each ACL has a list of `AclEntry` objects. An `AclEntry` associates a principal, such as the user `rhelton`, with a permission object, such as `read`. An `AclEntry` has a positive number if it grants permission and a negative number to deny the permission. This paradigm can also be displayed in the form of tables, not just objects. A table can have the ACL IDs and normalize to an `AclEntry` that can then normalize to a table of principals and permissions. Figure 20-2 illustrates this relationship.

If the user, or the group to which the user belongs, has the correct rights, the user can perform the desired operation. This security architecture is incorporated into the Java Development Kit 1.3 as a separate distributed package. The advantage of this architecture is that it decouples the authorization process from the authentication process. Decoupling the authentication protects the certificates from corruption if the authorization gets corrupted. This also provides a central location to store all access across the Enterprise system. The central location for storing information across an Enterprise system is typically referred to as a *Security Realm*.

Figure 20-3 shows how a Web Container can decouple the actions of authentication and authorization by using the Access Control List. Note that the ACL table is just an example to show the separation and is not normalized. The table stores relationships between principals and permissions. Even though the `AclEntry` is calculated by using positive and negative algorithms, the permissions are normally in the form of read, write, execute, and delete. As you can see from Figures 20-2 and 20-3, you load the principals, permissions, and resource names from the tables to check the user's access level.

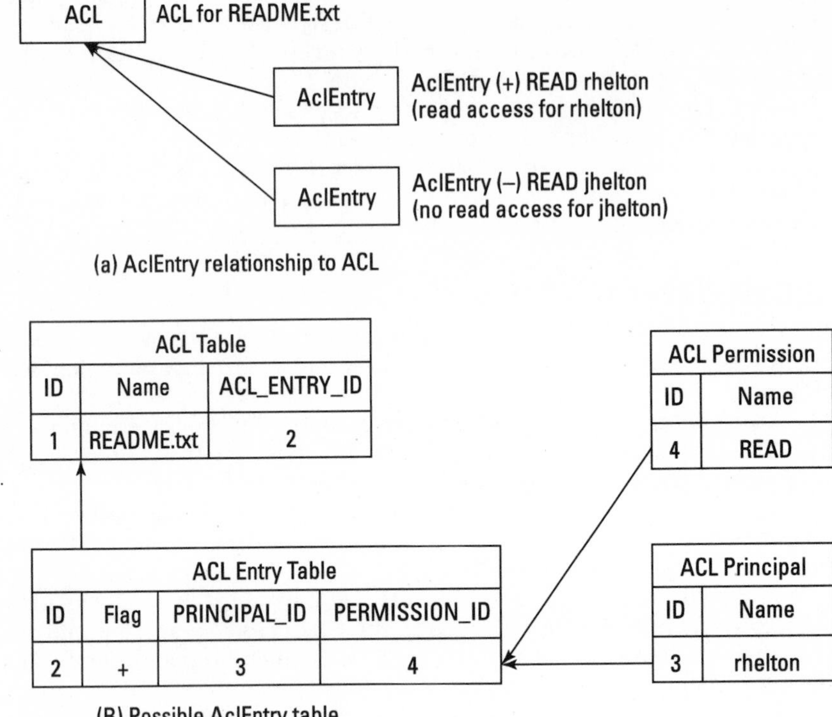

Figure 20-2: ACL and AclEntry objects

LDAP

Not long ago, most organizations had their own interfaces and schema for implementing access lists such as the one shown in the preceding figure. The problem was that there was no common interface to this data. Most organizations created these tables from scratch, which was a lot of work, and they could not reuse this work across organizations. That changed, however, with the implementation of *Lightweight Directory Access Protocol* (LDAP).

An LDAP service provides a generic directory service, which stores information of all sorts. LDAP was created to do much more than just store user and group information; it can store a server's configuration, certificates, EJB and JSP objects, file system information, and customer information. I believe, however, that it excels at authorization because it can centralize all the user information for an entire Enterprise. Using LDAP can be another centralized choke point for attackers. It can force the authorization into one point. Just as the firewall forces the attacker to enter at a predetermined point on the network, the LDAP server forces the attacker to use a predetermined store of user and group access. This can aid the system and network administrators to audit specific points and carefully monitor those points that the attacker is forced to go through to gain any control of the system.

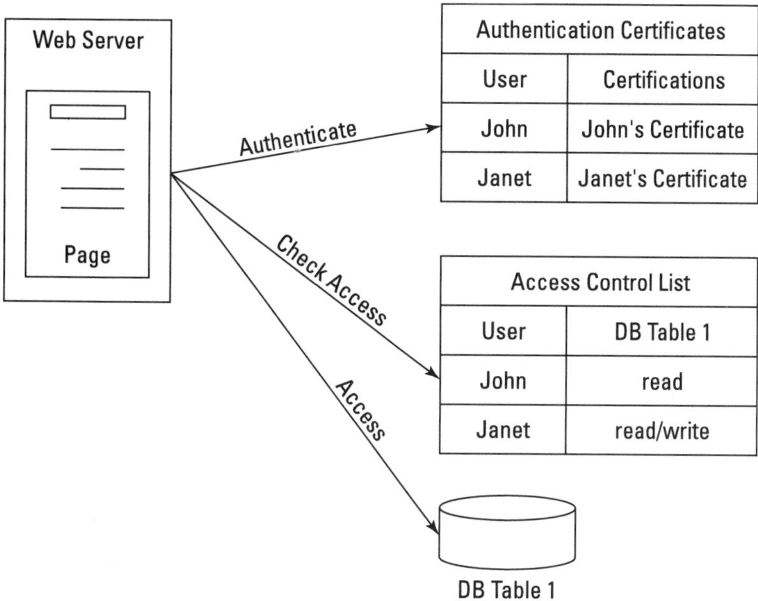

Figure 20-3: Access versus Authentication tables

Another feature in administrating the LDAP service is that owners can modify groups. Groups are a subset of any users, which can modify many users at the same time. The LDAP server itself has authorization for a user to modify these records, like an owner. The owner can add, modify, and delete any record by using the LDAP SDK or console. The console will change depending on the manufacturer, such as the Netscape's Directory Server or Active Directory from Microsoft. This gives the administrator a GUI-like tool for administrating user rights instead of traversing multiple UNIX stations and proprietary databases to accomplish the same goals.

LDAP was invented in 1995 with the release of RFC 1777 for version 2. Version 1 was the X.500 server that was created in 1993 with RFC 1487. This opened the doors to many possibilities for centralizing Enterprise directories. The motivation was to first store a distributed directory structure. But because a directory structure has attributes, files, and subdirectories in them, it formed a basis for storing information about machines, objects, and services. Tree-like directory structures and file systems are traversed like any other file system, as shown in Figure 20-4.

The first thing that you might notice in Figure 20-4 is some of the symbols used to define the structures. The symbol to define the overall organization that owns the Enterprise System is `o=richware.com`. Because there is normally one LDAP Server at a given organization, it uses the organization as the root and initial name. In this diagram, the organization is defined as `richware.com`. This folder can contain any number of attributes about the organization, such as the location of the headquarters, the CEO, and more. This is for referencing organizational data.

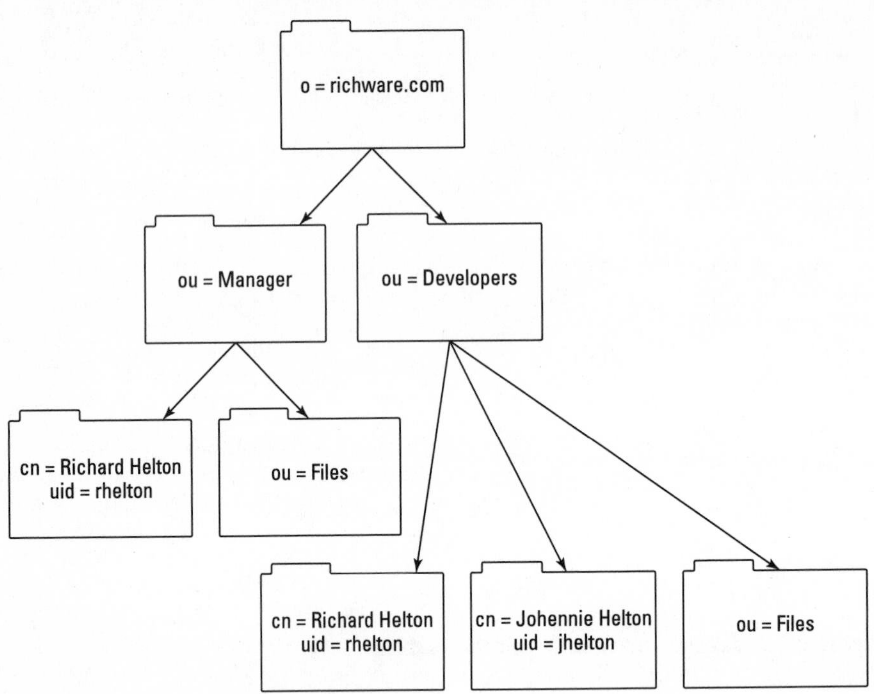

Figure 20-4: An LDAP directory structure

The next folder in the directory structure is `ou=Manager`, which belongs to the organization `richware.com` because it is part of the same tree. The `ou` in `ou=Manager` stands for organizational unit and acts as a directory, which can contain files, attributes, or users. This `ou` contains one user, which is `Richard Helton` and has the user identity of `rhelton`. This is the user's ID that is used so that the user may get a connection to the LDAP Service. In the figure, the user `Richard Helton` can get a connection from the `Manager` folder or the `Developers` folder. When logging in, this user can specify which `ou` that he is logging in under. Depending on which one he uses, he may set his permissions differently. Another `ou` is the `Files` subdirectory under the `Manager` `ou`. This `ou` contains all the manager's files (text or binary-based). If the user `Richard Helton` logged in under the `Manager` `ou` and had his permissions set, he may access these `Manager` files in the `ou=Files` subdirectory. These permissions are set through the LDAP service from an administrator. After `Richard Helton` logs in through the LDAP SDK, he can start accessing files if the permissions are set in the LDAP ACL table. The permissions that are allowed in LDAP are read, write, search, compare, selfwrite, delete, add, and proxy. These permissions can be applied to the `ou` folder or any resource that may belong to that `ou` folder. These resources can be in the form of files or even objects. In this scenario, an LDAP administrator had the role of an owner that set the permissions of the files for the `Richard Helton` user.

One of the biggest security features that should be mentioned about LDAP servers is that they have their own internal ACL for handling users and groups of the elements inside the LDAP directory tree. LDAP Servers have authentication protocols that they follow to get a *bind.* A bind is an association of a name with an object. An EJB client, for example, binds to an EJB's home name to access the home object. A single bind, or multiple binds, can be stored in a context object. To get a bind, there must be access to a *namespace*, which contains all the names within a naming system that can be used for the association. A namespace could be in the form of all the names in an LDAP directory tree. To get a specific name, normally you would have to traverse a namespace. In finding the file `etc/hosts` in Unix, for example, the traverse would need to start at the root directory, form the root, traverse to the subdirectory, `etc` and then traverse the file `hosts`. This is how directory trees are normally traversed.

As mentioned earlier, LDAP provides its own authentication mechanisms. These mechanisms can be anonymous, simple, none, and SASL. SASL is the most secure, and it stands for *Simple Authentication and Security Layer.* RFC 2222 defines SASL. LDAP uses this protocol to identify and authenticate a user in the server. The command built into LDAP requires that it specify the name and mechanism to use for authentication. When the client makes an authentication request of the server, the server can challenge the authentication. The client sends responses to the server, which can challenge as many times as it deems necessary. If the authentication succeeds, it will get a SUCCESS message, otherwise the client will receive an `INVALID CREDENTIALS` error. SASL is part of the JAAS product and further information can be found in the `javax.security.sasl` package.

This was a brief introduction to the LDAP server, but there are many other mechanisms that a Java Servlet, or EJB, may use to get permissions to resources. The most common are locally-stored deployment descriptors, which eliminate the need to make network calls to an LDAP server (you may, however, decide to put some of these resources in the LDAP server later because the maintenance of these files becomes complex). Because of such complexities, Sun has provided an architecture where both LDAP and file systems can be used interchangeably. This specification is called *Java Naming and Directory Interface* (JNDI).

JNDI

The purpose of the JNDI interface is to provide a single API to access different directory structures using different protocols. It hides the implementation details for accessing protocols such as LDAP. JNDI makes it possible to link different types of directories, such as a file directory on Unix and an LDAP service.

JNDI has a client API (shown in Figure 20-5) for getting the object from the contexts. It also has a Service Provider Interface that wraps around the various directory and naming services. Both the file system and LDAP server can act as a service provider.

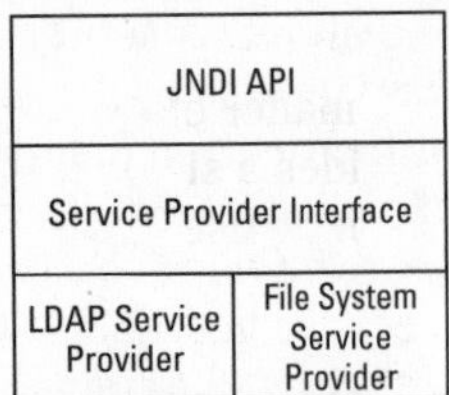

Figure 20-5: The JNDI API Layer

A code example of JNDI looks like the following:

```
// Start the environment settings
Hashtable env = new HashTable();
env. put(Context.INITIAL_CONTEXT_FACTORY,
"com.sun.jndi.ldap.LdapCtxFactory");
env.put(Context.PROVIDER_URL,"ldap://localhost:389/o=JNDIServer
");
// Authenticate user "Rich" with password "password".
// Start with Authentication Type
env.put(Context.SECURITY_AUTHENTICATION,"simple");
env.put(Context.SECURITY_PRINCIPAL","cn=Rich,ou=Author,o=richwa
re.com");
env.put(Context.SECURITY_CREDENTIALS,"password");
// Create the Initial Context
DirContext ctx = new InitialDirContext(env);
//  Work with the newly created Conext
```

In the preceding code, there is a communication directly to the LDAP server. To change the code to access the File System Provider, a file system in Unix, simply change two of the functions and reuse the rest of the code to produce the following code:

```
// Start the environment settings
Hashtable env = new HashTable();
env. put(Context.INITIAL_CONTEXT_FACTORY,
"com.sun.jndi.fscontext.LdapCtxFactory");
env.put(Context.PROVIDER_URL,"file:/tmp");
// Authenticate user "Rich" with password "password".
// Start with Authentication Type
env.put(Context.SECURITY_AUTHENTICATION,"simple");
env.put(Context.SECURITY_PRINCIPAL","cn=Rich,ou=Author,o=richwa
re.com");
env.put(Context.SECURITY_CREDENTIALS,"password");
// Create the Initial Context
DirContext ctx = new InitialDirContext(env);
//  Work with the newly created Conext
```

See Chapter 8 for additional LDAP programming examples.

JAAS

Introducing LDAP may be overkill for some applications or for smaller organizations. The Java Authentication and Authorization Service (JAAS) provides a simpler alternative for these situations. Because it is built into J2EE, JAAS can be used in a WebLogic environment without adding an additional server.

Just as the JDK 1.2 provides a `SecurityManager` class implementation that can enforce access control on source code and classes, there is a JAAS SecurityManager that augments the JDK 1.3 version that can enforce access control to sensitive resources. Augmenting the security in the newer versions of the JDK is just an example of how the Java 2 Security Manager from Sun continues to evolve.

To use the JAAS SecurityManager, a policy file must be maintained. This policy file is simply a variation of the JDK 1.2 `SecurityManager` policy file. This form of access control is referred to as *Principal-Based Access Control* because it is based on the policy file's principals. Only authorized principals may access the resources. You can, however, grant access to non-principals, as shown in the following code:

```
// Java 2 codesource-based policy
grant Codebase "http://richware.com", Signedby "rich" {
  permission java.io.FilePermission "/cdrom/-", "read";
}
```

In this example, because the policy file has `grant Codebase` instead of `grant Principal`, all Java code trying to access the CD-ROM through `http://richware.com` will have access to it. The files will have the signature of `rich` regardless of who executes it. To demonstrate a principal using JAAS, see the following policy file:

```
// Java 2 codesource-based policy
grant Principal com.sun.security.auth.SolarisPrincipal "rich" {
  permission java.io.FilePermission "/cdrom/-", "read";
}
```

In this example, only the subjects associated with the `SolarisPrincipal` principal type that has the name `rich` associated with it can have access to the CD-ROM. The `com.sun.security.auth.SolarisPrincipal` is a Sun principal for a Solaris user.

When accessing a resource, such as the CD-ROM in the preceding example, the JAAS API will need many properties in the policy file for the policy file to be sufficient. The properties that are needed are the subject, the set of name properties associated with the subject, called principals, and the security-related attributes called credentials. To execute the Subject, one of the easiest ways is to use the static function "doAs" that associates a function with a Subject:

```
class ExampleAction implements java.security.PrivilegedAction {
        public Object run() {
            java.io.File f = new java.io.File("/cdrom/-");

            // the following call invokes a security check
            if (f.exists()) {
```

```
                System.out.println("cdrom exists");
            }
            return null;
        }
    }

    public class Example1 {
        public static void main(String[] args) {

            // Authenticate the subject, "rich".
            // This process is described in the
            // LoginContext section.

            Subject rich;
            ...

            // perform "ExampleAction" as "rich"
            Subject.doAs(rich, new ExampleAction());
        }
}
```

The preceding code will check to see if it can read the CD-ROM as the user `rich`. If the user `rich` is logged into a Solaris machine, it will work.

Enterprise principals

As mentioned before, principals are used in other Enterprise System Architectures besides JAAS; they are also used in EJBs and Java Servlets. In EJB 1.1/2.0, you may get a principal by calling the function `getCallerPrincipal()`. After the principal is received, the name of the principal can be retrieved by calling the `getName()` function. You can see an example of this in the following code:

```
//Obtain the default initial JNDI context
Context initCtx = new InitialContext();
// get the home interface
Object result = initCtx.lookup("java:comp/env/ejb/UserRecord");
// narrow to the proper type
UserRecordHome userRecordHome = (UserRecordHome)
javax.rmi.PortableRemoteObject.narrow(result, UserRecordHome.class);
// get the caller principal
userPrincipal = ejbContext.getCallerPrincipal();
// get the user's name
String username = userPrincipal.getName();
// Lookup or execute something on the user's name
```

This code creates an EJB and retrieves the current user's name in the `getName()` function. After the user's name is returned, a lookup in the ACL, Database Server, or LDAP Server can be performed to get the permissions of this user. Another function, `isCallerInRole()`, is used to see if the current user is in the group that is authorized to perform actions on the resources in that thread of execution. Using it as `ejbContext.isCallerInRole("admin")` will return `true` if the user belongs to the admin group.

Java Servlets provide the same functionality as EJBs, but the method names are different. The method names servlets used to check the user's role and principal are `isUserInRole()` and `getUserPrincipal()`.

The focus of this section has been on authorization; but it has been very difficult to separate some of the other layers, such as authentication, because the security layers overlap each other and are needed to work with each other every step of the way.

Authorization can be implemented in various different methods, but they all implement the DAC model in various forms. Securing the organization's data is very important if that organization wants to stay in the market. I cannot think of a single company that can freely distribute its information and data and still survive the market. All companies have some form of data that it does not wish to distribute, such as financial records or the CEO's home phone number. Guarding that information should be of the utmost importance with several people allocated to it.

Integrity layer

Integrity is the assurance that data has not been modified without knowledge of its modification in an Enterprise system. Adding a signature to a document or having a digest to compare against provides data integrity. Data integrity is especially important for organizations that are disseminating files to the public. These organizations would not want to inadvertently transmit viruses in their files, as this could damage their credibility with the public.

Some of the concepts of digital signatures were already mentioned in the authentication layer section because these security principles constantly rely on each other for support.

Digital signatures

Digital signatures are based on the same concept as a person signing a document. If a person receives a document in the mail from a bank, signs it, and returns it to the bank, how does the bank know that it is a valid signature? Even if the person were authenticated (if, for example, a package sent by registered mail is signed for in the presence for the postal carrier), the signature might still be forged. If the bank has the person's signature on file for comparison purposes and the two signatures appear the same, this would furnish validation. Another validation method is to use a certified trusted third party. When the person seeking validation presents an ID to the trusted third party, he can put a seal on the document. The issue is that sometimes more than authentication is needed, as when there is no trust between the sender and the receiver, or when it is possible to forge the message.

Two types of digital signatures exist: *direct signatures* and *arbitrated signatures*. The direct digital signature is just between the sender and receiver; the arbitrated digital signature is between the sender, a trusted third party, and the receiver. The direct digital signature is the use of either a secret key or public key to decrypt a message. If the message uses a secret key, and if there are only two people in the group that share the key, then trusting that it came from the other person who has the secret key can be somewhat valid. If more than two people are involved, copies could start to appear and managing the keys becomes an issue.

One method of ensuring who encrypted a message is by applying the key pair algorithm. If a person receives a message from Jane, for example, as long as the message decrypts with Jane's public key, using the key pair algorithm, you can somewhat trust that Jane had to use her private key to encrypt the message, and therefore the message is considered valid. But what if the secret key or the private key were stolen? Messages could be sent and received, and the integrity of the message is compromised between parties.

The arbitrated digital signature has a trusted third party to ensure authenticity, such as a Certificate Authority in the Authentication Principle. The idea is that every signed message between the sender and receiver goes through an arbitrator. All parties must trust the arbitrator. The arbitrator will receive the message from the sender, validate that it came from the sender, sign it saying that it was verified, and forward it to the receiver. One method of verification is that the sender and the arbitrator share a secret key, and the arbitrator and the receiver share a different secret key. The arbitrator receives the message from the sender, decrypts it, and then encrypts it with the other secret key to send it to the sender, thus playing a middleman to ensure trust between the sender and the receiver. The man-in-the-middle becomes very difficult to implement with an arbitrator because all sets of keys would have to be impersonated, both from the receiver and the sender. Also, because there are trusted third-party servers used from the arbitrator to transport the certificate to both the receiver and the sender, impersonations are more complex because of information used to set up the HTTPS to the arbitrator to both the sender and receiver. The arbitrator establishes the connection between the sender and receiver. This makes destroying the integrity of the message a little more difficult.

Message digests

A Digital Signature Standard (DSS) exists to handle digital signatures, but to understand how an algorithm such as this one works, you need to know about the message digest.

A message digest, shown in Figure 20-6, is normally referred to as a digital fingerprint. Its purpose is to take a stream of data as the input to a hash algorithm, and produce an output called a *digest.* The digest is a representation of the input data and does not change unless the input data changes. This allows you compare the digests that are computed at different times to determine if the data has been altered. An example is the Java utility `jarsigner`. `Jarsigner` signs a Java Archive (JAR) file. A JAR contains resource files that are used in similar packages to extend the functionality of Java. An example is the JSSE (Java Secure Socket Extension) distribution from Sun in the jsse.jar. The `jarsigner` utility is advisable when extending the functionality of WLS and adding JAR files to created EJBs, Java files, and JSPs. When giving these files to a client as a deliverable, the creator of these files doesn't know if they have tampered with unless they were signed.

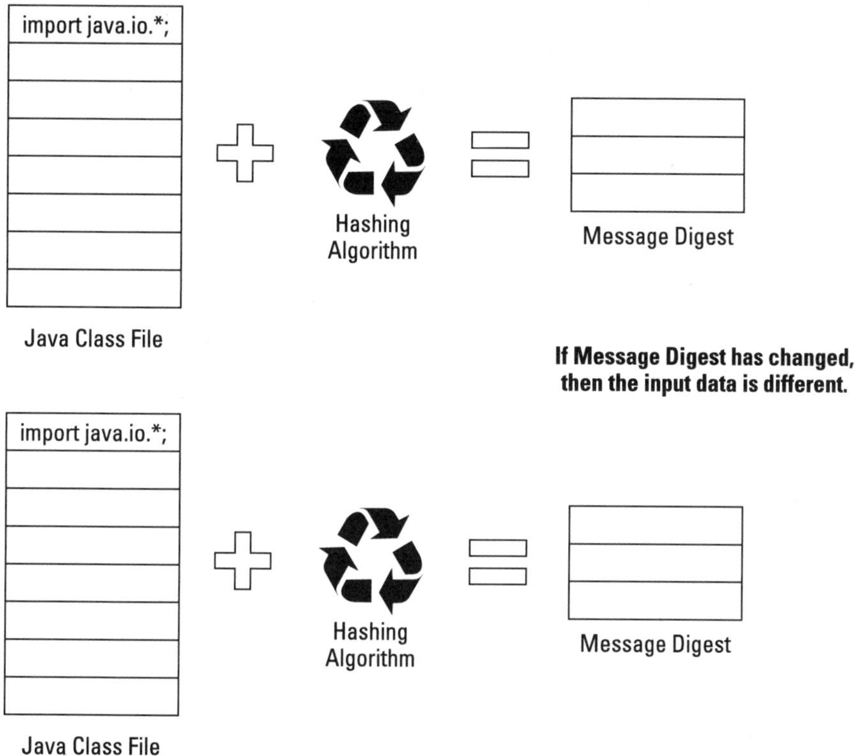

Figure 20-6: Using the message digest

Message digests are also called *one-way hash algorithms.* One-way hash algorithms work in only one direction, taking plaintext data and computing it into a unique hash. If one byte has changed in the plaintext, it will create a different hash than the previous hash. The same input will always produce the same hash. If the data is different, the hash output will be different. The hash will always be the same size regardless of the size of the data. The hash is also referred to as a digest because it is a digest of the data or, put simply, a description of the byte pattern that obscures the original data. Hash is taken from the hashing algorithms that are involved in producing the result. Most algorithms will iterate through the data, XORing each byte and then rehashing that result into the next byte. The hash is the result of the hashing algorithm. The digest, or hash, was originally used mostly in messaging protocols, like SSL, which coined its name: the message digest. The one-way hash is never reversed; the digest cannot create the original data. This ensures that the original data is never compromised.

Several message digest algorithms exist, including MD2, MD4, and MD5. Ron Rivest of RSA invented all these. MD stands for Message Digest. These algorithms produce 128-bit hash values. MD2 is used for Privacy Enhanced Mail (PEM). It's byte-oriented in its checksums calculations and requires input that is multiple of 16 bytes. Padding has to be done to ensure that it is a multiple. This algorithm has been cracked. The MD5 was created to enhance MD4 because it was rumored that it would be broken. MD5 is slower and more robust because it has more hashing loops than MD4. MD4 wasn't broken as promised and is still used today. MD5 and MD4 both use 512 bit blocks. These fit the block cipher paradigm as far as hashing a 64-bit block at a time. It has to be padded if not divisible by 64 bits. Both algorithms produce a 128-bit message digest.

Besides the MD series of message digests, there is another very common message digest called the *Secure Hash Algorithm* (SHA). The SHA was developed by the *National Institute of Standards and Technology* (NIST) and published as a federal information-processing standard in 1993. A revised copy, called SHA-1, was developed in 1995. SHA is based on the MD4 algorithm, and its design closely models MD4. SHA takes an input message with a maximum length of less than 2^{64} bits and produces as output a 160-bit message digest. The input is processed in 512-bit blocks. This produces a full 32 bits wider than the other hash algorithms, and because of this, it was invented to be stronger than the other hash algorithms.

Because the message digest is so widely used, it was included in the *Java Cryptography Architecture* (JCA) that will work with JDK 1.3. It is part of the JDK 1.4 distribution. WLS has support for this functionality in the `weblogic.security.MessageDigest` class. This class supports the SHA and MD5 algorithms. To use this class, first you get an instance of the class using the `MessageDigest.getInstance("MD5")` function. The input of this function is a case-insensitive string that states that it is either MD5 or SHA. A provider may also be included in this function if other algorithms are desired from a provider. Next you need to use an `update` function and pass in the input stream as a byte or byte array. After data has been inputted to the class, the digest is returned using the `digest` function. Here is a code example:

```
MessageDigest sha = MessageDigest.getInstance("SHA");
byte [] i1;
// Initialize i1with some data here
sha.update(i1);
byte[] hash = sha.digest();
```

Now that you have been given an introduction to message digest, you can move on to DSS. DSS was invented from the National Institute of Standards and Technology (NIST). NIST also developed SHA, so there is no wonder that DSS uses SHA. DSS was originally proposed in 1991, and its last minor change was 1996. DSS uses a key pair algorithm. The first thing that DSS does on a message is to get a digest of the message through the SHA algorithm. Then it encrypts the digest by using a private key to form a signature. Both message and signature are sent to the receiver. On the receiver's end, the receiver first produces a digest by using the SHA algorithm. Then the receiver decrypts the signature by using the public key of the sender. If both digests match, the one from the receiver and the one from the sender, then the message is considered valid. An example of DSS in Java code is as follows:

```
/* Get Signature object */
Signature sig = Signature.getInstance("DSS");
/* Initialize for signing */
sig.initSign(myPrivateKey);
/* Process the document */
sig.update(document);
/* Sign it */
byte[] signature = sig.sign();
```

Verifying the authenticity of a signed document in Java code looks like the following:

```
/* Get Signature object */
Signature sig = Signature.getInstance("DSS");
/* Initialize for verifying */
sig.initSign(myPublicKey);
/* Process the document */
sig.update(document);
/* Verify authenticity */
Boolean authentic = sig.verify(signature);
```

Auditing layer

Auditing is simply a practice of keeping records for the purpose of capturing security-related events. One purpose is to hold users or systems accountable, but most important, to know whether any damage is done to your systems if security has been breached. A lot of this functionality relies on the services and servers that you use in the organization's Enterprise system. All firewalls, application servers, Web servers, and LDAP servers come with logging and monitoring features. But when developing your Enterprise systems, a good place to start is to log any security exceptions that have taken place. When logging exceptions, capture the principal and user information when the exception happens. Ensure that these files are protected and trusted with integrity and review them constantly. Files like these will report issues across the Enterprise system.

Another approach is to try to break in the system while the auditing techniques are in place to ensure that they work. Many cracking packages are available on the Web. Try some out against an isolated section of you site—by isolated, I mean one that is in test and not production—and see what the log files generate. Try spoofing the firewall to see if the firewall catches it.

Security Perimeters

Before getting into a discussion about types of security attacks, I must discuss the perimeters within which these attacks can take place. Every organization has perimeters around its systems, with specific points where users can enter. There may be points where the customer enters the system through the Web farm, where other organizations enter the system, and where administrators enter to monitor system status.

It is to these entry points that most of the concentration of security techniques is usually applied. The premise is that if a hacker cannot enter the system, the system is safe. There are two tiers of concern: the outside world (the entry from the Internet), and the inside world (the entry from the internal servers). The internal servers must also have a form of security for securing the objects between each other.

Figure 20-7 shows a few entry points to the system; therefore, these entries must be protected against attackers. The most common technique is to install a firewall. A firewall provides a protective perimeter, preventing hackers from entering through the organization's front door. Such a perimeter is commonly known as a demilitarized zone (DMZ), a term borrowed from battlefield tactics. A DMZ blocks the enemy (hackers), although permitting access to allies (customers and other authorized users).

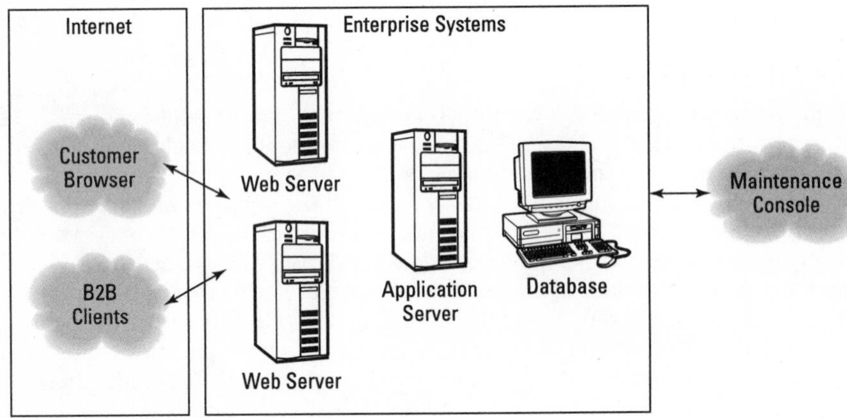

Figure 20-7: An organization's Enterprise

A DMZ is formed by the combination of two firewalls. One firewall is between the Web server and the outside world. The other firewall is between the Web and application servers; it prevents outside connections, other than that of the known Web server, from accessing the application server as a client. The *client* is the process that initiates the connection into the system. These firewalls can be implemented in hardware or software; they provide filters by port, protocol, or IP/DNS Name.

Port filtering allows certain network ports to be seen from the outside world, while rendering others invisible. Access is almost always provided for port 80, which is the default for Hypertext Transfer Protocol (HTTP). The firewall is supposed to block other ports to ensure that the attacker can only enter specific ports that are monitored.

The next concept is *protocol filtering*, which ensures that the only protocol entering the port is the protocol permitted by the firewall. In most cases, it is the HTTP protocol that is passed from the Web server to the application server via an application server port that is unknown to the outside world. Usually this port is an uncommon one; so it's hard to find.

One of the filters that most firewalls take into consideration is the knowledge of which originating machines allow connections to the application server. The knowledge is based on recognizing the DNS name of the client machine or its IP address; that is the basis for IP/DNS Name filtering. The firewall will check to see if the client originated on that machine inside the DMZ. This is to ensure that the connection to the application server doesn't originate outside of the DMZ. These machines that are in the perimeter of the firewall are considered *trusted* machines. Figure 20-8 shows the location of the two firewalls that make up the DMZ and shows a typical attack at this level.

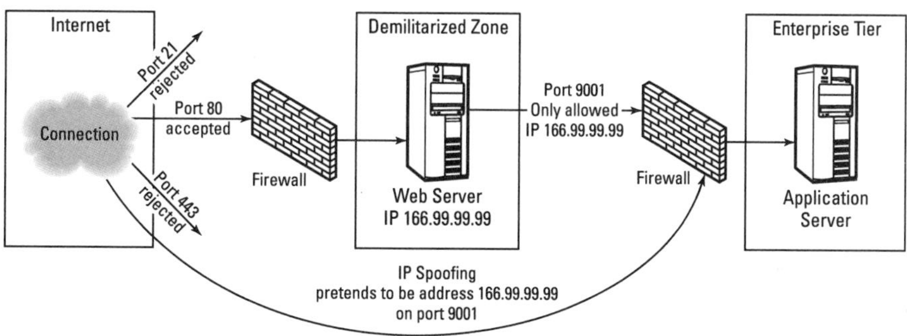

Figure 20-8: A DMZ with firewalls

The technique of a DMZ is fundamental to force attackers to enter through a single choking point in which they must apply their attack techniques. The entry points are the gate they must pass through to get into an organization's Enterprise world. There are other tactics that must be applied against hackers and their attacks; these will be discussed in the "Security Attacks" section. But it's quite obvious that the firewall must support auditing. If the attacker tries to gain any access, records need to be created to monitor the techniques. This not only gives a performance report of the existing firewall structure, but also gives information to network administrators on the directions that attackers are taking. It also provides information about the attackers that allows administrators to prepare for future attacks. It could even point out a specific tool that the attacker is using—it's useful to get details on such a tool and prevent its use. Integrity is used to ensure that no one is trying to change the startup information to the firewalls and, at various points, to ensure that attackers are not introducing their own files for an attack.

Another popular strategy is to attack well-known firewalls; the motivation could be to bring down the firewall or even change the startup of the firewall to be less secured. Not all the attacks are intended to reach valuable data on the other side; they might originate with a competitor trying to bring down an organizations site to get its business. The motivation of attackers is as diverse as the attacks themselves.

Security Attacks

Some people spend hours studying the specifications for a particular firewall and try to break it. Attackers are not limited to individuals sitting in their parents' basement with limited resources. Some may have bigger labs than the companies designing the firewalls! Some may be in the organization that they plan to attack. Some may be disgruntled employees who get laid off, and then develop a program to execute vengeance on the system. Some attackers even do it for fun, or just to see if they have the technical abilities to accomplish their tasks. In this section, I'll explore common techniques employed by attackers to gain unauthorized access to computers and data.

IP spoofing

In Figure 20-8, the firewall on the right is filtering all addresses and ports except port 9001 from host 166.99.99.99. An attack that circumvents this barrier is one where the attacking machine pretends to have the IP address 166.99.99.99, transmitting on port 9001. Such an attack is called *IP spoofing.*

The IP spoofing attack begins by knowing the address of the Web server. This can be easily found by doing a ping to the Web host if it is a direct connection. A ping establishes a short connection to a host to determine if it exists. A ping will only work if the Web server is the physical host to a WWW site and the ping port is active. In many systems, the Web server may not be connected directly to the Internet through the firewall. When you are accessing a Web host, it could be through a Load Balancing Router or proxy server. But after an IP address is found, the idea is to build an IP packet with the Web server's IP address as the return address to pretend that the packet originated on the Web server. After the address is inserted, and no other filtering is applied, the firewall believes that the packet is from the company's Web server. Usually the Web server is considered a *trusted machine* because it belongs to the company. IP spoofing breaks this trust between machines by pretending to be one of the trusted machines.

DNS spoofing

Firewalls may be configured to filter by hostname instead of IP address. In this case, if the intruder assumes the name of a trusted host, the intruder is performing *Domain Name Service (DNS) spoofing,* which has the same net effect as IP spoofing—unauthorized access to the protected machine.

A common way to affect DNS spoofing is to change the DNS entry to reflect that of the attacker's machine and fake the firewall into believing that this machine is valid. The DNS uses a table lookup usually found in the `etc/host` file on the network administration server. Changing the entry to this table to point to other machines triggers the spoof.

IP and DNS spoofing defeat firewall security only if the firewalls employ IP filtering exclusively. But most firewalls employ multiple layers of filtering, making spoofing difficult. Most firewalls, for example, employ an HTTP protocol filter, which permits HTTP connections only. The downside of such filters is that they restrict other potentially friendly protocols, such as RMI. The workaround for this is called *HTTP tunneling,* shown in Figure 20-9, in which the packets of a nonpermitted protocol (such as RMI) are wrapped within the packets of a permitted protocol (such as HTTP), causing the firewall to let them through. Of course, the recipient of these tunneled packets must be able to recognize them, unwrap them, and act on them accordingly.

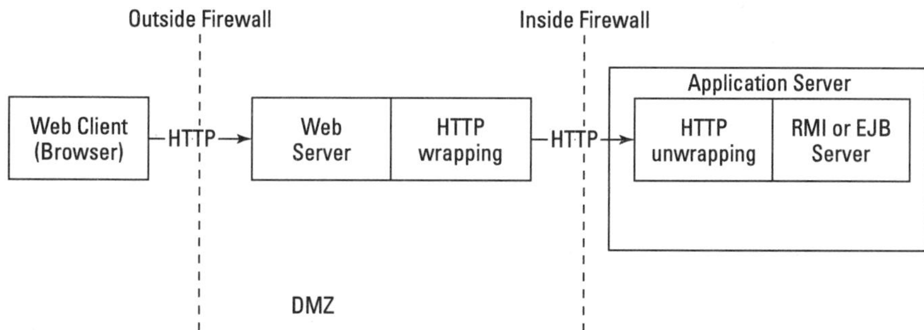

Figure 20-9: HTTP tunneling

Trapdoors

A *trapdoor,* also known as a *backdoor,* is a secret entry point into a system that allows someone access without going through the normal security routines. Developers have been adding trapdoors to systems for decades to help in the testing and debugging of programs. It may take time, for example, to go through the security setup; and because of time constraints, the developer will take shortcuts in testing. These developers may also be responsible for fixing bugs in the programs even after the testing phase, so they leave doors in the program to update classes to fix the bugs discovered at a later date. Some developers don't even consider them as trapdoors because the developers might be trying to build something that is experimental for dynamically configuring their system and its security to enhance system functionality.

An example of a trapdoor may be a database table that dynamically changes the organization's Enterprise system, and that database system has privileges set to bypass the system's security. A trapdoor is any door that can access the system without going through the normal security access procedure. The threat is that these doors allow accesses to the system without going through security, and the threat is extended if any of the developers with trapdoors ever leave the organization or let others know of them. The ex-employees that have access to the ex-employer's software are no longer be held responsible for the consequences, and they no longer have the threat of being fired from the organization. A disgruntled employee could be very dangerous with a trapdoor.

Logic bombs

The *logic bomb* is a program requiring that some condition be met in the program before the bomb explodes into the system to do some damage. An example is a program that deletes system files unless it is disabled before a particular date. The motivation here may be for an insecure contractor to ensure he gets paid; a logic bomb might go off if he doesn't turn it off. Again, it's important to have auditing in place to help monitor any of these possibilities. A very strong monitoring system would reveal improper logins and , if done at regular intervals, could catch changes in files that might indicate logic bombs.

Worms

A *worm* is a virus that crawls through the Internet to make its way to other systems. Worms are commonly spread via e-mail; the "Nimda" virus is a recent example. E-mail has become a popular delivery method for worms because it is easy to fool unwitting users into executing damaging programs disguised as harmless e-mail attachments. A common trick is for the worm to send itself to every address in the victim's e-mail address book. This not only causes the worm to propagate at an exponential rate, but it fools recipients into believing the worm is harmless, because it was apparently sent by someone they know.

Trojan horses

A *Trojan horse* does something harmful when invoked, but disguises itself as a valid program. This could be in the form of a useful utility program that, when executed, captures the keystrokes of the user and monitors for any sites that the user may be logging into at that time. These keystrokes could be saved to a file or be sent to a waiting server on the Internet to collect keystrokes from various users and organizations that use this utility. A database could be built from the number of users accessing this utility program. The utility program from ABCD.com might not even be from ABCD.com, but a modified version uploaded to a shareware site with a Trojan horse hidden in it. Anyone who uses it would invoke the Trojan horse. Integrity could help out in this area because of the capability to ensure that the version from the shareware site matches a valid version from ABCD.com.

I have introduced different types of security attacks. Books could easily be written about the many different attack types created. The attacks that were mentioned can also contain various combinations. A worm attack, for example, could easily contain a logic bomb that was transported to the machine by using the worm but set to explode based on a specific date.

Ciphers, Keys, and Secure Sockets

Before much more is said about security, you need to be a familiar with ciphers and keys.

Several components are involved in encryption, as shown in Figure 20-10. There is the *plaintext,* which is the input, or unencrypted data, to the encryption engine. The output, which is the encrypted data, is called *ciphertext.* The encryption/decryption algorithm is called a *cipher. Keys* are a block of bytes that will produce a ciphertext when used with the plaintext. When a different key is used with the same plaintext, it will produce a different ciphertext. Simply put, it's used to keep attackers guessing as to when they have access to the cipher. Because a key and cipher are used to create ciphertext, it's part of the measurement of most algorithms. Most ciphers' strength is measured against the *brute-force* attack. The brute-force attack is walking through all the possible keys in order until the ciphertext produces readable plaintext in the decryption cipher. Another measurement is the level of complexity involved with possible systems to break the algorithm; it sets the differentiation between strong and weak algorithms.

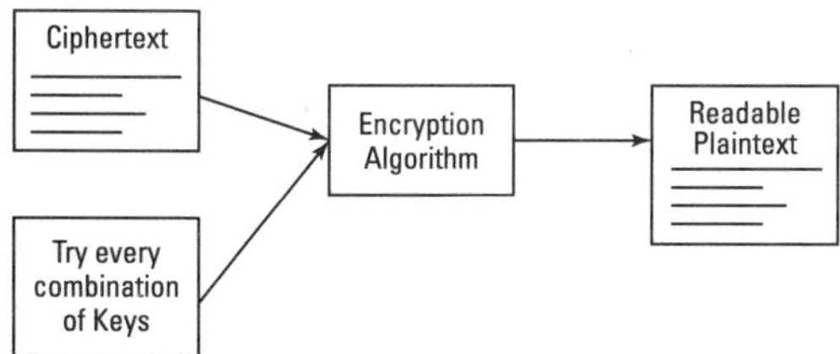

Figure 20-10: Brute force attack

The ciphers also exist in two forms, block and stream. The *block ciphers* operate on plaintext (and ciphertext), one block at a time. The block sizes are normally 64 bits or longer. *Stream ciphers* act on one byte or bit at a time, but execute through a continuous stream. A block cipher's encryption occurs independently of the data, while a stream cipher's encryption is based on the contents of the data itself.

A rough example of a cipher stream is XORing the bytes from beginning to end only padding the first byte to XOR at the beginning of the stream. XOR stands for an exclusive OR operation. The XOR operation is one among many Boolean operations in which two input bits are used to produce a single output bit. The XOR is when one bit is "1" and the other is "0," it will produce a "1" output; otherwise it will produce a "0" bit. A block may need padding because it is not divisible by 64 bits. The last bytes may have to be padded by adding the bytes needed to be divisible by 64. If the total blocks are 12 bytes, for example, the first 8 bytes will work, and then 4 bytes have to be added to the remaining 4 bytes to be divisible by 64. The last 4 bytes can be padded with zeros and a number size. An example is if the remaining block is 1111, the finished product can be 11110004 before encryption. When the message is decrypted, the 0004 states that the remaining padded zeros that equals 4 bytes need to be deleted. This can be an issue if the actual message ends with 0004; so there are several other techniques that can be applied to limit the issues. Another way would be to end all of the blocks with an end-of-file character to denote the final plaintext byte.

Keys, not just ciphers, also can take on many forms, as shown in Figure 20-11. The *secret key* is a key that a group agrees to use and not to change. A secret key is a key, such as 90909090, that Alice and John agree upon to decrypt and encrypt messages when communicating with each other.

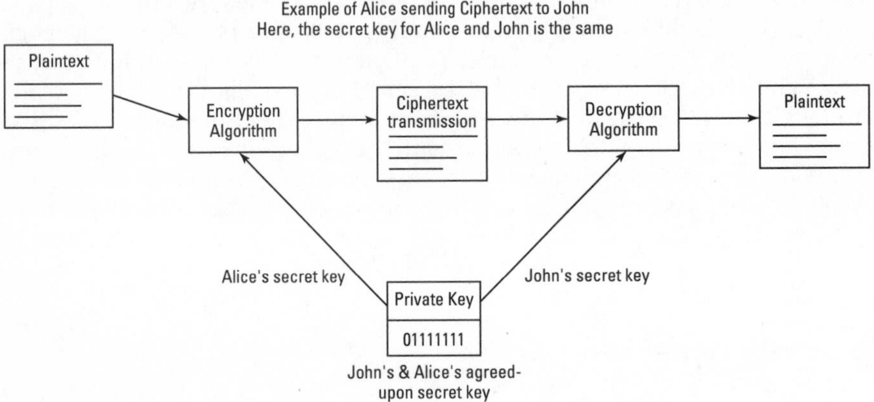

Figure 20-11: Secret key algorithm

The *key-pair*, sometimes called the public key algorithm or asymmetric ciphering, starts with two keys generated from a key utility, such as RIPEMD or the `KeyPairGenerator` class in the Java Cryptography Extension (JCE). Figure 20-12 illustrates the key-pair algorithm. The generated pair is made up of a public key and a private key. The public key is given out to people in your group to encrypt, and the private key is used to decrypt the message. This algorithm makes it infeasible to determine the private key, thus hiding half of the keying technology from anyone.

The key and cipher techniques are applied by using many algorithms; however, those techniques do not solve the problems of building programs that support network protocols. In the early 90s, the Socket Application Program Interface (API) was used to develop network protocols in the C language on Unix by using BSD Sockets, and later on the NT Operating System by using WinSock. Cipher libraries for programming were available at the time from different vendors. But they were not standardized at the time, and handshaking with the client and servers to exchange keys was not established as a standard in the protocols. There was no way of ensuring that the other client vendors were using the same package.

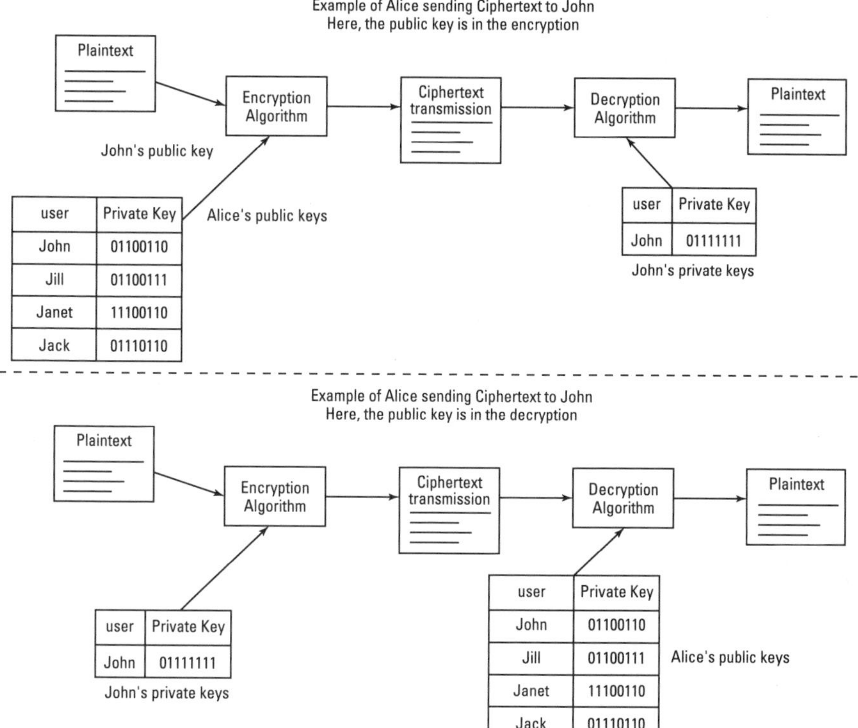

Figure 20-12: The key-pair algorithm

Netscape took the challenge in 1994 and created a wrapper on top of the Socket API that became known as Secure Socket Layer (SSL V1.0). This evolved into what is today the Secure Socket Layer (SSL V3.0) protocol. SSL is a security protocol that provides communications privacy over the Internet. The protocol allows client/server applications to communicate in a way that is designed to prevent eavesdropping, tampering, or message forgery. Figure 20-13 illustrates the Secure Sockets Layering.

<table>
<tr><td colspan="2">Secure Socket Layer (SSL)</td><td rowspan="4">Encryption Algorithms and Keying</td></tr>
<tr><td colspan="2">Socket Layer (BSD Sockets or WinSocks)</td></tr>
<tr><td>Transmission Control Protocol (TCP)</td><td>User Datagram Protocol (UDP)</td></tr>
<tr><td colspan="2">Internet Protocol (IP)</td></tr>
</table>

Figure 20-13: SSL layering

SSL was designed as a programming interface for network protocols that provided functionality for connecting and transporting data across TCP and UDP. TCP is a connection across the Internet that guarantees delivery; UDP does not guarantee delivery. UDP is used mostly in sending a one-way message or message broadcasting, such as used for a stock ticker. The SSL primary goal is to provide privacy and reliability between two communicating applications. The SSL has two layers: the SSL Record and the SSL Handshake Protocol. The SSL Record is at the lowest level that handles the transport of the data. The SSL Handshake Protocol allows the server and client to authenticate each other and to negotiate the keys before the data is transmitted and received. The advantage of SSL is that it is protocol independent.

The SSL protocol has many more properties. SSL can handshake by using the key-pair algorithm and encrypt by using a secret key. Its transport includes message integrity, and it can support digital signatures such as MD5 and SHA, which are discussed later. This makes SSL a very powerful instrument in the arsenal against attackers.

Summary

This was just a short introduction into some security fundamentals. Many organizations employ full-time security experts, because attackers are becoming more sophisticated and aggressive every day, and more data is at risk as organizations become more networked. To keep the site up and the data safe should be a daily goal in every organization. Some malicious people have nothing better to do than to get your data and bring your machines down. Disgruntled employees who start working for your competitors can probably do the most damage. The best advice is to have your security systems protected by people that you trust and who understand the hacker mentality and tool sets.

You may be asking yourself, how much security is enough? I recommend that all organizations have a security department whose job is to stay one step ahead of hackers. Just because you're not aware of any attacks doesn't mean that they didn't happen. It may be that the auditing is not adequate enough to discover attacks. The leadership in the organization needs to constantly ask the question about the value of the data in the organization being made public. Organizations need to have a set of procedures to follow when their sites have been hacked. It's better to be overprepared than to suffer the consequences. For a secure system, all layers and resources need to be marked off in a checklist as being secured.

✦ ✦ ✦

CHAPTER 21

Understanding WebLogic's Security Architecture

✦ ✦ ✦ ✦

In This Chapter

Introduction to WebLogic's security architecture

Understanding JAAS

Security realms

WebLogic Service Provider Interface

WebLogic Enterprise Connectivity

Authentication and authorization layers

✦ ✦ ✦ ✦

This chapter shows you how WebLogic Server implements some of the security fundamentals described in Chapter 20. WebLogic's security features enable you to establish secure connections with Web browsers, Web servers, Java applications, and other WebLogic servers. It also allows you to secure resources controlled by WebLogic Server by using a variety of methods.

Although security features are integrated into WebLogic Server, it's not a complete security package. The security you implement with WebLogic will need to be integrated with the rest of your organization's security infrastructure. WebLogic cannot, for example, protect your e-mail system, or restrict access to your network's perimeter. In many cases, however, WebLogic can cooperate with other systems to help an organization achieve its overall security goals.

Introduction to WebLogic Security Architecture

WebLogic Server uses some common principles for its different security layers, as illustrated in Figure 21-1. For the authorization layer, it predominately uses the Java Authentication and Authorization Service (JAAS). For the authorization layer, it uses JAAS, but has to wrap its own Service Provider Interface to handle the ACLs stored in its proprietary security realms. For data integrity, it uses the standard SSL protocol to protect its data. WebLogic has created the class `weblogic.security.audit` for its auditing capabilities.

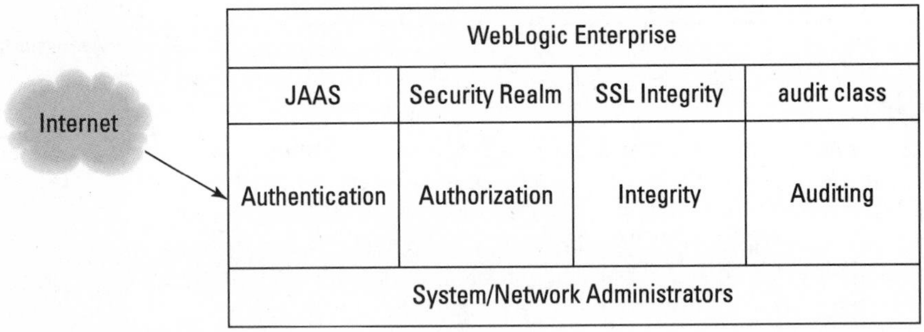

WebLogic Enterprise			
JAAS	Security Realm	SSL Integrity	audit class
Authentication	Authorization	Integrity	Auditing
System/Network Administrators			

Internet → Authentication

Figure 21-1: WebLogic Server security layers

Besides some extensions to the Java Security APIs such as JAAS, WebLogic Server follows many similar Security Architectures introduced in Chapter 20. Some of these extensions are needed for the WebLogic SPI to support the security realms. Other issues are the security between WebLogic Server and the WebLogic Enterprise Domain. The WebLogic Enterprise Domain is a group of objects, services, machines, and resources that you administer as a unit. Because the Enterprise Domain might include multiple WebLogic Servers and security realms, they will have to be synched up using the WebLogic Enterprise Connectivity (WLEC) that will be discussed later in this chapter. WLEC is the connectivity between WLS servers to authenticate each other.

WebLogic Server supports SSL with most of the cipher suites, X.509, JAAS, RSA protocols, key-pair algorithms with triple DES and RC4, MD5, and SHA. WebLogic Server can also be configured to support Certificate Authorities and HTTPS. In summary, WebLogic Server supports most standard security mechanisms that are needed for Internet development with some extensions to address enterprise security that are not addressed by the current Java standards.

Understanding JAAS

JAAS is an extension to the Java 2 Software Development Kit version 1.3 and it can be used with the WLS 6.1 server to authenticate Java servlets, Java Server Pages, Enterprise Java Beans, Remote Method Invocation Objects, and Java applications. The authentication part of JAAS provides the ability to reliably and securely maintain client identity. WebLogic Server extends the JAAS service to allow it to use the WebLogic Security Realm Architecture by layering it over the WebLogic Security Service Provider Interface (SPI). This provides a slightly modified version of JAAS and the differences will be demonstrated in Chapter 23. The Sun reference implementation uses a policy file to define the permission set on the principals that are authenticated. Since WebLogic Server does not implement the authentication through policy files, but through security realms, the Weblogic Server JAAS reference implementation will communicate to the realms that are defined in WebLogic Server, starting with the caching realm, then the file realm. The SPI layer in WebLogic Server provides the ability to use most methods and classes just as in the Sun implementation of JAAS but redirects the communication from policy files to the security realm.

Pluggable Authentication Modules

JAAS was built with the idea of being independent of different authentication technologies, such as RSA, DCE, Kerberos, S/Key, and smart card based authentication systems. This is known as the Pluggable Authentication Module (PAM) framework. The PAM framework is particularly useful for authentication because authentication can take on many forms, and both the client and the server must be prepared to handle the changes in protocols. Some of these protocols have been operating-system-specific, such as `rlogin`, and need to remain independent of the actual authentication mechanisms on that machine. PAM allows a system administrator to simply plug in a new authentication module without modifying any services. For authentication to be user friendly the authentication should be hidden from the user so that the user need not remember a password for each authentication protocol and authentication technique.

A user usually encounters multiple authentications when logging in to a system. A database connection and application server login might be used to give a user access to the resources he needs. In a lot of today's systems, these passwords are hard coded; after a user makes it through the front door, hard-coded passwords are utilized in the databases and other resources to give the user access to resources. This practice defeats the purpose of authentication because it doesn't layer authentication by the user's login. In fact, a lot of code is used to guess at the user's access level and to try to limit these accesses. But if any of the properties or class files are captured, they can easily be viewed along with the user ID and password. Not only does PAM alleviate these issues, but it also ensures that proper authentication layering is enforced. What's amazing about passwords used throughout systems is that in many of the files, there's usually just a properties file that has `prod` for the user ID and `prod` for the password for the production machines.

PAM does not address all authentication issues, such as the single-sign-on problem of securely transferring the identity of the caller to the remote site. By this, I mean that PAM works with authentication layering locally on the same machine and the PAM architecture is not handling logons at an enterprise level but at a system level. Because PAM protocol does not handle single-sign-on at an enterprise level of transferring login information, the use of enterprise authentication is still required. PAM is the connection of authentication protocols; however, some of the protocols that it supports could be enterprise-level authentication protocols such as Kerberos. However, there is no guarantee that the authentication that PAM is accessing is an enterprise protocol, and other authentication measures, like EJBs roles, might have to be used to compensate for this issue. What it does provide is the ability for the system administrator to install multiple authentication protocols for each application. It allows users to be authenticated from multiple protocols without retyping the password. The architecture provides a pluggable model for system authentication and related tasks such as password, account, and session management. Figure 21-2 shows how PAM is independent of an operating system.

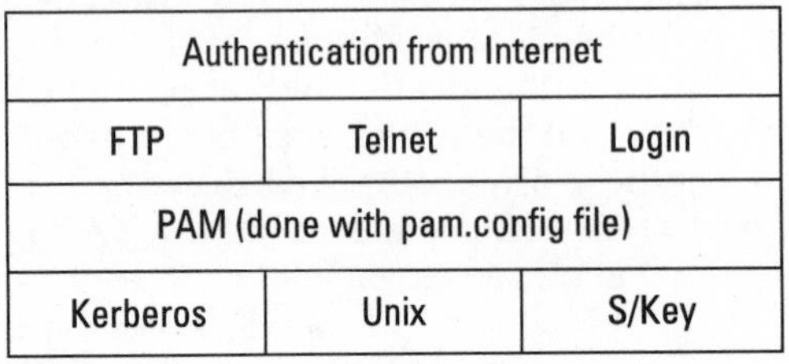

Authentication from Internet		
FTP	Telnet	Login
PAM (done with pam.config file)		
Kerberos	Unix	S/Key

Figure 21-2: The Pluggable Authentication Module

Figure 21-2 shows the PAM architecture and how it uses a `pam.config` file to store and configure the authentication modules. The configure modules are Kerberos, Unix authentication, and S/Key. These modules are set for the FTP, Telnet, and Login applications. As illustrated in Figure 21-3, PAM has four modules that can be configured independently: Authentication, Password, Session, and Account. The system administrator may, for example, add a Kerberos and password module and reuse the same session and account modules.

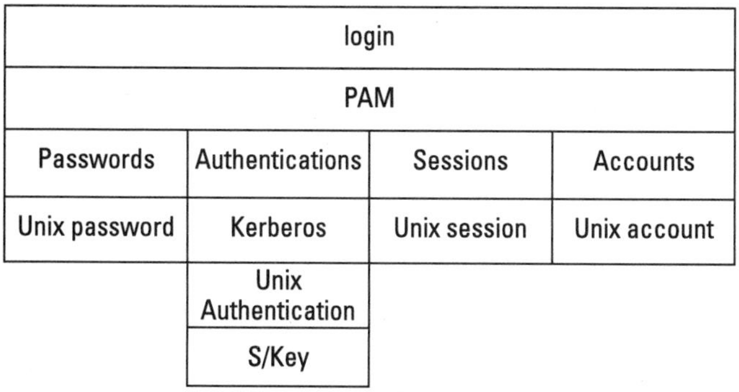

login			
PAM			
Passwords	Authentications	Sessions	Accounts
Unix password	Kerberos	Unix session	Unix account
	Unix Authentication		
	S/Key		

Figure 21-3: Adding modules to PAM

LoginContext

As mentioned earlier, PAM simply provides the pluggable interface. For most systems PAM is not part of Java, nor is it written in Java. In JAAS, the `LoginContext` represents the Java implementation of the PAM framework. The LoginContext uses policy files for configuring the one or many `LoginModules`. A `LoginModule` can best be described as a wrapper around an authentication technology provider, such as Kerberos. Applications write to the `LoginContext` API, while authentication providers implement the `LoginModule` interface that the configuration file will call to be used with the `LoginContext`. This enables different `LoginModules` to be plugged under the same application without modifications to the application. Only the configuration file needs to be changed.

```
public final class LoginContext {
  public LoginContext(String name) { }
  public void login() { }          // two phase process
  public void logout() { }
  public Subject getSubject() { } // get the authenticated user
}

public interface LoginModule {
  boolean login();   // 1st authentication phase
  boolean commit();  // 2nd authentication phase
  boolean abort();
  boolean logout();
}
```

The `LoginContext` is responsible for reading the configuration file and installing the correct `LoginModules`. Each `LoginModule` has a subject; each subject represents the user currently being authenticated and is updated with the proper credentials if the authentication succeeds.

For logging in, the `LoginContext`'s login function is invoked, which in turn invokes the appropriate `LoginModule`'s login method. The login method that is executed from the `LoginModule` class performs the login procedure, such as adding principals and credentials to the subject.

For logging out, the `LoginContext`'s logout function is invoked, which in turn invokes the `LoginModule`'s logout method. The logout method that is executed from the `LoginModule` class performs the logout procedure, such as removing principals and credentials from a subject.

One of the major components of JAAS is the use of Principal-Based Access Control (PBAC). The PBAC is defined as the ability for JAAS to give access to the system resource based on the principal defined in the grant entry for the permissions and resources that the defined principal may access. Since the WLS 6.1 does not use the policy file access, the PBAC must be defined in the WLS 6.1 security realm by the relationship of a principal that has permissions to a resource. These relationships are defined in the form of an ACL structure. WLS 6.1 does support PBAC, but it redefines it through the WLS 6.1 SPI layer to form these relationships without the use of a policy files.

Security realms

A security realm is a logical collection of groups, users, and Access Control Lists (ACLs) that are controlled by the same authentication or authorization policy. See Chapter 20 for some of the information on security realms. An ACL represents a resource, such as a file. That ACL can only live within a single security realm. That ACL can have multiple users, defined as `AclEntries`, but each user must be defined in the security realm. When the user tries to access the resource, WebLogic Server tries to authenticate and authorize the user by checking the corresponding ACL for that resource. If the user has the correct permissions to use that resource, such as + for a read action when the user is trying to read the file, then the resource is allowed to read the file. ACLs are composed of ACL Entries, which represent a set of principals and their credentials. Each ACL is considered a named system resource, such as CD-ROM. Each ACL entry has a permission associated to it and a permission flag, such as + and `read`, implying read permission. The ACL entry principal can be a User or Group, such as "system" that is defined as the administrator for WLS 6.1. Since the ACL contains a set of ACL Entries, there can be many mapped principals to a resource. For the CD-ROM ACL, there could be an ACL entry containing a read permission for the system principal, and an ACL entry for a group called `users` for a read permission. The way that the ACL code can tell the difference between Groups and Users is to check the class type being presented on the principal's behalf. In JAAS, this is also very similar to a grant entry in a policy file.

Figure 21-4 shows two ACL Entries that are related to an ACL. It also shows an example of a possible group, user, and permission table and the relationship that has been described. In this case, the credential is a password. In the WLS 6.1 example of storing passwords, it uses MD5 to hash the password and then compares them to see whether they match.

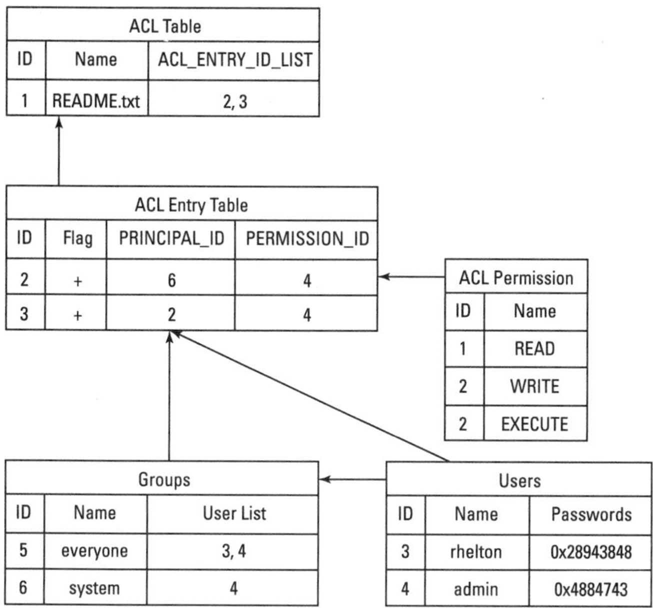

Figure 21-4: Security realm entries

The ACL is made available for applications (or objects), such as a Java servlet, to access them. If a servlet wanted, for example, to access the `README.txt` file, it would have to go through the security realm and access the ACL to see if the user had permission, as shown in Figure 21-5.

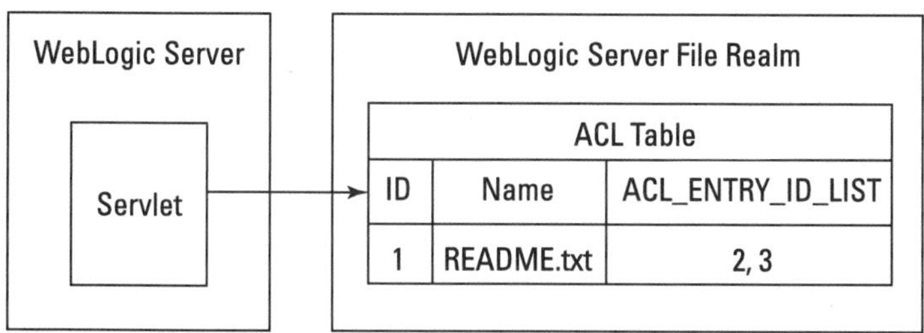

Figure 21-5: Accessing security realm entries

The File realm is the default security realm for WebLogic Server. It was designed for 1,000 or fewer users. The File realm is stored in the file `realm.properties` that installs users, groups, and ACL objects defined when WebLogic Server is first started. But reading from a file to look up ACLs can be very slow. For this reason, the servlet would normally communicate to a Caching realm first before accessing the File realm (see Figure 21-6). If the `README.txt` ACL is not loaded in the Caching realm, then it would load it up from the File realm into the Caching realm so that next time, it's loaded up in memory and doesn't have to read the File realm.

To further simplify the example, to define another security realm, such as an RDBMS realm, as a primary realm, it must be set as the current Caching realm through the WLS 6.1 console panel. It is set as a Caching realm because the Caching realm sits as a communication layer on top of the primary realm. The Caching realm is there to avoid too many calls to the primary realm by caching the ACLs that are frequently called and not doing a search on them unless there has been a change. In this example, a lookup is being done to get the permissions of the "system" principal, which is the root user for administration commands in the WLS 6.1 that is used for operations like changing settings to WLS 6.1 and having "modify" access for many permissions to system resources throughout the WLS 6.1. The "system" user should never be defined in any realm except the File realm, or else it will create authentication conflicts. Likewise, the "system" user in the File realm must always be present because the File realm is the one realm that is always available for performing lookups. After the RDBMS realm returns a null that it could not find the "system" user, then the WLS 6.1 will do a lookup on the File realm, and retrieve the permissions of the "system" user.

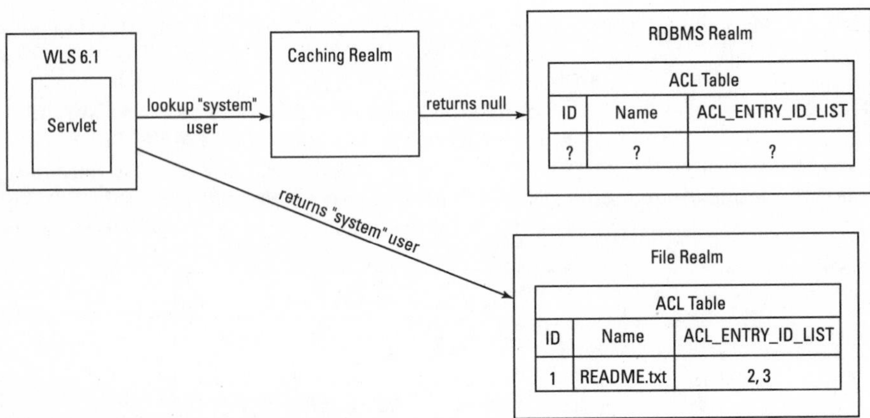

Figure 21-6: The Caching realm

So far, I've only discussed using ACLs as part of the authorization layer. But security realms may also be used in the authentication layer for the user to login in to the system. The security realms also contain user and group information, as well as passwords, for users to log in. This information is reused for authentication. But it might be desired that the authentication have different users than the authorization realm. In this case, the authentication realm can be a separate realm that the Caching realm uses to get authentication information.

Besides the File realm, it's possible to configure the security realm tables by using other technologies, such as Relational Database Management Systems (RDBMS),

Lightweight Directory Access Protocol (LDAP), Unix security realm, and Windows NT security realm. Even custom security realms can be created and used as security realms. In the Unix security realm, if PAM is available, it is used; otherwise, normal Unix login is used in this security realm. For the Windows NT security realm, the users and groups are defined in the Windows NT Operating System domain. For the LDAP and RDBMS security realms, the ACLs and table information is stored in the directory structures or tables.

WebLogic Service Provider Interface

WebLogic Server provides a WebLogic Service Provider Interface (SPI) to extend the JAAS to use the security realms provided by WebLogic Server. WebLogic Server may use the JAAS for authentication, but WebLogic Server's security realms must be incorporated into the JAAS. Much more detail of this SPI is covered in Chapter 22. In this section, I briefly mention the four packages in WebLogic Server Architecture that provide access to the functionality of the security realms. The four packages are `weblogic.security`, `weblogic.security.acl`, `weblogic.security.audit`, and `weblogic.security.net`. The purpose of the `weblogic.security` package is to map digital certificates from the Web browsers and Java Clients to WebLogic Server, so there's no need for a user to enter a username and password if there's a digital certificate. The next added class is the `weblogic.security.acl`, which is used for creating custom ACLs for purposes of the custom security realms and getting ACLs from an external store, such as LDAP. The next class is the `weblogic.security.audit`, which is for auditing security events. This class can filter authentications and authorizations requests and redirect them into a file for auditing. The last class of the SPI is the `weblogic.security.net` class. The purpose of this class is to allow or deny connections based on IP addresses, domain name, or protocol that the connection is using. This last class is similar to security mechanisms in firewalls.

WebLogic Enterprise Connectivity

Propagation of security from the authentication layer to the authorization layer can be accomplished by passing the security context from WebLogic Server security realms to the different WLS 6.1 domains across an enterprise system. This is done by using WebLogic Enterprise Connectivity (WLEC).

WLEC provides support for the Secure Socket Layer (SSL) and security context propagation from WebLogic Server to the WebLogic Enterprise Domain. Using WLEC allows SSL to be used between the Enterprise objects, such as EJBs, to authenticate through the WLEC connection pool to other Enterprise objects, such as servlets.

The security context propagation works only with the WLEC connection pool, as shown in Figure 21-7. A WLEC connection pool is a pool of Internet Inter-ORB Protocol (IIOP) connections. IIOP is a standard for Object Request Brokers (ORB) to communicate with other ORBs, even from different ORB vendors, across TCP.

Because EJBs only communicate with Remote Method Invocation (RMI), there is the RMI over IIOP specification for EJBs to run on top of ORBs. The IIOP protocol also uses principals and credentials, similar to the EJB specification. Each IIOP connection in the WLEC pool will be authenticated by using a particular principal identity specified by the system administrator. Either password authentication or certificates can be used in this authentication technique. The SSL protocol establishes secure communications between client and server applications. SSL is provided for IIOP requests to CORBA objects and for RMI on IIOP requests to EJBs or RMI objects.

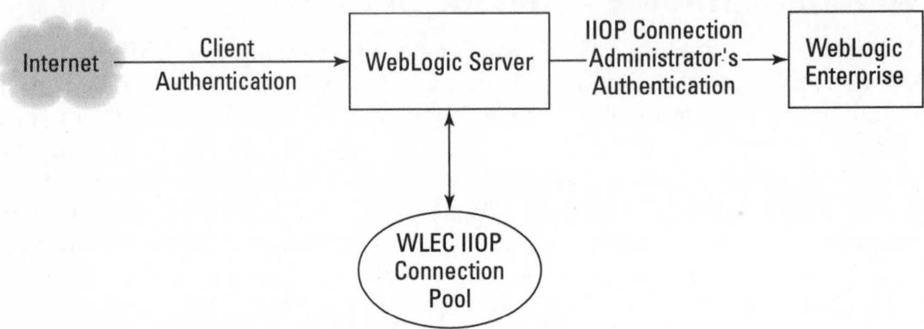

Figure 21-7: The WLEC security context propagation

Authentication layer

Authentication is the first layer of security in WebLogic Server. By default, WebLogic Server uses one-way authentication. One-way authentication is when a client needs to authenticate that it is contacting the correct server. Two-way authentication is when both the client and the server want to verify that the other entity is who they have identified themselves as being. You accomplish authentication by using a username and password combination, or digital certificates using the X.509 protocol. In the X.509 protocol, the client is authenticated by using the digital certificate as part of the Secure Socket Layer (SSL) handshaking. When using a set of digital certificates, the digital certificates must be received from a trusted Certificate Authority to verify the certificates presented by WebLogic Server. But you can configure the SSL to support mutual authentication through SSL where the client is also required to pass a chain of digital certificates.

The WebLogic Server is versatile because it may also be configured as a Web server. It also provides support for other Web servers from Apache, Netscape, and Microsoft IIS via plug-ins (see Figure 21-8). It supports plug-ins from Apache, Netscape, and Microsoft's IIS. For the support of Apache, it uses a straight plug-in. To support the Netscape Web server, it uses the Netscape Server Application Programming Interface (NSAPI). For the support of IIS, WebLogic Server uses the Internet Information Server Application Programming Interface (ISAPI).

One of purposes of the Web server plug-in is to integrate the authentication from the Web server to WebLogic Server by passing the user ID and password to WebLogic Server via the HTTP protocol. The plug-in is also used to support the WebLogic security mechanisms to have the ability to check to see of a resource is protected by an ACL in the WebLogic security realms. If the resource is protected, then the Web server uses the HTTP connection to request a user's ID and password. After this successful authentication, WebLogic Server will determine whether the user has the necessary permissions to access the resource. This is done through a Java servlet that resides on WebLogic Server.

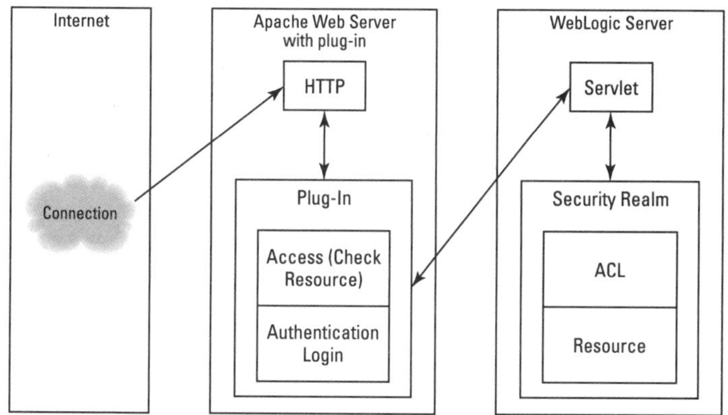

Figure 21-8: The Authentication plug-in

The WLS 6.1 server can be redirected through multiple Web servers. If the need arises, multiple plug-ins can call the servlet across HTTP, and they can be routed from port 80 as shown in Figure 21-9.

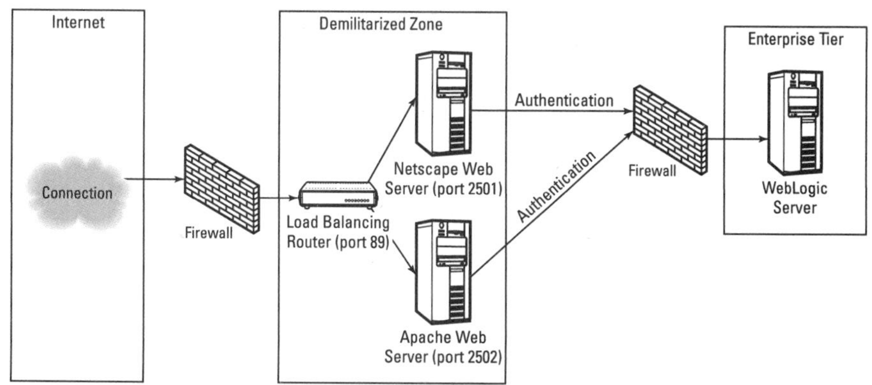

Figure 21-9: WebLogic Server with multiple Web servers

In Figure 21-9, a Load Balancing Router (LBR) receives the communication for the HTTP at port 80. It is the responsibility of the LBR to send this request to one of the Web servers, be it the Netscape Web server or the Apache Web server based on the balancing algorithm of the LBR. The idea is that if it is attached to another Web server besides the one included in WebLogic Server, the WebLogic server can still be authenticated as an application server. The securities of the Web servers are now a factor to the Enterprise Security outside of the scope of WebLogic Server. If a security breach occurs on the Apache Web server, such as the HTTP server being compromised, the application server may still be protected because it has its own security mechanisms. The reason for the architecture shown in Figure 21-9 is that a lot of organizations already have Web servers in place before installing an Application Server. Application Servers can also be more expensive than Web servers, so in order to save some money, they use different Web servers. Not all technologies can support DMZs, but WLS 6.1 Application Servers do.

WebLogic Server also has the ability to block client connections based on the client IP addresses. If the authentication does not come directly from the Web server or the firewall, then WebLogic Server may block the request and return a denial on the authentication. WebLogic Server may also block specific protocols. The Application Server may, for example, only allow messages implementing the HTTP protocol to pass to it.

JAAS authentication

WebLogic Server also supports JAAS for authentication. When using JAAS authentication (see Figure 21-10), Java clients enable the authentication process by instantiating a `LoginContext` object that in turn references a configuration file, or configuration object. A configuration object specifies the configured `LoginModule`s to be used for client authentication. The `LoginModule` object prompts for and verifies the client credentials. In WebLogic Server, the credentials will be retrieved from the security realm. In order to retrieve credentials through the security realm with JAAS, the WebLogic SPI is used to communicate with the security realm. The `LoginContext` will return the subject if the completion is normal, otherwise it will return a `LoginException`.

You need to write a `LoginModule` object for each type of authentication mechanism you want to use with WebLogic Server. If you want to use mutual authentication, for example, you need to provide a `LoginModule` object that both requests and provides credentials. WebLogic Server does not supply any `LoginModule` objects.

The security realms are used in authentication to store users, groups, and passwords. Many passwords are saved in a one-way hash algorithm using a seed to salt the algorithm so that it can't be read. Salts are values that are used to hide a password. The salt can be XORed with the password to make it more difficult to break when encrypted. A salt could also be considered a pass phrase that is masked with the password to hide it. After the password is hashed, there should be no way to programmatically recover the password. The more random the salt, the more difficult it is to crack because the salt must also be recovered to crack the password.

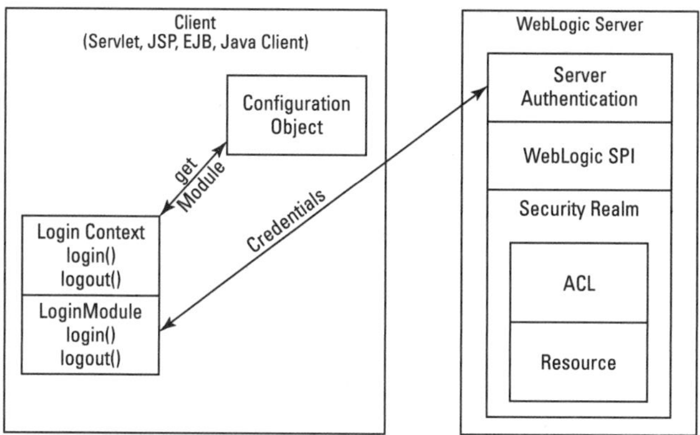

Figure 21-10: A JAAS scenario

Authentication is not just for Internet access anymore. Multiple WebLogic Servers within an organization must communicate with each other. When Application Servers communicate together, an attacker can intervene to take over the Application Server. Therefore, authentication between the servers can help avoid this situation. In the multiple WLS 6.1 servers used across an enterprise there is normally a single Application Server that administrates the other Application Servers; this is called an administration server, and the other servers are known as cluster or managed servers. The Application Servers that the administration server manages are called managed servers. By default, the connection between the administrator servers and the managed servers is not secure. The file that it uses to contain usernames and passwords is not encrypted, and they are sent in clear text over the connections when communicating. For these reasons, the SSL protocol and certificate authentication should be set up to protect the configuration information in WebLogic Servers. When the SSL protocol and certificate information is used, and the manager server is started, it receives the digital certificate from the administration server. Then the managed server authenticates the administration server with this certificate.

Comparing security realms

WebLogic Server has its own security realm, which is different from the WebLogic Enterprise Domain security realm. The only way to propagate the identity information of an authenticated user from WebLogic Server to the WebLogic Enterprise Domain is to use WLEC. This is called security context propagation. The security propagation is one-way, meaning that WebLogic Server contains the security information that will be retrieved by the WebLogic Enterprise Domain and not vice versa. That means that a trusted CORBA pool has to be formed containing the IIOP connections. The security context propagation is sent over the network connection from one of the connections in the IIOP connection pool. Each one of these network connections has been authenticated by using a defined user identity. A plug-in is used in the IIOP handler to change the principal to the tokens.

To pass the authentication and authorization of a user's identity (see Figure 21-11), a pair of tokens is used. These tokens propagate to the target WebLogic Server across the WebLogic Enterprise Domain for authentication and authorization. These tokens are then propagated to the EJB, or CORBA, object that needs to use them to access a resource. SSL can be used to protect the request sent from WebLogic Server security realm. As mentioned before, SSL can be used in IIOP requests and RMI requests. In order to use SSL, both the WebLogic Connectivity and the WebLogic Enterprise applications need to be configured to support this protocol.

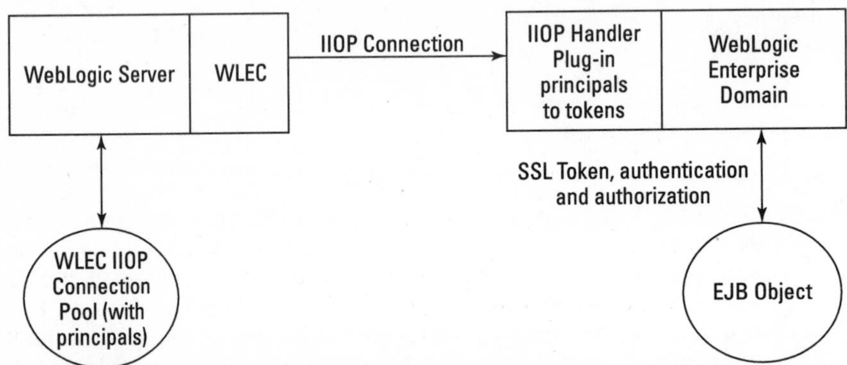

Figure 21-11: The WLEC security context propagation

Authorization layer

The next layer of security inside the WebLogic security model is authorization. WebLogic Server does authorization through the use of Access Control Lists (ACLs). The authorization lists in WebLogic Server are stored in security realms, which represent users, groups, and Access Control Lists for allowing users to access resources. By default, the WebLogic Server uses files for a security realm, but you may set it up for the Windows NT, Unix, LDAP, and custom developed security realms. In order to access a resource using a security realm, a user must be defined in a security realm with permissions for that resource. WebLogic Server determines the set of required permissions to invoke a method on a WebLogic Server resource. If the invoking user has at least one of the required permissions, WebLogic Server allows the method to be invoked.

Propagation of security from the authentication layer to the authorization layer can be accomplished by passing the security context from WebLogic Server security realms to the WebLogic Enterprise domains. This is done by using the WebLogic Enterprise Connectivity (WLEC).

Summary

WebLogic Server has security architecture that addresses common security concerns as well as providing support for the emerging Java and J2EE security APIs. BEA has done a good job supporting the current Java security APIs and protocols and extending them for the use in WLS 6.1. The JAAS example that was demonstrated in this chapter has shown that one of the differences was extending JAAS to support the WLS security realm instead of policy files. WLS distributes reference examples similar to Sun's reference implementations of the Java security protocols. This gives the architect the ability to incorporate future Java extensions in the current architecture.

Not many application servers currently support JAAS as much as WebLogic Server does. The only piece that seems lacking to support the entire enterprise security is the support for file integrity. That is simply because WebLogic Server is not a directory and file server, but an Application Server. This means that the organization is still responsible for some of its objects outside of WebLogic Server. Solving security issues is still a full-time job, and when you buy a tool like WebLogic Server, your specific organization still has a lot of setup and programming needs.

WebLogic Server is a tool and nothing more. If an attacker still makes it onto your system, it is not the tool's fault, but how it was implemented and the security policy that the organization has in place to prepare for attackers. This requires that the implementer of WLS 6.1 for security concerns cannot leave it at just using the product, but must spend time searching through newsgroups and calls to customer support to constantly keep the programs current and ensure that WLS and Java are being implemented properly. You can always make enhancements to ensure that the current threats of attackers are thwarted. A thorough understanding of the security features provided by the Application Server as well as the overall security approach for the enterprise is essential to obtaining the desired enterprise security.

✦ ✦ ✦

Securing a WebLogic Application

✦ ✦ ✦ ✦

In This Chapter

Introduction to JAAS programming

Building a custom RDBMS Security Realm

Auditing in WebLogic Server

✦ ✦ ✦ ✦

Now that you understand security fundamentals and how WebLogic implements them, it's time to see how to configure and program security for a WebLogic application. This chapter provides you with the configuration steps and source code required to effectively secure a WebLogic system.

Introduction to JAAS Programming

JAAS 1.0 is a separate software package provided by Sun to extend the Java Software Development Kit version 1.3 as an alternative to the JNDI authentication process. It comes standard with the Java SDK 1.4 Beta. This implies that at a minimum, version 1.3 of the Java Software Development Kit must be installed and used for development. The JAAS mechanism is used for authentication from the Java client through WebLogic Server to authenticate a subject. The authorization components are not provided in JAAS for the WebLogic Server because of the use of the security realms. To understand how to program to the WebLogic Server's implementation of JAAS, you must first understand how to program to Sun's implementation of JAAS.

Start the architecture by defining the various classes that make up JAAS in the following classes that compose the JAAS v1.0 architecture:

- `javax.security.auth.Subject`: Represents the source of the request that can be an individual or group with a set of public and private credentials. A `Subject` object is created at the completion of a successful user authentication or login.

- `javax.security.auth.login.LoginContext`: Provides the base API for initiating login, logout, and acquires the authenticated `Subject` for the purpose of authorization.
- `javax.security.auth.login.Configuration`: Is the configuration object that specifies which `LoginModule` to use from the `LoginConext`.
- `javax.security.auth.spi.LoginModule`: Is the object that provides a module for a specific implementation of an authentication technology from the providers that support JAAS. This object is also the actual object that performs the authentication.
- `javax.security.auth.callback.Callback`: Is the object that interfaces with the `CallbackHandler`. This allows the security services to interact with the calling application to retrieve specific data such as usernames and passwords. The type of `Callbacks` used is based on the type of `LoginModule`.
- `javax.security.auth.callback.Callback.CallbackHandler`: This is the object that is passed as a mechanism between the `LoginContext` and the `LoginModule` to communicate with a subject to obtain the authentication mechanism. This mechanism is used to both provide information and to get information to the `LoginModule`. The information is passed through the `Callback` object.

Writing and configuring the LoginContext

To create the Java Client for authentication, the first step is to associate the login mechanism to the `LoginContext`. The login mechanism is in an implementation of `LoginModule`. When the `LoginContext` is constructed, the `LoginModule` and `CallbackHandler` instances are associated with it at that time. The `LoginModule` is not hard coded to the `LoginContext` but is distributed through a `Configuration` object. All that will be called in the `LoginContext` is a reference that is stored in the config file to specify which login mechanism to install. This is so that login mechanisms can be plugged in without changing code, just the configuration. The following code starts the `LoginContext`:

```
/**
 * Sample client for JAAS user authentication
 */
public class Sample {

  /**
  * Attempt to authenticate the user.
  */
  public static void main(String[] args) {

    LoginContext loginContext = null;

    /**
```

```
    * Set JAAS server url system property and create a LoginContext
    */
    try {
      // Create LoginContext
      loginContext = new LoginContext("Sample",
        new MyCallbackHandler());
    } catch (SecurityException se) {
      se.printStackTrace();
    } catch (LoginException le) {
      le.printStackTrace();
    }

    /**
    * Attempt authentication
    */
    try {
      // If we return without an exception, authentication succeeded
      loginContext.login();
    } catch (FailedLoginException fle) {
      System.out.println("Authentication Failed, " +
        fle.getMessage());
    } catch (AccountExpiredException aee) {
        System.out.println("Authentication Failed: Account Expired");
    } catch (CredentialExpiredException cee) {
      System.out.println("Authentication Failed: CredentialsExpired");
    } catch (Exception e) {
      System.out.println("Authentication Failed: Unexpected Exception, "
        + e.getMessage());
      e.printStackTrace();
    }

    /**
    * Retrieve authenticated subject, perform SampleAction as Subject
    */
    Subject      subject      = loginContext.getSubject();
    SampleAction sampleAction = new SampleAction();
    Subject.doAs(subject, sampleAction);
    System.exit(0);
  }
}
```

Figure 22-1 shows a lot of work being done underneath the covers in the process of the `LoginContext` creation. The instance of the `CallbackHandler` is passed to the underlying `LoginModule` in order for the `Subject` and the `LoginModule` to communicate. The configuration of the `LoginModule` must succeed in order for the authentication to succeed. One thing that becomes clear regarding communication between the `LoginModule` and `LoginContext` is that they never interact directly, but through mediators such as the `Configuration` object and `CallbackHandler`.

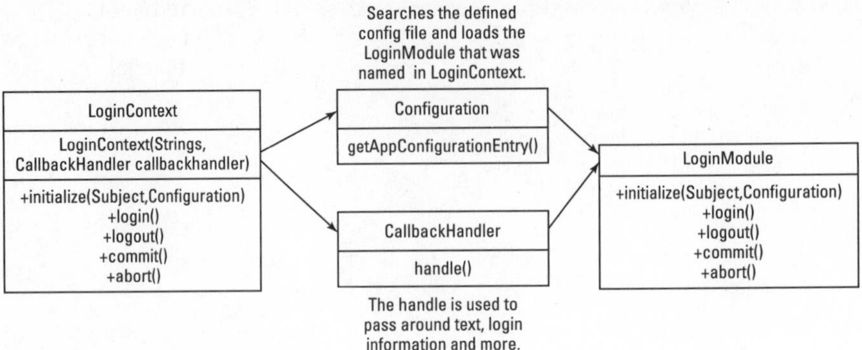

Figure 22-1: LoginContext

After the Java client creates the `LoginContext` object, it must then invoke the `login()` function. This `login()` function will, in turn, invoke the `login()` function from the each of the `LoginModule` objects defined in the creation of the `LoginContext`. Regardless of whether the `login()` function fails or succeeds, this method will complete a two-phase authentication process by calling either the commit or abort, functions of the `LoginModules`. The `commit()` function gets called for every successful authentication of the `login()` function to associate the `Principals` and `Credentials` to the `Subject`. The `abort()` function gets called for every unsuccessful attempt of the `login()` function to clean up any resources used for the verification. A successful `login()` of the `Subject` is when the `login()` function completes and no exception was thrown; otherwise the authentication was unsuccessful. After a successful authentication, a `getSubject()` function can be called on the `LoginContext` to get the current `Subject` that was authenticated in the Java client. To get the `Principals` on the `Subject`, a `getPrincipals()` function can be called on the `Subject` object. To get the current `Credentials`, a `getCredentials()` function can be called on the current `Subject` object.

The configuration determines the `LoginModule` that will be applied to the `LoginContext`. The configuration for the example is defined by the environment properties `-Djava.security.auth.login.config==sample_jaas.config`:

```
/** Login Configuration for the JAAS Sample Application **/

Sample {
  SampleLoginModule required debug=true;
};
```

The file is set for the `Sample` name, but more names can be named in this file for multiple configurations. The `java.auth.login.config` setting to define the configuration file can also be changed by overwriting the `Configuration` object's `getAppConfigurationEntry()` function. The `debug=true` is a name and value pair that are parameters that can be passed into the `LoginModule` initialization.

The SampleLoginModule is the class that will be loaded up and become the running instance of the LoginModule. It is normally referred to as the ModuleName. The Authentication Flag is required and is not case sensitive; its legal values are:

✦ **Required:** The associated LoginModule must succeed for the authentication to be considered successful. The next modules will still continue to load even if a failure condition is encountered.

✦ **Requisite:** The LoginModule must succeed for the authentication process to be considered successful, but the subsequent modules will not be attempted if a failure occurs.

✦ **Sufficient:** The LoginModule is not required to succeed. If it does succeed, it will not proceed to the next LoginModule. But if it doesn't succeed, it will proceed to the next LoginModule that is specified.

✦ **Optional:** The LoginModule is not required to succeed. Whether it succeeds or not, it will proceed to the next LoginModule down the chain.

This solves the issue of configuring the LoginModule. You can also give access to the SampleAction and the rest of the sample code by configuring policy files. You can use the policytool that comes with the JDK 1.3 to configure policy files. These policy files can grant permissions to JAR files, directories, or even URLs. The SampleAction was put into a JAR to assign the permissions and a principal to it:

```
/** Subject-Based Access Control Policy for the JAAS Sample Application **/

grant codebase "file:D:/Working/jaas/jaas/SampleAction.jar",
  Principal sample.SamplePrincipal "rich" {
  permission java.util.PropertyPermission "java.home", "read";
  permission java.util.PropertyPermission "user.home", "read";
  permission java.io.FilePermission "sample_jaas.config", "read";
};
```

Because the SampleAction.class is saved in the SampleAction.jar, and the Principal is set to rich, the user rich will have read permissions to the user.home and java.home properties and read permissions for the file sample jaas.config. The type of permissions that are allowed depends on the on the permission class name. The permission class name in the example given is java.io.FilePermission that can have a read, write, delete, and execute permission on a particular file. The same type of permission structure is applied to the rest of the JARs and sample code. It is recommended to keep the LoginModules in separate JARs for decoupling them from the rest of the sample code. Separating the LoginModules models maintains the pluggable behaviors of these authentication mechanisms. The other file that is part of the sample code is as follows:

```
/** Java 2 Access Control Policy for the JAAS Sample Application **/

/* grant the JAAS core library AllPermission */
```

```
grant codebase "file:D:/Working/jaas/jaas/jaas.jar" {
  permission java.security.AllPermission;
};

/* grant the sample LoginModule AllPermission */
grant codebase "file:D:/Working/jaas/jaas/LoginModule.jar" {
  permission java.security.AllPermission;
};

/*grant permissions for the Sample Class */
grant {
  permission javax.security.auth.AuthPermission "modifyPrincipals";
  permission javax.security.auth.AuthPermission "createLoginContext";
  permission javax.security.auth.AuthPermission "doAs";
  permission java.util.PropertyPermission "java.home", "read";
  permission java.util.PropertyPermission "user.home", "read";
  permission java.io.FilePermission "sample_jaas.config", "read";
};
```

To enable the use of loading property files, the `java.security.manager` must be enabled in the environment.

Writing a LoginModule

The first function in the `LoginModule` is the `initialize()` function. This function receives the `Subject`, `CallbackHandler`, and any shared states and options that were started from the `Configuration` object loading the configuration file. The `initialize()` function is associated with the `Configuration` object settings and the `CallbackHandler` functionality when it is started by the JVM. The `initialize()` function needs to set these parameters to the `LoginModule`'s global variables for future reference. The `LoginModule` will use the `CallbackHandler` to establish any interaction with the `LoginContext`, such as getting a password.

The next function is the `login()` function, which is called when the `login()` function of the `LoginContext` starts. In this code, a simple authentication was written to compare the username to `rich` and the password `richpass`. In the WebLogic implementation, WebLogic Server provides a helper class `weblogic.security.auth.Authenticate` that will be used with these principals to authenticate through WebLogic Server. The `Authenticate` class uses a JNDI `Environment` object and returns the authenticated subject. This implies that if the `Credential` and `Principals` are defined in the JNDI environment, it will associate those `Credentials` and `Principals` to that `Subject` after there is a successful login into WebLogic Server. This authentication method will interface to WebLogic's security realm to access the permissions and the authentication of the users. If the user is not defined in WebLogic Server security realm, or if the password is not valid, the user cannot be authenticated.

Using standard JAAS conventions would make the developer copy the `PasswordCallback` and `NameCallback` directly into the `Subject` object and start an authentication process. These are the callbacks that will retrieve the values from the `CallbackHandler` that interfaces between the Java client and the `LoginModule`. The `login()` function associates `Principals` and `Credentials` with the `Subject`. A `commit()` function is called if the login is successful, otherwise it is an `abort()` function. These functions simply finish the work of either continuing to notify the `LoginModule` to change to a confirmation state of a login or, in an abort, cleaning up the `Subject` to ensure that it returns that there were errors. Listing 22-1 is an example of the `login()` function:

Listing 22-1: Login example

```
/**
 * Authenticate the user by username and password passed in
 *
 * @return true in all cases
 *
 *
 * @exception LoginException if this LoginModule
 *            is unable to perform the authentication.
 */
public boolean login() throws LoginException {

  // Verify that the client supplied a callback handler
  if (callbackHandler == null) {
    throw new LoginException("No CallbackHandler Specified");
  }

  // Populate callback list
  Callback[] callbacks = new Callback[2];
  callbacks[0] = new NameCallback("username: ");
  callbacks[1] = new PasswordCallback("password: ", false);

  try {
    // Prompt for username and password
    callbackHandler.handle(callbacks);

    // Retrieve username
    username = ((NameCallback) callbacks[0]).getName();

    // Retrieve password, converting from char[] to String
    char[] charPassword = ((PasswordCallback) callbacks[1]).getPassword();

    if (charPassword == null) {
      // Treat a NULL password as an empty password, not NULL
      charPassword = new char[0];
    }

    password = new String(charPassword);
  } catch (IOException ioe) {
    throw new LoginException(ioe.toString());
```

Continued

Listing 22-1 *(continued)*

```
} catch (UnsupportedCallbackException uce) {
  throw new LoginException("Error: Callback "
    + uce.getCallback().toString() + " Not Available");
}

// Populate weblogic environment and authenticate
/* WebLogic Only */
//    Environment env = new Environment();
//    env.setProviderUrl(url);
//    env.setSecurityPrincipal(username);
//    env.setSecurityCredentials(password);
try {
  // Authenticate user credentials, populating Subject
  /* WebLogic Specific */
  //      Authenticate.authenticate(env, subject);

  /* Non-WebLogic Function for Login */
  authenticate(username, password);
} catch (LoginException le) {
  System.err.println("Error: Login Exception on authenticate, "
    + le.getMessage());
  throw new LoginException(le.toString());
}

// Successfully authenticated subject with supplied info
succeeded = true;
return succeeded;
}
```

The last function that the LoginModule needs to define is the logout() function. This function is called in the LoginModule when the LoginContext executes its logout() function. The purpose of this function is simply to release its resources by setting its global variables to null as Listing 22-2 shows.

Listing 22-2: Logout function example

```
/**
 * Logout the user.
 *
 * @exception LoginException if the logout fails.
 *
 * @return true in all cases since this LoginModule
 *         should not be ignored.
 */
public boolean logout() throws LoginException {
  succeeded = false;
```

```
    commitSucceeded = false;
    username = null;
    password = null;
    return true;
}
```

Writing the CallbackHandler

The CallbackHandler is the object that populates the callbacks from the Java client for the LoginModule to use for authentication. These include the ChoiceCallback, ConfirmationCallback, LocaleCallback, NameCallback, PasswordCallback, TextInputCallback, and TextOutPutCallback. These are all the callbacks for handling the various authentication mechanisms and their protocols for passing information from and to the Java client. The ones that are emphasized in most LoginModules are the NameCallback for the username and the PasswordCallback for retrieving the user's password. TextInputCallback retrieves arbitrary text from the user, and TextOutputCallback sends messages such as warnings back to the user. The ConfirmationCalllback asks for confirmation from the user to ensure that he is who he claims to be. If it's a choice selection and the LoginModule needs to examine the choice, it would use a ChoiceCallback. The LocaleCallback provides the LoginModule with locale information such as the current country being executed in for language constraints. Listing 22-3 shows an example of populating the callbacks.

Listing 22-3: Populating callbacks

```
/**
 * Implementation of the CallbackHandler Interface
 */
class MyCallbackHandler implements CallbackHandler {

    /**
     * Method handle
     *
     * @param callbacks
     *
     * @throws IOException
     * @throws UnsupportedCallbackException
     */
    public void handle(Callback[] callbacks)
            throws IOException, UnsupportedCallbackException {

        for (int i = 0; i < callbacks.length; i++) {
            if (callbacks[i] instanceof TextOutputCallback) {

                // Display the message according to the specified type
```

Continued

Listing 22-3 *(continued)*

```
                TextOutputCallback toc = (TextOutputCallback) callbacks[i];

                switch (toc.getMessageType()) {

                case TextOutputCallback.INFORMATION :
                    System.out.println(toc.getMessage());
                    break;

                case TextOutputCallback.ERROR :
                    System.out.println("ERROR: " + toc.getMessage());
                    break;

                case TextOutputCallback.WARNING :
                    System.out.println("WARNING: " + toc.getMessage());
                    break;

                default :
                    throw new IOException("Unsupported message type: "
                                          + toc.getMessageType());
                }
            } else if (callbacks[i] instanceof NameCallback) {

                // Prompt the user for the username
                NameCallback nc = (NameCallback) callbacks[i];

                System.err.print(nc.getPrompt());
                System.err.flush();
                nc.setName((new BufferedReader(new InputStreamReader(System
                    .in))).readLine());
            } else if (callbacks[i] instanceof PasswordCallback) {

                // Prompt the user for the password
                PasswordCallback pc = (PasswordCallback) callbacks[i];

                System.err.print(pc.getPrompt());
                System.err.flush();

// Note: JAAS specifies that the password is a char[] rather than a String
                String tmpPassword =
                    (new BufferedReader(new InputStreamReader(System.in)))
                        .readLine();
                int    passLen      = tmpPassword.length();
                char[] password     = new char[passLen];

                for (int passIdx = 0; passIdx < passLen; passIdx++) {
                    password[passIdx] = tmpPassword.charAt(passIdx);
                }

                pc.setPassword(password);
            } else {
```

```
                throw new UnsupportedCallbackException(
                    callbacks[i], "Unrecognized Callback");
            }
        }
    }
```

Writing JAAS for WebLogic Server

So far, the JAAS example has only been used for the JAAS v1.0 package. WebLogic Server extends this package for its use and the use of the WebLogic authentication and security realms. If you examine the code, you will notice several differences. One of the biggest differences is that the authentication for login uses URLs that hit WebLogic Server instead of a policy file and calls a WebLogic Server `Authenticate` class to authenticate the user through WebLogic Server, as Listing 22-4 demonstrates.

Listing 22-4: Login function example

```
/**
 * Authenticate the user by username and password passed in
 *
 * @return true in all cases
 *
 * @exception LoginException if this LoginModule
 * is unable to perform the authentication.
 */
public boolean login() throws LoginException {

  // Verify that the client supplied a callback handler
  if (callbackHandler == null) {
    throw new LoginException("No CallbackHandler Specified");
  }

  // Populate callback list
  Callback[] callbacks = new Callback[2];
  callbacks[0] = new NameCallback("username: ");
  callbacks[1] = new PasswordCallback("password: ", false);

  try {
    // Prompt for username and password
    callbackHandler.handle(callbacks);

    // Retrieve username
    username = ((NameCallback) callbacks[0]).getName();

    // Retrieve password, converting from char[] to String
```

Continued

Listing 22-4 (continued)

```
      char[] charPassword = ((PasswordCallback) callbacks[1]).getPassword();

      if (charPassword == null) {
        // Treat a NULL password as an empty password, not NULL
        charPassword = new char[0];
      }

      password = new String(charPassword);
    } catch (IOException ioe) {
      throw new LoginException(ioe.toString());
    } catch (UnsupportedCallbackException uce) {
      throw new LoginException("Error: Callback "
        + uce.getCallback().toString() + " Not Available");
    }

    // Populate weblogic environment and authenticate

    /* WebLogic Only */
    Environment env = new Environment();
    env.setProviderUrl(url);
    env.setSecurityPrincipal(username);
    env.setSecurityCredentials(password);
    try {
      // Authenticate user credentials, populating Subject

      /* WebLogic Specific */
      Authenticate.authenticate(env, subject);

      /* Non-WebLogic Function for Login */
      //authenticate(username, password);
    } catch(RemoteException re) {
      System.err.println("Error: Remote Exception on authenticate, " +
        re.getMessage());
      throw new LoginException(re.toString());
    } catch(IOException ioe) {
      System.err.println("Error: IO Exception on authenticate, " +
        ioe.getMessage());
      throw new LoginException(ioe.toString());
    } catch (LoginException le) {
      System.err.println("Error: Login Exception on authenticate, "
        + le.getMessage());
      throw new LoginException(le.toString());
    }

    // Successfully authenticated subject with supplied info
    succeeded = true;
    return succeeded;
  }
```

Listing 22-5 shows how to substitute the policy file; the `Configuration` object's `getAppConfigurationEntry()` function will be overridden to accept URLs instead of policy files.

Listing 22-5: Sample configuration class for JAAS user authentication

```
package com.hungryminds.wljaas;
/*
 * Class SampleAction
*/
import java.util.Hashtable;
import javax.security.auth.login.Configuration;
import javax.security.auth.login.AppConfigurationEntry;
import java.io.File;
import java.io.FileReader;
import java.io.IOException;
import java.io.InputStream;
import java.io.BufferedReader;
import java.io.FileInputStream;
import java.io.FileNotFoundException;

/**
 * Sample configuration class for JAAS user authentication.
 */

public class ConfigFile extends Configuration
{
  String configFileName = null;

  /**
   *
   * Create a new Configuration object.
   */
  public ConfigFile()
  {
  }

 /**
   * Retrieve an entry from the Configuration object
   * using an application name as an index.
   */
  public AppConfigurationEntry[] getAppConfigurationEntry(
    String applicationName)
  {
    AppConfigurationEntry[] list = new AppConfigurationEntry[1];
```

Continued

Listing 22-5 *(continued)*

```
AppConfigurationEntry entry = null;

/* Get the spcified configuration file */
configFileName = System.getProperty("weblogic.security.jaas.Policy");
try
{
  FileReader fr = new FileReader(configFileName);
  BufferedReader reader = new BufferedReader(fr);
  String line;

  line = reader.readLine();
  while(line != null)
  {
    // Skip lines until the line starting with a '{'
    if(line.length() == 0 || line.charAt(0) != '{')
    {
      line = reader.readLine();
      continue;
    }
    /* Read following line which contains the LoginModule configured */
    line = reader.readLine();

    int i;
    for(i = 0; i < line.length(); i++)
    {
      char c = line.charAt(i);
      if(c != ' ')
        break;
    }
    int sep = line.indexOf(' ', i);

    String LMName = line.substring(0, sep).trim();
    String LMFlag = line.substring(sep + 1,
      line.indexOf(' ', sep + 1));

    if(LMFlag.equalsIgnoreCase("OPTIONAL")) {
      entry = new AppConfigurationEntry(LMName,
        AppConfigurationEntry.LoginModuleControlFlag.OPTIONAL,
        new Hashtable());
      list[0] = entry;
    }
    else if(LMFlag.equalsIgnoreCase("REQUIRED"))
    {
      entry = new AppConfigurationEntry(LMName,
        AppConfigurationEntry.LoginModuleControlFlag.REQUIRED,
        new Hashtable());
      list[0] = entry;
    }
    else if(LMFlag.equalsIgnoreCase("REQUISITE"))
    {
```

```
          entry = new AppConfigurationEntry(LMName,
            AppConfigurationEntry.LoginModuleControlFlag.REQUISITE,
            new Hashtable());
          list[0] = entry;
        }
        else if(LMFlag.equalsIgnoreCase("SUFFICIENT"))
        {
          entry = new AppConfigurationEntry(LMName,
            AppConfigurationEntry.LoginModuleControlFlag.SUFFICIENT,
            new Hashtable());
          list[0] = entry;
        }
        else
        {
          throw new IllegalArgumentException("Invalid controlFlag");
        }
        line = reader.readLine();
      }
      reader.close();
    }
    catch(java.io.FileNotFoundException ioe)
    {
      System.out.println(ioe.toString());
    }
    catch(java.io.IOException ioe)
    {
      System.out.println(ioe.toString());
    }
    return list;
  }


  /**
   * Refresh and reload the Configuration object by reading
   * all of the login configurations again.
   */
  public void refresh()
  {
    // No Implementation
  }
}
```

These classes extend the login to log into WebLogic Server by using URLs instead of the getting this information through a JAAS policy file. Only rewriting the `Configuration` object can do this. For the user to login to WebLogic Server, a valid username and password must be entered into the `authenticate` function. In the sample code, this was hard coded as follows:

```
private final static String USERNAME        = "rich";
private final static String PASSWORD        = "richpass";
```

Figure 22-2 shows how users are added and their passwords are changed using the WebLogic Console.

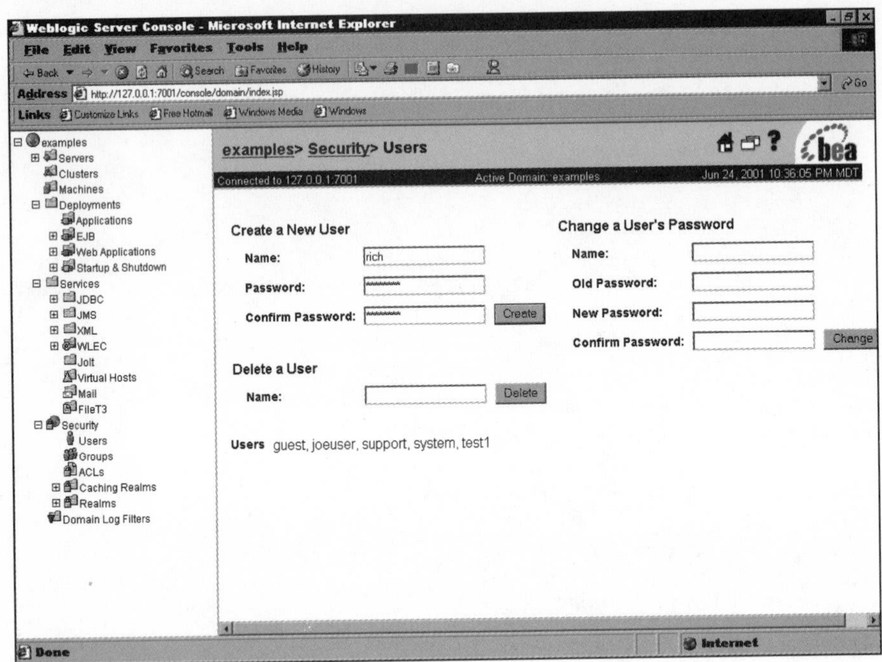

Figure 22-2: Installing a user

Listing 22-5 also illustrates how to test out the authentication and how a JAAS client can access WebLogic Server. The same process could be applied to a Java servlet or JSP page to authenticate a valid user. In many organizations, it is not usually up to the administrator to give access to a user for a first time login. Some systems require a new user to fill out a profile that can access the security realm classes, at a very basic level, to input a new user and password. Some systems require auditing new users for marketing or security reasons before they have too much access to a system. These new users can be defaulted to a new user group that, after a valid order, can be upgraded to a customer group. Listing 22-6 gives a quick example of an authentication process through a JAAS example.

Listing 22-6: SampleAction class

```
package com.hungryminds.wljaas;

import java.security.PrivilegedAction;
import javax.naming.Context;
import javax.naming.InitialContext;
import java.util.Hashtable;
```

```
import javax.naming.*;

public class SampleAction implements PrivilegedAction {

  public Object run() {

    Object  obj = null;
    Context ctx = null;
    String  url = null;

    try {
      // Retrieve WLS server URL string
      url = System.getProperty("weblogic.security.jaas.ServerURL");
    } catch (NullPointerException npe) {
      System.err.println("Error: ServerURL Not Specified");
      return null;
    } catch (IllegalArgumentException iae) {
      System.err.println("Error: ServerURL Not Specified");
      return null;
    } catch (SecurityException se) {
      System.err.println(
        "Error: Security Exception on accessing ServerURL Specification");
      return null;
    }

    // Populate environment
    Hashtable env = new Hashtable();
    env.put(Context.INITIAL_CONTEXT_FACTORY,
      "weblogic.jndi.WLInitialContextFactory");
    env.put(Context.PROVIDER_URL, url);

    try {
      // Create InitialContext
      ctx = new InitialContext(env);
      printBindingList("", ctx.listBindings(""));
      printNameList("", ctx.list(""));

      /**
       * Execute target EJB Frobable.frob() method. (This is left over from
       * the WLS example - it is intended to show that there is differences
       * and similarities to show that the same code slightly modified
       * works in both instances.)
       */
      System.out.println("JNDI Lists successfully");
    } catch (Throwable t) {
      t.printStackTrace();
      System.out.println("Failed to lists JNDI");
    } finally {
      try {
        // Close InitialContext
        ctx.close();
      } catch (Exception e) {
```

Continued

Listing 22-6 (continued)

```
        // Deal with any failures
      }
    }
    return obj;
  }

  void printNameList(String msg, NamingEnumeration nl) {
    System.out.println(msg);
    if (nl == null) {
      System.out.println("No items in name list");
    } else {
      try {
        while (nl.hasMore()) {
          System.out.println(nl.next());
        }
      } catch (NamingException e) {
        e.printStackTrace();
      }
    }
  }

  void printBindingList(String msg, NamingEnumeration bl) {
    System.out.println(msg);
    if (bl == null) {
      System.out.println("No items in binding list");
    } else {
      try {
        while (bl.hasMore()) {
          Binding b = (Binding) bl.next();
          System.out.println(b.getName() + "(" + b.getObject() + ")");
        }
      } catch (NamingException e) {
        e.printStackTrace();
      }
    }
  }
}
```

The following example will list the names and bindings in the JNDI services if the user has access. Because everyone has permissions by default to list and modify the JNDI entries, the lists will look like Figure 22-3.

Having the default permissions structured like this can create security risks. Every user can lookup, modify, and list the JNDI services. Some of these types of services should be restricted to the system user.

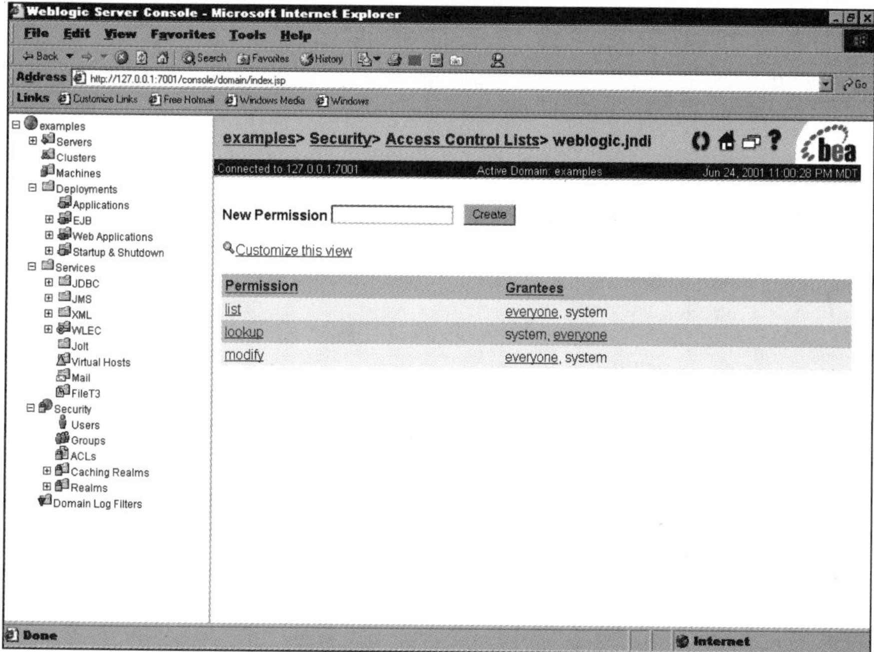

Figure 22-3: The JNDI permissions

Authorization and the Security Realm

Because WebLogic Server has its own type of security realms, it also uses its own ACL interface to communicate with it. This class is the `weblogic.security.acl.Security` and is only available in server-side code. This class may only be executed in WebLogic Server VM. This class requires access to the security realm that the client class cannot access.

You first need to know how to program the `weblogic.security.acl.Security` class. This class has many functions. The `Security.getRealm()` function is a static function that returns an instance of the `BasicRealm`. The `BasicRealm` offers a minimum interface to the security realms. This class has the capability to list all the instances managed by the realm and the capability to create and destroy instances. After the `BasicRealm` is accessed, users can be retrieved from the security realm by using the `getUser()` function, and permissions can be retrieved with `getPermission()`.

Let's start with the `Security.hasPermission()` and `Security.checkPermission()` methods, which are static functions defined in `weblogjc.security.acl.Security` class. These methods enable you to test whether a user has the correct permissions to access a resource. The two methods are similar except that the `Security.checkPermission()` throws a `java.lang.SecurityException` if the user does not have permission, whereas the `Security.checkPermission()` returns a `false` if the user does not have permission.

Building a Custom RDBMS Security Realm

WebLogic provides the capability to create a custom security realm. You can create a custom security realm in various ways; the example that I run through is the RDBMS example. The difference between a custom security realm and the relational database management system (RDBMS) example that ships with WebLogic Server 6.1 is that the RDBMS example uses a schema, which it retrieves from the Administration Console. This adds a lot of flexibility to the RDBMS realm example. The tables, however, should be static; and the code should use a referenced implementation for these static tables. The custom realm example that was produced was geared towards how Cloudscape (the RDBMS shipped with WLS 6.1) works. The biggest difference between the RDBMS realm example and the custom realm example is that the custom realm example also implements the create group, change password, create ACL, remove ACL, add ACL member, and remove ACL member functionality that the RDBMS realm example does not implement. The custom realm example was created for educational purposes and is not recommended for production.

Define the data store

For running code examples that allow you to run with a functional RDBMS, WebLogic Server 6.1 ships with an evaluation of the Cloudscape database. The Cloudscape database is a pure-Java relational database management system (RDBMS). In order to use Cloudscape with WebLogic Server, you must add the Cloudscape library `cloudscape.jar` to the `CLASSPATH` of WebLogic Server. The `cloudscape.system.home` Java system property will have to be set to the directory that contains the Cloudscape databases. Figure 22-4 shows the Cloudscape tables to support the custom RDBMS code.

users	
NAME	PASSWORD
alice	123456
janet	123456
john	123456

aclentries		
NAME	PRINCIPAL	PERMISSION
disk	user	read
disk	alice	write

groupmembers	
GROUP	MEMBER
user	alice
user	janet
user	john

Figure 22-4: The Cloudscape tables

You create a database that contains the tables that are part of the security realm using a DDL file. The DDL file defines the table structure and initial information to store in the database. To run the DDL script to initialize the database, a command to use the `rdbmsrealm.ddl` is as follows:

```
$ java utils.Schema jdbc:cloudscape:demo;create=true
COM.cloudscape.core.JDBCDriver -verbose rdbmsrealm.ddl
```

Define the custom classes

You're going to be working with four classes in your example (see Figure 22-5): `CustomRDBMSRealm`, `RDBMSUser`, `RDBMSGroup`, `RDBMSAcl` and `RDBMSStore`. The `CustomRDBMSRealm` is a class that works directly with WebLogic Server and, therefore, must implement the `AbstractManageableRealm` interface. The `RDBMSStore` class interfaces through a JDBC connection to the database. The `RDBMSUser` represents a row in the users database table. The `RDBMSAcl` class represents a row in the `ACLentries` table. The `RDBMSGroup` class represents a row in the `groupmembers` table. The `CustomRDBMSRealm` class controls the users, groups, permissions, and ACLs that can all be represented as enumerations. The `CustomRDBMSRealm` uses the `RDBMSStore` to populate the permissions, groups, users, and ACLs from the database.

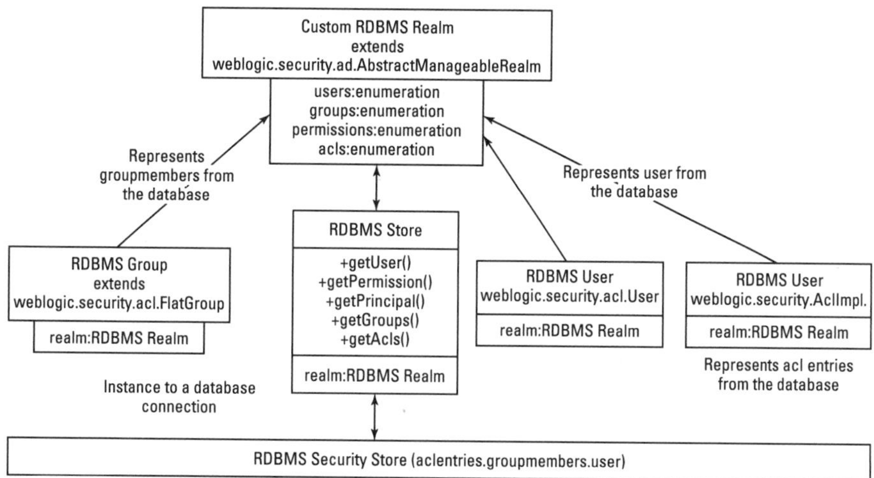

Figure 22-5: The CustomRDBMSRealm class

Define a class for users

The first class that interfaces to the `CustomRDBMSRealm` class is the `RDBMSUser` class. This class is extended from the `weblogic.security.acl.bUser` class that is used as an extension from WebLogic Server to include users in the security realms. The purpose of the `RDBMSUser` class is to create a user for the `RDBMSRealm`. The user class is mapped to the users table in the `rdbmsrealm` table. The users table has name and password fields; Listing 22-7 shows a code representation of the user information from the database.

Listing 22-7: User example

```
package com.hungryminds.customrealms;

import java.io.BufferedReader;
import java.io.IOException;
import java.io.InputStreamReader;

import java.security.MessageDigest;
import java.security.NoSuchAlgorithmException;

import weblogic.security.acl.BasicRealm;
import weblogic.security.acl.User;

import weblogic.utils.encoders.BASE64Encoder;

import weblogic.security.acl.DefaultUserImpl;
import weblogic.security.acl.CredentialChanger;
import weblogic.security.acl.DefaultUserInfoImpl;

/**
 * Class RDBMSUser
 * Description: The instance of a Custom User.
 *
 * Copyright:    Copyright (c) 2001
 * Company:      HungryMinds
 * @author Rich Helton <rhelton@richware.com>
 * @version 1.0  16-JUL-2001
 */
class RDBMSUser extends DefaultUserImpl implements CredentialChanger {

    /**
     * The default password generation algorithm.
     */
    public static final String HASH_ALGORITHM = "MD5";

    /**
     * The user's name that created this user object.
     */
    private transient String name;

    /**
     * The realm that created this user object.
     */
    private transient CustomRDBMSRealm realm;

    /**
```

```
     * The user's password. If the password is hashed, the md field will
     * contain an instance of an object that performs the hashing
     * algorithm.
     */
    private transient String passwd;

    /**
     * The digest algorithm used to one-way hash the user's password.
     * If the password is not hashed with a known algorithm, or is in
     * plain text, this will be null.
     */
    private transient MessageDigest md;

    /**
     * Constructor RDBMSUser
     *
     *
     * @param name is the name of the User.
     * @param passwd is the password of the User. Defaulted to MD5 hashing.
     * @param realm is the instance of the Custom Realm.
     *
     */
    RDBMSUser(String name, Object credential, CustomRDBMSRealm realm) {

        super(name, credential, realm);

        this.realm = realm;
        this.name  = name;

        /**
         *  Stores the password and the MD5 instance.
         */
        if (passwd != null) {
            this.passwd = passwd;

            try {
                md = MessageDigest.getInstance(HASH_ALGORITHM.toUpperCase());

                /**
                 * Catches
                 */
            } catch (NoSuchAlgorithmException nosuchalgorithmexception) {
                if (realm.isDebug) {
                    realm.debug(
                        "digest algorithm \"MD5\" not found - assuming plaintext
password");
                } else {
                    System.err.println(
                        "Error: digest algorithm \"MD5\" not found - assuming
plaintext password");
```

Continued

Listing 22-7 (continued)

```
                }
            }
        }
    }

    /**
     * Method getRealm
     * Description:  Returns the Custom Realm Instance.
     *
     *
     * @return the realm that created this object.
     */
    public BasicRealm getRealm() {
        return realm;
    }

    /**
     * Method changeCredential
     *
     *
     * @param obj
     * @param obj1
     *
     * @throws SecurityException
     *
     */
    public void changeCredential(Object obj, Object obj1)
            throws SecurityException {

        if (realm.isDebug) {
            realm.debug("RDBMSUser:changeCredential " + obj + " " + obj1);
        }

        if (authenticate((String) (obj))) {
            String hashed = hash(md, (String) obj1);

            setCredential(hashed);
        }
    }

    /**
     * Method hash
     * Description: Hashes the given plain text with the given digest algorithm,
and
     * base64-encode the result.
     *
     * @param md message digest algorithm to hash with
```

```
     * @param plaintext text to hash
     * @return base64-encoded hashed text
     */
    static public String hash(MessageDigest md, String plaintext) {

        BASE64Encoder enc = new BASE64Encoder();

        return enc.encodeBuffer(md.digest(plaintext.getBytes()));
    }

    /**
     * Method authenticate
     * Description: Checks a plain text password against the user's password. If
the
     * object containing the password is not known, authentication will
     * fail.
     *
     * @param plaintext the plaintext password to check
     * @return true if matched, false otherwise
     */
    public boolean authenticate(String plaintext) {

        String hashed = (md != null)
                        ? hash(md, plaintext)
                        : plaintext;

        if (realm.isDebug) {
            realm.debug("RDBMSUser:authticate: " + name + "  " + hashed
                        + " into principals..");

            if (hashed.equals(passwd)) {
                realm.debug("RDBMSUser:authticate:TRUE");
            } else {
                realm.debug("RDBMSUser:authticate:FALSE");
            }
        }

        return hashed.equals(passwd);
    }
}
```

The username in the class is simply a string. But storing the password in the database of a user is a security risk because anyone that has read access to the table could get the password. To solve this problem, the password should be stored in a ciphertext of some form. The easiest method is to use `java.security.MessageDigest` and hash the password in the form of the SHA algorithm.

Define a class for groups

The next class that interfaces to the CustomRDBMSRealm class is the RDBMSGroup class. It is used to map to the groupmembers table in the rdbmsrealm table. Groups are used in security systems because they make it easier to manage security. Permissions can be applied to a set of users, instead of an individual user, to ease the concern to subsets of users instead of managing every user individually. To implement the RDBMSGroup class, extend the weblogic.security.acl.FlatGroup class to create a group with no membership information. The RDBMSGroup class uses a Hash table to keep track of the members defined in the rdbmsrealm table. The members can be users or different groups. The constructor for this class takes the input: the name of the desired group to create, the realm that the groups are used in, and the member's table such as the following:

```
public class RDBMSGroup
  extends FlatGroup
{
  private RDBMSRealm realm;


  RDBMSGroup(String name, RDBMSRealm realm, Hashtable members)
  {
    super(name, realm, members);
    this.realm = realm;
  }


  RDBMSGroup(String name, RDBMSRealm realm)
  {
    super(name, realm);
    this.realm = realm;
  }
```

The weblogic.security.acl.FlatGroup is extended because it is designed to work with custom security realms. The FlatGroup maintains its group members in a cache instead of a never-changing set. The cache has a time to live, and when it expires, the group will query the CustomRDBMSRealm to obtain the most recent member information. The default time to live is five minutes. The weblogic.security.acl.AbstractListableRealm class implements this query. This caching mechanism keeps up-to-date member information when its backing store changes to keep the FlatGroup class and the rdbmsrealm table in synch.

The RDBMSGroup class has little other functionality besides adding and removing a member from the member table, as shown in Listing 22-8.

Listing 22-8: Adding and removing a member

```
public boolean addMember(Principal principal)
{
  if (!(principal instanceof RDBMSUser) && !(principal instanceof RDBMSGroup))
```

```
    {
      throw new SecurityException("attempt to add non-RDBMS principal");
    }

    if (this.equals(principal))
    {
      throw new SecurityException("adding group to self");
    }

    if (isMember(principal))
    {
      return false;
    }

    return realm.addGroupMember(this, principal) &&
addMemberInternal(principal);
  }


  public boolean removeMember(Principal principal)
  {
    if (!(principal instanceof RDBMSUser) && !(principal instanceof RDBMSGroup))
    {
      throw new SecurityException("attempt to remove non-RDBMS principal");
    }

    if (this.equals(principal))
    {
      throw new SecurityException("removing group from self");
    }

    if (isMember(principal))
    {
      return false;
    }

    return realm.removeGroupMember(this, principal) &&
      removeMemberInternal(principal);
  }
```

Define the enumeration classes for the result sets

So far the discussion has revolved around getting individual users and groups. To store the entire set of the results, however, you need a data structure for the store and the ability to access individual elements. Implementing the `weblogic.security.acl.ClosableEnumeration` class provides this functionality. The `ClosableEnumeration` class is just an implementation of the enumeration interface with a close function to release the resources. By using this data structure, you don't need to create a user or group object for every user and group in the security realm. The use of the enumeration class follows the database cursor algorithm. The database cursor algorithm provides the capability to divide the work of the result set into sections instead of pulling over all users and groups at once. The idea is to get a section of users and groups, and then query again to get the next set, and continue in this fashion until the class is finished with the set or there is no more to receive. The database cursor algorithm avoids the possibility of pulling all the data into a result set at once, which could be more than can fit into memory. The database cursor is an incremental algorithm that uses the incremental attributes of the enumeration data structure. Listing 22-9 shows an example of custom enumeration code.

Listing 22-9: Custom enumeration example

```
/**
 * The base class for enumerating over a ResultSet.
 * It is passed as a handler which figures out what to do with
 * the current item in the result set.
 */
private class RDBMSEnumeration implements ClosableEnumeration
{
  boolean           closed = false;
  ResultSet         resultSet;
  RDBMSNextHandler  handler;

  RDBMSEnumeration(ResultSet resultSet, RDBMSNextHandler handler)
  {
    this.resultSet = resultSet;
    this.handler   = handler;
    increment();
  }

  private void increment()
  {
    try {
      if (!resultSet.next()) {
        close();
      }
    } catch (SQLException e) {
      // When getting groups & acls, someone else is incrementing without
      // notifying us. Therefore, when we go to the next, an exception is
      // thrown since we're already at the end of the list. So, if we
      // get an exception here, just assume it's because we're trying to
      // go past the end of the list, and flag this enumerator as "done".
      close();
    }
  }

  public boolean hasMoreElements()
  {
    return (closed) ? false : true;
```

```
    }

    public Object nextElement()
    {
      if (closed) {
        throw new NoSuchElementException("RDBMEnumeration.nextElement");
      }
      try {
        Object results = handler.handle(resultSet);
        increment();
        return results;
      } catch (SQLException e) {
        throw new RDBMSException("RDBMSEnumeration.nextElement failed", e);
      }
    }

    public void close()
    {
      if (closed) {
        return;
      }
      try {
        closed = true;
        resultSet.close();
      } catch (SQLException e) {
        throw new RDBMSException("RDBMSEnumeration.close failed", e);
      }
    }
  }
```

Authenticate users

To this point, classes and functions have been created to develop a custom security realm. But the function of the security realm is to authenticate and authorize users and groups within the system. To do that, functions need to be created for the system to accomplish the authentication. To do so, the `CustomRDBMSRealm` class must explicitly implement the `authUserPassword()` to authenticate the users. The `authUserPassword()` calls the `RDBMSUser` class, which currently contains the password for that user. When the password in the `RDBMSUser` object is compared with the password of the user logging in and they match, the `RDBMSUser` object is returned to the security realm as a valid user, allowing access to the system. The code for the `authUserPassword` appears as follows:

```
/**
   * Authenticates the given user. If authentication is successful,
   * a User object is returned for that user. Otherwise, null is
   * returned.
   *
```

```
 * @return the authenticated user, or null
 * @exception RDBMSException an error occurred in communicating with
 * the database
 */
protected User authUserPassword(String name, String passwd)
{
  RDBMSUser user = (RDBMSUser) getUser(name);

  if (user != null && user.authenticate(passwd) == false)
  {
    user = null;
  }

  return user;
}
```

If the user does not exist or the password is incorrect, a null object is returned to from the CustomRDBMSRealm object to the system to tell it that there is no valid user within WebLogic Server.

Determining if the user belongs to a group

After the user logs into a system, the system must reconcile to which group the user belongs; all access permissions are associated with groups. The user may belong to the development group and require write permissions to all of the EJBs. WebLogic Server will use the getGroupMembersInternal() function from the CustomRDBMSRealm class to return the populated members of the group so that a lookup can be accomplished on those members later. This method is called if the membership cache of a FlatGroup object expires. The function looks as follows:

```
protected Hashtable getGroupMembersInternal(String name)
  {x
    // It's easiest to just call getGroup and use RDBMSGroup's
    // getMembers method to return the membership of this group.

    RDBMSGroup grp = (RDBMSGroup) getGroup(name);

    if (grp == null)
    {
      return null;
    } else {
      return grp.getMembers();
    }
  }
```

Get users and groups from security store

The purpose of the preceding section was to create a Hash Table to populate the members of the group to the CustomRDBMSGroup class. The next step, shown in

Listing 22-10, is to allow access to WebLogic Server to enable access to the user and the group using the `getUser()` and `getGroup()` methods. This method also extends the `weblogic.security.acl.AbstractListableRealm` class to retrieve information from the security store into the custom security realm. Extending these functions in the `CustomRDBMSRealm` class that uses the abstract class of `weblogic.security.acl.AbstractListableRealm` allows this system to interact with the security realm. This interaction now allows the users and groups to be viewed through the Administration Console.

Listing 22-10: Returning the group

```
/**
 * Returns the group with the given name. Returns null if the group does
 * not exist in the database.
 *
 * @param name the name to obtain
 * @return the group, or null if none
 * @exception RealmException an error occurred in communicating with
 * the database
 */
public Group getGroup(String name)
{
  RDBMSStore connection = getConnection();

  try
  {
    return connection.getGroup(name);
  }
  catch (SQLException e)
  {
    connection.close();
    connection = null;

    throw new RealmException("caught SQL exception", e);
  }
  finally
  {
    returnConnection(connection);
  }
}

/**
 * Returns the user with the given name. Returns null if the user does not
 * exist in the database.
 *
 * @param name the name to obtain
 * @return the user, or null if none
 * @exception RealmException an error occurred in communicating with
```

Continued

Listing 22-10 (continued)

```
 * the database
 */
public User getUser(String name)
{
  // Most of the other methods in this class are patterned after
  // this one. The connection does all of the actual work. These
  // methods simply obtain a connection from the pool, call through to
  // it, and handle any errors that arise.

  // Obtains a connection to talk to.
  RDBMSStore connection = getConnection();

  try
  {
    return connection.getUser(name);
  }
  catch (SQLException e)
  {
    // If the connection throws an exception, the connection to the
    // database may be in an unsafe state. Make sure we don't use
    // this connection again.

    connection.close();
    connection = null;

    throw new RealmException("caught SQL exception", e);
  }
  finally
  {
    // This will do nothing if the reference to the connection has
    // been set to null because of an error, so the connection will
    // not be returned to the pool.

    returnConnection(connection);
  }
}
```

Defining the custom realm in WebLogic Server is associating the class `CustomRDMSRealm` in the Administration Console. The class must be defined in WebLogic Server's `CLASSPATH`, as shown in Figure 22-6.

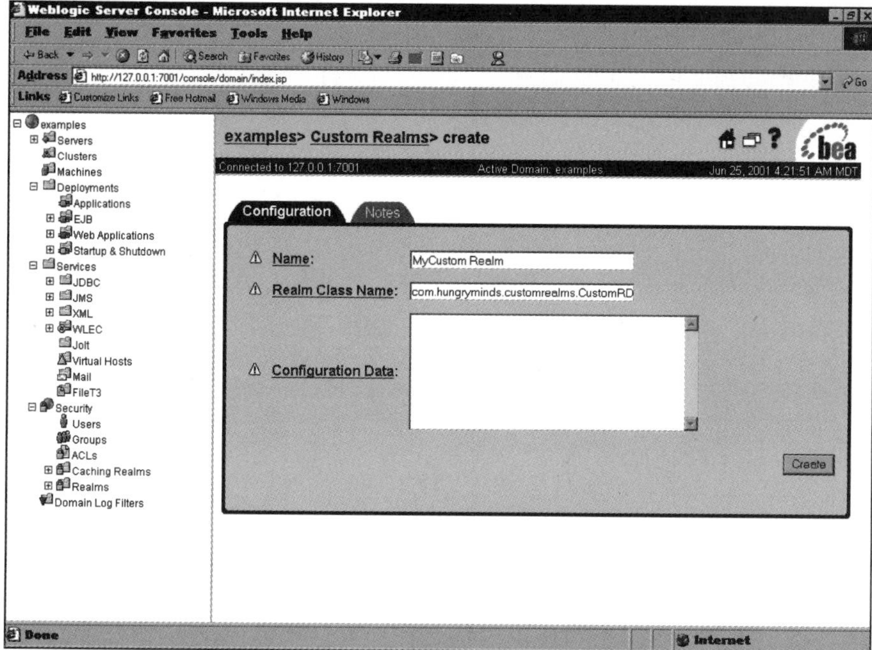

Figure 22-6: Configuring the custom realm

Auditing in WebLogic Server

WebLogic Server provides a Service Provider Interface for auditing security events by using the `weblogic.security.audit.Audit` and `weblogic.security.audit.AuditProvider` class. The `AuditProvider` is the class that actually implements the location to where and how the audit logs are stored in WebLogic Server. The `Audit` class is the entry point for the security subsystems that will perform the auditing operations (see Figure 22-7). The Audit function controls the audit destination to the correct `AuditProvider`, as long as the `AuditProvider` is defined in WebLogic Server through the Administrator's Console. The `Audit` class is a static class that can be called directly from a security service to log the event. The `AuditProvider` is a logging mechanism and should operate as other logging systems. This means that no value normally returns, no exceptions are thrown, null elements are used for objects, and a string should be passed in to point towards an issue that is easy to understand and find in WebLogic Server. Some of the logging mechanisms include logging the results of checking the permissions of a user and the results of authenticating a user.

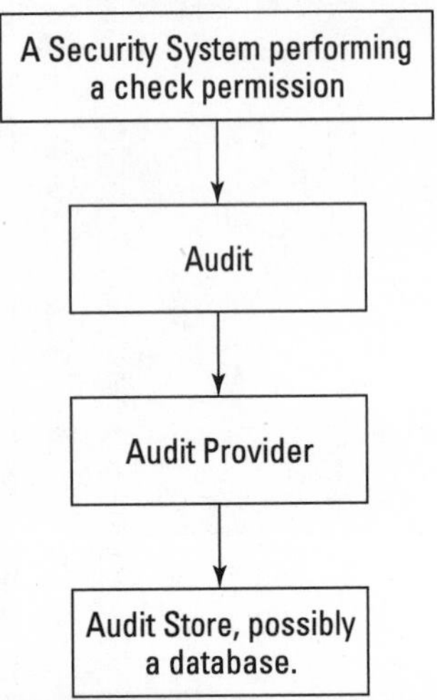

Figure 22-7: The layers of the AuditProvider

After building the `AuditProvider`, it must be defined in WebLogic Server through the Administration Console through the Security Configuration.

To write an `AuditProvider` is a simple task of implementing the `AuditProvider` functions of `authenticateUser`, `certificateInvalid`, `checkPermission`, and `rootCAInvalid` with the underlying layers to save it to a file or RDBMS. An example of the `LogAuditProvider` code can be found in the examples shipped with WebLogic Server.

An example of a `AuditProvider` function is the following:

```
User p = Security.getCurrentUser();
BasicRealm realm = Realm.getBasicRealm();
Acl acl = realm.getAcl(ACL_NAME);
Permission perm = realm.getPermission(PERMISSION_NAME);
boolean result = acl == null || !acl.checkPermission(p, perm);

Audit.checkPermission("Rich", acl, p, perm, !result);
```

Summary

In this chapter, we have seen how WLS uses a generic implementation of JAAS and how to build a custom implementation of a RDBMS realm. WebLogic Server has standard security development for JAAS support, except for extensions into the security realm. These extensions just provide a basis for developing security systems. By starting to develop in these extensions, you can save a lot of work and extend more security to your applications.

✦ ✦ ✦

WebLogic Server Administration

P A R T

VII

✦ ✦ ✦ ✦

In This Part

✦ ✦ ✦ ✦

Working with WebLogic's Administration Tools

✦ ✦ ✦ ✦

In This Chapter

Understanding the WebLogic Server Console

Administering domain information, servers, clusters, and machines from the console

Administering deployments, services, security, and domain log filters from the console

Administering WebLogic Server using command-line tools

✦ ✦ ✦ ✦

WebLogic Server provides two separate methods for accessing the WebLogic Server administration tools and configuration settings. The primary administration tool available to WebLogic developers and administrators is the WebLogic Console. The console, which is a Web application implemented by using JSPs, was introduced with WebLogic 6.0 and has been improved with the release of WebLogic 6.1. The console provides an easy-to-use interface that replaces the old, error-prone method of directly editing XML or properties files.

The majority of this chapter explores the console and the different WebLogic services that can be administered and monitored with it. The console section is broken down into the different major headings of the console and the subsections of those headings. These subheadings are then explained and their use is demonstrated.

The second method of accessing the WebLogic Server administration tools is from the command line. WebLogic offers extensive command-line support for most major functionality. But because the server console is the main tool for administering a WebLogic environment, it's covered in greater detail.

Note

Many aspects of WebLogic Server administration and the WebLogic Console have already been covered in other chapters (such as JDBC in Chapter 5 and JMS in Chapter 9). Therefore, if the console settings for a particular section are covered in a previous chapter, I will give a short description and a reference to that chapter, rather than duplicating the material here.

Administering WebLogic Server Using the WebLogic Console

When you open the WebLogic Console, a screen similar to the one shown in Figure 23-1 appears. The left side of the screen is a view of the current WebLogic Server domain, organized in a tree structure. This is called, appropriately enough, the *domain tree*. The right side of the screen is where configuration information appears for the item you have selected in the domain tree. Initially, no item is selected on the left, so the right side contains links to common functions, organized by topic.

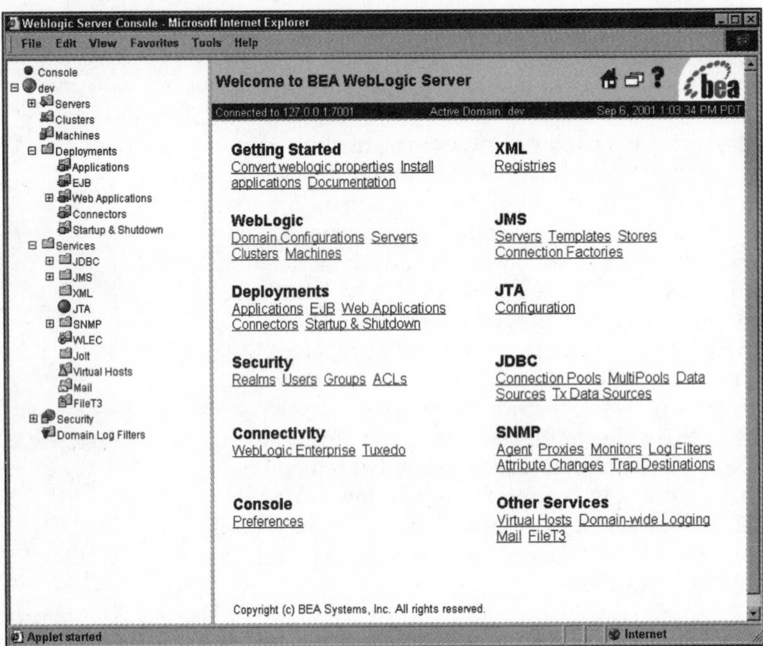

Figure 23-1: WebLogic Console opening screen

The following sections discuss the items in the domain tree in the order in which they appear.

Console

The Console node is for configuring the appearance of the console itself, as well as for viewing version information about the console and WebLogic Server. Figure 23-2 shows the Preferences tab of the Console Preferences page. Notice the red question mark icons next to the entry fields. Clicking one of these icons brings up a context-sensitive, online help screen for that topic.

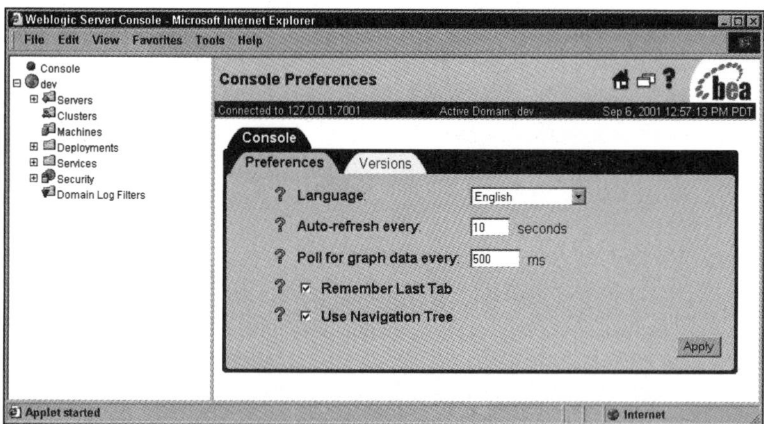

Figure 23-2: The Preferences page of Console Preferences

The entries on this page are as follows (click the question marks for more information):

- **Language:** The language in which you want the console and its help system displayed. The choices are English and Japanese, with the default being English.
- **Auto-refresh every:** The console screens automatically refresh themselves at the interval, in seconds, given by this number. The default is 10 seconds.
- **Poll for graph data every:** The console includes graphical monitoring screens, discussed later in this chapter, that give real-time displays of server traffic and memory usage. This setting determines the interval, in milliseconds, at which the graphs poll the server for data. The default is 500 milliseconds (½ second).
- **Remember Last Tab:** Many console pages, including this one, contain multiple configuration tabs. If this option is checked, the console remembers which tab you last visited for each node in the domain tree, and returns you to that tab the next time you go to that node. If unchecked, you will always be sent to the first (leftmost) tab. The default is checked.
- **Use Navigation Tree:** If checked, the console displays the navigation (domain) tree on the left side. If unchecked, the navigation tree disappears, and you must navigate using the menu on the opening screen (see Figure 23-1). I find it much easier to navigate by using the tree, which is the default.

Figure 23-3 shows the Versions tab of the Console Preferences page, which shows version information for the console and the underlying WebLogic Server.

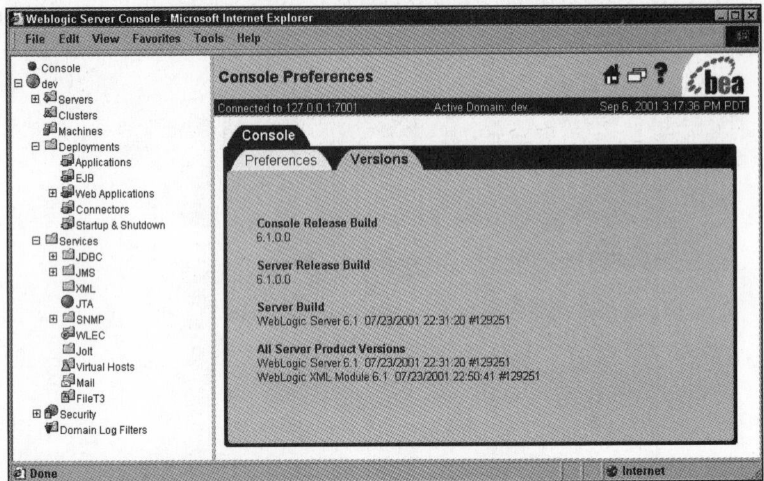

Figure 23-3: The Versions page of Console Preferences

Domain information

The node below Console is the node for the WebLogic domain you are administering. My domain is called `dev`. This node contains subnodes for administering all aspects of the domain.

See Chapter 4 for information on how to set up and configure WebLogic domains.

Clicking the name of the domain itself brings up several pages for adjusting domain-wide preferences. These pages are organized under three tabs: Configuration, Security, and Notes.

Configuration

The Configuration tab contains general domain settings, as well as settings for JTA, SNMP, Logging, and Applications.

General

Figure 23-4 shows the General page. You should never have to change the settings on this page. Notice, however, the yellow, triangular caution icons that appear next to the entry fields. These icons indicate that changes to those attributes require a restart of the affected WebLogic Server.

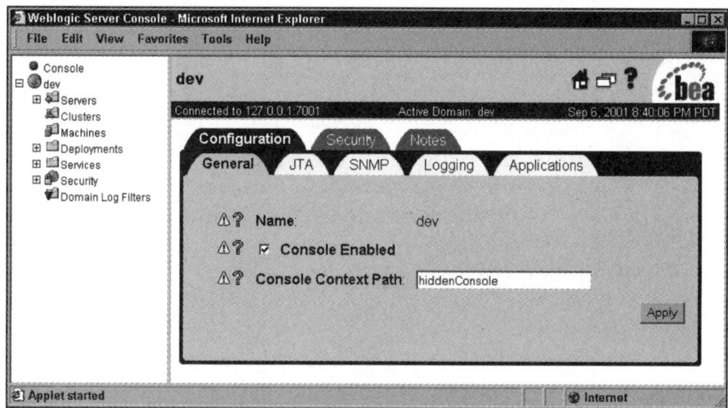

Figure 23-4: General configuration page for the domain

The entries on this page are as follows:

✦ **Name:** The name of the domain. This attribute cannot be changed. Nevertheless, a caution icon appears next to it, presumably in case you figure out how to hack it.

✦ **Console Enabled:** If checked, the domain can be managed with the WebLogic Console. Otherwise, you must manage the domain by using command-line tools. This is a primarily a security feature.

✦ **Console Context Path:** This allows you to change the servlet context for the console application itself. The default is `console`, which means that when you invoke the console in a Web browser, you enter `http://127.0.0.1:7001/console`. If you change this value, say, to `hiddenconsole`, the required URL becomes `http://127.0.0.1:7001/hiddenconsole`. The value you enter is case-sensitive.

This feature doesn't appear to work with WebLogic 6.1. In my testing, no matter what value I entered, the URL to bring up the console remained `http://127.0.0.1:7001/console`.

JTA

This tab, shown in Figure 23-5, contains configuration settings for the Java Transaction API (JTA), which is the J2EE component that manages user transactions.

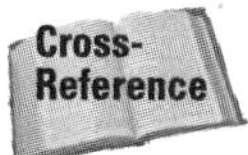

For more information about JTA, see Chapter 6.

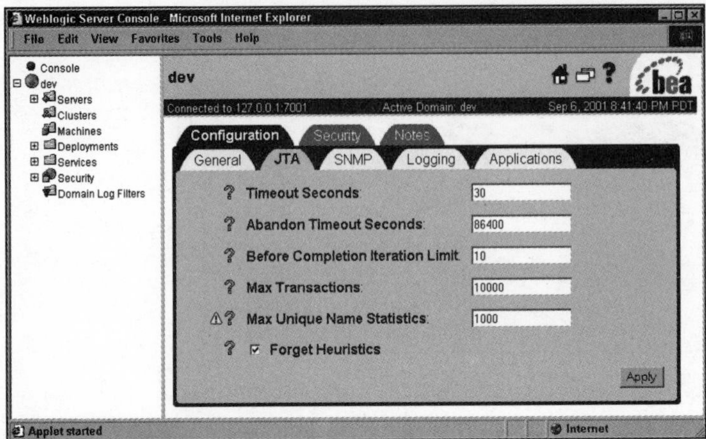

Figure 23-5: JTA configuration page

The entries on this page are as follows:

✦ **Timeout Seconds:** The number of seconds that must elapse before a transaction is rolled back automatically by WebLogic. The default is 30 seconds. When testing your applications, you will need to adjust this value to be greater than your longest-running transaction, or that transaction will never commit.

✦ **Abandon Timeout Seconds:** This is the maximum amount of time a transaction coordinator will attempt to complete a transaction before abandoning it. The default is 86,400 seconds, or 24 hours. Whereas `Timeout Seconds` controls how long WebLogic waits *each time* it tries to commit a transaction, `Abandon Timeout Seconds` controls how long WebLogic will keep trying, even in the face of timeouts, before it completely gives up.

✦ **Before Completion Iteration Limit:** The number of `beforeCompletion()` callbacks (implemented by EJB developers using the `javax.ejb.SessionSynchronization` interface) that WebLogic will process before forcing the rollback of a transaction. This setting prevents the server from getting bogged down with too many `beforeCompletion()` calls.

✦ **Max Transactions:** The maximum number of transactions that may be active on a server at one time. The default is 10,000. The setting you choose will depend on a number of factors, including the traffic on your site, the availability of licenses for databases and drivers, and performance.

✦ **Max Unique Name Statistics:** Programmers have the option of giving their transactions unique names. This setting determines how many such names the server will track when collecting performance statistics.

✦ **Forget Heuristics:** This tells the transaction manager not to track heuristic completions of transactions for monitoring purposes. Heuristic completions are those that occur outside the control of the transaction manager.

SNMP

Figure 23-6 shows the SNMP page, which contains configuration settings for WebLogic's Simple Network Management Protocol (SNMP) agent. The agent runs on the administration server for the domain and reports information for every server and/or cluster in the domain to a third-party SNMP management tool, which you must purchase separately.

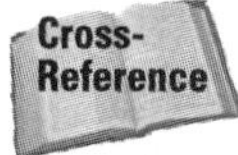

See Chapter 4 for more information on WebLogic administration servers.

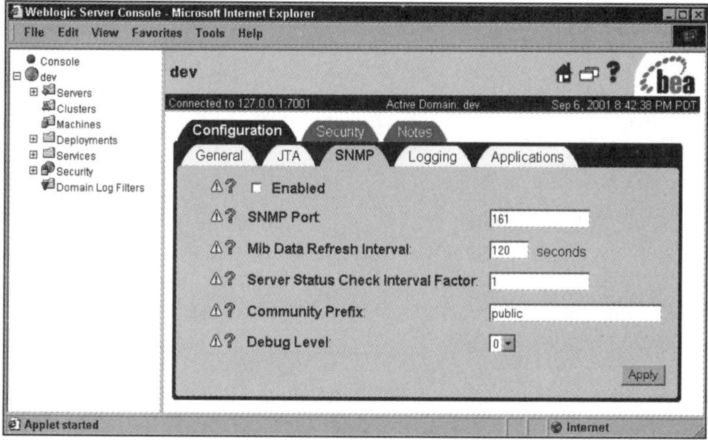

Figure 23-6: SNMP agent configuration page

The entries on this page are as follows:

- **Enabled:** If checked, the SNMP agent is enabled and will transmit data to the BEA management information base (MIB), which is the database that contains information about the WebLogic Server's state.
- **SNMP Port:** The network port on which the WebLogic SNMP agent listens for requests from SNMP managers. The default is 161.
- **Mib Data Refresh Interval:** The amount of time that elapses, in seconds, between updates to the MIB. The data in the MIB is what gets transferred to the SNMP agent when it makes a request. The default is 120.
- **Server Status Check Interval Factor:** The SNMP agent multiplies this number by the Mib Data Refresh Interval to determine how often to check whether managed servers in the domain are up or down. If this value is set to 2, for example, and the Mib Data Refresh Interval is 120, the SNMP agent polls the managed servers every 240 seconds. The default is 1.

✦ **Community Prefix:** This is a string that's used to determine what level of information is sent back to the SNMP manager. The default value is `public`, which means that the agent retrieves data only for the WebLogic administration server running in the `public` community. You can change this to any community name and the effect will be the same. If this value is of the form `community_prefix@server_name`, WebLogic returns data for that managed server only; if it is of the form `community_prefix@domain_name`, WebLogic returns data for the entire domain.

✦ **Debug Level:** An integer between 0 and 3 that determines how verbose the SNMP debugging messages will be. A value of 0 means no debugging messages are written, while a value of 3 means the messages will be most verbose. The default is 0.

Logging

Figure 23-7 shows the configuration page for the domain log file.

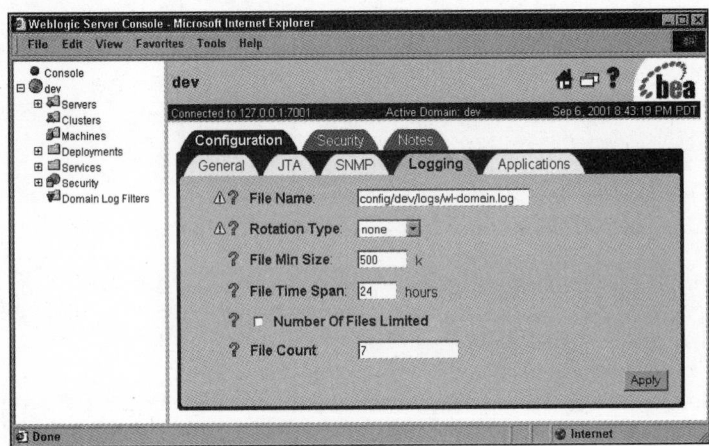

Figure 23-7: Logging configuration page

The entries on this page are as follows:

✦ **File Name:** The full pathname of the file to which WebLogic Server writes domain log messages. The default is `config/<domain-name>/logs/wl-domain.log`.

✦ **Rotation Type:** Determines how additional log files are created over time. The default is `none`, which means all messages are written to the same login perpetuity. The other options are `by Size`, which means a new log file is created once the current log file reaches a given size, and `by Time`, which means a new log file is created every time a certain number of hours passes.

✦ **File Min Size:** If Rotation Type is set to `by Size`, then this is the file size (in kilobytes) that must be exceeded by the current log file in order for the next log file to be created. The default is 500k.

✦ **File Time Span:** If Rotation Type is set to `by Time`, then this is the number of hours that will elapse between the creation of each additional log file. The default is 24 hours.

✦ **Number of Files Limited:** If this is checked, then the total number of log files created is limited to the number given by File Count; otherwise, there is no limit. Once the limit is reached, logging to files stops. Default is not checked.

✦ **File Count:** If Number of Files Limited is checked, this gives the total number of files that will be created before logging to files stops. The default is 7.

Applications

Figure 23-8 shows the Applications configuration page.

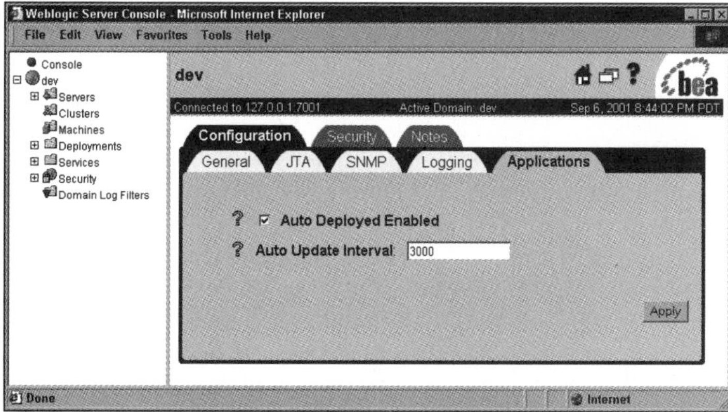

Figure 23-8: Applications configuration page

The entries on this page are as follows:

✦ **Auto Deployed Enabled:** When this is checked (the default), applications can be automatically deployed, without restarting WebLogic.

✦ **Auto Update Interval:** WebLogic Server checks for newly deployed applications at this interval, expressed in milliseconds. The default is 3,000 (3 seconds).

Security

The security pages are where you manage auditing, file realms, passwords, and other related parameters for WebLogic Server.

General

Figure 23-9 shows the General configuration page for WebLogic security.

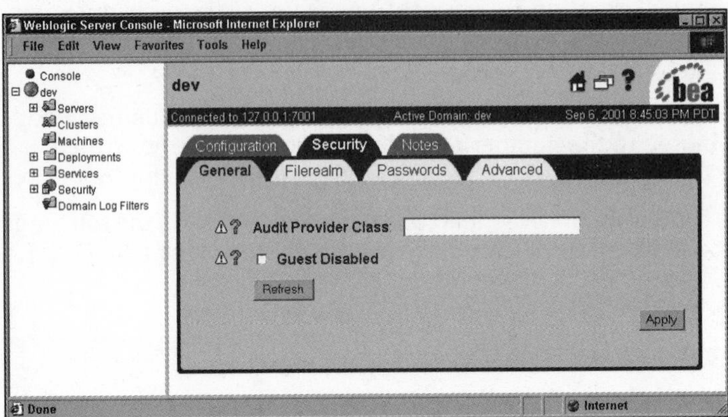

Figure 23-9: Configuring general security parameters

The entries on this page are as follows:

✦ **Audit Provider Class:** The fully qualified name of the Java class you have written to provide auditing services for the domain, such as writing login attempts to a log file, and so on.

You can find more information about this feature in Chapter 22.

✦ **Guest Disabled:** Checking this box disables the domain's built-in `guest` account, for increased security.

Filerealm

Figure 23-10 shows the Filerealm configuration page.

The entries on this page are as follows:

✦ **Caching Realm:** The fully qualified name of the Java class that is providing auditing services for the domain, such as writing all login attempts to a log file, and so on.

✦ **Max Users:** The maximum number of users supported by the realm, which must be an integer between 1 and 10,000. The default is 1000. Exceeding the maximum has no effect except to generate a warning.

✦ **Max Groups:** The maximum number of groups supported by the realm, which must be an integer between 1 and 10,000. The default is 1000. Exceeding the maximum has no effect except to generate a warning.

✦ **Max ACLs:** The maximum number of access control lists supported by the realm, which must be an integer between 1 and 10,000. The default is 1000. Exceeding the maximum has no effect except to generate a warning.

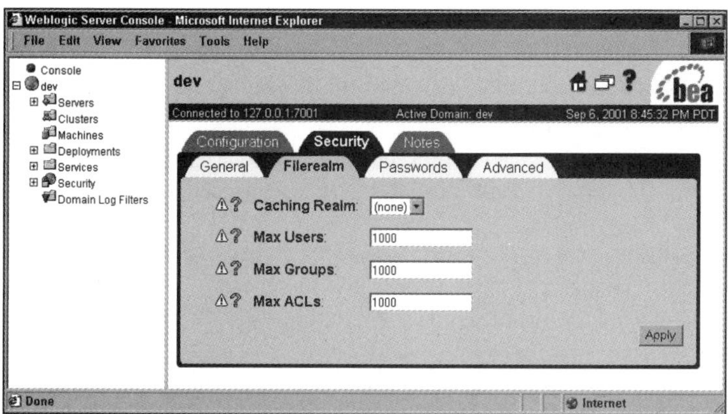

Figure 23-10: Configuring the Filerealm tab

Passwords

Figure 23-11 shows the Passwords configuration page.

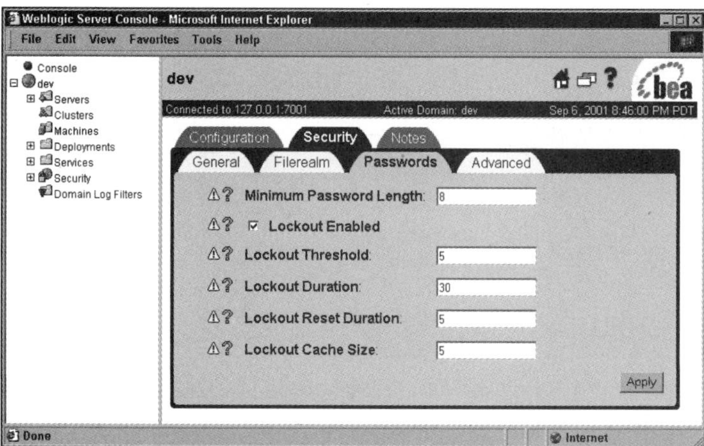

Figure 23-11: Configuring the Password tab

The entries on this page are as follows:

✦ **Minimum Password Length:** The minimum number of characters user passwords must contain. It must be an integer greater than or equal to 8, and the default is 8.

✦ **Lockout Enabled:** When checked, user accounts will be automatically disabled (the user will be locked out) after a certain number of failed login attempts. This is checked by default.

✦ **Lockout Threshold:** The number of failed login attempts that causes a user to be locked out. The default is 5.

✦ **Lockout Duration:** The length of time, in minutes, a user will be locked out after exceeding the lockout threshold. The default is 30. During this time, all login attempts (even with a correct username and password) will generate security exceptions, unless the system administrator explicitly unlocks the account.

✦ **Lockout Reset Duration:** The length of time, in minutes, within which failed login attempts count against the lockout threshold. The default is 5. Therefore, if five failed login attempts occur within five minutes, the account is locked.

✦ **Lockout Cache Size:** The total number of failed login attempts WebLogic Server will track across all user accounts. The default is 5.

Advanced

Figure 23-12 shows the Advanced security configuration page.

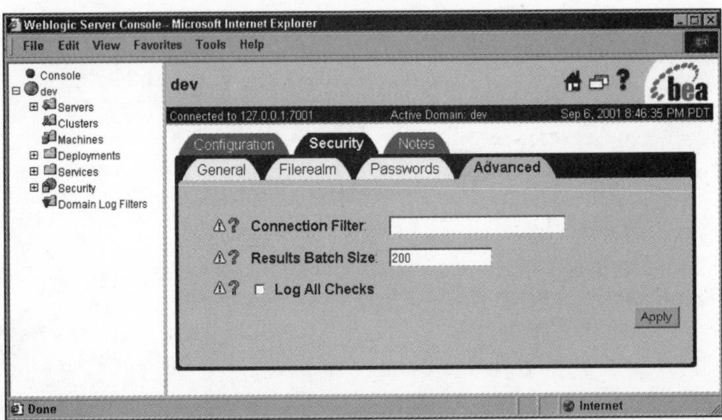

Figure 23-12: Configuring advanced security settings

The entries on this page are as follows:

✦ **Connection Filter:** According to the WebLogic documentation, "This attribute allows you to select the connection filter for your security realm." The documentation also says that you choose this item from a list, but the console displays an editable text area, not a list. I haven't received any clarification on this from BEA, so there you have it.

✦ **Results Batch Size and Log All Checks:** The meanings of these top-secret settings are known only to the engineers at BEA, as they are completely undocumented.

Notes

The Notes page allows you to enter administrative notes about the domain configuration. The field accepts free-form text, up to 32,000 characters. Every Notes page in the console works the same way, so I won't describe any of the others in the rest of this chapter.

Servers

Clicking the Servers node brings up a page that allows you to add new WebLogic servers to your domain, or to edit the settings of existing servers. You can also monitor the state of existing servers via the simple display that shows whether they are running or not. Figure 23-13 shows the Servers page.

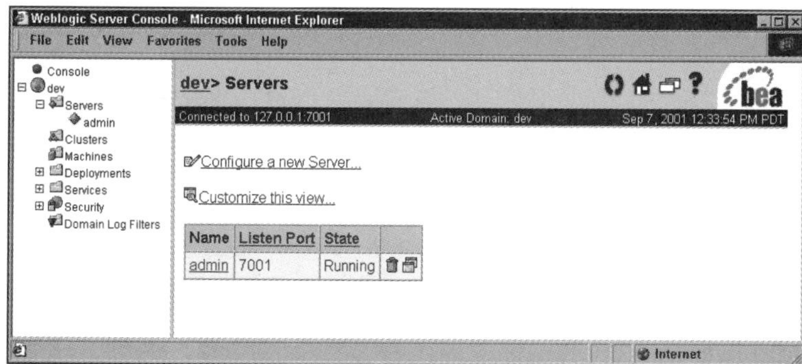

Figure 23-13: The Servers page

My domain contains only one server, admin, which you can see listed below the Servers node on the left, and also in the list of servers on the right. Clicking the name admin in either location brings up the server configuration page, shown in Figure 23-14. This page contains several tabs and subtabs for configuring all aspects of the server, which I'll now explain.

Configuration

The Configuration tab is where you manage the runtime aspects of your WebLogic Server, including its network identity, clustering behavior, HTTP support, and so on.

General

Figure 23-14 shows the General configuration page for a server.

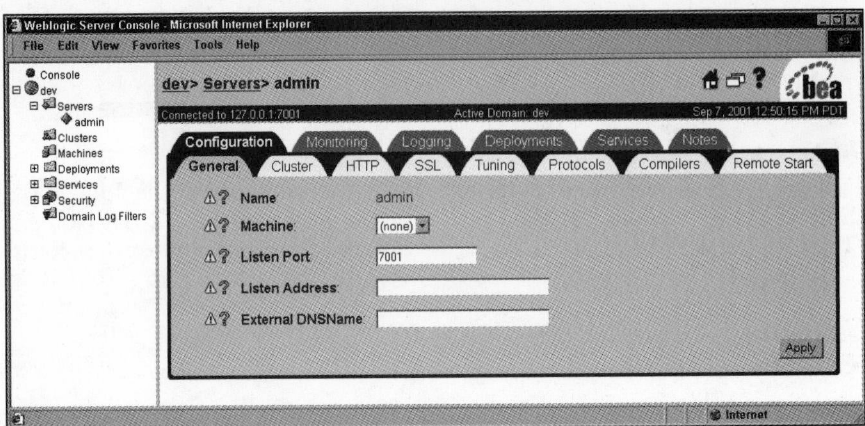

Figure 23-14: The General configuration page for a server

The entries on this page are as follows:

- ✦ **Name:** The name of the server, which must be unique within the WebLogic domain, and which cannot contain spaces or commas. This name is set when you create a new server and cannot be changed after the server is defined.
- ✦ **Machine:** The name of the machine on which the server runs. This attribute is not required to have a value, and the default is `none`. Machine names and the requirements for their usage are covered later in this chapter.
- ✦ **Listen Port:** The network port on which the server runs. This must be unique for each listen address; no two WebLogic servers running on the same listen address can listen on the same port. The default is 7001, but you can change it to any valid port that is not in use by other software on the machine.
- ✦ **Listen Address:** The IP address on which the server is listening for requests. You are not required to enter a value for this attribute, but if the computer running your WebLogic servers contains multiple network interface cards (each with a separate IP), you may want to map different servers to different cards. Addresses are entered in standard IP format (such as 192.168.0.10). The default is blank (no address).
- ✦ **External DNSName:** If the WebLogic Server sits behind a firewall that performs network address translation, enter the DNS name defined for the server on the public side of the firewall.

Cluster

Figure 23-15 shows the Cluster configuration page for a server.

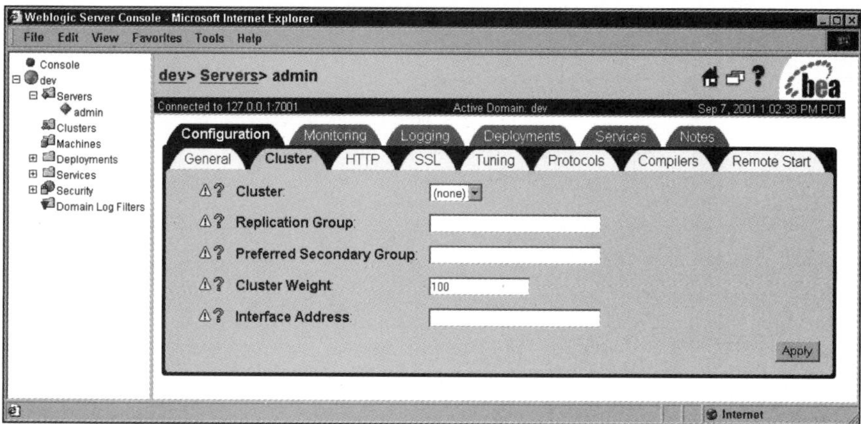

Figure 23-15: The Cluster configuration page for a server

The entries on this page are as follows:

- **Cluster:** The name of the cluster, if any, to which this server belongs. The default is `none`.
- **Replication Group:** The replication group within the cluster to which this server belongs.
- **Preferred Secondary Group:** The preferred replication group to be used as a backup if the primary replication group fails.
- **Cluster Weight:** The percentage of work to be performed by this server within the cluster. The default is 100. If all servers have equal cluster weights, the workload is split evenly among them.
- **Interface Address:** This server's physical IP address.

HTTP

Figure 23-16 shows the HTTP configuration page for a server.

The entries on this page are as follows:

- **Default Web Application:** The name of the Web application that serves as the default application for the server. This application must already be deployed to the server. Its home page will be displayed when the user accesses the server with the default URL (`http://localhost:<weblogic-port>`). `DefaultWebApp`, an application provided by BEA, displays the Web Server Index Page shown in Figure 23-17.

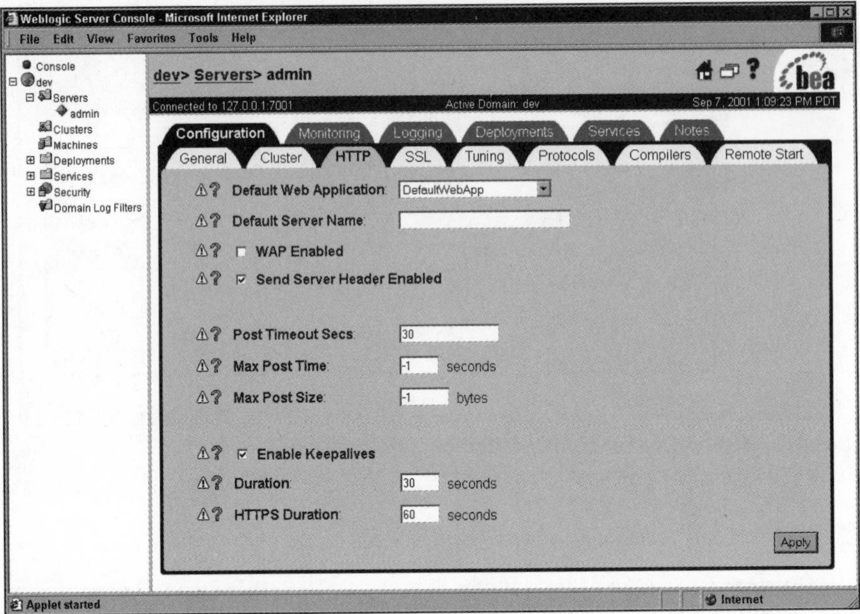

Figure 23-16: The HTTP configuration page for a server

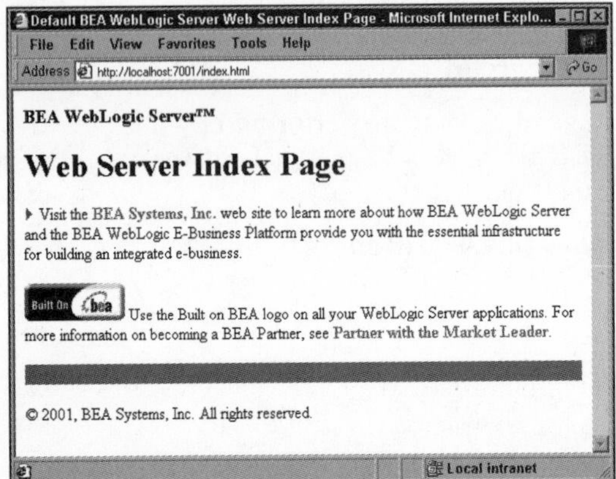

Figure 23-17: The home page for DefaultWebApp

✦ **Default Server Name:** The name entered in this field, if any, will be returned as the host name in the HTTP response header.

✦ **WAP Enabled:** When checked, WebLogic uses truncated session IDs (omitting its JVM information) to accommodate WAP devices that may limit URL lengths to 128 characters. The default is unchecked.

Using this feature may adversely affect the use of replicated sessions in a cluster. See the WebLogic documentation for more details.

✦ **Send Server Header Enabled:** When checked, WebLogic Server returns server information in the HTTP response header. The default is checked.

✦ **Post Timeout Secs:** Sets the amount of time, in seconds, that WebLogic waits between receiving HTTP POST requests. BEA added this feature to help administrators prevent denial-of-service attacks that are caused by flooding the server with POST requests. The default value is zero, which makes the server vulnerable to attack. Increasing positive values make the server less vulnerable, but slower under heavy loads.

✦ **Max Post Time:** Sets the amount of time, in seconds, that WebLogic waits for individual HTTP POST requests to complete. The default value is zero, which means WebLogic will wait indefinitely.

✦ **Max Post Size:** This is the maximum size, in bytes, of an HTTP POST request that will be accepted by WebLogic Server. POSTs larger than this size are truncated. A value of –1 (the default) indicates the server accepts POSTs of any size.

✦ **Enable Keepalives:** Check this option if you want the HTTP responses generated by WebLogic to contain HTTP 1.0-compliant Keep-Alive headers. This option is not required for HTTP 1.1 (which *always* uses Keep-Alives), but you may want to keep it checked for backward compatibility.

✦ **Duration:** This is the number of seconds WebLogic's HTTP listener waits before closing an inactive HTTP connection.

✦ **HTTPS Duration:** This is the number of seconds WebLogic's HTTPS listener waits before closing an inactive HTTPS connection.

SSL

Figure 23-18 shows the SSL configuration page for a server.

The entries on this page are as follows:

✦ **Enabled:** If checked (the default), SSL is enabled for this server.

✦ **Listen Port:** The network port on which to handle SSL requests. This port must be different from the server's HTTP port, as well as all other ports in use on the server's network interface. The default is 7002.

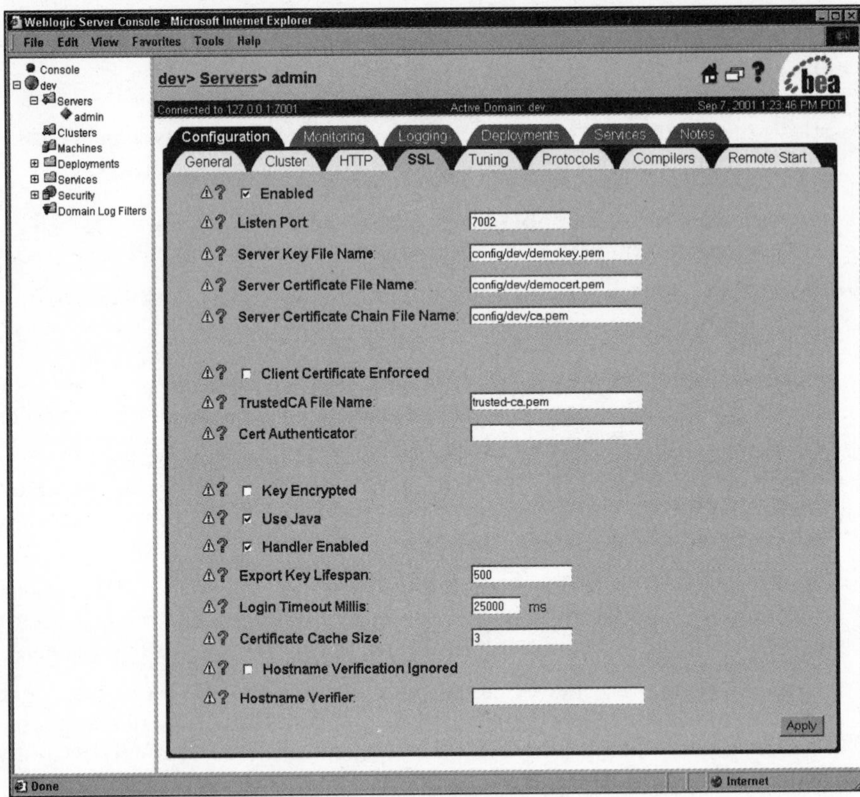

Figure 23-18: The SSL configuration page for a server

✦ **Server Key File Name:** The pathname of the file containing the server's security key. The default is config/<domain-name>/demokey.pem.

✦ **Server Certificate File Name:** The pathname to the file containing the server's private key file. The default is config/<domain-name>/demokey.pem.

✦ **Server Certificate Chain File Name:** The pathname to the file containing the server's digital certificate. The default is config/<domain-name>/ca.pem.

✦ **Client Certificate Enforced:** When checked, WebLogic Server enforces mutual authentication with clients. The default is not checked.

✦ **Trusted CA File Name:** The pathname to the file containing the digital certificate provided by a certificate authority that is trusted by WebLogic Server. The default is trusted-ca.pem.

- **Cert Authenticator:** The name of the Java class that implements the `CertAuthenticator` interface. The default is `null`.
- **Key Encrypted:** When checked, indicates that WebLogic Server's private key is encrypted with a password. The default is not checked.
- **Use Java:** When checked (the default), enables the use of WebLogic's Java libraries for SSL operations. Uncheck this if you prefer to use faster, native SSL libraries on the Solaris, Windows NT, and IBM AIX platforms.
- **Handler Enabled:** When checked (the default), WebLogic Server rejects SSL connections that fail client authentication.
- **Export Key Lifespan:** Sets the number of times WebLogic Server uses an exportable (40-bit) key when communicating with a client using export-strength encryption before generating a new key. The smaller the number, the more secure the communication. The premise is that 40-bit keys can be hacked within relatively short time frames. The default is 500.
- **Login Timeout Millis:** The number of seconds WebLogic Server waits for an SSL connection before timing out. The default is 25,000.
- **Certificate Cache Size:** The number of digital certificates that are tokenized and stored by WebLogic Server. The default is 3.
- **Hostname Verification Ignored** and **Hostname Verifier:** These two attributes are currently undocumented.

Tuning

Figure 23-19 shows the Tuning configuration page for a server.

The entries on this page are as follows:

- **Socket Readers:** The percentage of WebLogic threads to be allocated as socket readers. The default is 33.
- **Login Timeout:** The number of milliseconds WebLogic waits before timing out a login attempt. The default is 1000 (1 second).
- **Accept Backlog:** The number of connections WebLogic Server allows to "stack up" when the server is too busy to accept them. The default is 50. Backlogged connections become active when existing active connections drop.
- **Reverse DNS Allowed:** When checked, indicates that reverse DNS lookups are allowed on this server. The default is unchecked.
- **Enable Native IO:** When checked, instructs WebLogic Server to use the native operating system's I/O routines, instead of Java's. Native I/O is always faster, so the default is checked.

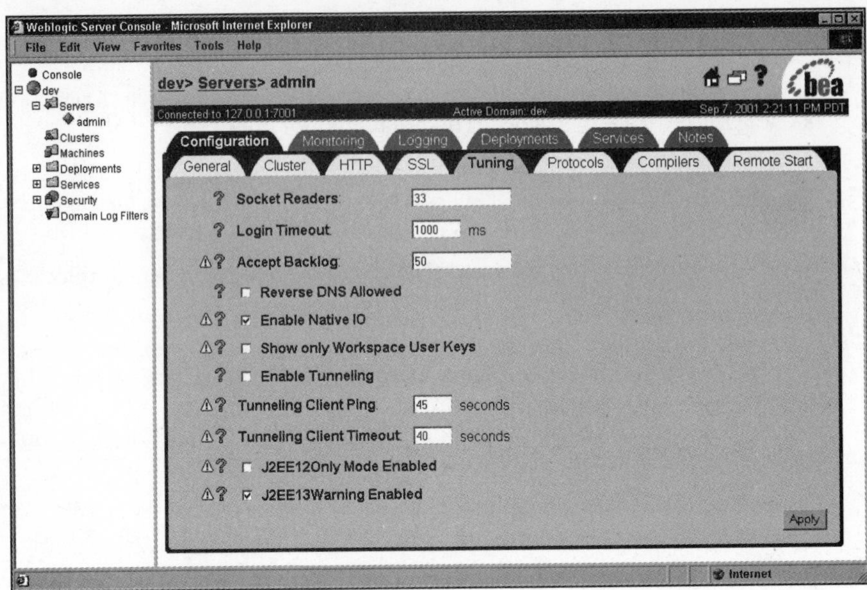

Figure 23-19: The Tuning configuration page for a server Protocols

- ✦ **Show only Workspace User Keys:** According to the WebLogic documentation, this attribute "determines whether or not the User Keys will be shown." I haven't received further clarification on this from BEA.
- ✦ **Enable Tunneling:** When checked, all client interactions with WebLogic Server will be tunneled through the HTTP and HTTPS ports on which WebLogic is listening. This feature is useful if you are trying to support RMI clients through a firewall. The default is not checked.
- ✦ **Tunneling Client Ping:** When a client is tunneling to WebLogic, the server pings the client every few seconds to make sure they are still connected. This is where you set the number of seconds between pings. The default is 45.
- ✦ **Tunneling Client Timeout:** This is the number of seconds WebLogic waits for a client ping to return before disconnecting the client. The default is 40.
- ✦ **J2EE12Only Mode Enabled:** Check this box if you want WebLogic Server to support J2EE version 1.2 only. Calls that don't comply with this specification (i.e., J2EE 1.3 calls) will cause exceptions to be thrown. The default is not checked.

✦ **J2EE13Warning Enabled:** This feature was intended to warn developers when they made J2EE 1.3 calls, back in the days before the specification was finalized. Now that the specification is finalized, this feature is obsolete. The default is checked, but starting with WebLogic Server 6.1 service pack 1, no warnings are given.

Figure 23-20 shows the Protocols configuration page for a server.

The entries on this page are as follows:

✦ **Default Protocol:** Select the protocol you would like WebLogic Server to use for its internal communications. The choices are t3, t3s, http, https, and IIOP. The default is t3, a BEA-proprietary protocol optimized for WebLogic Server.

✦ **Default Secure Protocol:** Select the secure protocol you would like WebLogic Server to use for its internal secure communications. The choices are t3s and https. The default is t3s, a BEA-proprietary protocol optimized for WebLogic Server.

✦ **T3 Max Message Size:** If the t3 protocol is used, this is the maximum message size WebLogic will use for communicating. The default is 10,000,000 bytes.

✦ **T3 Message Timeout:** This is the number of seconds WebLogic waits before giving up on an unacknowledged t3 message. The default is 480.

✦ **HTTP Max Message Size:** Same as T3 Max Message Size, but for HTTP.

✦ **HTTP Message Timeout:** Same as the T3 Message Timeout, but for HTTP.

✦ **Enable IIOP:** What does this mean? When checked, IIOP is enabled for this WebLogic Server instance. The default is checked.

✦ **IIOP Max Message Size:** Same as T3 Max Message Size, but for IIOP.

✦ **IIOP Message Timeout:** Same as the T3 Message Timeout, but for IIOP.

✦ **Default IIOP Password:** Sets the IIOP password for this server, if any. The default is `null`.

✦ **Default IIOP User:** Sets the default IIOP user for this server, if any. The default is `guest`.

Compilers

Figure 23-21 shows the Compilers configuration page for a server. WebLogic uses these settings when generating RMI stubs for EJBs and RMI servers.

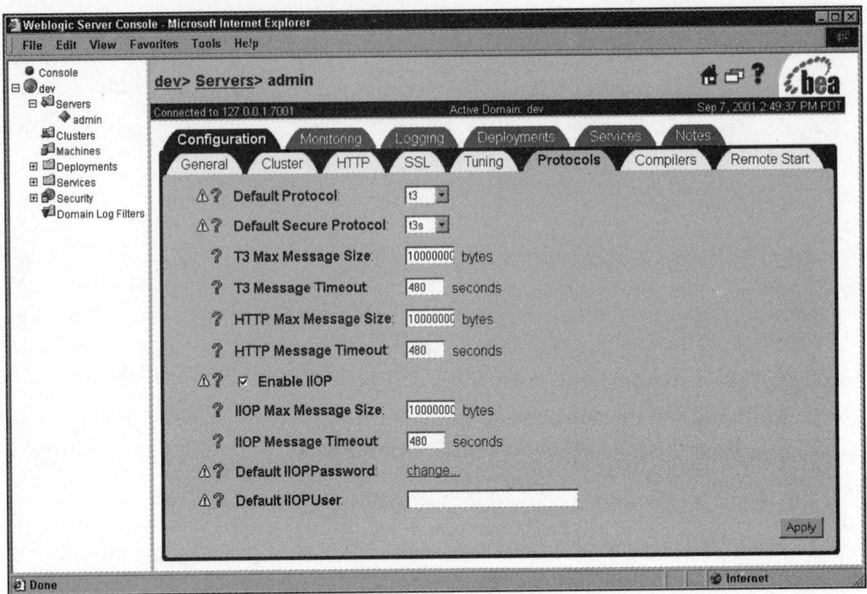

Figure 23-20: The Protocols configuration page for a server

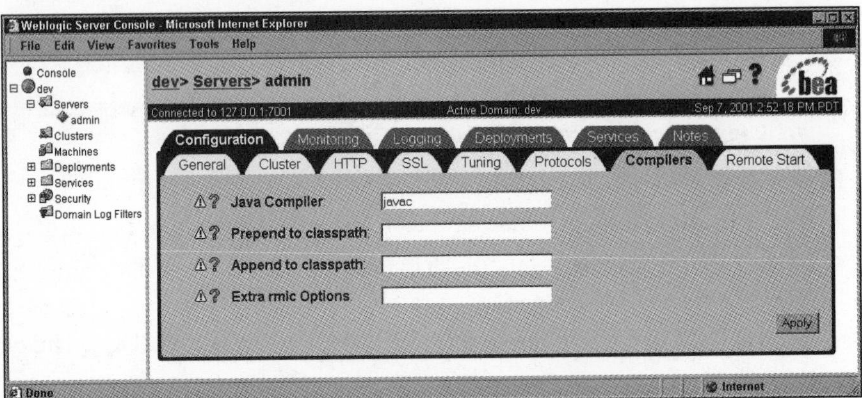

Figure 23-21: The Compilers configuration page for a server

The entries on this page are as follows:

✦ **Java Compiler:** The name of the Java compiler to use. This compiler must reside within your classpath. The default is `javac`.

✦ **Prepend to classpath:** Type directories into this space, separated by semi-colons, that you would like inserted before WebLogic's classpath when invoking the compiler. The default is blank.

✦ **Append to classpath:** Type directories into this space, separated by semi-colons, that you would like inserted after WebLogic's classpath when invoking the compiler. The default is blank.

✦ **Extra rmic Options:** Type extra command-line options you would like WebLogic to pass to the RMI compiler (rmic) when compiling EJBs and RMI servers.

Remote Start

Figure 23-22 shows the Remote Start configuration page for a server. This page is used to configure a managed server so it can be remotely started by Node Manager.

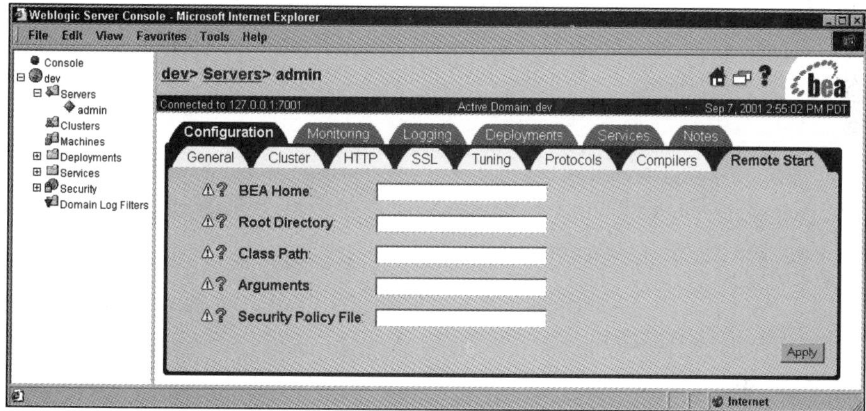

Figure 23-22: The Remote Start configuration page for a server

The entries on this page are as follows:

✦ **BEA Home:** The full pathname to the BEA Home directory; for example, `c:\bea\wlserver6.1`.

✦ **Root Directory:** The full pathname to the managed server's directory; for example, `c:\bea\wlserver6.1\config\dev`.

✦ **Class Path:** A valid classpath for use by this server instance. If none is provided, the machine's classpath will be used.

✦ **Arguments:** Command-line arguments you would like Node Manager to pass to the `weblogic.Server` executable.

✦ **Security Policy File:** The full pathname to the security policy file you would like Node Manager to pass to the `weblogic.Server` executable; for example, `c:\bea\wlserver6.1/lib/weblogic.policy`.

Monitoring

General

Figure 23-23 shows the General monitoring page for a server.

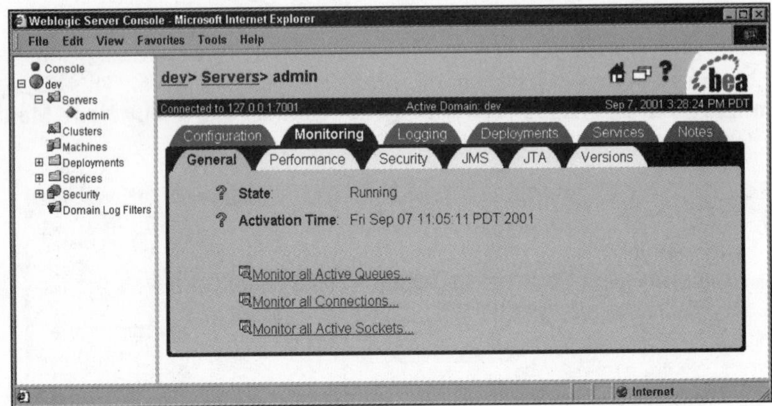

Figure 23-23: The General monitoring page for a server

The entries on this page are as follows:

- ✦ **State:** The server's current state; either Running or Stopped.
- ✦ **Activation Time:** The date and time the server was started.

There are additional links to monitor the server's active execution queues, monitor connections to the server, and monitor active network sockets. For more information on these options, see the WebLogic documentation.

Performance

Figure 23-24 shows the Performance monitoring page for a server.

The entries on this page are as follows:

- ✦ **Idle Threads:** The number of execution threads that are idle and available for immediate use.
- ✦ **Pending Request Oldest Time:** This is the start time of the oldest pending request that has not been processed by the server.
- ✦ **Throughput:** This is the amount of data passing through the server, expressed in kilobytes per second.
- ✦ **Queue Length:** This is the number of pending requests waiting for execution threads to become available. For optimal performance, you want this number to be as close to zero as possible.

✦ **Memory Usage:** The number of megabytes of RAM currently being used by WebLogic Server.

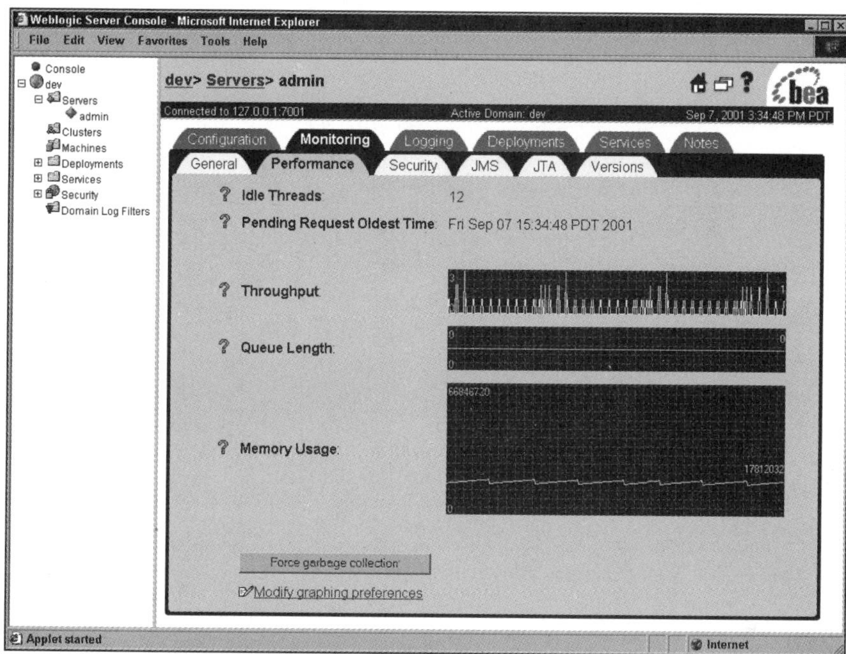

Figure 23-24: The Performance monitoring page for a server

In addition, there is a button to instantly force garbage collection within the server's JVM, and a link to modify the graphing preferences. You can find more information on these features in the WebLogic documentation.

Security

Figure 23-25 shows the Security monitoring page for a server.

The entries on this page are as follows:

✦ **Total Users Locked Out:** The number of users locked out at this because of too many failed login attempts.

✦ **Invalid Logins Total:** The total number of failed logins logged by the server.

✦ **Total Login Attempts while Locked:** The number of times users who were locked out attempted to log in while still locked out.

✦ **Total Users Unlocked:** The number of users who have been unlocked by the administrator, or who became unlocked because their lockout interval expired.

✦ **Invalid Logins High:** The highest number of failed logins for any one user account.

✦ **Locked Users:** The number of users locked out at this moment because of too many failed login attempts.

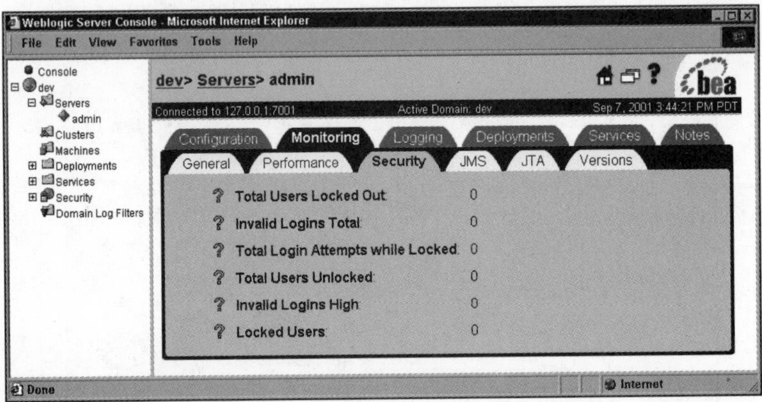

Figure 23-25: The Security monitoring page for a server

JMS

Figure 23-26 shows the JMS monitoring page for a server.

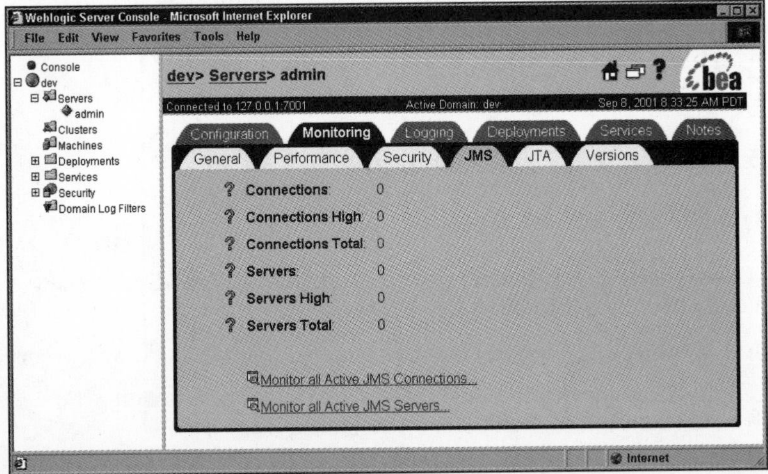

Figure 23-26: The JMS monitoring page for a server

The entries on this page are as follows:

✦ **Connections:** The number of JMS connections currently in use.

✦ **Connections High:** The peak number of JMS connections since the last server restart.

✦ **Connections Total:** The total number of JMS connections that have been made to the server since the last server restart.

✦ **Servers:** The number of JMS servers that are currently active.

✦ **Servers High:** The peak number of active JMS servers since the last server restart.

✦ **Servers Total:** The total number of JMS servers that have been created since the last server restart.

Additionally, the page contains links to monitor all active JMS connections and servers. See the WebLogic documentation for more information about these links.

For more information about JMS, see Chapter 9.

JTA

Figure 23-27 shows the JTA monitoring page for a server.

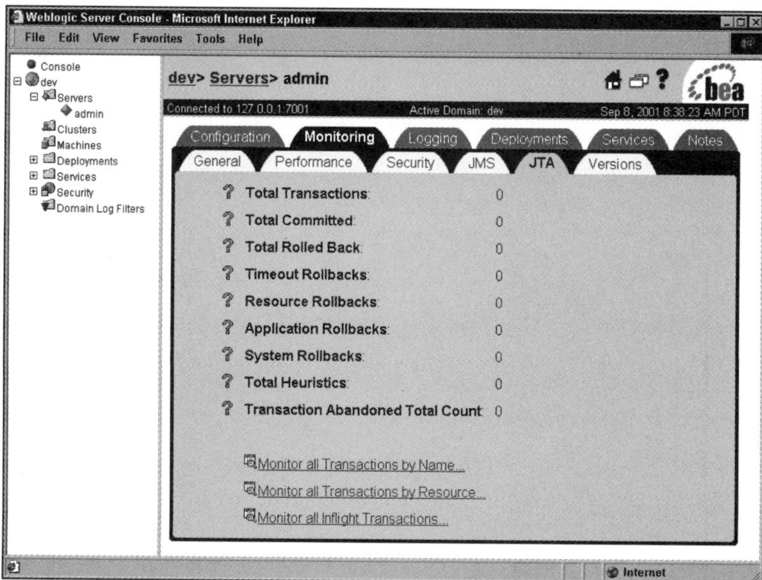

Figure 23-27: The JTA monitoring page for a server

The entries on this page are as follows:

- **Total Transactions:** The total number of transactions that have been initiated since server restart. This includes container-managed transactions as well as transactions initiated in code.
- **Total Committed:** The total number of transactions that have been committed since server restart.
- **Total Rolled Back:** The total number of transactions that have been rolled back since server restart.
- **Timeout Rollbacks:** The total number of transactions that have been rolled back due to timeouts since server restart.
- **Resource Rollbacks:** The total number of transactions that have been rolled back by participating resources since server restart.
- **Application Rollbacks:** The total number of transactions that have been rolled back by application code since server restart.
- **System Rollbacks:** The total number of transactions that have been rolled back by WebLogic's transaction manager since server restart.
- **Total Heuristics:** This is the total number of heuristic completions that have been reported by the transaction manager in response to transactions that were manually completed outside the transaction manager. This usually occurs when there is a problem with a transaction and a system administrator intervenes to end the transaction.
- **Transaction Abandoned Total Count:** The total number of transactions that were abandoned before being committed since server restart.

Additionally, the page contains links to monitor transactions based on various criteria. See the WebLogic documentation for more information about these links.

For more information about JTA, see Chapter 6.

Versions

Figure 23-28 shows the Versions monitoring page for a server. It simply displays version information for WebLogic Server, the JDK WebLogic Server is using, and the host operating system.

Logging

WebLogic Server provides separate logging for many of its services, including the Application Server itself, the server's domain, HTTP, JDBC, and JTA. In addition, the server can log debugging messages for remote exceptions and stack traces.

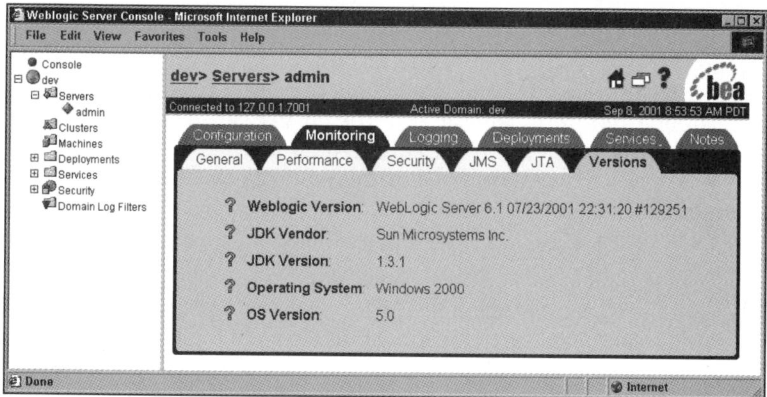

Figure 23-28: The Versions monitoring page for a server

General

Figure 23-29 shows the General logging page for a server. This is where logging options for the Application Server are set.

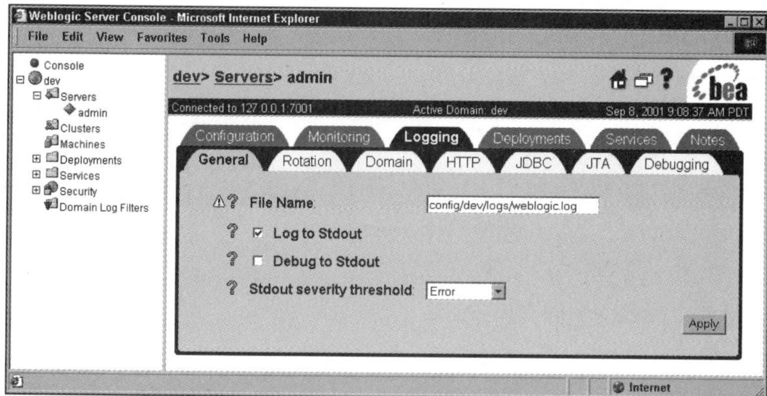

Figure 23-29: The General logging page for a server

The entries on this page are as follows:

✦ **File Name:** This is the pathname to the log file for the Application Server. The default is `config/<domain-name>/logs/weblogic.log`.

✦ **Log to Stdout:** If checked (the default), log messages are written to standard output — the WebLogic Server command window.

✦ **Debug to Stdout:** If checked, debug messages are written to standard output. The default is not checked.

✦ **Stdout severity threshold:** This determines the severity of messages that are logged to standard output. Messages of the chosen severity and higher are written logged to standard output. The severity levels, from highest to lowest, are `Emergency`, `Alert`, `Critical`, `Notice`, `Error`, `Warning`, and `Info`. The default setting is `Error`.

Rotation

Figure 23-30 shows the Rotation logging page for a server. This page allows you to configure the rotation scheme for the Application Server's log file.

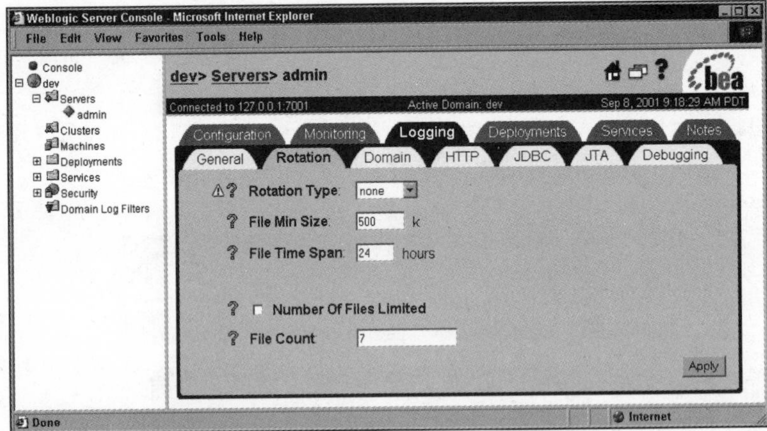

Figure 23-30: The Rotation logging page for a server

The entries on this page are as follows:

✦ **Rotation Type:** Determines how log files are created over time. The default is `none`, which means all messages are written to the same log in perpetuity. The other options are `by Size`, which means a new log file is created once the current log file reaches a given size, and `by Time`, which means a new log file is created every time a certain number of hours passes.

✦ **File Min Size:** If Rotation Type is set to `by Size`, then this is the file size (in kilobytes) that must be exceeded by the current log file in order for the next log file to be created. The default is 500k.

✦ **File Time Span:** If Rotation Type is set to `by Time`, then this is the number of hours that will elapse between the creation of each additional log file. The default is 24 hours.

✦ **Number of Files Limited:** If this is checked, then the total number of log files created is limited to the number given by File Count; otherwise, there is no limit. Once the limit is reached, logging to files stops. Default is not checked.

✦ **File Count:** If Number of Files Limited is checked, this gives the total number of files that will be created before logging to files stops. The default is 7.

Domain

Figure 23-31 shows the Rotation logging page for a server. This page allows you to configure the rotation scheme for the Application Server's log file.

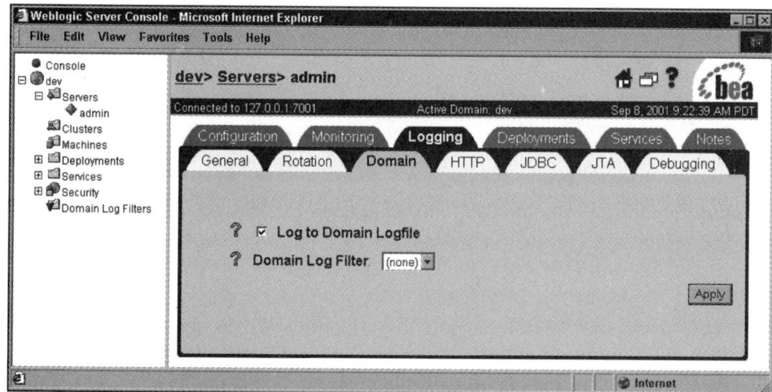

Figure 23-31: The Rotation logging page for a server

The entries on this page are as follows:

✦ **Log to Domain Logfile:** If checked, log messages for the domain are written to a log file.

✦ **Domain Log Filter:** Domain log filters that you have previously defined, if any, appear in this list. Select one to use for the domain. The default is `none`. The configuration of Domain Log Filters is covered later in this chapter.

HTTP

Figure 23-32 shows the HTTP logging page for a server. This page allows you to configure the logging and rotation scheme for WebLogic's HTTP server log.

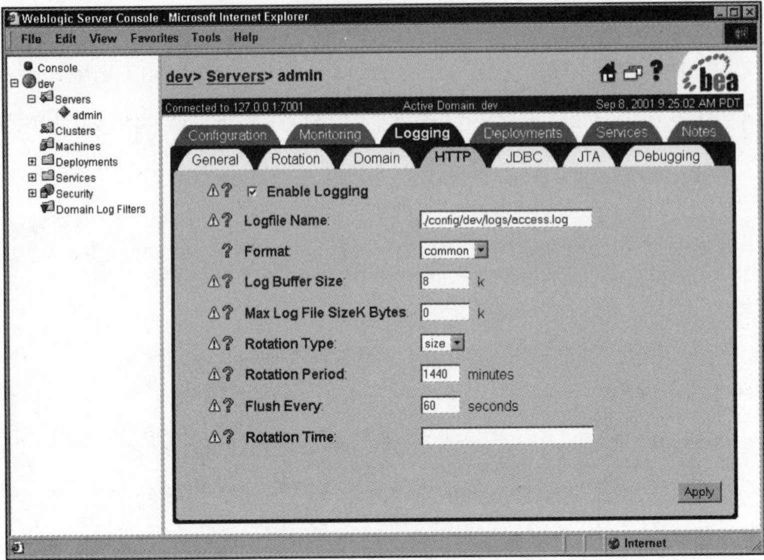

Figure 23-32: The HTTP logging page for a server

The entries on this page are as follows:

✦ **Enable Logging:** If checked (the default), logging is enabled for the HTTP server.

✦ **Logfile Name:** The pathname of the file to which HTTP log messages are written. The default is `/config/<domain-name>/logs/access.log`.

✦ **Format:** The HTTP log format. The choices are `common` (the default), and `extended`, which provides additional information.

✦ **Log Buffer Size:** This is the size, in kilobytes, of the in-memory buffer used for HTTP logging. When the buffer reaches this size, its contents are flushed to the log file on disk. This option is provided for increased performance. Generally speaking, the larger the buffer, the better the performance, because expensive writes to disk will be minimized. But you stand to lose more information with large buffer sizes if the server crashes before the buffer is flushed to disk. The default size is 8k.

✦ **Max Log File SizeK Bytes:** This is the maximum size, in kilobytes, to which the log file can grow. Once this size is reached, the contents of the log are overwritten.

✦ **Rotation Type, Period, and Time:** This appears to be an unfinished version of WebLogic's standard log file rotation scheme, as described in earlier sections of this chapter. I, therefore, recommend that you leave the values at their defaults, which are `size`, `1440 seconds`, and `null`, respectively.

✦ **Flush Every:** At this interval, given as a number of seconds, the log file will be flushed to disk, regardless of how full the log buffer is. The default is 60.

JDBC

Figure 23-33 shows the JDBC logging page for a server.

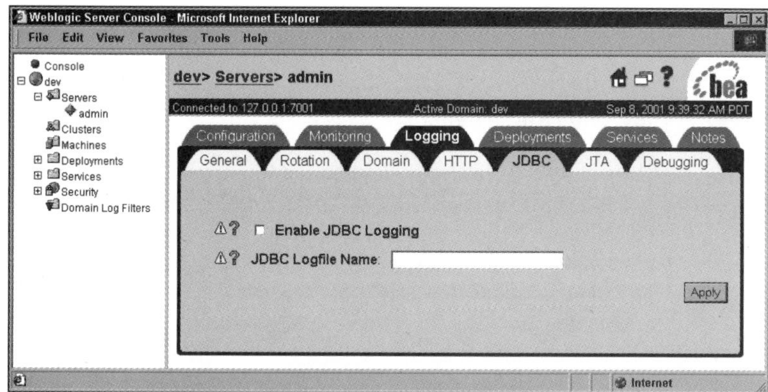

Figure 23-33: The JDBC logging page for a server

The entries on this page are as follows:

- ✦ **Enable JDBC Logging:** If checked, logging is enabled for JDBC. The default is not checked.
- ✦ **JDBC Logfile Name:** The pathname of the file to which JDBC log messages are written. There is no default. I suggest using /config/<domain-name>/logs/jdbc.log.

JTA

Figure 23-34 shows the JTA logging page for a server.

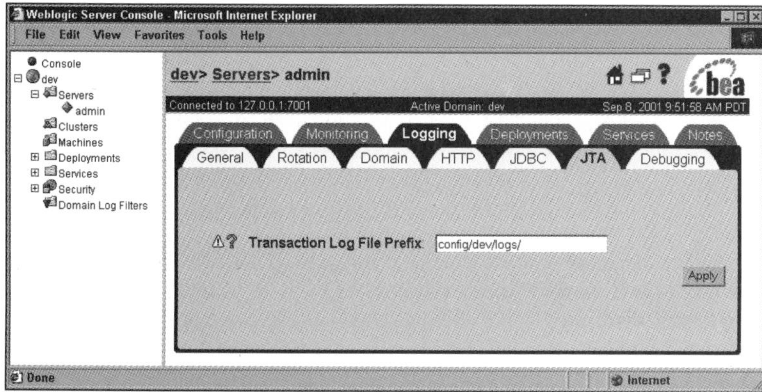

Figure 23-34: The JTA logging page for a server

This page contains only one entry:

✦ **Transaction Log File Prefix:** This is the pathname to the folder that contains the JTA logs. It should *not* include the file name. The default is `config/<domain-name>/logs/`.

Debugging

Figure 23-35 shows the Debugging logging page for a server.

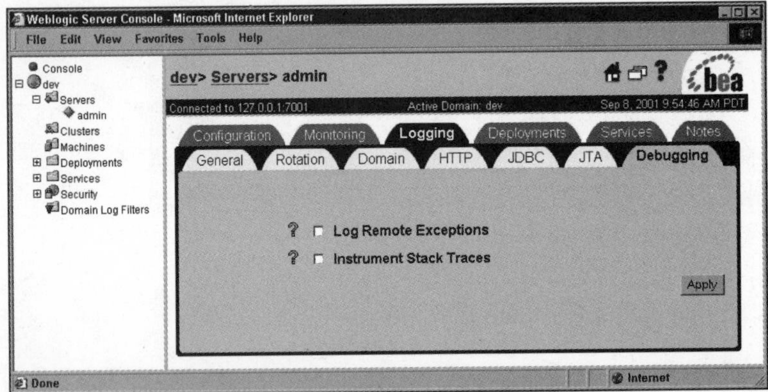

Figure 23-35: The Debugging logging page for a server

The entries on this page are as follows:

✦ **Log Remote Exceptions:** If checked, remote exceptions are logged to the debugging log. The default is not checked.

✦ **Instrument Stack Traces:** If checked, stack traces are logged to the debugging log. The default is not checked.

Deployments

The Deployments section contains pages for EJB, Web Applications, Java Connector Architecture (JCA), and Startup and Shutdown classes. These configuration options are covered elsewhere in this book, under the relevant topics.

Services

The Services tab for a server allows you to configure attributes related to JDBC, JMS, XML, WebLogic Enterprise Connectivity (WLEC), WebLogic Jolt, WebLogic File T3, virtual hosts, and mail.

JDBC

The JDBC page allows you to activate and deactivate JDBC connection pools. This functionality is fully described in Chapter 5.

JMS

Figure 23-36 shows the JMS services page for a server.

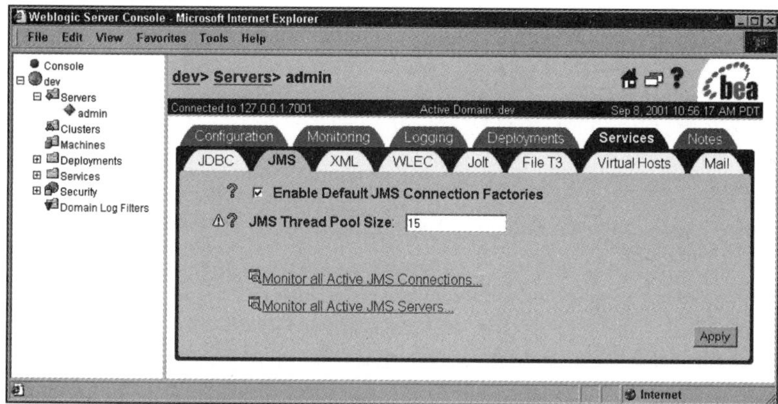

Figure 23-36: The JMS services page for a server

The entries on this page are as follows:

- **Enable Default JMS Connection Factories:** If checked (the default), WebLogic Server creates a default JMS connection factory at startup for use by applications. This factory is accessible through the `weblogic.jms.connectionfactory` interface. Otherwise, you must create your own connection factories with the console.
- **JMS Thread Pool Size:** This is the number of free threads WebLogic Server allocates for JMS requests at startup. The default is 15.

For more information about JMS, see Chapter 9.

XML

The XML page allows you to configure the XML registry and cache for your server. This functionality is covered later in this chapter.

WLEC

The WLEC page allows you to activate and deactivate WebLogic Enterprise Connectivity (WLEC) connection pools. These pools are used to connect to CORBA objects running within BEA Tuxedo. WLEC and Tuxedo are beyond the scope of this book.

Jolt

The Jolt page allows you to activate and deactivate Jolt connection pools. These pools are used to connect to BEA Tuxedo, which is a dedicated transaction server. Jolt and Tuxedo are beyond the scope of this book.

File T3

The File T3 page allows you to activate and deactivate File T3 connections. This functionality is described later in this chapter.

Virtual Hosts

The Virtual Hosts page allows you to activate and deactivate virtual hosts. This functionality is described later in this chapter.

Mail

The Mail page allows you to activate and deactivate JavaMail sessions. This functionality is fully described in Chapter 10.

Clusters

This node allows you to create and configure clusters of WebLogic servers.

See Chapter 24 for information on how to create and configure WebLogic clusters.

Machines

This panel is used to create entries for the physical machines that will participate in a cluster. WebLogic servers, configured by using the Server node, are assigned to these machines. WebLogic uses this information to determine whether or not server instances reside on the same machine. If you don't map servers to machines, WebLogic assumes each server runs on separate physical hardware. This may negatively impact the way WebLogic selects servers to host secondary HTTP session replicas, so you should always define machines for your clusters and map your WebLogic server instances to the appropriate machines.

The machines you define should map precisely to the physical machines in your installation. If two WebLogic Server instances are running on the same physical machine, map them to the same machine in the console as well.

Creating a machine

Figure 23-37 shows the console page for creating a machine.

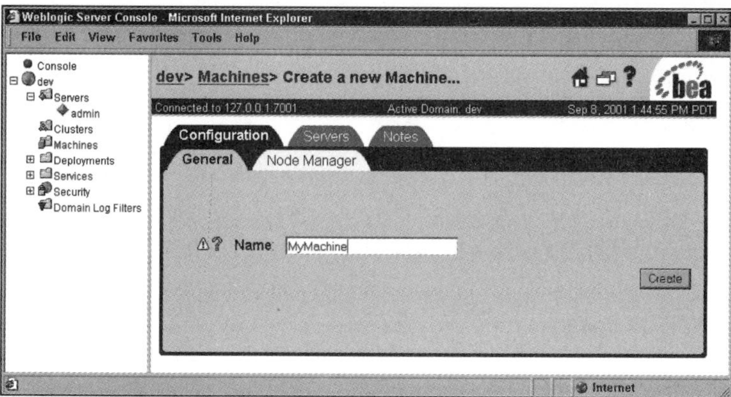

Figure 23-37: Creating a new machine

When you create a machine in the console, you give it a logical name. You can give any name you want; the name doesn't have to match the machine's physical or DNS name. But the name must be unique among the machines present in your cluster.

Configuring Node Manager for a machine

After creating the machine, you can move to the Node Manager tab to configure Node Manager settings. Node Manager is a Java program, new with WebLogic 6.1, which allows you to start and kill WebLogic managed servers remotely from the console. You use Node Manager when a server has hung or has become unresponsive. Figure 23-38 shows the Node Manager configuration page.

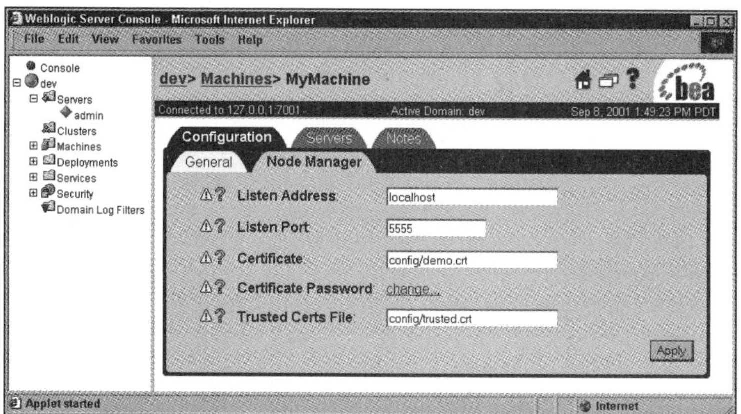

Figure 23-38: Node Manager configuration page for a machine

The entries on this page are as follows:

✦ **Listen Address and Port:** The IP address and port on which Node Manager listens for commands to start or kill a server.

✦ **Certificate:** The pathname to the file containing Node Manager's digital certificate. The default is `config/demo.crt`.

✦ **Certificate Password:** If Node Manager's digital certificate is encrypted with a password, provide that password here. The default is `null`.

✦ **Trusted Certs File:** The pathname to the file containing a digital certificate for Node Manager that is provided by a trusted certificate authority, such as VeriSign. The default is `config/trusted.crt`.

Assigning servers to a machine

After creating a machine and configuring Node Manager for it, use the Servers tab to assign existing WebLogic server instances to the machine.

Deployments

The configuration steps for all types of deployments are covered elsewhere in this book. See the relevant chapters for more information.

Services

The configuration steps for JDBC, JMS, JTA, and Mail have been covered elsewhere in this chapter or in this book, and will not be covered here. This section focuses on the remaining services—XML, SNMP, WLEC, Jolt, Virtual Hosts, and File T3—that have not yet been discussed in this book. Administration nodes for these services can be found by expanding the Services node in WebLogic Console's domain tree.

XML

The XML section is where you configure XML registries, parsers, transformers, and so on for servers in your WebLogic domain.

Creating a new XML registry

By default, WebLogic uses Apache's implementations of DocumentBuilderFactory, SAXParserFactory, and TransformerFactory to parse and transform XML documents. But you can create your own XML registries that substitute alternative implementations of DocumentBuilderFactory, SAXParserFactory and TransformerFactory. You can create any number of registries, but only one can be active per WebLogic Server. Figure 23-39 shows the configuration page for defining a new XML registry.

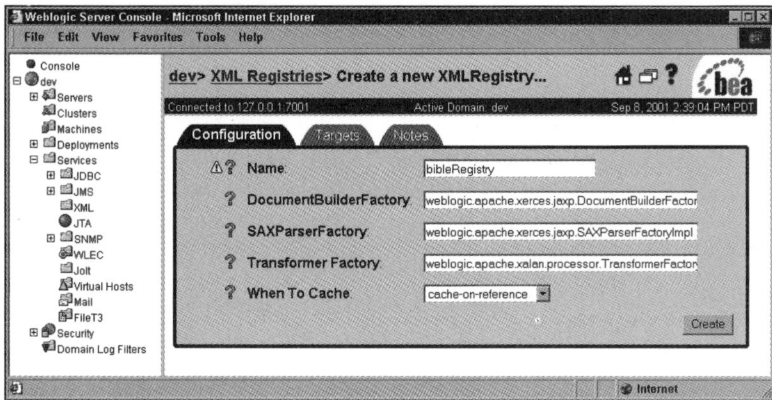

Figure 23-39: Configuring a new XML registry

To create a new XML registry, follow these steps:

1. Start WebLogic Server and WebLogic Console.
2. Expand the Services node in the domain tree and click the XML node.
3. Click the Create a New XML Registry link on the right side of the console. The screen in Figure 23-40 appears.
4. Give the new registry a unique name.
5. Enter a value for DocumentBuilderFactory if this XML registry will be used to produce `org.w3c.Document` objects, or leave the default in place, which is `weblogic.apache.xerces.jaxp.DocumentBuilderFactoryImpl`. You can also leave the field blank, which instructs WebLogic to use the default.
6. Enter a value for SAXParserFactory if this XML registry will be used to parse XML documents on an event-driven basis. The default is `weblogic.apache.xerces.jaxp.SAXParserFactoryImpl`, or you can leave the field blank to use the default.
7. Enter a value for TransformerFactory if this XML registry will be used to apply XSL stylesheets to XML documents. The default is `weblogic.apache.xalan.processor.TransformerFactoryImpl`, or you can leave the field blank to use the default.
8. Choose whether to have your XML components cache on reference or cache on initialization.
9. Click Create.
10. Click the Targets tab and move the desired server into the Chosen column.

11. Expand the Servers node in the domain tree and the click the server that will host the new XML registry.

12. Click the Services tab and then click the XML subtab. Figure 23-40 shows the resulting configuration page.

13. Use the drop-down list to select the XML registry to be associated with this server, and then enter values for Cache Memory Size, Cache Disk Size, and Cache Timeout Interval. These values are defined in kilobytes, megabytes, and seconds, respectively.

14. Click Apply.

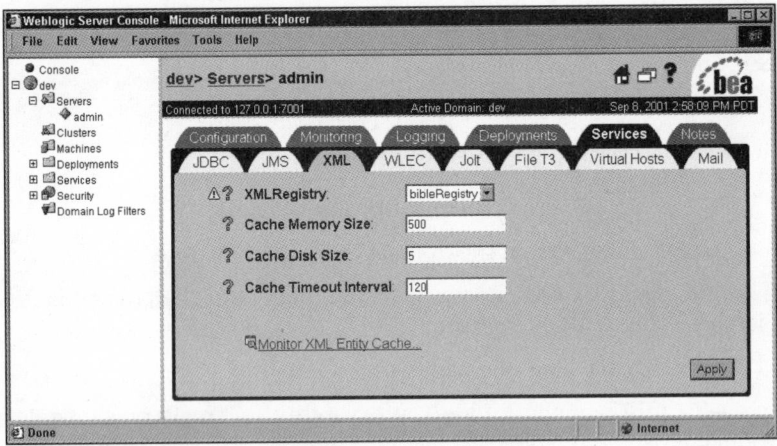

Figure 23-40: Assigning an XML registry to a server

Configuring an alternative parser for use with specific document types

Sometimes it's desirable to have certain XML documents processed by a particular parser. To have WebLogic use an alternative parser automatically with certain XML documents, do the following:

1. Follow the preceding steps to create a new XML registry and associate it with a WebLogic Server.

2. Under the XML node in the domain tree, expand the node of the XML registry with which this parser is to be associated. Click the XML Parser Select Registry Entries node, and then click the Configure a New XML Parser Select Registry Entry link on the right side of the console. Figure 23-41 shows the configuration page that appears.

3. Use either Public Id or System Id to specify the document type that will use the parser. Alternatively, a Root Element Tag can be specified for the parser. Only one of the three fields needs to have data.

4. Enter the class name for the parser that is to be used with the specified document type. Enter data either for DocumentBuilderFactory or SAXParserFactory, but not both. Parser Class Name is for backward compatibility with older versions of WebLogic. In this example, only when a document uses the Bible DTD will the WebLogic fast parser be used.

5. Click the Create button.

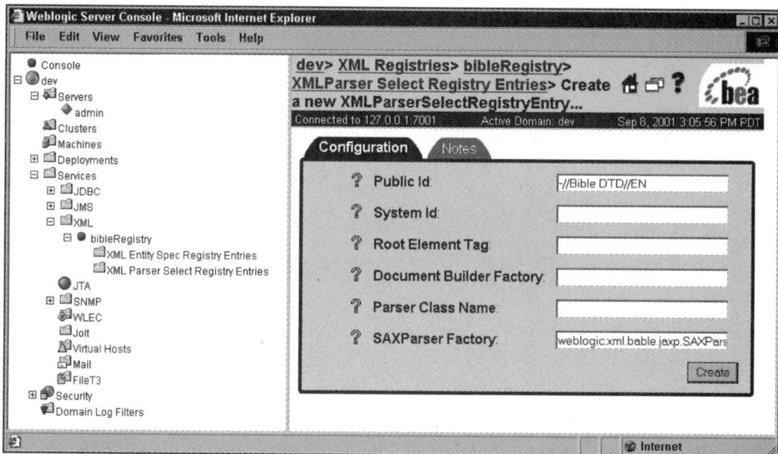

Figure 23-41: Configuring a different SAX parser to use with the Bible DTD

Configuring an external entity

External entities are XML entities that live outside of the XML document that references them. DTDs are an example, as are namespaces or other XML documents. Usually, these documents are accessed remotely via the Internet. But WebLogic Server enables the user to specify different locations for these entities. Users can also configure and monitor the caching of these entities.

To configure a new external entity resolution, follow these steps:

1. Follow the steps above to create a XML registry and associate it with a WebLogic Server.

2. Expand the new XML registry in the domain tree, and then click XML Entity Spec Registry Entries. Click the Create a New XML Entity Spec Registry Entry link on the right side of the console. Figure 23-42 shows the resulting configuration page.

3. Enter the Public Id or System Id that will cause the external entity to be referenced. In the example, this is a reference to `bible.dtd`.

4. Enter the EntityURI. This is the path to the file containing the external entity. If the entity resides on the administration WebLogic Server, then the entry

should be relative to the registries entity directory. This directory is BEAHome/wlserver6.1/config/<domain-name>/xml/registries/ <XML Registry name>.

5. If the entity is accessed over the Internet, then a fully qualified URL is required. The entity can also be accessed from databases by using a JDBC connection. The entity can only be accessed by URIs that start with these qualifiers: http://, ftp://, file://, and jdbc:. In this example, the DTD is accessed at the URL http://www.zeeware.com/dtds/bible.dtd.

6. Click Create.

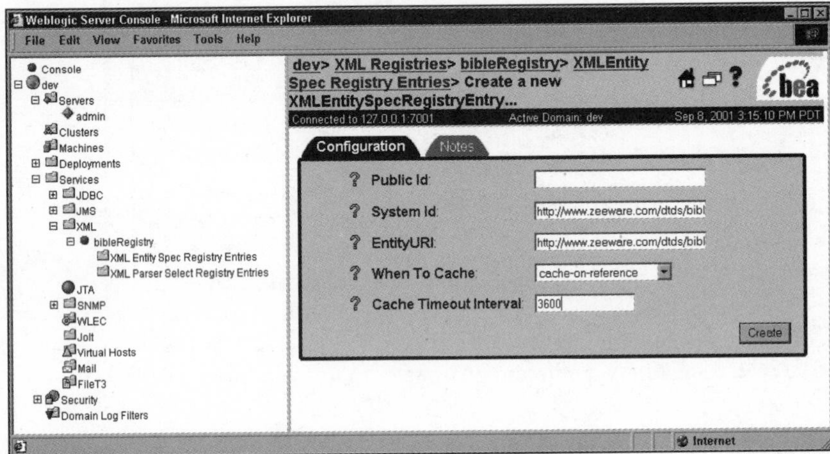

Figure 23-42: Creating a new external entity resolution

SNMP

Before creating a SNMP trap, you need to enable the SNMP service in WebLogic Server. To do so, follow these steps:

1. Load the WebLogic MIB (file name: BEA-WEBLOGIC-MIB.ansi) into the SNMP management system. Consult your SNMP vendor documentation for directions on how to do this.

2. In the domain tree, expand the SNMP node and click the Trap Destination node.

3. The right side of the console shows all SNMP Trap Destinations that exist for this WebLogic Server. Click the Configure a New SNMP Trap Destination link. Figure 23-43 shows the resulting configuration page and its default values.

4. Define the destination where trap notification will be sent.

   Name is a unique identifier for this SNMP trap and should describe what the trap is doing.

   Community is the name of the group of managed machines to which this trap should be mapped by the SNMP management software.

Host is either the hostname or IP address of the SNMP management station.

Port is the port number on which the SNMP management station listens. The default is 162.

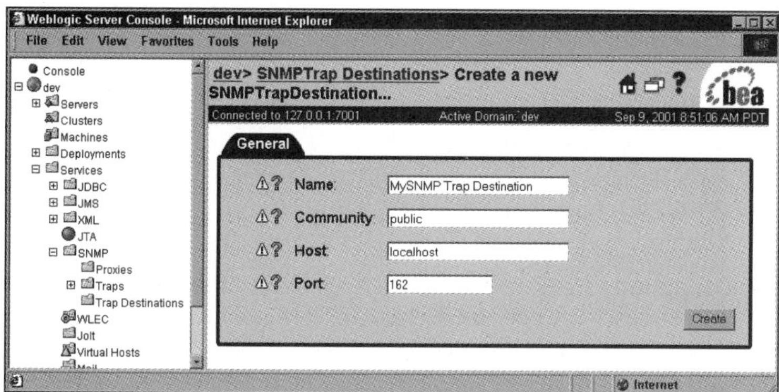

Figure 23-43: Configuring a new SNMP trap destination

5. Click Create.
6. In the domain tree, click the SNMP node. This takes you to the SNMP configuration tab for the domain, shown in Figure 23-44 (this screen is also shown in Figure 23-6, along with complete definitions of its entry fields).

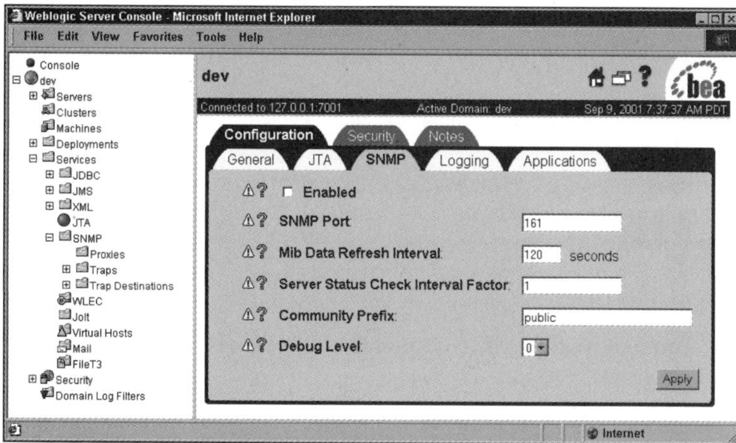

Figure 23-44: Configuring a SNMP trap for the domain

7. Enter values for the following fields:

Check the Enabled box. The SNMP agent will not be activated until this box is checked.

Set SNMP Port to the port number the SNMP agent listens on.

The Mib Data Refresh Interval is the interval that the SNMP Service updates its cache of WebLogic Server attribute values. The default value is 120 seconds, and the minimum value is 30 seconds. The closer the value is to 30 seconds, the worse performance will be, because the console does a `GET` for each WebLogic attribute in the MIB.

The Status Check Interval Factor is the interval that the SNMP Service checks to see if any managed servers are up or down. The Mib Data Refresh Interval is multiplied by this number, and status checks occur at that interval. The minimum value is 1; you will probably want to use a value between 1 and 3.

Community Prefix is the SNMP community that the manager will be using for requests sent to the WebLogic SNMP agent.

Set the Debug Level to the desired level, as described earlier in this chapter.

8. Click Apply.

WLEC

WebLogic Enterprise Connectivity is a component of WebLogic Server that allows you to create a pool of WLEC connections to WebLogic Tuxedo CORBA objects. WLEC connection pools operate under the same theory as JDBC connection pools; creating connections is expensive, so do it once at server startup, then share the connections among clients who need them.

To create a new WLEC connection pool, follow these steps:

1. In the domain tree, click the WLEC node. The right side of the console displays all existing WLEC connection pools.
2. Click the Configure a New WLEC Connection Pool link. Figure 23-45 shows the General tab of the WLEC connection pool configuration page, which appears when you click the link.
3. Enter values for:

   Name: A name for the connection pool that is unique within the WebLogic domain.

   Primary Addresses: A comma-separated list of addresses for IIOP listeners/handlers that are used to create the connection pool between WebLogic Server and the Tuxedo domain. The format for each address is `//hostname:port`; for example, `//tuxedo.zeeware.com:1024`.

Failover Addresses: A comma-separated list of addresses for IIOP listeners/handlers that are to be used if connections cannot be established with any of the addresses in the primary field. The entry format is the same. Entering data for this field is optional.

Domain: The name of the WebLogic Tuxedo domain to which this connection pool connects. There can be only one connection pool per domain.

Minimum Pool Size: The minimum number of IIOP connections that are to be created at startup. The default is 1.

Maximum Pool Size: The maximum number of IIOP connections that are allowed. The default is 1.

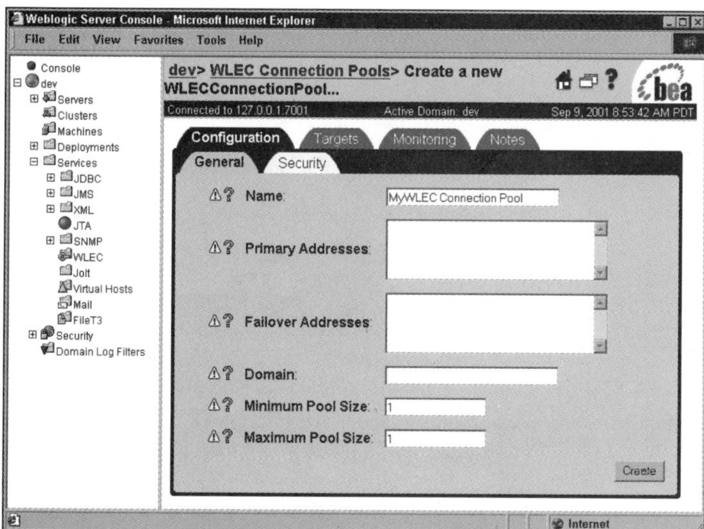

Figure 23-45: Configuring a WLEC connection pool

4. Click Create.
5. Click the Security tab to propagate the security context for a WebLogic user to the BEA Tuxedo domain. This is only needed if the security level in Tuxedo is `USER_AUTH`, `ACL`, and `MANDATORY_ACL`. Figure 23-46 shows the configuration page.
6. Enter values for:

   User Name: A BEA Tuxedo username.

   User Password: The password for the username given.

User Role: The BEA Tuxedo user role, chosen from among the roles defined in your Tuxedo installation.

Application Password: The password for the BEA Tuxedo CORBA application.

Minimum Encryption Level: The minimum SSL encryption level that WebLogic Server is allowed to communicate with Tuxedo. If this level is not met then the connection process will fail. Possible values are 0, 40, 56, and 128.

Maximum Encryption Level: The maximum SSL encryption level that WebLogic Server is allowed to communicate with BEA Tuxedo.

Enable Certificate Authentication: Check this box if certificates are to be used.

Enable Security Context: Check this box if the user security information provided is to be passed to BEA Tuxedo.

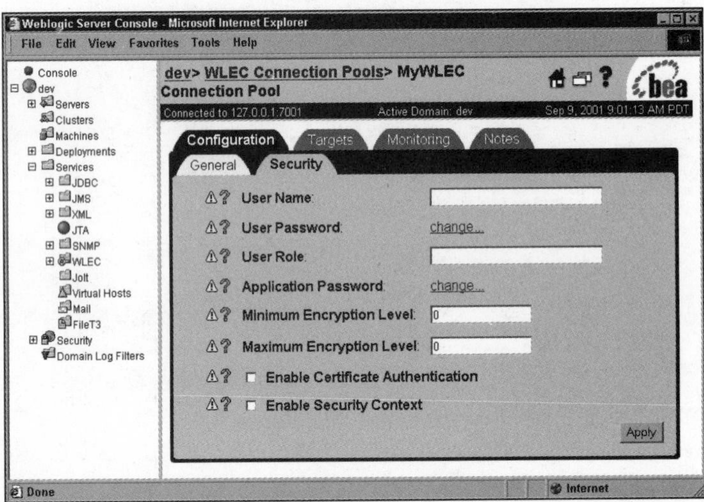

Figure 23-46: Configuring security for a WLEC connection pool

7. Click Apply.
8. Run the `tpuseradd` command to define the WebLogic user as an authorized user in the BEA Tuxedo domain.
9. Set the `-E` option of the ISL command to propagate the User information for the WebLogic server to the Tuxedo domain. The `-E` option requires that a principal username be provided. This is the same as the username entry above.

Jolt

BEA Jolt provides generic access to BEA Tuxedo. Jolt creates a pool of connections at startup, providing the same benefits as a JDBC connection pool.

To create a new Jolt connection pool, follow these steps:

1. In the domain tree, click the Jolt node. This displays all existing Jolt connection pools in the right side of the console.
2. Click the Configure a New JOLT Connection Pool link. The configuration page shown in Figure 23-47 appears.

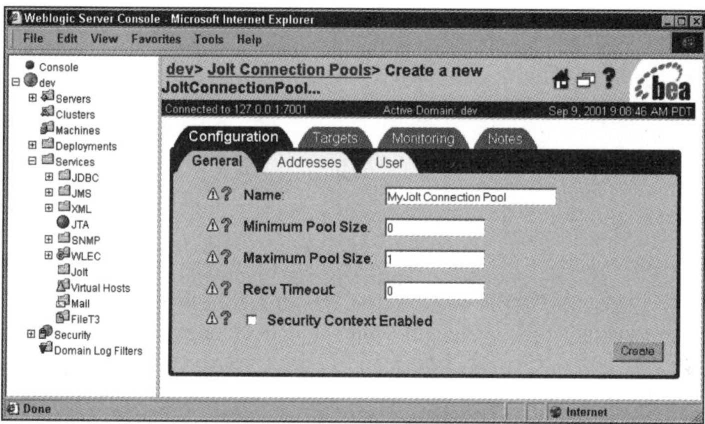

Figure 23-47: Configuring a Jolt connection pool

3. Enter values for the following parameters:

   Name: A unique identifier for this connection pool within the domain.

   Minimum Pool Size: The initial number of Tuxedo connections to create at startup. The default is 0.

   Maximum Pool Size: The maximum number of connections allowed. The default is 1.

   Recv Timeout: The amount of time to wait for a response from Tuxedo before timing out. The default is 0.

   Security Context Enabled: Check this box to enable WebLogic's security context for this connection pool.
4. Click Create.
5. Click the Addresses tab. Figure 23-48 shows the resulting configuration page.

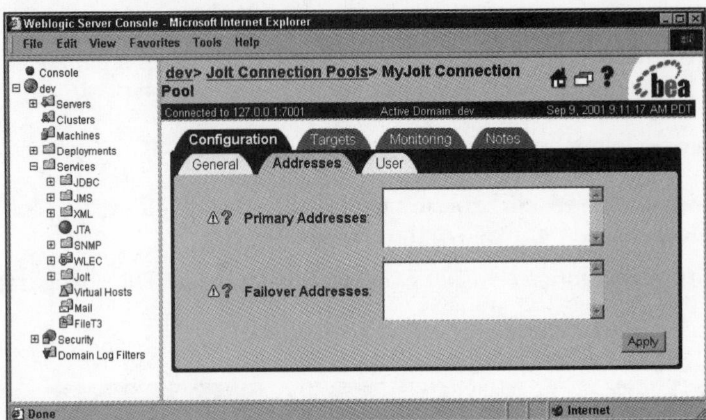

Figure 23-48: Configuring addresses for the Jolt connection pool

6. Enter primary and failover connection addresses for the Tuxedo domain. Failover addresses are optional. The format for each address is `//hostname:port`; for example, `//tuxedo.zeeware.com:1024`.
7. Click Apply.
8. Click the User tab. These fields must be set if you enabled the WebLogic security context on the General page. The user must be a known BEA Tuxedo domain user; provide valid entries for User Name, User Role, User Password, and Application Password, as described in Figure 23-46.
9. Click Apply.
10. Click the Targets tab, and move the WebLogic servers and/or clusters for which you would like to activate the Jolt connection pool into the Chosen list. Click Apply.

Virtual hosts

Virtual hosts are host names that WebLogic servers or clusters respond to. They allow you to have different Web applications respond to different host names, even if those applications are deployed on the same physical hardware. A retail banking application, for example, might respond to `www.onlinebanking.com`, while a stock trading application might respond to `www.onlinetrading.com`. The virtual host configuration screens allow you to define host names and map them to WebLogic Web applications.

Follow these steps to configure a new virtual host:

1. In the domain tree, click the Virtual Hosts node.
2. The right side of the console displays all existing virtual hosts for this server. Click the Configure a New Virtual Host link at the top. Figure 23-49 shows the resulting configuration page with its default values.

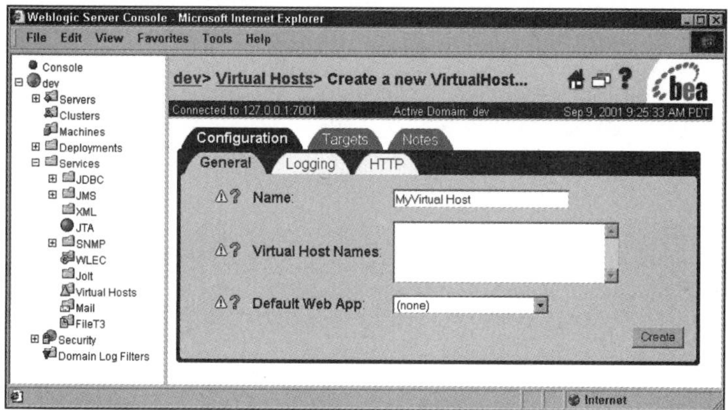

Figure 23-49: Configuring a new virtual host

3. The entries on this page are as follows:

   Name: The administrative name of the virtual host. This name must be unique within the WebLogic domain.

   Virtual Host Names: Enter one or more virtual host names for the application, one per line. Example: `www.onlinebanking.com`.

   Default Web App: Choose a deployed Web application from this list that will be invoked when the virtual host name is entered.

4. Click Create.

5. Enter the data for the Logging and HTTP tabs as you would for a normal WebLogic Server deployment. These configuration steps were described earlier in this chapter.

6. Click the Targets tab, and move the WebLogic servers and/or clusters for which you would like to activate the virtual host into the Chosen list. Click Apply.

Mail

This node is used to configure JavaMail sessions.

For more information on configuring mail, see Chapter 10.

File T3

File T3 allows WebLogic Server to create high-speed client access to native operating system files. The API extends the lowest common denominator Java classes (`java.io.InputStream`, `java.io.OutputStream`), thus allowing for seamless integration with a preexisting code base. In several ways, WebLogic file services provide superior network performance compared with the standard Java implementation:

✦ Data is transmitted in buffers whose size is independent of the request that was sent. Thus, clients can send several small requests and not affect performance.

✦ Read-ahead buffering allows the WebLogic server to load a buffer of data before it is actively processed by the application.

✦ Write-behind buffering allows the WebLogic application to write to a buffer beyond what has been flushed to disk. While the application writes to a buffer, other buffers are being written to disk. A flush operation blocks on the client until an acknowledgement is sent that all buffers have been written to disk.

Follow these steps to create and assign a File T3:

1. Click the File T3 node in the domain tree. The right side of the console shows all File T3 definitions that exist on WebLogic Server.
2. Click the Configure a New File T3 link. Figure 23-50 shows the resulting configuration page.

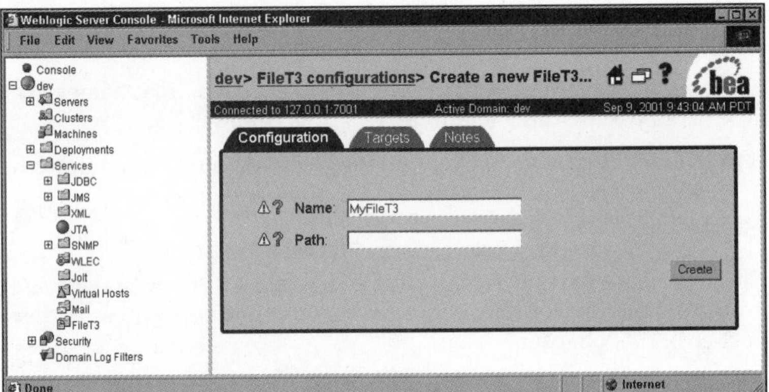

Figure 23-50: Configuring a File T3 entry

3. Enter a unique administrative name for the File T3, and a valid path to the file.
4. Click Create.
5. Click the Targets tab and moved the desired server and or cluster name into the Chosen list.
6. Click Apply.

The new File T3 is now created and deployed.

Security

The configuration steps for security are covered elsewhere in this book. See Chapter 25 for more information.

Domain log filters

Domain log filters allow you to customize the information written to WebLogic Server's domain log. This is a useful feature for troubleshooting problems you may be having with a domain. You are allowed to have one active domain log filter per domain. You can, however, create multiple filters for different purposes, and then swap them in and out depending on the troubleshooting you are trying to perform.

To create a domain log filter, click the Domain Log Filter node at the bottom of the domain tree. Figure 23-51 shows the resulting configuration screen.

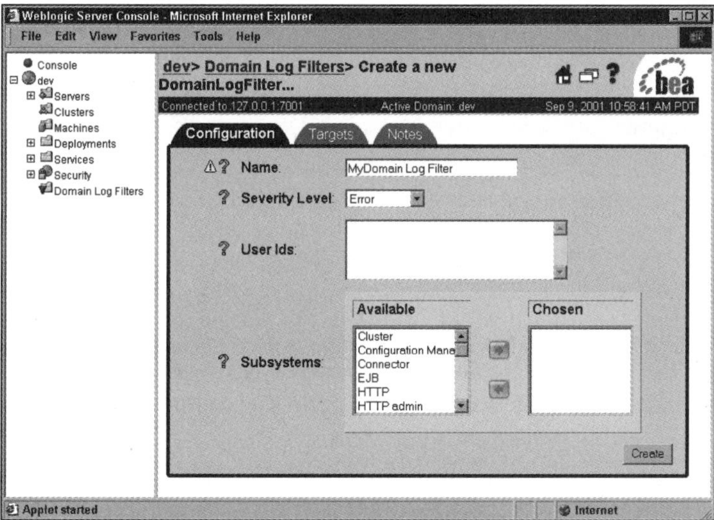

Figure 23-51: Configuring a domain log filter

The entries on this screen are as follows:

- **Name:** The administrative name for the filter. It must be unique within the domain.
- **Severity Level:** Select a level from the drop-down list. Errors of this severity or higher are written to the log.
- **User Ids:** Enter one or more WebLogic user IDs, one per line. This causes logging to happen only for sessions that can be tracked to those IDs.
- **Subsystems:** A list of WebLogic Server's subsystems is given. You can move any number of these subsystems into the Chosen list. Logging occurs only for the subsystems you choose.

Click Create after configuring the filter. Then click the Targets tab, and select the WebLogic servers or clusters in the domain to which you would like to apply the filter.

Administering WebLogic Using Command-Line Tools

WebLogic Server also provides a command-line interface to its administration tools, along with many configuration and runtime management bean (Mbean) properties, for the following reasons:

- ✦ Command scripts for management and administration efficiency.
- ✦ Users who cannot access the administration console via a browser.
- ✦ Users who prefer a command-line interface to a graphical user interface.

To use WebLogic Server's command-line interface, do one of the following:

- ✦ Enable the command-line interface by starting WebLogic Server from its install directory.
- ✦ Enable the command-line interface by adding `Dweblogic.system.home=c:\bea`. `C:\bea` is the default installation location and might be different on your system. It is easiest to add this to `startWeblogic.cmd` file in the `mydomain` directory.

To execute a WebLogic command from the command line, perform these steps:

1. Start WebLogic Server. This is most easily done by running the `startWeblogic.cmd` script.
2. Open a new command window.
3. Run the `setEnv.cmd` script that resides in the `mydomain` directory or add the necessary data to the classpath system environment variable. At the very least, classpath needs `weblogic\lib\weblogic.jar` and `weblogic\lib\weblogic_sp.jar`, where `weblogic` is the location of the WebLogic installation (usually the `bea\wlserver6.1` directory). Any other classes that might be accessed from the command line also need to be added to the classpath variable.
4. Run the WebLogic Server command. These are always in the form `java weblogic.Admin [-url URL] [-username username] [-password password] COMMAND parameters`, where:

   `url` is the URL that is used to access the WebLogic Server. By default, this is `localhost:7001`.

   `username` is a valid user on the WebLogic Server. This parameter is optional and defaults to `guest` if not provided.

   `password` is the password for the username provided. This is also optional.

These commands can be combined into command scripts. The following one-line command script, for example, shuts down the server specified in the `URL` parameter:

```
@rem shutdown the localhost server running on port 7001
java weblogic.Admin -url localhost:7001 -username bible -
password zeeware SHUTDOWN 200 "Server localhost is shutting
down."
```

The following debug script pings the WebLogic server to see if it is still up, and then prints several pieces of information to the command screen:

```
@rem Ping the WebLogic Server to see if it is still running
java weblogic.Admin -url localhost:7001 -username bible -
password zeeware PING 10

@rem print out the WebLogic Server JNDI binding list for the
@rem weblogic context
java weblogic.Admin -url localhost:7001 -username bible -
password zeeware LIST weblogic

@rem dump the server threads to the console
java weblogic.Admin -url localhost:7001 -username bible -
password zeeware THREAD_DUMP

@rem print out the server logs contents for 10 AM till 2 PM
@rem on August 1 2001.
java weblogic.Admin -url localhost:7001 -username bible -
password zeeware SERVERLOG "2001/08/01 10:00" "2001/08/01
14:00"
```

Most common administration and configuration duties can be performed from the command line. But coverage of all of the commands and their parameters is beyond the scope of this chapter. For more information on available command-line commands, see the WebLogic Documentation at `http://e-docs.bea.com/wls/docs61/adminguide/cli.html`.

Summary

Administering and configuring WebLogic Server is made considerably easier with the WebLogic Server console. The console provides a user-friendly GUI that eliminates the need for direct editing of XML configuration documents. This prevents validation errors that can occur when users are forced to edit XML documents. For those who prefer command-line tools to GUI tools, WebLogic Server has extensive command-line support. Most major configuration and administration operations can be performed form the command line. Common administration tasks can thus be automated by using scripts that contain these commands. Because of these two powerful features, administering a WebLogic Server is a relatively simple task.

✦ ✦ ✦

CHAPTER 24

Working with WebLogic Clusters

✦ ✦ ✦ ✦

In This Chapter

Building a simple cluster

Accessing a cluster through an HTTP proxy

Deploying a Web application to a cluster

Testing a clustered Web application

Session state persistence strategies

Clusters and J2EE services

Clustering of RMI objects and EJBs

✦ ✦ ✦ ✦

Have you ever found yourself with so much work to do that you wish you could clone yourself and delegate some of the work to the clone? Or maybe you've fallen ill with an important deadline looming, and you wish you had a clone that could finish the job while you recover. This kind of "cloning" is what WebLogic clusters are all about, except that clusters contain clones of WebLogic Servers, not people. A WebLogic cluster is a group of WebLogic servers working together to help your applications withstand heavier workloads and to continue functioning in the event of server failures.

Servers in a cluster cooperate in two ways. First, they share the workload of responding to incoming requests, allowing greater numbers of requests to be handled. This feature is typically called *load balancing*. Second, they cover for each other, so if one server "falls ill," the other servers in the cluster can instantly and transparently assume its workload, resulting in no service disruption to users. This is commonly called *failover*.

Load balancing and failover imply *scalability* and *availability*, and you sometimes hear the terms used interchangeably in discussions about clusters. Scalability is an application's capability to handle any number of users with no appreciable degradation in performance, and clusters provide this by distributing the workload across multiple servers. If traffic increases, simply add more servers to the cluster. Availability is an application's capability to "be there" for the user, even in the face of hardware or network failures. Clusters provide this through their failover capability.

Clustering is a simple concept, but it can be quite complicated in practice. One issue is that clusters can be designed lots of different ways, with some approaches working better than others for various types of applications. Another issue is that you must deal with a few gotchas when building even the simplest clusters, due to practical realities and limitations inherent in the J2EE architecture and computer networks.

BEA's documentation on clusters, which you can find online at `http://edocs.bea.com/wls/docs61/adminguide/config.html#1008419`, is essential reading and is especially strong at explaining cluster design strategies and their networking implications. I'm not going to waste paper by regurgitating that information here. What's missing from the documentation, however, is a concise, step-by-step description of how to set up a cluster and verify that it's functioning correctly. Nothing will solidify your understanding of clusters more than actually building a cluster and watching it work. Therefore, in this chapter I walk you through the process of building a simple, two-server cluster that is accessed through a third WebLogic Server instance acting as a proxy. I also show you how to deploy a Web application to this cluster, and I demonstrate how HTTP session replication works even in the face of server failures. Toward the end of the chapter I give you a brief overview of how J2EE services such as JDBC and JMS behave in clusters, and I close by explaining the clustering implications behind RMI objects and EJBs.

By the time you finish reading this chapter, you will have the hands-on ability to deploy a session-based Web application to a simple WebLogic cluster. This will give you a strong foundation of knowledge and experience for building clusters of arbitrary complexity, and designing applications to leverage their power.

Building a Simple Cluster

Probably the best way to learn about clusters is to build one. In this section, I demonstrate how to build a two-server WebLogic cluster, deployed on three physical machines. This is the simplest WebLogic cluster possible, and understanding how to build such a simple cluster makes it easier to work with more complex clustering arrangements.

Designing the cluster topology

A two-server WebLogic cluster actually requires three WebLogic instances: one for each participant in the cluster, and one to be the administration point for the cluster. The latter server is configured as a WebLogic administration server, and the cluster participants (also called *nodes*) are configured as managed servers that "belong" to the administration server. This arrangement is illustrated in Figure 24-1.

Administration and managed servers are explained in Chapter 4.

The administration server cannot participate in the cluster. This makes sense if you think about it — if the administration server belonged to the cluster, it would have to be a managed server as well, and WebLogic does not permit this.

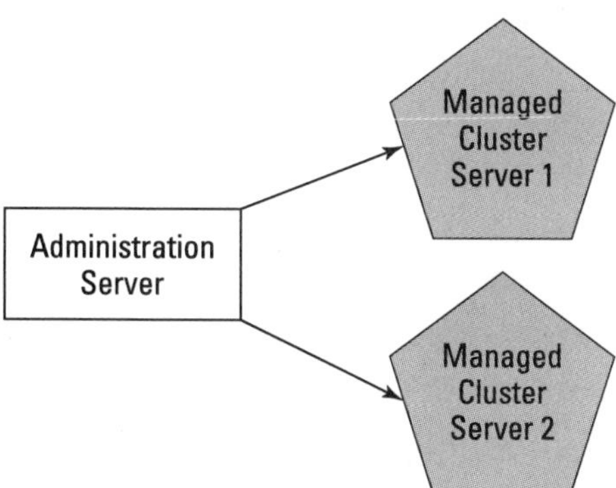

Figure 24-1: Administration and managed servers in a WebLogic cluster

The administration server, however, can still perform a useful role when it's not being used to manage the cluster: It can be used as an HTTP proxy to the servers in the cluster, at least for development purposes. I'll get back to that a little later in the chapter, in the section "Accessing a Cluster through an HTTP Proxy."

The machines themselves must be configured on the network according to a few simple rules:

1. Each machine must have a static IP address. Machines participating in clusters must not have their IP addresses assigned dynamically with DHCP or any other method. Otherwise, the participants in the cluster will suddenly be unable to communicate with each other if the addresses change.
2. All machines participating in a cluster must be on the same local area network and must be reachable by IP multicast. Although not a requirement, it is best if the machines are on the same subnet as well. This greatly simplifies troubleshooting and eliminates the possibility that you will have to reconfigure bridges or routers to support IP multicast.
3. All machines participating in the cluster must be running the same version of WebLogic Server. Note, however, that the machines can be running different operating systems, as long as those operating systems are supported by WebLogic.

Figure 24-2 shows the cluster from Figure 24-1 assigned to specific machines on my network. I'm running the administration server on a laptop called Vaio, and I'm running both managed servers on a multihomed server called Prosignia. (A *multihomed* server is simply a single computer with a network interface card mapped to multiple IP addresses. Multihomed servers are great for authors working from home with limited hardware.)

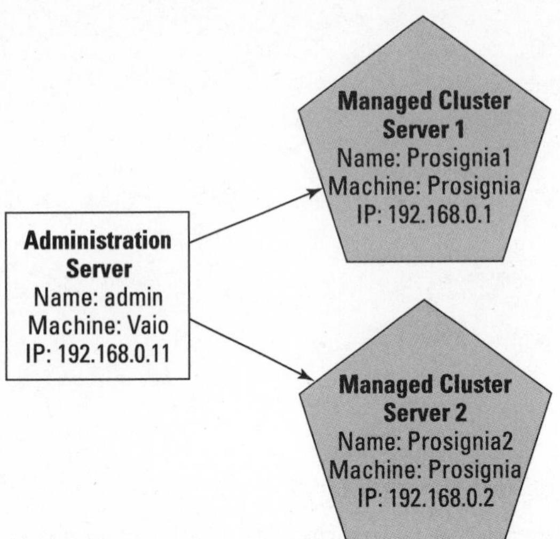

Figure 24-2: A cluster mapped to specific machines on the network

Creating the cluster

To create a cluster like this, follow these steps:

1. Install identical versions of WebLogic Server on each of the three machines.

   The domain names you assign don't matter, and they don't even have to match. The important thing is that you install a functional WebLogic runtime environment on each machine, because server and domain properties for the cluster will be established in startup scripts. I installed the administration server as described in Chapter 4; its domain name is `dev`, and the server name is `admin`. On the cluster machines, I performed default WebLogic installations. The domain names on both boxes are `myDomain`, and the server names are `myServer`.

2. On the administration server, define machine names for the server hardware participating in the cluster. Do this by choosing *<Domain>* ➪ Machines ➪ Configure a New Machine in the WebLogic Console.

   For my installation, I defined two machine names: Vaio and Prosignia. Note that Prosignia still qualifies as a single machine, even though it has multiple IP addresses. This is because all instances of WebLogic Server running on that machine will execute within the same JVM, which is what machine names are really designed to track.

3. Create server entries for the clustered servers. This is done in the WebLogic Console by choosing Domain ➪ Servers ➪ Configure a New Server. Figure 24-3 shows the configuration screens for both of my clustered servers.

The only differences are their names and listen addresses. *The listen ports must be the same.* Because I don't have DNS running on my network, I'm using IP addresses instead of host names and DNS entries on the configuration screens.

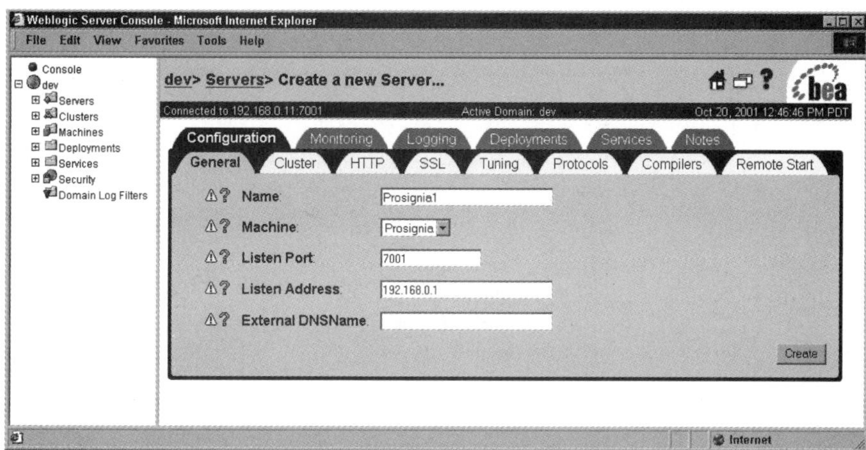

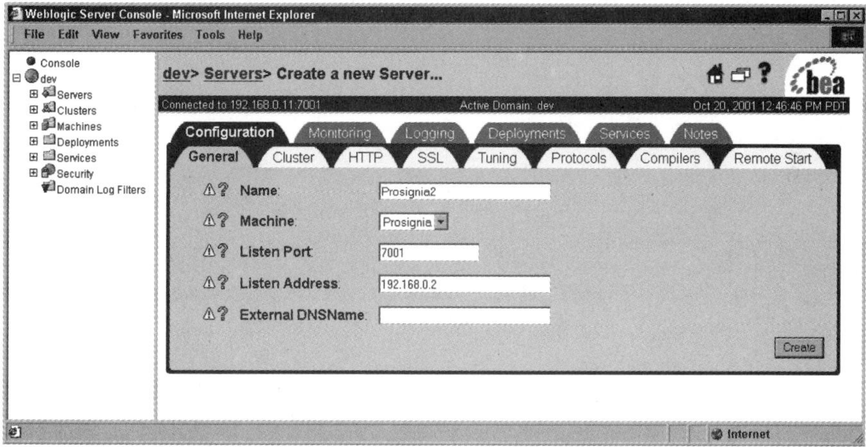

Figure 24-3: Configuring WebLogic Server instances for the cluster

4. Define the cluster by choosing *<Domain>* ⇨ Clusters ⇨ Configure a New Cluster. Figure 24-4 shows the settings for my cluster in the WebLogic Console.

   Because I'm using IP addresses instead of DNS, I enter a comma-separated list of the IP addresses to be used by servers in the cluster. If I were using DNS, I could map a single DNS name to all these addresses and then use the name in the Console instead. I could also enter a comma-separated list of my servers' DNS names.

The default load algorithm is `round-robin`, which means that requests made to the cluster are distributed among the cluster members in alternating fashion. Other options are `weight-based`, in which requests are distributed according to numeric weights you assign to each server, and `random`, which is self-explanatory. I chose `round-robin` for my cluster, because all my participating machines/servers are equal in terms of power and performance.

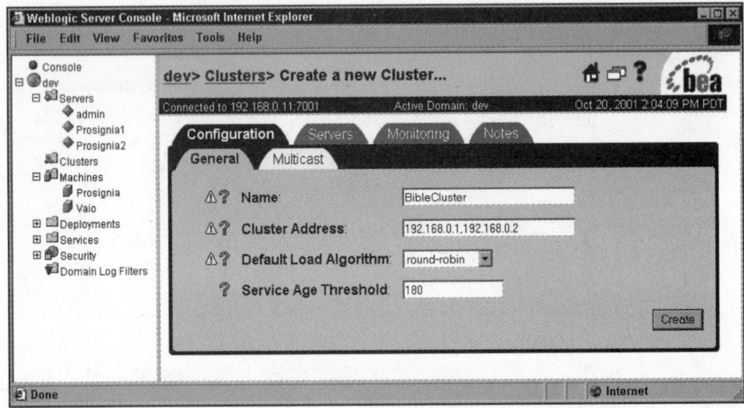

Figure 24-4: Defining a cluster in the WebLogic Console

After creating the cluster, use the Servers tab to assign servers to the cluster, as shown in Figure 24-5.

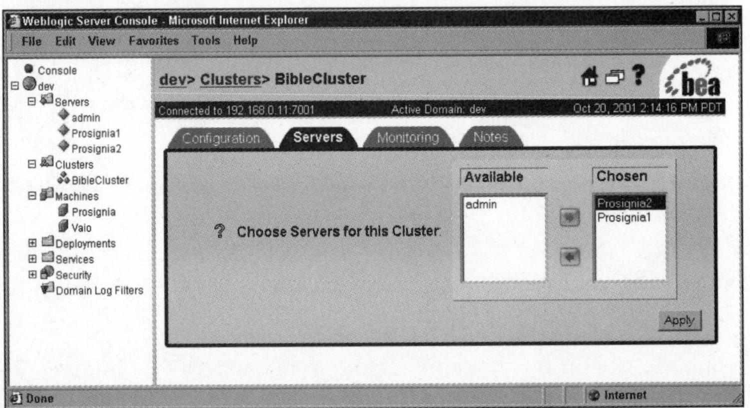

Figure 24-5: Assigning WebLogic Server instances to the cluster

Creating a cluster in the WebLogic Console has no effect on the target machines or servers unless managed WebLogic instances are up and running on the IP addresses and ports that you've specified for the cluster.

5. Create managed WebLogic Server instances on the target machines.

   To do so, I created a directory called `dev` in the `/bea/wlserver6.1/config` directory of my Prosignia machine (the directory name can be whatever you want), and I created an empty applications directory within this directory, as explained in Chapter 4. I also pasted two copies of `/bea/wlserver6.1/config/myDomain/startManagedWebLogic.cmd` into this directory. I renamed these command scripts `StartProsignia1.cmd` and `StartProsignia2.cmd`, as shown in Figure 24-6.

   WebLogic has no magic command for starting a cluster. Instead, you must start each participating server separately, and it will join the cluster on its own. The usual sequence is to start the administration server first, then the managed servers. You can do this using startup scripts or Node Manager; in this chapter I use startup scripts.

See the WebLogic Administration Guide for more information about using Node Manager.

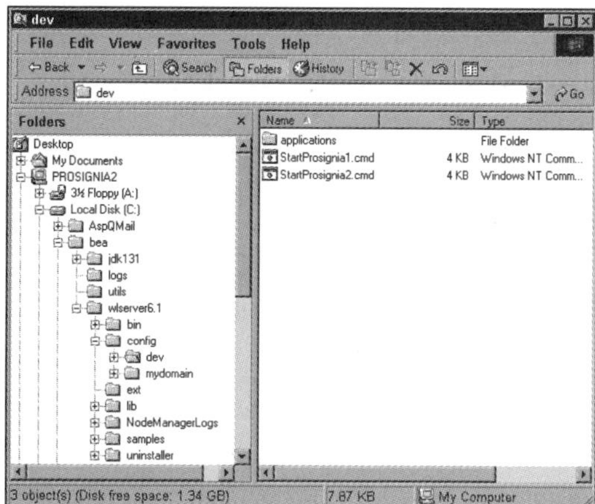

Figure 24-6: Creating directories and startup scripts for managed WebLogic Server instances in a cluster

Listing 24-1 shows the contents of `StartProsignia1.cmd`. This script starts up a managed WebLogic Server in Development mode. After setting the path to the JDK and checking that the script is being run from the proper directory, the script sets the execution parameters for the server instance. It assigns it to the `dev` domain and gives it a name equal to one of the two server names I defined for the cluster (`Prosignia1` or `Prosignia2`). The `ADMIN_URL` parameter is especially important: It tells this managed server where its administration server lives, so it can establish communications with that server. Finally, the script starts the server.

Listing 24-1: StartProsignia1.cmd, a command script for starting a managed WebLogic Server instance

```
@echo off
SETLOCAL
cd ..\..

set JAVA_HOME=C:\bea\jdk131

if not exist lib\weblogic.jar goto wrongplace
goto checkJDK

:wrongplace
echo startManagedWebLogic.cmd must be run from the config\dev
directory. 1>&2
goto finish

:checkJDK
if exist "%JAVA_HOME%/bin/javac.exe" goto setServerInfo
goto finish

:setServerInfo
set WEBLOGIC_DOMAIN=dev
set SERVER_NAME=Prosignia1
set ADMIN_URL=http://192.168.0.11:7001
set PATH=.\bin;%PATH%
set CLASSPATH=.;.\lib\weblogic_sp.jar;.\lib\weblogic.jar
set WLS_PW=password
set STARTMODE=false

echo on
"%JAVA_HOME%\bin\java" -hotspot -ms64m -mx64m -classpath
%CLASSPATH% -Dweblogic.Domain=%WEBLOGIC_DOMAIN% -
Dbea.home="C:\bea" -Dweblogic.management.password=%WLS_PW%
-Dweblogic.ProductionModeEnabled=%STARTMODE% -
Dweblogic.Name=%SERVER_NAME%
-Dweblogic.management.server=%ADMIN_URL% "-
Djava.security.policy==C:\bea\wlserver6.1/lib/weblogic.policy"
weblogic.Server
goto finish

:finish
cd config\dev
ENDLOCAL
```

`StartProsignia2.cmd` is identical to `StartProsignia1.cmd`, except `SERVER_NAME` is set to `Prosignia2`. Of course, you could write a single script that accepts values for SERVER_NAME and ADMIN_URL from the command line, but I'll leave that as an exercise for the reader (I've been wanting to write that phrase ever since I saw it in one of my electrical engineering textbooks in college).

Accessing a Cluster through an HTTP Proxy

At this point, if you start the administration server and the managed servers, you will technically have a cluster in place, but it won't be easy to reach for your clients. Think about it: If you were to deploy a Web application to the cluster, what URL would you give clients to point them to the application? Which IP address should it resolve to?

You have many ways to solve this problem, some of which I discuss later in this chapter. But one approach is to insert an *HTTP proxy* between clients and the cluster. This server receives requests from clients and dispatches them to servers in the cluster according to the load-balancing algorithm specified in Step 4 of the preceding section. The proxy can either be a WebLogic 6.1 server with the HttpClusterServlet installed, or a third-party HTTP server with the WebLogic Proxy plug-in installed. Figure 24-7 illustrates these options.

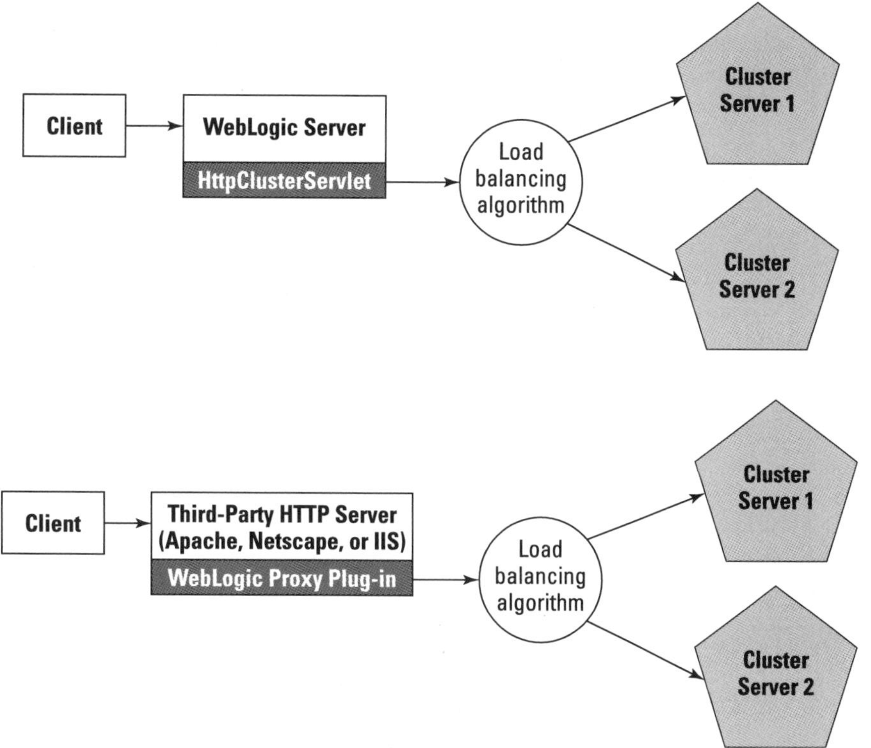

Figure 24-7: HTTP proxy server configurations for WebLogic clusters

For this example, I will install the `HttpClusterServlet` into my `admin` server and use it as an HTTP proxy for my cluster.

Configuring your administration server to perform double duty as an HTTP proxy is fine for development, but in production you will probably want your HTTP proxy server(s) to be separate from your administration server. I discuss different ways of doing this later in this chapter.

To install the `HttpClusterServlet` on the administration server, follow these steps:

1. Open the WebLogic Console for the administration server.
2. The `HttpClusterServlet` must be attached to a default Web application for the server. Therefore, attach it to `DefaultWebApp`, which is the default Web application for all freshly installed WebLogic servers. To do so, choose *<Domain>* ⇨ Deployments ⇨ Web Applications ⇨ DefaultWebApp, and then click the Edit Web Application Descriptor link on the right side of the screen.
3. Choose Servlets ⇨ Configure a New Servlet. Set Servlet Name to `HttpClusterServlet` and Servlet Class to `weblogic.servlet.internal.HttpClusterServlet`, as shown in Figure 24-8. Click Create.

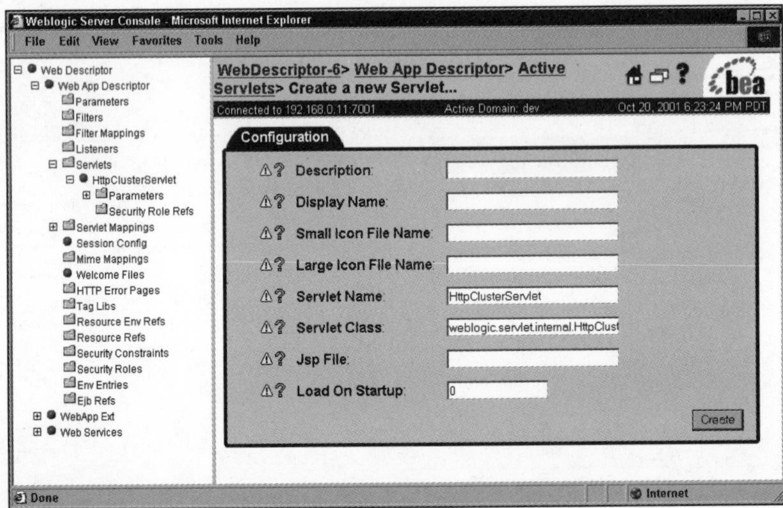

Figure 24-8: Configuring HttpClusterServlet

4. Expand the HttpClusterServlet node you just created. Click Parameters, and then click Configure a New Parameter. Set Param Name to defaultServers and Param Value to the IP addresses and ports of the clustered servers, separated by the pipe (|) character. The format for each entry is *<IP address>:<HTTP port>:<HTTPS port>*. For this example, the entry is 192.168.0.1:7001:7002| 192.168.0.2:7001:7002. Click Create.
5. Configure an additional parameter. Its name is DebugConfigInfo, and its value is ON. This allows you to request debugging information from HttpClusterServlet by appending the request parameter ?_WebLogicBridgeConfig to any request. Be sure to turn this parameter OFF for production environments.
6. Click Servlet Mappings, and then click Configure a New Servlet Mapping. Set Servlet to HttpClusterServlet (choose it from the drop-down menu), and set URL pattern to / (forward slash). Click Create. This tells WebLogic to invoke HttpClusterServlet for all servlet requests, which is necessary for it to function correctly.
7. Add three more servlet mappings for HttpClusterServlet: *.htm, *.html, and *.jsp. This ensures that HttpClusterServlet is invoked for all requests for HTML files and JSPs.
8. **Important!** Click the Web Descriptor node at the top left corner of the screen, and then click the Validate button on the right. You should get the message Validation was successful. Click the Web Descriptor node again, and then click the Persist button. *You must do this, or all the changes you made in this window will be lost!*

If, for some reason, validation was not successful, persist the changes, then shut down the administration server and your cluster. Use a text editor to manually repair the domain's config.xml file on the administration server. If you're not an XML expert, you'll need to find someone who is, as the only other way to repair the file is to throw it away and let WebLogic create a new, empty one.

Figure 24-9 shows the deployment descriptor editor after making the changes I just described. Note the entries under HttpClusterServlet and ServletMappings in the domain tree on the left side of the figure.

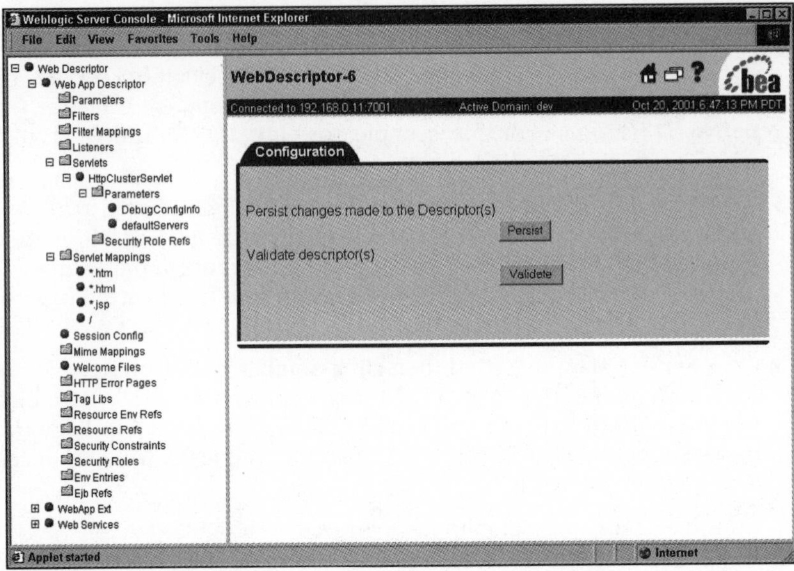

Figure 24-9: The deployment descriptor editor showing the completed configuration of HttpClusterServlet, along with its parameters and servlet mappings

Deploying a Web Application to the Cluster

Now that the pieces of the cluster are in place, it's time to deploy a Web application to the cluster to see how everything works. I will deploy `BibleServlets`, the servlet example I created in Chapter 11 (you may want to refer to Chapter 11 as you read this to understand the functioning of the application). Recall that `BibleServlets` makes extensive use of HTTP sessions and the servlet context; deploying such an application gives you a chance to see how sessions and context are handled by the cluster.

`BibleServlets` is already deployed to my administration server, so all I need to do is remove it from that server and deploy it to the cluster. Here's how to do it:

1. Start the administration server and open the WebLogic Console against it.
2. On the Prosignia machine, run the startup scripts for the managed servers, `StartProsignia1.cmd` and `StartProsignia2.cmd`. Figure 24-10 shows the command window after `Prosignia1` has started (the command window for `Prosignia2` is identical, with the exception of the server name and IP address).

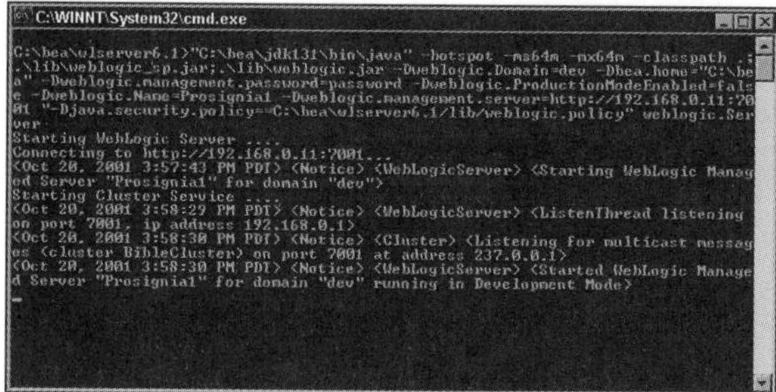

Figure 24-10: The WebLogic command window for the Prosignia1 clustered server

There are several things to notice about this window — it's not your typical WebLogic startup sequence. First, right after the startup begins, you see this line:

```
Connecting to http://192.168.0.11:7001...
```

Here you see the managed server attempting to contact its administration server in order to receive the latest configuration information and deployments. If contact cannot be made, the managed server won't start; without an administration server, the managed server cannot function.

Next you see an entry indicating the server is starting as a managed server called `Prosignia1` in the domain `dev`.

After that, the cluster service attempts to start. If the server's IP address and multicast address match those expected by the administration server, the cluster service will start successfully.

Finally, you see messages indicating that the cluster service is listening on the appointed IP addresses and ports, and that the WebLogic managed server is up and running under its given name and domain. Success!

3. Return to the WebLogic Console on the administration server. Here you can deploy a Web application to the cluster, just as you would to a single WebLogic server instance. But first, it might be wise to verify that the administration server is aware of the cluster nodes. To do so, choose *<Domain>* ➪ Servers, and click a server name that is a node in the cluster. On the right side of the display, click the Monitoring tab. Figure 24-11 shows the display for `Prosignia1`, the first node in my cluster. An indication that the server is running means that the administration server is indeed aware of its existence on the network.

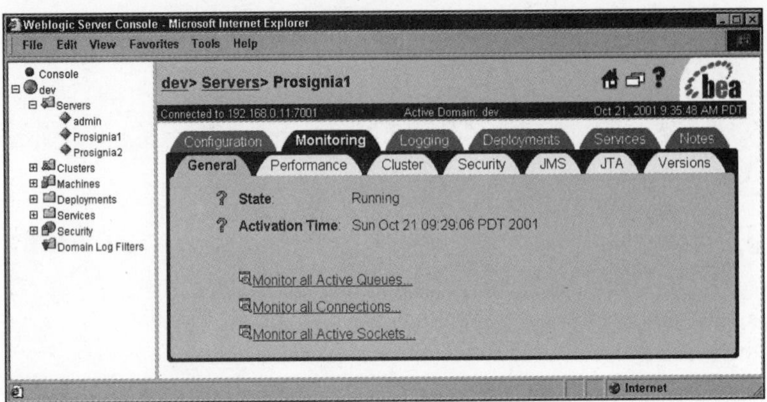

Figure 24-11: Using the WebLogic Console to verify that a cluster node is running

4. To deploy a Web application to the cluster, you can either install and deploy a new application (following the steps given in Chapter 11), or you can redeploy an existing application. Since `BibleServlets` is already deployed on my administration server, I'll perform the latter operation by choosing *<Domain>* ➪ Deployments ➪ Web Applications ➪ BibleServlets, and then clicking the Targets tab. Figure 24-12 shows the initial state of my deployment: `BibleServlets` is already deployed to the admin server.

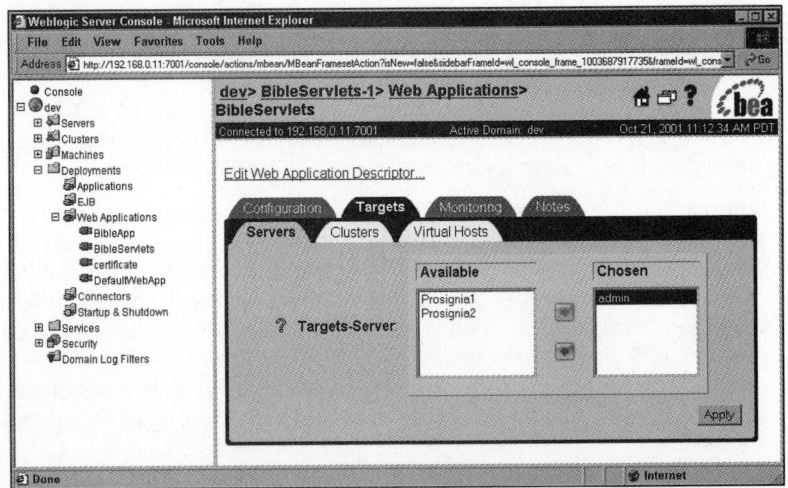

Figure 24-12: BibleServlets is already deployed on the admin server

I remove admin from the Chosen list and then click Apply. Figure 24-13 shows the result.

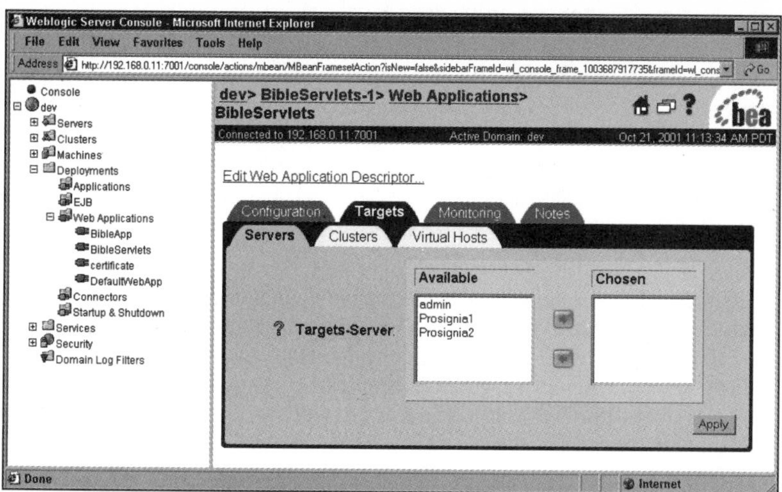

Figure 24-13: Now BibleServlets is not deployed to any server

Next, click the Clusters tab, and move `BibleCluster` from the Available list to the Chosen list, as shown in Figure 24-14. Click Apply.

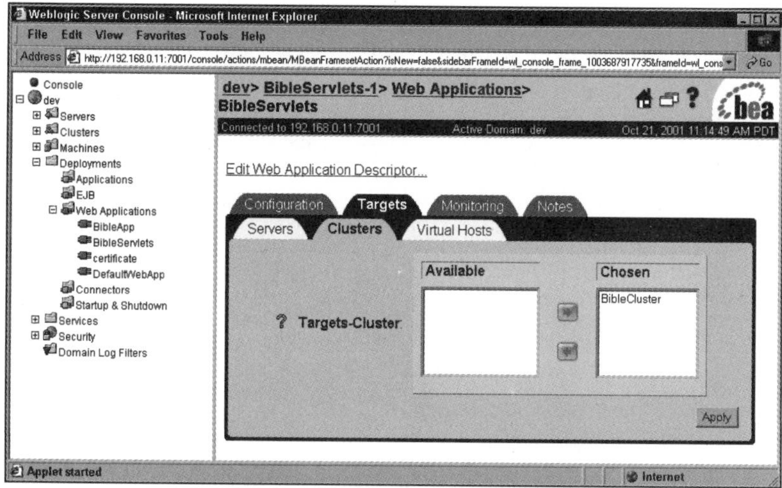

Figure 24-14: BibleServlets is now deployed to BibleCluster

When you click Apply, WebLogic Server copies the Web application (either its exploded directory format or its `.war` file, depending on what you've installed) to every server in the cluster. It also sets up the runtime infrastructure to support clustered execution of the application. Your servers will chug along for a few moments while this happens.

5. The final step is to configure session replication for the application. Because `BibleServlets`'s execution relies heavily on session management, it's a good idea to configure the cluster to replicate session state, so if one server fails, another server can pick up the user's session data. To better understand what I mean, imagine a shopping cart application that stores the user's purchases in the session. If the clustered server maintaining the session fails, the user is automatically routed to another server in the cluster, but without session replication, the contents of their shopping cart are lost. Session replication prevents this malady.

   Session state is maintained by a *primary cluster node,* which is the node to which the user initially connected. It is replicated to a *secondary node,* which is either the next node in round-robin sequence or the highest-ranked node as determined by the replication groups in effect for the cluster. (For more information about configuring replication groups, see the WebLogic documentation.)

   In order to replicate session state, you must somehow persist the state so it is available to the secondary node, in case the primary node fails. WebLogic Server provides five types of persistence for session state: *none, memory-based, file-based, JDBC-based,* and *cookie-based.* In this example, I will configure memory-based persistence.

   Note

   I discuss the pros and cons of the various persistence types later in this chapter.

   You specify the type of persistence you want in the `weblogic.xml` deployment descriptor for the application. You can use the WebLogic Console to make this change. To configure in-memory replication for `BibleServlets`, choose <*Domain*> ➪ Deployments ➪ Web Applications ➪ BibleServlets, and then click Edit Web Application Descriptor on the right side of the screen. In the secondary browser that appears, choose Web Descriptor ➪ WebApp Ext ➪ Session Descriptor. On the right side of the screen, use the drop-down menu to set Persistent Store Type to `replicated`, and then click Apply. Figure 24-15 shows the resulting display.

   Don't be fooled into selecting `memory` if you want in-memory replication—the correct choice is `replicated`. Selecting `memory` is equivalent to selecting none—the user's session is maintained on the node they are interacting with, but it is not persisted in any way, so it cannot be picked up by the other nodes if the user's node fails.

6. Stop and restart the administration server and the cluster nodes (this is good practice any time you change a deployment descriptor for a Web application or an EJB component).

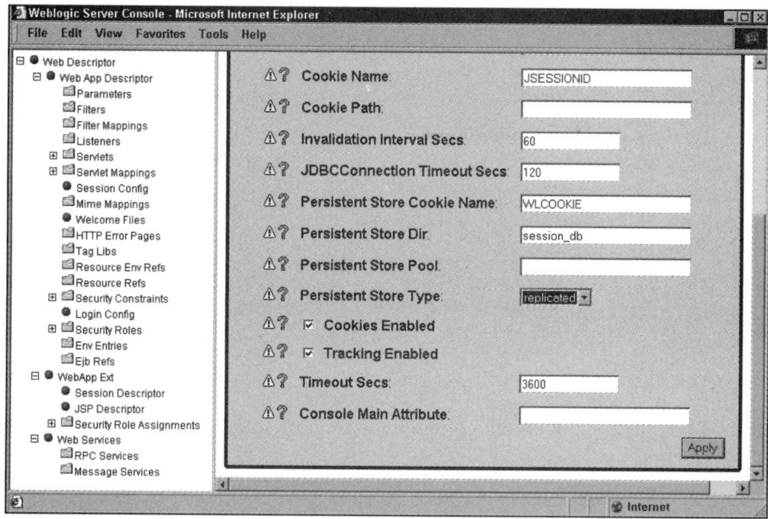

Figure 24-15: Configuring in-memory session state persistence for BibleServlets

Testing a Clustered Web Application

With the cluster up and running again, it's time to test the application by bringing it up in a Web browser. On my system, which has no DNS, I must navigate to the IP address and port of my proxy server. The full URL to `BibleServlets` on my system is

```
http://192.168.0.11:7001/BibleServlets
```

This brings up the home page for `BibleServlets`, as shown in Figure 24-16. I have great confidence that my proxy server and cluster are working. Why? Because `BibleServlets` is not physically deployed to my proxy server, so the request must have been forwarded to one of the servers in my cluster. Pretty cool, huh?

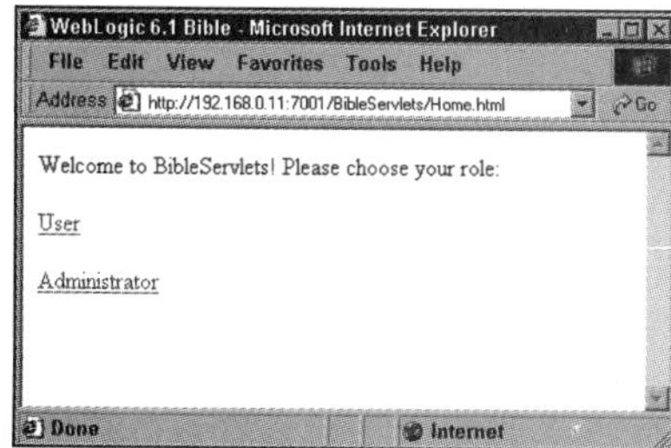

Figure 24-16: Navigating to the clustered version of BibleServlets

I tested this application by connecting two users and one administrator, and then I observed the application's behavior when I brought down and restarted nodes in the cluster. The results are enlightening, especially if you've never worked with clusters before.

First, I found a bug in the `BibleServlets` code that prevented it from working properly in a clustered environment. The problem was that user sessions were being created and maintained by `ApplicationServlet`, but changes in session state weren't being picked up by `AdminServlet`. In the application, this was reflected by individual users' pages properly showing which page they were on, but the administrator's page always showing that the user was on page 1. Why on earth would this happen?

Recall that `ApplicationServlet` tracks session state in a `Hashtable`, which it stores in the `HttpSession`. In my code, I was updating the `Hashtable` with the new page number every time the user switched pages, but I wasn't updating the session with a call to `setAttribute()` after making these changes. This works fine in a single-server application, but it fails in a cluster because WebLogic's session replication engine has no way of knowing that I changed the `Hashtable`, and therefore the changes don't get replicated. To fix this, simply be sure to call `setAttribute()` after every change to the session, and this will trigger replication of the session data to the other nodes.

The bold text in Listing 24-2 shows additions I made to the body of `ApplicationServlet` to fix this bug. For good measure, I added calls to `setAttribute()` for the servlet context as well.

Listing 24-2: Fixing ApplicationServlet so it works in the cluster

```
// Returning user. Retrieve their state from the session.
sessionInfo = (Hashtable)
  session.getAttribute("sessionInfo");
Integer pageNumber = (Integer)sessionInfo.get("pageNumber");
int nextPage = pageNumber.intValue();
pageNumber = null;
// Read the query string to determine the user's desired
// action. Update their state in the session accordingly.
if (request.getParameter("action").equals("next")) {
  // Go to the next page. Wrap around to the
  // first page after passing the last page.
  nextPage++;
  if (nextPage > LAST_PAGE) {
    nextPage = FIRST_PAGE;
  }
  sessionInfo.put("pageNumber", new Integer(nextPage));
  session.setAttribute("sessionInfo", sessionInfo);
```

```
      ctx.setAttribute("session_" + userName, sessionInfo);
    } else if (request.getParameter("action").equals("previous")) {
      // Go to the previous page. Wrap around to the last page
      // after passing the first page.
      nextPage--;
      if (nextPage < FIRST_PAGE) {
        nextPage = LAST_PAGE;
      }
      sessionInfo.put("pageNumber", new Integer(nextPage));
      session.setAttribute("sessionInfo", sessionInfo);
      ctx.setAttribute("session_" + userName, sessionInfo);
    } else if (request.getParameter("action").equals("logoff")) {
      ...
    }
```

With these changes in place, I tested the cluster by executing various sequences of steps. These steps involved invoking servlets from multiple clients while stopping and restarting the two nodes in the cluster. Note that the `HttpClusterServlet` and the WebLogic proxy plug-ins always load-balance HTTP sessions using the round-robin algorithm, with cluster nodes being served in the order in which they join the cluster. `Prosignia1` joined my cluster first (because I started it first). With that in mind, here is what happens and why:

1. User A logs into `BibleServlets` and is proxied to `Prosignia1`.
2. User B logs into `BibleServlets` and is proxied to `Prosignia2`.
3. Administrator A logs into `BibleServlets` and is proxied to `Prosignia1`. The only active session showing in the administrator's window is that of user A. But what about user B? Recall that `AdminServlet` uses the servlet context to display this information. Each node in the cluster has its own servlet context, separate from the others, which is why administrator A cannot "see" user B.
4. `Prosignia2` goes down when I shut down its WebLogic instance. User B, however, continues to use the application normally, because the cluster service transparently fails them over to `Prosignia1`.
5. Administrator A refreshes the screen, and now both users appear! This is because when `Prosignia2` fails, the cluster service merges its servlet context with that of `Prosignia1`. It is able to do this because the servlet contexts are replicated along with the sessions — they're just not combined unless a server fails.

I continued to experiment by restarting `Prosignia2` and stopping `Prosignia1`, and then restarting `Prosignia1` and stopping `Prosignia2`. As expected, my three users were able to continue their sessions without interruption, and their session states were accurately preserved. This is the power of clustering.

Session State Persistence Strategies

As I mentioned earlier, HTTP session state (and also session state for stateful session EJBs) can be persisted in five ways:

- **None:** No persistence
- **Memory-based:** Session state is maintained in active memory and replicated to in-memory caches on secondary replication nodes
- **File-based:** Session state is maintained in disk files that are stored in shared directories accessible to all nodes in the cluster
- **JDBC-based:** Session state is maintained in a JDBC-compliant database that is accessed via an associated connection pool created on each node of the cluster
- **Cookie-based:** Session state is maintained in client-side cookies

Each persistence type comes with its own tradeoffs in terms of reliability and performance. With no persistence, reliability is zero but performance is spectacular, because the overhead of persisting data is completely eliminated. Memory-based replication has excellent performance and good reliability, although session state can't survive server restarts or power outages. File-based and JDBC-based replication have mediocre performance but exceptional reliability, because changes to session state are immediately written to disk. Cookie-based replication works OK if users have cookies enabled, but it's useless if they don't.

I suggest you plug your cluster nodes into UPSs and go with memory-based replication. If you're really paranoid, or if your session data is really important enough to warrant the significant performance hit, go with JDBC-based replication. I wouldn't bother with any of the other choices for production systems.

Clusters and J2EE Services

WebLogic clusters affect the way certain J2EE services behave, and you must take this into account if your clustered applications use these services. In this section, I give you an overview of clustering's impact on JNDI, JDBC, and JMS.

Cluster-wide JNDI tree

Recall that the JNDI tree enables you to look up objects and services that reside on a WebLogic server instance. A cluster-wide JNDI tree provides this capability as well, but it lists objects and services that reside on all nodes of a WebLogic cluster.

As you might imagine, WebLogic manages cluster-wide JNDI trees somewhat differently from single-server trees. Each node in a cluster builds and maintains its own local copy of the cluster-wide tree. When the node boots, or if a service is added to the node while it is running, it first binds its services to its local copy of the tree. Then it uses IP multicast to broadcast availability of its clustered services to the other nodes in the cluster, and they add its services to their local copies of the tree. Meanwhile, the newly booted node receives notifications of services residing on the other nodes' trees, and it adds them to its local copy of the tree. The net effect is that all servers in the cluster maintain synchronized copies of the cluster-wide JNDI tree.

Of course, there are exceptions and caveats regarding the behavior of the cluster-wide JNDI tree, and you should study the WebLogic documentation to gain a better understanding of what they are.

Load balancing JDBC connections

WebLogic clusters do not provide failover support for JDBC connections, but you can configure a cluster to provide limited load-balancing support for JDBC connection pools. To configure a cluster this way, simply create identically-named JDBC data sources on each node, but have the data sources point to different connection pools. Figure 24-17 shows such an arrangement.

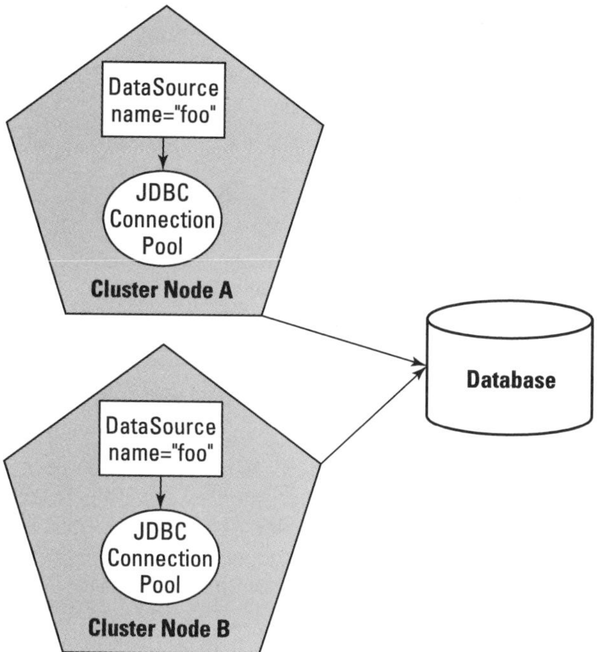

Figure 24-17: Load balancing JDBC connections in a cluster

As with unclustered JDBC, however, WebLogic has no way of knowing whether a pool has available connections or not, so your code may block if it's unlucky enough to execute on a node whose connection pool has run out of connections.

Load balancing JMS connection factories

Clustering support for JMS is similar to that for JDBC. Failover support is not provided for queues and topics, because they are pinned to specific WebLogic instances. But connection factories pointing to the same queues and topics can be deployed on multiple cluster nodes, allowing you to load-balance access to the queues and topics. Figure 24-18 illustrates one way to do this.

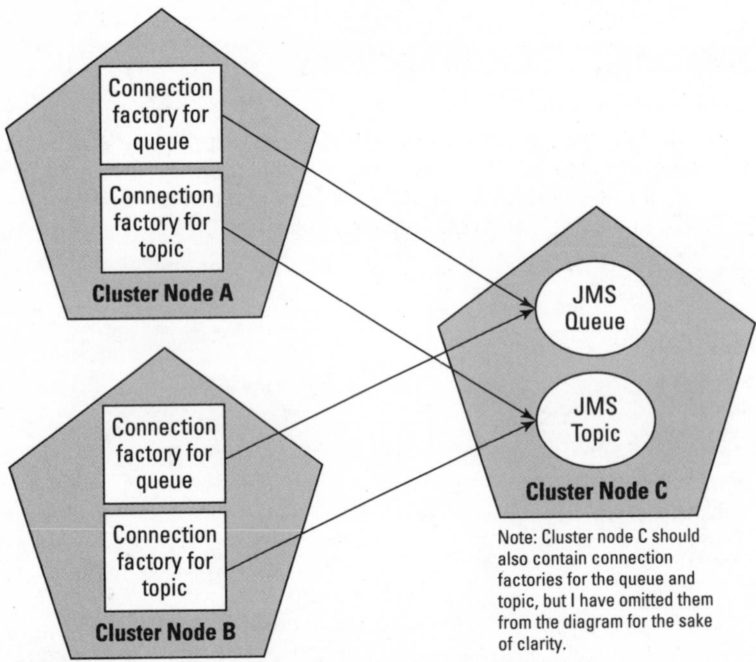

Figure 24-18: Load balancing JMS connection factories

The problem with this approach is that cluster node C becomes a single point of failure; if it goes down, no messages can be delivered. A better option is to create a JMS server on each cluster node, create identical copies of the queues and topics on each node, and then have the connection factory target the cluster. Figure 24-19 shows this arrangement.

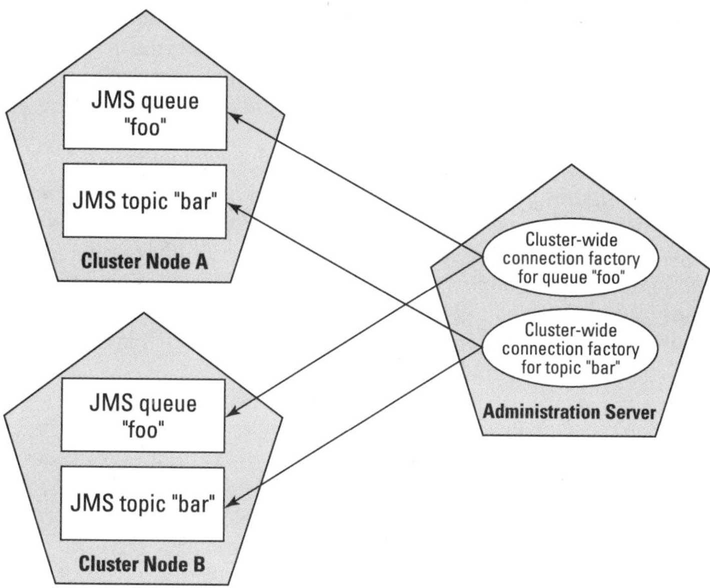

Figure 24-19: Redundant load balancing of JMS connection factories

Clustering of RMI Objects and EJBs

RMI objects and EJBs can be deployed to clusters, and WebLogic Server supports their runtime invocation through the use of *replica-aware stubs*. To calling clients, replica-aware stubs look the same as normal stubs, but they have embedded within them logic for finding all the instances of the objects they represent within the cluster, and also for implementing the load-balancing strategy that is being used by the cluster. Replica-aware stubs also provide failover capability by automatically rerouting calls to different object instances when runtime failures occur.

Generating replica-aware stubs for RMI objects is accomplished by invoking the RMI compiler (`rmic`) with the appropriate command-line options. For EJBs, the EJB compiler (`ejbc`) does this for you automatically if you send it a bean whose deployment descriptor specifies that it is cluster-aware.

When you invoke RMI objects, replica-aware stubs are returned for the local and remote interfaces, which allows load balancing and failover to occur for object lookups *and* method invocations.

For EJBs, replica-aware stubs are returned for all `EJBHome` interfaces. This provides load balancing and failover for EJB lookups. Whether you receive replica-aware stubs for `EJBObject` interfaces depends on the type of the bean. Replica-aware stubs are always returned for the `EJBObject` interfaces of stateless session beans, providing load balancing and failover for bean method invocations. The same applies for stateful session beans, but only if you specify that stateful session replication should be used for the bean. If not, the stub you receive is pinned to whatever bean instance was returned by the `EJBHome`.

Note: The load-balancing algorithm used for stateful EJB session replication is the same one used for HTTP session replication; primary session state is maintained on the node the client connected to, and secondary state on some other node, as determined by the round-robin algorithm or the replication groups in effect. This means the load-balancing logic embedded in replica-aware stubs for stateful session EJBs is different from that in the stubs for stateless session EJBs, which implements the load-balancing algorithm assigned to the cluster.

For entity EJBs, the type of `EJBObject` stub you receive depends on whether the bean is read-only or read/write. If the bean is read-only, you will always receive a replica-aware stub. This stub provides load balancing for method calls, but it does not provide failover capability. Why not? Because entity EJBs are pinned to JDBC connections, for which there is no failover support. For the same reason, `EJBObject` stubs returned for read/write beans are always pinned to a specific bean instance.

Summary

WebLogic clusters are an essential tool for building scalable, fault-tolerant J2EE applications. Although the concepts behind clusters are simple, the mechanics of setting up even a simple cluster are fairly complex, especially when you include the effort required to properly deploy applications in a clustered environment. Clustering requires application designers and developers to rethink everything, from HTTP session management to EJB deployment, and all the J2EE services in between. But the sturdiness of clustered applications, along with the peace-of-mind they offer to overworked developers, makes the effort more than worthwhile.

I hope you made the effort to set up your own cluster while you were reading this chapter. If you did so (and if you succeeded!), you'll have a major advantage when it comes time to build bigger, more complex clusters in your production environment.

✦ ✦ ✦

CHAPTER 25

Managing WebLogic Security

✦ ✦ ✦ ✦

In This Chapter

Configuring the File realm

Configuring the NT realm

Configuring the Unix realm

Configuring the LDAP realm

✦ ✦ ✦ ✦

When working with application servers, such as WebLogic Server, it is important to understand the security features before making a purchasing decision. The security features are responsible for protecting the organization's information and assets, so it is important to understand how to set up and configure these features. The purpose of security is not to understand how EJBs or JSPs work for the sake of understanding how to develop them, but to explore possible holes and crevices where attacks can happen. Some of the best attackers have very limited development skills, but they understand the tools and Application Servers at their disposal and explore every possibility to break into the system. The administrators who test out an enterprise system to find possible ways to attack it or to bring it down should make an effort to be just as clever and dedicated to finding holes and issues.

A test environment should mirror a production environment as much as possible as not to interfere with production systems, and it should be tested against virus makers, homegrown software to log in with the same user's names from multiple places simultaneously. Default passwords and usernames should be tried; you should even try to run a WebLogic example server remotely by using defaults. You should try to reach a certain level of effort to see what the system does based on a security checklist. A security checklist should list all of the things described. The checklist should be updated and a security specialist should always stay in touch with various organizations such as Cypherpunks, `www.cert.org`, `www.cryptography.com`, and `www.counterpane.com` to name a few.

For most organizations, this is a full-time job, where an active participant needs to observe the architecture documents, network and database mappings, and other artifacts to keep the organization vigilant in the proper methods to keep the systems secure. This not only requires someone who understands administration of Application Servers, but protocol and application specifications, such as Simple Network Management Protocol (SNMP) and EJB. An organization may, for example, have issues getting a DMZ in place due to some of the technology that the organization has used in the past, and a person with administration skills might understand the issues, but it would take someone with excellent development skills to offer a rewrite of the software to work around the software issues. Protecting an organization's data and keeping the systems up and running even if attacks are encountered should be a very skilled and diligent job. Doing so in an effective manner requires the cooperation of an entire organization.

Configuring the File Realm

As mentioned before, a security realm is a logical grouping of users, groups, and ACLs. Every resource that is secured in WebLogic Server is secured under a security realm by a single ACL in that security realm. ACLs in WebLogic Server are normally used for administration of WebLogic Server for associating permissions with resources. For a user to access the resource, that user must be defined in the security realm and have permissions to that resource. The default security realm inside the WebLogic Server is the File realm. When the WebLogic Server is first started, the File realm creates users, groups, and ACL objects in the `fileRealm.properties` file. The File realm is designed for use with less than 1,000 users. If more than 1,000 users are needed, then it is suggested that another type of security realm be used. You can set the maximum number of users, groups, and ACLs in the console panel by choosing Security ➪ Configuration ➪ Filerealm Properties. If for any reason the `fileRealm.properties` file gets corrupted or destroyed, all the security information must be reconfigured for WebLogic Server. It is recommended that regular backups be made. The associated `SerializedSystemIni.dat` file must also be backed up. `SerializedSystemIni.dat` and `fileRealm.properties` are located in WebLogic Server's domain configuration directory. If the domain's name is `mydomain`, for example, then it will be located under the subdirectory `bea\wlserver6.0\config\mydomain` (see Figure 25-1).

If your organization has already done development on a WebLogic Server that predates WLS 6.1, the WLS 6.1 comes with a conversion utility to convert the files that need to be updated to be used in WLS 6.1. The conversion program will convert security files, the `weblogic.properties` file, and the `config.xml` file to be used in the WLS 6.1. The `config.xml` file is used to store global information for WebLogic Server 6.1. As shown in Figure 25-2, the convert utility is found in the WebLogic Console.

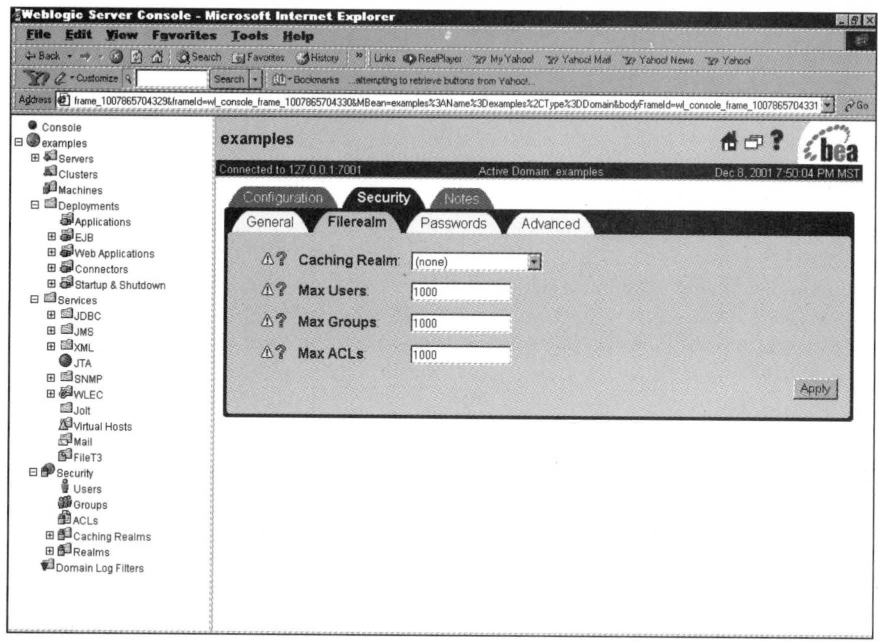

Figure 25-1: File realm maximum users

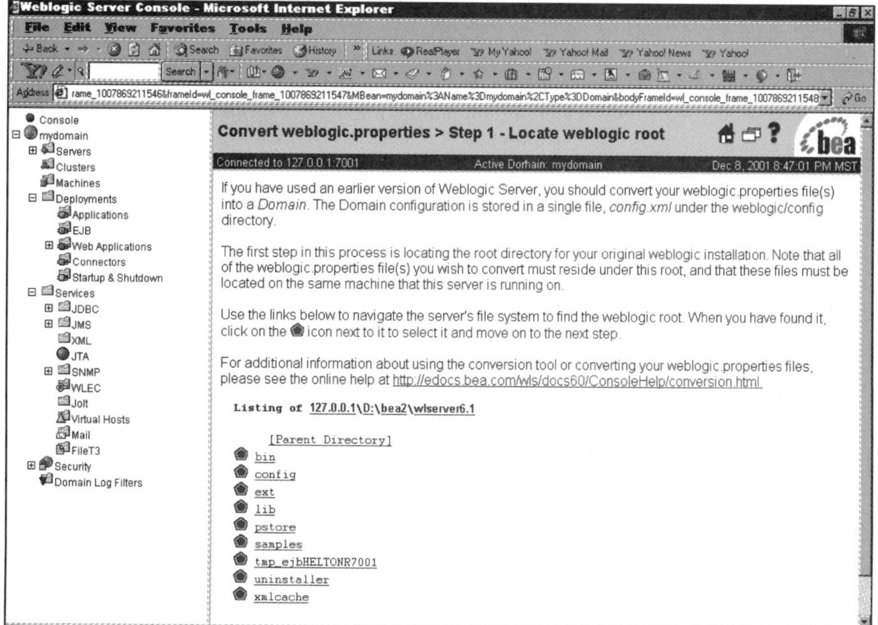

Figure 25-2: WebLogic Server 6.1 conversion from other WebLogic versions

These are just a couple of the configurations that must be maintained to ensure that the security is properly configured. Another configuration is for the password in the WebLogic Console (see Figure 25-3) that will include Minimum Password Length, Lockout Enabled, Lockout Threshold, Lockout Duration, Lockout Reset Duration, and Lockout Cache Size. The Minimum Password Length is the minimum length that the password must be to be considered valid, which is defaulted to 8. The Lockout Enabled requests the locking of a user account when an invalid attempt is made to log in to that account. This field is defaulted to enable. The Lockout Threshold sets the number of failed entries for a user that can be tried to log in to a user account before the account is locked. The Lockout Duration is the number of minutes that a user's account remains inaccessible after being locked in response to several invalid login attempts within the amount of time specified by the Lockout Reset Duration field. The default is 30 minutes. The Lockout Reset Duration is the number of minutes within which valid login attempts must occur in order for the user's account to be locked. The Lockout Cache Size specifies the intended cache size of unused and invalid login attempts.

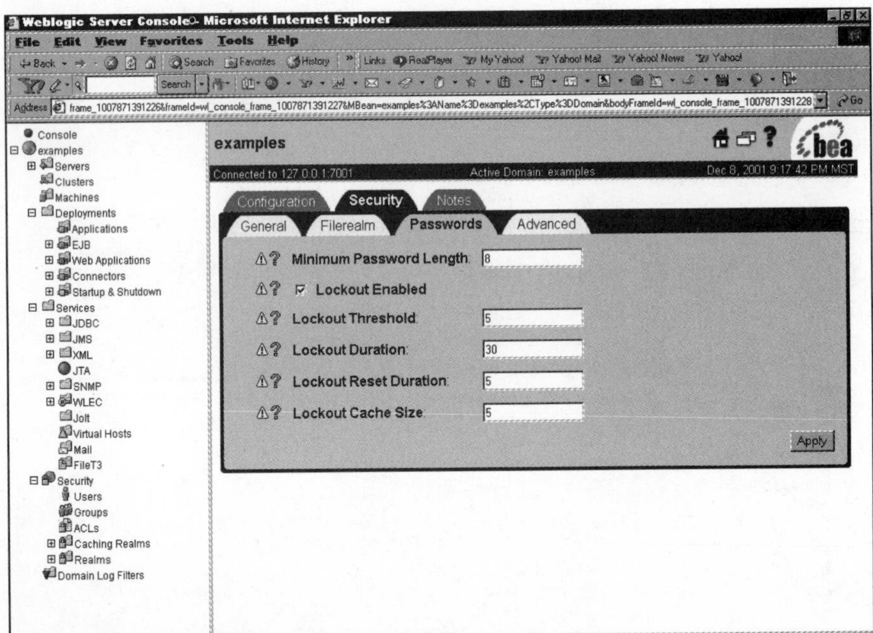

Figure 25-3: The Passwords configuration

It has been mentioned that `fileRealm.properties` contains ACLs. Some of these resources that are controlled by permissions are the administration resources, such as the weblogic.server utility that controls the booting of WebLogic Server. Some of these resources can be viewed in fileRealm.properties that is distributed with the example server of the WebLogic 6.1 package:

```
#Sat Jun 16 18:36:43 MDT 2001
acl.modify.weblogic.management=system,everyone
acl.lookup.weblogic.jndi.weblogic.ejb=system,everyone
user.system=0xf4a515d3b762a1649c48630e4489a56ba9174de8
user.support=0xa227185fac962e564de4796154a80757860e32d4
acl.lookup.weblogic.jndi.weblogic.rmi=system,everyone
acl.frob.acl.frob.aclexample=joeuser
acl.modify.weblogic.jndi.weblogic.ejb=system,everyone
acl.modify.weblogic.jndi.weblogic.fileSystem=everyone
acl.reserve.weblogic.jdbc.connectionPool.oraclepool=system,ever
yone
acl.modify.weblogic.jndi=system,everyone
acl.modify.weblogic.jndi.weblogic.rmi=system,everyone
acl.create.weblogic.jms.ConnectionConsumer=guest
acl.list.weblogic.jndi.weblogic.ejb=system,everyone
acl.admin.weblogic.jdbc.connectionPoolcreate=system,guest
acl.list.weblogic.jndi.weblogic.rmi=system,everyone
acl.shutdown.weblogic.admin=system,guest
acl.modify.weblogic.admin.acl=system,guest
acl.lookup.weblogic.jndi.weblogic=system,everyone
acl.list.weblogic.jndi=system,everyone
acl.boot.weblogic.server=system,everyone
acl.execute.weblogic.servlet=everyone
acl.list.weblogic.jndi.weblogic=system,everyone
acl.read.managedObject=system,guest
acl.reset.weblogic.jdbc.connectionPool=system
user.joeuser=0x5923f72dc88665f59c119a2a965897fc28a2feaa
acl.modify.weblogic.jndi.weblogic=system,everyone
acl.reserve.weblogic.jdbc.connectionPool.demopool=system,everyo
ne
acl.write.managedObject=system,guest
acl.lookup.weblogic.management=system,everyone
acl.lookup.weblogic.jndi=system,everyone
acl.unlockServer.weblogic.admin=system,guest
acl.lockServer.weblogic.admin=system,guest
acl.lookup.weblogic.jndi.weblogic.fileSystem=everyone
acl.frob.aclexample=joeuser
acl.list.weblogic.jndi.weblogic.fileSystem=everyone
```

In acl.boot.weblogic.server, it shows that the system and everyone has permission to boot the server. Some of the properties that the system and any guests have access to for administration utilities are the abilities to shut down, lock the server, and unlock the server. This can be seen in the respective entries acl.shutdown.weblogic.admin, acl.lockServer.weblogic.admin, and acl.unlockServer.weblogic.admin. Giving a guest that logs in to WebLogic Server permission to control WebLogic Server at this level is a big security risk and many administrators forget to turn off this feature. In the preceding example, only a specific user (called joeuser) is given specific information to an rmi object called acl.frob.acl.frob.aclexample. The acl.joeuser field contains the encrypted password of joeuser. WebLogic Server documents contain information the above ACL fields. But giving everyone information to some of these fields can provide an attacker with information into the system to discover further risks. The WebLogic Server for JAAS example gave a list of JNDI services; a part of this list gives information such as:

```
SubClass: weblogic.jndi.internal.ServerNamingNode

weblogic: weblogic.jndi.internal.ServerNamingNode

examples: weblogic.jndi.internal.ServerNamingNode

Weblogic: weblogic.jndi.internal.ServerNamingNode

xml-xslt-ContentHome_EO: weblogic.rmi.cluster.ClusterableRemoteObject

jta-jmsjdbc-ReceiveInTxHome_EO: weblogic.rmi.cluster.ClusterableRemoteObject

readMostly: weblogic.jndi.internal.ServerNamingNode

statelessSession: weblogic.jndi.internal.ServerNamingNode

statefulSession: weblogic.jndi.internal.ServerNamingNode
```

This type of information gives services that are available through JNDI, and in themselves do not appear to be a security risk. But it gives an attacker possibilities of places to look for a possible attack on a service within WebLogic Server. In the example, joeuser had access to display the information because the group for everyone had access to display the JNDI lists. This shows that giving a group access to something that is very innocent at first can be used to find places to initiate an attack. This just reinforces the need to have people carefully manage the resources in the Application Server of any type. The fileRealms.properties file was shown earlier, but there is no need to administrate the file itself. The management of this file is done in the WebLogic Console, as shown in Figure 25-4.

Notice that the parameters and resources in the console match the filerealms.properties file exactly. That is because the console is reading this properties file for the information needed in the console. As Figure 25-5 illustrates, the users are entered in the File realm through the Users window in the Security directory of the WebLogic Console.

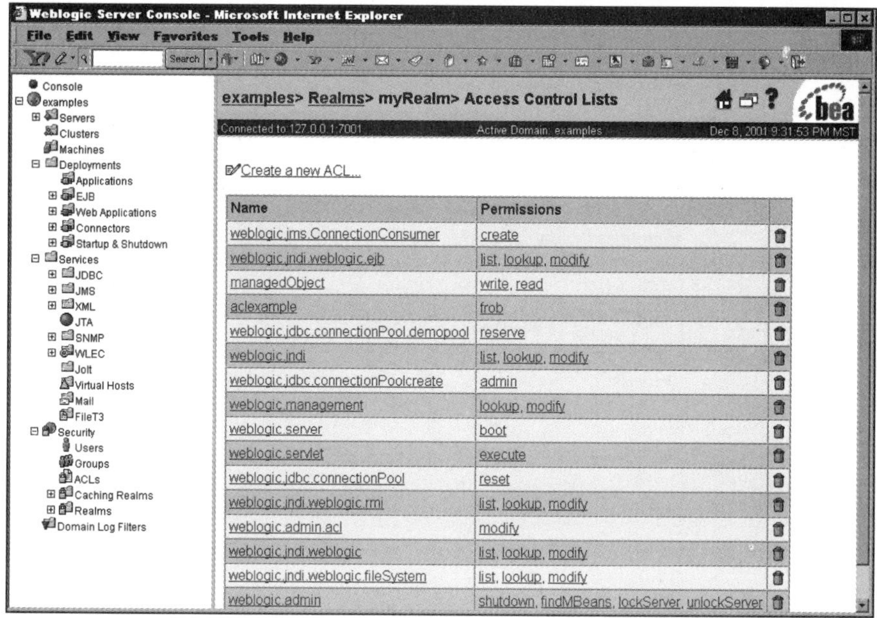

Figure 25-4: ACL panel

Figure 25-5: The Users configuration pane

You can set the Groups page in a similar way in the Security directory of the WebLogic Console (see Figure 25-6).

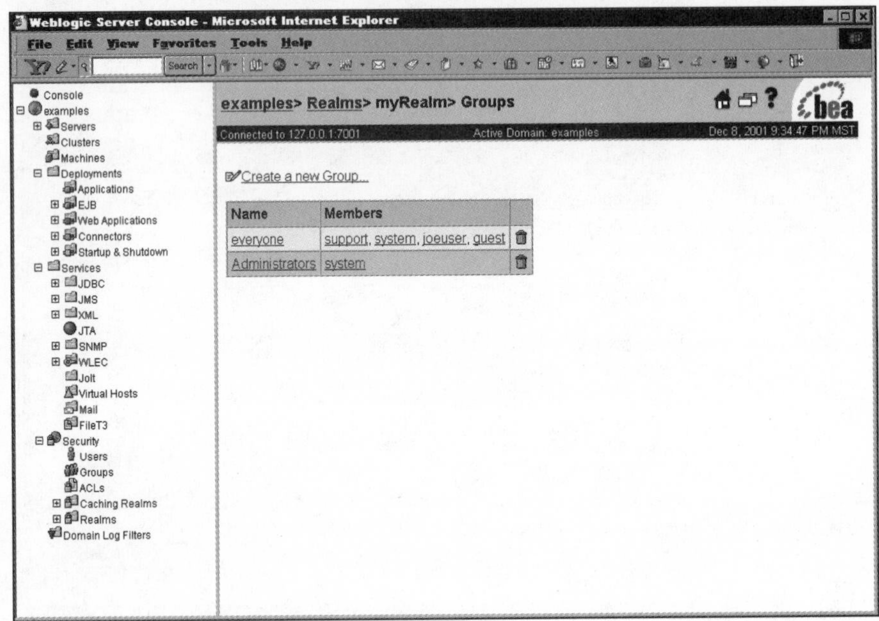

Figure 25-6: The Groups configuration pane

Configuring the NT Realm

Since the creation of Windows NT, Windows NT system has been using ACLs for managing permissions of resources. But instead of `AclEntries`, which were introduced as a JAAS concept, it uses ACEs. ACE stands for *Access Control Entries.* Just as the `ACLEntry` represents the principal, the ACE represents the user or group that has access to the resource. If an ACE has the user `rich` and it is set for read access for the ACL that represents a file, it's normally termed an access allowed ACE. An access denied ACE is an ACE that explicitly denies access to specific users for a particular ACL. These ACLs in the WinNT system are called *Discretionary Access Control Lists* (DACLs) because it is up to the owner to specify the resources and ACEs. Another version in the WinNT system is the *System Access Control Lists* (SACL). The SACL also contains the ACE. But these ACEs determine auditing. They determine who and why a user or group will be audited. The ACE consists of three parts: a security identifier (SID), an access mask, and a header. The SID is a value stored in the registry that defines users and groups that are used by the User Manager administration tool. The header states the type of ACE it is, such as access allowed or denied. The 32-bit mask will give the permission allowed or denied to the user, such as read, write, execute, and more.

WebLogic Server can use these ACLs that are defined in an NT domain server for specifying which users and groups are allowed authentication. The users and groups can be viewed through the WebLogic Console, but the User Manager tool on the WinNT domain server must manage them. WebLogic Server does not use the WinNT security realm, referred to as the NT realm, for authorization. The system user, which WebLogic Server uses for administration purposes, must be defined in the WinNT domain server so that the system user can log in to administrate WebLogic Server. This user must have administrative privileges to the NT operating system so that the user may read security-related information from the WinNT domain controller. But WebLogic Server does not need to be installed on the domain server. Before using the NT realm, the Caching realm must be enabled by using the class name of the security realm, `weblogic.security.ntrealm.NTRealm`, in the Basic Realm field.

To define the NT realm in WebLogic Server, a primary domain must be specified that contains the ACLs. As shown in Figure 25-7, this is the Windows NT domain server WebLogic Server will be getting the ACL information from.

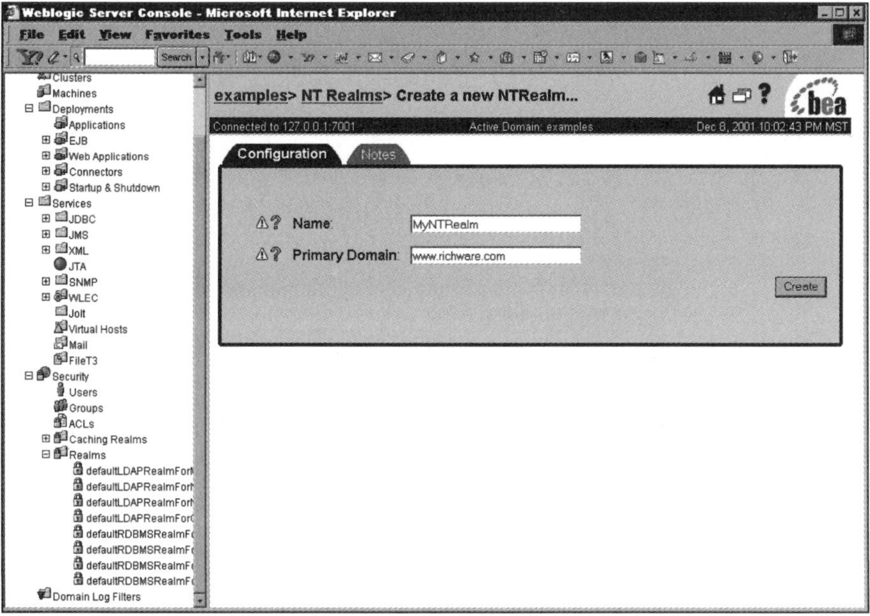

Figure 25-7: The NT realm configuration pane

The NT realm is given a name and needs to be specified as the primary Security realm. Make sure that the `Wlntrealm.dll` from the `bea\wlserver6.0\bin` directory is in the PATH of the WinNT environment. This DLL must be loaded in order for the NT realm to operate.

Configuring the Unix Realm

The Unix security realm is the foundation for providing permissions for resources based on users and groups. For every resource in Unix, there are assigned permissions for read, write, and execute for a user, group, and owner. These users have a login username and password in order to enter the Unix system. In order for WebLogic Server to pick up these usernames and groups, it must execute a Unix program called `wlauth`. This is used to authenticate users based on their login names and passwords. On some platforms, `wlauth` can interface with PAM, described in Chapter 21, to configure different authentication mechanisms; otherwise, just standard login mechanisms are supported. Because WebLogic Server reads ACLs from the `fileRealm.properties` file for authorization at startup time, it must be restarted after managing an ACL for it to take effect.

The `wlauth` program runs with the root user permissions because this program must interact with user and group information that only the root has access to in the Unix operating system.

To set up the Unix security realm (see Figure 25-8) on the Unix machine, copy the `wlauth` program to the file system on the computer that executes WebLogic Server. You can find the `wlauth` program the `bea/weblogic/lib/arch` directory, where `arch` is the name of the platform.

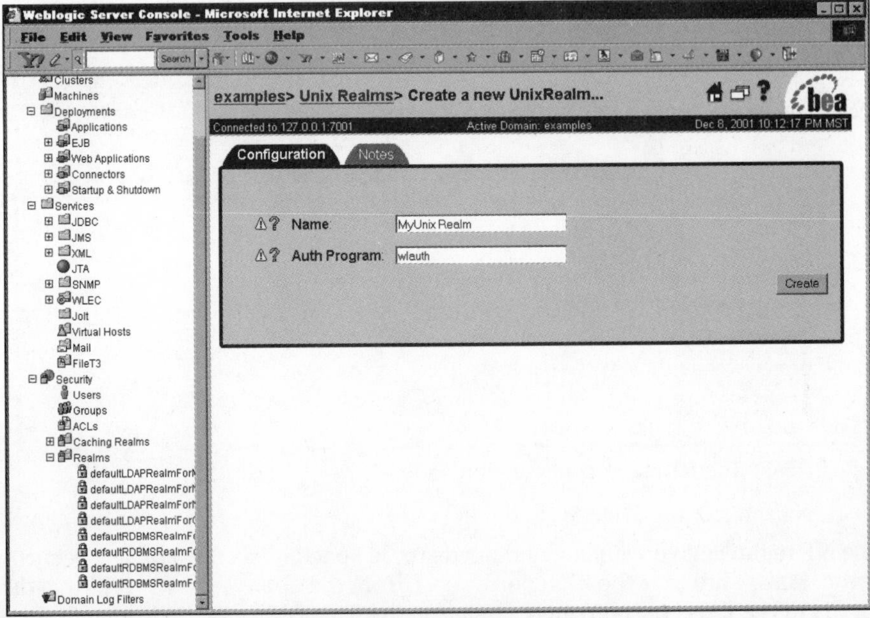

Figure 25-8: The Unix realm configuration pane

Configuring the LDAP Realm

The Lightweight Directory Access Protocol (LDAP) security realm provides authentication. The LDAP server allows the users for the entire organization to be managed in a centralized directory. Many companies and organizations use LDAP to store information about their employees, customers, and partners. In WLS 6.1, two versions of the LDAP security realms are supported, LDAP v1 realm and LDAP v2 realm. LDAP v1 realm is currently being deprecated but can be used by organizations that used previous LDAP realms in WLS 6.0. LDAP v2 realm was developed to improve performance and configurability. The v2 does not support the `getUsers()` or `getGroups()` methods that v1 supports. When running Windows 2000, BEA does recommend using LDAP realm v2. To fully understand how the LDAP security realm works, both v1 and v2 need to be discussed in detail. Understanding how v1 has evolved into v2 is crucial in understanding the dynamics of the LDAP realms. WebLogic Server 6.1 LDAP realm v1 is configured through the administration console and fully supports the Netscape Directory Server (now known as the iPlanet Directory Server), the Microsoft Site Server, and the Novell NDS. First, I'll discuss WebLogic Server 6.1 LDAP realm v1.

Because there is no standardized schema for storing access control information in LDAP directories, the ACLs must still be stored in the `filerealm.properties` file for WebLogic Server. These ACLs can refer to the users and groups defined in the LDAP server. The LDAP security realm currently supports only the password authentication of users and the groups to which they belong. The denial-of-service (DoS) attacks can be caused if authentication fails many times and the authentication for that user can no longer be processed. The LDAP security realm is not managed through the administration console of WebLogic Server, but must be managed by the LDAP server. If a user needs to be created, for example, it is created through the LDAP server's console.

To configure the LDAP security realm inside WebLogic, you must define how the users and groups are stored in the LDAP directory. Before you can use the LDAP security realm, you must enable the Caching realm and enter the class name of the LDAP security realm in the Basic Realm field of the Caching realm. This is the class name that is defined during the creation of the LDAP security realm. To create the LDAP security realm, choose Security ➪ Realms in the left pane of the administration console. In the right pane of the administration console, click the Create a New LDAP realm link. You can create, remove, and clone an LDAP security realm. The name specifies the name of the LDAP security realm. This can be up to 256 alphanumeric characters that cannot contain commas or spaces. The Realm Class Name specifies the name of the Java class that contains the LDAP security realm. This Java class name has to be included in the classpath of WebLogic Server. Shown in Figure 25-9, this field cannot be changed.

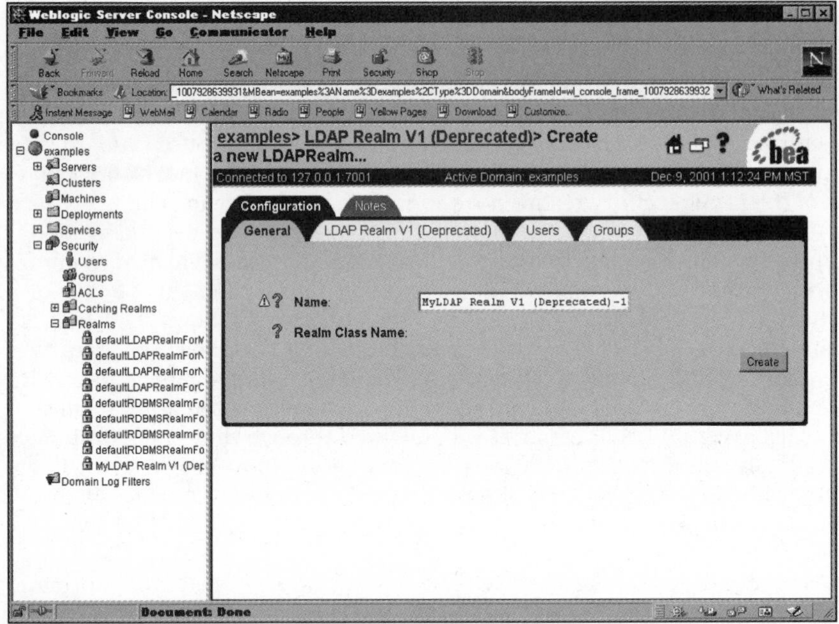

Figure 25-9: The LDAP security realm name

LDAPURL is the location of the LDAP server. The default Port for SSL is port 389. For SSL connections into the LDAP server, the default port is 636. These ports may be configurable in the LDAP server. It is better not use default ports when trying to hide servers. But this requires expertise in knowing the ports in your domain, and mapping them out explicitly — a task that I have not seen done very often, due to the administrators only knowing how to set up default ports. The LDAP URL defined by RFC 2255 is composed of the following:

```
"ldap://" [ hostname [":" portnumber] ] "/" baseDN ["?"
attributeList ["?" scope "?" filterString ["?" extensions ]]]
```

A complex example is `ldap://myhost.richware.com:389/o=richware.com??one`. This URL requests all immediate children under `o=richware.com` but not `richware.com` on the LDAP server running on `myhost.richware.com`. It returns all entries found. A simple example is `ldap://ldapserver:389`.

The principal is the distinguished name (DN) of the LDAP user used to connect to the LDAP server. The DN in this case is just a uid, which stands for user identification, which has the ability to list the LDAP users and groups. The Credential is the password that authenticates the Principal. The Enable SSL is set to `true` to enable the SSL protocol to protect the communication between the LDAP server and WebLogic Server. The LDAP server must be set up to support the SSL protocol. The Auth Protocol field is the type of authentication used to authenticate the LDAP server. The simple selection is just for password authentication. The iPlanet Directory Server can also support CRAM-MD5, which is used for certificate authentication to the LDAP server. A sample of this appears in Figure 25-10.

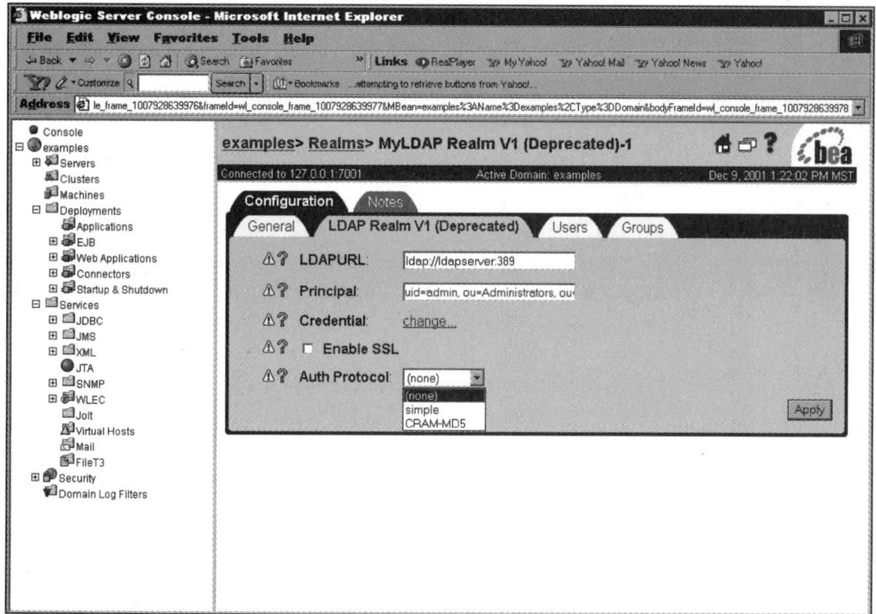

Figure 25-10: The LDAP security realm authentication

The next window that needs to be set up is the authentication of users logging in to the system. The Users window sets up these properties. The first field is the User Authentication type. Selecting Local specifies that the LDAP security realm retrieves the user information, including the password, from the LDAP directory server and checks the password in WebLogic Server. The iPlanet Directory Server and the Microsoft Site Server normally support the Local field. Selecting external in the Authentication type uses the SSL protocol, and is normally supported by the Novell NDS server. The Authentication type specifies that the LDAP security realm authenticates a user attempting to bind to the LDAP directory server with the username and password supplied by WebLogic Server. The User Password Attribute field sets the field to find the user's password in the LDAP directory server. The User DN field defines the location in the directory tree where the users will be found. The User Name Attribute defines the attribute field in LDAP that defines the identity of the user. In Figure 25-11, the User Name Attribute field is set to `uid`; this will inform the realm that when looking for the user's name, use the uid in the LDAP tree. The DN field is set to `ou=people, o=beasys.com`, which means that the users will be located under the organization `beasys.com` and under the `ou` node for people. The combination of these two fields is used to specify where and in which field users will be identified. This User DN field specifies the placement of the users by organization and organizational unit to retrieve the users' information. The User Name Attribute field specifies in which field of the LDAP directory server that you can find the usernames. Setting it `cn`, for example, specifies that the common name in the LDAP server contains the user's name, or `uid` meaning that the user's ID contains the user's name. In the example server, it's similar to Figure 25-11.

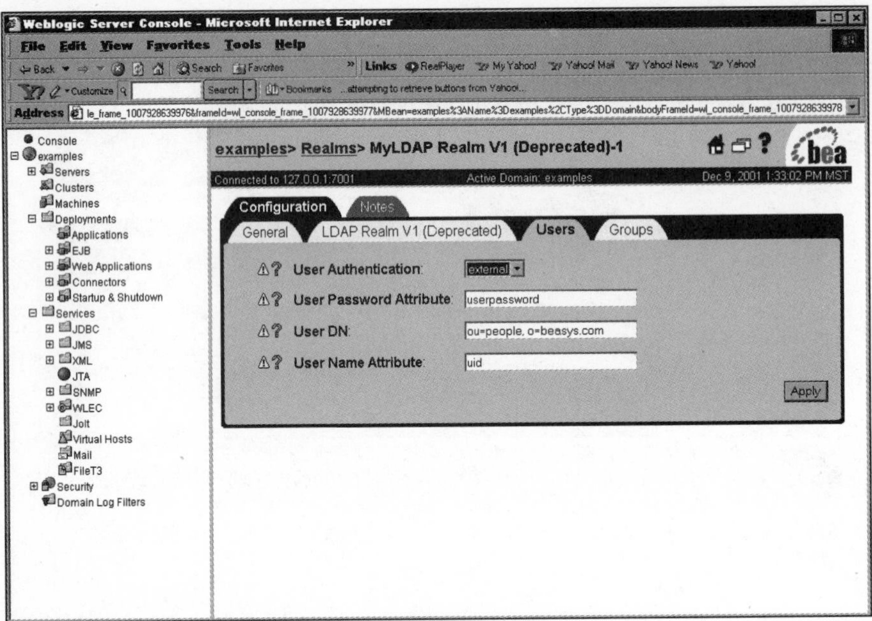

Figure 25-11: The LDAP security realm user's location

In Figure 25-11, the organization is `richware.com` and that organizational unit is set to People. By default in the iPlanet Directory Service, the organization unit is People. Figure 25-12 is a sample of NDS 5.1 with Rich Helton as the user and the uid, or User ID, set to RHelton.

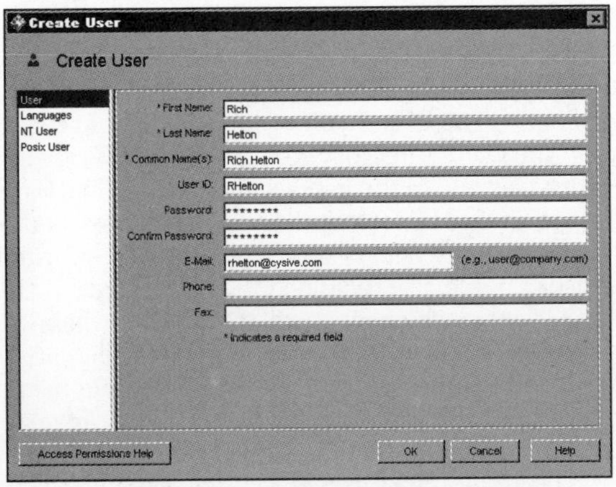

Figure 25-12: iPlanet Directory Service 5.1

After the user's information is specified in the LDAP server, the next information that WebLogic Server needs to know how to find is the group's information. The biggest difference between the Users panel and the Groups panel is that the group does not require password information. Just as a set of combination fields defines the Users panel, so, too, do the combination fields of Group DN and Group Name Attribute. They define the location of the group's name. Group DN defines the organization and organization unit that is the folder that defines the group names. Group Name Attribute defines the field name that the group names are defined in, such as `cn` for common name. Group IS Context is a Boolean field that you select. Selecting this option specifies that each group entry contains one user. Deselecting this option ensures that there is one group entry containing an attribute for each group member. The Group Username Attribute field is set to the name of the LDAP attribute that contains a group member in a group entry. This needs to contain a valid group member name. The Groups window looks like Figure 25-13.

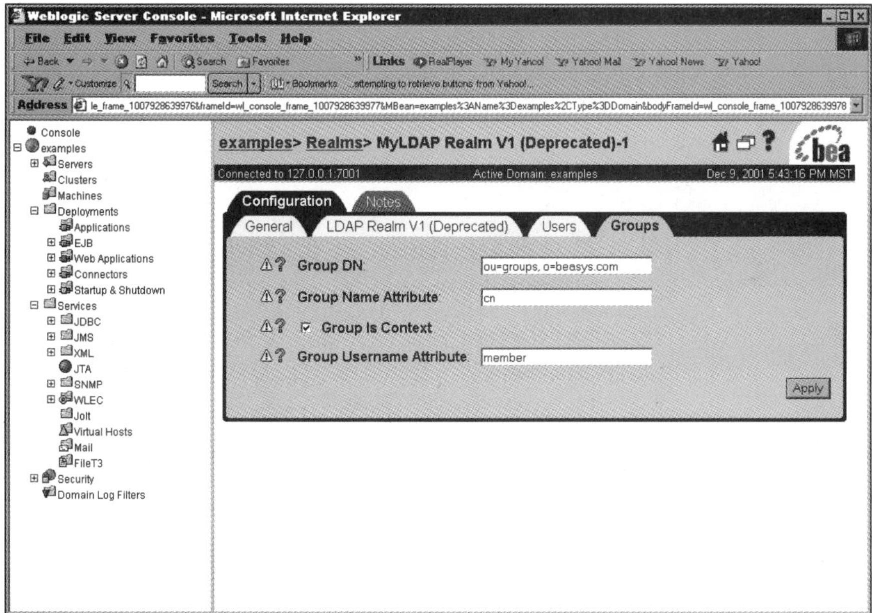

Figure 25-13: The LDAP security realm Groups location

In Figure 25-14, the organization is still `richware.com` and the organization unit changes to Groups. This is the default group area in iPlanet Directory Service 5.1.

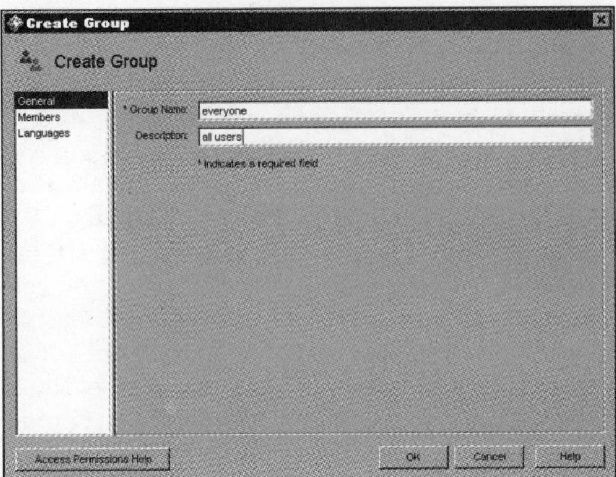

Figure 25-14: The Groups area in iPlanet Directory Service 5.1

You can also use the Notes window, shown in Figure 25-15, for any user-supplied information.

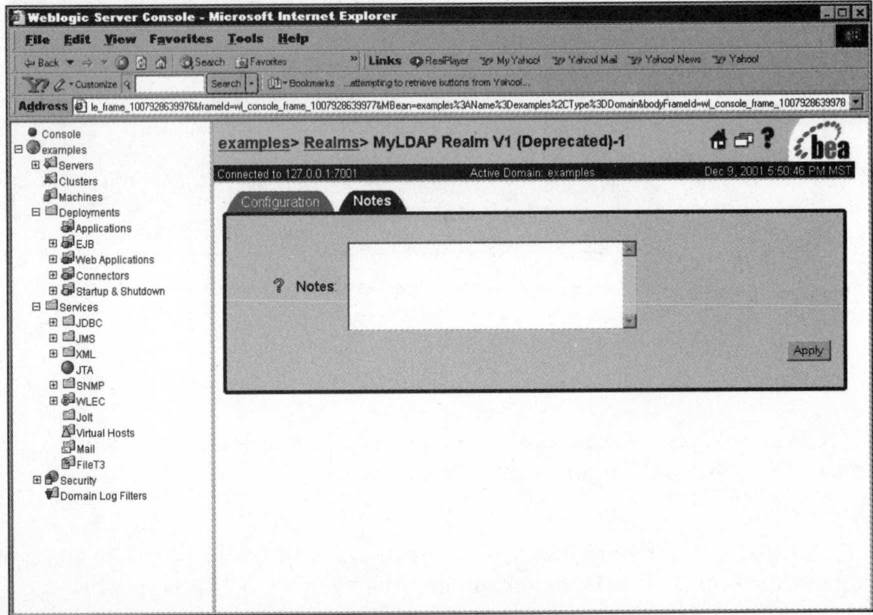

Figure 25-15: The LDAP security realm Notes location

Using the LDAP security realm for WebLogic Server allows users to be authenticated and for authorization of services. The LDAP security realm in WebLogic has been tested with the iPlanet Directory Server, the Microsoft Site Server, and the OpenLDAP server. WebLogic Server LDAP security realm has been improved to provide better performance and configurability. After configuring a LDAP v1 realm, the deprecated LDAP realm will appear like Figure 25-16. Notice the Realm Class Name is set to "weblogic.security.ldaprealmv1.LDAPRealm" in the MyLDAP Realm.

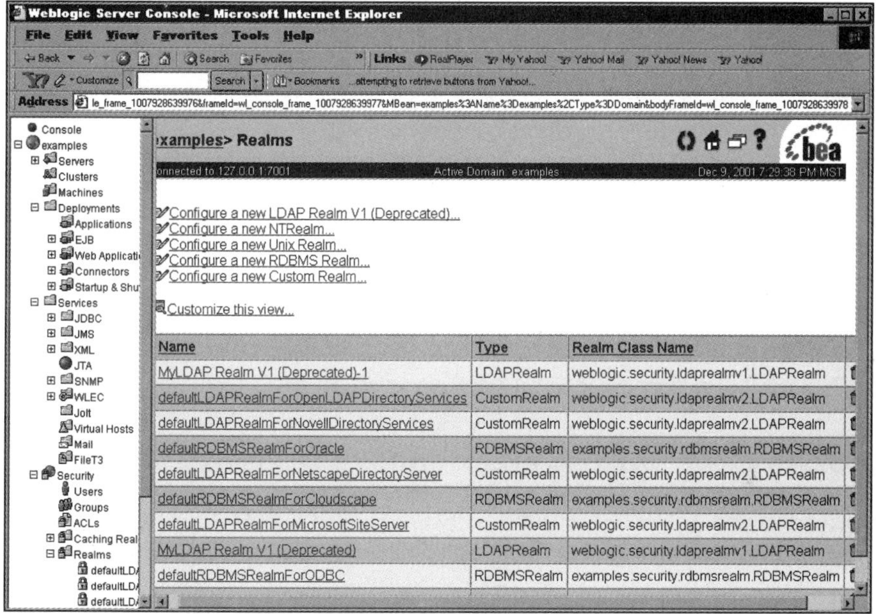

Figure 25-16: The LDAP v1 security realm configured

In the v2 of the LDAP realm, the iPlanet Directory Server 5.1 will be configured in the same manner. While the v2 has changed to improve performance, other sacrifices have been made in functionality, such as listing all Users, listing the members of a Group, and the `authProtocol` and `userAuthentication` mechanisms have been removed. The `authProtocol` and `userAuthentication` mechanisms are replaced by using the JNDI `bind` mechanism to pass security credentials to the LDAP server. There are several examples of LDAP v2 included in WLS 6.1. The example in Figure 25-17 demonstrates the LDAP v2 realm with the Netscape Directory Server.

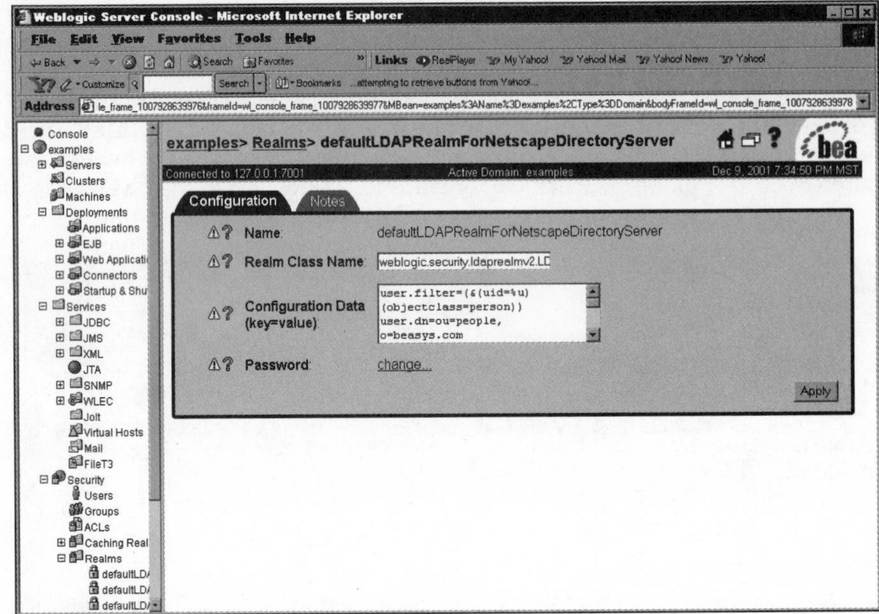

Figure 25-17: The LDAP v2 security realm

The Name field is a unique name that is used to identify the LDAP v2 realm. The Realm Class Name for LDAP v2 realm by default is set to `weblogic.security.ldaprealmv2.LDAPRealm` to use the default classes for LDAP v2 realm. It can be altered to support custom LDAP classes developed internally or by other vendors. The Configuration Data sets the Users and Groups similar to the settings in the LDAP v1 realm, except that all of the settings are set in a key/value pair in the Configuration Data field:

```
user.filter=(&(uid=%u)(objectclass=person))
user.dn=ou=people, o=beasys.com
server.principal=uid=admin, ou=Administrators, ou=TopologyManagement,
o=NetscapeRoot
membership.filter=(&(uniquemember=%M)(objectclass=groupofuniquenames))
group.filter=(&(cn=%g)(objectclass=groupofuniquenames))
server.host=ldapserver.example.com
group.dn=ou=groups, o=beasys.com
```

The `user.dn=` setting is set to `ou=people, o=beasys.com`, which was demonstrated in the User DN field in Figure 25-11. In the same figure, the User Name Attribute field was defined as `uid`, which matched the setting in LDAP v2 realm as the user.filter as user.filter=(&(uid=%u)(objectclass=person)) that also defines that the attribute for the user is uid. The Group DN is also defined in the above setting for v2 as group.dn=ou=groups, o=beasys.com, and in v1 it is defined as shown in Figure 25-13. In the same figure in v1, the Group Attribute was defined as cn for the field, or filter, to use for the location on the field to use for group as common name. This field is also defined in v2 in the above setting as cn in the following string, group.filter=(&(cn=%g)(objectclass=groupofuniquenames)). The only other fields in the preceding setting are the server.host and server.principal. These can be seen in v1 in Figure 25-10 as the LDAP Principal field and the LDAP URL. The only difference is that the entire URL is not put in the server.host setting and automatically assumes that the LDAP protocol will be port 389 unless otherwise specified. Almost every field in v1 maps to a given field in v2, except that all the entries are entered in the Configuration Data at once and not in individual field locations using multiple windows. This makes it a little more complex but centralizes all of the settings into one location. It should be noted that v2 provides less functionality and centralizes the settings into one location for better performance.

Configuring the RDBMS realm

In looking at weblogic.jar, you may notice various packages that implement the security realms. For the LDAP security realm, there is the weblogic.security.ldaprealm package. For the NT realm security realm, there is the weblogic.security.ntrealm package. For the Unix realm security realm, there is the weblogic.security.unixrealm package. And for the Cache realm, File realm, and Custom realm security realm, you can find various classes in the weblogic.security.acl package. But I never mentioned the RDBMS realm, because it doesn't exist in the weblogic.jar. The example for configuring the RDBMS realm security realm provided by BEA is in examples.security.rdbmsrealm.RDBMSRealm. This example, however, does not support change password, create group, create ACL, remove ACL, add ACL member, or remove ACL member. This example will be used to describe the setup of an RDBMS realm security realm. I want to emphasize that this is just an example that BEA provides and should be treated as such. The Cloudscape evaluation that is shipped with WebLogic will be described during the program's setup. The compiled code that comes shipped with WebLogic for this example is stored in the bea/weblogic/config/examples/serverclasses/examples/security/rdbmsrealm directory to be used with the example server. You can find the Cloudscape evaluation in the bea/weblogic/samples/eval/cloudscape directory. You find the demo store under the data subdirectory in the same tree. To start the Cloudscape view to view the database, ensure that cloudscape.jar and tools.jar in the lib subdirectory are included in the system's classpath. Then execute Java COM.cloudscape.tools.cview to view a database. To create the entries of users, ACLentries, and groups again, execute the rdbmsrealm.ddl found in the `bea/wlserver6.0sp1/samples/examples/security` directory on the demo store. Move the `rdbmsrealm.ddl` file to the demo store's directory and execute:

```
java utils.Schema jdbc:cloudscape:demo;create=true
     COM.cloudscape.core.JDBCDriver
     -verbose rdbmsrealm.ddl
```

This DDL will create the ACLENTRIES, GROUPMEMBERS, and USERS tables inside Cloudscape, as shown in Figures 25-18, 25-19, and 25-20.

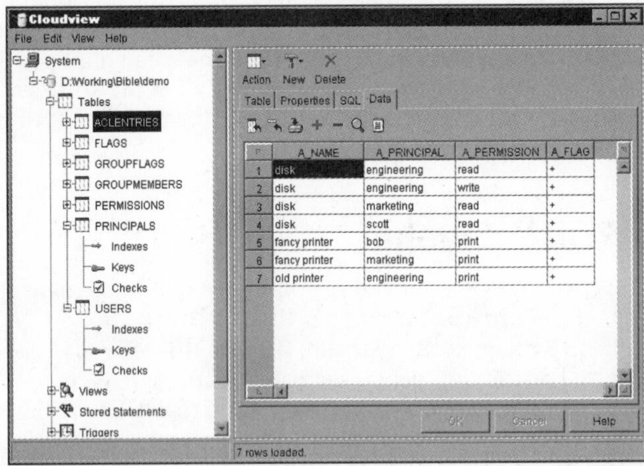

Figure 25-18: The ACLENTRIES table

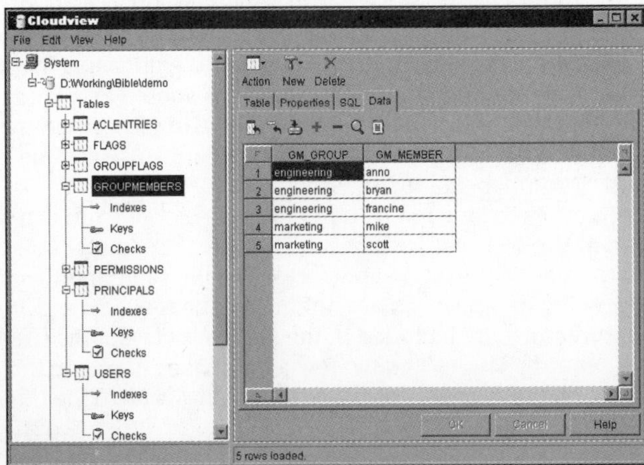

Figure 25-19: The GROUPMEMBERS table

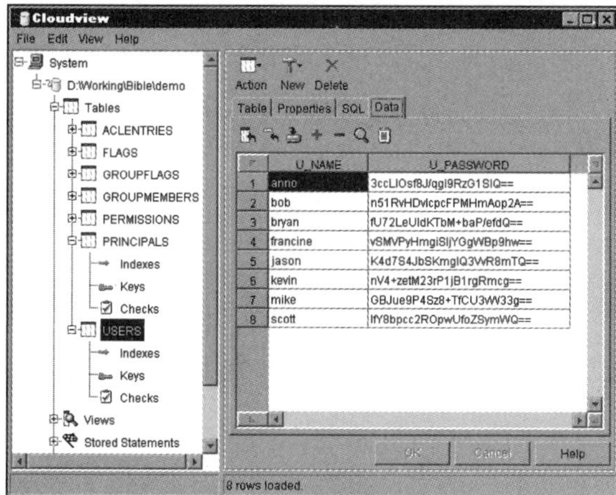
Figure 25-20: The USERS table

To add the RDBMS realm security realm into WebLogic Server, you must add it to the Caching Realm field in the Security pane, as shown in Figure 25-21.

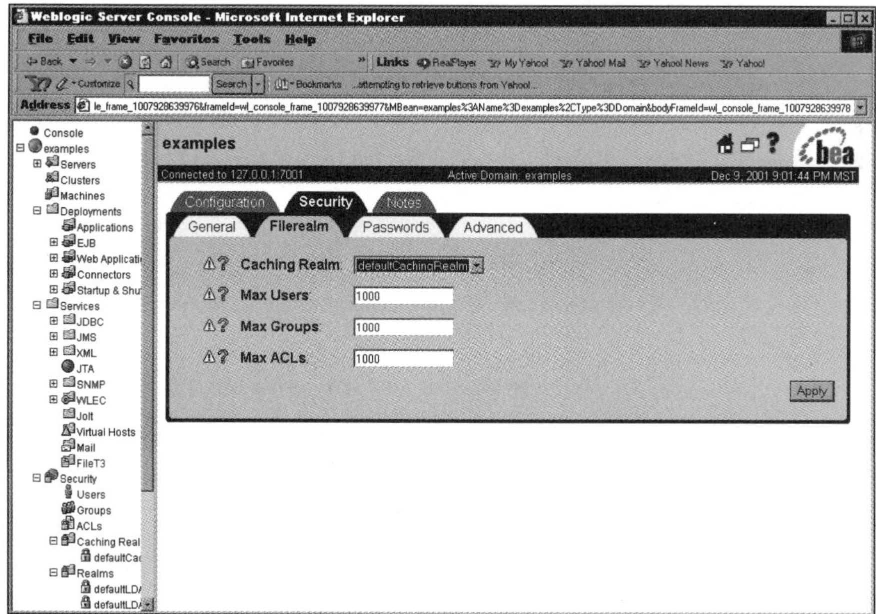
Figure 25-21: Setting the Caching Realm in the Security pane

The `defaultCachingRealm` has the `defaultRDBMSRealmForCloudscape` set in it as the RDBMS realm to use for the alternative security realm instead of the File realm. The File realm will be considered backup for ACLs and authorization. The RDBMS realm will be considered primary and WebLogic Server will check the RDBMS realm for the user first. If the user doesn't exist there, then it will check the File realm. The only ones that come close to handling ACLs are the RDBMS realm and any Custom realm that implements that ACLs in the `weblogic.security.acl.AbstractManageable` interface. Figure 25-22 shows that the `defaultRDBMSRealmForCloudscape` is defined in the Caching realm.

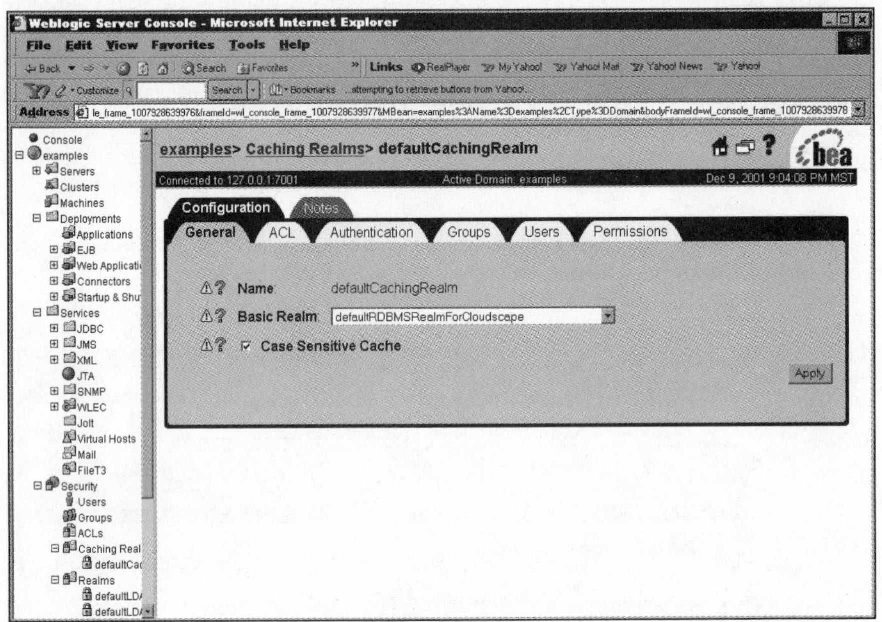

Figure 25-22: The Caching realm containing the defaultRDBMSRealmForCloudscape

The File realm is a fall-through check after authenticating any type of other security realm. Additionally, there cannot be duplicates in the File realm and another security realm for them to function properly. Also, in most cases the other security realm is used mostly used for authentication, while most authorization is handled through the File realm. This is simply because WebLogic is not aware of how the other security realms are configured to handle authorization to handle permissions. The other security realms always need to be aware of users and groups, along with passwords for authentication. In the RDBMS realm, the user and group statements will be defined in the Schema panel that the class will use for prepared statements. First, you must define the `defaultRDBMSRealmForCloudscape` class in the Realms window by selecting Create a New RDBMS Realm, as shown in Figure 25-23.

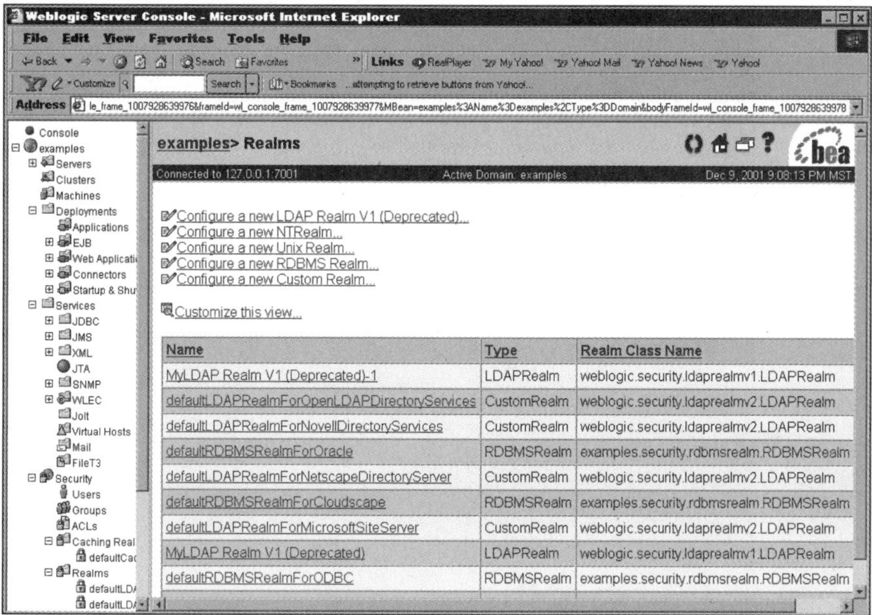

Figure 25-23: Creating a new RDBMS realm

When starting a new RDBMS security realm, you need a unique name defined to call this realm. Then you must select the class that executes the RDBMS realm functions that will extend the `AbstractManageableRealm` for creating and removing users, groups, and ACLs. Not all are supported in the example shown in Figure 25-24, but the class needs to be associated.

The first operation for a database of any database communication is to establish a database connection. Just like in JDBC, a JDBC driver, a URL, a username, and a password must be supplied to the connection parameters to specify how to connect to the database (see Figure 25-25). The driver needs to be specified in the classpath, in this case the start-up script specifies `.\samples\eval\cloudscape\lib\cloudscape.jar` for the cloudscape JDBC driver. One of the parameters in the URL is `jdbc:cloudscape:demo;create=true`; it specifies that if the table does not exist, then create it. Another parameter, `autocommit=false`, defines that after every operation don't commit, but explicitly commit with the `commit()` method. When auto-commit mode is set, it means that each individual SQL statement is treated as a transaction and will be automatically committed after it is executed. The start-up script for the example WebLogic Server also specifies `cloudscape.system.home=./samples/eval/cloudscape/data`, which is the directory where the demo database will be created. User ID and Password are the login for the database connection, if one is needed. Because this is an example, one is not used, but all database connections should require a secure authentication.

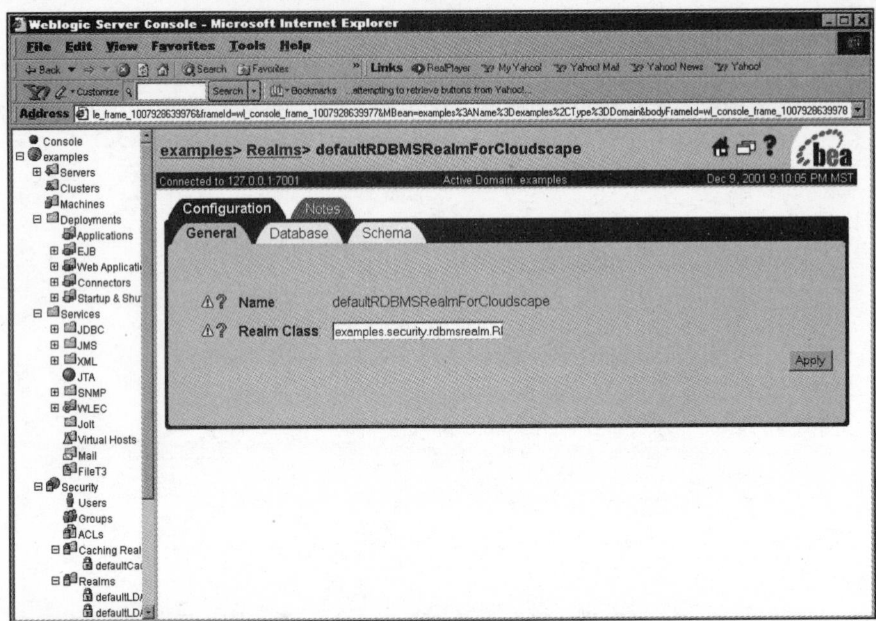

Figure 25-24: Associating the class name with the RDBMS realm

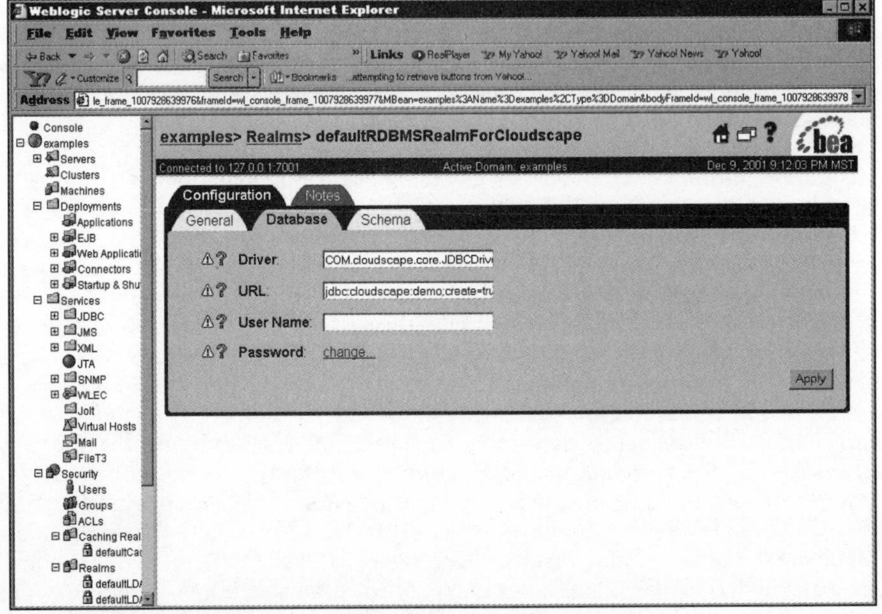

Figure 25-25: The database connection for the RDBMS realm

The last pane that is required to configure for the RDBMS realm is the Schema pane. This pane defines the statements needed for the prepared statements that the `examples.security.rdbmsrealm.RDBMSRealm` defines. These fields include getUser, getGroups, getPermissions, and more. The following is the example used with the Cloudscape database:

```
getGroupMembers=SELECT GM_GROUP, GM_MEMBER from groupmembers WHERE GM_GROUP = ?
deleteGroup2=DELETE FROM aclentries WHERE A_PRINCIPAL = ?
deleteGroup1=DELETE FROM groupmembers WHERE GM_GROUP = ?
addGroupMember=INSERT INTO groupmembers VALUES ( ? , ? )
getUser=SELECT U_NAME, U_PASSWORD FROM users WHERE U_NAME = ?
getPermission=SELECT DISTINCT A_PERMISSION FROM aclentries WHERE A_PERMISSION =
?
deleteUser3=DELETE FROM aclentries WHERE A_PRINCIPAL = ?
getGroupNewStatement=true
deleteUser2=DELETE FROM groupmembers WHERE GM_MEMBER = ?
deleteUser1=DELETE FROM users WHERE U_NAME = ?
getAcls=SELECT A_NAME, A_PRINCIPAL, A_PERMISSION FROM aclentries ORDER BY
A_NAME, A_PRINCIPAL
getUsers=SELECT U_NAME, U_PASSWORD FROM users
getGroups=SELECT GM_GROUP, GM_MEMBER FROM groupmembers
getPermissions=SELECT DISTINCT A_PERMISSION FROM aclentries
getAclEntries=SELECT A_NAME, A_PRINCIPAL, A_PERMISSION FROM aclentries WHERE
A_NAME = ? ORDER BY A_PRINCIPAL
newUser=INSERT INTO users VALUES ( ? , ? )
removeGroupMember=DELETE FROM groupmembers WHERE GM_GROUP = ? AND GM_MEMBER = ?
```

The Notes pane is simply an area to keep any administration notes associated with this RDBMS realm.

Configuring the Secure Socket Layers (SSL) protocol

The SSL protocol offers a mechanism that the applications can use to implement mutual authentication. It also offers a mechanism of encrypting data that is being transported to and from WebLogic Server. For one-way authentication, the client communicating with WebLogic Server is given authentication that this WebLogic Server is valid for the transaction. In the mutual authentication of SSL, WebLogic Server also validates that the client is whom it claims to be representing. Encryption of the data that is being transported avoids eavesdroppers from seeing the data by using the keys of the client and the server.

Server authentication occurs when the server provides a digital certificate issued by a Certificate Authority (CA) to a client during an SSL handshake. Client, or two-way, authentication occurs when the client provides the digital certificate as part of the SSL handshake. Data integrity is provided by SSL by providing digital signatures of the data being transmitted, and the data is encrypted by using keys that are passed by the CA. HTTP browsers connect to WebLogic Server by using the HTTPS protocol, where a browser uses a URL of the form `http://myserver.com/mypage.html` for SSL3. Java clients connecting to WebLogic Server with the SSL protocol other than the browser must tunnel over BEA's multiplexed T3 protocol, such as `t3s://myserver.com:7002/mypage.html`. Clients can use two methods to access WebLogic Server through SSL.

WebLogic Server supports exportable and domestic encryptions. Domestic encryptions have larger certificates and keys and cannot leave the United States or Canada under penalty of treason. When exporting a strong encryption, it is handled under the same laws as exporting a nuclear weapon. So, it's well advised that the laws are adhered to and understood. These laws apply to any digital means of encryption; even a strong encryption described on a book in CD form. The exportable SSL that WebLogic Server supports is the 512-bit certificate and 40-bit bulk data encryption. The domestic SSL supports the 768-bit certificate, 1024-bit certificate, 56-bit, and 128-bit bulk data encryption. The bulk data encryption is the bit size of a key that is not a digital certificate. The standard WebLogic Server distribution supports exportable-strength SSL only. The domestic SSL version must be arranged through a BEA representative directly so that they can ensure where they are shipping the software. The United States has been relaxing the encryption laws and the domestic version can be used in more countries, but a BEA representative should be consulted for which countries. If the version that is being supported is the exportable-strength SSL, then some high-strength SSL connections coming from the domestic-strength clients cannot be supported.

WebLogic Server's SSL protocol cannot be configured without first providing a key and digital certificate. Both will be required for each WebLogic Server that will use the SSL protocol. The key and digital certificate must be stored. To acquire a digital certificate from a CA, a request must be submitted in the form of a Certificate Signature Request (CSR). As shown in Figure 25-26, WebLogic Server has a Certificate Request Generator servlet (CRGS) that creates a CSR. This servlet collects the information from information that the administrator provides and generates a private key file and a certificate request file. This is the information that can be sent to a CA, such as VeriSign, to request the digital certificate. To access the CRGS from the local machine, use `https://localhost:7002/certificate`. The CRGS is installed by default and the administrator must be able to log in to WebLogic Server to access this servlet. For a remote machine, substitute the localhost with the host name.

After filling out the Host Name, User Information, E-mail Address, Organization, and Key Information fields, the request is generated as a private key file. The file is saved as a `www_mydomain-key.der` file, where `mydomain` is the WebLogic Server domain that this file is generated on. This file name should then be set into the Server Key File Name on the SSL tab in the administration console, as shown in Figure 25-27.

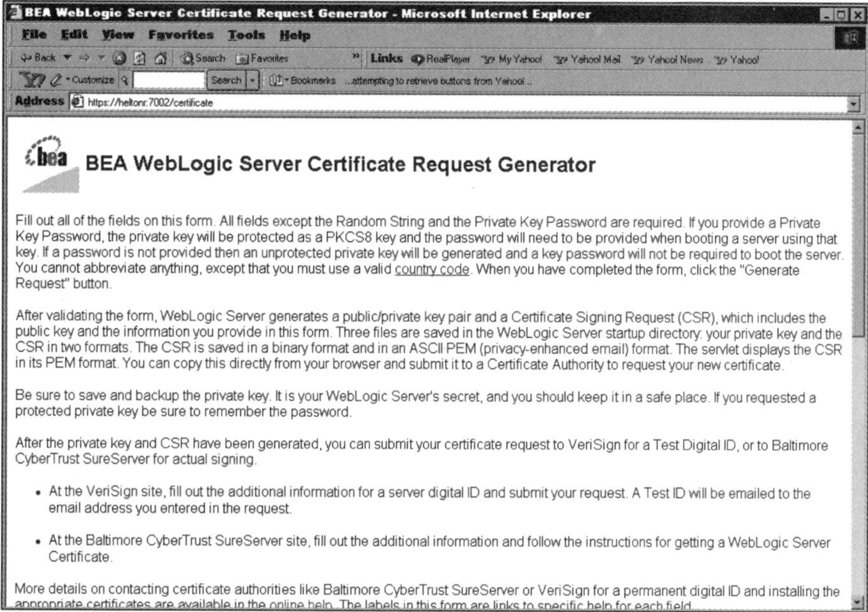

Figure 25-26: The Certificate Request Generator servlet

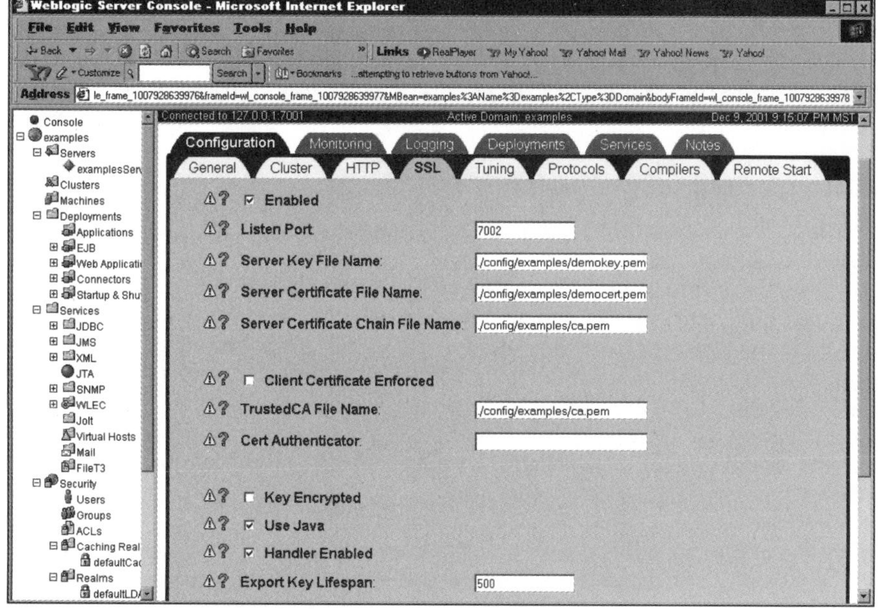

Figure 25-27: SSL configuration

A www_mydomain_com-request.dem file is also generated that contains ASCII data. ASCII can be pasted to an e-mail or Web form for submission into VeriSign. Both VeriSign and Entrust offer a 128-bit encryption for domestic Web services and a 40-bit encryption for export Web services.

When the digital certificate is received from a CA, it needs to be stored in the selected WebLogic Server's config directory, or the path that is defined to contain the CA certificates. If the default domain of mydomain is used, then it needs to be saved in the \wlserver6.0sp1\config\mydomain directory. In the Server Certificate File Name field of the SSL tab, you need to enter the full directory location and name of the digital certificate. The directory location and name of the digital certificate must be entered in the Trusted CA File Name field for the CA. The private key file name must be entered in the Server Key File Name field.

After the appropriate fields are filled out in the SSL tab, you need to start WebLogic Server with a command option that defines the password for logging into the CA and requesting the digital certificate. This is done by using the -Dweblogic.management.pkpassword=password command. To configure for mutual authentication, the Client Certificate Enforced option on the SSL tab must be checked.

Private key files and digital certificates are stored in either a .pem or .der file. A .der file format contains binary data, and a .pem file contains ASCII data. A .pem file for the private key will have a BEGIN ENCRYPTED PRIVATE KEY section and an END ENCRYPTED PRIVATE KEY section with the private key stored in between. A .pem file for the digital certificate will have a BEGIN CERTIFICATE section and an END CERTIFICATE section with the digital certificate stored in between. These files should be stored so that only the *system* user of WebLogic Server has read-only access to these files. No other user should have access to these files.

Configuring the connection filter

As mentioned as a perimeter defense beginning in Chapter 20, a firewall can reject or accept a connection based on the client's origin and protocol. WebLogic Server also has this feature built in. When WebLogic Server accepts a connection, it examines the client's IP number that is passed in the IP stack, and then checks the protocol used based on the data and handshaking mechanism. Some of the protocols that it will look for in various filtering techniques are HTTP, HTTPS, T3 (the WebLogic protocol), T3S (the WebLogic Secure protocol), and IIOP (the CORBA Internet Inter-ORB Protocol). If the client's IP or protocol seems to be untrusted, then the examining program should throw a FilterException to terminate the connection.

To build a connection filter program, the interface weblogic.security.net.ConnectionFilter needs to be implemented in one of the classes in the program. The class that implements this interface needs to be associated in the Connection Filter field in the Security pane (see Figure 25-28). An example class called examples.security.net.SimpleConnectionFilter is distributed with WebLogic Server.

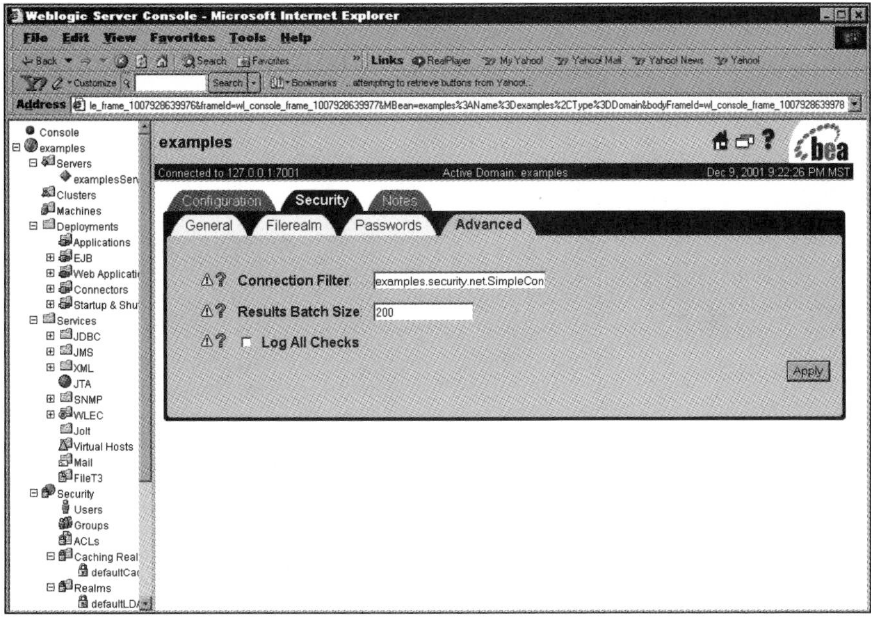

Figure 25-28: Connection filter

You can find this example in the `bea/wlserver6.1/samples/examples/security/net` directory. This example uses a filter file that provides rules for which clients are denied services to WebLogic Server and which protocols are allowed. An example of the rules will filter and deny all services from the address 192.168.0.0:

```
192.168.0.0/16 deny
```

Host names may be used instead of hard-coded addresses. This can thwart many attackers, but this means that the attacker must also mask as a different client and possibly a different protocol that makes it a little more difficult to break into WebLogic Server. The heart of the `SimpleConnectionFilter` class is the `accept()` function. This function acts in many ways like the socket `accept()` function that receives a connection from a client. This example receives a `ConnectionEvent` from the client, to which it will apply the rules and see if it needs to deny a service based on the protocol or the remote address. The remote address is the client's address.

```
/**
   * Filters a client connection event.  If the connection should be
   * allowed, this method returns normally.
   *
   * @param evt the connection event
   * @exception FilterException the connection should be rejected by
   * the server
   */
  public void accept(ConnectionEvent evt)
```

```
  throws FilterException
{
  InetAddress remoteAddress = evt.getRemoteAddress();
  String protocol = evt.getProtocol().toLowerCase();
  int bit = protocolToMaskBit(protocol);

  if (bit == 0xdeadbeef)
  {
    bit = 0;
  }

  // Check rules in the order in which they were written.

  for (int i = 0; i < rules.length; i++)
  {
    switch (rules[i].check(remoteAddress, bit))
    {
    case FilterEntry.ALLOW:
return;
    case FilterEntry.DENY:
throw new FilterException("rule " + (i + 1));
    case FilterEntry.IGNORE:
break;
    default:
throw new RuntimeException("connection filter internal error!");
    }
  }

  // If no rule matched, we allow the connection to succeed.

  return;
}
```

Summary

WebLogic Server becomes as secure as the weakest link in an enterprise system. Many cases exist of using the most secure database and Application Server security software, yet not having firewalls in place. The enterprise security of an organization depends on the organization's defense perimeter. Even though an organization such as the one described might have millions of dollars worth of security systems, it becomes weaker than most because of the lack of firewalls.

Other organizations have network diagrams, database models, and UML diagrams tacked on walls throughout their buildings. But when asked if there are enterprise diagrams describing the firewalls, security realms, and other security measures, they will most likely point at a physical architecture or network diagram. Security has layering across a system just as other enterprise components work across an organization's enterprise system. There should be models just as detailed as the others describing the authentication, authorization, auditing, and integrity schemes. These models might span from Change Management to the Network Architecture; however, they should be maintained and owned by the department that oversees the security requirements and checklist.

Organizations should perform random acts of testing the system for possible attacks. Usually the systems are most vulnerable during a release cycle. Some release cycles of software are well known and are even made public to the community through marketing ads. These are the times to be most diligent.

It should be a constant duty to ensure that the current Application Servers, and other software used in an organization, are constantly being tested and checked for security restrictions, and that these restrictions are always considered into the architectural documents and diagrams. The software in the industry is becoming more and more useful for breaking into systems, even for the novice. Enforcing security measures, like much of the terminology that has been adapted, should always be seen as trying to fight a war, usually a battle at a time. The price of the war is the systems and data of the organization. The enemy is usually anyone who can access something valuable that can cause harm to the company.

Probably the worst thing for an organization on the issue of security is to not be aware that someone has gained access to the systems. Even if someone has temporary access, there should auditing procedures to close the hole next time, and the most sensitive resources should never be seen. Even as a test, leaving a small hole into a temporary system with no data on it, isolated from the other systems, just to check out the auditing can be viable. By war, it means that there will be small battles lost in every system, but a good leader knows how to fake the enemy out and how to manipulate the attacker's offenses to focus on a particular area that is defended well. What makes an organization is its data, and the best way to defend it is to be prepared. Knowing the attacker's methods and the strengths of the systems at hand is the best way to be prepared.

✦ ✦ ✦

PART

VIII

Enterprise Application Integration

✦ ✦ ✦ ✦

In This Part

✦ ✦ ✦ ✦

CHAPTER 26

Working with Web Services, SOAP, and WSDL

In This Chapter

Understanding Web Services

How Web Services work in WebLogic

Building Web Services

Other Web-service technologies

A *Web service* is a general-purpose application that performs well-defined tasks and is invoked by other applications using common networking and communications protocols. Web Services are self-contained, self-describing, modular applications that can be accessed from any point on the Internet. They provide specific functionality that performs discrete tasks. These tasks can range from the trivial, such as reading the time from an atomic clock, to the complex, such as making an online mortgage payment.

Web Services are based on the client-server architecture model. However, there is an important difference with previous client-server architectures. Web Services were designed with the idea of insulating clients from the implementation details of the service and also for allowing heterogeneous clients to access the Web service. This means that a client written in one programming language may use a Web service written in a different language. The only requirement is that the client must be able to exchange information with the Web service by using the agreed-upon data format and networking protocol.

Web Services and Java Data Type Restrictions

Web Services solve an important problem in the world of modern distributed computing: how to allow a maximum number of clients to use an application. To solve this problem, the clients and application need a common language for communication, a common transmission standard, and a method of describing what a Web service does and how to invoke it. This is accomplished through the use of a few widely implemented standards. The communication language is Extensible Markup Language (XML), which has rapidly become the language of choice for sending data across the Internet. All Web Services use XML to exchange data, in conjunction with the Simple Object Access Protocol (SOAP), which is used to encode and decode data. Transmission of data is the very essence of the Internet, so there are many reliable protocols available. The one most commonly used for Web Services is HTTP. The description of what a Web service does and how to invoke it is contained within a Web Services Description Language (WSDL) document. I'll discuss WSDL in detail later in this chapter.

Figure 26-1 illustrates the basic architecture of Web Services. The user client can potentially be written by developers independently of the Web service's developers. It must contain the ability to parse XML data received from the Web service in the agreed-upon format and also be able to transmit XML data to the Web service for processing.

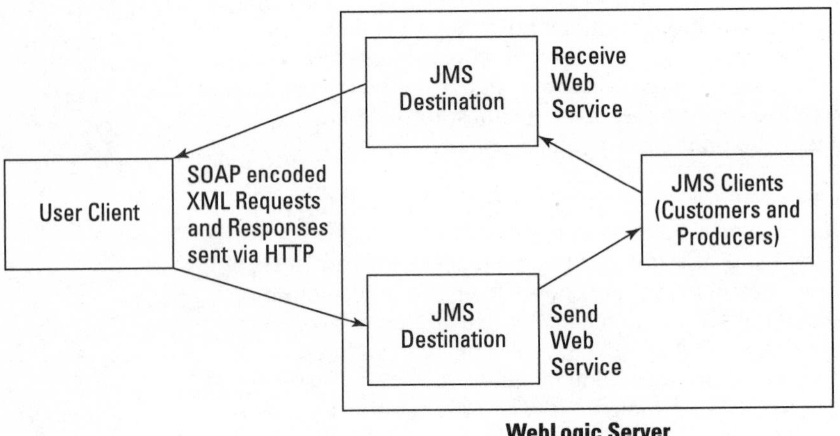

Figure 26-1: Web service architecture

Web Services run within the context of application servers (such as WebLogic Server), and their functioning within the server occurs in two or three distinct layers. The first is a Web protocol listening layer, which listens for arriving messages on the network port and protocol specified by the WSDL document. The second is the business-logic layer, which implements the service's functionality and returns results. There may also be a third layer between the listener and the business-logic that acts as a façade to the business logic, but this layer is not required. XML parsing usually occurs at this layer, relieving the business-logic layer of this responsibility.

Although all WebLogic components are J2EE-compliant, it is not necessary for Web service clients to be written in Java. Because clients can be written in languages different from the Web service, the SOAP specification places restrictions on the Java data types that can be transmitted as parameters or responses. The Java data types that can be encoded within a SOAP envelope are:

- Java primitive types: `int`, `short`, `long`, `double`, `float`, `boolean`
- `java.lang.Integer`
- `java.lang.Short`
- `java.lang.Long`
- `java.lang.Double`
- `java.lang.Float`
- `java.lang.Boolean`
- `java.lang.String`
- JavaBeans whose supported data types are in this list or another JavaBean
- Single-dimensional arrays of any supported data type except Object representations of primitive types. Example: A Web service can return an array of `ints` but not of Integers.
- `org.w3c.dom.Document`
- `org.w3c.dom.DocumentFragment`
- `org.w3c.dom.Element`

How Web Services Work in WebLogic

Now that you have a basic understanding of what a Web service is, it is time to see how all of this works in WebLogic Server. WebLogic's Web Services rely on the industry standards discussed previously for data interchange, data transmission, and self-description. WebLogic uses XML messages that are wrapped within a SOAP envelope. These are sent via HTTP and described in WSDL. This section explores these technologies in more detail, along with Jakarta Ant, a tool that automates the construction of Web Services.

WebLogic Web Services use J2EE components to form the core functionality of a Web service. A WebLogic Web service is packaged as a Web Application Archive (`.war`) file. War files can either be deployed as part of an Enterprise Application Archive (`.ear`) or as a standalone Web application. This makes deployment to multiple WebLogic servers a routine matter. Packaging is accomplished with the Jakarta Ant build tool using a special taskdef from WebLogic. Every section on constructing a Web service has a section on packaging and deploying an `.ear` file. Any service-type-specific information is given in these sections; also, there is a section on Jakarta Ant that has general information on how to use Ant with WebLogic.

For more information on deploying `.ear` files, see Chapter 18.

When the `.war` file is generated, two important files are automatically created and packaged inside of it by Ant and the WebLogic `wsgen` task definition. The first is the WSDL of the Web service. This eliminates the need for a developer to manually create the extensive and complicated XML document. The other file is a `client.jar` file that contains the necessary functionality to generate and send XML messages wrapped inside SOAP envelopes. It also contains the Java class files that are required as either parameters or return values from the Web service.

XML

Extensible Markup Language (XML) is used to describe a document's content and structure. XML is a standard for delivering data across the Internet. Like HTML, XML is a subset of the Standard Generalized Markup Language (SGML), meaning it uses `begin` and `end` tags to enclose data. Because XML allows for user-defined tags, it is also extensible.

XML is the standard language used for encoding Web-service requests and responses. It is also used to describe the Web service to remote clients who wish to use the service.

For the complete XML specification, see `http://www.w3.org/TR/REC-xml`.

HTTP

The Hypertext Transfer Protocol (HTTP) is an application-level protocol for distributed, collaborative, hypermedia information systems. It is a generic, stateless protocol that can be used for many tasks beyond the transmission of hypertext. Examples include name servers and distributed object management systems, through extension of its request methods, error codes, and headers. Although there is no requirement for Web Services to use HTTP, most major vendors do because of HTTP's ubiquity and stability. WebLogic Server uses HTTP for the transmission of data for Web Services, so we restrict our attention to this protocol.

For the complete HTTP 1.1 specification, see `http://www.ietf.org/rfc/rfc2616.txt`.

SOAP

Simple Object Access Protocol (SOAP) has become the *de-facto* standard for encoding the sending and receiving of Web-service information. SOAP uses small XML documents to exchange information in a decentralized and distributed manner.

The protocol consists of the following elements that can be embedded in a MIME-encoded package and transmitted via HTTP or another Web protocol:

✦ A SOAP envelope that contains the body of the message, who should process the message, and how to process it

✦ A set of encoding rules for representing application-specific data types

✦ A convention for representing remote procedure calls and responses

WebLogic 6.1 provides a built-in implementation of SOAP 1.1 for both the parsing of received XML messages and for the encoding of sent messages. Application developers are not required to do any low-level SOAP development if they use the WebLogic Web Services Programming Model.

For the complete SOAP specification, see `http://www.w3.org/TR/SOAP/`.

WSDL

Web Services Description Language (WSDL) is a way of describing a Web service using an XML document. The WSDL of a Web service describes how to invoke a Web service, what it does, and where it resides. Although WSDL is SOAP- and HTTP-independent, it makes the most sense to use it in a SOAP/HTTP/MIME architecture. This has evolved as the *de-facto* standard and is what WebLogic has adopted.

WSDL defines services as collections of network endpoints or *ports*. In WSDL, the abstract definition of endpoints and messages is separated from their concrete network deployment or data-format bindings. This allows the reuse of abstract definitions of messages, which are abstract descriptions of the data being exchanged, and port types, which are abstract collections of operations. The concrete protocol and data-format specifications for a particular port type constitute a reusable binding. A port is defined by associating a network address with a reusable binding; a collection of ports defines a service. This means that WSDL is a description of how clients may access and use the service.

For the complete WSDL specification, see `http://www.w3.org/TR/wsdl`.

Jakarta Ant

Jakarta Ant is a Java-based build tool developed and maintained by the Apache group under the Jakarta name. Ant uses XML files, by default called `build.xml`, to execute all recognized Java-build tasks included in the `build.xml` file. Ant comes with several built-in tasks for compiling and packaging Java projects. It also provides interfaces for creating user-defined build tasks that can be incorporated within the user's build process. WebLogic provides a vendor-specific task for generating and packaging Enterprise Application archive (`.ear`) files called wsgen. This WebLogic build task is the only way to construct a WebLogic Web service that makes use of all the features that WebLogic provides. For more information about using Jakarta Ant to construct WebLogic Web Services, see the Jakarta Ant section at the end of this chapter.

Building Web Services

Now that you understand what a Web service is, how it works, and what technologies it uses, it is time to start building Web services. The following sections discuss the different types of Web services available with WebLogic, how to get the files needed before building a Web service client, and finally a step-by-step guide to building each type of Web service.

Types of Web services

WebLogic Server supports two types of Web services: *Remote Procedure Call* (RPC) and *Message Style*. These two styles offer developers and service providers two approaches to solving different types of problems. RPC-style services resemble a conversation between two parties in which a client sends a request to the Web service and then waits until the service sends a response. Message-style services work in an asynchronous manner, where clients either send or receive messages from a JMS destination.

RPC-style Web services use a stateless session bean as the entry point to the Web service. The client invokes publicly available methods that are listed in the WSDL of the Web service with the correct parameters. Since the SOAP specification does not make use of method signatures, only method names for identification, method overloading is not available. Different method names need to be used instead of an overloaded method.

Figure 26-2 shows the architecture of a RPC style Web service. After the user client sends its XML message to the WebLogic Server, it is routed to a special servlet. This is the SOAP servlet that exists within the Servlet context of the Web application associated with the Web service. This RPC SOAP servlet is analogous to the Web Protocol Listener in the basic Web service architecture. It also performs all of the necessary parsing of XML messages wrapped within the SOAP envelope. It then passes along all the necessary parameters to the stateless Session Bean that resides within the EJB container. The Session Bean performs all necessary processing of the data and then sends its return value back to the SOAP servlet. The servlet then encodes the return value(s) in an XML message that is wrapped in a SOAP envelope. This envelope is then transmitted back to the client.

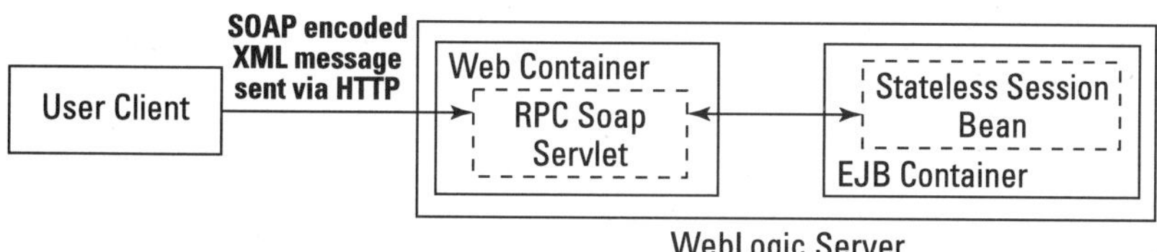

Figure 26-2: RPC-style Web service architecture

Message-style Web services work in fundamentally different ways than do RPC-style Web services while still using J2EE components. Message Web services are data-document driven instead of interface driven, like an RPC Web service. This means that when a client invokes a Message Web service, he or she sends or receives an entire document as opposed to a few parameters. Also, once the data has been sent/received, the relationship between the client and service is complete. This asynchronous relationship allows for a looser binding between the client and the Web service. This has many advantages, since the processing of the data may take an extended amount of time during which the RPC client would have to wait until the service had completed and returned a response. With a message-style Web service, the client is allowed to proceed to other work.

Figure 26-3 shows the architecture for both types of Message-style Web services. Each Web service has its own SOAP servlet, JMS destination, and client. The image demonstrates the one way movement of data in a Message-style Web service. There is no request and response processing in this model, only send or receive.

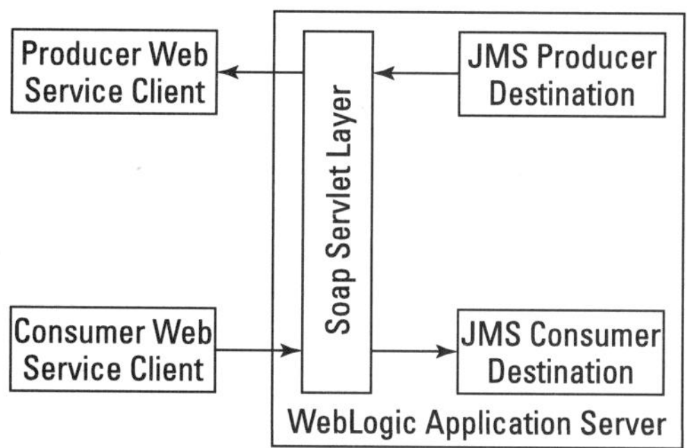

Figure 26-3: Message-Style Web service architecture

Message Web services are built upon the J2EE JMS technology. JMS destinations come in two varieties: topics and queues. All JMS components can be set up from the WebLogic Console. User clients can interact only with a JMS destination in one direction. Either messages are sent or they are received. All user interaction proceeds through a Soap servlet. Any messages that are sent to a JMS destination are placed on the destination as an object that implements the `javax.jms.ObjectMessage` interface.

See Chapter 9 for more information about JMS and JMS destinations.

The J2EE components that do the processing of the messages sent to a JMS destination can be of two varieties. JMS consumers can be either message-driven beans or simple JMS consumers. A message-driven bean is a new type of EJB that was introduced with the EJB 2.0 specification. All business logic for a message-driven bean resides in the `onMessage()` method. Message-driven beans are completely managed by the EJB container and are bound to the correct JMS destination based upon the bean's deployment descriptor. The advantage of a message-driven bean is that most of the code for connecting to a JMS destination is performed by the EJB container. Also, a message-driven bean is instantiated as soon as a message appears on a queue or topic. The bean's `onMessage()` method is then called and processing of the new message begins. This eliminates the need to have a JMS application consumer start after a specified time to consume some or all of the new messages that are in a destination. This significantly decreases the complexity and time involved in building and deploying a JMS-based application.

See Chapter 17 for more information about message-driven beans.

The J2EE component used to populate a JMS destination is still limited to an ordinary JMS applications publisher. Message-driven beans cannot place new messages on a destination without new a message first being placed on the destination to which the bean is bound.

Now that the two types of Web services available in WebLogic have been described, pick which one is right for your needs. Table 26-1 provides a few short questions to ask about your Web service and, based on your answer, which type of service to use.

Table 26-1
Deciding Which Type of Web Service to Build

If...	*write a(n)...*
the client invoking the Web service requires an immediate response	RPC Web service
the Web service functions in an asynchronous environment	message-style Web service
the behavior of the Web service can be expressed as an interface	RPC Web service
the Web service is process-oriented	RPC Web service
the Web service is data-driven	message-style Web service

Getting the Client.jar file and the WSDL

The WebLogic Web services home page lists the services available for a particular servlet context. This page also has links to the WSDL and client.jar files for each Web service defined in that context. To view the WebLogic Web services home page, use the following convention to build the correct URL to plug into your favorite Web browser:

```
[protocol]://[host]:[port][context]/index.html
```

Where

- protocol is the value defined as the protocol attribute of the <wsgen> element of a build.xml file that Ant uses to construct a Web services .ear file. There are only two valid values for this in WebLogic http (default) and https.
- host is the value defined as host in the <wsgen> element of the build.xml for that Web service. This refers to the name of the computer on which WebLogic Server is running.
- port refers to the port number upon which WebLogic Server is listening. This value is also specified as the port attribute of the <wsgen> element in the build.xml file.
- context refers to the context attribute of the <wsgen> element defined in the build.xml file for that Web service.

```
<project name="calculator" default="wsgen">
  <target name="wsgen">
    <wsgen destpath="calculator.ear"
      port="7001"
      host="localhost"
      context="/calculator"
      protocol="http">
      <rpcservices path="calculatorEJB.jar">
        <rpcservice bean="Calculator" URI="/calculator/"/>
      </rpcservices>
    </wsgen>
  </target>
</project>
```

Based upon the example build.xml file, the URL for invoking a WebLogic Web Services home page is:

```
http://localhost:7001/calculator/index.html
```

This page lists all of the Web services available under this context. They are separated into RPC and message-style services. There is a link for each service that takes it to the individual service home page. This link takes you to a page that has links to the individual services WSDL and its client.jar file. The WSDL of a Web service is a machine-readable description of a Web service. The `client.jar` file is a `.jar` file that is autogenerated by the WebLogic Server during the creation of the Web services `.ear` file. The `.jar` file is designed to allow the developer to quickly build, test, and deploy a client that uses a Web service on WebLogic Server. The `client.jar` file contains some or all of the following interfaces and classes:

- ✦ WebLogic's proprietary high-performance XML parser
- ✦ WebLogic's implementation of the SOAP 1.1 client API
- ✦ Remote interface of the RPC session bean
- ✦ Class files for any JavaBeans used as parameters or return values from the RPC session bean
- ✦ Additional class files specified by the `client.jar` element of the `build.xml` file used by Ant to build the `.ear` file for the Web service
- ✦ The necessary class files for sending or receiving information from the correct JMS destination as specified in the `build.xml` file

After downloading the `client.jar` file from the WebLogic Server, add it to your classpath before it can be used to develop a Web services client.

The `client.jar` file is only for use with JDK 1.3 or higher Java clients. If a developer wishes to write a client in another language, he or she must implement all of the features that WebLogic automatically provides in the `client.jar` file. There are also several third-party SOAP toolkits available.

Creating a Remote Procedure Call Web service

Remote Procedure Call (RPC) Web services use a stateless session bean, what we'll refer to as the interface bean, which receives the parsed XML information from the client and processes the XML information. The client calls a specific method on the bean based upon the WSDL of the service. The interface bean may then use any supporting beans or services to complete the processing of the request. After processing is finished, an XML response is HTTP encoded and sent back to the client.

The next section gives a detailed, four-step process on how to create an RPC-style Web service. The process covers creating the application server code, generating the Web service `.ear` file with Ant, and finally writing a static and dynamic client that interacts with the Web service.

Step 1: Design the Web service

This is where the interface for accessing the RPC service from the client should be designed. Also, any helper beans, database tables, or other services should be designed during Step 1.

Example: For the RPC service example, a simple calculator is built. The calculator has four public methods: add, subtract, multiply, and divide. Each method accepts two parameters and has a return parameter. Add and subtract accept longs and return a long. Multiply and divide both accept doubles and return a double. The following code shows the remote interface for the Calculator Session Bean:

```
package bible.webservices.rpc;

import java.rmi.*;
import javax.ejb.*;

public interface CalculatorRemote extends EJBObject {
  public double multiply(double amount, double factor)
    throws RemoteException;
  public double divide(double amount, double divisor)
    throws RemoteException;
  public long add(long amount1,long amount2)
    throws RemoteException;
  public long subtract(long amount1,long amount2)
    throws RemoteException;
}
```

Step 2: Build the session bean and supporting functionality

Step 2 is merely the implementation of Step 1. The RPC Session Bean, along with supporting beans and services, should be built and tested during this step. At the conclusion of Step 2, the RPC Session Bean and any supporting functionality should be packaged into a `.jar` file.

Example: Continuing with the calculator example, the functionality of the four worker methods is shown in the following code. All of the methods do simple arithmetic on the inputs and return the result.

```
package bible.webservices.rpc;

import java.rmi.*;
import javax.ejb.*;

public class Calculator implements SessionBean {
  private SessionContext sessionContext;
  public void ejbCreate() {}
  public void ejbRemove()
    throws RemoteException {}
  public void ejbActivate()
    throws RemoteException {}
  public void ejbPassivate()
    throws RemoteException {}
  public void setSessionContext(SessionContext
    sessionContext) throws RemoteException {
    this.sessionContext = sessionContext;
```

```
  }
  public long add(long amount1, long amount2) {
    return amount1 + amount2;
  }
  public long subtract(long amount1, long amount2) {
    return amount1 - amount2;
  }
  public double multiply(double amount, double factor) {
    return amount * factor;
  }
  public double divide(double amount, double divisor) {
    return amount / divisor;
  }
}
```

Step 3: Build and deploy the Enterprise Application (*.ear) file

To build a Web Service Enterprise Application (`*.ear`) file for WebLogic Server, use the Ant build utility with a properly constructed `build.xml` file.

Example: This simple `build.xml` file uses the wsgen taskdef provided by WebLogic to build a Web service called calculator from the `calculatorEJB.jar` file:

```
<target name="rpc.ws">
  <wsgen destpath="Calculator.ear" context="/calculator">
    <rpcservices path="rpc/Calculator.jar">
      <rpcservice bean="Calculator" URI="/calculator/" />
    </rpcservices>
  </wsgen>
</target>
```

See the Jakarta Ant section for more information on how to run an Ant build file.

Step 4: Build a client

To build a client for a WebLogic Web service, get the autogenerated `client.jar` file from the WebLogic server. This `.jar` file is created during the `.ear` file creation process when Ant is started (see Step 3).

See "Getting the Client.jar file and the WSDL" for more information on how to download the `client.jar` file.

When invoking an RPC Web service, you have two options for what kind of client to build: a static client or a dynamic client using a WSDL. Static clients use the actual remote interface of the RPC session bean to call methods. Dynamic clients use the Web Service's WSDL to describe what methods are available and then create a proxy to the session bean.

Example: A static client calling the Calculator Session Bean:

✦ Import the standard JNDI and Properties interfaces and classes, along with the remote interface for the RPC Session Bean:

```
import javax.naming.Context;
import javax.naming.InitialContext;
import java.util.Properties;
import bible.ws.rpc.CalculatorRemote;
```

✦ Initialize the client so that it can communicate with the Web service:

```
Properties props = new Properties ();
props.put(Context.INITIAL_CONTEXT_FACTORY,
  "weblogic.soap.http.SoapInitialContextFactory");
props.put("weblogic.soap.wsdl.interface",
  CalculatorRemote.class.getName());
Context context = new InitialContext(props);
CalculatorRemote calc =
(CalculatorRemote)context.lookup("http://localhost:7001/
calculator/Calculator/Calculator.wsdl");
```

✦ Invoke a public method on the RPC Session Bean:

```
double multReturn = calc.multiply(amount,action);
```

Here the Calculator Web service calculates the product of the two amounts passed to it and returns that amount to the client.

✦ Process the returned information:

```
System.out.println("The return value " +
  "from the calculator web service when multiplying " +
  amount + " and " + action + " is " + multReturn);
```

Here the client simply outputs the returned value to `System.out`. However, it is not too difficult to imagine a client performing more complicated processing of the return value.

The following code shows the entire code for the static client:

```
package bible.webservices.rpc.client;

import javax.naming.Context;
import javax.naming.InitialContext;
import java.util.Properties;
//the remote interface is included in the client.jar file
import bible. webservices.rpc.CalculatorRemote;

public class StaticClient {
  public StaticClient() {}

  public static void main (String[] args) throws Exception {
    Properties props = new Properties ();
    props.put(Context.INITIAL_CONTEXT_FACTORY,
```

```
      "weblogic.soap.http.SoapInitialContextFactory");
    props.put("weblogic.soap.wsdl.interface",
      CalculatorRemote.class.getName());

    Context context = new InitialContext(props);

    CalculatorRemote calc = (CalculatorRemote)context.lookup(
      "http://localhost:7001/calculator/Calculator/Calculator.wsdl");

    double amount = 34.839283;
    double action = 324232.3432;

    double multReturn = calc.multiply(amount,action);
    System.out.println("The return value from the calculator " +
      "web service when multiplying " + amount + " and " + action +
      " is " + multReturn);
  }
}
```

Example: A dynamic client that uses WSDL:

✦ Import the standard JNDI and Properties interfaces and classes along with two WebLogic SOAP classes:

```
import java.util.Properties;
import javax.naming.Context;
import javax.naming.InitialContext;
import weblogic.soap.WebServiceProxy;
import weblogic.soap.SoapMethod;
```

✦ Initialize the client so that it can communicate with the Web service:

```
Properties props = new Properties();
props.put(Context.INITIAL_CONTEXT_FACTORY,
  "weblogic.soap.http.SoapInitialContextFactory");

Context context = new InitialContext(props);
WebServiceProxy proxy =
  (WebServiceProxy)context.lookup(
    "http://localhost:7001/calculator/" +
    "Calculator/Calculator.wsdl");
```

Notice here that the client uses the context to create a new `WebServiceProxy`. The `WebServiceProxy` is a WebLogic class that is a generic wrapper that can go around any Web service EJB. This allows for the client to be more dynamic but constrains what the client can pass to the Web service as parameters.

✦ Invoke a public method on the RPC Session Bean by creating a `SoapMethod` object. The WSDL of the Web service is used to lookup names of available methods.

```
SoapMethod add = proxy.getMethod("add");
Long sum = (Long)add.invoke(new Object[] {new Long(add1),
  new Long(add2)});
```

Because the client uses a `SoapMethod` to be more dynamic, it must pass an array of objects to the Web service, so new `Long` objects have to be created in the example. Also, the `SoapMethod` class only returns `java.lang.Objects`, so there must be an explicit downcast into the appropriate Java object.

✦ Process the return data:

```
System.out.println("adding " +  add1 +
  " and " + add2 + " results in " + sum);
```

The following code shows the complete dynamic client:

```
package bible.webservices.rpc.client;

import java.util.Properties;
import javax.naming.Context;
import javax.naming.InitialContext;
import weblogic.soap.WebServiceProxy;
import weblogic.soap.SoapMethod;

public class DynamicClient {
  public DynamicClient() {}

  public static void main (String[] args) throws Exception {
    Properties props = new Properties();
    props.put(Context.INITIAL_CONTEXT_FACTORY,
      "weblogic.soap.http.SoapInitialContextFactory");
    Context context = new InitialContext(props);

    WebServiceProxy proxy = (WebServiceProxy)context.lookup(
      "http://localhost:7001/calculator/Calculator/Calculator.wsdl");

    SoapMethod add = proxy.getMethod("add");

    long add1 = 346;
    long add2 = 5623;

    //a weblogic SoapMethod only returns objects and only
    //takes objects thus the casting into Long
    Long sum = (Long)add.invoke(new Object[] {new Long(add1),
      new Long(add2)} );

    System.out.println("adding " +  add1 +
      " and " + add2 + " results in " + sum);
  }
}
```

Creating a Consumer Message-Style Web service

This section describes how to build, deploy, and invoke a Consumer Message-Style Web service. This is a five-step process and requires a little more design time than does a RPC-style service. Consumer Web Services receive messages off of either a JMS queue or topic and then process that message.

Step 1: Design the Web service

The first decision that you must make when designing a message-style Web service is whether to use a queue or a topic as your JMS destination. Queues implement a point-to-point messaging model that delivers the message to exactly one recipient. Topics use a publish/subscribe model, where a message is delivered to multiple recipients. A second concern should be whether your service should send the document to or receive it from the user client. If you want the service to do both, create two separate JMS destinations and two separate JMS listeners.

Example: The sending of a message by a client and the subsequent server-side processing is demonstrated. Notice that the client doesn't wait for a reply from the Web service when sending a message. It is free to continue processing other data separate from the Web Services server. This a good example of the asynchronous behavior of message-style Web Services. A queue is used as the JMS destination in this example.

Step 2: Set up the JMS Service on WebLogic Server

This is a multi-step process where you define several services that are interrelated. This can all be accomplished from the WebLogic Server Console. For more information on setting up a JMS destination, see Chapter 9.

Example: The JMS queue for this example has the JNDI names defined in Table 26-2.

Table 26-2
JNDI Names for Example 2's Components

JMS Component	*JNDI Name*
`ConnectionFactory`	`bible/ws/message/SendConnectionFactory`
`JMSServer`	`WSJMSSendServer`
`JMSDestination`	`SendQueue`

Step 3: Build the server-side components that interact with JMS

The developer has two choices when deciding what components to use to listen to a JMS destination: either a client application JMS consumer class or a message-driven bean. *Example:* In this portion of the example, a message-driven bean is used to consume messages that the user client, which we discuss in Step 5, sends to the appropriate JMS destination. In the following example, the `QueueReader` bean simply prints the value of the message to `System.out`:

```
package bible.webservices.message.consumer;

import javax.jms.*;
import javax.naming.*;
```

```
import javax.ejb.CreateException;
import javax.ejb.MessageDrivenContext;
import javax.ejb.MessageDrivenBean;
import java.rmi.RemoteException;


public class QueueReader implements MessageDrivenBean,
MessageListener {
  private transient MessageDrivenContext mdc = null;
  private Context context;

  public QueueReader() {
  }

  public void setMessageDrivenContext(MessageDrivenContext mdc)
{
    this.mdc = mdc;
  }

  public void ejbCreate() {
  }

  public void ejbRemove() {
  }

  public void onMessage(Message message) {
    ObjectMessage tm = (ObjectMessage)message;
try {
System.out.println(
"The text in the message was "
+ tm.getObject());
    }catch (Exception e) {
      e.printStackTrace();
    }
  }
}
```

Step 4: Build and deploy the .ear file

To build a Web Service Enterprise Application (`.ear`) file for WebLogic Server, use the Ant build utility with a properly constructed `build.xml` file.

Example: This `build.xml` file constructs an `.ear` file called `messageWS` that runs on port 7001 under the `messageWS` context. It uses the queue and `connectionFactory` named to create and place the message received from the client in the correct destination.

```
<wsgen destpath="Consumer.ear"
       context="/consumerWS"
       webapp="consumer.war">
  <messageservices>
    <messageservice
        action="send"
```

```
            name="consumer"
            destination="SendQueue"
            destinationtype="queue"
            uri="/sendMsg"
            ConnectionFactory=
              "bible/ws/message/SendConnectionFactory"/>
    </messageservices>
  </wsgen>
```

See Jakarta Ant for more information on creating and running a `build.xml` file.

Step 5: Build a client

To build a client for a WebLogic Web service, get the autogenerated `client.jar` file from the WebLogic server. This `.jar` file is created during the `.ear` file creation process when Ant is started. (See Step 4.) See "Getting the Client.jar file and the WSDL" for more information on how to download the `client.jar` file.

A message-style Web service only has one type of client that can be used with it. Message Web Services define only one method name based on whether the client sends or receives data. Aptly, these methods are named "send" for clients that send data and "receive" for those that receive data. Any kind of data can be sent to the Web service from the client, such as a simple String, an ArrayList, or a JavaBean. When the JMS consumer gets the data, the data is wrapped in a `javax.jms.ObjectMessage`.

Example: This simple client gets a handle on the correct JMS destination and then places a simple string message on the queue.

✦ Import the standard JNDI, Properties, and URL interfaces and classes, along with several WebLogic, SOAP, and Codec classes:

```
import javax.naming.Context;
import javax.naming.InitialContext;
import java.net.URL;
import java.util.Properties;
import weblogic.soap.WebServiceProxy;
import weblogic.soap.SoapMethod;
import weblogic.soap.SoapType;
import weblogic.soap.codec.CodecFactory;
import weblogic.soap.codec.SoapEncodingCodec;
```

✦ Create a `Codec` Factory and register `SoapEncodingCodec`:

```
CodecFactory factory = CodecFactory.newInstance();
factory.register( new SoapEncodingCodec());
```

✦ Initialize the client so that it can communicate with the WebLogic Web Services server, and parse the SOAP messages:

```
WebServiceProxy proxy = WebServiceProxy.createService(
  new URL("http://localhost:7001/consumerWS/sendMsg"));
proxy.setCodecFactory(factory);
proxy.setVerbose(true);
```

✦ Create a new SoapType and SoapMethod. The SoapType is used as a parameter to the Web service.

```
SoapType param = new SoapType( "message", String.class);
proxy.addMethod("send", null, new SoapType[] {param});
SoapMethod method = proxy.getMethod("send");
```

✦ Invoke the SoapMethod to send the data to the JMS destination that has been specified:

```
String message =
  "Sending data to the JMS queueReader from the client";
Object result = method.invoke(new Object[] {message});
```

The following code shows the entire client for sending data to the Web service:

```
package bible.webservices.message.consumer;

import javax.naming.Context;
import javax.naming.InitialContext;
import java.net.URL;
import java.util.Properties;
import weblogic.soap.WebServiceProxy;
import weblogic.soap.SoapMethod;
import weblogic.soap.SoapType;
import weblogic.soap.codec.CodecFactory;
import weblogic.soap.codec.SoapEncodingCodec;
import weblogic.soap.codec.LiteralCodec;

public class Client {

  public Client() {}

  public static void main (String[] args) {
    try {
      CodecFactory factory = CodecFactory.newInstance();
      factory.register( new SoapEncodingCodec());
      factory.register( new LiteralCodec());

      WebServiceProxy proxy = WebServiceProxy.createService(
        new URL("http://localhost:7001/consumerWS/sendMsg"));
      proxy.setCodecFactory(factory);
      proxy.setVerbose(true);

      SoapType param = new SoapType( "message", String.class);
      proxy.addMethod("send", null, new SoapType[] {param});
      SoapMethod method = proxy.getMethod("send");

      String message =
        "Sending data to the JMS queueReader from the client";
      Object result = method.invoke(new Object[] {message});
```

```
      } catch (Exception e) {
        e.printStackTrace();
      }
    }
  }
```

Building a Message-Style producer Web service

This section discusses how to build a message-style Web service that places a message on a JMS destination. The user client then actively goes to the JMS destination and consumes the message.

Step 1: Design the Web service

The first decision that you must make when designing a message-style Web service is whether to use a queue or a topic as your JMS destination. Queues implement a point-to-point messaging model that delivers the message to exactly one recipient. Topics use a publish/subscribe model, where a message is delivered to multiple recipients. A second concern should be whether your service should send or receive the document to the user client. If you want the service to do both, create two separate JMS destinations and two separate JMS listeners.

Example: In this example, a client receives messages placed on a JMS queue by a simple publishing application. The asynchronous behavior of message-style Web Services is highlighted by the fact that the `QueueFiller` class can be run a significant amount of time ahead of when the client retrieves the messages.

Step 2: Set up the JMS service on WebLogic Server

This is a multi-step process where you define several services that are interrelated. This can all be accomplished from the WebLogic Server Console. For more information on setting up a JMS destination, see Chapter 9.

Example: The JMS queue for this example has the JNDI names defined in Table 26-3.

Table 26-3
JNDI Names for Example 3's Components

JMS Component	*JNDI Name*
`ConnectionFactory`	`bible/ws/message/ReceiveConnectionFactory`
`JMSServer`	`WSJMSReceiveServer`
`JMSDestination`	`ReceiveQueue`

Step 3: Build the server-side components that interact with JMS

When the Web service needs to place messages on a JMS destination, only normal JMS client applications work. Message-driven beans currently do not have the capability to place information on a JMS destination; they can only consume. So this obviously limits the types of components that the developer can create. For more information on creating clients for sending information to a JMS destination, see Chapter 9.

Example: This JMS application simply fills a JMS queue with several trivial messages that have simple strings that identify the message number. Please see Chapter 9 for more information on the functioning of this class.

```
package bible.webservices.message.producer;

import javax.naming.*;
import javax.jms.*;
import java.util.*;

public class QueueFiller {

  public QueueFiller() {}

  public static void main(String[] args) {
    Context ctx = null;
    QueueConnectionFactory qConnectionFactory = null;
    QueueConnection qConnection = null;
    QueueSession qSession = null;
    QueueSender qSender = null;

    try {
      Properties props = new Properties();
      props.put(Context.INITIAL_CONTEXT_FACTORY,
        "weblogic.jndi.WLInitialContextFactory");
      props.put(Context.PROVIDER_URL,
        "t3://localhost:7001");
      ctx = new InitialContext(props);
      qConnectionFactory = (QueueConnectionFactory)
        ctx.lookup("bible/ws/message/ReceiveConnectionFactory");
      qConnection = qConnectionFactory.createQueueConnection();
      qSession = qConnection.createQueueSession(false,
        javax.jms.QueueSession.AUTO_ACKNOWLEDGE);
      Queue q = (Queue)ctx.lookup("ReceiveQueue");
      qSender = qSession.createSender(q);

      System.out.println("Sending messages to the client...");
      ObjectMessage message = qSession.createObjectMessage();

      for (int i=0; i<10; i++) {
        message.clearBody();
        message.setObject("Message #" + i + " data to the client");
        System.out.println("Sending message #" + i);
        qSender.send(message);
```

```
      }
      message.clearBody();
      message.setObject("Stop");
      System.out.println("Sending message " + message.getObject());
      qSender.send(message);
    } catch (Exception e) {
      e.printStackTrace();
    } finally {
      try {
        qSender.close();
        qSession.close();
        qConnection.close();
      } catch (Exception ex) {
      }
    }
  }
}
```

Step 4: Build and deploy the .ear file

To build a Web Service Enterprise Application (`.ear`) file for WebLogic Server, use the Ant build utility with a properly constructed `build.xml` file.

Example: This `build.xml` file constructs a `.ear` file named `messageWS` that runs on port 7001 under the `messageWS` context. Its uses the destination and connection factory listed for retrieving messages placed in the named JMS destination.

```
<wsgen destpath="Producer.ear"
       context="/producerWS"
       webapp="producer.war">
  <messageservices>
    <messageservice
      action="receive"
      name="producer"
      destination="ReceiveQueue"
      destinationtype="queue"
      uri="/receiveMsg"
      ConnectionFactory=
        "bible/ws/message/ReceiveConnectionFactory"/>
  </messageservices>
</wsgen>
```

See Jakarta Ant for more information on creating and running a `build.xml` file.

Step 5: Build a client

To build a client for a WebLogic Web service, get the autogenerated `client.jar` file from the WebLogic server. This `.jar` file is created during the `.ear` file creation process when Ant is started. (See Step 4.)

See "Getting the Client.jar file and the WSDL" for more information on how to download the `client.jar` file.

Message-style Web Services only have one type of client that can be used with them. Message Web Services define only one method name based on whether the client sends or receives data. Aptly, these methods are named "send" for clients that send data and "receive" for those that receive data. When a JMS producer creates a message that goes on a JMS destination, the data that the producer creates gets wrapped in a `javax.jms.ObjectMessage`. Thus, when a user client receives messages from a JMS destination, the return type is a `java.lang.Object` and must be downcast before any nontrivial processing may begin on it.

Example: This client gets a handle on the JMS destination and then continues to simply print the contents until the queue is empty.

- Import the standard JNDI, Properties, and URL interfaces and classes, along with the necessary WebLogic, SOAP, and Codec classes:

```
import javax.naming.Context;
import javax.naming.InitialContext;
import java.net.URL;
import java.util.Properties;
import weblogic.soap.WebServiceProxy;
import weblogic.soap.SoapMethod;
import weblogic.soap.SoapType;
import weblogic.soap.codec.CodecFactory;
import weblogic.soap.codec.SoapEncodingCodec;
```

- Create a `CodecFactory` and register the `SoapEncodingCodec`:

```
CodecFactory factory = CodecFactory.newInstance();
factory.register(new SoapEncodingCodec());
```

- Initialize the client for communication with the WebLogic Server:

```
WebServiceProxy proxy = WebServiceProxy.createService(
  new URL("http://localhost:7001/producerWS/receiveMsg"));
proxy.setCodecFactory(factory);
proxy.setVerbose(false);
```

  Note that since the client does not use the WSDL of the Web service, the URL that is created is for the actual Web service instead of its WSDL, such as an RPC-style client.

- Create a `SoapMethod` wrapper around the service's receive method:

```
SoapType ret = new SoapType( "result", String.class);
proxy.addMethod("receive", ret, null);
SoapMethod method = proxy.getMethod("receive");
```

✦ Receive the necessary data from the JMS destination that is specified in the `build.xml` file:

```
while(true) {
  Object result = method.invoke(null);
  System.out.println(
  "The message passed returned from the web service queue:
  " + result);
  if (result.equals("Stop"))
    break;
}
```

✦ This client continually invokes the receive method and prints out the result until the queue is empty.

The following code shows the entire receiver client:

```
package bible.webservices.message.producer.client;

import javax.naming.Context;
import javax.naming.InitialContext;
import java.net.URL;
import java.util.Properties;
import weblogic.soap.WebServiceProxy;
import weblogic.soap.SoapMethod;
import weblogic.soap.SoapType;
import weblogic.soap.codec.CodecFactory;
import weblogic.soap.codec.SoapEncodingCodec;
import weblogic.soap.codec.LiteralCodec;

public class ReaderClient {

  public ReaderClient() {}

  public static void main(String[] args) {

    try {
      CodecFactory factory = CodecFactory.newInstance();

      factory.register(new SoapEncodingCodec());

      WebServiceProxy proxy = WebServiceProxy.createService(
        new URL("http://localhost:7001/producerWS/receiveMsg"));

      proxy.setCodecFactory(factory);
      proxy.setVerbose(false);

      SoapType ret = new SoapType("result", String.class);

      proxy.addMethod("receive", ret, null);

      SoapMethod method = proxy.getMethod("receive");

      while (true){
```

```
        Object result = method.invoke(null);

        System.out.println("The message returned from "
                           + "the web service queue: " + result);
        if (result.equals("Stop"))
          break;
      }
    } catch (Exception e) {
      e.printStackTrace();
    }
  }
```

Other Web-Service Technologies

The following sections discuss several technologies that relate to Web Services in general and in some cases to WebLogic specifically. Although none of these technologies are required for Web Services to work, they increase the power and ease of building and deploying new Web Services.

Jakarta Ant

Jakarta Ant is a Java-based build tool from the Apache group. Because it is Java based, Ant is platform independent. This independence eliminates many of the headaches associated with OS-dependent make files or other build processes that are merely extensions of command-shell operations. Instead, Ant uses Java classes that read configuration build files that are XML based and use target trees of various tasks that get executed. An object that implements a particular Task interface runs each task. WebLogic has created a task object called `wsgen` that performs the creation of Web service `.ear` files and all other autogenerated files within the `.ear`.

Ant requires that an XML file describing the tasks to be performed be available prior to execution. By default Ant build files are called `build.xml` but the name of build files can be specified with the `-buildfile` command-line argument. To execute an Ant build task, do the following:

1. Create a staging directory where Ant can be run.
2. Copy the necessary source files such as EJB `.jar` files and other application code that needs to be included in the Web service `.ear` file.
3. Construct a well-formed `build.xml` file in the root of the staging directory.
4. Open a new command prompt.
5. Run the `setEnv.cmd` script for to setup the necessary classpath variables that Ant needs. `SetEnv.cmd` is located in the `%WL_HOME%/config/mydomain` directory. `%WL_HOME%` is the location of the WebLogic Server installation, for example, `c:/bea/wlserver6.1/config/mydomain` on a Windows system.

6. Run "ant" in the directory where you have constructed your `build.xml` file. The Ant build utility should construct an `.ear` file that has all of the necessary components to run the Web service.

Ant can be downloaded from the Jakarta Web site at the following URL: `http://jakarta.apache.org/ant/index.html`.

For a more complete tutorial on Ant, see the documentation included with the downloaded package from Jakarta.

The following is a listing of all possible elements and attributes that can go in an Ant `build.xml` file for a WebLogic Web service.

wsgen

The `wsgen` element is the root element of the WebLogic-specific information in the `build.xml` file. Its attributes specify information common to all Web Services described in the file. The `wsgen` element can have any number of `rpcservices` elements, one (optional) `messageservices` element, and one (optional) `client.jar` subelements. This element is the only one required by the `wsgen` build task and contains the attributes shown in Table 26-4.

Table 26-4
wsgen Attributes

Attributes	*Attribute Description*	*Required?*
`basepath`	Location of the input Enterprise Application archive file (`*.ear`) or exploded directory that contains the EJB `.jar` files for the entry point and supporting EJBs of RPC-style Web Services. Be sure to specify the full pathname of the file or directory if it is not located in the same directory as the `build.xml` file. Default value is null.	No
`destpath`	Type and location of the output Enterprise Application archive. To create an actual Enterprise Application archive file (`*.ear`), specify the `.ear` suffix; to create an exploded Enterprise Application directory, specify a directory name. Specify the full pathname of the file or directory if you do not want the Ant task to create the archive in the local directory. Default value is `basepath` if you have specified the `basepath` attribute; otherwise, it is null.	Yes
`context`	Context root of the Web Services. You later use this value to access the deployed Web service with a URL.	Yes
`protocol`	Protocol by which clients' access the Web service. There are two possible values: http or https. The default value is http.	No

Attributes	Attribute Description	Required?
host	Name of the host that is running the WebLogic Server instance that is hosting the Web service; for example, www.bea.com. If you do not specify this attribute, the host in the WSDL JSP is generated from the *hostname* section of the URL used to retrieve the WSDL.	No
port	Port number of WebLogic Server. Default value is 7001. If you do not specify this attribute, the port in the WSDL JSP is generated from the *port* section of the URL used to retrieve the WSDL.	No
webapp	URI that specifies the path to a Web Application module used to expose a Web service. Default value is web-services.war.	No
classpath	Semicolon-separated list of directories or JAR files that contain Java classes (such as utility classes) needed by the stateless session EJB that implements an RPC-style Web service.	No

Referenced from `http://edocs.bea.com/wls/docs61/webServices/build_xml.html`

rpcservices

The `rpcservices` element specifies an EJB archive that contains the entry-point stateless session EJBs and supporting EJBs that make up RPC-style Web services. This element can have any number of rpcservice subelements that describe each individual RPC-style Web service. This element contains the attributes listed in Table 26-5.

Table 26-5
rpcservices Attributes

Attributes	Attribute Description	Required?
module	If the `basepath` attribute of the `wsgen` element is set, this attribute specifies the URI of the Enterprise Application module that corresponds to an EJB archive contained by the Enterprise Application archive.	Only if the `basepath` attribute of the `wsgen` element is set.
path	If the `basepath` attribute of the `wsgen` element is not set, this attribute specifies the location of an existing EJB archive that contains the EJBs, either archive as a `*.jar` file or as an exploded directory.	Only if the `basepath` attribute of the `wsgen` element is *not* set.

Referenced from `http://edocs.bea.com/wls/docs61/webServices/build_xml.html`

rpcservice

The `rpcservice` element specifies a specific RPC-style Web service. This element does not have any subelements. This element contains the attributes listed in Table 26-6.

Table 26-6
rpcservice Attributes

Attributes	*Attribute Description*	*Required?*
`bean`	Name of the stateless session EJB that implements the RPC-style Web service. This name corresponds to the `ejb-name` element in the `ejb-jar.xml` file of the EJB archive in which the EJB is contained. The path to the EJB archive is specified in the parent `rpcservices` element.	Yes
`uri`	Part of the URL used by clients to invoke the Web service. The full URL to access the Web service is: [*protocol*]://[*host*]:[*port*][*context*][*uri*] where *protocol* refers to the protocol attribute of the `wsgen` element. *host* refers to the hostname of the computer upon which the WebLogic Server hosting the service is running. *port* refers to the port of WebLogic Server. *context* refers to the context attribute of the `wsgen` element. *uri* refers to this attribute. For example, the URL that accesses the RPC-style Web service in the example in Example of a `build.xml` file is: `http://www.myHost.com:7001/myContext/rpc_URI`	Yes

Referenced from `http://edocs.bea.com/wls/docs61/webServices/build_xml.html`

messageservices

The `messageservices` element acts as a container for any number of `messageservice` subelements. This element does not have any attributes.

messageservice

The `messageservice` element describes a specific message-style Web service by specifying a JMS destination that receives or sends XML data. This element does not have any subelements. This element contains the attributes shown in Table 26-7.

Table 26-7
messageservice Attributes

Attributes	*Attribute Description*	*Required?*
`name`	Name of the message-style Web service.	Yes
`destination`	JNDI name of a JMS topic or queue.	Yes
`destination` type	Type of JMS destination. Values: topic or queue	Yes
`action`	Specifies whether the client that invokes this message-style Web service sends or receives XML data to the JMS destination. Values: send or receive. Specify send if the client sends XML data to the JMS destination and receive if the client receives XML data from the JMS destination.	Yes
`connectionfactory`	JNDI name of the `ConnectionFactory` used to create a connection to the JMS destination	Yes
`uri`	Part of the URL used by clients to invoke the Web service. The full URL to access the Web service is: `[`*`protocol`*`]://[`*`host`*`]:[`*`port`*`]` `[`*`context`*`][`*`uri`*`]` where *protocol* refers to the protocol attribute of the `wsgen` element. *host* refers to the hostname of the computer upon which the WebLogic Server hosting the service is running. *port* refers to the port of WebLogic Server. *context* refers to the context attribute of the `wsgen` element. *uri* refers to this attribute. For example, the URL that accesses the first message-style Web service in the example in Example of a `build.xml` file is: `http://www.myHost.com:7001/myContext/sendMsg`	Yes

Referenced from `http://edocs.bea.com/wls/docs61/webServices/build_xml.html`

clientjar

Use the `clientjar` element to specify the name for the generated Java client `.jar` file. You can also use it to specify other arbitrary files that you want to add to the generated Java client `.jar` file. This element can have one subelement: manifest. Its attributes appear in Table 26-8.

Table 26-8
clientjar Attributes

Attribute	Attribute Description	Required?
`path`	URI for the generated Java client JAR file that contains all the Java classes and interfaces needed to invoke the Web Services	No

Referenced from `http://edocs.bea.com/wls/docs61/webServices/build_xml.html`

manifest

The `manifest` element is a container for additional header entries to the manifest file (`MANIFEST.MF`) included in the generated Java client JAR file. This element can have any number of entry subelements that describe the additional headers to the manifest file. This element does not have any attributes.

entry

The `entry` element specifies the name and value of an additional header to the manifest file (`MANIFEST.MF`) included in the generated Java client JAR file. This element does not have any subelements. This element contains the attributes listed in Table 26-9.

Table 26-9
entry Attributes

Attributes	Attribute Description	Required?
`name`	Name of the additional header that appears in the manifest file (`MANIFEST.MF`) of the generated Java client JAR file	Yes
`value`	Value of the additional header that appears in the manifest file (`MANIFEST.MF`) of the generated Java client JAR file	Yes

Referenced from `http://edocs.bea.com/wls/docs61/webServices/build_xml.html`

UDDI

Universal Description, Discovery and Integration Service (UDDI) can be thought of as directory service for Web Services. Clients can use the UDDI service to dynamically link to listed Web Services. UDDI has two types of users. The first type is Web service providers who wish to register their service for public use. The UDDI links users to the WSDL for a particular registered Web service. Obviously, the second type of user of UDDI is clients looking for a certain type of Web service and how to use the Web service. UDDI's major supporters include Microsoft, IBM, and Ariba.

Future J2EE and IDE support

Currently, the Java 2 Enterprise Edition (J2EE) specification makes no use of Web Services. However, Sun Microsystems has promised to incorporate Web Services technologies into the next major revision of the specification. Until that revision, Sun will provide, in incremental releases, a J2EE Web Services developer kit. Although it is not clear exactly what will be provided in this kit, many of its features are already present in the WebLogic platform.

Borland, IBM, and several other J2EE Integrated Development Environment (IDE) providers promise to incorporate Web-Services technologies in the next major releases of their respective products. It is likely that IDEs that integrate with WebLogic will also provide support for WebLogic-based Web Services.

Summary

Web Services are an exiting and challenging new technology. The decoupling of the client and server from each other through standard-transmission technologies allows for development in any language that implements the necessary technologies. Developers can now select the best language and environment independently for both servers and clients, instead of selecting the language and environment that was the best fit for both needs. WebLogic Server provides the developer with a huge benefit with its built-in support for the most popular Web Services technologies. Since WebLogic Web Services wrap around J2EE components, existing J2EE component functionality can be exposed. By streamlining the creation process and making it easy and fast to deploy both clients and server applications, WebLogic has removed most of the major barriers to Web service development. This allows WebLogic users to deploy their Web service before their competitors do and gain an advantage.

✦ ✦ ✦

Working with WebLogic and the J2EE Connector Architecture

CHAPTER 27

✦ ✦ ✦ ✦

In This Chapter

Understanding the J2EE Connector Architecture

Using the J2EE Connector Architecture in WebLogic

✦ ✦ ✦ ✦

This chapter provides a brief introduction into the world of the J2EE Connector Architecture and API. In many companies, and from experience in telecommunications, there are many third-party applications that must be used that are added to a system. An example of such a system is an OSS (Operational Support Systems) system. An OSS is a telecommunications system that can interface with other telecommunications systems and ordering systems to provide a customer with the ability to subscribe to a telecommunication service. These third-party components are needed to provide business objects that are necessary to complete the system.

An example of a third-party component is the Oracle ERP. It can process an Order Entry, the ERP notion of an ordering process, from end to end in out-of-the-box functionality. The business logic is proprietary to Oracle and the effort of building a system to implement and order ERP would take more time and effort than any mid-size company could afford. Tables and fields that provide the end-to-end ordering in the Oracle ERP system are proprietary to Oracle and cannot be discussed without Oracle's consent. Other pieces of an OSS could be a NightFire solution for communicating to other telecommunication companies through a proprietary communication network. NightFire and companies like it have given a large effort to understanding the interfaces between telecommunication companies, and reproducing some of their efforts requires a lot of money and time. In many of these cases, it's better to buy some of these products than to have a company produce them. Many companies that use these products don't necessarily need to produce each and every one. This allows the organization using the products to concentrate on their core products and services.

Third-party products are needed to connect the organization's enterprise systems. The organization's enterprise system may not be standardized with the third-party applications. Connecting them so that they work together may require significant effort and negotiation of various standards and technologies between many APIs. Some of these systems exist on multiple platforms. Some situations require that ports be made across COM (Component Object Model) and CORBA (Common Object Request Broker Architecture) for various systems to communicate to each other. Sometimes multiple hops and software have to be invented to read a single entry across a proprietary system. Without a single standard that can work across multiple machines and with multiple enterprise applications, building the entire OSS becomes a difficult exercise in matching APIs to other APIs and messaging data that can work across multiple domains and work in the same manner.

Countless millions have been used in such efforts, and many see XML as a relief to move their data internally through their systems. To parse a single data element multiple times to move that data item from one end of the room to the other is time consuming. It's even worse when it becomes so open that anyone that looks at the XML stream can read it in text form and gain access to data elements throughout the enterprise system. Selling a secure enterprise system is difficult when most of the data that is transmitted in the system is in human-readable form. Some of the benefits of the Connector API include Connection Management, Security Management, and Transaction Management. These topics are discussed in detail in later sections. But these management systems are the heart of the Connector API and they are needed infrastructure building blocks for providing a robust system.

Understanding the J2EE Connector Architecture

With many different products and specializations with e-commerce and back-end systems on the market, it has become imperative to find ways to have disparate systems communicate with each other effectively. An example of such a system is a J2EE-compliant system like WebLogic that uses EJBs and a non-J2EE-compliant system such as Siebel that has proprietary information for order processing. Both of these systems use data, even somewhat differently, but to one system there is data known as an order and to the other system there is also data known as an order. The two systems must somehow map what one system refers to as an order to what the other system refers to as an order. Accomplishing this task requires a common framework where both systems can communicate (thus the term *connector*) and where they can map one form of data to the other. This is the motivation behind the Connector API is to provide the framework and architecture to connect different third-party systems to each other. To understand the connector architecture, you must first understand some of the key concepts.

Key concepts

The Connector API version 1.0 was built to accommodate the mapping of data between various EAI and EIS systems. It has system contracts on how data must be mapped between systems. For any data manipulation, it must maintain transactional integrity to ensure that rollbacks and commits can be supported. Security must ensure that the data does not get manipulated during movement and is protected from eavesdropping. Resources must be managed to ensure that the movement of data can be accomplished without running out of resources before the task has been accomplished. The following sections examine the key concepts in detail to see how they fit together.

EAI and EIS

Many pieces make up the Connector API version 1.0. The emphasis of the Connector API is to provide a generic framework that is not specific to the Enterprise Information System (EIS), the application server, and the application component. Without the Connector API, it would be difficult to decouple the different APIs. Even if they were decoupled, there would be no other specification that is vender neutral that would avoid a rewrite every time a new component is added from a different company.

The EIS makes up the data information on the back end that is being accessed for processing information and business logic across an organization's enterprise (see Figure 27-1). In a pure J2EE architecture, this is the piece that normally contains the legacy system or proprietary data system. One of the systems that also make up the EIS is the Enterprise Application Integration (EAI) system. The connector architecture could be considered a type of EAI. The purpose of an EAI is to integrate multiple third-party applications and sometimes just multiple types of business logic into a centralized enterprise form of connectivity. The idea of an EAI system is to be able to process XML systems for B2B and back-end systems of different integrators for business logic. One of these systems could consist of Oracle's ERP (Enterprise Resource Planning) to plan a system across an enterprise to provide end-to-end processing of an order, billing, and product catalog system. A typical EAI system comes from systems such as Tuxedo, Vitria's BusinessWare, and TibCo. A lot of these systems provide asynchronous transactions for publishing and subscribing messages that are separated from the application servers.

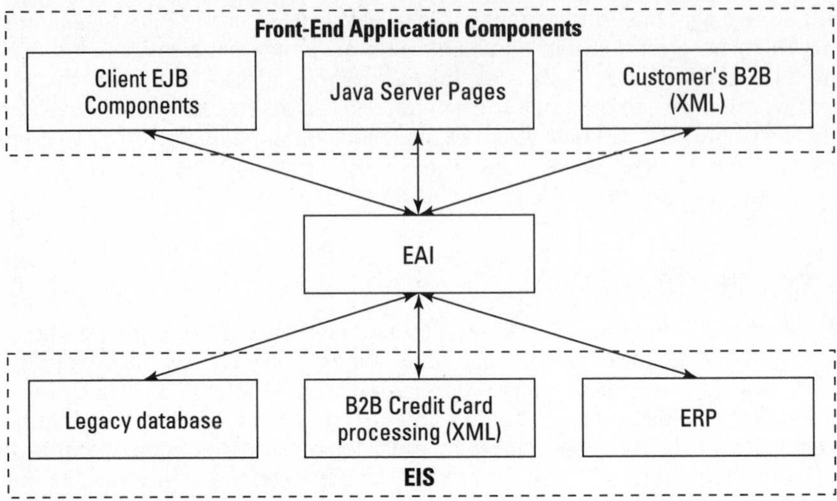

Figure 27-1: Enterprise Information System

The problem with this type of architecture is that it separates the EAI from the application servers. For some EAI systems, the Java Server Page (JSP) would have to be translated into XML (Extensible Markup Language) and then stored on a message queue similar to JMS (Java Message Service), and then translated again into the EIS system. Because there are multiple translations and parsing, this type of system could have a slow reaction. Another issue, if an EIS system is decoupled from the application server's security management, transaction management, and connection management, is that it would have to implement its own services of these management systems, as well as synchronize with the application server's form of these managers to work across an enterprise and to coordinate the application's components. If an EJB needs to perform a commit on the client side, for example, then the EAI system needs to synchronize that commit to the appropriate EIS system with the EAI's transaction management and the application server's transaction management to ensure the resource's transactional integrity. Managing multiple systems in this architecture can get complicated very easily. To simplify these types of issues, it's better to use the EAI as an application server, or an application server as an EAI to avoid the issues between communicating between the different managers.

The Connector API is a mechanism to turn the application server into an EAI system. This makes the application server solely responsible for the security management, transaction management, and connection management. It also transforms the EAI system from a separate server and vendor into an extension of the application server.

Resource adapter

You must add several parts to the application server to implement the Connector API. Figure 27-2 shows how the application component, such as an EJB, will communicate to the resource adapter through a Common Client Interface (CCI). The purpose of the CCI is to provide a generic Connector implementation independent of the application server. This connection is not aware of the security management, the transaction management, or the connection management. The CCI only needs some information of executing functions to a specific EIS system with data and getting data back. The resource adapter is responsible for managing the connection, which is aptly called a `ManagedConnection`. The application server has to interface into the resource adapter to provide the security management, the transaction management, and the connection management. The common interface for the interaction between the application server and the resource adapter is called the Service Provider Interface (SPI). The SPI interfaces between the providers, or in this case the application server and the resource adapter.

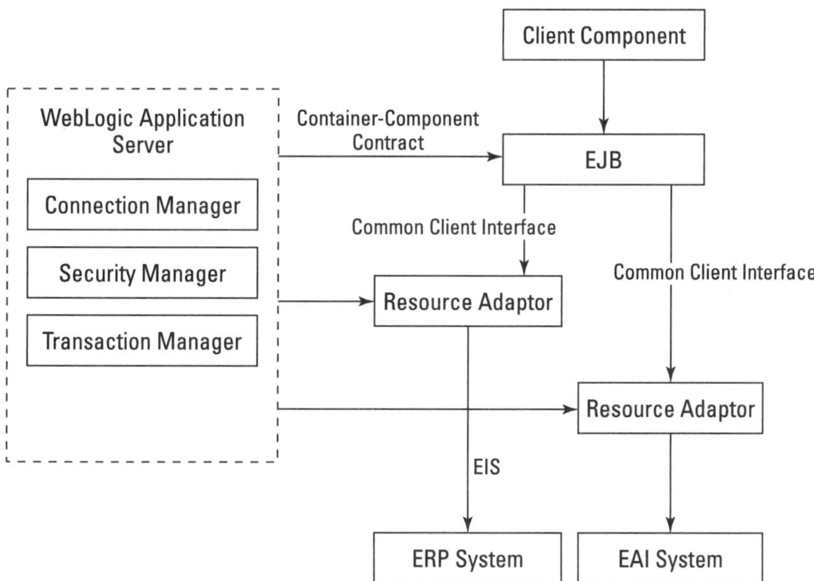

Figure 27-2: Resource adapter

The interaction between the application server and the resource adapters provide the security management, transaction management, and connection management (see Figure 27-3). The `ConnectionFactory` will interact with the `ConnectionManager` of the application server. The interaction and workings of the security management, transaction management, and connection management internal to the application server is application server specific and not defined in the connector specification. What is defined is the interaction between the resource adapter and the application server. Some of the information for operation of the resource adapter will be defined in the resource adapter's deployment descriptor. Some of the things defined are the EIS system to interact with, the security authentication type, and the transaction demarcation type, such as XA and Local Transaction. The application server will get these instances of the transaction,

ManagedConnectionFactory, and security instance from the resource connector. The application server will be listening for information from the ManagedConnection through the ConnectionEventListener that is created as part of the application server. The purpose of the ManagedConnectionFactory is to create an instance of a ManagedConnection that the application component will use to access the EIS, but will be managed by the managers of the application server based on the information provided in the deployment descriptor.

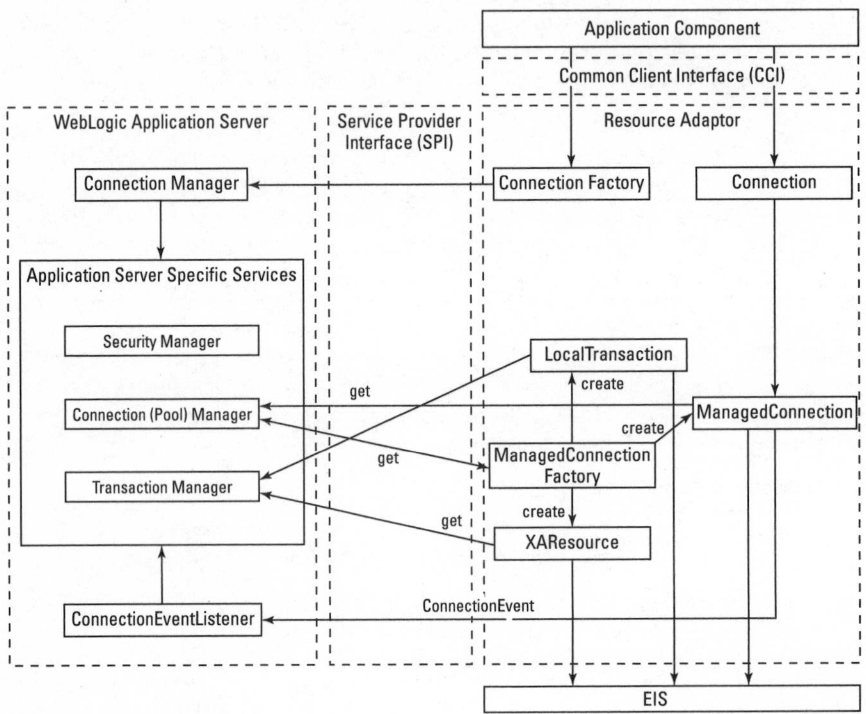

Figure 27-3: Common interfaces

System contracts

What has been discussed so far are some of the components that make up the Connector API. The heart of the matter is mapping data from one system to another and negotiating the interface between the two systems. The negotiation, or handshaking in between systems combined with the negotiation of data and the integrity of that data is commonly known as the system contracts. This includes the management of the transactions and connections involved with the movement of the data between systems.

Connection Management contract

One of the features of the Connector API is the support of Connection Management. Connection Management enables you to pool connections for reuse without the delay of allocating and deallocating the instance for each connection. It does this by providing a connection factory. Connection Management is a consistent application-programming model for acquiring connections for both managed and nonmanaged applications. It provides a generic mechanism for providing different quality of service (QoS) for transactions, security, error logging, and many more enhancements into the same connector. The connection pool can be application server specific. In the WebLogic Server, a maximum and minimum number of connections are prepopulated.

A resource adapter provides interfaces for both connections and connection factories. Examples of JDBC-based interfaces for database connectivity are `javax.sql.DataSource` and `java.sql.Connection`. The connection and connection factory are defined for the CCI with the interfaces `javax.resources.cci.ConnectionFactory` and `javax.resources.cci.Connection`.

The application component, such as an EJB or servlet, first gets the connection by getting a lookup of a connection factory in JNDI of a `javax.resource.cci.ConnectionFactory`. Then the connection factory instance calls the `ConnectionManager` to request a `Connection` from the application server by using the `allocateConnection` function. The `ConnectionManager` provides the QoS based on the application server. No specification exists for how the application server implements these services. The `ConnectionManager` will call the Connection Pool Manager internal to the application server. The application's Connection Pool Manager will call the `ManagedConnectionFactory` to get a `ManagedConnection`. A `ManagedConnection` is a `Connection` that is managed as a transaction through a `ConnectionEventListener` in the application server. Each `ConnectionEventListener` is registered with the `ManagedConnection` enabling it to receive events. Depending on the type of transaction, it will call the `LocalTransaction` interfaces or the `XAResource` interface, or even possibly none of those for no transaction handling. The resource adapter calls the `XAResource` or `LocalTransaction`. The Transaction Manager of the Application Server will get the `LocalTransaction` or `XAResource` class that the `ManagedConnectionFactory` created. Whenever a `ManagedConnection` is created, the security management of the Application Server sends a JAAS `Subject` as part of the method invocation.

To simplify the preceding process, it's easier to say that the Application Server will use its Pool Manager, which is part of the Connection Manager, to interface to the `ManagedConnectionFactory`, which will create the `ManagedConnection`. The `ManagedConnection` is created or found in a pool that will have an associated transaction. This transaction is either XA, local, or none, depending on how it was defined. The Transaction Manager of the Application Server gets these transaction interfaces of the `ManagedConnection` to handle the transactions internally so that it may perform commits and rollbacks based on the other `ManagedConnections` and resources. The `ConnectionEventListener` is also associated with the `ManagedConnection` so that it may provide feedback to the Application Server if manual rollbacks and commits are performed from the EIS. These events that are sent to the `ConnectionEventListener` are defined in the `ConnectionEvent` class. The `ConnectionManager` is the interface that is implemented by the Application Server for the resource adapter to get the original `Connection` that starts this process.

Transaction Management contract

The purpose of the Transaction Management is to manage a transaction. Transactions are defined and discussed in Chapter 6, but I review the key characteristics of transactions here as well.

What is a transaction?

A transaction is a unit of work composed of several operations made on one or more shared system resources that are governed by ACID properties. The acronym ACID stands for Atomicity, Consistency, Isolation, and Durability, and was originally defined by Andreas Reuter.

Atomicity—The unit of work performed in the transaction is identified as one atomic entity. In the case of failure, changes that occur due to this unit of work are either made permanent or are reversed to restore to the prior state before the transaction commences. Examples are database updates and message queue operations.

Consistency—When a transaction execution is completed, the system is left in a stable condition. If the system is left in an inconsistent state, the unit of work done as part of this transaction should be reversed to restore the system to its initial state. An example is database referential integrity constraints.

Isolation—The correctness of the unit of work performed within a transaction is not compromised when another concurrent transaction accesses the same set of resources as the current transaction. The changes that were made to the shared resources as part of the current transaction will not be visible to other transactions that are accessing the shared resources concurrently. An example is a "withdraw" activity from the same account by two concurrent transactions. Only the first transaction that gets access to the data will succeed, and the update to the account is not visible to others until the transaction commits.

Durability—The changes that are made as part of the transaction is made persistent once it is committed. This requires that the behavior should be repeatable in the case of a system failure. An example is a "withdraw" operation from a bank account that has been performed and the system crashes during the commit transaction. If the information about this transaction is not made persistent to the disk, the changes that were made as part of this transaction could be lost. This would result is a data integrity situation. The database and TP monitors typically solve this problem by logging a "commit" operation. In the case of a failure, the information is retrieved from the system log during recovery and the operation is replayed to produce the correct results.

The Transaction Management for the Connector API supports the XA interface, the `LocalTransaction`, or no transactions.

XA interface

The XA (X/Open Architecture) interface is a bidirectional interface between a Transaction Manager and Resource Managers. The X/Open group is now called the Open Group, and can be found at `www.opengroup.org`.

The XA interface supports global transactions, that is, transactions that can happen across multiple EIS systems.

X/Open is a standards organization whose goal it to standardize several interfaces between components in a distributed transaction processing framework. The X/Open consortium was initially formed to promote the Open Systems Computing paradigm and application portability. X/Open specified the most popular Distributed Transaction Processing Model (DTP) in 1991. It defines the three basic modules: Application Program (AP), Transaction Manager (TM), and Resource Manager (RM). AP is just the application component, which uses the libraries provided by TM and RM to interact with them. The TM is responsible for transaction coordination and control of execution of transactions. The RM is responsible for managing the access to the shared resources, such as files and databases.

Interaction exists between the AP and the TM, commonly known as TX; examples include `begin`, `commit`, `rollback`, and `info`:

```
Begin - starts a transaction
Commit - commits a transaction
Rollback - aborts a transaction
Info - gets the status of a transaction
```

The interface that defines the interaction between the TM and the RM is commonly known as XA. The Transaction Manager and the Resource Manager modules have to implement the interface bidirectionally to allow the Transaction Manager to interact with any Resource Manager.

```
Start - starts a transaction
Prepare - prepares a transaction in a 2PC.
End - ends the association of the transaction.
Commit - commits the transaction
Reg - registers the transaction with a TM.
```

XA allows a transaction to be managed by a TM external to the resource adapter and EIS. A resource adapter defines the type of transaction support by specifying the transaction-support element in the `ra.xml` file. A resource adapter can only support one type. When an application component demarcates an EIS connection request as part of a transaction, the Application Server is responsible for enlisting the XA resource with the Transaction Manager. When the application component closes the connection, the Application Server delists the XA resource from the TM and cleans up the EIS connection after the transaction is complete. Part of the XA interface is to implement a two-phase commit protocol to ensure there is synchronization between shared resources to ensure that they do not write at the same time.

Two-phase commit protocol

The steps of the two-phase commit protocol involve an interaction between an application, a Transaction Manager, and a Resource Manager, which in this case is part of the Data Transaction Manager in the following order:

Phase One:

The Transaction Manager issues the command to each Resource Manager to prepare to commit.

If all Resource Managers reply that they can commit, processing proceeds to Phase Two.

If any of the Resource Managers reply that they cannot commit, the Transaction Manager contacts all the Resource Managers to force an abort, and instructs them to discard all updates in waiting for that transaction.

If any of the Resource Managers cannot be contacted, then those Resource Managers that could not be contacted could not be told to abort. The abort command is then stored in the Transaction Manager log awaiting the restart of the Resource Managers to be recontacted. After the Resource Managers are up and running again, the abort is forced.

Phase Two:

If all Resource Managers confirm that they can commit, the commit message is broadcast to each of the Resource Managers by the Transaction Manager.

If all Resource Managers are still active, they commit the updates.

If any of the Resource Managers fail to respond, it could be for two reasons — either there was a communication failure or the Resource Manager failed. The Resource Manager is termed to be "in doubt" about the outcome. It will keep locks on the data until notification is received. Once the line is up and running, the Transaction Manager will commit the transaction.

If the Resource Manager fails and then restarts, the Resource Manager must reconstruct the committed state of the resources that it manages. If it does fail, all the enlisted transactions are aborted, except those that prepared or committed prior to the failure. When the Resource Manager restarts, it asks the Transaction Manager about the outcome of the "in doubt" transactions in which it enlisted. The Transaction Manager then tells the Resource Manager the outcome of each "in-doubt" transaction, and the Resource Manager commits or aborts accordingly.

Local Transaction

A Local Transaction is associated with a single physical connection and can be shared by multiple EJB components. To share a physical connection in the local transaction scope, the container assumes the connection to be shareable unless it has been marked unshareable in the `<res-sharing-scope>` tag of the deployment descriptor. The Local Transaction support allows an Application Server to manage resources that are only local to the resource adapter. They cannot manage the EIS resources and cannot participate in a two-phase commit protocol (2PC). When the support is defined for the Local Transaction, and the component requests an EIS connection, the application server starts a Local Transaction based on the current transaction context. When the application component closes that connection, the Application Server does a commit on the Local Transaction and also cleans up the EIS connection after the transaction has completed.

The transaction process starts by first getting a connection handle that is returned by calling `ManagedConnection.getConnection`, which in turn calls `LocalTransaction.begin`. The EJB gets a connection handle and performs a unit of work on EIS Resource Manager.

For Local Transactions, the Application Server implements the `javax.spi.LocalTransaction` to define the transaction contract between the Application Server and the resource adapter. The resource adapter supports the local transaction with the `javax.resource.cci.LocalTransaction` as defined in the CCI. The Application Server implements the Local Transaction with the `javax.resource.spi.ConnectionEventListener` interface.

The function used in the `ConnectionEventListener` for starting the Local Transaction is `localTransactionStarted` using the `ManagedConnection` instance. Notifying that the connection was committed in the `ManagedConnection` is done by using the `localTransactionCommitted`. Notifying that a Local Transaction is rolled back in the `ManagedConnection` is done by using the `localTransactionRolledBack` method.

To support the Local Transaction, the Application Server must support the `ConnectionEventListener` interface. This enables the Application Server to achieve Local Transaction cleanup and transaction serial interleaving. Resource adapter is required to send Local Transaction events through the `ConnectionEventListener` interface when an application starts a Local Transaction. The `ManagedConnection` registers this listener instance by using `ManagedConnection.addConnectionEventListener`.

If neither XA nor Local Transaction is set in the `ra.xml`, it means that a resource adapter does not support XA or Local Transactions. That means that if an application component needs to use that resource adapter, the application component must not involve any connections to the EIS, represented by the resource adapter, in a transaction. But if an application component needs to involve EIS connections in a transaction, the application component must interact with a resource adapter that supports XA or Local Transactions.

Security Management contract

The PasswordCredential class is a holder for the username and password. The GenericCredential interface is used for accessing the security credential of a resource principal. A GenericCredential interface can be used to wrap Kerberos credentials. Some EISs can support the GSS-API that is defined in rfc2078.txt. You can find all rfcs at www.ietf.org. The security over the communications between the Application Server and the EIS can be done with SSL. The username and password can be passed into the properties of the JNDI context during the getConnection method invocation. This is termed component-managed sign-on. Container-managed sign-on is when the authorization is specific in the deployment descriptor of the EJB or servlet.

For EIS sign-on, a basic password containing username and password, or a Kerberos version 5 authentication mechanism can be used from the resource adapter to the EIS system. The authentication is specified in the <authentication-mechanism-type> tag of the deployment descriptor of the resource adapter. Authorization to an EIS resource can be applied at the Application Server, at the EIS, or neither.

Communication between the Application Server and the EIS is subject to threats, such as a man-in-the-middle attack, loss of data, data modification, and rerouting. The Connector API allows EIS sign-on by propagating the security context, consisting of a JAAS Subject with Principal and Credentials from the Application Server to the resource adapter in the createManagedConnection method. A Subject represents a person or a group. It can contain multiple passwords and keys. A Subject can have multiple Principals and Credentials. Principals are passed through the Subject during the getConnection.

The Application Server uses the createManagedConnection when it requests a resource adapter to create a new connection. It can pass in the Subject by using either the component or container-managed sign-on. In the container-managed sign-on, the Application Server is responsible for filling the Subject. Adding credentials can be done through the Subject class.

The Connector API does not define a standard format and requirements for security mechanism for specific credentials, but it does offer a GenericCredential interface to wrap Credentials as a Java and Kerberos wrapper. This allows the resource adapter to get the information about the Credential, as well as EIS sign-on. The only other mechanism for the Connector API is the GSS-API. GSS-API is the Generic Security Service Application Programming Interface. A Subject class can contain one to many PasswordCredentials, one to many GenericCredentials, or one to many Principals for sign-on. If the Application Server invokes the createManagedConnection with one or more PasswordCredentials in the Subject, the resource adapter will use this information to sign on to the EIS. The PasswordCredentials are set in the private credential set. The resource adapter extracts the username and password and uses this information for EIS sign-on.

The Application Server can invoke the createManagedConnection with one or more GenericCredentials passed in the Subject. The resource adapter will use this information as private or public keys. These could contain Kerberos keys. This could also be used to process EIS sign-on. The resource adapter will extract these `Credentials`, and if Kerberos is selected as the authentication mechanism type, then it will get this information out of the private `Credential` as Kerberos-based keys.

Another option is where the Application Server does not provide any security information by passing a null `Subject`. Then the component is responsible for the security in a component sign-on. This security can be placed in a `ConnectionRequestInfo` for component information; however, the Application Server cannot read this information because the `ConnectionRequestInfo` is a data structure for the resource adapter to pass information for its own data in the connection request. If the resource adapter does not find information in the `ConnectionRequestInfo`, then it will use default security configuration.

Common Client Interface

The Common Client Interface (CCI) defines a standard client API for an application component, and EAI, to create and manage connections to heterogeneous EISs. The purpose of the CCI is to provide a generic framework that is independent of a particular EIS or EAI system. Not only is it a generic API, but data can also drive various aspects of the EAI system. A Metadata repository (see Figure 27-4) can be used to drive the CCI. An example is when a connector can decide to go to either an EIS system or ERP system depending on the order type and format. The transaction can have a type value of batch or single to route the direction of the transaction. You don't want to hard code this information because it can limit the capabilities of upgrading the system. This also limits adding more systems in the transaction routing when adding more transactions. To avoid hard-coded transactions, a connection can contain Metadata specific to itself. It can look up in a routing table and have a new connection to route to that is based on that connection. One of the new connections leads to a legacy system, and one leads to the ERP system based on the type of order. Metadata has other purposes besides routing to EIS systems; another use could be to route messages that contain log information into a log file.

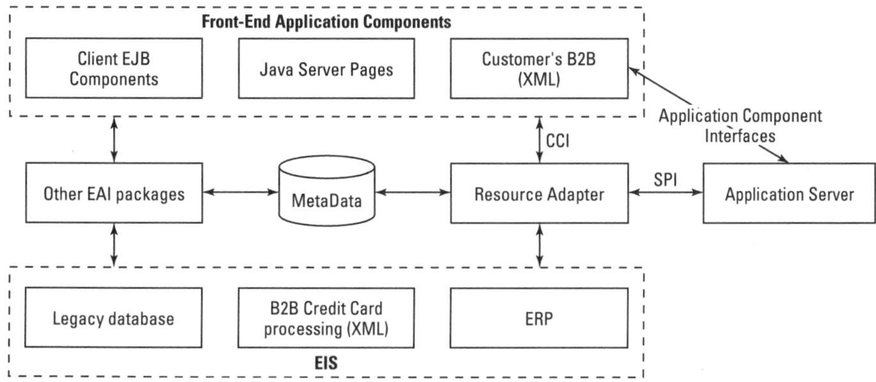

Figure 27-4: Metadata diagram

The use of Metadata allows EJBs, Java servlets, and other systems to get records results of data from an EIS system. Just as a JDBC connection can retrieve a `ResultSet` from a database, a CCI connection can retrieve a set of data from an EIS system such as ERP. Other records (see Figure 27-5) are `IndexedRecords` and `MappedRecords`. The `ResultSet` uses the SQL `ResultSet` interface, the `IndexedRecord` implements the `java.util.list` interface, and the `MappedRecord` implements the `java.util.map` interface.

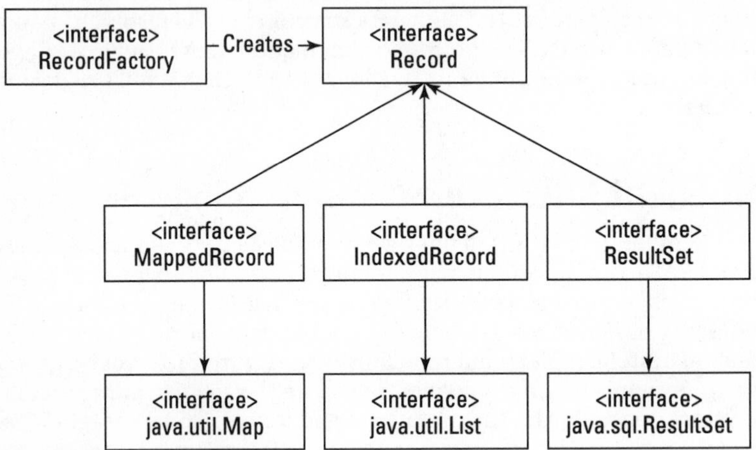

Figure 27-5: Record sets

The package that makes up the CCI is found under `javax.resource.cci`. The classes can be divided into interfaces to handle connections, interactions, and metadata, plus structures to handle records. The `RecordFactory` creates the generic `MappedRecord` and `IndexedRecord` on demand.

The Connection interface

The Connection interface consists of `Connection`, the `ConnectionFactory`, the `ConnectionSpec`, and `LocalTransaction`. The purpose of the `javax.resource.cci.ConnectionFactory` is to provide an interface for getting a connection to an EIS instance. The component will first get an instance from a JNDI namespace to look up a `ConnectionFactory` instance, and then use this instance to establish a connection. The `getConnection` method, from the `ConnectionFactory`, will then be used to get a connection to an EIS instance. The `getConnection` method may also take a `ConnectionSpec` class that contains resource adapter-specific properties such as component sign-on. Some of the parameters that are defined in the `ConnectionSpec` are username and password. This `ConnectionFactory` interface also provides a method to get the `RecordFactory`.

Another class of the Connection interface is the `javax.resource.cci.Connection`, which represents an application-level connection handle. This is used by the application component to access an EIS instance. A `ManagedConnection` through the `ManagedFactory` later represents the physical connection. The `ManagedConnection` is simply the connection that is managed through the application server for transaction integrity. The `Connection` can create an `Interaction` instance associated with the current `Connection` instance. This `Interaction` instance is for enabling the component to access the EIS components and data. An instance of the `getResultInfo` can also be used to get the `ResultSet` information for data access from the EIS instance. Metadata is can also be retrieved in the `Connection` to provide instance-specific data for itself. The Local Transaction can be retrieved, if one is available, for managing transactions locally, meaning that the resource is local to the managing agent and non-global to the enterprise.

Just as a `Connection` in the JDBC interface, auto-commit can be set in the CCI Connection. This means that there is an implicit commit called on the transactions, which is `AutoCommit`. By default, this is set to `false`, which means not to implicitly commit.

The Interaction interface

The `Interaction` interface is used for moving data between the application component and the EIS instance. The `Interaction` is created by the `Connection` instance. The core of the `Interaction` interface is the `javax.resource.cci.Interaction` interface, the `javax.resource.cci.InteractionSpec` instance, and the data structures used to interact with the EIS instance. The main interface for the EIS instance is the `javax.resource.cci.Record`. Some of the interfaces that extended from the record are `MappedRecord`, `IndexedRecord`, and `ResultSet`. These records are passed through the `Interaction` by using the `Interaction` execute method. The `InteractionSpec` is also passed through these methods. The `InteractionSpec` holds properties for driving an `Interaction` instance to an EIS instance. These are properties for the underlying EIS.

The properties for the `InteractionSpec` consist of two parts, the standard properties and the `ResultSet` properties. The standard properties define interaction with the EIS instance. There are two parts of the standard properties: a `FunctionName` and an `InteractionVerb`. The `FunctionName` represents the name of the EIS function, such as a business object function. The `InteractionVerb` represents the mode of interaction with the EIS instance. There are three possible `InteractionVerbs`: `SYNC_SEND`, `SYNC_SEND_RECEIVE`, and `SYNC_RECEIVE`. `SYNC_SEND` specifies to only send a data to the EIS instance. `SYNC_SEND_RECEIVE` specifies to send a record to the EIS instance and receive information in the form of a record or `ResultSet`. `SYNC_RECEIVE` can be used to specify to receive a record from a messaging system like a message queue. The `ResultSet` properties give information about the `ResultSet` record, which consist of `FetchSize`, `FetchDirection`, `MaxFieldSize`, `ResultSetType`, and `ResultSetConcurrency`. They define the size and types of the `ResultSet` for the direction.

The Metadata interface

There are two main interfaces for the `Metadata` interface, the `ConnectionMetaData` interface and the `ResourceAdapterMetaData` interface. The purpose of the `ConnectionMetaData` interface, `javax.resource.cci.ConnectionMetaData`, is to give information about the EIS instance that is accessed through the `Connection` instance. The `ConnectionMetaData` interface is retrieved through the `getMetaData` method. Some of the information that can be reviewed by the `Metadata` interface is the product name and version of the EIS. The `ConnectionMetaData` interface is required to be implemented for the `Connection`.

The purpose of the `ResourceAdapterMetaData` interface is to contain information about the resource adapter implementation, not the EIS information. Because there is no EIS information, a connection does not have to be established to the EIS. Some of the functions of the `ResourceAdapterMetaData` interface are the version, name, vender name, and connector specification number of the adapter.

The record

A record is a data structure used as input and output to the EIS function. There are two types of records: generic and custom. A tool that uses the Metadata information from a repository at development time for information develops the custom record. The generic record is used at runtime from Metadata information to build the type of record. This Metadata is EIS specific.

Most ERP and EAI systems have their own descriptive information for records. A typical record could be an order record that gets sent to an ERP system for when an order is placed from a Web site. This Metadata information may not even be Java specific; it could be based on an older EIS system such as CICS. But if the EIS uses vendor-specific information, then the adapter must be able to understand this Metadata if it is passing records to and from an EIS system. So, the Metadata information must be available and understandable to the adapter vendor.

Connections may have to add a layer of translation to make the connectors record more generic. If a system, for example, is passing order information to either a CICS or an ERP system, an order record needs to be built that accommodates both systems, but not particular to any one system, so it can be used in both cases. This leads to the case of a component-view contract, which implies that the interface to the EIS from the application component is dependent on the component and not the EIS-specific information. To support this, a `RecordFactory` must be in place to provide a record that would be dependent on the EIS-specific data. The `RecordFactory` does a lookup based on the specific EIS and specific component and returns a record that maps to both parties. The component creates the custom record for the EIS-specific record.

Some of these records may become very complex because of the different technologies used. A situation could arise where an EJB has a connection to a CORBA object, which has a connection to an older TCP stream object. The benefit of the Connector interface is that it allows separate layers to focus on different aspects of the technology. In a scenario such as the one mentioned, an architect can work on the mapping of the records with the three different technical groups and focus on the data for the record and `RecordFactory`. Then the EJB and CORBA group can focus on the connectors through the ORB and EJB interfaces through their respective application servers, and the Socket developers could establish an EIS interface for integrating into the legacy system. Without the Connector API, there would be no common interfaces for this type of communication between systems.

XML is another alternative, but the support of the services, such as Transaction Management and security would have to be built independently of the Transaction Management and security extensions of the Application Servers for connectors. Using this methodology also allows individuals, such as an architect, to focus on the data independently of the transport. This mapping can take some time and effort on its own, because it is not just a mapping of data but of data types. The EJB uses the Java types, CORBA has its own types defined in the Interface Definition Language, and the Sockets could be defined in the C language. So, if the first field is an integer for the type of message, it needs to match the same type across all three technologies. This is commonly known as type mapping.

Because more complexity may be involved in the `Record` interface, the `Record` interface can be extended into an `IndexedRecord`, `MapRecord`, and `ResultSet`. The `MapRecord` is taken from the Java utilities interface for a map, which provides a key/value pair for storing data. Doing a lookup on a key returns the value. The `IndexedRecord` is taken from the Java utilities for a list that is a linked list implementation for dynamically providing an ordered and indexed set of data that is traversed through one at a time. The last is the `ResultSet`, which is taken from the SQL interface of a `ResultSet` that is normally returned in a database query. A lookup of the data is normally done by doing another lookup on the `ResultSet`, such as a `getString` function, used to return an entry in the column from the resulting set that still contains table information. Using these types of records together can produce a very complicated and robust set of organizing data that can be permutated into more types of records. Because the `ResultSet` is based on a return from a query, it is not generated from a `RecordFactory`. But the `RecordFactory` does support getting a generic `MappedRecord` and `IndexedRecord` with the `createMappedRecord` and `createIndexedRecord` functions. Sometimes, it might not be adequate to just work with a Recordset, but a stream of bytes, such as a file structure. For this reason, there is also a `Streamable` interface for the purpose of working with a stream of bytes from Java I/O.

As mentioned earlier in the chapter, the `Interaction` interface transports these records into and from the EIS instance (see Figure 27-6). The `Interaction` interface is retrieved from the `Connection`. Before the record is passed through the `Interaction`, it must be retrieved from a `RecordFactory`, such as a generic `MappedRecord` and `IndexedRecord`. Otherwise, a custom record can be passed through the execute method.

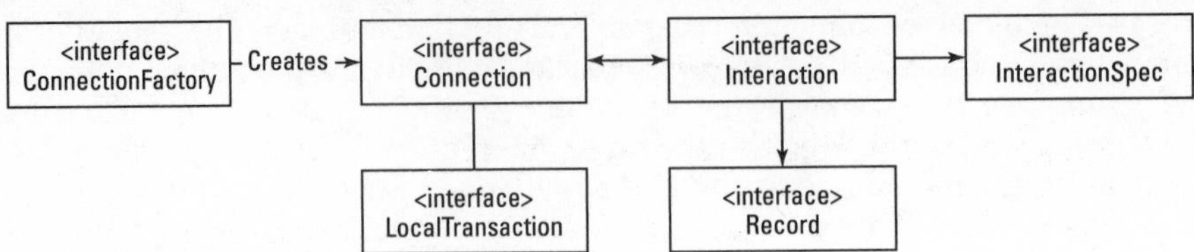

Figure 27-6: Common Component interface

Using the J2EE Connector Architecture in WebLogic

So far, I've discussed how most Application Servers can support the Connector API. The WebLogic Server has specific things that it can support out of the Connector API. Like all other Application Servers, it uses the `ra.xml` deployment descriptor, but the WebLogic Server extends some of these entries. To specify the minimum and maximum size of the connection pool, for example, it has an extra deployment descriptor called the `weblogic-ra.xml`. If the `weblogic-ra.xml` is not defined when running the `.rar` file, then a default one will be created from the WebLogic Application Server. The `.rar` file is the resource adapter archive that is a compressed file used to load classes and any other files that may be required to run the resource adapter. The `weblogic-ra.xml` file must be deployed in the `/META-INF/` subdirectory just as the `ra.xml` must be contained there. If a default `weblogic-ra.xml` file is automatically generated, the tags for `<connection-factory-name>` and the `<jndi-name>` need to be modified to point at the correct instance of the `ConnectionFactory`.

The WebLogic Application Server uses container-managed sign-on to sign on to the EIS. The WebLogic Server calls this the security principal map. This is a where the security principal is mapped from the `weblogic-ra.xml` entries. In the deployment descriptor of the `weblogic-ra.xml`, the element `security-principal-map` defines a relationship of the initiating-principal to the resource-principal. These are all optional entries in the WebLogic connector's deployment descriptor. The resource-principal defines the username and password, and the associated initiating-principal defines the caller's principal that initiated the process. A wildcard of * can be used in the initiating-principal to specify a resource-principal for all initiating-principals not defined explicitly. Because plaintext is not desirable for a password, BEA offers a password converter utility for setting a password to a ciphertext. The password converter tool is executed with the Java `weblogic.Connector.ConnecterXMLEncrypt` command. The entry for the principal can look like the following:

```
<security-principal-map>
        <map-entry>
                <initiating-principal>*</initiating-principal>
                <resource-principal>
```

```
                <resource-username>rich</resource-username>
                <resource-password>password</resource-password>
            </resource-principal>
        </map-entry>
</security-principal-map>
```

For transaction support, the ra.xml still defines an XA Transaction, Local Transaction, or neither. The error logging is handled through the weblogic-ra.xml file by the <logging-enabled> tag being set to true or false. The <log-file-name> tag is used to give the file name to save the log. The logging tags work with the features of the ManagedConnectionFactory set and getLogWriter functions. Another top-level XML tag for the WebLogic definition is the <jndi-name> tag that defines the name to bind the ConnectionFactory into the JNDI namespace. The WebLogic application components use this descriptor to find the ConnectionFactory.

By using the weblogic-ra.xml, there is also the possibility of generating multiple resource adapters inherited from a single deployed resource adapter. The new links to the single instance can have different pool information. All or none of the <pool-params> must be defined in the derived instances of the resource adapter. This helps with reusing the same resource adapter with only slight modifications to some of the attributes. The tag specified for this action is the <ra-link-ref>.

The next set of attributes in the deployment descriptor is for managing the WebLogic Server's connection pool. Depending on how these are set, it can maximize the connection resources while minimizing the creation time for each connection. The <initial-capacity> is the number of ManagedConnections that will be initialized at the startup of the WebLogic Server. This avoids creating all of the connections at runtime by initializing them ahead of time. But creating too many may cause too much memory usage, so a threshold is needed for a limit of the number of connections. The <max-capacity> tag is used to limit the number of connections running at a given instance. If new connections need to be created because there are none in the reuse pool, there is the option to create a set of connections at a time, instead of one at a time. This is done with the <capacity-increment> tag. At given intervals when connection resources are not being utilized, it might be desirable to free the resources used by the connectors if it seems like the resource adapter is no longer using them. The shrink properties are used to specify how long before an inactive connector should get taken out of the pool. This will reduce the size of the connection pool.

```
<pool-params>
    <initial-capacity>0</initial-capacity>
    <max-capacity>1</max-capacity>
    <capacity-increment>1</capacity-increment>
    <shrinking-enabled>false</shrinking-enabled>
    <shrink-period-minutes>200</shrink-period-minutes>
</pool-params>
```

Using the WebLogic administrator's console, you can monitor the connection pools. After accessing the domain name, choose Applications ⇨ MyConnector Component ⇨ Resource ⇨ Connectors. Select the Monitoring tab. In this example (shown in Figure 27-7), `MyConnector` is the deployed Connector.

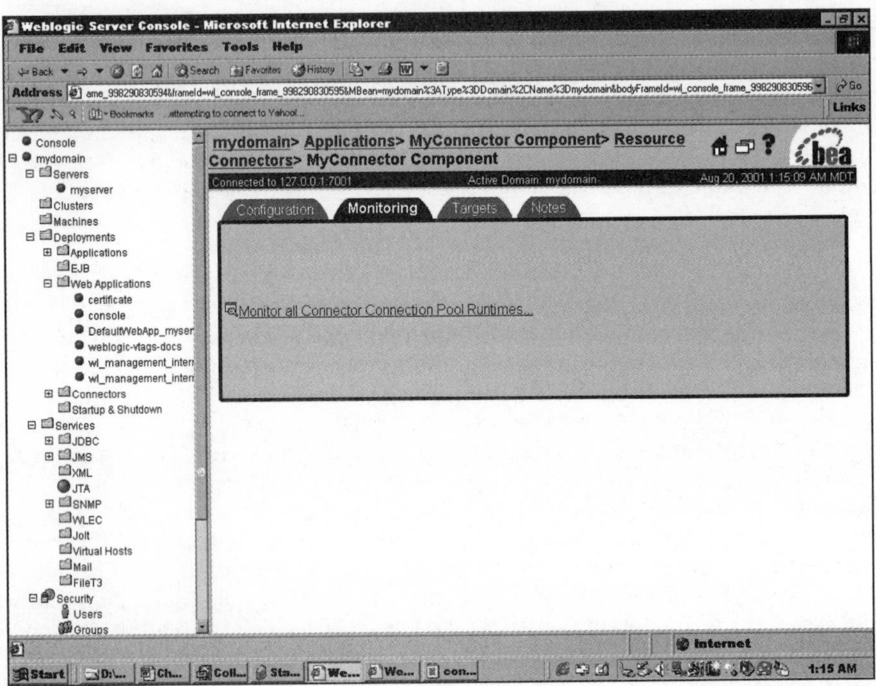

Figure 27-7: Monitoring entrance

You can view many attributes of the Connection Pool, such as Total Rejected Connections, and Free Connections (see Figure 27-8).

Configuration

Before viewing the Connection Pool of the Connector, a Connector Component has to be added into the WebLogic Server environment. This can be done through the Admin Console of the WebLogic Server, as shown in Figure 27-9.

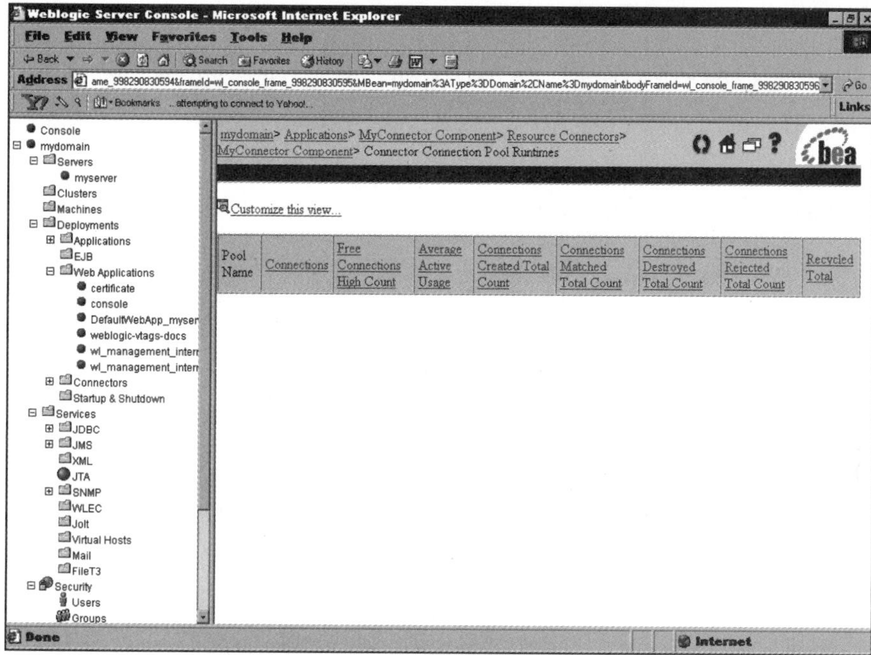

Figure 27-8: Monitoring connectors

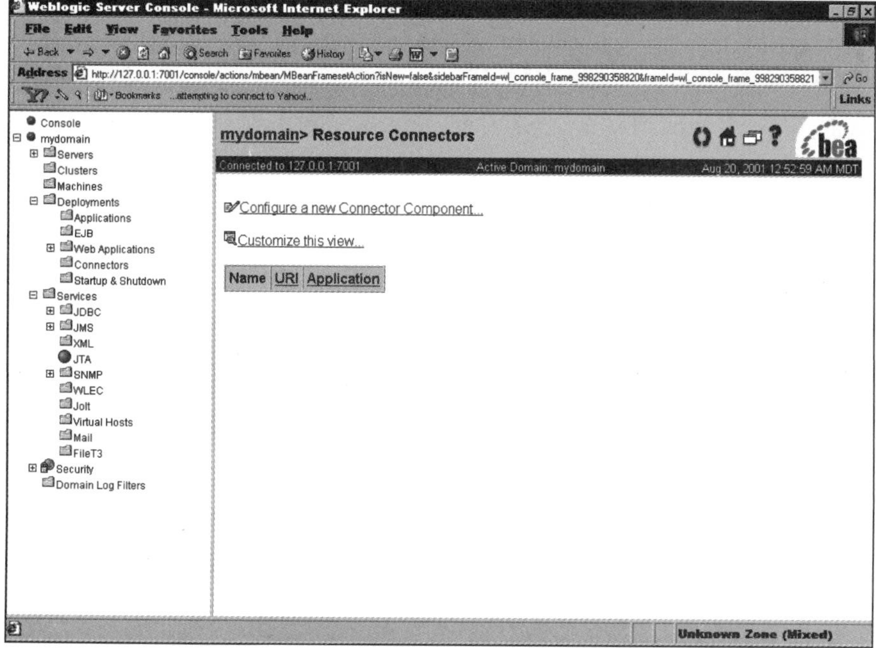

Figure 27-9: Configuring start

The following attributes need to be supplied in the WebLogic Console:

✦ **Name:** The name to be associated with the Connector Component.

✦ **URI (Uniform Resource Identifier):** The URI of the connection component.

✦ **Path:** The path that the RAR will be accessed from.

✦ **Deployed:** The RAR file should be deployed when created.

After clicking the Create button, and typing the correct information into the fields, the Connection Component should appear in the left pane. To undeploy the Connection Component, simply uncheck the Deployed check box, shown in Figure 27-10.

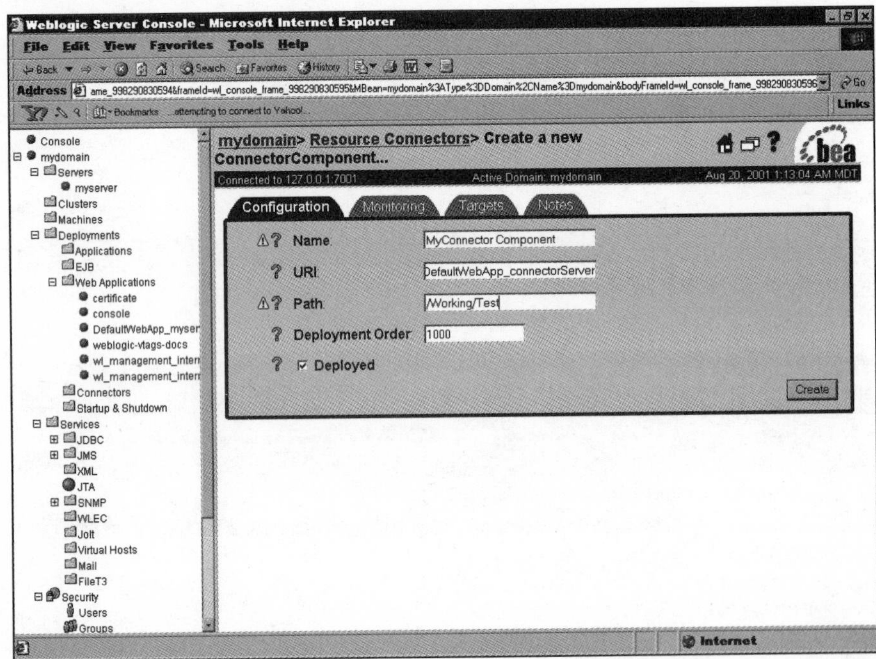

Figure 27-10: Configurations

Development

Developing a Connector is just like developing any other Java application in WebLogic 6.1. The `webLogic.jar` file that is included with the WebLogic 6.1 Application Server includes the Connector API files needed for development. Ensure that this file is in the classpath when developing with WebLogic 6.1. Logging routines are provided to help in the development process.

Logging

According to the J2EE Connector Specification, version 1.0, the Application Server must support the `getLogWriter` and `set` methods of the `ManagedConnectionFactory` to provide error logging and tracing for the resource adapter. The WebLogic Server supports this by its deployment descriptor, the `weblogic-ra.xml`. There are two fields that are of importance to the deployment descriptor for this support: logging-enabled and log-filename. The logging-enabled field defines whether logging is turned on or off. The log-filename field is to define the filename for where the log will be captured.

Deployment

The `Connection` is a J2EE component, and like most J2EE components it requires a deployment descriptor. The deployment descriptor is needed to load the Resource Adapter Module (RAM). The RAM contains the required files, such as the native files, images, Java files, and any other files for deploying the resource adapter. The deployment descriptor is a contract on how to deploy the RAM into the resource adapter for the connectors. Using a deployment descriptor and a RAM allows the resource adapter to be deployed as a stand-alone unit into an Application Server or with other J2EE modules, such as the EJB deployment. This implies that there is a generic deployment of a resource adapter for multiple application components that can be loaded separately, and the resource adapter that is deployed with specific application components as a package deployment.

The RAM must be packaged by using the Java utility JAR, Java Archive, to RAR file type, Resource Adapter Archive. This RAM must contain the deployment descriptor in the RAR file; like most deployment descriptors, it must be under the `/META-INF/` directory to become `/META-INF/ra.xml`. The utilities and program files that are programmed in Java to support and execute the resource adapter must further be distributed in the RAR file as separate JAR files. These are normally stored in the root subdirectory and can be separated into multiple JAR files based on their functionality. The RAR may contain an `ra.jar` and `cci.jar` in the base directory for the Common Client Components, and the resource adapter utilities for implementing the RAM. Other files that may typically be distributed in the RAR file are native library files for support of the EIS and image files for the graphical user interface of the application component. Any platform-specific files must be included in the RAR.

The deployer is a piece that is responsible for deploying the elements of the RAR. It will ensure that the JAR files are loaded in the environment of the resource adapter. If it is a stand-alone RAM, it must be deployed so that the required application components have access to the resource adapter. The deployment descriptor defines to the deployer how it will load the resource adapter. It uses the information as Metadata for declaring how to deploy. The deployment descriptor is configured in a XML file. The DTD (Document Type Definition) that defines the `ra.xml` file is connector_1_0.dtd. A DTD is needed to define the values that are acceptable for the ra.xml. But this information can be extended beyond the general information for more specific information that is meaningful for the specific Application Server that starts the deployer. The WebLogic 6.1 Application Server extends this functionality by adding an additional deployment descriptor specific to the Application Server called weblogic-ra.xml; a corresponding DTD, in the J2EE Connector Beta, is the weblogic600-ra.dtd that is later changed to weblogic-ra.dtd. The deployer can also be configured through the WebLogic Console, but I'll discuss that later.

The elements defined in the ra.xml are very important for the operation of the resource adapter. Some of the first fields that should be mentioned are the vendor name, the version number, any licensing information, and the Connector specification number. This is data to ensure that the correct resource adapter is being deployed. The next field that should be mentioned is the authentication mechanism. Defining the authentication-mechanism type to BasicPassword implies that the javax.resource.spi.security.PasswordCredential is being used. Setting the authentication-mechanism type to Kerbv5 implies that Kerberos version 5 is being used with Kerberos certificates and the javax.resource.spi.security.GenericCredential has been implemented in the resource adapter. So depending on the setting, authentication-mechanism type defines which authentication protocols will be implemented and the corresponding credential.

The config-property defines the properties for the ManagedConnectionFactory to use to connect to the EIS. These fields include port numbers, Connection URLs, server names, usernames, and passwords to establish connections to the ManagedConnectionFactory. The ManagedConnectionFactory is normally implemented as a JavaBean. This also means that it uses getter and setter methods for passing of data. When configuring the ra.xml, a property has three pieces: config-property-name to define the property name that is being set, such as the ServerName; the config-property-type that defines the Java type being set like a String; and the config-property-value, which contains the data being set such as MyServer. Following this convention, the server's name that is to be connected on the EIS is called MyServer.

```
<config-property>
     <config-property-name>ServerName</config-property-name>
     <config-property-type>java.lang.String</config-property-type>
     <config-property-value>MyServer</config-property-value>
      <config-property-description>This is the name of the EIS
Server</config-property-description>
</config-property>
```

Most of the Connector specifies the different interfaces that can be used to build the resource adapter and CCI components. One thing to note is that the ra.xml can redefine some of these interfaces. One such instance is the Connection interface that can be changed by defining it in <connection-interface>. This tag defines the Connection interface that the resource adapter will use. Another interface that can be defined is the ConnectionFactory interface.

Interfaces are not the only coding pieces that can be defined in the ra.xml, implementation classed for the Connection, ManagedConnectionFactory, and ConnectionFactory are also defined in the <connection-impl-class>, <managedconnectionfactory-impl>, and <connectionfactory-impl-class>. Other pieces that are specified in the ra.xml are the icons for the resource adapter, and EIS type for the resource adapter for connection.

To create a RAR file, first compile the Java class files and put them in a staging directory. A *staging directory* is a directory containing only the files that will be put into the RAR file. You may want to create multiple JAR files for some of these Java resources; an example is a CCI.jar for the CCI-specific files and a RA.jar for resource adapter-specific files. Create a META-INF subdirectory that the XML files will be stored in. Create the ra.xml and weblogic-ra.xml files. Ensure that the proper class implementations are defined for the ManagedConnectionFactory, ConnectionFactory, and Connection in the ra.xml file. Create a JAR file that contains these files. The following is an example:

```
jar cvf myRA.rar *
```

Deploy the RAR into the WebLogic Server by using the Admin Console. If the resource adapter is not a stand-alone resource adapter, meaning that it has associated EJB clients to be deployed with, the EJB files need to be deployed in an EAR (Enterprise Archive) file, and need to be JARed into the RAR as well with its deployment information. To add other files into the RAR file, simply copy them to the staging directory and add them to the RAR by using the JAR command:

```
jar xf myRA.rar *
```

Some things to consider when working with the WebLogic Server is that there is no support for the Kerberos authentication implementation. This means javax.resource.spi.security.GenericCredential is not supported. Also, only serializable ConnectionFactory implementations are supported.

Not everything has to be handled from the Admin Console. You can also view the deployed Connection Components, undeploy Connection Components, and deploy more Connection Components from the command prompt by using the java weblogic.deploy command.

Summary

One thing that can't be emphasized enough is the need for the Connector API. Without using the Connector API, it becomes difficult to provide a standard solution for interfacing to EIS systems. Most organizations use third-party, non-J2EE components to some degree. But developing proprietary solutions without a common architecture can be very time consuming and less reusable.

As time evolves and maintenance needs increase, standards provide a common ground for both developers and architects to communicate how to develop a common J2EE component. Using a standard, such as the Connector specification, provides out-of-the-box documentation that has the benefit of being proven in other development initiatives. An important aspect to this discussion is the need for EAI to be integrated into the Application Server. The Connector API enables the Application Server to become an EAI solution. The need for using the same management systems of security, transaction, and connection services is very important unless an organization wants to spend a great deal of time and effort in getting into how management systems manage each other.

A lot of work still needs to be offered in the study of Connectors, and it should be evident that the Application Servers could offer more tools for the building and deployment of Connectors. A need also exists for multiple sets of Connectors for different EIS systems so that organizations can plug their J2EE components into EISs from out-of-the-box components. From the specification and the motivation to try to standardize J2EE components into legacy systems, the Connector API is advantageous for moving data in between disparate systems and contributes significantly to the evolution of Enterprise Components and connecting them across a wide range of distributed architectures. Without the Connector specification, there would be a lot missing in architecture for the capability to provide interfaces into legacy systems and other third-party systems.

✦ ✦ ✦

Upgrading to WebLogic Server 6.1 from Earlier Versions

✦ ✦ ✦ ✦

In This Appendix

Upgrading WebLogic Server

Upgrading WebLogic applications

Removed and deprecated features

✦ ✦ ✦ ✦

Like all successful software products, WebLogic Server has evolved and improved with age. WebLogic Server's evolution is unique, however, because it is closely tied to the evolution of the J2EE specification. In fact, one of WebLogic Server's greatest strengths is its robust and timely adherence to the specification, because this permits WebLogic developers to take advantage of new J2EE features almost as soon as they hit the street.

The downside of this is that upgrading to a new version of WebLogic Server is a two-part process and can sometimes be quite involved. First, you must upgrade your server instances themselves, which usually entails conversions of license files and properties files. Then you must upgrade your applications, which is usually more complicated because you must update them to match new features both in WebLogic Server and in the J2EE specification. In this chapter, I give you some pointers and checklists on how to accomplish these tasks.

Upgrading WebLogic Server

A number of tasks are required in the process of upgrading your WebLogic server installation to WebLogic 6.1. BEA has provided a clear and simple upgrade path that involves only a few a steps:

Upgrading the WebLogic license file

Converting the `weblogic.properties` file

Of course, these simple points have a good bit of work behind them. But if you plan your server upgrade carefully, it should be an orderly and simple process.

The real work will come later when you upgrade your *applications* to function with WebLogic 6.1!

Upgrading the WebLogic license file

Depending on the version of WebLogic that you are running, this can be a multipart process. Start at the section that is appropriate for your server installation and continue from there.

Pre-WebLogic 4.0 installations

If you are currently running a version older than WebLogic 4.0, you must upgrade your license file from the `WebLogicLicense.class` file to a `WebLogicLicense.xml` file before proceeding.

For this you must use the license converter utility provided with WebLogic 6.1. The `WebLogicLicense.class` file should be located on your classpath, in the `WL_HOME` directory, or be in the directory in which you execute the `licenseConverter` utility.

From a command line, run the `setenv` script (`.cmd` or `.sh` depending on your platform) provided by WebLogic to properly set up your environment; then type

```
$ java utils.licenseConverter -w c:\bea
```

In this example, `c:\bea` is the directory where you want the new `WebLogicLicense.xml` file to be written.

WebLogic 4.0 to 5.1 installations

To upgrade your `WebLogicLicense.xml` file to the `license_wls61.bea` file, you must visit a special BEA Web site and follow the instructions given there. The URL for the site is:

```
http://websupport.beasys.com/custsupp/wls6_license.htm
```

You need to have a BEA WebSupport account to be able to submit this form, and you will be prompted for the name and password for that account. Once you have been authenticated, you can update as many as ten license files at a time. The new license files will be mailed to you at the e-mail account you specify.

Turnaround time can be anywhere from ten minutes to a day or more (so they say—it's always been rather quick in my experience). In any case, you should plan for a delay and be pleasantly surprised when it arrives early.

WebLogic 6.0 installations

Although the format for WebLogic 6.0 and 6.1 licenses is similar, you do need to update your 6.0 license to work with 6.1. The process is exactly the same as the WebLogic 4.0 to 5.1 update, but the URL to visit is different:

```
http://websupport.beasys.com/custsupp/wls60to61_license.htm
```

Place the converted license files you received from BEA in the BEA home directory (on Windows this is often `c:\bea`).

You can accomplish the license conversion with a simple command-line application provided by BEA. First, ensure that your environment is set up by using the WebLogic `setenv` script. Then, if you are running on Windows, go to the BEA home directory and execute the following command:

```
UpdateLicense.cmd license_update_file
```

If you are running on Unix, execute this command instead:

```
sh UpdateLicense.sh license_update_file
```

Converting the weblogic.properties file

In versions of WebLogic prior to 6.0, server and application properties were stored in a `weblogic.properties` file. With the support of J2EE applications in WebLogic 6.0 and 6.1, application configuration settings are stored separately from the server properties. They are now stored in XML deployment descriptor files associated with each J2EE application.

WebLogic provides a utility that parses existing `weblogic.properties` files and generates the appropriate XML files for each of your applications.

Using this converter utility creates a new WebLogic 6.1 domain and places the XML file for each of your applications in the new domain directory.

To use the converter, open the WebLogic Console home Web page (or from any page in the console, click the Home icon in the upper right) and click the Convert Weblogic.properties link under Getting Started on the main page. This takes you to the properties conversion page, as shown in Figure A-1.

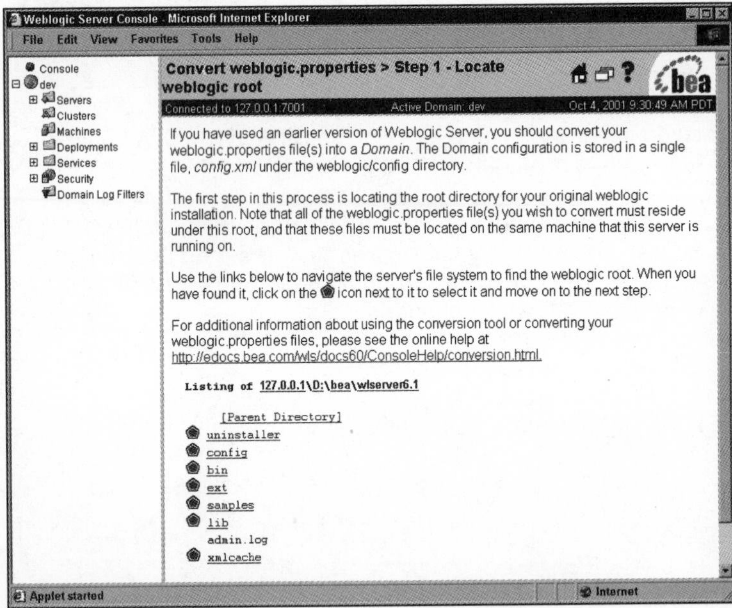

Figure A-1: Selecting the directory containing the weblogic.properties to convert

You will be asked to browse to the original installation directory, so be sure that you have network access to that original server installation. Note that if you have multiple servers running under your WebLogic home directory, you will need to convert those servers separately. Once you have navigated to the proper directory, click the orange pentagon next to the installation directory.

You will be asked to choose the server and cluster properties you want to convert. It is helpful at this point to have a text editor open so that you can view the contents of the `weblogic.properties` file; the selections on this screen do not always make sense out of context (see Figure A-2).

The following table (Table A-1) shows what values in the `weblogic.properties` file match which elements in your newly created `config.xml`. It may be worth your while to browse the newly converted properties to ensure the transfer occurred properly.

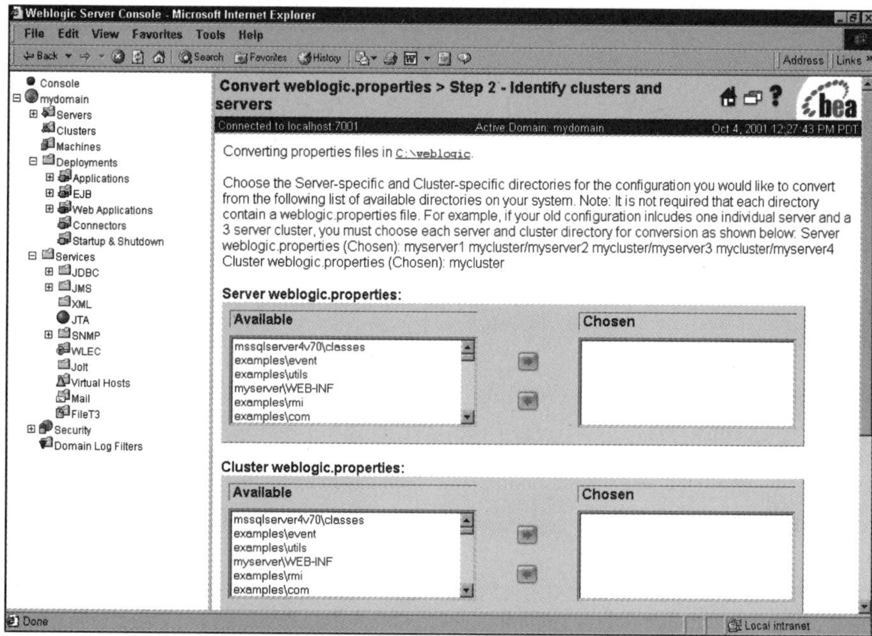

Figure A-2: The properties file conversion page in WebLogic Console

Table A-1
Config.xml Elements & weblogic.properties Entries

Element	*Attribute*	*weblogic.properties file entry*
Cluster		
	Cluster Address	weblogic.cluster.name
JDBC ConnectionPool		
	Name	weblogic.jdbc.connectionPool
	ShrinkingEnabled	weblogic.jdbc.connectionPool - allowShrinking
	CapacityIncrement	weblogic.jdbc.connectionPool - capacityIncrement
	DriverName	weblogic.jdbc.connectionPool - driver
	InitialCapacity	weblogic.jdbc.connectionPool - initialCapacity
	LoginDelaySeconds	weblogic.jdbc.connectionPool - loginDelaySecs
	MaxCapacity	weblogic.jdbc.connectionPool - maxCapacity
	Password	weblogic.jdbc.connectionPool - props
	Properties	weblogic.jdbc.connectionPool - props (password)
	RefreshMinutes	weblogic.jdbc.connectionPool - refreshTestMinutes
	ShrinkPeriodMinutes	weblogic.jdbc.connectionPool - shrinkPeriodMins
	TestConnectionsOnReserve	weblogic.jdbc.connectionPool - testConnsOnReserve
	TestConnectionsOnRelease	weblogic.jdbc.connectionPool - testConnsOnRelease
	TestTableName	weblogic.jdbc.connectionPool - testTable
	URL	weblogic.jdbc.connectionPool - url

Element	Attribute	weblogic.properties file entry
JMSConnection Consumer		
	Name	weblogic.jms. ConnectionConsumer
JMSDestination		
	Name	weblogic.jms.topic.<topic name>
LDAPRealm		
	LdapProvider	weblogic.security. ldaprealm.factory
Security		
	AuditProviderClassName	weblogic.security. audit.provider
Server		
	TunnelingEnabled	weblogic.httpd. tunnelingenabled
	AdministrationPort	weblogic.system. AdministrationPort
	TGIOPEnabled	weblogic.system.enableTGIOP
	HelpPageURL	weblogic.system.helpPageURL
	ListenPort	weblogic.system.ListenPort
	LoginTimeoutMillis	weblogic.system. readTimeoutMillis
	ClusterWeight	weblogic.system.weight
SSL		
	LoginTimeoutMillis	weblogic.login. readTimeoutMillisSSL
	ServerCertificateChain FileName	weblogic.security. certificate.authority
	Ciphersuites	weblogic.security. SSL.ciphersuite
	HostnameVerifier	weblogic.security. SSL.hostnameVerifier
	HostNameVerification Ignored	weblogic.security.SSL. ignoreHostnameVerification

Continued

Table A-1 *(continued)*

Element	***Attribute***	***weblogic.properties file entry***
StartupClass		
	FailureIsFatal	weblogic.system.startupFailureIsFatal
UnixMachine		
	PostBindGID	weblogic.system.nonPrivGroup
	PostBindUID	weblogic.system.nonPrivUser
WebServer		
	DefaultServerName	weblogic.httpd.defaultServerName
Administrator		
	EmailAddress	weblogic.administrator.email
	Name	weblogic.administrator.name
	PhoneNumber	weblogic.administrator.phone
	Notes **(freeform, optional)**	weblogic.administrator.location
CachingRealm		
	ACLCacheEnable	weblogic.security.realm.cache.acl.enable
	ACLCacheSize	weblogic.security.realm.cache.acl.size
	ACLCacheTTLNegative	weblogic.security.realm.cache.acl.ttl.negative
	ACLCacheTTLPositive	weblogic.security.realm.cache.acl.ttl.positive
	AuthenticationCacheEnable	weblogic.security.realm.cache.auth.enable
	AuthenticationCacheSize	weblogic.security.realm.cache.auth.size
	AuthenticationCacheTTLNegative	weblogic.security.realm.cache.auth.ttl.negative
	AuthenticationCacheTTLPositive	weblogic.security.realm.cache.auth.ttl.positive

Element	*Attribute*	*weblogic.properties file entry*
CachingRealm		
	CacheCaseSensitive	weblogic.security.realm.cache.caseSensitive
	GroupCacheEnable	weblogic.security.realm.cache.group.enable
	GroupCacheSize	weblogic.security.realm.cache.group.size
	GroupCacheTTLNegative	weblogic.security.realm.cache.group.ttl.negative
	GroupCacheTTLPositive	weblogic.security.realm.cache.group.ttl.positive
	PermissionCacheEnable	weblogic.security.realm.cache.perm.enable
	PermissionCacheSize	weblogic.security.realm.cache.perm.size
	PermissionCacheTTLNegative	weblogic.security.realm.cache.perm.ttl.negative
	PermissionCacheTTLPositive	weblogic.security.realm.cache.perm.ttl.positive
	UserCacheEnable	weblogic.security.realm.cache.user.enable
	UserCacheSize	weblogic.security.realm.cache.user.size
	UserCacheTTLNegative	weblogic.security.realm.cache.user.ttl.negative
	UserCacheTTLPositive	weblogic.security.realm.cache.user.ttl.positive
Cluster		
	DefaultLoadAlgorithm	weblogic.cluster.defaultLoadAlgorithm
	MulticastAddress	weblogic.cluster.multicastAddress
	MulticastTTL	weblogic.cluster.multicastTTL

Continued

Table A-1 *(continued)*

Element	*Attribute*	*weblogic.properties file entry*
JMSConnectionFactory		
	ClientID	weblogic.jms.connectionFactoryArgs.ClientID
	DefaultDeliveryMode	weblogic.jms.connectionFactoryArgs.DeliveryMode
	TransactionTimeout	weblogic.jms.connectionFactoryArgs.TransactionTimeout
	JNDIName	weblogic.jms.connectionFactoryName
JMSDestination		
	Name	weblogic.jms.queue
JMSJDBCStore		
	PrefixName	weblogic.jms.tableNamePrefix
JMSSessionPool		
	Name	weblogic.jms.queueSessionPool
	Name	weblogic.jms.topicSessionPool
Kernel		
	StdoutEnabled	weblogic.system.enableConsole
	ThreadPoolPercentSocketReaders	weblogic.system.percentSocketReaders
LDAPRealm		
	GroupNameAttribute	weblogic.security.ldaprealm.groupNameAttribute
	AuthProtocol	weblogic.security.ldaprealm.authentication
	Credential	weblogic.security.ldaprealm.credential
	GroupDN	weblogic.security.ldaprealm.groupDN
	GroupIsContext	weblogic.security.ldaprealm.groupIsContext
	GroupUsernameAttribute	weblogic.security.ldaprealm.groupUsernameAttribute

Element	*Attribute*	*weblogic.properties file entry*
LDAPRealm		
	Principal	weblogic.security.ldaprealm.principal
	SSLEnable	weblogic.security.ldaprealm.ssl
	LDAPURL	weblogic.security.ldaprealm.url
	UserAuthentication	weblogic.security.ldaprealm.userAuthentication
	UserDN	weblogic.security.ldaprealm.userDN
	UserNameAttribute	weblogic.security.ldaprealm.userNameAttribute
	UserPasswordAttribute	weblogic.security.ldaprealm.userPasswordAttribute
Log		
	FileName	weblogic.system.logFile
	FileMinxSize	weblogic.system.maxLogFileSize
NTRealm		
	PrimaryDomain	weblogic.security.ntrealm.domain
Security		
	GuestDisabled	weblogic.security.disableGuest
	ConnectionFilter	weblogic.security.net.connectionFilter
	SystemUser	weblogic.system.user
Server		
	HttpdEnabled	weblogic.httpd.enable
	TunnelingClientPingSecs	weblogic.httpd.tunneling.clientPingSecs
	TunnelingClient TimeoutSecs	weblogic.httpd.tunneling.clientTimeoutSecs
	DefaultIIOPPassword	weblogic.iiop.password
	DefaultIIOPUser	weblogic.iiop.user

Continued

Table A-1 *(continued)*

Element	***Attribute***	***weblogic.properties file entry***
Server		
	JDBCLoggingEnabled	weblogic.jdbc.enableLogFile
	JDBCLogFileName	weblogic.jdbc.logFileName
	JNDITransportable ObjectFactoryList	weblogic.jndi. transportableObjectFactories
	AdministrationPort	weblogic.system. AdministrationPort
	ListenAddress	weblogic.system.bindAddr
	DefaultProtocol	weblogic.system. defaultProtocol
	DefaultSecureProtocol	weblogic.system. defaultSecureProtocol
	IIOPEnabled	weblogic.system.enableIIOP
	ReverseDNSAllowed	weblogic.system. enableReverseDNSLookups
	RootDirectory	weblogic.system.home
	NativeIOEnabled	weblogic.system. nativeIO.enable
	LoginTimeoutMillis	weblogic.system. readTimeoutMillis
	WorkspaceShowUserKeys Only	weblogic.workspace. showUserKeysOnly
	ZACEnabled	weblogic.zac.enable
	ZACPublishRoot	weblogic.zac.publishRootProp
ServerDebug		
	MagicThreadDump BackToSocket	weblogic.system. MagicThreadBackToSocket
	MagicThreadDumpFile	weblogic.system. MagicThreadDumpFile
	MagicThreadDumpHost	weblogic.system. MagicThreadDumpHost
	MagicThreadDumpEnabled	weblogic.system. magicThreadDumps

Element	*Attribute*	*weblogic.properties file entry*
SSL		
	ServerCertificateFile Name	weblogic.security. certificate.server
	CertificateCacheSize	weblogic.security. certificateCacheSize
	TrustedCAFileName	weblogic.security.clientRootCA
	ClientCertificate Enforced	weblogic.security. enforceClientCert
	ExportKeyLifespan	weblogic.security.key. export.lifespan
	ServerKeyFileName	weblogic.security.key.server
	CertAuthenticator	weblogic.security. realm.certAuthenticator
	Enabled	weblogic.security.ssl.enable
	HandlerEnabled	weblogic.security. SSLHandler.enable
	UseJava	weblogic.system.SSL.useJava
	ListenPort	weblogic.system.SSLListenPort
UnixMachine		
	PostBindGID	weblogic.system.enableSetGID,
	PostBindUIDEnabled	weblogic.system.enableSetUID,
UnixRealm		
	AuthProgram	weblogic.security. unixrealm.authProgram
WebAppComponent		
	AuthRealmName	weblogic.httpd.authRealmName
	IndexDirectoryEnabled	weblogic.httpd. indexDirectories
	ServletExtensionCase Sensitive	weblogic.httpd.servlet. extensionCaseSensitive
	ServletReloadCheckSecs	weblogic.httpd.servlet. reloadCheckSecs
	SingleThreadedServlet PoolSize	weblogic.httpd.servlet. SingleThreadedModelPoolSize

Continued

Table A-1 *(continued)*

Element	*Attribute*	*weblogic.properties file entry*
WebServer		
	Charsets	weblogic.httpd.charsets
	ClusteringEnabled	weblogic.httpd.clustering.enable
	DefaultWebApp	weblogic.httpd.defaultWebApp
	LoggingEnabled	weblogic.httpd.enableLogFile
	KeepAliveSecs	weblogic.httpd.http.keepAliveSecs
	HttpsKeepAliveSecs	weblogic.httpd.https.keepAliveSecs
	KeepAliveEnabled	weblogic.httpd.keepAlive.enable
	LogFileBufferKBytes	weblogic.httpd.logFileBufferKBytes
	LogFileFlushSecs	weblogic.httpd.logFileFlushSecs
	LogFileFormat	weblogic.httpd.logFileFormat
	LogFileName	weblogic.httpd.logFileName
	LogRotationPeriodMins	weblogic.httpd.logRotationPeriodMins
	LogRotationTimeBegin	weblogic.httpd.logRotationPeriodMins
	LogRotationType	weblogic.httpd.logRotationType
	MaxLogFileSizeKBytes	weblogic.httpd.maxLogFileSizeKBytes
	PostTimeoutSecs	weblogic.httpd.postTimeoutSecs
	URLResource	weblogic.httpd.URLResource

Upgrading WebLogic Applications

Now that you have migrated your servers to WebLogic 6.1, you can migrate your applications into J2EE application formats that match the current version of the specification.

Migrating J2EE Web applications

The most commonly migrated applications are Web applications (possibly packaged into .war files).

Two files describe Web applications under WebLogic 6.1, the web.xml and weblogic.xml deployment descriptors. For more information on these files and on packaging and deploying Web applications on WebLogic in general, see Chapter 18.

Tables A-2 and A-3 show the mappings between name/value pairs in the weblogic.properties file and XML elements and attributes in the web.xml and weblogic.xml files, respectively. Skeletons of these files should have been created by the migration utility mentioned earlier and placed in your new domain directory. You should update these deployment descriptors by using the tools described in Chapter 18 to take full advantage of the configurations made available by WebLogic and the Servlet 2.3 Web application specification.

Only a single property from the weblogic.properties file maps to the J2EE web.xml file, as shown in Table A-2:

Table A-2
web.xml Elements & weblogic.properties Entries

Element	*Attribute*	*weblogic.properties file entry*
Mime-mapping		
	mime-type	weblogic.httpd.mimeType

All the other conversions deal with session management and are placed in the WebLogic-specific weblogic.xml file.

It should be noted that sessions created by previous versions of WebLogic Server are not recognized in WebLogic 6.0 and later, as the session cookie format has changed.

The entries listed in Table A-3 appear as <param-name>/<param-value> element pairs inside of a <session-param> element. For example:

```
<session-param>
  <param-name>TimeoutSecs</param-name>
  <param-value>3600</param-value>
</session-param>
```

sets the Web application session timeout to one hour.

Table A-3
Web Application Elements and weblogic.properties Entries

param-name	*weblogic.properties file entry*
mime-type	weblogic.httpd.mimeType
CacheSize	weblogic.httpd.session.cacheEntries
CookieComment	weblogic.httpd.session.cookie.comment
CookieDomain	weblogic.httpd.session.cookie.domain
CookieMaxAgeSecs	weblogic.httpd.session.cookie.maxAgeSecs
CookieName	weblogic.httpd.session.cookie.name
CookiePath	weblogic.httpd.session.cookie.path
CookiesEnabled	weblogic.httpd.session.cookies.enable
SessionDebuggable	weblogic.httpd.session.debug
SessionTrackingEnabled	weblogic.httpd.session.enable
InvalidationIntervalSecs	weblogic.httpd.session.invalidationintervalSecs
JDBCConnectionTimeoutSecs	weblogic.httpd.session.jdbc.connTimeoutSecs
PersistentStoreDir	weblogic.httpd.session.persistentStoreDir
PersistentStorePool	weblogic.httpd.session.persistentStorePool
SessionPersistentStoreShared	weblogic.httpd.session.persistentStoreShared
PersistentStoreType	weblogic.httpd.session.persistentStoreType
IDLength	weblogic.httpd.session.sessionIDLength
SwapIntervalSecs	weblogic.httpd.session.swapintervalSecs
TimeoutSecs	weblogic.httpd.session.timeoutSecs
URLRewritingEnabled	weblogic.httpd.session.URLRewriting.enable

Following is a list of some items to consider when upgrading to the Servlet 2.3 Web Application format:

- ✦ If you have hard-coded URLs in your servlets or HTML, you may need to change them to reflect the new Web application path:

  `http://myweblogic:7001/webappname/your_files_are_here.`

  If you have used relative URLs throughout your files, these changes should not be necessary.

- ✦ Objects stored in the session should be serializable if the application is going to run under WebLogic clustering. Also, dynamic classloading of your Web applications could cause `ClassCastExceptions` if nonserializable objects are stored in the session.

- ✦ Access Control Lists for you files are now security constraints defined in the `web.xml` file.

- ✦ Server-side includes (`.shtml`) are no longer supported. You will need to convert to JSP files to get this functionality.

Migrating EJB applications

WebLogic 6.1 supports both the Enterprise JavaBeans 1.1 and 2.0 specifications, so EJBs that you developed for WebLogic 5.1 should be easy to deploy on WebLogic 6.1. It is important to note that the XML deployment descriptor parser for 6.1 is a bit stricter that the one included in 5.1, so you might have to include a few new entries in the deployment descriptor of your 1.1 EJB. The server will tell you which ones you have to add at deployment time.

Unlike WebLogic 5.1, you no longer have to run the `ejbc` compiler on the EJB prior to deployment. If `ejbc` has not been run on a bean at deploy time, WebLogic 6.1 will do it automatically for you.

Some developers think it's good practice to run `ejbc` anyway—to expose possible problems with EJBs before they are deployed.

Only two features have been removed from EJB applications in WebLogic 6.1. The finder expressions used in the EJB 1.1 specification are no longer supported in 6.1. Also, the `weblogic.deploy` utility for deploying EJB to a running server is no longer supported.

See Chapters 14-17 for more information on how to deploy EJBs in WebLogic 6.1.

Migrating EJBs from 1.1 to 2.0

Should you want to upgrade existing EJB 1.1 beans to 2.0, WebLogic conveniently provides an upgrade utility called DDConverter to help you convert your deployment descriptors to the 2.0 specification.

You feed the DDConverter utility your 1.1 EJB JAR file that contains your bean classes and your deployment descriptors; DDConverter will output a JAR file containing the converted deployment descriptors.

Here's a sample command line:

```
$ java weblogic.ejb20.utils.ddconverter.DDConverter -d .\tmp
myEJB.jar
```

The package here is different than that listed in some WebLogic documentation (often listed as `weblogic.ejb20.utils.DDConverter`).

You should specify an output directory different than the current directory (using the required `-d` flag), as the output will be a file of the same name as the input.

After running the utility, you should repackage the original EJB classes with the new deployment descriptors (don't include classes generated by the WebLogic 5.1 `ejbc` compiler).

For session beans, this is all you should have to do to upgrade from 1.1 to 2.0. For CMP entity beans, however, there are several additional steps.

In EJB 2.0 CMP beans, all getter and setter methods for bean properties are abstract, and the container takes care of creating the concrete implementation class. So, if you had the following `setXXX` and `getXX` methods in your 1.1 CMP bean:

```
private String name;
public String getName() {
  return name;
}
public void setName(String newName) {
  name = newName;
}
```

you would change this to:

```
public abstract String getName();
public abstract void setName(String newName);
```

Any finders methods you have declared that have return values of `java.util.Enumeration` should be updated to return `java.util.Collection`, as CMP 2.0 can no longer return enumerations.

Migrating to Enterprise Applications

Something to note is the advent of the Enterprise Application Java application structure, which allows you to package many Java applications into a single deployable unit with a defined structure. This can support any number of Web applications, EJBs, and supporting files and classes bundled together in a single `.ear` file (packaged using the `.jar` format).

For more information on Enterprise Applications, see Chapter 18.

Removed and Deprecated Features

In the course of upgrading WebLogic Server to 6.1, BEA removed some features and deprecated others.

Removed APIs and features

The following features have been removed from WebLogic 6.1:

- ✦ Java-based Administration Console — Use the browser-based console instead.
- ✦ The Deployer Tool — You should now deploy applications via the WebLogic console.
- ✦ WebLogic/Tengah Beans — Use the latest JavaBean specification.
- ✦ WebLogic jHTML — Upgrade to JSP by using the jHTML JSP converter (see the WebLogic documentation on how to use this tool).
- ✦ WebLogic/Tengah Remote and Workspaces — Consider using JNDI and RMI for communication and object sharing (see Chapters 7 and 8 for details about these technologies).
- ✦ T3 Client and Remote T3 — Applications using this should change to RMI.
- ✦ WebLogic COM — Relied on the Microsoft JVM, which is no longer supported. Consider using a third-party Java-Com bridge if you need direct access to COM objects.
- ✦ SSI — Use JSPs and `<jsp:include>` instead.
- ✦ Jview and the Microsoft JVM are no longer supported.
- ✦ `weblogic.jdbc20.*` packages — Moved to `weblogic.jdbc.*`.

Deprecated APIs

If you are using any of the following features of WebLogic prior to version 6.1, you may wish to look into alternative processes, prior to or soon after upgrading to WebLogic 6.1, as it is likely that they will removed in a future release:

- **WebLogic Events**—Look into using unacknowledged JMS messages instead (see Chapter 9 on JMS).
- **WebLogic HTMLKona**—Consider upgrading servlets by using HTMLKona to JSP pages (see Chapters 12 and 13 on JSP and JSP Tag libraries).
- **T3 JDBC Driver**—You should use the RMI JDBC driver instead (see Chapter 5 on using JDBC with WebLogic).

Where to Find More Information

BEA provides two manuals to assist with the migration process:

- For more information about how to upgrade servers, go to `http://e-docs.bea.com/wls/docs61/notes/upgrade.html`
- For more information about how to upgrade applications, go to `http://e-docs.bea.com/wls/docs61/notes/migrate.html`

✦ ✦ ✦

Index

A

B

Continued

C

D

Continued

E

Continued

Continued

I

Continued

Continued

Continued

Continued

K

L

Continued

N

O

P

Q

R

Continued

Continued

Continued

Continued

U

Continued

X